THE OFFICIAL

1997 PRICE GUIDE TO

BASKETBALL CARDS

BY
DR. JAMES BECKETT

SIXTH EDITION

HOUSE OF COLLECTIBLES • NEW YORK

Important Notice: All of the information, including valuations, in this book has
been compiled from the most reliable sources, and every effort has been made
to eliminate errors and questionable data. Nevertheless, the possibility of error
in a work of such scope always exists. The publisher will not be held responsi-
ble for losses which may occur in the purchase, sale or other transaction of
items because of information contained herein. Readers who feel they have
discovered errors are invited to write and inform us, so that they may be
corrected in subsequent editions. Those seeking further information on the
topics covered in this book are advised to refer to the complete line of *Official
Price Guides* published by the House of Collectibles.

© 1996 by James Beckett III

All rights reserved under International
and Pan-American Copyright Conventions.

 This is a registered trademark of Random House, Inc.

Published by:
House of Collectibles
201 East 50th Street
New York, New York 10022

Distributed by Ballantine Books, a division of Random House, Inc.,
New York, and simultaneously in Canada by
Random House of Canada Limited, Toronto.

Manufactured in the United States of America

ISSN: 1062-6980

ISBN: 0-676-60021-2

Cover photo © Robert Beck / Sports Illustrated

Sixth Edition: December 1996

10 9 8 7 6 5 4 3 2 1

Table of Contents

About the Author

Jim Beckett, the leading authority on sport card values in the United States, maintains a wide range of activities in the world of sports. He possesses one of the finest collections of sports cards and autographs in the world, has made numerous appearances on radio and television, and has been frequently cited in many national publications. He was awarded the first "Special Achievement Award" for Contributions to the Hobby by the National Sports Collectors Convention in 1980, the "Jock-Jaspersen Award" for Hobby Dedication in 1983, and the "Buck Barker, Spirit of the Hobby Award" in 1991.

Dr. Beckett is the author of *Beckett Baseball Card Price Guide, The Official Price Guide to Baseball Cards, The Sport Americana Price Guide to Baseball Collectibles, The Sport Americana Baseball Memorabilia and Autograph Price Guide, Beckett Football Card Price Guide, The Official Price Guide to Football Cards, Beckett Hockey Card Price Guide, The Official Price Guide to Hockey Cards, Beckett Basketball Card Price Guide, The Official Price Guide to Basketball Cards, and The Sport Americana Baseball Card Alphabetical Checklist.* In addition, he is the founder, publisher, and editor of *Beckett Baseball Card Monthly, Beckett Basketball Monthly, Beckett Football Card Monthly, Beckett Hockey Monthly, Beckett Future Stars, Beckett Tribute,* and *Beckett Racing Monthly* magazines.

Jim Beckett received his Ph.D. in Statistics from Southern Methodist University in 1975. Prior to starting Beckett Publications in 1984, Dr. Beckett served as an Associate Professor of Statistics at Bowling Green State University and as a Vice President of a consulting firm in Dallas, Texas. He currently resides in Dallas with his wife, Patti, and their daughters, Christina, Rebecca, and Melissa.

How to Use This Book

Isn't it great? Every year this book gets bigger and bigger with all the new sets coming out. But even more exciting is that every year there are more attractive choices and, subsequently, more interest in the cards we love so much. This edition has been enhanced and expanded from the previous edition. The cards you collect — who appears on them, what they look like, where they are from, and (most important to most of you) what their current values are — are enumerated within. Many of the features contained in the other *Beckett Price Guides* have been incorporated into this volume since condition grading, terminology, and many other aspects of collecting are common to the card hobby in general. We hope you find the book both interesting and useful in your collecting pursuits.

The Beckett Guide has been successful where other attempts have failed because it is complete, current, and valid. This Price Guide contains not just one, but three prices by condition for all the basketball cards listed. These account for most of the basketball cards in existence. The prices were added to the card lists just prior to printing and reflect not the author's opinions or desires but the going retail prices for each card, based on the marketplace (sports memorabilia conventions and shows, sports card shops, hobby papers, current mail-order catalogs, local club meetings, auction results, and other firsthand reportings of actually realized prices).

What is the best price guide available on the market today? Of course card sellers will prefer the price guide with the highest prices, while card buyers will naturally prefer the one with the lowest prices. Accuracy, however, is the true test. Use the price guide used by more collectors and dealers than all the others combined. Look for the Beckett name. I won't put my name on anything I won't stake my reputation on. Not the lowest and not the highest — but the most accurate, with integrity.

To facilitate your use of this book, read the complete introductory section on the following pages before going to the pricing pages. Every collectible field has its own terminology; we've tried to capture most of these terms and definitions in our glossary. Please read carefully the section on grading and the condition of your cards, as you will not be able to determine which price column is appropriate for a given card without first knowing its condition.

Introduction

Welcome to the exciting world of sports card collecting, one of America's most popular avocations. You have made a good choice in buying this book, since it will open up to you the entire panorama of this field in the simplest, most concise way.

The growth of *Beckett Baseball Card Monthly*, *Beckett Basketball Monthly*, *Beckett Football Card Monthly*, *Beckett Hockey Monthly*, *Beckett Future Stars*, and *Beckett Racing Monthly* is another indication of the unprecedented popularity of sports cards. Founded in 1984 by Dr. James Beckett, the author of this Price Guide, *Beckett Baseball Card Monthly* contains the most extensive and accepted monthly Price Guide, collectible glossy superstar covers, colorful feature articles, "Hot List," Convention Calendar, tips for beginners, "Readers Write" letters to and responses from the editor, information on errors and varieties, autograph collecting tips and profiles of the sport's Hottest stars. Published every month, *BBCM* is the hobby's largest paid circulation periodical. The other five magazines were built on the success of *BBCM*.

So collecting sports cards — while still pursued as a hobby with youthful exuberance by kids in the neighborhood — has also taken on the trappings of an industry, with thousands of full- and part-time card dealers, as well as vendors of supplies, clubs and conventions. In fact, each year since 1980 thousands of hobbyists have assembled for a National Sports Collectors Convention, at which hundreds of dealers have displayed their wares, seminars have been conducted, autographs penned by sports notables, and millions of cards changed hands.

The Beckett Guide is the best annual guide available to the exciting world of basketball cards. Read it and use it. May your enjoyment and your card collection increase in the coming months and years.

How to Collect

Each collection is personal and reflects the individuality of its owner. There are no set rules on how to collect cards. Since card collecting is a hobby or leisure pastime, what you collect, how much you collect, and how much time and money you spend collecting are entirely up to you. The funds you have available for collecting and your own personal taste should determine how you collect. The information and ideas presented here are intended to help you get the most enjoyment from this hobby.

It is impossible to collect every card ever produced. Therefore, beginners as well as intermediate and advanced collectors usually specialize in some way. One of the reasons this hobby is popular is that individual collectors can define and tailor their collecting methods to match their own tastes. To give you some ideas of the various approaches to collecting, we will list some of the more popular areas of specialization.

Many collectors select complete sets from particular years. For example, they may concentrate on assembling complete sets from all the years since their birth or since they became avid sports fans. They may try to collect a card for every player during that specified period of time. Many others wish to acquire only certain players. Usually such players are the superstars of the sport, but occasionally collectors will specialize in all the cards of players who attended a particular college or came from a certain town. Some collectors are only interested in the first cards or Rookie Cards of certain players.

Another fun way to collect cards is by team. Most fans have a favorite team, and it is natural for that loyalty to be translated into a desire for cards of the players on that favorite team. For most of the recent years, team sets (all the cards from a given team for that year) are readily available at a reasonable price. *The Sport Americana Team Football* and *Basketball Card Checklist* will open up this field to the collector.

Obtaining Cards

Several avenues are open to card collectors. Cards still can be purchased in the traditional way: by the pack at the local discount, grocery or convenience stores. But there are also thousands of card shops across the country that specialize in selling cards individually or by the pack, box, or set. Another alternative is the thousands of card shows held each month around the country, which feature anywhere from five to 800 tables of sports cards and memorabilia for sale.

For many years, it has been possible to purchase complete sets of cards through mail-order advertisers found in traditional sports media publications, such as *The Sporting News, Football Digest, Street & Smith* yearbooks, and others. These sets also are advertised in the card collecting periodicals. Many collectors will begin by subscribing to at least one of the hobby periodicals, all with good up-to-date information. In fact, subscription offers can be found in the advertising section of this book.

Most serious card collectors obtain old (and new) cards from one or more of several main sources: (1) trading or buying from other collectors or dealers; (2) responding to sale or auction ads in the hobby publications; (3) buying at a local hobby store; and/or (4) attending sports collectibles shows or conventions.

We advise that you try all four methods since each has its own distinct advantages: (1) trading is a great way to make new friends; (2) hobby periodicals help you keep up with what's going on in the hobby (including when and where the conventions are happening); (3) stores provide the opportunity to enjoy personalized service and consider a great diversity of material in a relaxed sports-oriented atmosphere; and (4) shows allow you to choose from multiple dealers and thousands of cards under one roof in a competitive situation.

Preserving Your Cards

Cards are fragile. They must be handled properly in order to retain their value. Careless handling can easily result in creased or bent cards. It is, however, not recommended that tweezers or tongs be used to pick up your cards since such utensils might mar or indent card surfaces and thus reduce those cards' conditions and values. In general, your cards should be handled directly as little as possible. This is sometimes easier to say than to do.

Although there are still many who use custom boxes, storage trays, or even shoe boxes, plastic sheets are the preferred method of many collectors for storing cards. A collection stored in plastic pages in a three-ring album allows you to view your collection at any time without the need to touch the card itself. Cards can also be kept in single holders (of various types and thickness) designed for the enjoyment of each card individually. For a large collection, some collectors may use a combination of the above methods. When purchasing plastic sheets for your cards, be sure that you find the pocket size that fits the cards snugly. Don't put your 1969-70 Topps in a sheet designed to fit 1992-93 Topps.

Most hobby and collectibles shops and virtually all collectors' conventions will have these plastic pages available in quantity for the various sizes offered, or you can purchase them directly from the advertisers in this book. Also, remember that pocket size isn't the only factor to consider when looking for plastic sheets. Other factors such as safety, economy, appearance, availability, or personal preference also may indicate which types of sheets a collector may want to buy.

Damp, sunny and/or hot conditions — no, this is not a weather forecast — are three elements to avoid in extremes if you are interested in preserving your collection. Too much (or too little) humidity can cause gradual deterioration of a card. Direct, bright sun (or fluorescent light) over time will bleach out the color of a card. Extreme heat accelerates the decomposition of the card. On the other hand, many cards have lasted more than 50 years without much scientific intervention. So be cautious, even if the above factors typically present a problem only when present in the extreme. It never hurts to be prudent.

Collecting vs. Investing

Collecting individual players and collecting complete sets are both popular vehicles for investment and speculation. Most investors and speculators stock up on complete sets or on quantities of players they think have good investment potential.

There is obviously no guarantee in this book, or anywhere else for that matter, that cards will outperform the stock market or other investment alternatives in the future. After all, basketball cards do not pay quarterly dividends and cards cannot be sold at their "current values" as easily as stocks or bonds.

Nevertheless, investors have noticed a favorable long-term trend in the past performance of sports collectibles, and certain cards and sets have outperformed just about any other investment in some years. Many hobbyists maintain that the best investment is and always will be the building of a collection, which traditionally has held up better than outright speculation.

Some of the obvious questions are: Which cards? When to buy? When to sell? The best investment you can make is in your own education. The more you know about your collection and the hobby, the more informed the decisions you will be able to make. We're not selling investment tips. We're selling information about the current value of basketball cards. It's up to you to use that information to your best advantage.

Glossary/Legend

Our glossary defines terms frequently used in the card collecting hobby. Many of these terms are also common to other types of sports memorabilia collecting. Some terms may have several meanings depending on use and context.

ABA - American Basketball Association.

ACC - Accomplishment.

ACO - Assistant Coach Card.

AL - Active Leader.

ART - All-Rookie Team.

AS - All-Star.

ASA - All-Star Advice.

ASW - All-Star Weekend.

AUTO - Autograph.

AW - Award Winner.

BC - Bonus Card.

BRICK - A group or "lot" or cards, usually 50 or more having common characteristics, that is intended to be bought, sold, or traded as a unit.

BT - Beam Team or Breakaway Threats.

CBA - Continental Basketball Association.

CL - Checklist card. A card that lists in order the cards and players in the set or series. Older checklist cards in Mint condition that have not been checked off are very desirable and command large premiums.

CO - Coach card.

COIN - A small disc of metal or plastic portraying a player in its center.

COLLECTOR - A person who engages in the hobby of collecting cards primarily for his own enjoyment, with any profit motive being secondary.

COMBINATION CARD - A single card depicting two or more players (not including team cards).

COMMON CARD - The typical card of any set; it has no premium value accruing from subject matter, numerical scarcity, popular demand, or anomaly.

CONVENTION ISSUE - A set produced in conjunction with a sports collectibles convention to commemorate or promote the show. Most recent convention issues could also be classified as promo sets.

COR - Corrected card. A version of an error card that was fixed by the manufacturer.

COUPON - See Tab.

DEALER - A person who engages in buying, selling, and trading sports collectibles or supplies. A dealer may also be a collector, but as a dealer, he anticipates a profit.

DIE-CUT - A card with part of its stock partially cut for ornamental reasons.

DISC - A circular-shaped card.

DISPLAY SHEET - A clear, plastic page that is punched for insertion into a binder (with standard three-ring spacing) containing pockets for displaying cards. Many different styles of sheets exist with pockets of varying sizes to hold the many differing card formats. The vast majority of current cards measure 2 1/2 by 3 1/2 inches and fit in nine-pocket sheets.

DP - Double Print. A card that was printed in approximately double the quantity compared to other cards in the same series, or draft pick card.

ERR - Error card. A card with erroneous information, spelling, or depiction on either side of the card. Most errors are never corrected by the producing card company.

FIN - Finals.

FLB - Flashback.

FPM - Future Playoff MVP's.

FSL - Future Scoring Leaders.

FULL SHEET - A complete sheet of cards that has not been cut into individual cards by the manufacturer. Also called an uncut sheet.

GQ - Gentleman's Quarterly.

HL - Highlight card.

HOF - Hall of Fame, or Hall of Famer (also abbreviated HOFer).

HOR - Horizontal pose on a card as opposed to the standard vertical orientation found on most cards.

IA - In Action card. A special type of card depicting a player in an action photo, such as the 1982 Topps cards.

INSERT - A card of a different type, e.g., a poster, or any other sports collectible contained and sold in the same package along with a card or cards of a major set.

IS - Inside Stuff.

ISSUE - Synonymous with set, but usually used in conjunction with a manufacturer, e.g., a Topps issue.

JWA - John Wooden Award.

KID - Kid Picture card.

LEGITIMATE ISSUE - A set produced to promote or boost sales of a product or service, e.g., bubble gum, cereal, cigarettes, etc. Most collector issues are not legitimate issues in this sense.

LID - A circular-shaped card (possibly with tab) that forms the top of the container for the product being promoted.

MAG - Magic of SkyBox cards.

MAJOR SET - A set produced by a national manufacturer of cards, containing a large number of cards. Usually 100 or more different cards comprise a major set.

MC - Members Choice.

MEM - Memorial.

MO - McDonald's Open.

MINI - A small card or stamp (the 1991-92 SkyBox Canadian set, for example).

MVP - Most Valuable Player.

NNO - No number on back.

NY - New York.

OBVERSE - The front, face, or pictured side of the card.

OLY - Olympic card.

PANEL - An extended card that is composed of multiple individual cards.

PC - Poster card.

PERIPHERAL SET - A loosely defined term that applies to any non-regular issue set. This term most often is used to describe food issue, giveaway, regional or sendaway sets that contain a fairly small number of cards and are not accepted by the hobby as major sets.

PF - Pacific Finest.

POY - Player of the Year.

PREMIUM - A card, sometimes on photographic stock, that is purchased or obtained in conjunction with (or redeemed for) another card or product. This term applies mainly to older products, as newer cards distributed in this manner are generally lumped together as peripheral sets.

PREMIUM CARDS - A class of products introduced recently, intended to have higher quality card stock and photography than regular cards, but more limited production and higher cost. Defining what is and isn't a premium card is somewhat subjective.

PROMOTIONAL SET - A set, usually containing a small number of cards, issued by a national card producer and distributed in limited quantities or to a select group of people, such as major show attendees or dealers with wholesale accounts. Presumably, the purpose of a promo set is to stir up demand for an upcoming set. Also called a preview, prototype or test set.

RARE - A card or series of cards of very limited availability. Unfortunately, "rare" is a subjective term sometimes used indiscriminately. Using the strict definitions, rare cards are harder to obtain than scarce cards.

RC - Rookie Card. A player's first appearance on a regular issue card from one of the major card companies. Each company has only one regular issue set per season, and that is the widely available traditional set. With a few exceptions, each player has only one RC in any given set. A Rookie Card cannot be an All-Star, Highlight, In Action, League Leader, Super Action or Team Leader card. It can, however, be a coach card or draft pick card.

REGIONAL - A card issued and distributed only in a limited geographical area of the country. The producer may or may not be a major, national producer of trading cards. The key is whether the set was distributed nationally in any form or not.

REVERSE - The back or narrative side of the card.

REV NEG - Reversed or flopped photo side of the card. This is a major type of error card, but only some are corrected.

RIS - Rising Star.

ROY - Rookie of the Year.

SA - Super Action card. Similar to an In Action card.

SAL - SkyBox Salutes.

SASE - Self-addressed, stamped envelope.

SCARCE - A card or series of cards of limited availability. This subjective term is sometimes used indiscriminately to promote or hype value. Using strict definitions, scarce cards are easier to obtain than rare cards.

SERIES - The entire set of cards issued by a particular producer in a particular year, e.g., the 1978-79 Topps series. Also, within a particular set, series can refer to a group of (consecutively numbered) cards printed at the same time, e.g., the first series of the 1972-73 Topps set (#1 through #132).

SET - One each of an entire run of cards of the same type, produced by a particular manufacturer during a single season. In other words, if you have a complete set of 1989-90 Fleer cards, then you have every card from #1 up to and including #132; i.e., all the different cards that were produced.

SHOOT - Shooting Star.

SHOW - A large gathering of dealers and collectors at a single location for the purpose of buying, selling, and trading sorts cards and memorabilia. Conventions are open to the public and sometimes also feature autograph guests, door prizes, films, contests, etc.

SKED - Schedules.

SP - Single or Short Print. A card which was printed in lesser quantity compared to the other cards in the same series (also see DP). This term only can be used in a relative sense and in reference to one particular set. For instance, the 1989-90 Hoops Pistons Championship card (#353A) is less common than the other cards in that set, but it isn't necessarily scarcer than regular cards of any other set.

SPECIAL CARD - A card that portrays something other than a single player or team.

SS - Star Stats.

STANDARD SIZE - The standard size for sports cards is 2 1/2 by 3 1/2 inches. All exceptions, such as 1969-70 Topps, are noted in card descriptions.

STAR CARD - A card that portrays a player of some repute, usually determined by his ability, but sometimes referring to sheer popularity.

STAY - Stay in School.

STICKER - A card-like item with a removable layer that can be affixed to another surface. Example: 1986-87 through 1989-90 Fleer bonus cards.

STOCK - The cardboard or paper on which the card is printed.

SUPERSTAR CARD - A card that portrays a superstar, e.g., a Hall of Fame member or a player whose current performance may eventually warrant serious Hall of Fame consideration.

SY - Schoolyard Stars.

TC - Team card or team checklist card.

TD - Triple Double. A term used for having double digit totals in three categories.

TEAM CARD - A card that depicts an entire team, notably the 1989-90 and 1990-91 NBA Hoops Detroit Pistons championship cards and the 1991-92 NBA Hoops subset.

TEST SET - A set, usually containing a small number of cards, issued by a national producer and distributed in a limited section of the country or to a select group of people. Presumably, the purpose of a test set is to measure market appeal for a particular type of card. Also called a promo or prototype set.

TFC - Team Fact card.

TL - Team Leader.

TO - Tip-off.

TR - Traded card.

TRIB - Tribune.

TRV - Trivia.

TT - Team Tickets card.

UER - Uncorrected Error card.

USA - Team USA.

VAR - Variation card. One of two or more cards from the same series, with the same card number (or player with identical pose, if the series is unnumbered) differing from one another in some aspect, from the printing, stock or other feature of the card. This is often caused when the manufacturer of the cards notices an error in a particular card, corrects the error and then resumes the print run. In this case there will be two versions or variations of the same card. Sometimes one of the variations is relatively scarce. Variations also can result from accidental or deliberate design changes, information updates, photo substitutions, etc.

VERT - Vertical pose on a card.

XRC - Extended Rookie Card. A player's first appearance on a card, but issued in a set that was not distributed nationally nor in packs. In basketball sets, this term only refers to the 1983, '84 and '85 Star Company sets.

YB - Yearbook.

20A - Twenty assist club.

50P - Fifty point club.

6M - Sixth Man.

! - Condition sensitive card or set *(see Grading Your Cards)*.

* - Multi-sport set.

Understanding Card Values

Determining Value

Why are some cards more valuable than others? Obviously, the economic laws of supply and demand are applicable to card collecting just as they are to any other field where a commodity is bought, sold or traded in a free, unregulated market.

Supply (the number of cards available on the market) is less than the total number of cards originally produced since attrition diminishes that original quantity. Each year a percentage of cards is typically thrown away, destroyed or otherwise lost to collectors. This percentage is much, much smaller today than it was in the past because more and more people have become increasingly aware of the value of their cards.

For those who collect only Mint condition cards, the supply of older cards can be quite small indeed. Until recently, collectors were not so conscious of the need to preserve the condition of their cards. For this reason, it is difficult to know exactly how many 1957-58 Topps are currently available, Mint or otherwise. It is generally accepted that there are fewer 1957-58 Topps available than 1969-70, 1979-80 or 1992-93 Topps cards. If demand were equal for each of these sets, the law of supply and demand would increase the price for the least available sets.

Demand, however, is never equal for all sets, so price correlations can be complicated. The demand for a card is influenced by many factors. These include: (1) the age of the card; (2) the number of cards printed; (3) the player(s) portrayed on the card; (4) the attractiveness and popularity of the set; and (5) the physical condition of the card.

In general, (1) the older the card, (2) the fewer the number of the cards printed, (3) the more famous, popular and talented the player, (4) the more attractive and popular the set, and (5) the better the condition of the card, the higher the value of the card will be. There are exceptions to all but one of these factors: the condition of the card. Given two cards similar in all respects except condition, the one in the best condition will always be valued higher.

While those guidelines help to establish the value of a card, the countless exceptions and peculiarities make any simple, direct mathematical formula to determine card values impossible.

Regional Variation

Since the market varies from region to region, card prices of local players may be higher. This is known as a regional premium. How significant the premium is — and if there is any premium at all — depends on the local popularity of the team and the player.

The largest regional premiums usually do not apply to superstars, who often are so well known nationwide that the prices of their key cards are too high for local dealers to realize a premium.

Lesser stars often command the strongest premiums. Their popularity is concentrated in their home region, creating local demand that greatly exceeds overall demand.

Regional premiums can apply to popular retired players and sometimes can be found in the areas where the players grew up or starred in college.

A regional discount is the converse of a regional premium. Regional discounts occur when a player has been so popular in his region for so long that local collectors and dealers have accumulated quantities of his cards. The abundant supply may make the cards available in that area at the lowest prices anywhere.

Set Prices

A somewhat paradoxical situation exists in the price of a complete set vs. the combined cost of the individual cards in the set. In nearly every case, the sum of the prices for the individual cards is higher than the cost for the complete set. This is prevalent especially in the cards of the past few years. The reasons for this apparent anomaly stem from the habits of collectors and from the carrying costs to dealers. Today, each card in a set normally is produced in the same quantity as all others in its set.

Many collectors pick up only stars, superstars and particular teams. As a result, the dealer is left with a shortage of certain player cards and an abundance of others. He therefore incurs an expense in simply "carrying" these less desirable cards in stock. On the other hand, if he sells a complete set, he gets rid of large numbers of cards at one time. For this reason, he generally is willing to receive less money for a complete set. By doing this, he recovers all of his costs and also makes a profit.

Set prices do not include rare card varieties, unless specifically stated. Of course, the prices for sets do include one example of each type for the given set, but this is the least expensive variety.

Scarce Series

Only a select few basketball sets contain scarce series: 1948 Bowman, 1970-71 and 1972-73 Topps, 1983-84, 1984-85 and 1985-86 Star. The 1948 Bowman set was printed on two 36-card sheets, the second of which was issued in significantly lower quantities. The two Topps scarce series are only marginally tougher than the set as a whole. The Star Company scarcities relate to particular team sets that, to different extents, were less widely distributed.

We are always looking for information or photographs of printing sheets of cards for research. Each year, we try to update the hobby's knowledge of distribution anomalies. Please let us know at the address in this book if you have first-hand knowledge that would be helpful in this pursuit.

Grading Your Cards

Each hobby has its own grading terminology — stamps, coins, comic books, record collecting, etc. Collectors of sports cards are no exception. The one invariable criterion for determining the value of a card is its condition: the better the condition of the card, the more valuable it is. Condition grading, however, is subjective. Individual card dealers and collectors differ in the strictness of their grading, but the stated condition of a card should be determined without regard to whether it is being bought or sold.

No allowance is made for age. A 1961-62 Fleer card is judged by the same standards as a 1991-92 Fleer card. But there are specific sets and cards that are condition sensitive (marked with "!" in the Price Guide) because of their border color, consistently poor centering, etc. Such cards and sets sometimes command premiums above the listed percentages in Mint condition.

Centering

Current centering terminology uses numbers representing the percentage of border on either side of the main design. Obviously, centering is diminished in importance for borderless cards such as Stadium Club.

Slightly Off-Center (60/40): A slightly off-center card is one that upon close inspection is found to have one border bigger than the opposite border. This degree once was offensive to only purists, but now some hobbyists try to avoid cards that are anything other than perfectly centered.

Off-Center (70/30): An off-center card has one border that is noticeably more than twice as wide as the opposite border.

Badly Off-Center (80/20 or worse): A badly off-center card has virtually no border on one side of the card.

Miscut: A miscut card actually shows part of the adjacent card in its larger

Centering

Well-centered

Slightly off-centered

Off-centered

Badly off-centered

Miscut

border and consequently a corresponding amount of its card is cut off.

Corner Wear

Corner wear is the most scrutinized grading criteria in the hobby. These are the major categories of corner wear:

Corner with a slight touch of wear: The corner still is sharp, but there is a slight touch of wear showing. On a dark-bordered card, this shows as a dot of white.

Fuzzy corner: The corner still comes to a point, but the point has just begun to fray. A slightly "dinged" corner is considered the same as a fuzzy corner.

Slightly rounded corner: The fraying of the corner has increased to where there is only a hint of a point. Mild layering may be evident. A "dinged" corner is considered the same as a slightly rounded corner.

Rounded corner: The point is completely gone. Some layering is noticeable.

Badly rounded corner: The corner is completely round and rough. Severe layering is evident.

Creases

A third common defect is the crease. The degree of creasing in a card is difficult to show in a drawing or picture. On giving the specific condition of an expensive card for sale, the seller should note any creases additionally. Creases can be categorized as to severity according to the following scale.

Light Crease: A light crease is a crease that is barely noticeable upon close inspection. In fact, when cards are in plastic sheets or holders, a light crease may not be seen (until the card is taken out of the holder). A light crease on the front is much more serious than a light crease on the card back only.

Medium Crease: A medium crease is noticeable when held and studied at arm's length by the naked eye, but does not overly detract from the appearance of the card. It is an obvious crease, but not one that breaks the picture surface of the card.

Heavy Crease: A heavy crease is one that has torn or broken through the card's picture surface, e.g., puts a tear in the photo surface.

Alterations

Deceptive Trimming: This occurs when someone alters the card in order (1) to shave off edge wear, (2) to improve the sharpness of the corners, or (3) to improve centering — obviously their objective is to falsely increase the perceived value of the card to an unsuspecting buyer. The shrinkage usually is evident only if the trimmed card is compared to an adjacent full-sized card or if the trimmed card is itself measured.

Obvious Trimming: Obvious trimming is noticeable and unfortunate. It is usually performed by non-collectors who give no thought to the present or future value of their cards.

Deceptively Retouched Borders: This occurs when the borders (especially on those cards with dark borders) are touched up on the edges and corners with magic marker or crayons of appropriate color in order to make the card appear to be Mint.

Categorization of Defects

Miscellaneous Flaws

The following are common minor flaws that, depending on severity, lower a card's condition by one to four grades and often render it no better than Excellent-Mint: bubbles (lumps in surface), gum and wax stains, diamond cutting (slanted borders), notching, off-centered backs, paper wrinkles, scratched-off cartoons or puzzles on back, rubber band marks, scratches, surface

Corner Wear

The partial cards here have been photographed at 300%. This was done in order to magnify each card's corner wear to such a degree that differences could be shown on a printed page.

This 1986-87 Fleer Mark Aguirre card has a touch of wear. Notice the extremely slight fraying on the corner.

This 1986-87 Fleer Isiah Thomas card has a fuzzy corner. Notice that there is no longer a sharp corner.

This 1986-87 Fleer Wayman Tisdale card has a slightly rounded corner evident by the lack of a sharp point and heavy wear on both edges.

This 1986-87 Fleer Herb Williams card displays a badly rounded corner. Notice a large portion of missing cardboard accompanied by heavy wear and excessive fraying.

This 1986-87 Fleer Maurice Cheeks card displays several creases of varying degrees. Light creases (middle of the card) may not break the card's surface, while heavy creases (right side) will.

impressions and warping.

The following are common serious flaws that, depending on severity, lower a card's condition at least four grades and often render it no better than Good: chemical or sun fading, erasure marks, mildew, miscutting (severe off-centering), holes, bleached or retouched borders, tape marks, tears, trimming, water or coffee stains and writing.

Condition Guide

Grades

Mint (Mt) - A card with no flaws or wear. The card has four perfect corners, 60/40 or better centering from top to bottom and from left to right, original gloss, smooth edges and original color borders. A Mint card does not have print spots, color or focus imperfections.

Near Mint-Mint (NrMt-Mt) - A card with one minor flaw. Any one of the following would lower a Mint card to Near Mint-Mint: one corner with a slight touch of wear, barely noticeable print spots, color or focus imperfections. The card must have 60/40 or better centering in both directions, original gloss, smooth edges and original color borders.

Near Mint (NrMt) - A card with one minor flaw. Any one of the following would lower a Mint card to Near Mint: one fuzzy corner or two to four corners with slight touches of wear, 70/30 to 60/40 centering, slightly rough edges, minor print spots, color or focus imperfections. The card must have original gloss and original color borders.

Excellent-Mint (ExMt) - A card with two or three fuzzy, but not rounded, corners and centering no worse than 80/20. The card may have no more than two of the following: slightly rough edges, very slightly discolored borders, minor print spots, color or focus imperfections. The card must have original gloss.

Excellent (Ex) - A card with four fuzzy but definitely not rounded corners and centering no worse than 80/20. The card may have a small amount of original gloss lost, rough edges, slightly discolored borders and minor print spots, color or focus imperfections.

Very Good (Vg) - A card that has been handled but not abused: slightly rounded corners with slight layering, slight notching on edges, a significant amount of gloss lost from the surface but no scuffing and moderate discoloration of borders. The card may have a few light creases.

Good (G), Fair (F), Poor (P) - A well-worn, mishandled or abused card: badly rounded and layered corners, scuffing, most or all original gloss missing, seriously discolored borders, moderate or heavy creases, and one or more serious flaws. The grade of Good, Fair or Poor depends on the severity of wear and flaws. Good, Fair and Poor cards generally are used only as fillers.

The most widely used grades are defined above. Obviously, many cards will not perfectly fit one of the definitions.

Therefore, categories between the major grades known as in-between grades are used, such as Good to Very Good (G-Vg), Very Good to Excellent (VgEx), and Excellent-Mint to Near Mint (ExMt-NrMt). Such grades indicate a card with all qualities of the lower category but with at least a few qualities of the higher category.

This Price Guide book lists each card and set in three grades, with the middle grade valued at about 40-45% of the top grade, and the bottom grade valued at about 10-15% of the top grade.

The value of cards that fall between the listed columns can also be calculated using a percentage of the top grade. For example, a card that falls between the top and middle grades (Ex, ExMt or NrMt in most cases) will generally be valued at anywhere from 50% to 90% of the top grade.

Similarly, a card that falls between the middle and bottom grades (G-Vg, Vg or VgEx in most cases) will generally be valued at anywhere from 20% to 40% of the top grade.

There are also cases where cards are in better condition than the top grade or worse than the bottom grade. Cards that grade worse than the lowest grade are generally valued at 5-10% of the top grade.

When a card exceeds the top grade by one — such as NrMt-Mt when the top grade is NrMt, or Mint when the top grade is NrMt-Mt — a premium of up to 50% is possible, with 10-20% the usual norm.

When a card exceeds the top grade by two — such as Mint when the top grade is NrMt, or NrMt-Mt when the top grade is ExMt — a premium of 25-50% is the usual norm. But certain condition sensitive cards or sets, particularly those from the pre-war era, can bring premiums of up to 100% or even more.

Unopened packs, boxes and factory-collated sets are considered Mint in their unknown (and presumed perfect) state. Once opened, however, each card can be graded (and valued) in its own right by taking into account any defects that may be present in spite of the fact that the card has never been handled.

Selling Your Cards

Just about every collector sells cards or will sell cards eventually. Someday you may be interested in selling your duplicates or maybe even your whole collection. You may sell to other collectors, friends or dealers. You may even sell cards you purchased from a certain dealer back to that same dealer. In any event, it helps to know some of the mechanics of the typical transaction between buyer and seller.

Dealers will buy cards in order to resell them to other collectors who are interested in the cards. Dealers will always pay a higher percentage for items that (in their opinion) can be resold quickly, and a much lower percentage for those items that are perceived as having low demand and hence are slow moving. In either case, dealers must buy at a price that allows for the expense of doing business and a margin for profit.

If you have cards for sale, the best advice we can give is that you get several offers for your cards — either from card shops or at a card show — and take the best offer, all things considered. Note, the "best" offer may not be the one for the highest amount. And remember, if a dealer really wants your cards, he won't let you get away without making his best competitive offer. Another alternative is to place your cards in an auction as one or several lots.

Many people think nothing of going into a department store and paying $15 for an item of clothing for which the store paid $5. But if you were selling your $15 card to a dealer and he offered you $5 for it, you might think his mark-up unreasonable. To complete the analogy: most department stores (and card dealers) that consistently pay $10 for $15 items eventually go out of business. An exception is when the dealer has lined up a willing buyer for the item(s) you are attempting to sell, or if the cards are so Hot that it's likely he'll have to hold the cards for only a short period of time.

In those cases, an offer of up to 75 percent of book value still will allow the dealer to make a reasonable profit considering the short time he will need to hold the merchandise. In general, however, most cards and collections will bring offers in the range of 25 to 50 percent of retail price. Also consider that most material from the past five to 10 years is plentiful. If that's what you're selling, don't be surprised if your best offer is well below that range.

Interesting Notes

The first card numerically of an issue is the single card most likely to obtain excessive wear. Consequently, you typically will find the price on the #1 card (in NrMt or Mint condition) somewhat higher than might otherwise be the case. Similarly, but to a lesser extent (because normally the less important, reverse side of the card is the one exposed), the last card numerically in an issue also is prone to abnormal wear. This extra wear and tear occurs because the first and last cards are exposed to the elements (human element included) more than any other cards. They are generally end cards in any brick formations, rubber bandings, stackings on wet surfaces, and like activities.

Sports cards have no intrinsic value. The value of a card, like the value of other collectibles, can be determined only by you and your enjoyment in viewing and possessing these cardboard treasures.

Remember, the buyer ultimately determines the price of each card. You are the determining price factor because you have the ability to say "No" to the price of any card by not exchanging your hard-earned money for a given card. When the cost of a trading card exceeds the enjoyment you will receive from it, your answer should be "No." We assess and report the prices. You set them!

We are always interested in receiving the price input of collectors and dealers from around the country. We happily credit all contributors. We welcome your opinions, since your contributions assist us in ensuring a better guide each year. If you would like to join our survey list for the next editions of this book and others authored by Dr. Beckett, please send your name and address to Dr. James Beckett, 15850 Dallas Parkway, Dallas, Texas 75248.

History of Basketball Cards

The earliest basketball collectibles known are team postcards issued at the turn of the 20th century. Many of these postcards feature collegiate or high school teams of that day. Postcards were intermittently issued throughout the first half of the 20th century, with the bulk of them coming out in the 1920s and '30s. Unfortunately, the cataloging of these collectibles is sporadic at best. In addition, many collectors consider these postcards as memorabilia more so than trading cards, thus their exclusion from this book.

In 1910, College Athlete Felts (catalog number B-33) made their debut. Of a total of 270 felts, 20 featured basketball plays.

The first true basketball trading cards were issued by Murad cigarettes in 1911. The "College Series" cards depict a number of various sports and colleges, including four basketball cards (Luther, Northwestern, Williams and Xavier). In addition to these small (2-by-3 inch) cards, Murad issued a large (8-by-5 inch) basketball card featuring Williams college (catalog number T-6) as part of another multisport set.

The first basketball cards ever to be issued in gum packs were distributed in 1933 by Goudey in its multisport Sport Kings set, which was the first issue to list individual and professional players. Four cards from the complete 48-card set feature Boston Celtics basketball players Nat Holman, Ed Wachter, Joe Lapchick and Eddie Burke.

The period of growth that the NBA experienced from 1948 to 1951 marked the first initial boom, both for that sport and the cards that chronicle it. In 1948, Bowman created the first trading card set exclusively devoted to basketball cards, ushering in the modern era of hoops collectibles. The 72-card Bowman set contains the Rookie Card of HOFer George Mikan, one of the most valuable, and important, basketball cards in the hobby. Mikan, pro basketball's first dominant big man, set the stage for Bill Russell, Wilt Chamberlain and all the other legendary centers who have played the game since.

In addition to the Bowman release, Topps included 11 basketball cards in its 252-card multisport 1948 Magic Photo set. Five of the cards feature individual players (including collegiate great "Easy" Ed Macauley), another five feature colleges, and one additional card highlights a Manhattan-Dartmouth game. These 11 cards represent Topps first effort to produce basketball trading cards. Kellogg's also created an 18-card multisport set of trading cards in 1948 that were inserted into boxes of Pep cereal. The only basketball card in the set features Mikan. Throughout 1948 and 1949, the Exhibit Supply Company of Chicago issued oversized thick-stock multisport trading cards in conjunction with the 1948 Olympic games. Six basketball players were featured, including HOFers Mikan and Joe Fulks, among others. The cards were distributed through penny arcade machines.

In 1950-51, Scott's Chips issued a 13-card set featuring the Minneapolis Lakers. The cards were issued in Scott's Potato and Cheese Potato Chip boxes. The cards are extremely scarce today due to the fact that many were redeemed back in 1950-51 in exchange for game tickets and signed team pictures. This set contains possibly the scarcest Mikan issue in existence. In 1951, a Philadelphia-based meat company called Berk Ross issued a four-series, 72-card multisport set. The set contains five different basketball players, including the first cards of HOFers Bob Cousy and Bill Sharman.

Wheaties issued an oversized six-card multisport set on the backs of its cereal boxes in 1951. The only basketball player featured in the set is Mikan.

In 1952, Wheaties expanded the cereal box set to 30 cards, including six issues featuring basketball players of that day. Of these six cards, two feature Mikan (a portrait and an action shot). The 1952 cards are significantly smaller than the previous year's issue. That same year, the 32-card Bread for Health set was issued. The set was one of the few trading card issues of that decade exclusively devoted to the sport of basketball. The cards are actually bread end labels and were probably meant to be housed in an album. To date, the only companies known to have issued this set are Fisher's Bread in the New Jersey, New York and Pennsylvania areas and NBC Bread in the Michigan area.

One must skip ahead to 1957-58 to find the next major basketball issue, again produced by Topps. Its 80-card basketball set from that year is recognized within the hobby as the second major modern basketball issue, including Rookie Cards of all-time greats such as Bill Russell, Bob Cousy and Bob Pettit.

In 1960, Post cereal created a nine-card multisport set by devoting most of the back of the actual cereal boxes to full color picture frames of the athletes. HOFers Cousy and Pettit are the two featured basketball players.

In 1961-62, Fleer issued the third major basketball set. The 66-card set contains the Rookie Cards of all-time greats such as Wilt Chamberlain, Oscar Robertson and Jerry West. That same year, Bell Brand Potato Chips inserted trading cards (one per bag) featuring the L.A. Lakers team of that year and including scarce, early issues of HOFers West and Elgin Baylor.

From 1963 to 1968 no major companies manufactured basketball cards. Kahn's (an Ohio-based meat company) issued small regional basketball sets from 1957-58 through 1965-66 (including the first cards of Jerry West and

Oscar Robertson in its 1960-61 set). All the Kahn's sets feature members of the Cincinnati Royals, except for the few issues featuring the Lakers' West.

In 1968, Topps printed a very limited quantity of standard-size black-and-white test issue cards, preluding its 1969-70 nationwide return to the basketball card market.

The 1969-70 Topps set began a 13-year run of producing nationally distributed basketball card sets which ended in 1981-82. This was about the time the league's popularity bottomed out and was about to begin its ascent to the lofty level it's at today.

Topps' run included several sets that are troublesome for today's collectors. The 1969-70, 1970-71 and 1976-77 sets are larger than standard size, thus making them hard to store and preserve. The 1980-81 set consists of standard-size panels containing three cards each. Completing and cataloging the 1980-81 set (which features the classic Larry Bird RC/Magic Johnson RC/Julius Erving panel) is challenging, to say the least.

In 1983, this basketball card void was filled by the Star Company, a small company which issued three attractive sets of basketball cards, along with a plethora of peripheral sets. Star's 1983-84 premiere offering was issued in four groups, with the first series (cards 1-100) very difficult to obtain, as many of the early team subsets were miscut and destroyed before release. The 1984-85 and 1985-86 sets were more widely and evenly distributed. Even so, players' initial appearances on any of the three Star Company sets are considered Extended Rookie Cards, not regular Rookie Cards, because of the relatively limited distribution. Chief among these is Michael Jordan's 1984-85 Star XRC, the most valuable sports card issued in a 1980s major set.

Then, in 1986, Fleer took over the rights to produce cards for the NBA. Their 1986-87, 1987-88 and 1988-89 sets each contain 132 attractive, colorful cards depicting mostly stars and superstars. They were sold in the familiar wax pack format (12 cards and one sticker per pack). Fleer increased its set size to 168 in 1989-90, and was joined by NBA Hoops, which produced a 300-card first series (containing David Robinson's only Rookie Card) and a 52-card second series. The demand for all three Star Company sets, along with the first four Fleer sets and the premiere NBA Hoops set, skyrocketed during the early part of 1990.

The basketball card market stabilized somewhat in 1990-91, with both Fleer and Hoops stepping up production tremendously. A new major set, SkyBox, also made a splash in the market with its unique "high-tech" cards featuring computer-generated backgrounds. Because of overproduction, none of the three major 1990-91 sets have experienced significant price growth, although the increased competition has led to higher quality and more innovative products.

Another milestone in 1990-91 was the first-time inclusion of current rookies in update sets (NBA Hoops and SkyBox Series II, Fleer Update). The NBA Hoops and SkyBox issues contain just the 11 lottery picks, while Fleer's 100-card boxed set includes all rookies of any significance. A small company called "Star Pics" (not to be confused with Star Company) tried to fill this niche by printing a 70-card set in late 1990, but because the set was not licensed by the NBA, it is not considered a major set by the majority of collectors. It does, however, contain the first nationally distributed cards of 1990-91 rookies such as Derrick Coleman and Kendall Gill, among others.

In 1991-92, the draft pick set market that Star Pics opened in 1990-91 expanded to include several competitors. More significantly, that season brought with it the three established NBA card brands plus Upper Deck, known throughout the hobby for its high quality card stock and photography in other sports. Upper Deck's first basketball set probably captured NBA action better than any previous set. But its value — like all other major 1990-91 and 1991-92 NBA sets — declined because of overproduction.

On the bright side, the historic entrance of NBA players to Olympic competition kept interest in basketball cards going long after the Chicago Bulls won their second straight NBA championship. So for at least one year, the basketball card market — probably the most seasonal of the four major team sports — remained in the spotlight for an extended period of time.

The 1992-93 season will be remembered as the year of Shaq — the debut campaign of the most heralded rookie in many years. Shaquille O'Neal headlined the most promising rookie class in NBA history, sparking unprecedented interest in basketball cards. Among O'Neal's many talented rookie companions were Alonzo Mourning, Jim Jackson and Latrell Sprewell.

Classic Games, known primarily for producing draft picks and minor league baseball cards, signed O'Neal to an exclusive contract through 1992, thus postponing the appearances of O'Neal's NBA-licensed cards.

Shaquille's Classic and NBA cards, particularly the inserts, became some of the most sought-after collectibles in years. As a direct result of O'Neal and his fellow rookie standouts, the basketball card market achieved a new level of popularity in 1993.

The hobby rode that crest of popularity throughout the 1993-94 season. Michael Jordan may have retired, but his absence only spurred interest in some of his tougher inserts. Another strong rookie class followed Shaq, and Reggie Miller elevated his collectibility to a superstar level. Hakeem Olajuwon, by leading the Rockets to an NBA title, boosted his early cards to levels surpassed only by Jordan.

No new cardmakers came on board, but super premium Topps Finest raised the stakes, and the parallel set came into its own.

In 1994-95, the return of Michael Jordan, coupled with the high impact splash of Detroit Pistons rookie Grant Hill, kept collector interest high. In addition, the NBA granted all the licensed manufacturers the opportunity to create a fourth brand of basketball cards that year, allowing each company to create a selection of clearly defined niche products at different price points. The manufacturers also expanded the calendar release dates with 1994-95 cards being released on a consistent basis from August, 1994 all the way through June, 1995. The super-premium card market expanded greatly as the battle for the best selling five dollar (or more) pack reached epic levels by season's end. The key new super premium products included the premier of SP, Embossed and Emotion. This has continued through 1996 with the release of SPX, which contained only one card per pack.

Additional Reading

Each year Beckett Publications produces comprehensive annual price guides for each of the four major sports: *Beckett Baseball Card Price Guide, Beckett Football Card Price Guide, Beckett Basketball Card Price Guide,* and *Beckett Hockey Card Price Guide.* The aim of these annual guides is to provide information and accurate pricing on a wide array of sports cards, ranging from main issues by the major card manufacturers to various regional, promotional, and food issues. Also alphabetical checklists, such as *Sport Americana Baseball Card Alphabetical Checklist #6,* are published to assist the collector in identifying all the cards of a particular player. The seasoned collector will find these tools valuable sources of information that will enable him to pursue his hobby interests.

In addition, abridged editions of the Beckett Price Guides have been published for each of the four major sports as part of the House of Collectible series: *The Official Price Guide to Baseball Cards, The Official Price Guide to Football Cards, The Official Price Guide to Basketball Cards,* and *The Official Price Guide to Hockey Cards.* Published in a convenient mass-market paperback format, these price guides provide information and accurate pricing on all the main issues by the major card manufacturers.

Advertising

Within this Price Guide you will find advertisements for sports memorabilia material, mail order, and retail sports collectibles establishments. All advertisements were accepted in good faith based on the reputation of the advertiser; however, neither the author, the publisher, the distributors, nor the other advertisers in this Price Guide accept any responsibility for any particular advertiser not complying with the terms of his or her ad.

Readers also should be aware that prices in advertisements are subject to change over the annual period before a new edition of this volume is issued each spring. When replying to an advertisement late in the basketball year, the reader should take this into account, and contact the dealer by phone or in writing for up-to-date price information. Should you come into contact with any of the advertisers in this guide as a result of their advertisement herein, please mention this source as your contact.

Prices in This Guide

Prices found in this guide reflect current retail rates just prior to the printing of this book. They do not reflect the FOR SALE prices of the author, the publisher, the distributors, the advertisers, or any card dealers associated with this guide. No one is obligated in any way to buy, sell or trade his or her cards based on these prices. The price listings were compiled by the author from actual buy/sell transactions at sports conventions, sports card shops, buy/sell advertisements in the hobby papers, for sale prices from dealer catalogs and price lists, and discussions with leading hobbyists in the U.S. and Canada. All prices are in U.S. dollars.

Acknowledgments

A great deal of diligence, hard work, and dedicated effort went into this year's volume. The high standards to which we hold ourselves, however, could not have been met without the expert input and generous amount of time contributed by many people. Our sincere thanks are extended to each and every one of you.

A complete list of these invaluable contributors appears after the price guide.

1948 Bowman

The 1948 Bowman set of 72 cards was the company's only basketball issue. Five cards were issued in each pack. It was also the only major basketball issue until 1957-58 when Topps released a set. Cards in the set measure 2 1/16" by 2 1/2". The set is in color and features both player cards and diagram cards. The player cards in the second series are sometimes found without the red or blue printing on the card front, leaving only a gray background. These gray versions are more difficult to find, as they are printing errors where the printer apparently ran out of red or blue ink that was supposed to print on the player's uniform. The key Rookie Card in this set is George Mikan. Other Rookie Cards include Carl Braun, Joe Fulks, William "Red" Holzman, Jim Pollard, and Max Zaslofsky.

		EX-MT	VG-E	GOOD
COMPLETE SET (72)		8000.00	3600.00	1000.00
COMMON CARD (1-36)		60.00	27.00	7.50
COMMON CARD (37-72)		100.00	45.00	12.50
☐ 1	Ernie Calverley	250.00	75.00	25.00
☐ 2	Ralph Hamilton	60.00	27.00	7.50
☐ 3	Gale Bishop	60.00	27.00	7.50
☐ 4	Fred Lewis CO	70.00	32.00	8.75
☐ 5	Basketball Play	50.00	22.00	6.25
	Single cut off post			
☐ 6	Bob Ferrick	70.00	32.00	8.75
☐ 7	John Logan	60.00	27.00	7.50
☐ 8	Mel Riebe	60.00	27.00	7.50
☐ 9	Andy Phillip	150.00	70.00	19.00
☐ 10	Bob Davies	175.00	80.00	22.00
☐ 11	Basketball Play	50.00	22.00	6.25
	Single cut with			
	return pass to post			
☐ 12	Kenny Sailors	70.00	32.00	8.75
☐ 13	Paul Armstrong	60.00	27.00	7.50
☐ 14	Howard Dallmar	70.00	32.00	8.75
☐ 15	Bruce Hale	70.00	32.00	8.75
☐ 16	Sid Hertzberg	60.00	27.00	7.50
☐ 17	Basketball Play	50.00	22.00	6.25
	Single cut			
☐ 18	Red Rocha	60.00	27.00	7.50
☐ 19	Eddie Ehlers	60.00	27.00	7.50
☐ 20	Ellis(Gene) Vance	60.00	27.00	7.50
☐ 21	Andrew(Fuzzy) Levane	70.00	32.00	8.75
☐ 22	Earl Shannon	60.00	27.00	7.50
☐ 23	Basketball Play	50.00	22.00	6.25
	Double cut off post			
☐ 24	Leo(Crystal) Klier	60.00	27.00	7.50
☐ 25	George Senesky	60.00	27.00	7.50
☐ 26	Price Brookfield	60.00	27.00	7.50
☐ 27	John Norlander	60.00	27.00	7.50
☐ 28	Don Putman	60.00	27.00	7.50
☐ 29	Basketball Play	50.00	22.00	6.25
	Double post			
☐ 30	Jack Garfinkel	60.00	27.00	7.50
☐ 31	Chuck Gilmur	60.00	27.00	7.50
☐ 32	William Holzman	425.00	190.00	52.50
☐ 33	Jack Smiley	60.00	27.00	7.50
☐ 34	Joe Fulks	425.00	190.00	52.50
☐ 35	Basketball Play	50.00	22.00	6.25
	Screen play			
☐ 36	Hal Tidrick	60.00	27.00	7.50
☐ 37	Don(Swede) Carlson	100.00	45.00	12.50
☐ 38	Buddy Jeanette CO	150.00	70.00	19.00
☐ 39	Ray Kuka	100.00	45.00	12.50
☐ 40	Stan Miasek	100.00	45.00	12.50
☐ 41	Basketball Play	80.00	36.00	10.00
	Double screen			
☐ 42	George Nostrand	100.00	45.00	12.50
☐ 43	Chuck Halbert	125.00	55.00	15.50
☐ 44	Arnie Johnson	100.00	45.00	12.50
☐ 45	Bob Doll	100.00	45.00	12.50
☐ 46	Horace McKinney	140.00	65.00	17.50
☐ 47	Basketball Play	80.00	36.00	10.00
	Out of bounds			
☐ 48	Ed Sadowski	100.00	45.00	12.50
☐ 49	Bob Kinney	100.00	45.00	12.50
☐ 50	Charles(Hawk) Black	100.00	45.00	12.50
☐ 51	Jack Dwan	100.00	45.00	12.50
☐ 52	Cornelius Simmons	125.00	55.00	15.50
☐ 53	Basketball Play	80.00	36.00	10.00
	Out of bounds			
☐ 54	Bud Palmer	150.00	70.00	19.00
☐ 55	Max Zaslofsky	300.00	135.00	38.00
☐ 56	Lee Roy Robbins	100.00	45.00	12.50
☐ 57	Arthur Spector	100.00	45.00	12.50
☐ 58	Arnie Risen	150.00	70.00	19.00
☐ 59	Basketball Play	80.00	36.00	10.00
	Out of bounds play			
☐ 60	Ariel Maughan	100.00	45.00	12.50
☐ 61	Dick O'Keefe	100.00	45.00	12.50
☐ 62	Herman Schaefer	100.00	45.00	12.50
☐ 63	John Mahnken	100.00	45.00	12.50
☐ 64	Tommy Byrnes	100.00	45.00	12.50
☐ 65	Basketball Play	80.00	36.00	10.00
	Held ball			
☐ 66	Jim Pollard	425.00	190.00	52.50
☐ 67	Lee Mogus	100.00	45.00	12.50
☐ 68	Lee Knorek	100.00	45.00	12.50
☐ 69	George Mikan	4500.00	2000.00	550.00
☐ 70	Walter Budko	100.00	45.00	12.50
☐ 71	Basketball Play	80.00	36.00	10.00
	Guards Play			
☐ 72	Carl Braun	450.00	135.00	45.00

1994-95 Collector's Choice

These 420 standard-size cards, issued in two separate series of 210-cards each, comprise Upper Deck's '94-95 Collector's Choice set. Cards were issued in 12-card hobby packs (suggested retail of ninety-nine cents), 13-card retail packs (suggest-

ed retail of $1.18), and 20-card retail jumbo packs. White bordered fronts feature color player action shots. The player's name, team, and position appear in a lower corner. The back carries another color player action shot at the top, with statistics and career highlights displayed below. The following subsets are included in this set: Tip-Off (166-192), All-Star Advice (193-198), NBA Profiles (199-206), Blueprints (372-398), Trivia (399-406), and Draft Class (407-416). Rookie Cards in this set include Grant Hill, Juwan Howard, Eddie Jones, Jason Kidd and Glenn Robinson.

	MINT	NRMT	EXC
COMPLETE SET (420)	30.00	13.50	3.70
COMPLETE SERIES 1 (210)	12.00	5.50	1.50
COMPLETE SERIES 2 (210)	18.00	8.00	2.20
COMMON CARD (1-420)	.05	.02	.01

☐ 1	Anfernee Hardaway	1.25	.55	.16
☐ 2	Mark Macon	.05	.02	.01
☐ 3	Steve Smith	.10	.05	.01
☐ 4	Chris Webber	.25	.11	.03
☐ 5	Donald Royal	.05	.02	.01
☐ 6	Avery Johnson	.05	.02	.01
☐ 7	Kevin Johnson	.10	.05	.01
☐ 8	Doug Christie	.05	.02	.01
☐ 9	Derrick McKey	.05	.02	.01
☐ 10	Dennis Rodman	.75	.35	.09
☐ 11	Scott Skiles UER	.05	.02	.01
	(Listed as playing with Cavaliers instead of Pacers in '87-'88, '88-'89)			
☐ 12	Johnny Dawkins	.05	.02	.01
☐ 13	Kendall Gill	.05	.02	.01
☐ 14	Jeff Hornacek	.10	.05	.01
☐ 15	Latrell Sprewell	.30	.14	.04
☐ 16	Lucious Harris	.05	.02	.01
☐ 17	Chris Mullin	.10	.05	.01
☐ 18	John Williams	.05	.02	.01
☐ 19	Tony Campbell	.05	.02	.01
☐ 20	LaPhonso Ellis	.05	.02	.01
☐ 21	Gerald Wilkins	.05	.02	.01
☐ 22	Clyde Drexler	.25	.11	.03
☐ 23	Michael Jordan	2.50	1.10	.30
☐ 24	George Lynch	.05	.02	.01
☐ 25	Mark Price	.05	.02	.01
☐ 26	James Robinson	.05	.02	.01
☐ 27	Elmore Spencer	.05	.02	.01
☐ 28	Stacey King	.05	.02	.01
☐ 29	Corie Blount	.05	.02	.01
☐ 30	Dell Curry	.05	.02	.01
☐ 31	Reggie Miller	.25	.11	.03
☐ 32	Karl Malone	.20	.09	.03
☐ 33	Scottie Pippen	.60	.25	.07
☐ 34	Hakeem Olajuwon	.50	.23	.06
☐ 35	Clarence Weatherspoon	.05	.02	.01
☐ 36	Kevin Edwards	.05	.02	.01
☐ 37	Pete Myers	.05	.02	.01
☐ 38	Jeff Turner	.05	.02	.01
☐ 39	Ennis Whatley	.05	.02	.01
☐ 40	Calbert Cheaney	.10	.05	.01
☐ 41	Glen Rice	.10	.05	.01
☐ 42	Vin Baker	.25	.11	.03
☐ 43	Grant Long	.05	.02	.01
☐ 44	Derrick Coleman	.05	.02	.01
☐ 45	Rik Smits	.10	.05	.01
☐ 46	Chris Smith	.05	.02	.01
☐ 47	Carl Herrera	.05	.02	.01
☐ 48	Bob Martin	.05	.02	.01
☐ 49	Terrell Brandon	.10	.05	.01
☐ 50	David Robinson	.40	.18	.05
☐ 51	Danny Ferry	.05	.02	.01
☐ 52	Buck Williams	.10	.05	.01
☐ 53	Josh Grant	.05	.02	.01
☐ 54	Ed Pinckney	.05	.02	.01
☐ 55	Dikembe Mutombo	.10	.05	.01
☐ 56	Clifford Robinson	.10	.05	.01
☐ 57	Luther Wright	.05	.02	.01
☐ 58	Scott Burrell	.05	.02	.01
☐ 59	Stacey Augmon	.10	.05	.01
☐ 60	Jeff Malone	.05	.02	.01
☐ 61	Byron Houston	.05	.02	.01
☐ 62	Anthony Peeler	.05	.02	.01
☐ 63	Michael Adams	.05	.02	.01
☐ 64	Negele Knight	.05	.02	.01
☐ 65	Terry Cummings	.05	.02	.01
☐ 66	Christian Laettner	.10	.05	.01
☐ 67	Tracy Murray	.05	.02	.01
☐ 68	Sedale Threatt	.05	.02	.01
☐ 69	Dan Majerle	.10	.05	.01
☐ 70	Frank Brickowski	.05	.02	.01
☐ 71	Ken Norman	.05	.02	.01
☐ 72	Charles Smith	.05	.02	.01
☐ 73	Adam Keefe	.05	.02	.01
☐ 74	P.J. Brown	.05	.02	.01
☐ 75	Kevin Duckworth	.05	.02	.01
☐ 76	Shawn Bradley UER	.10	.05	.01
	Bradely on back			
☐ 77	Darnell Mee	.05	.02	.01
☐ 78	Nick Anderson	.10	.05	.01
☐ 79	Mark West	.05	.02	.01
☐ 80	B.J. Armstrong	.05	.02	.01
☐ 81	Dennis Scott	.10	.05	.01
☐ 82	Lindsey Hunter	.05	.02	.01
☐ 83	Derek Strong	.05	.02	.01
☐ 84	Mike Brown	.05	.02	.01
☐ 85	Antonio Harvey	.05	.02	.01
☐ 86	Anthony Bonner	.05	.02	.01
☐ 87	Sam Cassell	.10	.05	.01
☐ 88	Harold Miner	.05	.02	.01
☐ 89	Spud Webb	.10	.05	.01
☐ 90	Mookie Blaylock	.10	.05	.01
☐ 91	Greg Anthony	.05	.02	.01
☐ 92	Richard Petruska	.05	.02	.01
☐ 93	Sean Rooks	.05	.02	.01
☐ 94	Ervin Johnson	.05	.02	.01
☐ 95	Randy Brown	.05	.02	.01
☐ 96	Orlando Woolridge	.05	.02	.01
☐ 97	Charles Oakley	.10	.05	.01
☐ 98	Craig Ehlo	.05	.02	.01
☐ 99	Derek Harper	.05	.02	.01
☐ 100	Doug Edwards	.05	.02	.01
☐ 101	Muggsy Bogues	.10	.05	.01
☐ 102	Mitch Richmond	.15	.07	.02
☐ 103	Mahmoud Abdul-Rauf	.10	.05	.01
☐ 104	Joe Dumars	.10	.05	.01

#	Player			
☐ 105	Eric Riley	.05	.02	.01
☐ 106	Terry Mills	.05	.02	.01
☐ 107	Toni Kukoc	.15	.07	.02
☐ 108	Jon Koncak	.05	.02	.01
☐ 109	Haywoode Workman	.05	.02	.01
☐ 110	Todd Day	.05	.02	.01
☐ 111	Detlef Schrempf	.10	.05	.01
☐ 112	David Wesley	.05	.02	.01
☐ 113	Mark Jackson	.05	.02	.01
☐ 114	Doug Overton	.05	.02	.01
☐ 115	Vinny Del Negro	.05	.02	.01
☐ 116	Loy Vaught	.05	.02	.01
☐ 117	Mike Peplowski	.05	.02	.01
☐ 118	Bimbo Coles	.05	.02	.01
☐ 119	Rex Walters	.05	.02	.01
☐ 120	Sherman Douglas	.05	.02	.01
☐ 121	David Benoit	.05	.02	.01
☐ 122	John Salley	.05	.02	.01
☐ 123	Cedric Ceballos	.10	.05	.01
☐ 124	Chris Mills	.10	.05	.01
☐ 125	Robert Horry	.10	.05	.01
☐ 126	Johnny Newman	.05	.02	.01
☐ 127	Malcolm Mackey	.05	.02	.01
☐ 128	Terry Dehere	.05	.02	.01
☐ 129	Dino Radja	.10	.05	.01
☐ 130	Tree Rollins	.05	.02	.01
☐ 131	Xavier McDaniel	.05	.02	.01
☐ 132	Bobby Hurley	.05	.02	.01
☐ 133	Alonzo Mourning	.25	.11	.03
☐ 134	Isaiah Rider	.10	.05	.01
☐ 135	Antoine Carr	.05	.02	.01
☐ 136	Robert Pack	.05	.02	.01
☐ 137	Walt Williams	.10	.05	.01
☐ 138	Tyrone Corbin	.05	.02	.01
☐ 139	Popeye Jones	.05	.02	.01
☐ 140	Shawn Kemp	.60	.25	.07
☐ 141	Thurl Bailey	.05	.02	.01
☐ 142	James Worthy	.10	.05	.01
☐ 143	Scott Haskin	.05	.02	.01
☐ 144	Hubert Davis	.05	.02	.01
☐ 145	A.C. Green	.10	.05	.01
☐ 146	Dale Davis	.05	.02	.01
☐ 147	Nate McMillan	.05	.02	.01
☐ 148	Chris Morris	.05	.02	.01
☐ 149	Will Perdue	.05	.02	.01
☐ 150	Felton Spencer	.05	.02	.01
☐ 151	Rod Strickland	.05	.02	.01
☐ 152	Blue Edwards	.05	.02	.01
☐ 153	John Williams	.05	.02	.01
☐ 154	Rodney Rogers	.05	.02	.01
☐ 155	Acie Earl	.05	.02	.01
☐ 156	Hersey Hawkins	.05	.02	.01
☐ 157	Jamal Mashburn	.15	.07	.02
☐ 158	Don MacLean	.05	.02	.01
☐ 159	Micheal Williams	.05	.02	.01
☐ 160	Kenny Gattison	.05	.02	.01
☐ 161	Rich King	.05	.02	.01
☐ 162	Allan Houston	.15	.07	.02
☐ 163	Hoop-it up	.05	.02	.01
	Men's Champions			
☐ 164	Hoop-it up	.10	.05	.01
	Women's Champions			
	Lisa Harrison			
☐ 165	Hoop-it up	.10	.05	.01
	Slam-Dunk Champions			
	Corey Etheridge			
☐ 166	Danny Manning TO	.05	.02	.01
☐ 167	Robert Parish TO	.05	.02	.01
☐ 168	Alonzo Mourning TO	.10	.05	.01
☐ 169	Scottie Pippen TO	.30	.14	.04
☐ 170	Mark Price TO	.05	.02	.01
☐ 171	Jamal Mashburn TO	.10	.05	.01
☐ 172	Dikembe Mutombo TO	.05	.02	.01
☐ 173	Joe Dumars TO	.05	.02	.01
☐ 174	Chris Webber TO	.15	.07	.02
☐ 175	Hakeem Olajuwon TO	.25	.11	.03
☐ 176	Reggie Miller TO	.15	.07	.02
☐ 177	Ron Harper TO	.05	.02	.01
☐ 178	Nick Van Exel TO	.25	.11	.03
☐ 179	Steve Smith TO	.05	.02	.01
☐ 180	Vin Baker TO	.10	.05	.01
☐ 181	Isaiah Rider TO	.05	.02	.01
☐ 182	Derrick Coleman TO	.05	.02	.01
☐ 183	Patrick Ewing TO	.10	.05	.01
☐ 184	Shaquille O'Neal TO	.50	.23	.06
☐ 185	Clarence Weatherspoon TO	.05	.02	.01
☐ 186	Charles Barkley TO	.15	.07	.02
☐ 187	Clyde Drexler TO	.10	.05	.01
☐ 188	Mitch Richmond TO	.05	.02	.01
☐ 189	David Robinson TO	.20	.09	.03
☐ 190	Shawn Kemp TO	.30	.14	.04
☐ 191	Karl Malone TO	.10	.05	.01
☐ 192	Tom Gugliotta TO	.05	.02	.01
☐ 193	Kenny Anderson ASA	.05	.02	.01
☐ 194	Alonzo Mourning ASA	.10	.05	.01
☐ 195	Mark Price ASA	.05	.02	.01
☐ 196	John Stockton ASA	.10	.05	.01
☐ 197	Shaquille O'Neal ASA	.50	.23	.06
☐ 198	Latrell Sprewell ASA	.05	.02	.01
☐ 199	Charles Barkley PRO	.15	.07	.02
☐ 200	Chris Webber PRO	.15	.07	.02
☐ 201	Patrick Ewing PRO	.10	.05	.01
☐ 202	Dennis Rodman PRO	.40	.18	.05
☐ 203	Shawn Kemp PRO	.30	.14	.04
☐ 204	Michael Jordan PRO	1.25	.55	.16
☐ 205	Shaquille O'Neal PRO	.50	.23	.06
☐ 206	Larry Johnson PRO	.10	.05	.01
☐ 207	Tim Hardaway CL	.05	.02	.01
☐ 208	John Stockton CL	.10	.05	.01
☐ 209	Harold Miner CL	.05	.02	.01
☐ 210	B.J. Armstrong CL	.05	.02	.01
☐ 211	Vernon Maxwell	.05	.02	.01
☐ 212	John Stockton	.20	.09	.03
☐ 213	Luc Longley	.05	.02	.01
☐ 214	Sam Perkins	.05	.02	.01
☐ 215	Pooh Richardson	.05	.02	.01
☐ 216	Tyrone Corbin	.05	.02	.01
☐ 217	Mario Elie	.05	.02	.01
☐ 218	Bobby Phills	.05	.02	.01
☐ 219	Grant Hill	2.50	1.10	.30
☐ 220	Gary Payton	.30	.14	.04
☐ 221	Tom Hammonds	.05	.02	.01
☐ 222	Danny Ainge	.10	.05	.01
☐ 223	Gary Grant	.05	.02	.01
☐ 224	Jimmy Jackson	.30	.14	.04
☐ 225	Chris Gatling	.05	.02	.01
☐ 226	Sergei Bazarevich	.05	.02	.01
☐ 227	Tony Dumas	.10	.05	.01
☐ 228	Andrew Lang	.05	.02	.01
☐ 229	Wesley Person	.50	.23	.06
☐ 230	Terry Porter	.05	.02	.01
☐ 231	Duane Causwell	.05	.02	.01
☐ 232	Shaquille O'Neal	1.00	.45	.12
☐ 233	Antonio Davis	.05	.02	.01
☐ 234	Charles Barkley	.30	.14	.04
☐ 235	Tony Massenburg	.05	.02	.01
☐ 236	Ricky Pierce	.05	.02	.01
☐ 237	Scott Skiles	.05	.02	.01
☐ 238	Jalen Rose	.20	.09	.03
☐ 239	Charlie Ward	.10	.05	.01
☐ 240	Michael Jordan	1.25	.55	.16

#	Player			
☐ 241	Elden Campbell	.10	.05	.01
☐ 242	Bill Cartwright	.05	.02	.01
☐ 243	Armon Gilliam	.05	.02	.01
☐ 244	Rick Fox	.05	.02	.01
☐ 245	Tim Breaux	.05	.02	.01
☐ 246	Monty Williams	.05	.02	.01
☐ 247	Dominique Wilkins	.10	.05	.01
☐ 248	Robert Parish	.10	.05	.01
☐ 249	Mark Jackson	.05	.02	.01
☐ 250	Jason Kidd	1.50	.70	.19
☐ 251	Andres Guibert	.05	.02	.01
☐ 252	Matt Geiger	.05	.02	.01
☐ 253	Stanley Roberts	.05	.02	.01
☐ 254	Jack Haley	.05	.02	.01
☐ 255	David Wingate	.05	.02	.01
☐ 256	John Crotty	.05	.02	.01
☐ 257	Brian Grant	.30	.14	.04
☐ 258	Otis Thorpe	.10	.05	.01
☐ 259	Clifford Rozier	.05	.02	.01
☐ 260	Grant Long	.05	.02	.01
☐ 261	Eric Mobley	.05	.02	.01
☐ 262	Dickey Simpkins	.05	.02	.01
☐ 263	J.R. Reid	.05	.02	.01
☐ 264	Kevin Willis	.05	.02	.01
☐ 265	Scott Brooks	.05	.02	.01
☐ 266	Glenn Robinson	.75	.35	.09
☐ 267	Dana Barros	.05	.02	.01
☐ 268	Kenny Norman	.05	.02	.01
☐ 269	Herb Williams	.05	.02	.01
☐ 270	Dee Brown	.05	.02	.01
☐ 271	Steve Kerr	.10	.05	.01
☐ 272	Jon Barry	.05	.02	.01
☐ 273	Sean Elliott	.10	.05	.01
☐ 274	Elliot Perry	.05	.02	.01
☐ 275	Kenny Smith	.05	.02	.01
☐ 276	Sean Rooks	.05	.02	.01
☐ 277	Gheorghe Muresan	.10	.05	.01
☐ 278	Juwan Howard	1.50	.70	.19
☐ 279	Steve Smith	.10	.05	.01
☐ 280	Anthony Bowie	.05	.02	.01
☐ 281	Moses Malone	.15	.07	.02
☐ 282	Olden Polynice	.05	.02	.01
☐ 283	Jo Jo English	.05	.02	.01
☐ 284	Marty Conlon	.05	.02	.01
☐ 285	Sam Mitchell	.05	.02	.01
☐ 286	Doug West	.05	.02	.01
☐ 287	Cedric Ceballos	.10	.05	.01
☐ 288	Lorenzo Williams	.05	.02	.01
☐ 289	Harold Ellis	.05	.02	.01
☐ 290	Doc Rivers	.05	.02	.01
☐ 291	Keith Tower	.05	.02	.01
☐ 292	Mark Bryant	.05	.02	.01
☐ 293	Oliver Miller	.05	.02	.01
☐ 294	Michael Adams	.05	.02	.01
☐ 295	Tree Rollins	.05	.02	.01
☐ 296	Eddie Jones	.50	.23	.06
☐ 297	Malik Sealy	.05	.02	.01
☐ 298	Blue Edwards	.05	.02	.01
☐ 299	Brooks Thompson	.10	.05	.01
☐ 300	Benoit Benjamin	.05	.02	.01
☐ 301	Avery Johnson	.10	.05	.01
☐ 302	Larry Johnson	.20	.09	.03
☐ 303	John Starks	.05	.02	.01
☐ 304	Byron Scott	.10	.05	.01
☐ 305	Eric Murdock	.05	.02	.01
☐ 306	Jay Humphries	.05	.02	.01
☐ 307	Kenny Anderson	.10	.05	.01
☐ 308	Brian Williams	.05	.02	.01
☐ 309	Nick Van Exel	.20	.09	.03
☐ 310	Tim Hardaway	.10	.05	.01
☐ 311	Lee Mayberry	.05	.02	.01
☐ 312	Vlade Divac	.10	.05	.01
☐ 313	Donyell Marshall	.10	.05	.01
☐ 314	Anthony Mason	.05	.02	.01
☐ 315	Danny Manning	.10	.05	.01
☐ 316	Tyrone Hill	.05	.02	.01
☐ 317	Vincent Askew	.05	.02	.01
☐ 318	Khalid Reeves	.10	.05	.01
☐ 319	Ron Harper	.05	.02	.01
☐ 320	Brent Price	.05	.02	.01
☐ 321	Byron Houston	.05	.02	.01
☐ 322	Lamond Murray	.10	.05	.01
☐ 323	Bryant Stith	.05	.02	.01
☐ 324	Tom Gugliotta	.05	.02	.01
☐ 325	Jerome Kersey	.05	.02	.01
☐ 326	B.J. Tyler	.05	.02	.01
☐ 327	Antonio Lang	.05	.02	.01
☐ 328	Carlos Rogers	.05	.02	.01
☐ 329	Wayman Tisdale	.05	.02	.01
☐ 330	Kevin Gamble	.05	.02	.01
☐ 331	Eric Piatkowski	.05	.02	.01
☐ 332	Mitchell Butler	.05	.02	.01
☐ 333	Patrick Ewing	.20	.09	.03
☐ 334	Doug Smith	.05	.02	.01
☐ 335	Joe Kleine	.05	.02	.01
☐ 336	Keith Jennings	.05	.02	.01
☐ 337	Bill Curley	.05	.02	.01
☐ 338	Johnny Newman	.05	.02	.01
☐ 339	Howard Eisley	.05	.02	.01
☐ 340	Willie Anderson	.05	.02	.01
☐ 341	Aaron McKie	.10	.05	.01
☐ 342	Tom Chambers	.05	.02	.01
☐ 343	Scott Williams	.05	.02	.01
☐ 344	Harvey Grant	.05	.02	.01
☐ 345	Billy Owens	.05	.02	.01
☐ 346	Sharone Wright	.10	.05	.01
☐ 347	Michael Cage	.05	.02	.01
☐ 348	Vern Fleming	.05	.02	.01
☐ 349	Darrin Hancock	.05	.02	.01
☐ 350	Matt Fish	.05	.02	.01
☐ 351	Rony Seikaly	.05	.02	.01
☐ 352	Victor Alexander	.05	.02	.01
☐ 353	Anthony Miller	.05	.02	.01
☐ 354	Horace Grant	.10	.05	.01
☐ 355	Jayson Williams	.05	.02	.01
☐ 356	Dale Ellis	.05	.02	.01
☐ 357	Sarunas Marciulionis	.05	.02	.01
☐ 358	Anthony Avent	.05	.02	.01
☐ 359	Rex Chapman	.05	.02	.01
☐ 360	Askia Jones	.05	.02	.01
☐ 361	Charles Outlaw	.05	.02	.01
☐ 362	Chuck Person	.05	.02	.01
☐ 363	Dan Schayes	.05	.02	.01
☐ 364	Morlon Wiley	.05	.02	.01
☐ 365	Dontonio Wingfield	.05	.02	.01
☐ 366	Tony Smith	.05	.02	.01
☐ 367	Bill Wennington	.05	.02	.01
☐ 368	Bryon Russell	.05	.02	.01
☐ 369	Geert Hammink	.05	.02	.01
☐ 370	Eric Montross	.10	.05	.01
☐ 371	Cliff Levingston	.05	.02	.01
☐ 372	Stacey Augmon BP	.05	.02	.01
☐ 373	Eric Montross BP	.05	.02	.01
☐ 374	Alonzo Mourning BP	.10	.05	.01
☐ 375	Scottie Pippen BP	.30	.14	.04
☐ 376	Mark Price BP	.05	.02	.01
☐ 377	Jason Kidd BP	.60	.25	.07
☐ 378	Jalen Rose BP	.10	.05	.01
☐ 379	Grant Hill BP	1.00	.45	.12
☐ 380	Latrell Sprewell BP	.05	.02	.01
☐ 381	Hakeem Olajuwon BP	.25	.11	.03
☐ 382	Reggie Miller BP	.15	.07	.02

		MINT	NRMT	EXC
☐ 383	Lamond Murray BP	.05	.02	.01
☐ 384	Eddie Jones BP	.20	.09	.03
☐ 385	Khalid Reeves BP	.05	.02	.01
☐ 386	Glenn Robinson BP	.30	.14	.04
☐ 387	Donyell Marshall BP	.05	.02	.01
☐ 388	Derrick Coleman BP	.05	.02	.01
☐ 389	Patrick Ewing BP	.10	.05	.01
☐ 390	Shaquille O'Neal BP	.50	.23	.06
☐ 391	Sharone Wright BP	.05	.02	.01
☐ 392	Charles Barkley BP	.15	.07	.02
☐ 393	Aaron McKie BP	.05	.02	.01
☐ 394	Brian Grant BP	.10	.05	.01
☐ 395	David Robinson BP	.20	.09	.03
☐ 396	Shawn Kemp BP	.30	.14	.04
☐ 397	Karl Malone BP	.10	.05	.01
☐ 398	Tom Gugliotta BP	.05	.02	.01
☐ 399	Hakeem Olajuwon TRIV	.25	.11	.03
☐ 400	Shaquille O'Neal TRIV	.50	.23	.06
☐ 401	Chris Webber TRIV	.15	.07	.02
☐ 402	Michael Jordan TRIV	1.25	.55	.16
☐ 403	David Robinson TRIV	.20	.09	.03
☐ 404	Shawn Kemp TRIV	.30	.14	.04
☐ 405	Patrick Ewing TRIV	.10	.05	.01
☐ 406	Charles Barkley TRIV	.15	.07	.02
☐ 407	Glenn Robinson DC	.30	.14	.04
☐ 408	Jason Kidd DC	.60	.25	.07
☐ 409	Grant Hill DC	1.00	.45	.12
☐ 410	Donyell Marshall DC	.05	.02	.01
☐ 411	Sharone Wright DC	.05	.02	.01
☐ 412	Lamond Murray DC	.05	.02	.01
☐ 413	Brian Grant DC	.10	.05	.01
☐ 414	Eric Montross DC	.05	.02	.01
☐ 415	Eddie Jones DC	.20	.09	.03
☐ 416	Carlos Rogers DC	.05	.02	.01
☐ 417	Shawn Kemp CL	.10	.05	.01
☐ 418	Bobby Hurley CL	.05	.02	.01
☐ 419	Shawn Bradley CL	.05	.02	.01
☐ 420	Michael Jordan CL	.60	.25	.07

1994-95 Collector's Choice Silver Signature

Issued one per Collector's Choice 12-card hobby pack, two per 13-card retail pack, and three per 20-card retail jumbo pack, these 420 standard-size cards parallel that of the basic 1994-95 Collector's Choice set. The difference is the player's facsimile autograph appears in silver-foil near the bottom and the front borders are colored in silver. A handful of first year players were

not available for facsimile autographs and have team names scripted in silver foil instead. Please refer to the multiplier provided (and the values listed for the regular-issue 1994-95 Collector's Choice cards) to ascertain the value of the silver cards.

	MINT	NRMT	EXC
COMPLETE SET (420)	100.00	45.00	12.50
COMPLETE SERIES 1 (210)	40.00	18.00	5.00
COMPLETE SERIES 2 (210)	60.00	27.00	7.50
COMMON SILVER (1-420)	.10	.05	.01
SEMISTARS	.25	.11	.03
*STARS: 1.5X to 3X BASIC CARDS			
*ROOKIES: 1X to 2X BASIC CARDS			

1994-95 Collector's Choice Gold Signature

Issued one in every 36 first series 12-card hobby packs and 13-card retail packs, and one in every twenty 20-card retail jumbo packs, these 420 standard-size cards parallel that of the basic 1994-95 Collector's Choice set. The difference is the player's facsimile autograph which appears in gold-foil near the bottom and the front borders are colored in gold. Only the key cards within the set are listed below. Please refer to the multiplier provided (and the values listed for the regular-issue 1994-95 Collector's Choice cards) to ascertain the value of the other Gold cards within the set.

	MINT	NRMT	EXC
COMPLETE GOLD SET (420)	1000.00	450.00	125.00
COMPLETE SERIES 1 (210)	400.00	180.00	50.00
COMPLETE SERIES 2 (210)	600.00	275.00	75.00
COMMON GOLD (1-420)	1.50	.70	.19
SEMISTARS	4.00	1.80	.50
*STARS: 20X TO 40X VALUE			
*ROOKIES: 15X TO 30X VALUE			
☐ 1	Anfernee Hardaway	50.00	22.00	6.25
☐ 10	Dennis Rodman	30.00	13.50	3.70
☐ 23	Michael Jordan	100.00	45.00	12.50
☐ 33	Scottie Pippen	25.00	11.00	3.10
☐ 34	Hakeem Olajuwon	20.00	9.00	2.50
☐ 140	Shawn Kemp	25.00	11.00	3.10
☐ 184	Shaquille O'Neal TO	20.00	9.00	2.50
☐ 197	Shaquille O'Neal ASA	20.00	9.00	2.50

		MINT	NRMT	EXC
☐ 204	Michael Jordan PRO	50.00	22.00	6.25
☐ 205	Shaquille O'Neal PRO	20.00	9.00	2.50
☐ 219	Grant Hill	60.00	27.00	7.50
☐ 232	Shaquille O'Neal	40.00	18.00	5.00
☐ 240	Michael Jordan	50.00	22.00	6.25
☐ 250	Jason Kidd	40.00	18.00	5.00
☐ 266	Glenn Robinson	20.00	9.00	2.50
☐ 278	Juwan Howard	40.00	18.00	5.00
☐ 379	Grant Hill BP	25.00	11.00	3.10
☐ 390	Shaquille O'Neal BP	20.00	9.00	2.50
☐ 400	Shaquille O'Neal TRIV	20.00	9.00	2.50
☐ 402	Michael Jordan TRIV	50.00	22.00	6.25
☐ 409	Grant Hill DC	25.00	11.00	3.10
☐ 420	Michael Jordan CL	25.00	11.00	3.10

1994-95 Collector's Choice Blow-Ups

One of these oversized (5" by 7") cards was inserted exclusively into each series 2 hobby box. Each Blow-Up is identical in design and numbering to their corresponding basic issue card. According to information provided by Upper Deck at least 3,000 of these cards were autographed and randomly seeded into boxes. There are far fewer autographed Michael Jordan Blow-Ups than the other four players featured.

		MINT	NRMT	EXC
COMPLETE SET (5)		10.00	4.50	1.25
COMMON CARD (40/76/132)		.50	.23	.06
☐ 23	Michael Jordan BB	8.00	3.60	1.00
☐ 40	Calbert Cheaney	.50	.23	.06
☐ 76	Shawn Bradley	.50	.23	.06
☐ 132	Bobby Hurley	.50	.23	.06
☐ 140	Shawn Kemp	2.00	.90	.25
☐ A23	Michael Jordan AU	4000.00	1800.00	500.00
☐ A40	Calbert Cheaney AU	25.00	11.00	3.10
☐ A76	Shawn Bradley AU	25.00	11.00	3.10
☐ A132	Bobby Hurley AU	25.00	11.00	3.10
☐ A140	Shawn Kemp AU	150.00	70.00	19.00

1994-95 Collector's Choice Crash the Game Assists

These fifteen standard-size Crash the Game Assists cards were randomly insert-

ed exclusively into first series retail packs at a rate of one in 20. Cards that featured players who tallied 750 or more assists during the 1994-95 campaign were redeemable for a 15-card parallel Crash the Game Assists Redemption set. Only John Stockton eclipsed the mark. The fronts feature a color-action photo with the background of the game in black and white. The top has the player's name in a box the color of his team and the bottom has the words "You Crash The Game" in foil with the player's position behind it in his team's color. The back says 750 assists at the top below his name surrounded by the player's team color. There are instructions on how to redeem your cards if you win. The exchange deadline was June 16th, 1995. The redemption cards were delayed in shipping until late October, 1995. Please refer to the exchange header lines provided below to ascertain value of the exchange cards.

	MINT	NRMT	EXC
COMPLETE SET (15)	15.00	6.75	1.85
COMMON CARD (A1-A15)	.50	.23	.06
COMP. ASSTS EXCH. SET (15)	7.50	3.40	.95
*ASSISTS EXC. CARDS: 50% VALUE			
☐ A1 Michael Adams	.50	.23	.06
☐ A2 Kenny Anderson	1.00	.45	.12
☐ A3 Mookie Blaylock	1.00	.45	.12
☐ A4 Muggsy Bogues	1.00	.45	.12
☐ A5 Sherman Douglas	.50	.23	.06
☐ A6 Anfernee Hardaway	10.00	4.50	1.25
☐ A7 Tim Hardaway	1.00	.45	.12
☐ A8 Lindsey Hunter	.50	.23	.06
☐ A9 Mark Jackson	.50	.23	.06
☐ A10 Kevin Johnson	1.00	.45	.12
☐ A11 Eric Murdock	.50	.23	.06
☐ A12 Mark Price	.50	.23	.06
☐ A13 John Stockton	1.50	.70	.19
☐ A14 Rod Strickland	.50	.23	.06
☐ A15 Micheal Williams	.50	.23	.06

1994-95 Collector's Choice Crash the Game Rebounds

These fifteen standard-size Crash the Game Rebounds cards were randomly

inserted exclusively into second series retail packs at a rate of one in 20. Cards that featured players who grabbed 1,000 or more rebounds during the 1994-95 campaign were redeemable for a 15-card parallel Crash the Game Rebounds Redemption set. The card design is the same as the Assists set except on the back it says 1,000 Rebounds. Only Dikembe Mutombo eclipsed the mark. The exchange deadline was June 30, 1995. The redemption cards were delayed in shipping until late October, 1995. Please refer to the exchange header lines provided below to ascertain value of the exchange cards.

	MINT	NRMT	EXC
COMPLETE SET (15)	20.00	9.00	2.50
COMMON CARD (R1-R15)	.50	.23	.06
COMP. REB. EXCH. SET (15)	10.00	4.50	1.25
*REB. EXCH. CARDS: 50% VALUE...			
☐ R1 Derrick Coleman	.50	.23	.06
☐ R2 Patrick Ewing	1.25	.55	.16
☐ R3 Horace Grant	.75	.35	.09
☐ R4 Shawn Kemp	4.00	1.80	.50
☐ R5 Karl Malone	1.25	.55	.16
☐ R6 Alonzo Mourning	1.50	.70	.19
☐ R7 Dikembe Mutombo	1.00	.45	.12
☐ R8 Charles Oakley	.50	.23	.06
☐ R9 Hakeem Olajuwon	3.00	1.35	.35
☐ R10 Shaquille O'Neal	6.00	2.70	.75
☐ R11 Olden Polynice	.50	.23	.06
☐ R12 David Robinson	2.50	1.10	.30
☐ R13 Dennis Rodman	5.00	2.20	.60
☐ R14 Otis Thorpe	.50	.23	.06
☐ R15 Kevin Willis	.50	.23	.06

1994-95 Collector's Choice Crash the Game Rookie Scoring

These fifteen standard-size Crash the Game Rookie Scoring cards were randomly inserted exclusively into second series hobby packs at a rate of one in 20. Cards that featured rookies who scored more than 1,250 points during the 1994-95 campaign were redeemable for a 15-card parallel

Crash the Game Rookie Scoring Redemption set. The card design is the same as the Assists set except on the back it says 1,250 Points. Only Grant Hill and Glenn Robinson eclipsed the mark. The exchange deadline was June 30th, 1995. The redemption cards were delayed in shipping until late October, 1995. Please refer to the exchange header lines provided below to ascertain value of the exchange cards.

	MINT	NRMT	EXC
COMPLETE SET (15)	20.00	9.00	2.50
COMMON CARD (S1-S15)	.50	.23	.06
COMP. RKE SCO. EXCH. SET (15)	10.00	4.50	1.25
*ROOK. SCO. EXCH. CARDS: 50% VALUE			
☐ S1 Tony Dumas	.50	.23	.06
☐ S2 Brian Grant	.75	.35	.09
☐ S3 Grant Hill	6.00	2.70	.75
☐ S4 Juwan Howard	5.00	2.20	.60
☐ S5 Eddie Jones	1.50	.70	.19
☐ S6 Jason Kidd	5.00	2.20	.60
☐ S7 Donyell Marshall	.50	.23	.06
☐ S8 Eric Montross	.50	.23	.06
☐ S9 Lamond Murray	.50	.23	.06
☐ S10 Khalid Reeves	.50	.23	.06
☐ S11 Glenn Robinson	2.00	.90	.25
☐ S12 Jalen Rose	.75	.35	.09
☐ S13 Dickey Simpkins	.50	.23	.06
☐ S14 Charlie Ward	.75	.35	.09
☐ S15 Sharone Wright	.50	.23	.06

1994-95 Collector's Choice Crash the Game Scoring

These fifteen standard-size Crash the Game Scoring cards were randomly inserted exclusively into first series hobby packs at a rate of one in 20. Cards that featured players who posted 2,000 or more points during the 1994-95 campaign were redeemable for a 15-card parallel Crash the Game Scoring Redemption set. The card design is the same as the Assists set except on the back it says 2,000 Points. Karl Malone, Shaquille O'Neal, Hakeem Olajuwon and David Robinson all eclipsed the mark. The exchange deadline was June

30, 1995. The redemption cards were delayed in shipping until late October, 1995. Please refer to the exchange header lines provided below to ascertain value of the exchange cards.

	MINT	NRMT	EXC
COMPLETE SET (15)	25.00	11.00	3.10
COMMON CARD (S1-S15)	.50	.23	.06
COMP. SCOR. EXCH. SET (15)	15.00	6.75	1.85
*SCO. EXCH. CARDS: 50% VALUE...			

		MINT	NRMT	EXC
☐ S1	Charles Barkley	2.00	.90	.25
☐ S2	Derrick Coleman	.50	.23	.06
☐ S3	Joe Dumars	.75	.35	.09
☐ S4	Patrick Ewing	1.25	.55	.16
☐ S5	Karl Malone	1.25	.55	.16
☐ S6	Reggie Miller	1.50	.70	.19
☐ S7	Shaquille O'Neal	4.00	1.80	.50
☐ S8	Hakeem Olajuwon	3.00	1.35	.35
☐ S9	Scottie Pippen	4.00	1.80	.50
☐ S10	Glen Rice	.75	.35	.09
☐ S11	Mitch Richmond	1.00	.45	.12
☐ S12	David Robinson	2.50	1.10	.30
☐ S13	Latrell Sprewell	.75	.35	.09
☐ S14	Chris Webber	1.50	.70	.19
☐ S15	Dominique Wilkins	.75	.35	.09

1994-95 Collector's Choice Draft Trade

This 10-card set was available only by redeeming a Draft Trade card that was randomly seeded into one in every 36 first series Collector's Choice hobby or retail packs. The fronts have a color-action photo with the top-half having the background of the game in black and white. The bottom of the card has a white background. On the left side of the card are the words "NBA Draft Lottery Picks" with the player's name above it. The backs have the player's name and information set against the colors of his team. The expiration date on the redemption was June 16th, 1995.

	MINT	NRMT	EXC
COMPLETE SET (10)	8.00	3.60	1.00
COMMON CARD (1-10)	.25	.11	.03

		MINT	NRMT	EXC
☐ 1	Glenn Robinson	1.25	.55	.16
☐ 2	Jason Kidd	2.50	1.10	.30
☐ 3	Grant Hill	4.00	1.80	.50
☐ 4	Donyell Marshall	.25	.11	.03
☐ 5	Juwan Howard	2.50	1.10	.30
☐ 6	Sharone Wright	.25	.11	.03
☐ 7	Lamond Murray	.25	.11	.03
☐ 8	Brian Grant	.50	.23	.06
☐ 9	Eric Montross	.25	.11	.03
☐ 10	Eddie Jones	.75	.35	.09
☐ NNO	Draft Trade Card	.25	.11	.03

1995-96 Collector's Choice

These 410-standard size cards, issued in two seperate series of 210 and 200 cards respectively, comprise Upper Deck's 1995-96 Collector's Choice set. Cards were primarily issued in 12-card hobby and retail packs (suggested retail price of ninety-nine cents) and five-card retail mini-packs. In addition, large retail chain stores received complete factory sets around the end of the season (SRP $29.97). Each factory set contains a basic 410 card set, four Collector's Choice Jordan Collection inserts, four Player's Club Platinum inserts and a special 5" by 7" Bulls Commemorative card celebrating their 70 win season. Regular issue cards feature white-bordered fronts with color player action shots. The backs have a color photo and statistics. The following subsets are included: Fun Facts (166-194), Professor Dunk (195-208), Scouting Report (321-349), Playoff Time (350-365), I Love this Team (366-394), Photo Gallery (395-403) and Shawn Kemp's Top 40 (404-408). Special Crash Packs containing only inserts (an assortion of Player's Club, Player's Club Platinum and Crash the Game cards) were randomly inserted into one in every

175 12-card packs. Rookie Cards of note include Michael Finley, Kevin Garnett, Joe Smith, Jerry Stackhouse and Damon Stoudamire.

	MINT	NRMT	EXC
COMPLETE SET (410)	35.00	16.00	4.40
COMPLETE RACT. SET (419)	35.00	16.00	4.40
COMPLETE SERIES 1 (210)	15.00	6.75	1.85
COMPLETE SERIES 2 (200)	20.00	9.00	2.50
COMMON CARD (1-410)	.05	.02	.01

☐ 1	Rod Strickland	.05	.02	.01
☐ 2	Larry Johnson	.20	.09	.03
☐ 3	Mahmoud Abdul-Rauf	.05	.02	.01
☐ 4	Joe Dumars	.10	.05	.01
☐ 5	Jason Kidd	.50	.23	.06
☐ 6	Avery Johnson	.05	.02	.01
☐ 7	Dee Brown	.05	.02	.01
☐ 8	Brian Williams	.05	.02	.01
☐ 9	Nick Van Exel	.15	.07	.02
☐ 10	Dennis Rodman	.75	.35	.09
☐ 11	Rony Seikaly	.05	.02	.01
☐ 12	Harvey Grant	.05	.02	.01
☐ 13	Craig Ehlo	.05	.02	.01
☐ 14	Derek Harper	.05	.02	.01
☐ 15	Oliver Miller	.05	.02	.01
	Drafted by the Raptors			
☐ 16	Dennis Scott	.05	.02	.01
☐ 17	Ed Pinckney	.05	.02	.01
	Drafted by the Raptors			
☐ 18	Eric Piatkowski	.05	.02	.01
☐ 19	B.J. Armstrong	.05	.02	.01
☐ 20	Tyrone Hill	.05	.02	.01
☐ 21	Malik Sealy	.05	.02	.01
☐ 22	Clyde Drexler	.25	.11	.03
☐ 23	Aaron McKie	.05	.02	.01
☐ 24	Harold Miner	.05	.02	.01
☐ 25	Bobby Hurley	.05	.02	.01
☐ 26	Dell Curry	.05	.02	.01
☐ 27	Micheal Williams	.05	.02	.01
☐ 28	Adam Keefe	.05	.02	.01
☐ 29	Antonio Harvey	.05	.02	.01
	Drafted by the Grizzlies			
☐ 30	Billy Owens	.05	.02	.01
☐ 31	Nate McMillan	.05	.02	.01
☐ 32	J.R. Reid	.05	.02	.01
☐ 33	Grant Hill	.75	.35	.09
☐ 34	Charles Barkley	.30	.14	.04
☐ 35	Tyrone Corbin	.05	.02	.01
	Traded to the Kings			
☐ 36	Don MacLean	.05	.02	.01
☐ 37	Kenny Smith	.05	.02	.01
☐ 38	Juwan Howard	.50	.23	.06
☐ 39	Charles Smith	.05	.02	.01
☐ 40	Shawn Kemp	.60	.25	.07
☐ 41	Dana Barros	.05	.02	.01
☐ 42	Vin Baker	.20	.09	.03
☐ 43	Armon Gilliam	.05	.02	.01
☐ 44	Spud Webb	.10	.05	.01
	Traded to the Hawks			
☐ 45	Michael Jordan	2.50	1.10	.30
☐ 46	Scott Williams	.05	.02	.01
☐ 47	Vlade Divac	.10	.05	.01
☐ 48	Roy Tarpley	.05	.02	.01
☐ 49	Bimbo Coles	.05	.02	.01
☐ 50	David Robinson	.40	.18	.05
☐ 51	Terry Dehere	.05	.02	.01
☐ 52	Bobby Phills	.05	.02	.01
☐ 53	Sherman Douglas	.05	.02	.01
☐ 54	Rodney Rogers	.05	.02	.01

	Traded to the Clippers			
☐ 55	Detlef Schrempf	.10	.05	.01
☐ 56	Calbert Cheaney	.05	.02	.01
☐ 57	Tom Gugliotta	.10	.05	.01
☐ 58	Jeff Turner	.05	.02	.01
☐ 59	Mookie Blaylock	.10	.05	.01
☐ 60	Bill Curley	.05	.02	.01
☐ 61	Chris Dudley	.05	.02	.01
☐ 62	Popeye Jones	.05	.02	.01
☐ 63	Scott Burrell	.05	.02	.01
☐ 64	Dale Davis	.05	.02	.01
☐ 65	Mitchell Butler	.05	.02	.01
☐ 66	Pervis Ellison	.05	.02	.01
☐ 67	Todd Day	.05	.02	.01
☐ 68	Carl Herrera	.05	.02	.01
☐ 69	Jeff Hornacek	.05	.02	.01
☐ 70	Vincent Askew	.05	.02	.01
☐ 71	A.C. Green	.10	.05	.01
☐ 72	Kevin Gamble	.05	.02	.01
☐ 73	Chris Gatling	.05	.02	.01
☐ 74	Otis Thorpe	.10	.05	.01
☐ 75	Michael Cage	.05	.02	.01
☐ 76	Carlos Rogers	.05	.02	.01
☐ 77	Gheorghe Muresan	.10	.05	.01
☐ 78	Olden Polynice	.05	.02	.01
☐ 79	Grant Long	.05	.02	.01
☐ 80	Allan Houston	.10	.05	.01
☐ 81	Charles Outlaw	.05	.02	.01
☐ 82	Clarence Weatherspoon	.10	.05	.01
☐ 83	Tony Dumas	.05	.02	.01
☐ 84	Herb Williams	.05	.02	.01
☐ 85	P.J. Brown	.05	.02	.01
☐ 86	Robert Horry	.10	.05	.01
☐ 87	Byron Scott	.10	.05	.01
	Drafted by the Grizzlies			
☐ 88	Horace Grant	.10	.05	.01
☐ 89	Dominique Wilkins	.10	.05	.01
☐ 90	Doug West	.05	.02	.01
☐ 91	Antoine Carr	.05	.02	.01
☐ 92	Dickey Simpkins	.05	.02	.01
	Washington Bulls			
☐ 93	Elden Campbell	.10	.05	.01
☐ 94	Kevin Johnson	.10	.05	.01
☐ 95	Rex Chapman	.05	.02	.01
	Traded to the Heat			
☐ 96	John Williams	.05	.02	.01
☐ 97	Tim Hardaway	.10	.05	.01
☐ 98	Rik Smits	.10	.05	.01
☐ 99	Rex Walters	.05	.02	.01
☐ 100	Robert Parish	.10	.05	.01
☐ 101	Isaiah Rider	.10	.05	.01
☐ 102	Sarunas Marciulionis	.05	.02	.01
☐ 103	Andrew Lang	.05	.02	.01
☐ 104	Eric Mobley	.05	.02	.01
☐ 105	Randy Brown	.05	.02	.01
☐ 106	John Stockton	.20	.09	.03
☐ 107	Lamond Murray	.05	.02	.01
☐ 108	Will Perdue	.05	.02	.01
☐ 109	Wayman Tisdale	.05	.02	.01
☐ 110	John Starks	.05	.02	.01
☐ 111	John Salley	.05	.02	.01
☐ 112	Lucious Harris	.05	.02	.01
☐ 113	Jeff Malone	.05	.02	.01
☐ 114	Anthony Bowie	.05	.02	.01
☐ 115	Vinny Del Negro	.05	.02	.01
☐ 116	Michael Adams	.05	.02	.01
☐ 117	Chris Mullin	.10	.05	.01
☐ 118	Benoit Benjamin	.05	.02	.01
	Drafted by the Grizzlies			
☐ 119	Byron Houston	.05	.02	.01
☐ 120	LaPhonso Ellis	.05	.02	.01

#	Player			
☐ 121	Doug Overton	.05	.02	.01
☐ 122	Jerome Kersey	.05	.02	.01
	Drafted by the Grizzlies			
☐ 123	Greg Minor	.05	.02	.01
☐ 124	Christian Laettner	.10	.05	.01
☐ 125	Mark Price	.05	.02	.01
☐ 126	Kevin Willis	.05	.02	.01
☐ 127	Kenny Anderson	.10	.05	.01
☐ 128	Marty Conlon	.05	.02	.01
☐ 129	Blue Edwards	.05	.02	.01
	Drafted by the Grizzlies			
☐ 130	Dan Schayes	.05	.02	.01
☐ 131	Duane Ferrell	.05	.02	.01
☐ 132	Charles Oakley	.05	.02	.01
☐ 133	Brian Grant	.10	.05	.01
☐ 134	Reggie Williams	.05	.02	.01
☐ 135	Steve Kerr	.10	.05	.01
☐ 136	Khalid Reeves	.05	.02	.01
☐ 137	David Benoit	.05	.02	.01
☐ 138	Derrick Coleman	.05	.02	.01
☐ 139	Anthony Peeler	.05	.02	.01
☐ 140	Jim Jackson	.25	.11	.03
☐ 141	Stacey Augmon	.10	.05	.01
☐ 142	Sam Cassell	.05	.02	.01
☐ 143	Derrick McKey	.05	.02	.01
☐ 144	Danny Ferry	.05	.02	.01
☐ 145	Anfernee Hardaway	1.25	.55	.16
☐ 146	Clifford Robinson	.10	.05	.01
☐ 147	B.J. Tyler	.05	.02	.01
	Drafted by the Raptors			
☐ 148	Mark West	.05	.02	.01
☐ 149	David Wingate	.05	.02	.01
	Traded to the Sonics			
☐ 150	Willie Anderson	.05	.02	.01
	Drafted by the Raptors			
☐ 151	Hersey Hawkins	.10	.05	.01
	Traded to the Sonics			
☐ 152	Bryant Stith	.05	.02	.01
☐ 153	Dan Majerle	.10	.05	.01
☐ 154	Chris Smith	.05	.02	.01
☐ 155	Donyell Marshall	.05	.02	.01
☐ 156	Loy Vaught	.10	.05	.01
☐ 157	Reggie Miller	.25	.11	.03
☐ 158	Hubert Davis	.05	.02	.01
☐ 159	Ron Harper	.10	.05	.01
☐ 160	Lee Mayberry	.05	.02	.01
☐ 161	Eddie Jones	.15	.07	.02
☐ 162	Shawn Bradley	.10	.05	.01
☐ 163	Nick Anderson	.10	.05	.01
☐ 164	Ervin Johnson	.05	.02	.01
☐ 165	Walt Williams	.10	.05	.01
☐ 166	Steve Smith FF	.05	.02	.01
☐ 167	Dino Radja FF	.05	.02	.01
☐ 168	Alonzo Mourning FF	.10	.05	.01
☐ 169	Michael Jordan FF	1.25	.55	.16
☐ 170	Tyrone Hill FF	.05	.02	.01
☐ 171	Jamal Mashburn FF	.10	.05	.01
☐ 172	Dikembe Mutombo FF	.10	.05	.01
☐ 173	Grant Hill FF	.60	.25	.07
	with Michael Jordan			
☐ 174	Latrell Sprewell FF	.10	.05	.01
☐ 175	Hakeem Olajuwon FF	.25	.11	.03
☐ 176	Reggie Miller FF	.15	.07	.02
☐ 177	Pooh Richardson FF	.05	.02	.01
☐ 178	Cedric Ceballos FF	.10	.05	.01
☐ 179	Glen Rice FF	.10	.05	.01
☐ 180	Glenn Robinson FF	.15	.07	.02
☐ 181	Isaiah Rider FF	.05	.02	.01
☐ 182	Derrick Coleman FF	.05	.02	.01
☐ 183	Patrick Ewing FF	.10	.05	.01
☐ 184	Shaquille O'Neal FF	.50	.23	.06
☐ 185	Dana Barros FF	.05	.02	.01
☐ 186	Dan Majerle FF	.05	.02	.01
☐ 187	Clifford Robinson FF	.05	.02	.01
☐ 188	Mitch Richmond FF	.10	.05	.01
☐ 189	David Robinson FF	.20	.09	.03
☐ 190	Gary Payton FF	.15	.07	.02
☐ 191	Oliver Miller FF	.05	.02	.01
☐ 192	Karl Malone FF	.10	.05	.01
☐ 193	Kevin Pritchard FF	.05	.02	.01
☐ 194	Chris Webber FF	.10	.05	.01
☐ 195	Michael Jordan PD	1.25	.55	.16
☐ 196	Hakeem Olajuwon PD	.25	.11	.03
☐ 197	Vin Baker PD	.10	.05	.01
☐ 198	Grant Hill PD	.40	.18	.05
☐ 199	Clyde Drexler PD	.10	.05	.01
☐ 200	Chris Webber PD	.10	.05	.01
☐ 201	Shawn Kemp PD	.30	.14	.04
☐ 202	Shaquille O'Neal PD	.50	.23	.06
☐ 203	Stacey Augmon PD	.05	.02	.01
☐ 204	David Benoit PD	.05	.02	.01
☐ 205	Rodney Rogers PD	.05	.02	.01
☐ 206	Latrell Sprewell PD	.05	.02	.01
☐ 207	Brian Grant PD	.05	.02	.01
☐ 208	Lamond Murray PD	.05	.02	.01
☐ 209	Shawn Kemp CL	.15	.07	.02
☐ 210	Michael Jordan CL	.60	.25	.07
☐ 211	Cory Alexander	.05	.02	.01
☐ 212	Vernon Maxwell	.05	.02	.01
☐ 213	George Lynch	.05	.02	.01
☐ 214	Terry Mills	.05	.02	.01
☐ 215	Scottie Pippen	.60	.25	.07
☐ 216	Donald Royal	.05	.02	.01
☐ 217	Wesley Person	.10	.05	.01
☐ 218	Antonio Davis	.05	.02	.01
☐ 219	Glenn Robinson	.25	.11	.03
☐ 220	Jerry Stackhouse	1.50	.70	.19
☐ 221	James Robinson	.05	.02	.01
☐ 222	Chris Mills	.10	.05	.01
☐ 223	Chuck Person	.05	.02	.01
☐ 224	Duane Causwell	.05	.02	.01
☐ 225	Gary Payton	.30	.14	.04
☐ 226	Eric Montross	.05	.02	.01
☐ 227	Felton Spencer	.05	.02	.01
☐ 228	Scott Skiles	.05	.02	.01
☐ 229	Latrell Sprewell	.10	.05	.01
☐ 230	Sedale Threatt	.05	.02	.01
☐ 231	Mark Bryant	.05	.02	.01
☐ 232	Buck Williams	.10	.05	.01
☐ 233	Brian Williams	.05	.02	.01
☐ 234	Sharone Wright	.05	.02	.01
☐ 235	Karl Malone	.20	.09	.03
☐ 236	Kevin Edwards	.05	.02	.01
☐ 237	Muggsy Bogues	.10	.05	.01
☐ 238	Mario Elie	.05	.02	.01
☐ 239	Rasheed Wallace	.40	.18	.05
☐ 240	George Zidek	.10	.05	.01
☐ 241	Cedric Ceballos	.10	.05	.01
☐ 242	Alan Henderson	.15	.07	.02
☐ 243	Joe Kleine	.05	.02	.01
☐ 244	Patrick Ewing	.20	.09	.03
☐ 245	Sasha Danilovic	.10	.05	.01
☐ 246	Bill Wennington	.05	.02	.01
☐ 247	Steve Smith	.10	.05	.01
☐ 248	Bryant Stith	.05	.02	.01
☐ 249	Dino Radja	.10	.05	.01
☐ 250	Monty Williams	.05	.02	.01
☐ 251	Andrew DeClerq	.05	.02	.01
☐ 252	Sean Elliott	.10	.05	.01
☐ 253	Rick Fox	.05	.02	.01
☐ 254	Lionel Simmons	.05	.02	.01
☐ 255	Dikembe Mutombo	.10	.05	.01

□	256	Lindsey Hunter	.05	.02	.01
□	257	Terrell Brandon	.10	.05	.01
□	258	Shawn Respert	.10	.05	.01
□	259	Rodney Rogers	.05	.02	.01
□	260	Bryon Russell	.05	.02	.01
□	261	David Wesley	.05	.02	.01
□	262	Ken Norman	.05	.02	.01
□	263	Mitch Richmond	.15	.07	.02
□	264	Sam Perkins	.10	.05	.01
□	265	Hakeem Olajuwon	.50	.23	.06
□	266	Brian Shaw	.05	.02	.01
□	267	B.J. Armstrong	.05	.02	.01
□	268	Jalen Rose	.05	.02	.01
□	269	Bryant Reeves	.50	.23	.06
□	270	Cherokee Parks	.10	.05	.01
□	271	Dennis Rodman Bulls	1.25	.55	.16
□	272	Kendall Gill	.05	.02	.01
□	273	Elliot Perry	.05	.02	.01
□	274	Anthony Mason	.10	.05	.01
□	275	Kevin Garnett	2.50	1.10	.30
□	276	Damon Stoudamire	2.00	.90	.25
□	277	Lawrence Moten	.05	.02	.01
□	278	Ed O'Bannon	.30	.14	.04
□	279	Toni Kukoc	.15	.07	.02
□	280	Greg Ostertag	.05	.02	.01
□	281	Tom Hammonds	.05	.02	.01
□	282	Yinka Dare	.05	.02	.01
□	283	Michael Smith	.05	.02	.01
□	284	Clifford Rozier	.05	.02	.01
□	285	Gary Trent	.10	.05	.01
□	286	Shaquille O'Neal	1.00	.45	.12
□	287	Luc Longley	.10	.05	.01
□	288	Bob Sura	.15	.07	.02
□	289	Dana Barros	.05	.02	.01
□	290	Lorenzo Williams	.05	.02	.01
□	291	Haywoode Workman	.05	.02	.01
□	292	Randolph Childress	.05	.02	.01
□	293	Doc Rivers	.05	.02	.01
□	294	Chris Webber	.20	.09	.03
□	295	Kurt Thomas	.25	.11	.03
□	296	Greg Anthony	.05	.02	.01
□	297	Tyus Edney	.40	.18	.05
□	298	Danny Manning	.10	.05	.01
□	299	Brent Barry	.40	.18	.05
□	300	Joe Smith	1.00	.45	.12
□	301	Pooh Richardson	.05	.02	.01
□	302	Mark Jackson	.05	.02	.01
□	303	Richard Dumas	.05	.02	.01
□	304	Michael Finley	1.00	.45	.12
□	305	Theo Ratliff	.10	.05	.01
□	306	Gary Grant	.05	.02	.01
□	307	Jamal Mashburn	.15	.07	.02
□	308	Corliss Williamson	.15	.07	.02
□	309	Eric Williams	.15	.07	.02
□	310	Zan Tabak	.05	.02	.01
□	311	Eric Murdock	.05	.02	.01
□	312	Sherell Ford	.05	.02	.01
□	313	Terry Davis	.05	.02	.01
□	314	Vern Fleming	.05	.02	.01
□	315	Jason Caffey	.10	.05	.01
□	316	Mario Bennett	.05	.02	.01
□	317	David Vaughn	.05	.02	.01
□	318	Loren Meyer	.10	.05	.01
□	319	Travis Best	.15	.07	.02
□	320	Byron Scott	.15	.07	.02
□	321	Mookie Blaylock SR	.05	.02	.01
□	322	Dee Brown SR	.05	.02	.01
□	323	Alonzo Mourning SR	.10	.05	.01
□	324	Michael Jordan SR	1.25	.55	.16
□	325	Terrell Brandon SR	.05	.02	.01
□	326	Jim Jackson SR	.10	.05	.01

□	327	Dikembe Mutombo SR	.10	.05	.01
□	328	Grant Hill SR	.40	.18	.05
□	329	Joe Smith SR UER	.40	.18	.05
		Team stats say Seattle			
		Should be Golden State			
□	330	Clyde Drexler SR	.15	.07	.02
□	331	Reggie Miller SR	.15	.07	.02
□	332	Lamond Murray SR	.05	.02	.01
□	333	Nick Van Exel SR	.15	.07	.02
□	334	Glen Rice SR	.05	.02	.01
□	335	Glenn Robinson SR	.15	.07	.02
□	336	Christian Laettner SR	.10	.05	.01
□	337	Kenny Anderson SR	.10	.05	.01
□	338	Patrick Ewing SR	.10	.05	.01
□	339	Shaquille O'Neal SR	.50	.23	.06
□	340	Jerry Stackhouse SR	.60	.25	.07
□	341	Charles Barkley SR	.15	.07	.02
□	342	Clifford Robinson SR	.10	.05	.01
□	343	Brian Grant SR	.10	.05	.01
□	344	David Robinson SR	.20	.09	.03
□	345	Shawn Kemp SR	.30	.14	.04
□	346	Damon Stoudamire SR	.75	.35	.09
□	347	Karl Malone SR	.10	.05	.01
□	348	Bryant Reeves SR	.20	.09	.03
□	349	Juwan Howard SR	.25	.11	.03
□	350	Nick Anderson	.10	.05	.01
		Dee Brown PT			
		Orlando vs. Boston East Conf. 1st Round			
□	351	Rik Smits PT	.10	.05	.01
		Indiana vs Atlanta East Conf. 1st Round			
□	352	Herb Williams PT	.05	.02	.01
		Greg Dreiling PT			
		New York vs Cleveland East Conf. 1st Round			
□	353	Michael Jordan PT	1.25	.55	.16
		Chicago vs Charlotte East Conf. 1st Round			
□	354	David Robinson PT	.20	.09	.03
		San Antonio vs Denver West Conf. 1st Round			
□	355	Terry Porter	.05	.02	.01
		Kevin Johnson PT			
		Phoenix vs Portland West Conf. 1st Round			
□	356	Clyde Drexler PT	.15	.07	.02
		Houston vs Utah West Conf. 1st Round			
□	357	Cedric Ceballos PT	.05	.02	.01
		L.A. Lakers vs Seattle West Conf. 1st Round			
□	358	Horace Grant/Group PT	.10	.05	.01
		Orlando vs Chicago East Conf. Semifinals			
□	359	Reggie Miller PT	.15	.07	.02
		Indiana vs New York East Conf. Semifinals			
□	360	Avery Johnson	.05	.02	.01
		Nick Van Exel PT			
		SA vs L.A. Lakers West Conf. Semifinals			
□	361	Hakeem Olajuwon	.15	.07	.02
		Robert Horry PT			
		Houston vs Phoenix West Conf. Semifinals			
□	362	Rik Smits PT	.10	.05	.01
		Orlando vs Indiana East Conf. Finals			
□	363	David Robinson	.25	.11	.03
		Hakeem Olajuwon PT			
		Houston vs San Antonio West Conf. Finals			
□	364	Robert Horry PT	.10	.05	.01
		Houston vs Orlando NBA Finals			
□	365	Kenny Smith PT	.05	.02	.01
		Houston Rockets 1995 NBA Champs			
□	366	Stacey Augmon LOVE	.05	.02	.01
□	367	Sherman Douglas LOVE	.05	.02	.01
□	368	Larry Johnson LOVE	.10	.05	.01
□	369	Scottie Pippen LOVE	.30	.14	.04
□	370	Tyrone Hill LOVE	.05	.02	.01
□	371	Jamal Mashburn LOVE	.10	.05	.01
□	372	Mahmoud Abdul-Rauf LOVE	.10	.05	.01
□	373	Grant Hill LOVE	.40	.18	.05

☐	374	Latrell Sprewell LOVE ..	.10	.05	.01
☐	375	Sam Cassell LOVE	.05	.02	.01
☐	376	Rik Smits LOVE	.10	.05	.01
☐	377	Terry Dehere LOVE	.05	.02	.01
☐	378	Eddie Jones LOVE.........	.10	.05	.01
☐	379	Billy Owens LOVE.........	.05	.02	.01
☐	380	Vin Baker LOVE............	.10	.05	.01
☐	381	Isaiah Rider LOVE	.05	.02	.01
☐	382	Kenny Anderson LOVE..	.10	.05	.01
☐	383	John Starks LOVE	.05	.02	.01
☐	384	Anfernee Hardaway LOVE	.60	.25	.07
☐	385	Sharone Wright LOVE...	.05	.02	.01
☐	386	Charles Barkley LOVE ..	.15	.07	.02
☐	387	Clifford Robinson LOVE	.05	.02	.01
☐	388	Walt Williams LOVE......	.05	.02	.01
☐	389	Sean Elliott LOVE.........	.10	.05	.01
☐	390	Gary Payton LOVE	.15	.07	.02
☐	391	Carlos Rogers LOVE	.05	.02	.01
☐	392	John Stockton LOVE	.10	.05	.01
☐	393	Greg Anthony LOVE	.05	.02	.01
☐	394	Chris Webber LOVE	.10	.05	.01
☐	395	Gary Payton PG	.15	.07	.02
☐	396	Mookie Blaylock PG	.05	.02	.01
☐	397	Charles Barkley PG	.15	.07	.02
☐	398	Grant Hill PG	.40	.18	.05
☐	399	Anfernee Hardaway PG	.60	.25	.07
☐	400	Kenny Anderson PG......	.10	.05	.01
☐	401	Mark Jackson PG.........	.05	.02	.01
☐	402	Karl Malone PG	.10	.05	.01
☐	403	Avery Johnson PG	.05	.02	.01
☐	404	Larry Johnson 40.........	.10	.05	.01
		Top Scorers			
☐	405	Nick Van Exel 40	.10	.05	.01
		Top Shooters			
☐	406	Vin Baker 40	.10	.05	.01
		Top Rebounders			
☐	407	Jason Kidd 40..............	.25	.11	.03
		Top Passers			
☐	408	David Robinson 40	.20	.09	.03
		Top Defenders			
☐	409	Shawn Kemp CL	.15	.07	.02
☐	410	Michael Jordan CL	.60	.25	.07
☐	NNO	Bulls Fact.Set Comm.	6.00	2.70	.75

1995-96 Collector's Choice Player's Club

Issued one per pack in both first and second series Collector's Choice 12-card packs, these 410 standard-size cards par-

allel the basic 1995-96 Collector's Choice set. Unlike the basic issue cards, Player's Club card fronts feature silver borders (except on the borderless subset cards) and a silver foil facsimile autograph and Player's Club logo. Please refer to the multiplier provided below (and the values listed for the regular issue 1995-96 Collector's Choice cards) to ascertain the value of individual Player's Club cards.

	MINT	NRMT	EXC
COMPLETE SET (410)	70.00	32.00	8.75
COMPLETE SERIES 1 (210)...	30.00	13.50	3.70
COMPLETE SERIES 2 (200)..	40.00	18.00	5.00
COMMON CARD (1-410)	.10	.05	.01

*STARS: 1.25X to 2.5X BASIC CARDS
*ROOKIES: 1X to 2X BASIC CARDS.

1995-96 Collector's Choice Player's Club Platinum

Issued randomly one in every thirty-five first and second series 12-card packs (and also packaged four per retail factory set at the end of the season), these 410 standard-size cards parallel the basic 1995-96 Collector's Choice series. Unlike the basic issue cards, Player's Club Platinum card fronts feature a special silver-foil paper stock and a silver foil facsimile autograph and Player's Club Platinum logo. Please refer to the multiplier provided below (and the values listed for the regular-issue 1995-96 Collector's Choice cards) to ascertain the value of individual Player's Club Platinum cards.

	MINT	NRMT	EXC
COMPLETE SET (410)	800.00	350.00	100.00
COMPLETE SERIES 1 (210).	300.00	135.00	38.00
COMPLETE SERIES 2 (200).	500.00	220.00	60.00
COMMON CARD (1-410)	1.00	.45	.12

*STARS: 15X to 30X BASIC CARDS.
*ROOKIES: 10X to 20X BASIC CARDS

☐	5	Jason Kidd..................	15.00	6.75	1.85
☐	10	Dennis Rodman............	25.00	11.00	3.10
☐	33	Grant Hill...................	25.00	11.00	3.10
☐	38	Juwan Howard............	15.00	6.75	1.85

☐ 40	Shawn Kemp	20.00	9.00	2.50
☐ 45	Michael Jordan	100.00	45.00	12.50
☐ 145	Anfernee Hardaway	40.00	18.00	5.00
☐ 169	Michael Jordan FF	50.00	22.00	6.25
☐ 173	Grant Hill FF	30.00	13.50	3.70
	Michael Jordan			
☐ 195	Michael Jordan PD	50.00	22.00	6.25
☐ 210	Michael Jordan CL	25.00	11.00	3.10
☐ 215	Scottie Pippen	20.00	9.00	2.50
☐ 220	Jerry Stackhouse	30.00	13.50	3.70
☐ 265	Hakeem Olajuwon	15.00	6.75	1.85
☐ 271	Dennis Rodman Bulls	40.00	18.00	5.00
☐ 275	Kevin Garnett	50.00	22.00	6.25
☐ 276	Damon Stoudamire	40.00	18.00	5.00
☐ 286	Shaquille O'Neal	30.00	13.50	3.70
☐ 300	Joe Smith	20.00	9.00	2.50
☐ 304	Michael Finley	20.00	9.00	2.50
☐ 324	Michael Jordan SR	50.00	22.00	6.25
☐ 346	D.Stoudamire SR	15.00	6.75	1.85
☐ 353	Michael Jordan PT	50.00	22.00	6.25
	Chicago vs Charlotte East Conf. 1st Round			
☐ 384	A.Hardaway LOVE	20.00	9.00	2.50
☐ 399	A.Hardaway PG	20.00	9.00	2.50
☐ 410	Michael Jordan CL	25.00	11.00	3.10

1995-96 Collector's Choice Crash the Game Assists/Rebounds

Issued randomly into one in every five second series 12-card packs, cards from this 90-card set feature three separate versions of thirty different player cards. Each player was given three separate specific game dates. If the player depicted on the card tallied 10 or more assists or rebounds on that date, the card was redeemable for for a special 30-card Crash the Game Assists/Rebounds Silver Trade set. Scarcer parallel gold versions of each card were also seeded one in every forty-nine second series packs. Winning gold cards were redeemable for a special 30-card Crash the Game Assists/Rebounds Gold Trade set. Both silver and gold cards had an expiration date of May 8th, 1996. Please refer to the multipliers provided within the header below for gold, gold exchange and silver

exchange card values. Losing cards are signified with an "L" and winning cards with a "W". The winning cards are actually in shorter supply than losing cards due to the fact that many of them were mailed in for redemption and then destroyed.

	MINT	NRMT	EXC
COMPLETE SILVER SET (90)	60.00	27.00	7.50
COMMON SILVER (C1-C30)	.25	.11	.03
*GOLD: 2X TO 4X VALUE			
COMP. SILVER EXCH. SET (30)	8.00	3.60	1.00
*SIL. EXCH. CARDS: 50% OF VALUE			
*GOLD EXCH.: 2X TO 4X SIL. EXCH.			

☐ C1	Michael Jordan 1/30 L	8.00	3.60	1.00
☐ C1B	Michael Jordan 2/22 L	8.00	3.60	1.00
☐ C1C	Michael Jordan 3/19 L	8.00	3.60	1.00
☐ C2	Tim Hardaway 2/4 L	.25	.11	.03
☐ C2B	Tim Hardaway 3/12 L	.25	.11	.03
☐ C2C	Tim Hardaway 4/11 W	.50	.23	.06
☐ C3	Juwan Howard 2/2 L	1.50	.70	.19
☐ C3B	Juwan Howard 2/21 L	.75	.35	.09
☐ C3C	Juwan Howard 3/30 L	.75	.35	.09
☐ C4	Shawn Kemp 1/29 L	2.00	.90	.25
☐ C4B	Shawn Kemp 3/15 W	5.00	2.20	.60
☐ C4C	Shawn Kemp 4/3 L	2.00	.90	.25
☐ C5	Nick Van Exel 2/4 L	.50	.23	.06
☐ C5B	Nick Van Exel 2/21 L	.75	.35	.09
☐ C5C	Nick Van Exel 4/14 L	1.00	.45	.12
☐ C6	Mookie Blaylock 2/15 L	.25	.11	.03
☐ C6B	Mookie Blaylock 3/8 L	.25	.11	.03
☐ C6C	Mookie Blaylock 4/20 L	.50	.23	.06
☐ C7	John Stockton 2/13 W	.60	.25	.07
☐ C7B	John Stockton 3/6 W	4.00	1.80	.50
☐ C7C	John Stockton 4/14 W	.75	.35	.09
☐ C8	Scottie Pippen 1/28 L	2.00	.90	.25
☐ C8B	Scottie Pippen 3/15 L	1.00	.45	.12
☐ C8C	Scottie Pippen 4/11 L	1.25	.55	.16
☐ C9	Vin Baker 2/3 L	.60	.25	.07
☐ C9B	Vin Baker 3/4 W	3.00	1.35	.35
☐ C9C	Vin Baker 4/5 W	.60	.25	.07
☐ C10	Lamond Murray 2/3 L	.25	.11	.03
☐ C10B	Lamond Murray 2/17 L	.25	.11	.03
☐ C10C	Lamond Murray 3/30 L	.25	.11	.03
☐ C11	D. Robinson 2/15 W	1.25	.55	.16
☐ C11B	D. Robinson 3/14 W	4.00	1.80	.50
☐ C11C	D. Robinson 4/13 W	1.50	.70	.19
☐ C12	Jason Kidd 2/6 L	1.50	.70	.19
☐ C12B	Jason Kidd 3/19 L	1.50	.70	.19
☐ C12C	Jason Kidd 4/13 W	2.00	.90	.25
☐ C13	Rod Strickland 2/15 L	.25	.11	.03
☐ C13B	Rod Strickland 3/8 W	3.00	1.35	.35
☐ C13C	Rod Strickland 4/5 L	.50	.23	.06
☐ C14	Glen Rice 1/29 L	.25	.11	.03
☐ C14B	Glen Rice 2/28 L	.25	.11	.03
☐ C14C	Glen Rice 4/2 L	.50	.23	.06
☐ C15	A. Hardaway 2/4 W	4.00	1.80	.50
☐ C15B	A. Hardaway 3/31 L	3.00	1.35	.35
☐ C15C	A. Hardaway 4/21 W	4.00	1.80	.50
☐ C16	H. Olajuwon 2/15 L	1.50	.70	.19
☐ C16B	H. Olajuwon 3/8 L	1.50	.70	.19
☐ C16C	H. Olajuwon 4/15 W	2.00	.90	.25
☐ C17	K. Anderson 2/14 W	3.00	1.35	.35
☐ C17B	K. Anderson 2/29 W	3.00	1.35	.35
☐ C17C	K. Anderson 3/29 L	.25	.11	.03
☐ C18	Sharone Wright 2/14 L	.25	.11	.03
☐ C18B	Sharone Wright 3/22 L	.25	.11	.03
☐ C18C	Sharone Wright 4/17 L	.50	.23	.06
☐ C19	D. Mutombo 2/16 L	.25	.11	.03
☐ C19B	D. Mutombo 3/2 W	3.00	1.35	.35

		MINT	NRMT	EXC
☐ C19C D. Mutombo 4/5 W.....		.50	.23	.06
☐ C20 Muggsy Bogues 2/1.....		.25	.11	.03
☐ C20B Muggsy Bogues 2/21 L		.25	.11	.03
☐ C20C Muggsy Bogues 3/20 L		.25	.11	.03
☐ C21 Reggie Miller 2/18 L		.75	.35	.09
☐ C21B Reggie Miller 3/5 L		.75	.35	.09
☐ C21C Reggie Miller 4/8 L....		1.00	.45	.12
☐ C22 Danny Manning 2/6 L		.25	.11	.03
☐ C22B Danny Manning 3/3 L ..		.25	.11	.03
☐ C22C Danny Manning 4/16 L		.50	.23	.06
☐ C23 C. Laettner 2/5 L		.25	.11	.03
☐ C23B C. Laettner 3/10 L.......		.25	.11	.03
☐ C23C C. Laettner 3/27 W ..		3.00	1.35	.35
☐ C24 Eric Montross 2/14 L		.25	.11	.03
☐ C24B Eric Montross 3/8 L.....		.25	.11	.03
☐ C24C Eric Montross 3/31 L...		.25	.11	.03
☐ C25 Patrick Ewing 2/21 L......		.60	.25	.07
☐ C25B Patrick Ewing 3/29 W		3.00	1.35	.35
☐ C25C Patrick Ewing 4/3 W...		.75	.35	.09
☐ C26 D. Stoudamire 1/30 L		4.00	1.80	.50
☐ C26B D. Stoudamire 3/10 L		4.00	1.80	.50
☐ C26C D. Stoudamire 3/22 W		6.00	2.70	.75
☐ C27 Bryant Reeves 2/28 L		1.00	.45	.12
☐ C27B Bryant Reeves 3/31 L		1.00	.45	.12
☐ C27C Bryant Reeves 4/9 L		1.25	.55	.16
☐ C28 Joe Dumars 2/15 L		.25	.11	.03
☐ C28B Joe Dumars 3/22 L		.25	.11	.03
☐ C28C Joe Dumars 4/13 L		.50	.23	.06
☐ C29 Tyrone Hill 2/6 L.............		.25	.11	.03
☐ C29B Tyrone Hill 3/10 L........		.25	.11	.03
☐ C29C Tyrone Hill 4/20 L........		.50	.23	.06
☐ C30 Brian Grant 2/13 L		.25	.11	.03
☐ C30B Brian Grant 3/20 L		.25	.11	.03
☐ C30C Brian Grant 4/21 L......		.50	.23	.06

1995-96 Collector's Choice Crash the Game Scoring

Issued randomly into one in every five first series 12-card packs, cards from this 81-card set features three separate versions of twenty-seven different player cards. Each player is matched up against three different teams (two within their conference and one outside of their conference). If the player depicted on the card scored 30 or more points, versus the team depicted on the card, the card was redeemable for a special 30-card Crash the Game Scoring Silver Trade set. Exchange sets consist of parallel versions of the 27 players originally depicted plus three additional cards (D.Stoudamire, B.Reeves & M.Jordan) available exclusively in the exchange set. Scarcer parallel gold versions of each card were also seeded one in every forty-nine first series packs. Winning gold cards were redeemable for a special 30-card Crash the Game Scoring Gold Trade set. Both regular and gold Crash the Game cards had an expiration date of May 8th, 1996. Please refer to the multipliers provided within the header below for gold, gold exchange and silver exchange card values. Losing cards are signified with an "L" and winning cards are signified with a "W". The winning cards are actually in shorter supply than losing cards due to the fact that many of them were mailed in for redemption and then destroyed.

	MINT	NRMT	EXC
COMPLETE SILVER SET (81)	60.00	27.00	7.50
COMMON SILVER (C1-C27)	.25	.11	.03
*GOLD: 2X to 4X VALUE			
COMPLETE SILVER EXCHANGE SET (30)	10.00	4.50	1.25
*SILVER EXCH. CARDS: 50% OF VALUE			
*GOLD EXCH.: 2X to 4X SILVER EXCH.			

		MINT	NRMT	EXC
☐ C1 Michael Jordan HOU W		8.00	3.60	1.00
☐ C1B Michael Jordan NY W		15.00	6.75	1.85
☐ C1C Michael Jordan ORL W		15.00	6.75	1.85
☐ C2 Kenny Anderson CLE L		1.00	.45	.12
☐ C2B Kenny Anderson LAC L		.25	.11	.03
☐ C2C Kenny Anderson MIA L		1.00	.45	.12
☐ C3 Charles Barkley CLE L...		1.00	.45	.12
☐ C3B Charles Barkley GS W		3.00	1.35	.35
☐ C3C Charles Barkley SA W		3.00	1.35	.35
☐ C4 Dana Barros ATL L		.25	.11	.03
☐ C4B Dana Barros BOS W ..		1.00	.45	.12
☐ C4C Dana Barros LAL L		.25	.11	.03
☐ C5 A.Hardaway CHI W		4.00	1.80	.50
☐ C5B A.Hardaway SA W		5.00	2.20	.60
☐ C5C A.Hardaway MIL W......		5.00	2.20	.60
☐ C6 Mookie Blaylock DAL L...		.25	.11	.03
☐ C6B Mookie Blaylock DET L		.25	.11	.03
☐ C6C Mookie Blaylock TOR L		.25	.11	.03
☐ C7 Lamond Murray ATL L.....		.25	.11	.03
☐ C7B Lamond Murray MIN L		.25	.11	.03
☐ C7C Lamond Murray VAN L		1.00	.45	.12
☐ C8 Karl Malone HOU L.........		.60	.25	.07
☐ C8B Karl Malone NY L		1.50	.70	.19
☐ C8C Karl Malone POR W......		1.50	.70	.19
☐ C9 A.Mourning CHI L............		.60	.25	.07
☐ C9B A.Mourning IND L..........		1.50	.70	.19
☐ C9C A.Mourning WASH W....		1.50	.70	.19
☐ C10 H.Olajuwon LAL W........		1.50	.70	.19
☐ C10B H.Olajuwon ORL W......		4.00	1.80	.50
☐ C10C H.Olajuwon POR W......		4.00	1.80	.50
☐ C11 Mark Price CHI L............		1.00	.45	.12
☐ C11B Mark Price NJ L...........		.25	.11	.03
☐ C11C Mark Price SEA L		.25	.11	.03
☐ C12 Isaiah Rider BOS L		.25	.11	.03
☐ C12B Isaiah Rider PHO L......		.25	.11	.03
☐ C12C Isaiah Rider SAC L		.25	.11	.03
☐ C13 Glen Rice NJ W.............		1.00	.45	.12
☐ C13B Glen Rice SAC W........		1.00	.45	.12
☐ C13C Glen Rice WASH W.....		1.00	.45	.12
☐ C14 M.Richmond LAL L.........		.50	.23	.06
☐ C14B M.Richmond MIN W.....		1.00	.45	.12

☐ C14C M.Richmond NJ L	1.00	.45	.12
☐ C15 Chris Webber GS W	.60	.25	.07
☐ C15B Chris Webber IND L	1.50	.70	.19
☐ C15C Chris Webber PHI L	1.50	.70	.19
☐ C16 Nick Van Exel DAL L	.50	.23	.06
☐ C16B Nick Van Exel MIL L	2.00	.90	.25
☐ C16C Nick Van Exel SAC L	2.00	.90	.25
☐ C17 M.Abdul-Rauf CHA L	.25	.11	.03
☐ C17B M.Abdul-Rauf PHO W	1.00	.45	.12
☐ C17C M.Abdul-Rauf SEA	1.00	.45	.12
☐ C18 D.Wilkins PHI L	.25	.11	.03
☐ C18B D.Wilkins ORL L	.25	.11	.03
☐ C18C D.Wilkins TOR L	.25	.11	.03
☐ C19 Patrick Ewing BOS W	.60	.25	.07
☐ C19B Patrick Ewing CHA L	1.50	.70	.19
☐ C19C Patrick Ewing PHO L	1.50	.70	.19
☐ C20 D.Robinson DEN	1.25	.55	.16
☐ C20B D.Robinson SEA	3.00	1.35	.35
☐ C20C D.Robinson WASH W	3.00	1.35	.35
☐ C21 Shawn Kemp DEN L	2.00	.90	.25
☐ C21B Shawn Kemp DET L	3.00	1.35	.35
☐ C21C Shawn Kemp UTAH L	3.00	1.35	.35
☐ C22 Jason Kidd IND W	1.50	.70	.19
☐ C22B Jason Kidd LAC L	5.00	2.20	.60
☐ C22C Jason Kidd SA L	5.00	2.20	.60
☐ C23 G.Robinson ATL W	.75	.35	.09
☐ C23B G.Robinson CHA L	5.00	2.20	.60
☐ C23C G.Robinson VAN L	5.00	2.20	.60
☐ C24 Reggie Miller MIN L	.75	.35	.09
☐ C24B Reggie Miller NY L	1.50	.70	.19
☐ C24C Reggie Miller ORL L	1.50	.70	.19
☐ C25 Joe Dumars CLE L	1.00	.45	.12
☐ C25B Joe Dumars MIL L	1.00	.45	.12
☐ C25C Joe Dumars UTAH L	.25	.11	.03
☐ C26 L. Sprewell DAL L	1.50	.70	.19
☐ C26B L.Sprewell HOU L	1.50	.70	.19
☐ C26C L.Sprewell MIA L	1.50	.70	.19
☐ C27 C.Robinson LAC L	1.00	.45	.12
☐ C27B C.Robinson PHI L	.25	.11	.03
☐ C27C C.Robinson UTAH W	1.00	.45	.12
☐ XC28 D.Stoudamire EXCH	2.00	.90	.25
☐ XC29 Bryant Reeves EXCH	.50	.23	.06
☐ XC30 Michael Jordan EXCH	4.00	1.80	.50

1995-96 Collector's Choice Debut Trade

This 30-card set was only available by redeeming one of the Collector's Choice Debut Trade cards, which were randomly seeded into second series 12-card packs. In all, there were three versions of the Debut Trade card issued - regular issue (1:30 packs), Player's Club (1:144 packs)

and Player's Club Platinum (1:720 packs). The 30-card set primarily consists of a selection of player's traded during the 1995-96 season. The prices listed below are for the more common regular issue cards. Please refer to the multiplier's provided below to find values on the Player's Club and Player's Club Platinum versions. The Debut Trade card program expired on May 8th, 1996. Collectors started receiving their cards around late June, 1996. It's interesting to note that rookies Antonio McDyess and Arvydas Sabonis were left out of the regular issue Collector's Choice set but included here in the Debut Trade set.

	MINT	NRMT	EXC
COMPLETE SET (30)	4.00	1.80	.50
COMMON CARD (T1-T30)	.05	.02	.01
COMP. PLAY. CLUB SET (30)	10.00	4.50	1.25
COMMON PLAY. CLUB (T1-T30)	.10	.04	.02
*PLAYER'S CLUB: 1X to 2X BASIC CARDS			
*PLAYER'S CLUB RKES: .75X to 1.5X BASIC CARDS			
COMP. PLAY. CB.PLAT. SET (30)	40.00	18.00	5.00
COMMON PLAY. CB.PLAT. (T1-T30)	1.00	.45	.12
*PLAYER'S CLUB PLAT.: 10X to 20X BASIC CARDS			
*PLAYER'S CLUB PLAT. RKES.			
6X to 12X VALUE			

☐ T1 Magic Johnson	1.00	.45	.12
☐ T2 Arvydas Sabonis	1.00	.45	.12
☐ T3 Kenny Anderson	.15	.07	.02
☐ T4 Hersey Hawkins	1.25	.55	.16
☐ T5 Sherman Douglas	.05	.02	.01
☐ T6 Spud Webb	.15	.07	.02
☐ T7 Glen Rice	.25	.11	.03
☐ T8 Todd Day	.05	.02	.01
☐ T9 John Williams	.05	.02	.01
☐ T10 Chris Morris	.05	.02	.01
☐ T11 Shawn Bradley	.15	.07	.02
☐ T12 Dan Majerle	.15	.07	.02
☐ T13 George McCloud	.05	.02	.01
☐ T14 Derrick Coleman	.05	.02	.01
☐ T15 Kendall Gill	.05	.02	.01
☐ T16 Ricky Pierce	.05	.02	.01
☐ T17 Robert Pack	.05	.02	.01
☐ T18 Alonzo Mourning	.30	.14	.04
☐ T19 Matt Geiger	.05	.02	.01
☐ T20 Don MacLean	.05	.02	.01
☐ T21 Willie Anderson	.05	.02	.01
☐ T22 Oliver Miller	.05	.02	.01
☐ T23 Tracy Murray	.05	.02	.01
☐ T24 Ed Pinckney	.05	.02	.01
☐ T25 Alvin Robertson	.05	.02	.01
☐ T26 Anthony Avent	.05	.02	.01
☐ T27 Blue Edwards	.05	.02	.01
☐ T28 Kenny Gattison	.05	.02	.01
☐ T29 Chris King	.05	.02	.01
☐ T30 Eric Murdock	.05	.02	.01

1995-96 Collector's Choice Draft Trade

This 10-card set was only available by redeeming a Collector's Choice Draft Trade card, which was randomly inserted into series one packs at a rate of one in 144 packs. The 10-card set consists of the top

rookies from the 1995-96 season. Card fronts contain a photo with the player's name, draft pick number and position. Card backs contain biographical and statistical information from the player's college/high school year(s) and are numbered with a "D" prefix. The Draft Trade card program expired on June 7, 1996.

	MINT	NRMT	EXC
COMPLETE SET (10)	15.00	6.75	1.85
COMMON CARD (D1-D10)	.25	.11	.03
☐ D1 Joe Smith	2.50	1.10	.30
☐ D2 Antonio McDyess	2.00	.90	.25
☐ D3 Jerry Stackhouse	4.00	1.80	.50
☐ D4 Rasheed Wallace	1.00	.45	.12
☐ D5 Kevin Garnett	6.00	2.70	.75
☐ D6 Bryant Reeves	1.25	.55	.16
☐ D7 Damon Stoudamire	5.00	2.20	.60
☐ D8 Shawn Respert	.25	.11	.03
☐ D9 Ed O'Bannon	.75	.35	.09
☐ D10 Kurt Thomas	.25	.11	.03

1995-96 Collector's Choice Jordan Collection

Randomly inserted into one in every 11 first and second series 12-card packs, these eight standard-size cards comprise the first and third parts of a 24-card set, spanning across all of Upper Deck's 1995-96 basketball products, highlighting the career of Michael Jordan. The fronts have a full-color photo with a gold-foil picture of Jordan in the lower left hand corner wearing number 45. The backs have a color photo at the top with information about the highlight and statistics from that year at the bottom.

	MINT	NRMT	EXC
COMPLETE SER.1 SET (4)	10.00	4.50	1.25
COMPLETE SER.2 SET (4)	10.00	4.50	1.25
COMMON SER.1 (JC1-JC4)	3.00	1.35	.35
COMMON SER.2 (JC9-JC12)	3.00	1.35	.35
☐ JC1 Michael Jordan 1985 NBA ROY	3.00	1.35	.35
☐ JC2 Michael Jordan 1986-87 3000 Points	3.00	1.35	.35
☐ JC3 Michael Jordan '88 NBA Defensive POY	3.00	1.35	.35
☐ JC4 Michael Jordan Jordan Collection CL	3.00	1.35	.35
☐ JC9 Michael Jordan 7 Consecutive Scoring Titles	3.00	1.35	.35
☐ JC10 Michael Jordan 50 Point Games	3.00	1.35	.35
☐ JC11 Michael Jordan Career NBA Playoff SL	3.00	1.35	.35
☐ JC12 Michael Jordan The Scoring Records	3.00	1.35	.35
☐ JC24 Michael Jordan Championship Seasons.	3.00	1.35	.35

1996-97 Collector's Choice

These 200-standard size cards, comprise Upper Deck's 1995-96 Collector's Choice series one set. Cards were primarily issued in 12-card hobby and retail packs with a suggested retail price of ninety-nine cents. Regular issue cards feature white-bordered fronts with color player action shots. The backs have a color photo and statistics. The following subsets are included: Bulls Victory Tour (25-29), Penny! (113-117) and NBA Fundamentals (166-195). A Draft Trade card (exchangeable for a 10-card set of 1996-97 rookies) was also randomly inserted into packs at a rate of one in 144 packs. The expiration date for the Draft Trade card is May 9, 1997.

	MINT	NRMT	EXC
COMPLETE SERIES 1 (200)	15.00	6.75	1.85
COMMON CARD (1-200)	.05	.02	.01
☐ 1 Mookie Blaylock	.10	.05	.01
☐ 2 Grant Long	.05	.02	.01
☐ 3 Christian Laettner	.10	.05	.01
☐ 4 Craig Ehlo	.05	.02	.01
☐ 5 Ken Norman	.05	.02	.01
☐ 6 Stacey Augmon	.10	.05	.01
☐ 7 Dana Barros	.05	.02	.01

#	Player			
☐ 8	Dino Radja	.10	.05	.01
☐ 9	Rick Fox	.05	.02	.01
☐ 10	Eric Montross	.05	.02	.01
☐ 11	David Wesley	.05	.02	.01
☐ 12	Eric Williams	.05	.02	.01
☐ 13	Glen Rice	.10	.05	.01
☐ 14	Dell Curry	.05	.02	.01
☐ 15	Matt Geiger	.05	.02	.01
☐ 16	Scott Burrell	.05	.02	.01
☐ 17	George Zidek	.05	.02	.01
☐ 18	Muggsy Bogues	.10	.05	.01
☐ 19	Ron Harper	.10	.05	.01
☐ 20	Steve Kerr	.05	.02	.01
☐ 21	Toni Kukoc	.10	.05	.01
☐ 22	Dennis Rodman	1.00	.45	.12
☐ 23	Michael Jordan	2.50	1.10	.30
☐ 24	Luc Longley	.05	.02	.01
☐ 25	Michael Jordan	1.25	.55	.16
	Vlade Divac VT			
☐ 26	M.Jordan Bulls VT	1.25	.55	.16
☐ 27	Luc Longley VT	.05	.02	.01
☐ 28	Scottie Pippen VT	.30	.14	.04
☐ 29	Toni Kukoc VT	.20	.09	.03
	Juwan Howard VT			
☐ 30	Terrell Brandon	.10	.05	.01
☐ 31	Bobby Phills	.05	.02	.01
☐ 32	Tyrone Hill	.05	.02	.01
☐ 33	Michael Cage	.05	.02	.01
☐ 34	Bob Sura	.05	.02	.01
☐ 35	Tony Dumas	.05	.02	.01
☐ 36	Jim Jackson	.10	.05	.01
☐ 37	Loren Meyer	.05	.02	.01
☐ 38	Cherokee Parks	.05	.02	.01
☐ 39	Jamal Mashburn	.10	.05	.01
☐ 40	Popeye Jones	.05	.02	.01
☐ 41	LaPhonso Ellis	.05	.02	.01
☐ 42	Jalen Rose	.05	.02	.01
☐ 43	Antonio McDyess	.25	.11	.03
☐ 44	Tom Hammonds	.05	.02	.01
☐ 45	Mahmoud Abdul-Rauf	.05	.02	.01
☐ 46	Dale Ellis	.05	.02	.01
☐ 47	Joe Dumars	.10	.05	.01
☐ 48	Theo Ratliff	.05	.02	.01
☐ 49	Lindsey Hunter	.05	.02	.01
☐ 50	Terry Mills	.05	.02	.01
☐ 51	Don Reid	.05	.02	.01
☐ 52	B.J. Armstrong	.05	.02	.01
☐ 53	Bimbo Coles	.05	.02	.01
☐ 54	Joe Smith	.30	.14	.04
☐ 55	Chris Mullin	.05	.02	.01
☐ 56	Rony Seikaly	.05	.02	.01
☐ 57	Donyell Marshall	.05	.02	.01
☐ 58	Hakeem Olajuwon	.50	.23	.06
☐ 59	Robert Horry	.10	.05	.01
☐ 60	Mario Elie	.05	.02	.01
☐ 61	Mark Bryant	.05	.02	.01
☐ 62	Chucky Brown	.05	.02	.01
☐ 63	Rik Smits	.10	.05	.01
☐ 64	Derrick McKey	.05	.02	.01
☐ 65	Eddie Johnson	.05	.02	.01
☐ 66	Mark Jackson	.05	.02	.01
☐ 67	Ricky Pierce	.05	.02	.01
☐ 68	Travis Best	.05	.02	.01
☐ 69	Rodney Rogers	.05	.02	.01
☐ 70	Brent Barry	.15	.07	.02
☐ 71	Lamond Murray	.05	.02	.01
☐ 72	Eric Piatkowski	.05	.02	.01
☐ 73	Pooh Richardson	.05	.02	.01
☐ 74	Cedric Ceballos	.10	.05	.01
☐ 75	Eddie Jones	.15	.07	.02
☐ 76	Anthony Peeler	.05	.02	.01
☐ 77	George Lynch	.05	.02	.01
☐ 78	Vlade Divac	.10	.05	.01
☐ 79	Rex Chapman	.05	.02	.01
☐ 80	Sasha Danilovic	.05	.02	.01
☐ 81	Kurt Thomas	.05	.02	.01
☐ 82	Keith Askins	.05	.02	.01
☐ 83	Walt Williams	.05	.02	.01
☐ 84	Vin Baker	.15	.07	.02
☐ 85	Shawn Respert	.05	.02	.01
☐ 86	Sherman Douglas	.05	.02	.01
☐ 87	Marty Conlon	.05	.02	.01
☐ 88	Johnny Newman	.05	.02	.01
☐ 89	Kevin Garnett	.75	.35	.09
☐ 90	Andrew Lang	.05	.02	.01
☐ 91	Terry Porter	.05	.02	.01
☐ 92	Sam Mitchell	.05	.02	.01
☐ 93	Tom Gugliotta	.10	.05	.01
☐ 94	Spud Webb	.05	.02	.01
☐ 95	Kendall Gill	.05	.02	.01
☐ 96	Vern Fleming	.05	.02	.01
☐ 97	Shawn Bradley	.10	.05	.01
☐ 98	Yinka Dare	.05	.02	.01
☐ 99	Jayson Williams	.05	.02	.01
☐ 100	Kevin Edwards	.05	.02	.01
☐ 101	Charles Oakley	.05	.02	.01
☐ 102	Anthony Mason	.05	.02	.01
☐ 103	John Starks	.10	.05	.01
☐ 104	J.R. Reid	.05	.02	.01
☐ 105	Hubert Davis	.05	.02	.01
☐ 106	Gary Grant	.05	.02	.01
☐ 107	Nick Anderson	.10	.05	.01
☐ 108	Donald Royal	.05	.02	.01
☐ 109	Brian Shaw	.05	.02	.01
☐ 110	Brooks Thompson	.05	.02	.01
☐ 111	Anfernee Hardaway	1.25	.55	.16
☐ 112	Dennis Scott	.10	.05	.01
☐ 113	Anfernee Hardaway PEN	.50	.23	.06
☐ 114	Anfernee Hardaway PEN	.50	.23	.06
☐ 115	Anfernee Hardaway PEN	.50	.23	.06
☐ 116	Anfernee Hardaway PEN	.50	.23	.06
☐ 117	Anfernee Hardaway PEN	.50	.23	.06
☐ 118	Derrick Coleman	.10	.05	.01
☐ 119	Rex Walters	.05	.02	.01
☐ 120	Sean Higgins	.05	.02	.01
☐ 121	Clarence Weatherspoon	.10	.05	.01
☐ 122	Jerry Stackhouse	.50	.23	.06
☐ 123	Elliot Perry	.05	.02	.01
☐ 124	Wayman Tisdale	.05	.02	.01
☐ 125	Wesley Person	.05	.02	.01
☐ 126	Charles Barkley	.30	.14	.04
☐ 127	A.C. Green	.05	.02	.01
☐ 128	Harvey Grant	.05	.02	.01
☐ 129	Arvydas Sabonis	.20	.09	.03
☐ 130	Aaron McKie	.05	.02	.01
☐ 131	Gary Trent	.05	.02	.01
☐ 132	Buck Williams	.05	.02	.01
☐ 133	Billy Owens	.05	.02	.01
☐ 134	Brian Grant	.05	.02	.01
☐ 135	Corliss Williamson	.05	.02	.01
☐ 136	Tyus Edney	.15	.07	.02
☐ 137	Olden Polynice	.05	.02	.01
☐ 138	Avery Johnson	.05	.02	.01
☐ 139	Vinny Del Negro	.05	.02	.01
☐ 140	Sean Elliott	.10	.05	.01
☐ 141	Chuck Person	.05	.02	.01
☐ 142	Will Perdue	.05	.02	.01
☐ 143	Nate McMillan	.05	.02	.01
☐ 144	Vincent Askew	.05	.02	.01
☐ 145	Detlef Schrempf	.10	.05	.01
☐ 146	Hersey Hawkins	.10	.05	.01
☐ 147	Sharone Wright	.05	.02	.01

		MINT	NRMT	EXC
☐ 148	Zan Tabak	.05	.02	.01
☐ 149	Oliver Miller	.05	.02	.01
☐ 150	Doug Christie	.05	.02	.01
☐ 151	Damon Stoudamire	.60	.25	.07
☐ 152	Jeff Hornacek	.10	.05	.01
☐ 153	Chris Morris	.05	.02	.01
☐ 154	Antoine Carr	.05	.02	.01
☐ 155	Karl Malone	.20	.09	.03
☐ 156	Adam Keefe	.05	.02	.01
☐ 157	Greg Anthony	.05	.02	.01
☐ 158	Blue Edwards	.05	.02	.01
☐ 159	Bryant Reeves	.15	.07	.02
☐ 160	Anthony Avent	.05	.02	.01
☐ 161	Lawrence Moten	.05	.02	.01
☐ 162	Calbert Cheaney	.05	.02	.01
☐ 163	Chris Webber	.15	.07	.02
☐ 164	Tim Legler	.05	.02	.01
☐ 165	Gheorghe Muresan	.10	.05	.01
☐ 166	Stacey Augmon FUND	.05	.02	.01
☐ 167	Dee Brown FUND	.05	.02	.01
☐ 168	Glen Rice FUND	.05	.02	.01
☐ 169	Scottie Pippen FUND	.30	.14	.04
☐ 170	Danny Ferry FUND	.05	.02	.01
☐ 171	Jason Kidd FUND	.20	.09	.03
☐ 172	LaPhonso Ellis FUND	.05	.02	.01
☐ 173	Grant Hill FUND	.30	.14	.04
☐ 174	Chris Mullin FUND	.05	.02	.01
☐ 175	Clyde Drexler FUND	.15	.07	.02
☐ 176	Rik Smits FUND	.05	.02	.01
☐ 177	Loy Vaught FUND	.05	.02	.01
☐ 178	Nick Van Exel FUND	.10	.05	.01
☐ 179	Alonzo Mourning FUND	.10	.05	.01
☐ 180	Glenn Robinson FUND	.10	.05	.01
☐ 181	Isaiah Rider FUND	.05	.02	.01
☐ 182	Ed O'Bannon FUND	.05	.02	.01
☐ 183	Patrick Ewing FUND	.10	.05	.01
☐ 184	Shaquille O'Neal FUND	.50	.23	.06
☐ 185	Derrick Coleman FUND	.05	.02	.01
☐ 186	Danny Manning FUND	.05	.02	.01
☐ 187	Clifford Robinson FUND	.05	.02	.01
☐ 188	Mitch Richmond FUND	.10	.05	.01
☐ 189	David Robinson FUND	.20	.09	.03
☐ 190	Shawn Kemp FUND	.30	.14	.04
☐ 191	Oliver Miller FUND	.05	.02	.01
☐ 192	John Stockton FUND	.10	.05	.01
☐ 193	Greg Anthony FUND	.05	.02	.01
☐ 194	Rasheed Wallace FUND	.10	.05	.01
☐ 195	Michael Jordan FUND	1.25	.55	.16
☐ 196	Michael Jordan	.25	.11	.03
	Matt Geiger CL			
☐ 197	Eddie Jones	.05	.02	.01
	Antonio McDyess CL			
☐ 198	Anfernee Hardaway	.05	.02	.01
	Kevin Garnett CL			
☐ 199	Damon Stoudamire CL	.05	.02	.01
	Avery Johnson CL			
☐ 200	David Robinson CL	.05	.02	.01
	Chris Mullin CL			
☐ NNO	Draft Trade Card	15.00	6.75	1.85

1996-97 Collector's Choice Crash the Game Scoring

Randomly inserted into first series packs at a rate of one in 5, this 60-card silver set

features two separate versions of thirty different player cards. Each player is given two seperate weeks to score 30 points in any given game during that time period. If the player depicted on the card scores 30 or more points in the given week, the card can be redeemed for one premium quality silver card of the depicted player. The expiration date for the cards is May 9, 1997.

		MINT	NRMT	EXC
	COMPLETE SILVER SET (60)	60.00	27.00	7.50
	COMMON SILVER (C1-C30)	.75	.35	.09
☐ C1A	Mookie Blaylock 11/4	.75	.35	.09
☐ C1B	Mookie Blaylock 12/16	.75	.35	.09
☐ C2A	Dino Radja 11/18	.75	.35	.09
☐ C2B	Dino Radja 1/6	.75	.35	.09
☐ C3A	Glen Rice 11/18	.75	.35	.09
☐ C3B	Glen Rice 1/27	.75	.35	.09
☐ C4A	Scottie Pippen 12/2	3.00	1.35	.35
☐ C4B	Scottie Pippen 1/13	3.00	1.35	.35
☐ C5A	Terrell Brandon 11/4	.75	.35	.09
☐ C5B	Terrell Brandon 1/13	.75	.35	.09
☐ C6A	Jason Kidd 12/9	2.00	.90	.25
☐ C6B	Jason Kidd 12/23	2.00	.90	.25
☐ C7A	A.McDyess 11/11	1.25	.55	.16
☐ C7B	A.McDyess 12/23	1.25	.55	.16
☐ C8A	Joe Dumars 12/9	.75	.35	.09
☐ C8B	Joe Dumars 1/13	.75	.35	.09
☐ C9A	Joe Smith 12/2	1.50	.70	.19
☐ C9B	Joe Smith 12/23	1.50	.70	.19
☐ C10A	H.Olajuwon 11/4	2.50	1.10	.30
☐ C10B	H.Olajuwon 12/23	2.50	1.10	.30
☐ C11A	Reggie Miller 12/9	1.25	.55	.16
☐ C11B	Reggie Miller 1/27	1.25	.55	.16
☐ C12A	Loy Vaught 11/18	.75	.35	.09
☐ C12B	Loy Vaught 1/6	.75	.35	.09
☐ C13A	Cedric Ceballos 12/2	.75	.35	.09
☐ C13B	Cedric Ceballos 1/27	.75	.35	.09
☐ C14A	A.Mourning 11/11	1.00	.45	.12
☐ C14B	A.Mourning 1/6	1.00	.45	.12
☐ C15A	Vin Baker 12/9	1.00	.45	.12
☐ C15B	Vin Baker 1/27	1.00	.45	.12
☐ C16A	Kevin Garnett 11/18	4.00	1.80	.50
☐ C16B	Kevin Garnett 1/13	4.00	1.80	.50
☐ C17A	Ed O'Bannon 12/2	.75	.35	.09
☐ C17B	Ed O'Bannon 1/6	.75	.35	.09
☐ C18A	Patrick Ewing 11/4	1.00	.45	.12
☐ C18B	Patrick Ewing 1/13	1.00	.45	.12
☐ C19A	A.Hardaway 12/23	6.00	2.70	.75
☐ C19B	A.Hardaway 1/27	6.00	2.70	.75
☐ C20A	C.Weatherspoon 12/16	.75	.35	.09
☐ C20B	C.Weatherspoon 1/13	.75	.35	.09
☐ C21A	Kevin Johnson 11/11	.75	.35	.09
☐ C21B	Kevin Johnson 1/27	.75	.35	.09
☐ C22A	C.Robinson 12/16	.75	.35	.09

		MINT	NRMT	EXC
☐ C22B	C.Robinson 1/6	.75	.35	.09
☐ C23A	Mitch Richmond 12/16	1.00	.45	.12
☐ C23B	Mitch Richmond 1/27	1.00	.45	.12
☐ C24A	Sean Elliott 11/4	.75	.35	.09
☐ C24B	Sean Elliott 1/6	.75	.35	.09
☐ C25A	Shawn Kemp 12/16.	3.00	1.35	.35
☐ C25B	Shawn Kemp 1/13..	3.00	1.35	.35
☐ C26A	D.Stoudamire 12/9..	3.00	1.35	.35
☐ C26B	D.Stoudamire 1/6 ...	3.00	1.35	.35
☐ C27A	John Stockton 11/11	1.00	.45	.12
☐ C27B	John Stockton 12/23	1.00	.45	.12
☐ C28A	Bryant Reeves 2/2 ..	1.00	.45	.12
☐ C28B	Bryant Reeves 1/27 .	1.00	.45	.12
☐ C29A	R.Wallace 11/18	.75	.35	.09
☐ C29B	R.Wallace 1/13	.75	.35	.09
☐ C30A	Michael Jordan 11/11	12.00	5.50	1.50
☐ C30B	Michael Jordan 12/23	12.00	5.50	1.50

1996-97 Collector's Choice Crash the Game Scoring Gold

Randomly inserted in packs at a rate of one in 49, this 60-card gold set features parallels the more common silver version. Each player is given two seperate weeks to score 30 points in any given game during that time period. If the player depicted on the card scores 30 or more points in the given week, the card an be redeemed for one premium quality gold card of the depicted player. The expiration date for the cards is May 9, 1997. Please refer to the multipliers provided within the header below for gold values.

	MINT	NRMT	EXC
COMPLETE GOLD SET (60) .	300.00	135.00	38.00
COMMON GOLD (C1-C30)......	3.75	1.70	.45
*GOLD CARDS: 2.5X to 5X VALUE...			

1996-97 Collector's Choice Game Face

Inserted one per special retail pack, this 10-card set is standard-sized with white bordered fronts and the logo "Game Face" in

gold on the front. Card backs include a inset photo of the player with commentary. Cards are numbered with a "GF" prefix.

	MINT	NRMT	EXC
COMPLETE SET (10)	8.00	3.60	1.00
COMMON CARD (GF1-GF10).....	.25	.11	.03
☐ GF1 Anfernee Hardaway....	2.00	.90	.25
☐ GF2 Michael Jordan..........	4.00	1.80	.50
☐ GF3 Shawn Kemp	1.00	.45	.12
☐ GF4 Alonzo Mourning.........	.40	.18	.05
☐ GF5 Cherokee Parks..........	.25	.11	.03
☐ GF6 Avery Johnson	.25	.11	.03
☐ GF7 LaPhonso Ellis	.25	.11	.03
☐ GF8 Rasheed Wallace	.25	.11	.03
☐ GF9 Jim Jackson	.25	.11	.03
☐ GF10 Larry Johnson	.40	.18	.05

1996-97 Collector's Choice Jordan A Cut Above

One of these ten Jordan ACA cards was inserted into every special Wal-Mart ninety-nine cent series one retail pack. This 10-card set focuses on Michael Jordan's career feats. Each card front is die cut at the top with the set name "A Cut Above" in gold foil. Card backs feature a head shot with a summary of each feat.

	MINT	NRMT	EXC
COMPLETE SET (10)	8.00	3.60	1.00
COMMON CARD (CA1-CA10) ..	1.00	.45	.12
☐ CA1 Michael Jordan	1.00	.45	.12
1985 Rookie of the Year			
☐ CA2 Michael Jordan	1.00	.45	.12
8-Time Scoring Leader			

			MINT	NRMT	EXC
☐	CA3	Michael Jordan	1.00	.45	.12
		8-Time All-NBA First Team			
☐	CA4	Michael Jordan	1.00	.45	.12
		Defensive POY			
☐	CA5	Michael Jordan	1.00	.45	.12
		10-Time All-Star			
☐	CA6	Michael Jordan	1.00	.45	.12
		2-Time All-Star Game MVP			
☐	CA7	Michael Jordan	1.00	.45	.12
		4-Time MVP			
☐	CA8	Michael Jordan	1.00	.45	.12
		4-Time Champion			
☐	CA9	Michael Jordan	1.00	.45	.12
		4-Time Finals MVP			
☐	CA10	Michael Jordan	1.00	.45	.12
		Continuing Excellence			

1996-97 Collector's Choice Mini-Cards

Inserted at a rate of one per series one pack, this 30-card set is comprised of 90 different "mini-cards". Three of these mini-cards form one standard-sized card and are issued in that form. Card fronts feature perforated panels of three players with silver foil. Card backs feature a brief commentary on each player. Each card contains it's own individual number, with an "M" prefix and is ordered below by the far left number on the card back.

		MINT	NRMT	EXC
COMPLETE SET (30)		8.00	3.60	1.00
COMMON CARD (1-30)		.10	.05	.01
☐ M2	Rex Walters	.10	.05	.01
	Jeff Hornacek			
	Mookie Blaylock			
☐ M5	Detlef Schrempf	.10	.05	.01
	Toni Kukoc			
	Dino Radja			
☐ M6	Ashraf Amaya	.10	.05	.01
	Sharone Wright			
	Eric Williams			
☐ M10	Tyus Edney	.20	.09	.03
	Ed O'Bannon			
	George Zidek			
☐ M13	Theo Ratliff	.10	.05	.01
	Shawn Bradley			
	Luc Longley			
☐ M22	Bobby Phills	.10	.05	.01

		MINT	NRMT	EXC
	Avery Johnson			
	Mahmoud Abdul-Rauf			
☐ M23	Popeye Jones	.10	.05	.01
	Chris Morris			
	Tom Hammonds			
☐ M25	Bobby Hurley	.75	.35	.09
	Christian Laettner			
	Grant Hill			
☐ M28	Sherman Douglas	.10	.05	.01
	Derrick Coleman			
	Rony Seikaly			
☐ M30	Nick Van Exel	.20	.09	.03
	John Starks			
	Sam Cassell			
☐ M33	Matt Geiger	.10	.05	.01
	Dennis Scott			
	Travis Best			
☐ M36	Cedric Ceballos	.20	.09	.03
	Isaiah Rider			
	Brent Barry			
☐ M37	Jason Kidd	.50	.23	.06
	Kevin Johnson			
	Lamond Murray			
☐ M38	Chris Mullin	.10	.05	.01
	Jayson Williams			
	Terry Dehere			
☐ M39	Arvydas Sabonis	.25	.11	.03
	Sasha Danilovic			
	Vlade Divac			
☐ M43	Tyrone Hill	.10	.05	.01
	Brian Grant			
	Kurt Thomas			
☐ M44	Derrick McKey	.10	.05	.01
	Robert Horry			
	Keith Askins			
☐ M46	Randolph Childress	.50	.23	.06
	David Robinson			
	Shawn Respert			
☐ M49	Todd Day	.10	.05	.01
	Oliver Miller			
	Andrew Lang			
☐ M56	Dell Curry	.10	.05	.01
	Bimbo Coles			
	Charles Oakley			
☐ M57	Rasheed Wallace	.60	.25	.07
	Jerry Stackhouse			
	J.R. Reid			
☐ M66	Joe Dumars	.30	.14	.04
	Clyde Drexler			
	A.C. Green			
☐ M67	Kendall Gill	.10	.05	.01
	Nick Anderson			
	Aaron McKie			
☐ M75	Danny Ferry	.10	.05	.01
	Mark Jackson			
	Doc Rivers			
☐ M78	Michael Jordan	5.00	2.20	.60
	Anfernee Hardaway			
	Shawn Kemp			
☐ M79	Jalen Rose	.20	.09	.03
	Chris Webber			
	Jimmy King			
☐ M83	Dennis Rodman	2.00	.90	.25
	Charles Barkley			
	Karl Malone			
☐ M85	Stacey Augmon	.25	.11	.03
	Larry Johnson			
	Greg Anthony			
☐ M86	Nate McMillan	.10	.05	.01
	Tom Gugliotta			
	Blue Edwards			

☐ M90 Jimmy Jackson............25 .11 .03
Glenn Robinson
Calbert Cheaney

1996-97 Collector's Choice Mini-Cards Gold

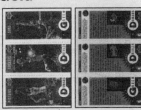

Randomly inserted into first series packs at a rate of one in 35, this 30-card set is comprised of 90 different "mini-cards" and parallels the more common silver foil version. Please refer to the multipliers provided within the header below for gold card values.

	MINT	NRMT	EXC
COMPLETE SET (30)	80.00	36.00	10.00
COMMON CARD (1-30)	1.00	.45	.12
*GOLD CARDS: 6X to 12X VALUE....			

1996-97 Collector's Choice Stick-Ums

Randomly inserted into first series packs at a rate of one in 4, this 30-card set features separate removable stickers of the actual player, the player's name and the given statistical categories. Card backs are black and white and feature set information including the complete Stick-Um checklist. Card stock is noticeably thin. Cards are numbered with an "S" prefix.

	MINT	NRMT	EXC
COMPLETE SET (30)	10.00	4.50	1.25
COMMON CARD (S1-S30)	.15	.07	.02
☐ S1 Mookie Blaylock	.15	.07	.02
☐ S2 Dana Barros	.15	.07	.02
☐ S3 Scott Burrell	.15	.07	.02
☐ S4 Dennis Rodman	1.50	.70	.19
☐ S5 Terrell Brandon	.15	.07	.02
☐ S6 Jamal Mashburn	.15	.07	.02
☐ S7 LaPhonso Ellis	.15	.07	.02
☐ S8 Grant Hill	1.00	.45	.12
☐ S9 Joe Smith	.50	.23	.06
☐ S10 Hakeem Olajuwon	.75	.35	.09
☐ S11 Rik Smits	.15	.07	.02
☐ S12 Brent Barry	.20	.09	.03
☐ S13 Nick Van Exel	.20	.09	.03
☐ S14 Sasha Danilovic	.15	.07	.02
☐ S15 Vin Baker	.25	.11	.03
☐ S16 Kevin Garnett	1.25	.55	.16
☐ S17 Shawn Bradley	.15	.07	.02
☐ S18 Patrick Ewing	.30	.14	.04
☐ S19 Anfernee Hardaway	2.00	.90	.25
☐ S20 Clarence Weatherspoon	.15	.07	.02
☐ S21 Charles Barkley	.50	.23	.06
☐ S22 Clifford Robinson	.15	.07	.02
☐ S23 Mitch Richmond	.25	.11	.03
☐ S24 David Robinson	.60	.25	.07
☐ S25 Shawn Kemp	1.00	.45	.12
☐ S26 Damon Stoudamire	1.00	.45	.12
☐ S27 Karl Malone	.30	.14	.04
☐ S28 Bryant Reeves	.25	.11	.03
☐ S29 Gheorghe Muresan	.15	.07	.02
☐ S30 Michael Jordan	5.00	2.20	.60

1994-95 Embossed

Featuring 121 double-sided, standard-size embossed cards, the 1994-95 Embossed set marks the premier of a new product for Topps. Each six-card pack contained five basic cards and one Golden Idols parallel gold foil card, with a suggested retail of 3.00 per pack. The fronts display a color embossed player photo framed by a textured border. The backs carry a second embossed player photo, biography, statistics, and a special "Did You Know" section containing unique information not found on other Topps cards. The cards are grouped alphabetically within teams. The set closes with a silver foil Draft Picks subset (101-120) followed by a Michael Jordan card that was added at the last minute. In addition to

the Draft Picks, all of the Houston Rockets cards were given a foil background treatment. Rookie Cards of note in this set include Grant Hill, Juwan Howard, Jason Kidd and Glenn Robinson.

	MINT	NRMT	EXC
COMPLETE SET (121)	30.00	13.50	3.70
COMMON CARD (1-121)	.10	.05	.01

		MINT	NRMT	EXC
☐ 1	Stacey Augmon	.15	.07	.02
☐ 2	Mookie Blaylock	.15	.07	.02
☐ 3	Ken Norman	.10	.05	.01
☐ 4	Steve Smith	.15	.07	.02
☐ 5	Dee Brown	.10	.05	.01
☐ 6	Blue Edwards	.10	.05	.01
☐ 7	Dino Radja	.25	.11	.03
☐ 8	Dominique Wilkins	.25	.11	.03
☐ 9	Muggsy Bogues	.15	.07	.02
☐ 10	Dell Curry	.10	.05	.01
☐ 11	Larry Johnson	.50	.23	.06
☐ 12	Alonzo Mourning	.60	.25	.07
☐ 13	B.J. Armstrong	.10	.05	.01
☐ 14	Ron Harper	.10	.05	.01
☐ 15	Toni Kukoc	.40	.18	.05
☐ 16	Scottie Pippen	1.50	.70	.19
☐ 17	Tyrone Hill	.10	.05	.01
☐ 18	Mark Price	.10	.05	.01
☐ 19	John Williams	.10	.05	.01
☐ 20	Jim Jackson	1.00	.45	.12
☐ 21	Popeye Jones	.10	.05	.01
☐ 22	Jamal Mashburn	.40	.18	.05
☐ 23	Mahmoud Abdul-Rauf	.15	.07	.02
☐ 24	LaPhonso Ellis	.10	.05	.01
☐ 25	Dikembe Mutombo	.25	.11	.03
☐ 26	Rodney Rogers	.10	.05	.01
☐ 27	Joe Dumars	.25	.11	.03
☐ 28	Lindsey Hunter	.10	.05	.01
☐ 29	Oliver Miller	.10	.05	.01
☐ 30	Terry Mills	.10	.05	.01
☐ 31	Tom Gugliotta	.10	.05	.01
☐ 32	Tim Hardaway	.25	.11	.03
☐ 33	Chris Mullin	.25	.11	.03
☐ 34	Latrell Sprewell	1.00	.45	.12
☐ 35	Sam Cassell FOIL	.25	.11	.03
☐ 36	Robert Horry FOIL	.30	.14	.04
☐ 37	Vernon Maxwell FOIL	.10	.05	.01
☐ 38	Hakeem Olajuwon FOIL	1.25	.55	.16
☐ 39	Otis Thorpe FOIL	.15	.07	.02
☐ 40	Mark Jackson	.10	.05	.01
☐ 41	Reggie Miller	.60	.25	.07
☐ 42	Rik Smits	.25	.11	.03
☐ 43	Terry Dehere	.10	.05	.01
☐ 44	Stanley Roberts	.10	.05	.01
☐ 45	Loy Vaught	.10	.05	.01
☐ 46	Vlade Divac	.25	.11	.03
☐ 47	George Lynch	.10	.05	.01
☐ 48	Nick Van Exel	.50	.23	.06
☐ 49	Billy Owens	.10	.05	.01
☐ 50	Glen Rice	.25	.11	.03
☐ 51	Kevin Willis	.10	.05	.01
☐ 52	Vin Baker	.60	.25	.07
☐ 53	Todd Day	.10	.05	.01
☐ 54	Eric Murdock	.10	.05	.01
☐ 55	Christian Laettner	.25	.11	.03
☐ 56	Isaiah Rider	.25	.11	.03
☐ 57	Micheal Williams	.10	.05	.01
☐ 58	Kenny Anderson	.25	.11	.03
☐ 59	P.J. Brown	.10	.05	.01
☐ 60	Derrick Coleman	.10	.05	.01
☐ 61	Chris Morris	.10	.05	.01
☐ 62	Patrick Ewing	.50	.23	.06
☐ 63	Derek Harper	.10	.05	.01
☐ 64	Anthony Mason	.15	.07	.02
☐ 65	Charles Oakley	.15	.07	.02
☐ 66	John Starks	.15	.07	.02
☐ 67	Horace Grant	.25	.11	.03
☐ 68	Anfernee Hardaway	3.00	1.35	.35
☐ 69	Shaquille O'Neal	2.50	1.10	.30
☐ 70	Dennis Scott	.15	.07	.02
☐ 71	Shawn Bradley	.25	.11	.03
☐ 72	Jeff Malone	.10	.05	.01
☐ 73	Clarence Weatherspoon	.15	.07	.02
☐ 74	Charles Barkley	.75	.35	.09
☐ 75	Kevin Johnson	.25	.11	.03
☐ 76	Dan Majerle	.15	.07	.02
☐ 77	Danny Manning	.15	.07	.02
☐ 78	Wayman Tisdale	.10	.05	.01
☐ 79	Clyde Drexler	.60	.25	.07
☐ 80	Clifford Robinson	.25	.11	.03
☐ 81	Rod Strickland	.10	.05	.01
☐ 82	Bobby Hurley	.10	.05	.01
☐ 83	Olden Polynice	.10	.05	.01
☐ 84	Mitch Richmond	.40	.18	.05
☐ 85	Spud Webb	.15	.07	.02
☐ 86	Sean Elliott	.25	.11	.03
☐ 87	Chuck Person	.10	.05	.01
☐ 88	David Robinson	1.00	.45	.12
☐ 89	Dennis Rodman	2.00	.90	.25
☐ 90	Kendall Gill	.10	.05	.01
☐ 91	Shawn Kemp	1.50	.70	.19
☐ 92	Sarunas Marciulionis	.10	.05	.01
☐ 93	Gary Payton	.75	.35	.09
☐ 94	Detlef Schrempf	.15	.07	.02
☐ 95	Jeff Hornacek	.15	.07	.02
☐ 96	Karl Malone	.50	.23	.06
☐ 97	John Stockton	.50	.23	.06
☐ 98	Don MacLean	.10	.05	.01
☐ 99	Scott Skiles	.10	.05	.01
☐ 100	Chris Webber	.60	.25	.07
☐ 101	Glenn Robinson FOIL	2.00	.90	.25
☐ 102	Jason Kidd FOIL	4.00	1.80	.50
☐ 103	Grant Hill FOIL	6.00	2.70	.75
☐ 104	Donyell Marshall FOIL	.15	.07	.02
☐ 105	Juwan Howard FOIL	4.00	1.80	.50
☐ 106	Sharone Wright FOIL	.15	.07	.02
☐ 107	Lamond Murray FOIL	.15	.07	.02
☐ 108	Brian Grant FOIL	.75	.35	.09
☐ 109	Eric Montross FOIL	.15	.07	.02
☐ 110	Eddie Jones FOIL	1.25	.55	.16
☐ 111	Carlos Rogers FOIL	.10	.05	.01
☐ 112	Khalid Reeves FOIL	.10	.05	.01
☐ 113	Jalen Rose FOIL	.50	.23	.06
☐ 114	Yinka Dare FOIL	.10	.05	.01
☐ 115	Eric Piatkowski FOIL	.10	.05	.01
☐ 116	Clifford Rozier FOIL	.15	.07	.02
☐ 117	Aaron McKie FOIL	.15	.07	.02
☐ 118	Eric Mobley FOIL	.10	.05	.01
☐ 119	Tony Dumas FOIL	.15	.07	.02
☐ 120	B.J. Tyler FOIL	.10	.05	.01
☐ 121	Michael Jordan	10.00	4.50	1.25

1994-95 Embossed Golden Idols

Inserted one per pack, this 121-card set parallels the regular 1994-95 Embossed

issue. The only difference is the full gold foil treatment on each card front. Please refer to the multipliers provided below for individual card values.

	MINT	NRMT	EXC
COMPLETE SET (120)	80.00	36.00	10.00
COMMON CARD (1-120)	.25	.11	.03
SEMISTARS	.60	.25	.07

*GOLD STARS: 1.25X TO 2.5X BASIC CARDS
*GOLD ROOKIES: 1X TO 2X BASIC CARDS

1994-95 Emotion

The complete 1994-95 Emotion set (produced by SkyBox) consists of 121 standard size cards. The cards were issued in eight-card packs with 36 packs per box. Suggested retail price was $4.99 per pack. The fronts have full-bleed color photos. Predominantly placed in the middle is a one word description of the player. The backs have career statistics and player information against a two photo background. The cards are grouped alphabetically within teams. The set closes with two topical subsets: Rookies (101-110) and Masters (111-120). A Grant Hill SkyMotion card was offered to those who sent in two wrappers and a check or money order for 24.99 before December 31st, 1995. The card shows three seconds of a Hill dunk. Rookie Cards of note in this set include Grant Hill, Juwan Howard, Eddie Jones, Jason Kidd and Glenn Robinson.

	MINT	NRMT	EXC
COMPLETE SET (121)	50.00	22.00	6.25
COMMON CARD (1-121)	.15	.07	.02
☐ 1 Stacey Augmon	.20	.09	.03
☐ 2 Mookie Blaylock	.20	.09	.03
☐ 3 Steve Smith	.30	.14	.04

☐ 4 Greg Minor	.15	.07	.02
☐ 5 Eric Montross	.30	.14	.04
☐ 6 Dino Radja	.30	.14	.04
☐ 7 Dominique Wilkins	.30	.14	.04
☐ 8 Muggsy Bogues	.20	.09	.03
☐ 9 Larry Johnson	.60	.25	.07
☐ 10 Alonzo Mourning	.75	.35	.09
☐ 11 B.J. Armstrong	.15	.07	.02
☐ 12 Toni Kukoc	.50	.23	.06
☐ 13 Scottie Pippen	2.00	.90	.25
☐ 14 Dickey Simpkins	.20	.09	.03
☐ 15 Tyrone Hill	.15	.07	.02
☐ 16 Chris Mills	.30	.14	.04
☐ 17 Mark Price	.15	.07	.02
☐ 18 Tony Dumas	.30	.14	.04
☐ 19 Jim Jackson	1.25	.55	.16
☐ 20 Jason Kidd	5.00	2.20	.60
☐ 21 Jamal Mashburn	.50	.23	.06
☐ 22 LaPhonso Ellis	.15	.07	.02
☐ 23 Dikembe Mutombo	.30	.14	.04
☐ 24 Rodney Rogers	.30	.14	.04
☐ 25 Jalen Rose	.60	.25	.07
☐ 26 Bill Curley	.15	.07	.02
☐ 27 Joe Dumars	.30	.14	.04
☐ 28 Grant Hill	8.00	3.60	1.00
☐ 29 Tim Hardaway	.30	.14	.04
☐ 30 Donyell Marshall	.20	.09	.03
☐ 31 Chris Mullin	.30	.14	.04
☐ 32 Carlos Rogers	.15	.07	.02
☐ 33 Clifford Rozier	.20	.09	.03
☐ 34 Latrell Sprewell	1.25	.55	.16
☐ 35 Sam Cassell	.30	.14	.04
☐ 36 Clyde Drexler	2.50	1.10	.30
☐ 37 Robert Horry	.40	.18	.05
☐ 38 Hakeem Olajuwon	1.50	.70	.19
☐ 39 Mark Jackson	.15	.07	.02
☐ 40 Reggie Miller	.75	.35	.09
☐ 41 Rik Smits	.30	.14	.04
☐ 42 Lamond Murray	.15	.07	.02
☐ 43 Eric Piatkowski	.15	.07	.02
☐ 44 Loy Vaught	.15	.07	.02
☐ 45 Cedric Ceballos	.40	.18	.05
☐ 46 Eddie Jones	1.50	.70	.19
☐ 47 George Lynch	.15	.07	.02
☐ 48 Nick Van Exel	.60	.25	.07
☐ 49 Harold Miner	.15	.07	.02
☐ 50 Khalid Reeves	.15	.07	.02
☐ 51 Glen Rice	.30	.14	.04
☐ 52 Kevin Willis	.15	.07	.02
☐ 53 Vin Baker	.75	.35	.09
☐ 54 Eric Mobley	.15	.07	.02
☐ 55 Eric Murdock	.15	.07	.02
☐ 56 Glenn Robinson	2.50	1.10	.30
☐ 57 Tom Gugliotta	.15	.07	.02
☐ 58 Christian Laettner	.30	.14	.04
☐ 59 Isaiah Rider	.30	.14	.04
☐ 60 Kenny Anderson	.30	.14	.04
☐ 61 Derrick Coleman	.15	.07	.02
☐ 62 Yinka Dare	.15	.07	.02
☐ 63 Patrick Ewing	.60	.25	.07
☐ 64 John Starks	.15	.07	.02
☐ 65 Charlie Ward	.20	.09	.03
☐ 66 Monty Williams	.15	.07	.02
☐ 67 Nick Anderson	.30	.14	.04
☐ 68 Horace Grant	.30	.14	.04
☐ 69 Anfernee Hardaway	4.00	1.80	.50
☐ 70 Shaquille O'Neal	3.00	1.35	.35
☐ 71 Brooks Thompson	.20	.09	.03
☐ 72 Dana Barros	.15	.07	.02
☐ 73 Shawn Bradley	.30	.14	.04
☐ 74 B.J. Tyler	.15	.07	.02

			MINT	NRMT	EXC
☐	75	Clarence Weatherspoon	.20	.09	.03
☐	76	Sharone Wright	.20	.09	.03
☐	77	Charles Barkley	1.00	.45	.12
☐	78	Kevin Johnson	.30	.14	.04
☐	79	Dan Majerle	.20	.09	.03
☐	80	Danny Manning	.20	.09	.03
☐	81	Wesley Person	1.50	.70	.19
☐	82	Aaron McKie	.30	.14	.04
☐	83	Clifford Robinson	.30	.14	.04
☐	84	Rod Strickland	.15	.07	.02
☐	85	Brian Grant	1.00	.45	.12
☐	86	Bobby Hurley	.20	.09	.03
☐	87	Mitch Richmond	.50	.23	.06
☐	88	Sean Elliott	.30	.14	.04
☐	89	David Robinson	1.25	.55	.16
☐	90	Dennis Rodman	2.50	1.10	.30
☐	91	Shawn Kemp	2.00	.90	.25
☐	92	Gary Payton	1.00	.45	.12
☐	93	Dontonio Wingfield	.15	.07	.02
☐	94	Jeff Hornacek	.20	.09	.03
☐	95	Karl Malone	.60	.25	.07
☐	96	John Stockton	.60	.25	.07
☐	97	Calbert Cheaney	.30	.14	.04
☐	98	Juwan Howard	5.00	2.20	.60
☐	99	Chris Webber	.75	.35	.09
☐	100	Michael Jordan	12.00	5.50	1.50
☐	101	Brian Grant ROO	.30	.14	.04
☐	102	Grant Hill ROO	3.00	1.35	.35
☐	103	Juwan Howard ROO	2.00	.90	.25
☐	104	Eddie Jones ROO	.60	.25	.07
☐	105	Jason Kidd ROO	2.00	.90	.25
☐	106	Eric Montross ROO	.15	.07	.02
☐	107	Lamond Murray ROO	.15	.07	.02
☐	108	Wesley Person ROO	.30	.14	.04
☐	109	Glenn Robinson ROO	1.00	.45	.12
☐	110	Sharone Wright ROO	.15	.07	.02
☐	111	Anfernee Hardaway MAS	2.00	.90	.25
☐	112	Shawn Kemp MAS	1.00	.45	.12
☐	113	Karl Malone MAS	.30	.14	.04
☐	114	Alonzo Mourning MAS	.40	.18	.05
☐	115	Shaquille O'Neal MAS	1.50	.70	.19
☐	116	Hakeem Olajuwon MAS	.75	.35	.09
☐	117	Scottie Pippen MAS	.30	.14	.04
☐	118	David Robinson MAS	.60	.25	.07
☐	119	Latrell Sprewell MAS	.20	.09	.03
☐	120	Chris Webber MAS	.40	.18	.05
☐	121	Checklist	.15	.07	.02
☐	NNO	Grant Hill SkyMotion Exchange	60.00	27.00	7.50

1994-95 Emotion N-Tense

Cards from this 10-card standard-size set were randomly inserted in Emotion packs at a rate of one in 18. The set contains a selection of some of the top players in the NBA. The fronts have full-bleed color photos and the player's name down the left in a hologram set against a sparkling gold background. The backs have two color action photos with the players name across the middle against a black background. The set is sequenced in alphabetical order.

	MINT	NRMT	EXC
COMPLETE SET (10)	100.00	45.00	12.50
COMMON CARD (N1-N10)	4.00	1.80	.50

			MINT	NRMT	EXC
☐	N1	Charles Barkley	6.00	2.70	.75
☐	N2	Patrick Ewing	4.00	1.80	.50
☐	N3	Michael Jordan	50.00	22.00	6.25
☐	N4	Shawn Kemp	12.00	5.50	1.50
☐	N5	Karl Malone	4.00	1.80	.50
☐	N6	Alonzo Mourning	5.00	2.20	.60
☐	N7	Shaquille O'Neal	20.00	9.00	2.50
☐	N8	Hakeem Olajuwon	10.00	4.50	1.25
☐	N9	David Robinson	8.00	3.60	1.00
☐	N10	Glenn Robinson	6.00	2.70	.75

1994-95 Emotion X-Cited

Cards from this 20-card standard-size set were randomly inserted in Emotion packs at a rate of one in four. The set features a selection of the top guards and small forwards in the NBA. The fronts have full-bleed color photos and the player's last name across the top set against a sparkling background. The backs have two color action photos set against a black background. The set is sequenced in alphabetical order.

	MINT	NRMT	EXC
COMPLETE SET (20)	50.00	22.00	6.25
COMMON CARD (X1-X20)	.75	.35	.09

			MINT	NRMT	EXC
☐	X1	Kenny Anderson	1.50	.70	.19
☐	X2	Anfernee Hardaway	15.00	6.75	1.85
☐	X3	Tim Hardaway	1.50	.70	.19
☐	X4	Grant Hill	15.00	6.75	1.85
☐	X5	Jimmy Jackson	1.50	.70	.19
☐	X6	Eddie Jones	3.00	1.35	.35
☐	X7	Jason Kidd	10.00	4.50	1.25

		MINT	NRMT	EXC
☐ X8	Dan Majerle	1.50	.70	.19
☐ X9	Jamal Mashburn	2.00	.90	.25
☐ X10	Lamond Murray	.75	.35	.09
☐ X11	Gary Payton	4.00	1.80	.50
☐ X12	Wesley Person	1.50	.70	.19
☐ X13	Scottie Pippen	8.00	3.60	1.00
☐ X14	Mark Price	.75	.35	.09
☐ X15	Mitch Richmond	2.00	.90	.25
☐ X16	Isaiah Rider	1.50	.70	.19
☐ X17	Latrell Sprewell	1.50	.70	.19
☐ X18	John Stockton	2.50	1.10	.30
☐ X19	Rod Strickland	.75	.35	.09
☐ X20	Nick Van Exel	2.50	1.10	.30

1993-94 Finest

The premier edition of the 1993-94 Finest basketball set (produced by Topps) contains 220 standard-size cards. The set is comprised of 180 player cards and a 40-card subset of ten of the best players in each of the four divisions as follows: Atlantic (90-99), Central (100-109), Midwest (110-119), and Pacific (120-129). These subset cards are commonly referred to as "brick" cards due to their brick wall background design. The seven-card packs (24 per box) included six player cards plus one subset card and had a suggested retail price of 3.99. Topps also issued a 14-card jumbo pack for 7.99, which included 11 regulars, two subsets, and a jumbo-only Main Attraction chase card. Packs hit the market upon release well above the aforementioned prices. The rainbow colored metallic front features a color action cutout on a metallic marble background. The white bordered back features a color player cutout on the left inset in a marble textured background. Rookie Cards of note include Vin Baker, Anfernee Hardaway, Jamal Mashburn and Chris Webber.

		MINT	NRMT	EXC
COMPLETE SET (220)		100.00	45.00	12.50
COMMON CARD (1-220)		.25	.11	.03
☐ 1	Michael Jordan TRIB	20.00	9.00	2.50
☐ 2	Larry Bird TRIB	5.00	2.20	.60
☐ 3	Shaquille O'Neal	8.00	3.60	1.00
☐ 4	Benoit Benjamin	.25	.11	.03
☐ 5	Ricky Pierce	.25	.11	.03
☐ 6	Ken Norman	.25	.11	.03

		MINT	NRMT	EXC
☐ 7	Victor Alexander	.25	.11	.03
☐ 8	Mark Jackson	.25	.11	.03
☐ 9	Mark West	.25	.11	.03
☐ 10	Don MacLean	.25	.11	.03
☐ 11	Reggie Miller	1.50	.70	.19
☐ 12	Sarunas Marciulionis	.25	.11	.03
☐ 13	Craig Ehlo	.25	.11	.03
☐ 14	Toni Kukoc	3.00	1.35	.35
☐ 15	Glen Rice	.75	.35	.09
☐ 16	Otis Thorpe	.50	.23	.06
☐ 17	Reggie Williams	.25	.11	.03
☐ 18	Charles Smith	.25	.11	.03
☐ 19	Micheal Williams	.25	.11	.03
☐ 20	Tom Chambers	.25	.11	.03
☐ 21	David Robinson	2.50	1.10	.30
☐ 22	Jamal Mashburn	3.00	1.35	.35
☐ 23	Clifford Robinson	.50	.23	.06
☐ 24	Acie Earl	.25	.11	.03
☐ 25	Danny Ferry	.25	.11	.03
☐ 26	Bobby Hurley	.50	.23	.06
☐ 27	Eddie Johnson	.25	.11	.03
☐ 28	Detlef Schrempf	.25	.11	.03
☐ 29	Mike Brown	.25	.11	.03
☐ 30	Latrell Sprewell	1.00	.45	.12
☐ 31	Derek Harper	.25	.11	.03
☐ 32	Stacey Augmon	.25	.11	.03
☐ 33	Pooh Richardson	.25	.11	.03
☐ 34	Larry Krystkowiak	.25	.11	.03
☐ 35	Pervis Ellison	.25	.11	.03
☐ 36	Jeff Malone	.25	.11	.03
☐ 37	Sean Elliott	.50	.23	.06
☐ 38	John Paxson	.50	.23	.06
☐ 39	Robert Parish	.50	.23	.06
☐ 40	Mark Aguirre	.50	.23	.06
☐ 41	Danny Ainge	.50	.23	.06
☐ 42	Brian Shaw	.25	.11	.03
☐ 43	LaPhonso Ellis	.25	.11	.03
☐ 44	Carl Herrera	.25	.11	.03
☐ 45	Terry Cummings	.25	.11	.03
☐ 46	Chris Dudley	.25	.11	.03
☐ 47	Anthony Mason	.25	.11	.03
☐ 48	Chris Morris	.25	.11	.03
☐ 49	Todd Day	.25	.11	.03
☐ 50	Nick Van Exel	4.00	1.80	.50
☐ 51	Larry Nance	.25	.11	.03
☐ 52	Derrick McKey	.25	.11	.03
☐ 53	Muggsy Bogues	.50	.23	.06
☐ 54	Andrew Lang	.25	.11	.03
☐ 55	Chuck Person	.25	.11	.03
☐ 56	Michael Adams	.25	.11	.03
☐ 57	Spud Webb	.25	.11	.03
☐ 58	Scott Skiles	.25	.11	.03
☐ 59	A.C. Green	.50	.23	.06
☐ 60	Terry Mills	.25	.11	.03
☐ 61	Xavier McDaniel	.25	.11	.03
☐ 62	B.J. Armstrong	.25	.11	.03
☐ 63	Donald Hodge	.25	.11	.03
☐ 64	Gary Grant	.25	.11	.03
☐ 65	Billy Owens	.25	.11	.03
☐ 66	Greg Anthony	.25	.11	.03
☐ 67	Jay Humphries	.25	.11	.03
☐ 68	Lionel Simmons	.25	.11	.03
☐ 69	Dana Barros	.25	.11	.03
☐ 70	Steve Smith	.50	.23	.06
☐ 71	Ervin Johnson	.50	.23	.06
☐ 72	Sleepy Floyd	.25	.11	.03
☐ 73	Blue Edwards	.25	.11	.03
☐ 74	Clyde Drexler	1.50	.70	.19
☐ 75	Elden Campbell	.25	.11	.03
☐ 76	Hakeem Olajuwon	3.00	1.35	.35
☐ 77	Clarence Weatherspoon	.50	.23	.06

#	Player			
☐ 78	Kevin Willis	.25	.11	.03
☐ 79	Isaiah Rider	1.50	.70	.19
☐ 80	Derrick Coleman	.25	.11	.03
☐ 81	Nick Anderson	.50	.23	.06
☐ 82	Bryant Stith	.25	.11	.03
☐ 83	Johnny Newman	.25	.11	.03
☐ 84	Calbert Cheaney	1.25	.55	.16
☐ 85	Oliver Miller	.25	.11	.03
☐ 86	Loy Vaught	.25	.11	.03
☐ 87	Isiah Thomas	.75	.35	.09
☐ 88	Dee Brown	.25	.11	.03
☐ 89	Horace Grant	.75	.35	.09
☐ 90	Patrick Ewing AF	.75	.35	.09
☐ 91	Clarence Weatherspoon AF	.25	.11	.03
☐ 92	Rony Seikaly AF	.25	.11	.03
☐ 93	Dino Radja AF	.50	.23	.06
☐ 94	Kenny Anderson AF	.25	.11	.03
☐ 95	John Starks AF	.25	.11	.03
☐ 96	Tom Gugliotta AF	.50	.23	.06
☐ 97	Steve Smith AF	.50	.23	.06
☐ 98	Derrick Coleman AF	.25	.11	.03
☐ 99	Shaquille O'Neal AF	5.00	2.20	.60
☐ 100	Brad Daugherty CF	.25	.11	.03
☐ 101	Horace Grant CF	.50	.23	.06
☐ 102	Dominique Wilkins CF	.50	.23	.06
☐ 103	Joe Dumars CF	.50	.23	.06
☐ 104	Alonzo Mourning CF	1.25	.55	.16
☐ 105	Scottie Pippen CF	2.50	1.10	.30
☐ 106	Reggie Miller CF	1.00	.45	.12
☐ 107	Mark Price CF	.25	.11	.03
☐ 108	Ken Norman CF	.25	.11	.03
☐ 109	Larry Johnson CF	1.00	.45	.12
☐ 110	Jamal Mashburn MF	1.25	.55	.16
☐ 111	Christian Laettner MF	.50	.23	.06
☐ 112	Karl Malone MF	.75	.35	.09
☐ 113	Dennis Rodman MF	3.00	1.35	.35
☐ 114	Mahmoud Abdul-Rauf MF	.50	.23	.06
☐ 115	Hakeem Olajuwon MF	2.00	.90	.25
☐ 116	Jim Jackson MF	1.00	.45	.12
☐ 117	John Stockton MF	.75	.35	.09
☐ 118	David Robinson MF	1.50	.70	.19
☐ 119	Dikembe Mutombo MF	.50	.23	.06
☐ 120	Vlade Divac PF	.50	.23	.06
☐ 121	Dan Majerle PF	.25	.11	.03
☐ 122	Chris Mullin PF	.25	.11	.03
☐ 123	Shawn Kemp PF	2.50	1.10	.30
☐ 124	Danny Manning PF	.25	.11	.03
☐ 125	Charles Barkley PF	1.25	.55	.16
☐ 126	Mitch Richmond PF	.50	.23	.06
☐ 127	Tim Hardaway PF	.25	.11	.03
☐ 128	Detlef Schrempf PF	.25	.11	.03
☐ 129	Clyde Drexler PF	1.00	.45	.12
☐ 130	Christian Laettner	.25	.11	.03
☐ 131	Rodney Rogers	.75	.35	.09
☐ 132	Rik Smits	.25	.11	.03
☐ 133	Chris Mills	2.00	.90	.25
☐ 134	Corie Blount	.25	.11	.03
☐ 135	Mookie Blaylock	.50	.23	.06
☐ 136	Jim Jackson	1.50	.70	.19
☐ 137	Tom Gugliotta	.50	.23	.06
☐ 138	Dennis Scott	.50	.23	.06
☐ 139	Vin Baker	5.00	2.20	.60
☐ 140	Gary Payton	2.00	.90	.25
☐ 141	Sedale Threatt	.25	.11	.03
☐ 142	Orlando Woolridge	.25	.11	.03
☐ 143	Avery Johnson	.25	.11	.03
☐ 144	Charles Oakley	.25	.11	.03
☐ 145	Harvey Grant	.25	.11	.03
☐ 146	Bimbo Coles	.25	.11	.03
☐ 147	Vernon Maxwell	.25	.11	.03
☐ 148	Danny Manning	.25	.11	.03
☐ 149	Hersey Hawkins	.25	.11	.03
☐ 150	Kevin Gamble	.25	.11	.03
☐ 151	Johnny Dawkins	.25	.11	.03
☐ 152	Olden Polynice	.25	.11	.03
☐ 153	Kevin Edwards	.25	.11	.03
☐ 154	Willie Anderson	.25	.11	.03
☐ 155	Wayman Tisdale	.25	.11	.03
☐ 156	Popeye Jones	.75	.35	.09
☐ 157	Dan Majerle	.50	.23	.06
☐ 158	Rex Chapman	.25	.11	.03
☐ 159	Shawn Kemp	4.00	1.80	.50
☐ 160	Eric Murdock	.25	.11	.03
☐ 161	Randy White	.25	.11	.03
☐ 162	Larry Johnson	1.50	.70	.19
☐ 163	Dominique Wilkins	.50	.23	.06
☐ 164	Dikembe Mutombo	.75	.35	.09
☐ 165	Patrick Ewing	1.25	.55	.16
☐ 166	Jerome Kersey	.25	.11	.03
☐ 167	Dale Davis	.25	.11	.03
☐ 168	Ron Harper	.25	.11	.03
☐ 169	Sam Cassell	2.00	.90	.25
☐ 170	Bill Cartwright	.25	.11	.03
☐ 171	John Williams	.25	.11	.03
☐ 172	Dino Radja	1.50	.70	.19
☐ 173	Dennis Rodman	5.00	2.20	.60
☐ 174	Kenny Anderson	.50	.23	.06
☐ 175	Robert Horry	.75	.35	.09
☐ 176	Chris Mullin	.50	.23	.06
☐ 177	John Salley	.25	.11	.03
☐ 178	Scott Burrell	.75	.35	.09
☐ 179	Mitch Richmond	1.00	.45	.12
☐ 180	Lee Mayberry	.25	.11	.03
☐ 181	James Worthy	.50	.23	.06
☐ 182	Rick Fox	.25	.11	.03
☐ 183	Kevin Johnson	.50	.23	.06
☐ 184	Lindsey Hunter	.50	.23	.06
☐ 185	Marlon Maxey	.25	.11	.03
☐ 186	Sam Perkins	.25	.11	.03
☐ 187	Kevin Duckworth	.25	.11	.03
☐ 188	Jeff Hornacek	.25	.11	.03
☐ 189	Anfernee Hardaway	40.00	18.00	5.00
☐ 190	Rex Walters	.25	.11	.03
☐ 191	Mahmoud Abdul-Rauf	.50	.23	.06
☐ 192	Terry Dehere	.25	.11	.03
☐ 193	Brad Daugherty	.25	.11	.03
☐ 194	John Starks	.25	.11	.03
☐ 195	Rod Strickland	.25	.11	.03
☐ 196	Luther Wright	.25	.11	.03
☐ 197	Vlade Divac	.50	.23	.06
☐ 198	Tim Hardaway	.50	.23	.06
☐ 199	Joe Dumars	.50	.23	.06
☐ 200	Charles Barkley	2.00	.90	.25
☐ 201	Alonzo Mourning	2.00	.90	.25
☐ 202	Doug West	.25	.11	.03
☐ 203	Anthony Avent	.25	.11	.03
☐ 204	Lloyd Daniels	.25	.11	.03
☐ 205	Mark Price	.25	.11	.03
☐ 206	Rumeal Robinson	.25	.11	.03
☐ 207	Kendall Gill	.25	.11	.03
☐ 208	Scottie Pippen	4.00	1.80	.50
☐ 209	Kenny Smith	.25	.11	.03
☐ 210	Walt Williams	.50	.23	.06
☐ 211	Hubert Davis	.25	.11	.03
☐ 212	Chris Webber	6.00	2.70	.75
☐ 213	Rony Seikaly	.25	.11	.03
☐ 214	Sam Bowie	.25	.11	.03
☐ 215	Karl Malone	1.25	.55	.16
☐ 216	Malik Sealy	.25	.11	.03
☐ 217	Dale Ellis	.25	.11	.03
☐ 218	Harold Miner	.25	.11	.03

		MINT	NRMT	EXC
☐	219 John Stockton	1.25	.55	.16
☐	220 Shawn Bradley	1.50	.70	.19

1993-94 Finest Refractors

This set of Refractor cards parallels that of the 220-card Finest set. Information provided by Topps indicated the cards were randomly inserted at a rate of one in every nine seven-card packs and one in approximately four 14-card jumbo packs. However, widespread evidence indicates the cards are easier to obtain. In addition, a good amount of the cards were included in retail "re-packs" at chains like Wal-Mart and Sams. The only difference in design to the basic cards is refracting foil that creates a glossy shine to the card fronts when held under light. Cards with an asterisk next to their listing signify that it is currently perceived to be in shorter supply.

		MINT	NRMT	EXC
	COMPLETE SET (220)	3000.00	1350.00	375.00
	COMMON CARD (1-220)	5.00	2.20	.60
☐	1 Michael Jordan TRIB	400.00	180.00	50.00
☐	2 Larry Bird TRIB	50.00	22.00	6.25
☐	3 Shaquille O'Neal	300.00	135.00	38.00
☐	4 Benoit Benjamin	5.00	2.20	.60
☐	5 Ricky Pierce	5.00	2.20	.60
☐	6 Ken Norman	5.00	2.20	.60
☐	7 Victor Alexander *	25.00	11.00	3.10
☐	8 Mark Jackson	5.00	2.20	.60
☐	9 Mark West	5.00	2.20	.60
☐	10 Don MacLean *	15.00	6.75	1.85
☐	11 Reggie Miller	60.00	27.00	7.50
☐	12 Sarunas Marciulionis *	40.00	18.00	5.00
☐	13 Craig Ehlo	5.00	2.20	.60
☐	14 Toni Kukoc	40.00	18.00	5.00
☐	15 Glen Rice	12.00	5.50	1.50
☐	16 Otis Thorpe	8.00	3.60	1.00
☐	17 Reggie Williams	5.00	2.20	.60
☐	18 Charles Smith	5.00	2.20	.60
☐	19 Micheal Williams	5.00	2.20	.60
☐	20 Tom Chambers	8.00	3.60	1.00
☐	21 David Robinson	50.00	22.00	6.25
☐	22 Jamal Mashburn	40.00	18.00	5.00
☐	23 Clifford Robinson	12.00	5.50	1.50
☐	24 Acie Earl	5.00	2.20	.60
☐	25 Danny Ferry	8.00	3.60	1.00
☐	26 Bobby Hurley	12.00	5.50	1.50
☐	27 Eddie Johnson	5.00	2.20	.60
☐	28 Detlef Schrempf *	15.00	6.75	1.85
☐	29 Mike Brown	5.00	2.20	.60
☐	30 Latrell Sprewell	20.00	9.00	2.50
☐	31 Derek Harper	8.00	3.60	1.00
☐	32 Stacey Augmon	8.00	3.60	1.00
☐	33 Pooh Richardson	25.00	11.00	3.10
☐	34 Larry Krystkowiak	5.00	2.20	.60
☐	35 Pervis Ellison	15.00	6.75	1.85
☐	36 Jeff Malone	25.00	11.00	3.10
☐	37 Sean Elliott	12.00	5.50	1.50
☐	38 John Paxson	8.00	3.60	1.00
☐	39 Robert Parish	12.00	5.50	1.50
☐	40 Mark Aguirre *	15.00	6.75	1.85
☐	41 Danny Ainge *	25.00	11.00	3.10
☐	42 Brian Shaw	5.00	2.20	.60
☐	43 LaPhonso Ellis	8.00	3.60	1.00
☐	44 Carl Herrera	5.00	2.20	.60
☐	45 Terry Cummings	8.00	3.60	1.00
☐	46 Chris Dudley	5.00	2.20	.60
☐	47 Anthony Mason *	15.00	6.75	1.85
☐	48 Chris Morris *	30.00	13.50	3.70
☐	49 Todd Day	15.00	6.75	1.85
☐	50 Nick Van Exel	60.00	27.00	7.50
☐	51 Larry Nance	8.00	3.60	1.00
☐	52 Derrick McKey	5.00	2.20	.60
☐	53 Muggsy Bogues *	15.00	6.75	1.85
☐	54 Andrew Lang	5.00	2.20	.60
☐	55 Chuck Person	8.00	3.60	1.00
☐	56 Michael Adams *	15.00	6.75	1.85
☐	57 Spud Webb *	15.00	6.75	1.85
☐	58 Scott Skiles	5.00	2.20	.60
☐	59 A.C. Green	8.00	3.60	1.00
☐	60 Terry Mills	5.00	2.20	.60
☐	61 Xavier McDaniel	5.00	2.20	.60
☐	62 B.J. Armstrong	8.00	3.60	1.00
☐	63 Donald Hodge	5.00	2.20	.60
☐	64 Gary Grant *	40.00	18.00	5.00
☐	65 Billy Owens	8.00	3.60	1.00
☐	66 Greg Anthony *	25.00	11.00	3.10
☐	67 Jay Humphries	5.00	2.20	.60
☐	68 Lionel Simmons	5.00	2.20	.60
☐	69 Dana Barros	8.00	3.60	1.00
☐	70 Steve Smith	12.00	5.50	1.50
☐	71 Ervin Johnson	8.00	3.60	1.00
☐	72 Sleepy Floyd	5.00	2.20	.60
☐	73 Blue Edwards	5.00	2.20	.60
☐	74 Clyde Drexler *	60.00	27.00	7.50
☐	75 Elden Campbell	8.00	3.60	1.00
☐	76 Hakeem Olajuwon	60.00	27.00	7.50
☐	77 Clarence Weatherspoon	8.00	3.60	1.00
☐	78 Kevin Willis *	25.00	11.00	3.10
☐	79 Isaiah Rider	20.00	9.00	2.50
☐	80 Derrick Coleman	8.00	3.60	1.00
☐	81 Nick Anderson	8.00	3.60	1.00
☐	82 Bryant Stith	8.00	3.60	1.00
☐	83 Johnny Newman	5.00	2.20	.60
☐	84 Calbert Cheaney *	60.00	27.00	7.50
☐	85 Oliver Miller	8.00	3.60	1.00
☐	86 Loy Vaught	8.00	3.60	1.00
☐	87 Isiah Thomas	15.00	6.75	1.85
☐	88 Dee Brown	5.00	2.20	.60
☐	89 Horace Grant *	25.00	11.00	3.10
☐	90 Patrick Ewing AF	12.00	5.50	1.50
☐	91 C. Weatherspoon AF	25.00	11.00	3.10
☐	92 Rony Seikaly AF	5.00	2.20	.60
☐	93 Dino Radja AF	8.00	3.60	1.00
☐	94 Kenny Anderson AF	8.00	3.60	1.00
☐	95 John Starks AF	5.00	2.20	.60

☐ 96	Tom Gugliotta AF	8.00	3.60	1.00
☐ 97	Steve Smith AF	8.00	3.60	1.00
☐ 98	Derrick Coleman AF	5.00	2.20	.60
☐ 99	Shaquille O'Neal AF	75.00	34.00	9.50
☐ 100	Brad Daugherty CF	5.00	2.20	.60
☐ 101	Horace Grant CF	8.00	3.60	1.00
☐ 102	Dominique Wilkins CF	8.00	3.60	1.00
☐ 103	Joe Dumars CF	8.00	3.60	1.00
☐ 104	Alonzo Mourning CF	20.00	9.00	2.50
☐ 105	Scottie Pippen CF *	60.00	27.00	7.50
☐ 106	Reggie Miller CF *	35.00	16.00	4.40
☐ 107	Mark Price CF *	15.00	6.75	1.85
☐ 108	Ken Norman CF	5.00	2.20	.60
☐ 109	Larry Johnson CF	15.00	6.75	1.85
☐ 110	Jamal Mashburn MF	15.00	6.75	1.85
☐ 111	Christian Laettner MF.	8.00	3.60	1.00
☐ 112	Karl Malone MF	12.00	5.50	1.50
☐ 113	Dennis Rodman MF * !	125.0055.00		15.50
☐ 114	Mahmoud Abdul-Rauf MF	5.00	2.20	.60
☐ 115	Hakeem Olajuwon MF	30.00	13.50	3.70
☐ 116	Jim Jackson MF *	30.00	13.50	3.70
☐ 117	John Stockton MF	12.00	5.50	1.50
☐ 118	David Robinson MF *	60.00	27.00	7.50
☐ 119	Dikembe Mutombo MF	8.00	3.60	1.00
☐ 120	Vlade Divac PF	8.00	3.60	1.00
☐ 121	Dan Majerle PF	8.00	3.60	1.00
☐ 122	Chris Mullin PF	8.00	3.60	1.00
☐ 123	Shawn Kemp PF	35.00	16.00	4.40
☐ 124	Danny Manning PF	8.00	3.60	1.00
☐ 125	Charles Barkley PF	20.00	9.00	2.50
☐ 126	Mitch Richmond PF	8.00	3.60	1.00
☐ 127	Tim Hardaway PF	8.00	3.60	1.00
☐ 128	Detlef Schrempf PF *	25.00	11.00	3.10
☐ 129	Clyde Drexler PF	15.00	6.75	1.85
☐ 130	Christian Laettner	15.00	6.75	1.85
☐ 131	Rodney Rogers	8.00	3.60	1.00
☐ 132	Rik Smits	12.00	5.50	1.50
☐ 133	Chris Mills *	80.00	36.00	10.00
☐ 134	Corie Blount	5.00	2.20	.60
☐ 135	Mookie Blaylock	8.00	3.60	1.00
☐ 136	Jim Jackson	30.00	13.50	3.70
☐ 137	Tom Gugliotta	12.00	5.50	1.50
☐ 138	Dennis Scott	8.00	3.60	1.00
☐ 139	Vin Baker *	100.00	45.00	12.50
☐ 140	Gary Payton *	80.00	36.00	10.00
☐ 141	Sedale Threatt	5.00	2.20	.60
☐ 142	Orlando Woolridge *	25.00	11.00	3.10
☐ 143	Avery Johnson	8.00	3.60	1.00
☐ 144	Charles Oakley	8.00	3.60	1.00
☐ 145	Harvey Grant	5.00	2.20	.60
☐ 146	Bimbo Coles	5.00	2.20	.60
☐ 147	Vernon Maxwell *	25.00	11.00	3.10
☐ 148	Danny Manning	8.00	3.60	1.00
☐ 149	Hersey Hawkins	8.00	3.60	1.00
☐ 150	Kevin Gamble	5.00	2.20	.60
☐ 151	Johnny Dawkins	5.00	2.20	.60
☐ 152	Olden Polynice	5.00	2.20	.60
☐ 153	Kevin Edwards	5.00	2.20	.60
☐ 154	Willie Anderson	5.00	2.20	.60
☐ 155	Wayman Tisdale *	25.00	11.00	3.10
☐ 156	Popeye Jones	12.00	5.50	1.50
☐ 157	Dan Majerle	8.00	3.60	1.00
☐ 158	Rex Chapman	5.00	2.20	.60
☐ 159	Shawn Kemp UER *	75.00	34.00	9.50
	(Misnumbered 136)			
☐ 160	Eric Murdock	5.00	2.20	.60
☐ 161	Randy White	5.00	2.20	.60
☐ 162	Larry Johnson	30.00	13.50	3.70
☐ 163	Dominique Wilkins	12.00	5.50	1.50
☐ 164	Dikembe Mutombo	15.00	6.75	1.85
☐ 165	Patrick Ewing *	50.00	22.00	6.25

☐ 166	Jerome Kersey	5.00	2.20	.60
☐ 167	Dale Davis	5.00	2.20	.60
☐ 168	Ron Harper	8.00	3.60	1.00
☐ 169	Sam Cassell	25.00	11.00	3.10
☐ 170	Bill Cartwright *	30.00	13.50	3.70
☐ 171	John Williams	5.00	2.20	.60
☐ 172	Dino Radja	20.00	9.00	2.50
☐ 173	Dennis Rodman *	150.00	70.00	19.00
☐ 174	Kenny Anderson	8.00	3.60	1.00
☐ 175	Robert Horry	15.00	6.75	1.85
☐ 176	Chris Mullin	12.00	5.50	1.50
☐ 177	John Salley	5.00	2.20	.60
☐ 178	Scott Burrell	8.00	3.60	1.00
☐ 179	Mitch Richmond	25.00	11.00	3.10
☐ 180	Lee Mayberry *	25.00	11.00	3.10
☐ 181	James Worthy	12.00	5.50	1.50
☐ 182	Rick Fox *	30.00	13.50	3.70
☐ 183	Kevin Johnson	12.00	5.50	1.50
☐ 184	Lindsey Hunter	8.00	3.60	1.00
☐ 185	Marlon Maxey	5.00	2.20	.60
☐ 186	Sam Perkins	8.00	3.60	1.00
☐ 187	Kevin Duckworth	5.00	2.20	.60
☐ 188	Jeff Hornacek	8.00	3.60	1.00
☐ 189	Anfernee Hardaway	400.00	180.00	50.00
☐ 190	Rex Walters	15.00	6.75	1.85
☐ 191	Mahmoud Abdul-Rauf	8.00	3.60	1.00
☐ 192	Terry Dehere	5.00	2.20	.60
☐ 193	Brad Daugherty	8.00	3.60	1.00
☐ 194	John Starks	8.00	3.60	1.00
☐ 195	Rod Strickland	12.00	5.50	1.50
☐ 196	Luther Wright	5.00	2.20	.60
☐ 197	Vlade Divac	8.00	3.60	1.00
☐ 198	Tim Hardaway	12.00	5.50	1.50
☐ 199	Joe Dumars	12.00	5.50	1.50
☐ 200	Charles Barkley	40.00	18.00	5.00
☐ 201	Alonzo Mourning	40.00	18.00	5.00
☐ 202	Doug West	5.00	2.20	.60
☐ 203	Anthony Avent	5.00	2.20	.60
☐ 204	Lloyd Daniels	15.00	6.75	1.85
☐ 205	Mark Price	8.00	3.60	1.00
☐ 206	Rumeal Robinson	5.00	2.20	.60
☐ 207	Kendall Gill	5.00	2.20	.60
☐ 208	Scottie Pippen *	125.00	55.00	15.50
☐ 209	Kenny Smith	5.00	2.20	.60
☐ 210	Walt Williams	8.00	3.60	1.00
☐ 211	Hubert Davis *	25.00	11.00	3.10
☐ 212	Chris Webber *	140.00	65.00	17.50
☐ 213	Rony Seikaly	5.00	2.20	.60
☐ 214	Sam Bowie	12.00	5.50	1.50
☐ 215	Karl Malone	25.00	11.00	3.10
☐ 216	Malik Sealy	5.00	2.20	.60
☐ 217	Dale Ellis *	25.00	11.00	3.10
☐ 218	Harold Miner	15.00	6.75	1.85
☐ 219	John Stockton	25.00	11.00	3.10
☐ 220	Shawn Bradley	20.00	9.00	2.50

1993-94 Finest Main Attraction

Distributed one per 14-card jumbo pack, a player from each of the 27 NBA teams is represented in this standard size set. The rainbow colored metallic front features a semi-embossed color action cutout on textured metallic background. The brick textured bordered back features a color action

shot with a gold border. Player's statistics and profile appear below the photo. The cards are numbered on the back "X of 27."

	MINT	NRMT	EXC
COMPLETE SET (27)	75.00	34.00	9.50
COMMON CARD (1-27)	1.00	.45	.12
☐ 1 Dominique Wilkins	1.50	.70	.19
☐ 2 Dino Radja	2.50	1.10	.30
☐ 3 Larry Johnson	4.00	1.80	.50
☐ 4 Scottie Pippen	10.00	4.50	1.25
☐ 5 Mark Price	1.00	.45	.12
☐ 6 Jamal Mashburn	6.00	2.70	.75
☐ 7 Mahmoud Abdul-Rauf	1.50	.70	.19
☐ 8 Joe Dumars	1.50	.70	.19
☐ 9 Chris Webber	8.00	3.60	1.00
☐ 10 Hakeem Olajuwon	8.00	3.60	1.00
☐ 11 Reggie Miller	4.00	1.80	.50
☐ 12 Danny Manning	1.00	.45	.12
☐ 13 Doug Christie	1.00	.45	.12
☐ 14 Steve Smith	1.50	.70	.19
☐ 15 Eric Murdock	1.00	.45	.12
☐ 16 Isaiah Rider	2.50	1.10	.30
☐ 17 Derrick Coleman	1.00	.45	.12
☐ 18 Patrick Ewing	3.00	1.35	.35
☐ 19 Shaquille O'Neal	20.00	9.00	2.50
☐ 20 Shawn Bradley	2.50	1.10	.30
☐ 21 Charles Barkley	5.00	2.20	.60
☐ 22 Clyde Drexler	4.00	1.80	.50
☐ 23 Mitch Richmond	2.50	1.10	.30
☐ 24 David Robinson	6.00	2.70	.75
☐ 25 Shawn Kemp	10.00	4.50	1.25
☐ 26 Karl Malone	3.00	1.35	.35
☐ 27 Tom Gugliotta	1.50	.70	.19

1994-95 Finest

This 331-card standard size set was issued in two series of 165 and 166 cards each.

Cards were distributed in 7-card packs carrying a suggested retail price of $5.00 each. Metallic silver fronts feature a color player photo against a prismatic background. The backs have a small photo, stats, bio and a "Finest Moment `93-94". The backs have blue borders with the player's name and position at the top. Topical subsets featured are City Legend-NYC (1-10), City Legend-Balt/DC (51-55), City Legend-Detroit (101-105), City Legend-Chicago (106-110), City Legend/LA (151-155), Finest's ACC's Best (201-209), Finest's Big East's Best (226-234), Finest's Big Ten's Best (250-259), and Finest's SEC's Best (275-284). Each card features a protective coating on front that was designed to protect the card from problems that may arise from handling. The coating can be removed by carefully peeling it from the card. Values provided below are for unpeeled cards. Peeled cards generally trade for about ten to twenty-five percent less. Rookie Cards of note include Grant Hill, Juwan Howard, Eddie Jones, Jason Kidd and Glenn Robinson.

	MINT	NRMT	EXC
COMPLETE SET (1-331)	190.00	85.00	24.00
COMPLETE SERIES 1 (165)	100.00	45.00	12.50
COMPLETE SERIES 2 (166)	90.00	40.00	11.00
COMMON CARD (1-165)	.50	.23	.06
COMMON CARD (166-331)	.25	.11	.03
☐ 1 Chris Mullin CY	.75	.35	.09
☐ 2 Anthony Mason CY	.50	.23	.06
☐ 3 John Salley CY	.50	.23	.06
☐ 4 Jamal Mashburn CY	1.25	.55	.16
☐ 5 Mark Jackson CY	.50	.23	.06
☐ 6 Mario Elie CY	.50	.23	.06
☐ 7 Kenny Anderson CY	.75	.35	.09
☐ 8 Rod Strickland CY	.50	.23	.06
☐ 9 Kenny Smith CY	.50	.23	.06
☐ 10 Olden Polynice CY	.50	.23	.06
☐ 11 Derek Harper	.50	.23	.06
☐ 12 Danny Ainge	1.25	.55	.16
☐ 13 Dino Radja	1.25	.55	.16
☐ 14 Eric Murdock	.50	.23	.06
☐ 15 Sean Rooks	.50	.23	.06
☐ 16 Dell Curry	.50	.23	.06
☐ 17 Victor Alexander	.50	.23	.06
☐ 18 Rodney Rogers	.50	.23	.06
☐ 19 John Salley	.50	.23	.06
☐ 20 Brad Daugherty	.50	.23	.06
☐ 21 Elmore Spencer	.50	.23	.06
☐ 22 Mitch Richmond	2.00	.90	.25
☐ 23 Rex Walters	.50	.23	.06
☐ 24 Antonio Davis	.50	.23	.06
☐ 25 B.J. Armstrong	.50	.23	.06
☐ 26 Andrew Lang	.50	.23	.06
☐ 27 Carl Herrera	.50	.23	.06
☐ 28 Kevin Edwards	.50	.23	.06
☐ 29 Micheal Williams	.50	.23	.06
☐ 30 Clyde Drexler	3.00	1.35	.35
☐ 31 Dana Barros	.50	.23	.06
☐ 32 Shaquille O'Neal	12.00	5.50	1.50
☐ 33 Patrick Ewing	2.50	1.10	.30
☐ 34 Charles Barkley	4.00	1.80	.50
☐ 35 J.R. Reid	.50	.23	.06
☐ 36 Lindsey Hunter	.50	.23	.06
☐ 37 Jeff Malone	.50	.23	.06

#	Player			
☐ 38	Rik Smits	1.25	.55	.16
☐ 39	Brian Williams	.50	.23	.06
☐ 40	Shawn Kemp	8.00	3.60	1.00
☐ 41	Terry Porter	.50	.23	.06
☐ 42	James Worthy	1.25	.55	.16
☐ 43	Rex Chapman	.50	.23	.06
☐ 44	Stanley Roberts	.50	.23	.06
☐ 45	Chris Smith	.50	.23	.06
☐ 46	Dee Brown	.50	.23	.06
☐ 47	Chris Gatling	.50	.23	.06
☐ 48	Donald Hodge	.50	.23	.06
☐ 49	Bimbo Coles	.50	.23	.06
☐ 50	Derrick Coleman	.50	.23	.06
☐ 51	Muggsy Bogues CY	.50	.23	.06
☐ 52	Reggie Williams CY	.50	.23	.06
☐ 53	David Wingate CY	.50	.23	.06
☐ 54	Sam Cassell CY	.75	.35	.09
☐ 55	Sherman Douglas CY	.50	.23	.06
☐ 56	Keith Jennings	.50	.23	.06
☐ 57	Kenny Gattison	.50	.23	.06
☐ 58	Brent Price	.50	.23	.06
☐ 59	Luc Longley	.50	.23	.06
☐ 60	Jamal Mashburn	2.00	.90	.25
☐ 61	Doug West	.50	.23	.06
☐ 62	Walt Williams	.75	.35	.09
☐ 63	Tracy Murray	.50	.23	.06
☐ 64	Robert Pack	.50	.23	.06
☐ 65	Johnny Dawkins	.50	.23	.06
☐ 66	Vin Baker	3.00	1.35	.35
☐ 67	Sam Cassell	1.25	.55	.16
☐ 68	Dale Davis	.50	.23	.06
☐ 69	Terrell Brandon	1.25	.55	.16
☐ 70	Billy Owens	.50	.23	.06
☐ 71	Ervin Johnson	.50	.23	.06
☐ 72	Allan Houston	1.50	.70	.19
☐ 73	Craig Ehlo	.50	.23	.06
☐ 74	Loy Vaught	.50	.23	.06
☐ 75	Scottie Pippen	8.00	3.60	1.00
☐ 76	Sam Bowie	.50	.23	.06
☐ 77	Anthony Mason	.75	.35	.09
☐ 78	Felton Spencer	.50	.23	.06
☐ 79	P.J. Brown	.50	.23	.06
☐ 80	Christian Laettner	1.25	.55	.16
☐ 81	Todd Day	.50	.23	.06
☐ 82	Sean Elliott	1.25	.55	.16
☐ 83	Grant Long	.50	.23	.06
☐ 84	Xavier McDaniel	.50	.23	.06
☐ 85	David Benoit	.50	.23	.06
☐ 86	Larry Stewart	.50	.23	.06
☐ 87	Donald Royal	.50	.23	.06
☐ 88	Duane Causwell	.50	.23	.06
☐ 89	Vlade Divac	1.25	.55	.16
☐ 90	Derrick McKey	.50	.23	.06
☐ 91	Kevin Johnson	1.25	.55	.16
☐ 92	LaPhonso Ellis	.50	.23	.06
☐ 93	Jerome Kersey	.50	.23	.06
☐ 94	Muggsy Bogues	.75	.35	.09
☐ 95	Tom Gugliotta	.50	.23	.06
☐ 96	Jeff Hornacek	.75	.35	.09
☐ 97	Kevin Willis	.50	.23	.06
☐ 98	Chris Mills	.50	.55	.16
☐ 99	Sam Perkins	.75	.35	.09
☐ 100	Alonzo Mourning	3.00	1.35	.35
☐ 101	Derrick Coleman CY	.50	.23	.06
☐ 102	Glen Rice CY	.50	.23	.06
☐ 103	Kevin Willis CY	.50	.23	.06
☐ 104	Chris Webber CY	1.50	.70	.19
☐ 105	Terry Mills CY	.50	.23	.06
☐ 106	Tim Hardaway CY	.50	.23	.06
☐ 107	Nick Anderson CY	.50	.23	.06
☐ 108	Terry Cummings CY	.50	.23	.06
☐ 109	Hersey Hawkins CY	.50	.23	.06
☐ 110	Ken Norman CY	.50	.23	.06
☐ 111	Nick Anderson	1.25	.55	.16
☐ 112	Tim Perry	.50	.23	.06
☐ 113	Terry Dehere	.50	.23	.06
☐ 114	Chris Morris	.50	.23	.06
☐ 115	John Williams	.50	.23	.06
☐ 116	Jon Barry	.50	.23	.06
☐ 117	Rony Seikaly	.50	.23	.06
☐ 118	Detlef Schrempf	.75	.35	.09
☐ 119	Terry Cummings	.50	.23	.06
☐ 120	Chris Webber	3.00	1.35	.35
☐ 121	David Wingate	.50	.23	.06
☐ 122	Popeye Jones	.50	.23	.06
☐ 123	Sherman Douglas	.50	.23	.06
☐ 124	Greg Anthony	.50	.23	.06
☐ 125	Mookie Blaylock	.75	.35	.09
☐ 126	Don MacLean	.50	.23	.06
☐ 127	Lionel Simmons	.50	.23	.06
☐ 128	Scott Brooks	.50	.23	.06
☐ 129	Jeff Turner	.50	.23	.06
☐ 130	Bryant Stith	.50	.23	.06
☐ 131	Shawn Bradley	1.25	.55	.16
☐ 132	Byron Scott	1.25	.55	.16
☐ 133	Doug Christie	.50	.23	.06
☐ 134	Dennis Rodman	10.00	4.50	1.25
☐ 135	Dan Majerle	.75	.35	.09
☐ 136	Gary Grant	.50	.23	.06
☐ 137	Bryon Russell	.50	.23	.06
☐ 138	Will Perdue	.50	.23	.06
☐ 139	Gheorghe Muresan	1.25	.55	.16
☐ 140	Kendall Gill	.50	.23	.06
☐ 141	Isaiah Rider	1.25	.55	.16
☐ 142	Terry Mills	.50	.23	.06
☐ 143	Willie Anderson	.50	.23	.06
☐ 144	Hubert Davis	.50	.23	.06
☐ 145	Lucious Harris	.50	.23	.06
☐ 146	Spud Webb	.75	.35	.09
☐ 147	Glen Rice	1.25	.55	.16
☐ 148	Dennis Scott	.75	.35	.09
☐ 149	Robert Horry	1.00	.45	.12
☐ 150	John Stockton	2.50	1.10	.30
☐ 151	Stacey Augmon CY	.50	.23	.06
☐ 152	Chris Mills CY	.50	.23	.06
☐ 153	Elden Campbell CY	.50	.23	.06
☐ 154	Jay Humphries CY	.50	.23	.06
☐ 155	Reggie Miller CY	1.50	.70	.19
☐ 156	George Lynch	.50	.23	.06
☐ 157	Tyrone Hill	.50	.23	.06
☐ 158	Lee Mayberry	.50	.23	.06
☐ 159	Jon Koncak	.50	.23	.06
☐ 160	Joe Dumars	1.25	.55	.16
☐ 161	Vernon Maxwell	.50	.23	.06
☐ 162	Joe Kleine	.50	.23	.06
☐ 163	Acie Earl	.50	.23	.06
☐ 164	Steve Kerr	.75	.35	.09
☐ 165	Rod Strickland	.50	.23	.06
☐ 166	Glenn Robinson	5.00	2.20	.60
☐ 167	Anfernee Hardaway	10.00	4.50	1.25
☐ 168	Latrell Sprewell	2.00	.90	.25
☐ 169	Sergei Bazarevich	.25	.11	.03
☐ 170	Hakeem Olajuwon	3.00	1.35	.35
☐ 171	Nick Van Exel	1.25	.55	.16
☐ 172	Buck Williams	.40	.18	.05
☐ 173	Antoine Carr	.25	.11	.03
☐ 174	Corie Blount	.25	.11	.03
☐ 175	Dominique Wilkins	.60	.25	.07
☐ 176	Yinka Dare	.25	.11	.03
☐ 177	Byron Houston	.25	.11	.03
☐ 178	LaSalle Thompson	.25	.11	.03
☐ 179	Doug Smith	.25	.11	.03

☐	180	David Robinson	2.50	1.10	.30	☐	251	Kevin Willis FB	.25	.11	.03
☐	181	Eric Piatkowski	.25	.11	.03	☐	252	B.J. Armstrong FB	.25	.11	.03
☐	182	Scott Skiles	.25	.11	.03	☐	253	Jim Jackson FB	.60	.25	.07
☐	183	Scott Burrell	.25	.11	.03	☐	254	Steve Smith FB	.25	.11	.03
☐	184	Mark West	.25	.11	.03	☐	255	Chris Webber FB	.75	.35	.09
☐	185	Billy Owens	.25	.11	.03	☐	256	Glen Rice FB	.25	.11	.03
☐	186	Brian Grant	2.00	.90	.25	☐	257	Derek Harper FB	.25	.11	.03
☐	187	Scott Williams	.25	.11	.03	☐	258	Jalen Rose FB	.25	.11	.03
☐	188	Gerald Madkins	.25	.11	.03	☐	259	Juwan Howard FB	4.00	1.80	.50
☐	189	Reggie Williams	.25	.11	.03	☐	260	Kenny Anderson	.60	.25	.07
☐	190	Danny Manning	.40	.18	.05	☐	261	Calbert Cheaney	.40	.18	.05
☐	191	Mike Brown	.25	.11	.03	☐	262	Bill Cartwright	.25	.11	.03
☐	192	Charles Smith	.25	.11	.03	☐	263	Mario Elie	.25	.11	.03
☐	193	Elden Campbell	.40	.18	.05	☐	264	Chris Dudley	.25	.11	.03
☐	194	Ricky Pierce	.25	.11	.03	☐	265	Jim Jackson	2.00	.90	.25
☐	195	Karl Malone	1.25	.55	.16	☐	266	Antonio Harvey	.25	.11	.03
☐	196	Brooks Thompson	.40	.18	.05	☐	267	Bill Curley	.25	.11	.03
☐	197	Alaa Abdelnaby	.25	.11	.03	☐	268	Moses Malone	.75	.35	.09
☐	198	Tyrone Corbin	.25	.11	.03	☐	269	A.C. Green	.60	.25	.07
☐	199	Johnny Newman	.25	.11	.03	☐	270	Larry Johnson	1.25	.55	.16
☐	200	Grant Hill FB	6.00	2.70	.75	☐	271	Marty Conlon	.25	.11	.03
☐	201	Kenny Anderson FB	.25	.11	.03	☐	272	Greg Graham	.25	.11	.03
☐	202	Olden Polynice FB	.25	.11	.03	☐	273	Eric Montross	.40	.18	.05
☐	203	Horace Grant FB	.25	.11	.03	☐	274	Stacey King	.25	.11	.03
☐	204	Muggsy Bogues FB	.25	.11	.03	☐	275	Charles Barkley FB	1.00	.45	.12
☐	205	Mark Price FB	.25	.11	.03	☐	276	Chris Morris FB	.25	.11	.03
☐	206	Tom Gugliotta FB	.25	.11	.03	☐	277	Robert Horry FB	.60	.25	.07
☐	207	Christian Laettner FB	.40	.18	.05	☐	278	Dominique Wilkins FB	.40	.18	.05
☐	208	Eric Montross FB	.25	.11	.03	☐	279	Latrell Sprewell FB	.40	.18	.05
☐	209	Sam Cassell FB	.25	.11	.03	☐	280	Shaquille O'Neal FB	3.00	1.35	.35
☐	210	Charles Oakley	.40	.18	.05	☐	281	Wesley Person FB	.60	.25	.07
☐	211	Harold Ellis	.25	.11	.03	☐	282	Mahmoud Abdul-Rauf FB	.25	.11	.03
☐	212	Nate McMillan	.25	.11	.03	☐	283	Jamal Mashburn FB	.60	.25	.07
☐	213	Chuck Person	.25	.11	.03	☐	284	Dale Ellis FB	.25	.11	.03
☐	214	Harold Miner	.25	.11	.03	☐	285	Gary Payton	2.00	.90	.25
☐	215	Clarence Weatherspoon	.40	.18	.05	☐	286	Jason Kidd	10.00	4.50	1.25
☐	216	Robert Parish	.60	.25	.07	☐	287	Ken Norman	.25	.11	.03
☐	217	Michael Cage	.25	.11	.03	☐	288	Juwan Howard	12.00	5.50	1.50
☐	218	Kenny Smith	.25	.11	.03	☐	289	Lamond Murray	.25	.11	.03
☐	219	Larry Krystkowiak	.25	.11	.03	☐	290	Clifford Robinson	.60	.25	.07
☐	220	Dikembe Mutombo	.60	.25	.07	☐	291	Frank Brickowski	.25	.11	.03
☐	221	Wayman Tisdale	.25	.11	.03	☐	292	Adam Keefe	.25	.11	.03
☐	222	Kevin Duckworth	.25	.11	.03	☐	293	Ron Harper	.40	.18	.05
☐	223	Vern Fleming	.25	.11	.03	☐	294	Tom Hammonds	.25	.11	.03
☐	224	Eric Mobley	.25	.11	.03	☐	295	Otis Thorpe	.40	.18	.05
☐	225	Patrick Ewing FB	.60	.25	.07	☐	296	Rick Mahorn	.25	.11	.03
☐	226	Clifford Robinson FB	.25	.11	.03	☐	297	Alton Lister	.25	.11	.03
☐	227	Eric Murdock FB	.25	.11	.03	☐	298	Vinny Del Negro	.25	.11	.03
☐	228	Derrick Coleman FB	.25	.11	.03	☐	299	Danny Ferry	.25	.11	.03
☐	229	Otis Thorpe FB	.25	.11	.03	☐	300	John Starks	.25	.11	.03
☐	230	Alonzo Mourning FB	1.00	.45	.12	☐	301	Duane Ferrell	.25	.11	.03
☐	231	Donyell Marshall FB	.25	.11	.03	☐	302	Hersey Hawkins	.25	.11	.03
☐	232	Dikembe Mutombo FB	.40	.18	.05	☐	303	Khalid Reeves	.40	.18	.05
☐	233	Rony Seikaly FB	.25	.11	.03	☐	304	Anthony Peeler	.25	.11	.03
☐	234	Chris Mullin FB	.25	.11	.03	☐	305	Tim Hardaway	.60	.25	.07
☐	235	Reggie Miller	1.50	.70	.19	☐	306	Rick Fox	.25	.11	.03
☐	236	Benoit Benjamin	.25	.11	.03	☐	307	Jay Humphries	.25	.11	.03
☐	237	Sean Rooks	.25	.11	.03	☐	308	Brian Shaw	.25	.11	.03
☐	238	Terry Davis	.25	.11	.03	☐	309	Dan Schayes	.25	.11	.03
☐	239	Anthony Avent	.25	.11	.03	☐	310	Stacey Augmon	.40	.18	.05
☐	240	Grant Hill	25.00	11.00	3.10	☐	311	Oliver Miller	.25	.11	.03
☐	241	Randy Woods	.25	.11	.03	☐	312	Pooh Richardson	.25	.11	.03
☐	242	Tom Chambers	.25	.11	.03	☐	313	Donyell Marshall	.40	.18	.05
☐	243	Michael Adams	.25	.11	.03	☐	314	Aaron McKie	.40	.18	.05
☐	244	Monty Williams	.25	.11	.03	☐	315	Mark Price	.25	.11	.03
☐	245	Chris Mullin	.60	.25	.07	☐	316	B.J. Tyler	.25	.11	.03
☐	246	Bill Wennington	.25	.11	.03	☐	317	Olden Polynice	.25	.11	.03
☐	247	Mark Jackson	.25	.11	.03	☐	318	Avery Johnson	.40	.18	.05
☐	248	Blue Edwards	.25	.11	.03	☐	319	Derek Strong	.25	.11	.03
☐	249	Jalen Rose	1.25	.55	.16	☐	320	Toni Kukoc	1.00	.45	.12
☐	250	Glenn Robinson FB	2.00	.90	.25	☐	321	Charlie Ward	.60	.25	.07

			MINT	NRMT	EXC
☐	322	Wesley Person	2.50	1.10	.30
☐	323	Eddie Jones	5.00	2.20	.60
☐	324	Horace Grant	.60	.25	.07
☐	325	Mahmoud Abdul-Rauf..	.40	.18	.05
☐	326	Sharone Wright	.60	.25	.07
☐	327	Kevin Gamble	.25	.11	.03
☐	328	Sarunas Marciulionis..	.25	.11	.03
☐	329	Harvey Grant	.25	.11	.03
☐	330	Bobby Hurley	.25	.11	.03
☐	331	Michael Jordan	30.00	13.50	3.70

1994-95 Finest Refractors

Parallel to the basic set, Refractors were randomly inserted in first and second packs at a rate of one in 12. Refractors are distinguished from the basic cards by their rainbow-like appearance that refracts more light. Just like regular issue Finest cards, each Refractor comes with a protective coating designed to protect the card from wear and tear. Values provided below are for unpeeled cards. Peeled cards trade for about twenty-five to fifty percent less.

	MINT	NRMT	EXC
COMPLETE SET (331)	4800.00	2200.00	600.00
COMPLETE SERIES 1 (165)	1800.00	800.00	220.00
COMPLETE SERIES 2 (166)	3000.00	1350.00	375.00
COMMON CARD (1-331)	6.00	2.70	.75

			MINT	NRMT	EXC
☐	1	Chris Mullin CY	8.00	3.60	1.00
☐	2	Anthony Mason CY	6.00	2.70	.75
☐	3	John Salley CY	6.00	2.70	.75
☐	4	Jamal Mashburn CY	15.00	6.75	1.85
☐	5	Mark Jackson CY	6.00	2.70	.75
☐	6	Mario Elie CY	6.00	2.70	.75
☐	7	Kenny Anderson CY	6.00	2.70	.75
☐	8	Rod Strickland CY	6.00	2.70	.75
☐	9	Kenny Smith CY	6.00	2.70	.75
☐	10	Olden Polynice CY	6.00	2.70	.75
☐	11	Derek Harper	8.00	3.60	1.00
☐	12	Danny Ainge	8.00	3.60	1.00
☐	13	Dino Radja	10.00	4.50	1.25
☐	14	Eric Murdock	6.00	2.70	.75
☐	15	Sean Rooks	6.00	2.70	.75
☐	16	Dell Curry	6.00	2.70	.75
☐	17	Victor Alexander	6.00	2.70	.75
☐	18	Rodney Rogers	6.00	2.70	.75
☐	19	John Salley	6.00	2.70	.75
☐	20	Brad Daugherty	8.00	3.60	1.00
☐	21	Elmore Spencer	6.00	2.70	.75
☐	22	Mitch Richmond	25.00	11.00	3.10
☐	23	Rex Walters	6.00	2.70	.75
☐	24	Antonio Davis	6.00	2.70	.75
☐	25	B.J. Armstrong	8.00	3.60	1.00
☐	26	Andrew Lang	6.00	2.70	.75
☐	27	Carl Herrera	6.00	2.70	.75
☐	28	Kevin Edwards	6.00	2.70	.75
☐	29	Micheal Williams	6.00	2.70	.75
☐	30	Clyde Drexler	30.00	13.50	3.70
☐	31	Dana Barros	8.00	3.60	1.00
☐	32	Shaquille O'Neal	225.00	100.00	28.00
☐	33	Patrick Ewing	25.00	11.00	3.10
☐	34	Charles Barkley	40.00	18.00	5.00
☐	35	J.R. Reid	6.00	2.70	.75
☐	36	Lindsey Hunter	6.00	2.70	.75
☐	37	Jeff Malone	6.00	2.70	.75
☐	38	Rik Smits	10.00	4.50	1.25
☐	39	Brian Williams	6.00	2.70	.75
☐	40	Shawn Kemp	100.00	45.00	12.50
☐	41	Terry Porter	6.00	2.70	.75
☐	42	James Worthy	10.00	4.50	1.25
☐	43	Rex Chapman	6.00	2.70	.75
☐	44	Stanley Roberts	6.00	2.70	.75
☐	45	Chris Smith	6.00	2.70	.75
☐	46	Dee Brown	6.00	2.70	.75
☐	47	Chris Gatling	6.00	2.70	.75
☐	48	Donald Hodge	6.00	2.70	.75
☐	49	Bimbo Coles	6.00	2.70	.75
☐	50	Derrick Coleman	8.00	3.60	1.00
☐	51	Muggsy Bogues CY	6.00	2.70	.75
☐	52	Reggie Williams CY	6.00	2.70	.75
☐	53	David Wingate CY	6.00	2.70	.75
☐	54	Sam Cassell CY	8.00	3.60	1.00
☐	55	Sherman Douglas CY..	6.00	2.70	.75
☐	56	Keith Jennings	6.00	2.70	.75
☐	57	Kenny Gattison	6.00	2.70	.75
☐	58	Brent Price	6.00	2.70	.75
☐	59	Luc Longley	6.00	2.70	.75
☐	60	Jamal Mashburn	35.00	16.00	4.40
☐	61	Doug West	6.00	2.70	.75
☐	62	Walt Williams	8.00	3.60	1.00
☐	63	Tracy Murray	6.00	2.70	.75
☐	64	Robert Pack	6.00	2.70	.75
☐	65	Johnny Dawkins	6.00	2.70	.75
☐	66	Vin Baker	35.00	16.00	4.40
☐	67	Sam Cassell	10.00	4.50	1.25
☐	68	Dale Davis	6.00	2.70	.75
☐	69	Terrell Brandon	8.00	3.60	1.00
☐	70	Billy Owens	8.00	3.60	1.00
☐	71	Ervin Johnson	6.00	2.70	.75
☐	72	Allan Houston	60.00	27.00	7.50
☐	73	Craig Ehlo	6.00	2.70	.75
☐	74	Loy Vaught	8.00	3.60	1.00
☐	75	Scottie Pippen	140.00	65.00	17.50
☐	76	Sam Bowie	6.00	2.70	.75
☐	77	Anthony Mason	8.00	3.60	1.00
☐	78	Felton Spencer	6.00	2.70	.75
☐	79	P.J. Brown	6.00	2.70	.75
☐	80	Christian Laettner	8.00	3.60	1.00
☐	81	Todd Day	6.00	2.70	.75
☐	82	Sean Elliott	10.00	4.50	1.25
☐	83	Grant Long	6.00	2.70	.75
☐	84	Xavier McDaniel	6.00	2.70	.75
☐	85	David Benoit	6.00	2.70	.75
☐	86	Larry Stewart	6.00	2.70	.75
☐	87	Donald Royal	6.00	2.70	.75
☐	88	Duane Causwell	6.00	2.70	.75
☐	89	Vlade Divac	8.00	3.60	1.00
☐	90	Derrick McKey	6.00	2.70	.75
☐	91	Kevin Johnson	10.00	4.50	1.25

☐ 92	LaPhonso Ellis	6.00	2.70	.75
☐ 93	Jerome Kersey	6.00	2.70	.75
☐ 94	Muggsy Bogues	8.00	3.60	1.00
☐ 95	Tom Gugliotta	10.00	4.50	1.25
☐ 96	Jeff Hornacek	8.00	3.60	1.00
☐ 97	Kevin Willis	6.00	2.70	.75
☐ 98	Chris Mills	10.00	4.50	1.25
☐ 99	Sam Perkins	8.00	3.60	1.00
☐ 100	Alonzo Mourning	30.00	13.50	3.70
☐ 101	Derrick Coleman CY	6.00	2.70	.75
☐ 102	Glen Rice CY	8.00	3.60	1.00
☐ 103	Kevin Willis CY	6.00	2.70	.75
☐ 104	Chris Webber CY	40.00	18.00	5.00
☐ 105	Terry Mills CY	6.00	2.70	.75
☐ 106	Tim Hardaway CY	8.00	3.60	1.00
☐ 107	Nick Anderson CY	6.00	2.70	.75
☐ 108	Terry Cummings CY	6.00	2.70	.75
☐ 109	Hersey Hawkins CY	6.00	2.70	.75
☐ 110	Ken Norman CY	6.00	2.70	.75
☐ 111	Nick Anderson	8.00	3.60	1.00
☐ 112	Tim Perry	6.00	2.70	.75
☐ 113	Terry Dehere	6.00	2.70	.75
☐ 114	Chris Morris	6.00	2.70	.75
☐ 115	John Williams	6.00	2.70	.75
☐ 116	Jon Barry	6.00	2.70	.75
☐ 117	Rony Seikaly	6.00	2.70	.75
☐ 118	Detlef Schrempf	10.00	4.50	1.25
☐ 119	Terry Cummings	8.00	3.60	1.00
☐ 120	Chris Webber	90.00	40.00	11.00
☐ 121	David Wingate	6.00	2.70	.75
☐ 122	Popeye Jones	6.00	2.70	.75
☐ 123	Sherman Douglas	6.00	2.70	.75
☐ 124	Greg Anthony	6.00	2.70	.75
☐ 125	Mookie Blaylock	8.00	3.60	1.00
☐ 126	Don MacLean	6.00	2.70	.75
☐ 127	Lionel Simmons	6.00	2.70	.75
☐ 128	Scott Brooks	6.00	2.70	.75
☐ 129	Jeff Turner	6.00	2.70	.75
☐ 130	Bryant Stith	6.00	2.70	.75
☐ 131	Shawn Bradley	8.00	3.60	1.00
☐ 132	Byron Scott	8.00	3.60	1.00
☐ 133	Doug Christie	6.00	2.70	.75
☐ 134	Dennis Rodman	180.00	80.00	22.00
☐ 135	Dan Majerle	8.00	3.60	1.00
☐ 136	Gary Grant	6.00	2.70	.75
☐ 137	Bryon Russell	6.00	2.70	.75
☐ 138	Will Perdue	6.00	2.70	.75
☐ 139	Gheorghe Muresan	10.00	4.50	1.25
☐ 140	Kendall Gill	6.00	2.70	.75
☐ 141	Isaiah Rider	10.00	4.50	1.25
☐ 142	Terry Mills	6.00	2.70	.75
☐ 143	Willie Anderson	6.00	2.70	.75
☐ 144	Hubert Davis	6.00	2.70	.75
☐ 145	Lucious Harris	6.00	2.70	.75
☐ 146	Spud Webb	8.00	3.60	1.00
☐ 147	Glen Rice	10.00	4.50	1.25
☐ 148	Dennis Scott	8.00	3.60	1.00
☐ 149	Robert Horry	15.00	6.75	1.85
☐ 150	John Stockton	25.00	11.00	3.10
☐ 151	Stacey Augmon CY	6.00	2.70	.75
☐ 152	Chris Mills CY	8.00	3.60	1.00
☐ 153	Elden Campbell CY	6.00	2.70	.75
☐ 154	Jay Humphries CY	6.00	2.70	.75
☐ 155	Reggie Miller CY	18.00	8.00	2.20
☐ 156	George Lynch	6.00	2.70	.75
☐ 157	Tyrone Hill	6.00	2.70	.75
☐ 158	Lee Mayberry	6.00	2.70	.75
☐ 159	Jon Koncak	6.00	2.70	.75
☐ 160	Joe Dumars	10.00	4.50	1.25
☐ 161	Vernon Maxwell	6.00	2.70	.75
☐ 162	Joe Kleine	6.00	2.70	.75
☐ 163	Acie Earl	6.00	2.70	.75
☐ 164	Steve Kerr	6.00	2.70	.75
☐ 165	Rod Strickland	8.00	3.60	1.00
☐ 166	Glenn Robinson	80.00	36.00	10.00
☐ 167	Anfernee Hardaway	400.00	180.00	50.00
☐ 168	Latrell Sprewell	18.00	8.00	2.20
☐ 169	Sergei Bazarevich	6.00	2.70	.75
☐ 170	Hakeem Olajuwon	65.00	29.00	8.00
☐ 171	Nick Van Exel	25.00	11.00	3.10
☐ 172	Buck Williams	8.00	3.60	1.00
☐ 173	Antoine Carr	6.00	2.70	.75
☐ 174	Corie Blount	6.00	2.70	.75
☐ 175	Dominique Wilkins	10.00	4.50	1.25
☐ 176	Yinka Dare	6.00	2.70	.75
☐ 177	Byron Houston	6.00	2.70	.75
☐ 178	LaSalle Thompson	6.00	2.70	.75
☐ 179	Doug Smith	6.00	2.70	.75
☐ 180	David Robinson	50.00	22.00	6.25
☐ 181	Eric Piatkowski	6.00	2.70	.75
☐ 182	Scott Skiles	6.00	2.70	.75
☐ 183	Scott Burrell	10.00	4.50	1.25
☐ 184	Mark West	6.00	2.70	.75
☐ 185	Billy Owens	8.00	3.60	1.00
☐ 186	Brian Grant	25.00	11.00	3.10
☐ 187	Scott Williams	6.00	2.70	.75
☐ 188	Gerald Madkins	6.00	2.70	.75
☐ 189	Reggie Williams	6.00	2.70	.75
☐ 190	Danny Manning	8.00	3.60	1.00
☐ 191	Mike Brown	6.00	2.70	.75
☐ 192	Charles Smith	6.00	2.70	.75
☐ 193	Elden Campbell	8.00	3.60	1.00
☐ 194	Ricky Pierce	6.00	2.70	.75
☐ 195	Karl Malone	25.00	11.00	3.10
☐ 196	Brooks Thompson	6.00	2.70	.75
☐ 197	Alaa Abdelnaby	6.00	2.70	.75
☐ 198	Tyrone Corbin	6.00	2.70	.75
☐ 199	Johnny Newman	6.00	2.70	.75
☐ 200	Grant Hill FB	125.00	55.00	15.50
☐ 201	Kenny Anderson FB	6.00	2.70	.75
☐ 202	Olden Polynice FB	6.00	2.70	.75
☐ 203	Horace Grant FB	8.00	3.60	1.00
☐ 204	Muggsy Bogues FB	8.00	3.60	1.00
☐ 205	Mark Price FB	6.00	2.70	.75
☐ 206	Tom Gugliotta FB	8.00	3.60	1.00
☐ 207	Christian Laettner FB	8.00	3.60	1.00
☐ 208	Eric Montross FB	8.00	3.60	1.00
☐ 209	Sam Cassell FB	8.00	3.60	1.00
☐ 210	Charles Oakley	8.00	3.60	1.00
☐ 211	Harold Ellis	6.00	2.70	.75
☐ 212	Nate McMillan	6.00	2.70	.75
☐ 213	Chuck Person	6.00	2.70	.75
☐ 214	Harold Miner	6.00	2.70	.75
☐ 215	Clarence Weatherspoon	8.00	3.60	1.00
☐ 216	Robert Parish	10.00	4.50	1.25
☐ 217	Michael Cage	6.00	2.70	.75
☐ 218	Kenny Smith	6.00	2.70	.75
☐ 219	Larry Krystkowiak	6.00	2.70	.75
☐ 220	Dikembe Mutombo	10.00	4.50	1.25
☐ 221	Wayman Tisdale	8.00	3.60	1.00
☐ 222	Kevin Duckworth	6.00	2.70	.75
☐ 223	Vern Fleming	6.00	2.70	.75
☐ 224	Eric Mobley	6.00	2.70	.75
☐ 225	Patrick Ewing FB	10.00	4.50	1.25
☐ 226	Clifford Robinson FB	8.00	3.60	1.00
☐ 227	Eric Murdock FB	6.00	2.70	.75
☐ 228	Derrick Coleman FB	6.00	2.70	.75
☐ 229	Otis Thorpe FB	6.00	2.70	.75
☐ 230	Alonzo Mourning FB	15.00	6.75	1.85
☐ 231	Donyell Marshall FB	6.00	2.70	.75
☐ 232	Dikembe Mutombo FB	8.00	3.60	1.00
☐ 233	Rony Seikaly FB	6.00	2.70	.75

☐ 234	Chris Mullin FB	8.00	3.60	1.00
☐ 235	Reggie Miller FB	30.00	13.50	3.70
☐ 236	Benoit Benjamin	6.00	2.70	.75
☐ 237	Sean Rooks	6.00	2.70	.75
☐ 238	Terry Davis	6.00	2.70	.75
☐ 239	Anthony Avent	6.00	2.70	.75
☐ 240	Grant Hill	500.00	220.00	60.00
☐ 241	Randy Woods	6.00	2.70	.75
☐ 242	Tom Chambers	8.00	3.60	1.00
☐ 243	Michael Adams	6.00	2.70	.75
☐ 244	Monty Williams	6.00	2.70	.75
☐ 245	Chris Mullin	8.00	3.60	1.00
☐ 246	Bill Wennington	6.00	2.70	.75
☐ 247	Mark Jackson	6.00	2.70	.75
☐ 248	Blue Edwards	6.00	2.70	.75
☐ 249	Jalen Rose	8.00	3.60	1.00
☐ 250	Glenn Robinson FB	30.00	13.50	3.70
☐ 251	Kevin Willis FB	6.00	2.70	.75
☐ 252	B.J. Armstrong FB	6.00	2.70	.75
☐ 253	Jim Jackson FB	10.00	4.50	1.25
☐ 254	Steve Smith FB	8.00	3.60	1.00
☐ 255	Chris Webber FB	40.00	18.00	5.00
☐ 256	Glen Rice FB	8.00	3.60	1.00
☐ 257	Derek Harper FB	6.00	2.70	.75
☐ 258	Jalen Rose FB	8.00	3.60	1.00
☐ 259	Juwan Howard FB	75.00	34.00	9.50
☐ 260	Kenny Anderson	8.00	3.60	1.00
☐ 261	Calbert Cheaney	8.00	3.60	1.00
☐ 262	Bill Cartwright	6.00	2.70	.75
☐ 263	Mario Elie	6.00	2.70	.75
☐ 264	Chris Dudley	6.00	2.70	.75
☐ 265	Jim Jackson	20.00	9.00	2.50
☐ 266	Antonio Harvey	6.00	2.70	.75
☐ 267	Bill Curley	6.00	2.70	.75
☐ 268	Moses Malone	15.00	6.75	1.85
☐ 269	A.C. Green	8.00	3.60	1.00
☐ 270	Larry Johnson	30.00	13.50	3.70
☐ 271	Marty Conlon	6.00	2.70	.75
☐ 272	Greg Graham	6.00	2.70	.75
☐ 273	Eric Montross	10.00	4.50	1.25
☐ 274	Stacey King	6.00	2.70	.75
☐ 275	Charles Barkley FB	15.00	6.75	1.85
☐ 276	Chris Morris FB	6.00	2.70	.75
☐ 277	Robert Horry FB	8.00	3.60	1.00
☐ 278	Dominique Wilkins FB	8.00	3.60	1.00
☐ 279	Latrell Sprewell FB	8.00	3.60	1.00
☐ 280	Shaquille O'Neal FB	70.00	32.00	8.75
☐ 281	Wesley Person FB	8.00	3.60	1.00
☐ 282	Mahmoud Abdul-Rauf FB	6.00	2.70	.75
☐ 283	Jamal Mashburn FB	15.00	6.75	1.85
☐ 284	Dale Ellis FB	6.00	2.70	.75
☐ 285	Gary Payton	50.00	22.00	6.25
☐ 286	Jason Kidd	175.00	80.00	22.00
☐ 287	Ken Norman	6.00	2.70	.75
☐ 288	Juwan Howard	200.00	90.00	25.00
☐ 289	Lamond Murray	10.00	4.50	1.25
☐ 290	Clifford Robinson	10.00	4.50	1.25
☐ 291	Frank Brickowski	6.00	2.70	.75
☐ 292	Adam Keefe	6.00	2.70	.75
☐ 293	Ron Harper	8.00	3.60	1.00
☐ 294	Tom Hammonds	6.00	2.70	.75
☐ 295	Otis Thorpe	8.00	3.60	1.00
☐ 296	Rick Mahorn	6.00	2.70	.75
☐ 297	Alton Lister	6.00	2.70	.75
☐ 298	Vinny Del Negro	8.00	3.60	1.00
☐ 299	Danny Ferry	6.00	2.70	.75
☐ 300	John Starks	8.00	3.60	1.00
☐ 301	Duane Ferrell	6.00	2.70	.75
☐ 302	Hersey Hawkins	8.00	3.60	1.00
☐ 303	Khalid Reeves	8.00	3.60	1.00
☐ 304	Anthony Peeler	6.00	2.70	.75
☐ 305	Tim Hardaway	10.00	4.50	1.25
☐ 306	Rick Fox	6.00	2.70	.75
☐ 307	Jay Humphries	6.00	2.70	.75
☐ 308	Brian Shaw	6.00	2.70	.75
☐ 309	Dan Schayes	6.00	2.70	.75
☐ 310	Stacey Augmon	8.00	3.60	1.00
☐ 311	Oliver Miller	6.00	2.70	.75
☐ 312	Pooh Richardson	6.00	2.70	.75
☐ 313	Donyell Marshall	6.00	2.70	.75
☐ 314	Aaron McKie	10.00	4.50	1.25
☐ 315	Mark Price	8.00	3.60	1.00
☐ 316	B.J. Tyler	6.00	2.70	.75
☐ 317	Olden Polynice	6.00	2.70	.75
☐ 318	Avery Johnson	8.00	3.60	1.00
☐ 319	Derek Strong	6.00	2.70	.75
☐ 320	Toni Kukoc	25.00	11.00	3.10
☐ 321	Charlie Ward	8.00	3.60	1.00
☐ 322	Wesley Person	10.00	4.50	1.25
☐ 323	Eddie Jones	110.00	50.00	14.00
☐ 324	Horace Grant	10.00	4.50	1.25
☐ 325	Mahmoud Abdul-Rauf	8.00	3.60	1.00
☐ 326	Sharone Wright	10.00	4.50	1.25
☐ 327	Kevin Gamble	6.00	2.70	.75
☐ 328	Sarunas Marciulionis	6.00	2.70	.75
☐ 329	Harvey Grant	6.00	2.70	.75
☐ 330	Bobby Hurley	8.00	3.60	1.00
☐ 331	Michael Jordan	700.00	325.00	90.00

1994-95 Finest Cornerstone

Randomly inserted in second series packs at a rate of one in every 24, cards from this 15-card standard-size set highlight players who are foundations of their respective teams. The fronts have a color-action photo set against a multi-colored background. The backs have a color-photo and player information. Values provided below are for unpeeled cards. Peeled cards generally trade for ten to twenty-five percent less.

	MINT	NRMT	EXC
COMPLETE SET (15)	125.00	55.00	15.50
COMMON CARD (1-15)	3.00	1.35	.35
☐ CS1 Shaquille O'Neal	30.00	13.50	3.70
☐ CS2 Alonzo Mourning	8.00	3.60	1.00
☐ CS3 Patrick Ewing	6.00	2.70	.75
☐ CS4 Karl Malone	6.00	2.70	.75
☐ CS5 Kenny Anderson	3.00	1.35	.35
☐ CS6 Latrell Sprewell	4.00	1.80	.50

		MINT	NRMT	EXC
☐ CS7	Dikembe Mutombo....	3.00	1.35	.35
☐ CS8	Charles Barkley........	10.00	4.50	1.25
☐ CS9	John Stockton	6.00	2.70	.75
☐ CS10	Reggie Miller	8.00	3.60	1.00
☐ CS11	Jamal Mashburn.......	5.00	2.20	.60
☐ CS12	Anfernee Hardaway	40.00	18.00	5.00
☐ CS13	Jim Jackson	4.00	1.80	.50
☐ CS14	David Robinson	12.00	5.50	1.50
☐ CS15	Hakeem Olajuwon..	15.00	6.75	1.85

1994-95 Finest Iron Men

Randomly inserted in first series packs at a rate of one in 24, cards from this 10-card standard-size set spotlight players who played at least 3,000 minutes during the 1993-94 NBA season. These transparent cards have a front design much like the basic Finest cards with "Iron Man" at the top. The only design element on back is a small stat box at the bottom. Unlike most other 1994-95 Finest cards, Iron Men inserts have no protective coating.

		MINT	NRMT	EXC
	COMPLETE SET (10)	50.00	22.00	6.25
	COMMON CARD (1-10)	1.00	.45	.12
☐ 1	Shaquille O'Neal...........	15.00	6.75	1.85
☐ 2	Kenny Anderson	1.50	.70	.19
☐ 3	Jim Jackson	2.00	.90	.25
☐ 4	Clarence Weatherspoon	1.00	.45	.12
☐ 5	Karl Malone	3.00	1.35	.35
☐ 6	Dan Majerle	1.50	.70	.19
☐ 7	Anfernee Hardaway	20.00	9.00	2.50
☐ 8	David Robinson	6.00	2.70	.75
☐ 9	Latrell Sprewell	1.50	.70	.19
☐ 10	Hakeem Olajuwon	8.00	3.60	1.00

1994-95 Finest Lottery Prize

Randomly inserted in second series packs at a rate of one in six, cards from this 22-card standard-size set showcase lottery picks who went on to become impact players. The fronts have a color-action photo with background having a large basketball

surrounded by a variety of colors and stars. The backs have a color photo and player information with the words "Lottery Prize" set against a basketball. Values provided below are for unpeeled cards. Peeled cards generally trade for ten to twenty-five percent less.

		MINT	NRMT	EXC
	COMPLETE SET (22)	50.00	22.00	6.25
	COMMON CARD (1-22)	.75	.35	.09
☐ LP1	Patrick Ewing................	2.50	1.10	.30
☐ LP2	Chris Mullin.................	1.25	.55	.16
☐ LP3	David Robinson	5.00	2.20	.60
☐ LP4	Scottie Pippen	8.00	3.60	1.00
☐ LP5	Kevin Johnson	1.25	.55	.16
☐ LP6	Danny Manning	1.25	.55	.16
☐ LP7	Mitch Richmond	1.25	.55	.16
☐ LP8	Derrick Coleman	.75	.35	.09
☐ LP9	Gary Payton	4.00	1.80	.50
☐ LP10	Mahmoud Abdul-Rauf	1.25	.55	.16
☐ LP11	Larry Johnson	2.50	1.10	.30
☐ LP12	Kenny Anderson	1.25	.55	.16
☐ LP13	Dikembe Mutombo ..	1.25	.55	.16
☐ LP14	Stacey Augmon	1.25	.55	.16
☐ LP15	Shaquille O'Neal	12.00	5.50	1.50
☐ LP16	Alonzo Mourning	3.00	1.35	.35
☐ LP17	Clarence Weatherspoon	.75	.35	.09
☐ LP18	Robert Horry................	1.25	.55	.16
☐ LP19	Chris Webber...............	3.00	1.35	.35
☐ LP20	Anfernee Hardaway	15.00	6.75	1.85
☐ LP21	Jamal Mashburn	2.00	.90	.25
☐ LP22	Vin Baker	3.00	1.35	.35

1994-95 Finest Marathon Men

Randomly inserted into first series packs at a rate of one in 12, cards from this 12-card

standard-size set highlight players who played in all 82 games during the 1993-94 NBA season. These transparent cards have a design on front that is similar to the basic issue with the words "Marathon Man" at the top. The back contains a small stat box at the bottom. Unlike most other 1994-95 Finest cards, Marathon Men inserts have no protective coatings.

	MINT	NRMT	EXC
COMPLETE SET (20)	50.00	22.00	6.25
COMMON CARD (1-20)	1.50	.70	.19
☐ 1 Latrell Sprewell	4.00	1.80	.50
☐ 2 Gary Payton	10.00	4.50	1.25
☐ 3 Kenny Anderson	3.00	1.35	.35
☐ 4 Jim Jackson	4.00	1.80	.50
☐ 5 Lindsey Hunter	1.50	.70	.19
☐ 6 Rod Strickland	1.50	.70	.19
☐ 7 Hersey Hawkins	1.50	.70	.19
☐ 8 Gerald Wilkins	1.50	.70	.19
☐ 9 B.J. Armstrong	1.50	.70	.19
☐ 10 Anfernee Hardaway	40.00	18.00	5.00
☐ 11 Stacey Augmon	3.00	1.35	.35
☐ 12 Eric Murdock	1.50	.70	.19
☐ 13 Clarence Weatherspoon	1.50	.70	.19
☐ 14 Karl Malone	6.00	2.70	.75
☐ 15 Charles Oakley	1.50	.70	.19
☐ 16 Rick Fox	1.50	.70	.19
☐ 17 Otis Thorpe	1.50	.70	.19
☐ 18 Dikembe Mutombo	3.00	1.35	.35
☐ 19 Mike Brown	1.50	.70	.19
☐ 20 A.C. Green	3.00	1.35	.35

1994-95 Finest Rack Pack

Randomly inserted in second series packs at a rate of one in every 72, cards from this seven-card standard-size set spotlight a selection of top performers from the 1994 NBA draft class. The fronts have a color-action photo with a basketball hoop and lights in the background. The words "Rack Pack" appear at the top in a red-foil. The backs have player information inside of a computer monitor. Like many of the Finest cards, these cards also came with a protective covering. The prices listed below are for peeled cards. Unpeeled cards are worth about 20 percent less and are also rarely seen or traded in the secondary market.

	MINT	NRMT	EXC
COMPLETE SET (7)	125.00	55.00	15.50
COMMON CARD (1-7)	2.00	.90	.25
☐ RP1 Grant Hill	60.00	27.00	7.50
☐ RP2 Wesley Person	15.00	6.75	1.85
☐ RP3 Juwan Howard	30.00	13.50	3.70
☐ RP4 Lamond Murray	12.00	5.50	1.50
☐ RP5 Glenn Robinson	15.00	6.75	1.85
☐ RP6 Donyell Marshall	2.00	.90	.25
☐ RP7 Jason Kidd	30.00	13.50	3.70

1995-96 Finest

The 1995-96 Topps Finest set was issued in two separate series of 140 and 111 standard-size cards. Cards for both series were issued in 6-card packs (suggested retail price of $5.00). Each pack contained five basic cards and one Mystery insert card. Basic player cards feature blue-bordered metallic fronts and cut-out action shots set against a swirling court background. The Rookie subset cards (111-139) feature orange-bordered cards. Magic Johnson's card (#252) was added very late in the production schedule and unlike other player cards features a red border on front instead of blue. The checklist card (#111) has an uncorrected error - it should have been numbered 140 as the last card in the first series. Also, card #251, originally scheduled to be a checklist for the second series set, was never printed. Each card features an opaque coating that can be carefully peeled off designed to protect the card front from problems that may arise from handling. Values provided below are for unpeeled cards. Peeled cards generally trade for ten to twenty-five percent less. Noteworthy Rookie Cards include Michael Finley, Kevin Garnett, Joe Smith, Jerry Stackhouse and Damon Stoudamire.

	MINT	NRMT	EXC
COMPLETE SET (251)	150.00	70.00	19.00
COMPLETE SERIES 1 (140)	100.00	45.00	12.50
COMPLETE SERIES 2 (111)	50.00	22.00	6.25
COMMON CARD (1-250/252)	.25	.11	.03
☐ 1 Hakeem Olajuwon	3.00	1.35	.35
☐ 2 Stacey Augmon	.35	.16	.04
☐ 3 John Starks	.25	.11	.03
☐ 4 Sharone Wright	.25	.11	.03
☐ 5 Jason Kidd	3.00	1.35	.35

#	Player			
☐ 6	Lamond Murray	.25	.11	.03
☐ 7	Kenny Anderson	.50	.23	.06
☐ 8	James Robinson	.25	.11	.03
☐ 9	Wesley Person	.25	.11	.03
☐ 10	Latrell Sprewell	.50	.23	.06
☐ 11	Sean Elliott	.50	.23	.06
☐ 12	Greg Anthony	.25	.11	.03
☐ 13	Kendall Gill	.25	.11	.03
☐ 14	Mark Jackson	.25	.11	.03
☐ 15	John Stockton	1.25	.55	.16
☐ 16	Steve Smith	.50	.23	.06
☐ 17	Bobby Hurley	.25	.11	.03
☐ 18	Ervin Johnson	.25	.11	.03
☐ 19	Elden Campbell	.35	.16	.04
☐ 20	Vin Baker	1.25	.55	.16
☐ 21	Micheal Williams	.25	.11	.03
☐ 22	Steve Kerr	.35	.16	.04
☐ 23	Kevin Duckworth	.25	.11	.03
☐ 24	Willie Anderson	.25	.11	.03
☐ 25	Joe Dumars	.50	.23	.06
☐ 26	Dale Ellis	.25	.11	.03
☐ 27	Bimbo Coles	.25	.11	.03
☐ 28	Nick Anderson	.50	.23	.06
☐ 29	Dee Brown	.25	.11	.03
☐ 30	Tyrone Hill	.25	.11	.03
☐ 31	Reggie Miller	1.50	.70	.19
☐ 32	Shaquille O'Neal	6.00	2.70	.75
☐ 33	Brian Grant	.25	.11	.03
☐ 34	Charles Barkley	2.00	.90	.25
☐ 35	Cedric Ceballos	.60	.25	.07
☐ 36	Rex Walters	.25	.11	.03
☐ 37	Kenny Smith	.25	.11	.03
☐ 38	Popeye Jones	.25	.11	.03
☐ 39	Harvey Grant	.25	.11	.03
☐ 40	Gary Payton	2.00	.90	.25
☐ 41	John Williams	.25	.11	.03
☐ 42	Sherman Douglas	.25	.11	.03
☐ 43	Oliver Miller	.25	.11	.03
☐ 44	Kevin Willis	.25	.11	.03
☐ 45	Isaiah Rider	.50	.23	.06
☐ 46	Gheorghe Muresan	.50	.23	.06
☐ 47	Blue Edwards	.25	.11	.03
☐ 48	Jeff Hornacek	.35	.16	.04
☐ 49	J.R. Reid	.25	.11	.03
☐ 50	Glenn Robinson	1.50	.70	.19
☐ 51	Dell Curry	.25	.11	.03
☐ 52	Greg Graham	.25	.11	.03
☐ 53	Ron Harper	.35	.16	.04
☐ 54	Derek Harper	.25	.11	.03
☐ 55	Dikembe Mutombo	.50	.23	.06
☐ 56	Terry Mills	.25	.11	.03
☐ 57	Victor Alexander	.25	.11	.03
☐ 58	Malik Sealy	.25	.11	.03
☐ 59	Vincent Askew	.25	.11	.03
☐ 60	Mitch Richmond	1.00	.45	.12
☐ 61	Duane Ferrell	.25	.11	.03
☐ 62	Dickey Simpkins	.25	.11	.03
☐ 63	Pooh Richardson	.25	.11	.03
☐ 64	Khalid Reeves	.25	.11	.03
☐ 65	Dino Radja	.35	.16	.04
☐ 66	Lee Mayberry	.25	.11	.03
☐ 67	Kenny Gattison	.25	.11	.03
☐ 68	Joe Kleine	.25	.11	.03
☐ 69	Tony Dumas	.25	.11	.03
☐ 70	Nick Van Exel	1.00	.45	.12
☐ 71	Armon Gilliam	.35	.16	.04
☐ 72	Craig Ehlo	.25	.11	.03
☐ 73	Adam Keefe	.25	.11	.03
☐ 74	Chris Dudley	.25	.11	.03
☐ 75	Clyde Drexler	1.50	.70	.19
☐ 76	Jeff Turner	.25	.11	.03
☐ 77	Calbert Cheaney	.25	.11	.03
☐ 78	Vinny Del Negro	.25	.11	.03
☐ 79	Tim Perry	.25	.11	.03
☐ 80	Tim Hardaway	.50	.23	.06
☐ 81	B.J. Armstrong	.25	.11	.03
☐ 82	Muggsy Bogues	.35	.16	.04
☐ 83	Mark Macon	.25	.11	.03
☐ 84	Doug West	.25	.11	.03
☐ 85	Jalen Rose	.25	.11	.03
☐ 86	Chris Mills	.50	.23	.06
☐ 87	Charles Oakley	.35	.16	.04
☐ 88	Andrew Lang	.25	.11	.03
☐ 89	Olden Polynice	.25	.11	.03
☐ 90	Sam Cassell	.50	.23	.06
☐ 91	Todd Day	.25	.11	.03
☐ 92	P.J. Brown	.25	.11	.03
☐ 93	Benoit Benjamin	.25	.11	.03
☐ 94	Sam Perkins	.25	.11	.03
☐ 95	Eddie Jones	1.00	.45	.12
☐ 96	Robert Parish	.50	.23	.06
☐ 97	Avery Johnson	.35	.16	.04
☐ 98	Lindsey Hunter	.25	.11	.03
☐ 99	Billy Owens	.25	.11	.03
☐ 100	Shawn Bradley	.50	.23	.06
☐ 101	Dale Davis	.25	.11	.03
☐ 102	Terry Dehere	.25	.11	.03
☐ 103	A.C. Green	.50	.23	.06
☐ 104	Christian Laettner	.50	.23	.06
☐ 105	Horace Grant	.50	.23	.06
☐ 106	Rony Seikaly	.25	.11	.03
☐ 107	Reggie Williams	.25	.11	.03
☐ 108	Toni Kukoc	.75	.35	.09
☐ 109	Terrell Brandon	.50	.23	.06
☐ 110	Clifford Robinson	.50	.23	.06
☐ 111	Joe Smith	6.00	2.70	.75
☐ 112	Antonio McDyess	5.00	2.20	.60
☐ 113	Jerry Stackhouse	10.00	4.50	1.25
☐ 114	Rasheed Wallace	2.50	1.10	.30
☐ 115	Kevin Garnett	30.00	13.50	3.70
☐ 116	Bryant Reeves	3.00	1.35	.35
☐ 117	Damon Stoudamire..	12.00	5.50	1.50
☐ 118	Shawn Respert	1.00	.45	.12
☐ 119	Ed O'Bannon	2.00	.90	.25
☐ 120	Kurt Thomas	1.50	.70	.19
☐ 121	Gary Trent	1.00	.45	.12
☐ 122	Cherokee Parks	1.00	.45	.12
☐ 123	Corliss Williamson	1.00	.45	.12
☐ 124	Eric Williams	1.00	.45	.12
☐ 125	Brent Barry	2.50	1.10	.30
☐ 126	Alan Henderson	.75	.35	.09
☐ 127	Bob Sura	1.00	.45	.12
☐ 128	Theo Ratliff	1.00	.45	.12
☐ 129	Randolph Childress	.25	.11	.03
☐ 130	Jason Caffey	.35	.16	.04
☐ 131	Michael Finley	6.00	2.70	.75
☐ 132	George Zidek	.60	.25	.07
☐ 133	Travis Best	.75	.35	.09
☐ 134	Loren Meyer	.50	.23	.06
☐ 135	David Vaughn	.25	.11	.03
☐ 136	Sherell Ford	.25	.11	.03
☐ 137	Mario Bennett	.25	.11	.03
☐ 138	Greg Ostertag	.25	.11	.03
☐ 139	Cory Alexander	.25	.11	.03
☐ 140	Checklist UER #111	.25	.11	.03
☐ 141	Chucky Brown	.25	.11	.03
☐ 142	Eric Mobley	.25	.11	.03
☐ 143	Tom Hammonds	.25	.11	.03
☐ 144	Chris Webber	1.25	.55	.16
☐ 145	Carlos Rogers	.25	.11	.03
☐ 146	Chuck Person	.25	.11	.03
☐ 147	Brian Williams	.25	.11	.03

☐ 148	Kevin Gamble	.25	.11	.03
☐ 149	Dennis Rodman Bulls	8.00	3.60	1.00
☐ 150	Pervis Ellison	.25	.11	.03
☐ 151	Jayson Williams	.25	.11	.03
☐ 152	Buck Williams	.25	.11	.03
☐ 153	Allan Houston	.50	.23	.06
☐ 154	Tom Gugliotta	.50	.23	.06
☐ 155	Charles Smith	.25	.11	.03
☐ 156	Chris Gatling	.25	.11	.03
☐ 157	Darrin Hancock	.25	.11	.03
☐ 158	Blue Edwards	.25	.11	.03
☐ 159	Shawn Kemp	4.00	1.80	.50
☐ 160	Michael Cage	.25	.11	.03
☐ 161	Sedale Threatt	.25	.11	.03
☐ 162	Byron Scott	.35	.16	.04
☐ 163	Elliot Perry	.25	.11	.03
☐ 164	Jim Jackson	.50	.23	.06
☐ 165	Wayman Tisdale	.25	.11	.03
☐ 166	Vernon Maxwell	.25	.11	.03
☐ 167	Brian Shaw	.25	.11	.03
☐ 168	Haywoode Workman	.25	.11	.03
☐ 169	Mookie Blaylock	.35	.16	.04
☐ 170	Donald Royal	.25	.11	.03
☐ 171	Lorenzo Williams	.25	.11	.03
☐ 172	Eric Piatkowski UER	.25	.11	.03
	Name spelled Paitkowski on back			
☐ 173	Sarunas Marciulionis	.25	.11	.03
☐ 174	Otis Thorpe	.35	.16	.04
☐ 175	Rex Chapman	.25	.11	.03
☐ 176	Felton Spencer	.25	.11	.03
☐ 177	John Salley	.25	.11	.03
☐ 178	Pete Chilcutt	.25	.11	.03
☐ 179	Scottie Pippen	4.00	1.80	.50
☐ 180	Robert Pack	.25	.11	.03
☐ 181	Dana Barros	.25	.11	.03
☐ 182	Mahmoud Abdul-Rauf.	.25	.11	.03
☐ 183	Eric Murdock	.25	.11	.03
☐ 184	Anthony Mason	.25	.11	.03
☐ 185	Will Perdue	.25	.11	.03
☐ 186	Jeff Malone	.25	.11	.03
☐ 187	Anthony Peeler	.25	.11	.03
☐ 188	Chris Childs	.25	.11	.03
☐ 189	Glen Rice	.50	.23	.06
☐ 190	Grant Hill	5.00	2.20	.60
☐ 191	Michael Smith	.25	.11	.03
☐ 192	Sean Rooks	.25	.11	.03
☐ 193	Clifford Rozier	.25	.11	.03
☐ 194	Rik Smits	.50	.23	.06
☐ 195	Spud Webb	.35	.16	.04
☐ 196	Aaron McKie	.25	.11	.03
☐ 197	Nate McMillan	.25	.11	.03
☐ 198	Bobby Phills	.25	.11	.03
☐ 199	Dennis Scott	.50	.23	.06
☐ 200	Mark West	.25	.11	.03
☐ 201	George McCloud	.25	.11	.03
☐ 202	B.J. Tyler	.25	.11	.03
☐ 203	Lionel Simmons	.25	.11	.03
☐ 204	Loy Vaught	.35	.16	.04
☐ 205	Kevin Edwards	.25	.11	.03
☐ 206	Eric Montross	.25	.11	.03
☐ 207	Kenny Gattison	.25	.11	.03
☐ 208	Mario Elie	.25	.11	.03
☐ 209	Karl Malone	1.25	.55	.16
☐ 210	Ken Norman	.25	.11	.03
☐ 211	Antonio Davis	.25	.11	.03
☐ 212	Doc Rivers	.25	.11	.03
☐ 213	Hubert Davis	.25	.11	.03
☐ 214	Jamal Mashburn	.75	.35	.09
☐ 215	Donyell Marshall	.25	.11	.03
☐ 216	Sasha Danilovic	.25	.11	.03
☐ 217	Danny Manning	.25	.11	.03
☐ 218	Scott Burrell	.25	.11	.03
☐ 219	Vlade Divac	.50	.23	.06
☐ 220	Marty Conlon	.25	.11	.03
☐ 221	Clarence Weatherspoon	.50	.23	.06
☐ 222	Terry Porter	.25	.11	.03
☐ 223	Luc Longley	.35	.16	.04
☐ 224	Juwan Howard	3.00	1.35	.35
☐ 225	Danny Ferry	.25	.11	.03
☐ 226	Rod Strickland	.25	.11	.03
☐ 227	Bryant Stith	.25	.11	.03
☐ 228	Derrick McKey	.25	.11	.03
☐ 229	Michael Jordan	15.00	6.75	1.85
☐ 230	Jamie Watson	.25	.11	.03
☐ 231	Rick Fox	.25	.11	.03
☐ 232	Scott Williams	.25	.11	.03
☐ 233	Larry Johnson	1.25	.55	.16
☐ 234	Anfernee Hardaway	8.00	3.60	1.00
☐ 235	Hersey Hawkins	.35	.16	.04
☐ 236	Robert Horry	.35	.16	.04
☐ 237	Kevin Johnson	.50	.23	.06
☐ 238	Rodney Rogers	.25	.11	.03
☐ 239	Detlef Schrempf	.50	.23	.06
☐ 240	Derrick Coleman	.35	.16	.04
☐ 241	Walt Williams	.25	.11	.03
☐ 242	LaPhonso Ellis	.25	.11	.03
☐ 243	Patrick Ewing	1.25	.55	.16
☐ 244	Grant Long	.25	.11	.03
☐ 245	David Robinson	2.50	1.10	.30
☐ 246	Chris Mullin	.35	.16	.04
☐ 247	Alonzo Mourning	1.25	.55	.16
☐ 248	Dan Majerle	.35	.16	.04
☐ 249	Johnny Newman	.25	.11	.03
☐ 250	Chris Morris	.25	.11	.03
☐ 252	Magic Johnson	4.00	1.80	.50

1995-96 Finest Refractors

Parallel to cards 1-110, 141-250 and 252, Refractors were randomly inserted into first and second series packs at a rate of one in 12. For the first time ever, Topps decided to randomly seed entire 24-pack boxes full of Refractors into their cases. The insertion ratio of these Refractor "Hot Boxes" is one in every 450 boxes. None of the regular issue first series Rookie Cards (111-139) were given parallel Refractor cards, thus the first series is complete at 110 cards. In addition, card #251 does not exist, thus the second series set is complete at 111 cards. The Magic Johnson card (#252) was insert-

ed into one in every 216 packs, making it approximately six time easier to pull than other second series Refractors. Refractors are distinguished from the basic cards by their rainbow-like appearance that refracts more light. Just like regular issue cards, each Refractor comes with a protective coating to protect the card from wear and tear. Values provided below are for unpeeled cards. Peeled cards generally trade for twenty-five to fifty percent less.

	MINT	NRMT	EXC
COMPLETE SET (221)	2000.00	900.00	250.00
COMPLETE SERIES 1 (110)	800.00	350.00	100.00
COMPLETE SERIES 2 (111)	1200.00	550.00	150.00
COMMON CARD (1-110)	5.00	2.20	.60
COMMON CARD (141-252)	4.00	1.80	.50

☐ 1 Hakeem Olajuwon	60.00	27.00	7.50
☐ 2 Stacey Augmon	10.00	4.50	1.25
☐ 3 John Starks	10.00	4.50	1.25
☐ 4 Sharone Wright	5.00	2.20	.60
☐ 5 Jason Kidd	60.00	27.00	7.50
☐ 6 Lamond Murray	10.00	4.50	1.25
☐ 7 Kenny Anderson	10.00	4.50	1.25
☐ 8 James Robinson	5.00	2.20	.60
☐ 9 Wesley Person	10.00	4.50	1.25
☐ 10 Latrell Sprewell	12.00	5.50	1.50
☐ 11 Sean Elliott	12.00	5.50	1.50
☐ 12 Greg Anthony	5.00	2.20	.60
☐ 13 Kendall Gill	5.00	2.20	.60
☐ 14 Mark Jackson	5.00	2.20	.60
☐ 15 John Stockton	25.00	11.00	3.10
☐ 16 Steve Smith	10.00	4.50	1.25
☐ 17 Bobby Hurley	10.00	4.50	1.25
☐ 18 Ervin Johnson	5.00	2.20	.60
☐ 19 Elden Campbell	5.00	2.20	.60
☐ 20 Vin Baker	25.00	11.00	3.10
☐ 21 Micheal Williams	5.00	2.20	.60
☐ 22 Steve Kerr	10.00	4.50	1.25
☐ 23 Kevin Duckworth	5.00	2.20	.60
☐ 24 Willie Anderson	5.00	2.20	.60
☐ 25 Joe Dumars	12.00	5.50	1.50
☐ 26 Dale Ellis	10.00	4.50	1.25
☐ 27 Bimbo Coles	5.00	2.20	.60
☐ 28 Nick Anderson	10.00	4.50	1.25
☐ 29 Dee Brown	5.00	2.20	.60
☐ 30 Tyrone Hill	5.00	2.20	.60
☐ 31 Reggie Miller	30.00	13.50	3.70
☐ 32 Shaquille O'Neal	125.00	55.00	15.50
☐ 33 Brian Grant	12.00	5.50	1.50
☐ 34 Charles Barkley	40.00	18.00	5.00
☐ 35 Cedric Ceballos	12.00	5.50	1.50
☐ 36 Rex Walters	5.00	2.20	.60
☐ 37 Kenny Smith	5.00	2.20	.60
☐ 38 Popeye Jones	5.00	2.20	.60
☐ 39 Harvey Grant	5.00	2.20	.60
☐ 40 Gary Payton	40.00	18.00	5.00
☐ 41 John Williams	5.00	2.20	.60
☐ 42 Sherman Douglas	5.00	2.20	.60
☐ 43 Oliver Miller	5.00	2.20	.60
☐ 44 Kevin Willis	10.00	4.50	1.25
☐ 45 Isaiah Rider	10.00	4.50	1.25
☐ 46 Gheorghe Muresan	12.00	5.50	1.50
☐ 47 Blue Edwards	5.00	2.20	.60
☐ 48 Jeff Hornacek	10.00	4.50	1.25
☐ 49 J.R. Reid	5.00	2.20	.60
☐ 50 Glenn Robinson	30.00	13.50	3.70
☐ 51 Dell Curry	5.00	2.20	.60
☐ 52 Greg Graham	5.00	2.20	.60

☐ 53 Ron Harper	10.00	4.50	1.25
☐ 54 Derek Harper	10.00	4.50	1.25
☐ 55 Dikembe Mutombo	12.00	5.50	1.50
☐ 56 Terry Mills	5.00	2.20	.60
☐ 57 Victor Alexander	5.00	2.20	.60
☐ 58 Malik Sealy	5.00	2.20	.60
☐ 59 Vincent Askew	5.00	2.20	.60
☐ 60 Mitch Richmond	25.00	11.00	3.10
☐ 61 Duane Ferrell	5.00	2.20	.60
☐ 62 Dickey Simpkins	5.00	2.20	.60
☐ 63 Pooh Richardson	5.00	2.20	.60
☐ 64 Khalid Reeves	5.00	2.20	.60
☐ 65 Dino Radja	10.00	4.50	1.25
☐ 66 Lee Mayberry	5.00	2.20	.60
☐ 67 Kenny Gattison	5.00	2.20	.60
☐ 68 Joe Kleine	5.00	2.20	.60
☐ 69 Tony Dumas	5.00	2.20	.60
☐ 70 Nick Van Exel	20.00	9.00	2.50
☐ 71 Armon Gilliam	10.00	4.50	1.25
☐ 72 Craig Ehlo	5.00	2.20	.60
☐ 73 Adam Keefe	5.00	2.20	.60
☐ 74 Chris Dudley	5.00	2.20	.60
☐ 75 Clyde Drexler	30.00	13.50	3.70
☐ 76 Jeff Turner	5.00	2.20	.60
☐ 77 Calbert Cheaney	10.00	4.50	1.25
☐ 78 Vinny Del Negro	5.00	2.20	.60
☐ 79 Tim Perry	5.00	2.20	.60
☐ 80 Tim Hardaway	12.00	5.50	1.50
☐ 81 B.J. Armstrong	10.00	4.50	1.25
☐ 82 Muggsy Bogues	10.00	4.50	1.25
☐ 83 Mark Macon	5.00	2.20	.60
☐ 84 Doug West	5.00	2.20	.60
☐ 85 Jalen Rose	10.00	4.50	1.25
☐ 86 Chris Mills	10.00	4.50	1.25
☐ 87 Charles Oakley	10.00	4.50	1.25
☐ 88 Andrew Lang	5.00	2.20	.60
☐ 89 Olden Polynice	5.00	2.20	.60
☐ 90 Sam Cassell	10.00	4.50	1.25
☐ 91 Todd Day	5.00	2.20	.60
☐ 92 P.J. Brown	5.00	2.20	.60
☐ 93 Benoit Benjamin	5.00	2.20	.60
☐ 94 Sam Perkins	10.00	4.50	1.25
☐ 95 Eddie Jones	20.00	9.00	2.50
☐ 96 Robert Parish	12.00	5.50	1.50
☐ 97 Avery Johnson	10.00	4.50	1.25
☐ 98 Lindsey Hunter	5.00	2.20	.60
☐ 99 Billy Owens	10.00	4.50	1.25
☐ 100 Shawn Bradley	10.00	4.50	1.25
☐ 101 Dale Davis	5.00	2.20	.60
☐ 102 Terry Dehere	5.00	2.20	.60
☐ 103 A.C. Green	10.00	4.50	1.25
☐ 104 Christian Laettner	10.00	4.50	1.25
☐ 105 Horace Grant	12.00	5.50	1.50
☐ 106 Rony Seikaly	5.00	2.20	.60
☐ 107 Reggie Williams	5.00	2.20	.60
☐ 108 Toni Kukoc	20.00	9.00	2.50
☐ 109 Terrell Brandon	10.00	4.50	1.25
☐ 110 Clifford Robinson	12.00	5.50	1.50
☐ 141 Chucky Brown	4.00	1.80	.50
☐ 142 Eric Mobley	4.00	1.80	.50
☐ 143 Tom Hammonds	4.00	1.80	.50
☐ 144 Chris Webber	35.00	16.00	4.40
☐ 145 Carlos Rogers	4.00	1.80	.50
☐ 146 Chuck Person	4.00	1.80	.50
☐ 147 Brian Williams	4.00	1.80	.50
☐ 148 Kevin Gamble	4.00	1.80	.50
☐ 149 Dennis Rodman Bulls	135.00	60.00	17.00
☐ 150 Pervis Ellison	4.00	1.80	.50
☐ 151 Jayson Williams	4.00	1.80	.50
☐ 152 Buck Williams	4.00	1.80	.50
☐ 153 Allan Houston	20.00	9.00	2.50

☐ 154	Tom Gugliotta	12.00	5.50	1.50
☐ 155	Charles Smith	4.00	1.80	.50
☐ 156	Chris Gatling	4.00	1.80	.50
☐ 157	Darrin Hancock	4.00	1.80	.50
☐ 158	Blue Edwards	4.00	1.80	.50
☐ 159	Shawn Kemp	60.00	27.00	7.50
☐ 160	Michael Cage	4.00	1.80	.50
☐ 161	Sedale Threatt	4.00	1.80	.50
☐ 162	Byron Scott	10.00	4.50	1.25
☐ 163	Elliot Perry	4.00	1.80	.50
☐ 164	Jim Jackson	12.00	5.50	1.50
☐ 165	Wayman Tisdale	10.00	4.50	1.25
☐ 166	Vernon Maxwell	4.00	1.80	.50
☐ 167	Brian Shaw	4.00	1.80	.50
☐ 168	Haywoode Workman	4.00	1.80	.50
☐ 169	Mookie Blaylock	10.00	4.50	1.25
☐ 170	Donald Royal	4.00	1.80	.50
☐ 171	Lorenzo Williams	4.00	1.80	.50
☐ 172	Eric Piatkowski	4.00	1.80	.50
☐ 173	Sarunas Marciulionis	4.00	1.80	.50
☐ 174	Otis Thorpe	10.00	4.50	1.25
☐ 175	Rex Chapman	4.00	1.80	.50
☐ 176	Felton Spencer	4.00	1.80	.50
☐ 177	John Salley	4.00	1.80	.50
☐ 178	Pete Chilcutt	4.00	1.80	.50
☐ 179	Scottie Pippen	90.00	40.00	11.00
☐ 180	Robert Pack	4.00	1.80	.50
☐ 181	Dana Barros	4.00	1.80	.50
☐ 182	Mahmoud Abdul-Rauf	4.00	1.80	.50
☐ 183	Eric Murdock	4.00	1.80	.50
☐ 184	Anthony Mason	10.00	4.50	1.25
☐ 185	Will Perdue	4.00	1.80	.50
☐ 186	Jeff Malone	4.00	1.80	.50
☐ 187	Anthony Peeler	4.00	1.80	.50
☐ 188	Chris Childs	4.00	1.80	.50
☐ 189	Glen Rice	12.00	5.50	1.50
☐ 190	Grant Hill	110.00	50.00	14.00
☐ 191	Michael Smith	4.00	1.80	.50
☐ 192	Sean Rooks	4.00	1.80	.50
☐ 193	Clifford Rozier	4.00	1.80	.50
☐ 194	Rik Smits	12.00	5.50	1.50
☐ 195	Spud Webb	10.00	4.50	1.25
☐ 196	Aaron McKie	4.00	1.80	.50
☐ 197	Nate McMillan	4.00	1.80	.50
☐ 198	Bobby Phills	4.00	1.80	.50
☐ 199	Dennis Scott	12.00	5.50	1.50
☐ 200	Mark West	4.00	1.80	.50
☐ 201	Geroge McCloud	4.00	1.80	.50
☐ 202	B.J. Tyler	4.00	1.80	.50
☐ 203	Lionel Simmons	4.00	1.80	.50
☐ 204	Loy Vaught	10.00	4.50	1.25
☐ 205	Kevin Edwards	4.00	1.80	.50
☐ 206	Eric Montross	4.00	1.80	.50
☐ 207	Kenny Gattison	4.00	1.80	.50
☐ 208	Mario Elie	4.00	1.80	.50
☐ 209	Karl Malone	20.00	9.00	2.50
☐ 210	Ken Norman	4.00	1.80	.50
☐ 211	Antonio Davis	4.00	1.80	.50
☐ 212	Doc Rivers	4.00	1.80	.50
☐ 213	Hubert Davis	4.00	1.80	.50
☐ 214	Jamal Mashburn	20.00	9.00	2.50
☐ 215	Donyell Marshall	4.00	1.80	.50
☐ 216	Sasha Danilovic	4.00	1.80	.50
☐ 217	Danny Manning	10.00	4.50	1.25
☐ 218	Scott Burrell	4.00	1.80	.50
☐ 219	Vlade Divac	10.00	4.50	1.25
☐ 220	Marty Conlon	4.00	1.80	.50
☐ 221	Clarence Weatherspoon	10.00	4.50	1.25
☐ 222	Terry Porter	4.00	1.80	.50
☐ 223	Luc Longley	10.00	4.50	1.25
☐ 224	Juwan Howard	60.00	27.00	7.50
☐ 225	Danny Ferry	4.00	1.80	.50
☐ 226	Rod Strickland	4.00	1.80	.50
☐ 227	Bryant Stith	4.00	1.80	.50
☐ 228	Derrick McKey	4.00	1.80	.50
☐ 229	Michael Jordan	550.00	250.00	70.00
☐ 230	Jamie Watson	4.00	1.80	.50
☐ 231	Rick Fox	4.00	1.80	.50
☐ 232	Scott Williams	4.00	1.80	.50
☐ 233	Larry Johnson	20.00	9.00	2.50
☐ 234	Anfernee Hardaway	250.00	110.00	31.00
☐ 235	Hersey Hawkins	10.00	4.50	1.25
☐ 236	Robert Horry	10.00	4.50	1.25
☐ 237	Kevin Johnson	12.00	5.50	1.50
☐ 238	Rodney Rogers	4.00	1.80	.50
☐ 239	Detlef Schrempf	10.00	4.50	1.25
☐ 240	Derrick Coleman	4.00	1.80	.50
☐ 241	Walt Williams	10.00	4.50	1.25
☐ 242	LaPhonso Ellis	10.00	4.50	1.25
☐ 243	Patrick Ewing	20.00	9.00	2.50
☐ 244	Grant Long	4.00	1.80	.50
☐ 245	David Robinson	40.00	18.00	5.00
☐ 246	Chris Mullin	10.00	4.50	1.25
☐ 247	Alonzo Mourning	20.00	9.00	2.50
☐ 248	Dan Majerle	10.00	4.50	1.25
☐ 249	Johnny Newman	4.00	1.80	.50
☐ 250	Chris Morris	4.00	1.80	.50
☐ 251	Checklist	4.00	1.80	.50
☐ 252	Magic Johnson 6P	25.00	11.00	3.10

1995-96 Finest
Dish and Swish

Randomly inserted into first series packs at a rate of one in 24, cards from this dual-sided, 29-card standard-size set feature combinations of two key players from each NBA team. Each side feature one of the two players in game action, with the words "Dish" or "Swish" along the bottom. Values provided below are for unpeeled cards. Peeled cards generally trade for ten to twenty-five percent less. The set is sequenced in alphabetical order by team.

	MINT	NRMT	EXC
COMPLETE SET (29)	450.00	200.00	55.00
COMMON CARD (DS1-DS29)	5.00	2.20	.60
☐ DS1 Mookie Blaylock Steve Smith	5.00	2.20	.60
☐ DS2 Sherman Douglas Dino Radja	5.00	2.20	.60
☐ DS3 Muggsy Bogues Larry Johnson	10.00	4.50	1.25

			MINT	NRMT	EXC
☐ DS4	Scottie Pippen.......	200.00	90.00	25.00	
	Michael Jordan				
☐ DS5	Mark Price.................	5.00	2.20	.60	
	Chris Mills				
☐ DS6	Jason Kidd	30.00	13.50	3.70	
	Jamal Mashburn				
☐ DS7	Mahmoud Abdul-Rauf	5.00	2.20	.60	
	Dikembe Mutombo				
☐ DS8	Grant Hill..................	40.00	18.00	5.00	
	Joe Dumars				
☐ DS9	Tim Hardaway	5.00	2.20	.60	
	Chris Mullin				
☐ DS10	Clyde Drexler.........	40.00	18.00	5.00	
	Hakeem Olajuwon				
☐ DS11	Mark Jackson........	12.00	5.50	1.50	
	Reggie Miller				
☐ DS12	Pooh Richardson	5.00	2.20	.60	
	Lamond Murray				
☐ DS13	Nick Van Exel	8.00	3.60	1.00	
	Cedric Ceballos				
☐ DS14	Glen Rice.................	5.00	2.20	.60	
	Khalid Reeves				
☐ DS15	Glenn Robinson	12.00	5.50	1.50	
	Eric Murdock				
☐ DS16	Tom Gugliotta	5.00	2.20	.60	
	Christian Laettner				
☐ DS17	Kenny Anderson......	5.00	2.20	.60	
	Derrick Coleman				
☐ DS18	Patrick Ewing	10.00	4.50	1.25	
	Derek Harper				
☐ DS19	Anfernee Hardaway	120.00	55.00	15.00	
	Shaquille O'Neal				
☐ DS20	Dana Barros	5.00	2.20	.60	
	Clarence Weatherspoon				
☐ DS21	Kevin Johnson	15.00	6.75	1.85	
	Charles Barkley				
☐ DS22	Rod Strickland	5.00	2.20	.60	
	Clifford Robinson				
☐ DS23	Mitch Richmond......	8.00	3.60	1.00	
	Walt Williams				
☐ DS24	Avery Johnson	20.00	9.00	2.50	
	David Robinson				
☐ DS25	Gary Payton	40.00	18.00	5.00	
	Shawn Kemp				
☐ DS26	B.J.Armstrong..........	5.00	2.20	.60	
	Oliver Miller				
☐ DS27	John Stockton.......	20.00	9.00	2.50	
	Karl Malone				
☐ DS28	Greg Anthony	5.00	2.20	.60	
	Byron Scott				
☐ DS29	Juwan Howard	30.00	13.50	3.70	
	Chris Webber				

1995-96 Finest
Hot Stuff

Randomly inserted into first series packs at a rate of one in nine, cards from this 15-card standard-size set highlight some of the NBA's top stars in slam-dunk action. Orange-bordered fronts feature game action shots. The words "Hot Stuff" run down the left hand side of the card front. Values provided below are for unpeeled cards. Peeled cards generally trade for ten to twenty-five percent less.

		MINT	NRMT	EXC
COMPLETE SET (15)		75.00	34.00	9.50
COMMON CARD (HS1-HS15)..		1.00	.45	.12
☐ HS1	Michael Jordan........	30.00	13.50	3.70
☐ HS2	Grant Hill.................	10.00	4.50	1.25
☐ HS3	Clyde Drexler..............	3.00	1.35	.35
☐ HS4	Anfernee Hardaway ..	15.00	6.75	1.85
☐ HS5	Sean Elliott................	1.00	.45	.12
☐ HS6	Latrell Sprewell	1.00	.45	.12
☐ HS7	Larry Johnson	2.50	1.10	.30
☐ HS8	Eddie Jones..............	2.00	.90	.25
☐ HS9	Karl Malone	2.50	1.10	.30
☐ HS10	John Starks.............	1.00	.45	.12
☐ HS11	Scottie Pippen.........	8.00	3.60	1.00
☐ HS12	Shawn Kemp...........	6.00	2.70	.75
☐ HS13	Chris Webber...........	2.50	1.10	.30
☐ HS14	Isaiah Rider.............	1.00	.45	.12
☐ HS15	Robert Horry............	1.00	.45	.12

1995-96 Finest
Mystery

Inserted at a rate of one in every first and second series pack, cards from this 44-

piece standard-size set were 1.25 times easier to pull than regular issue cards. The set contains a selection of some of the NBA's top stars and rookies. The first twenty-two cards, issued exclusively in first series packs, were designed in three different parallel styles (Bordered, Borderless and Borderless Refractors). The last twenty-two cards, issued exclusively in second series packs, were also designed in three different parallel styles (Bronze, Silver and Gold). Collectors had to peel off a dark protective coating to find out what version of the card they had obtained. The first series Mystery cards feature a radically different design to the second series. Each first series Bordered card front features a bronze outline, framing a cut-out action shot of the player against a metallic basketball background. The second series Bronze cards feature a mosaic-style, tiled border with bronze-colored features, framing a cut-out action shot of the player. The prices listed below are for the more common Bordered and Bronze cards. There have been isolated cases of first series Bordered Refractor versions in circulation but the cards are too scarce to establish common secondary market trading values. Values provided below are for peeled cards.

	MINT	NRMT	EXC
COMPLETE SET (44)	50.00	22.00	6.25
COMP. BORDERED SER. 1 (22)	30.00	13.50	3.70
COMP. BRONZE SER. 2 (22)	20.00	9.00	2.50
COMMON BORDERED (M1-M22)	.50	.23	.06
COMMON BRONZE (M23-M44)	.40	.18	.05

		MINT	NRMT	EXC
☐ M1	Michael Jordan	12.00	5.50	1.50
☐ M2	Grant Hill	4.00	1.80	.50
☐ M3	Anfernee Hardaway	6.00	2.70	.75
☐ M4	Shawn Kemp	3.00	1.35	.35
☐ M5	Kenny Anderson	.50	.23	.06
☐ M6	Charles Barkley	1.50	.70	.19
☐ M7	Latrell Sprewell	.50	.23	.06
☐ M8	Chris Webber	1.00	.45	.12
☐ M9	Jason Kidd	2.50	1.10	.30
☐ M10	Glenn Robinson	1.25	.55	.16
☐ M11	David Robinson	2.00	.90	.25
☐ M12	Karl Malone	1.00	.45	.12
☐ M13	Larry Johnson	1.00	.45	.12
☐ M14	Reggie Miller	1.25	.55	.16
☐ M15	Scottie Pippen	3.00	1.35	.35
☐ M16	Patrick Ewing	1.00	.45	.12
☐ M17	Mitch Richmond	.75	.35	.09
☐ M18	Glen Rice	.50	.23	.06
☐ M19	Jamal Mashburn	.60	.25	.07
☐ M20	Juwan Howard	2.50	1.10	.30
☐ M21	Hakeem Olajuwon	2.50	1.10	.30
☐ M22	Shaquille O'Neal	5.00	2.20	.60
☐ M23	Alonzo Mourning	.75	.35	.09
☐ M24	Dennis Rodman Bulls	5.00	2.20	.60
☐ M25	Joe Dumars	.40	.18	.05
☐ M26	Tim Hardaway	.40	.18	.05
☐ M27	Clyde Drexler	1.00	.45	.12
☐ M28	Jerry Stackhouse	5.00	2.20	.60
☐ M29	John Stockton	.75	.35	.09
☐ M30	Derrick Coleman	.40	.18	.05
☐ M31	Michael Finley	3.00	1.35	.35
☐ M32	Glen Rice	.40	.18	.05
☐ M33	Mahmoud Abdul-Rauf	.40	.18	.05
☐ M34	Anthony Mason	.40	.18	.05
☐ M35	Nick Van Exel	.60	.25	.07
☐ M36	Vin Baker	.75	.35	.09
☐ M37	Horace Grant	.40	.18	.05
☐ M38	John Starks	.40	.18	.05
☐ M39	Clarence Weatherspoon	.40	.18	.05
☐ M40	Kevin Johnson	.40	.18	.05
☐ M41	Joe Smith	3.00	1.35	.35
☐ M42	Dikembe Mutombo	.40	.18	.05
☐ M43	Damon Stoudamire	6.00	2.70	.75
☐ M44	Antonio McDyess	2.50	1.10	.30

1995-96 Finest Mystery Borderless/Silver

Randomly inserted into first and second series hobby packs at a rate of one in 24 and retail at one in 20, cards from this 44-card set parallel the more common Mystery Bordered/Bronze issue. Unlike the first series bordered cards, Borderless card fronts feature an action cutout against a full-bleed background. The second series Silver cards differ from the common second series Bronze cards with their silver framed front borders. Please refer to the multipliers provided below to ascertain values for singles. Values provided below are for peeled cards.

	MINT	NRMT	EXC
COMPLETE SET (44)	325.00	145.00	40.00
COMP. BDLS. 1 (22)	200.00	90.00	25.00
COMP. SILVER SER. 2 (22)	125.00	55.00	15.50
COMMON BDLS. (M1-M22)	2.00	.90	.25

COMMON SILVER (M23-M44) 1.50 .70 .19
*BORDERLESS/SIL.: 2.5X to 5X VALUE
*SILVER ROOKIES: 2X to 4X VALUE

1995-96 Finest Mystery Borderless Refractors/Gold

Randomly inserted into first and second series hobby packs at a rate of one in 96 and retail at one in 80, cards from this 44-card set parallel the more common Mystery Bordered/Bronze issue. Unlike the first series bordered cards, Borderless Refractor card fronts feature an action cutout against a full-bleed, prismatic, metallic basketball background. The second series Gold cards differ from the common second series Bronze cards with their brighter Gold framed front borders. Also, the words "gold" run in small repetitive type diagonally across the background of each card front. The more common Bronze cards have the word "bronze" running across the card fronts. Values provided below are for peeled cards.

	MINT	NRMT	EXC
COMPLETE SET (44)	3000.00	1350.00	375.00
COMP.BDLS.REF.SER.1 (22)	2500.00	1100.00	300.00
COMP. GOLD SERIES 2 (22)	500.00	220.00	60.00
COMMON BDLS REF. (M1-M22)	25.00	11.00	3.10
COMMON GOLD (M23-M44)	10.00	4.50	1.25

☐	M1 Michael Jordan	800.00	350.00	100.00
☐	M2 Grant Hill	180.00	80.00	22.00
☐	M3 Anfernee Hardaway	325.00	145.00	40.00
☐	M4 Shawn Kemp	120.00	55.00	15.00
☐	M5 Kenny Anderson	25.00	11.00	3.10
☐	M6 Charles Barkley	60.00	27.00	7.50
☐	M7 Latrell Sprewell	25.00	11.00	3.10
☐	M8 Chris Webber	80.00	36.00	10.00
☐	M9 Jason Kidd	100.00	45.00	12.50
☐	M10 Glenn Robinson	50.00	22.00	6.25
☐	M11 David Robinson	75.00	34.00	9.50
☐	M12 Karl Malone	40.00	18.00	5.00
☐	M13 Larry Johnson	40.00	18.00	5.00
☐	M14 Reggie Miller	50.00	22.00	6.25
☐	M15 Scottie Pippen	150.00	70.00	19.00
☐	M16 Patrick Ewing	40.00	18.00	5.00
☐	M17 Mitch Richmond	40.00	18.00	5.00
☐	M18 Glen Rice	25.00	11.00	3.10
☐	M19 Jamal Mashburn	35.00	16.00	4.40
☐	M20 Juwan Howard	125.00	55.00	15.50
☐	M21 Hakeem Olajuwon	100.00	45.00	12.50
☐	M22 Shaquille O'Neal	200.00	90.00	25.00
☐	M25 Joe Dumars	10.00	4.50	1.25
☐	M26 Tim Hardaway	10.00	4.50	1.25
☐	M27 Clyde Drexler	25.00	11.00	3.10
☐	M28 Jerry Stackhouse	75.00	34.00	9.50
☐	M29 John Stockton	20.00	9.00	2.50
☐	M30 Derrick Coleman	10.00	4.50	1.25
☐	M31 Michael Finley	50.00	22.00	6.25
☐	M32 Glen Rice	10.00	4.50	1.25
☐	M33 M.Abdul-Rauf	10.00	4.50	1.25
☐	M34 Anthony Mason	10.00	4.50	1.25
☐	M35 Nick Van Exel	15.00	6.75	1.85
☐	M36 Vin Baker	20.00	9.00	2.50
☐	M37 Horace Grant	10.00	4.50	1.25
☐	M38 John Starks	10.00	4.50	1.25
☐	M39 C.Weatherspoon	10.00	4.50	1.25
☐	M40 Kevin Johnson	10.00	4.50	1.25
☐	M41 Joe Smith	50.00	22.00	6.25
☐	M42 Dikembe Mutombo	10.00	4.50	1.25
☐	M43 Damon Stoudamire	100.00	45.00	12.50
☐	M44 Antonio McDyess	40.00	18.00	5.00

1995-96 Finest Rack Pack

Randomly inserted into packs at a rate of one in 72, cards from this 7-card set features a selection of top rookies from the 1995-96 campaign. Card fronts feature a colorful "swirl-like" background with a player photo and the set name "Rack Pack" underneath the photo. Card backs feature biographical information, a headshot and a brief commentary. Values below are for

unpeeled cards. Peeled cards generally trade for about 75% of the listed prices.

	MINT	NRMT	EXC
COMPLETE SET (7)	125.00	55.00	15.50
COMMON CARD (RP1-RP7)	8.00	3.60	1.00
☐ RP1 Jerry Stackhouse	30.00	13.50	3.70
☐ RP2 Brent Barry	8.00	3.60	1.00
☐ RP3 Damon Stoudamire	40.00	18.00	5.00
☐ RP4 Joe Smith	20.00	9.00	2.50
☐ RP5 Michael Finley	20.00	9.00	2.50
☐ RP6 Antonio McDyess	15.00	6.75	1.85
☐ RP7 Rasheed Wallace	8.00	3.60	1.00

1995-96 Finest Veteran/Rookie

Randomly inserted in second series packs at a rate of one in 24, this 29-card set features rookie/veteran duos from a selection of NBA teams. The cards are dual-sided with each player getting a full photo on a separate side. Prices provided below are for unpeeled cards. Peeled cards generally trade for about 75 % of the listed prices.

	MINT	NRMT	EXC
COMPLETE SET (29)	450.00	200.00	55.00
COMMON CARD (RV1-RV29)	5.00	2.20	.60
☐ RV1 Joe Smith Latrell Sprewell	25.00	11.00	3.10
☐ RV2 Antonio McDyess Dikembe Mutombo	20.00	9.00	2.50
☐ RV3 Jerry Stackhouse Clarence Weatherspoon	40.00	18.00	5.00
☐ RV4 Rasheed Wallace Chris Webber	12.00	5.50	1.50
☐ RV5 Kevin Garnett Tim Gugliotta	60.00	27.00	7.50
☐ RV6 Bryant Reeves Greg Anthony	12.00	5.50	1.50
☐ RV7 Damon Stoudamire Willie Anderson	50.00	22.00	6.25
☐ RV8 Shawn Respert Vin Baker	10.00	4.50	1.25
☐ RV9 Ed O'Bannon Armon Gilliam	8.00	3.60	1.00
☐ RV10 Kurt Thomas Alonzo Mourning	10.00	4.50	1.25
☐ RV11 Gary Trent Rod Strickland	5.00	2.20	.60

☐ RV12 Cherokee Parks Jamal Mashburn	6.00	2.70	.75
☐ RV13 Corliss Williamson Mitch Richmond	8.00	3.60	1.00
☐ RV14 Eric Williams Dino Radja	5.00	2.20	.60
☐ RV15 Brent Barry Loy Vaught	10.00	4.50	1.25
☐ RV16 Alan Henderson Mookie Blaylock	5.00	2.20	.60
☐ RV17 Bobby Sura Terrell Brandon	5.00	2.20	.60
☐ RV18 Theo Ratliff Rod Strickland	40.00	18.00	5.00
☐ RV19 Randolph Childress	5.00	2.20	.60
☐ RV20 Jason Caffey Michael Jordan	130.00	57.50	16.00
☐ RV21 Michael Finley Kevin Johnson	25.00	11.00	3.10
☐ RV22 George Zidek Larry Johnson	10.00	4.50	1.25
☐ RV23 Travis Best Reggie Miller	12.00	5.50	1.50
☐ RV24 Loren Meyer Jason Kidd	25.00	11.00	3.10
☐ RV25 David Vaughn Shaquille O'Neal	50.00	22.00	6.25
☐ RV26 Sherell Ford Shawn Kemp	30.00	13.50	3.70
☐ RV27 Mario Bennett Charles Barkley	15.00	6.75	1.85
☐ RV28 Greg Ostertag Karl Malone	10.00	4.50	1.25
☐ RV29 Cory Alexander David Robinson	20.00	9.00	2.50

1994-95 Flair

This 326-card super-premium standard-size set (made by Fleer) was issued in two series. The first series contains 175 cards while the second has 151 cards (including the late addition of Michael Jordan as card #326). Cards were distributed in 10-card "hardpacks" (featuring a two-piece protective design wrapper), each with a suggested retail price of $4.00. The cards have a polyester laminate protective coating on both sides and are made with extra thick 30 point stock. The front has two color action photos blended. The back has one full color action photo with the player's statistics laid on top. Both sides have the player's name *stamped in gold foil along with his team. The cards are numbered on the back and checklisted below alphabetically within teams. The first series includes a "Dream Team II" subset (159-172) commemorating the USA's team victory at the 1994 World Championships in Toronto. Rookie Cards of note in this set include Grant Hill, Juwan Howard, Eddie Jones, Jason Kidd, and Glenn Robinson.*

	MINT	NRMT	EXC
COMPLETE SET (326)	80.00	36.00	10.00
COMPLETE SERIES 1 (175)	30.00	13.50	3.70
COMPLETE SERIES 2 (151)	50.00	22.00	6.25
COMMON CARD (1-325)	.20	.09	.03
COMMON CARD (176-325)	.20	.09	.03

#	Player	MINT	NRMT	EXC
1	Stacey Augmon	.35	.16	.04
2	Mookie Blaylock	.35	.16	.04
3	Craig Ehlo	.20	.09	.03
4	Jon Koncak	.20	.09	.03
5	Andrew Lang	.20	.09	.03
6	Dee Brown	.20	.09	.03
7	Sherman Douglas	.20	.09	.03
8	Acie Earl	.20	.09	.03
9	Rick Fox	.20	.09	.03
10	Kevin Gamble	.20	.09	.03
11	Xavier McDaniel	.20	.09	.03
12	Dino Radja	.50	.23	.06
13	Tony Bennett	.20	.09	.03
14	Dell Curry	.20	.09	.03
15	Kenny Gattison	.20	.09	.03
16	Hersey Hawkins	.20	.09	.03
17	Larry Johnson	.75	.35	.09
18	Alonzo Mourning	1.00	.45	.12
19	David Wingate	.20	.09	.03
20	B.J. Armstrong	.20	.09	.03
21	Steve Kerr	.35	.16	.04
22	Toni Kukoc	.60	.25	.07
23	Pete Myers	.20	.09	.03
24	Scottie Pippen	2.50	1.10	.30
25	Bill Wennington	.20	.09	.03
26	Terrell Brandon	.50	.23	.06
27	Brad Daugherty	.20	.09	.03
28	Tyrone Hill	.20	.09	.03
29	Bobby Phills	.20	.09	.03
30	Mark Price	.20	.09	.03
31	Gerald Wilkins	.20	.09	.03
32	John Williams	.20	.09	.03
33	Lucious Harris	.20	.09	.03
34	Jim Jackson	1.50	.70	.19
35	Jamal Mashburn	.60	.25	.07
36	Sean Rooks	.20	.09	.03
37	Doug Smith	.20	.09	.03
38	Mahmoud Abdul-Rauf	.35	.16	.04
39	LaPhonso Ellis	.20	.09	.03
40	Dikembe Mutombo	.50	.23	.06
41	Robert Pack	.20	.09	.03
42	Rodney Rogers	.20	.09	.03
43	Brian Williams	.20	.09	.03
44	Reggie Williams	.20	.09	.03
45	Joe Dumars	.50	.23	.06
46	Allan Houston	.50	.23	.06
47	Lindsey Hunter	.20	.09	.03
48	Terry Mills	.20	.09	.03
49	Victor Alexander	.20	.09	.03
50	Chris Gatling	.20	.09	.03
51	Billy Owens	.20	.09	.03
52	Latrell Sprewell	1.50	.70	.19
53	Chris Webber	1.00	.45	.12
54	Sam Cassell	.50	.23	.06
55	Carl Herrera	.20	.09	.03
56	Robert Horry	.50	.23	.06
57	Hakeem Olajuwon	2.00	.90	.25
58	Kenny Smith	.20	.09	.03
59	Otis Thorpe	.35	.16	.04
60	Antonio Davis	.20	.09	.03
61	Dale Davis	.20	.09	.03
62	Reggie Miller	1.00	.45	.12
63	Byron Scott	.50	.23	.06
64	Rik Smits	.50	.23	.06
65	Haywoode Workman	.20	.09	.03
66	Terry Dehere	.20	.09	.03
67	Harold Ellis	.20	.09	.03
68	Gary Grant	.20	.09	.03
69	Elmore Spencer	.20	.09	.03
70	Loy Vaught	.20	.09	.03
71	Elden Campbell	.20	.09	.03
72	Doug Christie	.20	.09	.03
73	Vlade Divac	.50	.23	.06
74	George Lynch	.20	.09	.03
75	Anthony Peeler	.20	.09	.03
76	Nick Van Exel	.75	.35	.09
77	James Worthy	.50	.23	.06
78	Bimbo Coles	.20	.09	.03
79	Harold Miner	.20	.09	.03
80	John Salley	.20	.09	.03
81	Rony Seikaly	.20	.09	.03
82	Steve Smith	.50	.23	.06
83	Vin Baker	1.00	.45	.12
84	Jon Barry	.20	.09	.03
85	Todd Day	.20	.09	.03
86	Lee Mayberry	.20	.09	.03
87	Eric Murdock	.20	.09	.03
88	Mike Brown	.20	.09	.03
89	Christian Laettner	.50	.23	.06
90	Isaiah Rider	.50	.23	.06
91	Doug West	.20	.09	.03
92	Micheal Williams	.20	.09	.03
93	Kenny Anderson	.50	.23	.06
94	Benoit Benjamin	.20	.09	.03
95	P.J. Brown	.20	.09	.03
96	Derrick Coleman	.20	.09	.03
97	Kevin Edwards	.20	.09	.03
98	Hubert Davis	.20	.09	.03
99	Patrick Ewing	.75	.35	.09
100	Derek Harper	.20	.09	.03
101	Anthony Mason	.20	.09	.03
102	Charles Oakley	.35	.16	.04
103	Charles Smith	.20	.09	.03
104	John Starks	.20	.09	.03
105	Nick Anderson	.50	.23	.06
106	Anfernee Hardaway	5.00	2.20	.60
107	Shaquille O'Neal	4.00	1.80	.50
108	Dennis Scott	.35	.16	.04
109	Jeff Turner	.20	.09	.03
110	Dana Barros	.20	.09	.03
111	Shawn Bradley	.50	.23	.06
112	Jeff Malone	.20	.09	.03
113	Tim Perry	.20	.09	.03
114	Clarence Weatherspoon	.20	.09	.03
115	Danny Ainge	.50	.23	.06
116	Charles Barkley	1.25	.55	.16
117	A.C. Green	.50	.23	.06
118	Kevin Johnson	.50	.23	.06
119	Dan Majerle	.35	.16	.04
120	Clyde Drexler	1.00	.45	.12
121	Harvey Grant	.20	.09	.03
122	Jerome Kersey	.20	.09	.03
123	Clifford Robinson	.50	.23	.06
124	Rod Strickland	.20	.09	.03

#	Player			
☐ 125	Buck Williams	.35	.16	.04
☐ 126	Randy Brown	.20	.09	.03
☐ 127	Olden Polynice	.20	.09	.03
☐ 128	Mitch Richmond	.60	.25	.07
☐ 129	Lionel Simmons	.20	.09	.03
☐ 130	Spud Webb	.35	.16	.04
☐ 131	Walt Williams	.50	.23	.06
☐ 132	Willie Anderson	.20	.09	.03
☐ 133	Vinny Del Negro	.20	.09	.03
☐ 134	Sean Elliott	.50	.23	.06
☐ 135	Avery Johnson	.35	.16	.04
☐ 136	J.R. Reid	.20	.09	.03
☐ 137	David Robinson	1.50	.70	.19
☐ 138	Dennis Rodman	3.00	1.35	.35
☐ 139	Kendall Gill	.20	.09	.03
☐ 140	Ervin Johnson	.20	.09	.03
☐ 141	Shawn Kemp	2.50	1.10	.30
☐ 142	Nate McMillan	.20	.09	.03
☐ 143	Gary Payton	1.25	.55	.16
☐ 144	Sam Perkins	.20	.09	.03
☐ 145	David Benoit	.20	.09	.03
☐ 146	Jeff Hornacek	.35	.16	.04
☐ 147	Jay Humphries	.20	.09	.03
☐ 148	Karl Malone	.75	.35	.09
☐ 149	Bryon Russell	.20	.09	.03
☐ 150	Felton Spencer	.20	.09	.03
☐ 151	John Stockton	.75	.35	.09
☐ 152	Rex Chapman	.20	.09	.03
☐ 153	Calbert Cheaney	.35	.16	.04
☐ 154	Tom Gugliotta	.35	.16	.04
☐ 155	Don MacLean	.20	.09	.03
☐ 156	Gheorghe Muresan	.50	.23	.06
☐ 157	Doug Overton	.20	.09	.03
☐ 158	Brent Price	.20	.09	.03
☐ 159	Derrick Coleman USA	.20	.09	.03
☐ 160	Joe Dumars USA	.35	.16	.04
☐ 161	Tim Hardaway USA	.20	.09	.03
☐ 162	Kevin Johnson USA	.35	.16	.04
☐ 163	Larry Johnson USA	.50	.23	.06
☐ 164	Shawn Kemp USA	1.25	.55	.16
☐ 165	Dan Majerle USA	.20	.09	.03
☐ 166	Reggie Miller USA	.50	.23	.06
☐ 167	Alonzo Mourning USA	.50	.23	.06
☐ 168	Shaquille O'Neal USA	2.00	.90	.25
☐ 169	Mark Price USA	.20	.09	.03
☐ 170	Steve Smith USA	.20	.09	.03
☐ 171	Isiah Thomas USA	.35	.16	.04
☐ 172	Dominique Wilkins USA	.35	.16	.04
☐ 173	Checklist	.20	.09	.03
☐ 174	Checklist	.20	.09	.03
☐ 175	Checklist	.20	.09	.03
☐ 176	Tyrone Corbin	.20	.09	.03
☐ 177	Grant Long	.20	.09	.03
☐ 178	Ken Norman	.20	.09	.03
☐ 179	Steve Smith	.40	.18	.05
☐ 180	Blue Edwards	.20	.09	.03
☐ 181	Pervis Ellison	.20	.09	.03
☐ 182	Greg Minor	.20	.09	.03
☐ 183	Eric Montross	.40	.18	.05
☐ 184	Derek Strong	.20	.09	.03
☐ 185	David Wesley	.20	.09	.03
☐ 186	Dominique Wilkins	.40	.18	.05
☐ 187	Michael Adams	.20	.09	.03
☐ 188	Muggsy Bogues	.30	.14	.04
☐ 189	Scott Burrell	.20	.09	.03
☐ 190	Darrin Hancock	.20	.09	.03
☐ 191	Robert Parish	.40	.18	.05
☐ 192	Jud Buechler	.20	.09	.03
☐ 193	Ron Harper	.30	.14	.04
☐ 194	Larry Krystkowiak	.20	.09	.03
☐ 195	Will Perdue	.20	.09	.03
☐ 196	Dickey Simpkins	.20	.09	.03
☐ 197	Michael Cage	.20	.09	.03
☐ 198	Tony Campbell	.20	.09	.03
☐ 199	Danny Ferry	.20	.09	.03
☐ 200	Chris Mills	.40	.18	.05
☐ 201	Popeye Jones	.20	.09	.03
☐ 202	Jason Kidd	6.00	2.70	.75
☐ 203	Roy Tarpley	.20	.09	.03
☐ 204	Lorenzo Williams	.20	.09	.03
☐ 205	Dale Ellis	.20	.09	.03
☐ 206	Tom Hammonds	.20	.09	.03
☐ 207	Jalen Rose	.75	.35	.09
☐ 208	Reggie Slater	.20	.09	.03
☐ 209	Bryant Stith	.20	.09	.03
☐ 210	Rafael Addison	.20	.09	.03
☐ 211	Bill Curley	.20	.09	.03
☐ 212	Johnny Dawkins	.20	.09	.03
☐ 213	Grant Hill	10.00	4.50	1.25
☐ 214	Mark Macon	.20	.09	.03
☐ 215	Oliver Miller	.20	.09	.03
☐ 216	Ivano Newbill	.20	.09	.03
☐ 217	Mark West	.20	.09	.03
☐ 218	Tom Gugliotta	.30	.14	.04
☐ 219	Tim Hardaway	.40	.18	.05
☐ 220	Keith Jennings	.20	.09	.03
☐ 221	Dwayne Morton	.20	.09	.03
☐ 222	Chris Mullin	.40	.18	.05
☐ 223	Ricky Pierce	.20	.09	.03
☐ 224	Carlos Rogers	.20	.09	.03
☐ 225	Clifford Rozier	.30	.14	.04
☐ 226	Rony Seikaly	.20	.09	.03
☐ 227	Tim Breaux	.20	.09	.03
☐ 228	Scott Brooks	.20	.09	.03
☐ 229	Mario Elie	.20	.09	.03
☐ 230	Vernon Maxwell	.20	.09	.03
☐ 231	Zan Tabak	.20	.09	.03
☐ 232	Mark Jackson	.20	.09	.03
☐ 233	Derrick McKey	.20	.09	.03
☐ 234	Tony Massenburg	.20	.09	.03
☐ 235	Lamond Murray	.30	.14	.04
☐ 236	Charles Outlaw	.20	.09	.03
☐ 237	Eric Piatkowski	.20	.09	.03
☐ 238	Pooh Richardson	.20	.09	.03
☐ 239	Malik Sealy	.20	.09	.03
☐ 240	Cedric Ceballos	.40	.18	.05
☐ 241	Eddie Jones	2.00	.90	.25
☐ 242	Anthony Miller	.20	.09	.03
☐ 243	Tony Smith	.20	.09	.03
☐ 244	Sedale Threatt	.20	.09	.03
☐ 245	Ledell Eackles	.20	.09	.03
☐ 246	Kevin Gamble	.20	.09	.03
☐ 247	Matt Geiger	.20	.09	.03
☐ 248	Brad Lohaus	.20	.09	.03
☐ 249	Billy Owens	.20	.09	.03
☐ 250	Khalid Reeves	.20	.09	.03
☐ 251	Glen Rice	.40	.18	.05
☐ 252	Kevin Willis	.20	.09	.03
☐ 253	Marty Conlon	.20	.09	.03
☐ 254	Eric Mobley	.20	.09	.03
☐ 255	Johnny Newman	.20	.09	.03
☐ 256	Ed Pinckney	.20	.09	.03
☐ 257	Glenn Robinson	3.00	1.35	.35
☐ 258	Pat Durham	.20	.09	.03
☐ 259	Howard Eisley	.20	.09	.03
☐ 260	Winston Garland	.20	.09	.03
☐ 261	Stacey King	.20	.09	.03
☐ 262	Donyell Marshall	.30	.14	.04
☐ 263	Sean Rooks	.20	.09	.03
☐ 264	Chris Smith	.20	.09	.03
☐ 265	Chris Childs	1.00	.45	.12
☐ 266	Sleepy Floyd	.20	.09	.03

			MINT	NRMT	EXC
☐	267	Armon Gilliam	.20	.09	.03
☐	268	Sean Higgins	.20	.09	.03
☐	269	Rex Walters	.20	.09	.03
☐	270	Greg Anthony	.20	.09	.03
☐	271	Charlie Ward	.40	.18	.05
☐	272	Herb Williams	.20	.09	.03
☐	273	Monty Williams	.20	.09	.03
☐	274	Anthony Avent	.20	.09	.03
☐	275	Anthony Bowie	.20	.09	.03
☐	276	Horace Grant	.40	.18	.05
☐	277	Donald Royal	.20	.09	.03
☐	278	Brian Shaw	.20	.09	.03
☐	279	Brooks Thompson	.30	.14	.04
☐	280	Derrick Alston	.20	.09	.03
☐	281	Willie Burton	.20	.09	.03
☐	282	Greg Graham	.20	.09	.03
☐	283	B.J. Tyler	.20	.09	.03
☐	284	Scott Williams	.20	.09	.03
☐	285	Sharone Wright	.40	.18	.05
☐	286	Joe Kleine	.20	.09	.03
☐	287	Danny Manning	.30	.14	.04
☐	288	Elliot Perry	.20	.09	.03
☐	289	Wesley Person	1.50	.70	.19
☐	290	Trevor Ruffin	.40	.18	.05
☐	291	Wayman Tisdale	.20	.09	.03
☐	292	Mark Bryant	.20	.09	.03
☐	293	Chris Dudley	.20	.09	.03
☐	294	Aaron McKie	.40	.18	.05
☐	295	Tracy Murray	.20	.09	.03
☐	296	Terry Porter	.20	.09	.03
☐	297	James Robinson	.20	.09	.03
☐	298	Alaa Abdelnaby	.20	.09	.03
☐	299	Duane Causwell	.20	.09	.03
☐	300	Brian Grant	1.25	.55	.16
☐	301	Bobby Hurley	.20	.09	.03
☐	302	Michael Smith	.40	.18	.05
☐	303	Terry Cummings	.20	.09	.03
☐	304	Moses Malone	.60	.25	.07
☐	305	Julius Nwosu	.20	.09	.03
☐	306	Chuck Person	.20	.09	.03
☐	307	Doc Rivers	.20	.09	.03
☐	308	Vincent Askew	.20	.09	.03
☐	309	Sarunas Marciulionis	.20	.09	.03
☐	310	Detlef Schrempf	.30	.14	.04
☐	311	Dontonio Wingfield	.20	.09	.03
☐	312	Antoine Carr	.20	.09	.03
☐	313	Tom Chambers	.20	.09	.03
☐	314	John Crotty	.20	.09	.03
☐	315	Adam Keefe	.20	.09	.03
☐	316	Jamie Watson	.20	.09	.03
☐	317	Mitchell Butler	.20	.09	.03
☐	318	Kevin Duckworth	.20	.09	.03
☐	319	Juwan Howard	6.00	2.70	.75
☐	320	Jim McIlvaine	.30	.14	.04
☐	321	Scott Skiles	.20	.09	.03
☐	322	Anthony Tucker	.20	.09	.03
☐	323	Chris Webber	1.00	.45	.12
☐	324	Checklist	.20	.09	.03
☐	325	Checklist	.20	.09	.03
☐	326	Michael Jordan	15.00	6.75	1.85

1994-95 Flair
Center Spotlight

Randomly inserted at a rate of one in every 25 first series packs, cards from this 6-card

set features dominant centers. The fronts have a 100% etched-foil design with a full color action photo with three shadows of him in red, green and blue. The back also has a color photo with the red, green and blue shadowing on a white background along with player information. The cards are numbered on the back as "X of 6" and are sequenced in alphabetical order.

		MINT	NRMT	EXC
	COMPLETE SET (6)	50.00	22.00	6.25
	COMMON CARD (1-6)	5.00	2.20	.60
☐	1 Patrick Ewing	5.00	2.20	.60
☐	2 Alonzo Mourning	6.00	2.70	.75
☐	3 Hakeem Olajuwon	12.00	5.50	1.50
☐	4 Shaquille O'Neal	25.00	11.00	3.10
☐	5 David Robinson	10.00	4.50	1.25
☐	6 Chris Webber	6.00	2.70	.75

1994-95 Flair
Hot Numbers

Randomly inserted into first series packs at a rate of one in six, cards from this 20-card standard-size set feature a selection of players who consistently produce big statistics. The player's top statistical numbers are shown on the front of the card without identifying which category. While some numbers are obvious, like the player's points per game, other statistics are not, like steals and blocks, particularly for multi-talented players. The fronts also have full-color action photos with the team's colors used as the background along with the words "Hot Numbers". The backs also have

a color picture with information on what type of player he is. The cards are numbered on the back as "X of 20" and are sequenced in alphabetical order.

	MINT	NRMT	EXC
COMPLETE SET (20)	60.00	27.00	7.50
COMMON CARD (1-20)	1.00	.45	.12

		MINT	NRMT	EXC
☐ 1	Vin Baker	3.00	1.35	.35
☐ 2	Sam Cassell	1.50	.70	.19
☐ 3	Patrick Ewing	2.50	1.10	.30
☐ 4	Anfernee Hardaway	15.00	6.75	1.85
☐ 5	Robert Horry	1.50	.70	.19
☐ 6	Shawn Kemp	8.00	3.60	1.00
☐ 7	Toni Kukoc	2.00	.90	.25
☐ 8	Jamal Mashburn	2.00	.90	.25
☐ 9	Reggie Miller	3.00	1.35	.35
☐ 10	Dikembe Mutombo	1.50	.70	.19
☐ 11	Hakeem Olajuwon	6.00	2.70	.75
☐ 12	Shaquille O'Neal	12.00	5.50	1.50
☐ 13	Scottie Pippen	8.00	3.60	1.00
☐ 14	Isaiah Rider	1.50	.70	.19
☐ 15	David Robinson	5.00	2.20	.60
☐ 16	Latrell Sprewell	1.50	.70	.19
☐ 17	John Starks	1.00	.45	.12
☐ 18	John Stockton	2.50	1.10	.30
☐ 19	Nick Van Exel	2.50	1.10	.30
☐ 20	Chris Webber	3.00	1.35	.35

1994-95 Flair Playmakers

Randomly inserted into second series packs at a rate of one in four, cards from this 10-card standard-size set feature a selection of the best assist men in the NBA. The fronts have a full color action photo with a hardwood floor in the background. The back also has a color photo with player information set against a hardwood floor. The cards are numbered on the back as "X of 10" and are sequenced in alphabetical order.

	MINT	NRMT	EXC
COMPLETE SET (10)	12.00	5.50	1.50
COMMON CARD (1-10)	.50	.23	.06

		MINT	NRMT	EXC
☐ 1	Kenny Anderson	.75	.35	.09
☐ 2	Mookie Blaylock	.75	.35	.09
☐ 3	Sam Cassell	.75	.35	.09
☐ 4	Anfernee Hardaway	8.00	3.60	1.00
☐ 5	Robert Pack	.50	.23	.06
☐ 6	Scottie Pippen	4.00	1.80	.50
☐ 7	Mark Price	.50	.23	.06
☐ 8	Mitch Richmond	.75	.35	.09
☐ 9	John Stockton	1.25	.55	.16
☐ 10	Nick Van Exel	1.25	.55	.16

1994-95 Flair Rejectors

Randomly inserted into second series packs at a rate of one in 25, cards from this six-card standard-size set feature a selection of top shot blockers in basketball. The fronts are 100% etched foil that have a full color action photo of the player. The background is three hands in red, green and blue seemingly up to reject a shot. The back also has a player photo along with information on him, such as his blocks per game. The background is nearly identical to the background on the front. The cards are numbered on the back as "X of 6" and are sequenced in alphabetical order.

	MINT	NRMT	EXC
COMPLETE SET (6)	60.00	27.00	7.50
COMMON CARD (1-6)	3.00	1.35	.35

		MINT	NRMT	EXC
☐ 1	Patrick Ewing	6.00	2.70	.75
☐ 2	Alonzo Mourning	8.00	3.60	1.00
☐ 3	Dikembe Mutombo	3.00	1.35	.35
☐ 4	Hakeem Olajuwon	15.00	6.75	1.85
☐ 5	Shaquille O'Neal	30.00	13.50	3.70
☐ 6	David Robinson	12.00	5.50	1.50

1994-95 Flair Scoring Power

Randomly inserted into first series packs at a rate of one in eight, cards from this 20-card standard-size set feature a selection of perennial NBA scoring leaders. The fronts emphasize the words scoring power as they are the size of the card laid out horizontally against a black background. There

is a player photo in front of the words and another inside. The back also says "Scoring Power" across the entire card horizontally. There is also a player photo with information on it, namely about his scoring. The cards are numbered on the back as "X of 10" and are sequenced in alphabetical order.

	MINT	NRMT	EXC
COMPLETE SET (10)	30.00	13.50	3.70
COMMON CARD (1-10)	1.00	.45	.12
☐ 1 Charles Barkley	4.00	1.80	.50
☐ 2 Patrick Ewing	2.50	1.10	.30
☐ 3 Karl Malone	2.50	1.10	.30
☐ 4 Hakeem Olajuwon	6.00	2.70	.75
☐ 5 Shaquille O'Neal	12.00	5.50	1.50
☐ 6 Scottie Pippen	8.00	3.60	1.00
☐ 7 Mitch Richmond	2.00	.90	.25
☐ 8 David Robinson	5.00	2.20	.60
☐ 9 Latrell Sprewell	1.00	.45	.12
☐ 10 Dominique Wilkins	1.00	.45	.12

1994-95 Flair
Wave of the Future

Randmly inserted into second series packs at a rate of one in seven, cards from this 10-card standard-size set feature a selection of top rookies from the 1994-95 season. Card fronts are laid out horizontally with three color photos of the player. The one in the middle has yellow glow surrounding it and the picture on the left is the same as the middle. The one on the left is a head shot of the color photo used on the back of the card. The back has player infor-

mation including some college statistics. Both sides of the card have a wave in the background in the team's colors. The cards are numbered on the back as "X of 10" and are sequenced in alphabetical order.

	MINT	NRMT	EXC
COMPLETE SET (10)	40.00	18.00	5.00
COMMON CARD (1-10)	1.00	.45	.12
☐ 1 Brian Grant	2.50	1.10	.30
☐ 2 Grant Hill	20.00	9.00	2.50
☐ 3 Juwan Howard	12.00	5.50	1.50
☐ 4 Eddie Jones	4.00	1.80	.50
☐ 5 Jason Kidd	12.00	5.50	1.50
☐ 6 Donyell Marshall	1.00	.45	.12
☐ 7 Eric Montross	1.00	.45	.12
☐ 8 Lamond Murray	1.00	.45	.12
☐ 9 Wesley Person	2.00	.90	.25
☐ 10 Glenn Robinson	6.00	2.70	.75

1995-96 Flair

These 250-standard size cards comprise Fleer's premium 1995-96 Flair set which was issued in two separate series of 150 and 100 cards respectively. Cards were issued in 9-card "hardpacks" (featuring a two-piece protective design wrapper) with a suggested retail price of $4.99. Player selection was restricted to recognized starters, top rookies and top players off the bench. Card fronts were upgraded from the previous year, each featuring 100% etched foil designs. Like the previous year, each card was printed on 30-point stock, giving the card twice the thickness of regular issue cards. First and second series cards are numbered alphabetically by team. Two subsets are included in the set: Rookies (199-228) and Style (229-248). Noteworthy Rookie Cards in this set include Michael Finley, Kevin Garnett, Antonio McDyess, Joe Smith, Jerry Stackhouse and Damon Stoudamire.

	MINT	NRMT	EXC
COMPLETE SET (250)	80.00	36.00	10.00
COMPLETE SERIES 1 (150)	40.00	18.00	5.00
COMPLETE SERIES 2 (100)	40.00	18.00	5.00
COMMON CARD (1-150)	.25	.11	.03
☐ 1 Stacey Augmon	.15	.07	.02
☐ 2 Mookie Blaylock	.15	.07	.02

	Player			
☐	3	Grant Long	.25	.11	.03
☐	4	Steve Smith	.50	.23	.06
☐	5	Dee Brown	.25	.11	.03
☐	6	Sherman Douglas	.25	.11	.03
☐	7	Eric Montross	.25	.11	.03
☐	8	Dino Radja	.15	.07	.02
☐	9	David Wesley	.25	.11	.03
☐	10	Muggsy Bogues	.15	.07	.02
☐	11	Scott Burrell	.25	.11	.03
☐	12	Dell Curry	.25	.11	.03
☐	13	Larry Johnson	1.00	.45	.12
☐	14	Alonzo Mourning	1.00	.45	.12
☐	15	Michael Jordan	12.00	5.50	1.50
☐	16	Steve Kerr	.15	.07	.02
☐	17	Toni Kukoc	.60	.25	.07
☐	18	Scottie Pippen	3.00	1.35	.35
☐	19	Terrell Brandon	.50	.23	.06
☐	20	Tyrone Hill	.25	.11	.03
☐	21	Chris Mills	.50	.23	.06
☐	22	Bobby Phills	.25	.11	.03
☐	23	Mark Price	.25	.11	.03
☐	24	John Williams	.25	.11	.03
☐	25	Jim Jackson	.60	.25	.07
☐	26	Popeye Jones	.25	.11	.03
☐	27	Jason Kidd	2.50	1.10	.30
☐	28	Jamal Mashburn	.60	.25	.07
☐	29	Lorenzo Williams	.25	.11	.03
☐	30	Mahmoud Abdul-Rauf	.15	.07	.02
☐	31	Dikembe Mutombo	.50	.23	.06
☐	32	Robert Pack	.25	.11	.03
☐	33	Jalen Rose	.15	.07	.02
☐	34	Bryant Stith	.25	.11	.03
☐	35	Reggie Williams	.25	.11	.03
☐	36	Joe Dumars	.50	.23	.06
☐	37	Grant Hill	4.00	1.80	.50
☐	38	Allan Houston	.50	.23	.06
☐	39	Lindsey Hunter	.25	.11	.03
☐	40	Terry Mills	.25	.11	.03
☐	41	Chris Gatling	.25	.11	.03
☐	42	Tim Hardaway	.50	.23	.06
☐	43	Donyell Marshall	.25	.11	.03
☐	44	Chris Mullin	.50	.23	.06
☐	45	Carlos Rogers	.25	.11	.03
☐	46	Clifford Rozier	.25	.11	.03
☐	47	Latrell Sprewell	.50	.23	.06
☐	48	Sam Cassell	.50	.23	.06
☐	49	Clyde Drexler	1.25	.55	.16
☐	50	Mario Elie	.25	.11	.03
☐	51	Robert Horry	.50	.23	.06
☐	52	Hakeem Olajuwon	2.50	1.10	.30
☐	53	Kenny Smith	.25	.11	.03
☐	54	Antonio Davis	.25	.11	.03
☐	55	Dale Davis	.25	.11	.03
☐	56	Mark Jackson	.25	.11	.03
☐	57	Derrick McKey	.25	.11	.03
☐	58	Reggie Miller	1.25	.55	.16
☐	59	Rik Smits	.50	.23	.06
☐	60	Lamond Murray	.25	.11	.03
☐	61	Pooh Richardson	.25	.11	.03
☐	62	Malik Sealy	.25	.11	.03
☐	63	Loy Vaught	.25	.11	.03
☐	64	Elden Campbell	.15	.07	.02
☐	65	Cedric Ceballos	.60	.25	.07
☐	66	Vlade Divac	.50	.23	.06
☐	67	Eddie Jones	.75	.35	.09
☐	68	Nick Van Exel	.75	.35	.09
☐	69	Bimbo Coles	.25	.11	.03
☐	70	Billy Owens	.25	.11	.03
☐	71	Khalid Reeves	.25	.11	.03
☐	72	Glen Rice	.50	.23	.06
☐	73	Kevin Willis	.25	.11	.03
☐	74	Vin Baker	1.00	.45	.12
☐	75	Todd Day	.25	.11	.03
☐	76	Eric Murdock	.25	.11	.03
☐	77	Glenn Robinson	1.25	.55	.16
☐	78	Tom Gugliotta	.50	.23	.06
☐	79	Christian Laettner	.50	.23	.06
☐	80	Isaiah Rider	.25	.11	.03
☐	81	Doug West	.25	.11	.03
☐	82	Kenny Anderson	.50	.23	.06
☐	83	P.J. Brown	.25	.11	.03
☐	84	Derrick Coleman	.25	.11	.03
☐	85	Armon Gilliam	.15	.07	.02
☐	86	Chris Morris	.25	.11	.03
☐	87	Hubert Davis	.25	.11	.03
☐	88	Patrick Ewing	1.00	.45	.12
☐	89	Derek Harper	.25	.11	.03
☐	90	Anthony Mason	.15	.07	.02
☐	91	Charles Oakley	.15	.07	.02
☐	92	Charles Smith	.25	.11	.03
☐	93	John Starks	.25	.11	.03
☐	94	Nick Anderson	.50	.23	.06
☐	95	Horace Grant	.50	.23	.06
☐	96	Anfernee Hardaway	6.00	2.70	.75
☐	97	Shaquille O'Neal	5.00	2.20	.60
☐	98	Dennis Scott	.50	.23	.06
☐	99	Brian Shaw	.25	.11	.03
☐	100	Dana Barros	.25	.11	.03
☐	101	Shawn Bradley	.50	.23	.06
☐	102	Clarence Weatherspoon	.25	.11	.03
☐	103	Sharone Wright	.25	.11	.03
☐	104	Charles Barkley	1.50	.70	.19
☐	105	A.C. Green	.50	.23	.06
☐	106	Kevin Johnson	.50	.23	.06
☐	107	Dan Majerle	.15	.07	.02
☐	108	Danny Manning	.50	.23	.06
☐	109	Elliot Perry	.25	.11	.03
☐	110	Wesley Person	.25	.11	.03
☐	111	Terry Porter	.25	.11	.03
☐	112	Clifford Robinson	.50	.23	.06
☐	113	Rod Strickland	.25	.11	.03
☐	114	Otis Thorpe	.15	.07	.02
☐	115	Buck Williams	.15	.07	.02
☐	116	Brian Grant	.25	.11	.03
☐	117	Bobby Hurley	.25	.11	.03
☐	118	Olden Polynice	.25	.11	.03
☐	119	Mitch Richmond	.75	.35	.09
☐	120	Walt Williams	.50	.23	.06
☐	121	Vinny Del Negro	.25	.11	.03
☐	122	Sean Elliott	.50	.23	.06
☐	123	Avery Johnson	.15	.07	.02
☐	124	David Robinson	2.00	.90	.25
☐	125	Dennis Rodman	4.00	1.80	.50
☐	126	Shawn Kemp	3.00	1.35	.35
☐	127	Nate McMillan	.25	.11	.03
☐	128	Gary Payton	1.50	.70	.19
☐	129	Sam Perkins	.25	.11	.03
☐	130	Detlef Schrempf	.15	.07	.02
☐	131	B.J. Armstrong	.25	.11	.03
☐	132	Jerome Kersey	.25	.11	.03
☐	133	Oliver Miller	.25	.11	.03
☐	134	John Salley	.25	.11	.03
☐	135	David Benoit	.25	.11	.03
☐	136	Antoine Carr	.25	.11	.03
☐	137	Jeff Hornacek	.15	.07	.02
☐	138	Karl Malone	1.00	.45	.12
☐	139	John Stockton	1.00	.45	.12
☐	140	Greg Anthony	.25	.11	.03
☐	141	Benoit Benjamin	.25	.11	.03
☐	142	Blue Edwards	.25	.11	.03
☐	143	Byron Scott	.50	.23	.06
☐	144	Calbert Cheaney	.25	.11	.03

☐ 145	Juwan Howard	2.50	1.10	.30
☐ 146	Gheorghe Muresan	.50	.23	.06
☐ 147	Scott Skiles	.25	.11	.03
☐ 148	Chris Webber	1.00	.45	.12
☐ 149	Checklist	.25	.11	.03
☐ 150	Checklist	.25	.11	.03
☐ 151	Stacey Augmon	.15	.07	.02
☐ 152	Mookie Blaylock	.15	.07	.02
☐ 153	Andrew Lang	.25	.11	.03
☐ 154	Steve Smith	.50	.23	.06
☐ 155	Dana Barros	.25	.11	.03
☐ 156	Rick Fox	.25	.11	.03
☐ 157	Kendall Gill	.25	.11	.03
☐ 158	Khalid Reeves	.25	.11	.03
☐ 159	Glen Rice	.50	.23	.06
☐ 160	Dennis Rodman Bulls	4.00	1.80	.50
☐ 161	Dan Majerle	.15	.07	.02
☐ 162	Tony Dumas	.25	.11	.03
☐ 163	Dale Ellis	.25	.11	.03
☐ 164	Otis Thorpe	.15	.07	.02
☐ 165	Rony Seikaly	.25	.11	.03
☐ 166	Sam Cassell	.50	.23	.06
☐ 167	Clyde Drexler	.75	.35	.09
☐ 168	Robert Horry	.50	.23	.06
☐ 169	Hakeem Olajuwon	1.50	.70	.19
☐ 170	Ricky Pierce	.25	.11	.03
☐ 171	Rodney Rogers	.25	.11	.03
☐ 172	Brian Williams	.25	.11	.03
☐ 173	Magic Johnson	2.00	.90	.25
☐ 174	Alonzo Mourning	.60	.25	.07
☐ 175	Lee Mayberry	.25	.11	.03
☐ 176	Terry Porter	.25	.11	.03
☐ 177	Shawn Bradley	.50	.23	.06
☐ 178	Jayson Williams	.25	.11	.03
☐ 179	Gary Grant	.25	.11	.03
☐ 180	Jon Koncak	.25	.11	.03
☐ 181	Derrick Coleman	.25	.11	.03
☐ 182	Vernon Maxwell	.25	.11	.03
☐ 183	John Williams	.25	.11	.03
☐ 184	Aaron McKie	.25	.11	.03
☐ 185	Michael Smith	.25	.11	.03
☐ 186	Chuck Person	.25	.11	.03
☐ 187	Hersey Hawkins	.25	.11	.03
☐ 188	Shawn Kemp	2.00	.90	.25
☐ 189	Gary Payton	1.00	.45	.12
☐ 190	Detlef Schrempf	.15	.07	.02
☐ 191	Chris Morris	.25	.11	.03
☐ 192	Robert Pack	.25	.11	.03
☐ 193	Willie Anderson EXP	.25	.11	.03
☐ 194	Oliver Miller EXP	.25	.11	.03
☐ 195	Alvin Robertson EXP	.25	.11	.03
☐ 196	Greg Anthony EXP	.25	.11	.03
☐ 197	Blue Edwards EXP	.25	.11	.03
☐ 198	Byron Scott EXP	.50	.23	.06
☐ 199	Cory Alexander	.25	.11	.03
☐ 200	Brent Barry	1.25	.55	.16
☐ 201	Travis Best	.40	.18	.05
☐ 202	Jason Caffey	.25	.11	.03
☐ 203	Sasha Danilovic	.50	.23	.06
☐ 204	Tyus Edney	1.25	.55	.16
☐ 205	Michael Finley	3.00	1.35	.35
☐ 206	Kevin Garnett	8.00	3.60	1.00
☐ 207	Alan Henderson	.40	.18	.05
☐ 208	Antonio McDyess	2.50	1.10	.30
☐ 209	Loren Meyer	.50	.23	.06
☐ 210	Lawrence Moten	.25	.11	.03
☐ 211	Ed O'Bannon	1.00	.45	.12
☐ 212	Greg Ostertag	.25	.11	.03
☐ 213	Cherokee Parks	.50	.23	.06
☐ 214	Theo Ratliff	.50	.23	.06
☐ 215	Bryant Reeves	1.50	.70	.19
☐ 216	Shawn Respert	.50	.23	.06
☐ 217	Arvydas Sabonis	2.00	.90	.25
☐ 218	Joe Smith	3.00	1.35	.35
☐ 219	Jerry Stackhouse	5.00	2.20	.60
☐ 220	Damon Stoudamire	6.00	2.70	.75
☐ 221	Bob Sura	.50	.23	.06
☐ 222	Kurt Thomas	.75	.35	.09
☐ 223	Gary Trent	.50	.23	.06
☐ 224	David Vaughn	.25	.11	.03
☐ 225	Rasheed Wallace	1.25	.55	.16
☐ 226	Eric Williams	.50	.23	.06
☐ 227	Corliss Williamson	.50	.23	.06
☐ 228	George Zidek	.50	.23	.06
☐ 229	Vin Baker STY	.50	.23	.06
☐ 230	Charles Barkley STY	.50	.23	.06
☐ 231	Patrick Ewing STY	.50	.23	.06
☐ 232	Anfernee Hardaway STY	2.00	.90	.25
☐ 233	Grant Hill STY	1.25	.55	.16
☐ 234	Larry Johnson STY	.50	.23	.06
☐ 235	Michael Jordan STY	4.00	1.80	.50
☐ 236	Jason Kidd STY	.75	.35	.09
☐ 237	Karl Malone STY	.50	.23	.06
☐ 238	Jamal Mashburn STY	.15	.07	.02
☐ 239	Reggie Miller STY	.40	.18	.05
☐ 240	Shaquille O'Neal STY	1.50	.70	.19
☐ 241	Scottie Pippen STY	1.00	.45	.12
☐ 242	Mitch Richmond STY	.15	.07	.02
☐ 243	Clifford Robinson STY	.25	.11	.03
☐ 244	David Robinson STY	.60	.25	.07
☐ 245	Glenn Robinson STY	.40	.18	.05
☐ 246	John Stockton STY	.50	.23	.06
☐ 247	Nick Van Exel STY	.50	.23	.06
☐ 248	Chris Webber STY	.15	.07	.02
☐ 249	Checklist	.25	.11	.03
☐ 250	Checklist	.25	.11	.03

1995-96 Flair Anticipation

Randomly inserted in second series packs at a rate of one in 36, cards from this ten card standard-size set feature a collection of fan favorites. Borderless fronts have a full-color action raised cutouts and two ghosted images of the same shot in the player's team colors. Backs have a close-up color shot and a player profile. The set is sequenced in alphabetical order.

	MINT	NRMT	EXC
COMPLETE SET (10)	175.00	80.00	22.00
COMMON CARD (1-10)	5.00	2.20	.60

		MINT	NRMT	EXC
☐ 1	Grant Hill	20.00	9.00	2.50
☐ 2	Michael Jordan	75.00	34.00	9.50
☐ 3	Shawn Kemp	15.00	6.75	1.85
☐ 4	Jason Kidd	12.00	5.50	1.50
☐ 5	Alonzo Mourning	5.00	2.20	.60
☐ 6	Hakeem Olajuwon	12.00	5.50	1.50
☐ 7	Shaquille O'Neal	25.00	11.00	3.10
☐ 8	Glenn Robinson	6.00	2.70	.75
☐ 9	Joe Smith	12.00	5.50	1.50
☐ 10	Jerry Stackhouse	25.00	11.00	3.10

1995-96 Flair
Center Spotlight

Randomly inserted in first series packs at a
rate of one in 18, cards from this 6-card
standard-size set feature a selection of the
game's dominant centers. This was the
second year in a row Flair included a
Center Spotlight insert within their first
series product. Each card is printed on
clear plastic, with a full color action photo
layered on top of a circular designed background. Backs are numbered in left in
gold foil and the player's blue silhouette
serves as a background for biography and
career highlights which are printed in white.
The set is sequenced in alphabetical order.

		MINT	NRMT	EXC
COMPLETE SET (6)		30.00	13.50	3.70
COMMON CARD (1-6)		1.25	.55	.16
☐ 1	Vlade Divac	1.25	.55	.16
☐ 2	Patrick Ewing	4.00	1.80	.50
☐ 3	Alonzo Mourning	4.00	1.80	.50
☐ 4	Hakeem Olajuwon	8.00	3.60	1.00
☐ 5	Shaquille O'Neal	15.00	6.75	1.85
☐ 6	David Robinson	6.00	2.70	.75

1995-96 Flair
Class of '95

Seeded in first series packs at the same
rate as regular issue cards, these 15-cards
were added to the first series Flair product
just prior to release. Each card features one

of the top rookies from the 1995 NBA draft
in their new pro uniforms. Full color, cutout
player action shots are placed against a
glowing orange basketball backdrop. The
set is sequenced in alphabetical order.

		MINT	NRMT	EXC
COMPLETE SET (15)		40.00	18.00	5.00
COMMON CARD (R1-R15)		1.00	.45	.12
☐ R1	Brent Barry	2.00	.90	.25
☐ R2	Kevin Garnett	12.00	5.50	1.50
☐ R3	Antonio McDyess	4.00	1.80	.50
☐ R4	Ed O'Bannon	1.50	.70	.19
☐ R5	Cherokee Parks	1.00	.45	.12
☐ R6	Bryant Reeves	2.50	1.10	.30
☐ R7	Shawn Respert	1.00	.45	.12
☐ R8	Joe Smith	5.00	2.20	.60
☐ R9	Jerry Stackhouse	8.00	3.60	1.00
☐ R10	Damon Stoudamire	10.00	4.50	1.25
☐ R11	Kurt Thomas	1.00	.45	.12
☐ R12	Gary Trent	1.00	.45	.12
☐ R13	Rasheed Wallace	2.00	.90	.25
☐ R14	Eric Williams	1.00	.45	.12
☐ R15	Corliss Williamson	1.00	.45	.12

1995-96 Flair
Hot Numbers

Randomly inserted in first series packs at
rate of one in 36, cards from this 15-card
standard-size set showcase the game's top
players. Each card is given a three-dimensional effect by the addition of a special
lenticular coating (a ribbed plastic material)
on the front. The full color player photos are
placed against a swirling background of
numbers. The backs continue with the num-

bers motif that serve as a background for the full-color player cutout. Player's name and short biography are printed in white. The set is sequenced in alphabetical order.

	MINT	NRMT	EXC
COMPLETE SET (15)	200.00	90.00	25.00
COMMON CARD (1-15)	5.00	2.20	.60
☐ 1 Charles Barkley	12.00	5.50	1.50
☐ 2 Grant Hill	30.00	13.50	3.70
☐ 3 Eddie Jones	6.00	2.70	.75
☐ 4 Michael Jordan	100.00	45.00	12.50
☐ 5 Shawn Kemp	20.00	9.00	2.50
☐ 6 Jason Kidd	20.00	9.00	2.50
☐ 7 Karl Malone	8.00	3.60	1.00
☐ 8 Alonzo Mourning	8.00	3.60	1.00
☐ 9 Dikembe Mutombo	5.00	2.20	.60
☐ 10 Hakeem Olajuwon	20.00	9.00	2.50
☐ 11 Shaquille O'Neal	40.00	18.00	5.00
☐ 12 Glenn Robinson	10.00	4.50	1.25
☐ 13 Dennis Rodman	30.00	13.50	3.70
☐ 14 Latrell Sprewell	5.00	2.20	.60
☐ 15 Chris Webber	8.00	3.60	1.00

1995-96 Flair
New Heights

Randomly inserted in second series hobby packs only at a rate of one in 18, cards from this 10-card standard-size set feature some of the more popular players in the hobby. Borderless fronts have a full-color action cutout with a ghosted image trailing behind. Backs have player profile and biographies. The set is sequenced in alphabetical order.

	MINT	NRMT	EXC
COMPLETE SET (10)	75.00	34.00	9.50
COMMON CARD (1-10)	3.00	1.35	.35
☐ 1 Anfernee Hardaway	20.00	9.00	2.50
☐ 2 Grant Hill	12.00	5.50	1.50
☐ 3 Larry Johnson	3.00	1.35	.35
☐ 4 Michael Jordan	40.00	18.00	5.00
☐ 5 Shawn Kemp	10.00	4.50	1.25
☐ 6 Karl Malone	3.00	1.35	.35
☐ 7 Hakeem Olajuwon	8.00	3.60	1.00
☐ 8 David Robinson	6.00	2.70	.75
☐ 9 Glenn Robinson	4.00	1.80	.50
☐ 10 Chris Webber	4.00	1.80	.50

1995-96 Flair
Perimeter Power

Randomly inserted in first series packs at a rate of one in 6, cards from this 15-card set feature players that dominate play from the perimeter. Full-bleed team-color backgrounds include a player cutout with silver foil printing on the front. Backs are printed on a white background with another full-color action player shot.

	MINT	NRMT	EXC
COMPLETE SET (15)	20.00	9.00	2.50
COMMON CARD (1-15)	.75	.35	.09
☐ 1 Dana Barros	.75	.35	.09
☐ 2 Clyde Drexler	2.50	1.10	.30
☐ 3 Anfernee Hardaway	12.00	5.50	1.50
☐ 4 Tim Hardaway	1.50	.70	.19
☐ 5 Dan Majerle	1.50	.70	.19
☐ 6 Jamal Mashburn	1.25	.55	.16
☐ 7 Reggie Miller	2.50	1.10	.30
☐ 8 Gary Payton	3.00	1.35	.35
☐ 9 Scottie Pippen	5.00	2.20	.60
☐ 10 Glen Rice	1.50	.70	.19
☐ 11 Mitch Richmond	1.50	.70	.19
☐ 12 Steve Smith	1.50	.70	.19
☐ 13 John Starks	.75	.35	.09
☐ 14 John Stockton	2.00	.90	.25
☐ 15 Nick Van Exel	1.50	.70	.19

1995-96 Flair
Play Makers

Randomly inserted in second series packs at a rate of one in 54 packs, this set of ten standard-size cards features a selection of some of the league's top playmakers.

Fronts are printed in a 3-D lenticular format and feature the player in a full-color action shot. The background is a three-color chalkboard diagram. The diagram background continues on the back and a player profile appears in a screened box next to a full-color action player cutout. The set is sequenced in alphabetical order.

	MINT	NRMT	EXC
COMPLETE SET (10)	275.00	125.00	34.00
COMMON CARD (1-10)	12.00	5.50	1.50

		MINT	NRMT	EXC
☐ 1	Clyde Drexler	20.00	9.00	2.50
☐ 2	Anfernee Hardaway	120.00	55.00	15.00
☐ 3	Jamal Mashburn	12.00	5.50	1.50
☐ 4	Reggie Miller	20.00	9.00	2.50
☐ 5	Gary Payton	25.00	11.00	3.10
☐ 6	Scottie Pippen	50.00	22.00	6.25
☐ 7	Mitch Richmond	15.00	6.75	1.85
☐ 8	David Robinson	30.00	13.50	3.70
☐ 9	Jerry Stackhouse	50.00	22.00	6.25
☐ 10	Nick Van Exel	12.00	5.50	1.50

1995-96 Flair Stackhouse's Scrapbook

Randomly inserted into one in every 24 second series packs, these two cards continue the cross-brand set of Fleer spokesperson Jerry Stackhouse. The two Flair cards represent the third of a four series, eight card set. Card fronts feature a full-color action shot framed by a ghosted white border.

	MINT	NRMT	EXC
COMPLETE SET (2)	15.00	6.75	1.85
COMMON CARD (S5-S6)	8.00	3.60	1.00

		MINT	NRMT	EXC
☐ S5	Jerry Stackhouse Flair	8.00	3.60	1.00
☐ S6	Jerry Stackhouse Flair	8.00	3.60	1.00

1995-96 Flair Wave of the Future

The 10 cards in this standard-size set were randomly inserted at a rate of one in 12

second series packs and feature rookie NBA players with potential for greatness. A full-color player action cutout appears on the front with a watercolor background painted in a wave pattern. Backs continue with the wave pattern background and have another full-color action cutout. The cards are sequenced in alphabetical order.

	MINT	NRMT	EXC
COMPLETE SET (10)	40.00	18.00	5.00
COMMON CARD (1-10)	1.50	.70	.19

		MINT	NRMT	EXC
☐ 1	Tyus Edney	2.00	.90	.25
☐ 2	Michael Finley	5.00	2.20	.60
☐ 3	Kevin Garnett	15.00	6.75	1.85
☐ 4	Antonio McDyess	4.00	1.80	.50
☐ 5	Ed O'Bannon	1.50	.70	.19
☐ 6	Arvydas Sabonis	3.00	1.35	.35
☐ 7	Joe Smith	5.00	2.20	.60
☐ 8	Jerry Stackhouse	8.00	3.60	1.00
☐ 9	Damon Stoudamire	10.00	4.50	1.25
☐ 10	Rasheed Wallace	2.00	.90	.25

1961-62 Fleer

The 1961-62 Fleer set was the company's only major basketball issue until the 1986-87 season. The cards were issued in five-cent wax packs. The cards in the set measure the standard 2 1/2" by 3 1/2". Cards numbered 45 to 66 are action shots (designated IA) of players elsewhere in the set. Both the regular cards and the IA cards are numbered alphabetically within that particular subset. No known scarcities exist, although the set is quite popular since it contains the first mainstream basketball cards of many of the game's all-time greats including Elgin Baylor, Wilt Chamberlain,

Oscar Robertson and Jerry West. Most cards are frequently found with centering problems

	NRMT	VG-E	GOOD
COMPLETE SET (66)	4000.00	1800.00	500.00
COMMON CARD (1-44)	15.00	6.75	1.85
COMMON CARD (45-66)	15.00	6.75	1.85
☐ 1 Al Attles	100.00	30.00	10.00
☐ 2 Paul Arizin	40.00	18.00	5.00
☐ 3 Elgin Baylor	300.00	135.00	38.00
☐ 4 Walt Bellamy	60.00	27.00	7.50
☐ 5 Arlen Bockhorn	15.00	6.75	1.85
☐ 6 Bob Boozer	20.00	9.00	2.50
☐ 7 Carl Braun	15.00	6.75	1.85
☐ 8 Wilt Chamberlain	1200.00	550.00	150.00
☐ 9 Larry Costello	15.00	6.75	1.85
☐ 10 Bob Cousy	250.00	110.00	31.00
☐ 11 Walter Dukes	15.00	6.75	1.85
☐ 12 Wayne Embry	25.00	11.00	3.10
☐ 13 Dave Gambee	15.00	6.75	1.85
☐ 14 Tom Gola	40.00	18.00	5.00
☐ 15 Sihugo Green	15.00	6.75	1.85
☐ 16 Hal Greer	80.00	36.00	10.00
☐ 17 Richie Guerin	40.00	18.00	5.00
☐ 18 Cliff Hagan	45.00	20.00	5.50
☐ 19 Tom Heinsohn	90.00	40.00	11.00
☐ 20 Bailey Howell	40.00	18.00	5.00
☐ 21 Rod Hundley	50.00	22.00	6.25
☐ 22 K.C. Jones	100.00	45.00	12.50
☐ 23 Sam Jones	100.00	45.00	12.50
☐ 24 Phil Jordan	15.00	6.75	1.85
☐ 25 John Kerr	40.00	18.00	5.00
☐ 26 Rudy LaRusso	35.00	16.00	4.40
☐ 27 George Lee	15.00	6.75	1.85
☐ 28 Bob Leonard	15.00	6.75	1.85
☐ 29 Clyde Lovellette	50.00	22.00	6.25
☐ 30 John McCarthy	15.00	6.75	1.85
☐ 31 Tom Meschery	25.00	11.00	3.10
☐ 32 Willie Naulls	25.00	11.00	3.10
☐ 33 Don Ohl	20.00	9.00	2.50
☐ 34 Bob Pettit	80.00	36.00	10.00
☐ 35 Frank Ramsey	40.00	18.00	5.00
☐ 36 Oscar Robertson	450.00	200.00	55.00
☐ 37 Guy Rodgers	25.00	11.00	3.10
☐ 38 Bill Russell	500.00	220.00	60.00
☐ 39 Dolph Schayes	55.00	25.00	7.00
☐ 40 Frank Selvy	15.00	6.75	1.85
☐ 41 Gene Shue	25.00	11.00	3.10
☐ 42 Jack Twyman	40.00	18.00	5.00
☐ 43 Jerry West	650.00	300.00	80.00
☐ 44 Len Wilkens UER	150.00	70.00	19.00
(Misspelled Wilkins on card front)			
☐ 45 Paul Arizin IA	25.00	11.00	3.10
☐ 46 Elgin Baylor IA	100.00	45.00	12.50
☐ 47 Wilt Chamberlain IA	350.00	160.00	45.00
☐ 48 Larry Costello IA	15.00	6.75	1.85
☐ 49 Bob Cousy IA	120.00	55.00	15.00
☐ 50 Walter Dukes IA	15.00	6.75	1.85
☐ 51 Tom Gola IA	25.00	11.00	3.10
☐ 52 Richie Guerin IA	20.00	9.00	2.50
☐ 53 Cliff Hagan IA	25.00	11.00	3.10
☐ 54 Tom Heinsohn IA	40.00	18.00	5.00
☐ 55 Bailey Howell IA	20.00	9.00	2.50
☐ 56 John Kerr IA	25.00	11.00	3.10
☐ 57 Rudy LaRusso IA	15.00	6.75	1.85
☐ 58 Clyde Lovelliette IA	30.00	13.50	3.70
☐ 59 Bob Pettit IA	40.00	18.00	5.00
☐ 60 Frank Ramsey IA	25.00	11.00	3.10
☐ 61 Oscar Robertson IA	160.00	70.00	20.00
☐ 62 Bill Russell IA	225.00	100.00	28.00
☐ 63 Dolph Schayes IA	30.00	13.50	3.70
☐ 64 Gene Shue IA	15.00	6.75	1.85
☐ 65 Jack Twyman IA	25.00	11.00	3.10
☐ 66 Jerry West IA	300.00	90.00	30.00

1986-87 Fleer

This 132-card standard-size set marks Fleer's return to the basketball card industry after a 25-year hiatus. It also marks what is considered to be the beginning of the modern era of basketball cards. The cards were issued in 12-card wax packs (11 cards plus a sticker) that retailed for 50 cents. Wax boxes consisted of 36 packs. A stick of gum was also included in each pack. The set is checklisted alphabetically by the player's last name. Since only the Star Company had been issuing basketball cards nationally since 1983, most of the players in this Fleer set already had cards which are considered Extended Rookie Cards. However, since this Fleer set was the first nationally distributed through wax packs since the 1981-82 Topps issue, most of the players in the set are considered Rookie Cards including Michael Jordan. Other Rookie Cards, of those that had Star Company cards include Charles Barkley, Clyde Drexler, Patrick Ewing, Hakeem Olajuwon, Isiah Thomas and Dominique Wilkins. Rookie Cards of those that did not previously appear in a set include Joe Dumars, Karl Malone, Chris Mullin and Charles Oakley. Red, white and blue borders surround a color photo that contains a Fleer "Premier" logo in an upper corner. The card backs are printed in red and blue on white card stock. Several cards have "Traded" notations on them if the player was traded subsequent to the photo selection process. It's important to note that some of the more expensive cards in this set (especially Michael Jordan) have been counterfeited in the past few years. Checking key detailed printing areas such as the "Fleer Premier" logo on the front and the players' association logo on the back under eight or ten power magnification usually detects the legitimate from the counterfeits. The cards are condition sensitive due to dark borders and centering problems.

		NRMT-MT	EXC	G-VG
	COMP. w/Stickers (143)	1350.00	600.00	170.00
	COMPLETE SET (132)	1250.00	550.00	160.00
	COMMON CARD (1-132)	1.50	.70	.19

	#	Player	NRMT-MT	EXC	G-VG
☐	1	Kareem Abdul-Jabbar ..	12.00	5.50	1.50
☐	2	Alvan Adams	2.00	.90	.25
☐	3	Mark Aguirre...............	2.50	1.10	.30
☐	4	Danny Ainge	5.00	2.20	.60
☐	5	John Bagley	1.50	.70	.19
☐	6	Thurl Bailey	2.00	.90	.25
☐	7	Charles Barkley	80.00	36.00	10.00
☐	8	Benoit Benjamin	2.00	.90	.25
☐	9	Larry Bird...................	50.00	22.00	6.25
☐	10	Otis Birdsong.............	2.00	.90	.25
☐	11	Rolando Blackman	2.50	1.10	.30
☐	12	Manute Bol	2.00	.90	.25
☐	13	Sam Bowie.................	2.00	.90	.25
☐	14	Joe Barry Carroll	2.00	.90	.25
☐	15	Tom Chambers	4.00	1.80	.50
☐	16	Maurice Cheeks	2.00	.90	.25
☐	17	Michael Cooper	2.00	.90	.25
☐	18	Wayne Cooper	1.50	.70	.19
☐	19	Pat Cummings	1.50	.70	.19
☐	20	Terry Cummings	2.00	.90	.25
☐	21	Adrian Dantley	2.50	1.10	.30
☐	22	Brad Davis	2.00	.90	.25
☐	23	Walter Davis	2.50	1.10	.30
☐	24	Darryl Dawkins	2.00	.90	.25
☐	25	Larry Drew	1.50	.70	.19
☐	26	Clyde Drexler.............	60.00	27.00	7.50
☐	27	Joe Dumars	15.00	6.75	1.85
☐	28	Mark Eaton	2.00	.90	.25
☐	29	James Edwards............	1.50	.70	.19
☐	30	Alex English	2.50	1.10	.30
☐	31	Julius Erving	15.00	6.75	1.85
☐	32	Patrick Ewing	50.00	22.00	6.25
☐	33	Vern Fleming	2.00	.90	.25
☐	34	Sleepy Floyd	1.50	.70	.19
☐	35	World B. Free..............	2.00	.90	.25
☐	36	George Gervin	4.00	1.80	.50
☐	37	Artis Gilmore..............	2.50	1.10	.30
☐	38	Mike Gminski	2.00	.90	.25
☐	39	Rickey Green..............	2.00	.90	.25
☐	40	Sidney Green	1.50	.70	.19
☐	41	David Greenwood	1.50	.70	.19
☐	42	Darrell Griffith	2.00	.90	.25
☐	43	Bill Hanzlik	1.50	.70	.19
☐	44	Derek Harper	4.00	1.80	.50
☐	45	Gerald Henderson	1.50	.70	.19
☐	46	Roy Hinson	1.50	.70	.19
☐	47	Craig Hodges	1.50	.70	.19
☐	48	Phil Hubbard	1.50	.70	.19
☐	49	Jay Humphries	1.50	.70	.19
☐	50	Dennis Johnson	2.00	.90	.25
☐	51	Eddie Johnson	2.00	.90	.25
☐	52	Frank Johnson	1.50	.70	.19
☐	53	Magic Johnson	40.00	18.00	5.00
☐	54	Marques Johnson	2.50	1.10	.30
		(Decimal point missing, rookie year scoring avg.)			
☐	55	Steve Johnson UER	1.50	.70	.19
		(photo actually David Greenwood)			
☐	56	Vinnie Johnson	2.00	.90	.25
☐	57	Michael Jordan	1000.00	450.00	125.00
☐	58	Clark Kellogg..............	2.50	1.10	.30
☐	59	Albert King	1.50	.70	.19
☐	60	Bernard King..............	2.50	1.10	.30
☐	61	Bill Laimbeer..............	2.50	1.10	.30
☐	62	Allen Leavell..............	1.50	.70	.19

	#	Player	NRMT-MT	EXC	G-VG
☐	63	Lafayette Lever	2.00	.90	.25
☐	64	Alton Lister	2.00	.90	.25
☐	65	Lewis Lloyd................	1.50	.70	.19
☐	66	Maurice Lucas	2.50	1.10	.30
☐	67	Jeff Malone	1.50	.70	.19
☐	68	Karl Malone................	50.00	22.00	6.25
☐	69	Moses Malone	5.00	2.20	.60
☐	70	Cedric Maxwell	1.50	.70	.19
☐	71	Rodney McCray	2.00	.90	.25
☐	72	Xavier McDaniel	2.00	.90	.25
☐	73	Kevin McHale	5.00	2.20	.60
☐	74	Mike Mitchell	1.50	.70	.19
☐	75	Sidney Moncrief...........	2.00	.90	.25
☐	76	Johnny Moore	1.50	.70	.19
☐	77	Chris Mullin	15.00	6.75	1.85
☐	78	Larry Nance	4.00	1.80	.50
☐	79	Calvin Natt	1.50	.70	.19
☐	80	Norm Nixon	1.50	.70	.19
☐	81	Charles Oakley	5.00	2.20	.60
☐	82	Hakeem Olajuwon	125.00	55.00	15.50
☐	83	Louis Orr...................	1.50	.70	.19
☐	84	Robert Parish UER	3.00	1.35	.35
		(Misspelled Parrish on both sides)			
☐	85	Jim Paxson	1.50	.70	.19
☐	86	Sam Perkins	5.00	2.20	.60
☐	87	Ricky Pierce	2.00	.90	.25
☐	88	Paul Pressey	1.50	.70	.19
☐	89	Kurt Rambis	2.00	.90	.25
☐	90	Robert Reid................	1.50	.70	.19
☐	91	Doc Rivers	2.00	.90	.25
☐	92	Alvin Robertson	2.00	.90	.25
☐	93	Cliff Robinson	1.50	.70	.19
☐	94	Tree Rollins	2.00	.90	.25
☐	95	Dan Roundfield	2.00	.90	.25
☐	96	Jeff Ruland	2.00	.90	.25
☐	97	Ralph Sampson	2.00	.90	.25
☐	98	Danny Schayes	2.00	.90	.25
☐	99	Byron Scott	4.00	1.80	.50
☐	100	Purvis Short	1.50	.70	.19
☐	101	Jerry Sichting	1.50	.70	.19
☐	102	Jack Sikma	2.50	1.10	.30
☐	103	Derek Smith	1.50	.70	.19
☐	104	Larry Smith	1.50	.70	.19
☐	105	Rory Sparrow	1.50	.70	.19
☐	106	Steve Stipanovich.........	1.50	.70	.19
☐	107	Terry Teagle	1.50	.70	.19
☐	108	Reggie Theus	2.50	1.10	.30
☐	109	Isiah Thomas	25.00	11.00	3.10
☐	110	LaSalle Thompson	1.50	.70	.19
☐	111	Mychal Thompson	2.00	.90	.25
☐	112	Sedale Threatt............	2.00	.90	.25
☐	113	Wayman Tisdale	2.00	.90	.25
☐	114	Andrew Toney	1.50	.70	.19
☐	115	Kelly Tripucka	2.00	.90	.25
☐	116	Mel Turpin	2.00	.90	.25
☐	117	Kiki Vandeweghe.........	2.00	.90	.25
☐	118	Jay Vincent	1.50	.70	.19
☐	119	Bill Walton	5.00	2.20	.60
		(Missing decimal points on four lines of FG Percentage)			
☐	120	Spud Webb................	4.00	1.80	.50
☐	121	Dominique Wilkins........	20.00	9.00	2.50
☐	122	Gerald Wilkins.............	2.00	.90	.25
☐	123	Buck Williams..............	4.00	1.80	.50
☐	124	Gus Williams...............	2.00	.90	.25
☐	125	Herb Williams.............	2.00	.90	.25
☐	126	Kevin Willis	3.00	1.35	.35
☐	127	Randy Wittman	1.50	.70	.19
☐	128	Al Wood	1.50	.70	.19

☐	129 Mike Woodson	1.50	.70	.19
☐	130 Orlando Woolridge	2.00	.90	.25
☐	131 James Worthy	15.00	6.75	1.85
☐	132 Checklist 1-132	10.00	4.50	1.25

1986-87 Fleer Stickers

One of these eleven different stickers was inserted into each 1986-87 Fleer wax pack. The stickers are 2 1/2" by 3 1/2". The backs of the sticker cards are printed in blue and red on white card stock. The set numbering of the stickers is alphabetical by player's name. Based on the one-to-twelve proportion of stickers to regular cards in the wax packs, there are theoretically an equal number of sticker sets and regular sets. The cards are frequently found off-centered and most card backs are found with wax stains due to packaging.

	NRMT-MT	EXC	G-VG
COMPLETE SET (11)	140.00	65.00	17.50
COMMON STICKER (1-11)	1.50	.70	.19

☐	1 Kareem Abdul-Jabbar	4.00	1.80	.50
☐	2 Larry Bird	15.00	6.75	1.85
☐	3 Adrian Dantley	1.50	.70	.19
☐	4 Alex English	1.50	.70	.19
☐	5 Julius Erving	5.00	2.20	.60
☐	6 Patrick Ewing	8.00	3.60	1.00
☐	7 Magic Johnson	12.00	5.50	1.50
☐	8 Michael Jordan	100.00	45.00	12.50
☐	9 Hakeem Olajuwon	20.00	9.00	2.50
☐	10 Isiah Thomas	4.00	1.80	.50
☐	11 Dominique Wilkins	2.50	1.10	.30

1987-88 Fleer

The 1987-88 Fleer basketball set contains 132 standard-size cards. The cards were issued in 12-card wax packs that retailed for 50 cents. A wax box consisted of 36 packs. A sticker card and stick of gum were included. The fronts are white with gray horizontal stripes. The backs are red, white and blue and show each player's complete NBA statistics. The cards are numbered in alphabetical order by last name. Rookie Cards include Brad Daugherty, A.C. Green, Chuck Person, Terry Porter, Detlef Schrempf and Hot Rod Williams. Other key Rookie Cards in this set, who had already had cards in previous Star sets, are Dale Ellis, John Paxson, and Otis Thorpe. The cards are frequently found off-centered.

	MINT	NRMT	EXC
COMPLETE w/Stickers (143)	300.00	135.00	38.00
COMPLETE SET (132)	250.00	110.00	31.00
COMMON CARD (1-132)	1.00	.45	.12

☐	1 Kareem Abdul-Jabbar	8.00	3.60	1.00
☐	2 Alvan Adams	1.50	.70	.19
☐	3 Mark Aguirre	1.50	.70	.19
☐	4 Danny Ainge	2.00	.90	.25
☐	5 John Bagley	1.00	.45	.12
☐	6 Thurl Bailey UER	1.00	.45	.12
	(reverse negative)			
☐	7 Greg Ballard	1.00	.45	.12
☐	8 Gene Banks	1.00	.45	.12
☐	9 Charles Barkley	20.00	9.00	2.50
☐	10 Benoit Benjamin	1.00	.45	.12
☐	11 Larry Bird	30.00	13.50	3.70
☐	12 Rolando Blackman	1.50	.70	.19
☐	13 Manute Bol	1.00	.45	.12
☐	14 Tony Brown	1.00	.45	.12
☐	15 Michael Cage	1.00	.45	.12
☐	16 Joe Barry Carroll	1.00	.45	.12
☐	17 Bill Cartwright	1.50	.70	.19
☐	18 Terry Catledge	1.00	.45	.12
☐	19 Tom Chambers	1.50	.70	.19
☐	20 Maurice Cheeks	2.00	.90	.25
☐	21 Michael Cooper	2.00	.90	.25
☐	22 Dave Corzine	1.00	.45	.12
☐	23 Terry Cummings	1.50	.70	.19
☐	24 Adrian Dantley	2.00	.90	.25
☐	25 Brad Daugherty	2.50	1.10	.30
☐	26 Walter Davis	2.00	.90	.25
☐	27 Johnny Dawkins	1.00	.45	.12
☐	28 James Donaldson	1.00	.45	.12
☐	29 Larry Drew	1.00	.45	.12
☐	30 Clyde Drexler	15.00	6.75	1.85
☐	31 Joe Dumars	3.00	1.35	.35
☐	32 Mark Eaton	1.50	.70	.19
☐	33 Dale Ellis	2.50	1.10	.30
☐	34 Alex English	2.00	.90	.25
☐	35 Julius Erving	10.00	4.50	1.25
☐	36 Mike Evans	1.00	.45	.12
☐	37 Patrick Ewing	12.00	5.50	1.50
☐	38 Vern Fleming	1.00	.45	.12
☐	39 Sleepy Floyd	1.00	.45	.12
☐	40 Artis Gilmore	2.00	.90	.25
☐	41 Mike Gminski UER	1.00	.45	.12

(reversed negative)

☐ 42	A.C. Green	6.00	2.70	.75
☐ 43	Rickey Green	1.00	.45	.12
☐ 44	Sidney Green	1.00	.45	.12
☐ 45	David Greenwood	1.00	.45	.12
☐ 46	Darrell Griffith	1.50	.70	.19
☐ 47	Bill Hanzlik	1.00	.45	.12
☐ 48	Derek Harper	2.00	.90	.25
☐ 49	Ron Harper	6.00	2.70	.75
☐ 50	Gerald Henderson	1.00	.45	.12
☐ 51	Roy Hinson	1.00	.45	.12
☐ 52	Craig Hodges	1.00	.45	.12
☐ 53	Phil Hubbard	1.00	.45	.12
☐ 54	Dennis Johnson	2.00	.90	.25
☐ 55	Eddie Johnson	1.50	.70	.19
☐ 56	Magic Johnson	25.00	11.00	3.10
☐ 57	Steve Johnson	1.00	.45	.12
☐ 58	Vinnie Johnson	1.50	.70	.19
☐ 59	Michael Jordan	180.00	80.00	22.00
☐ 60	Jerome Kersey	1.50	.70	.19
☐ 61	Bill Laimbeer	1.50	.70	.19
☐ 62	Lafayette Lever UER	1.50	.70	.19

(Photo actually
Otis Smith)

☐ 63	Cliff Levingston	1.00	.45	.12
☐ 64	Alton Lister	1.00	.45	.12
☐ 65	John Long	1.00	.45	.12
☐ 66	John Lucas	1.50	.70	.19
☐ 67	Jeff Malone	1.50	.70	.19
☐ 68	Karl Malone	12.00	5.50	1.50
☐ 69	Moses Malone	3.00	1.35	.35
☐ 70	Cedric Maxwell	1.00	.45	.12
☐ 71	Tim McCormick	1.00	.45	.12
☐ 72	Rodney McCray	1.00	.45	.12
☐ 73	Xavier McDaniel	1.50	.70	.19
☐ 74	Kevin McHale	3.00	1.35	.35
☐ 75	Nate McMillan	2.00	.90	.25
☐ 76	Sidney Moncrief	2.00	.90	.25
☐ 77	Chris Mullin	3.00	1.35	.35
☐ 78	Larry Nance	2.00	.90	.25
☐ 79	Charles Oakley	2.00	.90	.25
☐ 80	Hakeem Olajuwon	30.00	13.50	3.70
☐ 81	Robert Parish UER	2.00	.90	.25

(Misspelled Parrish
on both sides)

☐ 82	Jim Paxson	1.00	.45	.12
☐ 83	John Paxson	2.50	1.10	.30
☐ 84	Sam Perkins	2.00	.90	.25
☐ 85	Chuck Person	2.50	1.10	.30
☐ 86	Jim Peterson	1.00	.45	.12
☐ 87	Ricky Pierce	1.50	.70	.19
☐ 88	Ed Pinckney	1.50	.70	.19
☐ 89	Terry Porter	2.50	1.10	.30

(College Wisconsin,
should be Wisconsin -
Stevens Point)

☐ 90	Paul Pressey	1.00	.45	.12
☐ 91	Robert Reid	1.00	.45	.12
☐ 92	Doc Rivers	1.00	.45	.12
☐ 93	Alvin Robertson	1.50	.70	.19
☐ 94	Tree Rollins	1.00	.45	.12
☐ 95	Ralph Sampson	1.50	.70	.19
☐ 96	Mike Sanders	1.00	.45	.12
☐ 97	Detlef Schrempf	10.00	4.50	1.25
☐ 98	Byron Scott	2.00	.90	.25
☐ 99	Jerry Sichting	1.00	.45	.12
☐ 100	Jack Sikma	1.50	.70	.19
☐ 101	Larry Smith	1.00	.45	.12
☐ 102	Rory Sparrow	1.00	.45	.12
☐ 103	Steve Stipanovich	1.00	.45	.12
☐ 104	Jon Sundvold	1.00	.45	.12
☐ 105	Reggie Theus	1.50	.70	.19
☐ 106	Isiah Thomas	6.00	2.70	.75
☐ 107	LaSalle Thompson	1.00	.45	.12
☐ 108	Mychal Thompson	1.00	.45	.12
☐ 109	Otis Thorpe	5.00	2.20	.60
☐ 110	Sedale Threatt	1.50	.70	.19
☐ 111	Waymon Tisdale	1.50	.70	.19
☐ 112	Kelly Tripucka	1.50	.70	.19
☐ 113	Trent Tucker	1.00	.45	.12
☐ 114	Terry Tyler	1.00	.45	.12
☐ 115	Darnell Valentine	1.00	.45	.12
☐ 116	Kiki Vandeweghe	1.50	.70	.19
☐ 117	Darrell Walker	1.00	.45	.12
☐ 118	Dominique Wilkins	4.00	1.80	.50
☐ 119	Gerald Wilkins	1.50	.70	.19
☐ 120	Buck Williams	2.00	.90	.25
☐ 121	Herb Williams	1.00	.45	.12
☐ 122	John Williams	1.00	.45	.12
☐ 123	John Williams	2.50	1.10	.30
☐ 124	Kevin Willis	1.50	.70	.19
☐ 125	David Wingate	1.00	.45	.12
☐ 126	Randy Wittman	1.00	.45	.12
☐ 127	Leon Wood	1.00	.45	.12
☐ 128	Mike Woodson	1.00	.45	.12
☐ 129	Orlando Woolridge	1.00	.45	.12
☐ 130	James Worthy	4.00	1.80	.50
☐ 131	Danny Young	1.00	.45	.12
☐ 132	Checklist 1-132	3.00	1.35	.35

1987-88 Fleer Stickers

The 1987-88 Fleer Stickers is an 11-card standard-size set inserted one per wax pack. The fronts are red, white, blue and yellow. The backs are white and blue and contain career highlights. Based on the one-to-twelve proportion of stickers to regular cards in the wax packs, there are theoretically an equal number of sticker sets and regular sets. Virtually all cards from this set have wax-stained backs as a result of the packaging.

	MINT	NRMT	EXC
COMPLETE SET (11)	60.00	27.00	7.50
COMMON STICKER (1-11)	.50	.23	.06

☐ 1	Magic Johnson	6.00	2.70	.75
☐ 2	Michael Jordan	40.00	18.00	5.00

(In text, votes mis-
spelled as voites)

		MINT	NRMT	EXC
☐ 3	Hakeem Olajuwon UER .. (Misspelled Olajuwan on card back)	8.00	3.60	1.00
☐ 4	Larry Bird	8.00	3.60	1.00
☐ 5	Kevin McHale	.50	.23	.06
☐ 6	Charles Barkley	5.00	2.20	.60
☐ 7	Dominique Wilkins	1.00	.45	.12
☐ 8	Kareem Abdul-Jabbar	2.00	.90	.25
☐ 9	Mark Aguirre	.50	.23	.06
☐ 10	Chuck Person	.50	.23	.06
☐ 11	Alex English	.50	.23	.06

1988-89 Fleer

The 1988-89 Fleer basketball set contains 132 standard-size cards. There are 119 regular cards, plus 12 All-Star cards and a checklist. This set was issued in wax packs of 12 cards, gum and a sticker. Wax boxes contained 36 wax packs. The outer borders are white and gray, while the inner borders correspond to the team colors. The backs are greenish and show full NBA statistics with limited biographical information. The set is ordered alphabetically by team with a few exceptions due to late trades. The only subset is All-Stars (120-131). Rookie Cards of note include Muggsy Bogues, Dell Curry, Horace Grant, Mark Jackson, Reggie Miller, Derrick McKey, Scottie Pippen, Mark Price and Dennis Rodman. There is also a Rookie Card of John Stockton who had previously only appeared in Star Company sets.

		MINT	NRMT	EXC
COMPLETE w/Stickers (143)		210.00	95.00	26.00
COMPLETE SET (132)		185.00	85.00	23.00
COMMON CARD (1-132)		.25	.11	.03

		MINT	NRMT	EXC
☐ 1	Antoine Carr	.75	.35	.09
☐ 2	Cliff Levingston	.25	.11	.03
☐ 3	Doc Rivers	.25	.11	.03
☐ 4	Spud Webb	.50	.23	.06
☐ 5	Dominique Wilkins	2.00	.90	.25
☐ 6	Kevin Willis	.50	.23	.06
☐ 7	Randy Wittman	.25	.11	.03
☐ 8	Danny Ainge	.75	.35	.09
☐ 9	Larry Bird	12.00	5.50	1.50
☐ 10	Dennis Johnson	.75	.35	.09
☐ 11	Kevin McHale	1.25	.55	.16
☐ 12	Robert Parish	.75	.35	.09
☐ 13	Tyrone Bogues	2.00	.90	.25
☐ 14	Dell Curry	1.50	.70	.19
☐ 15	Dave Corzine	.25	.11	.03

		MINT	NRMT	EXC
☐ 16	Horace Grant	10.00	4.50	1.25
☐ 17	Michael Jordan	50.00	22.00	6.25
☐ 18	Charles Oakley	.50	.23	.06
☐ 19	John Paxson	.50	.23	.06
☐ 20	Scottie Pippen UER (Misspelled Pippin on card back)	50.00	22.00	6.25
☐ 21	Brad Sellers	.25	.11	.03
☐ 22	Brad Daugherty	.25	.11	.03
☐ 23	Ron Harper	.50	.23	.06
☐ 24	Larry Nance	.50	.23	.06
☐ 25	Mark Price	2.00	.90	.25
☐ 26	Hot Rod Williams	.25	.11	.03
☐ 27	Mark Aguirre	.50	.23	.06
☐ 28	Rolando Blackman	.50	.23	.06
☐ 29	James Donaldson	.25	.11	.03
☐ 30	Derek Harper	.50	.23	.06
☐ 31	Sam Perkins	.50	.23	.06
☐ 32	Roy Tarpley	.75	.35	.09
☐ 33	Michael Adams	.75	.35	.09
☐ 34	Alex English	.50	.23	.06
☐ 35	Lafayette Lever	.25	.11	.03
☐ 36	Blair Rasmussen	.25	.11	.03
☐ 37	Danny Schayes	.25	.11	.03
☐ 38	Jay Vincent	.25	.11	.03
☐ 39	Adrian Dantley	.50	.23	.06
☐ 40	Joe Dumars	2.00	.90	.25
☐ 41	Vinnie Johnson	.50	.23	.06
☐ 42	Bill Laimbeer	.50	.23	.06
☐ 43	Dennis Rodman	50.00	22.00	6.25
☐ 44	John Salley	.25	.11	.03
☐ 45	Isiah Thomas	1.50	.70	.19
☐ 46	Winston Garland	.25	.11	.03
☐ 47	Rod Higgins	.25	.11	.03
☐ 48	Chris Mullin	.75	.35	.09
☐ 49	Ralph Sampson	.25	.11	.03
☐ 50	Joe Barry Carroll	.25	.11	.03
☐ 51	Sleepy Floyd	.25	.11	.03
☐ 52	Rodney McCray	.25	.11	.03
☐ 53	Hakeem Olajuwon	8.00	3.60	1.00
☐ 54	Purvis Short	.25	.11	.03
☐ 55	Vern Fleming	.25	.11	.03
☐ 56	John Long	.25	.11	.03
☐ 57	Reggie Miller	30.00	13.50	3.70
☐ 58	Chuck Person	.50	.23	.06
☐ 59	Steve Stipanovich	.25	.11	.03
☐ 60	Waymon Tisdale	.50	.23	.06
☐ 61	Benoit Benjamin	.25	.11	.03
☐ 62	Michael Cage	.25	.11	.03
☐ 63	Mike Woodson	.25	.11	.03
☐ 64	Kareem Abdul-Jabbar	4.00	1.80	.50
☐ 65	Michael Cooper	.50	.23	.06
☐ 66	A.C. Green	.75	.35	.09
☐ 67	Magic Johnson	10.00	4.50	1.25
☐ 68	Byron Scott	.50	.23	.06
☐ 69	Mychal Thompson	.50	.23	.06
☐ 70	James Worthy	.75	.35	.09
☐ 71	Duane Washington	.25	.11	.03
☐ 72	Kevin Williams	.25	.11	.03
☐ 73	Randy Breuer	.25	.11	.03
☐ 74	Terry Cummings	.50	.23	.06
☐ 75	Paul Pressey	.25	.11	.03
☐ 76	Jack Sikma	.50	.23	.06
☐ 77	John Bagley	.25	.11	.03
☐ 78	Roy Hinson	.25	.11	.03
☐ 79	Buck Williams	.50	.23	.06
☐ 80	Patrick Ewing	3.00	1.35	.35
☐ 81	Sidney Green	.25	.11	.03
☐ 82	Mark Jackson	1.50	.70	.19
☐ 83	Kenny Walker	.25	.11	.03
☐ 84	Gerald Wilkins	.25	.11	.03

		MINT	NRMT	EXC
☐ 85	Charles Barkley	5.00	2.20	.60
☐ 86	Maurice Cheeks	.50	.23	.06
☐ 87	Mike Gminski	.50	.23	.06
☐ 88	Cliff Robinson	.25	.11	.03
☐ 89	Armon Gilliam	2.00	.90	.25
☐ 90	Eddie Johnson	.50	.23	.06
☐ 91	Mark West	.25	.11	.03
☐ 92	Clyde Drexler	4.00	1.80	.50
☐ 93	Kevin Duckworth	.25	.11	.03
☐ 94	Steve Johnson	.25	.11	.03
☐ 95	Jerome Kersey	.25	.11	.03
☐ 96	Terry Porter	.25	.11	.03
	(College Wisconsin, should be Wisconsin Stevens Point)			
☐ 97	Joe Kleine	.75	.35	.09
☐ 98	Reggie Theus	.50	.23	.06
☐ 99	Otis Thorpe	.50	.23	.06
☐ 100	Kenny Smith	1.50	.70	.19
	(College NC State, should be North Carolina)			
☐ 101	Greg Anderson	.25	.11	.03
☐ 102	Walter Berry	.25	.11	.03
☐ 103	Frank Brickowski	.25	.11	.03
☐ 104	Johnny Dawkins	.50	.23	.06
☐ 105	Alvin Robertson	.50	.23	.06
☐ 106	Tom Chambers	.50	.23	.06
	(Born 6/2/59, should be 6/21/59)			
☐ 107	Dale Ellis	.50	.23	.06
☐ 108	Xavier McDaniel	.25	.11	.03
☐ 109	Derrick McKey	1.50	.70	.19
☐ 110	Nate McMillan UER	.25	.11	.03
	(Photo actually Kevin Williams)			
☐ 111	Thurl Bailey	.25	.11	.03
☐ 112	Mark Eaton	.50	.23	.06
☐ 113	Bobby Hansen	.25	.11	.03
☐ 114	Karl Malone	3.00	1.35	.35
☐ 115	John Stockton	25.00	11.00	3.10
☐ 116	Bernard King	.50	.23	.06
☐ 117	Jeff Malone	.25	.11	.03
☐ 118	Moses Malone	1.25	.55	.16
☐ 119	John Williams	.25	.11	.03
☐ 120	Michael Jordan AS	20.00	9.00	2.50
☐ 121	Mark Jackson AS	.25	.11	.03
☐ 122	Byron Scott AS	.25	.11	.03
☐ 123	Magic Johnson AS	4.00	1.80	.50
☐ 124	Larry Bird AS	5.00	2.20	.60
☐ 125	Dominique Wilkins AS	.25	.23	.06
☐ 126	Hakeem Olajuwon AS	3.00	1.35	.35
☐ 127	John Stockton AS	5.00	2.20	.60
☐ 128	Alvin Robertson AS	.25	.11	.03
☐ 129	Charles Barkley AS	2.00	.90	.25
	(Back says Buck Williams is member of Jets, should be Nets)			
☐ 130	Patrick Ewing AS	1.25	.55	.16
☐ 131	Mark Eaton AS	.25	.11	.03
☐ 132	Checklist 1-132	.50	.23	.06

1988-89 Fleer Stickers

The 1988-89 Fleer Stickers is an 11-card standard-size set issued as a one per pack insert along with 12 cards from the regular 132-card set. The fronts are baby blue, red, and white. The backs are blue and pink and contain career highlights. The set is ordered alphabetically. Based on the one-to-twelve proportion of stickers to regular cards in the wax packs, there are theoretically an equal number of sticker sets and regular sets. Virtually all cards from this set have wax-stained backs as a result of the packaging.

		MINT	NRMT	EXC
COMPLETE SET (11)		25.00	11.00	3.10
COMMON STICKER (1-11)		.25	.11	.03
☐ 1	Mark Aguirre	.25	.11	.03
☐ 2	Larry Bird	5.00	2.20	.60
☐ 3	Clyde Drexler	1.50	.70	.19
☐ 4	Alex English	.25	.11	.03
☐ 5	Patrick Ewing	1.25	.55	.16
☐ 6	Magic Johnson	4.00	1.80	.50
☐ 7	Michael Jordan	20.00	9.00	2.50
☐ 8	Karl Malone	1.25	.55	.16
☐ 9	Kevin McHale	.35	.16	.04
☐ 10	Isiah Thomas	.60	.25	.07
☐ 11	Dominique Wilkins	.75	.35	.09

1989-90 Fleer

The 1989-90 Fleer basketball set consists of 168 standard-size cards. The cards were distributed in 15-card wax packs (and one sticker) and in 36-card rack packs. Wax boxes contained 36 packs. The fronts feature color action player photos, with various color borders between white inner and outer borders. The player's name and position appear in the upper left corner, with the team logo superimposed over the upper right corner of the picture. The horizontally

oriented backs have black lettering on red, pink, and white background and present career statistics, biographical information, and a performance index. The set is ordered alphabetically in team subsets (with a few exceptions due to late trades). The only subset is All-Star Game Combos (163-167). Rookie Cards of note in this set include Hersey Hawkins, Jeff Hornacek, Kevin Johnson, Reggie Lewis, Dan Majerle, Danny Manning, Mitch Richmond,, Rik Smits, and Rod Strickland. Cards from this set are frequently found off-center.

	MINT	NRMT	EXC
COMPLETE w/Stickers (179) .	30.00	13.50	3.70
COMPLETE SET (168)	25.00	11.00	3.10
COMMON CARD (1-168)	.10	.05	.01
☐ 1 John Battle........................	.10	.05	.01
☐ 2 Jon Koncak	.20	.09	.03
☐ 3 Cliff Levingston	.10	.05	.01
☐ 4 Moses Malone	.50	.23	.06
☐ 5 Doc Rivers	.10	.05	.01
☐ 6 Spud Webb UER	.20	.09	.03
(Points per 48 minutes incorrect at 2.6)			
☐ 7 Dominique Wilkins.........	.35	.16	.04
☐ 8 Larry Bird	3.00	1.35	.35
☐ 9 Dennis Johnson	.35	.16	.04
☐ 10 Reggie Lewis	.75	.35	.09
☐ 11 Kevin McHale	.35	.16	.04
☐ 12 Robert Parish	.35	.16	.04
☐ 13 Ed Pinckney	.10	.05	.01
☐ 14 Brian Shaw	.50	.23	.06
☐ 15 Rex Chapman	.50	.23	.06
☐ 16 Kurt Rambis	.10	.05	.01
☐ 17 Robert Reid	.10	.05	.01
☐ 18 Kelly Tripucka	.10	.05	.01
☐ 19 Bill Cartwright UER	.10	.05	.01
(First season 1978-80, should be 1979-80)			
☐ 20 Horace Grant...............	1.00	.45	.12
☐ 21 Michael Jordan	10.00	4.50	1.25
☐ 22 John Paxson	.20	.09	.03
☐ 23 Scottie Pippen	5.00	2.20	.60
☐ 24 Brad Sellers	.10	.05	.01
☐ 25 Brad Daugherty...........	.10	.05	.01
☐ 26 Craig Ehlo	.20	.09	.03
☐ 27 Ron Harper	.20	.09	.03
☐ 28 Larry Nance	.20	.09	.03
☐ 29 Mark Price	.20	.09	.03
☐ 30 Mike Sanders	.10	.05	.01
☐ 31A John Williams ERR.....	.50	.23	.06
☐ 31B John Williams COR.....	.20	.09	.03
☐ 32 Rolando Blackman UER .	.20	.09	.03
(Career blocks and points listed as 1961 and 2127, should be 196 and 12,127)			
☐ 33 Adrian Dantley	.35	.16	.04
☐ 34 James Donaldson	.10	.05	.01
☐ 35 Derek Harper	.20	.09	.03
☐ 36 Sam Perkins	.20	.09	.03
☐ 37 Herb Williams	.10	.05	.01
☐ 38 Michael Adams	.10	.05	.01
☐ 39 Walter Davis	.35	.16	.04
☐ 40 Alex English	25.00	11.00	3.10
☐ 41 Lafayette Lever	.10	.05	.01
☐ 42 Blair Rasmussen	.10	.05	.01
☐ 43 Dan Schayes	.10	.05	.01
☐ 44 Mark Aguirre	.20	.09	.03

☐ 45 Joe Dumars	.35	.16	.04
☐ 46 James Edwards............	.20	.09	.03
☐ 47 Vinnie Johnson............	.20	.09	.03
☐ 48 Bill Laimbeer	.20	.09	.03
☐ 49 Dennis Rodman	6.00	2.70	.75
☐ 50 Isiah Thomas	.50	.23	.06
☐ 51 John Salley	.20	.09	.03
☐ 52 Manute Bol	.10	.05	.01
☐ 53 Winston Garland	.10	.05	.01
☐ 54 Rod Higgins	.10	.05	.01
☐ 55 Chris Mullin	.20	.09	.03
☐ 56 Mitch Richmond	4.00	1.80	.50
☐ 57 Terry Teagle	.10	.05	.01
☐ 58 Derrick Chievous UER...	.10	.05	.01
(Stats correctly say 81 games in '88-89, text says 82)			
☐ 59 Sleepy Floyd	.10	.05	.01
☐ 60 Tim McCormick	.10	.05	.01
☐ 61 Hakeem Olajuwon	2.00	.90	.25
☐ 62 Otis Thorpe	.20	.09	.03
☐ 63 Mike Woodson	.10	.05	.01
☐ 64 Vern Fleming	.10	.05	.01
☐ 65 Reggie Miller	2.50	1.10	.30
☐ 66 Chuck Person	.20	.09	.03
☐ 67 Detlef Schrempf	.50	.23	.06
☐ 68 Rik Smits	1.50	.70	.19
☐ 69 Benoit Benjamin..........	.10	.05	.01
☐ 70 Gary Grant	.10	.05	.01
☐ 71 Danny Manning	1.00	.45	.12
☐ 72 Ken Norman	.20	.09	.03
☐ 73 Charles Smith	.35	.16	.04
☐ 74 Reggie Williams	.20	.09	.03
☐ 75 Michael Cooper	.35	.16	.04
☐ 76 A.C. Green	.20	.09	.03
☐ 77 Magic Johnson	2.50	1.10	.30
☐ 78 Byron Scott	.20	.09	.03
☐ 79 Mychal Thompson	.10	.05	.01
☐ 80 James Worthy	.35	.16	.04
☐ 81 Kevin Edwards	.10	.05	.01
☐ 82 Grant Long	.50	.23	.06
☐ 83 Rony Seikaly	.50	.23	.06
☐ 84 Rory Sparrow	.10	.05	.01
☐ 85 Greg Anderson UER......	.10	.05	.01
(Stats show 1988-89 as 19888-89)			
☐ 86 Jay Humphries.............	.10	.05	.01
☐ 87 Larry Krystkowiak	.10	.05	.01
☐ 88 Ricky Pierce	.10	.05	.01
☐ 89 Paul Pressey	.10	.05	.01
☐ 90 Alvin Robertson	.10	.05	.01
☐ 91 Jack Sikma	.20	.09	.03
☐ 92 Steve Johnson	.10	.05	.01
☐ 93 Rick Mahorn	.10	.05	.01
☐ 94 David Rivers	.10	.05	.01
☐ 95 Joe Barry Carroll.........	.10	.05	.01
☐ 96 Lester Conner UER	.10	.05	.01
(Garden State in stats, should be Golden State)			
☐ 97 Roy Hinson	.10	.05	.01
☐ 98 Mike McGee	.10	.05	.01
☐ 99 Chris Morris	.50	.23	.06
☐ 100 Patrick Ewing	.75	.35	.09
☐ 101 Mark Jackson	.10	.05	.01
☐ 102 Johnny Newman	.20	.09	.03
☐ 103 Charles Oakley	.20	.09	.03
☐ 104 Rod Strickland	2.00	.90	.25
☐ 105 Trent Tucker	.10	.05	.01
☐ 106 Kiki Vandeweghe........	.20	.09	.03
☐ 107A Gerald Wilkins	.20	.09	.03
(U. of Tennessee)			

☐ 107B	Gerald Wilkins (U. of Tenn.)	.20	.09	.03
☐ 108	Terry Catledge	.10	.05	.01
☐ 109	Dave Corzine	.10	.05	.01
☐ 110	Scott Skiles	.10	.05	.01
☐ 111	Reggie Theus	.20	.09	.03
☐ 112	Ron Anderson	.10	.05	.01
☐ 113	Charles Barkley	1.25	.55	.16
☐ 114	Scott Brooks	.10	.05	.01
☐ 115	Maurice Cheeks	.20	.09	.03
☐ 116	Mike Gminski	.10	.05	.01
☐ 117	Hersey Hawkins UER (Born 9/29/65, should be 9/9/65)	1.00	.45	.12
☐ 118	Christian Welp	.10	.05	.01
☐ 119	Tom Chambers	.10	.05	.01
☐ 120	Armon Gilliam	.20	.09	.03
☐ 121	Jeff Hornacek	1.00	.45	.12
☐ 122	Eddie Johnson	.10	.05	.01
☐ 123	Kevin Johnson	1.50	.70	.19
☐ 124	Dan Majerle	.75	.35	.09
☐ 125	Mark West	.10	.05	.01
☐ 126	Richard Anderson	.10	.05	.01
☐ 127	Mark Bryant	.20	.09	.03
☐ 128	Clyde Drexler	1.00	.45	.12
☐ 129	Kevin Duckworth	.10	.05	.01
☐ 130	Jerome Kersey	.10	.05	.01
☐ 131	Terry Porter	.10	.05	.01
☐ 132	Buck Williams	.20	.09	.03
☐ 133	Danny Ainge	.35	.16	.04
☐ 134	Ricky Berry	.10	.05	.01
☐ 135	Rodney McCray	.10	.05	.01
☐ 136	Jim Petersen	.10	.05	.01
☐ 137	Harold Pressley	.10	.05	.01
☐ 138	Kenny Smith	.10	.05	.01
☐ 139	Wayman Tisdale	.20	.09	.03
☐ 140	Willie Anderson	.10	.05	.01
☐ 141	Frank Brickowski	.10	.05	.01
☐ 142	Terry Cummings	.10	.05	.01
☐ 143	Johnny Dawkins	.10	.05	.01
☐ 144	Vern Maxwell	.50	.23	.06
☐ 145	Michael Cage	.10	.05	.01
☐ 146	Dale Ellis	.20	.09	.03
☐ 147	Alton Lister	.10	.05	.01
☐ 148	Xavier McDaniel UER (All-Rookie team in 1985, not 1988)	.10	.05	.01
☐ 149	Derrick McKey	.10	.05	.01
☐ 150	Nate McMillan	.10	.05	.01
☐ 151	Thurl Bailey	.10	.05	.01
☐ 152	Mark Eaton	.10	.05	.01
☐ 153	Darrell Griffith	.20	.09	.03
☐ 154	Eric Leckner	.10	.05	.01
☐ 155	Karl Malone	.75	.35	.09
☐ 156	John Stockton	2.00	.90	.25
☐ 157	Mark Alarie	.10	.05	.01
☐ 158	Ledell Eackles	.10	.05	.01
☐ 159	Bernard King	.20	.09	.03
☐ 160	Jeff Malone	.10	.05	.01
☐ 161	Darrell Walker	.10	.05	.01
☐ 162A	John Williams ERR	.50	.23	.06
☐ 162B	John Williams COR	.20	.09	.03
☐ 163	Karl Malone AS John Stockton Mark Eaton	.50	.23	.06
☐ 164	Hakeem Olajuwon AS Clyde Drexler AS	1.00	.45	.12
☐ 165	Dominique Wilkins AS Moses Malone AS	.20	.09	.03
☐ 166	Brad Daugherty AS Mark Price AS	.10	.05	.01

	Larry Nance AS UER Bio says Nance had 204 blocks, should be 206)				
☐ 167	Patrick Ewing AS Mark Jackson AS	.20	.09	.03
☐ 168	Checklist 1-168	.10	.05	.01

1989-90 Fleer Stickers

This set of 11 insert standard-size stickers features NBA All-Stars. One All-Star sticker was inserted in each 12-card wax pack. The front has a color action player photo. An aqua stripe with dark blue stars traverses the card top, and the same pattern reappears about halfway down the card face. The words "Fleer '89 All-Stars" appear at the top of the picture, with the player's name and position immediately below the picture. The back has a star pattern similar to the front. A career summary is printed in blue on a white background. Most card backs have problems with wax stains as a result of packaging.

	MINT	NRMT	EXC
COMPLETE SET (11)	6.00	2.70	.75
COMMON STICKER (1-11)	.10	.05	.01
☐ 1 Karl Malone	.40	.18	.05
☐ 2 Hakeem Olajuwon	1.00	.45	.12
☐ 3 Michael Jordan	5.00	2.20	.60
☐ 4 Charles Barkley	.60	.25	.07
☐ 5 Magic Johnson	1.25	.55	.16
☐ 6 Isiah Thomas	.25	.11	.03
☐ 7 Patrick Ewing	.40	.18	.05
☐ 8 Dale Ellis	.10	.05	.01
☐ 9 Chris Mullin	.15	.07	.02
☐ 10 Larry Bird	1.50	.70	.19
☐ 11 Tom Chambers	.15	.07	.02

1990-91 Fleer

The 1990-91 Fleer set contains 198 standard-size cards. The cards were available in 15-card wax packs, 23-card cello packs and 36-card rack packs. Wax boxes contained 36 wax packs. There were also 43-

card pre-priced packs ($1.49) which contained Rookie Sensation inserts. The fronts feature a color action player photo, with a white inner border and a two-color (red on top and bottom, blue on sides) outer border on a white card face. The team logo is superimposed at the upper left corner of the picture, with the player's name and position appearing below the picture. The backs are printed in black, gray, and yellow, and present biographical and statistical information. The set is ordered alphabetically in team subsets (with a few exceptions due to late trades). The description, All-American, is properly capitalized on the back of cards 134 and 144, but is not capitalized on cards 20, 29, 51, 53, 59, 70, 119, 130, 178, and 192. Rookie Cards of note in the set include Nick Anderson, Mookie Blaylock, Vlade Divac, Sean Elliott, Tim Hardaway, Shawn Kemp, Glen Rice, and Clifford Robinson.

	MINT	NRMT	EXC
COMPLETE SET (198)	6.00	2.70	.75
COMMON CARD (1-198)	.05	.02	.01
☐ 1 John Battle UER	.05	.02	.01
(Drafted in '84, should be '85)			
☐ 2 Cliff Levingston	.05	.02	.01
☐ 3 Moses Malone	.10	.05	.01
☐ 4 Kenny Smith	.05	.02	.01
☐ 5 Spud Webb	.08	.04	.01
☐ 6 Dominique Wilkins	.08	.04	.01
☐ 7 Kevin Willis	.05	.02	.01
☐ 8 Larry Bird	.60	.25	.07
☐ 9 Dennis Johnson	.08	.04	.01
☐ 10 Joe Kleine	.05	.02	.01
☐ 11 Reggie Lewis	.08	.04	.01
☐ 12 Kevin McHale	.08	.04	.01
☐ 13 Robert Parish	.08	.04	.01
☐ 14 Jim Paxson	.05	.02	.01
☐ 15 Ed Pinckney	.05	.02	.01
☐ 16 Muggsy Bogues	.08	.04	.01
☐ 17 Rex Chapman	.05	.02	.01
☐ 18 Dell Curry	.05	.02	.01
☐ 19 Armon Gilliam	.05	.02	.01
☐ 20 J.R. Reid	.08	.04	.01
☐ 21 Kelly Tripucka	.05	.02	.01
☐ 22 B.J. Armstrong	.08	.04	.01
☐ 23A Bill Cartwright ERR	.50	.03	.06
(No decimal points in FGP and FTP)			
☐ 23B Bill Cartwright COR	.05	.02	.01
☐ 24 Horace Grant	.10	.05	.01
☐ 25 Craig Hodges	.05	.02	.01
☐ 26 Michael Jordan UER	2.00	.90	.25
(Led NBA in scoring 4 years, not 3)			
☐ 27 Stacey King UER	.05	.02	.01
(Comma missing between progressed and Stacy)			
☐ 28 John Paxson	.08	.04	.01
☐ 29 Will Perdue	.05	.02	.01
☐ 30 Scottie Pippen UER	.60	.25	.07
(Born AR, not AK)			
☐ 31 Brad Daugherty	.05	.02	.01
☐ 32 Craig Ehlo	.05	.02	.01
☐ 33 Danny Ferry	.15	.07	.02
☐ 34 Steve Kerr	.05	.02	.01
☐ 35 Larry Nance	.05	.02	.01
☐ 36 Mark Price UER	.05	.02	.01
(Drafted by Cleveland, should be Dallas)			
☐ 37 Hot Rod Williams	.05	.02	.01
☐ 38 Rolando Blackman	.08	.04	.01
☐ 39A Adrian Dantley ERR	.40	.18	.05
(No decimal points in FGP and FTP)			
☐ 39B Adrian Dantley COR	.08	.04	.01
☐ 40 Brad Davis	.05	.02	.01
☐ 41 James Donaldson UER	.05	.02	.01
(Text says in committed, should be is committed)			
☐ 42 Derek Harper	.08	.04	.01
☐ 43 Sam Perkins UER	.05	.02	.01
(First line of text should be intact)			
☐ 44 Bill Wennington	.05	.02	.01
☐ 45 Herb Williams	.05	.02	.01
☐ 46 Michael Adams	.05	.02	.01
☐ 47 Walter Davis	.08	.04	.01
☐ 48 Alex English UER	.08	.04	.01
(Stats missing from '76-77 through '79-80)			
☐ 49 Bill Hanzlik	.05	.02	.01
☐ 50 Lafayette Lever UER	.05	.02	.01
(Born AR, not AK)			
☐ 51 Todd Lichti	.05	.02	.01
☐ 52 Blair Rasmussen	.05	.02	.01
☐ 53 Dan Schayes	.05	.02	.01
☐ 54 Mark Aguirre	.08	.04	.01
☐ 55 Joe Dumars	.08	.04	.01
☐ 56 James Edwards	.05	.02	.01
☐ 57 Vinnie Johnson	.05	.02	.01
☐ 58 Bill Laimbeer	.05	.02	.01
☐ 59 Dennis Rodman UER	.75	.35	.09
(College misspelled as coilege on back)			
☐ 60 John Salley	.05	.02	.01
☐ 61 Isiah Thomas	.10	.05	.01
☐ 62 Manute Bol	.05	.02	.01
☐ 63 Tim Hardaway	.40	.18	.05
☐ 64 Rod Higgins	.05	.02	.01
☐ 65 Sarunas Marciulionis	.05	.02	.01
☐ 66 Chris Mullin	.08	.04	.01
☐ 67 Mitch Richmond	.20	.09	.03
☐ 68 Terry Teagle	.05	.02	.01
☐ 69 Anthony Bowie UER	.05	.02	.01
(Seasons, not seasons)			
☐ 70 Sleepy Floyd	.05	.02	.01
☐ 71 Buck Johnson	.05	.02	.01
☐ 72 Vernon Maxwell	.05	.02	.01
☐ 73 Hakeem Olajuwon	.40	.18	.05
☐ 74 Otis Thorpe	.08	.04	.01
☐ 75 Mitchell Wiggins	.05	.02	.01
☐ 76 Vern Fleming	.05	.02	.01

□	77	George McCloud	.15	.07	.02
□	78	Reggie Miller	.25	.11	.03
□	79	Chuck Person	.05	.02	.01
□	80	Mike Sanders	.05	.02	.01
□	81	Detlef Schrempf	.05	.02	.01
□	82	Rik Smits	.08	.04	.01
□	83	LaSalle Thompson	.05	.02	.01
□	84	Benoit Benjamin	.05	.02	.01
□	85	Winston Garland	.05	.02	.01
□	86	Ron Harper	.05	.02	.01
□	87	Danny Manning	.08	.04	.01
□	88	Ken Norman	.05	.02	.01
□	89	Charles Smith	.05	.02	.01
□	90	Michael Cooper	.08	.04	.01
□	91	Vlade Divac	.25	.11	.03
□	92	A.C. Green	.08	.04	.01
□	93	Magic Johnson	.50	.23	.06
□	94	Byron Scott	.08	.04	.01
□	95	Mychal Thompson UER	.05	.02	.01

(Missing '78-79 stats from Portland)

□	96	Orlando Woolridge	.05	.02	.01
□	97	James Worthy	.08	.04	.01
□	98	Sherman Douglas	.05	.02	.01
□	99	Kevin Edwards	.05	.02	.01
□	100	Grant Long	.05	.02	.01
□	101	Glen Rice	.50	.23	.06
□	102	Rony Seikaly UER	.05	.02	.01

(Ron on front)

□	103	Billy Thompson	.05	.02	.01
□	104	Jeff Grayer	.05	.02	.01
□	105	Jay Humphries	.05	.02	.01
□	106	Ricky Pierce	.05	.02	.01
□	107	Paul Pressey	.05	.02	.01
□	108	Fred Roberts	.05	.02	.01
□	109	Alvin Robertson	.05	.02	.01
□	110	Jack Sikma	.08	.04	.01
□	111	Randy Breuer	.05	.02	.01
□	112	Tony Campbell	.05	.02	.01
□	113	Tyrone Corbin	.05	.02	.01
□	114	Sam Mitchell UER	.05	.02	.01

(Mercer University, not Mercer College)

□	115	Tod Murphy UER	.05	.02	.01

(Born Long Beach, not Lakewood)

□	116	Pooh Richardson	.08	.04	.01
□	117	Mookie Blaylock	.30	.14	.04
□	118	Sam Bowie	.05	.02	.01
□	119	Lester Conner	.05	.02	.01
□	120	Dennis Hopson	.05	.02	.01
□	121	Chris Morris	.05	.02	.01
□	122	Charles Shackleford	.05	.02	.01
□	123	Purvis Short	.05	.02	.01
□	124	Maurice Cheeks	.08	.04	.01
□	125	Patrick Ewing	.15	.07	.02
□	126	Jack Haley	.05	.02	.01
□	127A	Johnny Newman ERR	.50	.23	.06

(Jr. misprinted as J. on card back)

□	127B	Johnny Newman COR	.05	.02	.01
□	128	Charles Oakley	.05	.02	.01
□	129	Trent Tucker	.05	.02	.01
□	130	Kenny Walker	.05	.02	.01
□	131	Gerald Wilkins	.05	.02	.01
□	132	Nick Anderson	.30	.14	.04
□	133	Terry Catledge	.05	.02	.01
□	134	Sidney Green	.05	.02	.01
□	135	Otis Smith	.05	.02	.01
□	136	Reggie Theus	.08	.04	.01
□	137	Sam Vincent	.05	.02	.01

□	138	Ron Anderson	.05	.02	.01
□	139	Charles Barkley UER	.25	.11	.03

(FG Percentage .545.)

□	140	Scott Brooks UER	.05	.02	.01

('89-89 Philadelphia in wrong typeface)

□	141	Johnny Dawkins	.05	.02	.01
□	142	Mike Gminski	.05	.02	.01
□	143	Hersey Hawkins	.05	.02	.01
□	144	Rick Mahorn	.05	.02	.01
□	145	Derek Smith	.05	.02	.01
□	146	Tom Chambers	.05	.02	.01
□	147	Jeff Hornacek	.05	.02	.01
□	148	Eddie Johnson	.05	.02	.01
□	149	Kevin Johnson	.08	.04	.01
□	150A	Dan Majerle ERR	.50	.23	.06

(Award in 1988; three-time selection)

□	150B	Dan Majerle COR	.08	.04	.01

(Award in 1989; three-time selection)

□	151	Tim Perry	.05	.02	.01
□	152	Kurt Rambis	.05	.02	.01
□	153	Mark West	.05	.02	.01
□	154	Clyde Drexler	.20	.09	.03
□	155	Kevin Duckworth	.05	.02	.01
□	156	Byron Irvin	.05	.02	.01
□	157	Jerome Kersey	.05	.02	.01
□	158	Terry Porter	.05	.02	.01
□	159	Clifford Robinson	.40	.18	.05
□	160	Buck Williams	.08	.04	.01
□	161	Danny Young	.05	.02	.01
□	162	Danny Ainge	.08	.04	.01
□	163	Antoine Carr	.05	.02	.01
□	164	Pervis Ellison	.08	.04	.01
□	165	Rodney McCray	.05	.02	.01
□	166	Harold Pressley	.05	.02	.01
□	167	Wayman Tisdale	.05	.02	.01
□	168	Willie Anderson	.05	.02	.01
□	169	Frank Brickowski	.05	.02	.01
□	170	Terry Cummings	.05	.02	.01
□	171	Sean Elliott	.50	.23	.06
□	172	David Robinson	.60	.25	.07
□	173	Rod Strickland	.05	.02	.01
□	174	David Wingate	.05	.02	.01
□	175	Dana Barros	.15	.07	.02
□	176	Michael Cage UER	.05	.02	.01

(Born AR, not AK)

□	177	Dale Ellis	.05	.02	.01
□	178	Shawn Kemp	3.00	1.35	.35
□	179	Xavier McDaniel	.05	.02	.01
□	180	Derrick McKey	.05	.02	.01
□	181	Nate McMillan	.05	.02	.01
□	182	Thurl Bailey	.05	.02	.01
□	183	Mike Brown	.05	.02	.01
□	184	Mark Eaton	.05	.02	.01
□	185	Blue Edwards	.08	.04	.01
□	186	Bob Hansen	.05	.02	.01
□	187	Eric Leckner	.05	.02	.01
□	188	Karl Malone	.15	.07	.02
□	189	John Stockton	.20	.09	.03
□	190	Mark Alarie	.05	.02	.01
□	191	Ledell Eackles	.05	.02	.01
□	192A	Harvey Grant	1.00	.45	.13

(First name on card front in black)

□	192B	Harvey Grant	.05	.02	.01

(First name on card front in white)

□	193	Tom Hammonds	.05	.02	.01
□	194	Bernard King	.08	.04	.01

☐ 195	Jeff Malone	.05	.02	.01
☐ 196	Darrell Walker	.05	.02	.01
☐ 197	Checklist 1-99	.05	.02	.01
☐ 198	Checklist 100-198	.05	.02	.01

1990-91 Fleer All-Stars

The 12-card All-Star insert standard-size set was randomly inserted in 1990-91 Fleer 12-card packs at a rate of one in five. The fronts feature a color action photo, framed by a basketball hoop and net on an aqua background. An orange stripe at the top represents the bottom of the backboard and has the words "Fleer '90 All-Stars." The player's name and position are given at the bottom between stars. The backs are printed in blue and pink with white borders and have career summaries.

	MINT	NRMT	EXC
COMPLETE SET (12)	8.00	3.60	1.00
COMMON CARD (1-12)	.15	.07	.02
☐ 1 Charles Barkley	.75	.35	.09
☐ 2 Larry Bird	2.00	.90	.25
☐ 3 Hakeem Olajuwon	1.25	.55	.16
☐ 4 Magic Johnson	1.50	.70	.19
☐ 5 Michael Jordan	6.00	2.70	.75
☐ 6 Isiah Thomas	.30	.14	.04
☐ 7 Karl Malone	.50	.23	.06
☐ 8 Tom Chambers	.15	.07	.02
☐ 9 John Stockton	.60	.25	.07
☐ 10 David Robinson	2.00	.90	.25
☐ 11 Clyde Drexler	.60	.25	.07
☐ 12 Patrick Ewing	.50	.23	.06

1990-91 Fleer Roo“kie Sensations

Randomly inserted in 23-card cello packs, the 1990-91 Fleer Rookie Sensations set consists of 10 standard-size cards. Cards were inserted at a rate of approximately one in five packs. The fronts feature color action player photos, with white and red

borders on an aqua background. A basket-ball overlays the lower left corner of the picture, with the words "Rookie Sensation" in yellow lettering, and the player's name appearing in white lettering in the bottom red border. The backs are printed in black and red on gray background (with white borders) and present summaries of their college careers and rookie seasons. The key card is David Robinson's first insert.

	MINT	NRMT	EXC
COMPLETE SET (10)	30.00	13.50	3.70
COMMON CARD (1-10)	1.00	.45	.12
☐ 1 David Robinson UER	20.00	9.00	2.50
(Text has 1988-90 season, should be 1989-90)			
☐ 2 Sean Elliott UER	5.00	2.20	.60
(Misspelled Elliot on card front)			
☐ 3 Glen Rice	5.00	2.20	.60
☐ 4 J.R.Reid	2.00	.90	.25
☐ 5 Stacey King	1.00	.45	.12
☐ 6 Pooh Richardson	2.00	.90	.25
☐ 7 Nick Anderson	3.00	1.35	.35
☐ 8 Tim Hardaway	4.00	1.80	.50
☐ 9 Vlade Divac	2.50	1.10	.30
☐ 10 Sherman Douglas	1.00	.45	.12

1990-91 Fleer Update

These cards are the same size and design as the regular issue yet were issued only in complete set form. Factory sets were dis-tributed exclusively through hobby dealers. The set numbering is arranged alphabeti-

cally by team. The card numbers have a
"U" prefix. Rookie Cards of note include
Dee Brown, Elden Campbell, Cedric
Ceballos, Derrick Coleman, Kendall Gill,
Chris Jackson, Gary Payton, Drazen
Petrovic, Dennis Scott and Loy Vaught. It's
interesting to note that this is one of the first
sets to actually get current year rookies pic-
tured on trading cards.

	MINT	NRMT	EXC
COMPLETE SET (100)	5.00	2.20	.60
COMMON CARD (U1-U100)	.05	.02	.01
☐ U1 Jon Koncak	.05	.02	.01
☐ U2 Tim McCormick	.05	.02	.01
☐ U3 Doc Rivers	.05	.02	.01
☐ U4 Rumeal Robinson	.05	.02	.01
☐ U5 Trevor Wilson	.05	.02	.01
☐ U6 Dee Brown	.30	.14	.04
☐ U7 Dave Popson	.05	.02	.01
☐ U8 Kevin Gamble	.05	.02	.01
☐ U9 Brian Shaw	.05	.02	.01
☐ U10 Michael Smith	.05	.02	.01
☐ U11 Kendall Gill	.20	.09	.03
☐ U12 Johnny Newman	.05	.02	.01
☐ U13 Steve Scheffler	.05	.02	.01
☐ U14 Dennis Hopson	.05	.02	.01
☐ U15 Cliff Levingston	.05	.02	.01
☐ U16 Chucky Brown	.05	.02	.01
☐ U17 John Morton	.05	.02	.01
☐ U18 Gerald Paddio	.05	.02	.01
☐ U19 Alex English	.15	.07	.02
☐ U20 Fat Lever	.05	.02	.01
☐ U21 Rodney McCray	.05	.02	.01
☐ U22 Roy Tarpley	.05	.02	.01
☐ U23 Randy White	.05	.02	.01
☐ U24 Anthony Cook	.05	.02	.01
☐ U25 Chris Jackson	.50	.23	.06
☐ U26 Marcus Liberty	.05	.02	.01
☐ U27 Orlando Woolridge	.05	.02	.01
☐ U28 William Bedford	.05	.02	.01
☐ U29 Lance Blanks	.05	.02	.01
☐ U30 Scott Hastings	.05	.02	.01
☐ U31 Tyrone Hill	.25	.11	.03
☐ U32 Les Jepsen	.05	.02	.01
☐ U33 Steve Johnson	.05	.02	.01
☐ U34 Kevin Pritchard	.05	.02	.01
☐ U35 Dave Jamerson	.05	.02	.01
☐ U36 Kenny Smith	.05	.02	.01
☐ U37 Greg Dreiling	.05	.02	.01
☐ U38 Kenny Williams	.05	.02	.01
☐ U39 Micheal Williams UER	.05	.02	.01
☐ U40 Gary Grant	.05	.02	.01
☐ U41 Bo Kimble	.05	.02	.01
☐ U42 Loy Vaught	.75	.35	.09
☐ U43 Elden Campbell	.75	.35	.09
☐ U44 Sam Perkins	.10	.05	.01
☐ U45 Tony Smith	.05	.02	.01
☐ U46 Terry Teagle	.05	.02	.01
☐ U47 Willie Burton	.10	.05	.01
☐ U48 Bimbo Coles	.05	.02	.01
☐ U49 Terry Davis	.05	.02	.01
☐ U50 Alec Kessler	.05	.02	.01
☐ U51 Greg Anderson	.05	.02	.01
☐ U52 Frank Brickowski	.05	.02	.01
☐ U53 Steve Henson	.05	.02	.01
☐ U54 Brad Lohaus	.05	.02	.01
☐ U55 Dan Schayes	.05	.02	.01
☐ U56 Gerald Glass	.05	.02	.01
☐ U57 Felton Spencer	.05	.02	.01

☐ U58 Doug West	.10	.05	.01
☐ U59 Jud Buechler	.05	.02	.01
☐ U60 Derrick Coleman	.50	.23	.06
☐ U61 Tate George	.05	.02	.01
☐ U62 Reggie Theus	.15	.07	.02
☐ U63 Greg Grant	.05	.02	.01
☐ U64 Jerrod Mustaf	.05	.02	.01
☐ U65 Eddie Lee Wilkins	.05	.02	.01
☐ U66 Michael Ansley	.05	.02	.01
☐ U67 Jerry Reynolds	.05	.02	.01
☐ U68 Dennis Scott	.50	.23	.06
☐ U69 Manute Bol	.10	.05	.01
☐ U70 Armon Gilliam	.10	.05	.01
☐ U71 Brian Oliver	.05	.02	.01
☐ U72 Kenny Payne	.05	.02	.01
☐ U73 Jayson Williams	.15	.07	.02
☐ U74 Kenny Battle	.05	.02	.01
☐ U75 Cedric Ceballos	1.00	.45	.12
☐ U76 Negele Knight	.05	.02	.01
☐ U77 Xavier McDaniel	.05	.02	.01
☐ U78 Alaa Abdelnaby	.05	.02	.01
☐ U79 Danny Ainge	.15	.07	.02
☐ U80 Mark Bryant	.05	.02	.01
☐ U81 Drazen Petrovic	.25	.11	.03
☐ U82 Anthony Bonner	.05	.02	.01
☐ U83 Duane Causwell	.05	.02	.01
☐ U84 Bobby Hansen	.05	.02	.01
☐ U85 Eric Leckner	.05	.02	.01
☐ U86 Travis Mays	.05	.02	.01
☐ U87 Lionel Simmons	.05	.02	.01
☐ U88 Sidney Green	.05	.02	.01
☐ U89 Tony Massenburg	.05	.02	.01
☐ U90 Paul Pressey	.05	.02	.01
☐ U91 Dwayne Schintzius	.05	.02	.01
☐ U92 Gary Payton	2.50	1.10	.30
☐ U93 Olden Polynice	.05	.02	.01
☐ U94 Jeff Malone	.05	.02	.01
☐ U95 Walter Palmer	.05	.02	.01
☐ U96 Delaney Rudd	.05	.02	.01
☐ U97 Pervis Ellison	.10	.05	.01
☐ U98 A.J. English	.05	.02	.01
☐ U99 Greg Foster	.05	.02	.01
☐ U100 Checklist 1-100	.05	.02	.01

1991-92 Fleer

The complete 1991-92 Fleer basketball
card set contains 400 standard-size cards.
The set was distributed in two series of 240
and 160 cards, respectively. The cards
were distributed in 12-card wax packs, 23-
card cello packs and 36-card rack packs.
Wax boxes contained 36 packs. The fronts
feature color action player photos, bordered

by a red stripe on the bottom, and gray and red stripes on the top. A 3/4" blue stripe checkered with black NBA logos runs the length of the card and serves as the left border of the picture. The team logo, player's name, and position are printed in white lettering in this stripe. The picture is bordered on the right side by a thin gray stripe and a thicker blue one. The backs present career summaries and are printed with black lettering on various pastel colors, superimposed over a wooden basketball floor background. The cards are numbered and checklisted below alphabetically according to teams within each series. Subsets include All-Stars (210-219), League Leaders (220-226), Slam Dunk (227-232), All Star Game Highlights (233-238) and Team Leaders (372-398). Rookie Cards of note include Kenny Anderson, Stacey Augmon, Terrell Brandon, Larry Johnson, Anthony Mason, Dikembe Mutombo, Steve Smith, and John Starks.

	MINT	NRMT	EXC
COMPLETE SET (400)	10.00	4.50	1.25
COMPLETE SERIES 1 (240)	5.00	2.20	.60
COMPLETE SERIES 2 (160)	5.00	2.20	.60
COMMON CARD (1-400)	.05	.02	.01

		MINT	NRMT	EXC
☐ 1	John Battle	.05	.02	.01
☐ 2	Jon Koncak	.05	.02	.01
☐ 3	Rumeal Robinson	.05	.02	.01
☐ 4	Spud Webb	.08	.04	.01
☐ 5	Bob Weiss CO	.05	.02	.01
☐ 6	Dominique Wilkins	.08	.04	.01
☐ 7	Kevin Willis	.05	.02	.01
☐ 8	Larry Bird	.60	.25	.07
☐ 9	Dee Brown	.05	.02	.01
☐ 10	Chris Ford CO	.05	.02	.01
☐ 11	Kevin Gamble	.05	.02	.01
☐ 12	Reggie Lewis	.08	.04	.01
☐ 13	Kevin McHale	.08	.04	.01
☐ 14	Robert Parish	.08	.04	.01
☐ 15	Ed Pinckney	.05	.02	.01
☐ 16	Brian Shaw	.05	.02	.01
☐ 17	Muggsy Bogues	.08	.04	.01
☐ 18	Rex Chapman	.05	.02	.01
☐ 19	Dell Curry	.05	.02	.01
☐ 20	Kendall Gill	.05	.02	.01
☐ 21	Eric Leckner	.05	.02	.01
☐ 22	Gene Littles CO	.05	.02	.01
☐ 23	Johnny Newman	.05	.02	.01
☐ 24	J.R. Reid	.05	.02	.01
☐ 25	B.J. Armstrong	.05	.02	.01
☐ 26	Bill Cartwright	.05	.02	.01
☐ 27	Horace Grant	.08	.04	.01
☐ 28	Phil Jackson CO	.08	.04	.01
☐ 29	Michael Jordan	2.00	.90	.25
☐ 30	Cliff Levingston	.05	.02	.01
☐ 31	John Paxson	.08	.04	.01
☐ 32	Will Perdue	.05	.02	.01
☐ 33	Scottie Pippen	.50	.23	.06
☐ 34	Brad Daugherty	.05	.02	.01
☐ 35	Craig Ehlo	.05	.02	.01
☐ 36	Danny Ferry	.05	.02	.01
☐ 37	Larry Nance	.08	.04	.01
☐ 38	Mark Price	.05	.02	.01
☐ 39	Darnell Valentine	.05	.02	.01
☐ 40	Hot Rod Williams	.05	.02	.01
☐ 41	Lenny Wilkens CO	.08	.04	.01
☐ 42	Richie Adubato CO	.05	.02	.01
☐ 43	Rolando Blackman	.08	.04	.01
☐ 44	James Donaldson	.05	.02	.01
☐ 45	Derek Harper	.08	.04	.01
☐ 46	Rodney McCray	.05	.02	.01
☐ 47	Randy White	.05	.02	.01
☐ 48	Herb Williams	.05	.02	.01
☐ 49	Chris Jackson	.08	.04	.01
☐ 50	Marcus Liberty	.05	.02	.01
☐ 51	Todd Lichti	.05	.02	.01
☐ 52	Blair Rasmussen	.05	.02	.01
☐ 53	Paul Westhead CO	.05	.02	.01
☐ 54	Reggie Williams	.05	.02	.01
☐ 55	Joe Wolf	.05	.02	.01
☐ 56	Orlando Woolridge	.05	.02	.01
☐ 57	Mark Aguirre	.08	.04	.01
☐ 58	Chuck Daly CO	.08	.04	.01
☐ 59	Joe Dumars	.08	.04	.01
☐ 60	James Edwards	.05	.02	.01
☐ 61	Vinnie Johnson	.05	.02	.01
☐ 62	Bill Laimbeer	.05	.02	.01
☐ 63	Dennis Rodman	.60	.25	.07
☐ 64	Isiah Thomas	.10	.05	.01
☐ 65	Tim Hardaway	.08	.04	.01
☐ 66	Rod Higgins	.05	.02	.01
☐ 67	Tyrone Hill	.05	.02	.01
☐ 68	Sarunas Marciulionis	.05	.02	.01
☐ 69	Chris Mullin	.08	.04	.01
☐ 70	Don Nelson CO	.08	.04	.01
☐ 71	Mitch Richmond	.15	.07	.02
☐ 72	Tom Tolbert	.05	.02	.01
☐ 73	Don Chaney CO	.05	.02	.01
☐ 74	Eric(Sleepy) Floyd	.05	.02	.01
☐ 75	Buck Johnson	.05	.02	.01
☐ 76	Vernon Maxwell	.05	.02	.01
☐ 77	Hakeem Olajuwon	.40	.18	.05
☐ 78	Kenny Smith	.05	.02	.01
☐ 79	Larry Smith	.05	.02	.01
☐ 80	Otis Thorpe	.08	.04	.01
☐ 81	Vern Fleming	.05	.02	.01
☐ 82	Bob Hill CO	.05	.02	.01
☐ 83	Reggie Miller	.20	.09	.03
☐ 84	Chuck Person	.08	.04	.01
☐ 85	Detlef Schrempf	.08	.04	.01
☐ 86	Rik Smits	.08	.04	.01
☐ 87	LaSalle Thompson	.05	.02	.01
☐ 88	Micheal Williams	.05	.02	.01
☐ 89	Gary Grant	.05	.02	.01
☐ 90	Ron Harper	.05	.02	.01
☐ 91	Bo Kimble	.05	.02	.01
☐ 92	Danny Manning	.08	.04	.01
☐ 93	Ken Norman	.05	.02	.01
☐ 94	Olden Polynice	.05	.02	.01
☐ 95	Mike Schuler CO	.05	.02	.01
☐ 96	Charles Smith	.05	.02	.01
☐ 97	Vlade Divac	.08	.04	.01
☐ 98	Mike Dunleavy CO	.05	.02	.01
☐ 99	A.C. Green	.08	.04	.01
☐ 100	Magic Johnson	.50	.23	.06
☐ 101	Sam Perkins	.05	.02	.01
☐ 102	Byron Scott	.08	.04	.01
☐ 103	Terry Teagle	.05	.02	.01
☐ 104	James Worthy	.08	.04	.01
☐ 105	Willie Burton	.05	.02	.01
☐ 106	Bimbo Coles	.05	.02	.01
☐ 107	Sherman Douglas	.05	.02	.01
☐ 108	Kevin Edwards	.05	.02	.01
☐ 109	Grant Long	.05	.02	.01
☐ 110	Kevin Loughery CO	.05	.02	.01
☐ 111	Glen Rice	.10	.05	.01
☐ 112	Rony Seikaly	.05	.02	.01

☐ 113 Frank Brickowski	.05	.02	.01
☐ 114 Dale Ellis	.05	.02	.01
☐ 115 Del Harris CO	.05	.02	.01
☐ 116 Jay Humphries	.05	.02	.01
☐ 117 Fred Roberts	.05	.02	.01
☐ 118 Alvin Robertson	.05	.02	.01
☐ 119 Dan Schayes	.05	.02	.01
☐ 120 Jack Sikma	.08	.04	.01
☐ 121 Tony Campbell	.05	.02	.01
☐ 122 Tyrone Corbin	.05	.02	.01
☐ 123 Sam Mitchell	.05	.02	.01
☐ 124 Tod Murphy	.05	.02	.01
☐ 125 Pooh Richardson	.05	.02	.01
☐ 126 Jim Rodgers CO	.05	.02	.01
☐ 127 Felton Spencer	.05	.02	.01
☐ 128 Mookie Blaylock	.08	.04	.01
☐ 129 Sam Bowie	.05	.02	.01
☐ 130 Derrick Coleman	.05	.02	.01
☐ 131 Chris Dudley	.05	.02	.01
☐ 132 Bill Fitch CO	.05	.02	.01
☐ 133 Chris Morris	.05	.02	.01
☐ 134 Drazen Petrovic	.08	.04	.01
☐ 135 Maurice Cheeks	.08	.04	.01
☐ 136 Patrick Ewing	.15	.07	.02
☐ 137 Mark Jackson	.05	.02	.01
☐ 138 Charles Oakley	.05	.02	.01
☐ 139 Pat Riley CO	.08	.04	.01
☐ 140 Trent Tucker	.05	.02	.01
☐ 141 Kiki Vandeweghe	.05	.02	.01
☐ 142 Gerald Wilkins	.05	.02	.01
☐ 143 Nick Anderson	.08	.04	.01
☐ 144 Terry Catledge	.05	.02	.01
☐ 145 Matt Guokas CO	.05	.02	.01
☐ 146 Jerry Reynolds	.05	.02	.01
☐ 147 Dennis Scott	.08	.04	.01
☐ 148 Scott Skiles	.05	.02	.01
☐ 149 Otis Smith	.05	.02	.01
☐ 150 Ron Anderson	.05	.02	.01
☐ 151 Charles Barkley	.25	.11	.03
☐ 152 Johnny Dawkins	.05	.02	.01
☐ 153 Armon Gilliam	.05	.02	.01
☐ 154 Hersey Hawkins	.05	.02	.01
☐ 155 Jim Lynam CO	.05	.02	.01
☐ 156 Rick Mahorn	.05	.02	.01
☐ 157 Brian Oliver	.05	.02	.01
☐ 158 Tom Chambers	.05	.02	.01
☐ 159 Cotton Fitzsimmons CO	.05	.02	.01
☐ 160 Jeff Hornacek	.05	.02	.01
☐ 161 Kevin Johnson	.08	.04	.01
☐ 162 Negele Knight	.05	.02	.01
☐ 163 Dan Majerle	.05	.02	.01
☐ 164 Xavier McDaniel	.05	.02	.01
☐ 165 Mark West	.05	.02	.01
☐ 166 Rick Adelman CO	.05	.02	.01
☐ 167 Danny Ainge	.08	.04	.01
☐ 168 Clyde Drexler	.20	.09	.03
☐ 169 Kevin Duckworth	.05	.02	.01
☐ 170 Jerome Kersey	.05	.02	.01
☐ 171 Terry Porter	.05	.02	.01
☐ 172 Clifford Robinson	.05	.02	.01
☐ 173 Buck Williams	.08	.04	.01
☐ 174 Antoine Carr	.05	.02	.01
☐ 175 Duane Causwell	.05	.02	.01
☐ 176 Jim Les	.05	.02	.01
☐ 177 Travis Mays	.05	.02	.01
☐ 178 Dick Motta CO	.05	.02	.01
☐ 179 Lionel Simmons	.05	.02	.01
☐ 180 Rory Sparrow	.05	.02	.01
☐ 181 Wayman Tisdale	.05	.02	.01
☐ 182 Willie Anderson	.05	.02	.01
☐ 183 Larry Brown CO	.08	.04	.01
☐ 184 Terry Cummings	.05	.02	.01
☐ 185 Sean Elliott	.10	.05	.01
☐ 186 Paul Pressey	.05	.02	.01
☐ 187 David Robinson	.40	.18	.05
☐ 188 Rod Strickland	.08	.04	.01
☐ 189 Benoit Benjamin	.05	.02	.01
☐ 190 Eddie Johnson	.05	.02	.01
☐ 191 K.C. Jones CO	.08	.04	.01
☐ 192 Shawn Kemp	.75	.35	.09
☐ 193 Derrick McKey	.05	.02	.01
☐ 194 Gary Payton	.40	.18	.05
☐ 195 Ricky Pierce	.05	.02	.01
☐ 196 Sedale Threatt	.05	.02	.01
☐ 197 Thurl Bailey	.05	.02	.01
☐ 198 Mark Eaton	.05	.02	.01
☐ 199 Blue Edwards	.05	.02	.01
☐ 200 Jeff Malone	.05	.02	.01
☐ 201 Karl Malone	.15	.07	.02
☐ 202 Jerry Sloan CO	.08	.04	.01
☐ 203 John Stockton	.15	.07	.02
☐ 204 Ledell Eackles	.05	.02	.01
☐ 205 Pervis Ellison	.05	.02	.01
☐ 206 A.J. English	.05	.02	.01
☐ 207 Harvey Grant	.05	.02	.01
☐ 208 Bernard King	.08	.04	.01
☐ 209 Wes Unseld CO	.08	.04	.01
☐ 210 Kevin Johnson AS	.08	.04	.01
☐ 211 Michael Jordan AS	1.00	.45	.12
☐ 212 Dominique Wilkins AS	.08	.04	.01
☐ 213 Charles Barkley AS	.15	.07	.02
☐ 214 Hakeem Olajuwon AS	.20	.09	.03
☐ 215 Patrick Ewing AS	.08	.04	.01
☐ 216 Tim Hardaway AS	.08	.04	.01
☐ 217 John Stockton AS	.08	.04	.01
☐ 218 Chris Mullin AS	.08	.04	.01
☐ 219 Karl Malone AS	.08	.04	.01
☐ 220 Michael Jordan LL	1.00	.45	.12
☐ 221 John Stockton LL	.08	.04	.01
☐ 222 Alvin Robertson LL	.05	.02	.01
☐ 223 Hakeem Olajuwon LL	.20	.09	.03
☐ 224 Buck Williams LL	.05	.02	.01
☐ 225 David Robinson LL	.20	.09	.03
☐ 226 Reggie Miller LL	.10	.05	.01
☐ 227 Blue Edwards SD	.05	.02	.01
☐ 228 Dee Brown SD	.05	.02	.01
☐ 229 Rex Chapman SD	.05	.02	.01
☐ 230 Kenny Smith SD	.05	.02	.01
☐ 231 Shawn Kemp SD	.40	.18	.05
☐ 232 Kendall Gill SD	.05	.02	.01
☐ 233 '91 All Star Game	.50	.23	.06
	Enemies - A Love Story			
	(East Bench Scene)			
☐ 234 Clyde Drexler ASG	.08	.04	.01
	Kevin McHale ASG			
☐ 235 Alvin Robertson ASG	.05	.02	.01
☐ 236 Patrick Ewing ASG	.10	.05	.01
	Karl Malone ASG			
☐ 237 '91 All Star Game	.25	.11	.03
	Just Me and the Boys			
	Michael Jordan			
	Magic Johnson			
	David Robinson			
	Patrick Ewing			
☐ 238 Michael Jordan ASG	.50	.23	.06
☐ 239 Checklist 1-120	.05	.02	.01
☐ 240 Checklist 121-240	.05	.02	.01
☐ 241 Stacey Augmon	.20	.09	.03
☐ 242 Maurice Cheeks	.08	.04	.01
☐ 243 Paul Graham	.05	.02	.01
☐ 244 Rodney Monroe	.05	.02	.01
☐ 245 Blair Rasmussen	.05	.02	.01

#	Player			
☐ 246	Alexander Volkov	.05	.02	.01
☐ 247	John Bagley	.05	.02	.01
☐ 248	Rick Fox	.10	.05	.01
☐ 249	Rickey Green	.05	.02	.01
☐ 250	Joe Kleine	.05	.02	.01
☐ 251	Stojko Vrankovic	.05	.02	.01
☐ 252	Allan Bristow CO	.05	.02	.01
☐ 253	Kenny Gattison	.05	.02	.01
☐ 254	Mike Gminski	.05	.02	.01
☐ 255	Larry Johnson	1.00	.45	.12
☐ 256	Bobby Hansen	.05	.02	.01
☐ 257	Craig Hodges	.05	.02	.01
☐ 258	Stacey King	.05	.02	.01
☐ 259	Scott Williams	.05	.02	.01
☐ 260	John Battle	.05	.02	.01
☐ 261	Winston Bennett	.05	.02	.01
☐ 262	Terrell Brandon	.40	.18	.05
☐ 263	Henry James	.05	.02	.01
☐ 264	Steve Kerr	.08	.04	.01
☐ 265	Jimmy Oliver	.05	.02	.01
☐ 266	Brad Davis	.05	.02	.01
☐ 267	Terry Davis	.05	.02	.01
☐ 268	Donald Hodge	.05	.02	.01
☐ 269	Mike Iuzzolino	.05	.02	.01
☐ 270	Fat Lever	.05	.02	.01
☐ 271	Doug Smith	.05	.02	.01
☐ 272	Greg Anderson	.05	.02	.01
☐ 273	Kevin Brooks	.05	.02	.01
☐ 274	Walter Davis	.08	.04	.01
☐ 275	Winston Garland	.05	.02	.01
☐ 276	Mark Macon	.05	.02	.01
☐ 277	Dikembe Mutombo	.50	.23	.06
	(Fleer '91 on front)			
☐ 277B	Dikembe Mutombo	1.00	.45	.12
	(Fleer '91-92 on front)			
☐ 278	William Bedford	.05	.02	.01
☐ 279	Lance Blanks	.05	.02	.01
☐ 280	John Salley	.05	.02	.01
☐ 281	Charles Thomas	.05	.02	.01
☐ 282	Darrell Walker	.05	.02	.01
☐ 283	Orlando Woolridge	.05	.02	.01
☐ 284	Victor Alexander	.05	.02	.01
☐ 285	Vincent Askew	.05	.02	.01
☐ 286	Mario Elie	.20	.09	.03
☐ 287	Alton Lister	.05	.02	.01
☐ 288	Billy Owens	.15	.07	.02
☐ 289	Matt Bullard	.05	.02	.01
☐ 290	Carl Herrera	.05	.02	.01
☐ 291	Tree Rollins	.05	.02	.01
☐ 292	John Turner	.05	.02	.01
☐ 293	Dale Davis UER	.15	.07	.02
	(Photo on back actually Sean Green)			
☐ 294	Sean Green	.05	.02	.01
☐ 295	Kenny Williams	.05	.02	.01
☐ 296	James Edwards	.05	.02	.01
☐ 297	LeRon Ellis	.05	.02	.01
☐ 298	Doc Rivers	.05	.02	.01
☐ 299	Loy Vaught	.08	.04	.01
☐ 300	Elden Campbell	.08	.04	.01
☐ 301	Jack Haley	.05	.02	.01
☐ 302	Keith Owens	.05	.02	.01
☐ 303	Tony Smith	.05	.02	.01
☐ 304	Sedale Threatt	.05	.02	.01
☐ 305	Keith Askins	.05	.02	.01
☐ 306	Alec Kessler	.05	.02	.01
☐ 307	John Morton	.05	.02	.01
☐ 308	Alan Ogg	.05	.02	.01
☐ 309	Steve Smith	.40	.18	.05
☐ 310	Lester Conner	.05	.02	.01
☐ 311	Jeff Grayer	.05	.02	.01
☐ 312	Frank Hamblen CO	.05	.02	.01
☐ 313	Steve Henson	.05	.02	.01
☐ 314	Larry Krystkowiak	.05	.02	.01
☐ 315	Moses Malone	.10	.05	.01
☐ 316	Thurl Bailey	.05	.02	.01
☐ 317	Randy Breuer	.05	.02	.01
☐ 318	Scott Brooks	.05	.02	.01
☐ 319	Gerald Glass	.05	.02	.01
☐ 320	Luc Longley	.20	.09	.03
☐ 321	Doug West	.05	.02	.01
☐ 322	Kenny Anderson	.30	.14	.04
☐ 323	Tate George	.05	.02	.01
☐ 324	Terry Mills	.08	.04	.01
☐ 325	Greg Anthony	.15	.07	.02
☐ 326	Anthony Mason	.25	.11	.03
☐ 327	Tim McCormick	.05	.02	.01
☐ 328	Xavier McDaniel	.05	.02	.01
☐ 329	Brian Quinnett	.05	.02	.01
☐ 330	John Starks	.20	.09	.03
☐ 331	Stanley Roberts	.05	.02	.01
☐ 332	Jeff Turner	.05	.02	.01
☐ 333	Sam Vincent	.05	.02	.01
☐ 334	Brian Williams	.10	.05	.01
☐ 335	Manute Bol	.05	.02	.01
☐ 336	Kenny Payne	.05	.02	.01
☐ 337	Charles Shackleford	.05	.02	.01
☐ 338	Jayson Williams	.05	.02	.01
☐ 339	Cedric Ceballos	.10	.05	.01
☐ 340	Andrew Lang	.05	.02	.01
☐ 341	Jerrod Mustaf	.05	.02	.01
☐ 342	Tim Perry	.05	.02	.01
☐ 343	Kurt Rambis	.05	.02	.01
☐ 344	Alaa Abdelnaby	.05	.02	.01
☐ 345	Robert Pack	.05	.02	.01
☐ 346	Danny Young	.05	.02	.01
☐ 347	Anthony Bonner	.05	.02	.01
☐ 348	Pete Chilcutt	.05	.02	.01
☐ 349	Rex Hughes CO	.05	.02	.01
☐ 350	Mitch Richmond	.15	.07	.02
☐ 351	Dwayne Schintzius	.05	.02	.01
☐ 352	Spud Webb	.08	.04	.01
☐ 353	Antoine Carr	.05	.02	.01
☐ 354	Sidney Green	.05	.02	.01
☐ 355	Vinnie Johnson	.05	.02	.01
☐ 356	Greg Sutton	.05	.02	.01
☐ 357	Dana Barros	.05	.02	.01
☐ 358	Michael Cage	.05	.02	.01
☐ 359	Marty Conlon	.05	.02	.01
☐ 360	Rich King	.05	.02	.01
☐ 361	Nate McMillan	.05	.02	.01
☐ 362	David Benoit	.08	.04	.01
☐ 363	Mike Brown	.05	.02	.01
☐ 364	Tyrone Corbin	.05	.02	.01
☐ 365	Eric Murdock	.05	.02	.01
☐ 366	Delaney Rudd	.05	.02	.01
☐ 367	Michael Adams	.05	.02	.01
☐ 368	Tom Hammonds	.05	.02	.01
☐ 369	Larry Stewart	.05	.02	.01
☐ 370	Andre Turner	.05	.02	.01
☐ 371	David Wingate	.05	.02	.01
☐ 372	Dominique Wilkins TL	.08	.04	.01
☐ 373	Larry Bird TL	.30	.14	.04
☐ 374	Rex Chapman TL	.05	.02	.01
☐ 375	Michael Jordan TL	1.00	.45	.12
☐ 376	Brad Daugherty TL	.05	.02	.01
☐ 377	Derek Harper TL	.05	.02	.01
☐ 378	Dikembe Mutombo TL	.10	.05	.01
☐ 379	Joe Dumars TL	.08	.04	.01
☐ 380	Chris Mullin TL	.05	.02	.01
☐ 381	Hakeem Olajuwon TL	.20	.09	.03
☐ 382	Chuck Person TL	.05	.02	.01

		MINT	NRMT	EXC
☐ 383	Charles Smith TL	.05	.02	.01
☐ 384	James Worthy TL	.08	.04	.01
☐ 385	Glen Rice TL	.05	.02	.01
☐ 386	Alvin Robertson TL	.05	.02	.01
☐ 387	Tony Campbell TL	.05	.02	.01
☐ 388	Derrick Coleman TL	.05	.02	.01
☐ 389	Patrick Ewing TL	.08	.04	.01
☐ 390	Scott Skiles TL	.05	.02	.01
☐ 391	Charles Barkley TL	.15	.07	.02
☐ 392	Kevin Johnson TL	.08	.04	.01
☐ 393	Clyde Drexler TL	.08	.04	.01
☐ 394	Lionel Simmons TL	.05	.02	.01
☐ 395	David Robinson TL	.20	.09	.03
☐ 396	Ricky Pierce TL	.05	.02	.01
☐ 397	John Stockton TL	.08	.04	.01
☐ 398	Michael Adams TL	.05	.02	.01
☐ 399	Checklist	.05	.02	.01
☐ 400	Checklist	.05	.02	.01

1991-92 Fleer Dikembe Mutombo

This 12-card standard-size set was randomly inserted in 1991-92 Fleer second series 12-card wax packs at a rate of approximately one in six. The set highlights the accomplishments of then Denver Nuggets' rookie Dikembe Mutombo. The front borders are dark red and checkered with miniature NBA logos. The background of the color action photo is ghosted so that the featured player stands out, and the color of the lettering on the front is mustard. On a pink background, the back has a color close-up photo and a summary of the player's performance. Mutombo autographed over 2,000 of these cards which were also randomly inserted into packs. Those cards inserted in packs feature embossed Fleer logos for authenticity.

	MINT	NRMT	EXC
COMPLETE SET (12)	5.00	2.20	.60
COMMON MUTOMBO (1-12)	.50	.23	.06
☐ 1 Dikembe Mutombo Childhood in Zaire	.50	.23	.06
☐ 2 Dikembe Mutombo Georgetown Start	.50	.23	.06
☐ 3 Dikembe Mutombo Arrival on	.50	.23	.06
college scene			
☐ 4 Dikembe Mutombo Capping college career	.50	.23	.06
☐ 5 Dikembe Mutombo NBA Draft	.50	.23	.06
☐ 6 Dikembe Mutombo First NBA games	.50	.23	.06
☐ 7 Dikembe Mutombo Offensive skills	.50	.23	.06
☐ 8 Dikembe Mutombo What he has meant to the Nuggets	.50	.23	.06
☐ 9 Dikembe Mutombo Work Habits	.50	.23	.06
☐ 10 Dikembe Mutombo Charmed Denver	.50	.23	.06
☐ 11 Dikembe Mutombo The Future	.50	.23	.06
☐ 12 Dikembe Mutombo The Mutombo Legend	.50	.23	.06
☐ AU Dikembe Mutombo (Certified autograph)	75.00	34.00	9.50

1991-92 Fleer Pro-Visions

This six-card standard-size set showcases outstanding NBA players. The set was distributed as a random insert in 1991-92 Fleer first series 12-card plastic-wrap packs at a rate of approximately one per six packs. The fronts feature a color player portrait by sports artist Terry Smith. The portrait is bordered on all sides by white, with the player's name in red lettering below the picture. The backs present biographical information and career summary in black lettering on a color background (with white borders).

	MINT	NRMT	EXC
COMPLETE SET (6)	5.00	2.20	.60
COMMON CARD (1-6)	.30	.14	.04
☐ 1 David Robinson	.75	.35	.09
☐ 2 Michael Jordan	4.00	1.80	.50
☐ 3 Charles Barkley	.50	.23	.06
☐ 4 Patrick Ewing	.30	.14	.04
☐ 5 Karl Malone	.30	.14	.04
☐ 6 Magic Johnson	1.00	.45	.12

1991-92 Fleer Rookie Sensations

This 10-card standard-size set showcases outstanding rookies from the 1990-91 season. The set was distributed as a random insert in 1991-92 Fleer 23-card cello packs at a rate of approximately two in every three packs. The card fronts feature a color player photo inside a basketball rim and net. The picture is bordered in magenta on all sides. The words "Rookie Sensations" appear above the picture, and player information is given below the picture. An orange basketball with the words "Fleer '91" appears in the upper left corner on both sides of the card. The back has a magenta border and includes highlights of the player's rookie season.

	MINT	NRMT	EXC
COMPLETE SET (10)	8.00	3.60	1.00
COMMON CARD (1-10)	.50	.23	.06
☐ 1 Lionel Simmons	.50	.23	.06
☐ 2 Dennis Scott	1.25	.55	.16
☐ 3 Derrick Coleman	1.25	.55	.16
☐ 4 Kendall Gill	1.00	.45	.12
☐ 5 Travis Mays	.50	.23	.06
☐ 6 Felton Spencer	.50	.23	.06
☐ 7 Willie Burton	.50	.23	.06
☐ 8 Chris Jackson	1.25	.55	.16
☐ 9 Gary Payton	6.00	2.70	.75
☐ 10 Dee Brown	1.00	.45	.12

1991-92 Fleer Schoolyard

This six-card standard-size set of "Schoolyard Stars" was inserted one per 1991-92 Fleer 36-card rack packs. The card front features color action player photos. The photos are bordered on the left and bottom by a black stripe and a broken pink stripe. Yellow stripes traverse the card top and bottom, and the background is a gray cement-colored design. The back has a similar layout and presents a basketball tip in black lettering on white.

	MINT	NRMT	EXC
COMPLETE SET (6)	8.00	3.60	1.00
COMMON CARD (1-6)	.75	.35	.09
☐ 1 Chris Mullin	1.50	.70	.19
☐ 2 Isiah Thomas	2.50	1.10	.30
☐ 3 Kevin McHale	1.50	.70	.19
☐ 4 Kevin Johnson	4.00	1.80	.50
☐ 5 Karl Malone	4.00	1.80	.50
☐ 6 Alvin Robertson	.75	.35	.09

1991-92 Fleer Dominique Wilkins

Cards from this 12-card insert standard-size set were randomly inserted in 1991-92 Fleer second series 12-card wax packs at a rate of approximately one per six. The set highlights the career of superstar Dominique Wilkins. The front borders are dark red and checkered with miniature black NBA logos. The background of the color action photo is ghosted so that the featured player stands out, and the color of the lettering on the front is mustard. On a pink background, the back has a color close-up photo and a summary of the player's performance. Wilkins personally autographed over 2,000 of these cards which were also randomly inserted in packs. Those cards inserted in packs feature embossed Fleer logos for authenticity.

	MINT	NRMT	EXC
COMPLETE SET (12)	4.00	1.80	.50
COMMON D.WILKINS (1-12)	.40	.18	.05
☐ 1 Dominique Wilkins Overview	.40	.18	.05

		MINT	NRMT	EXC
☐ 2	Dominique Wilkins College	.40	.18	.05
☐ 3	Dominique Wilkins Early years	.40	.18	.05
☐ 4	Dominique Wilkins Early Career	.40	.18	.05
☐ 5	Dominique Wilkins Dominique Emerges	.40	.18	.05
☐ 6	Dominique Wilkins Another milestone	.40	.18	.05
☐ 7	Dominique Wilkins Wilkins continues to shine	.40	.18	.05
☐ 8	Dominique Wilkins Best all-round season	.40	.18	.05
☐ 9	Dominique Wilkins Charitable Causes	.40	.18	.05
☐ 10	Dominique Wilkins Durability	.40	.18	.05
☐ 11	Dominique Wilkins Career Numbers	.40	.18	.05
☐ 12	Dominique Wilkins Future	.40	.18	.05
☐ AU	Dominique Wilkins (Certified autograph)	75.00	34.00	9.50

1992-93 Fleer

The complete 1992-93 Fleer basketball set contains 444 standard-size cards. The set was distributed in two series of 264 and 180 cards, respectively. First series cards were distributed in 17-card plastic-wrap packs, 32-card cello packs, and 42-card rack packs. Second series cards were distributed in 15-card plastic-wrap packs and 32-card cello packs. The fronts display color action player photos, enclosed by metallic bronze borders and accented on the right by two pebble-grain colored stripes. On a tan pebble-grain background, the horizontally oriented backs have a color close-up photo in the shape of the lane under the basket. Biography, career statistics, and player profile are included on the backs. The cards are numbered on the back and checklisted below alphabetically according to teams. Subsets include League Leaders (238-245), Award Winners (246-249), Pro-Visions (250-255), Schoolyard Stars (256-264) and Slam Dunk (265-300). The Slam Dunk subset is divided into five categories: Power, Grace, Champions, Little Big Men, and Great Defenders. Randomly inserted throughout the packs were more than 3,000 (Slam

Dunk subset) cards signed by former NBA players Darryl Dawkins and Kenny Walker as well as by current NBA star Shawn Kemp. According to Fleer's advertising material, odds of finding a signed Slam Dunk card are one in 5,000 packs. Rookie Cards of note include Tom Gugliotta, Robert Horry, Christian Laettner, Alonzo Mourning, Shaquille O'Neal, Latrell Sprewell and Clarence Weatherspoon. A second series mail-in offer featuring an "All-Star Slam Dunk Team" card and an issue of Inside Stuff was available (expiring 6/30/93) in return for ten second series wrappers plus a dollar.

		MINT	NRMT	EXC
COMPLETE SET (444)		30.00	13.50	3.70
COMPLETE SERIES 1 (264)		15.00	6.75	1.85
COMPLETE SERIES 2 (180)		15.00	6.75	1.85
COMMON CARD (1-444)		.05	.02	.01
☐ 1	Stacey Augmon	.10	.05	.01
☐ 2	Duane Ferrell	.05	.02	.01
☐ 3	Paul Graham	.05	.02	.01
☐ 4A	Jon Koncak (Shooting pose on back)	.05	.02	.01
☐ 4B	Jon Koncak (No ball visible in photo on back)	.05	.02	.01
☐ 5	Blair Rasmussen	.05	.02	.01
☐ 6	Rumeal Robinson	.05	.02	.01
☐ 7	Bob Weiss CO	.05	.02	.01
☐ 8	Dominique Wilkins	.10	.05	.01
☐ 9	Kevin Willis	.05	.02	.01
☐ 10	John Bagley	.05	.02	.01
☐ 11	Larry Bird	1.00	.45	.12
☐ 12	Dee Brown	.05	.02	.01
☐ 13	Chris Ford CO	.05	.02	.01
☐ 14	Rick Fox	.05	.02	.01
☐ 15	Kevin Gamble	.05	.02	.01
☐ 16	Reggie Lewis	.10	.05	.01
☐ 17	Kevin McHale	.10	.05	.01
☐ 18	Robert Parish	.10	.05	.01
☐ 19	Ed Pinckney	.05	.02	.01
☐ 20	Muggsy Bogues	.10	.05	.01
☐ 21	Allan Bristow CO	.05	.02	.01
☐ 22	Dell Curry	.05	.02	.01
☐ 23	Kenny Gattison	.05	.02	.01
☐ 24	Kendall Gill	.05	.02	.01
☐ 25	Larry Johnson	.50	.23	.06
☐ 26	Johnny Newman	.05	.02	.01
☐ 27	J.R. Reid	.05	.02	.01
☐ 28	B.J. Armstrong	.05	.02	.01
☐ 29	Bill Cartwright	.05	.02	.01
☐ 30	Horace Grant	.10	.05	.01
☐ 31	Phil Jackson CO	.10	.05	.01
☐ 32	Michael Jordan	3.00	1.35	.35
☐ 33	Stacey King	.05	.02	.01
☐ 34	Cliff Levingston	.05	.02	.01
☐ 35	John Paxson	.10	.05	.01
☐ 36	Scottie Pippen	.75	.35	.09
☐ 37	Scott Williams	.05	.02	.01
☐ 38	John Battle	.05	.02	.01
☐ 39	Terrell Brandon	.10	.05	.01
☐ 40	Brad Daugherty	.05	.02	.01
☐ 41	Craig Ehlo	.05	.02	.01
☐ 42	Larry Nance	.05	.02	.01
☐ 43	Mark Price	.10	.05	.01
☐ 44	Mike Sanders	.05	.02	.01
☐ 45	Lenny Wilkens CO	.10	.05	.01

☐ 46	John Hot Rod Williams ..	.05	.02	.01
☐ 47	Richie Adubato CO	.05	.02	.01
☐ 48	Terry Davis	.05	.02	.01
☐ 49	Derek Harper	.05	.02	.01
☐ 50	Donald Hodge	.05	.02	.01
☐ 51	Mike Iuzzolino	.05	.02	.01
☐ 52	Rodney McCray	.05	.02	.01
☐ 53	Doug Smith	.05	.02	.01
☐ 54	Greg Anderson	.05	.02	.01
☐ 55	Winston Garland	.05	.02	.01
☐ 56	Dan Issel CO	.10	.05	.01
☐ 57	Chris Jackson	.10	.05	.01
☐ 58	Marcus Liberty..............	.05	.02	.01
☐ 59	Mark Macon	.05	.02	.01
☐ 60	Dikembe Mutombo	.25	.11	.03
☐ 61	Reggie Williams	.05	.02	.01
☐ 62	Mark Aguirre	.10	.05	.01
☐ 63	Joe Dumars	.10	.05	.01
☐ 64	Bill Laimbeer	.05	.02	.01
☐ 65	Olden Polynice..............	.05	.02	.01
☐ 66	Dennis Rodman	1.00	.45	.12
☐ 67	Ron Rothstein CO	.05	.02	.01
☐ 68	John Salley	.05	.02	.01
☐ 69	Isiah Thomas	.15	.07	.02
☐ 70	Darrell Walker	.05	.02	.01
☐ 71	Orlando Woolridge.........	.05	.02	.01
☐ 72	Victor Alexander	.05	.02	.01
☐ 73	Mario Elie	.05	.02	.01
☐ 74	Tim Hardaway	.10	.05	.01
☐ 75	Tyrone Hill	.05	.02	.01
☐ 76	Sarunas Marciulionis	.05	.02	.01
☐ 77	Chris Mullin	.10	.05	.01
☐ 78	Don Nelson CO	.10	.05	.01
☐ 79	Billy Owens	.05	.02	.01
☐ 80	Sleepy Floyd UER..........	.05	.02	.01
	(Went past 4000 assist			
	mark, not 2000)			
☐ 81	Avery Johnson	.05	.02	.01
☐ 82	Buck Johnson	.05	.02	.01
☐ 83	Vernon Maxwell	.05	.02	.01
☐ 84	Hakeem Olajuwon	.60	.25	.07
☐ 85	Kenny Smith	.05	.02	.01
☐ 86	Otis Thorpe	.10	.05	.01
☐ 87	Rudy Tomjanovich CO ...	.10	.05	.01
☐ 88	Dale Davis	.05	.02	.01
☐ 89	Vern Fleming	.05	.02	.01
☐ 90	Bob Hill CO	.05	.02	.01
☐ 91	Reggie Miller	.30	.14	.04
☐ 92	Chuck Person	.05	.02	.01
☐ 93	Detlef Schrempf	.10	.05	.01
☐ 94	Rik Smits	.10	.05	.01
☐ 95	LaSalle Thompson	.05	.02	.01
☐ 96	Micheal Williams	.05	.02	.01
☐ 97	Larry Brown CO	.10	.05	.01
☐ 98	James Edwards	.05	.02	.01
☐ 99	Gary Grant	.05	.02	.01
☐ 100	Ron Harper	.05	.02	.01
☐ 101	Danny Manning	.10	.05	.01
☐ 102	Ken Norman	.05	.02	.01
☐ 103	Doc Rivers	.05	.02	.01
☐ 104	Charles Smith	.05	.02	.01
☐ 105	Loy Vaught	.10	.05	.01
☐ 106	Elden Campbell.............	.10	.05	.01
☐ 107	Vlade Divac	.10	.05	.01
☐ 108	A.C. Green...................	.10	.05	.01
☐ 109	Sam Perkins	.05	.02	.01
☐ 110	Randy Pfund CO	.05	.02	.01
☐ 111	Byron Scott	.10	.05	.01
☐ 112	Terry Teagle	.05	.02	.01
☐ 113	Sedale Threatt..............	.05	.02	.01
☐ 114	James Worthy...............	.10	.05	.01
☐ 115	Willie Burton	.05	.02	.01
☐ 116	Bimbo Coles	.05	.02	.01
☐ 117	Kevin Edwards	.05	.02	.01
☐ 118	Grant Long	.05	.02	.01
☐ 119	Kevin Loughery CO	.05	.02	.01
☐ 120	Glen Rice	.10	.05	.01
☐ 121	Rony Seikaly	.05	.02	.01
☐ 122	Brian Shaw	.05	.02	.01
☐ 123	Steve Smith	.10	.05	.01
☐ 124	Frank Brickowski..........	.05	.02	.01
☐ 125	Mike Dunleavy CO.........	.05	.02	.01
☐ 126	Blue Edwards...............	.05	.02	.01
☐ 127	Moses Malone	.15	.07	.02
☐ 128	Eric Murdock	.05	.02	.01
☐ 129	Fred Roberts	.05	.02	.01
☐ 130	Alvin Robertson	.05	.02	.01
☐ 131	Thurl Bailey.................	.05	.02	.01
☐ 132	Tony Campbell	.05	.02	.01
☐ 133	Gerald Glass	.05	.02	.01
☐ 134	Luc Longley	.05	.02	.01
☐ 135	Sam Mitchell................	.05	.02	.01
☐ 136	Pooh Richardson	.05	.02	.01
☐ 137	Jimmy Rodgers CO	.05	.02	.01
☐ 138	Felton Spencer	.05	.02	.01
☐ 139	Doug West	.05	.02	.01
☐ 140	Kenny Anderson	.10	.05	.01
☐ 141	Mookie Blaylock...........	.10	.05	.01
☐ 142	Sam Bowie...................	.05	.02	.01
☐ 143	Derrick Coleman	.05	.02	.01
☐ 144	Chuck Daly CO	.10	.05	.01
☐ 145	Terry Mills...................	.05	.02	.01
☐ 146	Chris Morris	.05	.02	.01
☐ 147	Drazen Petrovic............	.10	.05	.01
☐ 148	Greg Anthony	.05	.02	.01
☐ 149	Rolando Blackman........	.05	.02	.01
☐ 150	Patrick Ewing...............	.25	.11	.03
☐ 151	Mark Jackson	.05	.02	.01
☐ 152	Anthony Mason.............	.10	.05	.01
☐ 153	Xavier McDaniel	.05	.02	.01
☐ 154	Charles Oakley	.05	.02	.01
☐ 155	Pat Riley CO.................	.10	.05	.01
☐ 156	John Starks..................	.10	.05	.01
☐ 157	Gerald Wilkins..............	.05	.02	.01
☐ 158	Nick Anderson	.10	.05	.01
☐ 159	Anthony Bowie..............	.05	.02	.01
☐ 160	Terry Catledge	.05	.02	.01
☐ 161	Matt Guokas CO	.05	.02	.01
☐ 162	Stanley Roberts	.05	.02	.01
☐ 163	Dennis Scott	.10	.05	.01
☐ 164	Scott Skiles.................	.05	.02	.01
☐ 165	Brian Williams	.05	.02	.01
☐ 166	Ron Anderson	.05	.02	.01
☐ 167	Manute Bol	.05	.02	.01
☐ 168	Johnny Dawkins	.05	.02	.01
☐ 169	Armon Gilliam	.05	.02	.01
☐ 170	Hersey Hawkins	.10	.05	.01
☐ 171	Jeff Hornacek...............	.10	.05	.01
☐ 172	Andrew Lang	.05	.02	.01
☐ 173	Doug Moe CO	.05	.02	.01
☐ 174	Tim Perry	.05	.02	.01
☐ 175	Jeff Ruland	.05	.02	.01
☐ 176	Charles Shackleford	.05	.02	.01
☐ 177	Danny Ainge	.10	.05	.01
☐ 178	Charles Barkley............	.40	.18	.05
☐ 179	Cedric Ceballos	.10	.05	.01
☐ 180	Tom Chambers	.05	.02	.01
☐ 181	Kevin Johnson	.10	.05	.01
☐ 182	Dan Majerle.................	.10	.05	.01
☐ 183	Mark West UER	.05	.02	.01
	(Needs 33 blocks to			
	reach 1000, not 31)			

#	Player			
☐ 184	Paul Westphal CO	.05	.02	.01
☐ 185	Rick Adelman CO	.05	.02	.01
☐ 186	Clyde Drexler	.30	.14	.04
☐ 187	Kevin Duckworth	.05	.02	.01
☐ 188	Jerome Kersey	.05	.02	.01
☐ 189	Robert Pack	.05	.02	.01
☐ 190	Terry Porter	.05	.02	.01
☐ 191	Clifford Robinson	.10	.05	.01
☐ 192	Rod Strickland	.05	.02	.01
☐ 193	Buck Williams	.10	.05	.01
☐ 194	Anthony Bonner	.05	.02	.01
☐ 195	Duane Causwell	.05	.02	.01
☐ 196	Mitch Richmond	.20	.09	.03
☐ 197	Garry St. Jean CO	.05	.02	.01
☐ 198	Lionel Simmons	.05	.02	.01
☐ 199	Wayman Tisdale	.05	.02	.01
☐ 200	Spud Webb	.10	.05	.01
☐ 201	Willie Anderson	.05	.02	.01
☐ 202	Antoine Carr	.05	.02	.01
☐ 203	Terry Cummings	.05	.02	.01
☐ 204	Sean Elliott	.05	.02	.01
☐ 205	Dale Ellis	.05	.02	.01
☐ 206	Vinnie Johnson	.05	.02	.01
☐ 207	David Robinson	.50	.23	.06
☐ 208	Jerry Tarkanian CO	.15	.07	.02
☐ 209	Benoit Benjamin	.05	.02	.01
☐ 210	Michael Cage	.05	.02	.01
☐ 211	Eddie Johnson	.05	.02	.01
☐ 212	George Karl CO	.05	.02	.01
☐ 213	Shawn Kemp	1.00	.45	.12
☐ 214	Derrick McKey	.05	.02	.01
☐ 215	Nate McMillan	.05	.02	.01
☐ 216	Gary Payton	.50	.23	.06
☐ 217	Ricky Pierce	.05	.02	.01
☐ 218	David Benoit	.05	.02	.01
☐ 219	Mike Brown	.05	.02	.01
☐ 220	Tyrone Corbin	.05	.02	.01
☐ 221	Mark Eaton	.05	.02	.01
☐ 222	Jay Humphries	.05	.02	.01
☐ 223	Larry Krystkowiak	.05	.02	.01
☐ 224	Jeff Malone	.05	.02	.01
☐ 225	Karl Malone	.25	.11	.03
☐ 226	Jerry Sloan CO	.10	.05	.01
☐ 227	John Stockton	.25	.11	.03
☐ 228	Michael Adams	.05	.02	.01
☐ 229	Rex Chapman	.05	.02	.01
☐ 230	Ledell Eackles	.05	.02	.01
☐ 231	Pervis Ellison	.05	.02	.01
☐ 232	A.J. English	.05	.02	.01
☐ 233	Harvey Grant	.05	.02	.01
☐ 234	LaBradford Smith	.05	.02	.01
☐ 235	Larry Stewart	.05	.02	.01
☐ 236	Wes Unseld CO	.10	.05	.01
☐ 237	David Wingate	.05	.02	.01
☐ 238	Michael Jordan LL Scoring	1.50	.70	.19
☐ 239	Dennis Rodman LL Rebounding	.50	.23	.06
☐ 240	John Stockton LL Assists/Steals	.10	.05	.01
☐ 241	Buck Williams LL Field Goal Percentage	.05	.02	.01
☐ 242	Mark Price LL Free Throw Percentage	.05	.02	.01
☐ 243	Dana Barros LL Three Point Percentage	.05	.02	.01
☐ 244	David Robinson LL Shots Blocked	.25	.11	.03
☐ 245	Chris Mullin LL Minutes Played	.05	.02	.01
☐ 246	Michael Jordan MVP	1.50	.70	.19
☐ 247	Larry Johnson ROY UER (Scoring average was 19.2, not 19.7)	.25	.11	.03
☐ 248	David Robinson Defensive Player of the Year	.25	.11	.03
☐ 249	Detlef Schrempf Sixth Man of the Year	.05	.02	.01
☐ 250	Clyde Drexler PV	.10	.05	.01
☐ 251	Tim Hardaway PV	.05	.02	.01
☐ 252	Kevin Johnson PV	.05	.02	.01
☐ 253	Larry Johnson PV UER (Scoring average was 19.2, not 19.7)	.25	.11	.03
☐ 254	Scottie Pippen PV	.40	.18	.05
☐ 255	Isiah Thomas PV	.10	.05	.01
☐ 256	Larry Bird SY	.50	.23	.06
☐ 257	Brad Daugherty SY	.05	.02	.01
☐ 258	Kevin Johnson SY	.05	.02	.01
☐ 259	Larry Johnson SY	.25	.11	.03
☐ 260	Scottie Pippen SY	.40	.18	.05
☐ 261	Dennis Rodman SY	.50	.23	.06
☐ 262	Checklist 1	.05	.02	.01
☐ 263	Checklist 2	.05	.02	.01
☐ 264	Checklist 3	.05	.02	.01
☐ 265	Charles Barkley SD	.20	.09	.03
☐ 266	Shawn Kemp SD	.50	.23	.06
☐ 267	Dan Majerle SD	.05	.02	.01
☐ 268	Karl Malone SD	.10	.05	.01
☐ 269	Buck Williams SD	.05	.02	.01
☐ 270	Clyde Drexler SD	.10	.05	.01
☐ 271	Sean Elliott SD	.05	.02	.01
☐ 272	Ron Harper SD	.05	.02	.01
☐ 273	Michael Jordan SD	1.50	.70	.19
☐ 274	James Worthy SD	.10	.05	.01
☐ 275	Cedric Ceballos SD	.05	.02	.01
☐ 276	Larry Nance SD	.05	.02	.01
☐ 277	Kenny Walker SD	.05	.02	.01
☐ 278	Spud Webb SD	.05	.02	.01
☐ 279	Dominique Wilkins SD	.10	.05	.01
☐ 280	Terrell Brandon SD	.05	.02	.01
☐ 281	Dee Brown SD	.05	.02	.01
☐ 282	Kevin Johnson SD	.05	.02	.01
☐ 283	Doc Rivers SD	.05	.02	.01
☐ 284	Byron Scott SD	.05	.02	.01
☐ 285	Manute Bol SD	.05	.02	.01
☐ 286	Dikembe Mutombo SD	.10	.05	.01
☐ 287	Robert Parish SD	.10	.05	.01
☐ 288	David Robinson SD	.25	.11	.03
☐ 289	Dennis Rodman SD	.50	.23	.06
☐ 290	Blue Edwards SD	.05	.02	.01
☐ 291	Patrick Ewing SD	.10	.05	.01
☐ 292	Larry Johnson SD	.25	.11	.03
☐ 293	Jerome Kersey SD	.05	.02	.01
☐ 294	Hakeem Olajuwon SD	.30	.14	.04
☐ 295	Stacey Augmon SD	.05	.02	.01
☐ 296	Derrick Coleman SD	.05	.02	.01
☐ 297	Kendall Gill SD	.05	.02	.01
☐ 298	Shaquille O'Neal SD	1.50	.70	.19
☐ 299	Scottie Pippen SD	.40	.18	.05
☐ 300	Darryl Dawkins SD	.05	.02	.01
☐ 301	Mookie Blaylock	.10	.05	.01
☐ 302	Adam Keefe	.10	.05	.01
☐ 303	Travis Mays	.05	.02	.01
☐ 304	Morlon Wiley	.05	.02	.01
☐ 305	Sherman Douglas	.05	.02	.01
☐ 306	Joe Kleine	.05	.02	.01
☐ 307	Xavier McDaniel	.05	.02	.01
☐ 308	Tony Bennett	.05	.02	.01
☐ 309	Tom Hammonds	.05	.02	.01
☐ 310	Kevin Lynch	.05	.02	.01

#	Player			
311	Alonzo Mourning	1.25	.55	.16
312	David Wingate	.05	.02	.01
313	Rodney McCray	.05	.02	.01
314	Will Perdue	.05	.02	.01
315	Trent Tucker	.05	.02	.01
316	Corey Williams	.05	.02	.01
317	Danny Ferry	.05	.02	.01
318	Jay Guidinger	.05	.02	.01
319	Jerome Lane	.05	.02	.01
320	Gerald Wilkins	.05	.02	.01
321	Stephen Bardo	.05	.02	.01
322	Walter Bond	.05	.02	.01
323	Brian Howard	.05	.02	.01
324	Tracy Moore	.05	.02	.01
325	Sean Rooks	.05	.02	.01
326	Randy White	.05	.02	.01
327	Kevin Brooks	.05	.02	.01
328	LaPhonso Ellis	.20	.09	.03
329	Scott Hastings	.05	.02	.01
330	Todd Lichti	.05	.02	.01
331	Robert Pack	.05	.02	.01
332	Bryant Stith	.20	.09	.03
333	Gerald Glass	.05	.02	.01
334	Terry Mills	.05	.02	.01
335	Isaiah Morris	.05	.02	.01
336	Mark Randall	.05	.02	.01
337	Danny Young	.05	.02	.01
338	Chris Gatling	.05	.02	.01
339	Jeff Grayer	.05	.02	.01
340	Byron Houston	.05	.02	.01
341	Keith Jennings	.05	.02	.01
342	Alton Lister	.05	.02	.01
343	Latrell Sprewell	.60	.25	.07
344	Scott Brooks	.05	.02	.01
345	Matt Bullard	.05	.02	.01
346	Carl Herrera	.05	.02	.01
347	Robert Horry	.50	.23	.06
348	Tree Rollins	.05	.02	.01
349	Greg Dreiling	.05	.02	.01
350	George McCloud	.05	.02	.01
351	Sam Mitchell	.05	.02	.01
352	Pooh Richardson	.05	.02	.01
353	Malik Sealy	.10	.05	.01
354	Kenny Williams	.05	.02	.01
355	Jaren Jackson	.05	.02	.01
356	Mark Jackson	.05	.02	.01
357	Stanley Roberts	.05	.02	.01
358	Elmore Spencer	.05	.02	.01
359	Kiki Vandeweghe	.05	.02	.01
360	John S. Williams	.05	.02	.01
361	Randy Woods	.05	.02	.01
362	Duane Cooper	.05	.02	.01
363	James Edwards	.05	.02	.01
364	Anthony Peeler	.05	.02	.01
365	Tony Smith	.05	.02	.01
366	Keith Askins	.05	.02	.01
367	Matt Geiger	.05	.02	.01
368	Alec Kessler	.05	.02	.01
369	Harold Miner	.10	.05	.01
370	John Salley	.05	.02	.01
371	Anthony Avent	.05	.02	.01
372	Todd Day	.10	.05	.01
373	Blue Edwards	.05	.02	.01
374	Brad Lohaus	.05	.02	.01
375	Lee Mayberry	.05	.02	.01
376	Eric Murdock	.05	.02	.01
377	Dan Schayes	.05	.02	.01
378	Lance Blanks	.05	.02	.01
379	Christian Laettner	.40	.18	.05
380	Bob McCann	.05	.02	.01
381	Chuck Person	.05	.02	.01
382	Brad Sellers	.05	.02	.01
383	Chris Smith	.05	.02	.01
384	Micheal Williams	.05	.02	.01
385	Rafael Addison	.05	.02	.01
386	Chucky Brown	.05	.02	.01
387	Chris Dudley	.05	.02	.01
388	Tate George	.05	.02	.01
389	Rick Mahorn	.05	.02	.01
390	Rumeal Robinson	.05	.02	.01
391	Jayson Williams	.05	.02	.01
392	Eric Anderson	.05	.02	.01
393	Rolando Blackman	.05	.02	.01
394	Tony Campbell	.05	.02	.01
395	Hubert Davis	.10	.05	.01
396	Doc Rivers	.05	.02	.01
397	Charles Smith	.05	.02	.01
398	Herb Williams	.05	.02	.01
399	Litterial Green	.05	.02	.01
400	Greg Kite	.05	.02	.01
401	Shaquille O'Neal	5.00	2.20	.60
402	Jerry Reynolds	.05	.02	.01
403	Jeff Turner	.05	.02	.01
404	Greg Grant	.05	.02	.01
405	Jeff Hornacek	.05	.02	.01
406	Andrew Lang	.05	.02	.01
407	Kenny Payne	.05	.02	.01
408	Tim Perry	.05	.02	.01
409	Clarence Weatherspoon	.40	.18	.05
410	Danny Ainge	.10	.05	.01
411	Charles Barkley	.40	.18	.05
412	Negele Knight	.05	.02	.01
413	Oliver Miller	.25	.11	.03
414	Jerrod Mustaf	.05	.02	.01
415	Mark Bryant	.05	.02	.01
416	Mario Elie	.05	.02	.01
417	Dave Johnson	.05	.02	.01
418	Tracy Murray	.10	.05	.01
419	Reggie Smith	.05	.02	.01
420	Rod Strickland	.05	.02	.01
421	Randy Brown	.05	.02	.01
422	Pete Chilcutt	.05	.02	.01
423	Jim Les	.05	.02	.01
424	Walt Williams	.60	.25	.07
425	Lloyd Daniels	.05	.02	.01
426	Vinny Del Negro	.05	.02	.01
427	Dale Ellis	.05	.02	.01
428	Sidney Green	.05	.02	.01
429	Avery Johnson	.05	.02	.01
430	Dana Barros	.05	.02	.01
431	Rich King	.05	.02	.01
432	Isaac Austin	.05	.02	.01
433	John Crotty	.05	.02	.01
434	Stephen Howard	.05	.02	.01
435	Jay Humphries	.05	.02	.01
436	Larry Krystkowiak	.05	.02	.01
437	Tom Gugliotta	.40	.18	.05
438	Buck Johnson	.05	.02	.01
439	Charles Jones	.05	.02	.01
440	Don MacLean	.10	.05	.01
441	Doug Overton	.05	.02	.01
442	Brent Price	.05	.02	.01
443	Checklist 1	.05	.02	.01
444	Checklist 2	.05	.02	.01
SD266	Shawn Kemp AU (Certified Autograph)	200.00	90.00	25.00
SD277	Darrell Walker AU (Certified Autograph)	20.00	9.00	2.50
SD300	Darryl Dawkins AU (Certified Autograph)	40.00	18.00	5.00
NNO	Slam Dunk Wrapper Exchange	3.00	1.35	.35

1992-93 Fleer All-Stars

This 24-card standard-size set was randomly inserted in first series 17-card packs and features outstanding players from the Eastern (1-12) and Western (13-24) Conference. According to Fleer's advertising materials, the odds of pulling an All-Star insert are approximately one per nine packs. The horizontal fronts display two color images of the featured player against a gradated silver-blue background. The cards are bordered by a darker silver-blue, and the player's name is gold-foil stamped at the lower right corner. The Orlando All-Star Weekend logo is in the upper right and the team logo in the lower left corner. The backs are white with silver-blue borders and present career highlights, the player's name, and the Orlando All-Star Weekend logo. The cards are numbered on the back in alphabetical order.

		MINT	NRMT	EXC
COMPLETE SET (24)		120.00	55.00	15.00
COMMON CARD (1-24)		1.00	.45	.12
☐ 1	Michael Adams	1.00	.45	.12
☐ 2	Charles Barkley	8.00	3.60	1.00
☐ 3	Brad Daugherty	1.00	.45	.12
☐ 4	Joe Dumars	2.00	.90	.25
☐ 5	Patrick Ewing	5.00	2.20	.60
☐ 6	Michael Jordan	60.00	27.00	7.50
☐ 7	Reggie Lewis	2.00	.90	.25
☐ 8	Scottie Pippen	15.00	6.75	1.85
☐ 9	Mark Price	1.00	.45	.12
☐ 10	Dennis Rodman	20.00	9.00	2.50
☐ 11	Isiah Thomas	3.00	1.35	.35
☐ 12	Kevin Willis	1.00	.45	.12
☐ 13	Clyde Drexler	6.00	2.70	.75
☐ 14	Tim Hardaway	2.00	.90	.25
☐ 15	Jeff Hornacek	1.00	.45	.12
☐ 16	Dan Majerle	2.00	.90	.25
☐ 17	Karl Malone	5.00	2.20	.60
☐ 18	Chris Mullin	1.00	.45	.12
☐ 19	Dikembe Mutombo	3.00	1.35	.35
☐ 20	Hakeem Olajuwon	12.00	5.50	1.50
☐ 21	David Robinson	10.00	4.50	1.25
☐ 22	John Stockton	5.00	2.20	.60
☐ 23	Otis Thorpe	1.00	.45	.12
☐ 24	James Worthy	2.00	.90	.25

1992-93 Fleer Larry Johnson

Larry Johnson, the 1991-92 NBA Rookie of the Year, is featured in this 15-card signature series. The first 12 cards are available as random inserts in all forms of Fleer's first series packaging. The odds of pulling a Larry Johnson insert from a 17-card pack were one in 18, from a 32-card cello pack were one in 13 and from a 42-card rack pack were one in six. In addition, Larry personally autographed more than 2,000 of these cards, which were randomly inserted in the wax packs. These cards feature embossed Fleer logos on front for authenticity. According to Fleer's advertising materials, the odds of finding a signed Larry Johnson were approximately one in 15,000 packs. Collectors were also able to receive three additional Johnson cards and the premiere edition of NBA Inside Stuff magazine by sending in ten wrappers and 1.00 in a mail-in offer expiring 6/30/93. These standard-size cards feature color player photos framed by thin orange and blue borders on a silver-blue card face. The player's name and the words "NBA Rookie of the Year" are gold foil-stamped at the top. The backs feature an orange panel that summarizes Johnson's game and demeanor. His name and "NBA Rookie of the Year" appear at the top in a lighter orange.

	MINT	NRMT	EXC
COMPLETE SET (12)	12.00	5.50	1.50
COMMON L.JOHNSON (1-12)	1.50	.70	.19
COMMON SEND-OFF (13-15)	4.00	1.80	.50
☐ 1 Larry Johnson (Holding up Hornets' home jersey)	1.50	.70	.19
☐ 2 Larry Johnson (Driving through traffic against Knicks)	1.50	.70	.19
☐ 3 Larry Johnson (Turned to the side, holding ball over head)	1.50	.70	.19
☐ 4 Larry Johnson (Shooting jumpshot)	1.50	.70	.19
☐ 5 Larry Johnson (Smiling, holding ball at chest level)	1.50	.70	.19

		MINT	NRMT	EXC
☐ 6	Larry Johnson (Dribbling into a no-look pass)	1.50	.70	.19
☐ 7	Larry Johnson (Posting up down low)	1.50	.70	.19
☐ 8	Larry Johnson (Shooting ball in lane)	1.50	.70	.19
☐ 9	Larry Johnson (Going for tip-in in home jersey)	1.50	.70	.19
☐ 10	Larry Johnson (In warm-up suit)	1.50	.70	.19
☐ 11	Larry Johnson (High-fiving during pre-game introductions)	1.50	.70	.19
☐ 12	Larry Johnson (Dribbling with his left hand)	1.50	.70	.19
☐ 13	Larry Johnson (Going up for a rebound)	4.00	1.80	.50
☐ 14	Larry Johnson (Away from ball photo)	4.00	1.80	.50
☐ 15	Larry Johnson (Charlotte skyline in background)	4.00	1.80	.50
☐ AU	Larry Johnson AU (Certified autograph)	100.00	45.00	12.50

1992-93 Fleer Rookie Sensations

Randomly inserted in first series 32-card cello packs, this set features 12 of the top rookies from the 1991-92 season. According to information released by Fleer, the odds of pulling a Rookie Sensation is approximately one per five packs. Measuring the standard size, the cards feature the player in action against a computer generated team emblem on a gradated purple background. The words "Rookie Sensations" and the player's name are gold foil-stamped at the bottom. The backs display career highlights on a mint-green face with a purple border. The cards are numbered on the back in alphabetical order.

	MINT	NRMT	EXC
COMPLETE SET (12)	25.00	11.00	3.10
COMMON CARD (1-12)	1.00	.45	.12
☐ 1 Greg Anthony	1.00	.45	.12
☐ 2 Stacey Augmon	2.00	.90	.25

	MINT	NRMT	EXC
☐ 3 Terrell Brandon	4.00	1.80	.50
☐ 4 Rick Fox	1.00	.45	.12
☐ 5 Larry Johnson	10.00	4.50	1.25
☐ 6 Mark Macon	1.00	.45	.12
☐ 7 Dikembe Mutombo	5.00	2.20	.60
☐ 8 Billy Owens	5.00	2.20	.60
☐ 9 Stanley Roberts	1.00	.45	.12
☐ 10 Doug Smith	1.00	.45	.12
☐ 11 Steve Smith	4.00	1.80	.50
☐ 12 Larry Stewart	1.00	.45	.12

1992-93 Fleer Sharpshooters

Randomly inserted in second series 15-card plastic-wrap packs, these 18 standard-size cards feature some of the NBA's best shooters. According to Fleer's advertising materials, the odds of finding a Sharpshooter card are approximately one in three packs. The color action photos on the fronts are odd-shaped, overlaying a purple geometric shape and resting on a silver card face. The "Sharp Shooter" logo is gold-foil stamped at the upper left corner, while the player's name is gold-foil stamped below the picture. On a wheat-colored panel inside blue borders, the backs present a player profile.

	MINT	NRMT	EXC
COMPLETE SET (18)	20.00	9.00	2.50
COMMON CARD (1-18)	.50	.23	.06
☐ 1 Reggie Miller	5.00	2.20	.60
☐ 2 Dana Barros	.50	.23	.06
☐ 3 Jeff Hornacek	.50	.23	.06
☐ 4 Drazen Petrovic	1.00	.45	.12
☐ 5 Glen Rice	2.50	1.10	.30
☐ 6 Terry Porter	.50	.23	.06
☐ 7 Mark Price	.50	.23	.06
☐ 8 Michael Adams	.50	.23	.06
☐ 9 Hersey Hawkins	.50	.23	.06
☐ 10 Chuck Person	.50	.23	.06
☐ 11 John Stockton	4.00	1.80	.50
☐ 12 Dale Ellis	.50	.23	.06
☐ 13 Clyde Drexler	5.00	2.20	.60
☐ 14 Mitch Richmond	3.00	1.35	.35
☐ 15 Craig Ehlo	.50	.23	.06
☐ 16 Dell Curry	.50	.23	.06
☐ 17 Chris Mullin	.50	.23	.06
☐ 18 Rolando Blackman	.50	.23	.06

1992-93 Fleer Team Leaders

The 1992-93 Fleer Team Leaders were inserted into five of every six first series 42-card rack packs. A Larry Johnson Signature Series insert card replaced a Team Leader in every sixth rack pack. These 27 standard size cards feature a key member of each NBA team. The color action photos on the front are surrounded by thick dark blue borders, covered by a slick UV coating and stamped with gold foil printing. Because of the dark borders, these cards are condition sensitive. The full-color card backs include a player head shot accompanied by written text summarizing the player's career. The cards are numbered on the back in alphabetical order by team. A low production run of rack packs has contributed largely to the popularity of this set.

		MINT	NRMT	EXC
	COMPLETE SET (27)	300.00	135.00	38.00
	COMMON CARD (1-27)	2.50	1.10	.30
☐ 1	Dominique Wilkins	5.00	2.20	.60
☐ 2	Reggie Lewis	5.00	2.20	.60
☐ 3	Larry Johnson	15.00	6.75	1.85
☐ 4	Michael Jordan	150.00	70.00	19.00
☐ 5	Mark Price	2.50	1.10	.30
☐ 6	Terry Davis	2.50	1.10	.30
☐ 7	Dikembe Mutombo	8.00	3.60	1.00
☐ 8	Isiah Thomas	8.00	3.60	1.00
☐ 9	Chris Mullin	5.00	2.20	.60
☐ 10	Hakeem Olajuwon	30.00	13.50	3.70
☐ 11	Reggie Miller	15.00	6.75	1.85
☐ 12	Danny Manning	5.00	2.20	.60
☐ 13	James Worthy	5.00	2.20	.60
☐ 14	Glen Rice	8.00	3.60	1.00
☐ 15	Alvin Robertson	2.50	1.10	.30
☐ 16	Tony Campbell	2.50	1.10	.30
☐ 17	Derrick Coleman	2.50	1.10	.30
☐ 18	Patrick Ewing	12.00	5.50	1.50
☐ 19	Scott Skiles	2.50	1.10	.30
☐ 20	Hersey Hawkins	2.50	1.10	.30
☐ 21	Kevin Johnson	5.00	2.20	.60
☐ 22	Clyde Drexler	15.00	6.75	1.85
☐ 23	Mitch Richmond	10.00	4.50	1.25
☐ 24	David Robinson	25.00	11.00	3.10
☐ 25	Ricky Pierce	2.50	1.10	.30
☐ 26	Karl Malone	12.00	5.50	1.50
☐ 27	Pervis Ellison	2.50	1.10	.30

1992-93 Fleer Total D

The 1992-93 Fleer Total D cards were randomly inserted into second series 32-card cello packs. According to Fleer's advertising materials, the odds of pulling a Total D card were approximately one per five packs. These 15 standard size cards feature some of the NBA's top defensive players. Card fronts feature colorized players against a black border, covered with a slick UV coating and gold stamped lettering. Because of these black borders, the cards are condition sensitive. The full-color card backs feature small player head shots accompanied by text describing the player's defensive abilities.

		MINT	NRMT	EXC
	COMPLETE SET (15)	140.00	65.00	17.50
	COMMON CARD (1-15)	1.50	.70	.19
☐ 1	David Robinson	12.00	5.50	1.50
☐ 2	Dennis Rodman	25.00	11.00	3.10
☐ 3	Scottie Pippen	20.00	9.00	2.50
☐ 4	Joe Dumars	3.00	1.35	.35
☐ 5	Michael Jordan	80.00	36.00	10.00
☐ 6	John Stockton	6.00	2.70	.75
☐ 7	Patrick Ewing	6.00	2.70	.75
☐ 8	Micheal Williams	1.50	.70	.19
☐ 9	Larry Nance	1.50	.70	.19
☐ 10	Buck Williams	1.50	.70	.19
☐ 11	Alvin Robertson	1.50	.70	.19
☐ 12	Dikembe Mutombo	4.00	1.80	.50
☐ 13	Mookie Blaylock	3.00	1.35	.35
☐ 14	Hakeem Olajuwon	15.00	6.75	1.85
☐ 15	Rony Seikaly	1.50	.70	.19

1993-94 Fleer

The 1993-94 Fleer basketball card set contains 400 standard-size cards. The set was issued in two series consisting of 240 and 160 cards. Cards were primarily distributed in 15-card wax packs (1.29 suggested retail) and 21-card cello packs (1.99). Unlike the first series packs, all second series packs contained an insert card. There are 36 packs per wax box. The fronts are UV-coated and feature color action player photos and are enclosed by white

borders. The player's name appears in the lower left and is superimposed over a colorful florescent background. The backs feature full-color printing and bold graphics combining the player's picture, name, and complete statistics. With the exception of card numbers 131, 174, and 216, the cards are numbered and checklisted below alphabetically in team order. Subsets are NBA League Leaders (221-228), NBA Award Winners (229-232), Pro-Visions (223-237), and checklists (238-240). Players traded since the first series are pictured with their new team in a 160-card second series (241-400) offering. Rookie Cards of note include Vin Baker, Anfernee Hardaway, Jamal Mashburn, Nick Van Exel and Chris Webber.

	MINT	NRMT	EXC
COMPLETE SET (400)	20.00	9.00	2.50
COMPLETE SERIES 1 (240)	10.00	4.50	1.25
COMPLETE SERIES 2 (160)	10.00	4.50	1.25
COMMON CARD (1-400)	.05	.02	.01

☐	1 Stacey Augmon	.10	.05	.01
☐	2 Mookie Blaylock	.10	.05	.01
☐	3 Duane Ferrell	.05	.02	.01
☐	4 Paul Graham	.05	.02	.01
☐	5 Adam Keefe	.05	.02	.01
☐	6 Jon Koncak	.05	.02	.01
☐	7 Dominique Wilkins	.10	.05	.01
☐	8 Kevin Willis	.05	.02	.01
☐	9 Alaa Abdelnaby	.05	.02	.01
☐	10 Dee Brown	.05	.02	.01
☐	11 Sherman Douglas	.05	.02	.01
☐	12 Rick Fox	.05	.02	.01
☐	13 Kevin Gamble	.05	.02	.01
☐	14 Reggie Lewis	.10	.05	.01
☐	15 Xavier McDaniel	.05	.02	.01
☐	16 Robert Parish	.10	.05	.01
☐	17 Muggsy Bogues	.10	.05	.01
☐	18 Dell Curry	.05	.02	.01
☐	19 Kenny Gattison	.05	.02	.01
☐	20 Kendall Gill	.05	.02	.01
☐	21 Larry Johnson	.30	.14	.04
☐	22 Alonzo Mourning	.40	.18	.05
☐	23 Johnny Newman	.05	.02	.01
☐	24 David Wingate	.05	.02	.01
☐	25 B.J. Armstrong	.05	.02	.01
☐	26 Bill Cartwright	.05	.02	.01
☐	27 Horace Grant	.10	.05	.01
☐	28 Michael Jordan	3.00	1.35	.35
☐	29 Stacey King	.05	.02	.01
☐	30 John Paxson	.10	.05	.01
☐	31 Will Perdue	.05	.02	.01
☐	32 Scottie Pippen	.75	.35	.09
☐	33 Scott Williams	.05	.02	.01
☐	34 Terrell Brandon	.10	.05	.01
☐	35 Brad Daugherty	.05	.02	.01
☐	36 Craig Ehlo	.05	.02	.01
☐	37 Danny Ferry	.05	.02	.01
☐	38 Larry Nance	.05	.02	.01
☐	39 Mark Price	.05	.02	.01
☐	40 Mike Sanders	.05	.02	.01
☐	41 Gerald Wilkins	.05	.02	.01
☐	42 John(Hot Rod) Williams	.05	.02	.01
☐	43 Terry Davis	.05	.02	.01
☐	44 Derek Harper	.10	.05	.01
☐	45 Mike Iuzzolino	.05	.02	.01
☐	46 Jim Jackson	.30	.14	.04
☐	47 Sean Rooks	.05	.02	.01
☐	48 Doug Smith	.05	.02	.01
☐	49 Randy White	.05	.02	.01
☐	50 Mahmoud Abdul-Rauf	.10	.05	.01
☐	51 LaPhonso Ellis	.05	.02	.01
☐	52 Marcus Liberty	.05	.02	.01
☐	53 Mark Macon	.05	.02	.01
☐	54 Dikembe Mutombo	.10	.05	.01
☐	55 Robert Pack	.05	.02	.01
☐	56 Bryant Stith	.05	.02	.01
☐	57 Reggie Williams	.05	.02	.01
☐	58 Mark Aguirre	.10	.05	.01
☐	59 Joe Dumars	.10	.05	.01
☐	60 Bill Laimbeer	.10	.05	.01
☐	61 Terry Mills	.05	.02	.01
☐	62 Olden Polynice	.05	.02	.01
☐	63 Alvin Robertson	.05	.02	.01
☐	64 Dennis Rodman	1.00	.45	.12
☐	65 Isiah Thomas	.15	.07	.02
☐	66 Victor Alexander	.05	.02	.01
☐	67 Tim Hardaway	.10	.05	.01
☐	68 Tyrone Hill	.05	.02	.01
☐	69 Byron Houston	.05	.02	.01
☐	70 Sarunas Marciulionis	.05	.02	.01
☐	71 Chris Mullin	.10	.05	.01
☐	72 Billy Owens	.05	.02	.01
☐	73 Latrell Sprewell	.20	.09	.03
☐	74 Scott Brooks	.05	.02	.01
☐	75 Matt Bullard	.05	.02	.01
☐	76 Carl Herrera	.05	.02	.01
☐	77 Robert Horry	.10	.05	.01
☐	78 Vernon Maxwell	.05	.02	.01
☐	79 Hakeem Olajuwon	.60	.25	.07
☐	80 Kenny Smith	.05	.02	.01
☐	81 Otis Thorpe	.10	.05	.01
☐	82 Dale Davis	.05	.02	.01
☐	83 Vern Fleming	.05	.02	.01
☐	84 George McCloud	.05	.02	.01
☐	85 Reggie Miller	.30	.14	.04
☐	86 Sam Mitchell	.05	.02	.01
☐	87 Pooh Richardson	.05	.02	.01
☐	88 Detlef Schrempf	.10	.05	.01
☐	89 Rik Smits	.10	.05	.01
☐	90 Gary Grant	.05	.02	.01
☐	91 Ron Harper	.10	.05	.01
☐	92 Mark Jackson	.05	.02	.01
☐	93 Danny Manning	.10	.05	.01
☐	94 Ken Norman	.05	.02	.01
☐	95 Stanley Roberts	.05	.02	.01
☐	96 Loy Vaught	.10	.05	.01
☐	97 John Williams	.05	.02	.01
☐	98 Elden Campbell	.10	.05	.01
☐	99 Doug Christie	.05	.02	.01
☐	100 Duane Cooper	.05	.02	.01
☐	101 Vlade Divac	.10	.05	.01
☐	102 A.C. Green	.10	.05	.01
☐	103 Anthony Peeler	.05	.02	.01

☐ 104	Sedale Threatt	.05	.02	.01
☐ 105	James Worthy	.10	.05	.01
☐ 106	Bimbo Coles	.05	.02	.01
☐ 107	Grant Long	.05	.02	.01
☐ 108	Harold Miner	.05	.02	.01
☐ 109	Glen Rice	.10	.05	.01
☐ 110	John Salley	.05	.02	.01
☐ 111	Rony Seikaly	.05	.02	.01
☐ 112	Brian Shaw	.05	.02	.01
☐ 113	Steve Smith	.10	.05	.01
☐ 114	Anthony Avent	.05	.02	.01
☐ 115	Jon Barry	.05	.02	.01
☐ 116	Frank Brickowski	.05	.02	.01
☐ 117	Todd Day	.05	.02	.01
☐ 118	Blue Edwards	.05	.02	.01
☐ 119	Brad Lohaus	.05	.02	.01
☐ 120	Lee Mayberry	.05	.02	.01
☐ 121	Eric Murdock	.05	.02	.01
☐ 122	Thurl Bailey	.05	.02	.01
☐ 123	Christian Laettner	.10	.05	.01
☐ 124	Luc Longley	.05	.02	.01
☐ 125	Chuck Person	.05	.02	.01
☐ 126	Felton Spencer	.05	.02	.01
☐ 127	Doug West	.05	.02	.01
☐ 128	Micheal Williams	.05	.02	.01
☐ 129	Rafael Addison	.05	.02	.01
☐ 130	Kenny Anderson	.10	.05	.01
☐ 131	Sam Bowie	.05	.02	.01
☐ 132	Chucky Brown	.05	.02	.01
☐ 133	Derrick Coleman	.05	.02	.01
☐ 134	Chris Dudley	.05	.02	.01
☐ 135	Chris Morris	.05	.02	.01
☐ 136	Rumeal Robinson	.05	.02	.01
☐ 137	Greg Anthony	.05	.02	.01
☐ 138	Rolando Blackman	.05	.02	.01
☐ 139	Tony Campbell	.05	.02	.01
☐ 140	Hubert Davis	.05	.02	.01
☐ 141	Patrick Ewing	.25	.11	.03
☐ 142	Anthony Mason	.10	.05	.01
☐ 143	Charles Oakley	.10	.05	.01
☐ 144	Doc Rivers	.05	.02	.01
☐ 145	Charles Smith	.05	.02	.01
☐ 146	John Starks	.10	.05	.01
☐ 147	Nick Anderson	.10	.05	.01
☐ 148	Anthony Bowie	.05	.02	.01
☐ 149	Shaquille O'Neal	1.50	.70	.19
☐ 150	Donald Royal	.05	.02	.01
☐ 151	Dennis Scott	.10	.05	.01
☐ 152	Scott Skiles	.05	.02	.01
☐ 153	Tom Tolbert	.05	.02	.01
☐ 154	Jeff Turner	.05	.02	.01
☐ 155	Ron Anderson	.05	.02	.01
☐ 156	Johnny Dawkins	.05	.02	.01
☐ 157	Hersey Hawkins	.10	.05	.01
☐ 158	Jeff Hornacek	.10	.05	.01
☐ 159	Andrew Lang	.05	.02	.01
☐ 160	Tim Perry	.05	.02	.01
☐ 161	Clarence Weatherspoon	.10	.05	.01
☐ 162	Danny Ainge	.10	.05	.01
☐ 163	Charles Barkley	.40	.18	.05
☐ 164	Cedric Ceballos	.10	.05	.01
☐ 165	Tom Chambers	.05	.02	.01
☐ 166	Richard Dumas	.05	.02	.01
☐ 167	Kevin Johnson	.10	.05	.01
☐ 168	Negele Knight	.05	.02	.01
☐ 169	Dan Majerle	.10	.05	.01
☐ 170	Oliver Miller	.05	.02	.01
☐ 171	Mark West	.05	.02	.01
☐ 172	Mark Bryant	.05	.02	.01
☐ 173	Clyde Drexler	.30	.14	.04
☐ 174	Kevin Duckworth	.05	.02	.01
☐ 175	Mario Elie	.05	.02	.01
☐ 176	Jerome Kersey	.05	.02	.01
☐ 177	Terry Porter	.05	.02	.01
☐ 178	Clifford Robinson	.10	.05	.01
☐ 179	Rod Strickland	.05	.02	.01
☐ 180	Buck Williams	.10	.05	.01
☐ 181	Anthony Bonner	.05	.02	.01
☐ 182	Duane Causwell	.05	.02	.01
☐ 183	Mitch Richmond	.20	.09	.03
☐ 184	Lionel Simmons	.05	.02	.01
☐ 185	Wayman Tisdale	.05	.02	.01
☐ 186	Spud Webb	.10	.05	.01
☐ 187	Walt Williams	.10	.05	.01
☐ 188	Antoine Carr	.05	.02	.01
☐ 189	Terry Cummings	.05	.02	.01
☐ 190	Lloyd Daniels	.05	.02	.01
☐ 191	Vinny Del Negro	.05	.02	.01
☐ 192	Sean Elliott	.10	.05	.01
☐ 193	Dale Ellis	.05	.02	.01
☐ 194	Avery Johnson	.10	.05	.01
☐ 195	J.R. Reid	.05	.02	.01
☐ 196	David Robinson	.50	.23	.06
☐ 197	Michael Cage	.05	.02	.01
☐ 198	Eddie Johnson	.05	.02	.01
☐ 199	Shawn Kemp	.75	.35	.09
☐ 200	Derrick McKey	.05	.02	.01
☐ 201	Nate McMillan	.05	.02	.01
☐ 202	Gary Payton	.40	.18	.05
☐ 203	Sam Perkins	.05	.02	.01
☐ 204	Ricky Pierce	.05	.02	.01
☐ 205	David Benoit	.05	.02	.01
☐ 206	Tyrone Corbin	.05	.02	.01
☐ 207	Mark Eaton	.05	.02	.01
☐ 208	Jay Humphries	.05	.02	.01
☐ 209	Larry Krystkowiak	.05	.02	.01
☐ 210	Jeff Malone	.05	.02	.01
☐ 211	Karl Malone	.25	.11	.03
☐ 212	John Stockton	.25	.11	.03
☐ 213	Michael Adams	.05	.02	.01
☐ 214	Rex Chapman	.05	.02	.01
☐ 215	Pervis Ellison	.05	.02	.01
☐ 216	Harvey Grant	.05	.02	.01
☐ 217	Tom Gugliotta	.10	.05	.01
☐ 218	Buck Johnson	.05	.02	.01
☐ 219	LaBradford Smith	.05	.02	.01
☐ 220	Larry Stewart	.05	.02	.01
☐ 221	B.J. Armstrong LL 3-Pt Field Goal Percentage Leader	.05	.02	.01
☐ 222	Cedric Ceballos LL FG Percentage Leader	.05	.02	.01
☐ 223	Larry Johnson LL Minutes Played Leader	.10	.05	.01
☐ 224	Michael Jordan LL Scoring/Steals Leader	1.50	.70	.19
☐ 225	Hakeem Olajuwon LL Shot Block Leader	.30	.14	.04
☐ 226	Mark Price LL FT Percentage Leader	.05	.02	.01
☐ 227	Dennis Rodman LL Rebounding Leader	.50	.23	.06
☐ 228	John Stockton LL Assists Leader	.10	.05	.01
☐ 229	Charles Barkley AW Most Valuable Player	.20	.09	.03
☐ 230	Hakeem Olajuwon AW Defensive POY	.30	.14	.04
☐ 231	Shaquille O'Neal AW Rookie of the Year	.75	.35	.09
☐ 232	Clifford Robinson AW Sixth Man Award	.05	.02	.01

☐	233 Shawn Kemp PV	.40	.18	.05
☐	234 Alonzo Mourning PV	.20	.09	.03
☐	235 Hakeem Olajuwon PV	.30	.14	.04
☐	236 John Stockton PV	.10	.05	.01
☐	237 Dominique Wilkins PV	.10	.05	.01
☐	238 Checklist 1-85	.05	.02	.01
☐	239 Checklist 86-165	.05	.02	.01
☐	240 Checklist 166-240 UER	.05	.02	.01
	(237 listed as Cliff Robinson; should be Dominique Wilkins)			
☐	241 Doug Edwards	.05	.02	.01
☐	242 Craig Ehlo	.05	.02	.01
☐	243 Andrew Lang	.05	.02	.01
☐	244 Ennis Whatley	.05	.02	.01
☐	245 Chris Corchiani	.05	.02	.01
☐	246 Acie Earl	.05	.02	.01
☐	247 Jimmy Oliver	.05	.02	.01
☐	248 Ed Pinckney	.05	.02	.01
☐	249 Dino Radja	.30	.14	.04
☐	250 Matt Wenstrom	.05	.02	.01
☐	251 Tony Bennett	.05	.02	.01
☐	252 Scott Burrell	.10	.05	.01
☐	253 LeRon Ellis	.05	.02	.01
☐	254 Hersey Hawkins	.10	.05	.01
☐	255 Eddie Johnson	.05	.02	.01
☐	256 Corie Blount	.05	.02	.01
☐	257 Jo Jo English	.05	.02	.01
☐	258 Dave Johnson	.05	.02	.01
☐	259 Steve Kerr	.10	.05	.01
☐	260 Toni Kukoc	.60	.25	.07
☐	261 Pete Myers	.05	.02	.01
☐	262 Bill Wennington	.05	.02	.01
☐	263 John Battle	.05	.02	.01
☐	264 Tyrone Hill	.05	.02	.01
☐	265 Gerald Madkins	.05	.02	.01
☐	266 Chris Mills	.40	.18	.05
☐	267 Bobby Phills	.05	.02	.01
☐	268 Greg Dreiling	.05	.02	.01
☐	269 Lucious Harris	.10	.05	.01
☐	270 Donald Hodge	.05	.02	.01
☐	271 Popeye Jones	.10	.05	.01
☐	272 Tim Legler	.05	.02	.01
☐	273 Fat Lever	.05	.02	.01
☐	274 Jamal Mashburn	.60	.25	.07
☐	275 Darren Morningstar	.05	.02	.01
☐	276 Tom Hammonds	.05	.02	.01
☐	277 Darnell Mee	.05	.02	.01
☐	278 Rodney Rogers	.10	.05	.01
☐	279 Brian Williams	.05	.02	.01
☐	280 Greg Anderson	.05	.02	.01
☐	281 Sean Elliott	.10	.05	.01
☐	282 Alan Houston	.50	.23	.06
☐	283 Lindsey Hunter	.10	.05	.01
☐	284 Marcus Liberty	.05	.02	.01
☐	285 Mark Macon	.05	.02	.01
☐	286 David Wood	.05	.02	.01
☐	287 Jud Buechler	.05	.02	.01
☐	288 Chris Gatling	.05	.02	.01
☐	289 Josh Grant	.05	.02	.01
☐	290 Jeff Grayer	.05	.02	.01
☐	291 Avery Johnson	.10	.05	.01
☐	292 Chris Webber	1.00	.45	.12
☐	293 Sam Cassell	.40	.18	.05
☐	294 Mario Elie	.05	.02	.01
☐	295 Richard Petruska	.05	.02	.01
☐	296 Eric Riley	.05	.02	.01
☐	297 Antonio Davis	.05	.02	.01
☐	298 Scott Haskin	.05	.02	.01
☐	299 Derrick McKey	.05	.02	.01
☐	300 Byron Scott	.10	.05	.01
☐	301 Malik Sealy	.05	.02	.01

☐	302 LaSalle Thompson	.05	.02	.01
☐	303 Kenny Williams	.05	.02	.01
☐	304 Haywoode Workman	.05	.02	.01
☐	305 Mark Aguirre	.10	.05	.01
☐	306 Terry Dehere	.10	.05	.01
☐	307 Bob Martin	.05	.02	.01
☐	308 Elmore Spencer	.05	.02	.01
☐	309 Tom Tolbert	.05	.02	.01
☐	310 Randy Woods	.05	.02	.01
☐	311 Sam Bowie	.05	.02	.01
☐	312 James Edwards	.05	.02	.01
☐	313 Antonio Harvey	.05	.02	.01
☐	314 George Lynch	.05	.02	.01
☐	315 Tony Smith	.05	.02	.01
☐	316 Nick Van Exel	.75	.35	.09
☐	317 Manute Bol	.05	.02	.01
☐	318 Willie Burton	.05	.02	.01
☐	319 Matt Geiger	.05	.02	.01
☐	320 Alec Kessler	.05	.02	.01
☐	321 Vin Baker	1.00	.45	.12
☐	322 Ken Norman	.05	.02	.01
☐	323 Dan Schayes	.05	.02	.01
☐	324 Derek Strong	.05	.02	.01
☐	325 Mike Brown	.05	.02	.01
☐	326 Brian Davis	.05	.02	.01
☐	327 Tellis Frank	.05	.02	.01
☐	328 Marlon Maxey	.05	.02	.01
☐	329 Isaiah Rider	.30	.14	.04
☐	330 Chris Smith	.05	.02	.01
☐	331 Benoit Benjamin	.05	.02	.01
☐	332 P.J. Brown	.10	.05	.01
☐	333 Kevin Edwards	.05	.02	.01
☐	334 Armon Gilliam	.05	.02	.01
☐	335 Rick Mahorn	.05	.02	.01
☐	336 Dwayne Schintzius	.05	.02	.01
☐	337 Rex Walters	.05	.02	.01
☐	338 David Wesley	.05	.02	.01
☐	339 Jayson Williams	.05	.02	.01
☐	340 Anthony Bonner	.05	.02	.01
☐	341 Herb Williams	.05	.02	.01
☐	342 Litterial Green	.05	.02	.01
☐	343 Anfernee Hardaway	5.00	2.20	.60
☐	344 Greg Kite	.05	.02	.01
☐	345 Larry Krystkowiak	.05	.02	.01
☐	346 Todd Lichti	.05	.02	.01
☐	347 Keith Tower	.05	.02	.01
☐	348 Dana Barros	.05	.02	.01
☐	349 Shawn Bradley	.30	.14	.04
☐	350 Michael Curry	.05	.02	.01
☐	351 Greg Graham	.05	.02	.01
☐	352 Warren Kidd	.05	.02	.01
☐	353 Moses Malone	.15	.07	.02
☐	354 Orlando Woolridge	.05	.02	.01
☐	355 Duane Cooper	.05	.02	.01
☐	356 Joe Courtney	.05	.02	.01
☐	357 A.C. Green	.10	.05	.01
☐	358 Frank Johnson	.05	.02	.01
☐	359 Joe Kleine	.05	.02	.01
☐	360 Malcolm Mackey	.05	.02	.01
☐	361 Jerrod Mustaf	.05	.02	.01
☐	362 Chris Dudley	.05	.02	.01
☐	363 Harvey Grant	.05	.02	.01
☐	364 Tracy Murray	.05	.02	.01
☐	365 James Robinson	.10	.05	.01
☐	366 Reggie Smith	.05	.02	.01
☐	367 Kevin Thompson	.05	.02	.01
☐	368 Randy Breuer	.05	.02	.01
☐	369 Randy Brown	.05	.02	.01
☐	370 Evers Burns	.05	.02	.01
☐	371 Pete Chilcutt	.05	.02	.01
☐	372 Bobby Hurley	.10	.05	.01

☐	373	Jim Les	.05	.02	.01
☐	374	Mike Peplowski	.05	.02	.01
☐	375	Willie Anderson	.05	.02	.01
☐	376	Sleepy Floyd	.05	.02	.01
☐	377	Negele Knight	.05	.02	.01
☐	378	Dennis Rodman	1.00	.45	.12
☐	379	Chris Whitney	.05	.02	.01
☐	380	Vincent Askew	.05	.02	.01
☐	381	Kendall Gill	.05	.02	.01
☐	382	Ervin Johnson	.10	.05	.01
☐	383	Chris King	.05	.02	.01
☐	384	Rich King	.05	.02	.01
☐	385	Steve Scheffler	.05	.02	.01
☐	386	Detlef Schrempf	.10	.05	.01
☐	387	Tom Chambers	.05	.02	.01
☐	388	John Crotty	.05	.02	.01
☐	389	Bryon Russell	.05	.02	.01
☐	390	Felton Spencer	.05	.02	.01
☐	391	Luther Wright	.05	.02	.01
☐	392	Mitchell Butler	.05	.02	.01
☐	393	Calbert Cheaney	.25	.11	.03
☐	394	Kevin Duckworth	.05	.02	.01
☐	395	Don MacLean	.05	.02	.01
☐	396	Gheorghe Muresan	.40	.18	.05
☐	397	Doug Overton	.05	.02	.01
☐	398	Brent Price	.05	.02	.01
☐	399	Checklist	.05	.02	.01
☐	400	Checklist	.05	.02	.01

		MINT	NRMT	EXC
	COMPLETE SET (24)	90.00	40.00	11.00
	COMMON CARD (1-24)	1.00	.45	.12
☐ 1	Brad Daugherty	1.00	.45	.12
☐ 2	Joe Dumars	1.50	.70	.19
☐ 3	Patrick Ewing	3.00	1.35	.35
☐ 4	Larry Johnson	4.00	1.80	.50
☐ 5	Michael Jordan	40.00	18.00	5.00
☐ 6	Larry Nance	1.00	.45	.12
☐ 7	Shaquille O'Neal	20.00	9.00	2.50
☐ 8	Scottie Pippen UER	10.00	4.50	1.25
	(Name spelled Pipen on front)			
☐ 9	Mark Price	1.00	.45	.12
☐ 10	Detlef Schrempf	1.50	.70	.19
☐ 11	Isiah Thomas	1.50	.70	.19
☐ 12	Dominique Wilkins	1.50	.70	.19
☐ 13	Charles Barkley	5.00	2.20	.60
☐ 14	Clyde Drexler	4.00	1.80	.50
☐ 15	Sean Elliott	1.50	.70	.19
☐ 16	Tim Hardaway	1.50	.70	.19
☐ 17	Shawn Kemp	10.00	4.50	1.25
☐ 18	Dan Majerle	1.50	.70	.19
☐ 19	Karl Malone	3.00	1.35	.35
☐ 20	Danny Manning	1.50	.70	.19
☐ 21	Hakeem Olajuwon	8.00	3.60	1.00
☐ 22	Terry Porter	1.00	.45	.12
☐ 23	David Robinson	6.00	2.70	.75
☐ 24	John Stockton	3.00	1.35	.35

1993-94 Fleer All-Stars

Randomly inserted in 1993-94 Fleer first
series 15-card packs, this 24-card standard-size set features 12 players from the
Eastern Conference (1-12) and the
Western Conference (13-24) that participated in the 1992-93 All-Star Game in Salt
Lake City. According to wrapper information, All-Stars are randomly inserted into
one of every 10 packs. The fronts are UV-
coated and feature color action player photos enclosed by purple borders. The NBA
All-Star logo appears in the lower left or
right corner. The player's name is stamped
in gold foil and appears at the bottom. The
backs are also UV-coated and feature a
full-color shot of the player along with a statistical performance sketch from the previous year. Each division's All-Stars are in
alphabetical order.

1993-94 Fleer Clyde Drexler

Randomly inserted in all 1993-94 Fleer first
series packs at an approximate rate of one
in six, this 12-card standard-size set captures the greatest moments in Drexler's
career. Drexler autographed more than
2,000 of his cards. These cards are
embossed with Fleer logos for authenticity.
Odds of getting a signed card were approximately 1 in 7,000 packs. The collector
could acquire three additional cards and an
issue of NBA Inside Stuff magazine through
a mail-in for ten wrappers plus 1.50. The
offer expired June 10, 1994. An additional
card (No. 16) was offered free to collectors
who subscribed to NBA Inside Stuff magazine. Since 12 cards were issued through
packs, a 12-card set is considered complete. All 16 cards have the same basic
design with the front featuring a unique two

photo design, one color, and the other red-screened, serving as the background. The player's name as well as the Fleer logo appear at the top of the card in gold foil. The bottom of the card carries the words "Career Highlights," also stamped in gold foil. The back of the cards carry information about Drexler, with another red-screened photo again as the background. The cards are numbered on the back. The first twelve cards are numbered "X of 12" and the last four cards are simply numbered 13, 14, 15 and 16.

	MINT	NRMT	EXC
COMPLETE SET (12)	5.00	2.20	.60
COMMON DREXLER (1-12)	.50	.23	.06
COMMON SEND-OFF (13-15) ..	2.00	.90	.25
☐ 1 Clyde Drexler .... (Ball in right hand, pointing with left)	.50	.23	.06
☐ 2 Clyde Drexler .... (Holding ball aloft with right hand)	.50	.23	.06
☐ 3 Clyde Drexler .... (Wearing red shoes, left-hand dribble)	.50	.23	.06
☐ 4 Clyde Drexler .... (Wearing red shoes, right-hand dribble)	.50	.23	.06
☐ 5 Clyde Drexler .... (Making ready to slam dunk with both hands)	.50	.23	.06
☐ 6 Clyde Drexler .... (Wearing white shoes, right-hand dribble)	.50	.23	.06
☐ 7 Clyde Drexler .... (Right-hand dribble; half of ball visible)	.50	.23	.06
☐ 8 Clyde Drexler .... (Right hand under ball, left hand alongside)	.50	.23	.06
☐ 9 Clyde Drexler .... (Receiving or passing ball)	.50	.23	.06
☐ 10 Clyde Drexler .... (Both hands above head; right hand near ball)	.50	.23	.06
☐ 11 Clyde Drexler .... (Left foot off floor; right-hand dribble)	.50	.23	.06
☐ 12 Clyde Drexler .... (In NBA All-Star uniform)	.50	.23	.06
☐ 13 Clyde Drexler .... (Right-hand dribble, looking over defense)	2.00	.90	.25
☐ 14 Clyde Drexler .... (Dribbling down court with right hand)	2.00	.90	.25
☐ 15 Clyde Drexler .... (Shooting, with Pippen defending)	2.00	.90	.25
☐ 16 Clyde Drexler .... (Bringing ball upcourt black uniform)	5.00	2.20	.60
☐ AU Clyde Drexler AU ..... (Certified autograph)	125.00	55.00	15.50

1993-94 Fleer First Year Phenoms

These 10 standard-size cards feature top rookies from the 1993-94 season. Cards were randomly inserted in 1993-94 Fleer second-series 15-card wax and 21-card jumbo packs. The insertion rate was approximately one in four wax packs and one in three cello packs. The yellow-bordered fronts feature color player action cutouts superposed upon purple, yellow, and black florescent basketball court designs. The player's name appears vertically in gold foil near one corner, and the gold-foil set logo appears at the bottom left. The horizontal back sports a similar florescent design. A color player close-up cutout appears on one side; his name, team, and career highlights appear on the other. The cards are numbered on the back as "X of 10" and sequenced in alphabetical order.

	MINT	NRMT	EXC
COMPLETE SET (10)	8.00	3.60	1.00
COMMON CARD (1-10)	.25	.11	.03
☐ 1 Shawn Bradley	.30	.14	.04
☐ 2 Anfernee Hardaway	6.00	2.70	.75
☐ 3 Lindsey Hunter	.25	.11	.03
☐ 4 Bobby Hurley	.25	.11	.03
☐ 5 Toni Kukoc	.75	.35	.09
☐ 6 Jamal Mashburn	.75	.35	.09
☐ 7 Dino Radja	.40	.18	.05
☐ 8 Isaiah Rider	.40	.18	.05
☐ 9 Nick Van Exel	1.00	.45	.12
☐ 10 Chris Webber	1.25	.55	.16

1993-94 Fleer Internationals

This 12-card insert standard-size set features NBA players born outside the United States. The cards were randomly inserted in first series 15-card packs at a rate of one in 10. The fronts are UV-coated and feature a color player photo superimposed over a map of his country of origin. The player's name appears at the top of the

card and is gold foil stamped. The backs are also UV-coated and feature a color shot of the player along with a brief biographical sketch. The set is sequenced in alphabetical order.

	MINT	NRMT	EXC
COMPLETE SET (12)	4.00	1.80	.50
COMMON CARD (1-12)	.25	.11	.03
☐ 1 Alaa Abdelnaby	.25	.11	.03
☐ 2 Vlade Divac	.50	.23	.06
☐ 3 Patrick Ewing	1.25	.55	.16
☐ 4 Carl Herrera	.25	.11	.03
☐ 5 Luc Longley	.25	.11	.03
☐ 6 Sarunas Marciulionis	.25	.11	.03
☐ 7 Dikembe Mutombo	.75	.35	.09
☐ 8 Rumeal Robinson	.25	.11	.03
☐ 9 Detlef Schrempf	.50	.23	.06
☐ 10 Rony Seikaly	.25	.11	.03
☐ 11 Rik Smits	.50	.23	.06
☐ 12 Dominique Wilkins	.50	.23	.06

1993-94 Fleer
Living Legends

These six standard-size cards honoring veteran superstars were randomly inserted in 1993-94 Fleer second series 15-card (ratio of one in 37) and 21-card (one in 24) packs. The horizontal fronts feature color player action cutouts superimposed upon a borderless metallic motion-streaked background. The player's name and the set's logo appear at the bottom in gold foil. The horizontal back carries a color player close-up cutout on one side; his name, team, and career highlights appear on the other. The cards are numbered on the back as "X of 6" and are sequenced in alphabetical order

	MINT	NRMT	EXC
COMPLETE SET (6)	30.00	13.50	3.70
COMMON CARD (1-6)	.75	.35	.09
☐ 1 Charles Barkley	2.50	1.10	.30
☐ 2 Larry Bird	6.00	2.70	.75
☐ 3 Patrick Ewing	1.50	.70	.19
☐ 4 Michael Jordan	20.00	9.00	2.50
☐ 5 Hakeem Olajuwon	4.00	1.80	.50
☐ 6 Dominique Wilkins	.75	.35	.09

1993-94 Fleer
Lottery Exchange

This 11-card standard-size set features the top players from the 1993 NBA Draft. Card fronts resemble that of the basic Fleer issue with the exception of a notation of what number pick the player was. Backs have a photo and statistics. The set could be obtained in exchange for the Draft Exchange card that was randomly inserted (one in 180) in first series packs. The expiration date was April 1, 1994. The cards are numbered on the back in draft order.

	MINT	NRMT	EXC
COMPLETE SET (11)	20.00	9.00	2.50
COMMON CARD (1-11)	.50	.23	.06
☐ 1 Chris Webber	3.00	1.35	.35
☐ 2 Shawn Bradley	1.00	.45	.12
☐ 3 Anfernee Hardaway	15.00	6.75	1.85
☐ 4 Jamal Mashburn	2.00	.90	.25
☐ 5 Isaiah Rider	1.00	.45	.12
☐ 6 Calbert Cheaney	.75	.35	.09
☐ 7 Bobby Hurley	.50	.23	.06
☐ 8 Vin Baker	3.00	1.35	.35
☐ 9 Rodney Rogers	.50	.23	.06
☐ 10 Lindsey Hunter	.50	.23	.06
☐ 11 Allan Houston	1.50	.70	.19
☐ NNO Expired Exchange Card	.50	.23	.06

1993-94 Fleer
NBA Superstars

These 20 standard-size cards featuring NBA stars were randomly inserted in 1993-

94 Fleer second-series 15-card packs. The fronts feature color player action cutouts superimposed upon multiple color action shots on the right side and the player's name in team color-coded vertical block lettering on the left. The set's title appears vertically along the left edge in gold foil. The horizontal back carries a color player close-up cutout on one side; his name, team, and career highlights appear on the other. The cards are numbered on the back as "X of 20" and are sequenced in alphabetical order.

		MINT	NRMT	EXC
	COMPLETE SET (20)	20.00	9.00	2.50
	COMMON CARD (1-20)	.25	.11	.03
☐ 1	Mahmoud Abdul-Rauf	.40	.18	.05
☐ 2	Charles Barkley	1.25	.55	.16
☐ 3	Derrick Coleman	.25	.11	.03
☐ 4	Clyde Drexler	1.00	.45	.12
☐ 5	Joe Dumars	.40	.18	.05
☐ 6	Patrick Ewing	.75	.35	.09
☐ 7	Michael Jordan	10.00	4.50	1.25
☐ 8	Shawn Kemp	2.50	1.10	.30
☐ 9	Christian Laettner	.40	.18	.05
☐ 10	Karl Malone	.75	.35	.09
☐ 11	Danny Manning	.40	.18	.05
☐ 12	Reggie Miller	1.00	.45	.12
☐ 13	Alonzo Mourning	1.25	.55	.16
☐ 14	Chris Mullin	.40	.18	.05
☐ 15	Hakeem Olajuwon	2.00	.90	.25
☐ 16	Shaquille O'Neal	5.00	2.20	.60
☐ 17	Mark Price	.25	.11	.03
☐ 18	Mitch Richmond	.40	.18	.05
☐ 19	David Robinson	1.50	.70	.19
☐ 20	Dominique Wilkins	.40	.18	.05

1993-94 Fleer Rookie Sensations

Randomly inserted in 29-card series one jumbo packs, these 24 standard-size UV-coated cards feature top rookies from the 1992-93 season. Odds of finding a Rookie Sensations card are approximately one in every five packs. The cards feature color player action photos on the fronts within silver-colored borders. Each player photo is superimposed upon a card design that has a basketball "earth" at the card bottom radi-

ating "spotlight" beams that shade from yellow to magenta on a sky blue background. The player's name and the Rookie Sensations logo, both stamped in gold foil, appear in the lower left. Bordered in silver, the backs feature color close-ups of the players in the lower right or left. Blue "sky" and two intersecting yellow-to-magenta "spotlight" beams form the background. The player's name appears in silver-colored lettering at the top of the card above the player's NBA rookie-year highlights. The set is sequenced in alphabetical order.

		MINT	NRMT	EXC
	COMPLETE SET (24)	50.00	22.00	6.25
	COMMON CARD (1-24)	1.00	.45	.12
☐ 1	Anthony Avent	1.00	.45	.12
☐ 2	Doug Christie	1.00	.45	.12
☐ 3	Lloyd Daniels	1.00	.45	.12
☐ 4	Hubert Davis	1.50	.70	.19
☐ 5	Todd Day	1.00	.45	.12
☐ 6	Richard Dumas	1.00	.45	.12
☐ 7	LaPhonso Ellis	1.50	.70	.19
☐ 8	Tom Gugliotta	2.00	.90	.25
☐ 9	Robert Horry	2.50	1.10	.30
☐ 10	Byron Houston	1.00	.45	.12
☐ 11	Jim Jackson UER	5.00	2.20	.60
	(Text on back states he played in Big East; he played in Big Ten)			
☐ 12	Adam Keefe	1.00	.45	.12
☐ 13	Christian Laettner	2.00	.90	.25
☐ 14	Lee Mayberry	1.00	.45	.12
☐ 15	Oliver Miller	1.00	.45	.12
☐ 16	Harold Miner	1.00	.45	.12
☐ 17	Alonzo Mourning	6.00	2.70	.75
☐ 18	Shaquille O'Neal	25.00	11.00	3.10
☐ 19	Anthony Peeler	1.00	.45	.12
☐ 20	Sean Rooks	1.00	.45	.12
☐ 21	Latrell Sprewell	3.00	1.35	.35
☐ 22	Bryant Stith	1.00	.45	.12
☐ 23	Clarence Weatherspoon	1.50	.70	.19
☐ 24	Walt Williams	1.50	.70	.19

1993-94 Fleer Sharpshooters

These 10 standard-size cards were randomly inserted in 1993-94 Fleer second-series 15-card packs. The fronts feature color player action cutouts superposed

upon color-screened action shots. The player's name appears at the upper right in gold foil. The set's logo appears at the bottom left. The black horizontal back carries a color player close-up cutout on one side; his name, card title, and career highlights appear on the other. The cards are numbered on the back as "X of 10" and are sequenced in alphabetical order.

	MINT	NRMT	EXC
COMPLETE SET (10)	30.00	13.50	3.70
COMMON CARD (1-10)	1.00	.45	.12

		MINT	NRMT	EXC
☐ 1	Tom Gugliotta	1.50	.70	.19
☐ 2	Jim Jackson	2.50	1.10	.30
☐ 3	Michael Jordan	25.00	11.00	3.10
☐ 4	Dan Majerle	1.50	.70	.19
☐ 5	Mark Price	1.00	.45	.12
☐ 6	Glen Rice	1.50	.70	.19
☐ 7	Mitch Richmond	2.00	.90	.25
☐ 8	Latrell Sprewell	1.50	.70	.19
☐ 9	John Starks	1.00	.45	.12
☐ 10	Dominique Wilkins	1.50	.70	.19

background photo as the front and carries a color player cutout on one side, and his career highlights on the other. The cards are numbered on the back as "X of 30" and sequenced in alphabetical order.

		MINT	NRMT	EXC
COMPLETE SET (30)		50.00	22.00	6.25
COMMON CARD (1-30)		.75	.35	.09

		MINT	NRMT	EXC
☐ 1	Charles Barkley	4.00	1.80	.50
☐ 2	Shawn Bradley	2.00	.90	.25
☐ 3	Derrick Coleman	.75	.35	.09
☐ 4	Brad Daugherty	.75	.35	.09
☐ 5	Dale Davis	.75	.35	.09
☐ 6	Vlade Divac	1.25	.55	.16
☐ 7	Patrick Ewing	2.50	1.10	.30
☐ 8	Horace Grant	1.25	.55	.16
☐ 9	Tom Gugliotta	1.25	.55	.16
☐ 10	Larry Johnson	3.00	1.35	.35
☐ 11	Shawn Kemp	8.00	3.60	1.00
☐ 12	Christian Laettner	1.25	.55	.16
☐ 13	Karl Malone	2.50	1.10	.30
☐ 14	Danny Manning	1.25	.55	.16
☐ 15	Jamal Mashburn	4.00	1.80	.50
☐ 16	Oliver Miller	.75	.35	.09
☐ 17	Alonzo Mourning	4.00	1.80	.50
☐ 18	Dikembe Mutombo	1.50	.70	.19
☐ 19	Ken Norman	.75	.35	.09
☐ 20	Hakeem Olajuwon	6.00	2.70	.75
☐ 21	Shaquille O'Neal	15.00	6.75	1.85
☐ 22	Robert Parish	1.25	.55	.16
☐ 23	Olden Polynice	.75	.35	.09
☐ 24	Clifford Robinson	1.25	.55	.16
☐ 25	David Robinson	5.00	2.20	.60
☐ 26	Dennis Rodman	10.00	4.50	1.25
☐ 27	Rony Seikaly	.75	.35	.09
☐ 28	Wayman Tisdale	.75	.35	.09
☐ 29	Chris Webber	6.00	2.70	.75
☐ 30	Dominique Wilkins	1.25	.55	.16

1993-94 Fleer Towers Of Power

These 30 standard-size cards were randomly inserted in 1993-94 Fleer second series 21-card jumbo packs at an approximate rate of two in every three packs. The fronts feature color player action cutouts superposed upon borderless backgrounds of city skylines. The player's name appears in gold foil in a lower corner. The gold-foil set logo appears in an upper corner. The back has the same borderless skyline

1994-95 Fleer

The 390 cards comprising Fleer's '94-95 base-brand standard-size set were distributed in two separate series of 240 and 150 cards each. Cards were distributed in 15-card packs (SRP $1.29), 21-card magazine cello packs (SRP $1.99) and 23-card retail jumbo packs (SRP $2.27). The cards feature color player action shots on their white-bordered fronts. The player's name, team, and position appear in team-colored lettering set on an irregular team-colored foil patch at the lower left. The black-bordered back carries a color player action shot on the left side, with the player's name, biography, team logo, and statistics displayed on a team-colored background on the right. The cards are numbered on the back and grouped alphabetically within teams. Unlike previous years, there were no subset cards featured in this set. Each pack contained at least one insert card. One in every 72 packs (Hot Packs) contained only inserts. Rookie Cards of note in this set include Grant Hill, Juwan Howard, Eddie Jones, Jason Kidd and Glenn Robinson.

	MINT	NRMT	EXC
COMPLETE SET (390)	24.00	11.00	3.00
COMPLETE SERIES 1 (240)	12.00	5.50	1.50
COMPLETE SERIES 2 (150)	12.00	5.50	1.50
COMMON CARD (1-390)	.05	.02	.01

☐	1 Stacey Augmon	.10	.05	.01
☐	2 Mookie Blaylock	.10	.05	.01
☐	3 Craig Ehlo	.05	.02	.01
☐	4 Duane Ferrell	.05	.02	.01
☐	5 Adam Keefe	.05	.02	.01
☐	6 Jon Koncak	.05	.02	.01
☐	7 Andrew Lang	.05	.02	.01
☐	8 Danny Manning	.10	.05	.01
☐	9 Kevin Willis	.05	.02	.01
☐	10 Dee Brown	.05	.02	.01
☐	11 Sherman Douglas	.05	.02	.01
☐	12 Acie Earl	.05	.02	.01
☐	13 Rick Fox	.05	.02	.01
☐	14 Kevin Gamble	.05	.02	.01
☐	15 Xavier McDaniel	.05	.02	.01
☐	16 Robert Parish	.10	.05	.01
☐	17 Ed Pinckney	.05	.02	.01
☐	18 Dino Radja	.10	.05	.01
☐	19 Muggsy Bogues	.10	.05	.01
☐	20 Frank Brickowski	.05	.02	.01
☐	21 Scott Burrell	.05	.02	.01
☐	22 Dell Curry	.05	.02	.01
☐	23 Kenny Gattison	.05	.02	.01
☐	24 Hersey Hawkins	.05	.02	.01
☐	25 Eddie Johnson	.05	.02	.01
☐	26 Larry Johnson	.25	.11	.03
☐	27 Alonzo Mourning	.30	.14	.04
☐	28 David Wingate	.05	.02	.01
☐	29 B.J. Armstrong	.05	.02	.01
☐	30 Horace Grant	.10	.05	.01
☐	31 Steve Kerr	.05	.02	.01
☐	32 Toni Kukoc	.20	.09	.03
☐	33 Luc Longley	.05	.02	.01
☐	34 Pete Myers	.05	.02	.01
☐	35 Scottie Pippen	.75	.35	.09
☐	36 Bill Wennington	.05	.02	.01
☐	37 Scott Williams	.05	.02	.01
☐	38 Terrell Brandon	.10	.05	.01
☐	39 Brad Daugherty	.05	.02	.01
☐	40 Tyrone Hill	.05	.02	.01
☐	41 Chris Mills	.10	.05	.01
☐	42 Larry Nance	.05	.02	.01
☐	43 Bobby Phills	.05	.02	.01
☐	44 Mark Price	.05	.02	.01
☐	45 Gerald Wilkins	.05	.02	.01
☐	46 John Williams	.05	.02	.01
☐	47 Lucious Harris	.05	.02	.01
☐	48 Donald Hodge	.05	.02	.01
☐	49 Jim Jackson	.30	.14	.04
☐	50 Popeye Jones	.05	.02	.01
☐	51 Tim Legler	.05	.02	.01
☐	52 Fat Lever	.05	.02	.01
☐	53 Jamal Mashburn	.20	.09	.03
☐	54 Sean Rooks	.05	.02	.01
☐	55 Doug Smith	.05	.02	.01
☐	56 Mahmoud Abdul-Rauf	.10	.05	.01
☐	57 LaPhonso Ellis	.05	.02	.01
☐	58 Dikembe Mutombo	.10	.05	.01
☐	59 Robert Pack	.05	.02	.01
☐	60 Rodney Rogers	.05	.02	.01
☐	61 Bryant Stith	.05	.02	.01
☐	62 Brian Williams	.05	.02	.01
☐	63 Reggie Williams	.05	.02	.01
☐	64 Greg Anderson	.05	.02	.01
☐	65 Joe Dumars	.10	.05	.01
☐	66 Sean Elliott	.10	.05	.01
☐	67 Allan Houston	.15	.07	.02
☐	68 Lindsey Hunter	.05	.02	.01
☐	69 Terry Mills	.05	.02	.01
☐	70 Victor Alexander	.05	.02	.01
☐	71 Chris Gatling	.05	.02	.01
☐	72 Tim Hardaway	.10	.05	.01
☐	73 Keith Jennings	.05	.02	.01
☐	74 Avery Johnson	.05	.02	.01
☐	75 Chris Mullin	.10	.05	.01
☐	76 Billy Owens	.05	.02	.01
☐	77 Latrell Sprewell	.30	.14	.04
☐	78 Chris Webber	.30	.14	.04
☐	79 Scott Brooks	.05	.02	.01
☐	80 Sam Cassell	.10	.05	.01
☐	81 Mario Elie	.05	.02	.01
☐	82 Carl Herrera	.05	.02	.01
☐	83 Robert Horry	.10	.05	.01
☐	84 Vernon Maxwell	.05	.02	.01
☐	85 Hakeem Olajuwon	.60	.25	.07
☐	86 Kenny Smith	.05	.02	.01
☐	87 Otis Thorpe	.10	.05	.01
☐	88 Antonio Davis	.05	.02	.01
☐	89 Dale Davis	.05	.02	.01
☐	90 Vern Fleming	.05	.02	.01
☐	91 Derrick McKey	.05	.02	.01
☐	92 Reggie Miller	.30	.14	.04
☐	93 Pooh Richardson	.05	.02	.01
☐	94 Byron Scott	.10	.05	.01
☐	95 Rik Smits	.10	.05	.01
☐	96 Haywoode Workman	.05	.02	.01
☐	97 Terry Dehere	.05	.02	.01
☐	98 Harold Ellis	.05	.02	.01
☐	99 Gary Grant	.05	.02	.01
☐	100 Ron Harper	.05	.02	.01
☐	101 Mark Jackson	.05	.02	.01
☐	102 Stanley Roberts	.05	.02	.01
☐	103 Elmore Spencer	.05	.02	.01
☐	104 Loy Vaught	.05	.02	.01
☐	105 Dominique Wilkins	.10	.05	.01
☐	106 Elden Campbell	.10	.05	.01
☐	107 Doug Christie	.05	.02	.01
☐	108 Vlade Divac	.10	.05	.01
☐	109 George Lynch	.05	.02	.01
☐	110 Anthony Peeler	.05	.02	.01
☐	111 Tony Smith	.05	.02	.01
☐	112 Sedale Threatt	.05	.02	.01
☐	113 Nick Van Exel	.25	.11	.03
☐	114 James Worthy	.10	.05	.01
☐	115 Bimbo Coles	.05	.02	.01
☐	116 Grant Long	.05	.02	.01
☐	117 Harold Miner	.05	.02	.01
☐	118 Glen Rice	.10	.05	.01
☐	119 John Salley	.05	.02	.01
☐	120 Rony Seikaly	.05	.02	.01
☐	121 Brian Shaw	.05	.02	.01

□	Card				□	Card			
□	122 Steve Smith	.10	.05	.01	□	193 Bobby Hurley	.05	.02	.01
□	123 Vin Baker	.30	.14	.04	□	194 Olden Polynice	.05	.02	.01
□	124 Jon Barry	.05	.02	.01	□	195 Mitch Richmond	.20	.09	.03
□	125 Todd Day	.05	.02	.01	□	196 Lionel Simmons	.05	.02	.01
□	126 Blue Edwards	.05	.02	.01	□	197 Wayman Tisdale	.05	.02	.01
□	127 Lee Mayberry	.05	.02	.01	□	198 Spud Webb	.10	.05	.01
□	128 Eric Murdock	.05	.02	.01	□	199 Walt Williams	.10	.05	.01
□	129 Ken Norman	.05	.02	.01	□	200 Trevor Wilson	.05	.02	.01
□	130 Derek Strong	.05	.02	.01	□	201 Willie Anderson	.05	.02	.01
□	131 Thurl Bailey	.05	.02	.01	□	202 Antoine Carr	.05	.02	.01
□	132 Stacey King	.05	.02	.01	□	203 Terry Cummings	.05	.02	.01
□	133 Christian Laettner	.10	.05	.01	□	204 Vinny Del Negro	.05	.02	.01
□	134 Chuck Person	.05	.02	.01	□	205 Dale Ellis	.05	.02	.01
□	135 Isaiah Rider	.05	.02	.01	□	206 Negele Knight	.05	.02	.01
□	136 Chris Smith	.05	.02	.01	□	207 J.R. Reid	.05	.02	.01
□	137 Doug West	.05	.02	.01	□	208 David Robinson	.50	.23	.06
□	138 Micheal Williams	.05	.02	.01	□	209 Dennis Rodman	1.00	.45	.12
□	139 Kenny Anderson	.10	.05	.01	□	210 Vincent Askew	.05	.02	.01
□	140 Benoit Benjamin	.05	.02	.01	□	211 Michael Cage	.05	.02	.01
□	141 P.J. Brown	.05	.02	.01	□	212 Kendall Gill	.05	.02	.01
□	142 Derrick Coleman	.05	.02	.01	□	213 Shawn Kemp	.75	.35	.09
□	143 Kevin Edwards	.05	.02	.01	□	214 Nate McMillan	.05	.02	.01
□	144 Armon Gilliam	.05	.02	.01	□	215 Gary Payton	.40	.18	.05
□	145 Chris Morris	.05	.02	.01	□	216 Sam Perkins	.05	.02	.01
□	146 Johnny Newman	.05	.02	.01	□	217 Ricky Pierce	.05	.02	.01
□	147 Greg Anthony	.05	.02	.01	□	218 Detlef Schrempf	.10	.05	.01
□	148 Anthony Bonner	.05	.02	.01	□	219 David Benoit	.05	.02	.01
□	149 Hubert Davis	.05	.02	.01	□	220 Tom Chambers	.05	.02	.01
□	150 Patrick Ewing	.25	.11	.03	□	221 Tyrone Corbin	.05	.02	.01
□	151 Derek Harper	.05	.02	.01	□	222 Jeff Hornacek	.10	.05	.01
□	152 Anthony Mason	.10	.05	.01	□	223 Jay Humphries	.05	.02	.01
□	153 Charles Oakley	.10	.05	.01	□	224 Karl Malone	.25	.11	.03
□	154 Doc Rivers	.05	.02	.01	□	225 Bryon Russell	.05	.02	.01
□	155 Charles Smith	.05	.02	.01	□	226 Felton Spencer	.05	.02	.01
□	156 John Starks	.05	.02	.01	□	227 John Stockton	.25	.11	.03
□	157 Nick Anderson	.10	.05	.01	□	228 Michael Adams	.05	.02	.01
□	158 Anthony Avent	.05	.02	.01	□	229 Rex Chapman	.05	.02	.01
□	159 Anfernee Hardaway	1.50	.70	.19	□	230 Calbert Cheaney	.10	.05	.01
□	160 Shaquille O'Neal	1.25	.55	.16	□	231 Kevin Duckworth	.05	.02	.01
□	161 Donald Royal	.05	.02	.01	□	232 Pervis Ellison	.05	.02	.01
□	162 Dennis Scott	.10	.05	.01	□	233 Tom Gugliotta	.10	.05	.01
□	163 Scott Skiles	.05	.02	.01	□	234 Don MacLean	.05	.02	.01
□	164 Jeff Turner	.05	.02	.01	□	235 Gheorghe Muresan	.10	.05	.01
□	165 Dana Barros	.05	.02	.01	□	236 Brent Price	.05	.02	.01
□	166 Shawn Bradley	.10	.05	.01	□	237 Toronto Raptors	.10	.05	.01
□	167 Greg Graham	.05	.02	.01		Logo Card			
□	168 Eric Leckner	.05	.02	.01	□	238 Checklist	.05	.02	.01
□	169 Jeff Malone	.05	.02	.01	□	239 Checklist	.05	.02	.01
□	170 Moses Malone	.15	.07	.02	□	240 Checklist	.05	.02	.01
□	171 Tim Perry	.05	.02	.01	□	241 Sergei Bazarevich	.05	.02	.01
□	172 Clarence Weatherspoon	.05	.02	.01	□	242 Tyrone Corbin	.05	.02	.01
□	173 Orlando Woolridge	.05	.02	.01	□	243 Grant Long	.05	.02	.01
□	174 Danny Ainge	.10	.05	.01	□	244 Ken Norman	.05	.02	.01
□	175 Charles Barkley	.40	.18	.05	□	245 Steve Smith	.10	.05	.01
□	176 Cedric Ceballos	.10	.05	.01	□	246 Fred Vinson	.05	.02	.01
□	177 A.C. Green	.10	.05	.01	□	247 Blue Edwards	.05	.02	.01
□	178 Kevin Johnson	.10	.05	.01	□	248 Greg Minor	.05	.02	.01
□	179 Joe Kleine	.05	.02	.01	□	249 Eric Montross	.10	.05	.01
□	180 Dan Majerle	.10	.05	.01	□	250 Derek Strong	.05	.02	.01
□	181 Oliver Miller	.05	.02	.01	□	251 David Wesley	.05	.02	.01
□	182 Mark West	.05	.02	.01	□	252 Dominique Wilkins	.10	.05	.01
□	183 Clyde Drexler	.30	.14	.04	□	253 Michael Adams	.05	.02	.01
□	184 Harvey Grant	.05	.02	.01	□	254 Tony Bennett	.05	.02	.01
□	185 Jerome Kersey	.05	.02	.01	□	255 Darrin Hancock	.05	.02	.01
□	186 Tracy Murray	.05	.02	.01	□	256 Robert Parish	.10	.05	.01
□	187 Terry Porter	.05	.02	.01	□	257 Corie Blount	.05	.02	.01
□	188 Clifford Robinson	.10	.05	.01	□	258 Jud Buechler	.05	.02	.01
□	189 James Robinson	.05	.02	.01	□	259 Greg Foster	.05	.02	.01
□	190 Rod Strickland	.05	.02	.01	□	260 Ron Harper	.10	.05	.01
□	191 Buck Williams	.10	.05	.01	□	261 Larry Krystkowiak	.05	.02	.01
□	192 Duane Causwell	.05	.02	.01	□	262 Will Perdue	.05	.02	.01

☐ 263	Dickey Simpkins	.10	.05	.01
☐ 264	Michael Cage	.05	.02	.01
☐ 265	Tony Campbell	.05	.02	.01
☐ 266	Terry Davis	.05	.02	.01
☐ 267	Tony Dumas	.10	.05	.01
☐ 268	Jason Kidd	2.00	.90	.25
☐ 269	Roy Tarpley	.05	.02	.01
☐ 270	Morlon Wiley	.05	.02	.01
☐ 271	Lorenzo Williams	.05	.02	.01
☐ 272	Dale Ellis	.05	.02	.01
☐ 273	Tom Hammonds	.05	.02	.01
☐ 274	Cliff Levingston	.05	.02	.01
☐ 275	Darnell Mee	.05	.02	.01
☐ 276	Jalen Rose	.25	.11	.03
☐ 277	Reggie Slater	.05	.02	.01
☐ 278	Bill Curley	.05	.02	.01
☐ 279	Johnny Dawkins	.05	.02	.01
☐ 280	Grant Hill	3.00	1.35	.35
☐ 281	Eric Leckner	.05	.02	.01
☐ 282	Mark Macon	.05	.02	.01
☐ 283	Oliver Miller	.05	.02	.01
☐ 284	Mark West	.05	.02	.01
☐ 285	Manute Bol	.05	.02	.01
☐ 286	Tom Gugliotta	.10	.05	.01
☐ 287	Ricky Pierce	.05	.02	.01
☐ 288	Carlos Rogers	.05	.02	.01
☐ 289	Clifford Rozier	.10	.05	.01
☐ 290	Rony Seikaly	.05	.02	.01
☐ 291	Tim Breaux	.05	.02	.01
☐ 292	Chris Jent	.05	.02	.01
☐ 293	Eric Riley	.05	.02	.01
☐ 294	Zan Tabak	.05	.02	.01
☐ 295	Duane Ferrell	.05	.02	.01
☐ 296	Mark Jackson	.05	.02	.01
☐ 297	John Williams	.05	.02	.01
☐ 298	Matt Fish	.05	.02	.01
☐ 299	Tony Massenburg	.05	.02	.01
☐ 300	Lamond Murray	.05	.02	.01
☐ 301	Charles Outlaw	.05	.02	.01
☐ 302	Eric Piatkowski	.05	.02	.01
☐ 303	Pooh Richardson	.05	.02	.01
☐ 304	Randy Woods	.05	.02	.01
☐ 305	Sam Bowie	.05	.02	.01
☐ 306	Cedric Ceballos	.10	.05	.01
☐ 307	Antonio Harvey	.05	.02	.01
☐ 308	Eddie Jones	.60	.25	.07
☐ 309	Anthony Miller	.05	.02	.01
☐ 310	Ledell Eackles	.05	.02	.01
☐ 311	Kevin Gamble	.05	.02	.01
☐ 312	Brad Lohaus	.05	.02	.01
☐ 313	Billy Owens	.05	.02	.01
☐ 314	Khalid Reeves	.05	.02	.01
☐ 315	Kevin Willis	.05	.02	.01
☐ 316	Marty Conlon	.05	.02	.01
☐ 317	Eric Mobley	.05	.02	.01
☐ 318	Johnny Newman	.05	.02	.01
☐ 319	Ed Pinckney	.05	.02	.01
☐ 320	Glenn Robinson	1.00	.45	.12
☐ 321	Mike Brown	.05	.02	.01
☐ 322	Pat Durham	.05	.02	.01
☐ 323	Howard Eisley	.05	.02	.01
☐ 324	Andres Guibert	.05	.02	.01
☐ 325	Donyell Marshall	.10	.05	.01
☐ 326	Sean Rooks	.05	.02	.01
☐ 327	Yinka Dare	.05	.02	.01
☐ 328	Sleepy Floyd	.05	.02	.01
☐ 329	Sean Higgins	.05	.02	.01
☐ 330	Rick Mahorn	.05	.02	.01
☐ 331	Rex Walters	.05	.02	.01
☐ 332	Jayson Williams	.05	.02	.01
☐ 333	Charlie Ward	.10	.05	.01

☐ 334	Herb Williams	.05	.02	.01
☐ 335	Monty Williams	.05	.02	.01
☐ 336	Anthony Bowie	.05	.02	.01
☐ 337	Horace Grant	.10	.05	.01
☐ 338	Geert Hammink	.05	.02	.01
☐ 339	Tree Rollins	.05	.02	.01
☐ 340	Brian Shaw	.05	.02	.01
☐ 341	Brooks Thompson	.10	.05	.01
☐ 342	Derrick Alston	.05	.02	.01
☐ 343	Willie Burton	.05	.02	.01
☐ 344	Jaren Jackson	.05	.02	.01
☐ 345	B.J. Tyler	.05	.02	.01
☐ 346	Scott Williams	.05	.02	.01
☐ 347	Sharone Wright	.10	.05	.01
☐ 348	Antonio Lang	.05	.02	.01
☐ 349	Danny Manning	.10	.05	.01
☐ 350	Elliot Perry	.05	.02	.01
☐ 351	Wesley Person	.50	.23	.06
☐ 352	Trevor Ruffin	.10	.05	.01
☐ 353	Dan Schayes	.05	.02	.01
☐ 354	Aaron Swinson	.05	.02	.01
☐ 355	Wayman Tisdale	.05	.02	.01
☐ 356	Mark Bryant	.05	.02	.01
☐ 357	Chris Dudley	.05	.02	.01
☐ 358	James Edwards	.05	.02	.01
☐ 359	Aaron McKie	.10	.05	.01
☐ 360	Alaa Abdelnaby	.05	.02	.01
☐ 361	Frank Brickowski	.05	.02	.01
☐ 362	Randy Brown	.05	.02	.01
☐ 363	Brian Grant	.40	.18	.05
☐ 364	Michael Smith	.05	.02	.01
☐ 365	Henry Turner	.05	.02	.01
☐ 366	Sean Elliott	.10	.05	.01
☐ 367	Avery Johnson	.10	.05	.01
☐ 368	Moses Malone	.15	.07	.02
☐ 369	Julius Nwosu	.05	.02	.01
☐ 370	Chuck Person	.05	.02	.01
☐ 371	Chris Whitney	.05	.02	.01
☐ 372	Bill Cartwright	.05	.02	.01
☐ 373	Byron Houston	.05	.02	.01
☐ 374	Ervin Johnson	.05	.02	.01
☐ 375	Sarunas Marciulionis	.05	.02	.01
☐ 376	Antoine Carr	.05	.02	.01
☐ 377	John Crotty	.05	.02	.01
☐ 378	Adam Keefe	.05	.02	.01
☐ 379	Jamie Watson	.05	.02	.01
☐ 380	Mitchell Butler	.05	.02	.01
☐ 381	Juwan Howard	2.00	.90	.25
☐ 382	Jim McIlvaine	.10	.05	.01
☐ 383	Doug Overton	.05	.02	.01
☐ 384	Scott Skiles	.05	.02	.01
☐ 385	Larry Stewart	.05	.02	.01
☐ 386	Kenny Walker	.05	.02	.01
☐ 387	Chris Webber	.30	.14	.04
☐ 388	Vancouver Grizzlies	.10	.05	.01
	Logo Card			
☐ 389	Checklist	.05	.02	.01
☐ 390	Checklist	.05	.02	.01

1994-95 Fleer All-Defensive

Randomly inserted in all first-series packs at a rate of one in nine, these 10 standard-size cards feature first and second All-NBA Defensive teams. Card fronts are border-

less with color player action shots that have been faded to black-and-white. The player's name and first or second team designation appear in silver-foil lettering near the bottom. On a color-screened background, the back carries a color player cutout on one side and career highlights on the other. The cards are numbered on the back as "X of 10" and are sequenced in alphabetical order.

	MINT	NRMT	EXC
COMPLETE SET (10)	6.00	2.70	.75
COMMON CARD (1-10)	.25	.11	.03
☐ 1 Mookie Blaylock	.40	.18	.05
☐ 2 Charles Oakley	.40	.18	.05
☐ 3 Hakeem Olajuwon	2.00	.90	.25
☐ 4 Gary Payton	1.25	.55	.16
☐ 5 Scottie Pippen	2.50	1.10	.30
☐ 6 Horace Grant	.40	.18	.05
☐ 7 Nate McMillan	.25	.11	.03
☐ 8 David Robinson	1.50	.70	.19
☐ 9 Dennis Rodman	3.00	1.35	.35
☐ 10 Latrell Sprewell	.40	.18	.05

1994-95 Fleer All-Stars

Randomly inserted in 15-card first-series packs at a rate of one in two, these 26 standard-size cards feature borderless fronts with color player action shots and backgrounds that fade to black-and-white. The player's name and first or second team designation appear in silver-foil lettering near the bottom. On a color-screened background, the back carries a color player cutout on one side and career highlights on the other.

	MINT	NRMT	EXC
COMPLETE SET (26)	30.00	13.50	3.70
COMMON CARD (1-26)	.50	.23	.06
☐ 1 Kenny Anderson	.75	.35	.09
☐ 2 B.J. Armstrong	.50	.23	.06
☐ 3 Mookie Blaylock	.75	.35	.09
☐ 4 Derrick Coleman	.50	.23	.06
☐ 5 Patrick Ewing	1.50	.70	.19
☐ 6 Horace Grant	.75	.35	.09
☐ 7 Alonzo Mourning	2.00	.90	.25
☐ 8 Charles Oakley	.75	.35	.09
☐ 9 Shaquille O'Neal	8.00	3.60	1.00
☐ 10 Scottie Pippen	5.00	2.20	.60
☐ 11 Mark Price	.50	.23	.06
☐ 12 John Starks	.50	.23	.06
☐ 13 Dominique Wilkins	.75	.35	.09
☐ 14 Charles Barkley	2.50	1.10	.30
☐ 15 Clyde Drexler	2.00	.90	.25
☐ 16 Kevin Johnson	.75	.35	.09
☐ 17 Shawn Kemp	5.00	2.20	.60
☐ 18 Karl Malone	1.50	.70	.19
☐ 19 Danny Manning	.75	.35	.09
☐ 20 Hakeem Olajuwon	4.00	1.80	.50
☐ 21 Gary Payton	2.50	1.10	.30
☐ 22 Mitch Richmond	1.25	.55	.16
☐ 23 Clifford Robinson	.75	.35	.09
☐ 24 David Robinson	3.00	1.35	.35
☐ 25 Latrell Sprewell	.75	.35	.09
☐ 26 John Stockton	1.50	.70	.19

1994-95 Fleer Award Winners

These four standard-size cards were random inserts in all first series packs at an approximate rate of one in 22. The set highlights four NBA award winners from the 1993-94 season. The horizontal fronts feature multiple player images. The player's name and his award appear at the bottom in gold-foil lettering. The horizontal back carries a color player close-up on one side and career highlights on the other. The cards are numbered "X of 4" and are sequenced in alphabetical order.

	MINT	NRMT	EXC
COMPLETE SET (4)	4.00	1.80	.50
COMMON CARD (1-4)	.25	.11	.03

		MINT	NRMT	EXC
☐ 1	Dell Curry	.25	.11	.03
☐ 2	Don MacLean	.25	.11	.03
☐ 3	Hakeem Olajuwon	2.50	1.10	.30
☐ 4	Chris Webber	1.25	.55	.16

1994-95 Fleer Career Achievement

Randomly inserted in all first series packs at rate of one in 37, these six standard-size cards feature veteran NBA superstars. The fronts feature color player cutouts on their borderless metallic fronts. The player's name appears in gold-foil lettering in a lower corner. The back carries a color player close-up in a lower corner, with career highlights appearing above and alongside. The cards are numbered on the back as "X of 6" and are sequenced in alphabetical order.

		MINT	NRMT	EXC
COMPLETE SET (6)		20.00	9.00	2.50
COMMON CARD (1-6)		1.00	.45	.12
☐ 1	Patrick Ewing	3.00	1.35	.35
☐ 2	Karl Malone	3.00	1.35	.35
☐ 3	Hakeem Olajuwon	8.00	3.60	1.00
☐ 4	Robert Parish	1.00	.45	.12
☐ 5	Scottie Pippen	10.00	4.50	1.25
☐ 6	Dominique Wilkins	1.00	.45	.12

1994-95 Fleer First Year Phenoms

Randomly inserted into all second series packs at a rate of one in five, cards from

this 10-card standard-size set feature a selection of the top rookies from 1994. These borderless cards feature a full color, cut-out player photo bursting forth from the center of the card, against a multi-imaged, shaded photo background. Card backs feature brief text on each player. The set is sequenced in alphabetical order.

		MINT	NRMT	EXC
COMPLETE SET (10)		15.00	6.75	1.85
COMMON CARD (1-10)		.40	.18	.05
☐ 1	Grant Hill	8.00	3.60	1.00
☐ 2	Jason Kidd	5.00	2.20	.60
☐ 3	Donyell Marshall	.40	.18	.05
☐ 4	Eric Montross	.40	.18	.05
☐ 5	Lamond Murray	.40	.18	.05
☐ 6	Wesley Person	.75	.35	.09
☐ 7	Khalid Reeves	.40	.18	.05
☐ 8	Glenn Robinson	2.50	1.10	.30
☐ 9	Jalen Rose	.40	.18	.05
☐ 10	Sharone Wright	.40	.18	.05

1994-95 Fleer League Leaders

Randomly inserted in all first series Fleer packs at an approximate rate of one in 11, these eight standard-size cards showcase league statistical leaders from the 1993-94 season. Card fronts feature a horizontal design with color player cutouts set on hardwood backgrounds. The player's name and the category in which he led the NBA appear in gold-foil lettering at the bottom. On a hardwood background, the horizontal back carries a color player close-up on one side and career highlights on the other. The cards are numbered on the back as "X of 8" and are sequenced in alphabetical order.

		MINT	NRMT	EXC
COMPLETE SET (8)		8.00	3.60	1.00
COMMON CARD (1-8)		.25	.11	.03
☐ 1	Mahmoud Abdul-Rauf	.25	.11	.03
☐ 2	Nate McMillan	.25	.11	.03
☐ 3	Tracy Murray	.25	.11	.03
☐ 4	Dikembe Mutombo	.50	.23	.06
☐ 5	Shaquille O'Neal	4.00	1.80	.50
☐ 6	David Robinson	1.50	.70	.19

☐ 7	Dennis Rodman	3.00	1.35	.35
☐ 8	John Stockton	.75	.35	.09

1994-95 Fleer Lottery Exchange

This 11-card standard-size set was available exclusively by redeeming the Fleer Lottery Exchange card, which was randomly inserted into all first series packs at a rate of one in 175. The expiration date for the redemption was April 1st, 1995. Card design is very similar to the basic issue Fleer cards except for the Lottery Pick logo on front.

	MINT	NRMT	EXC
COMPLETE SET (11)	25.00	11.00	3.10
COMMON CARD (1-11)	.40	.18	.05

☐ 1	Glenn Robinson	3.00	1.35	.35
☐ 2	Jason Kidd	6.00	2.70	.75
☐ 3	Grant Hill	10.00	4.50	1.25
☐ 4	Donyell Marshall	.40	.18	.05
☐ 5	Juwan Howard	6.00	2.70	.75
☐ 6	Sharone Wright	.75	.35	.09
☐ 7	Lamond Murray	.40	.18	.05
☐ 8	Brian Grant	1.25	.55	.16
☐ 9	Eric Montross	.75	.35	.09
☐ 10	Eddie Jones	2.00	.90	.25
☐ 11	Carlos Rogers	.40	.18	.05
☐ NNO	Lottery Exchange Card	1.50	.70	.19

1994-95 Fleer Pro-Visions

Randomly inserted in all first-series packs at a rate of one in five, these nine standard-size cards highlight some top NBA stars. Borderless fronts feature color paintings of the players on fanciful backgrounds. The player's name appears in gold-foil lettering in a lower corner. The back carries career highlights on a colorful ghosted abstract background.

	MINT	NRMT	EXC
COMPLETE SET (9)	4.00	1.80	.50
COMMON CARD (1-9)	.15	.07	.02

☐ 1	Jamal Mashburn	.30	.14	.04
☐ 2	John Starks	.15	.07	.02
☐ 3	Toni Kukoc	.30	.14	.04
☐ 4	Derrick Coleman	.15	.07	.02
☐ 5	Chris Webber	.50	.23	.06
☐ 6	Dennis Rodman	1.50	.70	.19
☐ 7	Gary Payton	.60	.25	.07
☐ 8	Anfernee Hardaway	2.50	1.10	.30
☐ 9	Dan Majerle	.30	.14	.04

1994-95 Fleer Rookie Sensations

Randomly inserted at a rate of one in three first-series 21-card cello packs, these 25 standard-size cards feature a selection of the top rookies from the 1993-94 season. Card fronts feature color player action cutouts "breaking out" of borderless multi-colored backgrounds. The player's name appears in gold-foil lettering in a lower corner. The back carries another color player action cutout on one side, and career highlights within a colored panel on the other. The cards are numbered on the back as "X of 25" and are sequenced in alphabetical order.

	MINT	NRMT	EXC
COMPLETE SET (25)	25.00	11.00	3.10
COMMON CARD (1-25)	.50	.23	.06

☐ 1	Vin Baker	2.50	1.10	.30
☐ 2	Shawn Bradley	1.00	.45	.12
☐ 3	P.J. Brown	.50	.23	.06
☐ 4	Sam Cassell	1.00	.45	.12
☐ 5	Calbert Cheaney	1.00	.45	.12
☐ 6	Antonio Davis	.50	.23	.06
☐ 7	Acie Earl	.50	.23	.06
☐ 8	Harold Ellis	.50	.23	.06

		MINT	NRMT	EXC
☐ 9	Anfernee Hardaway	12.00	5.50	1.50
☐ 10	Allan Houston	1.25	.55	.16
☐ 11	Lindsey Hunter	.50	.23	.06
☐ 12	Bobby Hurley	1.00	.45	.12
☐ 13	Popeye Jones	.50	.23	.06
☐ 14	Toni Kukoc	1.50	.70	.19
☐ 15	George Lynch	.50	.23	.06
☐ 16	Jamal Mashburn	1.50	.70	.19
☐ 17	Chris Mills	1.00	.45	.12
☐ 18	Gheorghe Muresan	1.00	.45	.12
☐ 19	Dino Radja	1.00	.45	.12
☐ 20	Isaiah Rider	1.00	.45	.12
☐ 21	James Robinson	.50	.23	.06
☐ 22	Rodney Rogers	.50	.23	.06
☐ 23	Bryon Russell	.50	.23	.06
☐ 24	Nick Van Exel	2.00	.90	.25
☐ 25	Chris Webber	2.50	1.10	.30

1994-95 Fleer Sharpshooters

Randomly inserted exclusively into second series retail packs at a rate of one in seven, cards from this 10-card standard-size set feature a selection of the NBA's best long-distance shooters. Card fronts feature color player photos cut out against a neon basketball background overlapped by a basketball net. The set is sequenced in alphabetical order.

		MINT	NRMT	EXC
COMPLETE SET (10)		12.00	5.50	1.50
COMMON CARD (1-10)		1.00	.45	.12
☐ 1	Dell Curry	1.00	.45	.12
☐ 2	Joe Dumars	2.00	.90	.25
☐ 3	Dale Ellis	1.00	.45	.12
☐ 4	Dan Majerle	2.00	.90	.25
☐ 5	Reggie Miller	5.00	2.20	.60
☐ 6	Mark Price	1.00	.45	.12
☐ 7	Glen Rice	2.00	.90	.25
☐ 8	Mitch Richmond	3.00	1.35	.35
☐ 9	Dennis Scott	2.00	.90	.25
☐ 10	Latrell Sprewell	2.00	.90	.25

1994-95 Fleer Superstars

Randomly inserted into all second series packs at a rate of one in 37, cards from this

six-card set feature a selection of veteran NBA stars with true Hall of Fame potential. Card fronts feature psychedelic, etched-foil backgrounds against a full color, cut out player photo. The set is sequenced in alphabetical order.

		MINT	NRMT	EXC
COMPLETE SET (6)		20.00	9.00	2.50
COMMON CARD (1-6)		1.00	.45	.12
☐ 1	Charles Barkley	5.00	2.20	.60
☐ 2	Patrick Ewing	3.00	1.35	.35
☐ 3	Hakeem Olajuwon	8.00	3.60	1.00
☐ 4	Robert Parish	1.00	.45	.12
☐ 5	Scottie Pippen	10.00	4.50	1.25
☐ 6	Dominique Wilkins	1.00	.45	.12

1994-95 Fleer Team Leaders

Randomly inserted into all second series packs at a rate of one in three, cards from this nine-card standard-size set each feature three key players from an NBA team. Horizontal card fronts feature three full color, cut out player photos against a computer-enhanced graphic background. The backs have a head shot of all three players and infomation on them. The cards are numbered "X of 9." There are two variations of card #3. The error version lists Joe Dumars as a Houston Rocket. The corrected version lists him as a Detroit Piston. It appears that equal quantities of both versions exist.

	MINT	NRMT	EXC
COMPLETE SET (9)	4.00	1.80	.50
COMMON CARD (1-9)	.25	.11	.03

☐ 1 Mookie Blaylock	.50	.23	.06
Dominique Wilkins			
Alonzo Mourning			
☐ 2 Scottie Pippen	1.00	.45	.12
Mark Price			
Jamal Mashburn			
☐ 3A Dikembe Mutombo ERR	.50	.23	.06
Joe Dumars			
Detroit Pistons			
Latrell Sprewell			
Card has Dumars			
with Rockets			
☐ 3B Dikembe Mutombo COR	.50	.23	.06
Joe Dumars			
Latrell Sprewell			
☐ 4 Hakeem Olajuwon	1.00	.45	.12
Reggie Miller			
Loy Vaught			
☐ 5 Vlade Divac	.25	.11	.03
Glen Rice			
Vin Baker			
☐ 6 Isaiah Rider	.50	.23	.06
Kenny Anderson			
Patrick Ewing			
☐ 7 Shaquille O'Neal	1.50	.70	.19
Clarence Weatherspoon			
Charles Barkley			
☐ 8 Rod Strickland	.75	.35	.09
Mitch Richmond			
David Robinson			
☐ 9 Shawn Kemp	1.00	.45	.12
John Stockton			
Rex Chapman			

1994-95 Fleer Total D

Randomly inserted exclusively into second series hobby packs at a rate of one in seven, cards from this 10-card standard-size set feature a selection of the NBA's top defensive players. The fronts are laid out horizontally with a color photo and the player's name and team is in gold-foil at the bottom. "Total D" is in the background many times with a variety of colors set behind that. The backs have a head shot and information and why the player is so good defensively with a similar background to the front. The cards are numbered "X of 10" and are sequenced in alphabetical order.

	MINT	NRMT	EXC
COMPLETE SET (10)	10.00	4.50	1.25
COMMON CARD (1-10)	.50	.23	.06

☐ 1 Mookie Blaylock	.75	.35	.09
☐ 2 Nate McMillan	.50	.23	.06
☐ 3 Dikembe Mutombo	.75	.35	.09
☐ 4 Charles Oakley	.50	.23	.06
☐ 5 Hakeem Olajuwon	3.00	1.35	.35
☐ 6 Gary Payton	2.00	.90	.25
☐ 7 Scottie Pippen	4.00	1.80	.50
☐ 8 David Robinson	2.50	1.10	.30
☐ 9 Latrell Sprewell	.75	.35	.09
☐ 10 John Stockton	1.25	.55	.16

1994-95 Fleer Towers of Power

Randomly inserted exclusively into second series 21-card retail packs at a rate of one in five, cards from this 10-card standard-size set feature a selection of the top centers and power forwards in the NBA. The fronts have a color-action photo surrounded by a yellow glow with a tower in the background. The words "Tower of Power" are at the bottom in gold-foil. The backs are the same except for a different photo and player information at the bottom. The cards are numbered "X of 10" and are sequenced in alphabetical order.

	MINT	NRMT	EXC
COMPLETE SET (10)	30.00	13.50	3.70
COMMON CARD (1-10)	1.00	.45	.12

☐ 1 Charles Barkley	3.00	1.35	.35
☐ 2 Patrick Ewing	2.00	.90	.25
☐ 3 Shawn Kemp	6.00	2.70	.75
☐ 4 Karl Malone	2.00	.90	.25
☐ 5 Alonzo Mourning	2.50	1.10	.30
☐ 6 Dikembe Mutombo	1.00	.45	.12
☐ 7 Hakeem Olajuwon	5.00	2.20	.60
☐ 8 Shaquille O'Neal	10.00	4.50	1.25
☐ 9 David Robinson	4.00	1.80	.50
☐ 10 Chris Webber	2.50	1.10	.30

1994-95 Fleer Triple Threats

Randomly inserted in all first-series packs at an approximate rate of one in nine, these

10 standard-size cards spotlight some top NBA stars. Card fronts feature borderless fronts with multiple color player action cutouts on black backgrounds highlighted by colorful basketball court designs. The player's name appears in gold-foil lettering in a lower corner. This background design continues on the back, which carries a color player cutout on one side and career highlights in a ghosted strip on the other. The cards are numbered on the back as "X of 10" and are sequenced in alphabetical order.

	MINT	NRMT	EXC
COMPLETE SET (10)	6.00	2.70	.75
COMMON CARD (1-10)	.25	.11	.03
☐ 1 Mookie Blaylock	.25	.11	.03
☐ 2 Patrick Ewing	.50	.23	.06
☐ 3 Shawn Kemp	1.50	.70	.19
☐ 4 Karl Malone	.50	.23	.06
☐ 5 Reggie Miller	.60	.25	.07
☐ 6 Hakeem Olajuwon	1.25	.55	.16
☐ 7 Shaquille O'Neal	2.50	1.10	.30
☐ 8 Scottie Pippen	1.50	.70	.19
☐ 9 David Robinson	1.00	.45	.12
☐ 10 Latrell Sprewell	.25	.11	.03

1994-95 Fleer Young Lions

Randomly inserted into all second series packs at a rate of one in five, cards from this 6-card standard-size set feature a selection of popular players with three years or less of NBA experience. Fronts feature a player photo on the left and a lion photo on the right. In the bottom right corner there is gold-foil stamping of a lion, the term "Young Lion" and the player's name.

The back has a brief biography and another player photo. The card is numbered in the lower right as "X" of 6. The set is sequenced in alphabetical order.

	MINT	NRMT	EXC
COMPLETE SET (6)	10.00	4.50	1.25
COMMON CARD (1-6)	1.00	.45	.12
☐ 1 Vin Baker	1.00	.45	.12
☐ 2 Anfernee Hardaway	5.00	2.20	.60
☐ 3 Larry Johnson	1.00	.45	.12
☐ 4 Alonzo Mourning	1.00	.45	.12
☐ 5 Shaquille O'Neal	4.00	1.80	.50
☐ 6 Chris Webber	1.00	.45	.12

1995-96 Fleer

The 1995-96 Fleer set was issued in two separate series of 200 and 150 cards, respectively, for a total of 350. Cards were distributed in 11-card hobby and retail packs (SRP $1.49) and 17-card retail pre-priced packs (SRP $2.29). Each pack contains at least two insert cards. Special Hot Packs, containing a selection of only insert cards, were randomly seeded one to one in every 72 packs. The borderless fronts feature four different background designs (one for each division) against a cut-out color player action shot. The backs have a color-action photo and the same picture set against a pixeled background, along with statistics. The cards are grouped alphabetically within teams. The set concludes with the following topical subsets: Rookies (280-319) and Firm Foundations (320-348). Rookie Cards of note in this set include Michael Finley, Kevin Garnett, Antonio McDyess, Joe Smith, Jerry Stackhouse and Damon Stoudamire.

	MINT	NRMT	EXC
COMPLETE SET (350)	35.00	16.00	4.40
COMPLETE SERIES 1 (200)	15.00	6.75	1.85
COMPLETE SERIES 2 (150)	20.00	9.00	2.50
COMMON CARD (1-350)	.05	.02	.01
☐ 1 Stacey Augmon	.10	.05	.01
☐ 2 Mookie Blaylock	.10	.05	.01
☐ 3 Craig Ehlo	.05	.02	.01
☐ 4 Andrew Lang	.05	.02	.01
☐ 5 Grant Long	.05	.02	.01
☐ 6 Ken Norman	.05	.02	.01
☐ 7 Steve Smith	.10	.05	.01
☐ 8 Dee Brown	.05	.02	.01

☐ 9	Sherman Douglas	.05	.02	.01	☐ 80 Terry Dehere	.05	.02	.01
☐ 10	Eric Montross	.05	.02	.01	☐ 81 Tony Massenburg	.05	.02	.01
☐ 11	Dino Radja	.10	.05	.01	☐ 82 Lamond Murray	.05	.02	.01
☐ 12	David Wesley	.05	.02	.01	☐ 83 Pooh Richardson	.05	.02	.01
☐ 13	Dominique Wilkins	.10	.05	.01	☐ 84 Malik Sealy	.05	.02	.01
☐ 14	Muggsy Bogues	.10	.05	.01	☐ 85 Loy Vaught	.05	.02	.01
☐ 15	Scott Burrell	.05	.02	.01	☐ 86 Elden Campbell	.10	.05	.01
☐ 16	Dell Curry	.05	.02	.01	☐ 87 Cedric Ceballos	.10	.05	.01
☐ 17	Hersey Hawkins	.05	.02	.01	☐ 88 Vlade Divac	.10	.05	.01
☐ 18	Larry Johnson	.25	.11	.03	☐ 89 Eddie Jones	.20	.09	.03
☐ 19	Alonzo Mourning	.25	.11	.03	☐ 90 Anthony Peeler	.05	.02	.01
☐ 20	Robert Parish	.10	.05	.01	☐ 91 Sedale Threatt	.05	.02	.01
☐ 21	B.J. Armstrong	.05	.02	.01	☐ 92 Nick Van Exel	.20	.09	.03
☐ 22	Michael Jordan	3.00	1.35	.35	☐ 93 Bimbo Coles	.05	.02	.01
☐ 23	Steve Kerr	.10	.05	.01	☐ 94 Matt Geiger	.05	.02	.01
☐ 24	Toni Kukoc	.15	.07	.02	☐ 95 Billy Owens	.05	.02	.01
☐ 25	Will Perdue	.05	.02	.01	☐ 96 Khalid Reeves	.05	.02	.01
☐ 26	Scottie Pippen	.75	.35	.09	☐ 97 Glen Rice	.10	.05	.01
☐ 27	Terrell Brandon	.10	.05	.01	☐ 98 John Salley	.05	.02	.01
☐ 28	Tyrone Hill	.05	.02	.01	☐ 99 Kevin Willis	.05	.02	.01
☐ 29	Chris Mills	.10	.05	.01	☐ 100 Vin Baker	.25	.11	.03
☐ 30	Bobby Phills	.05	.02	.01	☐ 101 Marty Conlon	.05	.02	.01
☐ 31	Mark Price	.05	.02	.01	☐ 102 Todd Day	.05	.02	.01
☐ 32	John Williams	.05	.02	.01	☐ 103 Lee Mayberry	.05	.02	.01
☐ 33	Lucious Harris	.05	.02	.01	☐ 104 Eric Murdock	.05	.02	.01
☐ 34	Jim Jackson	.25	.11	.03	☐ 105 Glenn Robinson	.30	.14	.04
☐ 35	Popeye Jones	.05	.02	.01	☐ 106 Winston Garland	.05	.02	.01
☐ 36	Jason Kidd	.60	.25	.07	☐ 107 Tom Gugliotta	.10	.05	.01
☐ 37	Jamal Mashburn	.15	.07	.02	☐ 108 Christian Laettner	.10	.05	.01
☐ 38	George McCloud	.05	.02	.01	☐ 109 Isaiah Rider	.10	.05	.01
☐ 39	Roy Tarpley	.05	.02	.01	☐ 110 Sean Rooks	.05	.02	.01
☐ 40	Lorenzo Williams	.05	.02	.01	☐ 111 Doug West	.05	.02	.01
☐ 41	Mahmoud Abdul-Rauf	.10	.05	.01	☐ 112 Kenny Anderson	.10	.05	.01
☐ 42	Dale Ellis	.05	.02	.01	☐ 113 Benoit Benjamin	.05	.02	.01
☐ 43	LaPhonso Ellis	.05	.02	.01	☐ 114 P.J. Brown	.05	.02	.01
☐ 44	Dikembe Mutombo	.10	.05	.01	☐ 115 Derrick Coleman	.05	.02	.01
☐ 45	Robert Pack	.05	.02	.01	☐ 116 Armon Gilliam	.05	.02	.01
☐ 46	Rodney Rogers	.05	.02	.01	☐ 117 Chris Morris	.05	.02	.01
☐ 47	Jalen Rose	.05	.02	.01	☐ 118 Rex Walters	.05	.02	.01
☐ 48	Bryant Stith	.05	.02	.01	☐ 119 Hubert Davis	.05	.02	.01
☐ 49	Reggie Williams	.05	.02	.01	☐ 120 Patrick Ewing	.25	.11	.03
☐ 50	Joe Dumars	.10	.05	.01	☐ 121 Derek Harper	.05	.02	.01
☐ 51	Grant Hill	1.00	.45	.12	☐ 122 Anthony Mason	.10	.05	.01
☐ 52	Allan Houston	.05	.02	.01	☐ 123 Charles Oakley	.10	.05	.01
☐ 53	Lindsey Hunter	.05	.02	.01	☐ 124 Charles Smith	.05	.02	.01
☐ 54	Oliver Miller	.05	.02	.01	☐ 125 John Starks	.05	.02	.01
☐ 55	Terry Mills	.05	.02	.01	☐ 126 Nick Anderson	.05	.02	.01
☐ 56	Mark West	.05	.02	.01	☐ 127 Anthony Bowie	.05	.02	.01
☐ 57	Chris Gatling	.05	.02	.01	☐ 128 Horace Grant	.10	.05	.01
☐ 58	Tim Hardaway	.10	.05	.01	☐ 129 Anfernee Hardaway	1.50	.70	.19
☐ 59	Donyell Marshall	.05	.02	.01	☐ 130 Shaquille O'Neal	1.25	.55	.16
☐ 60	Chris Mullin	.10	.05	.01	☐ 131 Donald Royal	.05	.02	.01
☐ 61	Carlos Rogers	.05	.02	.01	☐ 132 Dennis Scott	.10	.05	.01
☐ 62	Clifford Rozier	.05	.02	.01	☐ 133 Brian Shaw	.05	.02	.01
☐ 63	Rony Seikaly	.05	.02	.01	☐ 134 Derrick Alston	.05	.02	.01
☐ 64	Latrell Sprewell	.10	.05	.01	☐ 135 Dana Barros	.05	.02	.01
☐ 65	Sam Cassell	.05	.02	.01	☐ 136 Shawn Bradley	.10	.05	.01
☐ 66	Clyde Drexler	.30	.14	.04	☐ 137 Willie Burton	.05	.02	.01
☐ 67	Mario Elie	.05	.02	.01	☐ 138 Clarence Weatherspoon	.05	.02	.01
☐ 68	Carl Herrera	.05	.02	.01	☐ 139 Scott Williams	.05	.02	.01
☐ 69	Robert Horry	.10	.05	.01	☐ 140 Sharone Wright	.05	.02	.01
☐ 70	Vernon Maxwell	.05	.02	.01	☐ 141 Danny Ainge	.10	.05	.01
☐ 71	Hakeem Olajuwon	.60	.25	.07	☐ 142 Charles Barkley	.40	.18	.05
☐ 72	Kenny Smith	.05	.02	.01	☐ 143 A.C. Green	.10	.05	.01
☐ 73	Dale Davis	.05	.02	.01	☐ 144 Kevin Johnson	.10	.05	.01
☐ 74	Mark Jackson	.05	.02	.01	☐ 145 Dan Majerle	.10	.05	.01
☐ 75	Derrick McKey	.05	.02	.01	☐ 146 Danny Manning	.10	.05	.01
☐ 76	Reggie Miller	.30	.14	.04	☐ 147 Elliot Perry	.05	.02	.01
☐ 77	Sam Mitchell	.05	.02	.01	☐ 148 Wesley Person	.10	.05	.01
☐ 78	Byron Scott	.10	.05	.01	☐ 149 Wayman Tisdale	.05	.02	.01
☐ 79	Rik Smits	.10	.05	.01	☐ 150 Chris Dudley	.05	.02	.01

☐ 151	Jerome Kersey	.05	.02	.01
☐ 152	Aaron McKie	.05	.02	.01
☐ 153	Terry Porter	.05	.02	.01
☐ 154	Clifford Robinson	.10	.05	.01
☐ 155	James Robinson	.05	.02	.01
☐ 156	Rod Strickland	.05	.02	.01
☐ 157	Otis Thorpe	.10	.05	.01
☐ 158	Buck Williams	.10	.05	.01
☐ 159	Brian Grant	.10	.05	.01
☐ 160	Bobby Hurley	.05	.02	.01
☐ 161	Olden Polynice	.05	.02	.01
☐ 162	Mitch Richmond	.20	.09	.03
☐ 163	Michael Smith	.05	.02	.01
☐ 164	Spud Webb	.05	.02	.01
☐ 165	Walt Williams	.10	.05	.01
☐ 166	Terry Cummings	.05	.02	.01
☐ 167	Vinny Del Negro	.05	.02	.01
☐ 168	Sean Elliott	.10	.05	.01
☐ 169	Avery Johnson	.10	.05	.01
☐ 170	Chuck Person	.05	.02	.01
☐ 171	J.R. Reid	.05	.02	.01
☐ 172	Doc Rivers	.05	.02	.01
☐ 173	David Robinson	.50	.23	.06
☐ 174	Dennis Rodman	1.00	.45	.12
☐ 175	Vincent Askew	.05	.02	.01
☐ 176	Kendall Gill	.05	.02	.01
☐ 177	Shawn Kemp	.75	.35	.09
☐ 178	Sarunas Marciulionis	.05	.02	.01
☐ 179	Nate McMillan	.05	.02	.01
☐ 180	Gary Payton	.40	.18	.05
☐ 181	Sam Perkins	.10	.05	.01
☐ 182	Detlef Schrempf	.10	.05	.01
☐ 183	David Benoit	.05	.02	.01
☐ 184	Antoine Carr	.05	.02	.01
☐ 185	Blue Edwards	.05	.02	.01
☐ 186	Jeff Hornacek	.10	.05	.01
☐ 187	Adam Keefe	.05	.02	.01
☐ 188	Karl Malone	.25	.11	.03
☐ 189	Felton Spencer	.05	.02	.01
☐ 190	John Stockton	.25	.11	.03
☐ 191	Rex Chapman	.05	.02	.01
☐ 192	Calbert Cheaney	.05	.02	.01
☐ 193	Juwan Howard	.60	.25	.07
☐ 194	Don MacLean	.05	.02	.01
☐ 195	Gheorge Muresan	.10	.05	.01
☐ 196	Scott Skiles	.05	.02	.01
☐ 197	Chris Webber	.25	.11	.03
☐ 198	Checklist	.05	.02	.01
☐ 199	Checklist	.05	.02	.01
☐ 200	Checklist	.05	.02	.01
☐ 201	Stacey Augmon	.10	.05	.01
☐ 202	Mookie Blaylock	.05	.02	.01
☐ 203	Grant Long	.05	.02	.01
☐ 204	Ken Norman	.05	.02	.01
☐ 205	Steve Smith	.10	.05	.01
☐ 206	Spud Webb	.10	.05	.01
☐ 207	Dana Barros	.05	.02	.01
☐ 208	Rick Fox	.05	.02	.01
☐ 209	Kendall Gill	.05	.02	.01
☐ 210	Khalid Reeves	.05	.02	.01
☐ 211	Glen Rice	.10	.05	.01
☐ 212	Luc Longley	.05	.02	.01
☐ 213	Dennis Rodman Bulls	1.50	.70	.19
☐ 214	Dan Majerle	.10	.05	.01
☐ 215	Tony Dumas	.05	.02	.01
☐ 216	Tom Hammonds	.05	.02	.01
☐ 217	Elmore Spencer	.05	.02	.01
☐ 218	Otis Thorpe	.10	.05	.01
☐ 219	B.J. Armstrong	.05	.02	.01
☐ 220	Sam Cassell	.10	.05	.01
☐ 221	Clyde Drexler	.30	.14	.04
☐ 222	Mario Elie	.05	.02	.01
☐ 223	Robert Horry	.10	.05	.01
☐ 224	Hakeem Olajuwon	.60	.25	.07
☐ 225	Kenny Smith	.05	.02	.01
☐ 226	Antonio Davis	.05	.02	.01
☐ 227	Eddie Johnson	.05	.02	.01
☐ 228	Ricky Pierce	.05	.02	.01
☐ 229	Eric Piatkowski	.05	.02	.01
☐ 230	Rodney Rogers	.05	.02	.01
☐ 231	Brian Williams	.05	.02	.01
☐ 232	Corie Blount	.05	.02	.01
☐ 233	George Lynch	.05	.02	.01
☐ 234	Kevin Gamble	.05	.02	.01
☐ 235	Alonzo Mourning	.25	.11	.03
☐ 236	Eric Mobley	.05	.02	.01
☐ 237	Terry Porter	.05	.02	.01
☐ 238	Micheal Williams	.05	.02	.01
☐ 239	Kevin Edwards	.05	.02	.01
☐ 240	Vern Fleming	.05	.02	.01
☐ 241	Charlie Ward	.10	.05	.01
☐ 242	Jon Koncak	.05	.02	.01
☐ 243	Richard Dumas	.05	.02	.01
☐ 244	Jeff Malone	.05	.02	.01
☐ 245	Vernon Maxwell	.05	.02	.01
☐ 246	John Williams	.05	.02	.01
☐ 247	Harvey Grant	.05	.02	.01
☐ 248	Dontonio Wingfield	.05	.02	.01
☐ 249	Tyrone Corbin	.05	.02	.01
☐ 250	Sarunas Marciulionis	.05	.02	.01
☐ 251	Will Perdue	.05	.02	.01
☐ 252	Hersey Hawkins	.05	.02	.01
☐ 253	Ervin Johnson	.05	.02	.01
☐ 254	Shawn Kemp	.75	.35	.09
☐ 255	Gary Payton	.40	.18	.05
☐ 256	Sam Perkins	.10	.05	.01
☐ 257	Detlef Schrempf	.10	.05	.01
☐ 258	Chris Morris	.05	.02	.01
☐ 259	Robert Pack	.05	.02	.01
☐ 260	Willie Anderson ET	.05	.02	.01
☐ 261	Jimmy King ET	.05	.02	.01
☐ 262	Oliver Miller ET	.05	.02	.01
☐ 263	Tracy Murray ET	.05	.02	.01
☐ 264	Ed Pinckney ET	.05	.02	.01
☐ 265	Alvin Robertson ET	.05	.02	.01
☐ 266	Carlos Rogers ET	.05	.02	.01
☐ 267	John Salley ET	.05	.02	.01
☐ 268	Damon Stoudamire ET	1.00	.45	.12
☐ 269	Zan Tabak ET	.05	.02	.01
☐ 270	Ashraf Amaya ET	.05	.02	.01
☐ 271	Greg Anthony ET	.05	.02	.01
☐ 272	Benoit Benjamin ET	.05	.02	.01
☐ 273	Blue Edwards ET	.05	.02	.01
☐ 274	Kenny Gattison ET	.05	.02	.01
☐ 275	Antonio Harvey ET	.05	.02	.01
☐ 276	Chris King ET	.05	.02	.01
☐ 277	Lawrence Moten ET	.05	.02	.01
☐ 278	Bryant Reeves ET	.25	.11	.03
☐ 279	Byron Scott ET	.10	.05	.01
☐ 280	Cory Alexander	.05	.02	.01
☐ 281	Jerome Allen	.10	.05	.01
☐ 282	Brent Barry	.50	.23	.06
☐ 283	Mario Bennett	.05	.02	.01
☐ 284	Travis Best	.15	.07	.02
☐ 285	Junior Burrough	.05	.02	.01
☐ 286	Jason Caffey	.10	.05	.01
☐ 287	Randolph Childress	.05	.02	.01
☐ 288	Sasha Danilovic	.15	.07	.02
☐ 289	Mark Davis	.05	.02	.01
☐ 290	Tyus Edney	.50	.23	.06
☐ 291	Michael Finley	1.25	.55	.16
☐ 292	Sherell Ford	.05	.02	.01

		MINT	NRMT	EXC
☐ 293	Kevin Garnett	3.00	1.35	.35
☐ 294	Alan Henderson	.15	.07	.02
☐ 295	Frankie King	.05	.02	.01
☐ 296	Jimmy King	.05	.02	.01
☐ 297	Donny Marshall	.05	.02	.01
☐ 298	Antonio McDyess	1.00	.45	.12
☐ 299	Loren Meyer	.10	.05	.01
☐ 300	Lawrence Moten	.05	.02	.01
☐ 301	Ed O'Bannon	.40	.18	.05
☐ 302	Greg Ostertag	.05	.02	.01
☐ 303	Cherokee Parks	.20	.09	.03
☐ 304	Theo Ratliff	.20	.09	.03
☐ 305	Bryant Reeves	.60	.25	.07
☐ 306	Shawn Respert	.20	.09	.03
☐ 307	Lou Roe	.05	.02	.01
☐ 308	Arvydas Sabonis	.75	.35	.09
☐ 309	Joe Smith	1.25	.55	.16
☐ 310	Jerry Stackhouse	2.00	.90	.25
☐ 311	Damon Stoudamire	2.50	1.10	.30
☐ 312	Bob Sura	.20	.09	.03
☐ 313	Kurt Thomas	.30	.14	.04
☐ 314	Gary Trent	.20	.09	.03
☐ 315	David Vaughn	.05	.02	.01
☐ 316	Rasheed Wallace	.50	.23	.06
☐ 317	Eric Williams	.20	.09	.03
☐ 318	Corliss Williamso	.20	.09	.03
☐ 319	George Zidek	.15	.07	.02
☐ 320	Mookie Blaylock FF	.05	.02	.01
☐ 321	Dino Radja FF	.05	.02	.01
☐ 322	Larry Johnson FF	.10	.05	.01
☐ 323	Michael Jordan FF	1.50	.70	.19
☐ 324	Tyrone Hill FF	.05	.02	.01
☐ 325	Jason Kidd FF	.30	.14	.04
☐ 326	Dikembe Mutombo FF	.10	.05	.01
☐ 327	Grant Hill FF	.50	.23	.06
☐ 328	Joe Smith FF	.50	.23	.06
☐ 329	Hakeem Olajuwon FF	.30	.14	.04
☐ 330	Reggie Miller FF	.15	.07	.02
☐ 331	Loy Vaught FF	.05	.02	.01
☐ 332	Nick Van Exel FF	.15	.07	.02
☐ 333	Alonzo Mourning FF	.10	.05	.01
☐ 334	Glenn Robinson FF	.15	.07	.02
☐ 335	Kevin Garnett FF	1.25	.55	.16
☐ 336	Kenny Anderson FF	.10	.05	.01
☐ 337	Patrick Ewing FF	.10	.05	.01
☐ 338	Shaquille O'Neal FF	.60	.25	.07
☐ 339	Jerry Stackhouse FF	.75	.35	.09
☐ 340	Charles Barkley FF	.20	.09	.03
☐ 341	Clifford Robinson FF	.05	.02	.01
☐ 342	Mitch Richmond FF	.05	.02	.01
☐ 343	David Robinson FF	.25	.11	.03
☐ 344	Shawn Kemp FF	.40	.18	.05
☐ 345	Damon Stoudamire FF	1.00	.45	.12
☐ 346	Karl Malone FF	.10	.05	.01
☐ 347	Bryant Reeves FF	.25	.11	.03
☐ 348	Chris Webber FF	.10	.05	.01
☐ 349	Checklist (201-319)	.05	.02	.01
☐ 350	Checklist (320-350/ins.)	.05	.02	.01

1995-96 Fleer All-Stars

Randomly inserted in all first series packs at an approximate rate of one in three, these thirteen dual-player, double-sided standard-size cards feature members of the 1994-95 Eastern and Western Conference All-Star squads. Only All-Star MVP Mitch

Richmond is given his own card. Both sides have a full-color action photo taken at the All-Star game with the West having a purple background and the East a green background. The bottoms have the Phoenix All-Star Weekend insignia with the player's name and conference in gold-foil. The cards are numbered "X of 13."

		MINT	NRMT	EXC
	COMPLETE SET (13)	5.00	2.20	.60
	COMMON CARD (1-13)	.25	.11	.03
☐ 1	Grant Hill	1.25	.55	.16
	Charles Barkley			
☐ 2	Scottie Pippen	1.50	.70	.19
	Shawn Kemp			
☐ 3	Shaquille O'Neal	2.00	.90	.25
	Hakeem Olajuwon			
☐ 4	Anfernee Hardaway	1.50	.70	.19
	Dan Majerle			
☐ 5	Reggie Miller	.50	.23	.06
	Latrell Sprewell			
☐ 6	Vin Baker	.25	.11	.03
	Cedric Ceballos			
☐ 7	Tyrone Hill	.25	.11	.03
	Karl Malone			
☐ 8	Larry Johnson	.25	.11	.03
	Detlef Schrempf			
☐ 9	Patrick Ewing	.75	.35	.09
	David Robinson			
☐ 10	Alonzo Mourning	.25	.11	.03
	Dikembe Mutombo			
☐ 11	Dana Barros	.25	.11	.03
	Gary Payton			
☐ 12	Joe Dumars	.25	.11	.03
	John Stockton			
☐ 13	Mitch Richmond AS MVP	.25	.11	.03

1995-96 Fleer Class Encounters

Randomly inserted in all second series packs at a rate of one in two, this 40-card standard-size set highlights the first 20 players of the 1995 draft and 20 of the most sucessful players from the 1994 draft. Full-bleed fronts have gold foil printing and one full-color action shot as the main background. Three head shots of the original appear in increasing size on the right side. Horizontal backs have a white-bordered, off-center head shot with a player profile

printed in black type on a red background. Each group of cards is sequenced in alphabetical order.

	MINT	NRMT	EXC
COMPLETE SET (40)	25.00	11.00	3.10
COMMON CARD (1-40)	.25	.11	.03
☐ 1 Derrick Alston	.25	.11	.03
☐ 2 Brian Grant	.25	.11	.03
☐ 3 Grant Hill	3.00	1.35	.35
☐ 4 Juwan Howard	2.00	.90	.25
☐ 5 Eddie Jones	.60	.25	.07
☐ 6 Jason Kidd	2.00	.90	.25
☐ 7 Donyell Marshall	.25	.11	.03
☐ 8 Anthony Miller	.25	.11	.03
☐ 9 Eric Mobley	.25	.11	.03
☐ 10 Eric Montross	.25	.11	.03
☐ 11 Lamond Murray	.25	.11	.03
☐ 12 Wesley Person	.25	.11	.03
☐ 13 Eric Piatkowski	.25	.11	.03
☐ 14 Khalid Reeves	.25	.11	.03
☐ 15 Glenn Robinson	1.00	.45	.12
☐ 16 Carlos Rogers	.25	.11	.03
☐ 17 Jalen Rose	.25	.11	.03
☐ 18 Clifford Rozier	.25	.11	.03
☐ 19 Michael Smith	.25	.11	.03
☐ 20 Sharone Wright	.25	.11	.03
☐ 21 Brent Barry	1.00	.45	.12
☐ 22 Jason Caffey	.25	.11	.03
☐ 23 Randolph Childress	.25	.11	.03
☐ 24 Kevin Garnett	6.00	2.70	.75
☐ 25 Alan Henderson	.50	.23	.06
☐ 26 Antonio McDyess	2.00	.90	.25
☐ 27 Ed O'Bannon	.75	.35	.09
☐ 28 Cherokee Parks	.40	.18	.05
☐ 29 Theo Ratliff			
☐ 30 Bryant Reeves	1.25	.55	.16
☐ 31 Shawn Respert	.40	.18	.05
☐ 32 Joe Smith	2.50	1.10	.30
☐ 33 Jerry Stackhouse	4.00	1.80	.50
☐ 34 Damon Stoudamire	5.00	2.20	.60
☐ 35 Bob Sura	.25	.11	.03
☐ 36 Kurt Thomas	.50	.23	.06
☐ 37 Gary Trent	.40	.18	.05
☐ 38 Rasheed Wallace	1.00	.45	.12
☐ 39 Eric Williams	.50	.23	.06
☐ 40 Corliss Williamson	.40	.18	.05

1995-96 Fleer Double Doubles

Randomly inserted in all first series packs at an approximate rate of one in three, these 12 cards feature players who averaged double figures per game in two statistical categories during the 1994-95 season. Full-bleed fronts features the player in two, split-shot color action photos separated by the words "Double Double" which are printed in the player's team colors. The player is again featured in full-color on the back with a career synopsis and '94-95 stats printed in black type. The set is sequenced in alphabetical order.

	MINT	NRMT	EXC
COMPLETE SET (12)	6.00	2.70	.75
COMMON CARD (1-12)	.25	.11	.03
☐ 1 Vin Baker	.40	.18	.05
☐ 2 Vlade Divac	.40	.18	.05
☐ 3 Patrick Ewing	.50	.23	.06
☐ 4 Tyrone Hill	.25	.11	.03
☐ 5 Popeye Jones	.25	.11	.03
☐ 6 Shawn Kemp	1.50	.70	.19
☐ 7 Karl Malone	.50	.23	.06
☐ 8 Dikembe Mutombo	.40	.18	.05
☐ 9 Hakeem Olajuwon	1.25	.55	.16
☐ 10 Shaquille O'Neal	2.50	1.10	.30
☐ 11 David Robinson	1.00	.45	.12
☐ 12 John Stockton	.50	.23	.06

1995-96 Fleer End to End

Randomly inserted in all second series packs at a rate of one in four, cards from this 20-card set focus on the NBA's leaders at both ends of the court. Borderless, horizontal fronts are split between two panels, one having a blue background with "End to

End" in repeating print, and the other with a full-color action player shot. A player cutout is placed in the middle of the two panels. Horizontal backs have a full-color action cutout and a player profile.

	MINT	NRMT	EXC
COMPLETE SET (20)	25.00	11.00	3.10
COMMON CARD (1-20)	.25	.11	.03

		MINT	NRMT	EXC
☐ 1	Mookie Blaylock	.40	.18	.05
☐ 2	Vlade Divac	.40	.18	.05
☐ 3	Clyde Drexler	1.00	.45	.12
☐ 4	Patrick Ewing	.75	.35	.09
☐ 5	Horace Grant	.40	.18	.05
☐ 6	Anfernee Hardaway	5.00	2.20	.60
☐ 7	Grant Hill	3.00	1.35	.35
☐ 8	Eddie Jones	.60	.25	.07
☐ 9	Michael Jordan	10.00	4.50	1.25
☐ 10	Jason Kidd	2.00	.90	.25
☐ 11	Alonzo Mourning	.75	.35	.09
☐ 12	Dikembe Mutombo	.40	.18	.05
☐ 13	Hakeem Olajuwon	2.00	.90	.25
☐ 14	Shaquille O'Neal	4.00	1.80	.50
☐ 15	Gary Payton	1.25	.55	.16
☐ 16	Scottie Pippen	2.50	1.10	.30
☐ 17	David Robinson	1.50	.70	.19
☐ 18	Latrell Sprewell	.40	.18	.05
☐ 19	John Stockton	.75	.35	.09
☐ 20	Rod Strickland	.25	.11	.03

		MINT	NRMT	EXC
☐ 1	Mookie Blaylock	.35	.16	.04
☐ 2	Dominique Wilkins	.35	.16	.04
☐ 3	Alonzo Mourning	.60	.25	.07
☐ 4	Michael Jordan	8.00	3.60	1.00
☐ 5	Mark Price	.25	.11	.03
☐ 6	Jim Jackson	.75	.35	.09
☐ 7	Dikembe Mutombo	.35	.16	.04
☐ 8	Grant Hill	2.50	1.10	.30
☐ 9	Tim Hardaway	.35	.16	.04
☐ 10	Hakeem Olajuwon	1.50	.70	.19
☐ 11	Reggie Miller	.75	.35	.09
☐ 12	Loy Vaught	.25	.11	.03
☐ 13	Cedric Ceballos	.25	.11	.03
☐ 14	Glen Rice	.35	.16	.04
☐ 15	Glenn Robinson	.75	.35	.09
☐ 16	Christian Laettner	.35	.16	.04
☐ 17	Derrick Coleman	.25	.11	.03
☐ 18	Patrick Ewing	.60	.25	.07
☐ 19	Shaquille O'Neal	3.00	1.35	.35
☐ 20	Dana Barros	.25	.11	.03
☐ 21	Charles Barkley	1.00	.45	.12
☐ 22	Clifford Robinson	.35	.16	.04
☐ 23	Mitch Richmond	.50	.23	.06
☐ 24	David Robinson	1.25	.55	.16
☐ 25	Gary Payton	1.00	.45	.12
☐ 26	Karl Malone	.60	.25	.07
☐ 27	Chris Webber	.60	.25	.07

1995-96 Fleer Flair Hardwood Leaders

Issued one per pack in all first series packs, these 27 super-premium, double-thick Flair style standard-size cards feature each team's statistical leader or award winner from the 1994-95 season. The fronts have a color action photo with the key as the background. The backs have a color photo with a hardwood background and player information. The entire 27-card set was also issued as a commemorative sheet most notably distributed as a wrapper redemption at the San Antonio All-Star Jam Session show. The set is sequenced in alphabetical order by team.

	MINT	NRMT	EXC
COMPLETE SET (27)	20.00	9.00	2.50
COMMON CARD (1-27)	.25	.11	.03

1995-96 Fleer Franchise Futures

Randomly inserted into all first series packs at an approximate rate of one in 37, these nine etched-foil standard-size cards feature a selection of the game's hottest young stars. The fronts have a full-color action photo with a huge basketball and fire underneath it in the background. The backs have a color photo with a similar yet less snazzy version of the front background. The set is sequenced in alphabetical order.

		MINT	NRMT	EXC
COMPLETE SET (9)		40.00	18.00	5.00
COMMON CARD (1-9)		1.50	.70	.19
☐ 1	Vin Baker	3.00	1.35	.35
☐ 2	Anfernee Hardaway	20.00	9.00	2.50
☐ 3	Jim Jackson	10.00	4.50	1.25
☐ 4	Jamal Mashburn	2.00	.90	.25
☐ 5	Alonzo Mourning	3.00	1.35	.35
☐ 6	Dikembe Mutombo	1.50	.70	.19

		MINT	NRMT	EXC
☐ 7	Shaquille O'Neal	15.00	6.75	1.85
☐ 8	Nick Van Exel	2.50	1.10	.30
☐ 9	Chris Webber	3.00	1.35	.35

1995-96 Fleer Rookie Phenoms

The 10 cards in this set were randomly inserted in second series hobby packs only at a rate of one in 24 and highlight the play of the NBA's best rookies. Borderless fronts are gold and silver foil finished with a full-color action cutout. Backs carry an extreme vertical color shot on the left and a player profile on the right. A collector could find a complete parallel Rookie Phenom set in hobby "Hot Packs". One in every 72 hobby packs was a Hot Pack (making the parallel Hot Pack cards four times easier to pull than corresponding regular Rookie Phenom inserts). These parallels are stamped with the words "Hot Pack" in red foil on the card fronts. Please refer to the percentages listed below to ascertain values for Hot Pack parallels.

	MINT	NRMT	EXC
COMPLETE SET (10)	75.00	34.00	9.50
COMMON CARD (1-10)	1.00	.45	.12
COMP. HOT PACK SET (10)	25.00	11.00	3.10
HP CARDS: 33% VALUE			

		MINT	NRMT	EXC
☐ 1	Kevin Garnett	25.00	11.00	3.10
☐ 2	Antonio McDyess	6.00	2.70	.75
☐ 3	Ed O'Bannon	2.50	1.10	.30
☐ 4	Bryant Reeves	4.00	1.80	.50
☐ 5	Shawn Respert	1.00	.45	.12
☐ 6	Joe Smith	8.00	3.60	1.00
☐ 7	Jerry Stackhouse	12.00	5.50	1.50
☐ 8	Damon Stoudamire	15.00	6.75	1.85
☐ 9	Gary Trent	1.00	.45	.12
☐ 10	Rasheed Wallace	3.00	1.35	.35

1995-96 Fleer Rookie Sensations

Randomly inserted exclusively into first series 17-card retail pre-priced packs at an approximate rate of one in five, these 15 cards spotlight the top rookies from the

1994-95 season. The fronts have a full-color action photo with the words "Rookie Sensation" in gold-foil around a basketball. The backs have a full-color photo with player information at the bottom in a yellow haze.

		MINT	NRMT	EXC
COMPLETE SET (15)		25.00	11.00	3.10
COMMON CARD (1-15)		.75	.35	.09
☐ 1	Brian Grant	1.50	.70	.19
☐ 2	Grant Hill	10.00	4.50	1.25
☐ 3	Juwan Howard	6.00	2.70	.75
☐ 4	Eddie Jones	2.00	.90	.25
☐ 5	Jason Kidd	6.00	2.70	.75
☐ 6	Donyell Marshall	.75	.35	.09
☐ 7	Eric Montross	.75	.35	.09
☐ 8	Lamond Murray	.75	.35	.09
☐ 9	Wesley Person	1.50	.70	.19
☐ 10	Khalid Reeves	.75	.35	.09
☐ 11	Glenn Robinson	3.00	1.35	.35
☐ 12	Jalen Rose	1.50	.70	.19
☐ 13	Clifford Rozier	.75	.35	.09
☐ 14	Michael Smith	.75	.35	.09
☐ 15	Sharone Wright	1.50	.70	.19

1995-96 Fleer Stackhouse's Scrapbook

Randomly inserted into all second series packs at a rate one in every 24, these two cards represent the first part of a multi-series, eight-card, cross-brand set devoted to Fleer spokesperson Jerry Stackhouse.

	MINT	NRMT	EXC
COMPLETE SET (2)	4.00	1.80	.50
COMMON CARD (S1-S2)	2.50	1.10	.30
☐ S1 Jerry Stackhouse Fleer	2.50	1.10	.30
☐ S2 Jerry Stackhouse Fleer	2.50	1.10	.30

1995-96 Fleer
Total D

Randomly inserted into first series 11-card hobby and retail packs at an approximate rate of one in five, these 12 standard-size cards feature a selection of the NBA's top defenders. The fronts have a color-action photo with the player's name and "Total D" on the side in gold-foil. The horizontal backs are split between a color action player photo on the left and a player profile printed in white and set against a gradated color background on the right. The set is sequenced in alphabetical order.

	MINT	NRMT	EXC
COMPLETE SET (12)	15.00	6.75	1.85
COMMON CARD (1-12)	.25	.11	.03
☐ 1 Mookie Blaylock	.25	.11	.03
☐ 2 Patrick Ewing	.60	.25	.07
☐ 3 Michael Jordan	8.00	3.60	1.00
☐ 4 Alonzo Mourning	.60	.25	.07
☐ 5 Dikembe Mutombo	.40	.18	.05
☐ 6 Hakeem Olajuwon	1.50	.70	.19
☐ 7 Shaquille O'Neal	3.00	1.35	.35
☐ 8 Gary Payton	1.00	.45	.12
☐ 9 Scottie Pippen	2.00	.90	.25
☐ 10 David Robinson	1.25	.55	.16
☐ 11 Dennis Rodman	2.50	1.10	.30
☐ 12 John Stockton	.60	.25	.07

1995-96 Fleer
Total O

Randomly inserted in second series retail packs only at a rate of one in 12, cards from this 10-card standard-size set spotlight the NBA's offensive talent. Borderless fronts capture the player in a full-color

action cutout with two red foil rings surrounding the image. All are on a backdrop of a basketball in the hands of a shooter and "Total O" is printed in silver foil on the ball. Backs are split between a full-color action player shot and a colored rock background containing a player profile printed in white type. A collector could find a complete parallel Total O set in retail "Hot Packs". One in every 72 retail packs was a Hot Pack (making the parallel Hot Pack cards approximately 1.6 times easier to pull than corresponding regular Total O inserts). These parallels are stamped with the words "Hot Pack" in red foil on the card fronts. Please refer to the percentages listed below to ascertain values for Hot Pack singles. The set is sequenced in alphabetical order.

	MINT	NRMT	EXC
COMPLETE SET (10)	40.00	18.00	5.00
COMMON CARD (1-10)	1.00	.45	.12
COMP. HOT PACK SET (10)	25.00	11.00	3.10
HP CARDS: 66% VALUE			
☐ 1 Grant Hill	6.00	2.70	.75
☐ 2 Michael Jordan	25.00	11.00	3.10
☐ 3 Jamal Mashburn	1.00	.45	.12
☐ 4 Reggie Miller	2.00	.90	.25
☐ 5 Hakeem Olajuwon	4.00	1.80	.50
☐ 6 Shaquille O'Neal	8.00	3.60	1.00
☐ 7 Mitch Richmond	1.25	.55	.16
☐ 8 David Robinson	3.00	1.35	.35
☐ 9 Glenn Robinson	2.00	.90	.25
☐ 10 Jerry Stackhouse	6.00	2.70	.75

1995-96 Fleer
Towers of Power

The big "Earth Shakers" of the NBA are represented in this 10-card set. Cards were randomly inserted into one in every 54 second series packs. Borderless fronts have etched copper foil designs and a full-color action player cutout. Backs are a three-tone color screen with a one-color action shot near the top right. A player profile appears in black type on the bottom half.

	MINT	NRMT	EXC
COMPLETE SET (10)	90.00	40.00	11.00
COMMON CARD (1-10)	5.00	2.20	.60

		MINT	NRMT	EXC
☐	1 Shawn Kemp	15.00	6.75	1.85
☐	2 Karl Malone	5.00	2.20	.60
☐	3 Antonio McDyess	10.00	4.50	1.25
☐	4 Alonzo Mourning	5.00	2.20	.60
☐	5 Hakeem Olajuwon	12.00	5.50	1.50
☐	6 Shaquille O'Neal	25.00	11.00	3.10
☐	7 David Robinson	10.00	4.50	1.25
☐	8 Glenn Robinson	6.00	2.70	.75
☐	9 Joe Smith	12.00	5.50	1.50
☐	10 Chris Webber	5.00	2.20	.60

1996-97 Fleer

The 1996-97 Fleer set will be issued in two series. The first series of 150 cards was issued in 11-card packs carrying a suggested retail price of $1.49 each. Card fronts contain a full-bleed photo with the player's last name in ghosted white letters and their first name in gold foil laid over it. The player's team name is also in gold foil under the player's first name. Card backs are horizontal with the team colors setting the background along with a basketball and the team logo. A photo of the player is provided along with statistical and biographical information. Cards are sequenced alphabetically within team order. The onky subset is Hardwood Leaders (120-148). No Rookie Cards are featured in the first series.

		MINT	NRMT	EXC
	COMPLETE SERIES 1 (150)	12.00	5.50	1.50
	COMMON CARD (1-150)	.05	.02	.01
☐	1 Stacey Augmon	.10	.05	.01
☐	2 Mookie Blaylock	.10	.05	.01
☐	3 Christian Laettner	.10	.05	.01
☐	4 Grant Long	.05	.02	.01

☐	5 Steve Smith	.10	.05	.01
☐	6 Rick Fox	.05	.02	.01
☐	7 Dino Radja	.10	.05	.01
☐	8 Eric Williams	.05	.02	.01
☐	9 Kenny Anderson	.10	.05	.01
☐	10 Dell Curry	.05	.02	.01
☐	11 Larry Johnson	.25	.11	.03
☐	12 Glen Rice	.10	.05	.01
☐	13 Michael Jordan	3.00	1.35	.35
☐	14 Toni Kukoc	.10	.05	.01
☐	15 Scottie Pippen	.75	.35	.09
☐	16 Dennis Rodman	1.25	.55	.16
☐	17 Terrell Brandon	.10	.05	.01
☐	18 Chris Mills	.05	.02	.01
☐	19 Bobby Phills	.05	.02	.01
☐	20 Bob Sura	.05	.02	.01
☐	21 Jim Jackson	.10	.05	.01
☐	22 Jason Kidd	.50	.23	.06
☐	23 Jamal Mashburn	.10	.05	.01
☐	24 George McCloud	.05	.02	.01
☐	25 Mahmoud Abdul-Rauf	.05	.02	.01
☐	26 Antonio McDyess	.30	.14	.04
☐	27 Dikembe Mutombo	.10	.05	.01
☐	28 Jalen Rose	.05	.02	.01
☐	29 Bryant Stith	.05	.02	.01
☐	30 Joe Dumars	.10	.05	.01
☐	31 Grant Hill	.75	.35	.09
☐	32 Allan Houston	.10	.05	.01
☐	33 Theo Ratliff	.05	.02	.01
☐	34 Otis Thorpe	.05	.02	.01
☐	35 Chris Mullin	.05	.02	.01
☐	36 Joe Smith	.40	.18	.05
☐	37 Latrell Sprewell	.10	.05	.01
☐	38 Kevin Willis	.05	.02	.01
☐	39 Sam Cassell	.10	.05	.01
☐	40 Clyde Drexler	.30	.14	.04
☐	41 Robert Horry	.10	.05	.01
☐	42 Hakeem Olajuwon	.60	.25	.07
☐	43 Dale Davis	.05	.02	.01
☐	44 Mark Jackson	.05	.02	.01
☐	45 Derrick McKey	.05	.02	.01
☐	46 Reggie Miller	.30	.14	.04
☐	47 Rik Smits	.10	.05	.01
☐	48 Brent Barry	.15	.07	.02
☐	49 Malik Sealy	.05	.02	.01
☐	50 Loy Vaught	.10	.05	.01
☐	51 Brian Williams	.05	.02	.01
☐	52 Elden Campbell	.10	.05	.01
☐	53 Cedric Ceballos	.10	.05	.01
☐	54 Vlade Divac	.10	.05	.01
☐	55 Eddie Jones	.15	.07	.02
☐	56 Nick Van Exel	.15	.07	.02
☐	57 Tim Hardaway	.10	.05	.01
☐	58 Alonzo Mourning	.25	.11	.03
☐	59 Kurt Thomas	.05	.02	.01
☐	60 Walt Williams	.05	.02	.01
☐	61 Vin Baker	.20	.09	.03
☐	62 Sherman Douglas	.05	.02	.01
☐	63 Glenn Robinson	.25	.11	.03
☐	64 Kevin Garnett	1.00	.45	.12
☐	65 Tom Gugliotta	.10	.05	.01
☐	66 Isaiah Rider	.10	.05	.01
☐	67 Shawn Bradley	.10	.05	.01
☐	68 Chris Childs	.05	.02	.01
☐	69 Armon Gilliam	.05	.02	.01
☐	70 Ed O'Bannon	.05	.02	.01
☐	71 Patrick Ewing	.25	.11	.03
☐	72 Derek Harper	.05	.02	.01
☐	73 Anthony Mason	.10	.05	.01
☐	74 Charles Oakley	.05	.02	.01
☐	75 John Starks	.10	.05	.01

☐ 76	Nick Anderson	.10	.05	.01
☐ 77	Horace Grant	.10	.05	.01
☐ 78	Anfernee Hardaway	1.50	.70	.19
☐ 79	Shaquille O'Neal	1.25	.55	.16
☐ 80	Dennis Scott	.10	.05	.01
☐ 81	Derrick Coleman	.10	.05	.01
☐ 82	Vernon Maxwell	.05	.02	.01
☐ 83	Jerry Stackhouse	.60	.25	.07
☐ 84	Clarence Weatherspoon	.10	.05	.01
☐ 85	Charles Barkley	.40	.18	.05
☐ 86	Michael Finley	.40	.18	.05
☐ 87	Kevin Johnson	.10	.05	.01
☐ 88	Wesley Person	.05	.02	.01
☐ 89	Clifford Robinson	.10	.05	.01
☐ 90	Arvydas Sabonis	.25	.11	.03
☐ 91	Rod Strickland	.10	.05	.01
☐ 92	Gary Trent	.05	.02	.01
☐ 93	Tyus Edney	.15	.07	.02
☐ 94	Brian Grant	.05	.02	.01
☐ 95	Billy Owens	.05	.02	.01
☐ 96	Mitch Richmond	.20	.09	.03
☐ 97	Vinny Del Negro	.05	.02	.01
☐ 98	Sean Elliott	.10	.05	.01
☐ 99	Avery Johnson	.05	.02	.01
☐ 100	David Robinson	.50	.23	.06
☐ 101	Hersey Hawkins	.10	.05	.01
☐ 102	Shawn Kemp	.75	.35	.09
☐ 103	Gary Payton	.30	.14	.04
☐ 104	Detlef Schrempf	.10	.05	.01
☐ 105	Oliver Miller	.05	.02	.01
☐ 106	Tracy Murray	.05	.02	.01
☐ 107	Damon Stoudamire	.75	.35	.09
☐ 108	Sharone Wright	.05	.02	.01
☐ 109	Jeff Hornacek	.10	.05	.01
☐ 110	Karl Malone	.25	.11	.03
☐ 111	John Stockton	.25	.11	.03
☐ 112	Greg Anthony	.05	.02	.01
☐ 113	Bryant Reeves	.20	.09	.03
☐ 114	Byron Scott	.05	.02	.01
☐ 115	Calbert Cheaney	.05	.02	.01
☐ 116	Juwan Howard	.50	.23	.06
☐ 117	Gheorghe Muresan	.10	.05	.01
☐ 118	Rasheed Wallace	.15	.07	.02
☐ 119	Chris Webber	.20	.09	.03
☐ 120	Mookie Blaylock HL	.05	.02	.01
☐ 121	Dino Radja HL	.05	.02	.01
☐ 122	Larry Johnson HL	.10	.05	.01
☐ 123	Michael Jordan HL	1.50	.70	.19
☐ 124	Terrell Brandon HL	.05	.02	.01
☐ 125	Jason Kidd HL	.25	.11	.03
☐ 126	Antonio McDyess HL	.15	.07	.02
☐ 127	Grant Hill HL	.40	.18	.05
☐ 128	Latrell Sprewell HL	.05	.02	.01
☐ 129	Hakeem Olajuwon HL	.30	.14	.04
☐ 130	Reggie Miller HL	.15	.07	.02
☐ 131	Loy Vaught HL	.05	.02	.01
☐ 132	Cedric Ceballos HL	.05	.02	.01
☐ 133	Alonzo Mourning HL	.10	.05	.01
☐ 134	Vin Baker HL	.10	.05	.01
☐ 135	Isaiah Rider HL	.05	.02	.01
☐ 136	Armon Gilliam HL	.05	.02	.01
☐ 137	Patrick Ewing HL	.10	.05	.01
☐ 138	Shaquille O'Neal HL	.60	.25	.07
☐ 139	Jerry Stackhouse HL	.30	.14	.04
☐ 140	Charles Barkley HL	.20	.09	.03
☐ 141	Clifford Robinson HL	.05	.02	.01
☐ 142	Mitch Richmond HL	.10	.05	.01
☐ 143	David Robinson HL	.25	.11	.03
☐ 144	Shawn Kemp HL	.40	.18	.05
☐ 145	Damon Stoudamire HL	.40	.18	.05
☐ 146	Karl Malone HL	.10	.05	.01

☐ 147	Bryant Reeves HL	.10	.05	.01
☐ 148	Juwan Howard HL	.25	.11	.03
☐ 149	Checklist	.05	.02	.01
☐ 150	Checklist	.05	.02	.01

1996-97 Fleer Decade of Excellence

Randomly inserted exclusively into first series hobby packs at a rate of one in 72, this 10-card set features reprints from the popular 1986-87 debut Fleer set. Card fronts are designated with the card name "Fleer Decade of Excellence 1986-1996" in gold foil to distinguish the card from the original issue. Card backs are identical to the 1986-87 release, but with a "1996" copyright.

	MINT	NRMT	EXC
COMPLETE SERIES 1 (10)	200.00	90.00	25.00
COMMON CARD (1-10)	8.00	3.60	1.00

☐ 1	Clyde Drexler	20.00	9.00	2.50
☐ 2	Joe Dumars	8.00	3.60	1.00
☐ 3	Derek Harper	8.00	3.60	1.00
☐ 4	Michael Jordan	150.00	70.00	19.00
☐ 5	Karl Malone	15.00	6.75	1.85
☐ 6	Chris Mullin	8.00	3.60	1.00
☐ 7	Charles Oakley	8.00	3.60	1.00
☐ 8	Sam Perkins	8.00	3.60	1.00
☐ 9	Ricky Pierce	8.00	3.60	1.00
☐ 10	Buck Williams	8.00	3.60	1.00

1996-97 Fleer Franchise Futures

Randomly inserted exclusively into first series hobby packs at a rate of one in 54, this 10-card set features young stars that may be the future of their respecive teams. Card fronts feature an embossed photo with the card name "Franchise Future" running along the left side of the card in silver foil. The player's name is also treated with silver foil at the bottom of the card. Card backs feature a brief commentary on the player and are numbered "X of 10".

	MINT	NRMT	EXC
COMPLETE SET (10)	130.00	57.50	16.00
COMMON CARD (1-10)	6.00	2.70	.75
☐ 1 Kevin Garnett	25.00	11.00	3.10
☐ 2 Anfernee Hardaway	35.00	16.00	4.40
☐ 3 Grant Hill	20.00	9.00	2.50
☐ 4 Juwan Howard	12.00	5.50	1.50
☐ 5 Jason Kidd	12.00	5.50	1.50
☐ 6 Antonio McDyess	8.00	3.60	1.00
☐ 7 Glenn Robinson	6.00	2.70	.75
☐ 8 Joe Smith	10.00	4.50	1.25
☐ 9 Jerry Stackhouse	15.00	6.75	1.85
☐ 10 Damon Stoudamire	20.00	9.00	2.50

1996-97 Fleer Game Breakers

Randomly inserted exclusively into first series retail packs at a rate of one in 48, this 15-card set features some of the top duos from the NBA. The card fronts are made of plastic and feature color action shots of both players represented. Both player's last names are in gold foil at the bottom under the Game Breakers card name. Card backs feature a background of the team's colors with a brief commentary on each individual player and are numbered "X of 15".

	MINT	NRMT	EXC
COMPLETE SET (15)	200.00	90.00	25.00
COMMON PAIR (1-15)	5.00	2.20	.60
☐ 1 Michael Jordan	70.00	32.00	8.75
Scottie Pippen			
☐ 2 Jim Jackson	10.00	4.50	1.25
Jason Kidd			
☐ 3 Grant Hill	15.00	6.75	1.85
Allan Houston			
☐ 4 Joe Smith	8.00	3.60	1.00
Latrell Sprewell			
☐ 5 Clyde Drexler	15.00	6.75	1.85
Hakeem Olajuwon			
☐ 6 Cedric Ceballos	5.00	2.20	.60
Nick Van Exel			
☐ 7 Tim Hardaway	5.00	2.20	.60
Alonzo Mourning			
☐ 8 Vin Baker	8.00	3.60	1.00
Glenn Robinson			
☐ 9 Kevin Garnett	20.00	9.00	2.50
Isaiah Rider			
☐ 10 Anfernee Hardaway	40.00	18.00	5.00
Shaquille O'Neal			
☐ 11 Jerry Stackhouse	10.00	4.50	1.25
Clarence Weahterspoon			
☐ 12 Charles Barkley	12.00	5.50	1.50
Michael Finley			
☐ 13 Sean Elliott	10.00	4.50	1.25
David Robinson			
☐ 14 Shawn Kemp	15.00	6.75	1.85
Gary Payton			
☐ 15 Karl Malone	8.00	3.60	1.00
John Stockton			

1996-97 Fleer Lucky 13

Randomly inserted into all first series packs at a rate of one in 30, this 13-card set features cards that are redeemable for the top 13 player's selected in the 1996 NBA Draft. Card fronts contain a colorful background with a number from 1-13. Whatever card number is on the front corresponds to the rookie selected at that spot in the 1996 NBA draft and can be redeemed for a special card featuring that player. The expiration date for this redemption was April 1, 1997. Cards are numbered on the back as "X of 13".

	MINT	NRMT	EXC
COMPLETE SET (13)	70.00	32.00	8.75
COMMON CARD (1-13)	1.50	.70	.19
☐ 1 Allen Iverson Trade	15.00	6.75	1.85
☐ 2 Marcus Camby Trade	12.00	5.50	1.50
☐ 3 Shareef Abdur-Rahim Trade	8.00	3.60	1.00
☐ 4 Stephon Marbury Trade	12.00	5.50	1.50
☐ 5 Ray Allen Trade	8.00	3.60	1.00
☐ 6 Antoine Walker Trade	6.00	2.70	.75
☐ 7 Lorenzen Wright Trade	2.50	1.10	.30
☐ 8 Kerry Kittles Trade	4.00	1.80	.50

		MINT	NRMT	EXC
☐ 9	Samaki Walker Trade	4.00	1.80	.50
☐ 10	Erick Dampier Trade	1.50	.70	.19
☐ 11	Todd Fuller Trade	1.50	.70	.19
☐ 12	Vitaly Potapenko Trade	1.50	.70	.19
☐ 13	Kobe Bryant Trade	15.00	6.75	1.85

1996-97 Fleer
Rookie Rewind

Randomly inserted in all first series packs at a rate of one in 24, this 15-card set takes a look back at the top rookies from the 1995-96 class. Card fronts contain team colors in the background with both the card name "Rookie Rewind" and the player's last name treated in gold foil. Card backs contain another player shot and a brief commentary. Card backs are numbered as "X of 15".

		MINT	NRMT	EXC
	COMPLETE SET (15)	40.00	18.00	5.00
	COMMON CARD (1-15)	1.00	.45	.12
☐ 1	Brent Barry	2.00	.90	.25
☐ 2	Tyus Edney	2.00	.90	.25
☐ 3	Michael Finley	5.00	2.20	.60
☐ 4	Kevin Garnett	12.00	5.50	1.50
☐ 5	Antonio McDyess	4.00	1.80	.50
☐ 6	Bryant Reeves	2.50	1.10	.30
☐ 7	Arvydas Sabonis	3.00	1.35	.35
☐ 8	Joe Smith	5.00	2.20	.60
☐ 9	Jerry Stackhouse	8.00	3.60	1.00
☐ 10	Damon Stoudamire	10.00	4.50	1.25
☐ 11	Bob Sura	1.50	.70	.19
☐ 12	Kurt Thomas	1.00	.45	.12
☐ 13	Gary Trent	1.00	.45	.12
☐ 14	Rasheed Wallace	2.00	.90	.25
☐ 15	Eric Williams	1.00	.45	.12

1996-97 Fleer
Stackhouse's
All-Fleer

Randomly inserted in first series nine-card packs at a rate of one in 12 and one per special first series retail pack, this 12-card set features some of the top player's in the NBA as seen through Fleer Spokesman

Jerry Stackhouse's eyes. Card fronts contain team colors in the background and have both the card name and the player's name running vertical in gold foil. Card backs contain a brief statistical summary and are numbered as "X of 12".

		MINT	NRMT	EXC
	COMPLETE SET (12)	30.00	13.50	3.70
	COMMON CARD (1-12)	1.00	.45	.12
☐ 1	Charles Barkley	1.50	.70	.19
☐ 2	Anfernee Hardaway	6.00	2.70	.75
☐ 3	Grant Hill	3.00	1.35	.35
☐ 4	Michael Jordan	12.00	5.50	1.50
☐ 5	Shawn Kemp	3.00	1.35	.35
☐ 6	Jason Kidd	2.00	.90	.25
☐ 7	Karl Malone	1.00	.45	.12
☐ 8	Hakeem Olajuwon	2.50	1.10	.30
☐ 9	Shaquille O'Neal	5.00	2.20	.60
☐ 10	Gary Payton	1.25	.55	.16
☐ 11	Scottie Pippen	3.00	1.35	.35
☐ 12	David Robinson	2.00	.90	.25

1996-97 Fleer
Stackhouse's
Scrapbook

Randomly inserted into all first series packs at a rate of one in 24, cards from this two-card set highlight moments from Stackhouse's rookie year. In addition, they are the last installment to the cross-brand insert from all of the 1995-96 Fleer products.

		MINT	NRMT	EXC
	COMPLETE SET (2)	5.00	2.20	.60
	COMMON CARD (S9-S10)	2.50	1.10	.30

		MINT	NRMT	EXC
☐ S9	Jerry Stackhouse	2.50	1.10	.30
☐ S10	Jerry Stackhouse	2.50	1.10	.30

1996 Fleer USA

The 1996 Fleer USA set was issued in one series totalling 52 cards. The 3-card packs retailed for $4.99 each during the summer of 1996. Each pack contained two super-premium and one lenticular card which resulted in the super-premium cards being triple-printed. The set contains the topical subsets: In the Beginning (1-10), By the Numbers (11-20), Defining Moment (21-30), Masters of the Game (31-40), Around the World (41-50). Each Around the World, In the Beginning and Defining Moments card features the lenticular technology with rotating images of the earth, pulsating player images and a USA/5-ring logo that changes color. Each By the Numbers and Masters of the Game card features super-premium UV-coating, foil-stamping and printing on thick, 20-point stock. Collectors were also offered the chance to receive a special 12-card exchange set by sending in 15 wrappers (along with $3.00 for postage and handling). The 12 cards consisted of three lenticular, two super-premium and one Heroes insert of both Charles Barkley and Mitch Richmond.

	MINT	NRMT	EXC
COMPLETE SET (52)	110.00	50.00	14.00
COMMON CARD (1-52)	.40	.18	.05
☐ 1 Anfernee Hardaway IB	8.00	3.60	1.00
☐ 2 Grant Hill IB	5.00	2.20	.60
☐ 3 Karl Malone IB	1.25	.55	.16
☐ 4 Reggie Miller IB	1.50	.70	.19
☐ 5 Hakeem Olajuwon IB	3.00	1.35	.35
☐ 6 Shaquille O'Neal IB	6.00	2.70	.75
☐ 7 Scottie Pippen IB	4.00	1.80	.50
☐ 8 David Robinson IB	2.50	1.10	.30
☐ 9 Glenn Robinson IB	1.50	.70	.19
☐ 10 John Stockton IB	1.25	.55	.16
☐ 11 Anfernee Hardaway BN	2.50	1.10	.30
☐ 12 Grant Hill BN	1.50	.70	.19
☐ 13 Karl Malone BN	.40	.18	.05
☐ 14 Reggie Miller BN	.50	.23	.06
☐ 15 Hakeem Olajuwon BN	1.00	.45	.12
☐ 16 Shaquille O'Neal BN	2.00	.90	.25
☐ 17 Scottie Pippen BN	1.25	.55	.16
☐ 18 David Robinson BN	.75	.35	.09
☐ 19 Glenn Robinson BN	.50	.23	.06
☐ 20 John Stockton BN	.40	.18	.05
☐ 21 Anfernee Hardaway DM	8.00	3.60	1.00
☐ 22 Grant Hill DM	5.00	2.20	.60
☐ 23 Karl Malone DM	1.25	.55	.16
☐ 24 Reggie Miller DM	1.50	.70	.19
☐ 25 Hakeem Olajuwon DM	3.00	1.35	.35
☐ 26 Shaquille O'Neal DM	6.00	2.70	.75
☐ 27 Scottie Pippen DM	4.00	1.80	.50
☐ 28 David Robinson DM	2.50	1.10	.30
☐ 29 Glenn Robinson DM	1.50	.70	.19
☐ 30 John Stockton DM	1.25	.55	.16
☐ 31 Anfernee Hardaway MAS	1.10		.30
☐ 32 Grant Hill MAS	1.50	.70	.19
☐ 33 Karl Malone MAS	.40	.18	.05
☐ 34 Reggie Miller MAS	.50	.23	.06
☐ 35 Hakeem Olajuwon MAS	1.00	.45	.12
☐ 36 Shaquille O'Neal MAS	2.00	.90	.25
☐ 37 Scottie Pippen MAS	1.25	.55	.16
☐ 38 David Robinson MAS	.75	.35	.09
☐ 39 Glenn Robinson MAS	.50	.23	.06
☐ 40 John Stockton MAS	.40	.18	.05
☐ 41 Anfernee Hardaway AW	8.00	3.60	1.00
☐ 42 Grant Hill AW	5.00	2.20	.60
☐ 43 Karl Malone AW	1.25	.55	.16
☐ 44 Reggie Miller AW	1.50	.70	.19
☐ 45 Hakeem Olajuwon AW	3.00	1.35	.35
☐ 46 Shaquille O'Neal AW	6.00	2.70	.75
☐ 47 Scottie Pippen AW	4.00	1.80	.50
☐ 48 David Robinson AW	2.50	1.10	.30
☐ 49 Glenn Robinson AW	1.50	.70	.19
☐ 50 John Stockton AW	1.25	.55	.16
☐ 51 Team USA CL	4.00	1.80	.50
☐ 52 Team USA CL	.40	.18	.05

1996 Fleer USA Heroes

Randomly inserted exclusively into hobby packs at a rate of one in 18, this 10-card set features the 10 original members of the 1996 USAB men's basketball team in a special die-cut design with the top left of the card clipped as the player is silhouetted across the American flag and extended out beyond the natural border of the card.

	MINT	NRMT	EXC
COMPLETE SET (10)	175.00	80.00	22.00
COMMON CARD (1-10)	8.00	3.60	1.00
☐ 1 Anfernee Hardaway	50.00	22.00	6.25
☐ 2 Grant Hill	30.00	13.50	3.70

		MINT	NRMT	EXC
☐ 3	Karl Malone	8.00	3.60	1.00
☐ 4	Reggie Miller	10.00	4.50	1.25
☐ 5	Hakeem Olajuwon	20.00	9.00	2.50
☐ 6	Shaquille O'Neal	40.00	18.00	5.00
☐ 7	Scottie Pippen	25.00	11.00	3.10
☐ 8	David Robinson	15.00	6.75	1.85
☐ 9	Glenn Robinson	10.00	4.50	1.25
☐ 10	John Stockton	8.00	3.60	1.00

1989-90 Hoops

*The 1989-90 Hoops set contains 352 stan-
dard-size cards. The cards were issued in
two series of 300 and 52 cards. Hoops' initial venture in the basketball market helped
spark the basketball card boom of 1989-90.
The cards were issued in 15-card packs.
The fronts feature color action player photos, bordered by a basketball lane in one of
the team's colors. On a white card face the
player's name appears in black lettering
above the picture. The backs have head
shots of the players, biographical information and statistics printed on a pale yellow
background with white borders. The cards
are numbered on the back. The key Rookie
Card in this set is David Robinson (138).
This is his lone Rookie Card. Beware of
Robinson counterfeits which are distin-
guishable primarily by comparison to a real
card or under magnification. Other Rookie
Cards of note include Hersey Hawkins, Jeff
Hornacek, Kevin Johnson, Steve Kerr,
Reggie Lewis, Dan Majerle, Danny
Manning, Mitch Richmond, Rik Smits and
Rod Strickland. The second series features
the premier cards of the expansion teams
(Minnesota and Orlando), traded players, a
special NBA Championship card of the
Detroit Pistons and a Robinson In Action
(310) card. Since the original Detroit
Pistons World Champs card (No. 353A)
was so difficult for collectors to find in
packs, Hoops produced another edition
(353B) of the card that was available direct
from the company free of charge. If a collector wished to acquire two or more from
the company, additional copies were available for 35 cents per card. The set is considered complete with the less difficult version. The short prints (SP below) in the first
series are those cards which were dropped
to make room for the new second series
cards on the printing sheet.*

		MINT	NRMT	EXC
COMPLETE SET (352)		25.00	11.00	3.10
COMPLETE SERIES 1 (300)		20.00	9.00	2.50
COMPLETE SERIES 2 (52)		5.00	2.20	.60
COMMON CARD (1-352)		.05	.02	.01
COMMON SP		.15	.07	.02
☐ 1	Joe Dumars	.10	.05	.01
☐ 2	Tree Rollins	.05	.02	.01
☐ 3	Kenny Walker	.05	.02	.01
☐ 4	Mychal Thompson	.05	.02	.01
☐ 5	Alvin Robertson SP	.15	.07	.02
☐ 6	Vinny Del Negro	.15	.07	.02
☐ 7	Greg Anderson SP	.15	.07	.02
☐ 8	Rod Strickland	.60	.25	.07
☐ 9	Ed Pinckney	.05	.02	.01
☐ 10	Dale Ellis	.05	.02	.01
☐ 11	Chuck Daly CO	.20	.09	.03
☐ 12	Eric Leckner	.05	.02	.01
☐ 13	Charles Davis	.05	.02	.01
☐ 14	Cotton Fitzsimmons CO	.05	.02	.01
	(No NBA logo on back in bottom right)			
☐ 15	Byron Scott	.10	.05	.01
☐ 16	Derrick Chievous	.05	.02	.01
☐ 17	Reggie Lewis	.25	.11	.03
☐ 18	Jim Paxson	.05	.02	.01
☐ 19	Tony Campbell	.05	.02	.01
☐ 20	Rolando Blackman	.10	.05	.01
☐ 21	Michael Jordan AS	1.50	.70	.19
☐ 22	Cliff Levingston	.05	.02	.01
☐ 23	Roy Tarpley	.05	.02	.01
☐ 24	Harold Pressley UER	.05	.02	.01
	(Cinderella misspelled as cindarella)			
☐ 25	Larry Nance	.05	.02	.01
☐ 26	Chris Morris	.15	.07	.02
☐ 27	Bob Hansen UER	.05	.02	.01
	(Drafted in '84, should say '83)			
☐ 28	Mark Price AS	.05	.02	.01
☐ 29	Reggie Miller	.75	.35	.09
☐ 30	Karl Malone	.25	.11	.03
☐ 31	Sidney Lowe SP	.15	.07	.02
☐ 32	Ron Anderson	.05	.02	.01
☐ 33	Mike Gminski	.05	.02	.01
☐ 34	Scott Brooks	.05	.02	.01
☐ 35	Kevin Johnson	.50	.23	.06
☐ 36	Mark Bryant	.05	.02	.01
☐ 37	Rik Smits	.50	.23	.06
☐ 38	Tim Perry	.05	.02	.01
☐ 39	Ralph Sampson	.05	.02	.01
☐ 40	Danny Manning UER	.30	.14	.04
	(Missing 1988 in draft info)			
☐ 41	Kevin Edwards	.05	.02	.01
☐ 42	Paul Mokeski	.05	.02	.01
☐ 43	Dale Ellis AS	.05	.02	.01
☐ 44	Walter Berry	.05	.02	.01
☐ 45	Chuck Person	.10	.05	.01
☐ 46	Rick Mahorn SP	.25	.11	.03
☐ 47	Joe Kleine	.05	.02	.01
☐ 48	Brad Daugherty AS	.05	.02	.01
☐ 49	Mike Woodson	.05	.02	.01
☐ 50	Brad Daugherty	.05	.02	.01
☐ 51	Shelton Jones SP	.15	.07	.02
☐ 52	Michael Adams	.05	.02	.01
☐ 53	Wes Unseld CO	.10	.05	.01
☐ 54	Rex Chapman	.15	.07	.02
☐ 55	Kelly Tripucka	.05	.02	.01
☐ 56	Rickey Green	.05	.02	.01

☐ 57 Frank Johnson SP	.15	.07	.02
☐ 58 Johnny Newman	.05	.02	.01
☐ 59 Billy Thompson	.05	.02	.01
☐ 60 Stu Jackson CO	.05	.02	.01
☐ 61 Walter Davis	.10	.05	.01
☐ 62 Brian Shaw SP UER	.25	.11	.03
(Gary Grant led rookies in assists, not Shaw)			
☐ 63 Gerald Wilkins	.05	.02	.01
☐ 64 Armon Gilliam	.05	.02	.01
☐ 65 Maurice Cheeks SP	.25	.11	.03
☐ 66 Jack Sikma	.10	.05	.01
☐ 67 Harvey Grant	.15	.07	.02
☐ 68 Jim Lynam CO	.05	.02	.01
☐ 69 Clyde Drexler AS	.15	.07	.02
☐ 70 Xavier McDaniel	.05	.02	.01
☐ 71 Danny Young	.05	.02	.01
☐ 72 Fennis Dembo	.05	.02	.01
☐ 73 Mark Acres SP	.15	.07	.02
☐ 74 Brad Lohaus SP	.15	.07	.02
☐ 75 Manute Bol	.05	.02	.01
☐ 76 Purvis Short	.05	.02	.01
☐ 77 Allen Leavell	.05	.02	.01
☐ 78 Johnny Dawkins SP	.15	.07	.02
☐ 79 Paul Pressey	.05	.02	.01
☐ 80 Patrick Ewing	.25	.11	.03
☐ 81 Bill Wennington	.10	.05	.01
☐ 82 Danny Schayes	.05	.02	.01
☐ 83 Derek Smith	.05	.02	.01
☐ 84 Moses Malone AS	.10	.05	.01
☐ 85 Jeff Malone	.05	.02	.01
☐ 86 Otis Smith SP	.15	.07	.02
☐ 87 Trent Tucker	.05	.02	.01
☐ 88 Robert Reid	.05	.02	.01
☐ 89 John Paxson	.10	.05	.01
☐ 90 Chris Mullin	.10	.05	.01
☐ 91 Tom Garrick	.05	.02	.01
☐ 92 Willis Reed CO SP UER	.25	.11	.03
(Gambling, should be Grambling)			
☐ 93 Dave Corzine SP	.15	.07	.02
☐ 94 Mark Alarie	.05	.02	.01
☐ 95 Mark Aguirre	.10	.05	.01
☐ 96 Charles Barkley AS	.20	.09	.03
☐ 97 Sidney Green SP	.15	.07	.02
☐ 98 Kevin Willis	.05	.02	.01
☐ 99 Dave Hoppen	.05	.02	.01
☐ 100 Terry Cummings SP	.15	.07	.02
☐ 101 Dwayne Washington SP	.15	.07	.02
☐ 102 Larry Brown CO	.05	.02	.01
☐ 103 Kevin Duckworth	.05	.02	.01
☐ 104 Uwe Blab SP	.15	.07	.02
☐ 105 Terry Porter	.05	.02	.01
☐ 106 Craig Ehlo	.05	.02	.01
☐ 107 Don Casey CO	.05	.02	.01
☐ 108 Pat Riley CO	.10	.05	.01
☐ 109 John Salley	.05	.02	.01
☐ 110 Charles Barkley	.40	.18	.05
☐ 111 Sam Bowie SP	.15	.07	.02
☐ 112 Earl Cureton	.05	.02	.01
☐ 113 Craig Hodges UER	.05	.02	.01
(3-pointing shooting)			
☐ 114 Benoit Benjamin	.05	.02	.01
☐ 115A Spud Webb ERR SP	.30	.14	.04
(Signed 9/27/89)			
☐ 115B Spud Webb COR	.10	.05	.01
(Second series; signed 9/26/85)			
☐ 116 Karl Malone AS	.10	.05	.01
☐ 117 Sleepy Floyd	.05	.02	.01
☐ 118 John Williams	.05	.02	.01
☐ 119 Michael Holton	.05	.02	.01
☐ 120 Alex English	.10	.05	.01
☐ 121 Dennis Johnson	.10	.05	.01
☐ 122 Wayne Cooper SP	.15	.07	.02
☐ 123A Don Chaney CO	.10	.05	.01
(Line next to NBA coaching record)			
☐ 123B Don Chaney CO	.10	.05	.01
(No line)			
☐ 124 A.C. Green	.10	.05	.01
☐ 125 Adrian Dantley	.10	.05	.01
☐ 126 Del Harris CO	.05	.02	.01
☐ 127 Dick Harter CO	.05	.02	.01
☐ 128 Reggie Williams	.05	.02	.01
☐ 129 Bill Hanzlik	.05	.02	.01
☐ 130 Dominique Wilkins	.10	.05	.01
☐ 131 Herb Williams	.05	.02	.01
☐ 132 Steve Johnson SP	.15	.07	.02
☐ 133 Alex English AS	.10	.05	.01
☐ 134 Darrell Walker	.05	.02	.01
☐ 135 Bill Laimbeer	.10	.05	.01
☐ 136 Fred Roberts	.05	.02	.01
☐ 137 Hersey Hawkins	.30	.14	.04
☐ 138 David Robinson SP	12.00	5.50	1.50
☐ 139 Brad Sellers SP	.15	.07	.02
☐ 140 John Stockton	.60	.25	.07
☐ 141 Grant Long	.15	.07	.02
☐ 142 Marc Iavaroni SP	.15	.07	.02
☐ 143 Steve Alford SP	.25	.11	.03
☐ 144 Jeff Lamp SP	.15	.07	.02
☐ 145 Buck Williams SP	.25	.11	.03
(Won ROY in '81, should say '82')			
☐ 146 Mark Jackson AS	.05	.02	.01
☐ 147 Jim Petersen	.05	.02	.01
☐ 148 Steve Stipanovich SP	.15	.07	.02
☐ 149 Sam Vincent SP	.15	.07	.02
☐ 150 Larry Bird	1.00	.45	.12
☐ 151 Jon Koncak	.05	.02	.01
☐ 152 Olden Polynice	.15	.07	.02
☐ 153 Randy Breuer	.05	.02	.01
☐ 154 John Battle	.05	.02	.01
☐ 155 Mark Eaton	.05	.02	.01
☐ 156 Kevin McHale AS UER	.10	.05	.01
(No TM on Celtics logo on back)			
☐ 157 Jerry Sichting SP	.15	.07	.02
☐ 158 Pat Cummings SP	.15	.07	.02
☐ 159 Patrick Ewing AS	.10	.05	.01
☐ 160 Mark Price	.10	.05	.01
☐ 161 Jerry Reynolds CO	.05	.02	.01
☐ 162 Ken Norman	.10	.05	.01
☐ 163 John Bagley SP UER	.15	.07	.02
(Picked in '83, should say '82')			
☐ 164 Christian Welp SP	.15	.07	.02
☐ 165 Reggie Theus SP	.25	.11	.03
☐ 166 Magic Johnson AS	.40	.18	.05
☐ 167 John Long UER	.05	.02	.01
(Picked in '79, should say '78')			
☐ 168 Larry Smith SP	.15	.07	.02
☐ 169 Charles Shackleford	.05	.02	.01
☐ 170 Tom Chambers	.10	.05	.01
☐ 171A John MacLeod CO SP	.10	.05	.01
ERR (NBA logo in wrong place)			
☐ 171B John MacLeod CO	.10	.05	.01
COR (Second series)			
☐ 172 Ron Rothstein CO	.05	.02	.01
☐ 173 Joe Wolf	.05	.02	.01

□	174	Mark Eaton AS	.05	.02	.01
□	175	Jon Sundvold	.05	.02	.01
□	176	Scott Hastings SP	.15	.07	.02
□	177	Isiah Thomas AS	.10	.05	.01
□	178	Hakeem Olajuwon AS...	.30	.14	.04
□	179	Mike Fratello CO	.05	.02	.01
□	180	Hakeem Olajuwon	.60	.25	.07
□	181	Randolph Keys	.05	.02	.01
□	182	Richard Anderson UER	.05	.02	.01
		(Trail Blazers on front			
		should be all caps)			
□	183	Dan Majerle	.25	.11	.03
□	184	Derek Harper	.10	.05	.01
□	185	Robert Parish	.10	.05	.01
□	186	Ricky Berry SP	.15	.07	.02
□	187	Michael Cooper	.10	.05	.01
□	188	Vinnie Johnson	.10	.05	.01
□	189	James Donaldson	.05	.02	.01
□	190	Clyde Drexler UER	.30	.14	.04
		(4th pick, should			
		be 14th)			
□	191	Jay Vincent SP	.15	.07	.02
□	192	Nate McMillan	.05	.02	.01
□	193	Kevin Duckworth AS	.05	.02	.01
□	194	Ledell Eackles	.05	.02	.01
□	195	Eddie Johnson	.05	.02	.01
□	196	Terry Teagle	.05	.02	.01
□	197	Tom Chambers AS	.05	.02	.01
□	198	Joe Barry Carroll	.05	.02	.01
□	199	Dennis Hopson	.05	.02	.01
□	200	Michael Jordan	3.00	1.35	.35
□	201	Jerome Lane	.05	.02	.01
□	202	Greg Kite	.05	.02	.01
□	203	David Rivers SP	.15	.07	.02
□	204	Sylvester Gray	.05	.02	.01
□	205	Ron Harper	.05	.02	.01
□	206	Frank Brickowski	.05	.02	.01
□	207	Rory Sparrow	.05	.02	.01
□	208	Gerald Henderson	.05	.02	.01
□	209	Rod Higgins UER	.05	.02	.01
		('85-86 stats should			
		also include San			
		Antonio and Seattle)			
□	210	James Worthy	.10	.05	.01
□	211	Dennis Rodman	2.00	.90	.25
□	212	Ricky Pierce	.05	.02	.01
□	213	Charles Oakley	.10	.05	.01
□	214	Steve Colter	.05	.02	.01
□	215	Danny Ainge	.10	.05	.01
□	216	Lenny Wilkens CO UER	.10	.05	.01
		(No NBA logo on back			
		in bottom right)			
□	217	Larry Nance AS	.05	.02	.01
□	218	Muggsy Bogues	.10	.05	.01
□	219	James Worthy AS	.10	.05	.01
□	220	Lafayette Lever	.05	.02	.01
□	221	Quintin Dailey SP	.15	.07	.02
□	222	Lester Conner	.05	.02	.01
□	223	Jose Ortiz	.05	.02	.01
□	224	Micheal Williams SP	.15	.07	.02
		UER (Misspelled			
		Michael on card)			
□	225	Wayman Tisdale	.05	.02	.01
□	226	Mike Sanders SP	.15	.07	.02
□	227	Jim Farmer SP	.15	.07	.02
□	228	Mark West	.05	.02	.01
□	229	Jeff Hornacek	.30	.14	.04
□	230	Chris Mullin AS	.05	.02	.01
□	231	Vern Fleming	.05	.02	.01
□	232	Kenny Smith	.05	.02	.01
□	233	Derrick McKey	.05	.02	.01
□	234	Dominique Wilkins AS	.10	.05	.01
□	235	Willie Anderson	.05	.02	.01
□	236	Keith Lee SP	.15	.07	.02
□	237	Buck Johnson	.05	.02	.01
□	238	Randy Wittman	.05	.02	.01
□	239	Terry Catledge SP	.15	.07	.02
□	240	Bernard King	.10	.05	.01
□	241	Darrell Griffith	.10	.05	.01
□	242	Horace Grant	.30	.14	.04
□	243	Rony Seikaly	.15	.07	.02
□	244	Scottie Pippen	1.50	.70	.19
□	245	Michael Cage UER	.05	.02	.01
		(Picked in '85,			
		should say '84)			
□	246	Kurt Rambis	.05	.02	.01
□	247	Morlon Wiley SP	.15	.07	.02
□	248	Ronnie Grandison	.05	.02	.01
□	249	Scott Skiles SP	.25	.11	.03
□	250	Isiah Thomas	.15	.07	.02
□	251	Thurl Bailey	.05	.02	.01
□	252	Doc Rivers	.05	.02	.01
□	253	Stuart Gray SP	.15	.07	.02
□	254	John Williams	.05	.02	.01
□	255	Bill Cartwright	.05	.02	.01
□	256	Terry Cummings AS	.05	.02	.01
□	257	Rodney McCray	.05	.02	.01
□	258	Larry Krystkowiak	.05	.02	.01
□	259	Will Perdue	.05	.02	.01
□	260	Mitch Richmond	1.25	.55	.16
□	261	Blair Rasmussen	.05	.02	.01
□	262	Charles Smith	.10	.05	.01
□	263	Tyrone Corbin SP	.15	.07	.02
□	264	Kelvin Upshaw	.05	.02	.01
□	265	Otis Thorpe	.10	.05	.01
□	266	Phil Jackson CO	.10	.05	.01
□	267	Jerry Sloan CO	.10	.05	.01
□	268	John Shasky	.05	.02	.01
□	269A	B. Bickerstaff CO SP	.30	.14	.04
		ERR (Born 2/11/44)			
□	269B	B. Bickerstaff CO	.05	.02	.01
		COR (Second series;			
		Born 11/2/43)			
□	270	Magic Johnson	.75	.35	.09
□	271	Vernon Maxwell	.15	.07	.02
□	272	Tim McCormick	.05	.02	.01
□	273	Don Nelson CO	.10	.05	.01
□	274	Gary Grant	.05	.02	.01
□	275	Sidney Moncrief SP	.25	.11	.03
□	276	Roy Hinson	.05	.02	.01
□	277	Jimmy Rodgers CO	.05	.02	.01
□	278	Antoine Carr	.05	.02	.01
□	279A	Orlando Woolridge SP	.15	.07	.02
		ERR (No Trademark)			
□	279B	Orlando Woolridge	.10	.05	.01
		COR (Second series)			
□	280	Kevin McHale	.10	.05	.01
□	281	LaSalle Thompson	.05	.02	.01
□	282	Detlef Schrempf	.15	.07	.02
□	283	Doug Moe CO	.05	.02	.01
□	284A	James Edwards	.30	.14	.04
		(Small black line			
		next to card number)			
□	284B	James Edwards	.10	.05	.01
		(No small black line)			
□	285	Jerome Kersey	.05	.02	.01
□	286	Sam Perkins	.05	.02	.01
□	287	Sedale Threatt	.05	.02	.01
□	288	Tim Kempton SP	.15	.07	.02
□	289	Mark McNamara	.05	.02	.01
□	290	Moses Malone	.15	.07	.02
□	291	Rick Adelman CO UER	.05	.02	.01

(Chemekata misspelled
as Chemketa)

☐ 292 Dick Versace CO	.05	.02	.01
☐ 293 Alton Lister SP	.15	.07	.02
☐ 294 Winston Garland	.05	.02	.01
☐ 295 Kiki Vandeweghe	.05	.02	.01
☐ 296 Brad Davis	.05	.02	.01
☐ 297 John Stockton AS	.30	.14	.04
☐ 298 Jay Humphries	.05	.02	.01
☐ 299 Dell Curry	.05	.02	.01
☐ 300 Mark Jackson	.05	.02	.01
☐ 301 Morlon Wiley	.05	.02	.01
☐ 302 Reggie Theus	.10	.05	.01
☐ 303 Otis Smith	.05	.02	.01
☐ 304 Tod Murphy	.05	.02	.01
☐ 305 Sidney Green	.05	.02	.01
☐ 306 Shelton Jones	.05	.02	.01
☐ 307 Mark Acres	.05	.02	.01
☐ 308 Terry Catledge	.05	.02	.01
☐ 309 Larry Smith	.05	.02	.01
☐ 310 David Robinson IA	2.00	.90	.25
☐ 311 Johnny Dawkins	.05	.02	.01
☐ 312 Terry Cummings	.05	.02	.01
☐ 313 Sidney Lowe	.05	.02	.01
☐ 314 Bill Musselman CO	.05	.02	.01
☐ 315 Buck Williams UER	.10	.05	.01

(Won ROY in '81,
should say '82)

☐ 316 Mel Turpin	.05	.02	.01
☐ 317 Scott Hastings	.05	.02	.01
☐ 318 Scott Skiles	.05	.02	.01
☐ 319 Tyrone Corbin	.05	.02	.01
☐ 320 Maurice Cheeks	.10	.05	.01
☐ 321 Matt Guokas CO	.05	.02	.01
☐ 322 Jeff Turner	.05	.02	.01
☐ 323 David Wingate	.05	.02	.01
☐ 324 Steve Johnson	.05	.02	.01
☐ 325 Alton Lister	.05	.02	.01
☐ 326 Ken Bannister	.05	.02	.01
☐ 327 Bill Fitch CO UER	.05	.02	.01

(Copyright missing
on bottom of back)

☐ 328 Sam Vincent	.05	.02	.01
☐ 329 Larry Drew	.05	.02	.01
☐ 330 Rick Mahorn	.05	.02	.01
☐ 331 Christian Welp	.05	.02	.01
☐ 332 Brad Lohaus	.05	.02	.01
☐ 333 Frank Johnson	.05	.02	.01
☐ 334 Jim Farmer	.05	.02	.01
☐ 335 Wayne Cooper	.05	.02	.01
☐ 336 Mike Brown	.05	.02	.01
☐ 337 Sam Bowie	.05	.02	.01
☐ 338 Kevin Gamble	.05	.02	.01
☐ 339 Jerry Ice Reynolds	.05	.02	.01
☐ 340 Mike Sanders	.05	.02	.01
☐ 341 Bill Jones UER	.05	.02	.01

(Center on front,
should be F)

☐ 342 Greg Anderson	.05	.02	.01
☐ 343 Dave Corzine	.05	.02	.01
☐ 344 Micheal Williams UER	.05	.02	.01

(Misspelled Michael
on card)

☐ 345 Jay Vincent	.05	.02	.01
☐ 346 David Rivers	.05	.02	.01
☐ 347 Caldwell Jones UER	.05	.02	.01

(He was not starting
center on '83 Sixers)

☐ 348 Brad Sellers	.05	.02	.01
☐ 349 Scott Roth	.05	.02	.01
☐ 350 Alvin Robertson	.05	.02	.01
☐ 351 Steve Kerr	.50	.23	.06
☐ 352 Stuart Gray	.05	.02	.01
☐ 353A World Champions SP	4.00	1.80	.50
☐ 353B World Champions UER	.50	.23	.06

(George Blaha mis-
spelled Blanha)

1989-90 Hoops
Checklists

*Hoops made available two different check-
lists to collectors, primarily by phone
request. The checklists are not actually
cards but are more like folded four-panel
booklets, although when folded they do
measure 2 1/2" by 3 1/2". The production
on these was rather limited.*

	MINT	NRMT	EXC
COMPLETE SET (2)	4.00	1.80	.50
COMMON CARD (1-2)	2.00	.90	.25
☐ CL1 Checklist 1-300	2.00	.90	.25
☐ CL2 Checklist 1-353	2.00	.90	.25

1990-91 Hoops

*The complete 1990-91 Hoops basketball
set contains 440 standard-size cards. The
set was distributed in two series of 336 and
104 cards, respectively. The cards were
issued in 15-card plastic-wrap packs which
came 36 to a box. On the front the color
action player photo appears in the shape of
a basketball lane, bordered by gold on the
All-Star cards (1-26) and by silver on the*

regular issues (27-331, 336). The player's name and the stripe below the picture are printed in one of the team's colors. The team logo at the lower right corner rounds out the card face. The back of the regular issue has a color head shot and biographical information as well as college and pro statistics, framed by a basketball lane. The set is arranged alphabetically according to teams. Subsets are Coaches (305-331/343-354), NBA Finals (337-342), Team checklists (355-381), Inside Stuff (382-385), Stay in School (386-387), Don't Foul Out (388-389), Lottery Selections (390-400), and Updates (401-438). Some of the All-Star cards (card numbers 2, 6, and 8) can be found with or without a printing mistake, i.e., no T in the trademark logo on the card back. A few of the cards (card numbers 14, 66, 144, and 279) refer to the player as "all America" rather than "All America." The following cards can be found with or without a black line under the card number, height, and birthplace: 20, 23, 24, 29, and 87. Rookie Cards of note included in the set are Nick Anderson, Mookie Blaylock, Derrick Coleman, Vlade Divac, Sean Elliott, Kendall Gill, Tim Hardaway, Chris Jackson, Shawn Kemp, Gary Payton, Drazen Petrovic, Glen Rice, Clifford Robinson, and Dennis Scott. The short prints (SP below) in the first series are those cards which were dropped to make room for the new second series cards on the printing sheet.

	MINT	NRMT	EXC
COMPLETE SET (440)	15.00	6.75	1.85
COMPLETE SERIES 1 (336)	10.00	4.50	1.25
COMPLETE SERIES 2 (104)	5.00	2.20	.60
COMMON CARD (1-440)	.05	.02	.01
COMMON SP	.10	.05	.01

☐ 1	Charles Barkley AS SP	.25	.11	.03
☐ 2	Larry Bird AS SP	.60	.25	.07
☐ 3	Joe Dumars AS SP	.15	.07	.02
☐ 4	Patrick Ewing AS SP	.15	.07	.02
	(A-S blocks listed as 1, should be 5) UER			
☐ 5	Michael Jordan AS SP	2.00	.90	.25
	(Won Slam Dunk in '87 and '88, not '86 and '88) UER			
☐ 6	Kevin McHale AS SP	.15	.07	.02
☐ 7	Reggie Miller AS SP	.25	.11	.03
☐ 8	Robert Parish AS SP	.10	.05	.01
☐ 9	Scottie Pippen AS SP	.60	.25	.07
☐ 10	Dennis Rodman AS SP	.75	.35	.09
☐ 11	Isiah Thomas AS SP	.10	.05	.01
☐ 12	Dominique Wilkins AS SP	.15	.07	.02
☐ 13A	All-Star Checklist SP ERR (No card number)	.50	.23	.06
☐ 13B	All-Star Checklist SP COR (Card number on back)	.10	.05	.01
☐ 14	Rolando Blackman AS SP	.10	.05	.01
☐ 15	Tom Chambers AS SP	.10	.05	.01
☐ 16	Clyde Drexler AS SP	.20	.09	.03
☐ 17	A.C. Green AS SP	.15	.07	.02
☐ 18	Magic Johnson AS SP	.50	.23	.06
☐ 19	Kevin Johnson AS SP	.15	.07	.02
☐ 20	Lafayette Lever AS SP	.10	.05	.01
☐ 21	Karl Malone AS SP	.15	.07	.02
☐ 22	Chris Mullin AS SP	.15	.07	.02
☐ 23	Hakeem Olajuwon AS SP	.40	.18	.05
☐ 24	David Robinson AS SP	.60	.25	.07
☐ 25	John Stockton AS SP	.20	.09	.03
☐ 26	James Worthy AS SP	.15	.07	.02
☐ 27	John Battle	.05	.02	.01
☐ 28	Jon Koncak	.05	.02	.01
☐ 29	Cliff Levingston SP	.10	.05	.01
☐ 30	John Long SP	.10	.05	.01
☐ 31	Moses Malone	.10	.05	.01
☐ 32	Doc Rivers	.05	.02	.01
☐ 33	Kenny Smith SP	.10	.05	.01
☐ 34	Alexander Volkov	.05	.02	.01
☐ 35	Spud Webb	.08	.04	.01
☐ 36	Dominique Wilkins	.08	.04	.01
☐ 37	Kevin Willis	.08	.04	.01
☐ 38	John Bagley	.05	.02	.01
☐ 39	Larry Bird	.60	.25	.07
☐ 40	Kevin Gamble	.05	.02	.01
☐ 41	Dennis Johnson SP	.15	.07	.02
☐ 42	Joe Kleine	.05	.02	.01
☐ 43	Reggie Lewis	.08	.04	.01
☐ 44	Kevin McHale	.08	.04	.01
☐ 45	Robert Parish	.08	.04	.01
☐ 46	Jim Paxson SP	.10	.05	.01
☐ 47	Ed Pinckney	.05	.02	.01
☐ 48	Brian Shaw	.05	.02	.01
☐ 49	Richard Anderson SP	.10	.05	.01
☐ 50	Muggsy Bogues	.08	.04	.01
☐ 51	Rex Chapman	.05	.02	.01
☐ 52	Dell Curry	.05	.02	.01
☐ 53	Kenny Gattison	.05	.02	.01
☐ 54	Armon Gilliam	.05	.02	.01
☐ 55	Dave Hoppen	.05	.02	.01
☐ 56	Randolph Keys	.05	.02	.01
☐ 57	J.R. Reid	.05	.02	.01
☐ 58	Robert Reid SP	.10	.05	.01
☐ 59	Kelly Tripucka	.05	.02	.01
☐ 60	B.J. Armstrong	.08	.04	.01
☐ 61	Bill Cartwright	.05	.02	.01
☐ 62	Charles Davis SP	.10	.05	.01
☐ 63	Horace Grant	.10	.05	.01
☐ 64	Craig Hodges	.05	.02	.01
☐ 65	Michael Jordan	2.00	.90	.25
☐ 66	Stacey King	.05	.02	.01
☐ 67	John Paxson	.08	.04	.01
☐ 68	Will Perdue	.05	.02	.01
☐ 69	Scottie Pippen	.60	.25	.07
☐ 70	Winston Bennett	.05	.02	.01
☐ 71	Chucky Brown	.05	.02	.01
☐ 72	Derrick Chievous	.05	.02	.01
☐ 73	Brad Daugherty	.05	.02	.01
☐ 74	Craig Ehlo	.05	.02	.01
☐ 75	Steve Kerr	.08	.04	.01
☐ 76	Paul Mokeski SP	.10	.05	.01
☐ 77	John Morton	.05	.02	.01
☐ 78	Larry Nance	.08	.04	.01
☐ 79	Mark Price	.05	.02	.01
☐ 80	Hot Rod Williams	.05	.02	.01
☐ 81	Steve Alford	.05	.02	.01
☐ 82	Rolando Blackman	.08	.04	.01
☐ 83	Adrian Dantley SP	.15	.07	.02
☐ 84	Brad Davis	.05	.02	.01
☐ 85	James Donaldson	.05	.02	.01
☐ 86	Derek Harper	.08	.04	.01
☐ 87	Sam Perkins SP	.10	.05	.01
☐ 88	Roy Tarpley	.05	.02	.01
☐ 89	Bill Wennington SP	.10	.05	.01
☐ 90	Herb Williams	.05	.02	.01
☐ 91	Michael Adams	.05	.02	.01

☐ 92	Joe Barry Carroll SP	.10	.05	.01
☐ 93	Walter Davis UER (Born NC, not PA)	.08	.04	.01
☐ 94	Alex English SP	.15	.07	.02
☐ 95	Bill Hanzlik	.05	.02	.01
☐ 96	Jerome Lane	.05	.02	.01
☐ 97	Lafayette Lever SP	.10	.05	.01
☐ 98	Todd Lichti	.05	.02	.01
☐ 99	Blair Rasmussen	.05	.02	.01
☐ 100	Danny Schayes SP	.10	.05	.01
☐ 101	Mark Aguirre	.08	.04	.01
☐ 102	William Bedford	.05	.02	.01
☐ 103	Joe Dumars	.08	.04	.01
☐ 104	James Edwards	.05	.02	.01
☐ 105	Scott Hastings	.05	.02	.01
☐ 106	Gerald Henderson SP	.10	.05	.01
☐ 107	Vinnie Johnson	.05	.02	.01
☐ 108	Bill Laimbeer	.08	.04	.01
☐ 109	Dennis Rodman	.75	.35	.09
☐ 110	John Salley	.05	.02	.01
☐ 111	Isiah Thomas UER (No position listed on the card)	.10	.05	.01
☐ 112	Manute Bol SP	.10	.05	.01
☐ 113	Tim Hardaway	.40	.18	.05
☐ 114	Rod Higgins	.05	.02	.01
☐ 115	Sarunas Marciulionis	.05	.02	.01
☐ 116	Chris Mullin UER (Born Brooklyn, NY, not New York, NY)	.08	.04	.01
☐ 117	Jim Petersen	.05	.02	.01
☐ 118	Mitch Richmond	.20	.09	.03
☐ 119	Mike Smrek	.05	.02	.01
☐ 120	Terry Teagle SP	.10	.05	.01
☐ 121	Tom Tolbert	.05	.02	.01
☐ 122	Christian Welp SP	.10	.05	.01
☐ 123	Byron Dinkins SP	.10	.05	.01
☐ 124	Eric(Sleepy) Floyd	.05	.02	.01
☐ 125	Buck Johnson	.05	.02	.01
☐ 126	Vernon Maxwell	.05	.02	.01
☐ 127	Hakeem Olajuwon	.40	.18	.05
☐ 128	Larry Smith	.05	.02	.01
☐ 129	Otis Thorpe	.08	.04	.01
☐ 130	Mitchell Wiggins SP	.10	.05	.01
☐ 131	Mike Woodson	.05	.02	.01
☐ 132	Greg Dreiling	.05	.02	.01
☐ 133	Vern Fleming	.05	.02	.01
☐ 134	Rickey Green SP	.10	.05	.01
☐ 135	Reggie Miller	.25	.11	.03
☐ 136	Chuck Person	.08	.04	.01
☐ 137	Mike Sanders	.05	.02	.01
☐ 138	Detlef Schrempf	.08	.04	.01
☐ 139	Rik Smits	.08	.04	.01
☐ 140	LaSalle Thompson	.05	.02	.01
☐ 141	Randy Wittman	.05	.02	.01
☐ 142	Benoit Benjamin	.05	.02	.01
☐ 143	Winston Garland	.05	.02	.01
☐ 144	Tom Garrick	.05	.02	.01
☐ 145	Gary Grant	.05	.02	.01
☐ 146	Ron Harper	.05	.02	.01
☐ 147	Danny Manning	.08	.04	.01
☐ 148	Jeff Martin	.05	.02	.01
☐ 149	Ken Norman	.05	.02	.01
☐ 150	David Rivers SP	.10	.05	.01
☐ 151	Charles Smith	.05	.02	.01
☐ 152	Joe Wolf SP	.10	.05	.01
☐ 153	Michael Cooper SP	.15	.07	.02
☐ 154	Vlade Divac UER (Height 6'11", should be 7'1")	.25	.11	.03
☐ 155	Larry Drew	.05	.02	.01
☐ 156	A.C. Green	.08	.04	.01
☐ 157	Magic Johnson	.50	.23	.06
☐ 158	Mark McNamara SP	.10	.05	.01
☐ 159	Byron Scott	.08	.04	.01
☐ 160	Mychal Thompson	.05	.02	.01
☐ 161	Jay Vincent SP	.10	.05	.01
☐ 162	Orlando Woolridge SP	.10	.05	.01
☐ 163	James Worthy	.08	.04	.01
☐ 164	Sherman Douglas	.10	.05	.01
☐ 165	Kevin Edwards	.05	.02	.01
☐ 166	Tellis Frank SP	.10	.05	.01
☐ 167	Grant Long	.05	.02	.01
☐ 168	Glen Rice	.50	.23	.06
☐ 169A	Rony Seikaly (Athens)	.08	.04	.01
☐ 169B	Rony Seikaly (Beirut)	.08	.04	.01
☐ 170	Rory Sparrow SP	.10	.05	.01
☐ 171A	Jon Sundvold (First series)	.05	.02	.01
☐ 171B	Billy Thompson (Second series)	.05	.02	.01
☐ 172A	Billy Thompson (First series)	.05	.02	.01
☐ 172B	Jon Sundvold (Second series)	.05	.02	.01
☐ 173	Greg Anderson	.05	.02	.01
☐ 174	Jeff Grayer	.05	.02	.01
☐ 175	Jay Humphries	.05	.02	.01
☐ 176	Frank Kornet	.05	.02	.01
☐ 177	Larry Krystkowiak	.05	.02	.01
☐ 178	Brad Lohaus	.05	.02	.01
☐ 179	Ricky Pierce	.05	.02	.01
☐ 180	Paul Pressey SP	.10	.05	.01
☐ 181	Fred Roberts	.05	.02	.01
☐ 182	Alvin Robertson	.05	.02	.01
☐ 183	Jack Sikma	.08	.04	.01
☐ 184	Randy Breuer	.05	.02	.01
☐ 185	Tony Campbell	.05	.02	.01
☐ 186	Tyrone Corbin	.05	.02	.01
☐ 187	Sidney Lowe SP	.10	.05	.01
☐ 188	Sam Mitchell	.05	.02	.01
☐ 189	Tod Murphy	.05	.02	.01
☐ 190	Pooh Richardson	.08	.04	.01
☐ 191	Scott Roth SP	.10	.05	.01
☐ 192	Brad Sellers SP	.10	.05	.01
☐ 193	Mookie Blaylock	.30	.14	.04
☐ 194	Sam Bowie	.05	.02	.01
☐ 195	Lester Conner	.05	.02	.01
☐ 196	Derrick Gervin	.05	.02	.01
☐ 197	Jack Haley	.05	.02	.01
☐ 198	Roy Hinson	.05	.02	.01
☐ 199	Dennis Hopson SP	.10	.05	.01
☐ 200	Chris Morris	.05	.02	.01
☐ 201	Purvis Short SP	.10	.05	.01
☐ 202	Maurice Cheeks	.08	.04	.01
☐ 203	Patrick Ewing	.15	.07	.02
☐ 204	Stuart Gray	.05	.02	.01
☐ 205	Mark Jackson	.05	.02	.01
☐ 206	Johnny Newman SP	.10	.05	.01
☐ 207	Charles Oakley	.05	.02	.01
☐ 208	Trent Tucker	.05	.02	.01
☐ 209	Kiki Vandeweghe	.05	.02	.01
☐ 210	Kenny Walker	.05	.02	.01
☐ 211	Eddie Lee Wilkins	.05	.02	.01
☐ 212	Gerald Wilkins	.05	.02	.01
☐ 213	Mark Acres	.05	.02	.01
☐ 214	Nick Anderson	.30	.14	.04
☐ 215	Michael Ansley UER (Ranked first, not third)	.05	.02	.01
☐ 216	Terry Catledge	.05	.02	.01

☐ 217 Dave Corzine SP	.10	.05	.01
☐ 218 Sidney Green SP	.10	.05	.01
☐ 219 Jerry Reynolds	.05	.02	.01
☐ 220 Scott Skiles	.05	.02	.01
☐ 221 Otis Smith	.05	.02	.01
☐ 222 Reggie Theus SP	.15	.07	.02
☐ 223A Sam Vincent	1.50	.70	.19
(First series, shows			
12 Michael Jordan)			
☐ 223B Sam Vincent	.08	.04	.01
(Second series, shows			
Sam dribbling)			
☐ 224 Ron Anderson	.05	.02	.01
☐ 225 Charles Barkley	.25	.11	.03
☐ 226 Scott Brooks SP UER	.10	.05	.01
(Born French Camp,			
not Lathron, Cal.)			
☐ 227 Johnny Dawkins	.05	.02	.01
☐ 228 Mike Gminski	.05	.02	.01
☐ 229 Hersey Hawkins	.05	.02	.01
☐ 230 Rick Mahorn	.05	.02	.01
☐ 231 Derek Smith SP	.10	.05	.01
☐ 232 Bob Thornton	.05	.02	.01
☐ 233 Kenny Battle	.05	.02	.01
☐ 234A Tom Chambers	.08	.04	.01
(First series;			
Forward on front)			
☐ 234B Tom Chambers	.08	.04	.01
(Second series;			
Guard on front)			
☐ 235 Greg Grant SP	.10	.05	.01
☐ 236 Jeff Hornacek	.08	.04	.01
☐ 237 Eddie Johnson	.05	.02	.01
☐ 238A Kevin Johnson	.08	.04	.01
(First series;			
Guard on front)			
☐ 238B Kevin Johnson	.08	.04	.01
(Second series;			
Forward on front)			
☐ 239 Dan Majerle	.08	.04	.01
☐ 240 Tim Perry	.05	.02	.01
☐ 241 Kurt Rambis	.05	.02	.01
☐ 242 Mark West	.05	.02	.01
☐ 243 Mark Bryant	.05	.02	.01
☐ 244 Wayne Cooper	.05	.02	.01
☐ 245 Clyde Drexler	.20	.09	.03
☐ 246 Kevin Duckworth	.05	.02	.01
☐ 247 Jerome Kersey	.05	.02	.01
☐ 248 Drazen Petrovic	.15	.07	.02
☐ 249A Terry Porter ERR	1.00	.45	.13
(No NBA symbol on back)			
☐ 249B Terry Porter COR	.05	.02	.01
☐ 250 Cliff Robinson	.40	.18	.05
☐ 251 Buck Williams	.05	.02	.01
☐ 252 Danny Young	.05	.02	.01
☐ 253 Danny Ainge SP UER	.08	.04	.01
(Middle name Ray mis-			
spelled as Rae on back)			
☐ 254 Randy Allen SP	.10	.05	.01
☐ 255 Antoine Carr	.05	.02	.01
☐ 256 Vinny Del Negro SP	.15	.07	.02
☐ 257 Pervis Ellison SP	.10	.05	.01
☐ 258 Greg Kite SP	.10	.05	.01
☐ 259 Rodney McCray SP	.10	.05	.01
☐ 260 Harold Pressley SP	.10	.05	.01
☐ 261 Ralph Sampson	.05	.02	.01
☐ 262 Wayman Tisdale	.05	.02	.01
☐ 263 Willie Anderson	.05	.02	.01
☐ 264 Uwe Blab SP	.10	.05	.01
☐ 265 Frank Brickowski SP	.10	.05	.01
☐ 266 Terry Cummings	.05	.02	.01
☐ 267 Sean Elliott	.50	.23	.06
☐ 268 Caldwell Jones SP	.10	.05	.01
☐ 269 Johnny Moore SP	.10	.05	.01
☐ 270 David Robinson	.60	.25	.07
☐ 271 Rod Strickland	.05	.02	.01
☐ 272 Reggie Williams	.05	.02	.01
☐ 273 David Wingate SP	.10	.05	.01
☐ 274 Dana Barros SP UER	.15	.07	.02
(Born April, not March)			
☐ 275 Michael Cage UER	.05	.02	.01
(Drafted '84, not '85)			
☐ 276 Quintin Dailey	.05	.02	.01
☐ 277 Dale Ellis	.05	.02	.01
☐ 278 Steve Johnson SP	.10	.05	.01
☐ 279 Shawn Kemp	3.00	1.35	.35
☐ 280 Xavier McDaniel	.05	.02	.01
☐ 281 Derrick McKey	.05	.02	.01
☐ 282 Nate McMillan	.05	.02	.01
☐ 283 Olden Polynice	.05	.02	.01
☐ 284 Sedale Threatt	.05	.02	.01
☐ 285 Thurl Bailey	.05	.02	.01
☐ 286 Mike Brown	.05	.02	.01
☐ 287 Mark Eaton UER	.05	.02	.01
(72nd pick, not 82nd)			
☐ 288 Blue Edwards	.05	.02	.01
☐ 289 Darrell Griffith	.05	.02	.01
☐ 290 Robert Hansen SP	.10	.05	.01
☐ 291 Eric Leckner SP	.10	.05	.01
☐ 292 Karl Malone	.15	.07	.02
☐ 293 Delaney Rudd	.05	.02	.01
☐ 294 John Stockton	.20	.09	.03
☐ 295 Mark Alarie	.05	.02	.01
☐ 296 Ledell Eackles SP	.10	.05	.01
☐ 297 Harvey Grant	.05	.02	.01
☐ 298A Tom Hammonds	.05	.02	.01
(No rookie logo on front)			
☐ 298B Tom Hammonds	.05	.02	.01
(Rookie logo on front)			
☐ 299 Charles Jones	.05	.02	.01
☐ 300 Bernard King	.08	.04	.01
☐ 301 Jeff Malone SP	.10	.05	.01
☐ 302 Mel Turpin SP	.10	.05	.01
☐ 303 Darrell Walker	.05	.02	.01
☐ 304 John Williams	.05	.02	.01
☐ 305 Bob Weiss CO	.05	.02	.01
☐ 306 Chris Ford CO	.05	.02	.01
☐ 307 Gene Littles CO	.05	.02	.01
☐ 308 Phil Jackson CO	.08	.04	.01
☐ 309 Lenny Wilkens CO	.08	.04	.01
☐ 310 Richie Adubato CO	.05	.02	.01
☐ 311 Doug Moe CO SP	.10	.05	.01
☐ 312 Chuck Daly CO	.08	.04	.01
☐ 313 Don Nelson CO	.08	.04	.01
☐ 314 Don Chaney CO	.05	.02	.01
☐ 315 Dick Versace CO	.05	.02	.01
☐ 316 Mike Schuler CO	.05	.02	.01
☐ 317 Pat Riley CO	.15	.07	.02
☐ 318 Ron Rothstein CO	.05	.02	.01
☐ 319 Del Harris CO	.05	.02	.01
☐ 320 Bill Musselman CO	.05	.02	.01
☐ 321 Bill Fitch CO	.05	.02	.01
☐ 322 Stu Jackson CO	.05	.02	.01
☐ 323 Matt Guokas CO	.05	.02	.01
☐ 324 Jim Lynam CO	.05	.02	.01
☐ 325 Cotton Fitzsimmons CO	.05	.02	.01
☐ 326 Rick Adelman CO	.05	.02	.01
☐ 327 Dick Motta CO	.05	.02	.01
☐ 328 Larry Brown CO	.08	.04	.01
☐ 329 K.C. Jones CO	.08	.04	.01
☐ 330 Jerry Sloan CO	.08	.04	.01
☐ 331 Wes Unseld CO	.08	.04	.01

☐ 332	Checklist 1 SP	.10	.05	.01
☐ 333	Checklist 2 SP	.10	.05	.01
☐ 334	Checklist 3 SP	.10	.05	.01
☐ 335	Checklist 4 SP	.10	.05	.01
☐ 336	Danny Ferry SP	.25	.11	.03
☐ 337	Pistons Celebrate	.08	.04	.01
	Dennis Rodman			
☐ 338	Buck Williams FIN	.08	.04	.01
	Dennis Rodman			
☐ 339	Joe Dumars FIN	.08	.04	.01
☐ 340	Jerome Kersey FIN	.08	.04	.01
	Isiah Thomas			
☐ 341A	Vinnie Johnson FIN ERR	.05	.02	.01
	No headline on back			
☐ 341B	Vinnie Johnson COR	.05	.02	.01
☐ 342	Pistons Celebrate UER	.05	.02	.01
	James Edwards			
	Player named as Sidney			
	Green is really			
	David Greenwood			
☐ 343	K.C. Jones CO	.08	.04	.01
☐ 344	Wes Unseld CO	.08	.04	.01
☐ 345	Don Nelson CO	.08	.04	.01
☐ 346	Bob Weiss CO	.05	.02	.01
☐ 347	Chris Ford CO	.05	.02	.01
☐ 348	Phil Jackson CO	.08	.04	.01
☐ 349	Lenny Wilkens CO	.08	.04	.01
☐ 350	Don Chaney CO	.05	.02	.01
☐ 351	Mike Dunleavy CO	.05	.02	.01
☐ 352	Matt Guokas CO	.05	.02	.01
☐ 353	Rick Adelman CO	.05	.02	.01
☐ 354	Jerry Sloan CO	.08	.04	.01
☐ 355	Dominique Wilkins TC	.08	.04	.01
☐ 356	Larry Bird TC	.30	.14	.04
☐ 357	Rex Chapman TC	.05	.02	.01
☐ 358	Michael Jordan TC	1.00	.45	.12
☐ 359	Mark Price TC	.05	.02	.01
☐ 360	Rolando Blackman TC	.05	.02	.01
☐ 361	Michael Adams TC UER	.05	.02	.01
	(Westhead should be			
	card 422, not 440)			
☐ 362	Joe Dumars TC UER	.08	.04	.01
	(Gerald Henderson's name			
	and number not listed)			
☐ 363	Chris Mullin TC	.05	.02	.01
☐ 364	Hakeem Olajuwon TC	.20	.09	.03
☐ 365	Reggie Miller TC	.15	.07	.02
☐ 366	Danny Manning TC	.05	.02	.01
☐ 367	Magic Johnson TC UER	.25	.11	.03
	(Dunleavy listed as 439,			
	should be 351)			
☐ 368	Rony Seikaly TC	.05	.02	.01
☐ 369	Alvin Robertson TC	.05	.02	.01
☐ 370	Pooh Richardson TC	.05	.02	.01
☐ 371	Chris Morris TC	.05	.02	.01
☐ 372	Patrick Ewing TC	.08	.04	.01
☐ 373	Nick Anderson TC	.15	.07	.02
☐ 374	Charles Barkley TC	.15	.07	.02
☐ 375	Kevin Johnson TC	.08	.04	.01
☐ 376	Clyde Drexler TC	.08	.04	.01
☐ 377	Wayman Tisdale TC	.05	.02	.01
☐ 378	David Robinson TC	.30	.14	.04
	(Basketball fully			
	visible)			
☐ 378B	David Robinson TC	.50	.23	.06
	(Basketball partially			
	visible)			
☐ 379	Xavier McDaniel TC	.05	.02	.01
☐ 380	Karl Malone TC	.08	.04	.01
☐ 381	Bernard King TC	.08	.04	.01
☐ 382	Michael Jordan	1.00	.45	.12
	Playground			
☐ 383	Karl Malone horseback	.08	.04	.01
☐ 384	European Imports	.05	.02	.01
	(Vlade Divac			
	Sarunas Marciulionis)			
☐ 385	Super Streaks	1.00	.45	.12
	Stay In School			
	(Magic Johnson and			
	Michael Jordan)			
☐ 386	Johnny Newman	.05	.02	.01
	(Stay in School)			
☐ 387	Dell Curry	.05	.02	.01
	(Stay in School)			
☐ 388	Patrick Ewing	.08	.04	.01
	(Don't Foul Out)			
☐ 389	Isiah Thomas	.08	.04	.01
	(Don't Foul Out)			
☐ 390	Derrick Coleman LS	.25	.11	.03
☐ 391	Gary Payton LS	1.25	.55	.16
☐ 392	Chris Jackson LS	.25	.11	.03
☐ 393	Dennis Scott LS	.25	.11	.03
☐ 394	Kendall Gill LS	.10	.05	.01
☐ 395	Felton Spencer LS	.05	.02	.01
☐ 396	Lionel Simmons LS	.05	.02	.01
☐ 397	Bo Kimble LS	.05	.02	.01
☐ 398	Willie Burton LS	.05	.02	.01
☐ 399	Rumeal Robinson LS	.05	.02	.01
☐ 400	Tyrone Hill LS	.15	.07	.02
☐ 401	Tim McCormick	.05	.02	.01
☐ 402	Sidney Moncrief	.08	.04	.01
☐ 403	Johnny Newman	.05	.02	.01
☐ 404	Dennis Hopson	.05	.02	.01
☐ 405	Cliff Levingston	.05	.02	.01
☐ 406A	Danny Ferry ERR	.50	.23	.06
	(No position on			
	front of card)			
☐ 406B	Danny Ferry COR	.08	.04	.01
☐ 407	Alex English	.08	.04	.01
☐ 408	Lafayette Lever	.05	.02	.01
☐ 409	Rodney McCray	.05	.02	.01
☐ 410	Mike Dunleavy CO	.05	.02	.01
☐ 411	Orlando Woolridge	.05	.02	.01
☐ 412	Joe Wolf	.05	.02	.01
☐ 413	Tree Rollins	.05	.02	.01
☐ 414	Kenny Smith	.05	.02	.01
☐ 415	Sam Perkins	.05	.02	.01
☐ 416	Terry Teagle	.05	.02	.01
☐ 417	Frank Brickowski	.05	.02	.01
☐ 418	Danny Schayes	.05	.02	.01
☐ 419	Scott Brooks	.05	.02	.01
☐ 420	Reggie Theus	.08	.04	.01
☐ 421	Greg Grant	.05	.02	.01
☐ 422	Paul Westhead CO	.05	.02	.01
☐ 423	Greg Kite	.05	.02	.01
☐ 424	Manute Bol	.05	.02	.01
☐ 425	Rickey Green	.05	.02	.01
☐ 426	Ed Nealy	.05	.02	.01
☐ 427	Danny Ainge	.08	.04	.01
☐ 428	Bobby Hansen	.05	.02	.01
☐ 429	Eric Leckner	.05	.02	.01
☐ 430	Rory Sparrow	.05	.02	.01
☐ 431	Bill Wennington	.05	.02	.01
☐ 432	Paul Pressey	.05	.02	.01
☐ 433	David Greenwood	.05	.02	.01
☐ 434	Mark McNamara	.05	.02	.01
☐ 435	Sidney Green	.05	.02	.01
☐ 436	Dave Corzine	.05	.02	.01
☐ 437	Jeff Malone	.05	.02	.01
☐ 438	Pervis Ellison	.05	.02	.01
☐ 439	Checklist 5	.05	.02	.01
☐ 440	Checklist 6	.05	.02	.01

		MINT	NRMT	EXC
☐ NNO David Robinson and All-Rookie Team (No stats on back)		1.50	.70	.19
☐ NNO David Robinson and All-Rookie Team (Stats on back)		6.00	2.70	.75

1991-92 Hoops

The complete 1991-92 Hoops basketball set contains 590 standard-size cards. The set was released in two series of 330 and 260 cards, respectively. For the first time, second series packs contained only second series cards. The fronts feature color action player photos, with different color borders on a white card face. The player's name is printed in black lettering in the upper left corner, and the team logo is superimposed over the lower left corner of the picture. In a horizontal format the backs have color head shots and biographical information on the left side, while the right side presents college and pro statistics. The cards are numbered on the back and checklisted below alphabetically within team order. Subsets are Coaches (221-247), All-Stars East (248-260), All-Stars West (261-273), Teams (274-300), Centennial Card honoring James Naismith (301), Inside Stuff (302-305), League Leaders (306-313), Milestones (314-318), NBA yearbook (319-324), Public Service messages (325-327/544/545), Supreme Court (449-502), Art Cards (503-529), Active Leaders (530-537), NBA Hoops Tribune (538-543), Draft Picks (546-556), USA Basketball 1976 (557), USA Basketball 1984 (558-564), USA Basketball 1988 (565-574) and USA Basketball 1992 (575-588). Rookie Cards of note include Kenny Anderson, Stacey Augmon, Terrell Brandon, Larry Johnson, Anthony Mason, Dikembe Mutombo, Steve Smith, and John Starks. A short-printed Naismith card, numbered CC1, was inserted into wax packs. It features a colorized photo of Dr. Naismith standing between two peach baskets like those used in the first basketball game. The back narrates the invention of the game of basketball. An unnumbered Centennial card featuring the Centennial logo was also available via a mail-in offer. Second series packs featured

a randomly inserted Gold Foil USA Basketball logo card. A special individually numbered (out of 10,000) "Head of the Class" (showing the top six draft picks from 1991) card was made available to the first 10,000 fans requesting one along with three wrappers from each series of 1991-92 Hoops cards. The card is numbered "of 10,000" and features tiny pictures of the top six players selected in the 1991 NBA draft.

		MINT	NRMT	EXC
	COMPLETE SET (590)	25.00	11.00	3.10
	COMPLETE SERIES 1 (330)	10.00	4.50	1.25
	COMPLETE SERIES 2 (260)	15.00	6.75	1.85
	COMMON CARD (1-590)	.05	.02	.01
☐ 1	John Battle	.05	.02	.01
☐ 2	Moses Malone UER (119 rebounds 1982-83, should be 1194)	.15	.07	.02
☐ 3	Sidney Moncrief	.10	.05	.01
☐ 4	Doc Rivers	.05	.02	.01
☐ 5	Rumeal Robinson UER (Back says 11th pick in 1990, should be 10th)	.05	.02	.01
☐ 6	Spud Webb	.10	.05	.01
☐ 7	Dominique Wilkins	.10	.05	.01
☐ 8	Kevin Willis	.05	.02	.01
☐ 9	Larry Bird	1.00	.45	.12
☐ 10	Dee Brown	.05	.02	.01
☐ 11	Kevin Gamble	.05	.02	.01
☐ 12	Joe Kleine	.05	.02	.01
☐ 13	Reggie Lewis	.10	.05	.01
☐ 14	Kevin McHale	.10	.05	.01
☐ 15	Robert Parish	.10	.05	.01
☐ 16	Ed Pinckney	.05	.02	.01
☐ 17	Brian Shaw	.05	.02	.01
☐ 18	Muggsy Bogues	.10	.05	.01
☐ 19	Rex Chapman	.05	.02	.01
☐ 20	Dell Curry	.05	.02	.01
☐ 21	Kendall Gill	.05	.02	.01
☐ 22	Mike Gminski	.05	.02	.01
☐ 23	Johnny Newman	.05	.02	.01
☐ 24	J.R. Reid	.05	.02	.01
☐ 25	Kelly Tripucka	.05	.02	.01
☐ 26	B.J. Armstrong (B.J. on front, Benjamin Roy on back)	.05	.02	.01
☐ 27	Bill Cartwright	.05	.02	.01
☐ 28	Horace Grant	.10	.05	.01
☐ 29	Craig Hodges	.05	.02	.01
☐ 30	Michael Jordan	3.00	1.35	.35
☐ 31	Stacey King	.05	.02	.01
☐ 32	Cliff Levingston	.05	.02	.01
☐ 33	John Paxson	.10	.05	.01
☐ 34	Scottie Pippen	.75	.35	.09
☐ 35	Chucky Brown	.05	.02	.01
☐ 36	Brad Daugherty	.05	.02	.01
☐ 37	Craig Ehlo	.05	.02	.01
☐ 38	Danny Ferry	.05	.02	.01
☐ 39	Larry Nance	.05	.02	.01
☐ 40	Mark Price	.05	.02	.01
☐ 41	Darnell Valentine	.05	.02	.01
☐ 42	Hot Rod Williams	.05	.02	.01
☐ 43	Rolando Blackman	.10	.05	.01
☐ 44	Brad Davis	.05	.02	.01
☐ 45	James Donaldson	.05	.02	.01
☐ 46	Derek Harper	.10	.05	.01
☐ 47	Fat Lever	.05	.02	.01

☐	48	Rodney McCray	.05	.02	.01
☐	49	Roy Tarpley	.05	.02	.01
☐	50	Herb Williams	.05	.02	.01
☐	51	Michael Adams	.05	.02	.01
☐	52	Chris Jackson UER	.10	.05	.01
		(Born in Mississippi,			
		not Michigan)			
☐	53	Jerome Lane	.05	.02	.01
☐	54	Todd Lichti	.05	.02	.01
☐	55	Blair Rasmussen	.05	.02	.01
☐	56	Reggie Williams	.05	.02	.01
☐	57	Joe Wolf	.05	.02	.01
☐	58	Orlando Woolridge	.05	.02	.01
☐	59	Mark Aguirre	.10	.05	.01
☐	60	Joe Dumars	.10	.05	.01
☐	61	James Edwards	.05	.02	.01
☐	62	Vinnie Johnson	.05	.02	.01
☐	63	Bill Laimbeer	.05	.02	.01
☐	64	Dennis Rodman	1.00	.45	.12
☐	65	John Salley	.05	.02	.01
☐	66	Isiah Thomas	.15	.07	.02
☐	67	Tim Hardaway	.10	.05	.01
☐	68	Rod Higgins	.05	.02	.01
☐	69	Tyrone Hill	.05	.02	.01
☐	70	Alton Lister	.05	.02	.01
☐	71	Sarunas Marciulionis	.05	.02	.01
☐	72	Chris Mullin	.10	.05	.01
☐	73	Mitch Richmond	.25	.11	.03
☐	74	Tom Tolbert	.05	.02	.01
☐	75	Eric(Sleepy) Floyd	.05	.02	.01
☐	76	Buck Johnson	.05	.02	.01
☐	77	Vernon Maxwell	.05	.02	.01
☐	78	Hakeem Olajuwon	.60	.25	.07
☐	79	Kenny Smith	.05	.02	.01
☐	80	Larry Smith	.05	.02	.01
☐	81	Otis Thorpe	.10	.05	.01
☐	82	David Wood	.05	.02	.01
☐	83	Vern Fleming	.05	.02	.01
☐	84	Reggie Miller	.30	.14	.04
☐	85	Chuck Person	.05	.02	.01
☐	86	Mike Sanders	.05	.02	.01
☐	87	Detlef Schrempf	.05	.02	.01
☐	88	Rik Smits	.10	.05	.01
☐	89	LaSalle Thompson	.05	.02	.01
☐	90	Micheal Williams	.05	.02	.01
☐	91	Winston Garland	.05	.02	.01
☐	92	Gary Grant	.05	.02	.01
☐	93	Ron Harper	.05	.02	.01
☐	94	Danny Manning	.10	.05	.01
☐	95	Jeff Martin	.05	.02	.01
☐	96	Ken Norman	.05	.02	.01
☐	97	Olden Polynice	.05	.02	.01
☐	98	Charles Smith	.05	.02	.01
☐	99	Vlade Divac	.10	.05	.01
☐	100	A.C. Green	.10	.05	.01
☐	101	Magic Johnson	.75	.35	.09
☐	102	Sam Perkins	.05	.02	.01
☐	103	Byron Scott	.10	.05	.01
☐	104	Terry Teagle	.05	.02	.01
☐	105	Mychal Thompson	.05	.02	.01
☐	106	James Worthy	.10	.05	.01
☐	107	Willie Burton	.05	.02	.01
☐	108	Bimbo Coles	.05	.02	.01
☐	109	Terry Davis	.05	.02	.01
☐	110	Sherman Douglas	.05	.02	.01
☐	111	Kevin Edwards	.05	.02	.01
☐	112	Alec Kessler	.05	.02	.01
☐	113	Glen Rice	.15	.07	.02
☐	114	Rony Seikaly	.05	.02	.01
☐	115	Frank Brickowski	.05	.02	.01
☐	116	Dale Ellis	.05	.02	.01
☐	117	Jay Humphries	.05	.02	.01
☐	118	Brad Lohaus	.05	.02	.01
☐	119	Fred Roberts	.05	.02	.01
☐	120	Alvin Robertson	.05	.02	.01
☐	121	Danny Schayes	.05	.02	.01
☐	122	Jack Sikma	.10	.05	.01
☐	123	Randy Breuer	.05	.02	.01
☐	124	Tony Campbell	.05	.02	.01
☐	125	Tyrone Corbin	.05	.02	.01
☐	126	Gerald Glass	.05	.02	.01
☐	127	Sam Mitchell	.05	.02	.01
☐	128	Tod Murphy	.05	.02	.01
☐	129	Pooh Richardson	.05	.02	.01
☐	130	Felton Spencer	.05	.02	.01
☐	131	Mookie Blaylock	.10	.05	.01
☐	132	Sam Bowie	.05	.02	.01
☐	133	Jud Buechler	.05	.02	.01
☐	134	Derrick Coleman	.05	.02	.01
☐	135	Chris Dudley	.05	.02	.01
☐	136	Chris Morris	.05	.02	.01
☐	137	Drazen Petrovic	.10	.05	.01
☐	138	Reggie Theus	.10	.05	.01
☐	139	Maurice Cheeks	.10	.05	.01
☐	140	Patrick Ewing	.25	.11	.03
☐	141	Mark Jackson	.05	.02	.01
☐	142	Charles Oakley	.05	.02	.01
☐	143	Trent Tucker	.05	.02	.01
☐	144	Kiki Vandeweghe	.05	.02	.01
☐	145	Kenny Walker	.05	.02	.01
☐	146	Gerald Wilkins	.05	.02	.01
☐	147	Nick Anderson	.10	.05	.01
☐	148	Michael Ansley	.05	.02	.01
☐	149	Terry Catledge	.05	.02	.01
☐	150	Jerry Reynolds	.05	.02	.01
☐	151	Dennis Scott	.10	.05	.01
☐	152	Scott Skiles	.05	.02	.01
☐	153	Otis Smith	.05	.02	.01
☐	154	Sam Vincent	.05	.02	.01
☐	155	Ron Anderson	.05	.02	.01
☐	156	Charles Barkley	.40	.18	.05
☐	157	Manute Bol	.05	.02	.01
☐	158	Johnny Dawkins	.05	.02	.01
☐	159	Armon Gilliam	.05	.02	.01
☐	160	Rickey Green	.05	.02	.01
☐	161	Hersey Hawkins	.05	.02	.01
☐	162	Rick Mahorn	.05	.02	.01
☐	163	Tom Chambers	.05	.02	.01
☐	164	Jeff Hornacek	.05	.02	.01
☐	165	Kevin Johnson	.10	.05	.01
☐	166	Andrew Lang	.05	.02	.01
☐	167	Dan Majerle	.10	.05	.01
☐	168	Xavier McDaniel	.05	.02	.01
☐	169	Kurt Rambis	.05	.02	.01
☐	170	Mark West	.05	.02	.01
☐	171	Danny Ainge	.10	.05	.01
☐	172	Mark Bryant	.05	.02	.01
☐	173	Walter Davis	.10	.05	.01
☐	174	Clyde Drexler	.30	.14	.04
☐	175	Kevin Duckworth	.05	.02	.01
☐	176	Jerome Kersey	.05	.02	.01
☐	177	Terry Porter	.05	.02	.01
☐	178	Cliff Robinson	.05	.02	.01
☐	179	Buck Williams	.10	.05	.01
☐	180	Anthony Bonner	.05	.02	.01
☐	181	Antoine Carr	.05	.02	.01
☐	182	Duane Causwell	.05	.02	.01
☐	183	Bobby Hansen	.05	.02	.01
☐	184	Travis Mays	.05	.02	.01
☐	185	Lionel Simmons	.05	.02	.01
☐	186	Rory Sparrow	.05	.02	.01
☐	187	Wayman Tisdale	.05	.02	.01

☐ 188	Willie Anderson	.05	.02	.01
☐ 189	Terry Cummings	.05	.02	.01
☐ 190	Sean Elliott	.15	.07	.02
☐ 191	Sidney Green	.05	.02	.01
☐ 192	David Greenwood	.05	.02	.01
☐ 193	Paul Pressey	.05	.02	.01
☐ 194	David Robinson	.60	.25	.07
☐ 195	Dwayne Schintzius	.05	.02	.01
☐ 196	Rod Strickland	.05	.02	.01
☐ 197	Benoit Benjamin	.05	.02	.01
☐ 198	Michael Cage	.05	.02	.01
☐ 199	Eddie Johnson	.05	.02	.01
☐ 200	Shawn Kemp	1.25	.55	.16
☐ 201	Derrick McKey	.05	.02	.01
☐ 202	Gary Payton	.60	.25	.07
☐ 203	Ricky Pierce	.05	.02	.01
☐ 204	Sedale Threatt	.05	.02	.01
☐ 205	Thurl Bailey	.05	.02	.01
☐ 206	Mike Brown	.05	.02	.01
☐ 207	Mark Eaton	.05	.02	.01
☐ 208	Blue Edwards UER	.05	.02	.01
	(Forward/guard on front, guard on back)			
☐ 209	Darrell Griffith	.10	.05	.01
☐ 210	Jeff Malone	.05	.02	.01
☐ 211	Karl Malone	.25	.11	.03
☐ 212	John Stockton	.25	.11	.03
☐ 213	Ledell Eackles	.05	.02	.01
☐ 214	Pervis Ellison	.05	.02	.01
☐ 215	A.J. English	.05	.02	.01
☐ 216	Harvey Grant	.05	.02	.01
	(Shown boxing out twin brother Horace)			
☐ 217	Charles Jones	.05	.02	.01
☐ 218	Bernard King	.10	.05	.01
☐ 219	Darrell Walker	.05	.02	.01
☐ 220	John Williams	.05	.02	.01
☐ 221	Bob Weiss CO	.05	.02	.01
☐ 222	Chris Ford CO	.05	.02	.01
☐ 223	Gene Littles CO	.05	.02	.01
☐ 224	Phil Jackson CO	.10	.05	.01
☐ 225	Lenny Wilkens CO	.10	.05	.01
☐ 226	Richie Adubato CO	.05	.02	.01
☐ 227	Paul Westhead CO	.05	.02	.01
☐ 228	Chuck Daly CO	.10	.05	.01
☐ 229	Don Nelson CO	.10	.05	.01
☐ 230	Don Chaney CO	.05	.02	.01
☐ 231	Bob Hill CO UER	.05	.02	.01
	(Coached under Ted Owens, not Ted Owen)			
☐ 232	Mike Schuler CO	.05	.02	.01
☐ 233	Mike Dunleavy CO	.05	.02	.01
☐ 234	Kevin Loughery CO	.05	.02	.01
☐ 235	Del Harris CO	.05	.02	.01
☐ 236	Jimmy Rodgers CO	.05	.02	.01
☐ 237	Bill Fitch CO	.05	.02	.01
☐ 238	Pat Riley CO	.10	.05	.01
☐ 239	Matt Guokas CO	.05	.02	.01
☐ 240	Jim Lynam CO	.05	.02	.01
☐ 241	Cotton Fitzsimmons CO	.05	.02	.01
☐ 242	Rick Adelman CO	.05	.02	.01
☐ 243	Dick Motta CO	.05	.02	.01
☐ 244	Larry Brown CO	.10	.05	.01
☐ 245	K.C. Jones CO	.10	.05	.01
☐ 246	Jerry Sloan CO	.10	.05	.01
☐ 247	Wes Unseld CO	.10	.05	.01
☐ 248	Charles Barkley AS	.20	.09	.03
☐ 249	Brad Daugherty AS	.05	.02	.01
☐ 250	Joe Dumars AS	.10	.05	.01
☐ 251	Patrick Ewing AS	.10	.05	.01
☐ 252	Hersey Hawkins AS	.05	.02	.01
☐ 253	Michael Jordan AS	1.50	.70	.19
☐ 254	Bernard King AS	.10	.05	.01
☐ 255	Kevin McHale AS	.10	.05	.01
☐ 256	Robert Parish AS	.10	.05	.01
☐ 257	Ricky Pierce AS	.05	.02	.01
☐ 258	Alvin Robertson AS	.05	.02	.01
☐ 259	Dominique Wilkins AS	.10	.05	.01
☐ 260	Chris Ford CO AS	.05	.02	.01
☐ 261	Tom Chambers AS	.05	.02	.01
☐ 262	Clyde Drexler AS	.10	.05	.01
☐ 263	Kevin Duckworth AS	.05	.02	.01
☐ 264	Tim Hardaway AS	.10	.05	.01
☐ 265	Kevin Johnson AS	.10	.05	.01
☐ 266	Magic Johnson AS	.40	.18	.05
☐ 267	Karl Malone AS	.10	.05	.01
☐ 268	Chris Mullin AS	.10	.05	.01
☐ 269	Terry Porter AS	.05	.02	.01
☐ 270	David Robinson AS	.30	.14	.04
☐ 271	John Stockton AS	.10	.05	.01
☐ 272	James Worthy AS	.10	.05	.01
☐ 273	Rick Adelman CO AS	.05	.02	.01
☐ 274	Atlanta Hawks	.05	.02	.01
	Team Card UER (Actually began as Tri-Cities Blackhawks)			
☐ 275	Boston Celtics	.05	.02	.01
	Team Card UER (No NBA Hoops logo on card front)			
☐ 276	Charlotte Hornets	.05	.02	.01
	Team Card			
☐ 277	Chicago Bulls	.05	.02	.01
	Team Card			
☐ 278	Cleveland Cavaliers	.05	.02	.01
	Team Card			
☐ 279	Dallas Mavericks	.05	.02	.01
	Team Card			
☐ 280	Denver Nuggets	.05	.02	.01
	Team Card			
☐ 281	Detroit Pistons	.05	.02	.01
	Team Card UER (Pistons not NBA Finalists until 1988; Ft. Ft. Wayne Pistons in Finals in 1955 and 1956)			
☐ 282	Golden State Warriors	.05	.02	.01
	Team Card			
☐ 283	Houston Rockets	.05	.02	.01
	Team Card			
☐ 284	Indiana Pacers	.05	.02	.01
	Team Card			
☐ 285	Los Angeles Clippers	.05	.02	.01
	Team Card			
☐ 286	Los Angeles Lakers	.05	.02	.01
	Team Card			
☐ 287	Miami Heat	.05	.02	.01
	Team Card			
☐ 288	Milwaukee Bucks	.05	.02	.01
	Team Card			
☐ 289	Minnesota Timberwolves	.05	.02	.01
	Team Card			
☐ 290	New Jersey Nets	.05	.02	.01
	Team Card			
☐ 291	New York Knicks	.05	.02	.01
	Team Card UER (Golden State not mentioned as an active charter member of NBA)			
☐ 292	Orlando Magic	.05	.02	.01
	Team Card			
☐ 293	Philadelphia 76ers	.05	.02	.01

☐ 294	Team Card Phoenix Suns	.05	.02	.01
☐ 295	Team Card Portland Trail Blazers	.05	.02	.01
☐ 296	Team Card Sacramento Kings	.05	.02	.01
☐ 297	Team Card San Antonio Spurs	.05	.02	.01
☐ 298	Team Card Seattle Supersonics	.05	.02	.01
☐ 299	Team Card Utah Jazz	.05	.02	.01
☐ 300	Team Card Washington Bullets	.05	.02	.01
☐ 301	Team Card James Naismith Centennial Card	.10	.05	.01
☐ 302	Kevin Johnson IS	.10	.05	.01
☐ 303	Reggie Miller IS	.15	.07	.02
☐ 304	Hakeem Olajuwon IS	.30	.14	.04
☐ 305	Robert Parish IS	.10	.05	.01
☐ 306	Scoring Leaders Michael Jordan Karl Malone	1.00	.45	.12
☐ 307	3-Point FG Percent League Leaders Jim Les Trent Tucker	.05	.02	.01
☐ 308	Free Throw Percent League Leaders Reggie Miller Jeff Malone	.08	.04	.01
☐ 309	Blocks League Leaders Hakeem Olajuwon David Robinson	.40	.18	.05
☐ 310	Steals League Leaders Alvin Robertson John Stockton	.10	.05	.01
☐ 311	Rebounds LL UER David Robinson Dennis Rodman (Robinson credited as playing for Houston)	.50	.23	.06
☐ 312	Assists League Leaders John Stockton Magic Johnson	.30	.14	.04
☐ 313	Field Goal Percent League Leaders Buck Williams Robert Parish	.10	.05	.01
☐ 314	Larry Bird UER Milestone (Should be card 315 to fit Milestone sequence)	.50	.23	.06
☐ 315	Alex English Moses Malone Milestone UER (Should be card 314 and be a League Leader card)	.10	.05	.01
☐ 316	Magic Johnson Milestone	.40	.18	.05
☐ 317	Michael Jordan Milestone	1.50	.70	.19
☐ 318	Moses Malone Milestone	.10	.05	.01
☐ 319	Larry Bird NBA Yearbook Look Back	.50	.23	.06
☐ 320	Maurice Cheeks NBA Yearbook Look Back	.10	.05	.01
☐ 321	Magic Johnson NBA Yearbook Look Back	.40	.18	.05
☐ 322	Bernard King NBA Yearbook Look Back	.10	.05	.01
☐ 323	Moses Malone NBA Yearbook Look Back	.10	.05	.01
☐ 324	Robert Parish NBA Yearbook Look Back	.10	.05	.01
☐ 325	All-Star Jam Jammin' With Will Smith (Stay in School)	.10	.05	.01
☐ 326	All-Star Jam Jammin' With The Boys and Will Smith (Stay in School)	.10	.05	.01
☐ 327	David Robinson Leave Alcohol Out	.30	.14	.04
☐ 328	Checklist 1	.05	.02	.01
☐ 329	Checklist 2 UER (Card front is from 330)	.05	.02	.01
☐ 330	Checklist 3 UER (Card front is from 329; card 327 listed oper- ation, should be celebration)	.05	.02	.01
☐ 331	Maurice Cheeks	.10	.05	.01
☐ 332	Duane Ferrell	.05	.02	.01
☐ 333	Jon Koncak	.05	.02	.01
☐ 334	Gary Leonard	.05	.02	.01
☐ 335	Travis Mays	.05	.02	.01
☐ 336	Blair Rasmussen	.05	.02	.01
☐ 337	Alexander Volkov	.05	.02	.01
☐ 338	John Bagley	.05	.02	.01
☐ 339	Rickey Green UER (Ricky on front)	.05	.02	.01
☐ 340	Derek Smith	.05	.02	.01
☐ 341	Stojko Vrankovic	.05	.02	.01
☐ 342	Anthony Frederick	.05	.02	.01
☐ 343	Kenny Gattison	.05	.02	.01
☐ 344	Eric Leckner	.05	.02	.01
☐ 345	Will Perdue	.05	.02	.01
☐ 346	Scott Williams	.05	.02	.01
☐ 347	John Battle	.05	.02	.01
☐ 348	Winston Bennett	.05	.02	.01
☐ 349	Henry James	.05	.02	.01
☐ 350	Steve Kerr	.05	.02	.01
☐ 351	John Morton	.05	.02	.01
☐ 352	Terry Davis	.05	.02	.01
☐ 353	Randy White	.05	.02	.01
☐ 354	Greg Anderson	.05	.02	.01
☐ 355	Anthony Cook	.05	.02	.01
☐ 356	Walter Davis	.10	.05	.01
☐ 357	Winston Garland	.05	.02	.01
☐ 358	Scott Hastings	.05	.02	.01
☐ 359	Marcus Liberty	.05	.02	.01
☐ 360	William Bedford	.05	.02	.01
☐ 361	Lance Blanks	.05	.02	.01
☐ 362	Brad Sellers	.05	.02	.01
☐ 363	Darrell Walker	.05	.02	.01
☐ 364	Orlando Woolridge	.05	.02	.01
☐ 365	Vincent Askew	.05	.02	.01
☐ 366	Mario Elie	.20	.09	.03
☐ 367	Jim Petersen	.05	.02	.01
☐ 368	Matt Bullard	.05	.02	.01
☐ 369	Gerald Henderson	.05	.02	.01
☐ 370	Dave Jamerson	.05	.02	.01
☐ 371	Tree Rollins	.05	.02	.01

#	Player			
☐ 372	Greg Dreiling	.05	.02	.01
☐ 373	George McCloud	.10	.05	.01
☐ 374	Kenny Williams	.05	.02	.01
☐ 375	Randy Wittman	.05	.02	.01
☐ 376	Tony Brown	.05	.02	.01
☐ 377	Lanard Copeland	.05	.02	.01
☐ 378	James Edwards	.05	.02	.01
☐ 379	Bo Kimble	.05	.02	.01
☐ 380	Doc Rivers	.05	.02	.01
☐ 381	Loy Vaught	.10	.05	.01
☐ 382	Elden Campbell	.10	.05	.01
☐ 383	Jack Haley	.05	.02	.01
☐ 384	Tony Smith	.05	.02	.01
☐ 385	Sedale Threatt	.05	.02	.01
☐ 386	Keith Askins	.05	.02	.01
☐ 387	Grant Long	.05	.02	.01
☐ 388	Alan Ogg	.05	.02	.01
☐ 389	Jon Sundvold	.05	.02	.01
☐ 390	Lester Conner	.05	.02	.01
☐ 391	Jeff Grayer	.05	.02	.01
☐ 392	Steve Henson	.05	.02	.01
☐ 393	Larry Krystkowiak	.05	.02	.01
☐ 394	Moses Malone	.15	.07	.02
☐ 395	Scott Brooks	.05	.02	.01
☐ 396	Tellis Frank	.05	.02	.01
☐ 397	Doug West	.05	.02	.01
☐ 398	Rafael Addison	.05	.02	.01
☐ 399	Dave Feitl	.05	.02	.01
☐ 400	Tate George	.05	.02	.01
☐ 401	Terry Mills	.10	.05	.01
☐ 402	Tim McCormick	.05	.02	.01
☐ 403	Xavier McDaniel	.05	.02	.01
☐ 404	Anthony Mason	.40	.18	.05
☐ 405	Brian Quinnett	.05	.02	.01
☐ 406	John Starks	.30	.14	.04
☐ 407	Mark Acres	.05	.02	.01
☐ 408	Greg Kite	.05	.02	.01
☐ 409	Jeff Turner	.05	.02	.01
☐ 410	Morlon Wiley	.05	.02	.01
☐ 411	Dave Hoppen	.05	.02	.01
☐ 412	Brian Oliver	.05	.02	.01
☐ 413	Kenny Payne	.05	.02	.01
☐ 414	Charles Shackleford	.05	.02	.01
☐ 415	Mitchell Wiggins	.05	.02	.01
☐ 416	Jayson Williams	.05	.02	.01
☐ 417	Cedric Ceballos	.10	.05	.01
☐ 418	Negele Knight	.05	.02	.01
☐ 419	Andrew Lang	.05	.02	.01
☐ 420	Jerrod Mustaf	.05	.02	.01
☐ 421	Ed Nealy	.05	.02	.01
☐ 422	Tim Perry	.05	.02	.01
☐ 423	Alaa Abdelnaby	.05	.02	.01
☐ 424	Wayne Cooper	.05	.02	.01
☐ 425	Danny Young	.05	.02	.01
☐ 426	Dennis Hopson	.05	.02	.01
☐ 427	Les Jepsen	.05	.02	.01
☐ 428	Jim Les	.05	.02	.01
☐ 429	Mitch Richmond	.25	.11	.03
☐ 430	Dwayne Schintzius	.05	.02	.01
☐ 431	Spud Webb	.10	.05	.01
☐ 432	Jud Buechler	.05	.02	.01
☐ 433	Antoine Carr	.05	.02	.01
☐ 434	Tom Garrick	.05	.02	.01
☐ 435	Sean Higgins	.05	.02	.01
☐ 436	Avery Johnson	.10	.05	.01
☐ 437	Tony Massenburg	.05	.02	.01
☐ 438	Dana Barros	.05	.02	.01
☐ 439	Quintin Dailey	.05	.02	.01
☐ 440	Bart Kofoed	.05	.02	.01
☐ 441	Nate McMillan	.05	.02	.01
☐ 442	Delaney Rudd	.05	.02	.01
☐ 443	Michael Adams	.05	.02	.01
☐ 444	Mark Alarie	.05	.02	.01
☐ 445	Greg Foster	.05	.02	.01
☐ 446	Tom Hammonds	.05	.02	.01
☐ 447	Andre Turner	.05	.02	.01
☐ 448	David Wingate	.05	.02	.01
☐ 449	Dominique Wilkins SC	.10	.05	.01
☐ 450	Kevin Willis SC	.05	.02	.01
☐ 451	Larry Bird SC	.50	.23	.06
☐ 452	Robert Parish SC	.10	.05	.01
☐ 453	Rex Chapman SC	.05	.02	.01
☐ 454	Kendall Gill SC	.05	.02	.01
☐ 455	Michael Jordan SC	1.50	.70	.19
☐ 456	Scottie Pippen SC	.40	.18	.05
☐ 457	Brad Daugherty SC	.05	.02	.01
☐ 458	Larry Nance SC	.05	.02	.01
☐ 459	Rolando Blackman SC	.10	.05	.01
☐ 460	Derek Harper SC	.10	.05	.01
☐ 461	Chris Jackson SC	.10	.05	.01
☐ 462	Todd Lichti SC	.05	.02	.01
☐ 463	Joe Dumars SC	.10	.05	.01
☐ 464	Isiah Thomas SC	.10	.05	.01
☐ 465	Tim Hardaway SC	.10	.05	.01
☐ 466	Chris Mullin SC	.10	.05	.01
☐ 467	Hakeem Olajuwon SC	.30	.14	.04
☐ 468	Otis Thorpe SC	.10	.05	.01
☐ 469	Reggie Miller SC	.15	.07	.02
☐ 470	Detlef Schrempf SC	.05	.02	.01
☐ 471	Ron Harper SC	.05	.02	.01
☐ 472	Charles Smith SC	.05	.02	.01
☐ 473	Magic Johnson SC	.40	.18	.05
☐ 474	James Worthy SC	.10	.05	.01
☐ 475	Sherman Douglas SC	.05	.02	.01
☐ 476	Rony Seikaly SC	.05	.02	.01
☐ 477	Jay Humphries SC	.05	.02	.01
☐ 478	Alvin Robertson SC	.05	.02	.01
☐ 479	Tyrone Corbin SC	.05	.02	.01
☐ 480	Pooh Richardson SC	.05	.02	.01
☐ 481	Sam Bowie SC	.05	.02	.01
☐ 482	Derrick Coleman SC	.05	.02	.01
☐ 483	Patrick Ewing SC	.10	.05	.01
☐ 484	Charles Oakley SC	.05	.02	.01
☐ 485	Dennis Scott SC	.10	.05	.01
☐ 486	Scott Skiles SC	.05	.02	.01
☐ 487	Charles Barkley SC	.20	.09	.03
☐ 488	Hersey Hawkins SC	.05	.02	.01
☐ 489	Tom Chambers SC	.05	.02	.01
☐ 490	Kevin Johnson SC	.10	.05	.01
☐ 491	Clyde Drexler SC	.10	.05	.01
☐ 492	Terry Porter SC	.05	.02	.01
☐ 493	Lionel Simmons SC	.05	.02	.01
☐ 494	Wayman Tisdale SC	.05	.02	.01
☐ 495	Terry Cummings SC	.05	.02	.01
☐ 496	David Robinson SC	.30	.14	.04
☐ 497	Shawn Kemp SC	.60	.25	.07
☐ 498	Ricky Pierce SC	.05	.02	.01
☐ 499	Karl Malone SC	.10	.05	.01
☐ 500	John Stockton SC	.10	.05	.01
☐ 501	Harvey Grant SC	.05	.02	.01
☐ 502	Bernard King SC	.10	.05	.01
☐ 503	Travis Mays Art	.05	.02	.01
☐ 504	Kevin McHale Art	.10	.05	.01
☐ 505	Muggsy Bogues Art	.10	.05	.01
☐ 506	Scottie Pippen Art	.40	.18	.05
☐ 507	Brad Daugherty Art	.05	.02	.01
☐ 508	Derek Harper Art	.10	.05	.01
☐ 509	Chris Jackson Art	.10	.05	.01
☐ 510	Isiah Thomas Art	.10	.05	.01
☐ 511	Tim Hardaway Art	.10	.05	.01
☐ 512	Otis Thorpe Art	.10	.05	.01
☐ 513	Chuck Person Art	.05	.02	.01

☐ 514	Ron Harper Art	.05	.02	.01
☐ 515	James Worthy Art	.10	.05	.01
☐ 516	Sherman Douglas Art	.05	.02	.01
☐ 517	Dale Ellis Art	.05	.02	.01
☐ 518	Tony Campbell Art	.05	.02	.01
☐ 519	Derrick Coleman Art	.05	.02	.01
☐ 520	Gerald Wilkins Art	.05	.02	.01
☐ 521	Scott Skiles Art	.05	.02	.01
☐ 522	Manute Bol Art	.05	.02	.01
☐ 523	Tom Chambers Art	.05	.02	.01
☐ 524	Terry Porter Art	.05	.02	.01
☐ 525	Lionel Simmons Art	.05	.02	.01
☐ 526	Sean Elliott Art	.10	.05	.01
☐ 527	Shawn Kemp Art	.60	.25	.07
☐ 528	John Stockton Art	.10	.05	.01
☐ 529	Harvey Grant Art	.05	.02	.01
☐ 530	Michael Adams	.05	.02	.01
	All-Time Active Leader			
	Three-Point Field Goals			
☐ 531	Charles Barkley	.20	.09	.03
	All-Time Active Leader			
	Field Goal Percentage			
☐ 532	Larry Bird	.50	.23	.06
	All-Time Active Leader			
	Free Throw Percentage			
☐ 533	Maurice Cheeks	.10	.05	.01
	All-Time Active Leader			
	Steals			
☐ 534	Mark Eaton	.05	.02	.01
	All-Time Active Leader			
	Blocks			
☐ 535	Magic Johnson	.40	.18	.05
	All-Time Active Leader			
	Assists			
☐ 536	Michael Jordan	1.50	.70	.19
	All-Time Active Leader			
	Scoring Average			
☐ 537	Moses Malone	.10	.05	.01
	All-Time Active Leader			
	Rebounds			
☐ 538	Sam Perkins FIN	.05	.02	.01
☐ 539	Scottie Pippen FIN	.25	.11	.03
	James Worthy			
☐ 540	Vlade Divac FIN	.10	.05	.01
☐ 541	John Paxson FIN	.10	.05	.01
☐ 542	Michael Jordan FIN	1.50	.70	.19
	Vlade Divac)			
☐ 543	Michael Jordan FIN	1.50	.70	.19
	kissing trophy)			
☐ 544	Otis Smith	.05	.02	.01
	Stay in School			
☐ 545	Jeff Turner	.05	.02	.01
	Stay in School			
☐ 546	Larry Johnson	1.50	.70	.19
☐ 547	Kenny Anderson	.50	.23	.06
☐ 548	Billy Owens	.25	.11	.03
☐ 549	Dikembe Mutombo	.75	.35	.09
☐ 550	Steve Smith	.60	.25	.07
☐ 551	Doug Smith	.05	.02	.01
☐ 552	Luc Longley	.30	.14	.04
☐ 553	Mark Macon	.05	.02	.01
☐ 554	Stacey Augmon	.30	.14	.04
☐ 555	Brian Williams	.15	.07	.02
☐ 556	Terrell Brandon	.60	.25	.07
☐ 557	Walter Davis	.10	.05	.01
	Team USA 1976			
☐ 558	Vern Fleming	.05	.02	.01
	Team USA 1984			
☐ 559	Joe Kleine	.05	.02	.01
	Team USA 1984			
☐ 560	Jon Koncak	.05	.02	.01

	Team USA 1984			
☐ 561	Sam Perkins	.05	.02	.01
	Team USA 1984			
☐ 562	Alvin Robertson	.05	.02	.01
	Team USA 1984			
☐ 563	Wayman Tisdale	.05	.02	.01
	Team USA 1984			
☐ 564	Jeff Turner	.05	.02	.01
	Team USA 1984			
☐ 565	Willie Anderson	.05	.02	.01
	Team USA 1988			
☐ 566	Stacey Augmon	.10	.05	.01
	Team USA 1988			
☐ 567	Bimbo Coles	.05	.02	.01
	Team USA 1988			
☐ 568	Jeff Grayer	.05	.02	.01
	Team USA 1988			
☐ 569	Hersey Hawkins	.05	.02	.01
	Team USA 1988			
☐ 570	Dan Majerle	.10	.05	.01
	Team USA 1988			
☐ 571	Danny Manning	.10	.05	.01
	Team USA 1988			
☐ 572	J.R. Reid	.05	.02	.01
	Team USA 1988			
☐ 573	Mitch Richmond	.10	.05	.01
	Team USA 1988			
☐ 574	Charles Smith	.05	.02	.01
	Team USA 1988			
☐ 575	Charles Barkley	.75	.35	.09
	Team USA 1992			
☐ 576	Larry Bird	2.00	.90	.25
	Team USA 1992			
☐ 577	Patrick Ewing	.50	.23	.06
	Team USA 1992			
☐ 578	Magic Johnson	1.50	.70	.19
	Team USA 1992			
☐ 579	Michael Jordan	6.00	2.70	.75
	Team USA 1992			
☐ 580	Karl Malone	.50	.23	.06
	Team USA 1992			
☐ 581	Chris Mullin	.10	.05	.01
	Team USA 1992			
☐ 582	Scottie Pippen	1.50	.70	.19
	Team USA 1992			
☐ 583	David Robinson	1.25	.55	.16
	Team USA 1992			
☐ 584	John Stockton	.50	.23	.06
	Team USA 1992			
☐ 585	Chuck Daly CO	.10	.05	.01
	Team USA 1992			
☐ 586	Lenny Wilkens CO	.10	.05	.01
	Team USA 1992			
☐ 587	P.J. Carlesimo CO	.10	.05	.01
	Team USA 1992			
☐ 588	Mike Krzyzewski CO	.40	.18	.05
	Team USA 1992			
☐ 589	Checklist Card 1	.05	.02	.01
☐ 590	Checklist Card 2	.05	.02	.01
☐ CC1	Dr.James Naismith	1.00	.45	.12
☐ XX	Head of the Class	20.00	9.00	2.50
	Kenny Anderson			
	Larry Johnson			
	Dikembe Mutombo			
	Billy Owens			
	Doug Smith			
	Steve Smith			
☐ NNO	Team USA SP	.50	.23	.06
	Title Card			
☐ NNO	Centennial Card	1.00	.45	.12
	(Sendaway)			

1991-92 Hoops All-Star MVP's

This six-card standard-size insert set commemorates the most valuable player of the NBA All-Star games from 1986 to 1991. Two cards were inserted in each second series rack pack. On a white card face, the front features non-action color photos framed by either a blue (7, 9, 12) or red (8, 10, 11) border. The top thicker border is jagged and displays the player's name, while the year the award was received appears in a colored box in the lower left corner. The backs have the same design and feature a color action photo from the All-Star game. The cards are numbered on the back by Roman numerals.

	MINT	NRMT	EXC
COMPLETE SET (6)	25.00	11.00	3.10
COMMON CARD (7-12)	.50	.23	.06
☐ 7 Isiah Thomas (Numbered VII)	1.00	.45	.12
☐ 8 Tom Chambers (Numbered VIII)	.50	.23	.06
☐ 9 Michael Jordan (Numbered IX)	20.00	9.00	2.50
☐ 10 Karl Malone (Numbered X)	1.50	.70	.19
☐ 11 Magic Johnson (Numbered XI)	5.00	2.20	.60
☐ 12 Charles Barkley (Numbered XII)	2.50	1.10	.30

1991-92 Hoops Slam Dunk

This six-card standard size insert set of "Slam Dunk Champions" features the winners of the All-Star weekend slam dunk competition from 1984 to 1991. The cards were issued two per first series 47-card rack pack. The front has a color photo of the player dunking the ball, with royal blue borders on a white card face. The player's name appears in orange lettering in a purple stripe above the picture, and the year

the player won is given in a "Slam Dunk Champion" emblem overlaying the lower left corner of the picture. The design of the back is similar to the front, only with an extended caption on a yellow-green background. A drawing of a basketball entering a rim appears at the upper left corner. The cards are numbered on the back by Roman numerals.

	MINT	NRMT	EXC
COMPLETE SET (6)	22.00	10.00	2.70
COMMON CARD (1-6)	.50	.23	.06
☐ 1 Larry Nance (Numbered I)	.50	.23	.06
☐ 2 Dominique Wilkins (Numbered II)	.75	.35	.09
☐ 3 Spud Webb (Numbered III)	.75	.35	.09
☐ 4 Michael Jordan (Numbered IV)	20.00	9.00	2.50
☐ 5 Kenny Walker (Numbered V)	.50	.23	.06
☐ 6 Dee Brown (Numbered VI)	.50	.23	.06

1992-93 Hoops

The complete 1992-93 Hoops basketball set contains 490 standard-size cards. The set was released in two series of 350 and 140 cards, respectively. Both series packs contained 12 cards each with a suggested retail price of 79 cents each. Reported production quantities were 20,000 20-box wax cases of the first series and approximately 14,000 20-box wax cases of the second series. The basic card fronts display color action player photos surrounded by white

borders. A color stripe reflecting one of the team's colors cuts across the picture and the player's name is printed vertically in a transparent stripe bordering the left side of the picture. The horizontally oriented backs carry a color head shot, biography, career highlights, and complete statistics (college and pro). The cards are checklisted below alphabetically according to teams. Subsets include Coaches (239-265), Team cards (266-292), NBA All-Stars East (293-305), NBA All-Stars West (306-319), League Leaders (320-327), Magic Moments (328-331), NBA Inside Stuff (332-333), NBA Stay in School (334-335), Basketball Tournament of the Americas (336-347) and Trivia (481-485). Rookie cards, scattered throughout the set, have a gold rather than a ghosted white stripe. The team logo appears in the lower left corner and intersects a team color-coded stripe that contains the player's position. The horizontal backs show a white background and include statistics (collegiate and pro), biographies, and career summaries. A close-up photo is at the upper left. Rookie Cards of note include Tom Gugliotta, Robert Horry, Christian Laettner, Alonzo Mourning, Shaquille O'Neal, Bobby Phills, Latrell Sprewell and Clarence Weatherspoon. A Magic Johnson "Commemorative Card" and a Patrick Ewing "Ultimate Game" card were randomly inserted in first series foil packs. One-thousand of each were autographed. The odds of pulling an autographed card were one in 14,400 packs. Also randomly inserted into second series foil packs were a Patrick Ewing Art card (reported odds were one per 21 packs), a Chicago Bulls Championship card (reported odds were one per 32 packs) and a John Stockton "Ultimate Game" card (reported odds were one per 92 packs). Stockton autographed 1,633 of these cards (reported odds were one per 5,732 packs). Also randomly inserted into first series packs was a USA Basketball Team card. A Barcelona Plastic card was also randomly inserted in first series packs at a rate of approximately one per 720 packs.

	MINT	NRMT	EXC
COMPLETE SET (490)	35.00	16.00	4.40
COMPLETE SERIES 1 (350)	15.00	6.75	1.85
COMPLETE SERIES 2 (140)	20.00	9.00	2.50
COMMON CARD (1-350)	.05	.02	.01
COMMON CARD (351-490)	.10	.05	.01

☐	1 Stacey Augmon	.10	.05	.01
☐	2 Maurice Cheeks	.10	.05	.01
☐	3 Duane Ferrell	.05	.02	.01
☐	4 Paul Graham	.05	.02	.01
☐	5 Jon Koncak	.05	.02	.01
☐	6 Blair Rasmussen	.05	.02	.01
☐	7 Rumeal Robinson	.05	.02	.01
☐	8 Dominique Wilkins	.10	.05	.01
☐	9 Kevin Willis	.05	.02	.01
☐	10 Larry Bird	1.00	.45	.12
☐	11 Dee Brown	.05	.02	.01
☐	12 Sherman Douglas	.05	.02	.01
☐	13 Rick Fox	.05	.02	.01
☐	14 Kevin Gamble	.05	.02	.01
☐	15 Reggie Lewis	.10	.05	.01
☐	16 Kevin McHale	.10	.05	.01
☐	17 Robert Parish	.10	.05	.01
☐	18 Ed Pinckney UER	.05	.02	.01
	(Wrong insert info, Kleine to Sacramento and Lohaus to Boston)			
☐	19 Muggsy Bogues	.10	.05	.01
☐	20 Dell Curry	.05	.02	.01
☐	21 Kenny Gattison	.05	.02	.01
☐	22 Kendall Gill	.05	.02	.01
☐	23 Mike Gminski	.05	.02	.01
☐	24 Larry Johnson	.50	.23	.06
☐	25 Johnny Newman	.05	.02	.01
☐	26 J.R. Reid	.05	.02	.01
☐	27 B.J. Armstrong	.05	.02	.01
☐	28 Bill Cartwright	.05	.02	.01
☐	29 Horace Grant	.10	.05	.01
☐	30 Michael Jordan	3.00	1.35	.35
☐	31 Stacey King	.05	.02	.01
☐	32 John Paxson	.10	.05	.01
☐	33 Will Perdue	.05	.02	.01
☐	34 Scottie Pippen	.75	.35	.09
☐	35 Scott Williams	.05	.02	.01
☐	36 John Battle	.05	.02	.01
☐	37 Terrell Brandon	.10	.05	.01
☐	38 Brad Daugherty	.05	.02	.01
☐	39 Craig Ehlo	.05	.02	.01
☐	40 Danny Ferry	.05	.02	.01
☐	41 Henry James	.05	.02	.01
☐	42 Larry Nance	.05	.02	.01
☐	43 Mark Price	.05	.02	.01
☐	44 Hot Rod Williams	.05	.02	.01
☐	45 Rolando Blackman	.05	.02	.01
☐	46 Terry Davis	.05	.02	.01
☐	47 Derek Harper	.05	.02	.01
☐	48 Mike Iuzzolino	.05	.02	.01
☐	49 Fat Lever	.05	.02	.01
☐	50 Rodney McCray	.05	.02	.01
☐	51 Doug Smith	.05	.02	.01
☐	52 Randy White	.05	.02	.01
☐	53 Herb Williams	.05	.02	.01
☐	54 Greg Anderson	.05	.02	.01
☐	55 Winston Garland	.05	.02	.01
☐	56 Chris Jackson	.10	.05	.01
☐	57 Marcus Liberty	.05	.02	.01
☐	58 Todd Lichti	.05	.02	.01
☐	59 Mark Macon	.05	.02	.01
☐	60 Dikembe Mutombo	.25	.11	.03
☐	61 Reggie Williams	.05	.02	.01
☐	62 Mark Aguirre	.10	.05	.01
☐	63 William Bedford	.05	.02	.01
☐	64 Joe Dumars	.10	.05	.01
☐	65 Bill Laimbeer	.05	.02	.01
☐	66 Dennis Rodman	1.00	.45	.12
☐	67 John Salley	.05	.02	.01
☐	68 Isiah Thomas	.15	.07	.02
☐	69 Darrell Walker	.05	.02	.01
☐	70 Orlando Woolridge	.05	.02	.01
☐	71 Victor Alexander	.05	.02	.01
☐	72 Mario Elie	.05	.02	.01
☐	73 Chris Gatling	.05	.02	.01
☐	74 Tim Hardaway	.10	.05	.01
☐	75 Tyrone Hill	.05	.02	.01
☐	76 Alton Lister	.05	.02	.01
☐	77 Sarunas Marciulionis	.05	.02	.01
☐	78 Chris Mullin	.10	.05	.01
☐	79 Billy Owens	.05	.02	.01
☐	80 Matt Bullard	.05	.02	.01

#	Player			
☐ 81	Sleepy Floyd	.05	.02	.01
☐ 82	Avery Johnson	.10	.05	.01
☐ 83	Buck Johnson	.05	.02	.01
☐ 84	Vernon Maxwell	.05	.02	.01
☐ 85	Hakeem Olajuwon	.60	.25	.07
☐ 86	Kenny Smith	.05	.02	.01
☐ 87	Larry Smith	.05	.02	.01
☐ 88	Otis Thorpe	.10	.05	.01
☐ 89	Dale Davis	.05	.02	.01
☐ 90	Vern Fleming	.05	.02	.01
☐ 91	George McCloud	.05	.02	.01
☐ 92	Reggie Miller	.30	.14	.04
☐ 93	Chuck Person	.05	.02	.01
☐ 94	Detlef Schrempf	.10	.05	.01
☐ 95	Rik Smits	.10	.05	.01
☐ 96	LaSalle Thompson	.05	.02	.01
☐ 97	Micheal Williams	.05	.02	.01
☐ 98	James Edwards	.05	.02	.01
☐ 99	Gary Grant	.05	.02	.01
☐ 100	Ron Harper	.05	.02	.01
☐ 101	Danny Manning	.10	.05	.01
☐ 102	Ken Norman	.05	.02	.01
☐ 103	Olden Polynice	.05	.02	.01
☐ 104	Doc Rivers	.05	.02	.01
☐ 105	Charles Smith	.05	.02	.01
☐ 106	Loy Vaught	.05	.02	.01
☐ 107	Elden Campbell	.10	.05	.01
☐ 108	Vlade Divac	.10	.05	.01
☐ 109	A.C. Green	.10	.05	.01
☐ 110	Sam Perkins	.05	.02	.01
☐ 111	Byron Scott	.10	.05	.01
☐ 112	Tony Smith	.05	.02	.01
☐ 113	Terry Teagle	.05	.02	.01
☐ 114	Sedale Threatt	.05	.02	.01
☐ 115	James Worthy	.10	.05	.01
☐ 116	Willie Burton	.05	.02	.01
☐ 117	Bimbo Coles	.05	.02	.01
☐ 118	Kevin Edwards	.05	.02	.01
☐ 119	Alec Kessler	.05	.02	.01
☐ 120	Grant Long	.05	.02	.01
☐ 121	Glen Rice	.10	.05	.01
☐ 122	Rony Seikaly	.05	.02	.01
☐ 123	Brian Shaw	.05	.02	.01
☐ 124	Steve Smith	.10	.05	.01
☐ 125	Frank Brickowski	.05	.02	.01
☐ 126	Dale Ellis	.05	.02	.01
☐ 127	Jeff Grayer	.05	.02	.01
☐ 128	Jay Humphries	.05	.02	.01
☐ 129	Larry Krystkowiak	.05	.02	.01
☐ 130	Moses Malone	.15	.07	.02
☐ 131	Fred Roberts	.05	.02	.01
☐ 132	Alvin Robertson	.05	.02	.01
☐ 133	Dan Schayes	.05	.02	.01
☐ 134	Thurl Bailey	.05	.02	.01
☐ 135	Scott Brooks	.05	.02	.01
☐ 136	Tony Campbell	.05	.02	.01
☐ 137	Gerald Glass	.05	.02	.01
☐ 138	Luc Longley	.05	.02	.01
☐ 139	Sam Mitchell	.05	.02	.01
☐ 140	Pooh Richardson	.05	.02	.01
☐ 141	Felton Spencer	.05	.02	.01
☐ 142	Doug West	.05	.02	.01
☐ 143	Rafael Addison	.05	.02	.01
☐ 144	Kenny Anderson	.10	.05	.01
☐ 145	Mookie Blaylock	.10	.05	.01
☐ 146	Sam Bowie	.05	.02	.01
☐ 147	Derrick Coleman	.05	.02	.01
☐ 148	Chris Dudley	.05	.02	.01
☐ 149	Terry Mills	.05	.02	.01
☐ 150	Chris Morris	.05	.02	.01
☐ 151	Drazen Petrovic	.10	.05	.01
☐ 152	Greg Anthony	.05	.02	.01
☐ 153	Patrick Ewing	.25	.11	.03
☐ 154	Mark Jackson	.05	.02	.01
☐ 155	Anthony Mason	.10	.05	.01
☐ 156	Xavier McDaniel	.05	.02	.01
☐ 157	Charles Oakley	.05	.02	.01
☐ 158	John Starks	.10	.05	.01
☐ 159	Gerald Wilkins	.05	.02	.01
☐ 160	Nick Anderson	.10	.05	.01
☐ 161	Terry Catledge	.05	.02	.01
☐ 162	Jerry Reynolds	.05	.02	.01
☐ 163	Stanley Roberts	.05	.02	.01
☐ 164	Dennis Scott	.10	.05	.01
☐ 165	Scott Skiles	.05	.02	.01
☐ 166	Jeff Turner	.05	.02	.01
☐ 167	Sam Vincent	.05	.02	.01
☐ 168	Brian Williams	.05	.02	.01
☐ 169	Ron Anderson	.05	.02	.01
☐ 170	Charles Barkley	.40	.18	.05
☐ 171	Manute Bol	.05	.02	.01
☐ 172	Johnny Dawkins	.05	.02	.01
☐ 173	Armon Gilliam	.05	.02	.01
☐ 174	Hersey Hawkins	.10	.05	.01
☐ 175	Brian Oliver	.05	.02	.01
☐ 176	Charles Shackleford	.05	.02	.01
☐ 177	Jayson Williams	.05	.02	.01
☐ 178	Cedric Ceballos	.10	.05	.01
☐ 179	Tom Chambers	.05	.02	.01
☐ 180	Jeff Hornacek	.05	.02	.01
☐ 181	Kevin Johnson	.10	.05	.01
☐ 182	Negele Knight	.05	.02	.01
☐ 183	Andrew Lang	.05	.02	.01
☐ 184	Dan Majerle	.10	.05	.01
☐ 185	Tim Perry	.05	.02	.01
☐ 186	Mark West	.05	.02	.01
☐ 187	Alaa Abdelnaby	.05	.02	.01
☐ 188	Danny Ainge	.10	.05	.01
☐ 189	Clyde Drexler	.30	.14	.04
☐ 190	Kevin Duckworth	.05	.02	.01
☐ 191	Jerome Kersey	.05	.02	.01
☐ 192	Robert Pack	.05	.02	.01
☐ 193	Terry Porter	.05	.02	.01
☐ 194	Clifford Robinson	.10	.05	.01
☐ 195	Buck Williams	.10	.05	.01
☐ 196	Anthony Bonner	.05	.02	.01
☐ 197	Duane Causwell	.05	.02	.01
☐ 198	Pete Chilcutt	.05	.02	.01
☐ 199	Dennis Hopson	.05	.02	.01
☐ 200	Mitch Richmond	.20	.09	.03
☐ 201	Lionel Simmons	.05	.02	.01
☐ 202	Wayman Tisdale	.05	.02	.01
☐ 203	Spud Webb	.10	.05	.01
☐ 204	Willie Anderson	.05	.02	.01
☐ 205	Antoine Carr	.05	.02	.01
☐ 206	Terry Cummings	.05	.02	.01
☐ 207	Sean Elliott	.10	.05	.01
☐ 208	Sidney Green	.05	.02	.01
☐ 209	David Robinson	.50	.23	.06
☐ 210	Rod Strickland	.05	.02	.01
☐ 211	Greg Sutton	.05	.02	.01
☐ 212	Dana Barros	.05	.02	.01
☐ 213	Benoit Benjamin	.05	.02	.01
☐ 214	Michael Cage	.05	.02	.01
☐ 215	Eddie Johnson	.05	.02	.01
☐ 216	Shawn Kemp	1.00	.45	.12
☐ 217	Derrick McKey	.05	.02	.01
☐ 218	Nate McMillan	.05	.02	.01
☐ 219	Gary Payton	.50	.23	.06
☐ 220	Ricky Pierce	.05	.02	.01
☐ 221	David Benoit	.05	.02	.01
☐ 222	Mike Brown	.05	.02	.01

☐ 223	Tyrone Corbin	.05	.02	.01	☐ 280	Milwaukee Bucks	.05	.02	.01
☐ 224	Mark Eaton	.05	.02	.01		Team Card			
☐ 225	Blue Edwards	.05	.02	.01	☐ 281	Minnesota Timberwolves	.05	.02	.01
☐ 226	Jeff Malone	.05	.02	.01		Team Card			
☐ 227	Karl Malone	.25	.11	.03	☐ 282	New Jersey Nets	.05	.02	.01
☐ 228	Eric Murdock	.05	.02	.01		Team Card			
☐ 229	John Stockton	.25	.11	.03	☐ 283	New York Knicks	.05	.02	.01
☐ 230	Michael Adams	.05	.02	.01		Team Card			
☐ 231	Rex Chapman	.05	.02	.01	☐ 284	Orlando Magic	.05	.02	.01
☐ 232	Ledell Eackles	.05	.02	.01		Team Card			
☐ 233	Pervis Ellison	.05	.02	.01	☐ 285	Philadelphia 76ers	.05	.02	.01
☐ 234	A.J. English	.05	.02	.01		Team Card			
☐ 235	Harvey Grant	.05	.02	.01	☐ 286	Phoenix Suns	.05	.02	.01
☐ 236	Charles Jones	.05	.02	.01		Team Card			
☐ 237	LaBradford Smith	.05	.02	.01	☐ 287	Portland Trail Blazers	.05	.02	.01
☐ 238	Larry Stewart	.05	.02	.01		Team Card			
☐ 239	Bob Weiss CO	.05	.02	.01	☐ 288	Sacramento Kings	.05	.02	.01
☐ 240	Chris Ford CO	.05	.02	.01		Team Card			
☐ 241	Allan Bristow CO	.05	.02	.01	☐ 289	San Antonio Spurs	.05	.02	.01
☐ 242	Phil Jackson CO	.10	.05	.01		Team Card			
☐ 243	Lenny Wilkens CO	.10	.05	.01	☐ 290	Seattle Supersonics	.05	.02	.01
☐ 244	Richie Adubato CO	.05	.02	.01		Team Card			
☐ 245	Dan Issel CO	.10	.05	.01	☐ 291	Utah Jazz	.05	.02	.01
☐ 246	Ron Rothstein CO	.05	.02	.01		Team Card			
☐ 247	Don Nelson CO	.10	.05	.01	☐ 292	Washington Bullets	.05	.02	.01
☐ 248	Rudy Tomjanovich CO	.10	.05	.01		Team Card			
☐ 249	Bob Hill CO	.05	.02	.01	☐ 293	Michael Adams AS	.05	.02	.01
☐ 250	Larry Brown CO	.10	.05	.01	☐ 294	Charles Barkley AS	.20	.09	.03
☐ 251	Randy Pfund CO	.05	.02	.01	☐ 295	Brad Daugherty AS	.05	.02	.01
☐ 252	Kevin Loughery CO	.05	.02	.01	☐ 296	Joe Dumars AS	.10	.05	.01
☐ 253	Mike Dunleavy CO	.05	.02	.01	☐ 297	Patrick Ewing AS	.10	.05	.01
☐ 254	Jimmy Rodgers CO	.05	.02	.01	☐ 298	Michael Jordan AS	1.50	.70	.19
☐ 255	Chuck Daly CO	.10	.05	.01	☐ 299	Reggie Lewis AS	.10	.05	.01
☐ 256	Pat Riley CO	.10	.05	.01	☐ 300	Scottie Pippen AS	.40	.18	.05
☐ 257	Matt Guokas CO	.05	.02	.01	☐ 301	Mark Price AS	.05	.02	.01
☐ 258	Doug Moe CO	.05	.02	.01	☐ 302	Dennis Rodman AS	.50	.23	.06
☐ 259	Paul Westphal CO	.05	.02	.01	☐ 303	Isiah Thomas AS	.10	.05	.01
☐ 260	Rick Adelman CO	.05	.02	.01	☐ 304	Kevin Willis AS	.05	.02	.01
☐ 261	Garry St. Jean CO	.05	.02	.01	☐ 305	Phil Jackson CO AS	.10	.05	.01
☐ 262	Jerry Tarkanian CO	.15	.07	.02	☐ 306	Clyde Drexler AS	.10	.05	.01
☐ 263	George Karl CO	.05	.02	.01	☐ 307	Tim Hardaway AS	.10	.05	.01
☐ 264	Jerry Sloan CO	.10	.05	.01	☐ 308	Jeff Hornacek AS	.05	.02	.01
☐ 265	Wes Unseld CO	.10	.05	.01	☐ 309	Magic Johnson AS	.40	.18	.05
☐ 266	Atlanta Hawks	.05	.02	.01	☐ 310	Dan Majerle AS	.10	.05	.01
	Team Card				☐ 311	Karl Malone AS	.10	.05	.01
☐ 267	Boston Celtics	.05	.02	.01	☐ 312	Chris Mullin AS	.05	.02	.01
	Team Card				☐ 313	Dikembe Mutombo AS	.10	.05	.01
☐ 268	Charlotte Hornets	.05	.02	.01	☐ 314	Hakeem Olajuwon AS	.30	.14	.04
	Team Card				☐ 315	David Robinson AS	.25	.11	.03
☐ 269	Chicago Bulls	.05	.02	.01	☐ 316	John Stockton AS	.10	.05	.01
	Team Card				☐ 317	Otis Thorpe AS	.10	.05	.01
☐ 270	Cleveland Cavaliers	.05	.02	.01	☐ 318	James Worthy AS	.10	.05	.01
	Team Card				☐ 319	Don Nelson CO AS	.05	.02	.01
☐ 271	Dallas Mavericks	.05	.02	.01	☐ 320	Scoring League Leaders	1.00	.45	.12
	Team Card					Michael Jordan			
☐ 272	Denver Nuggets	.05	.02	.01		Karl Malone			
	Team Card				☐ 321	Three-Point Field	.10	.05	.01
☐ 273	Detroit Pistons	.05	.02	.01		Goal Percent			
	Team Card					League Leaders			
☐ 274	Golden State Warriors	.05	.02	.01		Dana Barros			
	Team Card					Drazen Petrovic			
☐ 275	Houston Rockets	.05	.02	.01	☐ 322	Free Throw Percent	.30	.14	.04
	Team Card					League Leaders			
☐ 276	Indiana Pacers	.05	.02	.01		Mark Price			
	Team Card					Larry Bird			
☐ 277	Los Angeles Clippers	.05	.02	.01	☐ 323	Blocks League Leaders	.40	.18	.05
	Team Card					David Robinson			
☐ 278	Los Angeles Lakers	.05	.02	.01		Hakeem Olajuwon			
	Team Card				☐ 324	Steals League Leaders	.10	.05	.01
☐ 279	Miami Heat	.05	.02	.01		John Stockton			
	Team Card					Micheal Williams			

☐ 325	Rebounds League Leaders	.30	.14	.04
	Dennis Rodman			
	Kevin Willis			
☐ 326	Assists League Leaders	.10	.05	.01
	John Stockton			
	Kevin Johnson			
☐ 327	Field Goal Percent League Leaders	.05	.02	.01
	Buck Williams			
	Otis Thorpe			
☐ 328	Magic Moments 1980..	.50	.23	.06
☐ 329	Magic Moments 1985..	.50	.23	.06
☐ 330	Magic Moments 87,88.	.50	.23	.06
☐ 331	Magic Numbers	.50	.23	.06
☐ 332	Drazen Petrovic	.10	.05	.01
	Inside Stuff			
☐ 333	Patrick Ewing	.10	.05	.01
	Inside Stuff			
☐ 334	David Robinson	.25	.11	.03
	Stay in School			
☐ 335	Kevin Johnson	.10	.05	.01
	Stay in School			
☐ 336	Charles Barkley	.20	.09	.03
	Tournament of The Americas			
☐ 337	Larry Bird	.50	.23	.06
	Tournament of The Americas			
☐ 338	Clyde Drexler	.10	.05	.01
	Tournament of The Americas			
☐ 339	Patrick Ewing	.10	.05	.01
	Tournament of The Americas			
☐ 340	Magic Johnson	.40	.18	.05
	Tournament of The Americas			
☐ 341	Michael Jordan	1.50	.70	.19
	Tournament of The Americas			
☐ 342	Christian Laettner	.40	.18	.05
	Tournament of The Americas			
☐ 343	Karl Malone	.10	.05	.01
	Tournament of The Americas			
☐ 344	Chris Mullin	.05	.02	.01
	Tournament of The Americas			
☐ 345	Scottie Pippen	.40	.18	.05
	Tournament of The Americas			
☐ 346	David Robinson	.25	.11	.03
	Tournament of The Americas			
☐ 347	John Stockton	.10	.05	.01
	Tournament of The Americas			
☐ 348	Checklist 1	.05	.02	.01
☐ 349	Checklist 2	.05	.02	.01
☐ 350	Checklist 3	.05	.02	.01
☐ 351	Mookie Blaylock	.50	.23	.06
☐ 352	Adam Keefe	.50	.23	.06
☐ 353	Travis Mays	.10	.05	.01
☐ 354	Morlon Wiley	.10	.05	.01
☐ 355	Joe Kleine	.10	.05	.01
☐ 356	Bart Kofoed	.10	.05	.01
☐ 357	Xavier McDaniel	.10	.05	.01
☐ 358	Tony Bennett	.10	.05	.01
☐ 359	Tom Hammonds	.10	.05	.01
☐ 360	Kevin Lynch	.10	.05	.01
☐ 361	Alonzo Mourning	2.00	.90	.25
☐ 362	Rodney McCray	.10	.05	.01
☐ 363	Trent Tucker	.10	.05	.01
☐ 364	Corey Williams	.10	.05	.01
☐ 365	Steve Kerr	.10	.05	.01
	Traded to Orlando			
☐ 366	Jerome Lane	.10	.05	.01
☐ 367	Bobby Phills	.50	.23	.06
☐ 368	Mike Sanders	.10	.05	.01
☐ 369	Gerald Wilkins	.10	.05	.01
☐ 370	Donald Hodge	.10	.05	.01
☐ 371	Brian Howard	.10	.05	.01
☐ 372	Tracy Moore	.10	.05	.01
☐ 373	Sean Rooks	.10	.05	.01
☐ 374	Kevin Brooks	.10	.05	.01
☐ 375	LaPhonso Ellis	.30	.14	.04
☐ 376	Scott Hastings	.10	.05	.01
☐ 377	Robert Pack	.10	.05	.01
☐ 378	Bryant Stith	.30	.14	.04
☐ 379	Robert Werdann	.10	.05	.01
☐ 380	Lance Blanks	.10	.05	.01
	Traded to Minnesota			
☐ 381	Terry Mills	.10	.05	.01
☐ 382	Isaiah Morris	.10	.05	.01
☐ 383	Olden Polynice	.10	.05	.01
☐ 384	Brad Sellers	.10	.05	.01
	Traded to Minnesota			
☐ 385	Jud Buechler	.10	.05	.01
☐ 386	Jeff Grayer	.10	.05	.01
☐ 387	Byron Houston	.10	.05	.01
☐ 388	Keith Jennings	.10	.05	.01
☐ 389	Latrell Sprewell	1.00	.45	.12
☐ 390	Scott Brooks	.10	.05	.01
☐ 391	Carl Herrera	.10	.05	.01
☐ 392	Robert Horry	.75	.35	.09
☐ 393	Tree Rollins	.10	.05	.01
☐ 394	Kennard Winchester	.10	.05	.01
☐ 395	Greg Dreiling	.10	.05	.01
☐ 396	Sean Green	.10	.05	.01
☐ 397	Sam Mitchell	.10	.05	.01
☐ 398	Pooh Richardson	.10	.05	.01
☐ 399	Malik Sealy	.50	.23	.06
☐ 400	Kenny Williams	.10	.05	.01
☐ 401	Jaren Jackson	.10	.05	.01
☐ 402	Mark Jackson	.10	.05	.01
☐ 403	Stanley Roberts	.10	.05	.01
☐ 404	Elmore Spencer	.10	.05	.01
☐ 405	Kiki Vandeweghe	.10	.05	.01
☐ 406	John Williams	.10	.05	.01
☐ 407	Randy Woods	.10	.05	.01
☐ 408	Alex Blackwell	.10	.05	.01
☐ 409	Duane Cooper	.10	.05	.01
☐ 410	Anthony Peeler	.50	.23	.06
☐ 411	Keith Askins	.10	.05	.01
☐ 412	Matt Geiger	.10	.05	.01
☐ 413	Harold Miner	.10	.05	.01
☐ 414	John Salley	.10	.05	.01
☐ 415	Alaa Abdelnaby	.10	.05	.01
	Traded to Boston			
☐ 416	Todd Day	.50	.23	.06
☐ 417	Blue Edwards	.10	.05	.01
☐ 418	Brad Lohaus	.10	.05	.01
☐ 419	Lee Mayberry	.10	.05	.01
☐ 420	Eric Murdock	.10	.05	.01
☐ 421	Christian Laettner	.60	.25	.07
☐ 422	Bob McCann	.10	.05	.01
☐ 423	Chuck Person	.10	.05	.01
☐ 424	Chris Smith	.10	.05	.01
☐ 425	Gundars Vetra	.10	.05	.01
☐ 426	Micheal Williams	.10	.05	.01

☐ 427	Chucky Brown	.10	.05	.01
☐ 428	Tate George	.10	.05	.01
☐ 429	Rick Mahorn	.10	.05	.01
☐ 430	Rumeal Robinson	.10	.05	.01
☐ 431	Jayson Williams	.10	.05	.01
☐ 432	Eric Anderson	.10	.05	.01
☐ 433	Rolando Blackman	.10	.05	.01
☐ 434	Tony Campbell	.10	.05	.01
☐ 435	Hubert Davis	.50	.23	.06
☐ 436	Bo Kimble	.10	.05	.01
☐ 437	Doc Rivers	.10	.05	.01
☐ 438	Charles Smith	.10	.05	.01
☐ 439	Anthony Bowie	.10	.05	.01
☐ 440	Litterial Green	.10	.05	.01
☐ 441	Greg Kite	.10	.05	.01
☐ 442	Shaquille O'Neal	8.00	3.60	1.00
☐ 443	Donald Royal	.10	.05	.01
☐ 444	Greg Grant	.10	.05	.01
☐ 445	Jeff Hornacek	.10	.05	.01
☐ 446	Andrew Lang	.10	.05	.01
☐ 447	Kenny Payne	.10	.05	.01
☐ 448	Tim Perry	.10	.05	.01
☐ 449	Clarence Weatherspoon	.60	.25	.07
☐ 450	Danny Ainge	.50	.23	.06
☐ 451	Charles Barkley	.60	.25	.07
☐ 452	Tim Kempton	.10	.05	.01
☐ 453	Oliver Miller	.40	.18	.05
☐ 454	Mark Bryant	.10	.05	.01
☐ 455	Mario Elie	.10	.05	.01
☐ 456	Dave Jamerson	.10	.05	.01
☐ 457	Tracy Murray	.50	.23	.06
☐ 458	Rod Strickland	.10	.05	.01
☐ 459	Vincent Askew Traded to Seattle	.10	.05	.01
☐ 460	Randy Brown	.10	.05	.01
☐ 461	Marty Conlon	.10	.05	.01
☐ 462	Jim Les	.10	.05	.01
☐ 463	Walt Williams	1.00	.45	.12
☐ 464	William Bedford	.10	.05	.01
☐ 465	Lloyd Daniels	.10	.05	.01
☐ 466	Vinny Del Negro	.10	.05	.01
☐ 467	Dale Ellis	.10	.05	.01
☐ 468	Larry Smith	.10	.05	.01
☐ 469	David Wood	.10	.05	.01
☐ 470	Rich King	.10	.05	.01
☐ 471	Isaac Austin	.10	.05	.01
☐ 472	John Crotty	.10	.05	.01
☐ 473	Stephen Howard	.10	.05	.01
☐ 474	Jay Humphries	.10	.05	.01
☐ 475	Larry Krystowiak	.10	.05	.01
☐ 476	Tom Gugliotta	.60	.25	.07
☐ 477	Buck Johnson	.10	.05	.01
☐ 478	Don MacLean	.50	.23	.06
☐ 479	Doug Overton	.10	.05	.01
☐ 480	Brent Price	.10	.05	.01
☐ 481	David Robinson TRIV Blocks	.40	.18	.05
☐ 482	Magic Johnson TRIV Assists	.60	.25	.07
☐ 483	John Stockton TRIV Steals	.25	.11	.03
☐ 484	Patrick Ewing TRIV Points	.25	.11	.03
☐ 485	Answer Card TRIV Magic Johnson David Robinson Patrick Ewing John Stockton	.25	.11	.03
☐ 486	John Stockton Stay in School	.25	.11	.03
☐ 487	Ahmad Rashad	.50	.23	.06

	Willow Bay Inside Stuff			
☐ 488	Rookie Checklist	.10	.05	.01
☐ 489	Checklist 1	.10	.05	.01
☐ 490	Checklist 2	.10	.05	.01
☐ AC1	Patrick Ewing Art	.50	.23	.06
☐ SU1	John Stockton Game. His Ultimate Game	1.50	.70	.19
☐ SU1	John Stockton AU (Certified autograph)	100.00	45.00	12.50
☐ TR1	NBA Championship Michael Jordan Clyde Drexler	3.00	1.35	.35
☐ NNO	Barcelona Plastic	30.00	13.50	3.70
☐ NNO	Team USA	1.50	.70	.19
☐ NNO	M.Johnson Comm.	1.00	.45	.12
☐ NNO	M. Johnson AU	200.00	90.00	25.00
☐ NNO	Patrick Ewing AU (Certified autograph)	.50	.23	.06
☐ NNO	Team USA	100.00	45.00	12.50

1992-93 Hoops Draft Redemption

A "Lottery Exchange Card" randomly inserted (reportedly at a rate of one per 360 packs) in 1992-93 Hoops first series 12-card foil packs entitled the collector to receive this NBA Draft Redemption Lottery Exchange set. It consists of ten standard size cards of the top 1992 NBA Draft Picks. The first eleven players drafted are represented, with the exception of Jim Jackson, the late-signing fourth pick. Insert sets began to be mailed out during the week of January 4, 1993, and the redemption period expired on March 31, 1993. According to SkyBox International media releases a total of 25,876 sets were released to the public; 24,461 Lottery Exchange cards were redeemed. An additional 415 sets were claimed through a second chance drawing (selected from 149,166 mail-in entries). Finally, 1,000 more sets were released for public relations and promotional use. A reserve of 1,000 sets were held for replacement of damaged sets and 500 sets were kept for SkyBox International archives. In the color photos on the fronts, the players appear in dress attire in front of a gray studio background, except for cards C and J. The player's name is printed in white in a hardwood floor border design at the bottom of the card. A NBA Draft icon overlaps the border and the photo. A one inch tall hardwood design number at the upper left corner indicates the order the players were drafted. The horizontal backs display white backgrounds with a similar hardwood stripe containing the player's name across the top. A shadowed close-up photo is displayed next to college statistics and a player profile. The cards are lettered on the back. Sets still in the factory-sealed bags are valued at a premium of up to 20 percent above the complete set price below.

	MINT	NRMT	EXC
COMPLETE SET (10)	100.00	45.00	12.50
COMMON CARD (A-J)	1.50	.70	.19
☐ A Shaquille O'Neal	60.00	27.00	7.50
☐ B Alonzo Mourning	15.00	6.75	1.85
☐ C Christian Laettner	5.00	2.20	.60
☐ D LaPhonso Ellis	2.50	1.10	.30
☐ E Tom Gugliotta	5.00	2.20	.60
☐ F Walt Williams	6.00	2.70	.75
☐ G Todd Day	1.50	.70	.19
☐ H Clarence Weatherspoon	5.00	2.20	.60
☐ I Adam Keefe	1.50	.70	.19
☐ J Robert Horry	6.00	2.70	.75
☐ NNO Draft Redemption Card (Stamped)	.50	.23	.06
☐ NNO Draft Redemption Card (Unstamped)	2.00	.90	.25

1992-93 Hoops Magic's All-Rookies

This 10-card standard size set was randomly inserted into Hoops second series 12-card foil packs. They were inserted at a rate of one in 30 packs. The set features Magic Johnson's selections of the top rookies from the 1992-93 season. The cards show color action player photos and have a gold foil stripe containing the player's name down the left edge and a thinner stripe across the bottom printed with the city's name. The Magic's All-Rookie Team logo appears in the lower left corner. The backs display a small close-up picture of Magic Johnson in a yellow Los Angeles Lakers' warm-up jacket. A yellow stripe down the left edge contains the set name (Magic's

All-Rookie Team) and the card number. The white background is printed in black with Magic's evaluation of the player.

	MINT	NRMT	EXC
COMPLETE SET (10)	200.00	90.00	25.00
COMMON CARD (1-10)	3.00	1.35	.35
☐ 1 Shaquille O'Neal	120.00	55.00	15.00
☐ 2 Alonzo Mourning	30.00	13.50	3.70
☐ 3 Christian Laettner	10.00	4.50	1.25
☐ 4 LaPhonso Ellis	5.00	2.20	.60
☐ 5 Tom Gugliotta	10.00	4.50	1.25
☐ 6 Walt Williams	12.00	5.50	1.50
☐ 7 Todd Day	3.00	1.35	.35
☐ 8 Clarence Weatherspoon	10.00	4.50	1.25
☐ 9 Robert Horry	12.00	5.50	1.50
☐ 10 Harold Miner	3.00	1.35	.35

1992-93 Hoops More Magic Moments

Randomly inserted (at a reported rate of one card per 195 packs) into 1992-93 Hoops second series 12-card packs, this three-card standard-size set commemorates Magic Johnson's return to training camp and pre-season game action. Each card features a color player photo bordered in white. Team color-coded bars and lettering accent the picture on the left edge and below, and a team color-coded star overwritten with the words "More Magic" appears at the lower left corner. Over ghosted photos similar or identical to the front photos, the backs summarize Magic's return, his performance in his first game, his performance in his last game, and his decision to retire again. The cards are numbered on the back with an "M" prefix.

	MINT	NRMT	EXC
COMPLETE SET (3)	70.00	32.00	8.75
COMMON CARD (M1-M3)	25.00	11.00	3.10
☐ M1 Magic in Training Camp Fall 1992	25.00	11.00	3.10
☐ M2 L.A. Lakers vs. Philadelphia October 20, 1992	25.00	11.00	3.10
☐ M3 L.A. Lakers vs. Cleveland October 30, 1992	25.00	11.00	3.10

1992-93 Hoops Supreme Court

This 10-card, standard-size set was randomly inserted (at a reported rate of one card per 11 packs) in Hoops second series 12-card foil packs and features color action player photos on the front. A gold foil stripe frames the pictures which are surrounded by a hardwood floor design. The player's name is printed in gold foil down the left side. A gray and burnt-orange logo printed with the words "Supreme Court 1992-93" appears in the lower left corner. A purple stripe containing the phrase "The Fan's Choice" runs across the bottom of the picture. Hoops promoted The Supreme Court Sweepstakes, which offered fans the opportunity to select the ten players who appeared in this subset. The backs are white with black print. A small color player photo with rounded corners is displayed next to a personal profile. The cards are numbered on the back with an "SC" prefix.

	MINT	NRMT	EXC
COMPLETE SET (10)	30.00	13.50	3.70
COMMON CARD (SC1-SC10)	.60	.25	.07

		MINT	NRMT	EXC
☐ SC1	Michael Jordan	20.00	9.00	2.50
☐ SC2	Scottie Pippen	5.00	2.20	.60
☐ SC3	David Robinson	3.00	1.35	.35
☐ SC4	Patrick Ewing	1.50	.70	.19
☐ SC5	Clyde Drexler	2.00	.90	.25
☐ SC6	Karl Malone	1.50	.70	.19
☐ SC7	Charles Barkley	2.50	1.10	.30
☐ SC8	John Stockton	1.50	.70	.19
☐ SC9	Chris Mullin	.60	.25	.07
☐ SC10	Magic Johnson	5.00	2.20	.60

1993-94 Hoops

This 421-card standard-size set was issued in separate series of 300 and 121 cards. Cards were distributed in 13-card foil (12 basic cards plus one gold card) and 26-card jumbo (24 basic and two gold cards) packs. Cards feature full-bleed glossy color player photos on the fronts. Each player's name and team logo appear in team colors along a ghosted band at the bottom. The

back presents a color head shot of the player in a small rectangle bordered with a team color in the top right corner. Alongside is his jersey number and position within a team-colored bar. The player's name and a short biography are printed on a hardwood floor design at the top. Below, the player's college and NBA stats, displayed in separate tables on a white background, round out the card. The cards are numbered on the back and listed alphabetically within team order. Subsets are Coaches (230-256), All-Stars (257-282), League Leaders (283-290), Boys and Girls Club (291), Hoops Tribune (292-297), and Checklists (298-300/419-420). Rookie Cards of note include Vin Baker, Anfernee Hardaway, Jamal Mashburn, Nick Van Exel and Chris Webber.

	MINT	NRMT	EXC
COMPLETE SET (421)	20.00	9.00	2.50
COMPLETE SERIES 1 (300)	12.00	5.50	1.50
COMPLETE SERIES 2 (121)	8.00	3.60	1.00
COMMON CARD (1-421)	.05	.02	.01

		MINT	NRMT	EXC
☐ 1	Stacey Augmon	.10	.05	.01
☐ 2	Mookie Blaylock	.10	.05	.01
☐ 3	Duane Ferrell	.05	.02	.01
☐ 4	Paul Graham	.05	.02	.01
☐ 5	Adam Keefe	.05	.02	.01
☐ 6	Blair Rasmussen	.05	.02	.01
☐ 7	Dominique Wilkins	.10	.05	.01
☐ 8	Kevin Willis	.05	.02	.01
☐ 9	Alaa Abdelnaby	.05	.02	.01
☐ 10	Dee Brown	.05	.02	.01
☐ 11	Sherman Douglas	.05	.02	.01
☐ 12	Rick Fox	.05	.02	.01
☐ 13	Kevin Gamble	.05	.02	.01
☐ 14	Joe Kleine	.05	.02	.01
☐ 15	Xavier McDaniel	.05	.02	.01
☐ 16	Robert Parish	.10	.05	.01
☐ 17	Tony Bennett	.05	.02	.01
☐ 18	Muggsy Bogues	.10	.05	.01
☐ 19	Dell Curry	.05	.02	.01
☐ 20	Kenny Gattison	.05	.02	.01
☐ 21	Kendall Gill	.05	.02	.01
☐ 22	Larry Johnson	.30	.14	.04
☐ 23	Alonzo Mourning	.40	.18	.05
☐ 24	Johnny Newman	.05	.02	.01
☐ 25	B.J. Armstrong	.05	.02	.01
☐ 26	Bill Cartwright	.05	.02	.01
☐ 27	Horace Grant	.10	.05	.01
☐ 28	Michael Jordan	3.00	1.35	.35
☐ 29	Stacey King	.05	.02	.01
☐ 30	John Paxson	.10	.05	.01
☐ 31	Will Perdue	.05	.02	.01

#	Player			
☐ 32	Scottie Pippen	.75	.35	.09
☐ 33	Scott Williams	.05	.02	.01
☐ 34	Moses Malone	.15	.07	.02
☐ 35	John Battle	.05	.02	.01
☐ 36	Terrell Brandon	.10	.05	.01
☐ 37	Brad Daugherty	.05	.02	.01
☐ 38	Craig Ehlo	.05	.02	.01
☐ 39	Danny Ferry	.05	.02	.01
☐ 40	Larry Nance	.05	.02	.01
☐ 41	Mark Price	.05	.02	.01
☐ 42	Gerald Wilkins	.05	.02	.01
☐ 43	John Williams	.05	.02	.01
☐ 44	Terry Davis	.05	.02	.01
☐ 45	Derek Harper	.10	.05	.01
☐ 46	Donald Hodge	.05	.02	.01
☐ 47	Mike Iuzzolino	.05	.02	.01
☐ 48	Jim Jackson	.30	.14	.04
☐ 49	Sean Rooks	.05	.02	.01
☐ 50	Doug Smith	.05	.02	.01
☐ 51	Randy White	.05	.02	.01
☐ 52	Mahmoud Abdul-Rauf	.10	.05	.01
☐ 53	LaPhonso Ellis	.05	.02	.01
☐ 54	Marcus Liberty	.05	.02	.01
☐ 55	Mark Macon	.05	.02	.01
☐ 56	Dikembe Mutombo	.10	.05	.01
☐ 57	Robert Pack	.05	.02	.01
☐ 58	Bryant Stith	.05	.02	.01
☐ 59	Reggie Williams	.05	.02	.01
☐ 60	Mark Aguirre	.10	.05	.01
☐ 61	Joe Dumars	.10	.05	.01
☐ 62	Bill Laimbeer	.10	.05	.01
☐ 63	Terry Mills	.05	.02	.01
☐ 64	Olden Polynice	.05	.02	.01
☐ 65	Alvin Robertson	.05	.02	.01
☐ 66	Dennis Rodman	1.00	.45	.12
☐ 67	Isiah Thomas	.15	.07	.02
☐ 68	Victor Alexander	.05	.02	.01
☐ 69	Tim Hardaway	.10	.05	.01
☐ 70	Tyrone Hill	.05	.02	.01
☐ 71	Byron Houston	.05	.02	.01
☐ 72	Sarunas Marciulionis	.05	.02	.01
☐ 73	Chris Mullin	.10	.05	.01
☐ 74	Billy Owens	.05	.02	.01
☐ 75	Latrell Sprewell	.20	.09	.03
☐ 76	Scott Brooks	.05	.02	.01
☐ 77	Matt Bullard	.05	.02	.01
☐ 78	Carl Herrera	.05	.02	.01
☐ 79	Robert Horry	.10	.05	.01
☐ 80	Vernon Maxwell	.05	.02	.01
☐ 81	Hakeem Olajuwon	.60	.25	.07
☐ 82	Kenny Smith	.05	.02	.01
☐ 83	Otis Thorpe	.10	.05	.01
☐ 84	Dale Davis	.05	.02	.01
☐ 85	Vern Fleming	.05	.02	.01
☐ 86	George McCloud	.05	.02	.01
☐ 87	Reggie Miller	.30	.14	.04
☐ 88	Sam Mitchell	.05	.02	.01
☐ 89	Pooh Richardson	.05	.02	.01
☐ 90	Detlef Schrempf	.10	.05	.01
☐ 91	Malik Sealy	.05	.02	.01
☐ 92	Rik Smits	.10	.05	.01
☐ 93	Gary Grant	.05	.02	.01
☐ 94	Ron Harper	.05	.02	.01
☐ 95	Mark Jackson	.05	.02	.01
☐ 96	Danny Manning	.10	.05	.01
☐ 97	Ken Norman	.05	.02	.01
☐ 98	Stanley Roberts	.05	.02	.01
☐ 99	Elmore Spencer	.05	.02	.01
☐ 100	Loy Vaught	.10	.05	.01
☐ 101	John Williams	.05	.02	.01
☐ 102	Randy Woods	.05	.02	.01
☐ 103	Benoit Benjamin	.05	.02	.01
☐ 104	Elden Campbell	.10	.05	.01
☐ 105	Doug Christie UER	.05	.02	.01
	(Has uniform number on front and 35 on back)			
☐ 106	Vlade Divac	.10	.05	.01
☐ 107	Anthony Peeler	.05	.02	.01
☐ 108	Tony Smith	.05	.02	.01
☐ 109	Sedale Threatt	.05	.02	.01
☐ 110	James Worthy	.10	.05	.01
☐ 111	Bimbo Coles	.05	.02	.01
☐ 112	Grant Long	.05	.02	.01
☐ 113	Harold Miner	.05	.02	.01
☐ 114	Glen Rice	.10	.05	.01
☐ 115	John Salley	.05	.02	.01
☐ 116	Rony Seikaly	.05	.02	.01
☐ 117	Brian Shaw	.05	.02	.01
☐ 118	Steve Smith	.10	.05	.01
☐ 119	Anthony Avent	.05	.02	.01
☐ 120	Jon Barry	.05	.02	.01
☐ 121	Frank Brickowski	.05	.02	.01
☐ 122	Todd Day	.05	.02	.01
☐ 123	Blue Edwards	.05	.02	.01
☐ 124	Brad Lohaus	.05	.02	.01
☐ 125	Lee Mayberry	.05	.02	.01
☐ 126	Eric Murdock	.05	.02	.01
☐ 127	Derek Strong	.05	.02	.01
☐ 128	Thurl Bailey	.05	.02	.01
☐ 129	Christian Laettner	.10	.05	.01
☐ 130	Luc Longley	.05	.02	.01
☐ 131	Marlon Maxey	.05	.02	.01
☐ 132	Chuck Person	.05	.02	.01
☐ 133	Chris Smith	.05	.02	.01
☐ 134	Doug West	.05	.02	.01
☐ 135	Micheal Williams	.05	.02	.01
☐ 136	Rafael Addison	.05	.02	.01
☐ 137	Kenny Anderson	.10	.05	.01
☐ 138	Sam Bowie	.05	.02	.01
☐ 139	Chucky Brown	.05	.02	.01
☐ 140	Derrick Coleman	.05	.02	.01
☐ 141	Chris Morris	.05	.02	.01
☐ 142	Rumeal Robinson	.05	.02	.01
☐ 143	Greg Anthony	.05	.02	.01
☐ 144	Rolando Blackman	.05	.02	.01
☐ 145	Hubert Davis	.05	.02	.01
☐ 146	Patrick Ewing	.25	.11	.03
☐ 147	Anthony Mason	.10	.05	.01
☐ 148	Charles Oakley	.10	.05	.01
☐ 149	Doc Rivers	.05	.02	.01
☐ 150	Charles Smith	.05	.02	.01
☐ 151	John Starks	.05	.02	.01
☐ 152	Nick Anderson	.10	.05	.01
☐ 153	Anthony Bowie	.05	.02	.01
☐ 154	Litterial Green	.05	.02	.01
☐ 155	Shaquille O'Neal	1.50	.70	.19
☐ 156	Donald Royal	.05	.02	.01
☐ 157	Dennis Scott	.10	.05	.01
☐ 158	Scott Skiles	.05	.02	.01
☐ 159	Tom Tolbert	.05	.02	.01
☐ 160	Jeff Turner	.05	.02	.01
☐ 161	Ron Anderson	.05	.02	.01
☐ 162	Johnny Dawkins	.05	.02	.01
☐ 163	Hersey Hawkins	.05	.02	.01
☐ 164	Jeff Hornacek	.05	.02	.01
☐ 165	Andrew Lang	.05	.02	.01
☐ 166	Tim Perry	.05	.02	.01
☐ 167	Clarence Weatherspoon	.10	.05	.01
☐ 168	Danny Ainge	.10	.05	.01
☐ 169	Charles Barkley	.40	.18	.05
☐ 170	Cedric Ceballos	.10	.05	.01
☐ 171	Richard Dumas	.05	.02	.01

#	Player			
☐ 172	Kevin Johnson	.10	.05	.01
☐ 173	Dan Majerle	.10	.05	.01
☐ 174	Oliver Miller	.05	.02	.01
☐ 175	Mark West	.05	.02	.01
☐ 176	Clyde Drexler	.30	.14	.04
☐ 177	Kevin Duckworth	.05	.02	.01
☐ 178	Mario Elie	.05	.02	.01
☐ 179	Dave Johnson	.05	.02	.01
☐ 180	Jerome Kersey	.05	.02	.01
☐ 181	Tracy Murray	.05	.02	.01
☐ 182	Terry Porter	.05	.02	.01
☐ 183	Clifford Robinson	.10	.05	.01
☐ 184	Rod Strickland	.05	.02	.01
☐ 185	Buck Williams	.10	.05	.01
☐ 186	Anthony Bonner	.05	.02	.01
☐ 187	Randy Brown	.05	.02	.01
☐ 188	Duane Causwell	.05	.02	.01
☐ 189	Pete Chilcutt	.05	.02	.01
☐ 190	Mitch Richmond	.20	.09	.03
☐ 191	Lionel Simmons	.05	.02	.01
☐ 192	Wayman Tisdale	.05	.02	.01
☐ 193	Spud Webb	.10	.05	.01
☐ 194	Walt Williams	.10	.05	.01
☐ 195	Willie Anderson	.05	.02	.01
☐ 196	Antoine Carr	.05	.02	.01
☐ 197	Terry Cummings	.05	.02	.01
☐ 198	Lloyd Daniels	.05	.02	.01
☐ 199	Sean Elliott	.10	.05	.01
☐ 200	Dale Ellis	.05	.02	.01
☐ 201	Avery Johnson	.05	.02	.01
☐ 202	J.R. Reid	.05	.02	.01
☐ 203	David Robinson	.50	.23	.06
☐ 204	Dana Barros	.05	.02	.01
☐ 205	Michael Cage	.05	.02	.01
☐ 206	Eddie Johnson	.05	.02	.01
☐ 207	Shawn Kemp	.75	.35	.09
☐ 208	Derrick McKey	.05	.02	.01
☐ 209	Nate McMillan	.05	.02	.01
☐ 210	Gary Payton	.40	.18	.05
☐ 211	Sam Perkins	.05	.02	.01
☐ 212	Ricky Pierce	.05	.02	.01
☐ 213	David Benoit	.05	.02	.01
☐ 214	Tyrone Corbin	.05	.02	.01
☐ 215	Mark Eaton	.05	.02	.01
☐ 216	Jay Humphries	.05	.02	.01
☐ 217	Jeff Malone	.05	.02	.01
☐ 218	Karl Malone	.25	.11	.03
☐ 219	John Stockton	.25	.11	.03
☐ 220	Michael Adams	.05	.02	.01
☐ 221	Rex Chapman	.05	.02	.01
☐ 222	Pervis Ellison	.05	.02	.01
☐ 223	Harvey Grant	.05	.02	.01
☐ 224	Tom Gugliotta	.10	.05	.01
☐ 225	Don MacLean	.05	.02	.01
☐ 226	Doug Overton	.05	.02	.01
☐ 227	Brent Price	.05	.02	.01
☐ 228	LaBradford Smith	.05	.02	.01
☐ 229	Larry Stewart	.05	.02	.01
☐ 230	Lenny Wilkens CO	.10	.05	.01
☐ 231	Chris Ford CO	.05	.02	.01
☐ 232	Allan Bristow CO	.05	.02	.01
☐ 233	Phil Jackson CO	.10	.05	.01
☐ 234	Mike Fratello CO	.05	.02	.01
☐ 235	Quinn Buckner CO	.05	.02	.01
☐ 236	Dan Issel CO	.10	.05	.01
☐ 237	Don Chaney CO	.05	.02	.01
☐ 238	Don Nelson CO	.10	.05	.01
☐ 239	Rudy Tomjanovich CO	.10	.05	.01
☐ 240	Larry Brown CO	.10	.05	.01
☐ 241	Bob Weiss CO	.05	.02	.01
☐ 242	Randy Pfund CO	.05	.02	.01
☐ 243	Kevin Loughery CO	.05	.02	.01
☐ 244	Mike Dunleavy CO	.05	.02	.01
☐ 245	Sidney Lowe CO	.05	.02	.01
☐ 246	Chuck Daly CO	.10	.05	.01
☐ 247	Pat Riley CO	.10	.05	.01
☐ 248	Brian Hill CO	.05	.02	.01
☐ 249	Fred Carter CO	.05	.02	.01
☐ 250	Paul Westphal CO	.05	.02	.01
☐ 251	Rick Adelman CO	.05	.02	.01
☐ 252	Garry St. Jean CO	.05	.02	.01
☐ 253	John Lucas CO	.05	.02	.01
☐ 254	George Karl CO	.05	.02	.01
☐ 255	Jerry Sloan CO	.10	.05	.01
☐ 256	Wes Unseld CO	.10	.05	.01
☐ 257	Michael Jordan AS	1.50	.70	.19
☐ 258	Isiah Thomas AS	.10	.05	.01
☐ 259	Scottie Pippen AS	.40	.18	.05
☐ 260	Larry Johnson AS	.10	.05	.01
☐ 261	Dominique Wilkins AS	.10	.05	.01
☐ 262	Joe Dumars AS	.10	.05	.01
☐ 263	Mark Price AS	.05	.02	.01
☐ 264	Shaquille O'Neal AS	.75	.35	.09
☐ 265	Patrick Ewing AS	.10	.05	.01
☐ 266	Larry Nance AS	.05	.02	.01
☐ 267	Detlef Schrempf AS	.05	.02	.01
☐ 268	Brad Daugherty AS	.05	.02	.01
☐ 269	Charles Barkley AS	.20	.09	.03
☐ 270	Clyde Drexler AS	.10	.05	.01
☐ 271	Sean Elliott AS	.05	.02	.01
☐ 272	Tim Hardaway AS	.05	.02	.01
☐ 273	Shawn Kemp AS	.40	.18	.05
☐ 274	Dan Majerle AS	.05	.02	.01
☐ 275	Karl Malone AS	.10	.05	.01
☐ 276	Danny Manning AS	.05	.02	.01
☐ 277	Hakeem Olajuwon AS	.30	.14	.04
☐ 278	Terry Porter AS	.05	.02	.01
☐ 279	David Robinson AS	.25	.11	.03
☐ 280	John Stockton AS	.10	.05	.01
☐ 281	East Team Photo	.05	.02	.01
☐ 282	West Team Photo	.05	.02	.01
☐ 283	Scoring	.75	.35	.09
	Michael Jordan			
	Dominique Wilkins			
	Karl Malone			
☐ 284	Rebounding	.60	.25	.07
	Dennis Rodman			
	Shaquille O'Neal			
	Dikembe Mutombo			
☐ 285	Field Goal Percentage	.05	.02	.01
	Cedric Ceballos			
	Brad Daugherty			
	Dale Davis			
☐ 286	Assists	.10	.05	.01
	John Stockton			
	Tim Hardaway			
	Scott Skiles			
☐ 287	Free Throw Percentage	.05	.02	.01
	Mark Price			
	Mahmoud Abdul-Rauf			
	Eddie Johnson			
☐ 288	3-point FG Percentage	.05	.02	.01
	B.J. Armstrong			
	Chris Mullin			
	Kenny Smith			
☐ 289	Steals	.75	.35	.09
	Michael Jordan			
	Mookie Blaylock			
	John Stockton			
☐ 290	Blocks	.50	.23	.06
	Hakeem Olajuwon			
	Shaquille O'Neal			

	Dikembe Mutombo			
☐ 291	Boys and Girls Club	.25	.11	.03
	David Robinson			
☐ 292	B.J. Armstrong TRIB	.05	.02	.01
☐ 293	Scottie Pippen TRIB	.40	.18	.05
☐ 294	Kevin Johnson TRIB	.10	.05	.01
☐ 295	Charles Barkley TRIB	.20	.09	.03
☐ 296	Richard Dumas TRIB	.05	.02	.01
☐ 297	Horace Grant CL	.05	.02	.01
☐ 298	David Robinson CL	.10	.05	.01
☐ 299	David Robinson CL	.10	.05	.01
☐ 300	David Robinson CL	.10	.05	.01
☐ 301	Craig Ehlo	.05	.02	.01
☐ 302	Jon Koncak	.05	.02	.01
☐ 303	Andrew Lang	.05	.02	.01
☐ 304	Chris Corchiani	.05	.02	.01
☐ 305	Acie Earl	.05	.02	.01
☐ 306	Dino Radja	.30	.14	.04
☐ 307	Scott Burrell	.10	.05	.01
☐ 308	Hersey Hawkins	.05	.02	.01
☐ 309	Eddie Johnson	.05	.02	.01
☐ 310	David Wingate	.05	.02	.01
☐ 311	Corie Blount	.05	.02	.01
☐ 312	Steve Kerr	.10	.05	.01
☐ 313	Toni Kukoc	.60	.25	.07
☐ 314	Pete Myers	.05	.02	.01
☐ 315	Jay Guidinger	.05	.02	.01
☐ 316	Tyrone Hill	.05	.02	.01
☐ 317	Gerald Madkins	.05	.02	.01
☐ 318	Chris Mills	.40	.18	.05
☐ 319	Bobby Phills	.05	.02	.01
☐ 320	Lucious Harris	.10	.05	.01
☐ 321	Popeye Jones	.10	.05	.01
☐ 322	Fat Lever	.05	.02	.01
☐ 323	Jamal Mashburn	.60	.25	.07
☐ 324	Darren Morningstar	.05	.02	.01
	(See also 334)			
☐ 325	Kevin Brooks	.05	.02	.01
☐ 326	Tom Hammonds	.05	.02	.01
☐ 327	Darnell Mee	.05	.02	.01
☐ 328	Rodney Rodgers	.10	.05	.01
☐ 329	Brian Williams	.05	.02	.01
☐ 330	Greg Anderson	.05	.02	.01
☐ 331	Sean Elliott	.10	.05	.01
☐ 332	Allan Houston	.50	.23	.06
☐ 333	Lindsey Hunter	.10	.05	.01
☐ 334	David Wood UER	.05	.02	.01
	(Card misnumbered 324)			
☐ 335	Jud Buechler	.05	.02	.01
☐ 336	Chris Gatling	.05	.02	.01
☐ 337	Josh Grant	.05	.02	.01
☐ 338	Jeff Grayer	.05	.02	.01
☐ 339	Keith Jennings	.05	.02	.01
☐ 340	Avery Johnson	.05	.02	.01
☐ 341	Chris Webber	1.00	.45	.12
☐ 342	Sam Cassell	.40	.18	.05
☐ 343	Mario Elie	.05	.02	.01
☐ 344	Eric Riley	.05	.02	.01
☐ 345	Antonio Davis	.05	.02	.01
☐ 346	Scott Haskin	.05	.02	.01
☐ 347	Gerald Paddio	.05	.02	.01
☐ 348	LaSalle Thompson	.05	.02	.01
☐ 349	Ken Williams	.05	.02	.01
☐ 350	Mark Aguirre	.10	.05	.01
☐ 351	Terry Dehere	.05	.02	.01
☐ 352	Henry James	.05	.02	.01
☐ 353	Sam Bowie	.05	.02	.01
☐ 354	George Lynch	.05	.02	.01
☐ 355	Kurt Rambis	.05	.02	.01
☐ 356	Nick Van Exel	.75	.35	.09
☐ 357	Trevor Wilson	.05	.02	.01
☐ 358	Keith Askins	.05	.02	.01
☐ 359	Manute Bol	.05	.02	.01
☐ 360	Willie Burton	.05	.02	.01
☐ 361	Matt Geiger	.05	.02	.01
☐ 362	Alec Kessler	.05	.02	.01
☐ 363	Vin Baker	1.00	.45	.12
☐ 364	Ken Norman	.05	.02	.01
☐ 365	Dan Schayes	.05	.02	.01
☐ 366	Mike Brown	.05	.02	.01
☐ 367	Isaiah Rider	.30	.14	.04
☐ 368	Benoit Benjamin	.05	.02	.01
☐ 369	P.J. Brown	.05	.02	.01
☐ 370	Kevin Edwards	.05	.02	.01
☐ 371	Armon Gilliam	.05	.02	.01
☐ 372	Rick Mahorn	.05	.02	.01
☐ 373	Dwayne Schintzius	.05	.02	.01
☐ 374	Rex Walters	.05	.02	.01
☐ 375	Jayson Williams	.05	.02	.01
☐ 376	Eric Anderson	.05	.02	.01
☐ 377	Anthony Bonner	.05	.02	.01
☐ 378	Tony Campbell	.05	.02	.01
☐ 379	Herb Williams	.05	.02	.01
☐ 380	Anfernee Hardaway	5.00	2.20	.60
☐ 381	Greg Kite	.05	.02	.01
☐ 382	Larry Krystkowiak	.05	.02	.01
☐ 383	Todd Lichti	.05	.02	.01
☐ 384	Dana Barros	.05	.02	.01
☐ 385	Shawn Bradley	.30	.14	.04
☐ 386	Greg Graham	.05	.02	.01
☐ 387	Warren Kidd	.05	.02	.01
☐ 388	Eric Leckner	.05	.02	.01
☐ 389	Moses Malone	.15	.07	.02
☐ 390	A.C. Green	.10	.05	.01
☐ 391	Frank Johnson	.05	.02	.01
☐ 392	Joe Kleine	.05	.02	.01
☐ 393	Malcolm Mackey	.05	.02	.01
☐ 394	Jerrod Mustaf	.05	.02	.01
☐ 395	Mark Bryant	.05	.02	.01
☐ 396	Chris Dudley	.05	.02	.01
☐ 397	Harvey Grant	.05	.02	.01
☐ 398	James Robinson	.10	.05	.01
☐ 399	Reggie Smith	.05	.02	.01
☐ 400	Randy Brown	.05	.02	.01
☐ 401	Bobby Hurley	.10	.05	.01
☐ 402	Jim Les	.05	.02	.01
☐ 403	Vinny Del Negro	.05	.02	.01
☐ 404	Sleepy Floyd	.05	.02	.01
☐ 405	Dennis Rodman	1.00	.45	.12
☐ 406	Chris Whitney	.05	.02	.01
☐ 407	Vincent Askew	.05	.02	.01
☐ 408	Kendall Gill	.05	.02	.01
☐ 409	Ervin Johnson	.10	.05	.01
☐ 410	Rich King	.05	.02	.01
☐ 411	Detlef Schrempf	.10	.05	.01
☐ 412	Tom Chambers	.05	.02	.01
☐ 413	John Crotty	.05	.02	.01
☐ 414	Felton Spencer	.05	.02	.01
☐ 415	Luther Wright	.05	.02	.01
☐ 416	Calbert Cheaney	.25	.11	.03
☐ 417	Kevin Duckworth	.05	.02	.01
☐ 418	Gheorghe Muresan	.40	.18	.05
☐ 419	David Robinson CL	.05	.02	.01
☐ 420	David Robinson CL	.05	.02	.01
☐ 421	David Robinson CL	.05	.02	.01
☐ DR1	David Robinson	.50	.23	.06
	Commemorative 1989			
	Rookie Card			
☐ MB1	Magic Johnson	.50	.23	.06
	Larry Bird			
	Commemorative			
☐ NNO	D.Robinson AU	125.00	55.00	15.50

	MINT	NRMT	EXC
☐ NNO David Robinson Voucher	10.00	4.50	1.25
☐ NNO Magic Johnson Larry Bird Autograph Card	400.00	180.00	50.00
☐ NNO Magic Johnson Larry Bird Expired Voucher	35.00	16.00	4.40

1993-94 Hoops Fifth Anniversary Gold

Inserted one per 13-card pack and two per 26-card jumbo pack, this 421-card set parallels the regular 1993-94 Hoops issue. The only differences are the Fifth Anniversary embossed gold-foil seal, gold-foil stripes highlighting the player's name on the front and UV coating. The cards are numbered on the back. Please refer to the multiplier below (coupled with the corresponding regular issue cards) to ascertain value.

	MINT	NRMT	EXC
COMPLETE SET (421)	60.00	27.00	7.50
COMPLETE SERIES 1 (300)	35.00	16.00	4.40
COMPLETE SERIES 2 (121)	25.00	11.00	3.10
COMMON CARD (1-421)	.10	.05	.01
*STARS: 1.25X to 2.5X VALUE			
*ROOKIES: 1X to 2X VALUE			

1993-94 Hoops Admiral's Choice

Randomly inserted in second series 13-card foil and 26-card jumbo packs at a rate of one in 12, this five-card standard-size set features David Robinson's selection of the best starting five players in the game today. The cards have borderless fronts with color player photos. The player's name appears in gold-foil lettering at the top. The white back features a color player photo on the left with the player profile on the right. The cards are numbered on the back with an "AC" prefix.

	MINT	NRMT	EXC
COMPLETE SET (5)	4.00	1.80	.50
COMMON CARD (AC1-AC5)	.25	.11	.03
☐ AC1 Shawn Kemp	1.00	.45	.12
☐ AC2 Derrick Coleman	.25	.11	.03
☐ AC3 Kenny Anderson	.50	.23	.06
☐ AC4 Shaquille O'Neal	2.00	.90	.25
☐ AC5 Chris Webber	1.25	.55	.16

1993-94 Hoops David's Best

Inserted into one in every ten first series 1993-94 Hoops 13-card foil packs, these UV-coated cards feature color action photos of David Robinson against featured opponents. The "David's Best" logo runs across the bottom of the card in "golden crystal-foil" lettering. The back of the cards present Robinson's stat line from the selected game and a brief synopsis of the highlights. The cards are numbered on the back with a "DB" prefix.

	MINT	NRMT	EXC
COMPLETE SET (5)	2.00	.90	.25
COMMON ROBINSON (DB1-DB5)	.50	.23	.06
☐ DB1 David Robinson (Vs. Lakers)	.50	.23	.06
☐ DB2 David Robinson (Vs. Magic)	.50	.23	.06
☐ DB3 David Robinson (Vs. Trail Blazers)	.50	.23	.06
☐ DB4 David Robinson (Vs. Warriors)	.50	.23	.06

☐ DB5 David Robinson............ .50   .23   .06
   (Vs. Hornets)

1993-94 Hoops Draft Redemption

For the second consecutive year, a redemption card was randomly inserted into series one packs at a rate of one in 360. The card could be sent in for this 11-card standard-size set by March 31, 1994. The cards feature a full-color head photo on the front. The player's name appears centered at the top in gold foil. The player's draft number also appears in gold foil at the upper right. The horizontal back features a color player head shot on the left, with player statistics and biography alongside on the right. The cards are numbered on the back with an "LP" prefix and sequenced in draft lottery order.

	MINT	NRMT	EXC
COMPLETE SET (11)	50.00	22.00	6.25
COMMON CARD (LP1-LP11)...	1.00	.45	.12
☐ LP1 Chris Webber..............	6.00	2.70	.75
☐ LP2 Shawn Bradley............	2.00	.90	.25
☐ LP3 Anfernee Hardaway.....	30.00	13.50	3.70
☐ LP4 Jamal Mashburn.........	4.00	1.80	.50
☐ LP5 Isaiah Rider...............	2.00	.90	.25
☐ LP6 Calbert Cheaney.........	1.50	.70	.19
☐ LP7 Bobby Hurley..............	1.00	.45	.12
☐ LP8 Vin Baker	6.00	2.70	.75
☐ LP9 Rodney Rogers	1.00	.45	.12
☐ LP10 Lindsey Hunter	1.00	.45	.12
☐ LP11 Allan Houston	3.00	1.35	.35
☐ NNO Redeemed Lottery Card	.25	.11	.03
☐ NNO Unred. Lottery Card ..	1.50	.70	.19

1993-94 Hoops Face to Face

Randomly inserted in first series 13-card foil packs at a rate of one in 20, these 12 standard-size cards feature a standout rookie from 1992-93 on one side and a vet-

eran All-Star with similar skills on the other. The full-bleed glossy color player action photos on both sides are reproduced over metallic-type backgrounds. On both sides, the Face to Face logo and the player's name appears at the bottom. The cards are numbered on the second side with an "FTF" prefix.

	MINT	NRMT	EXC
COMPLETE SET (12)	35.00	16.00	4.40
COMMON CARD (1-12)	.75	.35	.09
☐ 1 Shaquille O'Neal............ David Robinson	10.00	4.50	1.25
☐ 2 Alonzo Mourning .... Patrick Ewing	3.00	1.35	.35
☐ 3 Christian Laettner .... Shawn Kemp	4.00	1.80	.50
☐ 4 Jim Jackson.................... Clyde Drexler	3.00	1.35	.35
☐ 5 LaPhonso Ellis .... Larry Johnson	1.50	.70	.19
☐ 6 Clarence Weatherspoon. Charles Barkley	2.50	1.10	.30
☐ 7 Tom Gugliotta................. Karl Malone	2.00	.90	.25
☐ 8 Walt Williams................. Magic Johnson	4.00	1.80	.50
☐ 9 Robert Horry................... Scottie Pippen	4.00	1.80	.50
☐ 10 Harold Miner .... Michael Jordan	15.00	6.75	1.85
☐ 11 Todd Day .... Chris Mullin	.75	.35	.09
☐ 12 Richard Dumas............. Dominique Wilkins	.75	.35	.09

1993-94 Hoops Magic's All-Rookies

Randomly inserted in second-series 13-card foil and 26-card jumbo packs at a rate of one in 30, this 10-card standard size set features Magic Johnson's projected All-Rookie team for 1993-94. The borderless front features a full-color action shot with the player's name in a gold-foil strip at the bottom. The borderless back features an italicized player profile written by Magic Johnson set against a ghosted background photo of Magic.

	MINT	NRMT	EXC
COMPLETE SET (10)	50.00	22.00	6.25
COMMON CARD (1-10)	1.00	.45	.12

		MINT	NRMT	EXC
☐ 1	Chris Webber	6.00	2.70	.75
☐ 2	Shawn Bradley	2.00	.90	.25
☐ 3	Anfernee Hardaway	30.00	13.50	3.70
☐ 4	Jamal Mashburn	5.00	2.20	.60
☐ 5	Isaiah Rider	2.00	.90	.25
☐ 6	Calbert Cheaney	1.50	.70	.19
☐ 7	Bobby Hurley	1.00	.45	.12
☐ 8	Vin Baker	6.00	2.70	.75
☐ 9	Lindsey Hunter	1.00	.45	.12
☐ 10	Toni Kukoc	4.00	1.80	.50

☐ HS1	Dominique Wilkins	.10	.05	.01
☐ HS2	Robert Parish	.10	.05	.01
☐ HS3	Alonzo Mourning	.25	.11	.03
☐ HS4	Scottie Pippen	.25	.11	.03
☐ HS5	Larry Nance	.05	.02	.01
☐ HS6	Derek Harper	.05	.02	.01
☐ HS7	Reggie Williams	.05	.02	.01
☐ HS8	Bill Laimbeer	.05	.02	.01
☐ HS9	Tim Hardaway	.10	.05	.01
☐ HS10	Hakeem Olajuwon UER	.25	.11	.03
	(Robert Horry is featured player)			
☐ HS11	LaSalle Thompson	.05	.02	.01
☐ HS12	Danny Manning	.05	.02	.01
☐ HS13	James Worthy	.10	.05	.01
☐ HS14	Grant Long	.05	.02	.01
☐ HS15	Blue Edwards	.05	.02	.01
☐ HS16	Christian Laettner	.10	.05	.01
☐ HS17	Derrick Coleman	.05	.02	.01
☐ HS18	Patrick Ewing	.25	.11	.03
☐ HS19	Nick Anderson	.05	.02	.01
☐ HS20	Clarence Weatherspoon	.05	.02	.01
☐ HS21	Charles Barkley	.25	.11	.03
☐ HS22	Clifford Robinson	.10	.05	.01
☐ HS23	Lionel Simmons	.05	.02	.01
☐ HS24	David Robinson	.25	.11	.03
☐ HS25	Shawn Kemp	.25	.11	.03
☐ HS26	Karl Malone	.25	.11	.03
☐ HS27	Rex Chapman	.05	.02	.01
☐ HS28	Answer Card	.05	.02	.01

1993-94 Hoops Scoops

Randomly inserted in second series 13-card foil packs, this 28-card set measures the standard size. Photos feature unique above the rim photography of a star player from each of the 27 NBA teams. Cards are either horizontal or vertical. The player's name, his team's name, and logo appear in a black bar under the photo, while the NBA Hoops Scoops logo appears in the upper right or left corner. On a white background, the backs carry trivia questions about the teams. The cards are numbered on the back with an "HS" prefix. These cards are as plentiful as the regular issue cards.

	MINT	NRMT	EXC
COMPLETE SET (28)	1.00	.45	.12
COMMON CARD (HS1-HS28)	.05	.02	.01

1993-94 Hoops Scoops Fifth Anniversary Gold

Randomly inserted in second series 13-card foil packs, this 28-card parallel set to the regular Hoops Scoops set measures the standard size. Aside from the gold-foil logo and UV coating, the cards are identical to the regular issue Hoops Scoops cards. The cards are numbered on the back with an "HS" prefix. Please refer to the multiplier below (coupled with the price of the corresponding regular issue scoops card) to ascertain value.

	MINT	NRMT	EXC
COMPLETE SET (28)	2.50	1.10	.30
COMMON CARD (HS1-HS28)	.10	.05	.01
*STARS: 1.25X to 2.5X VALUE			

1993-94 Hoops Supreme Court

Randomly inserted into second series 13-card foil and 26-card jumbo packs, this 11-card standard-size set reflects the All-NBA team as chosen by media members that report on the hobby. Card fronts feature full-color action player photos set against a wood grain vertical bar with the player's name centered at the top in silver-foil lettering. The backs carry color player action shots along the left side and player statistics along the right side. The cards are numbered on the back with an "SC" prefix.

	MINT	NRMT	EXC
COMPLETE SET (11)	12.00	5.50	1.50
COMMON CARD (SC1-SC11)	.50	.23	.06
☐ SC1 Charles Barkley............	.75	.35	.09
☐ SC2 David Robinson............	1.00	.45	.12
☐ SC3 Patrick Ewing..............	.50	.23	.06
☐ SC4 Shaquille O'Neal	3.00	1.35	.35
☐ SC5 Larry Johnson.............	.60	.25	.07
☐ SC6 Karl Malone	.50	.23	.06
☐ SC7 Alonzo Mourning	.75	.35	.09
☐ SC8 John Stockton	.50	.23	.06
☐ SC9 Hakeem Olajuwon UER	1.25	.55	.16
(Name spelled Olajwon on front)			
☐ SC10 Scottie Pippen	1.50	.70	.19
☐ SC11 Michael Jordan.........	6.00	2.70	.75

1994-95 Hoops

The 450 standard-size cards comprising the '94-95 Hoops set were distributed in two separate series of 300 and 150 cards each. Cards were issued in 12-card hobby and retail packs (suggested retail price first series $0.99, second series $1.19) and 24-card retail jumbo packs. All second series packs contained at least one insert card (12-card packs had one insert and 24-card jumbo packs had two). Cards feature borderless color player action shots on the front. The player's name, position, and team name appear in white lettering within a team colored stripe near the bottom. The white back carries a color player head shot at the upper left, with the player's name and brief biography appearing alongside to the right. Statistics and career highlights follow below. The cards are numbered on the back and grouped alphabetically within teams. Subsets include All-Stars (224-251), League Leaders (252-258), Award Winners (259-265), Tribune (266-273), Coaches (274-295/383-388), Team Cards (391-420), Top This (421-430) and Gold Mine (431-450). A special Shaquille O'Neal Press Sheet (featuring 100 of his previously issued Hoops and SkyBox cards in an uncut poster-size format) was available by sending in thirty-two first series wrappers along with a check or money order for $1.50. As a special bonus 100 Press Sheets were autographed by O'Neal and randomly mailed out to collectors who responded to the promotion, which expired on March 1st, 1995. A special Grant Hill Commemorative card was available by sending in two second series wrappers along with a check or money order for $3.00 before the June 15th expiration date. Rookie Cards of note include Grant Hill, Juwan Howard, Eddie Jones, Jason Kidd and Glenn Robinson.

	MINT	NRMT	EXC
COMPLETE SET (450)	24.00	11.00	3.00
COMPLETE SERIES 1 (300)....	12.00	5.50	1.50
COMPLETE SERIES 2 (150)....	12.00	5.50	1.50
COMMON CARD (1-450)	.05	.02	.01
☐ 1 Stacey Augmon...............	.10	.05	.01
☐ 2 Mookie Blaylock...............	.10	.05	.01
☐ 3 Doug Edwards.................	.05	.02	.01
☐ 4 Craig Ehlo	.05	.02	.01
☐ 5 Jon Koncak	.05	.02	.01
☐ 6 Danny Manning...............	.10	.05	.01
☐ 7 Kevin Willis	.05	.02	.01
☐ 8 Dee Brown	.05	.02	.01
☐ 9 Sherman Douglas...........	.05	.02	.01
☐ 10 Acie Earl....................	.05	.02	.01
☐ 11 Kevin Gamble...............	.05	.02	.01
☐ 12 Xavier McDaniel............	.05	.02	.01
☐ 13 Robert Parish	.10	.05	.01
☐ 14 Dino Radja	.10	.05	.01
☐ 15 Tony Bennett	.05	.02	.01
☐ 16 Muggsy Bogues............	.10	.05	.01
☐ 17 Scott Burrell...............	.05	.02	.01
☐ 18 Dell Curry...................	.05	.02	.01
☐ 19 Hersey Hawkins	.05	.02	.01
☐ 20 Eddie Johnson	.05	.02	.01
☐ 21 Larry Johnson..............	.25	.11	.03
☐ 22 Alonzo Mourning...........	.30	.14	.04
☐ 23 B.J. Armstrong	.05	.02	.01

☐ 24	Corie Blount	.05	.02	.01	☐ 95	Stanley Roberts	.05	.02	.01
☐ 25	Bill Cartwright	.05	.02	.01	☐ 96	Loy Vaught	.05	.02	.01
☐ 26	Horace Grant	.10	.05	.01	☐ 97	Dominique Wilkins	.10	.05	.01
☐ 27	Toni Kukoc	.20	.09	.03	☐ 98	Elden Campbell	.10	.05	.01
☐ 28	Luc Longley	.05	.02	.01	☐ 99	Doug Christie	.05	.02	.01
☐ 29	Pete Myers	.05	.02	.01	☐ 100	Vlade Divac	.10	.05	.01
☐ 30	Scottie Pippen	.75	.35	.09	☐ 101	Reggie Jordan	.05	.02	.01
☐ 31	Scott Williams	.05	.02	.01	☐ 102	George Lynch	.05	.02	.01
☐ 32	Terrell Brandon	.10	.05	.01	☐ 103	Anthony Peeler	.05	.02	.01
☐ 33	Brad Daugherty	.05	.02	.01	☐ 104	Sedale Threatt	.05	.02	.01
☐ 34	Tyrone Hill	.05	.02	.01	☐ 105	Nick Van Exel	.25	.11	.03
☐ 35	Chris Mills	.10	.05	.01	☐ 106	James Worthy	.10	.05	.01
☐ 36	Larry Nance	.05	.02	.01	☐ 107	Bimbo Coles	.05	.02	.01
☐ 37	Bobby Phills	.05	.02	.01	☐ 108	Matt Geiger	.05	.02	.01
☐ 38	Mark Price	.05	.02	.01	☐ 109	Grant Long	.05	.02	.01
☐ 39	Gerald Wilkins	.05	.02	.01	☐ 110	Harold Miner	.05	.02	.01
☐ 40	John(Hot Rod) Williams	.05	.02	.01	☐ 111	Glen Rice	.10	.05	.01
☐ 41	Terry Davis	.05	.02	.01	☐ 112	John Salley	.05	.02	.01
☐ 42	Lucious Harris	.05	.02	.01	☐ 113	Rony Seikaly	.05	.02	.01
☐ 43	Jim Jackson	.30	.14	.04	☐ 114	Brian Shaw	.05	.02	.01
☐ 44	Popeye Jones	.05	.02	.01	☐ 115	Steve Smith	.10	.05	.01
☐ 45	Tim Legler	.05	.02	.01	☐ 116	Vin Baker	.30	.14	.04
☐ 46	Jamal Mashburn	.20	.09	.03	☐ 117	Jon Barry	.05	.02	.01
☐ 47	Sean Rooks	.05	.02	.01	☐ 118	Todd Day	.05	.02	.01
☐ 48	Mahmoud Abdul-Rauf	.10	.05	.01	☐ 119	Lee Mayberry	.05	.02	.01
☐ 49	LaPhonso Ellis	.05	.02	.01	☐ 120	Eric Murdock	.05	.02	.01
☐ 50	Dikembe Mutombo	.10	.05	.01	☐ 121	Ken Norman	.05	.02	.01
☐ 51	Robert Pack	.05	.02	.01	☐ 122	Mike Brown	.05	.02	.01
☐ 52	Rodney Rogers	.05	.02	.01	☐ 123	Stacey King	.05	.02	.01
☐ 53	Bryant Stith	.05	.02	.01	☐ 124	Christian Laettner	.10	.05	.01
☐ 54	Brian Williams	.05	.02	.01	☐ 125	Chuck Person	.05	.02	.01
☐ 55	Reggie Williams	.05	.02	.01	☐ 126	Isaiah Rider	.10	.05	.01
☐ 56	Greg Anderson	.05	.02	.01	☐ 127	Chris Smith	.05	.02	.01
☐ 57	Joe Dumars	.10	.05	.01	☐ 128	Doug West	.05	.02	.01
☐ 58	Sean Elliott	.10	.05	.01	☐ 129	Micheal Williams	.05	.02	.01
☐ 59	Allan Houston	.15	.07	.02	☐ 130	Kenny Anderson	.10	.05	.01
☐ 60	Lindsey Hunter	.05	.02	.01	☐ 131	Benoit Benjamin	.05	.02	.01
☐ 61	Mark Macon	.05	.02	.01	☐ 132	P.J. Brown	.05	.02	.01
☐ 62	Terry Mills	.05	.02	.01	☐ 133	Derrick Coleman	.05	.02	.01
☐ 63	Victor Alexander	.05	.02	.01	☐ 134	Kevin Edwards	.05	.02	.01
☐ 64	Chris Gatling	.05	.02	.01	☐ 135	Armon Gilliam	.05	.02	.01
☐ 65	Tim Hardaway	.10	.05	.01	☐ 136	Chris Morris	.05	.02	.01
☐ 66	Avery Johnson	.05	.02	.01	☐ 137	Rex Walters	.05	.02	.01
☐ 67	Sarunas Marciulionis	.05	.02	.01	☐ 138	David Wesley	.05	.02	.01
☐ 68	Chris Mullin	.10	.05	.01	☐ 139	Greg Anthony	.05	.02	.01
☐ 69	Billy Owens	.05	.02	.01	☐ 140	Anthony Bonner	.05	.02	.01
☐ 70	Latrell Sprewell	.30	.14	.04	☐ 141	Hubert Davis	.05	.02	.01
☐ 71	Chris Webber	.30	.14	.04	☐ 142	Patrick Ewing	.25	.11	.03
☐ 72	Matt Bullard	.05	.02	.01	☐ 143	Derek Harper	.05	.02	.01
☐ 73	Sam Cassell	.10	.05	.01	☐ 144	Anthony Mason	.10	.05	.01
☐ 74	Mario Elie	.05	.02	.01	☐ 145	Charles Oakley	.10	.05	.01
☐ 75	Carl Herrera	.05	.02	.01	☐ 146	Charles Smith	.05	.02	.01
☐ 76	Robert Horry	.10	.05	.01	☐ 147	John Starks	.05	.02	.01
☐ 77	Vernon Maxwell	.05	.02	.01	☐ 148	Nick Anderson	.10	.05	.01
☐ 78	Hakeem Olajuwon	.60	.25	.07	☐ 149	Anthony Avent	.05	.02	.01
☐ 79	Kenny Smith	.05	.02	.01	☐ 150	Anthony Bowie	.05	.02	.01
☐ 80	Otis Thorpe	.10	.05	.01	☐ 151	Anfernee Hardaway	1.50	.70	.19
☐ 81	Antonio Davis	.05	.02	.01	☐ 152	Shaquille O'Neal	1.25	.55	.16
☐ 82	Dale Davis	.05	.02	.01	☐ 153	Donald Royal	.05	.02	.01
☐ 83	Vern Fleming	.05	.02	.01	☐ 154	Dennis Scott	.10	.05	.01
☐ 84	Scott Haskin	.05	.02	.01	☐ 155	Scott Skiles	.05	.02	.01
☐ 85	Derrick McKey	.05	.02	.01	☐ 156	Jeff Turner	.05	.02	.01
☐ 86	Reggie Miller	.30	.14	.04	☐ 157	Dana Barros	.05	.02	.01
☐ 87	Byron Scott	.10	.05	.01	☐ 158	Shawn Bradley	.10	.05	.01
☐ 88	Rik Smits	.10	.05	.01	☐ 159	Greg Graham	.05	.02	.01
☐ 89	Haywoode Workman	.05	.02	.01	☐ 160	Warren Kidd	.05	.02	.01
☐ 90	Terry Dehere	.05	.02	.01	☐ 161	Eric Leckner	.05	.02	.01
☐ 91	Harold Ellis	.05	.02	.01	☐ 162	Jeff Malone	.05	.02	.01
☐ 92	Gary Grant	.05	.02	.01	☐ 163	Tim Perry	.05	.02	.01
☐ 93	Ron Harper	.05	.02	.01	☐ 164	Clarence Weatherspoon	.05	.02	.01
☐ 94	Mark Jackson	.05	.02	.01	☐ 165	Danny Ainge	.10	.05	.01

☐ 166	Charles Barkley	.40	.18	.05
☐ 167	Cedric Ceballos	.10	.05	.01
☐ 168	A.C. Green	.10	.05	.01
☐ 169	Kevin Johnson	.10	.05	.01
☐ 170	Malcolm Mackey	.05	.02	.01
☐ 171	Dan Majerle	.10	.05	.01
☐ 172	Oliver Miller	.05	.02	.01
☐ 173	Mark West	.05	.02	.01
☐ 174	Clyde Drexler	.30	.14	.04
☐ 175	Chris Dudley	.05	.02	.01
☐ 176	Harvey Grant	.05	.02	.01
☐ 177	Tracy Murray	.05	.02	.01
☐ 178	Terry Porter	.05	.02	.01
☐ 179	Clifford Robinson	.10	.05	.01
☐ 180	James Robinson	.05	.02	.01
☐ 181	Rod Strickland	.05	.02	.01
☐ 182	Buck Williams	.10	.05	.01
☐ 183	Duane Causwell	.05	.02	.01
☐ 184	Bobby Hurley	.05	.02	.01
☐ 185	Olden Polynice	.05	.02	.01
☐ 186	Mitch Richmond	.20	.09	.03
☐ 187	Lionel Simmons	.05	.02	.01
☐ 188	Wayman Tisdale	.05	.02	.01
☐ 189	Spud Webb	.10	.05	.01
☐ 190	Walt Williams	.10	.05	.01
☐ 191	Willie Anderson	.05	.02	.01
☐ 192	Lloyd Daniels	.05	.02	.01
☐ 193	Vinny Del Negro	.05	.02	.01
☐ 194	Dale Ellis	.05	.02	.01
☐ 195	J.R. Reid	.05	.02	.01
☐ 196	David Robinson	.50	.23	.06
☐ 197	Dennis Rodman	1.00	.45	.12
☐ 198	Kendall Gill	.05	.02	.01
☐ 199	Ervin Johnson	.05	.02	.01
☐ 200	Shawn Kemp	.75	.35	.09
☐ 201	Chris King	.05	.02	.01
☐ 202	Nate McMillan	.05	.02	.01
☐ 203	Gary Payton	.40	.18	.05
☐ 204	Sam Perkins	.05	.02	.01
☐ 205	Ricky Pierce	.05	.02	.01
☐ 206	Detlef Schrempf	.10	.05	.01
☐ 207	David Benoit	.05	.02	.01
☐ 208	Tom Chambers	.05	.02	.01
☐ 209	Tyrone Corbin	.05	.02	.01
☐ 210	Jeff Hornacek	.10	.05	.01
☐ 211	Karl Malone	.25	.11	.03
☐ 212	Bryon Russell	.05	.02	.01
☐ 213	Felton Spencer	.05	.02	.01
☐ 214	John Stockton	.25	.11	.03
☐ 215	Luther Wright	.05	.02	.01
☐ 216	Michael Adams	.05	.02	.01
☐ 217	Mitchell Butler	.05	.02	.01
☐ 218	Rex Chapman	.05	.02	.01
☐ 219	Calbert Cheaney	.10	.05	.01
☐ 220	Pervis Ellison	.05	.02	.01
☐ 221	Tom Gugliotta	.10	.05	.01
☐ 222	Don MacLean	.05	.02	.01
☐ 223	Gheorghe Muresan	.10	.05	.01
☐ 224	Kenny Anderson AS	.05	.02	.01
☐ 225	B.J. Armstrong AS	.05	.02	.01
☐ 226	Mookie Blaylock AS	.05	.02	.01
☐ 227	Derrick Coleman AS	.05	.02	.01
☐ 228	Patrick Ewing AS	.10	.05	.01
☐ 229	Horace Grant AS	.05	.02	.01
☐ 230	Alonzo Mourning AS	.15	.07	.02
☐ 231	Shaquille O'Neal AS	.60	.25	.07
☐ 232	Charles Oakley AS	.05	.02	.01
☐ 233	Scottie Pippen AS	.40	.18	.05
☐ 234	Mark Price AS	.05	.02	.01
☐ 235	John Starks AS	.05	.02	.01
☐ 236	Dominique Wilkins AS	.10	.05	.01
☐ 237	East Team	.05	.02	.01
☐ 238	Charles Barkley AS	.20	.09	.03
☐ 239	Clyde Drexler AS	.10	.05	.01
☐ 240	Kevin Johnson AS	.10	.05	.01
☐ 241	Shawn Kemp AS	.40	.18	.05
☐ 242	Karl Malone AS	.10	.05	.01
☐ 243	Danny Manning AS	.05	.02	.01
☐ 244	Hakeem Olajuwon AS	.30	.14	.04
☐ 245	Gary Payton AS	.20	.09	.03
☐ 246	Mitch Richmond AS	.10	.05	.01
☐ 247	Clifford Robinson AS	.05	.02	.01
☐ 248	David Robinson AS	.25	.11	.03
☐ 249	Latrell Sprewell AS	.10	.05	.01
☐ 250	John Stockton AS	.10	.05	.01
☐ 251	West Team	.05	.02	.01
☐ 252	Tracy Murray LL B.J. Armstrong Reggie Miller	.05	.02	.01
☐ 253	John Stockton LL Muggsy Bogues Mookie Blaylock	.10	.05	.01
☐ 254	Dikembe Mutombo LL Hakeem Olajuwon Houston Rockets David Robinson	.25	.11	.03
☐ 255	Mahmoud Abdul-Rauf LL Reggie Miller Indiana Pacers Ricky Pierce	.05	.02	.01
☐ 256	Dennis Rodman LL Shaquille O'Neal Kevin Willis	.50	.23	.06
☐ 257	David Robinson LL Shaquille O'Neal Hakeem Olajuwon	.40	.18	.05
☐ 258	Nate McMillan LL Scottie Pippen Mookie Blaylock	.05	.02	.01
☐ 259	Chris Webber AW	.15	.07	.02
☐ 260	Hakeem Olajuwon AW	.30	.14	.04
☐ 261	Hakeem Olajuwon AW	.30	.14	.04
☐ 262	Dell Curry AW	.05	.02	.01
☐ 263	Scottie Pippen AW	.40	.18	.05
☐ 264	Anfernee Hardaway AW	.75	.35	.09
☐ 265	Don MacLean AW	.05	.02	.01
☐ 266	Hakeem Olajuwon FIN	.30	.14	.04
☐ 267	Derek Harper FIN	.05	.02	.01
☐ 268	Sam Cassell FIN	.10	.05	.01
☐ 269	John Starks FIN	.05	.02	.01
☐ 270	Patrick Ewing FIN Hakeem Olajuwon	.10	.05	.01
☐ 271	Carl Herrera FIN	.05	.02	.01
☐ 272	Vernon Maxwell FIN	.05	.02	.01
☐ 273	Hakeem Olajuwon FIN	.30	.14	.04
☐ 274	Lenny Wilkens CO	.10	.05	.01
☐ 275	Chris Ford CO	.05	.02	.01
☐ 276	Allan Bristow CO	.05	.02	.01
☐ 277	Phil Jackson CO	.10	.05	.01
☐ 278	Mike Fratello CO	.05	.02	.01
☐ 279	Dick Motta CO	.05	.02	.01
☐ 280	Dan Issel CO	.10	.05	.01
☐ 281	Don Chaney CO	.05	.02	.01
☐ 282	Don Nelson CO	.10	.05	.01
☐ 283	Rudy Tomjanovich CO	.10	.05	.01
☐ 284	Larry Brown CO	.10	.05	.01
☐ 285	Del Harris CO UER (Back refers to Ralph Sampson and Akeem Olajuwon as part of '80-'81 Rockets)	.05	.02	.01
☐ 286	Kevin Loughery CO	.05	.02	.01
☐ 287	Mike Dunleavy CO	.05	.02	.01
☐ 288	Sidney Lowe CO	.05	.02	.01

#	Player			
☐ 289	Pat Riley CO	.10	.05	.01
☐ 290	Brian Hill CO	.05	.02	.01
☐ 291	John Lucas CO	.05	.02	.01
☐ 292	Paul Westphal CO	.05	.02	.01
☐ 293	Garry St. Jean CO	.05	.02	.01
☐ 294	George Karl CO	.05	.02	.01
☐ 295	Jerry Sloan CO	.10	.05	.01
☐ 296	Magic Johnson Commemorative	.75	.35	.09
☐ 297	Denzel Washington	.15	.07	.02
☐ 298	Checklist	.05	.02	.01
☐ 299	Checklist	.05	.02	.01
☐ 300	Checklist	.05	.02	.01
☐ 301	Sergei Bazarevich	.05	.02	.01
☐ 302	Tyrone Corbin	.05	.02	.01
☐ 303	Grant Long	.05	.02	.01
☐ 304	Ken Norman	.05	.02	.01
☐ 305	Steve Smith	.10	.05	.01
☐ 306	Blue Edwards	.05	.02	.01
☐ 307	Greg Minor	.05	.02	.01
☐ 308	Eric Montross	.10	.05	.01
☐ 309	Dominique Wilkins	.10	.05	.01
☐ 310	Michael Adams	.05	.02	.01
☐ 311	Darrin Hancock	.05	.02	.01
☐ 312	Robert Parish	.10	.05	.01
☐ 313	Ron Harper	.10	.05	.01
☐ 314	Dickey Simpkins	.10	.05	.01
☐ 315	Michael Cage	.05	.02	.01
☐ 316	Tony Dumas	.10	.05	.01
☐ 317	Jason Kidd	2.00	.90	.25
☐ 318	Roy Tarpley	.05	.02	.01
☐ 319	Dale Ellis	.05	.02	.01
☐ 320	Jalen Rose	.25	.11	.03
☐ 321	Bill Curley	.05	.02	.01
☐ 322	Grant Hill	3.00	1.35	.35
☐ 323	Oliver Miller	.05	.02	.01
☐ 324	Mark West	.05	.02	.01
☐ 325	Tom Gugliotta	.10	.05	.01
☐ 326	Ricky Pierce	.05	.02	.01
☐ 327	Carlos Rogers	.05	.02	.01
☐ 328	Clifford Rozier	.10	.05	.01
☐ 329	Rony Seikaly	.05	.02	.01
☐ 330	Tim Breaux	.05	.02	.01
☐ 331	Duane Ferrell	.05	.02	.01
☐ 332	Mark Jackson	.05	.02	.01
☐ 333	Lamond Murray	.10	.05	.01
☐ 334	Charles Outlaw	.05	.02	.01
☐ 335	Eric Piatkowski	.05	.02	.01
☐ 336	Pooh Richardson	.05	.02	.01
☐ 337	Malik Sealy	.05	.02	.01
☐ 338	Cedric Ceballos	.10	.05	.01
☐ 339	Eddie Jones	.60	.25	.07
☐ 340	Anthony Miller	.05	.02	.01
☐ 341	Kevin Gamble	.05	.02	.01
☐ 342	Brad Lohaus	.05	.02	.01
☐ 343	Billy Owens	.05	.02	.01
☐ 344	Khalid Reeves	.05	.02	.01
☐ 345	Kevin Willis	.05	.02	.01
☐ 346	Eric Mobley	.10	.05	.01
☐ 347	Johnny Newman	.05	.02	.01
☐ 348	Ed Pinckney	.05	.02	.01
☐ 349	Glenn Robinson	1.00	.45	.12
☐ 350	Howard Eisley	.05	.02	.01
☐ 351	Donyell Marshall	.10	.05	.01
☐ 352	Yinka Dare	.05	.02	.01
☐ 353	Charlie Ward	.10	.05	.01
☐ 354	Monty Williams	.05	.02	.01
☐ 355	Horace Grant	.10	.05	.01
☐ 356	Brian Shaw	.05	.02	.01
☐ 357	Brooks Thompson	.10	.05	.01
☐ 358	Derrick Alston	.05	.02	.01
☐ 359	B.J. Tyler	.05	.02	.01
☐ 360	Scott Williams	.05	.02	.01
☐ 361	Sharone Wright	.10	.05	.01
☐ 362	Antonio Lang	.05	.02	.01
☐ 363	Danny Manning	.10	.05	.01
☐ 364	Wesley Person	.50	.23	.06
☐ 365	Wayman Tisdale	.05	.02	.01
☐ 366	Trevor Ruffin	.10	.05	.01
☐ 367	Aaron McKie	.10	.05	.01
☐ 368	Brian Grant	.40	.18	.05
☐ 369	Michael Smith	.05	.02	.01
☐ 370	Sean Elliott	.10	.05	.01
☐ 371	Avery Johnson	.05	.02	.01
☐ 372	Chuck Person	.05	.02	.01
☐ 373	Bill Cartwright	.05	.02	.01
☐ 374	Sarunas Marciulionis	.05	.02	.01
☐ 375	Dontonio Wingfield	.05	.02	.01
☐ 376	Antoine Carr	.05	.02	.01
☐ 377	Jamie Watson	.05	.02	.01
☐ 378	Juwan Howard	2.00	.90	.25
☐ 379	Jim McIlvaine	.10	.05	.01
☐ 380	Scott Skiles	.05	.02	.01
☐ 381	Anthony Tucker	.05	.02	.01
☐ 382	Chris Webber	.30	.14	.04
☐ 383	Bill Fitch CO	.05	.02	.01
☐ 384	Bill Blair CO	.05	.02	.01
☐ 385	Butch Beard CO	.05	.02	.01
☐ 386	P.J. Carlesimo CO	.10	.05	.01
☐ 387	Bob Hill CO	.05	.02	.01
☐ 388	Jim Lynam CO	.05	.02	.01
☐ 389	Checklist 4	.05	.02	.01
☐ 390	Checklist 5	.05	.02	.01
☐ 391	Atlanta Hawks TC	.05	.02	.01
☐ 392	Boston Celtics TC	.05	.02	.01
☐ 393	Charlotte Hornets TC	.05	.02	.01
☐ 394	Chicago Bulls TC	.05	.02	.01
☐ 395	Cleveland Cavaliers TC	.05	.02	.01
☐ 396	Dallas Mavericks TC	.05	.02	.01
☐ 397	Denver Nuggets TC	.05	.02	.01
☐ 398	Detroit Pistons TC	.05	.02	.01
☐ 399	Golden State Warriors TC	.05	.02	.01
☐ 400	Houston Rockets TC	.05	.02	.01
☐ 401	Indiana Pacers TC	.05	.02	.01
☐ 402	Los Angeles Clippers TC	.05	.02	.01
☐ 403	Los Angeles Lakers TC	.05	.02	.01
☐ 404	Miami Heat TC	.05	.02	.01
☐ 405	Milwaukee Bucks TC	.05	.02	.01
☐ 406	Minnesota Timberwolves TC	.05	.02	.01
☐ 407	New Jersey Nets TC	.05	.02	.01
☐ 408	New York Knicks TC	.05	.02	.01
☐ 409	Orlando Magic TC	.05	.02	.01
☐ 410	Philadelphia 76ers TC	.05	.02	.01
☐ 411	Phoenix Suns TC	.05	.02	.01
☐ 412	Portland Trail Blazers TC	.05	.02	.01
☐ 413	Sacramento Kings TC	.05	.02	.01
☐ 414	San Antonio Spurs TC	.05	.02	.01
☐ 415	Seattle Supersonics TC	.05	.02	.01
☐ 416	Utah Jazz TC	.05	.02	.01
☐ 417	Washington Bullets TC	.05	.02	.01
☐ 418	Toronto Raptors TC	.10	.05	.01
☐ 419	Vancouver Grizzlies TC	.10	.05	.01
☐ 420	NBA Logo Card	.05	.02	.01
☐ 421	Glenn Robinson TOP Chris Webber	.25	.11	.03
☐ 422	Jason Kidd TOP Shawn Bradley	.40	.18	.05
☐ 423	Grant Hill TOP Anfernee Hardaway	1.00	.45	.12

		MINT	NRMT	EXC
☐ 424	Donyell Marshall TOP .. Jamal Mashburn	.05	.02	.01
☐ 425	Juwan Howard TOP ..... Isaiah Rider	.40	.18	.05
☐ 426	Sharone Wright TOP .... Calbert Cheaney	.05	.02	.01
☐ 427	Lamond Murray TOP .... Bobby Hurley	.05	.02	.01
☐ 428	Brian Grant TOP.......... Vin Baker	.10	.05	.01
☐ 429	Eric Montross TOP...... Rodney Rogers	.05	.02	.01
☐ 430	Eddie Jones TOP......... Lindsey Hunter	.10	.05	.01
☐ 431	Craig Ehlo GM............	.05	.02	.01
☐ 432	Dino Radja GM............	.05	.02	.01
☐ 433	Toni Kukoc GM............	.10	.05	.01
☐ 434	Mark Price GM............	.05	.02	.01
☐ 435	Latrell Sprewell GM	.10	.05	.01
☐ 436	Sam Cassell GM..........	.10	.05	.01
☐ 437	Vernon Maxwell GM.....	.05	.02	.01
☐ 438	Haywoode Workman GM	.05	.02	.01
☐ 439	Harold Ellis GM...........	.05	.02	.01
☐ 440	Cedric Ceballos GM.....	.10	.05	.01
☐ 441	Vlade Divac GM...........	.10	.05	.01
☐ 442	Nick Van Exel GM........	.25	.11	.03
☐ 443	John Starks GM...........	.05	.02	.01
☐ 444	Scott Williams GM.......	.05	.02	.01
☐ 445	Clifford Robinson GM...	.05	.02	.01
☐ 446	Spud Webb GM	.05	.02	.01
☐ 447	Avery Johnson GM.......	.05	.02	.01
☐ 448	Dennis Rodman GM......	.50	.23	.06
☐ 449	Sarunas Marciulionis GM	.05	.02	.01
☐ 450	Nate McMillan GM........	.05	.02	.01
☐ NNO	G.Hill Wrapper Exch.	6.00	2.70	.75
☐ NNO	Shaq Sheet Wrapper Exchange Autograph	500.00	220.00	60.00
☐ NNO	Shaq Sheet Wrap.Exch.	30.00	13.50	3.70

1994-95 Hoops Big Numbers

Randomly inserted in first series hobby and retail foil packs at a rate of one in 30, this 12 standard-size set features color player action cutouts on their black horizontal and borderless fronts. The player's name and a number representing his Big Number accomplishment appear in silver-foil lettering offset to one side. The white horizontal back carries a color player head shot at the right, with a description of his Big Number

accomplishment appearing alongside. The cards are numbered on the back with a "BN" prefix.

		MINT	NRMT	EXC
COMPLETE SET (12)		60.00	27.00	7.50
COMMON CARD (BN1-BN12)..		1.50	.70	.19
☐ BN1	David Robinson.......	6.00	2.70	.75
☐ BN2	Jamal Mashburn	2.50	1.10	.30
☐ BN3	Hakeem Olajuwon	8.00	3.60	1.00
☐ BN4	Patrick Ewing	3.00	1.35	.35
☐ BN5	Shaquille O'Neal	15.00	6.75	1.85
☐ BN6	Latrell Sprewell	2.00	.90	.25
☐ BN7	Chris Webber	4.00	1.80	.50
☐ BN8	Anfernee Hardaway .	20.00	9.00	2.50
☐ BN9	Scottie Pippen	10.00	4.50	1.25
☐ BN10	Isaiah Rider	1.50	.70	.19
☐ BN11	Alonzo Mourning	4.00	1.80	.50
☐ BN12	Charles Barkley	5.00	2.20	.60

1994-95 Hoops Big Numbers Rainbow

Inserted one per first series special retail pack, these 12 standard-size (2 1/2" by 3 1/2") cards are identical to their Big Numbers Silver counterparts, except for their rainbow-colored foil numbers and highlights. The cards are numbered on the back with a "BN" prefix. Big Number Rainbow cards are valued equally to the regular issue silver-lettered "Big Numbers" inserts.

		MINT	NRMT	EXC
COMPLETE SET (12)		60.00	27.00	7.50
COMMON CARD (1-12)		1.50	.70	.19
*RAINBOW CARDS: EQUAL VALUE .				

1994-95 Hoops Draft Redemption

For the third straight year, a redemption card was randomly inserted into first series packs at a rate of one in 360. The card could be sent in for this 11-card standard size set on or before the June 15th, 1995 deadline. The cards feature a full-color player photo cut out against a computer-generated background with a big number (corresponding to the player's draft selection) zooming out of the side. This set is sequenced in draft order.

	MINT	NRMT	EXC
COMPLETE SET (11)	25.00	11.00	3.10
COMMON CARD (1-11)	.50	.23	.06
☐ 1 Glenn Robinson	4.00	1.80	.50
☐ 2 Jason Kidd	8.00	3.60	1.00
☐ 3 Grant Hill	12.00	5.50	1.50
☐ 4 Donyell Marshall	.50	.23	.06
☐ 5 Juwan Howard	8.00	3.60	1.00
☐ 6 Sharone Wright	1.00	.45	.12
☐ 7 Lamond Murray	.50	.23	.06
☐ 8 Brian Grant	1.50	.70	.19
☐ 9 Eric Montross	1.00	.45	.12
☐ 10 Eddie Jones	2.50	1.10	.30
☐ 11 Carlos Rogers	.50	.23	.06
☐ NNO Expired Exchange Card	1.50	.70	.19

1994-95 Hoops Magic's All-Rookies

Randomly inserted into all second series packs (12-card hobby and retail packs at a rate of one in twelve, 24-card retail jumbo packs at an approximate rate of slightly greater than one per pack), cards from this 12-card standard-size set feature a selection of top rookies from the 1994-95 season. The fronts have a color action photo with different color backgrounds for each card with designs in them. The word "Magic's" is in the upper right corner and "All-Rookie" is three-dimensionally encompassing the player. The backs have a picture of Magic Johnson holding the card showing the front. On the left side it says "Magic's All-Rookie Team" and the their is player commentary at the bottom.

	MINT	NRMT	EXC
COMPLETE SET (10)	20.00	9.00	2.50
COMMON CARD (AR1-AR10)	.50	.23	.06
☐ AR1 Glenn Robinson	2.50	1.10	.30
☐ AR2 Jason Kidd	5.00	2.20	.60
☐ AR3 Grant Hill	8.00	3.60	1.00
☐ AR4 Donyell Marshall	.50	.23	.06
☐ AR5 Juwan Howard	5.00	2.20	.60
☐ AR6 Sharone Wright	.50	.23	.06
☐ AR7 Brian Grant	1.00	.45	.12
☐ AR8 Eddie Jones	1.50	.70	.19
☐ AR9 Jalen Rose	.50	.23	.06
☐ AR10 Wesley Person	.50	.23	.06

1994-95 Hoops Magic's All-Rookies Foil-Tech

Randomly inserted into all series 2 packs at a rate of one in 36, these 10-cards parallel the basic Magic's All-Rookies insert cards. The difference is that each Foil-Tech card features a silver-foil background and has FAR numbering prefixes. Please refer to the multipliers provided below (coupled with the values of the basic Magic's All-Rookies inserts) to ascertain values.

	MINT	NRMT	EXC
COMPLETE SET (10)	50.00	22.00	6.25
COMMON CARD (1-10)	1.00	.45	.12
FOIL CARDS: 1.25X to 2.5X VALUE			

1994-95 Hoops Magic's All-Rookies Jumbos

One of these jumbo cards was inserted exclusively into second-series hobby boxes.

The cards are an exact parallel of the corresponding Magic's All-Rookie inserts except that these measure 5" by 7". Please refer to the multiplier provided below (coupled with the values of the regular Magic's All-Rookie inserts) to ascertain value.

	MINT	NRMT	EXC
COMPLETE SET (10)	40.00	18.00	5.00
COMMON CARD (AR1-AR10)	1.00	.45	.12
JUMBO CARDS: 1X to 2X VALUE			

1994-95 Hoops Power Ratings

Inserted one per pack into all second series packs, cards from this 54-card standard-size set feature a selection of the top players in the NBA. Cards feature a photo of the player silhouetted over flame-thrower graphics. Backs present a second photo and colorful bar chart of the players stats in seven key categories. Two players per team were included in this set.

		MINT	NRMT	EXC
	COMPLETE SET (54)	10.00	4.50	1.25
	COMMON CARD (PR1-PR54)	.10	.05	.01
☐	PR1 Mookie Blaylock	.25	.11	.03
☐	PR2 Stacey Augmon	.25	.11	.03
☐	PR3 Dino Radja	.25	.11	.03
☐	PR4 Dominique Wilkins	.35	.16	.04
☐	PR5 Larry Johnson	.50	.23	.06
☐	PR6 Alonzo Mourning	.60	.25	.07
☐	PR7 Toni Kukoc	.40	.18	.05
☐	PR8 Scottie Pippen	1.50	.70	.19
☐	PR9 John Williams	.10	.05	.01

☐	PR10 Mark Price	.10	.05	.01
☐	PR11 Jim Jackson	.60	.25	.07
☐	PR12 Jamal Mashburn	.40	.18	.05
☐	PR13 Dale Ellis	.10	.05	.01
☐	PR14 LaPhonso Ellis	.10	.05	.01
☐	PR15 Joe Dumars	.35	.16	.04
☐	PR16 Lindsey Hunter	.10	.05	.01
☐	PR17 Latrell Sprewell	.35	.16	.04
☐	PR18 Chris Mullin	.35	.16	.04
☐	PR19 Vernon Maxwell	.10	.05	.01
☐	PR20 Hakeem Olajuwon	1.25	.55	.16
☐	PR21 Mark Jackson	.10	.05	.01
☐	PR22 Reggie Miller	.60	.25	.07
☐	PR23 Pooh Richardson	.10	.05	.01
☐	PR24 Loy Vaught	.10	.05	.01
☐	PR25 Vlade Divac	.35	.16	.04
☐	PR26 Nick Van Exel	.50	.23	.06
☐	PR27 Glen Rice	.35	.16	.04
☐	PR28 Billy Owens	.10	.05	.01
☐	PR29 Vin Baker	.60	.25	.07
☐	PR30 Eric Murdock	.10	.05	.01
☐	PR31 Christian Laettner	.35	.16	.04
☐	PR32 Isaiah Rider	.35	.16	.04
☐	PR33 Kenny Anderson	.35	.16	.04
☐	PR34 Derrick Coleman	.10	.05	.01
☐	PR35 Patrick Ewing	.50	.23	.06
☐	PR36 John Starks	.10	.05	.01
☐	PR37 Nick Anderson	.35	.16	.04
☐	PR38 Anfernee Hardaway	3.00	1.35	.35
☐	PR39 Shawn Bradley	.35	.16	.04
☐	PR40 Clarence Weatherspoon	.25	.11	.03
☐	PR41 Charles Barkley	.75	.35	.09
☐	PR42 Kevin Johnson	.35	.16	.04
☐	PR43 Clyde Drexler	.60	.25	.07
☐	PR44 Clifford Robinson	.35	.16	.04
☐	PR45 Mitch Richmond	.35	.16	.04
☐	PR46 Olden Polynice	.10	.05	.01
☐	PR47 Sean Elliott	.35	.16	.04
☐	PR48 Chuck Person	.10	.05	.01
☐	PR49 Shawn Kemp	1.50	.70	.19
☐	PR50 Gary Payton	.75	.35	.09
☐	PR51 Jeff Hornacek	.25	.11	.03
☐	PR52 Karl Malone	.50	.23	.06
☐	PR53 Rex Chapman	.10	.05	.01
☐	PR54 Don MacLean	.10	.05	.01

1994-95 Hoops Predators

Randomly inserted into all second series packs (one in every twelve 12-card packs and two per 24-card jumbo pack), cards

from this 8-card standard-size set feature
eight league leaders from the 1993-94 season. Design is very similar to the Power
Ratings inserts. The set is sequenced in
alphabetical order.

	MINT	NRMT	EXC
COMPLETE SET (8)	4.00	1.80	.50
COMMON CARD (P1-P8)	.15	.07	.02
☐ P1 Mahmoud Abdul-Rauf	.25	.11	.03
☐ P2 Dikembe Mutombo	.25	.11	.03
☐ P3 Shaquille O'Neal	2.50	1.10	.30
☐ P4 Tracy Murray	.15	.07	.02
☐ P5 David Robinson	1.00	.45	.12
☐ P6 Dennis Rodman	2.00	.90	.25
☐ P7 Nate McMillan	.15	.07	.02
☐ P8 John Stockton	.50	.23	.06

1994-95 Hoops
Supreme Court

Randomly inserted in first series hobby and
retail packs at a rate of one in four, the 50
standard-size parallel cards comprising the
'94-95 Hoops Supreme Court set feature a
selection of the top stars within the basic
issue first series Hoops set. Unlike the regular issue cards, each Supreme Court
insert features a special embossed gold-foil
logo on the card front. The cards are also
numbered on the back with an "SC"
prefix.player head shot at the upper left,
with the player's name and brief biography
appearing alongside to the right. Statistics
and career highlights follow below. The
cards are numbered on the back with an
"SC" prefix.

	MINT	NRMT	EXC
COMPLETE SET (50)	20.00	9.00	2.50
COMMON CARD (SC1-SC50)	.25	.11	.03
☐ SC1 Mookie Blaylock	.50	.23	.06
☐ SC2 Danny Manning	.50	.23	.06
☐ SC3 Dino Radja	.50	.23	.06
☐ SC4 Larry Johnson	.75	.35	.09
☐ SC5 Alonzo Mourning	1.00	.45	.12
☐ SC6 B.J. Armstrong	.25	.11	.03
☐ SC7 Horace Grant	.50	.23	.06
☐ SC8 Toni Kukoc	.60	.25	.07
☐ SC9 Brad Daugherty	.25	.11	.03
☐ SC10 Mark Price	.25	.11	.03
☐ SC11 Jim Jackson	1.00	.45	.12
☐ SC12 Jamal Mashburn	.60	.25	.07
☐ SC13 Dikembe Mutombo	.50	.23	.06
☐ SC14 Joe Dumars	.50	.23	.06
☐ SC15 Lindsey Hunter	.25	.11	.03
☐ SC16 Tim Hardaway	.50	.23	.06
☐ SC17 Chris Mullin	.50	.23	.06
☐ SC18 Sam Cassell	.50	.23	.06
☐ SC19 Hakeem Olajuwon	2.00	.90	.25
☐ SC20 Reggie Miller	1.00	.45	.12
☐ SC21 Dominique Wilkins	.50	.23	.06
☐ SC22 Nick Van Exel	.75	.35	.09
☐ SC23 Harold Miner	.25	.11	.03
☐ SC24 Steve Smith	.50	.23	.06
☐ SC25 Vin Baker	1.00	.45	.12
☐ SC26 Christian Laettner	.50	.23	.06
☐ SC27 Isaiah Rider	.50	.23	.06
☐ SC28 Kenny Anderson	.50	.23	.06
☐ SC29 Derrick Coleman	.25	.11	.03
☐ SC30 Patrick Ewing	.75	.35	.09
☐ SC31 John Starks	.25	.11	.03
☐ SC32 Anfernee Hardaway	5.00	2.20	.60
☐ SC33 Shaquille O'Neal	4.00	1.80	.50
☐ SC34 Shawn Bradley	.50	.23	.06
☐ SC35 Clarence Weatherspoon	.50	.23	.06
☐ SC36 Charles Barkley	1.25	.55	.16
☐ SC37 Kevin Johnson	.50	.23	.06
☐ SC38 Oliver Miller	.25	.11	.03
☐ SC39 Clyde Drexler	1.00	.45	.12
☐ SC40 Clifford Robinson	.50	.23	.06
☐ SC41 Mitch Richmond	.60	.25	.07
☐ SC42 Bobby Hurley	.25	.11	.03
☐ SC43 David Robinson	1.50	.70	.19
☐ SC44 Dennis Rodman	3.00	1.35	.35
☐ SC45 Gary Payton	1.25	.55	.16
☐ SC46 Shawn Kemp	2.50	1.10	.30
☐ SC47 John Stockton	.75	.35	.09
☐ SC48 Karl Malone	.75	.35	.09
☐ SC49 Calbert Cheaney	.50	.23	.06
☐ SC50 Tom Gugliotta	.50	.23	.06

1995-96 Hoops

The 1995-96 Hoops basketball set was
issued in two series of 250 and 150 standard-size cards respectively for a total of
400. Series one cards were issued in 12-
card hobby and retail packs (SRP $1.29)
and 20-card retail jumbo packs (SRP
$1.99). Series two cards were issued in 8-
card hobby and retail packs for $.99 each.
Fronts have a full-color action photo with
the player's name in gold foil surrounded by

his team's color. The backs have a color photo with pro and college career statistics. Cards are grouped alphabetically within teams. The following subsets are featured: Coaches (171-197), Sizzlin' Sophs (198-207), Milestones (208-217), Buzzer Beaters (218-227), Pipeline (228-232), Class Acts (233-242), Triple Threats (243-247), Player/Coach Updates (291-333), Coaches (334-337), Expansion Teams (338-357), Earthshakers (358-372), Rock/House (373-387) and Wicked Dishes (388-397). A special Grant Hill Tribute card, featuring a clear acetate center, was randomly inserted into one in every 360 series one packs. All insert cards feature 3-D technology. A pair of Grant Hill 3-D glasses was available by sending in two first series wrappers and a check or money order for $3.50. In addition, a limited edition Grant Hill Commemorative Co-Rookie of the Year card was available by sending in a check or money order for $9.95 plus two series one wrappers. Both promotions were detailed on first series wrappers and both expired December 31, 1995. Rookie Cards of note in this set include Michael Finley, Kevin Garnett, Antonio McDyess, Joe Smith, Jerry Stackhouse and Damon Stoudamire.

	MINT	NRMT	EXC
COMPLETE SET (400)	30.00	13.50	3.70
COMPLETE SERIES 1 (250)	15.00	6.75	1.85
COMPLETE SERIES 2 (150)	15.00	6.75	1.85
COMMON CARD (1-400)	.05	.02	.01

☐ 1 Stacey Augmon	.10	.05	.01
☐ 2 Mookie Blaylock	.10	.05	.01
☐ 3 Craig Ehlo	.05	.02	.01
☐ 4 Andrew Lang	.05	.02	.01
☐ 5 Grant Long	.05	.02	.01
☐ 6 Ken Norman	.05	.02	.01
☐ 7 Steve Smith	.10	.05	.01
☐ 8 Dee Brown	.05	.02	.01
☐ 9 Sherman Douglas	.05	.02	.01
☐ 10 Pervis Ellison	.05	.02	.01
☐ 11 Eric Montross	.05	.02	.01
☐ 12 Dino Radja	.10	.05	.01
☐ 13 Dominique Wilkins	.10	.05	.01
☐ 14 Muggsy Bogues	.10	.05	.01
☐ 15 Scott Burrell	.05	.02	.01
☐ 16 Dell Curry	.05	.02	.01
☐ 17 Hersey Hawkins	.05	.02	.01
☐ 18 Larry Johnson	.25	.11	.03
☐ 19 Alonzo Mourning	.25	.11	.03
☐ 20 B.J. Armstrong	.05	.02	.01
☐ 21 Michael Jordan	3.00	1.35	.35
☐ 22 Toni Kukoc	.15	.07	.02
☐ 23 Will Perdue	.05	.02	.01
☐ 24 Scottie Pippen	.75	.35	.09
☐ 25 Dickey Simpkins	.05	.02	.01
☐ 26 Terrell Brandon	.10	.05	.01
☐ 27 Tyrone Hill	.05	.02	.01
☐ 28 Chris Mills	.10	.05	.01
☐ 29 Bobby Phills	.05	.02	.01
☐ 30 Mark Price	.05	.02	.01
☐ 31 John Williams	.05	.02	.01
☐ 32 Tony Dumas	.05	.02	.01
☐ 33 Jim Jackson	.25	.11	.03
☐ 34 Popeye Jones	.05	.02	.01
☐ 35 Jason Kidd	.60	.25	.07

☐ 36 Jamal Mashburn	.15	.07	.02
☐ 37 Roy Tarpley	.05	.02	.01
☐ 38 Mahmoud Abdul-Rauf	.10	.05	.01
☐ 39 LaPhonso Ellis	.05	.02	.01
☐ 40 Dikembe Mutombo	.10	.05	.01
☐ 41 Robert Pack	.05	.02	.01
☐ 42 Rodney Rogers	.05	.02	.01
☐ 43 Jalen Rose	.05	.02	.01
☐ 44 Bryant Stith	.05	.02	.01
☐ 45 Joe Dumars	.10	.05	.01
☐ 46 Grant Hill	1.00	.45	.12
☐ 47 Allan Houston	.10	.05	.01
☐ 48 Lindsey Hunter	.05	.02	.01
☐ 49 Oliver Miller	.05	.02	.01
☐ 50 Terry Mills	.05	.02	.01
☐ 51 Chris Gatling	.05	.02	.01
☐ 52 Tim Hardaway	.10	.05	.01
☐ 53 Donyell Marshall	.10	.05	.01
☐ 54 Chris Mullin	.10	.05	.01
☐ 55 Carlos Rogers	.05	.02	.01
☐ 56 Clifford Rozier	.05	.02	.01
☐ 57 Rony Seikaly	.05	.02	.01
☐ 58 Latrell Sprewell	.10	.05	.01
☐ 59 Sam Cassell	.10	.05	.01
☐ 60 Clyde Drexler	.30	.14	.04
☐ 61 Robert Horry	.10	.05	.01
☐ 62 Vernon Maxwell	.05	.02	.01
☐ 63 Hakeem Olajuwon	.60	.25	.07
☐ 64 Kenny Smith	.05	.02	.01
☐ 65 Dale Davis	.05	.02	.01
☐ 66 Mark Jackson	.05	.02	.01
☐ 67 Derrick McKey	.05	.02	.01
☐ 68 Reggie Miller	.30	.14	.04
☐ 69 Byron Scott	.10	.05	.01
☐ 70 Rik Smits	.10	.05	.01
☐ 71 Terry Dehere	.05	.02	.01
☐ 72 Lamond Murray	.05	.02	.01
☐ 73 Eric Piatkowski	.05	.02	.01
☐ 74 Pooh Richardson	.05	.02	.01
☐ 75 Malik Sealy	.05	.02	.01
☐ 76 Loy Vaught	.05	.02	.01
☐ 77 Elden Campbell	.10	.05	.01
☐ 78 Cedric Ceballos	.10	.05	.01
☐ 79 Vlade Divac	.10	.05	.01
☐ 80 Eddie Jones	.20	.09	.03
☐ 81 Sedale Threatt	.05	.02	.01
☐ 82 Nick Van Exel	.20	.09	.03
☐ 83 Bimbo Coles	.05	.02	.01
☐ 84 Harold Miner	.05	.02	.01
☐ 85 Billy Owens	.05	.02	.01
☐ 86 Khalid Reeves	.05	.02	.01
☐ 87 Glen Rice	.10	.05	.01
☐ 88 Kevin Willis	.05	.02	.01
☐ 89 Vin Baker	.25	.11	.03
☐ 90 Marty Conlon	.05	.02	.01
☐ 91 Todd Day	.05	.02	.01
☐ 92 Eric Mobley	.05	.02	.01
☐ 93 Eric Murdock	.05	.02	.01
☐ 94 Glenn Robinson	.30	.14	.04
☐ 95 Winston Garland	.05	.02	.01
☐ 96 Tom Gugliotta	.10	.05	.01
☐ 97 Christian Laettner	.10	.05	.01
☐ 98 Isaiah Rider	.10	.05	.01
☐ 99 Sean Rooks	.05	.02	.01
☐ 100 Doug West	.05	.02	.01
☐ 101 Kenny Anderson	.10	.05	.01
☐ 102 Benoit Benjamin	.05	.02	.01
☐ 103 Derrick Coleman	.05	.02	.01
☐ 104 Kevin Edwards	.05	.02	.01
☐ 105 Armon Gilliam	.05	.02	.01
☐ 106 Chris Morris	.05	.02	.01

☐ 107	Patrick Ewing	.25	.11	.03
☐ 108	Derek Harper	.05	.02	.01
☐ 109	Anthony Mason	.10	.05	.01
☐ 110	Charles Oakley	.10	.05	.01
☐ 111	Charles Smith	.05	.02	.01
☐ 112	John Starks	.05	.02	.01
☐ 113	Monty Williams	.05	.02	.01
☐ 114	Nick Anderson	.10	.05	.01
☐ 115	Horace Grant	.10	.05	.01
☐ 116	Anfernee Hardaway	1.50	.70	.19
☐ 117	Shaquille O'Neal	1.25	.55	.16
☐ 118	Dennis Scott	.10	.05	.01
☐ 119	Brian Shaw	.05	.02	.01
☐ 120	Dana Barros	.05	.02	.01
☐ 121	Shawn Bradley	.10	.05	.01
☐ 122	Willie Burton	.05	.02	.01
☐ 123	Jeff Malone	.05	.02	.01
☐ 124	Clarence Weatherspoon	.05	.02	.01
☐ 125	Sharone Wright	.05	.02	.01
☐ 126	Charles Barkley	.40	.18	.05
☐ 127	A.C. Green	.10	.05	.01
☐ 128	Kevin Johnson	.10	.05	.01
☐ 129	Dan Majerle	.10	.05	.01
☐ 130	Danny Manning	.10	.05	.01
☐ 131	Elliot Perry	.05	.02	.01
☐ 132	Wesley Person	.10	.05	.01
☐ 133	Chris Dudley	.05	.02	.01
☐ 134	Clifford Robinson	.10	.05	.01
☐ 135	James Robinson	.05	.02	.01
☐ 136	Rod Strickland	.05	.02	.01
☐ 137	Otis Thorpe	.10	.05	.01
☐ 138	Buck Williams	.05	.02	.01
☐ 139	Brian Grant	.10	.05	.01
☐ 140	Olden Polynice	.05	.02	.01
☐ 141	Mitch Richmond	.20	.09	.03
☐ 142	Michael Smith	.05	.02	.01
☐ 143	Spud Webb	.10	.05	.01
☐ 144	Walt Williams	.10	.05	.01
☐ 145	Vinny Del Negro	.05	.02	.01
☐ 146	Sean Elliott	.10	.05	.01
☐ 147	Avery Johnson	.10	.05	.01
☐ 148	Chuck Person	.05	.02	.01
☐ 149	David Robinson	.50	.23	.06
☐ 150	Dennis Rodman	1.00	.45	.12
☐ 151	Kendall Gill	.05	.02	.01
☐ 152	Ervin Johnson	.05	.02	.01
☐ 153	Shawn Kemp	.75	.35	.09
☐ 154	Nate McMillan	.05	.02	.01
☐ 155	Gary Payton	.40	.18	.05
☐ 156	Detlef Schrempf	.10	.05	.01
☐ 157	Dontonio Wingfield	.05	.02	.01
☐ 158	David Benoit	.05	.02	.01
☐ 159	Jeff Hornacek	.10	.05	.01
☐ 160	Karl Malone	.25	.11	.03
☐ 161	Felton Spencer	.05	.02	.01
☐ 162	John Stockton	.25	.11	.03
☐ 163	Jamie Watson	.05	.02	.01
☐ 164	Rex Chapman	.05	.02	.01
☐ 165	Calbert Cheaney	.05	.02	.01
☐ 166	Juwan Howard	.60	.25	.07
☐ 167	Don MacLean	.05	.02	.01
☐ 168	Gheorghe Muresan	.10	.05	.01
☐ 169	Scott Skiles	.05	.02	.01
☐ 170	Chris Webber	.25	.11	.03
☐ 171	Lenny Wilkens CO	.10	.05	.01
☐ 172	Allan Bristow CO	.05	.02	.01
☐ 173	Phil Jackson CO	.10	.05	.01
☐ 174	Mike Fratello CO	.05	.02	.01
☐ 175	Dick Motta CO	.05	.02	.01
☐ 176	Bernie Bickerstaff CO	.05	.02	.01
☐ 177	Doug Collins CO	.10	.05	.01
☐ 178	Rick Adelman CO	.05	.02	.01
☐ 179	Rudy Tomjanovich CO	.10	.05	.01
☐ 180	Larry Brown CO	.10	.05	.01
☐ 181	Bill Fitch CO	.05	.02	.01
☐ 182	Del Harris CO	.05	.02	.01
☐ 183	Mike Dunleavy CO	.05	.02	.01
☐ 184	Bill Blair CO	.05	.02	.01
☐ 185	Butch Beard CO	.05	.02	.01
☐ 186	Pat Riley CO	.10	.05	.01
☐ 187	Brian Hill CO	.05	.02	.01
☐ 188	John Lucas CO	.10	.05	.01
☐ 189	Paul Westphal CO	.10	.05	.01
☐ 190	P.J. Carlesimo CO	.10	.05	.01
☐ 191	Garry St. Jean CO	.05	.02	.01
☐ 192	Bob Hill CO	.05	.02	.01
☐ 193	George Karl CO	.05	.02	.01
☐ 194	Brendan Malone CO	.05	.02	.01
☐ 195	Jerry Sloan CO	.10	.05	.01
☐ 196	Kevin Pritchard	15.00	6.75	1.85
☐ 197	Jim Lynam CO	.05	.02	.01
☐ 198	Brian Grant SS	.05	.02	.01
☐ 199	Grant Hill SS	.50	.23	.06
☐ 200	Juwan Howard SS	.30	.14	.04
☐ 201	Eddie Jones SS	.10	.05	.01
☐ 202	Jason Kidd SS	.30	.14	.04
☐ 203	Donyell Marshall SS	.05	.02	.01
☐ 204	Eric Montross SS	.05	.02	.01
☐ 205	Glenn Robinson SS	.15	.07	.02
☐ 206	Jalen Rose SS	.05	.02	.01
☐ 207	Sharone Wright SS	.05	.02	.01
☐ 208	Dana Barros MS	.05	.02	.01
☐ 209	Joe Dumars MS	.10	.05	.01
☐ 210	A.C. Green MS	.10	.05	.01
☐ 211	Grant Hill MS	.50	.23	.06
☐ 212	Karl Malone MS	.10	.05	.01
☐ 213	Reggie Miller MS	.15	.07	.02
☐ 214	Glen Rice MS	.05	.02	.01
☐ 215	John Stockton MS	.10	.05	.01
☐ 216	Lenny Wilkens MS	.05	.02	.01
☐ 217	Dominique Wilkins MS	.10	.05	.01
☐ 218	Kenny Anderson BB	.05	.02	.01
☐ 219	Mookie Blaylock BB	.05	.02	.01
☐ 220	Larry Johnson BB	.10	.05	.01
☐ 221	Shawn Kemp BB	.40	.18	.05
☐ 222	Toni Kukoc BB	.10	.05	.01
☐ 223	Jamal Mashburn BB	.05	.02	.01
☐ 224	Glen Rice BB	.05	.02	.01
☐ 225	Mitch Richmond BB	.05	.02	.01
☐ 226	Latrell Sprewell BB	.05	.02	.01
☐ 227	Rod Strickland BB	.05	.02	.01
☐ 228	Michael Adams PL	.05	.02	.01
	Darrick Martin			
☐ 229	Craig Ehlo PL	.05	.02	.01
	Jerome Harmon			
☐ 230	Mario Elie PL	.05	.02	.01
	George McCloud			
☐ 231	Anthony Mason PL	.05	.02	.01
	Chucky Brown			
☐ 232	John Starks PL	.05	.02	.01
	Tim Legler			
☐ 233	Muggsy Bogues CA	.05	.02	.01
☐ 234	Joe Dumars CA	.10	.05	.01
☐ 235	LaPhonso Ellis CA	.05	.02	.01
☐ 236	Patrick Ewing CA	.10	.05	.01
☐ 237	Grant Hill CA	.50	.23	.06
☐ 238	Kevin Johnson CA	.10	.05	.01
☐ 239	Dan Majerle CA	.10	.05	.01
☐ 240	Karl Malone CA	.10	.05	.01
☐ 241	Hakeem Olajuwon CA	.30	.14	.04
☐ 242	David Robinson CA	.25	.11	.03
☐ 243	Dana Barros TT	.05	.02	.01

□	#	Player			
□	244	Scott Burrell TT	.05	.02	.01
□	245	Reggie Miller TT	.15	.07	.02
□	246	Glen Rice TT	.05	.02	.01
□	247	John Stockton TT	.10	.05	.01
□	248	Checklist #1	.05	.02	.01
□	249	Checklist #2	.05	.02	.01
□	250	Checklist #3	.05	.02	.01
□	251	Alan Henderson	.15	.07	.02
□	252	Junior Burrough	.05	.02	.01
□	253	Eric Williams	.20	.09	.03
□	254	George Zidek	.15	.07	.02
□	255	Jason Caffey	.10	.05	.01
□	256	Donny Marshall	.05	.02	.01
□	257	Bob Sura	.20	.09	.03
□	258	Loren Meyer	.15	.07	.02
□	259	Cherokee Parks	.20	.09	.03
□	260	Antonio McDyess	1.00	.45	.12
□	261	Theo Ratliff	.20	.09	.03
□	262	Lou Roe	.05	.02	.01
□	263	Andrew DeClerq	.05	.02	.01
□	264	Joe Smith	1.25	.55	.16
□	265	Travis Best	.15	.07	.02
□	266	Brent Barry	.50	.23	.06
□	267	Frankie King	.05	.02	.01
□	268	Sasha Danilovic	.15	.07	.02
□	269	Kurt Thomas	.30	.14	.04
□	270	Shawn Respert	.20	.09	.03
□	271	Jerome Allen	.10	.05	.01
□	272	Kevin Garnett	3.00	1.35	.35
□	273	Ed O'Bannon	.40	.18	.05
□	274	David Vaughn	.05	.02	.01
□	275	Jerry Stackhouse	2.00	.90	.25
□	276	Mario Bennett	.05	.02	.01
□	277	Michael Finley	1.25	.55	.16
□	278	Randolph Childress	.05	.02	.01
□	279	Arvydas Sabonis	.75	.35	.09
□	280	Gary Trent	.20	.09	.03
□	281	Tyus Edney	.50	.23	.06
□	282	Corliss Williamson	.20	.09	.03
□	283	Cory Alexander	.05	.02	.01
□	284	Sherell Ford	.05	.02	.01
□	285	Jimmy King	.05	.02	.01
□	286	Damon Stoudamire	2.50	1.10	.30
□	287	Greg Ostertag	.05	.02	.01
□	288	Lawrence Moten	.05	.02	.01
		Vancouver Grizzlies			
□	289	Bryant Reeves	.60	.25	.07
□	290	Rasheed Wallace	.50	.23	.06
□	291	Spud Webb	.10	.05	.01
□	292	Dana Barros	.05	.02	.01
□	293	Rick Fox	.05	.02	.01
□	294	Kendall Gill	.05	.02	.01
□	295	Khalid Reeves	.05	.02	.01
□	296	Glen Rice	.10	.05	.01
□	297	Luc Longley	.05	.02	.01
□	298	Dennis Rodman Bulls	1.50	.70	.19
□	299	Dan Majerle	.10	.05	.01
□	300	Lorenzo Williams	.05	.02	.01
□	301	Dale Ellis	.05	.02	.01
□	302	Reggie Williams	.05	.02	.01
□	303	Otis Thorpe	.10	.05	.01
□	304	B.J. Armstrong	.05	.02	.01
□	305	Pete Chilcutt	.05	.02	.01
□	306	Mario Elie	.05	.02	.01
□	307	Antonio Davis	.05	.02	.01
□	308	Ricky Pierce	.05	.02	.01
□	309	Rodney Rogers	.05	.02	.01
□	310	Brian Williams	.05	.02	.01
□	311	Corie Blount	.05	.02	.01
□	312	George Lynch	.05	.02	.01
□	313	Alonzo Mourning	.25	.11	.03
□	314	Lee Mayberry	.05	.02	.01
□	315	Terry Porter	.05	.02	.01
□	316	P.J. Brown	.05	.02	.01
□	317	Hubert Davis	.05	.02	.01
□	318	Charlie Ward	.10	.05	.01
□	319	Jon Koncak	.05	.02	.01
□	320	Derrick Coleman	.05	.02	.01
□	321	Richard Dumas	.05	.02	.01
□	322	Vernon Maxwell	.05	.02	.01
□	323	Wayman Tisdale	.05	.02	.01
□	324	Dontonio Wingfield	.05	.02	.01
□	325	Tyrone Corbin	.05	.02	.01
□	326	Bobby Hurley	.05	.02	.01
□	327	Will Perdue	.05	.02	.01
□	328	J.R. Reid	.05	.02	.01
□	329	Hersey Hawkins	.05	.02	.01
□	330	Sam Perkins	.10	.05	.01
□	331	Adam Keefe	.05	.02	.01
□	332	Chris Morris	.05	.02	.01
□	333	Robert Pack	.05	.02	.01
□	334	M.L. Carr CO	.05	.02	.01
□	335	Pat Riley CO	.10	.05	.01
□	336	Don Nelson CO	.10	.05	.01
□	337	Brian Winters CO	.05	.02	.01
□	338	Willie Anderson ET	.05	.02	.01
□	339	Acie Earl ET	.05	.02	.01
□	340	Jimmy King ET	.05	.02	.01
□	341	Oliver Miller ET	.05	.02	.01
□	342	Tracy Murray ET	.05	.02	.01
□	343	Ed Pinckney ET	.05	.02	.01
□	344	Alvin Robertson ET	.05	.02	.01
□	345	Carlos Rogers ET	.05	.02	.01
□	346	John Salley ET	.05	.02	.01
□	347	Damon Stoudamire ET	1.00	.45	.12
□	348	Zan Tabak ET	.05	.02	.01
□	349	Greg Anthony ET	.05	.02	.01
□	350	Blue Edwards ET	.05	.02	.01
□	351	Kenny Gattison ET	.05	.02	.01
□	352	Antonio Harvey ET	.05	.02	.01
□	353	Chris King ET	.05	.02	.01
□	354	Darrick Martin ET	.05	.02	.01
□	355	Lawrence Moten ET	.05	.02	.01
□	356	Bryant Reeves ET	.25	.11	.03
□	357	Byron Scott ET	.10	.05	.01
□	358	Michael Jordan ES	1.50	.70	.19
□	359	Dikembe Mutombo ES	.10	.05	.01
□	360	Grant Hill ES	.50	.23	.06
□	361	Robert Horry ES	.05	.02	.01
□	362	Alonzo Mourning ES	.10	.05	.01
□	363	Vin Baker ES	.10	.05	.01
□	364	Isaiah Rider ES	.05	.02	.01
□	365	Charles Oakley ES	.05	.02	.01
□	366	Shaquille O'Neal ES	.60	.25	.07
□	367	Jerry Stackhouse ES	.75	.35	.09
□	368	Clarence Weatherspoon ES	.05	.02	.01
□	369	Charles Barkley ES	.20	.09	.03
□	370	Sean Elliott ES	.10	.05	.01
□	371	Shawn Kemp ES	.40	.18	.05
□	372	Chris Webber ES	.10	.05	.01
□	373	Spud Webb RH	.10	.05	.01
□	374	Muggsy Bogues RH	.10	.05	.01
□	375	Toni Kukoc RH	.10	.05	.01
□	376	Dennis Rodman Bulls RH	.75	.35	.09
□	377	Jamal Mashburn RH	.10	.05	.01
□	378	Jalen Rose RH	.05	.02	.01
□	379	Clyde Drexler RH	.10	.05	.01
□	380	Mark Jackson RH	.05	.02	.01
□	381	Cedric Ceballos RH	.10	.05	.01
□	382	Nick Van Exel RH	.10	.05	.01
□	383	John Starks RH	.05	.02	.01
□	384	Vernon Maxwell RH	.05	.02	.01

		MINT	NRMT	EXC
☐ 385	Shawn Kemp RH	.40	.18	.05
☐ 386	Gary Payton RH	.20	.09	.03
☐ 387	Karl Malone RH	.10	.05	.01
☐ 388	Mookie Blaylock WD	.10	.05	.01
☐ 389	Muggsy Bogues WD	.10	.05	.01
☐ 390	Jason Kidd WD	.30	.14	.04
☐ 391	Tim Hardaway WD	.10	.05	.01
☐ 392	Nick Van Exel WD	.10	.05	.01
☐ 393	Kenny Anderson WD	.10	.05	.01
☐ 394	Anfernee Hardaway WD	.75	.35	.09
☐ 395	Rod Strickland WD	.05	.02	.01
☐ 396	Avery Johnson WD	.05	.02	.01
☐ 397	John Stockton WD	.10	.05	.01
☐ 398	Grant Hill SPEC	.50	.23	.06
☐ 399	Checklist (251-367)	.05	.02	.01
☐ 400	Checklist (368-400/Ins.)	.05	.02	.01
☐ NNO	G.Hill Co-ROY Exch.	15.00	6.75	1.85
☐ NNO	G.Hill Sweepstakes	1.00	.45	.12
☐ NNO	Grant Hill Tribute	40.00	18.00	5.00

1995-96 Hoops Block Party

Randomly inserted into all first series packs at an approximate rate of one in two packs, these 25 standard-size cards highlight the top shot-blockers in the NBA. The fronts have a full-color action photo with a multi-colored, computer-generated background and the words "Block Party" at the top in gold-foil. The backs have a color photo on the left side with a similar background to the front with player information and statistics on the right.

		MINT	NRMT	EXC
COMPLETE SET (25)		5.00	2.20	.60
COMMON CARD (1-25)		.15	.07	.02
☐ 1	Oliver Miller	.15	.07	.02
☐ 2	Dennis Rodman	1.50	.70	.19
☐ 3	Scottie Pippen	1.25	.55	.16
☐ 4	Dikembe Mutombo	.25	.11	.03
☐ 5	Vlade Divac	.25	.11	.03
☐ 6	Brian Grant	.25	.11	.03
☐ 7	Alonzo Mourning	.40	.18	.05
☐ 8	Hakeem Olajuwon	1.00	.45	.12
☐ 9	Patrick Ewing	.40	.18	.05
☐ 10	Shawn Kemp	1.25	.55	.16
☐ 11	Vin Baker	.25	.11	.03

		MINT	NRMT	EXC
☐ 12	Horace Grant	.25	.11	.03
☐ 13	Dale Davis	.15	.07	.02
☐ 14	Juwan Howard	1.00	.45	.12
☐ 15	Eddie Jones	.30	.14	.04
☐ 16	Eric Montross	.15	.07	.02
☐ 17	Tyrone Hill	.15	.07	.02
☐ 18	Tom Gugliotta	.25	.11	.03
☐ 19	Shawn Bradley	.25	.11	.03
☐ 20	Dan Majerle	.25	.11	.03
☐ 21	Loy Vaught	.15	.07	.02
☐ 22	Donyell Marshall	.15	.07	.02
☐ 23	Chris Webber	.40	.18	.05
☐ 24	Derrick Coleman	.15	.07	.02
☐ 25	Walt Williams	.25	.11	.03

1995-96 Hoops Grant Hill Dunks/Slams

Cards D1-D5 were randomly inserted exclusively into one in every 36 first series 12-card hobby packs, while cards S1-S5 were randomly inserted exclusively into one in every 36 first series retail 12-card packs. All cards are foil-coated, featuring an assortion of Grant Hill dunking and slamming photos. The fronts each carry an oversized letter, so that cards D1-D5 spell out "DUNK!!!," and cards S1-S5 spell out "SLAM!". All cards are designed to be viewed through special Grant Hill 3-D glasses which were available through an on-wrapper offer.

		MINT	NRMT	EXC
COMPLETE SET (10)		50.00	22.00	6.25
COMMON SLAM (S1-S5)		6.00	2.70	.75
COMMON DUNK (D1-D5)		6.00	2.70	.75
☐ S1	S-Card	6.00	2.70	.75
☐ S2	L-Card	6.00	2.70	.75
☐ S3	A-Card	6.00	2.70	.75
☐ S4	M-Card	6.00	2.70	.75
☐ S5	!-Card	6.00	2.70	.75
☐ D1	D-Card	6.00	2.70	.75
☐ D2	U-Card	6.00	2.70	.75
☐ D3	N-Card	6.00	2.70	.75
☐ D4	K-Card	6.00	2.70	.75
☐ D5	!!!-Card	6.00	2.70	.75

1995-96 Hoops Grant's All-Rookies

Randomly inserted in all second series packs at a rate of one in 64, this 10-card standard-size set continues the tradition of the Magic's All-Rookies sets featured in earlier Hoops products. New spokesperson Grant Hill replaces Magic Johnson, picking 10 players who may follow in his own foot-steps. Hill is pictured alongside the featured rookie on the horizontal fronts. The left side of the card contains a silver hologram strip with "Top 10" cut out to give the card a 3-D look when viewed with the Grant Hill 3-D glasses. Backs carry another full color cutout shot of the player set against the borderless color background. The "Top 10" logo is once again placed on the back. The player's name is printed across the top in gold and a player profile is printed in white. The set is sequenced in alphabetical order by team.

	MINT	NRMT	EXC
COMPLETE SET (10)	90.00	40.00	11.00
COMMON CARD (AR1-AR10) ..	2.00	.90	.25
☐ AR1 Cherokee Parks	2.00	.90	.25
☐ AR2 Antonio McDyess	10.00	4.50	1.25
☐ AR3 Theo Ratliff	2.00	.90	.25
☐ AR4 Joe Smith	12.00	5.50	1.50
☐ AR5 Shawn Respert	2.00	.90	.25
☐ AR6 Kevin Garnett	30.00	13.50	3.70
☐ AR7 Ed O'Bannon	4.00	1.80	.50
☐ AR8 Jerry Stackhouse	20.00	9.00	2.50
☐ AR9 Damon Stoudamire...	25.00	11.00	3.10
☐ AR10 Rasheed Wallace.....	2.00	2.20	.60

1995-96 Hoops HoopStars

Randomly inserted in all second series packs at a rate of one in 16, this 12-card standard-size set presents top players on multi-colored cards featuring color foils for the HoopStars logo and player name. The set is sequenced in alphabetical order by team.

	MINT	NRMT	EXC
COMPLETE SET (12)	20.00	9.00	2.50
COMMON CARD (HS1-HS12)	.75	.35	.09
☐ HS1 Scottie Pippen	4.00	1.80	.50
☐ HS2 Jim Jackson	.75	.35	.09
☐ HS3 Antonio McDyess	2.50	1.10	.30
☐ HS4 Clyde Drexler	1.50	.70	.19
☐ HS5 Alonzo Mourning	1.25	.55	.16
☐ HS6 Glenn Robinson	1.50	.70	.19
☐ HS7 Patrick Ewing	1.25	.55	.16
☐ HS8 Anfernee Hardaway	8.00	3.60	1.00
☐ HS9 Shawn Kemp	4.00	1.80	.50
☐ HS10 Karl Malone	1.25	.55	.16
☐ HS11 Juwan Howard	3.00	1.35	.35
☐ HS12 Rasheed Wallace.....	1.25	.55	.16

1995-96 Hoops Hot List

Randomly inserted in second series hobby packs only at a rate of one in 32, this 10-card standard-size set features full-bleed fronts with a full-color player cutout set against a blue foil background. Player's name is printed vertically in copper foil on a purple foil strip. HOT is printed diagonally across the front. Backs feature a full-color action shot with the player's stats printed below the photo. The set is sequenced in alphabetical order by team.

	MINT	NRMT	EXC
COMPLETE SET (10)	70.00	32.00	8.75
COMMON CARD (1-10)	1.25	.55	.16
☐ 1 Michael Jordan	25.00	11.00	3.10
☐ 2 Jason Kidd....................	5.00	2.20	.60

☐ 3 Jamal Mashburn	1.25	.55	.16
☐ 4 Grant Hill	8.00	3.60	1.00
☐ 5 Joe Smith	5.00	2.20	.60
☐ 6 Hakeem Olajuwon	5.00	2.20	.60
☐ 7 Glenn Robinson	2.50	1.10	.30
☐ 8 Shaquille O'Neal	10.00	4.50	1.25
☐ 9 Jerry Stackhouse	8.00	3.60	1.00
☐ 10 David Robinson	4.00	1.80	.50

1995-96 Hoops
Number Crunchers

Randomly inserted into all first series packs at an approximate rate of one in two packs, these 25 standard-size cards highlight players that attained notable statistical achievements during the 1994-95 season. The fronts have a color-action photo with the player's number in a multi-color background and the word "Crunchers" spelled out on a tic-tac-toe board in the lower left corner in gold-foil. The backs have a color-action photo with a huge multi-colored ball in the background along with player information and statistics.

	MINT	NRMT	EXC
COMPLETE SET (25)	10.00	4.50	1.25
COMMON CARD (1-25)	.15	.07	.02

☐ 1 Michael Jordan	5.00	2.20	.60
☐ 2 Shaquille O'Neal	2.00	.90	.25
☐ 3 Grant Hill	1.50	.70	.19
☐ 4 Detlef Schrempf	.15	.07	.02
☐ 5 Kenny Anderson	.15	.07	.02
☐ 6 Anfernee Hardaway	2.50	1.10	.30
☐ 7 Latrell Sprewell	.15	.07	.02
☐ 8 Jamal Mashburn	.25	.11	.03
☐ 9 Nick Van Exel	.30	.14	.04
☐ 10 Charles Barkley	.60	.25	.07
☐ 11 Mitch Richmond	.15	.07	.02
☐ 12 David Robinson	.75	.35	.09
☐ 13 Gary Payton	.60	.25	.07
☐ 14 Rod Strickland	.15	.07	.02
☐ 15 Glenn Robinson	.50	.23	.06
☐ 16 Reggie Miller	.50	.23	.06
☐ 17 Karl Malone	.40	.18	.05
☐ 18 Jim Jackson	.50	.23	.06
☐ 19 Clyde Drexler	.50	.23	.06
☐ 20 Glen Rice	.15	.07	.02
☐ 21 Isaiah Rider	.15	.07	.02
☐ 22 Cedric Ceballos	.20	.09	.03

☐ 23 John Stockton	.40	.18	.05
☐ 24 Jason Kidd	1.00	.45	.12
☐ 25 Mookie Blaylock	.15	.07	.02

1995-96 Hoops
Power Palette

Randomly inserted in second series retail packs only at a rate of one in 32, this 10-card set is a parallel version of the Hoops SkyView insert. Unlike the acetate-centered SkyView cards, the more common Power Palette's feature metallic foil backgrounds.

	MINT	NRMT	EXC
COMPLETE SET (10)	75.00	34.00	9.50
COMMON CARD (1-10)	3.00	1.35	.35

☐ 1 Michael Jordan	30.00	13.50	3.70
☐ 2 Jason Kidd	6.00	2.70	.75
☐ 3 Grant Hill	10.00	4.50	1.25
☐ 4 Joe Smith	6.00	2.70	.75
☐ 5 Hakeem Olajuwon	6.00	2.70	.75
☐ 6 Glenn Robinson	3.00	1.35	.35
☐ 7 Anfernee Hardaway	15.00	6.75	1.85
☐ 8 Shaquille O'Neal	12.00	5.50	1.50
☐ 9 Jerry Stackhouse	10.00	4.50	1.25
☐ 10 Charles Barkley	4.00	1.80	.50

1995-96 Hoops
SkyView

Randomly inserted in all second series packs at a rate of one in 480, cards from this 10-card standard-size set are extra-thick and replace two basic issue cards in the pack. The front of the card presents a die-cut action photo over a multi-color plastic acetate window. The set is sequenced in alphabetical order by team.

	MINT	NRMT	EXC
COMPLETE SET (10)	150.00	70.00	19.00
COMMON CARD (SV1-SV10)	6.00	2.70	.75

		MINT	NRMT	EXC
☐ SV1	Michael Jordan	75.00	34.00	9.50
☐ SV2	Jason Kidd	12.00	5.50	1.50
☐ SV3	Grant Hill	20.00	9.00	2.50
☐ SV4	Joe Smith	12.00	5.50	1.50
☐ SV5	Hakeem Olajuwon	12.00	5.50	1.50
☐ SV6	Glenn Robinson	6.00	2.70	.75
☐ SV7	Anfernee Hardaway	30.00	13.50	3.70
☐ SV8	Shaquille O'Neal	25.00	11.00	3.10
☐ SV9	Jerry Stackhouse	20.00	9.00	2.50
☐ SV10	Charles Barkley	8.00	3.60	1.00

1995-96 Hoops Slamland

Inserted into all second series packs at a rate of one per pack, cards from this 50-card standard-size set showcase top stars printed over one of five different animated "Slamland" backgrounds. The card fronts feature the player's name, area of expertise and a distinctive foil-stamped Slamland designation. The set is sequenced in alphabetical order by team.

	MINT	NRMT	EXC
COMPLETE SET (50)	8.00	3.60	1.00
COMMON CARD (SL1-SL50)	.10	.05	.01

		MINT	NRMT	EXC
☐ SL1	Stacey Augmon	.10	.05	.01
☐ SL2	Steve Smith	.20	.09	.03
☐ SL3	Eric Montross	.10	.05	.01
☐ SL4	Dino Radja	.10	.05	.01
☐ SL5	Dell Curry	.10	.05	.01
☐ SL6	Larry Johnson	.30	.14	.04
☐ SL7	Scottie Pippen	1.00	.45	.12
☐ SL8	Dennis Rodman Bulls	2.00	.90	.25
☐ SL9	Tyrone Hill	.10	.05	.01
☐ SL10	Jim Jackson	.25	.11	.03
☐ SL11	Jamal Mashburn	.20	.09	.03
☐ SL12	Dikembe Mutombo	.20	.09	.03
☐ SL13	Joe Dumars	.20	.09	.03
☐ SL14	Grant Hill	1.25	.55	.16

		MINT	NRMT	EXC
☐ SL15	Allan Houston	.20	.09	.03
☐ SL16	Donyell Marshall	.10	.05	.01
☐ SL17	Latrell Sprewell	.20	.09	.03
☐ SL18	Sam Cassell	.20	.09	.03
☐ SL19	Hakeem Olajuwon	.75	.35	.09
☐ SL20	Reggie Miller	.40	.18	.05
☐ SL21	Loy Vaught	.10	.05	.01
☐ SL22	Vlade Divac	.20	.09	.03
☐ SL23	Eddie Jones	.25	.11	.03
☐ SL24	Alonzo Mourning	.30	.14	.04
☐ SL25	Kevin Willis	.10	.05	.01
☐ SL26	Vin Baker	.30	.14	.04
☐ SL27	Glenn Robinson	.40	.18	.05
☐ SL28	Tom Gugliotta	.20	.09	.03
☐ SL29	Kenny Anderson	.20	.09	.03
☐ SL30	Derrick Coleman	.10	.05	.01
☐ SL31	Patrick Ewing	.30	.14	.04
☐ SL32	John Starks	.10	.05	.01
☐ SL33	Dennis Scott	.20	.09	.03
☐ SL34	Jerry Stackhouse	2.00	.90	.25
☐ SL35	Charles Barkley	.50	.23	.06
☐ SL36	Kevin Johnson	.20	.09	.03
☐ SL37	Danny Manning	.20	.09	.03
☐ SL38	Clifford Robinson	.20	.09	.03
☐ SL39	Brian Grant	.20	.09	.03
☐ SL40	Mitch Richmond	.25	.11	.03
☐ SL41	Walt Williams	.20	.09	.03
☐ SL42	David Robinson	.60	.25	.07
☐ SL43	Gary Payton	.50	.23	.06
☐ SL44	Detlef Schrempf	.20	.09	.03
☐ SL45	Damon Stoudamire	2.50	1.10	.30
☐ SL46	Karl Malone	.30	.14	.04
☐ SL47	John Stockton	.30	.14	.04
☐ SL48	Bryant Reeves	.60	.25	.07
☐ SL49	Juwan Howard	.75	.35	.09
☐ SL50	Chris Webber	.40	.18	.05

1995-96 Hoops Top Ten

Randomly inserted into all first series packs at an approximate rate of one in 12, these 10 standard-size cards feature a selection of former lottery picks that are on their way to or have already attained great success in the NBA. The fronts are laid out horizontally with a color-action photo and a wide strip down the left side that reads "Top" with 10 in the middle of the O. The background on each card is different and has a multi-colored cloudy look. The backs have the same background as the front with a color-action photo and player information at the top.

	MINT	NRMT	EXC
COMPLETE SET (10)	40.00	18.00	5.00
COMMON CARD (AR1-AR10)..	1.00	.45	.12

		MINT	NRMT	EXC
☐ AR1	Shaquille O'Neal.......	8.00	3.60	1.00
☐ AR2	Grant Hill.................	6.00	2.70	.75
☐ AR3	Chris Webber.............	1.50	.70	.19
☐ AR4	Jamal Mashburn........	1.00	.45	.12
☐ AR5	Anfernee Hardaway...	10.00	4.50	1.25
☐ AR6	Alonzo Mourning.......	1.50	.70	.19
☐ AR7	Michael Jordan..........	20.00	9.00	2.50
☐ AR8	Charles Barkley.........	2.50	1.10	.30
☐ AR9	Glenn Robinson.........	2.00	.90	.25
☐ AR10	Jason Kidd................	4.00	1.80	.50

1996-97 Hoops

The 1996-97 Hoops set will be issued in two series. The first series has a total of 200 cards. First series 9-card packs carry a suggested retail price of $1.29 each. Card fronts contain a full photo action shot with the player's name written in gold foil diagonally across the bottom right. Card backs have a small photo of the player in the top left corner with complete college and pro statistics as well as biographical information. The cards are grouped alphabetically within team order. The set contains the topical subset: The Big Finish (173-187). No Rookie Cards are included in the first series set. Also, a Grant Hill Z-Force Preview card was randomly inserted into series one packs at a rate of one in 360 packs. It previewed the inaugural edition of SkyBox Z-Force.

	MINT	NRMT	EXC
COMPLETE SERIES 1 (200)...	12.00	5.50	1.50
COMMON CARD (1-200)	.05	.02	.01

☐ 1	Stacey Augmon................	.10	.05	.01
☐ 2	Mookie Blaylock...............	.10	.05	.01
☐ 3	Alan Henderson...............	.05	.02	.01
☐ 4	Christian Laettner............	.10	.05	.01
☐ 5	Grant Long.......................	.05	.02	.01
☐ 6	Steve Smith......................	.10	.05	.01
☐ 7	Dana Barros.....................	.05	.02	.01
☐ 8	Todd Day..........................	.05	.02	.01
☐ 9	Rick Fox...........................	.05	.02	.01
☐ 10	Eric Montross...................	.05	.02	.01
☐ 11	Dino Radja........................	.10	.05	.01
☐ 12	Eric Williams....................	.05	.02	.01
☐ 13	Kenny Anderson................	.10	.05	.01
☐ 14	Scott Burrell.....................	.05	.02	.01
☐ 15	Dell Curry........................	.05	.02	.01
☐ 16	Matt Geiger......................	.05	.02	.01
☐ 17	Larry Johnson..................	.25	.11	.03
☐ 18	Glen Rice.........................	.10	.05	.01
☐ 19	Ron Harper.......................	.10	.05	.01
☐ 20	Michael Jordan.................	3.00	1.35	.35
☐ 21	Steve Kerr........................	.05	.02	.01
☐ 22	Toni Kukoc.......................	.10	.05	.01
☐ 23	Luc Longley......................	.05	.02	.01
☐ 24	Scottie Pippen..................	.75	.35	.09
☐ 25	Dennis Rodman................	1.25	.55	.16
☐ 26	Terrell Brandon................	.10	.05	.01
☐ 27	Danny Ferry......................	.05	.02	.01
☐ 28	Tyrone Hill.......................	.05	.02	.01
☐ 29	Chris Mills........................	.05	.02	.01
☐ 30	Bobby Phills.....................	.05	.02	.01
☐ 31	Bob Sura..........................	.05	.02	.01
☐ 32	Tony Dumas.....................	.05	.02	.01
☐ 33	Jim Jackson.....................	.10	.05	.01
☐ 34	Popeye Jones...................	.05	.02	.01
☐ 35	Jason Kidd.......................	.50	.23	.06
☐ 36	Jamal Mashburn...............	.10	.05	.01
☐ 37	George McCloud...............	.05	.02	.01
☐ 38	Cherokee Parks................	.05	.02	.01
☐ 39	Mahmoud Abdul-Rauf.......	.05	.02	.01
☐ 40	LaPhonso Ellis.................	.05	.02	.01
☐ 41	Antonio McDyess..............	.30	.14	.04
☐ 42	Dikembe Mutombo............	.10	.05	.01
☐ 43	Jalen Rose.......................	.05	.02	.01
☐ 44	Bryant Stith.....................	.05	.02	.01
☐ 45	Joe Dumars......................	.10	.05	.01
☐ 46	Grant Hill........................	.75	.35	.09
☐ 47	Allan Houston..................	.10	.05	.01
☐ 48	Lindsey Hunter.................	.05	.02	.01
☐ 49	Terry Mills.......................	.05	.02	.01
☐ 50	Theo Ratliff......................	.05	.02	.01
☐ 51	Otis Thorpe......................	.05	.02	.01
☐ 52	B.J. Armstrong.................	.05	.02	.01
☐ 53	Donyell Marshall..............	.05	.02	.01
☐ 54	Chris Mullin.....................	.05	.02	.01
☐ 55	Joe Smith.........................	.40	.18	.05
☐ 56	Rony Seikaly.....................	.05	.02	.01
☐ 57	Latrell Sprewell...............	.10	.05	.01
☐ 58	Mark Bryant.....................	.05	.02	.01
☐ 59	Sam Cassell......................	.10	.05	.01
☐ 60	Clyde Drexler....................	.30	.14	.04
☐ 61	Mario Elie........................	.05	.02	.01
☐ 62	Robert Horry.....................	.10	.05	.01
☐ 63	Hakeem Olajuwon.............	.60	.25	.07
☐ 64	Travis Best.......................	.05	.02	.01
☐ 65	Antonio Davis...................	.05	.02	.01
☐ 66	Mark Jackson....................	.05	.02	.01
☐ 67	Derrick McKey..................	.05	.02	.01
☐ 68	Reggie Miller....................	.30	.14	.04
☐ 69	Rik Smits..........................	.10	.05	.01
☐ 70	Brent Barry......................	.15	.07	.02
☐ 71	Terry Dehere....................	.05	.02	.01
☐ 72	Pooh Richardson...............	.05	.02	.01
☐ 73	Rodney Rodgers................	.05	.02	.01
☐ 74	Loy Vaught.......................	.10	.05	.01
☐ 75	Brian Williams..................	.05	.02	.01
☐ 76	Elden Campbell................	.10	.05	.01
☐ 77	Cedric Ceballos................	.10	.05	.01
☐ 78	Vlade Divac......................	.10	.05	.01
☐ 79	Eddie Jones......................	.15	.07	.02
☐ 80	Anthony Peeler.................	.05	.02	.01
☐ 81	Nick Van Exel...................	.15	.07	.02
☐ 82	Predrag Danilovic.............	.05	.02	.01
☐ 83	Tim Hardaway...................	.10	.05	.01
☐ 84	Alonzo Mourning	.25	.11	.03

☐ 85 Kurt Thomas	.05	.02	.01
☐ 86 Walt Williams	.05	.02	.01
☐ 87 Vin Baker	.20	.09	.03
☐ 88 Sherman Douglas	.05	.02	.01
☐ 89 Johnny Newman	.05	.02	.01
☐ 90 Shawn Respert	.05	.02	.01
☐ 91 Glenn Robinson	.25	.11	.03
☐ 92 Kevin Garnett	1.00	.45	.12
☐ 93 Tom Gugliotta	.10	.05	.01
☐ 94 Andrew Lang	.05	.02	.01
☐ 95 Sam Mitchell	.05	.02	.01
☐ 96 Isaiah Rider	.10	.05	.01
☐ 97 Shawn Bradley	.10	.05	.01
☐ 98 P.J. Brown	.05	.02	.01
☐ 99 Chris Childs	.05	.02	.01
☐ 100 Armon Gilliam	.05	.02	.01
☐ 101 Ed O'Bannon	.05	.02	.01
☐ 102 Jayson Williams	.05	.02	.01
☐ 103 Hubert Davis	.05	.02	.01
☐ 104 Patrick Ewing	.25	.11	.03
☐ 105 Anthony Mason	.05	.02	.01
☐ 106 Charles Oakley	.05	.02	.01
☐ 107 John Starks	.10	.05	.01
☐ 108 Charlie Ward	.05	.02	.01
☐ 109 Nick Anderson	.10	.05	.01
☐ 110 Horace Grant	.10	.05	.01
☐ 111 Anfernee Hardaway	1.50	.70	.19
☐ 112 Shaquille O'Neal	1.25	.55	.16
☐ 113 Dennis Scott	.10	.05	.01
☐ 114 Brian Shaw	.05	.02	.01
☐ 115 Derrick Coleman	.10	.05	.01
☐ 116 Vernon Maxwell	.05	.02	.01
☐ 117 Trevor Ruffin	.05	.02	.01
☐ 118 Jerry Stackhouse	.60	.25	.07
☐ 119 Clarence Weatherspoon	.10	.05	.01
☐ 120 Charles Barkley	.40	.18	.05
☐ 121 Michael Finley	.40	.18	.05
☐ 122 A.C. Green	.05	.02	.01
☐ 123 Kevin Johnson	.10	.05	.01
☐ 124 Danny Manning	.05	.02	.01
☐ 125 Wesley Person	.05	.02	.01
☐ 126 John Williams	.05	.02	.01
☐ 127 Harvey Grant	.05	.02	.01
☐ 128 Aaron McKie	.05	.02	.01
☐ 129 Clifford Robinson	.10	.05	.01
☐ 130 Arvydas Sabonis	.25	.11	.03
☐ 131 Rod Strickland	.10	.05	.01
☐ 132 Gary Trent	.05	.02	.01
☐ 133 Tyus Edney	.15	.07	.02
☐ 134 Brian Grant	.05	.02	.01
☐ 135 Billy Owens	.05	.02	.01
☐ 136 Olden Polynice	.05	.02	.01
☐ 137 Mitch Richmond	.20	.09	.03
☐ 138 Corliss Williamson	.05	.02	.01
☐ 139 Vinny Del Negro	.05	.02	.01
☐ 140 Sean Elliott	.10	.05	.01
☐ 141 Avery Johnson	.05	.02	.01
☐ 142 Chuck Person	.05	.02	.01
☐ 143 David Robinson	.50	.23	.06
☐ 144 Charles Smith	.05	.02	.01
☐ 145 Sherell Ford	.05	.02	.01
☐ 146 Hersey Hawkins	.10	.05	.01
☐ 147 Shawn Kemp	.75	.35	.09
☐ 148 Nate McMillan	.05	.02	.01
☐ 149 Gary Payton	.30	.14	.04
☐ 150 Detlef Schrempf	.10	.05	.01
☐ 151 Oliver Miller	.05	.02	.01
☐ 152 Tracy Murray	.05	.02	.01
☐ 153 Carlos Rogers	.05	.02	.01
☐ 154 Damon Stoudamire	.75	.35	.09
☐ 155 Zan Tabak	.05	.02	.01

☐ 156 Sharone Wright	.05	.02	.01
☐ 157 Antoine Carr	.05	.02	.01
☐ 158 Jeff Hornacek	.10	.05	.01
☐ 159 Adam Keefe	.05	.02	.01
☐ 160 Karl Malone	.25	.11	.03
☐ 161 Chris Morris	.05	.02	.01
☐ 162 John Stockton	.25	.11	.03
☐ 163 Greg Anthony	.05	.02	.01
☐ 164 Blue Edwards	.05	.02	.01
☐ 165 Chris King	.05	.02	.01
☐ 166 Lawrence Moten	.05	.02	.01
☐ 167 Bryant Reeves	.20	.09	.03
☐ 168 Byron Scott	.05	.02	.01
☐ 169 Calbert Cheaney	.05	.02	.01
☐ 170 Juwan Howard	.50	.23	.06
☐ 171 Tim Legler	.05	.02	.01
☐ 172 Gheorghe Muresan	.10	.05	.01
☐ 173 Rasheed Wallace	.15	.07	.02
☐ 174 Chris Webber	.20	.09	.03
☐ 175 Steve Smith BF	.05	.02	.01
☐ 176 Michael Jordan BF	1.50	.70	.19
☐ 177 Scottie Pippen BF	.40	.18	.05
☐ 178 Dennis Rodman BF	.60	.25	.07
☐ 179 Allan Houston BF	.10	.05	.01
☐ 180 Hakeem Olajuwon BF	.30	.14	.04
☐ 181 Patrick Ewing BF	.10	.05	.01
☐ 182 Anfernee Hardaway BF	.75	.35	.09
☐ 183 Shaquille O'Neal BF	.60	.25	.07
☐ 184 Charles Barkley BF	.20	.09	.03
☐ 185 Arvydas Sabonis BF	.05	.02	.01
☐ 186 David Robinson BF	.25	.11	.03
☐ 187 Shawn Kemp BF	.40	.18	.05
☐ 188 Gary Payton BF	.15	.07	.02
☐ 189 Karl Malone BF	.10	.05	.01
☐ 190 Kenny Anderson PLA	.05	.02	.01
☐ 191 Toni Kukoc PLA	.05	.02	.01
☐ 192 Brent Barry PLA	.05	.02	.01
☐ 193 Cedric Ceballos PLA	.05	.02	.01
☐ 194 Shawn Bradley PLA	.05	.02	.01
☐ 195 Charles Oakley PLA	.05	.02	.01
☐ 196 Dennis Scott PLA	.05	.02	.01
☐ 197 Clifford Robinson PLA	.05	.02	.01
☐ 198 Mitch Richmond PLA	.10	.05	.01
☐ 199 Checklist	.05	.02	.01
☐ 200 Checklist	.05	.02	.01
☐ NNO G.Hill Z-Force Preview	20.00	9.00	2.50

1996-97 Hoops Silver

Inserted at a rate of two per special retail box, and one per special retail pack, this set is a semi-parallel of the 200-card basic set even though the actual number of cards in the Silver set is 98. Card fronts are iden-

*tical to the regular issue except they have
the player's name in silver foil rather than
gold.*

		MINT	NRMT	EXC
	COMPLETE SERIES 1 (98)	40.00	18.00	5.00
	COMMON CARD (1-98)	.20	.09	.03
☐ 1	Stacey Augmon	.20	.09	.03
☐ 2	Mookie Blaylock	.30	.14	.04
☐ 3	Alan Henderson	.20	.09	.03
☐ 4	Christian Laettner	.30	.14	.04
☐ 5	Grant Long	.20	.09	.03
☐ 6	Steve Smith	.30	.14	.04
☐ 7	Dana Barros	.20	.09	.03
☐ 8	Todd Day	.20	.09	.03
☐ 9	Rick Fox	.20	.09	.03
☐ 10	Eric Montross	.20	.09	.03
☐ 11	Dino Radja	.30	.14	.04
☐ 12	Eric Williams	.20	.09	.03
☐ 13	Kenny Anderson	.30	.14	.04
☐ 14	Scott Burrell	.20	.09	.03
☐ 15	Dell Curry	.20	.09	.03
☐ 16	Matt Geiger	.20	.09	.03
☐ 17	Larry Johnson	.75	.35	.10
☐ 18	Glen Rice	.40	.18	.05
☐ 19	Ron Harper	.30	.14	.04
☐ 20	Michael Jordan	10.00	4.50	1.25
☐ 21	Steve Kerr	.30	.14	.04
☐ 22	Toni Kukoc	.40	.18	.05
☐ 23	Luc Longley	.30	.14	.04
☐ 24	Scottie Pippen	2.50	1.10	.30
☐ 25	Dennis Rodman	4.00	1.80	.50
☐ 26	Terrell Brandon	.40	.18	.05
☐ 27	Danny Ferry	.20	.09	.03
☐ 28	Tyrone Hill	.20	.09	.03
☐ 29	Chris Mills	.20	.09	.03
☐ 30	Bobby Phills	.20	.09	.03
☐ 31	Bob Sura	.20	.09	.03
☐ 32	Tony Dumas	.20	.09	.03
☐ 33	Jim Jackson	.40	.18	.05
☐ 34	Popeye Jones	.20	.09	.03
☐ 35	Jason Kidd	1.50	.70	.19
☐ 36	Jamal Mashburn	.20	.09	.03
☐ 37	George McCloud	.20	.09	.03
☐ 38	Cherokee Parks	.20	.09	.03
☐ 39	Mahmoud Abdul-Rauf	.20	.09	.03
☐ 40	LaPhonso Ellis	.20	.09	.03
☐ 41	Antonio McDyess	1.00	.45	.13
☐ 42	Dikembe Mutombo	.40	.18	.05
☐ 43	Jalen Rose	.20	.09	.03
☐ 44	Bryant Stith	.20	.09	.03
☐ 45	Joe Dumars	.40	.18	.05
☐ 46	Grant Hill	2.50	1.10	.30
☐ 47	Allan Houston	.40	.18	.05
☐ 48	Lindsey Hunter	.20	.09	.03
☐ 49	Terry Mills	.20	.09	.03
☐ 50	Theo Ratliff	.20	.09	.03
☐ 51	Otis Thorpe	.30	.14	.04
☐ 52	B.J. Armstrong	.20	.09	.03
☐ 53	Donyell Marshall	.20	.09	.03
☐ 54	Chris Mullin	.30	.14	.04
☐ 55	Joe Smith	1.25	.55	.15
☐ 56	Rony Seikaly	.20	.09	.03
☐ 57	Latrell Sprewell	.40	.18	.05
☐ 58	Mark Bryant	.20	.09	.03
☐ 59	Sam Cassell	.30	.14	.04
☐ 60	Clyde Drexler	1.00	.45	.13
☐ 61	Mario Elie	.20	.09	.03
☐ 62	Robert Horry	.40	.18	.05
☐ 63	Travis Best	.20	.09	.03
☐ 64	Antonio Davis	.20	.09	.03
☐ 65	Mark Jackson	.20	.09	.03
☐ 66	Derrick McKey	.20	.09	.03
☐ 67	Reggie Miller	1.00	.45	.13
☐ 68	Rik Smits	.40	.18	.05
☐ 69	Brent Barry	.50	.22	.06
☐ 70	Terry Dehere	.20	.09	.03
☐ 71	Pooh Richardson	.20	.09	.03
☐ 72	Rodney Rogers	.20	.09	.03
☐ 73	Loy Vaught	.30	.14	.04
☐ 74	Brian Williams	.20	.09	.03
☐ 75	Vin Baker	.60	.27	.08
☐ 76	Sherman Douglas	.20	.09	.03
☐ 77	Johnny Newman	.20	.09	.03
☐ 78	Shawn Respert	.20	.09	.03
☐ 79	Glenn Robinson	.75	.35	.10
☐ 80	Kevin Garnett	3.00	1.35	.40
☐ 81	Tom Gugliotta	.40	.18	.05
☐ 82	Andrew Lang	.20	.09	.03
☐ 83	Sam Mitchell	.20	.09	.03
☐ 84	Isaiah Rider	.30	.14	.04
☐ 85	Hubert Davis	.20	.09	.03
☐ 86	Patrick Ewing	.75	.35	.10
☐ 87	Anthony Mason	.20	.09	.03
☐ 88	Charles Oakley	.20	.09	.03
☐ 89	John Starks	.20	.09	.03
☐ 90	Charlie Ward	.20	.09	.03
☐ 91	Nick Anderson	.30	.14	.04
☐ 92	Charles Barkley	1.25	.55	.15
☐ 93	Michael Finley	1.25	.55	.15
☐ 94	A.C. Green	.30	.14	.04
☐ 95	Kevin Johnson	.40	.18	.05
☐ 96	Danny Manning	.30	.14	.04
☐ 97	Wesley Person	.20	.09	.03
☐ 98	John Williams	.20	.09	.03

1996-97 Hoops
Head to Head

*Randomly inserted at a rate of one in 24
packs, this 10-card set features dual-player
cards of either teammates or young players. Card fronts contain action photos of
both players and the logo "Head to Head"
in gold foil at the bottom of the card. In
addition, the logo and both of the player's
first names are treated with a diamond-like
element. Card backs are divided into four
quadrants with two of them featuring action
shots and the other two featuring a brief
commentary on each player. Card backs
are numbered with a "HH" prefix.*

	MINT	NRMT	EXC
COMPLETE SET (10)	70.00	32.00	8.75
COMMON PAIR (HH1-HH10)	3.00	1.35	.35
☐ HH1 Larry Johnson Glenn Rice	3.00	1.35	.35
☐ HH2 Michael Jordan Scottie Pippen	30.00	13.50	3.70
☐ HH3 Jason Kidd Grant Hill	10.00	4.50	1.25
☐ HH4 Clyde Drexler Hakeem Olajuwon	8.00	3.60	1.00
☐ HH5 Vin Baker Glenn Robinson	4.00	1.80	.50
☐ HH6 Anfernee Hardaway Shaquille O'Neal	20.00	9.00	2.50
☐ HH7 Antonio McDyess Jerry Stackhouse	8.00	3.60	1.00
☐ HH8 Sean Elliott David Robinson	5.00	2.20	.60
☐ HH9 Joe Smith Damon Stoudamire	8.00	3.60	1.00
☐ HH10 Karl Malone John Stockton	4.00	1.80	.50

1996-97 Hoops HIPnotized

Randomly inserted at a rate of one in four packs, this 20-card set features some of the top players in the game. Card fronts are full bleed action shots with a swirling background. The logo "HIPnotized" and the player's last name are in gold foil. Card backs are horizontal with statistical and biographical information as well as a having a brief commentary next to the photo. Cards are numbered with a "H" prefix.

	MINT	NRMT	EXC
COMPLETE SET (20)	15.00	6.75	1.85
COMMON CARD (H1-H20)	.30	.14	.04
☐ H1 Steve Smith	.60	.25	.07
☐ H2 Dana Barros	.30	.14	.04
☐ H3 Larry Johnson	.75	.35	.09
☐ H4 Dennis Rodman	4.00	1.80	.50
☐ H5 Terrell Brandon	.60	.25	.07
☐ H6 Jason Kidd	1.50	.70	.19
☐ H7 Grant Hill	2.50	1.10	.30
☐ H8 Clyde Drexler	1.00	.45	.12
☐ H9 Reggie Miller	1.00	.45	.12
☐ H10 Alonzo Mourning	.75	.35	.09
☐ H11 Glenn Robinson	.75	.35	.09
☐ H12 Patrick Ewing	.75	.35	.09
☐ H13 Shaquille O'Neal	4.00	1.80	.50
☐ H14 Jerry Stackhouse	2.00	.90	.25
☐ H15 Charles Barkley	1.25	.55	.16
☐ H16 Clifford Robinson	.60	.25	.07
☐ H17 Mitch Richmond	.60	.25	.07
☐ H18 David Robinson	1.50	.70	.19
☐ H19 Gary Payton	1.00	.45	.12
☐ H20 Juwan Howard	1.50	.70	.19

1996-97 Hoops Rookie Headliners

Randomly inserted at a rate of one in 72 hobby packs, this 10-card set focuses on some of the best rookies from the 1995-96 class. Card fronts are designed similar to a game ticket with both the left and right borders in gold foil. The action shot of the player is located between the two borders and the player's last name is in gold foil on top of the photo. Card backs have a shot of the player in the middle of the card against a light gold background along with a brief commentary on the player. The player's rookie statistics are located along the left border. Card backs are numbered as "X of 10".

	MINT	NRMT	EXC
COMPLETE SET (10)	125.00	55.00	15.50
COMMON CARD (1-10)	6.00	2.70	.75
☐ 1 Antonio McDyess	12.00	5.50	1.50
☐ 2 Joe Smith	15.00	6.75	1.85
☐ 3 Brent Barry	6.00	2.70	.75
☐ 4 Kevin Garnett	40.00	18.00	5.00
☐ 5 Jerry Stackhouse	25.00	11.00	3.10
☐ 6 Michael Finley	15.00	6.75	1.85
☐ 7 Arvydas Sabonis	10.00	4.50	1.25
☐ 8 Tyus Edney	6.00	2.70	.75
☐ 9 Damon Stoudamire	30.00	13.50	3.70
☐ 10 Bryant Reeves	8.00	3.60	1.00

1996-97 Hoops Superfeats

Randomly inserted at a rate of one in 36 retail packs, this 10-card set features play-

ers who had super "feats" during the 1995-96 NBA season. Card fronts feature a colorful background with a full color action shot of the player on top. The player's name and the logo "Superfeats" are treated with gold foil. Card backs feature another action shot of the player and a brief commentary on the extraordinary achievements the player had the previous season. Card backs are also numbered as "X of 10".

	MINT	NRMT	EXC
COMPLETE SET (10)	90.00	40.00	11.00
COMMON CARD (1-10)	2.00	.90	.25
☐ 1 Michael Jordan	40.00	18.00	5.00
☐ 2 Jason Kidd	6.00	2.70	.75
☐ 3 Grant Hill	10.00	4.50	1.25
☐ 4 Hakeem Olajuwon	8.00	3.60	1.00
☐ 5 Alonzo Mourning	3.00	1.35	.35
☐ 6 Anthony Mason	2.00	.90	.25
☐ 7 Anfernee Hardaway	20.00	9.00	2.50
☐ 8 Jerry Stackhouse	8.00	3.60	1.00
☐ 9 Shawn Kemp	10.00	4.50	1.25
☐ 10 Damon Stoudamire	10.00	4.50	1.25

1993-94 Jam Session

This 240-card set was issued in 1993 by Fleer and features oversized cards measuring approximately 2 1/2" by 4 3/4". Cards were issued in 12-card packs (36 per box) with a suggested retail pack price of 1.59. One insert card is included in every pack. The full-bleed fronts feature glossy color action player photos. Across the bottom edge of the picture appears a team color-coded bar with the player's name, position and team. The NBA Jam Session logo is superposed on the lower right corner. The backs are divided in half vertically with the left side carrying a second action shot and on the right side a panel with a background that fades from green to white. On the panel appears biography, career highlights, statistics and team logo. The cards are numbered on the back and checklisted below alphabetically within and according to teams. Rookie Cards of note include Anfernee Hardaway, Jamal Mashburn and Chris Webber.

	MINT	NRMT	EXC
COMPLETE SET (240)	30.00	13.50	3.70
COMMON CARD (1-240)	.10	.05	.01
☐ 1 Stacey Augmon	.15	.07	.02
☐ 2 Mookie Blaylock	.15	.07	.02
☐ 3 Doug Edwards	.10	.05	.01
☐ 4 Duane Ferrell	.10	.05	.01
☐ 5 Paul Graham	.10	.05	.01
☐ 6 Adam Keefe	.10	.05	.01
☐ 7 Jon Koncak	.10	.05	.01
☐ 8 Dominique Wilkins	.20	.09	.03
☐ 9 Kevin Willis	.10	.05	.01
☐ 10 Alaa Abdelnaby	.10	.05	.01
☐ 11 Dee Brown	.10	.05	.01
☐ 12 Sherman Douglas	.10	.05	.01
☐ 13 Rick Fox	.10	.05	.01
☐ 14 Kevin Gamble	.10	.05	.01
☐ 15 Xavier McDaniel	.10	.05	.01
☐ 16 Robert Parish	.20	.09	.03
☐ 17 Muggsy Bogues	.15	.07	.02
☐ 18 Scott Burrell	.20	.09	.03
☐ 19 Dell Curry	.10	.05	.01
☐ 20 Kenny Gattison	.10	.05	.01
☐ 21 Hersey Hawkins	.10	.05	.01
☐ 22 Eddie Johnson	.10	.05	.01
☐ 23 Larry Johnson	.60	.25	.07
☐ 24 Alonzo Mourning	.75	.35	.09
☐ 25 Johnny Newman	.10	.05	.01
☐ 26 David Wingate	.10	.05	.01
☐ 27 B.J. Armstrong	.10	.05	.01
☐ 28 Corie Blount	.10	.05	.01
☐ 29 Bill Cartwright	.10	.05	.01
☐ 30 Horace Grant	.20	.09	.03
☐ 31 Stacey King	.10	.05	.01
☐ 32 John Paxson	.15	.07	.02
☐ 33 Michael Jordan	6.00	2.70	.75
☐ 34 Scottie Pippen	1.50	.70	.19
☐ 35 Scott Williams	.10	.05	.01
☐ 36 Terrell Brandon	.20	.09	.03
☐ 37 Brad Daugherty	.10	.05	.01
☐ 38 Danny Ferry	.10	.05	.01
☐ 39 Tyrone Hill	.10	.05	.01
☐ 40 Chris Mills	.75	.35	.09
☐ 41 Larry Nance	.10	.05	.01
☐ 42 Mark Price	.10	.05	.01
☐ 43 Gerald Wilkins	.10	.05	.01
☐ 44 John Williams	.10	.05	.01
☐ 45 Terry Davis	.10	.05	.01
☐ 46 Derek Harper	.15	.07	.02
☐ 47 Donald Hodge	.10	.05	.01
☐ 48 Jim Jackson	.60	.25	.07
☐ 49 Jamal Mashburn	1.25	.55	.16
☐ 50 Sean Rooks	.10	.05	.01
☐ 51 Doug Smith	.10	.05	.01
☐ 52 Mahmoud Abdul-Rauf	.20	.09	.03

☐ 53 Kevin Brooks	.10	.05	.01
☐ 54 LaPhonso Ellis	.10	.05	.01
☐ 55 Mark Macon	.10	.05	.01
☐ 56 Dikembe Mutombo	.20	.09	.03
☐ 57 Rodney Rogers	.20	.09	.03
☐ 58 Bryant Stith	.10	.05	.01
☐ 59 Reggie Williams	.10	.05	.01
☐ 60 Joe Dumars	.20	.09	.03
☐ 61 Sean Elliott	.20	.09	.03
☐ 62 Bill Laimbeer	.15	.07	.02
☐ 63 Terry Mills	.10	.05	.01
☐ 64 Olden Polynice	.10	.05	.01
☐ 65 Alvin Robertson	.10	.05	.01
☐ 66 Isiah Thomas	.30	.14	.04
☐ 67 Victor Alexander	.10	.05	.01
☐ 68 Chris Gatling	.10	.05	.01
☐ 69 Tim Hardaway	.20	.09	.03
☐ 70 Byron Houston	.10	.05	.01
☐ 71 Sarunas Marciulionis	.10	.05	.01
☐ 72 Chris Mullin	.15	.07	.02
☐ 73 Billy Owens	.10	.05	.01
☐ 74 Latrell Sprewell	.40	.18	.05
☐ 75 Chris Webber	2.00	.90	.25
☐ 76 Scott Brooks	.10	.05	.01
☐ 77 Matt Bullard	.10	.05	.01
☐ 78 Sam Cassell	.75	.35	.09
☐ 79 Mario Elie	.10	.05	.01
☐ 80 Carl Herrera	.10	.05	.01
☐ 81 Robert Horry	.20	.09	.03
☐ 82 Vernon Maxwell	.10	.05	.01
☐ 83 Hakeem Olajuwon	1.25	.55	.16
☐ 84 Kenny Smith	.10	.05	.01
☐ 85 Otis Thorpe	.15	.07	.02
☐ 86 Dale Davis	.10	.05	.01
☐ 87 Vern Fleming	.10	.05	.01
☐ 88 Scott Haskin	.10	.05	.01
☐ 89 Reggie Miller	.60	.25	.07
☐ 90 Sam Mitchell	.10	.05	.01
☐ 91 Pooh Richardson	.10	.05	.01
☐ 92 Detlef Schrempf	.15	.07	.02
☐ 93 Malik Sealy	.10	.05	.01
☐ 94 Rik Smits	.20	.09	.03
☐ 95 Terry Dehere	.15	.07	.02
☐ 96 Ron Harper	.10	.05	.01
☐ 97 Mark Jackson	.10	.05	.01
☐ 98 Danny Manning	.15	.07	.02
☐ 99 Stanley Roberts	.10	.05	.01
☐ 100 Loy Vaught	.15	.07	.02
☐ 101 John Williams	.10	.05	.01
☐ 102 Sam Bowie	.10	.05	.01
☐ 103 Elden Campbell	.15	.07	.02
☐ 104 Doug Christie	.10	.05	.01
☐ 105 Vlade Divac	.20	.09	.03
☐ 106 James Edwards	.10	.05	.01
☐ 107 George Lynch	.10	.05	.01
☐ 108 Anthony Peeler	.10	.05	.01
☐ 109 Sedale Threatt	.10	.05	.01
☐ 110 James Worthy	.20	.09	.03
☐ 111 Bimbo Coles	.10	.05	.01
☐ 112 Grant Long	.10	.05	.01
☐ 113 Harold Miner	.10	.05	.01
☐ 114 Glen Rice	.20	.09	.03
☐ 115 John Salley	.10	.05	.01
☐ 116 Rony Seikaly	.10	.05	.01
☐ 117 Brian Shaw	.10	.05	.01
☐ 118 Steve Smith	.20	.09	.03
☐ 119 Anthony Avent	.10	.05	.01
☐ 120 Vin Baker	2.00	.90	.25
☐ 121 Jon Barry	.10	.05	.01
☐ 122 Frank Brickowski	.10	.05	.01
☐ 123 Todd Day	.10	.05	.01
☐ 124 Blue Edwards	.10	.05	.01
☐ 125 Brad Lohaus	.10	.05	.01
☐ 126 Lee Mayberry	.10	.05	.01
☐ 127 Eric Murdock	.10	.05	.01
☐ 128 Ken Norman	.10	.05	.01
☐ 129 Thurl Bailey	.10	.05	.01
☐ 130 Mike Brown	.10	.05	.01
☐ 131 Christian Laettner	.20	.09	.03
☐ 132 Luc Longley	.10	.05	.01
☐ 133 Chuck Person	.10	.05	.01
☐ 134 Chris Smith	.10	.05	.01
☐ 135 Doug West	.10	.05	.01
☐ 136 Micheal Williams	.10	.05	.01
☐ 137 Kenny Anderson	.20	.09	.03
☐ 138 Benoit Benjamin	.10	.05	.01
☐ 139 Derrick Coleman	.10	.05	.01
☐ 140 Armon Gilliam	.10	.05	.01
☐ 141 Rick Mahorn	.10	.05	.01
☐ 142 Chris Morris	.10	.05	.01
☐ 143 Rumeal Robinson	.10	.05	.01
☐ 144 Rex Walters	.10	.05	.01
☐ 145 Greg Anthony	.10	.05	.01
☐ 146 Rolando Blackman	.10	.05	.01
☐ 147 Tony Campbell	.10	.05	.01
☐ 148 Hubert Davis	.10	.05	.01
☐ 149 Patrick Ewing	.50	.23	.06
☐ 150 Anthony Mason	.20	.09	.03
☐ 151 Charles Oakley	.15	.07	.02
☐ 152 Doc Rivers	.10	.05	.01
☐ 153 Charles Smith	.10	.05	.01
☐ 154 John Starks	.15	.07	.02
☐ 155 Herb Williams	.10	.05	.01
☐ 156 Nick Anderson	.20	.09	.03
☐ 157 Anthony Bowie	.10	.05	.01
☐ 158 Litterial Green	.10	.05	.01
☐ 159 Anfernee Hardaway	10.00	4.50	1.25
☐ 160 Shaquille O'Neal	3.00	1.35	.35
☐ 161 Donald Royal	.10	.05	.01
☐ 162 Dennis Scott	.15	.07	.02
☐ 163 Scott Skiles	.10	.05	.01
☐ 164 Jeff Turner	.10	.05	.01
☐ 165 Dana Barros	.10	.05	.01
☐ 166 Shawn Bradley	.60	.25	.07
☐ 167 Johnny Dawkins	.10	.05	.01
☐ 168 Greg Graham	.10	.05	.01
☐ 169 Jeff Hornacek	.15	.07	.02
☐ 170 Moses Malone	.30	.14	.04
☐ 171 Tim Perry	.10	.05	.01
☐ 172 Clarence Weatherspoon	.20	.09	.03
☐ 173 Danny Ainge	.20	.09	.03
☐ 174 Charles Barkley	.75	.35	.09
☐ 175 Cedric Ceballos	.20	.09	.03
☐ 176 A.C. Green	.20	.09	.03
☐ 177 Frank Johnson	.10	.05	.01
☐ 178 Kevin Johnson	.20	.09	.03
☐ 179 Negele Knight	.10	.05	.01
☐ 180 Malcolm Mackey	.10	.05	.01
☐ 181 Dan Majerle	.15	.07	.02
☐ 182 Oliver Miller	.10	.05	.01
☐ 183 Mark West	.10	.05	.01
☐ 184 Clyde Drexler	.60	.25	.07
☐ 185 Chris Dudley	.10	.05	.01
☐ 186 Harvey Grant	.10	.05	.01
☐ 187 Jerome Kersey	.10	.05	.01
☐ 188 Terry Porter	.10	.05	.01
☐ 189 Clifford Robinson	.20	.09	.03
☐ 190 James Robinson	.15	.07	.02
☐ 191 Rod Strickland	.10	.05	.01
☐ 192 Buck Williams	.15	.07	.02
☐ 193 Randy Brown	.10	.05	.01
☐ 194 Duane Causwell	.10	.05	.01

□	195	Bobby Hurley	.20	.09	.03
□	196	Mitch Richmond	.40	.18	.05
□	197	Lionel Simmons	.10	.05	.01
□	198	Wayman Tisdale	.10	.05	.01
□	199	Spud Webb	.10	.05	.01
□	200	Walt Williams	.20	.09	.03
□	201	Willie Anderson	.10	.05	.01
□	202	Antoine Carr	.10	.05	.01
□	203	Terry Cummings	.10	.05	.01
□	204	Lloyd Daniels	.10	.05	.01
□	205	Vinny Del Negro	.10	.05	.01
□	206	Sleepy Floyd	.10	.05	.01
□	207	Avery Johnson	.15	.07	.02
□	208	J.R. Reid	.10	.05	.01
□	209	David Robinson	1.00	.45	.12
□	210	Dennis Rodman	2.00	.90	.25
□	211	Michael Cage	.10	.05	.01
□	212	Kendall Gill	.10	.05	.01
□	213	Ervin Johnson	.15	.07	.02
□	214	Shawn Kemp	1.50	.70	.19
□	215	Derrick McKey	.10	.05	.01
□	216	Nate McMillan	.10	.05	.01
□	217	Gary Payton	.75	.35	.09
□	218	Sam Perkins	.10	.05	.01
□	219	Ricky Pierce	.10	.05	.01
□	220	Isaac Austin	.10	.05	.01
□	221	David Benoit	.10	.05	.01
□	222	Tom Chambers	.10	.05	.01
□	223	Tyrone Corbin	.10	.05	.01
□	224	Mark Eaton	.10	.05	.01
□	225	Jay Humphries	.10	.05	.01
□	226	Jeff Malone	.10	.05	.01
□	227	Karl Malone	.50	.23	.06
□	228	John Stockton	.50	.23	.06
□	229	Luther Wright	.10	.05	.01
□	230	Michael Adams	.10	.05	.01
□	231	Calbert Cheaney	.50	.23	.06
□	232	Kevin Duckworth	.10	.05	.01
□	233	Pervis Ellison	.10	.05	.01
□	234	Tom Gugliotta	.20	.09	.03
□	235	Buck Johnson	.10	.05	.01
□	236	Doug Overton	.10	.05	.01
□	237	LaBradford Smith	.10	.05	.01
□	238	Larry Stewart	.10	.05	.01
□	239	Checklist	.10	.05	.01
□	240	Checklist	.10	.05	.01

	MINT	NRMT	EXC
COMPLETE SET (8)	4.00	1.80	.50
COMMON CARD (1-8)	.25	.11	.03

□	1	Charles Barkley	1.25	.55	.16
□	2	Tim Hardaway	.50	.23	.06
□	3	Kevin Johnson	.50	.23	.06
□	4	Dan Majerle	.50	.23	.06
□	5	Scottie Pippen	2.50	1.10	.30
□	6	Mark Price	.25	.11	.03
□	7	John Starks	.25	.11	.03
□	8	Dominique Wilkins	.50	.23	.06

1993-94 Jam Session Rookie Standouts

Randomly inserted in 12-card packs at a rate of one in four, this oversized (2 1/2" by 4 3/4") eight-card set features borderless fronts with full-color player action photos. The player's name appears in gold-foil lettering in the lower left corner. The back features a color player action head shot with the player's statistics below. The cards are numbered on the back as "X of 8."

	MINT	NRMT	EXC
COMPLETE SET (8)	20.00	9.00	2.50
COMMON CARD (1-8)	.50	.23	.06

□	1	Vin Baker	3.00	1.35	.35
□	2	Shawn Bradley	1.00	.45	.12
□	3	Calbert Cheaney	.75	.35	.09
□	4	Anfernee Hardaway UER	15.00	6.75	1.85
		Text states drafted after senior year instead of junior			

1993-94 Jam Session Gamebreakers

Randomly inserted into 12-card packs at a rate of one in four, this eight-card 2 1/2" by 4 3/4" set features some of the NBA's top players. The borderless fronts feature color action cutouts on multicolored backgrounds highlighted by grid lines. The player's name appears in gold foil at the lower left. The back features a color player head shot with a screened background similar to the front. The player's name appears above the photo, career highlights appear below. The cards are numbered on the back as "X of 8."

☐ 5 Bobby Hurley	.50	.23	.06
☐ 6 Jamal Mashburn	2.00	.90	.25
☐ 7 Rodney Rogers	.50	.23	.06
☐ 8 Chris Webber	3.00	1.35	.35

1993-94 Jam Session Second Year Stars

Randomly inserted into Jam Session 12-card packs at a rate of one in four, this eight-card 2 1/2" by 4 3/4" set features some of the NBA's top second-year players. The borderless fronts feature a color action cutout on a rainbow-colored background. The player's name appears in gold foil in the lower right. The back features a color player head shot with screened rainbow background. The players name appears above the photo with a player profile displayed below. The cards are numbered on the back as "X of 8.

	MINT	NRMT	EXC
COMPLETE SET (8)	8.00	3.60	1.00
COMMON CARD (1-8)	.25	.11	.03
☐ 1 Tom Gugliotta	.50	.23	.06
☐ 2 Jim Jackson	1.00	.45	.12
☐ 3 Christian Laettner	.50	.23	.06
☐ 4 Oliver Miller	.25	.11	.03
☐ 5 Harold Miner	.25	.11	.03
☐ 6 Alonzo Mourning	1.25	.55	.16
☐ 7 Shaquille O'Neal	5.00	2.20	.60
☐ 8 Walt Williams	.50	.23	.06

1993-94 Jam Session Slam Dunk Heroes

Randomly inserted in 12-card Jam Session packs at a rate of one in four, this eight-card 2 1/2" by 4 3/4" set features some of the NBA's top slam dunkers. The border-less fronts feature color action cutouts on

multicolored posterized background. The player's name appears vertically in gold foil near the bottom. The back features a color player head shot. The player's name appears above the photo, a player profile is displayed below. The cards are numbered on the back as "X of 8."

	MINT	NRMT	EXC
COMPLETE SET (8)	12.00	5.50	1.50
COMMON CARD (1-8)	.75	.35	.09
☐ 1 Patrick Ewing	.75	.35	.09
☐ 2 Larry Johnson	1.00	.45	.12
☐ 3 Shawn Kemp	2.50	1.10	.30
☐ 4 Karl Malone	.75	.35	.09
☐ 5 Alonzo Mourning	1.25	.55	.16
☐ 6 Hakeem Olajuwon	2.00	.90	.25
☐ 7 Shaquille O'Neal	5.00	2.20	.60
☐ 8 David Robinson	1.50	.70	.19

1994-95 Jam Session

The complete 1994-95 Jam Session set consists of 200 oversized (2 1/2" by 4 3/4") cards. The cards were issued in 12-card packs with 36 packs per box. Each pack has one card from one of the four insert sets. Suggested retail price was $1.59 per pack. Cello packs consisting of three player cards and a cover card were given away at McDonald's restaurants in the Phoenix area to promote the Jam Session featured at the NBA All-Star weekend. The fronts have full-bleed color action photos that are tightly cropped so the player takes up a larger percentage of the card than in most sets.

The NBA Jam Session logo is superim-posed on the lower right corner and the player's name and team is just above it in the teams color. The backs have color-action photos on the right side with statis-tics and information on the left that is set against the color of the player's team. The entire card is UV coated as are all the insert sets. The cards are numbered on the back and grouped alphabetically within teams. Rookie Cards of note in this set include Grant Hill, Eddie Jones and Jason Kidd.

	MINT	NRMT	EXC
COMPLETE SET (200)	30.00	13.50	3.70
COMMON CARD (1-200)	.10	.05	.01

1 Stacey Augmon	.15	.07	.02
2 Mookie Blaylock	.15	.07	.02
3 Tyrone Corbin	.10	.05	.01
4 Craig Ehlo	.10	.05	.01
5 Ken Norman	.10	.05	.01
6 Kevin Willis	.10	.05	.01
7 Dee Brown	.10	.05	.01
8 Sherman Douglas	.10	.05	.01
9 Acie Earl	.10	.05	.01
10 Blue Edwards	.10	.05	.01
11 Pervis Ellison	.10	.05	.01
12 Rick Fox	.10	.05	.01
13 Xavier McDaniel	.10	.05	.01
14 Eric Montross	.25	.11	.03
15 Dino Radja	.25	.11	.03
16 Dominique Wilkins	.25	.11	.03
17 Michael Adams	.10	.05	.01
18 Muggsy Bogues	.15	.07	.02
19 Dell Curry	.10	.05	.01
20 Kenny Gattison	.10	.05	.01
21 Hersey Hawkins	.10	.05	.01
22 Larry Johnson	.50	.23	.06
23 Alonzo Mourning	.60	.25	.07
24 Robert Parish	.25	.11	.03
25 B.J. Armstrong	.10	.05	.01
26 Ron Harper	.15	.07	.02
27 Steve Kerr	.15	.07	.02
28 Toni Kukoc	.40	.18	.05
29 Pete Myers	.10	.05	.01
30 Will Perdue	.10	.05	.01
31 Scottie Pippen	1.50	.70	.19
32 Terrell Brandon	.25	.11	.03
33 Michael Cage	.10	.05	.01
34 Brad Daugherty	.10	.05	.01
35 Chris Mills	.25	.11	.03
36 Bobby Phills	.10	.05	.01
37 Mark Price	.10	.05	.01
38 Gerald Wilkins	.10	.05	.01
39 John Williams	.10	.05	.01
40 Jim Jackson	.60	.25	.07
41 Jason Kidd	4.00	1.80	.50
42 Jamal Mashburn	.40	.18	.05
43 Sean Rooks	.10	.05	.01
44 Doug Smith	.10	.05	.01
45 Mahmoud Abdul-Rauf	.15	.07	.02
46 LaPhonso Ellis	.10	.05	.01
47 Dikembe Mutombo	.25	.11	.03
48 Robert Pack	.10	.05	.01
49 Rodney Rogers	.10	.05	.01
50 Jalen Rose	.50	.23	.06
51 Bryant Stith	.10	.05	.01
52 Reggie Williams	.10	.05	.01
53 Bill Curley	.10	.05	.01
54 Joe Dumars	.25	.11	.03
55 Grant Hill	6.00	2.70	.75
56 Allan Houston	.30	.14	.04
57 Lindsey Hunter	.10	.05	.01
58 Oliver Miller	.10	.05	.01
59 Terry Mills	.10	.05	.01
60 Mark West	.10	.05	.01
61 Chris Gatling	.10	.05	.01
62 Tim Hardaway	.25	.11	.03
63 Chris Mullin	.25	.11	.03
64 Billy Owens	.10	.05	.01
65 Ricky Pierce	.10	.05	.01
66 Latrell Sprewell	.60	.25	.07
67 Chris Webber	.60	.25	.07
68 Sam Cassell	.25	.11	.03
69 Mario Elie	.10	.05	.01
70 Carl Herrera	.10	.05	.01
71 Robert Horry	.20	.09	.03
72 Vernon Maxwell	.10	.05	.01
73 Hakeem Olajuwon	1.25	.55	.16
74 Kenny Smith	.10	.05	.01
75 Otis Thorpe	.15	.07	.02
76 Antonio Davis	.10	.05	.01
77 Dale Davis	.10	.05	.01
78 Mark Jackson	.10	.05	.01
79 Derrick McKey	.10	.05	.01
80 Reggie Miller	.60	.25	.07
81 Byron Scott	.25	.11	.03
82 Rik Smits	.25	.11	.03
83 Haywoode Workman	.10	.05	.01
84 Gary Grant	.10	.05	.01
85 Pooh Richardson	.10	.05	.01
86 Stanley Roberts	.10	.05	.01
87 Elmore Spencer	.10	.05	.01
88 Loy Vaught	.10	.05	.01
89 Elden Campbell	.15	.07	.02
90 Cedric Ceballos	.20	.09	.03
91 Doug Christie	.10	.05	.01
92 Vlade Divac	.25	.11	.03
93 Eddie Jones	1.25	.55	.16
94 George Lynch	.10	.05	.01
95 Anthony Peeler	.10	.05	.01
96 Nick Van Exel	.50	.23	.06
97 James Worthy	.25	.11	.03
98 Grant Long	.10	.05	.01
99 Harold Miner	.10	.05	.01
100 Glen Rice	.25	.11	.03
101 John Salley	.10	.05	.01
102 Rony Seikaly	.10	.05	.01
103 Steve Smith	.25	.11	.03
104 Vin Baker	.60	.25	.07
105 Jon Barry	.10	.05	.01
106 Todd Day	.10	.05	.01
107 Lee Mayberry	.10	.05	.01
108 Eric Murdock	.10	.05	.01
109 Stacey King	.10	.05	.01
110 Christian Laettner	.25	.11	.03
111 Donyell Marshall	.15	.07	.02
112 Isaiah Rider	.25	.11	.03
113 Doug West	.10	.05	.01
114 Micheal Williams	.10	.05	.01
115 Kenny Anderson	.25	.11	.03
116 P.J. Brown	.10	.05	.01
117 Derrick Coleman	.10	.05	.01
118 Yinka Dare	.10	.05	.01
119 Kevin Edwards	.10	.05	.01
120 Armon Gilliam	.10	.05	.01
121 Chris Morris	.10	.05	.01
122 Anthony Bonner	.10	.05	.01
123 Hubert Davis	.10	.05	.01
124 Patrick Ewing	.50	.23	.06

☐ 125	Derek Harper	.10	.05	.01
☐ 126	Anthony Mason	.15	.07	.02
☐ 127	Charles Oakley	.15	.07	.02
☐ 128	Doc Rivers	.10	.05	.01
☐ 129	Charles Smith	.10	.05	.01
☐ 130	John Starks	.10	.05	.01
☐ 131	Charlie Ward	.25	.11	.03
☐ 132	Nick Anderson	.25	.11	.03
☐ 133	Anthony Bowie	.10	.05	.01
☐ 134	Horace Grant	.25	.11	.03
☐ 135	Anfernee Hardaway	3.00	1.35	.35
☐ 136	Shaquille O'Neal	2.50	1.10	.30
☐ 137	Dennis Scott	.15	.07	.02
☐ 138	Jeff Turner	.10	.05	.01
☐ 139	Dana Barros	.10	.05	.01
☐ 140	Shawn Bradley	.25	.11	.03
☐ 141	Johnny Dawkins	.10	.05	.01
☐ 142	Jeff Malone	.10	.05	.01
☐ 143	Tim Perry	.10	.05	.01
☐ 144	Clarence Weatherspoon	.10	.05	.01
☐ 145	Scott Williams	.10	.05	.01
☐ 146	Danny Ainge	.25	.11	.03
☐ 147	Charles Barkley	.75	.35	.09
☐ 148	A.C. Green	.25	.11	.03
☐ 149	Kevin Johnson	.25	.11	.03
☐ 150	Joe Kleine	.10	.05	.01
☐ 151	Antonio Lang	.10	.05	.01
☐ 152	Dan Majerle	.15	.07	.02
☐ 153	Danny Manning	.15	.07	.02
☐ 154	Wayman Tisdale	.10	.05	.01
☐ 155	Clyde Drexler	.60	.25	.07
☐ 156	Harvey Grant	.10	.05	.01
☐ 157	Tracy Murray	.10	.05	.01
☐ 158	Terry Porter	.10	.05	.01
☐ 159	Clifford Robinson	.25	.11	.03
☐ 160	Rod Strickland	.10	.05	.01
☐ 161	Buck Williams	.15	.07	.02
☐ 162	Bobby Hurley	.10	.05	.01
☐ 163	Olden Polynice	.10	.05	.01
☐ 164	Mitch Richmond	.40	.18	.05
☐ 165	Lionel Simmons	.10	.05	.01
☐ 166	Spud Webb	.15	.07	.02
☐ 167	Walt Williams	.25	.11	.03
☐ 168	Willie Anderson	.10	.05	.01
☐ 169	Terry Cummings	.10	.05	.01
☐ 170	Vinny Del Negro	.10	.05	.01
☐ 171	Sean Elliott	.25	.11	.03
☐ 172	Avery Johnson	.15	.07	.02
☐ 173	Chuck Person	.10	.05	.01
☐ 174	J.R. Reid	.10	.05	.01
☐ 175	David Robinson	1.00	.45	.12
☐ 176	Dennis Rodman	2.00	.90	.25
☐ 177	Bill Cartwright	.10	.05	.01
☐ 178	Kendall Gill	.10	.05	.01
☐ 179	Shawn Kemp	1.50	.70	.19
☐ 180	Nate McMillan	.10	.05	.01
☐ 181	Gary Payton	.75	.35	.09
☐ 182	Sam Perkins	.10	.05	.01
☐ 183	Detlef Schrempf	.15	.07	.02
☐ 184	David Benoit	.10	.05	.01
☐ 185	Jeff Hornacek	.15	.07	.02
☐ 186	Jay Humphries	.10	.05	.01
☐ 187	Karl Malone	.50	.23	.06
☐ 188	Bryon Russell	.10	.05	.01
☐ 189	Felton Spencer	.10	.05	.01
☐ 190	John Stockton	.50	.23	.06
☐ 191	Mitchell Butler	.10	.05	.01
☐ 192	Rex Chapman	.10	.05	.01
☐ 193	Calbert Cheaney	.15	.07	.02
☐ 194	Tom Gugliotta	.15	.07	.02
☐ 195	Don MacLean	.10	.05	.01

☐ 196	Gheorghe Muresan	.25	.11	.03
☐ 197	Scott Skiles	.10	.05	.01
☐ 198	Checklist	.10	.05	.01
☐ 199	Checklist	.10	.05	.01
☐ 200	Checklist	.10	.05	.01

1994-95 Jam Session Flashing Stars

This eight card oversized (2 1/2" by 4 3/4") set was randomly inserted in 12-card packs at a rate of approximately one in two. The set is composed of the flashiest players in the game like Anfernee Hardaway and Reggie Miller. The fronts have full-bleed color action photos similar to the regular set but the background has swirling colors. The player's name and words "Flashing Star" are in gold foil at the bottom. The NBA Jam Session logo is superimposed on the upper right corner. The backs have color action photos and information explaining why he is a "Flashing star." The cards are numbered on the back as "X of 8" and are sequenced in alphabetical order.

	MINT	NRMT	EXC
COMPLETE SET (8)	6.00	2.70	.75
COMMON CARD (1-8)	.25	.11	.03

☐ 1	Anfernee Hardaway	5.00	2.20	.60
☐ 2	Robert Horry	.25	.11	.03
☐ 3	Dan Majerle	.50	.23	.06
☐ 4	Reggie Miller	1.00	.45	.12
☐ 5	Mitch Richmond	.50	.23	.06
☐ 6	Isaiah Rider	.25	.11	.03
☐ 7	Latrell Sprewell	.50	.23	.06
☐ 8	Dominique Wilkins	.50	.23	.06

1994-95 Jam Session Gamebreakers

This eight card oversized (2 1/2" by 4 3/4") set was randomly inserted in 12-card packs

Information on obtaining the set was on the packs and you had to pay $3.95 to receive the set. The wrapper offer expired on June 30th, 1995. The set contains a selection of the top rookies from the 1994-95 season. The fronts have full-bleed color action photos on a painted background with a black and white action photo in the looming behind. The NBA Jam Session logo is superimposed on the upper left corner. The player's name and the "Rookie Standout" with a basketball under it are in gold foil at the bottom of the card. The backs have a full color action photo also on a painted background and information on the rookie particularly about his college career. The cards are numbered on the back as "X of 20" and are sequenced in alphabetical order.

at a rate of one in four. The set is composed of players who can take control of the game. The fronts have full-bleed color action photos similar to the regular set but the background is a basketball going through a net. The player image is also pushed out slightly which can also be seen from the back to give it a 3-D look. The NBA Jam Session logo is superimposed on the upper right corner. The backs have three layers to it. The background has two colors that are different on each card. A full-color action photo of the player is the middle layer. Up front is the player name in the middle and player information is a hazy white box underneath. The cards are numbered on the back as "X of 8" and are sequenced in alphabetical order.

	MINT	NRMT	EXC
COMPLETE SET (20)	15.00	6.75	1.85
COMMON CARD (1-20)	.25	.11	.03
☐ 1 Brian Grant	.75	.35	.09
☐ 2 Grant Hill	6.00	2.70	.75
☐ 3 Juwan Howard	4.00	1.80	.50
☐ 4 Eddie Jones	1.25	.55	.16
☐ 5 Jason Kidd	4.00	1.80	.50
☐ 6 Donyell Marshall	.25	.11	.03
☐ 7 Eric Montross	.50	.23	.06
☐ 8 Lamond Murray	.25	.11	.03
☐ 9 Wesley Person	.50	.23	.06
☐ 10 Khalid Reeves	.25	.11	.03
☐ 11 Glenn Robinson	2.00	.90	.25
☐ 12 Carlos Rogers	.25	.11	.03
☐ 13 Jalen Rose	.50	.23	.06
☐ 14 Clifford Rozier	.25	.11	.03
☐ 15 Dickey Simpkins	.25	.11	.03
☐ 16 Michael Smith	.25	.11	.03
☐ 17 Anthony Tucker	.25	.11	.03
☐ 18 Charlie Ward	.50	.23	.06
☐ 19 Monty Williams	.25	.11	.03
☐ 20 Sharone Wright	.50	.23	.06

	MINT	NRMT	EXC
COMPLETE SET (8)	10.00	4.50	1.25
COMMON CARD (1-8)	.75	.35	.09
☐ 1 Charles Barkley	1.25	.55	.16
☐ 2 Patrick Ewing	.75	.35	.09
☐ 3 Karl Malone	.75	.35	.09
☐ 4 Alonzo Mourning	1.00	.45	.12
☐ 5 Hakeem Olajuwon	2.00	.90	.25
☐ 6 Shaquille O'Neal	4.00	1.80	.50
☐ 7 Scottie Pippen	2.50	1.10	.30
☐ 8 David Robinson	1.50	.70	.19

1994-95 Jam Session Rookie Standouts

1994-95 Jam Session Second Year Stars

This 20-card oversized (2 1/2" by 4 3/4") set was available exclusively via mail.

This eight card oversized (2 1/2" by 4 3/4") set was randomly inserted in 12-card packs at a rate of one in four. The set consists of the best rookies from the 93-94 crop. The fronts are laid out horizontally and have full-bleed color action photos. The player is surrounded by a glowing yellow. The background has a close-up of his face from the action shot and copies of the shot in television screens behind that. The bottom says the player's name and "Second Year Star" in gold foil. The backs are laid out vertically with a full color action photo also surrounded by a glowing yellow on the left with player information on the right. The background is the same player photo set in numerous television screens similar to the front. The cards are numbered on the back as "X of 8" and are sequenced in alphabetical order.

	MINT	NRMT	EXC
COMPLETE SET (8)	8.00	3.60	1.00
COMMON CARD (1-8)	.25	.11	.03
☐ 1 Vin Baker	1.00	.45	.12
☐ 2 Anfernee Hardaway	5.00	2.20	.60
☐ 3 Lindsey Hunter	.25	.11	.03
☐ 4 Toni Kukoc	.60	.25	.07
☐ 5 Jamal Mashburn	.60	.25	.07
☐ 6 Dino Radja	.50	.23	.06
☐ 7 Isaiah Rider	.50	.23	.06
☐ 8 Chris Webber	1.00	.45	.12

1994-95 Jam Session Slam Dunk Heroes

Cards from this eight-card oversized (2 1/2 by 4 3/4") set were randomly inserted in packs at a rate of one in 36. The set is made up of players who jam with authority, namely centers and forwards. The cards have a 100% etched foil design. The fronts have a full color action photo with the player's name and the words "Slam Dunk Hero" boxing in a net are at the bottom in gold foil. The backs have a fuller color action photo on the left with player information on the right. The background on both the fronts and backs have a psychedelic look to it with basketballs floating about. The cards are numbered on the back as "X of 8" and are sequenced in alphabetical order.

	MINT	NRMT	EXC
COMPLETE SET (8)	70.00	32.00	8.75
COMMON CARD (1-8)	3.00	1.35	.35
☐ 1 Charles Barkley	10.00	4.50	1.25
☐ 2 Larry Johnson	6.00	2.70	.75
☐ 3 Shawn Kemp	20.00	9.00	2.50
☐ 4 Jamal Mashburn	5.00	2.20	.60
☐ 5 Dikembe Mutombo	3.00	1.35	.35
☐ 6 Hakeem Olajuwon	15.00	6.75	1.85
☐ 7 Shaquille O'Neal	30.00	13.50	3.70
☐ 8 Chris Webber	8.00	3.60	1.00

1995-96 Jam Session

The 1995-96 NBA Jam Session regular card set was issued in one series of 118 cards with 2 checklist cards. Cards were distributed in eight card hobby and retail packs carrying a suggested retail price of $1.59. Forty of the cards are titled "Connection Collection" and feature two players that form a unique tandem. The 78 regular cards are full-bleed color player action photos with a strip at the top with the word "JAM" repeating. Backs include a full color action player shot with a screened strip containing the players biography, a short personality profile, a player rating and NBA career summary. The "Connection Collection" cards are borderless with one-color backgrounds and a full-color action player cutout. Backs of the Connection Collection cards feature an extreme vertical and skewed full-color action photo of the player with a player biography, career stats and a short player profile. Cards are grouped alphabetically by team name. There are no Rookie Cards in this set.

	MINT	NRMT	EXC
COMPLETE SET (120)	25.00	11.00	3.10
COMMON CARD (1-120)	.10	.05	.01
☐ 1 Stacey Augmon CC	.15	.07	.02
☐ 2 Mookie Blaylock	.15	.07	.02
☐ 3 Grant Long	.10	.05	.01
☐ 4 Steve Smith	.20	.09	.03
☐ 5 Dee Brown CC	.10	.05	.01
☐ 6 Sherman Douglas	.10	.05	.01
☐ 7 Eric Montross	.15	.07	.02

☐ 8 Dino Radja .15	.07	.02
☐ 9 Muggsy Bogues CC .15	.07	.02
☐ 10 Scott Burrell .10	.05	.01
☐ 11 Larry Johnson CC .40	.18	.05
☐ 12 Alonzo Mourning .40	.18	.05
☐ 13 Michael Jordan CC 5.00	2.20	.60
☐ 14 Steve Kerr .15	.07	.02
☐ 15 Toni Kukoc CC .25	.11	.03
☐ 16 Scottie Pippen 1.25	.55	.16
☐ 17 Terrell Brandon .20	.09	.03
☐ 18 Tyrone Hill .10	.05	.01
☐ 19 Mark Price CC .10	.05	.01
☐ 20 John Williams .10	.05	.01
☐ 21 Jim Jackson .25	.11	.03
☐ 22 Popeye Jones CC .10	.05	.01
☐ 23 Jason Kidd CC 1.00	.45	.12
☐ 24 Jamal Mashburn .25	.11	.03
☐ 25 Mahmoud Abdul-Rauf .15	.07	.02
☐ 26 Dikembe Mutombo CC .20	.09	.03
☐ 27 Robert Pack CC .10	.05	.01
☐ 28 Jalen Rose .15	.07	.02
☐ 29 Joe Dumars CC .20	.09	.03
☐ 30 Grant Hill CC 1.50	.70	.19
☐ 31 Allan Houston .20	.09	.03
☐ 32 Terry Mills .10	.05	.01
☐ 33 Chris Gatling .10	.05	.01
☐ 34 Tim Hardaway CC .20	.09	.03
☐ 35 Donyell Marshall .10	.05	.01
☐ 36 Chris Mullin CC .20	.09	.03
☐ 37 Latrell Sprewell .20	.09	.03
☐ 38 Sam Cassell .20	.09	.03
☐ 39 Clyde Drexler CC .50	.23	.06
☐ 40 Robert Horry .20	.09	.03
☐ 41 Hakeem Olajuwon CC 1.00	.45	.12
☐ 42 Kenny Smith .10	.05	.01
☐ 43 Dale Davis .10	.05	.01
☐ 44 Mark Jackson .10	.05	.01
☐ 45 Reggie Miller CC .50	.23	.06
☐ 46 Rik Smits .20	.09	.03
☐ 47 Lamond Murray .10	.05	.01
☐ 48 Pooh Richardson CC .10	.05	.01
☐ 49 Malik Sealy .10	.05	.01
☐ 50 Loy Vaught .10	.05	.01
☐ 51 Cedric Ceballos .25	.11	.03
☐ 52 Vlade Divac .20	.09	.03
☐ 53 Eddie Jones .30	.14	.04
☐ 54 Nick Van Exel .30	.14	.04
☐ 55 Billy Owens .10	.05	.01
☐ 56 Khalid Reeves .10	.05	.01
☐ 57 Glen Rice .20	.09	.03
☐ 58 Kevin Willis .10	.05	.01
☐ 59 Vin Baker .40	.18	.05
☐ 60 Todd Day .10	.05	.01
☐ 61 Eric Murdock .10	.05	.01
☐ 62 Glenn Robinson CC .50	.23	.06
☐ 63 Tom Gugliotta .20	.09	.03
☐ 64 Christian Laettner CC .20	.09	.03
☐ 65 Isaiah Rider CC .20	.09	.03
☐ 66 Doug West .10	.05	.01
☐ 67 Kenny Anderson .20	.09	.03
☐ 68 P.J. Brown .10	.05	.01
☐ 69 Derrick Coleman .10	.05	.01
☐ 70 Armon Gilliam .15	.07	.02
☐ 71 Patrick Ewing CC .40	.18	.05
☐ 72 Derek Harper .10	.05	.01
☐ 73 Charles Oakley .15	.07	.02
☐ 74 John Starks CC .10	.05	.01
☐ 75 Horace Grant CC .20	.09	.03
☐ 76 Anfernee Hardaway CC 2.50	1.10	.30
☐ 77 Shaquille O'Neal CC 2.00	.90	.25
☐ 78 Dennis Scott .15	.07	.02

☐ 79 Dana Barros CC .10	.05	.01
☐ 80 Shawn Bradley .20	.09	.03
☐ 81 Clarence Weatherspoon .10	.05	.01
☐ 82 Sharone Wright .10	.05	.01
☐ 83 Charles Barkley CC .60	.25	.07
☐ 84 Kevin Johnson CC .20	.09	.03
☐ 85 Dan Majerle CC .15	.07	.02
☐ 86 Wesley Person CC .15	.07	.02
☐ 87 Harvey Grant .10	.05	.01
☐ 88 Clifford Robinson .20	.09	.03
☐ 89 Rod Strickland .10	.05	.01
☐ 90 Buck Williams .15	.07	.02
☐ 91 Brian Grant .15	.07	.02
☐ 92 Olden Polynice .10	.05	.01
☐ 93 Mitch Richmond .30	.14	.04
☐ 94 Walt Williams .20	.09	.03
☐ 95 Sean Elliott .20	.09	.03
☐ 96 Avery Johnson .15	.07	.02
☐ 97 David Robinson CC .75	.35	.09
☐ 98 Dennis Rodman 1.50	.70	.19
☐ 99 Shawn Kemp CC 1.25	.55	.16
☐ 100 Nate McMillan .10	.05	.01
☐ 101 Gary Payton .60	.25	.07
☐ 102 Detlef Schrempf .15	.07	.02
☐ 103 Willie Anderson .10	.05	.01
☐ 104 Jerome Kersey .10	.05	.01
☐ 105 Oliver Miller .10	.05	.01
☐ 106 Ed Pinckney .10	.05	.01
☐ 107 David Benoit .10	.05	.01
☐ 108 Jeff Hornacek CC .15	.07	.02
☐ 109 Karl Malone .40	.18	.05
☐ 110 John Stockton .40	.18	.05
☐ 111 Greg Anthony .10	.05	.01
☐ 112 Benoit Benjamin .10	.05	.01
☐ 113 Blue Edwards .10	.05	.01
☐ 114 Kenny Gattison .10	.05	.01
☐ 115 Calbert Cheaney .10	.05	.01
☐ 116 Juwan Howard 1.00	.45	.12
☐ 117 Gheorghe Muresan CC .20	.09	.03
☐ 118 Chris Webber CC .40	.18	.05
☐ 119 Checklist .10	.05	.01
☐ 120 Checklist .10	.05	.01
☐ NNO G.Hill Foil Tribute 50.00	22.00	6.25

1995-96 Jam Session Die Cuts

This 120-card die cut set parallels the 1995-96 Jam Session set. One die cut card was inserted into each pack. These cards are identical to their regular issue counterparts except for the different die-cut styles

at the top (or bottom) of the card; in addition, these die-cut cards can be distinguished by a "D" prefix before the card number. Please refer to the multipliers provided in the header to ascertain values.

	MINT	NRMT	EXC
COMPLETE SET (120)	60.00	27.00	7.50
COMMON CARD (D1-D120)	.20	.09	.03

*STARS: 1.25X to 2.5X BASIC CARDS

1995-96 Jam Session Fuel Injectors

Randomly inserted into all packs at a rate of one in 36, these nine cards feature hot stars of the '90s. Borderless fronts have two-toned backgrounds with the player in a full-color action cutout. The player's image has a fuzzy outline, giving it an electric look. Numbered backs have the prefix "F" and another full-color action player cutout. A screened box contains the player's biography and a player profile. The player's career summary appears in black type near the bottom of the card. The set is sequenced in alphabetical order.

	MINT	NRMT	EXC
COMPLETE SET (9)	75.00	34.00	9.50
COMMON CARD (1-9)	2.50	1.10	.30
☐ 1 Grant Hill	20.00	9.00	2.50
☐ 2 Larry Johnson	5.00	2.20	.60
☐ 3 Eddie Jones	4.00	1.80	.50
☐ 4 Jason Kidd	12.00	5.50	1.50
☐ 5 Hakeem Olajuwon	12.00	5.50	1.50
☐ 6 Shaquille O'Neal	25.00	11.00	3.10
☐ 7 Scottie Pippen	15.00	6.75	1.85
☐ 8 Glenn Robinson	6.00	2.70	.75
☐ 9 Latrell Sprewell	2.50	1.10	.30

1995-96 Jam Session Pop-Ups

Seeded at a rate of one per pack these pop-up cards highlight the play of 25 NBA

standouts. Fronts feature the player in full-color action with a crowd background printed with horizontal lines. The cards are perforated around the player's image so that it can be separated from the rest of the card, popped out and displayed standing. Card backs give instructions on how to assemble the card for display. The set is sequenced in alphabetical order. Prices below are for mint unperforated cards.

	MINT	NRMT	EXC
COMPLETE SET (25)	8.00	3.60	1.00
COMMON CARD (1-25)	.15	.07	.02
☐ 1 Kenny Anderson	.25	.11	.03
☐ 2 Charles Barkley	1.00	.45	.12
☐ 3 Mookie Blaylock	.20	.09	.03
☐ 4 Muggsy Bogues	.20	.09	.03
☐ 5 Shawn Bradley	.20	.09	.03
☐ 6 Sam Cassell	.20	.09	.03
☐ 7 Clyde Drexler	.75	.35	.09
☐ 8 Brian Grant	.15	.07	.02
☐ 9 Horace Grant	.25	.11	.03
☐ 10 Tim Hardaway	.25	.11	.03
☐ 11 Michael Jordan	2.50	1.10	.30
☐ 12 Jim Jackson	.40	.18	.05
☐ 13 Shawn Kemp	2.00	.90	.25
☐ 14 Christian Laettner	.25	.11	.03
☐ 15 Dan Majerle	.20	.09	.03
☐ 16 Eric Montross	.15	.07	.02
☐ 17 Alonzo Mourning	.60	.25	.07
☐ 18 Gheorghe Muresan	.20	.09	.03
☐ 19 Lamond Murray	.15	.07	.02
☐ 20 Dikembe Mutombo	.25	.11	.03
☐ 21 Charles Oakley	.20	.09	.03
☐ 22 Scottie Pippen	2.00	.90	.25
☐ 23 Mark Price	.15	.07	.02
☐ 24 Glen Rice	.25	.11	.03
☐ 25 Clifford Robinson	.25	.11	.03

1995-96 Jam Session Pop-Ups Bonus

Randomly inserted exclusively in retail packs at a rate of one in 24, this five-card set features a selection of NBA stars. The card fronts are borderless with a full-color action shot set against a crowd background with horizontal fading lines. The player's

image is perforated for pop-out assembly. The unnumbered backs include instruction for assembly of the cards. The set is sequenced in alphabetical order. Prices below refer to mint unperforated cards.

	MINT	NRMT	EXC
COMPLETE SET (5)	30.00	13.50	3.70
COMMON CARD (1-5)	3.00	1.35	.35
☐ 1 Patrick Ewing	3.00	1.35	.35
☐ 2 Grant Hill	12.00	5.50	1.50
☐ 3 Glenn Robinson	4.00	1.80	.50
☐ 4 Jason Kidd	8.00	3.60	1.00
☐ 5 Jerry Stackhouse	12.00	5.50	1.50

1995-96 Jam Session Rookies

Randomly inserted in packs at a rate of one in six, cards from this 10-card set highlight the '95-96 freshman crop. Borderless fronts include a full-color player action cutout with stars winding around the player's image. "Rookie" is printed in a spiraling pattern and serves as the background. Numbered backs have the prefix "R" and feature the player in a full-color cutout pose standing on a hovering star and the background continues with the spiraling pattern with the word "rookie". The player's last name appears over his head.

	MINT	NRMT	EXC
COMPLETE SET (10)	20.00	9.00	2.50
COMMON CARD (1-10)	.75	.35	.09
☐ 1 Joe Smith	5.00	2.20	.60
☐ 2 Antonio McDyess	4.00	1.80	.50
☐ 3 Jerry Stackhouse	8.00	3.60	1.00

☐ 4 Rasheed Wallace	2.00	.90	.25
☐ 5 Bryant Reeves	2.50	1.10	.30
☐ 6 Shawn Respert	.75	.35	.09
☐ 7 Cherokee Parks	.75	.35	.09
☐ 8 Alan Henderson	.75	.35	.09
☐ 9 George Zidek	.75	.35	.09
☐ 10 Sherell Ford	.75	.35	.09

1995-96 Jam Session Show Stoppers

Randomly inserted exclusively in hobby packs at a rate of one in 48, this set of nine cards is the rarest of the '95-96 Jam Session collection and features some of the game's best players. The full-bleed, fronts show the player in a full-color cutout against a sparkling, etched blue-foil background The players name is stamped in gold foil at the bottom of the card in all caps. Backs are numbered with the prefix "S". A digital image of the player serves as a background and a smaller full-color action player shot appears on the bottom half of the card. The player's biography and profile wrap around the color shot and his NBA totals appear at the bottom of the card. The set is sequenced in alphabetical order and is condition sensitive due to the etched foil edges.

	MINT	NRMT	EXC
COMPLETE SET (9)	200.00	90.00	25.00
COMMON CARD (1-9)	4.00	1.80	.50
☐ 1 Anfernee Hardaway	60.00	27.00	7.50
☐ 2 Grant Hill	30.00	13.50	3.70
☐ 3 Michael Jordan	120.00	55.00	15.00
☐ 4 Karl Malone	6.00	2.70	.75
☐ 5 Jamal Mashburn	4.00	1.80	.50
☐ 6 Reggie Miller	8.00	3.60	1.00
☐ 7 David Robinson	12.00	5.50	1.50
☐ 8 John Stockton	6.00	2.70	.75
☐ 9 Chris Webber	8.00	3.60	1.00

1995-96 Metal

The 1995-96 premiere issue of Metal basketball by Fleer/SkyBox consists of 220

standard-size cards issued in two separate series of 120 and 100 cards respectively. The eight-card packs carried a suggested retail price of $2.49 each. Borderless fronts feature the player in a full-color action cutout against a multicolored, hand engraved, metallic foil background. Backs picture the player in a full-color action shot with his team's logo printed at the bottom. The only subset is Nuts and Bolts (209-218). Rookie Cards of note include Michael Finley, Kevin Garnett, Antonio McDyess, Joe Smith, Jerry Stackhouse and Damon Stoudamire.

	MINT	NRMT	EXC
COMPLETE SET (220)	50.00	22.00	6.25
COMPLETE SERIES 1 (120)	25.00	11.00	3.10
COMPLETE SERIES 2 (100)	25.00	11.00	3.10
COMMON CARD (1-220)	.10	.05	.01

☐ 1 Stacey Augmon	.15	.07	.02
☐ 2 Mookie Blaylock	.15	.07	.02
☐ 3 Grant Long	.10	.05	.01
☐ 4 Steve Smith	.25	.11	.03
☐ 5 Dee Brown	.10	.05	.01
☐ 6 Sherman Douglas	.10	.05	.01
☐ 7 Eric Montross	.10	.05	.01
☐ 8 Dino Radja	.15	.07	.02
☐ 9 Muggsy Bogues	.15	.07	.02
☐ 10 Scott Burrell	.10	.05	.01
☐ 11 Larry Johnson	.50	.23	.06
☐ 12 Alonzo Mourning	.50	.23	.06
☐ 13 Michael Jordan	6.00	2.70	.75
☐ 14 Toni Kukoc	.30	.14	.04
☐ 15 Scottie Pippen	1.50	.70	.19
☐ 16 Terrell Brandon	.25	.11	.03
☐ 17 Tyrone Hill	.10	.05	.01
☐ 18 Mark Price	.10	.05	.01
☐ 19 John Williams	.10	.05	.01
☐ 20 Jim Jackson	.30	.14	.04
☐ 21 Popeye Jones	.10	.05	.01
☐ 22 Jason Kidd	1.25	.55	.16
☐ 23 Jamal Mashburn	.30	.14	.04
☐ 24 Mahmoud Abdul-Rauf	.15	.07	.02
☐ 25 Dikembe Mutombo	.25	.11	.03
☐ 26 Robert Pack	.10	.05	.01
☐ 27 Jalen Rose	.10	.05	.01
☐ 28 Joe Dumars	.25	.11	.03
☐ 29 Grant Hill	2.00	.90	.25
☐ 30 Lindsey Hunter	.10	.05	.01
☐ 31 Terry Mills	.25	.11	.03
☐ 32 Tim Hardaway	.25	.11	.03
☐ 33 Donyell Marshall	.10	.05	.01
☐ 34 Chris Mullin	.25	.11	.03
☐ 35 Clifford Rozier	.10	.05	.01
☐ 36 Latrell Sprewell	.25	.11	.03
☐ 37 Sam Cassell	.25	.11	.03
☐ 38 Clyde Drexler	.60	.25	.07
☐ 39 Robert Horry	.25	.11	.03
☐ 40 Hakeem Olajuwon	1.25	.55	.16
☐ 41 Kenny Smith	.10	.05	.01
☐ 42 Dale Davis	.10	.05	.01
☐ 43 Mark Jackson	.10	.05	.01
☐ 44 Derrick McKey	.10	.05	.01
☐ 45 Reggie Miller	.60	.25	.07
☐ 46 Rik Smits	.25	.11	.03
☐ 47 Lamond Murray	.10	.05	.01
☐ 48 Pooh Richardson	.10	.05	.01
☐ 49 Malik Sealy	.10	.05	.01
☐ 50 Loy Vaught	.10	.05	.01
☐ 51 Elden Campbell	.15	.07	.02
☐ 52 Cedric Ceballos	.30	.14	.04
☐ 53 Vlade Divac	.25	.11	.03
☐ 54 Eddie Jones	.40	.18	.05
☐ 55 Nick Van Exel	.40	.18	.05
☐ 56 Bimbo Coles	.10	.05	.01
☐ 57 Billy Owens	.10	.05	.01
☐ 58 Khalid Reeves	.10	.05	.01
☐ 59 Glen Rice	.25	.11	.03
☐ 60 Kevin Willis	.10	.05	.01
☐ 61 Vin Baker	.50	.23	.06
☐ 62 Todd Day	.10	.05	.01
☐ 63 Eric Murdock	.10	.05	.01
☐ 64 Glenn Robinson	.60	.25	.07
☐ 65 Tom Gugliotta	.25	.11	.03
☐ 66 Christian Laettner	.25	.11	.03
☐ 67 Isaiah Rider	.25	.11	.03
☐ 68 Kenny Anderson	.25	.11	.03
☐ 69 P.J. Brown	.10	.05	.01
☐ 70 Derrick Coleman	.25	.11	.03
☐ 71 Patrick Ewing	.50	.23	.06
☐ 72 Anthony Mason	.15	.07	.02
☐ 73 Charles Oakley	.15	.07	.02
☐ 74 John Starks	.10	.05	.01
☐ 75 Nick Anderson	.25	.11	.03
☐ 76 Horace Grant	.25	.11	.03
☐ 77 Anfernee Hardaway	3.00	1.35	.35
☐ 78 Shaquille O'Neal	2.50	1.10	.30
☐ 79 Dennis Scott	.15	.07	.02
☐ 80 Dana Barros	.10	.05	.01
☐ 81 Shawn Bradley	.25	.11	.03
☐ 82 Clarence Weatherspoon	.10	.05	.01
☐ 83 Sharone Wright	.10	.05	.01
☐ 84 Charles Barkley	.75	.35	.09
☐ 85 Kevin Johnson	.25	.11	.03
☐ 86 Dan Majerle	.25	.11	.03
☐ 87 Danny Manning	.15	.07	.02
☐ 88 Wesley Person	.15	.07	.02
☐ 89 Clifford Robinson	.25	.11	.03
☐ 90 Rod Strickland	.10	.05	.01
☐ 91 Otis Thorpe	.15	.07	.02
☐ 92 Buck Williams	.15	.07	.02
☐ 93 Brian Grant	.15	.07	.02
☐ 94 Olden Polynice	.10	.05	.01
☐ 95 Mitch Richmond	.40	.18	.05
☐ 96 Walt Williams	.15	.11	.03
☐ 97 Sean Elliott	.25	.11	.03
☐ 98 Avery Johnson	.15	.07	.02
☐ 99 David Robinson	1.00	.45	.12
☐ 100 Dennis Rodman	2.00	.90	.25
☐ 101 Shawn Kemp	1.50	.70	.19
☐ 102 Nate McMillan	.10	.05	.01
☐ 103 Gary Payton	.75	.35	.09
☐ 104 Detlef Schempf	.15	.07	.02
☐ 105 B.J. Armstrong	.10	.05	.01
☐ 106 Oliver Miller	.10	.05	.01
☐ 107 John Salley	.10	.05	.01

☐ 108	David Benoit	.10	.05	.01
☐ 109	Jeff Hornacek	.15	.07	.02
☐ 110	Karl Malone	.50	.23	.06
☐ 111	John Stockton	.50	.23	.06
☐ 112	Greg Anthony	.10	.05	.01
☐ 113	Benoit Benjamin	.10	.05	.01
☐ 114	Byron Scott	.25	.11	.03
☐ 115	Calbert Cheaney	.10	.05	.01
☐ 116	Juwan Howard	1.25	.55	.16
☐ 117	Gheorghe Muresan	.25	.11	.03
☐ 118	Chris Webber	.50	.23	.06
☐ 119	Checklist	.10	.05	.01
☐ 120	Checklist	.10	.05	.01
☐ 121	Stacey Augmon	.15	.07	.02
☐ 122	Mookie Blaylock	.25	.11	.03
☐ 123	Alan Henderson	.25	.11	.03
☐ 124	Andrew Lang	.10	.05	.01
☐ 125	Ken Norman	.10	.05	.01
☐ 126	Steve Smith	.25	.11	.03
☐ 127	Dana Barros	.10	.05	.01
☐ 128	Rick Fox	.10	.05	.01
☐ 129	Eric Williams	.30	.14	.04
☐ 130	Kendall Gill	.10	.05	.01
☐ 131	Khalid Reeves	.10	.05	.01
☐ 132	Glen Rice	.25	.11	.03
☐ 133	George Zidek	.10	.05	.01
☐ 134	Dennis Rodman Bulls	2.50	1.10	.30
☐ 135	Danny Ferry	.10	.05	.01
☐ 136	Dan Majerle	.15	.07	.02
☐ 137	Chris Mills	.10	.05	.01
☐ 138	Bobby Phills	.10	.05	.01
☐ 139	Bob Sura	.30	.14	.04
☐ 140	Tony Dumas	.10	.05	.01
☐ 141	Dale Ellis	.10	.05	.01
☐ 142	Don MacLean	.10	.05	.01
☐ 143	Antonio McDyess	1.50	.70	.19
☐ 144	Bryant Stith	.10	.05	.01
☐ 145	Allan Houston	.25	.11	.03
☐ 146	Theo Ratliff	.15	.07	.02
☐ 147	Otis Thorpe	.15	.07	.02
☐ 148	B.J. Armstrong	.10	.05	.01
☐ 149	Rony Seikaly	.10	.05	.01
☐ 150	Joe Smith	2.00	.90	.25
☐ 151	Sam Cassell	.15	.07	.02
☐ 152	Clyde Drexler	.50	.23	.06
☐ 153	Robert Horry	.15	.07	.02
☐ 154	Hakeem Olajuwon	1.00	.45	.12
☐ 155	Antonio Davis	.10	.05	.01
☐ 156	Ricky Pierce	.10	.05	.01
☐ 157	Brent Barry	.75	.35	.09
☐ 158	Terry Dehere	.10	.05	.01
☐ 159	Rodney Rogers	.10	.05	.01
☐ 160	Brian Williams	.10	.05	.01
☐ 161	Magic Johnson	1.25	.55	.16
☐ 162	Sasha Danilovic	.10	.05	.01
☐ 163	Alonzo Mourning	.40	.18	.05
☐ 164	Kurt Thomas	.50	.23	.06
☐ 165	Sherman Douglas	.10	.05	.01
☐ 166	Shawn Respert	.10	.05	.01
☐ 167	Kevin Garnett	5.00	2.20	.60
☐ 168	Terry Porter	.10	.05	.01
☐ 169	Shawn Bradley	.25	.11	.03
☐ 170	Kevin Edwards	.10	.05	.01
☐ 171	Ed O'Bannon	.60	.25	.07
☐ 172	Jayson Williams	.10	.05	.01
☐ 173	Derek Harper	.10	.05	.01
☐ 174	Charles Smith	.10	.05	.01
☐ 175	Brian Shaw	.10	.05	.01
☐ 176	Derrick Coleman	.15	.07	.02
☐ 177	Vernon Maxwell	.10	.05	.01
☐ 178	Trevor Ruffin	.10	.05	.01

☐ 179	Jerry Stackhouse	3.00	1.35	.35
☐ 180	Michael Finley	2.00	.90	.25
☐ 181	A.C. Green	.15	.07	.02
☐ 182	John Williams	.10	.05	.01
☐ 183	Aaron McKie	.10	.05	.01
☐ 184	Arvydas Sabonis	1.25	.55	.16
☐ 185	Gary Trent	.10	.05	.01
☐ 186	Tyus Edney	.75	.35	.09
☐ 187	Sarunas Marciulionis	.10	.05	.01
☐ 188	Michael Smith	.10	.05	.01
☐ 189	Corliss Williamson	.30	.14	.04
☐ 190	Vinny Del Negro	.15	.07	.02
☐ 191	Hersey Hawkins	.15	.07	.02
☐ 192	Shawn Kemp	1.25	.55	.16
☐ 193	Gary Payton	.60	.25	.07
☐ 194	Sam Perkins	.15	.07	.02
☐ 195	Detlef Schrempf	.25	.11	.03
☐ 196	Willie Anderson	.10	.05	.01
☐ 197	Oliver Miller	.10	.05	.01
☐ 198	Tracy Murray	.10	.05	.01
☐ 199	Alvin Robertson	.10	.05	.01
☐ 200	Damon Stoudamire	4.00	1.80	.50
☐ 201	Chris Morris	.10	.05	.01
☐ 202	Greg Anthony	.10	.05	.01
☐ 203	Blue Edwards	.10	.05	.01
☐ 204	Eric Murdock	.10	.05	.01
☐ 205	Bryant Reeves	1.00	.45	.12
☐ 206	Byron Scott	.15	.07	.02
☐ 207	Robert Pack	.10	.05	.01
☐ 208	Rasheed Wallace	.75	.35	.09
☐ 209	Anfernee Hardaway NB	1.25	.55	.16
☐ 210	Grant Hill NB	.75	.35	.09
☐ 211	Larry Johnson NB	.15	.07	.02
☐ 212	Michael Jordan NB	2.50	1.10	.30
☐ 213	Jason Kidd NB	.50	.23	.06
☐ 214	Karl Malone NB	.15	.07	.02
☐ 215	Shaquille O'Neal NB	1.00	.45	.12
☐ 216	Scottie Pippen NB	.60	.25	.07
☐ 217	David Robinson NB	.40	.18	.05
☐ 218	Glenn Robinson NB	.25	.11	.03
☐ 219	Checklist	.10	.05	.01
☐ 220	Checklist	.10	.05	.01

1995-96 Metal Silver Spotlight

These 120 cards parallel the first series of Metal and were seeded at a rate of one per first series pack. The second series was discontinued due to lack of collector response. These "Silver Spotlight" cards are identical to the regular cards with the

exception of having etched pure silver foil backgrounds instead of the multi-colored backgrounds of the basic cards. Please refer to the multiplier listed below for values on singles.

	MINT	NRMT	EXC
COMPLETE SET (120)	90.00	40.00	11.00
COMMON CARD (1-120)	.25	.11	.03

* SIL. SPOT. STARS: 1.5X to 3X VALUE

1995-96 Metal Maximum Metal

Randomly inserted in all series one packs at a rate of one in 36, cards from this 10-card standard-size set highlight some NBA impact players. These cards have a basket-ball-shaped die cut design and feature a full-color player action cutout on the front. The background is a silver foil diamond-plate basketball going through a hoop. Backs continue with the diamond plate basketball and hoop background and also feature a full-color player cutout. The player's name and a player profile are printed on the back. The set is sequenced in alphabetical order.

	MINT	NRMT	EXC
COMPLETE SET (10)	90.00	40.00	11.00
COMMON CARD (1-10)	2.50	1.10	.30
☐ 1 Charles Barkley	5.00	2.20	.60
☐ 2 Patrick Ewing	3.00	1.35	.35
☐ 3 Grant Hill	12.00	5.50	1.50
☐ 4 Michael Jordan	40.00	18.00	5.00
☐ 5 Shawn Kemp	10.00	4.50	1.25
☐ 6 Karl Malone	3.00	1.35	.35
☐ 7 Hakeem Olajuwon	8.00	3.60	1.00
☐ 8 Shaquille O'Neal	15.00	6.75	1.85
☐ 9 Mitch Richmond	2.50	1.10	.30
☐ 10 David Robinson	6.00	2.70	.75

1995-96 Metal Metal Force

Randomly inserted exclusively in second series retail packs at a rate of one in 54, cards from this 15-card set feature a selection of the NBA's top stars and rookies.

Each card is made of a clear plastic materi-al and comes with a protective coating on front. Prices provided below refer to unpeeled cards. Peeled cards generally trade for ten to twenty-five percent less.

	MINT	NRMT	EXC
COMPLETE SET (15)	175.00	80.00	22.00
COMMON CARD (1-15)	3.00	1.35	.35
☐ 1 Vin Baker	6.00	2.70	.75
☐ 2 Charles Barkley	10.00	4.50	1.25
☐ 3 Cedric Ceballos	3.00	1.35	.35
☐ 4 Grant Hill	25.00	11.00	3.10
☐ 5 Larry Johnson	6.00	2.70	.75
☐ 6 Magic Johnson	20.00	9.00	2.50
☐ 7 Shawn Kemp	20.00	9.00	2.50
☐ 8 Karl Malone	6.00	2.70	.75
☐ 9 Jamal Mashburn	4.00	1.80	.50
☐ 10 Scottie Pippen	20.00	9.00	2.50
☐ 11 Glenn Robinson	8.00	3.60	1.00
☐ 12 Dennis Rodman Bulls	40.00	18.00	5.00
☐ 13 Joe Smith	12.00	5.50	1.50
☐ 14 Jerry Stackhouse	20.00	9.00	2.50
☐ 15 Chris Webber	8.00	3.60	1.00

1995-96 Metal Molten Metal

Randomly inserted in all series one packs at a rate of one in 72, cards from this 10-card standard-size set feature a selection of up and coming NBA stars. The fronts feature full-color action cutouts set against stamped multicolored laminated foil back-grounds. Borderless backs feature the play-er in a full-color action cutout and a white box surrounds a player profile which is printed in white type. The set is sequenced in alphabetical order.

	MINT	NRMT	EXC
COMPLETE SET (10)	180.00	80.00	22.00
COMMON CARD (1-10)	6.00	2.70	.75
☐ 1 Anfernee Hardaway	75.00	34.00	9.50
☐ 2 Grant Hill	50.00	22.00	6.25
☐ 3 Robert Horry	6.00	2.70	.75
☐ 4 Eddie Jones	10.00	4.50	1.25
☐ 5 Toni Kukoc	8.00	3.60	1.00
☐ 6 Jamal Mashburn	8.00	3.60	1.00
☐ 7 Alonzo Mourning	12.00	5.50	1.50
☐ 8 Glenn Robinson	15.00	6.75	1.85
☐ 9 Latrell Sprewell	6.00	2.70	.75
☐ 10 Chris Webber	12.00	5.50	1.50

1995-96 Metal Rookie Roll Call

Spotlighting the '95-96 rookie class, cards from this 10-card standard-size set were randomly inserted in both series one hobby and retail packs. Though these cards are considered inserts, they were distributed at the same rate as regular issue cards. The cards display hand-engraved, metalized foil designs and are numbered on the back. The set is sequenced in alphabetical order.

	MINT	NRMT	EXC
COMPLETE SET (10)	12.00	5.50	1.50
COMMON CARD (R1-R10)	.30	.14	.04
☐ R1 Brent Barry	1.00	.45	.12
☐ R2 Antonio McDyess	2.00	.90	.25
☐ R3 Ed O'Bannon	.75	.35	.09
☐ R4 Cherokee Parks	.30	.14	.04
☐ R5 Bryant Reeves	1.25	.55	.16
☐ R6 Shawn Respert	.30	.14	.04
☐ R7 Joe Smith	2.50	1.10	.30
☐ R8 Jerry Stackhouse	4.00	1.80	.50
☐ R9 Gary Trent	.30	.14	.04
☐ R10 Rasheed Wallace	1.00	.45	.12

1995-96 Metal Rookie Roll Call Silver Spotlight

These 10 cards parallel the more common Rookie Roll Call inserts. They are approximately eight times scarcer and were randomly seeded into first series packs. The cards are identical to their more common counterparts except for their pure silver foil backgrounds.

	MINT	NRMT	EXC
COMPLETE SET (10)			
COMMON CARD (R10-R10)			
* SILVER SPOTLIGHT: 1X to 2X VALUE			

1995-96 Metal Scoring Magnets

Randomly inserted exclusively into second series hobby packs at a rate of one in 54, cards from this 8-card set feature a selection of the NBA's top scoring threats. Card fronts have embossed player shots with the card name "Scoring Magnet" in silver foil running vertical along both sides of the player. Card backs contain a brief commentary and are numbered as "X of 8".

	MINT	NRMT	EXC
COMPLETE SET (8)	200.00	90.00	25.00
COMMON CARD (1-8)	12.00	5.50	1.50
☐ 1 Anfernee Hardaway	40.00	18.00	5.00
☐ 2 Grant Hill	25.00	11.00	3.10
☐ 3 Magic Johnson	20.00	9.00	2.50
☐ 4 Michael Jordan	75.00	34.00	9.50
☐ 5 Jason Kidd	15.00	6.75	1.85
☐ 6 Hakeem Olajuwon	15.00	6.75	1.85
☐ 7 Shaquille O'Neal	30.00	13.50	3.70
☐ 8 David Robinson	12.00	5.50	1.50

1995-96 Metal Slick Silver

Randomly inserted exclusively into first series hobby packs at a rate of one in seven, cards from this 10-card standard-size set highlight the league's premier point and shooting guards. The clear acetate cards feature the player in a full-color action shot with a trail of ghost images on the

front. Backs feature a player profile printed on the player's reverse silhouette. The set is sequenced in alphabetical order.

	MINT	NRMT	EXC
COMPLETE SET (10)	40.00	18.00	5.00
COMMON CARD (1-10)	1.00	.45	.12
☐ 1 Kenny Anderson	1.00	.45	.12
☐ 2 Anfernee Hardaway	12.00	5.50	1.50
☐ 3 Michael Jordan	25.00	11.00	3.10
☐ 4 Jason Kidd	5.00	2.20	.60
☐ 5 Reggie Miller	2.50	1.10	.30
☐ 6 Gary Payton	3.00	1.35	.35
☐ 7 Mitch Richmond	1.50	.70	.19
☐ 8 Latrell Sprewell	1.00	.45	.12
☐ 9 John Stockton	2.00	.90	.25
☐ 10 Nick Van Exel	1.50	.70	.19

1995-96 Metal Stackhouse's Scrapbook

Randomly inserted into one in every 24 second series packs, these two cards continue the eight-card, cross-brand set devoted Fleer spokesperson Jerry Stackhouse. Card #S7 often sells for a premium due to the appearance of Michael Jordan.

	MINT	NRMT	EXC
COMPLETE SET (2)	10.00	4.50	1.25
COMMON CARD (S7-S8)	4.00	1.80	.50
☐ S7 J.Stackhouse w/Jordan	8.00	3.60	1.00
☐ S8 Jerry Stackhouse Metal	4.00	1.80	.50

1995-96 Metal Steel Towers

Randomly inserted exclusively into series one retail and magazine packs at a rate of one in four, cards from this 10-card insert set focus on the leagues top big men. Full-bleed fronts have silver foil backgrounds and are stamped with skyscraper designs. Backs are two-toned according to player's team colors and feature a full-color action shot and a player profile printed next to it. Skyscraper designs also appear in the background on the backs. The set is sequenced in alphabetical order.

	MINT	NRMT	EXC
COMPLETE SET (10)	15.00	6.75	1.85
COMMON CARD (1-10)	.50	.23	.06
☐ 1 Shawn Bradley	.75	.35	.09
☐ 2 Vlade Divac	.75	.35	.09
☐ 3 Patrick Ewing	1.50	.70	.19
☐ 4 Alonzo Mourning	1.50	.70	.19
☐ 5 Dikembe Mutombo	.75	.35	.09
☐ 6 Hakeem Olajuwon	4.00	1.80	.50
☐ 7 Shaquille O'Neal	8.00	3.60	1.00
☐ 8 David Robinson	3.00	1.35	.35
☐ 9 Rik Smits	.75	.35	.09
☐ 10 Kevin Willis	.50	.23	.06

1995-96 Metal Tempered Steel

Randomly inserted into all second series packs at a rate of one in 12, cards from this 12-card set feature a selection of top rook-

ies from the 1995-96 season. Card fronts have a colorful foil-etched background with the "Tempered Steel" logo written in cursive running along the left side. Card backs feature an action shot and a brief commentary next to it. Card backs are numbered as "X of 12".

	MINT	NRMT	EXC
COMPLETE SET (12)	50.00	22.00	6.25
COMMON CARD (1-12)	1.50	.70	.19

		MINT	NRMT	EXC
☐ 1	Sasha Danilovic	1.50	.70	.19
☐ 2	Tyus Edney	2.50	1.10	.30
☐ 3	Michael Finley	6.00	2.70	.75
☐ 4	Kevin Garnett	15.00	6.75	1.85
☐ 5	Antonio McDyess	5.00	2.20	.60
☐ 6	Bryant Reeves	3.00	1.35	.35
☐ 7	Arvydas Sabonis	4.00	1.80	.50
☐ 8	Joe Smith	6.00	2.70	.75
☐ 9	Jerry Stackhouse	10.00	4.50	1.25
☐ 10	Damon Stoudamire	12.00	5.50	1.50
☐ 11	Rasheed Wallace	2.50	1.10	.30
☐ 12	Eric Williams	1.50	.70	.19

1996-97 Metal

Produced by Fleer/SkyBox, the 1996 Metal Series I set is comprised of 150 cards with eight-card packs carrying a suggested retail price of $2.49. Borderless fronts feature the player in a full-color action cutout against an etched color and silver foil background. The player's name is printed in silver foil and embossed along the right side of the card. Backs picture the player in a full-color action shot with his team's logo printed at the bottom against a "steel" background. The player's name and statistics run vertically along the right side of the card. The cards are grouped alphabetically within teams and checklisted below alphabetically according to team. The set also contains the topical subsets: On The Move (109-123), Metalized (124-133), Fresh Foundations (134-138) and Metal Shredders (139-148). The Fresh Foundation subset contains the Rookie Cards of Stephon Marbury, Shareef Abdur-Rahim, Ray Allen, Kobe Bryant and Steve Nash.

	MINT	NRMT	EXC
COMPLETE SERIES 1 (150)	25.00	11.00	3.10
COMMON CARD (1-150)	.10	.05	.01

		MINT	NRMT	EXC
☐ 1	Mookie Blaylock	.15	.07	.02
☐ 2	Christian Laettner	.10	.05	.01
☐ 3	Steve Smith	.15	.07	.02
☐ 4	Dana Barros	.10	.05	.01
☐ 5	Rick Fox	.10	.05	.01
☐ 6	Dino Radja	.10	.05	.01
☐ 7	Eric Williams	.10	.05	.01
☐ 8	Dell Curry	.10	.05	.01
☐ 9	Matt Geiger	.10	.05	.01
☐ 10	Glen Rice	.10	.05	.01
☐ 11	Michael Jordan	5.00	2.20	.60
☐ 12	Toni Kukoc	.15	.07	.02
☐ 13	Luc Longley	.10	.05	.01
☐ 14	Scottie Pippen	1.25	.55	.16
☐ 15	Dennis Rodman	2.00	.90	.25
☐ 16	Terrell Brandon	.20	.09	.03
☐ 17	Danny Ferry	.10	.05	.01
☐ 18	Chris Mills	.10	.05	.01
☐ 19	Bobby Phills	.10	.05	.01
☐ 20	Bob Sura	.10	.05	.01
☐ 21	Jim Jackson	.20	.09	.03
☐ 22	Jason Kidd	.75	.35	.09
☐ 23	Jamal Mashburn	.20	.09	.03
☐ 24	George McCloud	.10	.05	.01
☐ 25	LaPhonso Ellis	.10	.05	.01
☐ 26	Antonio McDyess	.50	.23	.06
☐ 27	Bryant Stith	.10	.05	.01
☐ 28	Joe Dumars	.20	.09	.03
☐ 29	Grant Hill	1.25	.55	.16
☐ 30	Theo Ratliff	.10	.05	.01
☐ 31	Otis Thorpe	.10	.05	.01
☐ 32	Chris Mullin	.10	.05	.01
☐ 33	Joe Smith	.60	.25	.07
☐ 34	Latrell Sprewell	.20	.09	.03
☐ 35	Sam Cassell	.15	.07	.02
☐ 36	Clyde Drexler	.50	.23	.06
☐ 37	Robert Horry	.20	.09	.03
☐ 38	Hakeem Olajuwon	1.00	.45	.12
☐ 39	Antonio Davis	.10	.05	.01
☐ 40	Dale Davis	.10	.05	.01
☐ 41	Derrick McKey	.10	.05	.01
☐ 42	Reggie Miller	.50	.23	.06
☐ 43	Rik Smits	.20	.09	.03
☐ 44	Brent Barry	.25	.11	.03
☐ 45	Malik Sealy	.10	.05	.01
☐ 46	Loy Vaught	.15	.07	.02
☐ 47	Elden Campbell	.10	.05	.01
☐ 48	Cedric Ceballos	.10	.05	.01
☐ 49	Eddie Jones	.25	.11	.03
☐ 50	Nick Van Exel	.25	.11	.03
☐ 51	Sasha Danilovic	.10	.05	.01
☐ 52	Tim Hardaway	.15	.07	.02
☐ 53	Alonzo Mourning	.40	.18	.05
☐ 54	Kurt Thomas	.10	.05	.01
☐ 55	Vin Baker	.30	.14	.04
☐ 56	Sherman Douglas	.10	.05	.01
☐ 57	Glenn Robinson	.40	.18	.05
☐ 58	Kevin Garnett	1.50	.70	.19
☐ 59	Tom Gugliotta	.20	.09	.03
☐ 60	Doug West	.10	.05	.01
☐ 61	Shawn Bradley	.15	.07	.02
☐ 62	Ed O'Bannon	.10	.05	.01
☐ 63	Jayson Williams	.10	.05	.01
☐ 64	Patrick Ewing	.40	.18	.05
☐ 65	Charles Oakley	.10	.05	.01
☐ 66	John Starks	.15	.07	.02
☐ 67	Nick Anderson	.20	.09	.03
☐ 68	Horace Grant	.10	.05	.01
☐ 69	Anfernee Hardaway	2.50	1.10	.30
☐ 70	Dennis Scott	.10	.05	.01
☐ 71	Brian Shaw	.10	.05	.01

☐ 72	Derrick Coleman	.10	.05	.01
☐ 73	Jerry Stackhouse	1.00	.45	.12
☐ 74	Clarence Weatherspoon	.10	.05	.01
☐ 75	Charles Barkley	.60	.25	.07
☐ 76	Michael Finley	.60	.25	.07
☐ 77	Kevin Johnson	.20	.09	.03
☐ 78	Wesley Person	.10	.05	.01
☐ 79	Aaron McKie	.10	.05	.01
☐ 80	Clifford Robinson	.20	.09	.03
☐ 81	Arvydas Sabonis	.40	.18	.05
☐ 82	Gary Trent	.10	.05	.01
☐ 83	Tyus Edney	.25	.11	.03
☐ 84	Brian Grant	.10	.05	.01
☐ 85	Billy Owens	.10	.05	.01
☐ 86	Olden Polynice	.10	.05	.01
☐ 87	Mitch Richmond	.30	.14	.04
☐ 88	Vinny Del Negro	.10	.05	.01
☐ 89	Sean Elliott	.20	.09	.03
☐ 90	Avery Johnson	.10	.05	.01
☐ 91	David Robinson	.75	.35	.09
☐ 92	Hersey Hawkins	.10	.05	.01
☐ 93	Shawn Kemp	1.25	.55	.16
☐ 94	Gary Payton	.60	.25	.07
☐ 95	Sam Perkins	.10	.05	.01
☐ 96	Detlef Schrempf	.10	.05	.01
☐ 97	Doug Christie	.10	.05	.01
☐ 98	Damon Stoudamire	1.25	.55	.16
☐ 99	Sharone Wright	.10	.05	.01
☐ 100	Jeff Hornacek	.15	.07	.02
☐ 101	Karl Malone	.40	.18	.05
☐ 102	John Stockton	.40	.18	.05
☐ 103	Greg Anthony	.10	.05	.01
☐ 104	Blue Edwards	.10	.05	.01
☐ 105	Bryant Reeves	.30	.14	.04
☐ 106	Juwan Howard	.75	.35	.09
☐ 107	Gheorghe Muresan	.15	.07	.02
☐ 108	Chris Webber	.30	.14	.04
☐ 109	Kenny Anderson OTM	.10	.05	.01
☐ 110	Stacey Augmon OTM	.10	.05	.01
☐ 111	Chris Childs OTM	.10	.05	.01
☐ 112	Vlade Divac OTM	.10	.05	.01
☐ 113	Allan Houston OTM	.15	.07	.02
☐ 114	Mark Jackson OTM	.10	.05	.01
☐ 115	Larry Johnson OTM	.15	.07	.02
☐ 116	Grant Long OTM	.10	.05	.01
☐ 117	Anthony Mason OTM	.10	.05	.01
☐ 118	Dikembe Mutombo OTM	.15	.07	.02
☐ 119	Shaquille O'Neal OTM	2.00	.90	.25
☐ 120	Isaiah Rider OTM	.10	.05	.01
☐ 121	Rod Strickland OTM	.10	.05	.01
☐ 122	Rasheed Wallace OTM	.10	.05	.01
☐ 123	Jalen Rose OTM	.10	.05	.01
☐ 124	Anfernee Hardaway MET	1.25	.55	.16
☐ 125	Tim Hardaway MET	.15	.07	.02
☐ 126	Allan Houston MET	.15	.07	.02
☐ 127	Eddie Jones MET	.15	.07	.02
☐ 128	Michael Jordan MET	2.50	1.10	.30
☐ 129	Reggie Miller MET	.25	.11	.03
☐ 130	Glen Rice MET	.15	.07	.02
☐ 131	Mitch Richmond MET	.15	.07	.02
☐ 132	Steve Smith MET	.10	.05	.01
☐ 133	John Stockton MET	.15	.07	.02
☐ 134	Stephon Marbury FF	3.00	1.35	.35
☐ 135	Shareef Abdur-Rahim FF	2.00	.90	.25
☐ 136	Ray Allen FF	2.00	.90	.25
☐ 137	Kobe Bryant FF	4.00	1.80	.50
☐ 138	Steve Nash FF	.60	.25	.07
☐ 139	Grant Hill MS	.60	.25	.07
☐ 140	Jason Kidd MS	.40	.18	.05
☐ 141	Karl Malone MS	.15	.07	.02
☐ 142	Hakeem Olajuwon MS	.50	.23	.06

☐ 143	Shaquille O'Neal MS	1.00	.45	.12
☐ 144	Gary Payton MS	.30	.14	.04
☐ 145	Scottie Pippen MS	.60	.25	.07
☐ 146	Jerry Stackhouse MS	.50	.23	.06
☐ 147	Damon Stoudamire MS	.60	.25	.07
☐ 148	Rod Strickland MS	.10	.05	.01
☐ 149	Checklist	.10	.05	.01
☐ 150	Checklist	.10	.05	.01

1990-91 SkyBox

This 1990-91 set marks SkyBox's entry into the basketball card market. The complete set contains 423 standard-size cards featuring NBA players. The set was released in two series of 300 and 123 cards, respectively. Foil packs for each series contained 15 cards. However, the second series packs contained a mix of players from both series. The second series cards replaced 123 cards from the first series, which then became short-prints compared to other cards in the first series. The front features an action shot of the player on a computer-generated background of various color schemes. The player's name appears in a black stripe at the bottom with the team logo superimposed at the left lower corner. The photo is bordered in gold. The back presents head shots of the player with gold borders on white background. Player statistics are given in a box below the photo. The cards are checklisted below alphabetically according to team. Subsets are Coaches (301-327), Team Checklists (328-354), Lottery Picks (355-365), Updates (366-420), and Checklists (421-423). Rookie Cards of note included in the set are Nick Anderson, Mookie Blaylock, Derrick Coleman, Vlade Divac, Sean Elliott, Danny Ferry, Kendall Gill, Tim Hardaway, Chris Jackson, Avery Johnson, Shawn Kemp, Gary Payton, Drazen Petrovic, Glen Rice, Clifford Robinson and Dennis Scott. First series single prints (SP) are noted below.

	MINT	NRMT	EXC
COMPLETE SET (423)	20.00	9.00	2.50
COMPLETE SERIES 1 (300)	12.00	5.50	1.50
COMPLETE SERIES 2 (123)	8.00	3.60	1.00
COMMON CARD (1-300)	.05	.02	.01
COMMON CARD (301-423)	.10	.05	.01
COMMON SP	.10	.05	.01

#	Player			
☐ 1	John Battle	.05	.02	.01
☐ 2	Duane Ferrell SP	.10	.05	.01
☐ 3	Jon Koncak	.05	.02	.01
☐ 4	Cliff Levingston SP	.10	.05	.01
☐ 5	John Long SP	.10	.05	.01
☐ 6	Moses Malone	.15	.07	.02
☐ 7	Doc Rivers	.05	.02	.01
☐ 8	Kenny Smith SP	.10	.05	.01
☐ 9	Alexander Volkov	.05	.02	.01
☐ 10	Spud Webb	.10	.05	.01
☐ 11	Dominique Wilkins	.10	.05	.01
☐ 12	Kevin Willis	.05	.02	.01
☐ 13	John Bagley	.05	.02	.01
☐ 14	Larry Bird	1.00	.45	.12
☐ 15	Kevin Gamble	.05	.02	.01
☐ 16	Dennis Johnson SP	.15	.07	.02
☐ 17	Joe Kleine	.05	.02	.01
☐ 18	Reggie Lewis	.10	.05	.01
☐ 19	Kevin McHale	.10	.05	.01
☐ 20	Robert Parish	.10	.05	.01
☐ 21	Jim Paxson SP	.10	.05	.01
☐ 22	Ed Pinckney	.05	.02	.01
☐ 23	Brian Shaw	.05	.02	.01
☐ 24	Michael Smith	.05	.02	.01
☐ 25	Richard Anderson SP	.10	.05	.01
☐ 26	Muggsy Bogues	.10	.05	.01
☐ 27	Rex Chapman	.05	.02	.01
☐ 28	Dell Curry	.05	.02	.01
☐ 29	Armon Gilliam	.05	.02	.01
☐ 30	Michael Holton SP	.10	.05	.01
☐ 31	Dave Hoppen	.05	.02	.01
☐ 32	J.R. Reid	.05	.02	.01
☐ 33	Robert Reid SP	.10	.05	.01
☐ 34	Brian Rowsom SP	.10	.05	.01
☐ 35	Kelly Tripucka	.05	.02	.01
☐ 36	Micheal Williams SP UER (Misspelled Michael on card)	.10	.05	.01
☐ 37	B.J. Armstrong	.10	.05	.01
☐ 38	Bill Cartwright	.05	.02	.01
☐ 39	Horace Grant	.15	.07	.02
☐ 40	Craig Hodges	.05	.02	.01
☐ 41	Michael Jordan	3.00	1.35	.35
☐ 42	Stacey King	.05	.02	.01
☐ 43	Ed Nealy SP	.10	.05	.01
☐ 44	John Paxson	.10	.05	.01
☐ 45	Will Perdue	.05	.02	.01
☐ 46	Scottie Pippen	1.00	.45	.12
☐ 47	Jeff Sanders SP	.10	.05	.01
☐ 48	Winston Bennett	.05	.02	.01
☐ 49	Chucky Brown	.05	.02	.01
☐ 50	Brad Daugherty	.05	.02	.01
☐ 51	Craig Ehlo	.05	.02	.01
☐ 52	Steve Kerr	.05	.02	.01
☐ 53	Paul Mokeski SP	.10	.05	.01
☐ 54	John Morton	.05	.02	.01
☐ 55	Larry Nance	.05	.02	.01
☐ 56	Mark Price	.05	.02	.01
☐ 57	Tree Rollins SP	.10	.05	.01
☐ 58	Hot Rod Williams	.05	.02	.01
☐ 59	Steve Alford	.05	.02	.01
☐ 60	Rolando Blackman	.05	.02	.01
☐ 61	Adrian Dantley SP	.15	.07	.02
☐ 62	Brad Davis	.05	.02	.01
☐ 63	James Donaldson	.05	.02	.01
☐ 64	Derek Harper	.10	.05	.01
☐ 65	Anthony Jones SP	.10	.05	.01
☐ 66	Sam Perkins SP	.15	.07	.02
☐ 67	Roy Tarpley	.05	.02	.01
☐ 68	Bill Wennington SP	.10	.05	.01
☐ 69	Randy White	.05	.02	.01
☐ 70	Herb Williams	.05	.02	.01
☐ 71	Michael Adams	.05	.02	.01
☐ 72	Joe Barry Carroll SP	.10	.05	.01
☐ 73	Walter Davis	.10	.05	.01
☐ 74	Alex English SP	.15	.07	.02
☐ 75	Bill Hanzlik	.05	.02	.01
☐ 76	Tim Kempton SP	.10	.05	.01
☐ 77	Jerome Lane	.05	.02	.01
☐ 78	Lafayette Lever SP	.10	.05	.01
☐ 79	Todd Lichti	.05	.02	.01
☐ 80	Blair Rasmussen	.05	.02	.01
☐ 81	Dan Schayes SP	.10	.05	.01
☐ 82	Mark Aguirre	.10	.05	.01
☐ 83	William Bedford	.05	.02	.01
☐ 84	Joe Dumars	.10	.05	.01
☐ 85	James Edwards	.05	.02	.01
☐ 86	David Greenwood SP	.10	.05	.01
☐ 87	Scott Hastings	.05	.02	.01
☐ 88	Gerald Henderson SP	.10	.05	.01
☐ 89	Vinnie Johnson	.05	.02	.01
☐ 90	Bill Laimbeer	.05	.02	.01
☐ 91	Dennis Rodman (SkyBox logo in upper right or left)	1.25	.55	.16
☐ 91B	Dennis Rodman (SkyBox logo in upper left corner)	.60	.25	.07
☐ 92	John Salley	.05	.02	.01
☐ 93	Isiah Thomas	.15	.07	.02
☐ 94	Manute Bol SP	.10	.05	.01
☐ 95	Tim Hardaway	.60	.25	.07
☐ 96	Rod Higgins	.05	.02	.01
☐ 97	Sarunas Marciulionis	.05	.02	.01
☐ 98	Chris Mullin	.05	.02	.01
☐ 99	Jim Petersen	.05	.02	.01
☐ 100	Mitch Richmond	.30	.14	.04
☐ 101	Mike Smrek	.05	.02	.01
☐ 102	Terry Teagle SP	.10	.05	.01
☐ 103	Tom Tolbert	.05	.02	.01
☐ 104	Kelvin Upshaw SP	.10	.05	.01
☐ 105	Anthony Bowie SP	.10	.05	.01
☐ 106	Adrian Caldwell	.05	.02	.01
☐ 107	Eric (Sleepy) Floyd	.05	.02	.01
☐ 108	Buck Johnson	.05	.02	.01
☐ 109	Vernon Maxwell	.05	.02	.01
☐ 110	Hakeem Olajuwon	.60	.25	.07
☐ 111	Larry Smith	.05	.02	.01
☐ 112A	Otis Thorpe ERR (Front photo actually Mitchell Wiggins)	.50	.23	.06
☐ 112B	Otis Thorpe COR	.10	.05	.01
☐ 113A	M. Wiggins SP ERR (Front photo actually Otis Thorpe)	.50	.23	.06
☐ 113B	M. Wiggins SP COR	.15	.07	.02
☐ 114	Vern Fleming	.05	.02	.01
☐ 115	Rickey Green SP	.10	.05	.01
☐ 116	George McCloud	.25	.11	.03
☐ 117	Reggie Miller	.40	.18	.05
☐ 118A	Dyron Nix SP ERR (Back photo actually Wayman Tisdale)	1.50	.65	.19
☐ 118B	Dyron Nix SP COR	.10	.05	.01
☐ 119	Chuck Person	.05	.02	.01
☐ 120	Mike Sanders	.05	.02	.01
☐ 121	Detlef Schrempf	.10	.05	.01
☐ 122	Rik Smits	.10	.05	.01
☐ 123	LaSalle Thompson	.05	.02	.01
☐ 124	Benoit Benjamin	.05	.02	.01
☐ 125	Winston Garland	.05	.02	.01
☐ 126	Tom Garrick	.05	.02	.01

☐ 127 Gary Grant	.05	.02	.01
☐ 128 Ron Harper	.05	.02	.01
☐ 129 Danny Manning	.10	.05	.01
☐ 130 Jeff Martin	.05	.02	.01
☐ 131 Ken Norman	.05	.02	.01
☐ 132 Charles Smith	.05	.02	.01
☐ 133 Joe Wolf SP	.10	.05	.01
☐ 134 Michael Cooper SP	.15	.07	.02
☐ 135 Vlade Divac	.40	.18	.05
☐ 136 Larry Drew	.05	.02	.01
☐ 137 A.C. Green	.10	.05	.01
☐ 138 Magic Johnson	.75	.35	.09
☐ 139 Mark McNamara SP	.10	.05	.01
☐ 140 Byron Scott	.10	.05	.01
☐ 141 Mychal Thompson	.05	.02	.01
☐ 142 Orlando Woolridge SP	.10	.05	.01
☐ 143 James Worthy	.10	.05	.01
☐ 144 Terry Davis	.05	.02	.01
☐ 145 Sherman Douglas	.10	.05	.01
☐ 146 Kevin Edwards	.05	.02	.01
☐ 147 Tellis Frank SP	.10	.05	.01
☐ 148 Scott Haffner SP	.10	.05	.01
☐ 149 Grant Long	.05	.02	.01
☐ 150 Glen Rice	.75	.35	.09
☐ 151 Rony Seikaly	.05	.02	.01
☐ 152 Rory Sparrow SP	.10	.05	.01
☐ 153 Jon Sundvold	.05	.02	.01
☐ 154 Billy Thompson	.05	.02	.01
☐ 155 Greg Anderson	.05	.02	.01
☐ 156 Ben Coleman SP	.10	.05	.01
☐ 157 Jeff Grayer	.05	.02	.01
☐ 158 Jay Humphries	.05	.02	.01
☐ 159 Frank Kornet	.05	.02	.01
☐ 160 Larry Krystkowiak	.05	.02	.01
☐ 161 Brad Lohaus	.05	.02	.01
☐ 162 Ricky Pierce	.05	.02	.01
☐ 163 Paul Pressey SP	.10	.05	.01
☐ 164 Fred Roberts	.05	.02	.01
☐ 165 Alvin Robertson	.05	.02	.01
☐ 166 Jack Sikma	.10	.05	.01
☐ 167 Randy Breuer	.05	.02	.01
☐ 168 Tony Campbell	.05	.02	.01
☐ 169 Tyrone Corbin	.05	.02	.01
☐ 170 Sidney Lowe SP	.10	.05	.01
☐ 171 Sam Mitchell	.05	.02	.01
☐ 172 Tod Murphy	.05	.02	.01
☐ 173 Pooh Richardson	.10	.05	.01
☐ 174 Donald Royal SP	.15	.07	.02
☐ 175 Brad Sellers SP	.10	.05	.01
☐ 176 Mookie Blaylock	.50	.23	.06
☐ 177 Sam Bowie	.05	.02	.01
☐ 178 Lester Conner	.05	.02	.01
☐ 179 Derrick Gervin	.05	.02	.01
☐ 180 Jack Haley	.05	.02	.01
☐ 181 Roy Hinson	.05	.02	.01
☐ 182 Dennis Hopson SP	.10	.05	.01
☐ 183 Chris Morris	.05	.02	.01
☐ 184 Pete Myers SP	.10	.05	.01
☐ 185 Purvis Short SP	.10	.05	.01
☐ 186 Maurice Cheeks	.10	.05	.01
☐ 187 Patrick Ewing	.25	.11	.03
☐ 188 Stuart Gray	.05	.02	.01
☐ 189 Mark Jackson	.05	.02	.01
☐ 190 Johnny Newman SP	.10	.05	.01
☐ 191 Charles Oakley	.05	.02	.01
☐ 192 Brian Quinnett	.05	.02	.01
☐ 193 Trent Tucker	.05	.02	.01
☐ 194 Kiki Vandeweghe	.05	.02	.01
☐ 195 Kenny Walker	.05	.02	.01
☐ 196 Eddie Lee Wilkins	.05	.02	.01
☐ 197 Gerald Wilkins	.05	.02	.01

☐ 198 Mark Acres	.05	.02	.01
☐ 199 Nick Anderson	.50	.23	.06
☐ 200 Michael Ansley	.05	.02	.01
☐ 201 Terry Catledge	.05	.02	.01
☐ 202 Dave Corzine SP	.10	.05	.01
☐ 203 Sidney Green SP	.10	.05	.01
☐ 204 Jerry Reynolds	.05	.02	.01
☐ 205 Scott Skiles	.05	.02	.01
☐ 206 Otis Smith	.05	.02	.01
☐ 207 Reggie Theus SP	.15	.07	.02
☐ 208 Jeff Turner	.05	.02	.01
☐ 209 Sam Vincent	.05	.02	.01
☐ 210 Ron Anderson	.05	.02	.01
☐ 211 Charles Barkley	.40	.18	.05
☐ 212 Scott Brooks SP	.10	.05	.01
☐ 213 Lanard Copeland SP	.10	.05	.01
☐ 214 Johnny Dawkins	.05	.02	.01
☐ 215 Mike Gminski	.05	.02	.01
☐ 216 Hersey Hawkins	.05	.02	.01
☐ 217 Rick Mahorn	.05	.02	.01
☐ 218 Derek Smith	.10	.05	.01
☐ 219 Bob Thornton	.05	.02	.01
☐ 220 Tom Chambers	.05	.02	.01
☐ 221 Greg Grant SP	.10	.05	.01
☐ 222 Jeff Hornacek	.05	.02	.01
☐ 223 Eddie Johnson	.05	.02	.01
☐ 224A Kevin Johnson	.10	.05	.01
(SkyBox logo in lower right corner)			
☐ 224B Kevin Johnson	.10	.05	.01
(SkyBox logo in upper right corner)			
☐ 225 Andrew Lang	.05	.02	.01
☐ 226 Dan Majerle	.10	.05	.01
☐ 227 Mike McGee SP	.10	.05	.01
☐ 228 Tim Perry	.05	.02	.01
☐ 229 Kurt Rambis	.05	.02	.01
☐ 230 Mark West	.05	.02	.01
☐ 231 Mark Bryant	.05	.02	.01
☐ 232 Wayne Cooper	.05	.02	.01
☐ 233 Clyde Drexler	.30	.14	.04
☐ 234 Kevin Duckworth	.05	.02	.01
☐ 235 Byron Irvin SP	.10	.05	.01
☐ 236 Jerome Kersey	.05	.02	.01
☐ 237 Drazen Petrovic	.25	.11	.03
☐ 238 Terry Porter	.05	.02	.01
☐ 239 Cliff Robinson	.60	.25	.07
☐ 240 Buck Williams	.10	.05	.01
☐ 241 Danny Young	.05	.02	.01
☐ 242 Danny Ainge SP	.15	.07	.02
☐ 243 Randy Allen SP	.10	.05	.01
☐ 244A Antoine Carr SP	.15	.07	.02
(Wearing Atlanta jersey on back)			
☐ 244B Antoine Carr	.05	.02	.01
(Wearing Sacramento jersey on back)			
☐ 245 Vinny Del Negro SP	.15	.07	.02
☐ 246 Pervis Ellison	.05	.02	.01
☐ 247 Greg Kite SP	.10	.05	.01
☐ 248 Rodney McCray SP	.10	.05	.01
☐ 249 Harold Pressley SP	.10	.05	.01
☐ 250 Ralph Sampson	.05	.02	.01
☐ 251 Wayman Tisdale	.05	.02	.01
☐ 252 Willie Anderson	.05	.02	.01
☐ 253 Uwe Blab SP	.10	.05	.01
☐ 254 Frank Brickowski SP	.10	.05	.01
☐ 255 Terry Cummings	.05	.02	.01
☐ 256 Sean Elliott	.75	.35	.09
☐ 257 Caldwell Jones SP	.10	.05	.01
☐ 258 Johnny Moore SP	.10	.05	.01

#	Player			
☐ 259	Zarko Paspalj SP	.10	.05	.01
☐ 260	David Robinson	1.00	.45	.12
☐ 261	Rod Strickland	.05	.02	.01
☐ 262	David Wingate SP	.10	.05	.01
☐ 263	Dana Barros	.25	.11	.03
☐ 264	Michael Cage	.05	.02	.01
☐ 265	Quintin Dailey	.05	.02	.01
☐ 266	Dale Ellis	.05	.02	.01
☐ 267	Steve Johnson SP	.10	.05	.01
☐ 268	Shawn Kemp	5.00	2.20	.60
☐ 269	Xavier McDaniel	.05	.02	.01
☐ 270	Derrick McKey	.05	.02	.01
☐ 271A	Nate McMillan SP ERR	.10	.05	.01
	(Back photo actually Olden Polynice; first series)			
☐ 271B	Nate McMillan COR	.05	.02	.01
	(second series)			
☐ 272	Olden Polynice	.05	.02	.01
☐ 273	Sedale Threatt	.05	.02	.01
☐ 274	Thurl Bailey	.05	.02	.01
☐ 275	Mike Brown	.05	.02	.01
☐ 276	Mark Eaton	.05	.02	.01
☐ 277	Blue Edwards	.05	.02	.01
☐ 278	Darrell Griffith	.10	.05	.01
☐ 279	Bobby Hansen SP	.10	.05	.01
☐ 280	Eric Johnson	.05	.02	.01
☐ 281	Eric Leckner SP	.10	.05	.01
☐ 282	Karl Malone	.25	.11	.03
☐ 283	Delaney Rudd	.05	.02	.01
☐ 284	John Stockton	.30	.14	.04
☐ 285	Mark Alarie	.05	.02	.01
☐ 286	Steve Colter SP	.10	.05	.01
☐ 287	Ledell Eackles SP	.10	.05	.01
☐ 288	Harvey Grant	.05	.02	.01
☐ 289	Tom Hammonds	.05	.02	.01
☐ 290	Charles Jones	.05	.02	.01
☐ 291	Bernard King	.10	.05	.01
☐ 292	Jeff Malone SP	.10	.05	.01
☐ 293	Darrell Walker	.05	.02	.01
☐ 294	John Williams	.05	.02	.01
☐ 295	Checklist 1 SP	.10	.05	.01
☐ 296	Checklist 2 SP	.10	.05	.01
☐ 297	Checklist 3 SP	.10	.05	.01
☐ 298	Checklist 4 SP	.10	.05	.01
☐ 299	Checklist 5 SP	.10	.05	.01
☐ 300	Danny Ferry SP	.50	.23	.06
☐ 301	Bob Weiss CO	.10	.05	.01
☐ 302	Chris Ford CO	.10	.05	.01
☐ 303	Gene Littles CO	.10	.05	.01
☐ 304	Phil Jackson CO	.15	.07	.02
☐ 305	Lenny Wilkens CO	.15	.07	.02
☐ 306	Richie Adubato CO	.10	.05	.01
☐ 307	Paul Westhead CO	.10	.05	.01
☐ 308	Chuck Daly CO	.15	.07	.02
☐ 309	Don Nelson CO	.15	.07	.02
☐ 310	Don Chaney CO	.10	.05	.01
☐ 311	Dick Versace CO	.10	.05	.01
☐ 312	Mike Schuler CO	.10	.05	.01
☐ 313	Mike Dunleavy CO	.10	.05	.01
☐ 314	Ron Rothstein CO	.10	.05	.01
☐ 315	Del Harris CO	.10	.05	.01
☐ 316	Bill Musselman CO	.10	.05	.01
☐ 317	Bill Fitch CO	.10	.05	.01
☐ 318	Stu Jackson CO	.10	.05	.01
☐ 319	Matt Guokas CO	.10	.05	.01
☐ 320	Jim Lynam CO	.10	.05	.01
☐ 321	Cotton Fitzsimmons CO	.10	.05	.01
☐ 322	Rick Adelman CO	.10	.05	.01
☐ 323	Dick Motta CO	.10	.05	.01
☐ 324	Larry Brown CO	.15	.07	.02
☐ 325	K.C. Jones CO	.15	.07	.02
☐ 326	Jerry Sloan CO	.15	.07	.02
☐ 327	Wes Unseld CO	.15	.07	.02
☐ 328	Atlanta Hawks TC	.10	.05	.01
☐ 329	Boston Celtics TC	.10	.05	.01
☐ 330	Charlotte Hornets TC	.10	.05	.01
☐ 331	Chicago Bulls TC	.10	.05	.01
☐ 332	Cleveland Cavaliers TC	.10	.05	.01
☐ 333	Dallas Mavericks TC	.10	.05	.01
☐ 334	Denver Nuggets TC	.10	.05	.01
☐ 335	Detroit Pistons TC	.10	.05	.01
☐ 336	Golden State Warriors TC	.10	.05	.01
☐ 337	Houston Rockets TC	.10	.05	.01
☐ 338	Indiana Pacers TC	.10	.05	.01
☐ 339	Los Angeles Clippers TC	.10	.05	.01
☐ 340	Los Angeles Lakers TC	.10	.05	.01
☐ 341	Miami Heat TC	.10	.05	.01
☐ 342	Milwaukee Bucks TC	.10	.05	.01
☐ 343	Minn. Timberwolves TC	.10	.05	.01
☐ 344	New Jersey Nets TC	.10	.05	.01
☐ 345	New York Knicks TC	.10	.05	.01
☐ 346	Orlando Magic TC	.10	.05	.01
☐ 347	Philadelphia 76ers TC	.10	.05	.01
☐ 348	Phoenix Suns TC	.10	.05	.01
☐ 349	Portland Trail Blazers TC	.10	.05	.01
☐ 350	Sacramento Kings TC	.10	.05	.01
☐ 351	San Antonio Spurs TC	.10	.05	.01
☐ 352	Seattle SuperSonics TC	.10	.05	.01
☐ 353	Utah Jazz TC	.10	.05	.01
☐ 354	Washington Bullets TC	.10	.05	.01
☐ 355	Rumeal Robinson	.10	.05	.01
☐ 356	Kendall Gill	.40	.18	.05
☐ 357	Chris Jackson	1.00	.45	.12
☐ 358	Tyrone Hill	.50	.23	.06
☐ 359	Bo Kimble	.10	.05	.01
☐ 360	Willie Burton	.10	.05	.01
☐ 361	Felton Spencer	.10	.05	.01
☐ 362	Derrick Coleman	1.00	.45	.12
☐ 363	Dennis Scott	1.00	.45	.12
☐ 364	Lionel Simmons	.25	.11	.03
☐ 365	Gary Payton	5.00	2.20	.60
☐ 366	Tim McCormick	.10	.05	.01
☐ 367	Sidney Moncrief	.15	.07	.02
☐ 368	Kenny Gattison	.10	.05	.01
☐ 369	Randolph Keys	.10	.05	.01
☐ 370	Johnny Newman	.10	.05	.01
☐ 371	Dennis Hopson	.10	.05	.01
☐ 372	Cliff Levingston	.10	.05	.01
☐ 373	Derrick Chievous	.10	.05	.01
☐ 374	Danny Ferry	.15	.07	.02
☐ 375	Alex English	.15	.07	.02
☐ 376	Lafayette Lever	.10	.05	.01
☐ 377	Rodney McCray	.10	.05	.01
☐ 378	T.R. Dunn	.10	.05	.01
☐ 379	Corey Gaines	.10	.05	.01
☐ 380	Avery Johnson	1.00	.45	.12
☐ 381	Joe Wolf	.10	.05	.01
☐ 382	Orlando Woolridge	.10	.05	.01
☐ 383	Tree Rollins	.10	.05	.01
☐ 384	Steve Johnson	.10	.05	.01
☐ 385	Kenny Smith	.10	.05	.01
☐ 386	Mike Woodson	.10	.05	.01
☐ 387	Greg Dreiling	.10	.05	.01
☐ 388	Micheal Williams	.10	.05	.01
☐ 389	Randy Wittman	.10	.05	.01
☐ 390	Ken Bannister	.10	.05	.01
☐ 391	Sam Perkins	.10	.05	.01
☐ 392	Terry Teagle	.10	.05	.01
☐ 393	Milt Wagner	.10	.05	.01
☐ 394	Frank Brickowski	.10	.05	.01
☐ 395	Dan Schayes	.10	.05	.01

		MINT	NRMT	EXC
☐ 396	Scott Brooks	.10	.05	.01
☐ 397	Doug West	.10	.05	.01
☐ 398	Chris Dudley	.10	.05	.01
☐ 399	Reggie Theus	.15	.07	.02
☐ 400	Greg Grant	.10	.05	.01
☐ 401	Greg Kite	.10	.05	.01
☐ 402	Mark McNamara	.10	.05	.01
☐ 403	Manute Bol	.10	.05	.01
☐ 404	Rickey Green	.10	.05	.01
☐ 405	Kenny Battle	.10	.05	.01
☐ 406	Ed Nealy	.10	.05	.01
☐ 407	Danny Ainge	.15	.07	.02
☐ 408	Steve Colter	.10	.05	.01
☐ 409	Bobby Hansen	.10	.05	.01
☐ 410	Eric Leckner	.10	.05	.01
☐ 411	Rory Sparrow	.10	.05	.01
☐ 412	Bill Wennington	.10	.05	.01
☐ 413	Sidney Green	.10	.05	.01
☐ 414	David Greenwood	.10	.05	.01
☐ 415	Paul Pressey	.10	.05	.01
☐ 416	Reggie Williams	.10	.05	.01
☐ 417	Dave Corzine	.10	.05	.01
☐ 418	Jeff Malone	.10	.05	.01
☐ 419	Pervis Ellison	.10	.05	.01
☐ 420	Byron Irvin	.10	.05	.01
☐ 421	Checklist 1	.10	.05	.01
☐ 422	Checklist 2	.10	.05	.01
☐ 423	Checklist 3	.10	.05	.01
☐ NNO	SkyBox Salutes the NBA	5.00	2.20	.60

1991-92 SkyBox

Earvin Johnson

The complete 1991-92 SkyBox basketball set contains 659 standard-size cards. The set was released in two series of 350 and 309 cards, respectively. This year SkyBox did not package both first and second series cards in second series packs. The cards were available in 15-card fin-sealed foil packs that feature four different mail-in offers on the back, or 62-card blister packs that contain two (of four) SkyBox logo cards not available in the 15-card foil packs. The fronts feature color action player photos overlaying multi-colored computer-generated geometric shapes and stripes. The pictures are borderless and the card face is white. The player's name appears in different color lettering at the bottom of each card, with the team logo in the lower right corner. In a trapezoid shape, the backs have non-action color player photos. At the bottom biographical and statistical informa-

tion appear inside a color-striped diagonal. The cards are numbered and checklisted below alphabetically within team order. Subsets are Stats (298-307), Best Single Game Performance (308-312), NBA All-Star Weekend Highlights (313-317), NBA All-Rookie Team (318-322), GQ's "NBA All-Star Style Team" (323-327), Centennial Highlights (328-332), Great Moments from the NBA Finals (333-337), Stay in School (338-344), Checklists (345-350), Team Logos (351-377), Coaches (378-404), Game Frames (405-431), Sixth Man (432-458), Teamwork (459-485), Rising Stars (486-512), Lottery Picks (513-523), Centennial (524-529), 1992 USA Basketball Team (530-546), 1988 USA Basketball Team (547-556), 1984 USA Basketball Team (557-563), The Magic of SkyBox (564-571), SkyBox Salutes (572-576), Skymasters (577-588), Shooting Stars (589-602), Small School Sensations (603-609), NBA Stay in School (610-614), Player Updates (615-653), and Checklists (654-659). As part of a promotion with Cheerios, four SkyBox cards from the basic set were inserted into specially marked 10-ounce and 15-ounce cereal boxes. These cereal boxes appeared on store shelves in December 1991 and January 1992, and they depicted images of SkyBox cards on the front, back, and side panels. An unnumbered gold foil-stamped 1992 USA Basketball Team photo card was randomly inserted into second series foil packs, while the blister packs featured two-card sets of NBA MVPs from the same team for consecutive years. As a mail-in offer a limited Clyde Drexler Olympic card was sent to the first 10,000 respondents in return for ten SkyBox wrappers and 1.00 for postage and handling. Rookie Cards of note include Kenny Anderson, Stacey Augmon, Terrell Brandon, Larry Johnson, Dikembe Mutombo, Steve Smith and John Starks.

		MINT	NRMT	EXC
	COMPLETE SET (659)	60.00	27.00	7.50
	COMPLETE SERIES 1 (350)	20.00	9.00	2.50
	COMPLETE SERIES 2 (309)	40.00	18.00	5.00
	COMMON CARD (1-659)	.05	.02	.01
☐ 1	John Battle	.05	.02	.01
☐ 2	Duane Ferrell	.05	.02	.01
☐ 3	Jon Koncak	.05	.02	.01
☐ 4	Moses Malone	.25	.11	.03
☐ 5	Tim McCormick	.05	.02	.01
☐ 6	Sidney Moncrief	.10	.05	.01
☐ 7	Doc Rivers	.05	.02	.01
☐ 8	Rumeal Robinson UER (Drafted 11th, should say 10th)	.05	.02	.01
☐ 9	Spud Webb	.10	.05	.01
☐ 10	Dominique Wilkins	.15	.07	.02
☐ 11	Kevin Willis	.10	.05	.01
☐ 12	Larry Bird	1.50	.70	.19
☐ 13	Dee Brown	.10	.05	.01
☐ 14	Kevin Gamble	.05	.02	.01
☐ 15	Joe Kleine	.05	.02	.01
☐ 16	Reggie Lewis	.10	.05	.01
☐ 17	Kevin McHale	.15	.07	.02

#	Player			
18	Robert Parish	.15	.07	.02
19	Ed Pinckney	.05	.02	.01
20	Brian Shaw	.05	.02	.01
21	Michael Smith	.05	.02	.01
22	Stojko Vrankovic	.05	.02	.01
23	Muggsy Bogues	.10	.05	.01
24	Rex Chapman	.05	.02	.01
25	Dell Curry	.05	.02	.01
26	Kenny Gattison	.05	.02	.01
27	Kendall Gill	.10	.05	.01
28	Mike Gminski	.05	.02	.01
29	Randolph Keys	.05	.02	.01
30	Eric Leckner	.05	.02	.01
31	Johnny Newman	.05	.02	.01
32	J.R. Reid	.05	.02	.01
33	Kelly Tripucka	.05	.02	.01
34	B.J. Armstrong	.10	.05	.01
35	Bill Cartwright	.05	.02	.01
36	Horace Grant	.15	.07	.02
37	Craig Hodges	.05	.02	.01
38	Dennis Hopson	.05	.02	.01
39	Michael Jordan	5.00	2.20	.60
40	Stacey King	.05	.02	.01
41	Cliff Levingston	.05	.02	.01
42	John Paxson	.10	.05	.01
43	Will Perdue	.05	.02	.01
44	Scottie Pippen	1.25	.55	.16
45	Winston Bennett	.05	.02	.01
46	Chucky Brown	.05	.02	.01
47	Brad Daugherty	.05	.02	.01
48	Craig Ehlo	.05	.02	.01
49	Danny Ferry	.05	.02	.01
50	Steve Kerr	.05	.02	.01
51	John Morton	.05	.02	.01
52	Larry Nance	.10	.05	.01
53	Mark Price	.05	.02	.01
54	Darnell Valentine	.05	.02	.01
55	John Williams	.05	.02	.01
56	Steve Alford	.10	.05	.01
57	Rolando Blackman	.10	.05	.01
58	Brad Davis	.05	.02	.01
59	James Donaldson	.05	.02	.01
60	Derek Harper	.10	.05	.01
61	Fat Lever	.05	.02	.01
62	Rodney McCray	.05	.02	.01
63	Roy Tarpley	.05	.02	.01
64	Kelvin Upshaw	.05	.02	.01
65	Randy White	.05	.02	.01
66	Herb Williams	.05	.02	.01
67	Michael Adams	.05	.02	.01
68	Greg Anderson	.05	.02	.01
69	Anthony Cook	.05	.02	.01
70	Chris Jackson	.15	.07	.02
71	Jerome Lane	.05	.02	.01
72	Marcus Liberty	.05	.02	.01
73	Todd Lichti	.05	.02	.01
74	Blair Rasmussen	.05	.02	.01
75	Reggie Williams	.05	.02	.01
76	Joe Wolf	.05	.02	.01
77	Orlando Woolridge	.05	.02	.01
78	Mark Aguirre	.10	.05	.01
79	William Bedford	.05	.02	.01
80	Lance Blanks	.05	.02	.01
81	Joe Dumars	.15	.07	.02
82	James Edwards	.05	.02	.01
83	Scott Hastings	.05	.02	.01
84	Vinnie Johnson	.05	.02	.01
85	Bill Laimbeer	.05	.02	.01
86	Dennis Rodman	1.50	.70	.19
87	John Salley	.05	.02	.01
88	Isiah Thomas	.25	.11	.03
89	Mario Elie	.30	.14	.04
90	Tim Hardaway	.15	.07	.02
91	Rod Higgins	.05	.02	.01
92	Tyrone Hill	.15	.07	.02
93	Les Jepsen	.05	.02	.01
94	Alton Lister	.05	.02	.01
95	Sarunas Marciulionis	.05	.02	.01
96	Chris Mullin	.10	.05	.01
97	Jim Petersen	.05	.02	.01
98	Mitch Richmond	.40	.18	.05
99	Tom Tolbert	.05	.02	.01
100	Adrian Caldwell	.05	.02	.01
101	Eric(Sleepy) Floyd	.05	.02	.01
102	Dave Jamerson	.05	.02	.01
103	Buck Johnson	.05	.02	.01
104	Vernon Maxwell	.05	.02	.01
105	Hakeem Olajuwon	1.00	.45	.12
106	Kenny Smith	.05	.02	.01
107	Larry Smith	.05	.02	.01
108	Otis Thorpe	.10	.05	.01
109	Kennard Winchester	.05	.02	.01
110	David Wood	.05	.02	.01
111	Greg Dreiling	.05	.02	.01
112	Vern Fleming	.05	.02	.01
113	George McCloud	.10	.05	.01
114	Reggie Miller	.50	.23	.06
115	Chuck Person	.05	.02	.01
116	Mike Sanders	.05	.02	.01
117	Detlef Schrempf	.10	.05	.01
118	Rik Smits	.15	.07	.02
119	LaSalle Thompson	.05	.02	.01
120	Kenny Williams	.05	.02	.01
121	Micheal Williams	.05	.02	.01
122	Ken Bannister	.05	.02	.01
123	Winston Garland	.05	.02	.01
124	Gary Grant	.05	.02	.01
125	Ron Harper	.05	.02	.01
126	Bo Kimble	.05	.02	.01
127	Danny Manning	.10	.05	.01
128	Jeff Martin	.05	.02	.01
129	Ken Norman	.05	.02	.01
130	Olden Polynice	.05	.02	.01
131	Charles Smith	.05	.02	.01
132	Loy Vaught	.10	.05	.01
133	Elden Campbell	.10	.05	.01
134	Vlade Divac	.15	.07	.02
135	Larry Drew	.05	.02	.01
136	A.C. Green	.05	.02	.01
137	Magic Johnson	1.25	.55	.16
138	Sam Perkins	.05	.02	.01
139	Byron Scott	.10	.05	.01
140	Tony Smith	.05	.02	.01
141	Terry Teagle	.05	.02	.01
142	Mychal Thompson	.05	.02	.01
143	James Worthy	.15	.07	.02
144	Willie Burton	.05	.02	.01
145	Bimbo Coles	.05	.02	.01
146	Terry Davis	.05	.02	.01
147	Sherman Douglas	.05	.02	.01
148	Kevin Edwards	.05	.02	.01
149	Alec Kessler	.05	.02	.01
150	Grant Long	.05	.02	.01
151	Glen Rice	.25	.11	.03
152	Rony Seikaly	.05	.02	.01
153	Jon Sundvold	.05	.02	.01
154	Billy Thompson	.05	.02	.01
155	Frank Brickowski	.05	.02	.01
156	Lester Conner	.05	.02	.01
157	Jeff Grayer	.05	.02	.01
158	Jay Humphries	.05	.02	.01
159	Larry Krystkowiak	.05	.02	.01

□	#	Player			
□	160	Brad Lohaus	.05	.02	.01
□	161	Dale Ellis	.05	.02	.01
□	162	Fred Roberts	.05	.02	.01
□	163	Alvin Robertson	.05	.02	.01
□	164	Danny Schayes	.05	.02	.01
□	165	Jack Sikma	.10	.05	.01
□	166	Randy Breuer	.05	.02	.01
□	167	Scott Brooks	.05	.02	.01
□	168	Tony Campbell	.05	.02	.01
□	169	Tyrone Corbin	.05	.02	.01
□	170	Gerald Glass	.05	.02	.01
□	171	Sam Mitchell	.05	.02	.01
□	172	Tod Murphy	.05	.02	.01
□	173	Pooh Richardson	.05	.02	.01
□	174	Felton Spencer	.05	.02	.01
□	175	Bob Thornton	.05	.02	.01
□	176	Doug West	.05	.02	.01
□	177	Mookie Blaylock	.15	.07	.02
□	178	Sam Bowie	.05	.02	.01
□	179	Jud Buechler	.05	.02	.01
□	180	Derrick Coleman	.05	.02	.01
□	181	Chris Dudley	.05	.02	.01
□	182	Tate George	.05	.02	.01
□	183	Jack Haley	.05	.02	.01
□	184	Terry Mills	.15	.07	.02
□	185	Chris Morris	.05	.02	.01
□	186	Drazen Petrovic	.10	.05	.01
□	187	Reggie Theus	.10	.05	.01
□	188	Maurice Cheeks	.10	.05	.01
□	189	Patrick Ewing	.40	.18	.05
□	190	Mark Jackson	.05	.02	.01
□	191	Jerrod Mustaf	.05	.02	.01
□	192	Charles Oakley	.05	.02	.01
□	193	Brian Quinnett	.05	.02	.01
□	194	John Starks	.50	.23	.06
□	195	Trent Tucker	.05	.02	.01
□	196	Kiki Vandeweghe	.05	.02	.01
□	197	Kenny Walker	.05	.02	.01
□	198	Gerald Wilkins	.05	.02	.01
□	199	Mark Acres	.05	.02	.01
□	200	Nick Anderson	.15	.07	.02
□	201	Michael Ansley	.05	.02	.01
□	202	Terry Catledge	.05	.02	.01
□	203	Greg Kite	.05	.02	.01
□	204	Jerry Reynolds	.05	.02	.01
□	205	Dennis Scott	.15	.07	.02
□	206	Scott Skiles	.05	.02	.01
□	207	Otis Smith	.05	.02	.01
□	208	Jeff Turner	.05	.02	.01
□	209	Sam Vincent	.05	.02	.01
□	210	Ron Anderson	.05	.02	.01
□	211	Charles Barkley	.60	.25	.07
□	212	Manute Bol	.05	.02	.01
□	213	Johnny Dawkins	.05	.02	.01
□	214	Armon Gilliam	.05	.02	.01
□	215	Rickey Green	.05	.02	.01
□	216	Hersey Hawkins	.10	.05	.01
□	217	Rick Mahorn	.05	.02	.01
□	218	Brian Oliver	.05	.02	.01
□	219	Andre Turner	.05	.02	.01
□	220	Jayson Williams	.05	.02	.01
□	221	Joe Barry Carroll	.05	.02	.01
□	222	Cedric Ceballos	.15	.07	.02
□	223	Tom Chambers	.05	.02	.01
□	224	Jeff Hornacek	.10	.05	.01
□	225	Kevin Johnson	.15	.07	.02
□	226	Negele Knight	.05	.02	.01
□	227	Andrew Lang	.05	.02	.01
□	228	Dan Majerle	.10	.05	.01
□	229	Xavier McDaniel	.05	.02	.01
□	230	Kurt Rambis	.05	.02	.01
□	231	Mark West	.05	.02	.01
□	232	Alaa Abdelnaby	.05	.02	.01
□	233	Danny Ainge	.15	.07	.02
□	234	Mark Bryant	.05	.02	.01
□	235	Wayne Cooper	.05	.02	.01
□	236	Walter Davis	.15	.07	.02
□	237	Clyde Drexler	.50	.23	.06
□	238	Kevin Duckworth	.05	.02	.01
□	239	Jerome Kersey	.05	.02	.01
□	240	Terry Porter	.05	.02	.01
□	241	Cliff Robinson	.05	.02	.01
□	242	Buck Williams	.10	.05	.01
□	243	Anthony Bonner	.05	.02	.01
□	244	Antoine Carr	.05	.02	.01
□	245	Duane Causwell	.05	.02	.01
□	246	Bobby Hansen	.05	.02	.01
□	247	Jim Les	.05	.02	.01
□	248	Travis Mays	.05	.02	.01
□	249	Ralph Sampson	.05	.02	.01
□	250	Lionel Simmons	.05	.02	.01
□	251	Rory Sparrow	.05	.02	.01
□	252	Wayman Tisdale	.05	.02	.01
□	253	Bill Wennington	.05	.02	.01
□	254	Willie Anderson	.05	.02	.01
□	255	Terry Cummings	.05	.02	.01
□	256	Sean Elliott	.25	.11	.03
□	257	Sidney Green	.05	.02	.01
□	258	David Greenwood	.05	.02	.01
□	259	Avery Johnson	.15	.07	.02
□	260	Paul Pressey	.05	.02	.01
□	261	David Robinson	1.00	.45	.12
□	262	Dwayne Schintzius	.05	.02	.01
□	263	Rod Strickland	.05	.02	.01
□	264	David Wingate	.05	.02	.01
□	265	Dana Barros	.10	.05	.01
□	266	Benoit Benjamin	.05	.02	.01
□	267	Michael Cage	.05	.02	.01
□	268	Quintin Dailey	.05	.02	.01
□	269	Ricky Pierce	.05	.02	.01
□	270	Eddie Johnson	.05	.02	.01
□	271	Shawn Kemp	2.00	.90	.25
□	272	Derrick McKey	.05	.02	.01
□	273	Nate McMillan	.05	.02	.01
□	274	Gary Payton	1.00	.45	.12
□	275	Sedale Threatt	.05	.02	.01
□	276	Thurl Bailey	.05	.02	.01
□	277	Mike Brown	.05	.02	.01
□	278	Tony Brown	.05	.02	.01
□	279	Mark Eaton	.05	.02	.01
□	280	Blue Edwards	.05	.02	.01
□	281	Darrell Griffith	.10	.05	.01
□	282	Jeff Malone	.05	.02	.01
□	283	Karl Malone	.40	.18	.05
□	284	Delaney Rudd	.05	.02	.01
□	285	John Stockton	.40	.18	.05
□	286	Andy Toolson	.05	.02	.01
□	287	Mark Alarie	.05	.02	.01
□	288	Ledell Eackles	.05	.02	.01
□	289	Pervis Ellison	.05	.02	.01
□	290	A.J. English	.05	.02	.01
□	291	Harvey Grant	.05	.02	.01
□	292	Tom Hammonds	.05	.02	.01
□	293	Charles Jones	.05	.02	.01
□	294	Bernard King	.15	.07	.02
□	295	Darrell Walker	.05	.02	.01
□	296	John Williams	.05	.02	.01
□	297	Haywoode Workman	.05	.02	.01
□	298	Muggsy Bogues	.10	.05	.01
		Assist-to-Turnover			
		Ratio Leader			
□	299	Lester Conner	.05	.02	.01

	Steal-to Turnover Ratio Leader			
☐ 300	Michael Adams	.05	.02	.01
	Largest One-Year Scoring Improvement			
☐ 301	Chris Mullin	.10	.05	.01
	Most Minutes Per Game			
☐ 302	Otis Thorpe	.10	.05	.01
	Most Consecutive Games Played			
☐ 303	Mitch Richmond	.10	.05	.01
	Chris Mullin Tim Hardaway Highest Scoring Trio			
☐ 304	Darrell Walker	.05	.02	.01
	Top Rebounding Guard			
☐ 305	Jerome Lane	.05	.02	.01
	Rebounds Per 48 Minutes			
☐ 306	John Stockton	.15	.07	.02
	Assists Per 48 Minutes			
☐ 307	Michael Jordan	2.50	1.10	.30
	Points Per 48 Minutes			
☐ 308	Michael Adams	.05	.02	.01
	Best Single Game Performance: Points			
☐ 309	Larry Smith	.05	.02	.01
	Jerome Lane Best Single Game Performance: Rebounds			
☐ 310	Scott Skiles	.05	.02	.01
	Best Single Game Performance: Assists			
☐ 311	Hakeem Olajuwon	1.00	.45	.12
	David Robinson Best Single Game Performance: Blocks			
☐ 312	Alvin Robertson	.05	.02	.01
	Best Single Game Performance: Steals			
☐ 313	Stay In School Jam	.05	.02	.01
☐ 314	Craig Hodges	.05	.02	.01
	Three-Point Shootout			
☐ 315	Dee Brown	.05	.02	.01
	Slam-Dunk Championship			
☐ 316	Charles Barkley	.30	.14	.04
	All-Star Game MVP			
☐ 317	Behind the Scenes	.10	.05	.01
	Charles Barkley Joe Dumars Kevin McHale			
☐ 318	Derrick Coleman ART	.05	.02	.01
☐ 319	Lionel Simmons ART	.05	.02	.01
☐ 320	Dennis Scott ART	.10	.05	.01
☐ 321	Kendall Gill ART	.05	.02	.01
☐ 322	Dee Brown ART	.05	.02	.01
☐ 323	Magic Johnson	.60	.25	.07
	GQ All-Star Style Team			
☐ 324	Hakeem Olajuwon	.50	.23	.06
	GQ All-Star Style Team			
☐ 325	Kevin Willis	.10	.05	.01
	Dominique Wilkins GQ All-Star Style Team			
☐ 326	Kevin Willis	.10	.05	.01
	Dominique Wilkins GQ All-Star Style Team			
☐ 327	Gerald Wilkins	.05	.02	.01
	GQ All-Star Style Team			
☐ 328	1891-1991 Basketball	.05	.02	.01
	Centennial Logo			
☐ 329	Old-Fashioned Ball	.05	.02	.01
☐ 330	Women Take the Court	.05	.02	.01
☐ 331	The Peach Basket	.05	.02	.01
☐ 332	James A. Naismith	.10	.05	.01
	Founder of Basketball			
☐ 333	Magic Johnson FIN	2.00	.90	.25
	Michael Jordan FIN			
☐ 334	Michael Jordan FIN	2.50	1.10	.30
☐ 335	Vlade Divac FIN	.10	.05	.01
☐ 336	John Paxson FIN	.10	.05	.01
☐ 337	Bulls Starting Five	1.25	.55	.16
	Great Moments from the NBA Finals			
☐ 338	Language Arts	.05	.02	.01
	Stay in School			
☐ 339	Mathematics	.05	.02	.01
	Stay in School			
☐ 340	Vocational Education	.05	.02	.01
	Stay in School			
☐ 341	Social Studies	.05	.02	.01
	Stay in School			
☐ 342	Physical Education	.05	.02	.01
	Stay in School			
☐ 343	Art	.05	.02	.01
	Stay in School			
☐ 344	Science	.05	.02	.01
	Stay in School			
☐ 345	Checklist 1 (1-60)	.05	.02	.01
☐ 346	Checklist 2 (61-120)	.05	.02	.01
☐ 347	Checklist 3 (121-180)	.05	.02	.01
☐ 348	Checklist 4 (181-244)	.05	.02	.01
☐ 349	Checklist 5 (245-305)	.05	.02	.01
☐ 350	Checklist 6 (306-350)	.05	.02	.01
☐ 351	Atlanta Hawks	.05	.02	.01
	Team Logo			
☐ 352	Boston Celtics	.05	.02	.01
	Team Logo			
☐ 353	Charlotte Hornets	.05	.02	.01
	Team Logo			
☐ 354	Chicago Bulls	.05	.02	.01
	Team Logo			
☐ 355	Cleveland Cavaliers	.05	.02	.01
	Team Logo			
☐ 356	Dallas Mavericks	.05	.02	.01
	Team Logo			
☐ 357	Denver Nuggets	.05	.02	.01
	Team Logo			
☐ 358	Detroit Pistons	.05	.02	.01
	Team Logo			
☐ 359	Golden State Warriors	.05	.02	.01
	Team Logo			
☐ 360	Houston Rockets	.05	.02	.01
	Team Logo			
☐ 361	Indiana Pacers	.05	.02	.01
	Team Logo			
☐ 362	Los Angeles Clippers	.05	.02	.01
	Team Logo			
☐ 363	Los Angeles Lakers	.05	.02	.01
	Team Logo			
☐ 364	Miami Heat	.05	.02	.01
	Team Logo			
☐ 365	Milwaukee Bucks	.05	.02	.01
	Team Logo			
☐ 366	Minnesota Timberwolves	.05	.02	.01
	Team Logo			
☐ 367	New Jersey Nets	.05	.02	.01
	Team Logo			
☐ 368	New York Knicks	.05	.02	.01
	Team Logo			
☐ 369	Orlando Magic	.05	.02	.01
	Team Logo			
☐ 370	Philadelphia 76ers	.05	.02	.01
	Team Logo			

☐ 371	Phoenix Suns .05 Team Logo	.02	.01
☐ 372	Portland Trail Blazers .05 Team Logo	.02	.01
☐ 373	Sacramento Kings .05 Team Logo	.02	.01
☐ 374	San Antonio Spurs .05 Team Logo	.02	.01
☐ 375	Seattle Supersonics .05 Team Logo	.02	.01
☐ 376	Utah Jazz .05 Team Logo	.02	.01
☐ 377	Washington Bullets .05 Team Logo	.02	.01
☐ 378	Bob Weiss CO .05	.02	.01
☐ 379	Chris Ford CO .05	.02	.01
☐ 380	Allan Bristow CO .05	.02	.01
☐ 381	Phil Jackson CO .10	.05	.01
☐ 382	Lenny Wilkens CO .10	.05	.01
☐ 383	Richie Adubato CO .05	.02	.01
☐ 384	Paul Westhead CO .05	.02	.01
☐ 385	Chuck Daly CO .10	.05	.01
☐ 386	Don Nelson CO .10	.05	.01
☐ 387	Don Chaney CO .05	.02	.01
☐ 388	Bob Hill CO .05	.02	.01
☐ 389	Mike Schuler CO .05	.02	.01
☐ 390	Mike Dunleavy CO .05	.02	.01
☐ 391	Kevin Loughery CO .05	.02	.01
☐ 392	Del Harris CO .05	.02	.01
☐ 393	Jimmy Rodgers CO .05	.02	.01
☐ 394	Bill Fitch CO .05	.02	.01
☐ 395	Pat Riley CO .10	.05	.01
☐ 396	Matt Guokas CO .05	.02	.01
☐ 397	Jim Lynam CO .05	.02	.01
☐ 398	Cotton Fitzsimmons CO .05	.02	.01
☐ 399	Rick Adelman CO .05	.02	.01
☐ 400	Dick Motta CO .05	.02	.01
☐ 401	Larry Brown CO .10	.05	.01
☐ 402	K.C. Jones CO .10	.05	.01
☐ 403	Jerry Sloan CO .10	.05	.01
☐ 404	Wes Unseld CO .10	.05	.01
☐ 405	Mo Cheeks GF .10	.05	.01
☐ 406	Dee Brown GF .05	.02	.01
☐ 407	Rex Chapman GF .05	.02	.01
☐ 408	Michael Jordan GF 2.50	1.10	.30
☐ 409	John Williams GF .05	.02	.01
☐ 410	James Donaldson GF .05	.02	.01
☐ 411	Dikembe Mutombo GF .40	.18	.05
☐ 412	Isiah Thomas GF .15	.07	.02
☐ 413	Tim Hardaway GF .10	.05	.01
☐ 414	Hakeem Olajuwon GF .50	.23	.06
☐ 415	Detlef Schrempf GF .05	.02	.01
☐ 416	Danny Manning GF .05	.02	.01
☐ 417	Magic Johnson GF .60	.25	.07
☐ 418	Bimbo Coles GF .05	.02	.01
☐ 419	Alvin Robertson GF .05	.02	.01
☐ 420	Sam Mitchell GF .05	.02	.01
☐ 421	Sam Bowie GF .05	.02	.01
☐ 422	Mark Jackson GF .05	.02	.01
☐ 423	Orlando Magic .05 Game Frame	.02	.01
☐ 424	Charles Barkley GF .30	.14	.04
☐ 425	Dan Majerle GF .10	.05	.01
☐ 426	Robert Pack GF .05	.02	.01
☐ 427	Wayman Tisdale GF .05	.02	.01
☐ 428	David Robinson GF .50	.23	.06
☐ 429	Nate McMillan GF .05 Seattle Supersonics)	.02	.01
☐ 430	Karl Malone GF .15	.07	.02
☐ 431	Michael Adams GF .05	.02	.01
☐ 432	Duane Ferrell SM .05	.02	.01
☐ 433	Kevin McHale SM .10	.05	.01
☐ 434	Dell Curry SM .05	.02	.01
☐ 435	B.J. Armstrong SM .05	.02	.01
☐ 436	John Williams SM .05	.02	.01
☐ 437	Brad Davis SM .05	.02	.01
☐ 438	Marcus Liberty SM .05	.02	.01
☐ 439	Mark Aguirre SM .05	.02	.01
☐ 440	Rod Higgins SM .05	.02	.01
☐ 441	Eric(Sleepy) Floyd SM .05	.02	.01
☐ 442	Detlef Schrempf SM .05	.02	.01
☐ 443	Loy Vaught SM .05	.02	.01
☐ 444	Terry Teagle SM .05	.02	.01
☐ 445	Kevin Edwards SM .05	.02	.01
☐ 446	Dale Ellis SM .05	.02	.01
☐ 447	Tod Murphy SM .05	.02	.01
☐ 448	Chris Dudley SM .05	.02	.01
☐ 449	Mark Jackson SM .05	.02	.01
☐ 450	Jerry Reynolds SM .05	.02	.01
☐ 451	Ron Anderson SM .05	.02	.01
☐ 452	Dan Majerle SM .10	.05	.01
☐ 453	Danny Ainge SM .15	.07	.02
☐ 454	Jim Les SM .05	.02	.01
☐ 455	Paul Pressey SM .05	.02	.01
☐ 456	Ricky Pierce SM .05	.02	.01
☐ 457	Mike Brown SM .05	.02	.01
☐ 458	Ledell Eackles SM .05	.02	.01
☐ 459	Atlanta Hawks .10 Teamwork (Dominique Wilkins and Kevin Willis)	.05	.01
☐ 460	Boston Celtics .40 Teamwork (Larry Bird and Robert Parish)	.18	.05
☐ 461	Charlotte Hornets .05 Teamwork (Rex Chapman and Kendall Gill)	.02	.01
☐ 462	Chicago Bulls 1.50 Teamwork (Michael Jordan and Scottie Pippen)	.70	.19
☐ 463	Cleveland Cavaliers .05 Teamwork (Craig Ehlo and Mark Price)	.02	.01
☐ 464	Dallas Mavericks .05 Teamwork (Derek Harper and Rolando Blackman)	.02	.01
☐ 465	Denver Nuggets .05 Teamwork (Reggie Williams and Chris Jackson)	.02	.01
☐ 466	Detroit Pistons .10 Teamwork (Isiah Thomas and Bill Laimbeer)	.05	.01
☐ 467	Golden State Warriors .10 Teamwork (Tim Hardaway and Chris Mullin)	.05	.01
☐ 468	Houston Rockets .05 Teamwork (Vernon Maxwell and Kenny Smith)	.02	.01
☐ 469	Indiana Pacers .05 Teamwork (Detlef Schrempf and Reggie Miller)	.02	.01
☐ 470	Los Angeles Clippers .05	.02	.01

Teamwork (Charles Smith and Danny Manning)

#	Player			
☐ 471	Los Angeles Lakers	.30	.14	.04
	Teamwork (Magic Johnson and James Worthy)			
☐ 472	Miami Heat	.05	.02	.01
	Teamwork (Glen Rice and Rony Seikaly)			
☐ 473	Milwaukee Bucks	.05	.02	.01
	Teamwork (Jay Humphries and Alvin Robertson)			
☐ 474	Minnesota Timberwolves	.05	.02	.01
	Teamwork (Tony Campbell and Pooh Richardson)			
☐ 475	New Jersey Nets	.05	.02	.01
	Teamwork (Derrick Coleman and Sam Bowie)			
☐ 476	New York Knicks	.10	.05	.01
	Teamwork (Patrick Ewing and Charles Oakley)			
☐ 477	Orlando Magic	.05	.02	.01
	Teamwork (Dennis Scott and Scott Skiles)			
☐ 478	Philadelphia 76ers	.15	.07	.02
	Teamwork (Charles Barkley and Hersey Hawkins)			
☐ 479	Phoenix Suns	.10	.05	.01
	Teamwork (Kevin Johnson and Tom Chambers)			
☐ 480	Portland Trail Blazers	.05	.02	.01
	Teamwork (Clyde Drexler and Terry Porter)			
☐ 481	Sacramento Kings	.05	.02	.01
	Teamwork (Lionel Simmons and Wayman Tisdale)			
☐ 482	San Antonio Spurs	.05	.02	.01
	Teamwork (Terry Cummings and Sean Elliott)			
☐ 483	Seattle Supersonics	.05	.02	.01
	Teamwork (Eddie Johnson and Ricky Pierce)			
☐ 484	Utah Jazz	.15	.07	.02
	Teamwork (Karl Malone and John Stockton)			
☐ 485	Washington Bullets	.10	.05	.01
	Teamwork (Harvey Grant and Bernard King)			
☐ 486	Rumeal Robinson RS	.05	.02	.01
☐ 487	Dee Brown RS	.05	.02	.01
☐ 488	Kendall Gill RS	.05	.02	.01
☐ 489	B.J. Armstrong RS	.05	.02	.01
☐ 490	Danny Ferry RS	.05	.02	.01
☐ 491	Randy White RS	.05	.02	.01
☐ 492	Chris Jackson RS	.10	.05	.01
☐ 493	Lance Blanks RS	.05	.02	.01
☐ 494	Tim Hardaway RS	.10	.05	.01
☐ 495	Vernon Maxwell RS	.05	.02	.01
☐ 496	Micheal Williams RS	.05	.02	.01
☐ 497	Charles Smith RS	.05	.02	.01
☐ 498	Vlade Divac RS	.10	.05	.01
☐ 499	Willie Burton RS	.05	.02	.01
☐ 500	Jeff Grayer RS	.05	.02	.01
☐ 501	Pooh Richardson RS	.05	.02	.01
☐ 502	Derrick Coleman RS	.05	.02	.01
☐ 503	John Starks RS	.15	.07	.02
☐ 504	Dennis Scott RS	.10	.05	.01
☐ 505	Hersey Hawkins RS	.10	.05	.01
☐ 506	Negele Knight RS	.05	.02	.01
☐ 507	Clifford Robinson RS	.10	.05	.01
☐ 508	Lionel Simmons RS	.05	.02	.01
☐ 509	David Robinson RS	.50	.23	.06
☐ 510	Gary Payton RS	.50	.23	.06
☐ 511	Blue Edwards RS	.05	.02	.01
☐ 512	Harvey Grant RS	.05	.02	.01
☐ 513	Larry Johnson	2.50	1.10	.30
☐ 514	Kenny Anderson	.75	.35	.09
☐ 515	Billy Owens	.40	.18	.05
☐ 516	Dikembe Mutombo	1.25	.55	.16
☐ 517	Steve Smith	1.00	.45	.12
☐ 518	Doug Smith	.05	.02	.01
☐ 519	Luc Longley	.50	.23	.06
☐ 520	Mark Macon	.05	.02	.01
☐ 521	Stacey Augmon	.50	.23	.06
☐ 522	Brian Williams	.25	.11	.03
☐ 523	Terrell Brandon	1.00	.45	.12
☐ 524	The Ball	.05	.02	.01
☐ 525	The Basket	.05	.02	.01
☐ 526	The 24-second Shot Clock	.05	.02	.01
☐ 527	The Game Program	.05	.02	.01
☐ 528	The Championship Gift	.05	.02	.01
☐ 529	Championship Trophy	.05	.02	.01
☐ 530	Charles Barkley USA	1.25	.55	.16
☐ 531	Larry Bird USA	3.00	1.35	.35
☐ 532	Patrick Ewing USA	.75	.35	.09
☐ 533	Magic Johnson USA	2.50	1.10	.30
☐ 534	Michael Jordan USA	10.00	4.50	1.25
☐ 535	Karl Malone USA	.75	.35	.09
☐ 536	Chris Mullin USA	.10	.05	.01
☐ 537	Scottie Pippen USA	2.50	1.10	.30
☐ 538	David Robinson USA	2.00	.90	.25
☐ 539	John Stockton USA	.75	.35	.09
☐ 540	Chuck Daly CO USA	.10	.05	.01
☐ 541	P.J. Carlesimo CO USA	.10	.05	.01
☐ 542	Mike Krzyzewski CO USA	.60	.25	.07
☐ 543	Lenny Wilkens CO USA	.10	.05	.01
☐ 544	Team USA Card 1	2.50	1.10	.30
☐ 545	Team USA Card 2	2.50	1.10	.30
☐ 546	Team USA Card 3	2.50	1.10	.30
☐ 547	Willie Anderson USA	.05	.02	.01
☐ 548	Stacey Augmon USA	.10	.05	.01
☐ 549	Bimbo Coles USA	.05	.02	.01
☐ 550	Jeff Grayer USA	.05	.02	.01
☐ 551	Hersey Hawkins USA	.05	.02	.01
☐ 552	Dan Majerle USA	.10	.05	.01
☐ 553	Danny Manning USA	.05	.02	.01
☐ 554	J.R. Reid USA	.05	.02	.01
☐ 555	Mitch Richmond USA	.10	.05	.01
☐ 556	Charles Smith USA	.05	.02	.01
☐ 557	Vern Fleming USA	.05	.02	.01
☐ 558	Joe Kleine USA	.05	.02	.01
☐ 559	Jon Koncak USA	.05	.02	.01
☐ 560	Sam Perkins USA	.05	.02	.01
☐ 561	Alvin Robertson USA	.05	.02	.01
☐ 562	Wayman Tisdale USA	.05	.02	.01
☐ 563	Jeff Turner USA	.05	.02	.01

☐ 564	Tony Campbell Magic of SkyBox	.05	.02	.01
☐ 565	Joe Dumars Magic of SkyBox	.10	.05	.01
☐ 566	Horace Grant Magic of SkyBox	.10	.05	.01
☐ 567	Reggie Lewis Magic of SkyBox	.10	.05	.01
☐ 568	Hakeem Olajuwon Magic of SkyBox	.50	.23	.06
☐ 569	Sam Perkins Magic of SkyBox	.05	.02	.01
☐ 570	Chuck Person Magic of SkyBox	.05	.02	.01
☐ 571	Buck Williams Magic of SkyBox	.05	.02	.01
☐ 572	Michael Jordan SkyBox Salutes	2.50	1.10	.30
☐ 573	Bernard King NBA All-Star SkyBox Salutes	.10	.05	.01
☐ 574	Moses Malone SkyBox Salutes	.10	.05	.01
☐ 575	Robert Parish SkyBox Salutes	.10	.05	.01
☐ 576	Pat Riley CO SkyBox Salutes	.10	.05	.01
☐ 577	Dee Brown SkyMaster	.05	.02	.01
☐ 578	Rex Chapman SkyMaster	.05	.02	.01
☐ 579	Clyde Drexler SkyMaster	.10	.05	.01
☐ 580	Blue Edwards SkyMaster	.05	.02	.01
☐ 581	Ron Harper SkyMaster	.05	.02	.01
☐ 582	Kevin Johnson SkyMaster	.10	.05	.01
☐ 583	Michael Jordan SkyMaster	2.50	1.10	.30
☐ 584	Shawn Kemp SkyMaster	1.00	.45	.12
☐ 585	Xavier McDaniel SkyMaster	.05	.02	.01
☐ 586	Scottie Pippen SkyMaster	.60	.25	.07
☐ 587	Kenny Smith SkyMaster	.05	.02	.01
☐ 588	Dominique Wilkins SkyMaster	.10	.05	.01
☐ 589	Michael Adams Shooting Star	.05	.02	.01
☐ 590	Danny Ainge Shooting Star	.10	.05	.01
☐ 591	Larry Bird Shooting Star	.75	.35	.09
☐ 592	Dale Ellis Shooting Star	.05	.02	.01
☐ 593	Hersey Hawkins Shooting Star	.05	.02	.01
☐ 594	Jeff Hornacek Shooting Star	.05	.02	.01
☐ 595	Jeff Malone Shooting Star	.05	.02	.01
☐ 596	Reggie Miller Shooting Star	.25	.11	.03
☐ 597	Chris Mullin Shooting Star	.10	.05	.01
☐ 598	John Paxson Shooting Star	.10	.05	.01
☐ 599	Drazen Petrovic Shooting Star	.10	.05	.01
☐ 600	Ricky Pierce Shooting Star	.05	.02	.01
☐ 601	Mark Price Shooting Star	.05	.02	.01
☐ 602	Dennis Scott Shooting Star	.10	.05	.01
☐ 603	Manute Bol Small School Sensation	.05	.02	.01
☐ 604	Jerome Kersey Small School Sensation	.05	.02	.01
☐ 605	Charles Oakley Small School Sensation	.05	.02	.01
☐ 606	Scottie Pippen Small School Sensation	.60	.25	.07
☐ 607	Terry Porter Small School Sensation	.05	.02	.01
☐ 608	Dennis Rodman Small School Sensation	.75	.35	.09
☐ 609	Sedale Threatt Small School Sensation	.05	.02	.01
☐ 610	Business Stay in School	.05	.02	.01
☐ 611	Engineering Stay in School	.05	.02	.01
☐ 612	Law Stay in School	.05	.02	.01
☐ 613	Liberal Arts Stay in School	.05	.02	.01
☐ 614	Medicine Stay in School	.05	.02	.01
☐ 615	Maurice Cheeks	.15	.07	.02
☐ 616	Travis Mays	.05	.02	.01
☐ 617	Blair Rasmussen	.05	.02	.01
☐ 618	Alexander Volkov	.05	.02	.01
☐ 619	Rickey Green	.05	.02	.01
☐ 620	Bobby Hansen	.05	.02	.01
☐ 621	John Battle	.05	.02	.01
☐ 622	Terry Davis	.05	.02	.01
☐ 623	Walter Davis	.15	.07	.02
☐ 624	Winston Garland	.05	.02	.01
☐ 625	Scott Hastings	.05	.02	.01
☐ 626	Brad Sellers	.05	.02	.01
☐ 627	Darrell Walker	.05	.02	.01
☐ 628	Orlando Woolridge	.05	.02	.01
☐ 629	Tony Brown	.05	.02	.01
☐ 630	James Edwards	.05	.02	.01
☐ 631	Doc Rivers	.05	.02	.01
☐ 632	Jack Haley	.05	.02	.01
☐ 633	Sedale Threatt	.05	.02	.01
☐ 634	Moses Malone	.25	.11	.03
☐ 635	Thurl Bailey	.05	.02	.01
☐ 636	Rafael Addison	.05	.02	.01
☐ 637	Tim McCormick	.05	.02	.01
☐ 638	Xavier McDaniel	.05	.02	.01
☐ 639	Charles Shackleford	.05	.02	.01
☐ 640	Mitchell Wiggins	.05	.02	.01
☐ 641	Jerrod Mustaf	.05	.02	.01
☐ 642	Dennis Hopson	.05	.02	.01
☐ 643	Les Jepsen	.05	.02	.01
☐ 644	Mitch Richmond	.40	.18	.05
☐ 645	Dwayne Schintzius	.05	.02	.01
☐ 646	Spud Webb	.10	.05	.01
☐ 647	Jud Buechler	.05	.02	.01
☐ 648	Antoine Carr	.05	.02	.01
☐ 649	Tyrone Corbin	.05	.02	.01
☐ 650	Michael Adams	.05	.02	.01
☐ 651	Ralph Sampson	.05	.02	.01
☐ 652	Andre Turner	.05	.02	.01
☐ 653	David Wingate	.05	.02	.01

		MINT	NRMT	EXC
☐ 654	Checklist "S" (351-404)	.05	.02	.01
☐ 655	Checklist "K" (405-458)	.05	.02	.01
☐ 656	Checklist "Y" (459-512)	.05	.02	.01
☐ 657	Checklist "B" (513-563)	.05	.02	.01
☐ 658	Checklist "O" (564-614)	.05	.02	.01
☐ 659	Checklist "X" (615-659)	.05	.02	.01
☐ NNO	Clyde Drexler USA.. (Send-away)	75.00	34.00	9.50
☐ NNO	Team USA Card	12.00	5.50	1.50

1991-92 SkyBox Blister Inserts

The first four inserts were featured in series one blister packs, while the last two were inserted in series two blister packs. The cards measure the standard size (2 1/2" by 3 1/2"). The first four have logos on their front and comments on the back. The last two are double-sided cards and display most valuable players from the same team for two consecutive years. The cards are numbered on the back with Roman numerals.

		MINT	NRMT	EXC
COMPLETE SET (6)		2.50	1.10	.30
COMMON CARD (1-4)		.25	.11	.03
COMMON CARD (5-6)		.50	.23	.06
☐ 1	USA Basketball (Numbered I)	.25	.11	.03
☐ 2	Stay in School It's Your Best Move (Numbered II)	.25	.11	.03
☐ 3	Orlando All-Star Weekend (Numbered III)	.25	.11	.03
☐ 4	Inside Shot (Numbered IV)	.25	.11	.03
☐ 5	Magic Johnson and James Worthy Back to Back NBA Finals MVP 1987/1988 (Numbered V)	1.00	.45	.12
☐ 6	Joe Dumars	.50	.23	.06

and Isiah Thomas
Back to Back
NBA Finals MVP 1989/1990
(Numbered VI)

1992-93 SkyBox

The complete 1992-93 SkyBox basketball set contains 413 standard-size cards. The set was released in two series of 327 and 86 cards, respectively. Both series foil packs contained 12 cards each with 36 packs to a box. Suggested retail price was 1.15 per pack. Reported production quantities were approximately 15,000 20-box cases for the first series and 15,000 20-box cases for the second series. The new front design features computer-generated screens of color blended with full-bleed color action photos. The backs carry full-bleed non-action close-up photos overlaid by a column displaying complete statistics and a color stripe with a personal "bio-bit." Cards of second series rookies have a gold seal in the other lower corner. In addition, the second series Draft Pick rookie cards were printed in shorter supply than the other cards in the second.series set. First series cards are checklisted below alphabetically according team order. Subsets are Coaches (255-281), Team Tix (282-308), 1992 NBA All-Star Weekend Highlights (309-313), 1992 NBA All-Star (314-318), 1992 NBA Finals (314-318), 1992 NBA All-Rookie Team (319), and Public Service (230-321). The set concludes with checklist cards (322-327). The cards are numbered on the back. Special gold-foil stamped cards of Magic Johnson and David Robinson, some personally autographed, were randomly inserted in first series foil packs. Versions of these Johnson and Robinson cards with sparkling silver foil were also produced and one of each accompanied the first 7,500 cases ordered exclusively by hobby accounts. According to SkyBox approximately one of every 36 packs contained either a Magic Johnson or David Robinson SP card. The "Head of the Class" mail-away card features the first six 1992 NBA draft picks. The card was made available to the first 20,000 fans through a mail-in offer for three wrappers from each series of 1992-93 SkyBox cards plus 3.25 for postage and handling.

The horizontal front features three color, cut-out player photos against a black background. Three wide vertical stripes in shades of red and violet run behind the players. A gold bar near the bottom carries the phrase "Head of the Class 1992 Top NBA Draft Picks." The back features three player photos similar to the ones on the front. The background design is the same except the wide stripes are green, orange, and blue. A white bar at the lower right corner carries the serial number and production run (20,000). Rookie Cards of note include Tom Gugliotta, Robert Horry, Christian Laettner, Alonzo Mourning, Shaquille O'Neal, Latrell Sprewell, and Clarence Weatherspoon.

	MINT	NRMT	EXC
COMPLETE SET (413)	50.00	22.00	6.25
COMPLETE SERIES 1 (327)	30.00	13.50	3.70
COMPLETE SERIES 2 (86)	20.00	9.00	2.50
COMMON CARD (1-413)	.10	.05	.01

#	Player	MINT	NRMT	EXC
1	Stacey Augmon	.15	.07	.02
2	Maurice Cheeks	.15	.07	.02
3	Duane Ferrell	.10	.05	.01
4	Paul Graham	.10	.05	.01
5	Jon Koncak	.10	.05	.01
6	Blair Rasmussen	.10	.05	.01
7	Rumeal Robinson	.10	.05	.01
8	Dominique Wilkins	.20	.09	.03
9	Kevin Willis	.10	.05	.01
10	Larry Bird	2.00	.90	.25
11	Dee Brown	.10	.05	.01
12	Sherman Douglas	.10	.05	.01
13	Rick Fox	.10	.05	.01
14	Kevin Gamble	.10	.05	.01
15	Reggie Lewis	.15	.07	.02
16	Kevin McHale	.20	.09	.03
17	Robert Parish	.20	.09	.03
18	Ed Pinckney	.10	.05	.01
19	Muggsy Bogues	.15	.07	.02
20	Dell Curry	.10	.05	.01
21	Kenny Gattison	.10	.05	.01
22	Kendall Gill	.10	.05	.01
23	Mike Gminski	.10	.05	.01
24	Tom Hammonds	.10	.05	.01
25	Larry Johnson	1.00	.45	.12
26	Johnny Newman	.10	.05	.01
27	J.R. Reid	.10	.05	.01
28	B.J. Armstrong	.10	.05	.01
29	Bill Cartwright	.10	.05	.01
30	Horace Grant	.20	.09	.03
31	Michael Jordan	6.00	2.70	.75
32	Stacey King	.10	.05	.01
33	John Paxson	.15	.07	.02
34	Will Perdue	.10	.05	.01
35	Scottie Pippen	1.50	.70	.19
36	Scott Williams	.10	.05	.01
37	John Battle	.10	.05	.01
38	Terrell Brandon	.20	.09	.03
39	Brad Daugherty	.10	.05	.01
40	Craig Ehlo	.10	.05	.01
41	Danny Ferry	.10	.05	.01
42	Henry James	.10	.05	.01
43	Larry Nance	.15	.07	.02
44	Mark Price	.10	.05	.01
45	Mike Sanders	.10	.05	.01
46	Hot Rod Williams	.10	.05	.01
47	Rolando Blackman	.15	.07	.02
48	Terry Davis	.10	.05	.01
49	Derek Harper	.15	.07	.02
50	Donald Hodge	.10	.05	.01
51	Mike Iuzzolino	.10	.05	.01
52	Fat Lever	.10	.05	.01
53	Rodney McCray	.10	.05	.01
54	Doug Smith	.10	.05	.01
55	Randy White	.10	.05	.01
56	Herb Williams	.10	.05	.01
57	Greg Anderson	.10	.05	.01
58	Walter Davis	.20	.09	.03
59	Winston Garland	.10	.05	.01
60	Chris Jackson	.20	.09	.03
61	Marcus Liberty	.10	.05	.01
62	Todd Lichti	.10	.05	.01
63	Mark Macon	.10	.05	.01
64	Dikembe Mutombo	.50	.23	.06
65	Reggie Williams	.10	.05	.01
66	Mark Aguirre	.15	.07	.02
67	William Bedford	.10	.05	.01
68	Lance Blanks	.10	.05	.01
69	Joe Dumars	.20	.09	.03
70	Bill Laimbeer	.15	.07	.02
71	Dennis Rodman	2.00	.90	.25
72	John Salley	.10	.05	.01
73	Isiah Thomas	.30	.14	.04
74	Darrell Walker	.10	.05	.01
75	Orlando Woolridge	.10	.05	.01
76	Victor Alexander	.10	.05	.01
77	Mario Elie	.10	.05	.01
78	Chris Gatling	.10	.05	.01
79	Tim Hardaway	.20	.09	.03
80	Tyrone Hill	.10	.05	.01
81	Alton Lister	.10	.05	.01
82	Sarunas Marciulionis	.10	.05	.01
83	Chris Mullin	.15	.07	.02
84	Billy Owens	.10	.05	.01
85	Matt Bullard	.10	.05	.01
86	Sleepy Floyd	.10	.05	.01
87	Avery Johnson	.15	.07	.02
88	Buck Johnson	.10	.05	.01
89	Vernon Maxwell	.10	.05	.01
90	Hakeem Olajuwon	1.25	.55	.16
91	Kenny Smith	.10	.05	.01
92	Larry Smith	.10	.05	.01
93	Otis Thorpe	.15	.07	.02
94	Dale Davis	.10	.05	.01
95	Vern Fleming	.10	.05	.01
96	George McCloud	.10	.05	.01
97	Reggie Miller	.60	.25	.07
98	Chuck Person	.10	.05	.01
99	Detlef Schrempf	.15	.07	.02
100	Rik Smits	.20	.09	.03
101	LaSalle Thompson	.10	.05	.01
102	Micheal Williams	.10	.05	.01
103	James Edwards	.10	.05	.01
104	Gary Grant	.10	.05	.01
105	Ron Harper	.10	.05	.01
106	Bo Kimble	.10	.05	.01
107	Danny Manning	.15	.07	.02
108	Ken Norman	.10	.05	.01
109	Olden Polynice	.10	.05	.01
110	Doc Rivers	.10	.05	.01
111	Charles Smith	.10	.05	.01
112	Loy Vaught	.10	.05	.01
113	Elden Campbell	.15	.07	.02
114	Vlade Divac	.20	.09	.03
115	A.C. Green	.20	.09	.03
116	Jack Haley	.10	.05	.01
117	Sam Perkins	.15	.07	.02
118	Byron Scott	.20	.09	.03

☐ 119	Tony Smith	.10	.05	.01	☐ 190	Jeff Hornacek	.15	.07	.02
☐ 120	Sedale Threatt	.10	.05	.01	☐ 191	Kevin Johnson	.20	.09	.03
☐ 121	James Worthy	.20	.09	.03	☐ 192	Negele Knight	.10	.05	.01
☐ 122	Keith Askins	.10	.05	.01	☐ 193	Andrew Lang	.10	.05	.01
☐ 123	Willie Burton	.10	.05	.01	☐ 194	Dan Majerle	.15	.07	.02
☐ 124	Bimbo Coles	.10	.05	.01	☐ 195	Jerrod Mustaf	.10	.05	.01
☐ 125	Kevin Edwards	.10	.05	.01	☐ 196	Tim Perry	.10	.05	.01
☐ 126	Alec Kessler	.10	.05	.01	☐ 197	Mark West	.10	.05	.01
☐ 127	Grant Long	.10	.05	.01	☐ 198	Alaa Abdelnaby	.10	.05	.01
☐ 128	Glen Rice	.20	.09	.03	☐ 199	Danny Ainge	.20	.09	.03
☐ 129	Rony Seikaly	.10	.05	.01	☐ 200	Mark Bryant	.10	.05	.01
☐ 130	Brian Shaw	.10	.05	.01	☐ 201	Clyde Drexler	.60	.25	.07
☐ 131	Steve Smith	.20	.09	.03	☐ 202	Kevin Duckworth	.10	.05	.01
☐ 132	Frank Brickowski	.10	.05	.01	☐ 203	Jerome Kersey	.10	.05	.01
☐ 133	Dale Ellis	.10	.05	.01	☐ 204	Robert Pack	.10	.05	.01
☐ 134	Jeff Grayer	.10	.05	.01	☐ 205	Terry Porter	.10	.05	.01
☐ 135	Jay Humphries	.10	.05	.01	☐ 206	Clifford Robinson	.20	.09	.03
☐ 136	Larry Krystkowiak	.10	.05	.01	☐ 207	Buck Williams	.15	.07	.02
☐ 137	Moses Malone	.30	.14	.04	☐ 208	Anthony Bonner	.10	.05	.01
☐ 138	Fred Roberts	.10	.05	.01	☐ 209	Randy Brown	.10	.05	.01
☐ 139	Alvin Robertson	.10	.05	.01	☐ 210	Duane Causwell	.10	.05	.01
☐ 140	Dan Schayes	.10	.05	.01	☐ 211	Pete Chilcutt	.10	.05	.01
☐ 141	Thurl Bailey	.10	.05	.01	☐ 212	Dennis Hopson	.10	.05	.01
☐ 142	Scott Brooks	.10	.05	.01	☐ 213	Jim Les	.10	.05	.01
☐ 143	Tony Campbell	.10	.05	.01	☐ 214	Mitch Richmond	.40	.18	.05
☐ 144	Gerald Glass	.10	.05	.01	☐ 215	Lionel Simmons	.10	.05	.01
☐ 145	Luc Longley	.10	.05	.01	☐ 216	Wayman Tisdale	.10	.05	.01
☐ 146	Sam Mitchell	.10	.05	.01	☐ 217	Spud Webb	.15	.07	.02
☐ 147	Pooh Richardson	.10	.05	.01	☐ 218	Willie Anderson	.10	.05	.01
☐ 148	Felton Spencer	.10	.05	.01	☐ 219	Antoine Carr	.10	.05	.01
☐ 149	Doug West	.10	.05	.01	☐ 220	Terry Cummings	.10	.05	.01
☐ 150	Rafael Addison	.10	.05	.01	☐ 221	Sean Elliott	.20	.09	.03
☐ 151	Kenny Anderson	.20	.09	.03	☐ 222	Sidney Green	.10	.05	.01
☐ 152	Mookie Blaylock	.20	.09	.03	☐ 223	Vinnie Johnson	.10	.05	.01
☐ 153	Sam Bowie	.10	.05	.01	☐ 224	David Robinson	1.00	.45	.12
☐ 154	Derrick Coleman	.10	.05	.01	☐ 225	Rod Strickland	.10	.05	.01
☐ 155	Chris Dudley	.10	.05	.01	☐ 226	Greg Sutton	.10	.05	.01
☐ 156	Tate George	.10	.05	.01	☐ 227	Dana Barros	.10	.05	.01
☐ 157	Terry Mills	.15	.07	.02	☐ 228	Benoit Benjamin	.10	.05	.01
☐ 158	Chris Morris	.10	.05	.01	☐ 229	Michael Cage	.10	.05	.01
☐ 159	Drazen Petrovic	.15	.07	.02	☐ 230	Eddie Johnson	.10	.05	.01
☐ 160	Greg Anthony	.10	.05	.01	☐ 231	Shawn Kemp	2.00	.90	.25
☐ 161	Patrick Ewing	.50	.23	.06	☐ 232	Derrick McKey	.10	.05	.01
☐ 162	Mark Jackson	.10	.05	.01	☐ 233	Nate McMillan	.10	.05	.01
☐ 163	Anthony Mason	.20	.09	.03	☐ 234	Gary Payton	1.00	.45	.12
☐ 164	Tim McCormick	.10	.05	.01	☐ 235	Ricky Pierce	.10	.05	.01
☐ 165	Xavier McDaniel	.10	.05	.01	☐ 236	David Benoit	.10	.05	.01
☐ 166	Charles Oakley	.15	.07	.02	☐ 237	Mike Brown	.10	.05	.01
☐ 167	John Starks	.20	.09	.03	☐ 238	Tyrone Corbin	.10	.05	.01
☐ 168	Gerald Wilkins	.10	.05	.01	☐ 239	Mark Eaton	.10	.05	.01
☐ 169	Nick Anderson	.20	.09	.03	☐ 240	Blue Edwards	.10	.05	.01
☐ 170	Terry Catledge	.10	.05	.01	☐ 241	Jeff Malone	.10	.05	.01
☐ 171	Jerry Reynolds	.10	.05	.01	☐ 242	Karl Malone	.50	.23	.06
☐ 172	Stanley Roberts	.10	.05	.01	☐ 243	Eric Murdock	.10	.05	.01
☐ 173	Dennis Scott	.20	.09	.03	☐ 244	John Stockton	.50	.23	.06
☐ 174	Scott Skiles	.10	.05	.01	☐ 245	Michael Adams	.10	.05	.01
☐ 175	Jeff Turner	.10	.05	.01	☐ 246	Rex Chapman	.10	.05	.01
☐ 176	Sam Vincent	.10	.05	.01	☐ 247	Ledell Eackles	.10	.05	.01
☐ 177	Brian Williams	.10	.05	.01	☐ 248	Pervis Ellison	.10	.05	.01
☐ 178	Ron Anderson	.10	.05	.01	☐ 249	A.J. English	.10	.05	.01
☐ 179	Charles Barkley	.75	.35	.09	☐ 250	Harvey Grant	.10	.05	.01
☐ 180	Manute Bol	.10	.05	.01	☐ 251	Charles Jones	.10	.05	.01
☐ 181	Johnny Dawkins	.10	.05	.01	☐ 252	Bernard King	.20	.09	.03
☐ 182	Armon Gilliam	.15	.07	.02	☐ 253	LaBradford Smith	.10	.05	.01
☐ 183	Greg Grant	.10	.05	.01	☐ 254	Larry Stewart	.10	.05	.01
☐ 184	Hersey Hawkins	.15	.07	.02	☐ 255	Bob Weiss CO	.10	.05	.01
☐ 185	Brian Oliver	.10	.05	.01	☐ 256	Chris Ford CO	.10	.05	.01
☐ 186	Charles Shackleford	.10	.05	.01	☐ 257	Allan Bristow CO	.10	.05	.01
☐ 187	Jayson Williams	.10	.05	.01	☐ 258	Phil Jackson CO	.15	.07	.02
☐ 188	Cedric Ceballos	.20	.09	.03	☐ 259	Lenny Wilkens CO	.15	.07	.02
☐ 189	Tom Chambers	.15	.07	.02	☐ 260	Richie Adubato CO	.10	.05	.01

☐ 261 Dan Issel CO	.15	.07	.02
☐ 262 Ron Rothstein CO	.10	.05	.01
☐ 263 Don Nelson CO	.15	.07	.02
☐ 264 Rudy Tomjanovich CO	.15	.07	.02
☐ 265 Bob Hill CO	.10	.05	.01
☐ 266 Larry Brown CO	.15	.07	.02
☐ 267 Randy Pfund CO	.10	.05	.01
☐ 268 Kevin Loughery CO	.10	.05	.01
☐ 269 Mike Dunleavy CO	.10	.05	.01
☐ 270 Jimmy Rodgers CO	.10	.05	.01
☐ 271 Chuck Daly CO	.15	.07	.02
☐ 272 Pat Riley CO	.15	.07	.02
☐ 273 Matt Guokas CO	.10	.05	.01
☐ 274 Doug Moe CO	.10	.05	.01
☐ 275 Paul Westphal CO	.10	.05	.01
☐ 276 Rick Adelman CO	.10	.05	.01
☐ 277 Garry St. Jean CO	.10	.05	.01
☐ 278 Jerry Tarkanian CO	.30	.14	.04
☐ 279 George Karl CO	.10	.05	.01
☐ 280 Jerry Sloan CO	.15	.07	.02
☐ 281 Wes Unseld CO	.15	.07	.02
☐ 282 Dominique Wilkins TT	.15	.07	.02
☐ 283 Reggie Lewis TT	.15	.07	.02
☐ 284 Kendall Gill TT	.10	.05	.01
☐ 285 Horace Grant TT	.15	.07	.02
☐ 286 Brad Daugherty TT	.10	.05	.01
☐ 287 Derek Harper TT	.10	.05	.01
☐ 288 Chris Jackson TT	.15	.07	.02
☐ 289 Isiah Thomas TT	.15	.07	.02
☐ 290 Chris Mullin TT	.10	.05	.01
☐ 291 Kenny Smith TT	.10	.05	.01
☐ 292 Reggie Miller TT	.30	.14	.04
☐ 293 Ron Harper TT	.10	.05	.01
☐ 294 Vlade Divac TT	.15	.07	.02
☐ 295 Glen Rice TT	.15	.07	.02
☐ 296 Moses Malone TT	.15	.07	.02
☐ 297 Doug West TT	.10	.05	.01
☐ 298 Derrick Coleman TT	.10	.05	.01
☐ 299 Patrick Ewing TT	.20	.09	.03
(See also card 305)			
☐ 300 Scott Skiles TT	.10	.05	.01
☐ 301 Hersey Hawkins TT	.10	.05	.01
☐ 302 Kevin Johnson TT	.15	.07	.02
☐ 303 Clifford Robinson TT	.15	.07	.02
☐ 304 Anthony Webb TT	.10	.05	.01
☐ 305 David Robinson TT COR	.50	.23	.06
☐ 305A David Robinson TT ERR	.50	.23	.06
(Card misnumbered as 299)			
☐ 306 Shawn Kemp TT	1.00	.45	.12
☐ 307 John Stockton	.20	.09	.03
☐ 308 Pervis Ellison TT	.10	.05	.01
☐ 309 Craig Hodges AS	.10	.05	.01
☐ 310 Magic Johnson A-S MVP	.75	.35	.09
☐ 311 Cedric Ceballos	.10	.05	.01
Slam Dunk Champ			
☐ 312 Karl Malone ASG	.50	.23	.06
☐ 313 Dennis Rodman ASG	.20	.09	.03
☐ 314 Michael Jordan MVP	3.00	1.35	.35
☐ 315 Clyde Drexler FIN	.20	.09	.03
☐ 316 Danny Ainge PO	.15	.07	.02
☐ 317 Scottie Pippen PO	.75	.35	.09
☐ 318 NBA Champs	.20	.09	.03
☐ 319 Larry Johnson ART	.50	.23	.06
Dikembe Mutombo			
☐ 320 NBA Stay in School	.10	.05	.01
☐ 321 Boys and Girls	.10	.05	.01
Clubs of America			
☐ 322 Checklist 1	.10	.05	.01
☐ 323 Checklist 2	.10	.05	.01
☐ 324 Checklist 3	.10	.05	.01
☐ 325 Checklist 4	.10	.05	.01

☐ 326 Checklist 5	.10	.05	.01
☐ 327 Checklist 6	.10	.05	.01
☐ 328 Adam Keefe	.20	.09	.03
☐ 329 Sean Rooks	.10	.05	.01
☐ 330 Xavier McDaniel	.10	.05	.01
☐ 331 Kiki Vandeweghe	.10	.05	.01
☐ 332 Alonzo Mourning	2.50	1.10	.30
☐ 333 Rodney McCray	.10	.05	.01
☐ 334 Gerald Wilkins	.10	.05	.01
☐ 335 Tony Bennett	.10	.05	.01
☐ 336 LaPhonso Ellis	.40	.18	.05
☐ 337 Bryant Stith	.40	.18	.05
☐ 338 Isaiah Morris	.10	.05	.01
☐ 339 Olden Polynice	.10	.05	.01
☐ 340 Jeff Grayer	.10	.05	.01
☐ 341 Byron Houston	.10	.05	.01
☐ 342 Latrell Sprewell	1.25	.55	.16
☐ 343 Scott Brooks	.10	.05	.01
☐ 344 Frank Johnson	.10	.05	.01
☐ 345 Robert Horry	1.00	.45	.12
☐ 346 David Wood	.10	.05	.01
☐ 347 Sam Mitchell	.10	.05	.01
☐ 348 Pooh Richardson	.10	.05	.01
☐ 349 Malik Sealy	.15	.07	.02
☐ 350 Morlon Wiley	.10	.05	.01
☐ 351 Mark Jackson	.10	.05	.01
☐ 352 Stanley Roberts	.10	.05	.01
☐ 353 Elmore Spencer	.10	.05	.01
☐ 354 John Williams	.10	.05	.01
☐ 355 Randy Woods	.10	.05	.01
☐ 356 James Edwards	.10	.05	.01
☐ 357 Jeff Sanders	.10	.05	.01
☐ 358 Magic Johnson	.75	.35	.09
☐ 359 Anthony Peeler	.15	.07	.02
☐ 360 Harold Miner	.15	.07	.02
☐ 361 John Salley	.10	.05	.01
☐ 362 Alaa Abdelnaby	.10	.05	.01
☐ 363 Todd Day	.20	.09	.03
☐ 364 Blue Edwards	.10	.05	.01
☐ 365 Lee Mayberry	.10	.05	.01
☐ 366 Eric Murdock	.10	.05	.01
☐ 367 Mookie Blaylock	.15	.07	.02
☐ 368 Anthony Avent	.10	.05	.01
☐ 369 Christian Laettner	.75	.35	.09
☐ 370 Chuck Person	.10	.05	.01
☐ 371 Chris Smith	.10	.05	.01
☐ 372 Micheal Williams	.10	.05	.01
☐ 373 Rolando Blackman	.10	.05	.01
☐ 374 Tony Campbell UER	.10	.05	.01
(Back photo actually			
Alvin Robertson)			
☐ 375 Hubert Davis	.20	.09	.03
☐ 376 Travis Mays	.10	.05	.01
☐ 377 Doc Rivers	.10	.05	.01
☐ 378 Charles Smith	.10	.05	.01
☐ 379 Rumeal Robinson	.10	.05	.01
☐ 380 Vinny Del Negro	.10	.05	.01
☐ 381 Steve Kerr	.10	.05	.01
☐ 382 Shaquille O'Neal	10.00	4.50	1.25
☐ 383 Donald Royal	.10	.05	.01
☐ 384 Jeff Hornacek	.15	.07	.02
☐ 385 Andrew Lang	.10	.05	.01
☐ 386 Tim Perry UER	.10	.05	.01
(Alvin Robertson pictured on back)			
☐ 387 Clarence Weatherspoon	.75	.35	.09
☐ 388 Danny Ainge	.20	.09	.03
☐ 389 Charles Barkley	.40	.18	.05
☐ 390 Tim Kempton	.10	.05	.01
☐ 391 Oliver Miller	.40	.18	.05
☐ 392 Dave Johnson	.10	.05	.01
☐ 393 Tracy Murray	.20	.09	.03

		MINT	NRMT	EXC
☐ 394	Rod Strickland	.10	.05	.01
☐ 395	Marty Conlon	.10	.05	.01
☐ 396	Walt Williams	1.00	.45	.12
☐ 397	Lloyd Daniels	.10	.05	.01
☐ 398	Dale Ellis	.10	.05	.01
☐ 399	Dave Hoppen	.10	.05	.01
☐ 400	Larry Smith	.10	.05	.01
☐ 401	Doug Overton	.10	.05	.01
☐ 402	Isaac Austin	.10	.05	.01
☐ 403	Jay Humphries	.10	.05	.01
☐ 404	Larry Krystkowiak	.10	.05	.01
☐ 405	Tom Gugliotta	.75	.35	.09
☐ 406	Buck Johnson	.10	.05	.01
☐ 407	Don MacLean	.20	.09	.03
☐ 408	Marlon Maxey	.10	.05	.01
☐ 409	Corey Williams	.10	.05	.01
☐ 410	Special Olympics	.20	.09	.03
	Dan Majerle			
☐ 411	Checklist 1	.10	.05	.01
☐ 412	Checklist 2	.10	.05	.01
☐ 413	Checklist 3	.10	.05	.01
☐ NNO	David Robinson	5.00	2.20	.60
	The Admiral Comes Prepared			
☐ NNO	Head of the Class	30.00	13.50	3.70
☐ NNO	Magic Johnson	8.00	3.60	1.00
	The Magic Never Ends			

1992-93 SkyBox Draft Picks

This 25-card standard-size insert set show-cases the first round picks from the 1992 NBA Draft. The cards were randomly inserted into 12-card (both series) foil packs. According to SkyBox, approximately one out of every eight packs contained a Draft Pick card. The card numbering (1-27) reflects the actual order in which each play-er was selected. Six players (2, 10-11, 15-16, 18) available by the first series cut-off date were issued in first series foil packs, while the rest of the first round picks who signed NBA contracts were issued in sec-ond series packs. DP4 and DP17, intended for Jim Jackson and Doug Christie respec-tively, were not issued with this set because neither player signed a professional con-tract in time to be included in the second series. They were issued in 1993-94 first series packs. The fronts display an opaque metallic gold rectangle set off from the play-er. On a gradated gold background, the backs present player profiles. A white rec-tangle that runs vertically the length of the card contains statistics. The team logo is superimposed on this rectangle. The cards are numbered on the back with a "DP" pre-fix.

		MINT	NRMT	EXC
COMPLETE SET (25)		45.00	20.00	5.50
COMPLETE SERIES 1 (6)		10.00	4.50	1.25
COMPLETE SERIES 2 (19)		35.00	16.00	4.40
COMMON (2/10/11/15/16/18)		.50	.23	.06
COMMON (1/3/5-9/12-14/19-27)		.50	.23	.06
☐ DP1	Shaquille O'Neal	25.00	11.00	3.10
☐ DP2	Alonzo Mourning	6.00	2.70	.75
☐ DP3	Christian Laettner	2.00	.90	.25
☐ DP4	Not issued			
	(Player unsigned)			
☐ DP5	LaPhonso Ellis	1.25	.55	.16
☐ DP6	Tom Gugliotta	2.00	.90	.25
☐ DP7	Walt Williams	3.00	1.35	.35
☐ DP8	Todd Day	.50	.23	.06
☐ DP9	Clarence Weatherspoon	2.00	.90	.25
☐ DP10	Adam Keefe	1.25	.55	.16
☐ DP11	Robert Horry	2.50	1.10	.30
☐ DP12	Harold Miner	1.25	.55	.16
☐ DP13	Bryant Stith	1.25	.55	.16
☐ DP14	Malik Sealy	1.25	.55	.16
☐ DP15	Anthony Peeler	1.25	.55	.16
☐ DP16	Randy Woods	.50	.23	.06
☐ DP17	Not issued			
	(Player unsigned)			
☐ DP18	Tracy Murray	1.25	.55	.16
☐ DP19	Don MacLean	1.25	.55	.16
☐ DP20	Hubert Davis	1.25	.55	.16
☐ DP21	Jon Barry	.50	.23	.06
☐ DP22	Oliver Miller	1.25	.55	.16
☐ DP23	Lee Mayberry	.50	.23	.06
☐ DP24	Latrell Sprewell	3.00	1.35	.35
☐ DP25	Elmore Spencer	.50	.23	.06
☐ DP26	Dave Johnson	.50	.23	.06
☐ DP27	Byron Houston	.50	.23	.06

1992-93 SkyBox Olympic Team

Each card in this 12-card standard-size set features an action photo of a team member and his complete statistics from the Olympic Games. According to SkyBox, the cards were randomly inserted into 12-card first series foil packs at a rate of approximately one per six. The backs tell the story of U.S. Men's Olympic Team, from scrimmage in Monte Carlo to the medal ceremony in Barcelona. The cards are numbered on the back with a "USA" prefix.

	MINT	NRMT	EXC
COMPLETE SET (12)	50.00	22.00	6.25
COMMON CARD (1-12)	1.00	.45	.12
☐ 1 Clyde Drexler	2.50	1.10	.30
☐ 2 Chris Mullin	1.00	.45	.12
☐ 3 John Stockton	2.00	.90	.25
☐ 4 Karl Malone	2.00	.90	.25
☐ 5 Scottie Pippen	6.00	2.70	.75
☐ 6 Larry Bird	8.00	3.60	1.00
☐ 7 Charles Barkley	3.00	1.35	.35
☐ 8 Patrick Ewing	2.00	.90	.25
☐ 9 Christian Laettner	2.00	.90	.25
☐ 10 David Robinson	4.00	1.80	.50
☐ 11 Michael Jordan	25.00	11.00	3.10
☐ 12 Magic Johnson	6.00	2.70	.75

1992-93 SkyBox
David Robinson

College

This ten-card standard-size insert set provides a look at Robinson at various stages of his life. Included are photos from his childhood, indulging in hobbies, with his family at the Naval Academy and his present day super stardom. The first five cards were randomly inserted in first series 12-card foil packs, while the second five were found in second series packs. According to SkyBox, approximately one of every eight packs contains a David Robinson insert card. The cards feature a different design than the regular issue cards. The fronts display color photos tilted slightly to the left with a special seal overlaying the upper left corner. The surrounding card face shows two colors.

	MINT	NRMT	EXC
COMPLETE SET (10)	4.00	1.80	.50
COMPLETE SERIES 1 (5)	2.00	.90	.25
COMPLETE SERIES 2 (5)	2.00	.90	.25
COMMON D.ROBINSON (R1-R10)	.50	.23	.06

☐ R1 David Robinson Childhood	.50	.23	.06
☐ R2 David Robinson At Ease	.50	.23	.06
☐ R3 David Robinson College	.50	.23	.06
☐ R4 David Robinson College	.50	.23	.06
☐ R5 David Robinson At Ease	.50	.23	.06
☐ R6 David Robinson College	.50	.23	.06
☐ R7 David Robinson College	.50	.23	.06
☐ R8 David Robinson Doug Drotman Awards	.50	.23	.06
☐ R9 David Robinson Awards	.50	.23	.06
☐ R10 David Robinson At Ease	.50	.23	.06

1992-93 SkyBox
School Ties

Randomly inserted in 1992-93 SkyBox second series 12-card foil packs at a reported rate of one per four, this 18-card standard-size set consists of six different three-card "School Ties" interlocking cards. When the three cards in each puzzle are placed together, they create a montage of active NBA players from one particular college. The fronts feature several color player photos that have team color-coded picture frames. The team logo appears in a team color-coded banner that is superimposed across the bottom of the picture. The backs have brightly colored backgrounds and display information about the college, the players, and a checklist of the players on the three-card puzzle. The cards are numbered on the back with an "ST" prefix.

	MINT	NRMT	EXC
COMPLETE SET (18)	15.00	6.75	1.85
COMMON CARD (ST1-ST18)	.25	.11	.03

☐ ST1 Patrick Ewing Alonzo Mourning Georgetown	2.50	1.10	.30
☐ ST2 Dikembe Mutombo Eric Floyd Georgetown	.35	.16	.04

☐ ST3	Reggie Williams..........David Wingate Georgetown	.25 .11	.03
☐ ST4	Kenny Anderson ....Duane Ferrell Georgia Tech	.40 .18	.05
☐ ST5	Tom Hammonds..........Jon Barry Mark Price Georgia Tech	.25 .11	.03
☐ ST6	John Salley..........Dennis Scott Georgia Tech	.40 .18	.05
☐ ST7	Rafael Addison ....Dave Johnson Syracuse	.25 .11	.03
☐ ST8	Billy Owens..........Derrick Coleman Rony Seikaly Syracuse	.25 .11	.03
☐ ST9	Sherman Douglas..........Danny Schayes Syracuse	.25 .11	.03
☐ ST10	Nick Anderson ....Kendall Gill Illinois	.40 .18	.05
☐ ST11	Derek Harper ....Eddie Johnson Illinois	.25 .11	.03
☐ ST12	Marcus Liberty ....Ken Norman Illinois	.25 .11	.03
☐ ST13	Greg Anthony ....Stacey Augmon Nevada-Las Vegas	.25 .11	.03
☐ ST14	Armon Gilliam..........Larry Johnson Sidney Green Nevada-Las Vegas	.75 .35	.09
☐ ST15	Elmore Spencer ....Gerald Paddio Nevada-Las Vegas	.25 .11	.03
☐ ST16	James Worthy ....Michael Jordan Sam Perkins North Carolina	12.00 5.50	1.50
☐ ST17	J.R. Reid..........Pete Chilcutt Brad Daugherty Rick Fox North Carolina	.25 .11	.03
☐ ST18	Hubert Davis..........Kenny Smith Scott Williams North Carolina	.25 .11	.03

1992-93 SkyBox Thunder and Lightning

Randomly inserted into second series 12-card foil packs at a reported rate of one per 40 packs, each card in this nine-card standard-size set features a pair of teammates. There is a photo on each side. The catch

word on the front is "Thunder", referring to a dominant power player, while "Lightning" on the back captures the speed of a guard. The cards are highlighted by a litho-foil printing which gives a foil-look to the graphics around the basketball. The cards have color action player photos against a dark background, with computer enhancement around the ball and player. On the front, the power player's name appears at the bottom and is underlined by a thin yellow stripe. The word "Thunder" appears below the stripe. On the horizontal backs, the speed player's name is displayed in the upper right with the same yellow underline, but the word "Lightning" appears below it. The cards are numbered on the back with a "TL" prefix.

	MINT	NRMT	EXC
COMPLETE SET (9)	40.00	18.00	5.00
COMMON PAIR (TL1-TL9).......	1.50	.70	.19
☐ TL1 Dikembe Mutombo .... Mark Macon	3.00	1.35	.35
☐ TL2 Buck Williams............ Clyde Drexler	6.00	2.70	.75
☐ TL3 Charles Barkley........... Kevin Johnson	8.00	3.60	1.00
☐ TL4 Pervis Ellison............. Michael Adams	1.50	.70	.19
☐ TL5 Larry Johnson............ Tyrone Bogues	6.00	2.70	.75
☐ TL6 Brad Daugherty.......... Mark Price	1.50	.70	.19
☐ TL7 Shawn Kemp............. Gary Payton	20.00	9.00	2.50
☐ TL8 Karl Malone............... John Stockton	10.00	4.50	1.25
☐ TL9 Billy Owens................ Tim Hardaway	1.50	.70	.19

1993-94 SkyBox

The 1993-94 SkyBox basketball set contains 341 standard-size cards that were issued in series of 191 and 150 respectively. Cards were issued in 12-card packs with 36 packs per box. The cards feature full-bleed color action photos with a wide white stripe down one side of the front containing the player's name, position, and team. The SkyBox Premium foil stamp logo appears superimposed on the front. The backs dis-

play a second player close-up shot on the top half, and the player's statistics and scouting report on the bottom half. The cards are numbered on the back and grouped alphabetically within team order. Subsets are Playoff Performances (4-21), Changing Faces (292-318), and Costacos Brothers Poster Cards (319-338). Rookie Cards of note include Vin Baker, Anfernee Hardaway, Allan Houston, Jamal Mashburn, Nick Van Exel and Chris Webber. The odds of finding a Head of the Class Exchange card are one in 360 first series packs. It was redeemable for a Head of the Class card featuring the top six 1993 draft picks. The redemption date was April 15, 1994.

	MINT	NRMT	EXC
COMPLETE SET (341)	30.00	13.50	3.70
COMPLETE SERIES 1 (191)	15.00	6.75	1.85
COMPLETE SERIES 2 (150)	15.00	6.75	1.85
COMMON CARD (1-341)	.05	.02	.01

☐ 1 Checklist	.05	.02	.01
☐ 2 Checklist	.05	.02	.01
☐ 3 Checklist	.05	.02	.01
☐ 4 Larry Johnson PO	.10	.05	.01
☐ 5 Alonzo Mourning PO	.25	.11	.03
☐ 6 Hakeem Olajuwon PO	.40	.18	.05
☐ 7 Brad Daugherty PO	.05	.02	.01
☐ 8 Oliver Miller PO	.05	.02	.01
☐ 9 David Robinson PO	.30	.14	.04
☐ 10 Patrick Ewing PO	.10	.05	.01
☐ 11 Ricky Pierce PO	.05	.02	.01
☐ 12 Sam Perkins PO	.05	.02	.01
☐ 13 John Starks PO	.05	.02	.01
☐ 14 Michael Jordan PO	2.00	.90	.25
☐ 15 Dan Majerle PO	.05	.02	.01
☐ 16 Scottie Pippen PO	.50	.23	.06
☐ 17 Shawn Kemp PO	.50	.23	.06
☐ 18 Charles Barkley PO	.25	.11	.03
☐ 19 Horace Grant PO	.05	.02	.01
☐ 20 Kevin Johnson PO	.10	.05	.01
☐ 21 John Paxson PO	.05	.02	.01
☐ 22 David Robinson IS	.05	.02	.01
☐ 23 NBA On NBC	.05	.02	.01
☐ 24 Stacey Augmon	.10	.05	.01
☐ 25 Mookie Blaylock	.10	.05	.01
☐ 26 Craig Ehlo	.05	.02	.01
☐ 27 Adam Keefe	.05	.02	.01
☐ 28 Dominique Wilkins	.15	.07	.02
☐ 29 Kevin Willis	.05	.02	.01
☐ 30 Dee Brown	.05	.02	.01
☐ 31 Sherman Douglas	.05	.02	.01
☐ 32 Rick Fox	.05	.02	.01
☐ 33 Kevin Gamble	.05	.02	.01
☐ 34 Xavier McDaniel	.05	.02	.01
☐ 35 Robert Parish	.15	.07	.02
☐ 36 Muggsy Bogues	.10	.05	.01
☐ 37 Dell Curry	.05	.02	.01
☐ 38 Kendall Gill	.05	.02	.01
☐ 39 Larry Johnson	.40	.18	.05
☐ 40 Alonzo Mourning	.50	.23	.06
☐ 41 Johnny Newman	.05	.02	.01
☐ 42 B.J. Armstrong	.05	.02	.01
☐ 43 Bill Cartwright	.05	.02	.01
☐ 44 Horace Grant	.15	.07	.02
☐ 45 Michael Jordan	4.00	1.80	.50
☐ 46 John Paxson	.10	.05	.01
☐ 47 Scottie Pippen	1.00	.45	.12
☐ 48 Scott Williams	.05	.02	.01
☐ 49 Terrell Brandon	.15	.07	.02
☐ 50 Brad Daugherty	.05	.02	.01
☐ 51 Larry Nance	.05	.02	.01
☐ 52 Mark Price	.05	.02	.01
☐ 53 Gerald Wilkins	.05	.02	.01
☐ 54 John Williams	.05	.02	.01
☐ 55 Terry Davis	.05	.02	.01
☐ 56 Derek Harper	.10	.05	.01
☐ 57 Jim Jackson	.40	.18	.05
☐ 58 Sean Rooks	.05	.02	.01
☐ 59 Doug Smith	.05	.02	.01
☐ 60 Mahmoud Abdul-Rauf	.15	.07	.02
☐ 61 LaPhonso Ellis	.05	.02	.01
☐ 62 Mark Macon	.05	.02	.01
☐ 63 Dikembe Mutombo	.15	.07	.02
☐ 64 Bryant Stith	.05	.02	.01
☐ 65 Reggie Williams	.05	.02	.01
☐ 66 Joe Dumars	.15	.07	.02
☐ 67 Bill Laimbeer	.10	.05	.01
☐ 68 Terry Mills	.05	.02	.01
☐ 69 Alvin Robertson	.05	.02	.01
☐ 70 Dennis Rodman	1.25	.55	.16
☐ 71 Isiah Thomas	.20	.09	.03
☐ 72 Victor Alexander	.05	.02	.01
☐ 73 Tim Hardaway	.10	.05	.01
☐ 74 Tyrone Hill	.05	.02	.01
☐ 75 Sarunas Marciulionis	.05	.02	.01
☐ 76 Chris Mullin	.10	.05	.01
☐ 77 Billy Owens	.05	.02	.01
☐ 78 Latrell Sprewell	.25	.11	.03
☐ 79 Robert Horry	.10	.05	.01
☐ 80 Vernon Maxwell	.05	.02	.01
☐ 81 Hakeem Olajuwon	.75	.35	.09
☐ 82 Kenny Smith	.05	.02	.01
☐ 83 Otis Thorpe	.10	.05	.01
☐ 84 Dale Davis	.05	.02	.01
☐ 85 Reggie Miller	.40	.18	.05
☐ 86 Pooh Richardson	.05	.02	.01
☐ 87 Detlef Schrempf	.10	.05	.01
☐ 88 Malik Sealy	.05	.02	.01
☐ 89 Rik Smits	.15	.07	.02
☐ 90 Ron Harper	.05	.02	.01
☐ 91 Mark Jackson	.05	.02	.01
☐ 92 Danny Manning	.10	.05	.01
☐ 93 Stanley Roberts	.05	.02	.01
☐ 94 Loy Vaught	.10	.05	.01
☐ 95 Randy Woods	.05	.02	.01
☐ 96 Sam Bowie	.05	.02	.01
☐ 97 Doug Christie	.05	.02	.01
☐ 98 Vlade Divac	.15	.07	.02
☐ 99 Anthony Peeler	.05	.02	.01
☐ 100 Sedale Threatt	.05	.02	.01
☐ 101 James Worthy	.15	.07	.02
☐ 102 Grant Long	.05	.02	.01
☐ 103 Harold Miner	.05	.02	.01
☐ 104 Glen Rice	.15	.07	.02

☐ 105	John Salley	.05	.02	.01
☐ 106	Rony Seikaly	.05	.02	.01
☐ 107	Steve Smith	.15	.07	.02
☐ 108	Anthony Avent	.05	.02	.01
☐ 109	Jon Barry	.05	.02	.01
☐ 110	Frank Brickowski	.05	.02	.01
☐ 111	Blue Edwards	.05	.02	.01
☐ 112	Todd Day	.05	.02	.01
☐ 113	Lee Mayberry	.05	.02	.01
☐ 114	Eric Murdock	.05	.02	.01
☐ 115	Thurl Bailey	.05	.02	.01
☐ 116	Christian Laettner	.15	.07	.02
☐ 117	Chuck Person	.05	.02	.01
☐ 118	Doug West	.05	.02	.01
☐ 119	Micheal Williams	.05	.02	.01
☐ 120	Kenny Anderson	.15	.07	.02
☐ 121	Benoit Benjamin	.05	.02	.01
☐ 122	Derrick Coleman	.05	.02	.01
☐ 123	Chris Morris	.05	.02	.01
☐ 124	Rumeal Robinson	.05	.02	.01
☐ 125	Rolando Blackman	.05	.02	.01
☐ 126	Patrick Ewing	.30	.14	.04
☐ 127	Anthony Mason	.15	.07	.02
☐ 128	Charles Oakley	.10	.05	.01
☐ 129	Doc Rivers	.05	.02	.01
☐ 130	Charles Smith	.05	.02	.01
☐ 131	John Starks	.10	.05	.01
☐ 132	Nick Anderson	.15	.07	.02
☐ 133	Shaquille O'Neal	2.00	.90	.25
☐ 134	Donald Royal	.05	.02	.01
☐ 135	Dennis Scott	.10	.05	.01
☐ 136	Scott Skiles	.05	.02	.01
☐ 137	Brian Williams	.05	.02	.01
☐ 138	Johnny Dawkins	.05	.02	.01
☐ 139	Hersey Hawkins	.05	.02	.01
☐ 140	Jeff Hornacek	.05	.02	.01
☐ 141	Andrew Lang	.05	.02	.01
☐ 142	Tim Perry	.05	.02	.01
☐ 143	Clarence Weatherspoon	.15	.07	.02
☐ 144	Danny Ainge	.15	.07	.02
☐ 145	Charles Barkley	.50	.23	.06
☐ 146	Cedric Ceballos	.15	.07	.02
☐ 147	Kevin Johnson	.15	.07	.02
☐ 148	Oliver Miller	.05	.02	.01
☐ 149	Dan Majerle	.10	.05	.01
☐ 150	Clyde Drexler	.40	.18	.05
☐ 151	Harvey Grant	.05	.02	.01
☐ 152	Jerome Kersey	.05	.02	.01
☐ 153	Terry Porter	.05	.02	.01
☐ 154	Clifford Robinson	.15	.07	.02
☐ 155	Rod Strickland	.05	.02	.01
☐ 156	Buck Williams	.10	.05	.01
☐ 157	Mitch Richmond	.25	.11	.03
☐ 158	Lionel Simmons	.05	.02	.01
☐ 159	Wayman Tisdale	.05	.02	.01
☐ 160	Spud Webb	.10	.05	.01
☐ 161	Walt Williams	.15	.07	.02
☐ 162	Antoine Carr	.05	.02	.01
☐ 163	Lloyd Daniels	.05	.02	.01
☐ 164	Sean Elliott	.15	.07	.02
☐ 165	Dale Ellis	.05	.02	.01
☐ 166	Avery Johnson	.10	.05	.01
☐ 167	J.R. Reid	.05	.02	.01
☐ 168	David Robinson	.60	.25	.07
☐ 169	Shawn Kemp	1.00	.45	.12
☐ 170	Derrick McKey	.05	.02	.01
☐ 171	Nate McMillan	.05	.02	.01
☐ 172	Gary Payton	.50	.23	.06
☐ 173	Sam Perkins	.05	.02	.01
☐ 174	Ricky Pierce	.05	.02	.01
☐ 175	Tyrone Corbin	.05	.02	.01
☐ 176	Jay Humphries	.05	.02	.01
☐ 177	Jeff Malone	.05	.02	.01
☐ 178	Karl Malone	.30	.14	.04
☐ 179	John Stockton	.30	.14	.04
☐ 180	Michael Adams	.05	.02	.01
☐ 181	Kevin Duckworth	.05	.02	.01
☐ 182	Pervis Ellison	.05	.02	.01
☐ 183	Tom Gugliotta	.15	.07	.02
☐ 184	Don MacLean	.05	.02	.01
☐ 185	Brent Price	.05	.02	.01
☐ 186	George Lynch	.05	.02	.01
☐ 187	Rex Walters	.05	.02	.01
☐ 188	Shawn Bradley	.40	.18	.05
☐ 189	Ervin Johnson	.10	.05	.01
☐ 190	Luther Wright	.05	.02	.01
☐ 191	Calbert Cheaney	.30	.14	.04
☐ 192	Craig Ehlo	.05	.02	.01
☐ 193	Duane Ferrell	.05	.02	.01
☐ 194	Paul Graham	.05	.02	.01
☐ 195	Andrew Lang	.05	.02	.01
☐ 196	Chris Corchiani	.05	.02	.01
☐ 197	Acie Earl	.05	.02	.01
☐ 198	Dino Radja	.40	.18	.05
☐ 199	Ed Pinckney	.05	.02	.01
☐ 200	Tony Bennett	.05	.02	.01
☐ 201	Scott Burrell	.15	.07	.02
☐ 202	Kenny Gattison	.05	.02	.01
☐ 203	Hersey Hawkins	.05	.02	.01
☐ 204	Eddie Johnson	.05	.02	.01
☐ 205	Corie Blount	.05	.02	.01
☐ 206	Steve Kerr	.10	.05	.01
☐ 207	Toni Kukoc	.75	.35	.09
☐ 208	Pete Myers	.05	.02	.01
☐ 209	Danny Ferry	.05	.02	.01
☐ 210	Tyrone Hill	.05	.02	.01
☐ 211	Gerald Madkins	.05	.02	.01
☐ 212	Chris Mills	.50	.23	.06
☐ 213	Lucious Harris	.15	.07	.02
☐ 214	Ron Jones	.15	.07	.02
☐ 215	Jamal Mashburn	.75	.35	.09
☐ 216	Darnell Mee	.05	.02	.01
☐ 217	Rodney Rodgers	.15	.07	.02
☐ 218	Brian Williams	.05	.02	.01
☐ 219	Greg Anderson	.05	.02	.01
☐ 220	Sean Elliott	.15	.07	.02
☐ 221	Allan Houston	.60	.25	.07
☐ 222	Lindsey Hunter	.10	.05	.01
☐ 223	Chris Gatling	.05	.02	.01
☐ 224	Josh Grant	.05	.02	.01
☐ 225	Keith Jennings	.05	.02	.01
☐ 226	Avery Johnson	.05	.02	.01
☐ 227	Chris Webber	1.25	.55	.16
☐ 228	Sam Cassell	.50	.23	.06
☐ 229	Mario Elie	.05	.02	.01
☐ 230	Richard Petruska	.05	.02	.01
☐ 231	Eric Riley	.05	.02	.01
☐ 232	Antonio Davis	.05	.02	.01
☐ 233	Scott Haskin	.05	.02	.01
☐ 234	Derrick McKey	.05	.02	.01
☐ 235	Mark Aguirre	.10	.05	.01
☐ 236	Terry Dehere	.10	.05	.01
☐ 237	Gary Grant	.05	.02	.01
☐ 238	Randy Woods	.05	.02	.01
☐ 239	Sam Bowie	.05	.02	.01
☐ 240	Elden Campbell	.10	.05	.01
☐ 241	Nick Van Exel	1.00	.45	.12
☐ 242	Manute Bol	.05	.02	.01
☐ 243	Brian Shaw	.05	.02	.01
☐ 244	Vin Baker	1.25	.55	.16
☐ 245	Brad Lohaus	.05	.02	.01
☐ 246	Ken Norman	.05	.02	.01

☐ 247	Derek Strong	.05	.02	.01
☐ 248	Dan Schayes	.05	.02	.01
☐ 249	Mike Brown	.05	.02	.01
☐ 250	Luc Longley	.05	.02	.01
☐ 251	Isaiah Rider	.40	.18	.05
☐ 252	Kevin Edwards	.05	.02	.01
☐ 253	Armon Gilliam	.05	.02	.01
☐ 254	Greg Anthony	.05	.02	.01
☐ 255	Anthony Bonner	.05	.02	.01
☐ 256	Tony Campbell	.05	.02	.01
☐ 257	Hubert Davis	.05	.02	.01
☐ 258	Litterial Green	.05	.02	.01
☐ 259	Anfernee Hardaway	6.00	2.70	.75
☐ 260	Larry Krystkowiak	.05	.02	.01
☐ 261	Todd Lichti	.05	.02	.01
☐ 262	Dana Barros	.05	.02	.01
☐ 263	Greg Graham	.05	.02	.01
☐ 264	Warren Kidd	.05	.02	.01
☐ 265	Moses Malone	.20	.09	.03
☐ 266	A.C. Green	.15	.07	.02
☐ 267	Joe Kleine	.05	.02	.01
☐ 268	Malcolm Mackey	.05	.02	.01
☐ 269	Mark Bryant	.05	.02	.01
☐ 270	Chris Dudley	.05	.02	.01
☐ 271	Harvey Grant	.05	.02	.01
☐ 272	James Robinson	.10	.05	.01
☐ 273	Duane Causwell	.05	.02	.01
☐ 274	Bobby Hurley	.15	.07	.02
☐ 275	Jim Les	.05	.02	.01
☐ 276	Willie Anderson	.05	.02	.01
☐ 277	Terry Cummings	.05	.02	.01
☐ 278	Vinny Del Negro	.05	.02	.01
☐ 279	Sleepy Floyd	.05	.02	.01
☐ 280	Dennis Rodman	1.25	.55	.16
☐ 281	Vincent Askew	.05	.02	.01
☐ 282	Kendall Gill	.05	.02	.01
☐ 283	Steve Scheffler	.05	.02	.01
☐ 284	Detlef Schrempf	.10	.05	.01
☐ 285	David Benoit	.05	.02	.01
☐ 286	Tom Chambers	.05	.02	.01
☐ 287	Felton Spencer	.05	.02	.01
☐ 288	Rex Chapman	.05	.02	.01
☐ 289	Kevin Duckworth	.05	.02	.01
☐ 290	Gheorghe Muresan	.50	.23	.06
☐ 291	Kenny Walker	.05	.02	.01
☐ 292	Andrew Lang CF	.05	.02	.01
	Craig Ehlo			
☐ 293	Dino Radja CF	.05	.02	.01
	Acie Earl			
☐ 294	Eddie Johnson CF	.05	.02	.01
	Hersey Hawkins			
☐ 295	Toni Kukoc CF	.20	.09	.03
	Corie Blount			
☐ 296	Tyrone Hill CF	.05	.02	.01
	Chris Mills			
☐ 297	Jamal Mashburn CF	.20	.09	.03
	Popeye Jones			
☐ 298	Darnell Mee CF	.05	.02	.01
	Rodney Rodgers			
☐ 299	Lindsey Hunter CF	.05	.02	.01
	Allan Houston			
☐ 300	Chris Webber CF	.30	.14	.04
	Avery Johnson			
☐ 301	Sam Cassell CF	.05	.02	.01
	Mario Elie			
☐ 302	Derrick McKey CF	.05	.02	.01
	Antonio Davis			
☐ 303	Terry Dehere CF	.05	.02	.01
	Mark Aguirre			
☐ 304	Nick Van Exel CF	.25	.11	.03
	George Lynch			

☐ 305	Harold Miner CF	.05	.02	.01
	Steve Smith			
☐ 306	Ken Norman CF	.10	.05	.01
	Vin Baker			
☐ 307	Mike Brown CF	.05	.02	.01
	Isaiah Rider			
☐ 308	Kevin Edwards CF	.05	.02	.01
	Rex Walters			
☐ 309	Hubert Davis CF	.05	.02	.01
	Anthony Bonner			
☐ 310	Anfernee Hardaway CF	1.50	.70	.19
	Larry Krystkowiak			
☐ 311	Moses Malone CF	.10	.05	.01
	Shawn Bradley			
☐ 312	Joe Kleine CF	.05	.02	.01
	A.C. Green			
☐ 313	Harvey Grant CF	.05	.02	.01
	Chris Dudley			
☐ 314	Bobby Hurley CF	.10	.05	.01
	Mitch Richmond			
☐ 315	Sleepy Floyd CF	.30	.14	.04
	Dennis Rodman			
☐ 316	Kendall Gill CF	.05	.02	.01
	Detlef Schrempf			
☐ 317	Felton Spencer CF	.05	.02	.01
	Luther Wright			
☐ 318	Calbert Cheaney CF	.05	.02	.01
	Kevin Duckworth			
☐ 319	Karl Malone PC	.15	.07	.02
☐ 320	Alonzo Mourning PC	.25	.11	.03
☐ 321	Scottie Pippen PC	.50	.23	.06
☐ 322	Mark Price PC	.05	.02	.01
☐ 323	LaPhonso Ellis PC	.05	.02	.01
☐ 324	Joe Dumars PC	.10	.05	.01
☐ 325	Chris Mullin PC	.05	.02	.01
☐ 326	Ron Harper PC	.05	.02	.01
☐ 327	Glen Rice PC	.05	.02	.01
☐ 328	Christian Laettner PC	.05	.02	.01
☐ 329	Kenny Anderson PC	.05	.02	.01
☐ 330	John Starks PC	.05	.02	.01
☐ 331	Shaquille O'Neal PC	1.00	.45	.12
☐ 332	Charles Barkley PC	.25	.11	.03
☐ 333	Clifford Robinson PC	.05	.02	.01
☐ 334	Clyde Drexler PC	.05	.02	.01
☐ 335	Mitch Richmond PC	.10	.05	.01
☐ 336	David Robinson PC	.30	.14	.04
☐ 337	Shawn Kemp PC	.50	.23	.06
☐ 338	John Stockton PC	.15	.07	.02
☐ 339	Checklist 4	.05	.02	.01
☐ 340	Checklist 5	.05	.02	.01
☐ 341	Checklist 6	.05	.02	.01
☐ DP4	Jim Jackson	2.50	1.10	.30
☐ DP17	Doug Christie	.20	.09	.03
☐ NNO	Expired Head of the ..	2.00	.90	.25
	Class Exchange Card			
☐ NNO	HOC Card	30.00	13.50	3.70

1993-94 SkyBox All-Rookies

Randomly inserted in first series 12-card packs at a rate of one in 36, this standard-size five-card set features top rookies from the 1992-93 season. The design features borderless fronts with color action player cutouts set against metallic game-crowd backgrounds. The player's name appears

in gold-foil lettering at the upper left. The white back carries a color player head shot along with career highlights.

	MINT	NRMT	EXC
COMPLETE SET (5)	20.00	9.00	2.50
COMMON CARD (AR1-AR5)	.75	.35	.09
☐ AR1 Shaquille O'Neal	15.00	6.75	1.85
☐ AR2 Alonzo Mourning	4.00	1.80	.50
☐ AR3 Christian Laettner	1.25	.55	.16
☐ AR4 Tom Gugliotta	1.25	.55	.16
☐ AR5 LaPhonso Ellis	.75	.35	.09

1993-94 SkyBox Center Stage

Randomly inserted in first series packs at a rate of one in 12, this 9-card standard-size set showcases some of the best players in the NBA. Card fronts feature are borderless fronts with color action player cutouts placed against black backgrounds. The player's name is centered at the top in prismatic silver-foil lettering. The white back features a color action player cutout and player biography.

	MINT	NRMT	EXC
COMPLETE SET (9)	40.00	18.00	5.00
COMMON CARD (CS1-CS9)	1.00	.45	.12
☐ CS1 Michael Jordan	25.00	11.00	3.10
☐ CS2 Shaquille O'Neal	12.00	5.50	1.50
☐ CS3 Charles Barkley	3.00	1.35	.35
☐ CS4 John Starks	1.00	.45	.12
☐ CS5 Larry Johnson	2.50	1.10	.30
☐ CS6 Hakeem Olajuwon	5.00	2.20	.60
☐ CS7 Kenny Anderson	1.75	.80	.22
☐ CS8 Mahmoud Abdul-Rauf	1.75	.80	.22
☐ CS9 Clifford Robinson	1.75	.80	.22

1993-94 SkyBox Draft Picks

These 26 standard-size cards were random inserts in both first series (Nos. 2, 6-8, 12, 15) and second series (the other 20) 12-card packs. The odds of finding one of these cards are one in every 12 packs. Card No. 26 was scheduled to be LSU center Geert Hammink. Hammink decided to play in Europe and his card was pulled. The fronts feature a color player action cutout set off to one side and superposed upon a ghosted posed color player photo. The player's name, the team that drafted him, and his draft pick number appear at the top. The white back carries the player's name, career highlights, and pre-NBA statistics. The cards are numbered on the back with a "DP" prefix. The set is sequenced in draft order.

	MINT	NRMT	EXC
COMPLETE SET (26)	50.00	22.00	6.25
COMPLETE SERIES 1 (9)	10.00	4.50	1.25
COMPLETE SERIES 2 (17)	40.00	18.00	5.00
COMMON 1 (2/6-8/12/15)	.50	.23	.06
COMMON 1 (16/18/23)	.50	.23	.06
COMMON 2 (1/3-5/9/10/13/14)	.50	.23	.06
COMMON 2 (17/19-22/24-27)	.50	.23	.06
☐ DP1 Chris Webber	6.00	2.70	.75
☐ DP2 Shawn Bradley	2.00	.90	.25
☐ DP3 Anfernee Hardaway	30.00	13.50	3.70
☐ DP4 Jamal Mashburn	4.00	1.80	.50
☐ DP5 Isaiah Rider	2.00	.90	.25
☐ DP6 Calbert Cheaney	1.50	.70	.19
☐ DP7 Bobby Hurley	1.00	.45	.12
☐ DP8 Vin Baker	6.00	2.70	.75
☐ DP9 Rodney Rodgers	1.00	.45	.12
☐ DP10 Lindsey Hunter	.50	.23	.06
☐ DP11 Allan Houston	3.00	1.35	.35
☐ DP12 George Lynch	.50	.23	.06
☐ DP13 Terry Dehere	1.00	.45	.12
☐ DP14 Scott Haskin	.50	.23	.06
☐ DP15 Doug Edwards	.50	.23	.06
☐ DP16 Rex Walters	.50	.23	.06
☐ DP17 Greg Graham	.50	.23	.06

		MINT	NRMT	EXC
☐	DP18 Luther Wright	.50	.23	.06
☐	DP19 Acie Earl	.50	.23	.06
☐	DP20 Scott Burrell	1.00	.45	.12
☐	DP21 James Robinson	.50	.23	.06
☐	DP22 Chris Mills	2.50	1.10	.30
☐	DP23 Ervin Johnson	1.00	.45	.12
☐	DP24 Sam Cassell	2.50	1.10	.30
☐	DP25 Corie Blount	.50	.23	.06
☐	DP26 Not Issued			
☐	DP27 Malcolm Mackey	.50	.23	.06

1993-94 SkyBox Dynamic Dunks

These nine standard-size cards were random inserts in second series 12-card packs. The odds of finding one of these cards are one in every 36 packs. The horizontal fronts feature color color dunking-action player cutouts superposed upon borderless black and gold metallic backgrounds. The player's name appears in gold lettering at the bottom right. The horizontal black back carries another color dunking-action player photo. The player's name and a comment on his dunking style appear in white lettering beneath the photo. The set is sequenced in alphabetical order.

		MINT	NRMT	EXC
	COMPLETE SET (9)	25.00	11.00	3.10
	COMMON CARD (D1-D9)	.50	.23	.06
☐	D1 Nick Anderson	.75	.35	.09
☐	D2 Charles Barkley	2.50	1.10	.30
☐	D3 Robert Horry	1.00	.45	.12
☐	D4 Michael Jordan	20.00	9.00	2.50
☐	D5 Shawn Kemp	5.00	2.20	.60
☐	D6 Anthony Mason	.50	.23	.06
☐	D7 Alonzo Mourning	2.00	.90	.25
☐	D8 Hakeem Olajuwon	4.00	1.80	.50
☐	D9 Dominique Wilkins	.75	.35	.09

1993-94 SkyBox Shaq Talk

The 1993-94 SkyBox Shaq Talk set consists of 10 cards that were randomly insert-

ed in first (cards 1-5) and second series (6-10) 12-card packs. The odds of finding one of these cards are reportedly one in every 36 packs. The standard size cards spotlight Shaquille O'Neal. The fronts feature cut-out action shots of Shaq over a ghosted background. The set title is superimposed across the top of the card in red lettering. The white backs have a ghosted SkyBox Premium logo. At the top is a quote from Shaquille regarding game strategy and below is player critique by a basketball analyst. The cards are numbered on the back with a "Shaq Talk" prefix.

		MINT	NRMT	EXC
	COMPLETE SET (10)	40.00	18.00	5.00
	COMPLETE SERIES 1 (5)	20.00	9.00	2.50
	COMPLETE SERIES 2 (5)	20.00	9.00	2.50
	COMMON O'NEAL (1-10)	5.00	2.20	.60
☐	1 Shaq Talk	5.00	2.20	.60
	The Rebound			
☐	2 Shaq Talk	5.00	2.20	.60
	The Block			
	(Blocking David			
	Robinson's shot)			
☐	3 Shaq Talk	5.00	2.20	.60
	The Postup			
☐	4 Shaq Talk	5.00	2.20	.60
	The Dunk			
☐	5 Shaq Talk	5.00	2.20	.60
	Defense			
☐	6 Shaq Talk	5.00	2.20	.60
	Scoring			
☐	7 Shaq Talk	5.00	2.20	.60
	Passing			
☐	8 Shaq Talk	5.00	2.20	.60
	Rejections			
☐	9 Shaq Talk	5.00	2.20	.60
	Confidence			
☐	10 Shaq Talk	5.00	2.20	.60
	Legends			

1993-94 SkyBox Showdown Series

These 12 standard-size cards were random inserts in first (cards 1-6) and second series (7-12) 12-card packs. The odds of finding one of these cards are one in every six packs. Each front features a borderless color action photo of the two players

involved in the "Showdown." Both players' names appear, one vs. the other, in gold lettering within a metallic black stripe near the bottom. The horizontal white back carries a color player close-up for each player on each side. The players' names appear beneath each photo. Comparative statistics fill in the area between the two player photos.

	MINT	NRMT	EXC
COMPLETE SET (12)	6.00	2.70	.75
COMPLETE SERIES 1 (6)	3.00	1.35	.35
COMPLETE SERIES 2 (6)	3.00	1.35	.35
COMMON PAIR (SS1-SS6)	.40	.18	.05
COMMON PAIR (SS7-SS12)	.25	.11	.03
☐ SS1 Alonzo Mourning Patrick Ewing	.40	.18	.05
☐ SS2 Shaquille O'Neal Patrick Ewing	1.00	.45	.12
☐ SS3 Alonzo Mourning Shaquille O'Neal	1.25	.55	.16
☐ SS4 Hakeem Olajuwon Dikembe Mutombo	.50	.23	.06
☐ SS5 David Robinson Hakeem Olajuwon	.75	.35	.09
☐ SS6 David Robinson Dikembe Mutombo	.40	.18	.05
☐ SS7 Shawn Kemp Karl Malone	.60	.25	.07
☐ SS8 Larry Johnson Charles Barkley	.40	.18	.05
☐ SS9 Dominique Wilkins Scottie Pippen	.50	.23	.06
☐ SS10 Joe Dumars Reggie Miller	.25	.11	.03
☐ SS11 Clyde Drexler Michael Jordan	2.00	.90	.25
☐ SS12 Magic Johnson Larry Bird	1.50	.70	.19

1993-94 SkyBox Thunder and Lightning

Randomly inserted in second series packs at a rate of one in 12 packs, this standard-size nine-card set features players pictured on both sides. On one side a guard would be featured and a forward or center on the other side. Borderless on either side, the color action player cutouts set against metallic backgrounds.

	MINT	NRMT	EXC
COMPLETE SET (9)	25.00	11.00	3.10
COMMON PAIR (1-9)	.50	.23	.06
☐ TL1 Jamal Mashburn Jim Jackson	2.50	1.10	.30
☐ TL2 Harold Miner Steve Smith	.50	.23	.06
☐ TL3 Isaiah Rider Micheal Williams	1.00	.45	.12
☐ TL4 Derrick Coleman Kenny Anderson	.50	.23	.06
☐ TL5 Patrick Ewing John Starks	1.00	.45	.12
☐ TL6 Shaquille O'Neal Anfernee Hardaway	20.00	9.00	2.50
☐ TL7 Shawn Bradley Jeff Hornacek	.50	.23	.06
☐ TL8 Walt Williams Bobby Hurley	.50	.23	.06
☐ TL9 Dennis Rodman David Robinson	6.00	2.70	.75

1993-94 SkyBox USA Tip-Off

The 13-card 1993-94 SkyBox USA Tip-Off set could be only acquired by sending in the USA Exchange card. The USA Exchange cards were randomly inserted in SkyBox series two packs. The Tip-Off redemption expiration was 6/15/94. It should be noted that Michael Jordan is not part of the set. Card fronts and backs feature studio photos of players in their USA Basketball uniforms.

	MINT	NRMT	EXC
COMPLETE SET (14)	25.00	11.00	3.10
COMMON CARD (1-13)	.75	.35	.09
☐ 1 Steve Smith	4.00	1.80	.50
Magic Johnson			
☐ 2 Larry Johnson	2.50	1.10	.30
Charles Barkley			
☐ 3 Patrick Ewing	2.50	1.10	.30
Alonzo Mourning			
☐ 4 Shawn Kemp	4.00	1.80	.50
Karl Malone			
☐ 5 Chris Mullin	.75	.35	.09
Dan Majerle			
☐ 6 John Stockton	1.25	.55	.16
Mark Price			
☐ 7 Christian Laettner	.75	.35	.09
Derrick Coleman			
☐ 8 Dominique Wilkins	1.50	.70	.19
Clyde Drexler			
☐ 9 Joe Dumars	3.00	1.35	.35
Scottie Pippen			
☐ 10 David Robinson	8.00	3.60	1.00
Shaquille O'Neal			
☐ 11 Reggie Miller	5.00	2.20	.60
Larry Bird			
☐ 12 Tim Hardaway	.75	.35	.09
☐ 13 Isiah Thomas	1.00	.45	.12
☐ NNO Checklist	.25	.11	.03
☐ NNO Expired USA Exchange	1.50	.70	.19

ber of other prizes including autographed Hakeem Olajuwon or David Robinson jerseys, a dual autographed Olajuwon /Robinson card or an exclusive Magic Johnson exchange card available only through this promotion. A special three-card panel featuring Johnson, Olajuwon and Robinson was available by mailing in forty first series wrappers before the June 30th, 1995 deadline. Also, three Master Series Preview Press Sheet Exchange cards were randomly seeded into one in every 360 first series packs. The cards were redeemable for 50-card uncut press sheets of SkyBox's new super-premium Emotion cards. The expiration date for the Emotion Press Sheets was March 1, 1995. As a final note, approximately one in every 360 first series retail packs contained an unannounced Hakeem Olajuwon Gold "stealth" card. Approximately one in every 360 second series retail packs contained an unannounced Grant Hill Gold "stealth" card. A standard-size promo card featuring Hakeem Olajuwon was issued to preview the set; a 3 1/2" by 5" jumbo version, distinguished by a gold foil autograph, was issued as a chiptopper in retail boxes. A 5" by 7" jumbo featuring Grant Hill (Slammin' Universe) was also issued as a chiptopper in retail boxes. Rookie Cards in this set include Grant Hill, Jason Kidd and Glenn Robinson.

1994-95 SkyBox

The 350 standard-size cards that comprise the 1994-95 SkyBox set were issued in two separate series of 200 and 150 cards respectively. Cards were distributed in 12-card hobby and retail packs with a suggested retail price of $1.99 each. Unlike first series packs, each second series pack contained an insert card. Card fronts feature full-bleed action photos with the player's name running down the upper-left corner. The cards are grouped alphabetically within teams and checklisted below alphabetically according to teams. Subsets are NBA on NBC (176-185), Dynamic Duals (186-197), USA Basketball (198), Checklists (298-300), SkySlams (301-313), SkyShots (314-325), SkySwats (326-338), and SkyPilots (339-350). Every first series pack contained an Action and Drama Instant Win game card, offering the chance to play one-on-one with Magic Johnson, or receive a num-

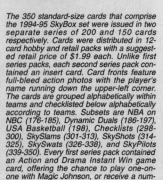

	MINT	NRMT	EXC
COMPLETE SET (350)	30.00	13.50	3.70
COMPLETE SERIES 1 (200)	15.00	6.75	1.85
COMPLETE SERIES 2 (150)	15.00	6.75	1.85
COMMON CARD (1-200)	.10	.05	.01
COMMON CARD (201-350)	.05	.02	.01
☐ 1 Stacey Augmon	.12	.05	.02
☐ 2 Mookie Blaylock	.12	.05	.02
☐ 3 Doug Edwards	.10	.05	.01
☐ 4 Craig Ehlo	.10	.05	.01
☐ 5 Adam Keefe	.10	.05	.01
☐ 6 Danny Manning	.15	.07	.02
☐ 7 Kevin Willis	.10	.05	.01
☐ 8 Dee Brown	.10	.05	.01
☐ 9 Sherman Douglas	.10	.05	.01
☐ 10 Acie Earl	.10	.05	.01
☐ 11 Kevin Gamble	.10	.05	.01
☐ 12 Xavier McDaniel	.10	.05	.01
☐ 13 Dino Radja	.15	.07	.02
☐ 14 Muggsy Bogues	.15	.07	.02
☐ 15 Scott Burrell	.10	.05	.01
☐ 16 Dell Curry	.10	.05	.01
☐ 17 LeRon Ellis	.10	.05	.01
☐ 18 Hersey Hawkins	.10	.05	.01
☐ 19 Larry Johnson	.40	.18	.05
☐ 20 Alonzo Mourning	.50	.23	.06
☐ 21 B.J. Armstrong	.10	.05	.01
☐ 22 Corie Blount	.10	.05	.01
☐ 23 Horace Grant	.20	.09	.03
☐ 24 Toni Kukoc	.30	.14	.04
☐ 25 Luc Longley	.10	.05	.01
☐ 26 Scottie Pippen	1.25	.55	.16
☐ 27 Scott Williams	.10	.05	.01
☐ 28 Terrell Brandon	.10	.05	.01
☐ 29 Brad Daugherty	.10	.05	.01
☐ 30 Tyrone Hill	.10	.05	.01

□	#	Player			
□	31	Chris Mills	.15	.07	.02
□	32	Bobby Phills	.10	.05	.01
□	33	Mark Price	.10	.05	.01
□	34	Gerald Wilkins	.10	.05	.01
□	35	Lucious Harris	.10	.05	.01
□	36	Jim Jackson	.50	.23	.06
□	37	Popeye Jones	.10	.05	.01
□	38	Jamal Mashburn	.30	.14	.04
□	39	Sean Rooks	.10	.05	.01
□	40	Mahmoud Abdul-Rauf	.12	.05	.02
□	41	LaPhonso Ellis	.10	.05	.01
□	42	Dikembe Mutombo	.25	.11	.03
□	43	Robert Pack	.10	.05	.01
□	44	Rodney Rogers	.10	.05	.01
□	45	Bryant Stith	.10	.05	.01
□	46	Reggie Williams	.10	.05	.01
□	47	Joe Dumars	.20	.09	.03
□	48	Sean Elliott	.12	.05	.02
□	49	Allan Houston	.25	.11	.03
□	50	Lindsey Hunter	.10	.05	.01
□	51	Terry Mills	.10	.05	.01
□	52	Victor Alexander	.10	.05	.01
□	53	Tim Hardaway	.15	.07	.02
□	54	Chris Mullin	.15	.07	.02
□	55	Billy Owens	.10	.05	.01
□	56	Latrell Sprewell	.50	.23	.06
□	57	Chris Webber	.50	.23	.06
□	58	Sam Cassell	.15	.07	.02
□	59	Carl Herrera	.10	.05	.01
□	60	Robert Horry	.15	.07	.02
□	61	Vernon Maxwell	.10	.05	.01
□	62	Hakeem Olajuwon	1.00	.45	.12
□	63	Kenny Smith	.10	.05	.01
□	64	Otis Thorpe	.12	.05	.02
□	65	Antonio Davis	.10	.05	.01
□	66	Dale Davis	.10	.05	.01
□	67	Derrick McKey	.10	.05	.01
□	68	Reggie Miller	.50	.23	.06
□	69	Pooh Richardson	.10	.05	.01
□	70	Rik Smits	.15	.07	.02
□	71	Haywoode Workman	.10	.05	.01
□	72	Terry Dehere	.10	.05	.01
□	73	Harold Ellis	.10	.05	.01
□	74	Ron Harper	.10	.05	.01
□	75	Mark Jackson	.10	.05	.01
□	76	Loy Vaught	.10	.05	.01
□	77	Dominique Wilkins	.20	.09	.03
□	78	Elden Campbell	.10	.05	.01
□	79	Doug Christie	.10	.05	.01
□	80	Vlade Divac	.15	.07	.02
□	81	George Lynch	.10	.05	.01
□	82	Anthony Peeler	.10	.05	.01
□	83	Sedale Threatt	.10	.05	.01
□	84	Nick Van Exel	.40	.18	.05
□	85	Harold Miner	.10	.05	.01
□	86	Glen Rice	.15	.07	.02
□	87	John Salley	.10	.05	.01
□	88	Rony Seikaly	.10	.05	.01
□	89	Brian Shaw	.10	.05	.01
□	90	Steve Smith	.12	.05	.02
□	91	Vin Baker	.50	.23	.06
□	92	Jon Barry	.10	.05	.01
□	93	Todd Day	.10	.05	.01
□	94	Blue Edwards	.10	.05	.01
□	95	Lee Mayberry	.10	.05	.01
□	96	Eric Murdock	.10	.05	.01
□	97	Mike Brown	.10	.05	.01
□	98	Stacey King	.10	.05	.01
□	99	Christian Laettner	.12	.05	.02
□	100	Isaiah Rider	.25	.11	.03
□	101	Doug West	.10	.05	.01
□	102	Micheal Williams	.10	.05	.01
□	103	Kenny Anderson	.15	.07	.02
□	104	P.J. Brown	.10	.05	.01
□	105	Derrick Coleman	.10	.05	.01
□	106	Kevin Edwards	.10	.05	.01
□	107	Chris Morris	.10	.05	.01
□	108	Rex Walters	.10	.05	.01
□	109	Hubert Davis	.10	.05	.01
□	110	Patrick Ewing	.40	.18	.05
□	111	Derek Harper	.10	.05	.01
□	112	Anthony Mason	.10	.05	.01
□	113	Charles Oakley	.12	.05	.02
□	114	Charles Smith	.10	.05	.01
□	115	John Starks	.10	.05	.01
□	116	Nick Anderson	.12	.05	.02
□	117	Anfernee Hardaway	2.50	1.10	.30
□	118	Shaquille O'Neal	2.00	.90	.25
□	119	Donald Royal	.10	.05	.01
□	120	Dennis Scott	.10	.05	.01
□	121	Scott Skiles	.10	.05	.01
□	122	Dana Barros	.10	.05	.01
□	123	Shawn Bradley	.15	.07	.02
□	124	Johnny Dawkins	.10	.05	.01
□	125	Greg Graham	.10	.05	.01
□	126	Clarence Weatherspoon	.10	.05	.01
□	127	Danny Ainge	.12	.05	.02
□	128	Charles Barkley	.60	.25	.07
□	129	Cedric Ceballos	.15	.07	.02
□	130	A.C. Green	.15	.07	.02
□	131	Kevin Johnson	.20	.09	.03
□	132	Dan Majerle	.12	.05	.02
□	133	Oliver Miller	.10	.05	.01
□	134	Clyde Drexler	.50	.23	.06
□	135	Harvey Grant	.10	.05	.01
□	136	Tracy Murray	.10	.05	.01
□	137	Terry Porter	.10	.05	.01
□	138	Clifford Robinson	.12	.05	.02
□	139	James Robinson	.10	.05	.01
□	140	Rod Strickland	.10	.05	.01
□	141	Bobby Hurley	.10	.05	.01
□	142	Olden Polynice	.10	.05	.01
□	143	Mitch Richmond	.30	.14	.04
□	144	Lionel Simmons	.10	.05	.01
□	145	Wayman Tisdale	.10	.05	.01
□	146	Spud Webb	.12	.05	.02
□	147	Walt Williams	.12	.05	.02
□	148	Willie Anderson	.10	.05	.01
□	149	Vinny Del Negro	.10	.05	.01
□	150	Dale Ellis	.10	.05	.01
□	151	J.R. Reid	.10	.05	.01
□	152	David Robinson	.75	.35	.09
□	153	Dennis Rodman	1.50	.70	.19
□	154	Kendall Gill	.10	.05	.01
□	155	Shawn Kemp	1.25	.55	.16
□	156	Nate McMillan	.10	.05	.01
□	157	Gary Payton	.60	.25	.07
□	158	Sam Perkins	.10	.05	.01
□	159	Ricky Pierce	.10	.05	.01
□	160	Detlef Schrempf	.15	.07	.02
□	161	David Benoit	.10	.05	.01
□	162	Tyrone Corbin	.10	.05	.01
□	163	Jeff Hornacek	.12	.05	.02
□	164	Jay Humphries	.10	.05	.01
□	165	Karl Malone	.40	.18	.05
□	166	Bryon Russell	.10	.05	.01
□	167	Felton Spencer	.10	.05	.01
□	168	John Stockton	.40	.18	.05
□	169	Michael Adams	.10	.05	.01
□	170	Rex Chapman	.10	.05	.01
□	171	Calbert Cheaney	.15	.07	.02
□	172	Pervis Ellison	.10	.05	.01

☐ 173 Tom Gugliotta	.12	.05	.02
☐ 174 Don MacLean	.10	.05	.01
☐ 175 Gheorghe Muresan	.12	.05	.02
☐ 176 Charles Barkley NBC	.30	.14	.04
☐ 177 Charles Oakley NBC	.10	.05	.01
☐ 178 Hakeem Olajuwon NBC	.50	.23	.06
☐ 179 Dikembe Mutombo NBC	.12	.05	.02
☐ 180 Scottie Pippen NBC	.60	.25	.07
☐ 181 Sam Cassell NBC	.10	.05	.01
☐ 182 Karl Malone NBC	.15	.07	.02
☐ 183 Reggie Miller PO	.25	.11	.03
☐ 184 Patrick Ewing NBC	.15	.07	.02
☐ 185 Vernon Maxwell NBC	.10	.05	.01
☐ 186 Anfernee Hardaway DD Steve Smith	.40	.18	.05
☐ 187 Chris Webber DD Shaquille O'Neal	.50	.23	.06
☐ 188 Jamal Mashburn DD Rodney Rogers	.10	.05	.01
☐ 189 Toni Kukoc DD Dino Radja	.12	.05	.02
☐ 190 Lindsey Hunter DD Kenny Anderson	.10	.05	.01
☐ 191 Latrell Sprewell DD Jimmy Jackson	.20	.09	.03
☐ 192 Clarence Weatherspoon Vin Baker DD	.12	.05	.02
☐ 193 Calbert Cheaney DD Chris Mills	.10	.05	.01
☐ 194 Isaiah Rider DD Robert Horry	.12	.05	.02
☐ 195 Sam Cassell DD Nick Van Exel	.15	.07	.02
☐ 196 Gheorghe Muresan DD Shawn Bradley	.10	.05	.01
☐ 197 LaPhonso Ellis DD Tom Gugliotta	.10	.05	.01
☐ 198 USA Basketball Card	.12	.05	.02
☐ 199 Checklist	.10	.05	.01
☐ 200 Checklist	.10	.05	.01
☐ 201 Sergei Bazarevich	.05	.02	.01
☐ 202 Tyrone Corbin	.05	.02	.01
☐ 203 Grant Long	.05	.02	.01
☐ 204 Ken Norman	.05	.02	.01
☐ 205 Steve Smith	.08	.04	.01
☐ 206 Blue Edwards	.05	.02	.01
☐ 207 Greg Minor	.05	.02	.01
☐ 208 Eric Montross	.40	.18	.05
☐ 209 Dominique Wilkins	.15	.07	.02
☐ 210 Michael Adams	.05	.02	.01
☐ 211 Kenny Gattison	.05	.02	.01
☐ 212 Darrin Hancock	.05	.02	.01
☐ 213 Robert Parish	.10	.05	.01
☐ 214 Ron Harper	.08	.04	.01
☐ 215 Steve Kerr	.05	.02	.01
☐ 216 Will Perdue	.05	.02	.01
☐ 217 Dickey Simpkins	.15	.07	.02
☐ 218 John Battle	.05	.02	.01
☐ 219 Michael Cage	.05	.02	.01
☐ 220 Tony Dumas	.07	.03	.01
☐ 221 Jason Kidd	2.00	.90	.25
☐ 222 Roy Tarpley	.05	.02	.01
☐ 223 Dale Ellis	.05	.02	.01
☐ 224 Jalen Rose	.25	.11	.03
☐ 225 Bill Curley	.05	.02	.01
☐ 226 Grant Hill	3.00	1.35	.35
☐ 227 Oliver Miller	.05	.02	.01
☐ 228 Mark West	.05	.02	.01
☐ 229 Tom Gugliotta	.08	.04	.01
☐ 230 Ricky Pierce	.05	.02	.01
☐ 231 Carlos Rogers	.05	.02	.01
☐ 232 Clifford Rozier	.20	.09	.03
☐ 233 Rony Seikaly	.05	.02	.01
☐ 234 Tim Breaux	.05	.02	.01
☐ 235 Duane Ferrell	.05	.02	.01
☐ 236 Mark Jackson	.05	.02	.01
☐ 237 Byron Scott	.08	.04	.01
☐ 238 John Williams	.05	.02	.01
☐ 239 Lamond Murray	.05	.02	.01
☐ 240 Eric Piatkowski	.05	.02	.01
☐ 241 Pooh Richardson	.05	.02	.01
☐ 242 Malik Sealy	.05	.02	.01
☐ 243 Cedric Ceballos	.10	.05	.01
☐ 244 Eddie Jones	.60	.25	.07
☐ 245 Anthony Miller	.05	.02	.01
☐ 246 Tony Smith	.05	.02	.01
☐ 247 Kevin Gamble	.05	.02	.01
☐ 248 Brad Lohaus	.05	.02	.01
☐ 249 Billy Owens	.05	.02	.01
☐ 250 Khalid Reeves	.05	.02	.01
☐ 251 Kevin Willis	.05	.02	.01
☐ 252 Eric Mobley	.15	.07	.02
☐ 253 Johnny Newman	.05	.02	.01
☐ 254 Ed Pinckney	.05	.02	.01
☐ 255 Glenn Robinson	1.00	.45	.12
☐ 256 Howard Eisley	.05	.02	.01
☐ 257 Donyell Marshall	.50	.23	.06
☐ 258 Yinka Dare	.05	.02	.01
☐ 259 Sean Higgins	.05	.02	.01
☐ 260 Jayson Williams	.05	.02	.01
☐ 261 Charlie Ward	.20	.09	.03
☐ 262 Monty Williams	.05	.02	.01
☐ 263 Horace Grant	.15	.07	.02
☐ 264 Brian Shaw	.05	.02	.01
☐ 265 Brooks Thompson	.07	.03	.01
☐ 266 Derrick Alston	.05	.02	.01
☐ 267 B.J. Tyler	.05	.02	.01
☐ 268 Scott Williams	.05	.02	.01
☐ 269 Sharone Wright	.30	.14	.04
☐ 270 Antonio Lang	.05	.02	.01
☐ 271 Danny Manning	.10	.05	.01
☐ 272 Wesley Person	.50	.23	.06
☐ 273 Trevor Ruffin	.07	.03	.01
☐ 274 Wayman Tisdale	.05	.02	.01
☐ 275 Jerome Kersey	.05	.02	.01
☐ 276 Aaron McKie	.20	.09	.03
☐ 277 Frank Brickowski	.05	.02	.01
☐ 278 Brian Grant	.40	.18	.05
☐ 279 Michael Smith	.05	.02	.01
☐ 280 Terry Cummings	.05	.02	.01
☐ 281 Sean Elliott	.08	.04	.01
☐ 282 Avery Johnson	.05	.02	.01
☐ 283 Moses Malone	.15	.07	.02
☐ 284 Chuck Person	.08	.04	.01
☐ 285 Vincent Askew	.05	.02	.01
☐ 286 Bill Cartwright	.05	.02	.01
☐ 287 Sarunas Marciulionis	.05	.02	.01
☐ 288 Dontonio Wingfield	.05	.02	.01
☐ 289 Jay Humphries	.05	.02	.01
☐ 290 Adam Keefe	.05	.02	.01
☐ 291 Jamie Watson	.05	.02	.01
☐ 292 Kevin Duckworth	.05	.02	.01
☐ 293 Juwan Howard	2.00	.90	.25
☐ 294 Jim McIlvaine	.05	.02	.01
☐ 295 Scott Skiles	.05	.02	.01
☐ 296 Anthony Tucker	.05	.02	.01
☐ 297 Chris Webber	.30	.14	.04
☐ 298 Checklist 201-265	.05	.02	.01
☐ 299 Checklist 266-345	.05	.02	.01
☐ 300 Checklist 346-350/Inserts	.05	.02	.01
☐ 301 Vin Baker SSL	.10	.05	.01
☐ 302 Charles Barkley SSL	.20	.09	.03

		MINT	NRMT	EXC
☐ 303	Derrick Coleman SSL	.05	.02	.01
☐ 304	Clyde Drexler SSL	.10	.05	.01
☐ 305	LaPhonso Ellis SSL	.05	.02	.01
☐ 306	Larry Johnson SSL	.08	.04	.01
☐ 307	Shawn Kemp SSL	.40	.18	.05
☐ 308	Karl Malone SSL	.10	.05	.01
☐ 309	Jamal Mashburn SSL	.25	.11	.03
☐ 310	Scottie Pippen SSL	.40	.18	.05
☐ 311	Dominique Wilkins SSL	.08	.04	.01
☐ 312	Walt Williams SSL	.05	.02	.01
☐ 313	Sharone Wright SSL	.05	.02	.01
☐ 314	B.J. Armstrong SSH	.05	.02	.01
☐ 315	Joe Dumars SSH	.08	.04	.01
☐ 316	Tony Dumas SSH	.05	.02	.01
☐ 317	Tim Hardaway SSH	.05	.02	.01
☐ 318	Toni Kukoc SSH	.05	.02	.01
☐ 319	Danny Manning SSH	.05	.02	.01
☐ 320	Reggie Miller SSH	.15	.07	.02
☐ 321	Chris Mullin SSH	.05	.02	.01
☐ 322	Wesley Person SSH	.20	.09	.03
☐ 323	John Starks SSH	.05	.02	.01
☐ 324	John Stockton SSH	.10	.05	.01
☐ 325	C. Weatherspoon SSH	.05	.02	.01
☐ 326	Shawn Bradley SSW	.05	.02	.01
☐ 327	Vlade Divac SSW	.05	.02	.01
☐ 328	Patrick Ewing SSW	.10	.05	.01
☐ 329	Christian Laettner SSW	.05	.02	.01
☐ 330	Eric Montross SSW	.05	.02	.01
☐ 331	Gheorghe Muresan SSW	.05	.02	.01
☐ 332	Dikembe Mutombo SSW	.08	.04	.01
☐ 333	Hakeem Olajuwon SSW	.30	.14	.04
☐ 334	Robert Parish SSW	.05	.02	.01
☐ 335	David Robinson SSW	.25	.11	.03
☐ 336	Dennis Rodman SSW	.50	.23	.06
☐ 337	Rony Seikaly SSW	.05	.02	.01
☐ 338	Rik Smits SSW	.05	.02	.01
☐ 339	Kenny Anderson SPI	.05	.02	.01
☐ 340	Dee Brown SPI	.05	.02	.01
☐ 341	Bobby Hurley SPI	.05	.02	.01
☐ 342	Kevin Johnson SPI	.08	.04	.01
☐ 343	Jason Kidd SPI	.75	.35	.09
☐ 344	Gary Payton SPI	.20	.09	.03
☐ 345	Mark Price SPI	.05	.02	.01
☐ 346	Khalid Reeves SPI	.05	.02	.01
☐ 347	Jalen Rose SPI	.05	.02	.01
☐ 348	Latrell Sprewell SPI	.05	.02	.01
☐ 349	B.J. Tyler SPI	.05	.02	.01
☐ 350	Charlie Ward SPI	.05	.02	.01
☐ GHO	Grant Hill SSW	30.00	13.50	3.70
☐ NNO	H.Olajuwon Gold	15.00	6.75	1.85
☐ NNO	Emotion Sheet A	30.00	13.50	3.70
☐ NNO	Emotion Sheet B	30.00	13.50	3.70
☐ NNO	Exp. Emotion Exch. A	1.50	.70	.19
☐ NNO	Exp. Emotion Exch. B	1.50	.70	.19
☐ NNO	Exp. Emotion Exch. C	1.50	.70	.19
☐ NNO	Exp. 3rd Prize Game Card	.25	.11	.03
☐ NNO	H. Olajuwon D. Robinson AU	250.00	110.00	31.00
☐ NNO	M.Johnson Exch. Card	5.00	2.20	.60
☐ NNO	Three-Card Panel Exch.	4.00	1.80	.50

1994-95 SkyBox Center Stage

Randomly inserted in all first series packs at a rate of one in 72, cards from this nine-

card standard-size set feature a selection of the game's top stars. Card fronts feature full-color player photos over etched-foil backgrounds.

	MINT	NRMT	EXC
COMPLETE SET (9)	70.00	32.00	8.75
COMMON CARD (CS1-CS9)	2.50	1.10	.30
☐ CS1 Hakeem Olajuwon	10.00	4.50	1.25
☐ CS2 Shaquille O'Neal	20.00	9.00	2.50
☐ CS3 Anfernee Hardaway	25.00	11.00	3.10
☐ CS4 Chris Webber	5.00	2.20	.60
☐ CS5 Scottie Pippen	12.00	5.50	1.50
☐ CS6 David Robinson	8.00	3.60	1.00
☐ CS7 Latrell Sprewell	2.50	1.10	.30
☐ CS8 Charles Barkley	6.00	2.70	.75
☐ CS9 Alonzo Mourning	5.00	2.20	.60

1994-95 SkyBox Draft Picks

These 27 standard-size cards were random inserts in both first series (Nos. 2, 9, 10, 14 and 23) and second series (the other 22) packs. The first series cards were randomly seeded into one in every 45 packs. The second series cards were randomly seeded into one in every 18 packs. The set features all twenty-seven first round draft selections from the 1994 NBA draft. The foil card fronts feature a head shot of each player. The cards are numbered with a "DP" prefix. The set is sequenced in draft order.

	MINT	NRMT	EXC
COMPLETE SET (27)	90.00	40.00	11.00
COMPLETE SERIES 1 (5)	25.00	11.00	3.10

		MINT	NRMT	EXC
COMPLETE SERIES 2 (22)		65.00	29.00	8.00
COMMON 1 (2/9/10/14/23)		1.00	.45	.12
COMMON 2 (1/3/5-8/11-13)		1.00	.45	.12
COMMON 2 (15-22/24-27)		1.00	.45	.12
☐ DP1	Glenn Robinson	10.00	4.50	1.25
☐ DP2	Jason Kidd	20.00	9.00	2.50
☐ DP3	Grant Hill	30.00	13.50	3.70
☐ DP4	Donyell Marshall	2.00	.90	.25
☐ DP5	Juwan Howard	20.00	9.00	2.50
☐ DP6	Sharone Wright	2.00	.90	.25
☐ DP7	Lamond Murray	1.00	.45	.12
☐ DP8	Brian Grant	4.00	1.80	.50
☐ DP9	Eric Montross	2.00	.90	.25
☐ DP10	Eddie Jones	6.00	2.70	.75
☐ DP11	Carlos Rogers	1.00	.45	.12
☐ DP12	Kahlid Reeves	1.00	.45	.12
☐ DP13	Jalen Rose	2.00	.90	.25
☐ DP14	Yinka Dare	1.00	.45	.12
☐ DP15	Eric Piatkowski	1.00	.45	.12
☐ DP16	Clifford Rozier	2.00	.90	.25
☐ DP17	Aaron McKie	2.00	.90	.25
☐ DP18	Eric Mobley	1.00	.45	.12
☐ DP19	Tony Dumas	2.00	.90	.25
☐ DP20	B.J. Tyler	1.00	.45	.12
☐ DP21	Dickey Simpkins	1.00	.45	.12
☐ DP22	Bill Curley	1.00	.45	.12
☐ DP23	Wesley Person	2.00	.90	.25
☐ DP24	Monty Williams	1.00	.45	.12
☐ DP25	Greg Minor	1.00	.45	.12
☐ DP26	Charlie Ward	2.00	.90	.25
☐ DP27	Brooks Thompson	1.00	.45	.12

1994-95 SkyBox
Grant Hill

Randomly inserted exclusively into one in every 36 second series hobby packs, cards from this 5-card standard-size set highlight the Detroit rookie, and SkyBox spokesperson, in various action shots. Full-color photos are set against a psychedelic background.

		MINT	NRMT	EXC
COMPLETE SET (5)		40.00	18.00	5.00
COMMON HILL (GH1-GH5)		10.00	4.50	1.25
☐ GH1	Grant Hill	10.00	4.50	1.25
	(Two-handed jam; back turned)			
☐ GH2	Grant Hill	10.00	4.50	1.25
	(One arm jam)			
☐ GH3	Grant Hill	10.00	4.50	1.25
	(Dribbling)			
☐ GH4	Grant Hill	10.00	4.50	1.25
	(Driving to hoop at left)			
☐ GH5	Grant Hill	10.00	4.50	1.25
	(Two-handed jam)			

1994-95 SkyBox
Head of the Class

This 6-card standard-size set was available exclusively by mailing in the SkyBox Head of the Class exchange card before the June 15th, 1995 deadline. The Head of the Class exchange card was randomly inserted into one in every 480 first series packs. SkyBox selected six top rookies from the 1994-95 NBA season to be featured in the set. Card fronts feature a full-color player photo against a computer generated textured background. The set is sequenced in alphabetical order.

		MINT	NRMT	EXC
COMPLETE SET (6)		50.00	22.00	6.25
COMMON CARD (1-6)		1.50	.70	.19
☐ 1	Grant Hill	25.00	11.00	3.10
☐ 2	Juwan Howard	15.00	6.75	1.85
☐ 3	Jason Kidd	15.00	6.75	1.85
☐ 4	Donyell Marshall	1.50	.70	.19
☐ 5	Glenn Robinson	8.00	3.60	1.00
☐ 6	Sharone Wright	1.50	.70	.19
☐ NNO	Checklist Card	.25	.11	.03
☐ NNO	Exp. HOC Exch. Card	3.00	1.35	.35

1994-95 SkyBox
Ragin' Rookies

Randomly inserted into all first series packs at a rate of one in five, cards from this 24-card set feature a selection of the top rookies from the 1993 NBA draft. Full-color action photos feature a scratched border design.

	MINT	NRMT	EXC
COMPLETE SET (24)	25.00	11.00	3.10
COMMON CARD (RR1-RR24)	.75	.35	.09

		MINT	NRMT	EXC
☐	RR1 Dino Radja	1.50	.70	.19
☐	RR2 Corie Blount	.75	.35	.09
☐	RR3 Toni Kukoc	2.00	.90	.25
☐	RR4 Chris Mills	1.50	.70	.19
☐	RR5 Jamal Mashburn	2.00	.90	.25
☐	RR6 Rodney Rogers	.75	.35	.09
☐	RR7 Allan Houston	1.50	.70	.19
☐	RR8 Lindsey Hunter	.75	.35	.09
☐	RR9 Chris Webber	3.00	1.35	.35
☐	RR10 Sam Cassell	1.50	.70	.19
☐	RR11 Antonio Davis	.75	.35	.09
☐	RR12 Terry Dehere	.75	.35	.09
☐	RR13 Nick Van Exel	2.50	1.10	.30
☐	RR14 George Lynch	.75	.35	.09
☐	RR15 Vin Baker	3.00	1.35	.35
☐	RR16 Isaiah Rider	.75	.35	.09
☐	RR17 P.J. Brown	.75	.35	.09
☐	RR18 Anfernee Hardaway	15.00	6.75	1.85
☐	RR19 Shawn Bradley	1.50	.70	.19
☐	RR20 James Robinson	.75	.35	.09
☐	RR21 Bobby Hurley	.75	.35	.09
☐	RR22 Ervin Johnson	.75	.35	.09
☐	RR23 Bryon Russell	.75	.35	.09
☐	RR24 Calbert Cheaney	1.50	.70	.19

1994-95 SkyBox Revolution

Randomly inserted into second series packs at a rate of one in 72, cards from this 10-card standard-size set feature a selection of NBA stars. The horizontal fronts feature full-color player photos against etched-foil backgrounds featuring team colors. The set is sequenced in alphabetical order.

	MINT	NRMT	EXC
COMPLETE SET (10)	75.00	34.00	9.50
COMMON CARD (R1-R10)	2.50	1.10	.30

		MINT	NRMT	EXC
☐	R1 Patrick Ewing	5.00	2.20	.60
☐	R2 Grant Hill	30.00	13.50	3.70
☐	R3 Jamal Mashburn	4.00	1.80	.50
☐	R4 Alonzo Mourning	6.00	2.70	.75
☐	R5 Dikembe Mutombo	2.50	1.10	.30
☐	R6 Shaquille O'Neal	25.00	11.00	3.10
☐	R7 Scottie Pippen	15.00	6.75	1.85
☐	R8 Glenn Robinson	10.00	4.50	1.25
☐	R9 Latrell Sprewell	2.50	1.10	.30
☐	R10 Chris Webber	6.00	2.70	.75

1994-95 SkyBox SkyTech Force

Randomly inserted into second series packs at a rate of one in two, cards from this 30-card standard-size set feature a selection of the NBA's top stars. Card fronts feature foil backgrounds. The player's name is in gold foil on the bottom while the words "SkyTech Force" is printed vertically on the right. The backs contain some career information as well as a color action photo. The cards are numbered in the upper right with an "SF" prefix and are sequenced in alphabetical order.

	MINT	NRMT	EXC
COMPLETE SET (30)	10.00	4.50	1.25
COMMON CARD (SF1-SF30)	.15	.07	.02

		MINT	NRMT	EXC
☐	SF1 Kenny Anderson	.40	.18	.05
☐	SF2 B.J. Armstrong	.15	.07	.02
☐	SF3 Charles Barkley	1.00	.45	.12
☐	SF4 Shawn Bradley	.40	.18	.05
☐	SF5 LaPhonso Ellis	.15	.07	.02
☐	SF6 Anfernee Hardaway	4.00	1.80	.50
☐	SF7 Bobby Hurley	.15	.07	.02
☐	SF8 Kevin Johnson	.40	.18	.05
☐	SF9 Larry Johnson	.60	.25	.07
☐	SF10 Shawn Kemp	2.00	.90	.25
☐	SF11 Jason Kidd	4.00	1.80	.50
☐	SF12 Christian Laettner	.40	.18	.05
☐	SF13 Karl Malone	.60	.25	.07
☐	SF14 Danny Manning	.40	.18	.05

		MINT	NRMT	EXC
☐ SF15	Chris Mills	.40	.18	.05
☐ SF16	Chris Mullin	.40	.18	.05
☐ SF17	Lamond Murray	.15	.07	.02
☐ SF18	Charles Oakley	.15	.07	.02
☐ SF19	Hakeem Olajuwon	1.50	.70	.19
☐ SF20	Gary Payton	1.00	.45	.12
☐ SF21	Mark Price	.15	.07	.02
☐ SF22	Dino Radja	.40	.18	.05
☐ SF23	Mitch Richmond	.50	.23	.06
☐ SF24	Clifford Robinson	.40	.18	.05
☐ SF25	David Robinson	1.25	.55	.16
☐ SF26	Dennis Rodman	2.50	1.10	.30
☐ SF27	Dickey Simpkins	.15	.07	.02
☐ SF28	John Starks	.15	.07	.02
☐ SF29	John Stockton	.60	.25	.07
☐ SF30	Charlie Ward	.40	.18	.05

		MINT	NRMT	EXC
☐ SU19	Shaquille O'Neal	3.00	1.35	.35
☐ SU20	Glen Rice	.40	.18	.05
☐ SU21	Isaiah Rider	.40	.18	.05
☐ SU22	Glenn Robinson	2.00	.90	.25
☐ SU23	Jalen Rose	.40	.18	.05
☐ SU24	Detlef Schrempf	.40	.18	.05
☐ SU25	Steve Smith	.40	.18	.05
☐ SU26	Latrell Sprewell	.40	.18	.05
☐ SU27	Rod Strickland	.15	.07	.02
☐ SU28	B.J. Tyler	.15	.07	.02
☐ SU29	Nick Van Exel	.60	.25	.07
☐ SU30	Dominique Wilkins	.40	.18	.05

1995-96 SkyBox

1994-95 SkyBox Slammin' Universe

Randomly inserted into second series packs at a rate of one in two, cards from this 30-card standard-size set feature a selection of the NBA's top dunkers. The horizontal card fronts feature full-color player action shots against a foil "galaxy" background. The cards are numbered with a "SU" prefix and are sequenced in alphabetical order.

The 1995-96 SkyBox set was issued in two series of 150 and 151 standard-size cards, for a total of 301. The cards were issued in 12-card regular packs at a suggested retail price of $1.99, and jumbo packs of 20 were sold at $3.99. Full-bleed fronts feature a full-color action player cutout against a one-color background of either blue, cyan, yellow or magenta. A computer-generated flame streaks out from the basketball the player is holding. Backs feature a one-color player action shot in a vertical strip on the right side of the cards and a full color close-up shot at the bottom left. The top right features a player biography and career stats. The set is arranged and checklisted below alphabetically according to teams by city. Subsets are Front and Center (125-133), Turning Point (134-142), Expansion Teams (143-148), Rookies (219-248), Honor Roll (249-298) and Checklists (299-300). Key Rookie Cards include Michael Finley, Kevin Garnett, Antonio McDyess, Joe Smith, Jerry Stackhouse and Damon Stoudamire. A 5" by 7" jumbo featuring Grant Hill (card #226) was issued as a chiptopper in retail boxes. In addition, parallel lenticular versions of the Grant Hill and Jerry Stackhouse Meltdown inserts were available through a second series wrapper offer. Both cards are unnumbered and feature nifty moving backgrounds in which a steel wall turns to goo as fireworks explode. Collectors had to send in two wrappers along with a check or money order for $9.99 per card before the December 31st, 1996 deadline.

		MINT	NRMT	EXC
COMPLETE SET (30)		15.00	6.75	1.85
COMMON CARD (SU1-SU30)		.15	.07	.02
☐ SU1	Vin Baker	.75	.35	.09
☐ SU2	Dee Brown	.15	.07	.02
☐ SU3	Derrick Coleman	.15	.07	.02
☐ SU4	Clyde Drexler	.75	.35	.09
☐ SU5	Joe Dumars	.40	.18	.05
☐ SU6	Tony Dumas	.15	.07	.02
☐ SU7	Patrick Ewing	.60	.25	.07
☐ SU8	Horace Grant	.40	.18	.05
☐ SU9	Tom Gugliotta	.40	.18	.05
☐ SU10	Grant Hill	6.00	2.70	.75
☐ SU11	Jim Jackson	.40	.18	.05
☐ SU12	Toni Kukoc	.50	.23	.06
☐ SU13	Donyell Marshall	.15	.07	.02
☐ SU14	Jamal Mashburn	.50	.23	.06
☐ SU15	Reggie Miller	.75	.35	.09
☐ SU16	Eric Montross	.15	.07	.02
☐ SU17	Alonzo Mourning	.75	.35	.09
☐ SU18	Dikembe Mutombo	.40	.18	.05

	MINT	NRMT	EXC
COMPLETE SET (301)	35.00	16.00	4.40
COMPLETE SERIES 1 (150)	15.00	6.75	1.85
COMPLETE SERIES 2 (151)	20.00	9.00	2.50
COMMON CARD (1-301)	.05	.02	.01
□ 1 Stacey Augmon	.10	.05	.01
□ 2 Mookie Blaylock	.10	.05	.01
□ 3 Grant Long	.05	.02	.01
□ 4 Steve Smith	.15	.07	.02
□ 5 Dee Brown	.05	.02	.01
□ 6 Sherman Douglas	.05	.02	.01
□ 7 Eric Montross	.05	.02	.01
□ 8 Dino Radja	.10	.05	.01
□ 9 Dominique Wilkins	.15	.07	.02
□ 10 Muggsy Bogues	.10	.05	.01
□ 11 Scott Burrell	.05	.02	.01
□ 12 Dell Curry	.05	.02	.01
□ 13 Larry Johnson	.30	.14	.04
□ 14 Alonzo Mourning	.30	.14	.04
□ 15 Michael Jordan UER	4.00	1.80	.50
Career block total is wrong			
□ 16 Steve Kerr	.10	.05	.01
□ 17 Toni Kukoc	.20	.09	.03
□ 18 Scottie Pippen	1.00	.45	.12
□ 19 Terrell Brandon	.15	.07	.02
□ 20 Tyrone Hill	.05	.02	.01
□ 21 Chris Mills	.15	.07	.02
□ 22 Mark Price	.05	.02	.01
□ 23 John Williams	.05	.02	.01
□ 24 Tony Dumas	.05	.02	.01
□ 25 Jim Jackson	.15	.07	.02
□ 26 Popeye Jones	.05	.02	.01
□ 27 Jason Kidd	.75	.35	.09
□ 28 Jamal Mashburn	.20	.09	.03
□ 29 LaPhonso Ellis	.05	.02	.01
□ 30 Dikembe Mutombo	.15	.07	.02
□ 31 Robert Pack	.05	.02	.01
□ 32 Jalen Rose	.10	.05	.01
□ 33 Bryant Stith	.05	.02	.01
□ 34 Joe Dumars	.15	.07	.02
□ 35 Grant Hill	1.25	.55	.16
□ 36 Allan Houston	.15	.07	.02
□ 37 Lindsey Hunter	.05	.02	.01
□ 38 Chris Gatling	.05	.02	.01
□ 39 Tim Hardaway	.15	.07	.02
□ 40 Donyell Marshall	.05	.02	.01
□ 41 Chris Mullin	.15	.07	.02
□ 42 Carlos Rogers	.05	.02	.01
□ 43 Latrell Sprewell	.15	.07	.02
□ 44 Sam Cassell	.15	.07	.02
□ 45 Clyde Drexler	.40	.18	.05
□ 46 Robert Horry	.15	.07	.02
□ 47 Hakeem Olajuwon	.75	.35	.09
□ 48 Kenny Smith	.05	.02	.01
□ 49 Dale Davis	.05	.02	.01
□ 50 Mark Jackson	.05	.02	.01
□ 51 Reggie Miller	.40	.18	.05
□ 52 Rik Smits	.15	.07	.02
□ 53 Lamond Murray	.05	.02	.01
□ 54 Eric Piatkowski	.05	.02	.01
□ 55 Pooh Richardson	.05	.02	.01
□ 56 Rodney Rogers	.05	.02	.01
□ 57 Loy Vaught	.05	.02	.01
□ 58 Elden Campbell	.10	.05	.01
□ 59 Cedric Ceballos	.15	.07	.02
□ 60 Vlade Divac	.15	.07	.02
□ 61 Eddie Jones	.25	.11	.03
□ 62 Anthony Peeler	.05	.02	.01
□ 63 Nick Van Exel	.25	.11	.03
□ 64 Bimbo Coles	.05	.02	.01
□ 65 Billy Owens	.05	.02	.01
□ 66 Khalid Reeves	.05	.02	.01
□ 67 Glen Rice	.15	.07	.02
□ 68 Kevin Willis	.05	.02	.01
□ 69 Vin Baker	.30	.14	.04
□ 70 Todd Day	.05	.02	.01
□ 71 Eric Murdock	.05	.02	.01
□ 72 Glenn Robinson	.40	.18	.05
□ 73 Tom Gugliotta	.15	.07	.02
□ 74 Christian Laettner	.15	.07	.02
□ 75 Isaiah Rider	.15	.07	.02
□ 76 Doug West	.05	.02	.01
□ 77 Kenny Anderson	.15	.07	.02
□ 78 P.J. Brown	.05	.02	.01
□ 79 Derrick Coleman	.05	.02	.01
□ 80 Armon Gilliam	.10	.05	.01
□ 81 Patrick Ewing	.30	.14	.04
□ 82 Derek Harper	.05	.02	.01
□ 83 Anthony Mason	.10	.05	.01
□ 84 Charles Oakley	.10	.05	.01
□ 85 John Starks	.05	.02	.01
□ 86 Nick Anderson	.15	.07	.02
□ 87 Horace Grant	.15	.07	.02
□ 88 Anfernee Hardaway	2.00	.90	.25
□ 89 Shaquille O'Neal	1.50	.70	.19
□ 90 Dana Barros	.05	.02	.01
□ 91 Shawn Bradley	.15	.07	.02
□ 92 Clarence Weatherspoon	.05	.02	.01
□ 93 Sharone Wright	.05	.02	.01
□ 94 Charles Barkley	.50	.23	.06
□ 95 Kevin Johnson	.15	.07	.02
□ 96 Dan Majerle	.10	.05	.01
□ 97 Danny Manning	.10	.05	.01
□ 98 Wesley Person	.10	.05	.01
□ 99 Clifford Robinson	.15	.07	.02
□ 100 Rod Strickland	.05	.02	.01
□ 101 Otis Thorpe	.10	.05	.01
□ 102 Buck Williams	.10	.05	.01
□ 103 Brian Grant	.15	.07	.02
□ 104 Olden Polynice	.05	.02	.01
□ 105 Mitch Richmond	.25	.11	.03
□ 106 Walt Williams	.15	.07	.02
□ 107 Vinny Del Negro	.05	.02	.01
□ 108 Sean Elliott	.15	.07	.02
□ 109 Avery Johnson	.10	.05	.01
□ 110 David Robinson	.60	.25	.07
□ 111 Dennis Rodman	1.25	.55	.16
□ 112 Shawn Kemp	1.00	.45	.12
□ 113 Gary Payton	.50	.23	.06
□ 114 Sam Perkins	.10	.05	.01
□ 115 Detlef Schrempf	.10	.05	.01
□ 116 David Benoit	.05	.02	.01
□ 117 Jeff Hornacek	.10	.05	.01
□ 118 Karl Malone	.30	.14	.04
□ 119 John Stockton	.30	.14	.04
□ 120 Calbert Cheaney	.10	.05	.01
□ 121 Juwan Howard	.75	.35	.09
□ 122 Don MacLean	.05	.02	.01
□ 123 Gheorghe Muresan	.15	.07	.02
□ 124 Chris Webber	.30	.14	.04
□ 125 Robert Horry FC	.10	.05	.01
□ 126 Mark Jackson FC	.05	.02	.01
□ 127 Steve Smith FC	.05	.02	.01
□ 128 Lamond Murray FC	.05	.02	.01
□ 129 Christian Laettner FC	.10	.05	.01
□ 130 Kenny Anderson FC	.10	.05	.01
□ 131 Anthony Mason FC	.05	.02	.01
□ 132 Kevin Johnson FC	.10	.05	.01
□ 133 Jeff Hornacek FC	.05	.02	.01
□ 134 Larry Johnson TP	.15	.07	.02
□ 135 Popeye Jones TP	.05	.02	.01

□	#	Card			
□	136	Allan Houston TP	.05	.02	.01
□	137	Chris Gatling TP	.05	.02	.01
□	138	Sam Cassell TP	.10	.05	.01
□	139	Anthony Peeler TP	.05	.02	.01
□	140	Vin Baker TP	.15	.07	.02
□	141	Dana Barros TP	.05	.02	.01
□	142	Gheorghe Muresan TP	.15	.07	.02
□	143	Toronto Raptors	.05	.02	.01
□	144	Vancouver Grizzlies	.05	.02	.01
□	145	Glen Rice EXP	.10	.05	.01
		Muggsy Bogues EXP			
□	146	Nick Anderson EXP	.10	.05	.01
		Christian Laettner EXP			
□	147	John Salley TF	.05	.02	.01
□	148	Greg Anthony TF	.05	.02	.01
□	149	Checklist #1	.05	.02	.01
□	150	Checklist #2	.05	.02	.01
□	151	Craig Ehlo	.05	.02	.01
□	152	Spud Webb	.10	.05	.01
□	153	Dana Barros	.05	.02	.01
□	155	Kendall Gill	.05	.02	.01
□	156	Khalid Reeves	.05	.02	.01
□	157	Glen Rice	.15	.07	.02
□	158	Luc Longley	.05	.02	.01
□	159	Dennis Rodman Bulls	2.00	.90	.25
□	160	Dickey Simpkins	.05	.02	.01
□	161	Danny Ferry	.05	.02	.01
□	162	Dan Majerle	.10	.05	.01
□	163	Bobby Phills	.05	.02	.01
□	164	Lucious Harris	.05	.02	.01
□	165	George McCloud	.05	.02	.01
□	166	Mahmoud Abdul-Rauf..	.10	.05	.01
□	167	Don MacLean	.05	.02	.01
□	168	Reggie Williams	.05	.02	.01
□	169	Terry Mills	.05	.02	.01
□	170	Otis Thorpe	.10	.05	.01
□	171	B.J. Armstrong	.10	.05	.01
□	172	Rony Seikaly	.05	.02	.01
□	173	Chucky Brown	.05	.02	.01
□	174	Mario Elie	.05	.02	.01
□	175	Antonio Davis	.05	.02	.01
□	176	Ricky Pierce	.05	.02	.01
□	177	Terry Dehere	.05	.02	.01
□	178	Rodney Rogers	.05	.02	.01
□	179	Malik Sealy	.05	.02	.01
□	180	Brian Williams	.05	.02	.01
□	181	Sedale Threatt	.05	.02	.01
□	182	Alonzo Mourning	.30	.14	.04
□	183	Lee Mayberry	.05	.02	.01
□	184	Sean Rooks	.05	.02	.01
□	185	Shawn Bradley	.15	.07	.02
□	186	Kevin Edwards	.05	.02	.01
□	187	Hubert Davis	.05	.02	.01
□	188	Charles Smith	.05	.02	.01
□	189	Charlie Ward	.10	.05	.01
□	190	Dennis Scott	.15	.07	.02
□	191	Brian Shaw	.05	.02	.01
□	192	Derrick Coleman	.05	.02	.01
□	193	Richard Dumas	.05	.02	.01
□	194	Vernon Maxwell	.05	.02	.01
□	195	A.C. Green	.15	.07	.02
□	196	Elliot Perry	.05	.02	.01
□	197	John Williams	.05	.02	.01
□	198	Aaron McKie	.05	.02	.01
□	199	Bobby Hurley	.05	.02	.01
□	200	Michael Smith	.05	.02	.01
□	201	J.R. Reid	.05	.02	.01
□	202	Hersey Hawkins	.05	.02	.01
□	203	Willie Anderson	.05	.02	.01
□	204	Oliver Miller	.05	.02	.01
□	205	Tracy Murray	.05	.02	.01
□	206	Alvin Robertson	.05	.02	.01
□	207	Carlos Rogers UER	.05	.02	.01
		Card says Rodney Rogers on front			
		with picture			
□	208	John Salley	.05	.02	.01
□	209	Zan Tabak	.05	.02	.01
□	210	Adam Keefe	.05	.02	.01
□	211	Chris Morris	.05	.02	.01
□	212	Greg Anthony	.05	.02	.01
□	213	Blue Edwards	.05	.02	.01
□	214	Kenny Gattison	.05	.02	.01
□	215	Antonio Harvey	.05	.02	.01
□	216	Chris King	.05	.02	.01
□	217	Byron Scott	.15	.07	.02
□	218	Robert Pack	.05	.02	.01
□	219	Alan Henderson	.20	.09	.03
□	220	Eric Williams	.25	.11	.03
□	221	George Zidek	.05	.02	.01
□	222	Jason Caffey	.05	.02	.01
□	223	Bob Sura	.25	.11	.03
□	224	Cherokee Parks	.15	.07	.02
□	225	Antonio McDyess	1.25	.55	.16
□	226	Theo Ratliff	.15	.07	.02
□	227	Joe Smith	1.50	.70	.19
□	228	Travis Best	.20	.09	.03
□	229	Brent Barry	.60	.25	.07
□	230	Sasha Danilovic	.15	.07	.02
□	231	Kurt Thomas	.40	.18	.05
□	232	Shawn Respert	.15	.07	.02
□	233	Kevin Garnett	4.00	1.80	.50
□	234	Ed O'Bannon	.50	.23	.06
□	235	Jerry Stackhouse	2.50	1.10	.30
□	236	Michael Finley	1.50	.70	.19
□	237	Mario Bennett	.05	.02	.01
□	238	Randolph Childress	.05	.02	.01
□	239	Arvydas Sabonis	1.00	.45	.12
□	240	Gary Trent	.15	.07	.02
□	241	Tyus Edney	.60	.25	.07
□	242	Corliss Williamson	.25	.11	.03
□	243	Cory Alexander	.15	.07	.02
□	244	Damon Stoudamire	3.00	1.35	.35
□	245	Greg Ostertag	.05	.02	.01
□	246	Lawrence Moten	.05	.02	.01
□	247	Bryant Reeves	.75	.35	.09
□	248	Rasheed Wallace	.60	.25	.07
□	249	Muggsy Bogues HR	.10	.05	.01
□	250	Dell Curry HR	.05	.02	.01
□	251	Scottie Pippen HR	.50	.23	.06
□	252	Danny Ferry HR	.05	.02	.01
□	253	Mahmoud Abdul-Rauf HR	.10	.05	.01
□	254	Joe Dumars HR	.10	.05	.01
□	255	Tim Hardaway HR	.10	.05	.01
□	256	Chris Mullin HR	.10	.05	.01
□	257	Hakeem Olajuwon HR ..	.40	.18	.05
□	258	Kenny Smith HR	.05	.02	.01
□	259	Reggie Miller HR	.20	.09	.03
□	260	Rik Smits HR	.10	.05	.01
□	261	Vlade Divac HR	.10	.05	.01
□	262	Doug West HR	.05	.02	.01
□	263	Patrick Ewing HR	.15	.07	.02
□	264	Charles Oakley HR	.05	.02	.01
□	265	Nick Anderson HR	.15	.07	.02
□	266	Dennis Scott HR	.15	.07	.02
□	267	Jeff Turner HR	.05	.02	.01
□	268	Charles Barkley HR	.25	.11	.03
□	269	Kevin Johnson HR	.10	.05	.01
□	270	Clifford Robinson HR..	.10	.05	.01
□	271	Buck Williams HR	.10	.05	.01
□	272	Lionel Simmons HR	.05	.02	.01
□	273	David Robinson HR	.30	.14	.04
□	274	Gary Payton HR	.25	.11	.03

☐ 275 Karl Malone HR	.15	.07	.02
☐ 276 John Stockton HR	.15	.07	.02
☐ 277 Steve Smith ELE	.10	.05	.01
☐ 278 Michael Jordan ELE	2.00	.90	.25
☐ 279 Jim Jackson ELE	.15	.07	.02
☐ 280 Jason Kidd ELE	.40	.18	.05
☐ 281 Jamal Mashburn ELE	.10	.05	.01
☐ 282 Dikembe Mutombo ELE	.15	.07	.02
☐ 283 Grant Hill ELE	.60	.25	.07
☐ 284 Tim Hardaway ELE	.15	.07	.02
☐ 285 Clyde Drexler ELE	.20	.09	.03
☐ 286 Cedric Ceballos ELE	.05	.02	.01
☐ 287 Gary Payton ELE	.25	.11	.03
☐ 288 Billy Owens ELE	.05	.02	.01
☐ 289 Vin Baker ELE	.15	.07	.02
☐ 290 Glenn Robinson ELE	.20	.09	.03
☐ 291 Kenny Anderson ELE	.15	.07	.02
☐ 292 Anfernee Hardaway ELE	1.00	.45	.12
☐ 293 Shaquille O'Neal ELE	.75	.35	.09
☐ 294 Charles Barkley ELE	.25	.11	.03
☐ 295 Rod Strickland ELE	.05	.02	.01
☐ 296 Mitch Richmond ELE	.10	.05	.01
☐ 297 Juwan Howard ELE	.40	.18	.05
☐ 298 Chris Webber ELE	.10	.05	.01
☐ 299 Checklist #1	.05	.02	.01
☐ 300 Checklist #2	.05	.02	.01
☐ 301 Magic Johnson	1.00	.45	.12
☐ PR Grant Hill JUMBO	10.00	4.50	1.25
☐ NNO Grant Hill Meltdown Exch	20.00	9.00	2.50
☐ NNO J.Stockhouse Meltdown Exch.	20.00	9.00	2.50

1995-96 SkyBox Atomic

Randomly inserted in all series one packs at a rate of one in four regular packs and one in three jumbo packs, this 15-card standard-size set highlights the play of the NBA's power men. Borderless fronts have etched foil backgrounds with a full-color action player cutout. An atomic symbol surrounds the ball the player is holding and the player's name, team and position are stamped in gold foil at the middle left of the card. Skybox's "Atomic" logo is printed at the bottom left. Backs are numbered with the prefix "A" and have a faded, one color action shot of the player and continues with the basketball as the center of an atomic symbol. Player biography and an inset color photo are set against red bars on the bottom half of the card.

	MINT	NRMT	EXC
COMPLETE SET (15)	8.00	3.60	1.00
COMMON CARD (A1-A15)	.30	.14	.04
☐ A1 Eric Montross	.30	.14	.04
☐ A2 Charles Oakley	.30	.14	.04
☐ A3 Rik Smits	.40	.18	.05
☐ A4 Vlade Divac	.40	.18	.05
☐ A5 Buck Williams	.40	.18	.05
☐ A6 Vin Baker	.75	.35	.09
☐ A7 Glenn Robinson	1.00	.45	.12
☐ A8 Isaiah Rider	.40	.18	.05
☐ A9 Derrick Coleman	.30	.14	.04
☐ A10 Clarence Weatherspoon	.30	.14	.04
☐ A11 Sharone Wright	.30	.14	.04
☐ A12 Brian Grant	.30	.14	.04
☐ A13 Jim Jackson	.50	.23	.06
☐ A14 Clyde Drexler	1.00	.45	.12
☐ A15 Anfernee Hardaway	5.00	2.20	.60

1995-96 SkyBox Close-Ups

A short player history is the focus of this nine-card standard-size set that features both established players and up-and-coming rookies. The cards were randomly inserted in all series one packs at a rate of one in nine regular packs and one in six jumbo packs. They were also inserted one per special series one Wal-Mart retail pack. Borderless fronts feature an extreme color close-up of the player's face set against an etched foil background. The player's first name is stamped in gold foil script against his last name which is printed larger and in full block letters. The SkyBox logo and "Close-Up" are stamped in gold foil at the bottom left of the card. The backs feature a stretched one-color player photo on the right side of the card. The left side has the player's name, team logo and a short player history printed in black type. The set is sequenced in alphabetical order by team.

	MINT	NRMT	EXC
COMPLETE SET (9)	20.00	9.00	2.50
COMMON CARD (C1-C9)	1.00	.45	.12
☐ C1 Scottie Pippen	6.00	2.70	.75
☐ C2 Grant Hill	8.00	3.60	1.00
☐ C3 Clyde Drexler	2.50	1.10	.30

		MINT	NRMT	EXC
☐ C4	Nick Van Exel	1.50	.70	.19
☐ C5	Tom Gugliotta	1.00	.45	.12
☐ C6	Patrick Ewing	2.00	.90	.25
☐ C7	Charles Barkley	3.00	1.35	.35
☐ C8	Karl Malone	2.00	.90	.25
☐ C9	Juwan Howard	5.00	2.20	.60

1995-96 SkyBox Dynamic

Randomly inserted at a rate of one in four series one regular packs and one in three series one jumbo packs, this 12-card standard-size set features the most intense NBA players. Fronts feature a full-color action player photo handling a ball that is exploding. The player is set against a bright red etched foil background with the "Dynamic" logo scrawled at an angle across the bottom. The player's name is printed on the bottom right of the card. Full-bleed, one-color backs are numbered with the prefix "D" and picture the player in an action shot and a full color close-up inset. The player's name is printed in white caps and a player profile is printed in black type on tilted red bars. The set is sequenced in alphabetical team order.

		MINT	NRMT	EXC
COMPLETE SET (12)		6.00	2.70	.75
COMMON CARD (D1-D12)		.25	.11	.03
☐ D1	Larry Johnson	.60	.25	.07
☐ D2	Alonzo Mourning	.60	.25	.07
☐ D3	Dikembe Mutombo	.40	.18	.05
☐ D4	Jalen Rose	.25	.11	.03
☐ D5	Grant Hill	2.50	1.10	.30
☐ D6	Latrell Sprewell	.40	.18	.05
☐ D7	Reggie Miller	.75	.35	.09
☐ D8	John Starks	.25	.11	.03
☐ D9	Calbert Cheaney	.25	.11	.03
☐ D10	Dennis Rodman	2.50	1.10	.30
☐ D11	Detlef Schrempf	.40	.18	.05
☐ D12	Chris Webber	.60	.25	.07

1995-96 SkyBox High Hopes

Randomly inserted in all second series packs at a rate of one in 18, this 20-card

set focuses on the hot young stars of the NBA. Borderless fronts feature the player in a full-color action cutout, with "High Hopes" spelled out in red and yellow spark and flame block letters on a black background. The player's name is printed in gold foil at the bottom. Backs have another full-color action cutout set against a back black-ground with a player profile printed in white type. "High Hopes" is printed vertically on the right side.

		MINT	NRMT	EXC
COMPLETE SET (20)		100.00	45.00	12.50
COMMON CARD (HH1-HH20)		1.00	.45	.12
☐ HH1	Alan Henderson	2.00	.90	.25
☐ HH2	Eric Williams	2.00	.90	.25
☐ HH3	George Zidek	1.00	.45	.12
☐ HH4	Bob Sura	1.00	.45	.12
☐ HH5	Cherokee Parks	1.00	.45	.12
☐ HH6	Antonio McDyess	8.00	3.60	1.00
☐ HH7	Joe Smith	10.00	4.50	1.25
☐ HH8	Brent Barry	4.00	1.80	.50
☐ HH9	Shawn Respert	1.00	.45	.12
☐ HH10	Kevin Garnett	25.00	11.00	3.10
☐ HH11	Ed O'Bannon	3.00	1.35	.35
☐ HH12	Jerry Stackhouse	15.00	6.75	1.85
☐ HH13	Michael Finley	10.00	4.50	1.25
☐ HH14	Arvydas Sabonis	6.00	2.70	.75
☐ HH15	Gary Trent	1.00	.45	.12
☐ HH16	Tyus Edney	4.00	1.80	.50
☐ HH17	Damon Stoudamire	20.00	9.00	2.50
☐ HH18	Greg Ostertag	1.00	.45	.12
☐ HH19	Bryant Reeves	5.00	2.20	.60
☐ HH20	Rasheed Wallace	4.00	1.80	.50

1995-96 SkyBox Hot Sparks

Randomly inserted in second series hobby packs only at a rate of one in 12, this 10-card set notes the players who make things happen in the NBA. Fronts have a full-color action cutout with the player's name printed vertically in gold foil on the right side. A mauve computerized image serves as a background. A similar but darker background appears on the back with another full-color action cutout and a player profile printed in white type.

	MINT	NRMT	EXC
COMPLETE SET (11)	40.00	18.00	5.00
COMMON CARD (HS1-HS11)	1.00	.45	.12

		MINT	NRMT	EXC
☐	HS1 Mookie Blaylock	1.00	.45	.12
☐	HS2 Jason Kidd	5.00	2.20	.60
☐	HS3 Tim Hardaway	1.00	.45	.12
☐	HS4 Nick Van Exel	1.50	.70	.19
☐	HS5 Kenny Anderson	1.00	.45	.12
☐	HS6 Anfernee Hardaway	12.00	5.50	1.50
☐	HS7 Rod Strickland	1.00	.45	.12
☐	HS8 Gary Payton	3.00	1.35	.35
☐	HS9 Damon Stoudamire	10.00	4.50	1.25
☐	HS10 John Stockton	2.00	.90	.25
☐	HS11 Magic Johnson	6.00	2.70	.75

1995-96 SkyBox
Kinetic

Randomly inserted in all first series at a rate of one in four (and one in three jumbo), cards from this 9-card standard-size set highlight the NBA's speed demons. Full-bleed fronts have swirling color swoops and surround a full-color player cutout against an etched foil background. Player's name and team name are printed in silver foil at the bottom. Borderless backs feature a one-color player cutout and continues with the swoosh patterns. A full-color head shot is inset with a white border and a player profile is printed in black type on gold bars.

		MINT	NRMT	EXC
	COMPLETE SET (9)	2.00	.90	.25
	COMMON CARD (K1-K9)	.25	.11	.03
☐	K1 Mookie Blaylock	.35	.16	.04
☐	K2 Tim Hardaway	.50	.23	.06
☐	K3 Lamond Murray UER	.25	.11	.03
	Mach is spelled Mock			
☐	K4 Stacey Augmon	.35	.16	.04
☐	K5 Nick Van Exel	.50	.23	.06

☐	K6 Khalid Reeves	.25	.11	.03
☐	K7 Kenny Anderson	.50	.23	.06
☐	K8 Rod Strickland	.25	.11	.03
☐	K9 Gary Payton	1.00	.45	.12

1995-96 SkyBox
Larger Than Life

Randomly inserted in first series regular and jumbo packs at a rate of one in 48 and one in 36 respectively, this 10-card standard-size set showcases those players who have established themselves in the NBA. A sunburst design is etched into gold foil and serves as a background for the fronts which include a full-color action player cutout. The "Larger Than Life" logo is printed diagonally and upwards from the bottom right and tapers up to the SkyBox logo. The player's first name is printed in lower case black type just above his last name which appears in all caps red type. Backs continue with the sunburst pattern on the gold type. A player profile is printed in black type on the right side and a full-color action cutout appears on the left side. The set is sequenced in alphabetical team order.

		MINT	NRMT	EXC
	COMPLETE SET (10)	150.00	70.00	19.00
	COMMON CARD (L1-L10)	6.00	2.70	.75
☐	L1 Michael Jordan	75.00	34.00	9.50
☐	L2 Jason Kidd	15.00	6.75	1.85
☐	L3 Grant Hill	25.00	11.00	3.10
☐	L4 Hakeem Olajuwon	15.00	6.75	1.85
☐	L5 Glenn Robinson	8.00	3.60	1.00
☐	L6 Patrick Ewing	6.00	2.70	.75
☐	L7 Shaquille O'Neal	30.00	13.50	3.70
☐	L8 Charles Barkley	10.00	4.50	1.25
☐	L9 David Robinson	12.00	5.50	1.50
☐	L10 John Stockton	6.00	2.70	.75

1995-96 SkyBox
Lottery Exchange

Hobbyists received this 13-card set after collecting the three separate Lottery

Exchange cards randomly inserted into first series packs (each card was seeded at a rate of 1:40 packs). The expiration date for exchanging the cards was June 15th, 1996. The set consists of the first thirteen players selected in the 1995 NBA draft. Card fronts feature a full-color player action cutout set against a murky colored background.

	Mint	Good	Poor
COMPLETE SET (13)	40.00	18.00	5.00
COMMON CARD (1-13)	1.00	.45	.12
☐ 1 Joe Smith	5.00	2.20	.60
☐ 2 Antonio McDyess	4.00	1.80	.50
☐ 3 Jerry Stackhouse	8.00	3.60	1.00
☐ 4 Rasheed Wallace	2.00	.90	.25
☐ 5 Kevin Garnett	12.00	5.50	1.50
☐ 6 Bryant Reeves	2.50	1.10	.30
☐ 7 Damon Stoudamire	10.00	4.50	1.25
☐ 8 Shawn Respert	1.00	.45	.12
☐ 9 Ed O'Bannon	1.50	.70	.19
☐ 10 Kurt Thomas	1.00	.45	.12
☐ 11 Gary Trent	1.00	.45	.12
☐ 12 Cherokee Parks	1.00	.45	.12
☐ 13 Corliss Williamson	1.00	.45	.12
☐ NNO Exchange Card 3	1.00	.45	.12
☐ NNO Exchange Card 2	1.00	.45	.12
☐ NNO Exchange Card 1	1.00	.45	.12

1995-96 SkyBox Meltdown

Randomly inserted in second series regular packs at a rate of one in 54 and jumbo packs at a rate of one in 48, this 10-card set is a tribute to the league's hottest scorers. Borderless fronts have a foil finish with

an image of green and blue melting metal. A full-color player cutout appears on the front with his name and team printed on the bottom. Blue metal showers down in a cascade on the back with a full-color action cutout and a player profile printed in white type.

	MINT	NRMT	EXC
COMPLETE SET (10)	175.00	80.00	22.00
COMMON CARD (M1-M10)	3.00	1.35	.35
☐ M1 Michael Jordan	75.00	34.00	9.50
☐ M2 Dan Majerle	3.00	1.35	.35
☐ M3 Jason Kidd	15.00	6.75	1.85
☐ M4 Antonio McDyess	12.00	5.50	1.50
☐ M5 Grant Hill	25.00	11.00	3.10
☐ M6 Joe Smith	15.00	6.75	1.85
☐ M7 Hakeem Olajuwon	15.00	6.75	1.85
☐ M8 Shaquille O'Neal	30.00	13.50	3.70
☐ M9 Jerry Stackhouse	25.00	11.00	3.10
☐ M10 David Robinson	12.00	5.50	1.50

1995-96 SkyBox Rookie Prevue

Randomly inserted in first series packs at a rate of one in nine, this 20-card standard-size set focuses on the hot rookies of 1994-95. The borderless fronts include a full-color action player cutout on the right. The player's last name is printed in gold foil across the top with his first name in smaller type underneath the last name. The background is a red and gold sunburst pattern with "Rookie Prevue" in bold block letters on the bottom left. Backs also carry the "Rookie Prevue" logo at the bottom left and a player action cutout on the right. The background continues the red and gold sunburst design and the player's name and a short profile is printed in black type on the upper left side of the back. The set is sequenced in dratt order.

	MINT	NRMT	EXC
COMPLETE SET (20)	80.00	36.00	10.00
COMMON CARD (RP1-RP20)	1.00	.45	.12
☐ RP1 Joe Smith	10.00	4.50	1.25
☐ RP2 Antonio McDyess	8.00	3.60	1.00
☐ RP3 Jerry Stackhouse	15.00	6.75	1.85

		MINT	NRMT	EXC
☐ RP4	Rasheed Wallace	4.00	1.80	.50
☐ RP5	Bryant Reeves	5.00	2.20	.60
☐ RP6	Damon Stoudamire	20.00	9.00	2.50
☐ RP7	Shawn Respert	1.00	.45	.12
☐ RP8	Ed O'Bannon	3.00	1.35	.35
☐ RP9	Kurt Thomas	1.00	.45	.12
☐ RP10	Gary Trent	1.00	.45	.12
☐ RP11	Cherokee Parks	1.00	.45	.12
☐ RP12	Corliss Williamson	1.00	.45	.12
☐ RP13	Eric Williams	1.00	.45	.12
☐ RP14	Brent Barry	4.00	1.80	.50
☐ RP15	Alan Henderson	1.00	.45	.12
☐ RP16	Bob Sura	1.00	.45	.12
☐ RP17	Theo Ratliff	2.00	.90	.25
☐ RP18	Randolph Childress	1.00	.45	.12
☐ RP19	Michael Finley	10.00	4.50	1.25
☐ RP20	George Zidek	1.00	.45	.12

1995-96 SkyBox
Standouts

Randomly inserted in first series packs at a rate of one in 18 regular packs and one in 36 jumbo packs, this 12-card standard-size set spotlights the play of the NBA's hot rookies. The fronts feature the player in a full-color action cutout set against a metallic copper foil. The player stands on top of a circular "Skybox Standouts" logo and his name is stamped in gold foil at the upper right corner. A full-color action player cutout appears on the back and is set against the "Standouts" logo. A player profile appears on the top left of the card and the player's name and team are printed in a reverse type process on a strip of light blue across the bottom.

		MINT	NRMT	EXC
COMPLETE SET (12)		40.00	18.00	5.00
COMMON CARD (S1-S12)		1.50	.70	.19
☐ S1	Alonzo Mourning	3.00	1.35	.35
☐ S2	Scottie Pippen	10.00	4.50	1.25
☐ S3	Danny Manning	1.50	.70	.19
☐ S4	Jamal Mashburn	2.00	.90	.25
☐ S5	Latrell Sprewell	1.50	.70	.19
☐ S6	Reggie Miller	4.00	1.80	.50
☐ S7	Anfernee Hardaway	20.00	9.00	2.50
☐ S8	Brian Grant	1.50	.70	.19
☐ S9	Shawn Kemp	10.00	4.50	1.25
☐ S10	Clifford Robinson	1.50	.70	.19

		MINT	NRMT	EXC
☐ S11	Joe Dumars	1.50	.70	.19
☐ S12	Chris Webber	3.00	1.35	.35

1995-96 SkyBox
Standouts Hobby

Randomly inserted exclusivelt into first series hobby packs at a rate of one in 18, this six-card set is a tribute to the league's best. Borderless fronts have gold foil paper and the player's name is stamped in the upper right in a lighter gold foil. A full-color action player cutout appears and a stand directly on a circular pattern that reads "Skybox Standouts." Backs have another full-color action cutout with a player profile, the Skybox medallion and a granite-like strip with the player's name and team etched inside.

		MINT	NRMT	EXC
COMPLETE SET (6)		80.00	36.00	10.00
COMMON CARD (SH1-SH6)		3.00	1.35	.35
☐ SH1	Michael Jordan	50.00	22.00	6.25
☐ SH2	Jason Kidd	10.00	4.50	1.25
☐ SH3	Hakeem Olajuwon	10.00	4.50	1.25
☐ SH4	Eddie Jones	3.00	1.35	.35
☐ SH5	Shaquille O'Neal	20.00	9.00	2.50
☐ SH6	Grant Hill	15.00	6.75	1.85

1995-96 SkyBox
USA Basketball

Randomly inserted in second series retail packs at a rate of one in 12 and one in every second series jumbo pack and one per series two special retail pack, this set features the first ten players selected to the 1996 USA men's basketball team. Card fronts feature full-color action cutouts of Team USA members pictured in their Olympic togs set against a gray background of a globe.

		MINT	NRMT	EXC
COMPLETE SET (10)		35.00	16.00	4.40
COMMON CARD (U1-U10)		1.50	.70	.19

		MINT	NRMT	EXC
☐ U1	Anfernee Hardaway ...	10.00	4.50	1.25
☐ U2	Grant Hill	6.00	2.70	.75
☐ U3	Karl Malone	1.50	.70	.19
☐ U4	Reggie Miller	2.00	.90	.25
☐ U5	Scottie Pippen	5.00	2.20	.60
☐ U6	Hakeem Olajuwon.......	4.00	1.80	.50
☐ U7	Shaquille O'Neal	8.00	3.60	1.00
☐ U8	David Robinson	3.00	1.35	.35
☐ U9	Glenn Robinson	2.00	.90	.25
☐ U10	John Stockton	1.50	.70	.19

1996-97 SkyBox Autographics

Randomly inserted in the following 1996-97 products: Hoops series one and two, SkyBox series one and two, SkyBox Z-Force series one and two and SkyBox E-XL all at a rate of one in 72, this set features autographs of some of the top stars in the NBA. Card design is identical for each issue and several players had their cards seeded into more than one of the aforementioned products. Card fronts feature a background in the particular player's team colors and an action shot of the player. Most of the cards were autographed vertically along the left side. Card backs are black with a spotlight photo, the player's name and career statistics. The first 100 cards of each player were autographed in blue ink and the remaining number were in black. The blue ink autographs generally trade at two times the value of the basic black. A couple exceptions include Hakeem Olajuwon and Scottie Pippen, who autographed all of their cards in blue ink only. Also, Kevin Garnett autographed two-thirds of his cards in blue and the rest in black. Cards below are designed with an abbreviation which determines where each autograph can be found. The cards below are not numbered and are listed alphabetically.

	MINT	NRMT	EXC
COMP.BLACK AU SET (70)	1000.00	450.00	125.00
COMMON BLACK AU CARD.....	8.00	3.60	1.00
*BLUE INK AU: 1X to 2X..................			

		MINT	NRMT	EXC
☐ 1	K.Anderson H1,Z1......	18.00	8.00	2.20
☐ 2	Nick Anderson H1	15.00	6.75	1.85
☐ 3	B.J. Armstrong H1	10.00	4.50	1.25
☐ 4	Dana Barros H1	10.00	4.50	1.25
☐ 5	Brent Barry Z1	20.00	9.00	2.50
☐ 6	Travis Best Z1	12.00	5.50	1.50
☐ 7	Muggsy Bogues H1	15.00	6.75	1.85
☐ 8	P.J. Brown H1,Z1.........	8.00	3.60	1.00
☐ 9	Randy Brown H1	8.00	3.60	1.00
☐ 10	Chris Childs H1	15.00	6.75	1.85
☐ 11	Dell Curry H1	10.00	4.50	1.25
☐ 12	Andrew DeClerq H1	8.00	3.60	1.00
☐ 13	Sherman Douglas Z1 .	10.00	4.50	1.25
☐ 14	Clyde Drexler Z1	60.00	27.00	7.50
☐ 15	Tyus Edney H1	18.00	8.00	2.20
☐ 16	Michael Finley H1,Z1..	50.00	22.00	6.25
☐ 17	Rick Fox H,Z1	10.00	4.50	1.25
☐ 18A	K.Garnett Black Z1 .	200.00	90.00	25.00
☐ 18B	K.Garnett Blue Z1 .	125.00	55.00	15.50
☐ 19	Kendall Gill Z1	12.00	5.50	1.50
☐ 20	Brian Grant H1,Z1	15.00	6.75	1.85
☐ 21	Matt Geiger H1............	8.00	3.60	1.00
☐ 22	Tim Hardaway H1,Z1 .	18.00	8.00	2.20
☐ 23	Grant Hill ALL	175.00	80.00	22.00
☐ 24	Tyrone Hill H1	8.00	3.60	1.00
☐ 25	Juwan Howard H1	80.00	36.00	10.00
☐ 26	Jim Jackson H1,Z1	25.00	11.00	3.10
☐ 27	Mark Jackson H1,Z1....	10.00	4.50	1.25
☐ 28	Eddie Jones Z1	30.00	13.50	3.70
☐ 29	Adam Keefe H1	8.00	3.60	1.00
☐ 30	Steve Kerr H1.............	18.00	8.00	2.20
☐ 31	Voshon Lenard H1	8.00	3.60	1.00
☐ 32	Grant Long Z1.............	8.00	3.60	1.00
☐ 33	Luc Longley H1,Z1	18.00	8.00	2.20
☐ 34	George Lynch H1	8.00	3.60	1.00
☐ 35	Don MacLean H1	10.00	4.50	1.25
☐ 36	Lee Mayberry H1,Z1 ...	8.00	3.60	1.00
☐ 37	Antonio McDyess Z1...	35.00	16.00	4.40
☐ 38	Nate McMillan Z1	8.00	3.60	1.00
☐ 39	Chris Mills Z1.............	12.00	5.50	1.50
☐ 40	Sam Mitchell Z1	8.00	3.60	1.00
☐ 41	Eric Montross H1	10.00	4.50	1.25
☐ 42	Lawrence Moten Z1	8.00	3.60	1.00
☐ 43	Alonzo Mourning Z1 ..	50.00	22.00	6.25
☐ 44	Gheorghe Muresan Z1	15.00	6.75	1.85
☐ 45	Ed O'Bannon Z1	15.00	6.75	1.85
☐ 46	Charles Oakley Z1	12.00	5.50	1.50
☐ 47	H.Olajuwon BLUE Z1 .	125.00	55.00	15.50
☐ 48	Greg Ostertag H1	8.00	3.60	1.00
☐ 49	Sam Perkins Z1	15.00	6.75	1.85
☐ 50	Wesley Person Z1.......	15.00	6.75	1.85
☐ 51	Bobby Phills H1,Z1	15.00	6.75	1.85
☐ 52	Theo Ratliff Z1	8.00	3.60	1.00
☐ 53	Glen Rice H1	25.00	11.00	3.10
☐ 54	Rodney Rogers H1.......	10.00	4.50	1.25
☐ 55	Dennis Scott H1	15.00	6.75	1.85
☐ 56	Joe Smith H1,Z1.........	50.00	22.00	6.25
☐ 57	Rik Smits H1	15.00	6.75	1.85
☐ 58	Eric Snow H1	8.00	3.60	1.00
☐ 59	Latrell Sprewell Z1.....	30.00	13.50	3.70

		MINT	NRMT	EXC
☐ 60	Jerry Stackhouse ALL	125.00	55.00	15.50
☐ 61	Bryant Stith Z1	10.00	4.50	1.25
☐ 62	Rod Strickland H1	18.00	8.00	2.20
☐ 63	Bob Sura H1	12.00	5.50	1.50
☐ 64	Loy Vaught Z1	15.00	6.75	1.85
☐ 65	Bill Wennington H1	12.00	5.50	1.50
☐ 66	David Wesley H1	8.00	3.60	1.00
☐ 67	Doug West Z1	8.00	3.60	1.00
☐ 68	Monty Williams H1	8.00	3.60	1.00
☐ 69	Joe Wolf H1,Z1	8.00	3.60	1.00
☐ 70	Sharone Wright Z1	10.00	4.50	1.25

1995-96 SkyBox E-XL

The 1995-96 Skybox E-XL set was issued in one series totalling 100 cards. Only the top veterans and rookies in the league were selected for inclusion within this premium brand set. The 6-card packs retailed for $4.99 each. Cards are numbered alphabetically within teams. The only subset is Untouchable (91-99). The product picks up where the 1994-95 SkyBox Emotion issue left off. Each player card features silhouetted action photo over a multi-colored background, framed by one of five different shaped die cut window designs. Only the player image and multi-colored backgrounds are UV coated. The rest of the card is non-UV coated, giving the card a unique look and feel.

		MINT	NRMT	EXC
	COMPLETE SET (100)	50.00	22.00	6.25
	COMMON CARD (1-100)	.15	.07	.02
☐ 1	Stacey Augmon	.20	.09	.03
☐ 2	Mookie Blaylock	.20	.09	.03
☐ 3	Christian Laettner	.20	.09	.03
☐ 4	Dana Barros	.15	.07	.02
☐ 5	Dino Radja	.15	.07	.02
☐ 6	Eric Williams	.50	.23	.06
☐ 7	Kenny Anderson	.20	.09	.03
☐ 8	Larry Johnson	.60	.25	.07
☐ 9	Glen Rice	.30	.14	.04
☐ 10	Michael Jordan	8.00	3.60	1.00
☐ 11	Toni Kukoc	.40	.18	.05
☐ 12	Scottie Pippen	2.00	.90	.25
☐ 13	Dennis Rodman Bulls	4.00	1.80	.50
☐ 14	Terrell Brandon	.30	.14	.04
☐ 15	Bobby Phills	.15	.07	.02
☐ 16	Bob Sura	.50	.23	.06
☐ 17	Jim Jackson	.30	.14	.04
☐ 18	Jason Kidd	1.50	.70	.19
☐ 19	Jamal Mashburn	.40	.18	.05
☐ 20	Mahmoud Abdul-Rauf	.15	.07	.02
☐ 21	Antonio McDyess	2.50	1.10	.30
☐ 22	Dikembe Mutombo	.30	.14	.04
☐ 23	Joe Dumars	.30	.14	.04
☐ 24	Grant Hill	2.50	1.10	.30
☐ 25	Allan Houston	.30	.14	.04
☐ 26	Joe Smith	3.00	1.35	.35
☐ 27	Latrell Sprewell	.30	.14	.04
☐ 28	Kevin Willis	.15	.07	.02
☐ 29	Sam Cassell	.20	.09	.03
☐ 30	Clyde Drexler	.75	.35	.09
☐ 31	Robert Horry	.20	.09	.03
☐ 32	Hakeem Olajuwon	1.50	.70	.19
☐ 33	Derrick McKey	.15	.07	.02
☐ 34	Reggie Miller	.75	.35	.09
☐ 35	Rik Smits	.30	.14	.04
☐ 36	Brent Barry	1.25	.55	.16
☐ 37	Loy Vaught	.20	.09	.03
☐ 38	Brian Williams	.15	.07	.02
☐ 39	Cedric Ceballos	.30	.14	.04
☐ 40	Magic Johnson	2.00	.90	.25
☐ 41	Nick Van Exel	.50	.23	.06
☐ 42	Tim Hardaway	.30	.14	.04
☐ 43	Alonzo Mourning	.60	.25	.07
☐ 44	Kurt Thomas	.75	.35	.09
☐ 45	Walt Williams	.15	.07	.02
☐ 46	Vin Baker	.60	.25	.07
☐ 47	Shawn Respert	.30	.14	.04
☐ 48	Glenn Robinson	.75	.35	.09
☐ 49	Kevin Garnett	8.00	3.60	1.00
☐ 50	Tom Gugliotta	.30	.14	.04
☐ 51	Isaiah Rider	.15	.07	.02
☐ 52	Shawn Bradley	.30	.14	.04
☐ 53	Chris Childs	.15	.07	.02
☐ 54	Ed O'Bannon	1.00	.45	.12
☐ 55	Patrick Ewing	.60	.25	.07
☐ 56	Anthony Mason	.15	.07	.02
☐ 57	Charles Oakley	.15	.07	.02
☐ 58	Horace Grant	.30	.14	.04
☐ 59	Anfernee Hardaway	4.00	1.80	.50
☐ 60	Shaquille O'Neal	3.00	1.35	.35
☐ 61	Derrick Coleman	.20	.09	.03
☐ 62	Jerry Stackhouse	5.00	2.20	.60
☐ 63	Clarence Weatherspoon	.30	.14	.04
☐ 64	Charles Barkley	1.00	.45	.12
☐ 65	Michael Finley	3.00	1.35	.35
☐ 66	Kevin Johnson	.30	.14	.04
☐ 67	Clifford Robinson	.30	.14	.04
☐ 68	Arvydas Sabonis	2.00	.90	.25
☐ 69	Rod Strickland	.20	.09	.03
☐ 70	Tyus Edney	1.50	.70	.19
☐ 71	Billy Owens	.15	.07	.02
☐ 72	Mitch Richmond	.50	.23	.06
☐ 73	Sean Elliott	.20	.09	.03
☐ 74	Avery Johnson	.20	.09	.03
☐ 75	David Robinson	1.25	.55	.16
☐ 76	Shawn Kemp	2.00	.90	.25
☐ 77	Gary Payton	1.00	.45	.12
☐ 78	Detlef Schrempf	.30	.14	.04
☐ 79	Tracy Murray	.15	.07	.02
☐ 80	Damon Stoudamire	6.00	2.70	.75
☐ 81	Sharone Wright	.15	.07	.02
☐ 82	Jeff Hornacek	.20	.09	.03
☐ 83	Karl Malone	.60	.25	.07
☐ 84	John Stockton	.60	.25	.07
☐ 85	Greg Anthony	.15	.07	.02
☐ 86	Bryant Reeves	1.50	.70	.19

		MINT	NRMT	EXC
☐ 87	Byron Scott	.20	.09	.03
☐ 88	Juwan Howard	1.50	.70	.19
☐ 89	Gheorghe Muresan	.30	.14	.04
☐ 90	Rasheed Wallace	1.25	.55	.16
☐ 91	Steve Smith UNT	.15	.07	.02
☐ 92	Dikembe Mutombo UNT	.20	.09	.03
☐ 93	Brent Barry UNT	.50	.23	.06
☐ 94	Glenn Robinson UNT	.40	.18	.05
☐ 95	Armon Gilliam UNT	.15	.07	.02
☐ 96	Nick Anderson UNT	.15	.07	.02
☐ 97	Gary Trent UNT	.15	.07	.02
☐ 98	Brian Grant UNT	.15	.07	.02
☐ 99	Bryant Reeves UNT	.60	.25	.07
☐ 100	Checklist	.15	.07	.02

1995-96 Skybox E-XL Blue

Randomly inserted at a rate of slightly more than one card per pack, this 100-card set is a parallel of the basic SkyBox E-XL set. Card fronts are identical to the basic issue except the black border is replaced with a blue border. Card backs are also identical. Please refer to the multipliers listed below to ascertain values.

	MINT	NRMT	EXC
COMPLETE SET (100)	100.00	45.00	12.50
COMMON CARD (1-100)	.30	.14	.04
*BLUE STARS: 1.25X to 2.5X VALUE			
*BLUE ROOKIES: 1X to 2X VALUE			

1995-96 SkyBox E-XL A Cut Above

Randomly inserted in hobby and retail packs at a rate of one in 130, this 10-card die-cut insert set features a selection of the NBA's elite stars. Each card front features a unique framing of two different, die-cut photos surrounded by a blue border. Card backs contain an action photo and brief commentary and are numbered as "X of 10".

	MINT	NRMT	EXC
COMPLETE SET (10)	250.00	110.00	31.00
COMMON CARD (1-10)	15.00	6.75	1.85

		MINT	NRMT	EXC
☐ 1	Scottie Pippen	40.00	18.00	5.00
☐ 2	Jason Kidd	25.00	11.00	3.10
☐ 3	Grant Hill	40.00	18.00	5.00
☐ 4	Joe Smith	20.00	9.00	2.50
☐ 5	Hakeem Olajuwon	25.00	11.00	3.10
☐ 6	Magic Johnson	30.00	13.50	3.70
☐ 7	Shaquille O'Neal	50.00	22.00	6.25
☐ 8	Jerry Stackhouse	30.00	13.50	3.70
☐ 9	Charles Barkley	15.00	6.75	1.85
☐ 10	David Robinson	20.00	9.00	2.50

1995-96 SkyBox E-XL Natural Born Thrillers

Randomly inserted in hobby and retail packs at a rate of one in 48, this 10-card set highlights a selection of crowd-pleasing players who do incredible things on the court. Each card features a multi-layered die-cut design. Card backs are black and textured with the player's name and a brief commentary in gold foil. The cards are numbered as "X of 10".

		MINT	NRMT	EXC
COMPLETE SET (10)		300.00	135.00	38.00
COMMON CARD (1-10)		12.00	5.50	1.50
☐ 1	Michael Jordan	125.00	55.00	15.50
☐ 2	Antonio McDyess	15.00	6.75	1.85
☐ 3	Grant Hill	30.00	13.50	3.70
☐ 4	Clyde Drexler	10.00	4.50	1.25
☐ 5	Kevin Garnett	50.00	22.00	6.25
☐ 6	Anfernee Hardaway	50.00	22.00	6.25
☐ 7	Jerry Stackhouse	30.00	13.50	3.70

☐ 8 Michael Finley	20.00	9.00	2.50
☐ 9 Shawn Kemp	25.00	11.00	3.10
☐ 10 Damon Stoudamire	40.00	18.00	5.00

1995-96 SkyBox E-XL No Boundaries

Randomly inserted exclusively in hobby packs at a rate of one in 18, this 10-card set features players that can bust open a game on a special die cut designed card. Card fronts have metallic backgrounds with an action shot of the player and the player's name which is written in gold foil. Card backs feature a head shot of the player in a die-cut circle. The cards are numbered as "X of 10".

	MINT	NRMT	EXC
COMPLETE SET (10)	125.00	55.00	15.50
COMMON CARD (1-10)	4.00	1.80	.50
☐ 1 Michael Jordan	50.00	22.00	6.25
☐ 2 Antonio McDyess	8.00	3.60	1.00
☐ 3 Hakeem Olajuwon	10.00	4.50	1.25
☐ 4 Magic Johnson	12.00	5.50	1.50
☐ 5 Vin Baker	4.00	1.80	.50
☐ 6 Patrick Ewing	4.00	1.80	.50
☐ 7 Anfernee Hardaway	25.00	11.00	3.10
☐ 8 Jerry Stackhouse	15.00	6.75	1.85
☐ 9 Gary Payton	6.00	2.70	.75
☐ 10 Damon Stoudamire	20.00	9.00	2.50

1995-96 SkyBox E-XL Unstoppable

Randomly inserted in hobby and retail packs at a rate of one in 6, this 20-card set features 10 players who are "unstoppable" inside the paint and 10 who are "unstoppable" from outside. Card fronts have a large action shot of the player with the player's name written vertically along the border. Card backs have a textured background photo with a brief commentary on the player. The cards are numbered as "X of 20".

	MINT	NRMT	EXC
COMPLETE SET (20)	70.00	32.00	8.75
COMMON CARD (1-20)	1.25	.55	.16
☐ 1 Alan Henderson	1.25	.55	.16
☐ 2 Glen Rice	2.50	1.10	.30
☐ 3 Scottie Pippen	8.00	3.60	1.00
☐ 4 Dennis Rodman Bulls	12.00	5.50	1.50
☐ 5 Terrell Brandon	1.25	.55	.16
☐ 6 Jason Kidd	6.00	2.70	.75
☐ 7 Grant Hill	10.00	4.50	1.25
☐ 8 Joe Smith	6.00	2.70	.75
☐ 9 Sam Cassell	1.25	.55	.16
☐ 10 Reggie Miller	3.00	1.35	.35
☐ 11 Alonzo Mourning	2.50	1.10	.30
☐ 12 Shaquille O'Neal	12.00	5.50	1.50
☐ 13 Charles Barkley	4.00	1.80	.50
☐ 14 Clifford Robinson	2.50	1.10	.30
☐ 15 Sean Elliott	2.50	1.10	.30
☐ 16 David Robinson	5.00	2.20	.60
☐ 17 Shawn Kemp	8.00	3.60	1.00
☐ 18 Karl Malone	2.50	1.10	.30
☐ 19 John Stockton	2.50	1.10	.30
☐ 20 Juwan Howard	6.00	2.70	.75

1996 SkyBox USA

The 1996 SkyBox USA set, featuring members of Dream Team 3, was issued in one series totalling 60 cards. The 6-card packs retailed for $1.99 each. The set features the topical subsets: Grant's Slant (1-10), Brag Book (11-20), Playing for Pride (21-30), Contribution (31-50), Coaches (51-54) and Awesome Duos (55-59). Card fronts feature an Olympic ring background with an action shot of the player.

	MINT	NRMT	EXC
COMPLETE SET (60)	15.00	6.75	1.85
COMMON CARD (1-60)	.15	.07	.02

		MINT	NRMT	EXC
☐ 1	Anfernee Hardaway GS	1.00	.45	.12
☐ 2	Grant Hill GS	.60	.25	.07
☐ 3	Karl Malone GS	.15	.07	.02
☐ 4	Reggie Miller GS	.20	.09	.03
☐ 5	Scottie Pippen GS	.50	.23	.06
☐ 6	Hakeem Olajuwon GS	.40	.18	.05
☐ 7	Shaquille O'Neal GS	.75	.35	.09
☐ 8	David Robinson GS	.30	.14	.04
☐ 9	Glenn Robinson GS	.20	.09	.03
☐ 10	John Stockton GS	.15	.07	.02
☐ 11	Anfernee Hardaway BB	1.00	.45	.12
☐ 12	Grant Hill BB	.60	.25	.07
☐ 13	Karl Malone BB	.15	.07	.02
☐ 14	Reggie Miller BB	.20	.09	.03
☐ 15	Scottie Pippen BB	.50	.23	.06
☐ 16	Hakeem Olajuwon BB	.40	.18	.05
☐ 17	Shaquille O'Neal BB	.75	.35	.09
☐ 18	David Robinson BB	.30	.14	.04
☐ 19	Glenn Robinson BB	.20	.09	.03
☐ 20	John Stockton BB	.15	.07	.02
☐ 21	Anfernee Hardaway PP	1.00	.45	.12
☐ 22	Grant Hill PP	.60	.25	.07
☐ 23	Karl Malone PP	.15	.07	.02
☐ 24	Reggie Miller PP	.20	.09	.03
☐ 25	Scottie Pippen PP	.50	.23	.06
☐ 26	Hakeem Olajuwon PP	.40	.18	.05
☐ 27	Shaquille O'Neal PP	.75	.35	.09
☐ 28	David Robinson PP	.30	.14	.04
☐ 29	Glenn Robinson PP	.20	.09	.03
☐ 30	John Stockton PP	.15	.07	.02
☐ 31	Anfernee Hardaway CON	1.00	.45	.12
☐ 32	Grant Hill CON	.60	.25	.07
☐ 33	Karl Malone CON	.15	.07	.02
☐ 34	Reggie Miller CON	.20	.09	.03
☐ 35	Scottie Pippen CON	.50	.23	.06
☐ 36	Hakeem Olajuwon CON	.40	.18	.05
☐ 37	Shaquille O'Neal CON	.75	.35	.09
☐ 38	David Robinson CON	.30	.14	.04
☐ 39	Glenn Robinson CON	.25	.11	.03
☐ 40	John Stockton CON	.15	.07	.02
☐ 41	Anfernee Hardaway CON	1.00	.45	.12
☐ 42	Grant Hill CON	.60	.25	.07
☐ 43	Karl Malone CON	.15	.07	.02
☐ 44	Reggie Miller CON	.20	.09	.03
☐ 45	Scottie Pippen CON	.50	.23	.06
☐ 46	Hakeem Olajuwon CON	.40	.18	.05
☐ 47	Shaquille O'Neal CON	.75	.35	.09
☐ 48	David Robinson CON	.30	.14	.04
☐ 49	Glenn Robinson CON	.20	.09	.03
☐ 50	John Stockton CON	.15	.07	.02
☐ 51	Lenny Wilkens CO	.15	.07	.02
☐ 52	Bobby Cremins CO	.15	.07	.02
☐ 53	Clem Haskins CO	.15	.07	.02
☐ 54	Jerry Sloan CO	.15	.07	.02
☐ 55	Shaquille O'Neal	1.00	.45	.12
	Anfernee Hardaway AD			
☐ 56	Karl Malone	.15	.07	.02
	John Stockton AD			
☐ 57	David Robinson	.25	.11	.03
	Hakeem Olajuwon AD			
☐ 58	Scottie Pippen	.40	.18	.05
	Grant Hill AD			
☐ 59	Reggie Miller	.15	.07	.02
	Glenn Robinson AD			
☐ 60	Checklist	.15	.07	.02

1996 SkyBox USA Bronze

Randomly inserted in hobby and retail packs at a rate of one in 12, this set features the first ten players selected to the 1996 USA men's basketball team. Card fronts feature foil printing and UV coating. A parallel version of the set entitled Bronze Sparkle, utilizing sparkling foil on the card fronts, was also created. These cards were exclusively seeded into hobby packs at a rate of 1:18. Please refer to the mulitplier provided below for values on the Sparkle cards.

	MINT	NRMT	EXC
COMPLETE SET (10)	30.00	13.50	3.70
COMMON CARD (B1-B10)	1.50	.70	.19
*SPARKLE CARDS: 1.5X VALUE			

		MINT	NRMT	EXC
☐ B1	Anfernee Hardaway	10.00	4.50	1.25
☐ B2	Grant Hill	6.00	2.70	.75
☐ B3	Karl Malone	1.50	.70	.19
☐ B4	Reggie Miller	2.00	.90	.25
☐ B5	Scottie Pippen	5.00	2.20	.60
☐ B6	Hakeem Olajuwon	4.00	1.80	.50
☐ B7	Shaquille O'Neal	8.00	3.60	1.00
☐ B8	David Robinson	3.00	1.35	.35
☐ B9	Glenn Robinson	2.00	.90	.25
☐ B10	John Stockton	1.50	.70	.19

1996 SkyBox USA Gold

Randomly inserted in hobby and retail packs at a rate of one in 120, this set features the first ten players selected to the 1996 men's USA basketball team. Card fronts feature foil printing and UV coating. A parallel version of the set entitled Gold Sparkle, utilizing sparkling foil on the card fronts, was also created. These cards were exclusively seeded into hobby packs at a rate of 1:180. Please refer to the multiplier provided below for values on the Sparkle cards.

	MINT	NRMT	EXC
COMPLETE SET (10)	225.00	100.00	28.00
COMMON CARD (G1-G10)	10.00	4.50	1.25
*SPARKLE: 1.5X VALUE			

		MINT	NRMT	EXC
☐	G1 Anfernee Hardaway	70.00	32.00	8.75
☐	G2 Grant Hill	40.00	18.00	5.00
☐	G3 Karl Malone	10.00	4.50	1.25
☐	G4 Reggie Miller	12.00	5.50	1.50
☐	G5 Scottie Pippen	30.00	13.50	3.70
☐	G6 Hakeem Olajuwon	25.00	11.00	3.10
☐	G7 Shaquille O'Neal	50.00	22.00	6.25
☐	G8 David Robinson	20.00	9.00	2.50
☐	G9 Glenn Robinson	12.00	5.50	1.50
☐	G10 John Stockton	10.00	4.50	1.25

1996 SkyBox USA Quads

Randomly inserted in packs at a rate of one in 3, this 15-card set features the first ten players selected to the 1996 USA men's basketball team. The standard-sized cards actually feature four preforated mini quadrant cards. These mini cards are replicas of the basic issue cards. Each of the original ten members of the team have their own quads. In addtion, the final five quads are based on the following themes: Power, Versatility, Passing, Defense and Scoring.

		MINT	NRMT	EXC
	COMPLETE SET (15)	15.00	6.75	1.85
	COMMON CARD (Q1-Q15)	.60	.25	.07
☐	Q1 Anfernee Hardaway	4.00	1.80	.50
☐	Q2 Grant Hill	2.50	1.10	.30
☐	Q3 Karl Malone	.60	.25	.07
☐	Q4 Reggie Miller	.75	.35	.09
☐	Q5 Scottie Pippen	2.00	.90	.25
☐	Q6 Hakeem Olajuwon	1.50	.70	.19
☐	Q7 Shaquille O'Neal	3.00	1.35	.35
☐	Q8 David Robinson	1.25	.55	.16
☐	Q9 Glenn Robinson	.75	.35	.09
☐	Q10 John Stockton	.60	.25	.07
☐	Q11 Karl Malone Power Shaquille O'Neal Hakeem Olajuwon David Robinson	.75	.35	.09
☐	Q12 Grant Hill Versatility Scottie Pippen Anfernee Hardaway Glenn Robinson	1.00	.45	.12
☐	Q13 A.Hardaway Passing John Stockton Grant Hill Reggie Miller	1.00	.45	.12
☐	Q14 Scottie Pippen Defense John Stockton Hakeem Olajuwon David Robinson	.75	.35	.09
☐	Q15 Karl Malone Scoring Reggie Miller Shaquille O'Neal Glenn Robinson	.75	.35	.09

1996 SkyBox USA Silver

Randomly inserted in hobby and retail packs at a rate of one in 48, this set features the first ten players selected to the 1996 men's USA basketball team. Card fronts feature foil printing and UV coating. A parallel version of the set entitled Silver Sparkle, utilizing sparkling foil on the card fronts, was also created. These cards were exclusively seeded into hobby packs at a rate of 1:72. Please refer to the mulitplier provided below for values on the Sparkle cards.

		MINT	NRMT	EXC
	COMPLETE SET (10)	100.00	45.00	12.50
	COMMON CARD (S1-S10)	5.00	2.20	.60
	*SPARKLE: 1.5X VALUE			
☐	S1 Anfernee Hardaway	30.00	13.50	3.70
☐	S2 Grant Hill	20.00	9.00	2.50
☐	S3 Karl Malone	5.00	2.20	.60
☐	S4 Reggie Miller	6.00	2.70	.75
☐	S5 Scottie Pippen	15.00	6.75	1.85
☐	S6 Hakeem Olajuwon	12.00	5.50	1.50
☐	S7 Shaquille O'Neal	25.00	11.00	3.10

		MINT	NRMT	EXC
☐	S8 David Robinson	10.00	4.50	1.25
☐	S9 Glenn Robinson	6.00	2.70	.75
☐	S10 John Stockton	5.00	2.20	.60

1996 SkyBox USA Wrapper Exchange

This 25-card set was available via a wrapper exchange program. Sets could be obtained by sending in 10 wrappers along with $3 for postage and handling before the December 31, 1996 deadline. The set contains cards for Charles Barkley and Mitch Richmond, two \late additions to the team, and has all of the subset and insert cards that they would have had if they were in the basic set.

		MINT	NRMT	EXC
	COMPLETE SET (25)	10.00	4.50	1.25
	*SPARKLE CARDS: SAME PRICE.....			
☐	61 Charles Barkley GS	.25	.11	.03
☐	62 Mitch Richmond GS	.15	.07	.02
☐	63 Charles Barkley BB	.25	.11	.03
☐	64 Mitch Richmond BB	.15	.07	.02
☐	65 Charles Barkley PP	.25	.11	.03
☐	66 Mitch Richmond PP	.15	.07	.02
☐	67 Charles Barkley CON	.25	.11	.03
☐	68 Mitch Richmond CON	.15	.07	.02
☐	69 Charles Barkley CON	.25	.11	.03
☐	70 Mitch Richmond CON	.15	.07	.02
☐	71 Charles Barkley	.15	.07	.02
	Mitch Richmond AD			
☐	B11 Charles Barkley Bronze	1.00	.45	.12
☐	B12 Mitch Richmond Bronze	.50	.23	.06
☐	G11 Charles Barkley Gold	2.00	.90	.25
☐	G12 Mitch Richmond Gold	1.00	.45	.12
☐	Q16 Charles Barkley Quad	.50	.23	.06
☐	Q17 Mitch Richmond Quad	.25	.11	.03
☐	S11 Charles Barkley Silver	1.50	.70	.19
☐	S12 Mitch Richmond Silver	.75	.35	.09

1996-97 SkyBox Z-Force

The inaugural edtion of SkyBox Z-Force series one has a total of 100 cards. The 8-card hobby and retail packs carry a suggested retail price of $2.49 each. Card fronts contain an action shot of the player

against an "explosive-type" background. The player's name is in block letters at the top of the card and the SkyBox Z-Force logo is outlined in gold foil along the bottom right of the card. Card backs contain a hardwood floor design in the background with a player shot over it. Statistical and biographical information is also located on the back. The cards are grouped alphabetically within teams. There are no Rookie Cards in the set.

		MINT	NRMT	EXC
	COMPLETE SERIES 1 (100)	20.00	9.00	2.50
	COMMON CARD (1-100)	.10	.05	.01
☐	1 Mookie Blaylock	.15	.07	.02
☐	2 Alan Henderson	.10	.05	.01
☐	3 Christian Laettner	.15	.07	.02
☐	4 Steve Smith	.15	.07	.02
☐	5 Rick Fox	.10	.05	.01
☐	6 Dino Radja	.20	.09	.03
☐	7 Eric Williams	.10	.05	.01
☐	8 Muggsy Bogues	.15	.07	.02
☐	9 Larry Johnson	.40	.18	.05
☐	10 Glen Rice	.20	.09	.03
☐	11 Michael Jordan	5.00	2.20	.60
☐	12 Toni Kukoc	.15	.07	.02
☐	13 Scottie Pippen	1.25	.55	.16
☐	14 Dennis Rodman	2.00	.90	.25
☐	15 Terrell Brandon	.20	.09	.03
☐	16 Bobby Phills	.10	.05	.01
☐	17 Bob Sura	.10	.05	.01
☐	18 Jim Jackson	.20	.09	.03
☐	19 Jason Kidd	.75	.35	.09
☐	20 Jamal Mashburn	.20	.09	.03
☐	21 George McCloud	.10	.05	.01
☐	22 Mahmoud Abdul-Rauf	.10	.05	.01
☐	23 Antonio McDyess	.50	.23	.06
☐	24 Dikembe Mutombo	.20	.09	.03
☐	25 Joe Dumars	.20	.09	.03
☐	26 Grant Hill	1.25	.55	.16
☐	27 Allan Houston	.20	.09	.03
☐	28 Otis Thorpe	.15	.07	.02
☐	29 Chris Mullin	.15	.07	.02
☐	30 Joe Smith	.60	.25	.07
☐	31 Latrell Sprewell	.20	.09	.03
☐	32 Sam Cassell	.15	.07	.02
☐	33 Clyde Drexler	.50	.23	.06
☐	34 Robert Horry	.20	.09	.03
☐	35 Hakeem Olajuwon	1.00	.45	.12
☐	36 Travis Best	.10	.05	.01
☐	37 Dale Davis	.10	.05	.01
☐	38 Reggie Miller	.50	.23	.06
☐	39 Rik Smits	.20	.09	.03
☐	40 Brent Barry	.25	.11	.03
☐	41 Loy Vaught	.15	.07	.02

☐ 42 Brian Williams	.10	.05	.01
☐ 43 Cedric Ceballos	.20	.09	.03
☐ 44 Eddie Jones	.25	.11	.03
☐ 45 Nick Van Exel	.25	.11	.03
☐ 46 Tim Hardaway	.20	.09	.03
☐ 47 Alonzo Mourning	.40	.18	.05
☐ 48 Kurt Thomas	.10	.05	.01
☐ 49 Walt Williams	.10	.05	.01
☐ 50 Vin Baker	.30	.14	.04
☐ 51 Glenn Robinson	.40	.18	.05
☐ 52 Kevin Garnett	1.50	.70	.19
☐ 53 Tom Gugliotta	.20	.09	.03
☐ 54 Isaiah Rider	.20	.09	.03
☐ 55 Shawn Bradley	.15	.07	.02
☐ 56 Chris Childs	.10	.05	.01
☐ 57 Jayson Williams	.10	.05	.01
☐ 58 Patrick Ewing	.40	.18	.05
☐ 59 Anthony Mason	.10	.05	.01
☐ 60 Charles Oakley	.10	.05	.01
☐ 61 Nick Anderson	.20	.09	.03
☐ 62 Horace Grant	.20	.09	.03
☐ 63 Anfernee Hardaway	2.50	1.10	.30
☐ 64 Shaquille O'Neal	2.00	.90	.25
☐ 65 Dennis Scott	.20	.09	.03
☐ 66 Jerry Stackhouse	1.00	.45	.12
☐ 67 Clarence Weatherspoon	.20	.09	.03
☐ 68 Charles Barkley	.60	.25	.07
☐ 69 Michael Finley	.60	.25	.07
☐ 70 Kevin Johnson	.20	.09	.03
☐ 71 Clifford Robinson	.20	.09	.03
☐ 72 Arvydas Sabonis	.40	.18	.05
☐ 73 Rod Strickland	.15	.07	.02
☐ 74 Tyus Edney	.25	.11	.03
☐ 75 Brian Grant	.10	.05	.01
☐ 76 Billy Owens	.10	.05	.01
☐ 77 Mitch Richmond	.30	.14	.04
☐ 78 Vinny Del Negro	.10	.05	.01
☐ 79 Sean Elliott	.20	.09	.03
☐ 80 Avery Johnson	.15	.07	.02
☐ 81 David Robinson	.75	.35	.09
☐ 82 Hersey Hawkins	.15	.07	.02
☐ 83 Shawn Kemp	1.25	.55	.16
☐ 84 Gary Payton	.60	.25	.07
☐ 85 Detlef Schrempf	.20	.09	.03
☐ 86 Doug Christie	.10	.05	.01
☐ 87 Damon Stoudamire	1.25	.55	.16
☐ 88 Sharone Wright	.10	.05	.01
☐ 89 Jeff Hornacek	.15	.07	.02
☐ 90 Karl Malone	.40	.18	.05
☐ 91 John Stockton	.40	.18	.05
☐ 92 Greg Anthony	.10	.05	.01
☐ 93 Bryant Reeves	.30	.14	.04
☐ 94 Byron Scott	.15	.07	.02
☐ 95 Juwan Howard	.75	.35	.09
☐ 96 Gheorghe Muresan	.20	.09	.03
☐ 97 Rasheed Wallace	.25	.11	.03
☐ 98 Chris Webber	.30	.14	.04
☐ 99 Checklist	.10	.05	.01
☐ 100 Checklist	.10	.05	.01

1996-97 SkyBox Z-Force Z-Cling

Inserted one per pack, this 100-card set is a semi-parallel to the regular set. The card fronts are identical to the basic issue, but the card backs are blank outside of the player's name and the card number. 96 of

the original 100 cards are parallels. The exceptions are Shaquille O'Neal, which has him in a Laker uniform on the parallel, the Byron Scott card (#94), which was never issued and the two checklist cards. The Byron Scott card and the two checklists were replaced with the following rookies: Ray Allen (#R1), Stephon Marbury (#R2) and Shareef Abdur-Rahim (#R3), thus making the set complete at 100 cards. Please refer to the multipliers provided below to ascertain values for all Z-Cling singles except for those players specifically listed below.

	MINT	NRMT	EXC
COMPLETE SET (100)	50.00	22.00	6.25
COMMON CARD (1-100)	.20	.09	.03
*Z-CLING CARDS: 1.25X to 2.5X BASIC			

☐ 64 Shaquille O'Neal Lakers	10.00	4.50	1.25
☐ R1 Ray Allen	5.00	2.20	.60
☐ R2 Stephon Marbury	8.00	3.60	1.00
☐ R3 Shareef Abdur-Rahim	5.00	2.20	.60

1996-97 SkyBox Z-Force Slam Cam

Randomly inserted in hobby and retail packs at a rate of one in 240, this 9-card set features some of the top slam dunkers in the game. Card fronts contain a kaleidoscopic color background with an action photo laid on top. The player's name and the set name "Slam Cam" are located above the photo. Card backs are horizontal with the set name in the background with another action shot of the player. The cards are numbered with a "SC" prefix.

	MINT	NRMT	EXC
COMPLETE SET (9)	450.00	200.00	55.00
COMMON CARD (SC1-SC9)	15.00	6.75	1.85
☐ SC1 Clyde Drexler	20.00	9.00	2.50
☐ SC2 Michael Finley	25.00	11.00	3.10
☐ SC3 Anfernee Hardaway	100.00	45.00	12.50
☐ SC4 Grant Hill	50.00	22.00	6.25
☐ SC5 Michael Jordan	225.00	100.00	28.00
☐ SC6 Shawn Kemp	50.00	22.00	6.25
☐ SC7 Karl Malone	15.00	6.75	1.85
☐ SC8 Antonio McDyess	20.00	9.00	2.50
☐ SC9 Shaquille O'Neal	75.00	34.00	9.50

1996-97 SkyBox Z-Force Swat Team

Randomly inserted in hobby packs only at a rate of one in 72, this 9-card set features some of the leagues best blockers. Card front backgrounds are prismatic with the logo "Swat Team" designed into it. An action shot of the player is laid on top with their names directly underneath. Card backs contain the same type background as the front, without the prismatic foil. The cards are numbered with a "ST" prefix.

	MINT	NRMT	EXC
COMPLETE SET (9)	125.00	55.00	15.50
COMMON CARD (ST1-ST9)	3.00	1.35	.35
☐ ST1 Patrick Ewing	6.00	2.70	.75
☐ ST2 Kevin Garnett	30.00	13.50	3.70
☐ ST3 Alonzo Mourning	6.00	2.70	.75
☐ ST4 Dikembe Mutombo	3.00	1.35	.35
☐ ST5 Hakeem Olajuwon	15.00	6.75	1.85
☐ ST6 Shaquille O'Neal	35.00	16.00	4.40
☐ ST7 David Robinson	12.00	5.50	1.50
☐ ST8 Dennis Rodman	40.00	18.00	5.00
☐ ST9 Joe Smith	10.00	4.50	1.25

1996-97 SkyBox Z-Force Vortex

Randomly inserted in retail packs only at a rate of one in 36, this 15-card set features

embossed card fronts with a swirl background. The action shot of the player is located in the middle of the card with the player's name in gold foil block letters directly below. Card backs are horizontal with a similar background and have a brief commentary along with another action shot. The cards are numbered as "Vortex/X".

	MINT	NRMT	EXC
COMPLETE SET (15)	160.00	70.00	20.00
COMMON CARD (V1-V15)	4.00	1.80	.50
☐ V1 Charles Barkley	8.00	3.60	1.00
☐ V2 Anfernee Hardaway	30.00	13.50	3.70
☐ V3 Grant Hill	15.00	6.75	1.85
☐ V4 Juwan Howard	10.00	4.50	1.25
☐ V5 Michael Jordan	60.00	27.00	7.50
☐ V6 Jason Kidd	10.00	4.50	1.25
☐ V7 Reggie Miller	6.00	2.70	.75
☐ V8 Gary Payton	8.00	3.60	1.00
☐ V9 Scottie Pippen	15.00	6.75	1.85
☐ V10 Mitch Richmond	4.00	1.80	.50
☐ V11 Glenn Robinson	5.00	2.20	.60
☐ V12 Arvydas Sabonis	5.00	2.20	.60
☐ V13 Jerry Stackhouse	12.00	5.50	1.50
☐ V14 John Stockton	5.00	2.20	.60
☐ V15 Damon Stoudamire	15.00	6.75	1.85

1994-95 SP

The complete 1994-95 SP set (issued by Upper Deck) consists of 165-card standard size cards issued in eight-card packs (suggested retail price $3.99). Boxes were distributed exclusively to hobby dealers. The set features full-bleed fronts with color action photos. There is a gold strip down the left side with the player name while the

team name is at the bottom. The backs feature another color action photo with the statistics at the bottom and a gold hologram at the bottom left. The only subset is Premier Prospects (1-30) which highlights rookies. Unlike the regular player cards, these rookie-focused cards have a full-bleed gold foil background with a silver foil pyramid at the bottom with the player's name in it. The backs have a vertical color photo on the right and statistics on the left. After the Premier Prospects subset, the cards are grouped alphabetically within teams. Two parallel Michael Jordan cards (red and silver), both numbered MJ1, were randomly inserted into packs. The cards feature feature photos from Jordan's return with the words "He's Back March 19, 1995" in red foil. The red version was inserted at a ratio of one in every 30 packs. The silver version was inserted at a ratio of one in every 192 packs. Rookie Cards of note in this set include Grant Hill, Juwan Howard, Eddie Jones, Jason Kidd and Glenn Robinson.

	MINT	NRMT	EXC
COMPLETE SET (165)	30.00	13.50	3.70
COMMON CARD (1-165)	.15	.07	.02
☐ 1 Glenn Robinson FOIL	2.50	1.10	.30
☐ 2 Jason Kidd FOIL	5.00	2.20	.60
☐ 3 Grant Hill FOIL	8.00	3.60	1.00
☐ 4 Donyell Marshall FOIL	.30	.14	.04
☐ 5 Juwan Howard FOIL	5.00	2.20	.60
☐ 6 Sharone Wright FOIL	.40	.18	.05
☐ 7 Lamond Murray FOIL	.30	.14	.04
☐ 8 Brian Grant FOIL	1.00	.45	.12
☐ 9 Eric Montross FOIL	.40	.18	.05
☐ 10 Eddie Jones FOIL	1.50	.70	.19
☐ 11 Carlos Rogers FOIL	.30	.14	.04
☐ 12 Khalid Reeves FOIL	.40	.18	.05
☐ 13 Jalen Rose FOIL	.60	.25	.07
☐ 14 Eric Piatkowski FOIL	.30	.14	.04
☐ 15 Clifford Rozier FOIL	.40	.18	.05
☐ 16 Aaron McKie FOIL	.40	.18	.05
☐ 17 Eric Mobley FOIL	.40	.18	.05
☐ 18 Tony Dumas FOIL	.40	.18	.05
☐ 19 B.J. Tyler FOIL	.30	.14	.04
☐ 20 Dickey Simpkins FOIL	.40	.18	.05
☐ 21 Bill Curley FOIL	.30	.14	.04
☐ 22 Wesley Person FOIL	.40	.18	.05
☐ 23 Monty Williams FOIL	.30	.14	.04
☐ 24 Greg Minor FOIL	.30	.14	.04
☐ 25 Charlie Ward FOIL	.40	.18	.05
☐ 26 Brooks Thompson FOIL	.30	.14	.04
☐ 27 Trevor Ruffin FOIL	.30	.14	.04
☐ 28 Derrick Alston FOIL	.30	.14	.04
☐ 29 Michael Smith FOIL	.30	.14	.04
☐ 30 Dontonio Wingfield FOIL	.30	.14	.04
☐ 31 Stacey Augmon	.30	.14	.04
☐ 32 Steve Smith	.40	.18	.05
☐ 33 Mookie Blaylock	.30	.14	.04
☐ 34 Grant Long	.15	.07	.02
☐ 35 Ken Norman	.15	.07	.02
☐ 36 Dominique Wilkins	.40	.18	.05
☐ 37 Dino Radja	.40	.18	.05
☐ 38 Dee Brown	.15	.07	.02
☐ 39 David Wesley	.15	.07	.02
☐ 40 Rick Fox	.15	.07	.02
☐ 41 Alonzo Mourning	.75	.35	.09
☐ 42 Larry Johnson	.60	.25	.07
☐ 43 Hersey Hawkins	.30	.14	.04
☐ 44 Scott Burrell	.15	.07	.02
☐ 45 Muggsy Bogues	.30	.14	.04
☐ 46 Scottie Pippen	2.00	.90	.25
☐ 47 Toni Kukoc	.50	.23	.06
☐ 48 B.J. Armstrong	.15	.07	.02
☐ 49 Will Perdue	.15	.07	.02
☐ 50 Ron Harper	.30	.14	.04
☐ 51 Mark Price	.15	.07	.02
☐ 52 Tyrone Hill	.15	.07	.02
☐ 53 Chris Mills	.40	.18	.05
☐ 54 John Williams	.15	.07	.02
☐ 55 Bobby Phills	.15	.07	.02
☐ 56 Jim Jackson	.40	.18	.05
☐ 57 Jamal Mashburn	.50	.23	.06
☐ 58 Popeye Jones	.15	.07	.02
☐ 59 Roy Tarpley	.15	.07	.02
☐ 60 Lorenzo Williams	.15	.07	.02
☐ 61 Mahmoud Abdul-Rauf	.30	.14	.04
☐ 62 Rodney Rogers	.15	.07	.02
☐ 63 Bryant Stith	.15	.07	.02
☐ 64 Dikembe Mutombo	.40	.18	.05
☐ 65 Robert Pack	.15	.07	.02
☐ 66 Joe Dumars	.40	.18	.05
☐ 67 Terry Mills	.15	.07	.02
☐ 68 Oliver Miller	.15	.07	.02
☐ 69 Lindsey Hunter	.15	.07	.02
☐ 70 Mark West	.15	.07	.02
☐ 71 Latrell Sprewell	.40	.18	.05
☐ 72 Tim Hardaway	.40	.18	.05
☐ 73 Ricky Pierce	.15	.07	.02
☐ 74 Rony Seikaly	.15	.07	.02
☐ 75 Tom Gugliotta	.40	.18	.05
☐ 76 Hakeem Olajuwon	1.50	.70	.19
☐ 77 Clyde Drexler	.75	.35	.09
☐ 78 Vernon Maxwell	.15	.07	.02
☐ 79 Robert Horry	.40	.18	.05
☐ 80 Sam Cassell	.40	.18	.05
☐ 81 Reggie Miller	.75	.35	.09
☐ 82 Rik Smits	.40	.18	.05
☐ 83 Derrick McKey	.15	.07	.02
☐ 84 Mark Jackson	.15	.07	.02
☐ 85 Dale Davis	.15	.07	.02
☐ 86 Loy Vaught	.30	.14	.04
☐ 87 Terry Dehere	.15	.07	.02
☐ 88 Malik Sealy	.15	.07	.02
☐ 89 Pooh Richardson	.15	.07	.02
☐ 90 Tony Massenburg	.15	.07	.02
☐ 91 Cedric Ceballos	.40	.18	.05
☐ 92 Nick Van Exel	.60	.25	.07
☐ 93 George Lynch	.15	.07	.02
☐ 94 Vlade Divac	.40	.18	.05
☐ 95 Elden Campbell	.30	.14	.04
☐ 96 Glen Rice	.40	.18	.05
☐ 97 Kevin Willis	.15	.07	.02
☐ 98 Billy Owens	.15	.07	.02
☐ 99 Bimbo Coles	.15	.07	.02
☐ 100 Harold Miner	.15	.07	.02
☐ 101 Vin Baker	.75	.35	.09
☐ 102 Todd Day	.15	.07	.02
☐ 103 Marty Conlon	.15	.07	.02
☐ 104 Lee Mayberry	.15	.07	.02
☐ 105 Eric Murdock	.15	.07	.02
☐ 106 Isaiah Rider	.40	.18	.05
☐ 107 Doug West	.15	.07	.02
☐ 108 Christian Laettner	.40	.18	.05
☐ 109 Sean Rooks	.15	.07	.02
☐ 110 Stacey King	.15	.07	.02
☐ 111 Derrick Coleman	.15	.07	.02
☐ 112 Kenny Anderson	.40	.18	.05
☐ 113 Chris Morris	.15	.07	.02

		MINT	NRMT	EXC
☐ 114	Armon Gilliam	.15	.07	.02
☐ 115	Benoit Benjamin	.15	.07	.02
☐ 116	Patrick Ewing	.60	.25	.07
☐ 117	Charles Oakley	.30	.14	.04
☐ 118	John Starks	.15	.07	.02
☐ 119	Derek Harper	.15	.07	.02
☐ 120	Charles Smith	.15	.07	.02
☐ 121	Shaquille O'Neal	3.00	1.35	.35
☐ 122	Anfernee Hardaway	4.00	1.80	.50
☐ 123	Nick Anderson	.40	.18	.05
☐ 124	Horace Grant	.40	.18	.05
☐ 125	Donald Royal	.15	.07	.02
☐ 126	Clarence Weatherspoon	.30	.14	.04
☐ 127	Dana Barros	.15	.07	.02
☐ 128	Jeff Malone	.15	.07	.02
☐ 129	Willie Burton	.15	.07	.02
☐ 130	Shawn Bradley	.40	.18	.05
☐ 131	Charles Barkley	1.00	.45	.12
☐ 132	Kevin Johnson	.40	.18	.05
☐ 133	Danny Manning	.30	.14	.04
☐ 134	Dan Majerle	.30	.14	.04
☐ 135	A.C. Green	.40	.18	.05
☐ 136	Otis Thorpe	.30	.14	.04
☐ 137	Clifford Robinson	.40	.18	.05
☐ 138	Rod Strickland	.15	.07	.02
☐ 139	Buck Williams	.30	.14	.04
☐ 140	James Robinson	.15	.07	.02
☐ 141	Mitch Richmond	.50	.23	.06
☐ 142	Walt Williams	.40	.18	.05
☐ 143	Olden Polynice	.15	.07	.02
☐ 144	Spud Webb	.30	.14	.04
☐ 145	Duane Causwell	.15	.07	.02
☐ 146	David Robinson	1.25	.55	.16
☐ 147	Dennis Rodman	2.50	1.10	.30
☐ 148	Sean Elliott	.40	.18	.05
☐ 149	Avery Johnson	.30	.14	.04
☐ 150	J.R. Reid	.15	.07	.02
☐ 151	Shawn Kemp	2.00	.90	.25
☐ 152	Gary Payton	1.00	.45	.12
☐ 153	Detlef Schrempf	.30	.14	.04
☐ 154	Nate McMillan	.15	.07	.02
☐ 155	Kendall Gill	.15	.07	.02
☐ 156	Karl Malone	.60	.25	.07
☐ 157	John Stockton	.60	.25	.07
☐ 158	Jeff Hornacek	.30	.14	.04
☐ 159	Felton Spencer	.15	.07	.02
☐ 160	David Benoit	.15	.07	.02
☐ 161	Chris Webber	.75	.35	.09
☐ 162	Rex Chapman	.15	.07	.02
☐ 163	Don MacLean	.15	.07	.02
☐ 164	Calbert Cheaney	.40	.18	.05
☐ 165	Scott Skiles	.15	.07	.02
☐ MJ1R	M.Jordan Red	8.00	3.60	1.00
☐ MJ1S	M.Jordan Silver	30.00	13.50	3.70

	MINT	NRMT	EXC
COMPLETE SET (165)	60.00	27.00	7.50
COMMON CARD (1-165)	.30	.14	.04

*DIE CUT STARS: 1.25X to 2.5X VALUE
*DIE CUT ROOKIES: 1X to 2X VALUE

1994-95 SP Holoviews

Cards from this 36-card standard size set were randomly inserted in packs at a rate of one in five. The set features a mixture of NBA stars coupled with a wide selection of 1994-95 rookies. The fronts feature color action photos with a hologram of company spokesperson Shawn Kemp on the left with the player's name in silver just to the right. In addition, a holographic head shot of each player is placed in the lower left corner. The backs have a black and white photo on the right and player information on the left.

1994-95 SP Die-Cuts

This is a parallel set to the regular SP issue. These die cuts appear one per pack. The only difference other than the die cut design is the silver hologram in the bottom left of the back instead of the gold hologram in the regular set and all cards are numbered with a "D" prefix. Please refer to the multipliers provided below (coupled with prices of the regular issue SP cards) to ascertain value.

		MINT	NRMT	EXC
COMPLETE SET (36)		75.00	34.00	9.50
COMMON CARD (PC1-PC36)		1.00	.45	.12
☐ PC1	Eric Montross	1.00	.45	.12
☐ PC2	Dominique Wilkins	2.00	.90	.25
☐ PC3	Larry Johnson	3.00	1.35	.35
☐ PC4	Dickey Simpkins	1.00	.45	.12
☐ PC5	Jalen Rose	1.50	.70	.19
☐ PC6	Latrell Sprewell	2.00	.90	.25
☐ PC7	Carlos Rogers	1.00	.45	.12
☐ PC8	Lamond Murray	1.00	.45	.12
☐ PC9	Eddie Jones	4.00	1.80	.50
☐ PC10	Cedric Ceballos	2.00	.90	.25
☐ PC11	Khalid Reeves	1.00	.45	.12

	MINT	NRMT	EXC
☐ PC12 Glenn Robinson	6.00	2.70	.75
☐ PC13 Christian Laettner	1.50	.70	.19
☐ PC14 Derrick Coleman	1.00	.45	.12
☐ PC15 Vin Baker	4.00	1.80	.50
☐ PC16 Donyell Marshall	1.00	.45	.12
☐ PC17 Kenny Anderson	1.50	.70	.19
☐ PC18 Sharone Wright	1.00	.45	.12
☐ PC19 Wesley Person	1.50	.70	.19
☐ PC20 Brian Grant	2.50	1.10	.30
☐ PC21 Mitch Richmond	2.50	1.10	.30
☐ PC22 Shawn Kemp	10.00	4.50	1.25
☐ PC23 Gary Payton	5.00	2.20	.60
☐ PC24 Juwan Howard	12.00	5.50	1.50
☐ PC25 Stacey Augmon	1.00	.45	.12
☐ PC26 Aaron McKie	1.00	.45	.12
☐ PC27 Clifford Rozier	1.00	.45	.12
☐ PC28 Eric Piatkowski	1.00	.45	.12
☐ PC29 Shaquille O'Neal	15.00	6.75	1.85
☐ PC30 Charlie Ward	1.50	.70	.19
☐ PC31 Monty Williams	1.00	.45	.12
☐ PC32 Jason Kidd	12.00	5.50	1.50
☐ PC33 Bill Curley	1.00	.45	.12
☐ PC34 Grant Hill	20.00	9.00	2.50
☐ PC35 Jamal Mashburn	2.00	.90	.25
☐ PC36 Nick Van Exel	3.00	1.35	.35

	MINT	NRMT	EXC
☐ 14 Derrick Coleman	4.00	1.80	.50
☐ 15 Vin Baker	20.00	9.00	2.50
☐ 16 Donyell Marshall	4.00	1.80	.50
☐ 17 Kenny Anderson	8.00	3.60	1.00
☐ 18 Sharone Wright	4.00	1.80	.50
☐ 19 Wesley Person	8.00	3.60	1.00
☐ 20 Brian Grant	12.00	5.50	1.50
☐ 21 Mitch Richmond	15.00	6.75	1.85
☐ 22 Shawn Kemp	50.00	22.00	6.25
☐ 23 Gary Payton	25.00	11.00	3.10
☐ 24 Juwan Howard	60.00	27.00	7.50
☐ 25 Stacey Augmon	4.00	1.80	.50
☐ 26 Aaron McKie	4.00	1.80	.50
☐ 27 Clifford Rozier	4.00	1.80	.50
☐ 28 Eric Piatkowski	4.00	1.80	.50
☐ 29 Shaquille O'Neal	100.00	45.00	12.50
☐ 30 Charlie Ward	8.00	3.60	1.00
☐ 31 Monty Williams	4.00	1.80	.50
☐ 32 Jason Kidd	60.00	27.00	7.50
☐ 33 Bill Curley	4.00	1.80	.50
☐ 34 Grant Hill	100.00	45.00	12.50
☐ 35 Jamal Mashburn	12.00	5.50	1.50
☐ 36 Nick Van Exel	15.00	6.75	1.85

1995-96 SP

1994-95 SP Holoview Die Cuts

This is a parallel set to the SP Holoviews. These die cuts appear one per 75 packs. The cards are similar to the regular Holoviews except for their die cut design and DPC prefixed numbering.

The 1995-96 Upper Deck SP set was issued in one series totalling 167 cards. The 8-card packs, distributed exclusively to hobby outlets, retailed for $4.19 each. The first 147 cards are grouped by team alphabetically by city. The set ends with the rookie-based subset Premier Prospects (148-167) which feature a totally different design to the basic cards. Card stock thickness was upgraded from the previous year. A special Hakeem Olajuwon Commemorative card (celebrating his achievement of becoming only the ninth player in NBA history to score 20,000 points and grab 10,000 rebounds) was randomly seeded into 1 in every 359 packs. Rookie Cards of note in this set include Michael Finley, Kevin Garnett, Antonio McDyess, Jerry Stackhouse and Damon Stoudamire.

	MINT	NRMT	EXC
COMPLETE SET (36)	450.00	200.00	55.00
COMMON CARD (1-36)	4.00	1.80	.50
☐ 1 Eric Montross	4.00	1.80	.50
☐ 2 Dominique Wilkins	8.00	3.60	1.00
☐ 3 Larry Johnson	15.00	6.75	1.85
☐ 4 Dickey Simpkins	4.00	1.80	.50
☐ 5 Jalen Rose	8.00	3.60	1.00
☐ 6 Latrell Sprewell	10.00	4.50	1.25
☐ 7 Carlos Rogers	4.00	1.80	.50
☐ 8 Lamond Murray	4.00	1.80	.50
☐ 9 Eddie Jones	20.00	9.00	2.50
☐ 10 Cedric Ceballos	8.00	3.60	1.00
☐ 11 Khalid Reeves	4.00	1.80	.50
☐ 12 Glenn Robinson	25.00	11.00	3.10
☐ 13 Christian Laettner	8.00	3.60	1.00

	MINT	NRMT	EXC
COMPLETE SET (167)	30.00	13.50	3.70
COMMON CARD (1-167)	.10	.05	.01
☐ 1 Stacey Augmon	.15	.07	.02
☐ 2 Mookie Blaylock	.15	.07	.02
☐ 3 Andrew Lang	.10	.05	.01

#	Player			
4	Steve Smith	.20	.09	.03
5	Spud Webb	.15	.07	.02
6	Dana Barros	.10	.05	.01
7	Dee Brown	.10	.05	.01
8	Todd Day	.10	.05	.01
9	Rick Fox	.10	.05	.01
10	Eric Montross	.10	.05	.01
11	Dino Radja	.20	.09	.03
12	Kenny Anderson	.15	.07	.02
13	Scott Burrell	.10	.05	.01
14	Dell Curry	.10	.05	.01
15	Matt Geiger	.10	.05	.01
16	Larry Johnson	.40	.18	.05
17	Glen Rice	.20	.09	.03
18	Steve Kerr	.15	.07	.02
19	Toni Kukoc	.25	.11	.03
20	Luc Longley	.15	.07	.02
21	Scottie Pippen	1.25	.55	.16
22	Dennis Rodman Bulls ..	3.00	1.35	.35
23	Michael Jordan	5.00	2.20	.60
24	Terrell Brandon	.20	.09	.03
25	Michael Cage	.10	.05	.01
26	Danny Ferry	.10	.05	.01
27	Chris Mills	.10	.05	.01
28	Bobby Phills	.10	.05	.01
29	Tony Dumas	.10	.05	.01
30	Jim Jackson	.20	.09	.03
31	Popeye Jones	.10	.05	.01
32	Jason Kidd	1.00	.45	.12
33	Jamal Mashburn	.25	.11	.03
34	Mahmoud Abdul-Rauf....	.10	.05	.01
35	LaPhonso Ellis	.10	.05	.01
36	Dikembe Mutombo	.20	.09	.03
37	Jalen Rose	.15	.07	.02
38	Bryant Stith	.10	.05	.01
39	Joe Dumars	.20	.09	.03
40	Grant Hill	1.50	.70	.19
41	Lindsey Hunter	.10	.05	.01
42	Allan Houston	.20	.09	.03
43	Otis Thorpe	.15	.07	.02
44	B.J. Armstrong	.10	.05	.01
45	Tim Hardaway	.20	.09	.03
46	Chris Mullin	.15	.07	.02
47	Latrell Sprewell	.20	.09	.03
48	Rony Seikaly	.10	.05	.01
49	Sam Cassell	.20	.09	.03
50	Clyde Drexler	.50	.23	.06
51	Robert Horry	.15	.07	.02
52	Hakeem Olajuwon	1.00	.45	.12
53	Kenny Smith	.10	.05	.01
54	Dale Davis	.10	.05	.01
55	Derrick McKey	.10	.05	.01
56	Reggie Miller	.50	.23	.06
57	Ricky Pierce	.10	.05	.01
58	Rik Smits	.20	.09	.03
59	Lamond Murray	.10	.05	.01
60	Rodney Rogers	.10	.05	.01
61	Malik Sealy	.10	.05	.01
62	Loy Vaught	.15	.07	.02
63	Brian Williams	.10	.05	.01
64	Elden Campbell	.10	.05	.01
65	Cedric Ceballos	.20	.09	.03
66	Magic Johnson	1.25	.55	.16
67	Eddie Jones	.30	.14	.04
68	Nick Van Exel	.30	.14	.04
69	Bimbo Coles	.10	.05	.01
70	Alonzo Mourning	.40	.18	.05
71	Billy Owens	.10	.05	.01
72	Kevin Willis	.10	.05	.01
73	Vin Baker	.40	.18	.05
74	Benoit Benjamin	.10	.05	.01
75	Sherman Douglas	.10	.05	.01
76	Lee Mayberry	.10	.05	.01
77	Glenn Robinson	.50	.23	.06
78	Tom Gugliotta	.20	.09	.03
79	Christian Laettner	.15	.07	.02
80	Sam Mitchell	.10	.05	.01
81	Terry Porter	.10	.05	.01
82	Isaiah Rider	.10	.05	.01
83	Shawn Bradley	.20	.09	.03
84	P.J. Brown	.10	.05	.01
85	Kendall Gill	.10	.05	.01
86	Armon Gilliam	.10	.05	.01
87	Jayson Williams	.10	.05	.01
88	Patrick Ewing	.40	.18	.05
89	Derek Harper	.10	.05	.01
90	Anthony Mason	.10	.05	.01
91	Charles Oakley	.10	.05	.01
92	John Starks	.15	.07	.02
93	Nick Anderson	.20	.09	.03
94	Horace Grant	.20	.09	.03
95	Anfernee Hardaway	2.50	1.10	.30
96	Shaquille O'Neal	2.00	.90	.25
97	Dennis Scott	.20	.09	.03
98	Derrick Coleman	.15	.07	.02
99	Vernon Maxwell	.10	.05	.01
100	Trevor Ruffin	.10	.05	.01
101	Clarence Weatherspoon	.20	.09	.03
102	Sharone Wright	.10	.05	.01
103	Charles Barkley	.60	.25	.07
104	A.C. Green	.15	.07	.02
105	Kevin Johnson	.20	.09	.03
106	Wesley Person	.10	.05	.01
107	John Williams	.10	.05	.01
108	Chris Dudley	.10	.05	.01
109	Harvey Grant	.10	.05	.01
110	Aaron McKie	.10	.05	.01
111	Clifford Robinson	.20	.09	.03
112	Rod Strickland	.10	.05	.01
113	Brian Grant	.10	.05	.01
114	Sarunas Marciulionis	.10	.05	.01
115	Olden Polynice	.10	.05	.01
116	Mitch Richmond	.30	.14	.04
117	Walt Williams	.10	.05	.01
118	Vinny Del Negro	.10	.05	.01
119	Sean Elliott	.15	.07	.02
120	Avery Johnson	.15	.07	.02
121	Chuck Person	.10	.05	.01
122	David Robinson	.75	.35	.09
123	Hersey Hawkins	.15	.07	.02
124	Shawn Kemp	1.25	.55	.16
125	Gary Payton	.60	.25	.07
126	Sam Perkins	.10	.05	.01
127	Detlef Schrempf	.10	.05	.01
128	Oliver Miller	.10	.05	.01
129	Tracy Murray	.10	.05	.01
130	Ed Pinckney	.10	.05	.01
131	Alvin Robertson	.10	.05	.01
132	Zan Tabak	.10	.05	.01
133	Jeff Hornacek	.10	.05	.01
134	Adam Keefe	.10	.05	.01
135	Karl Malone	.40	.18	.05
136	Chris Morris	.10	.05	.01
137	John Stockton	.40	.18	.05
138	Greg Anthony	.10	.05	.01
139	Blue Edwards	.10	.05	.01
140	Kenny Gattison	.10	.05	.01
141	Chris King	.10	.05	.01
142	Byron Scott	.15	.07	.02
143	Calbert Cheaney	.10	.05	.01
144	Juwan Howard	1.00	.45	.12
145	Gheorghe Muresan	.20	.09	.03

		MINT	NRMT	EXC
☐ 146	Robert Pack	.10	.05	.01
☐ 147	Chris Webber	.40	.18	.05
☐ 148	Alan Henderson PP	.25	.11	.03
☐ 149	Eric Williams PP	.30	.14	.04
☐ 150	George Zidek PP	.10	.05	.01
☐ 151	Bob Sura PP	.30	.14	.04
☐ 152	Antonio McDyess PP	1.50	.70	.19
☐ 153	Theo Ratliff PP	.15	.07	.02
☐ 154	Joe Smith PP	2.00	.90	.25
☐ 155	Brent Barry PP	.75	.35	.09
☐ 156	Sasha Danilovic PP	.10	.05	.01
☐ 157	Kurt Thomas PP	.50	.23	.06
☐ 158	Shawn Respert PP	.10	.05	.01
☐ 159	Kevin Garnett PP	5.00	2.20	.60
☐ 160	Ed O'Bannon PP	.60	.25	.07
☐ 161	Jerry Stackhouse PP	3.00	1.35	.35
☐ 162	Michael Finley PP	2.00	.90	.25
☐ 163	Arvydas Sabonis PP	1.25	.55	.16
☐ 164	Cory Alexander PP	.10	.05	.01
☐ 165	Damon Stoudamire PP	4.00	1.80	.50
☐ 166	Bryant Reeves PP	1.00	.45	.12
☐ 167	Rasheed Wallace PP	.75	.35	.09
☐ C1	H.Olajuwon Comm.	25.00	11.00	3.10

1995-96 SP All-Stars

Randomly inserted in packs at a rate of one in 5, this 30-card set features 24 players from the 1996 NBA All-Star game in addition to six future All-Star athletes. Each card features a double die-cut design and silver foil stamping.

		MINT	NRMT	EXC
	COMPLETE SET (30)	80.00	36.00	10.00
	COMMON CARD (AS1-AS30)	.75	.35	.09
☐ AS1	Anfernee Hardaway	10.00	4.50	1.25
☐ AS2	Michael Jordan	20.00	9.00	2.50
☐ AS3	Grant Hill	5.00	2.20	.60
☐ AS4	Scottie Pippen	4.00	1.80	.50
☐ AS5	Shaquille O'Neal	6.00	2.70	.75
☐ AS6	Vin Baker	1.25	.55	.16
☐ AS7	Terrell Brandon	.75	.35	.09
☐ AS8	Patrick Ewing	1.25	.55	.16
☐ AS9	Juwan Howard	3.00	1.35	.35
☐ AS10	Reggie Miller	1.50	.70	.19
☐ AS11	Alonzo Mourning	1.25	.55	.16
☐ AS12	Glen Rice	.75	.35	.09
☐ AS13	Clyde Drexler	1.50	.70	.19
☐ AS14	Jason Kidd	3.00	1.35	.35
☐ AS15	Charles Barkley	2.00	.90	.25
☐ AS16	Shawn Kemp	4.00	1.80	.50
☐ AS17	Hakeem Olajuwon	3.00	1.35	.35
☐ AS18	Sean Elliott	.75	.35	.09
☐ AS19	Karl Malone	1.25	.55	.16
☐ AS20	Dikembe Mutombo	.75	.35	.09
☐ AS21	Gary Payton	2.00	.90	.25
☐ AS22	Mitch Richmond	1.25	.55	.16
☐ AS23	David Robinson	2.50	1.10	.30
☐ AS24	John Stockton	1.25	.55	.16
☐ AS25	Jerry Stackhouse	5.00	2.20	.60
☐ AS26	Damon Stoudamire	6.00	2.70	.75
☐ AS27	Rasheed Wallace	1.25	.55	.16
☐ AS28	Kevin Garnett	10.00	4.50	1.25
☐ AS29	Antonio McDyess	2.50	1.10	.30
☐ AS30	Joe Smith	3.00	1.35	.35

1995-96 SP All-Stars Gold

Randomly inserted in packs at a rate of one in 61, this 30-card set parallels the more common silver All-Stars inserts. The main difference in design is the use of gold foil on the card fronts (rather than silver). Please refer to the multiplier provided below (coupled with All-Stars prices listed in the previous set) to ascertain value of Gold cards.

	MINT	NRMT	EXC
COMPLETE SET (30)	600.00	275.00	75.00
COMMON CARD (AS1-AS30)	2.00	.90	.25
*GOLD STARS: 4X to 8X VALUE			
*GOLD ROOKIES: 3X to 6X VALUE			

1995-96 SP Holoviews

Randomly inserted in packs at a rate of one in 7, this 40-card set features a selection of youngsters and veteran stars from all 29 teams. Each card utilizes the special Holoview technology and features four holographic head shot images in the background.

	MINT	NRMT	EXC
COMPLETE SET (40)	150.00	70.00	19.00
COMMON CARD (PC1-PC40)	1.25	.55	.16

☐	PC1	Mookie Blaylock	2.00	.90	.25
☐	PC2	Eric Williams	1.25	.55	.16
☐	PC3	Larry Johnson	2.50	1.10	.30
☐	PC4	George Zidek	1.25	.55	.16
☐	PC5	Michael Jordan	40.00	18.00	5.00
☐	PC6	Bob Sura	1.25	.55	.16
☐	PC7	Jason Kidd	6.00	2.70	.75
☐	PC8	Cherokee Parks	1.25	.55	.16
☐	PC9	Antonio McDyess	5.00	2.20	.60
☐	PC10	Grant Hill	10.00	4.50	1.25
☐	PC11	Theo Ratliff	1.25	.55	.16
☐	PC12	Joe Smith	6.00	2.70	.75
☐	PC13	Latrell Sprewell	2.00	.90	.25
☐	PC14	Hakeem Olajuwon	6.00	2.70	.75
☐	PC15	Travis Best	1.25	.55	.16
☐	PC16	Brent Barry	2.50	1.10	.30
☐	PC17	Nick Van Exel	2.00	.90	.25
☐	PC18	Kurt Thomas	1.25	.55	.16
☐	PC19	Shawn Respert	1.25	.55	.16
☐	PC20	Glenn Robinson	3.00	1.35	.35
☐	PC21	Christian Laettner	1.25	.55	.16
☐	PC22	Ed O'Bannon	2.00	.90	.25
☐	PC23	Patrick Ewing	2.50	1.10	.30
☐	PC24	Anfernee Hardaway	20.00	9.00	2.50
☐	PC25	Shaquille O'Neal	12.00	5.50	1.50
☐	PC26	Jerry Stackhouse	10.00	4.50	1.25
☐	PC27	Mario Bennett	1.25	.55	.16
☐	PC28	Michael Finley	6.00	2.70	.75
☐	PC29	Randolph Childress	1.25	.55	.16
☐	PC30	Brian Grant	1.25	.55	.16
☐	PC31	Mitch Richmond	2.50	1.10	.30
☐	PC32	Cory Alexander	1.25	.55	.16
☐	PC33	David Robinson	5.00	2.20	.60
☐	PC34	Sherell Ford	1.25	.55	.16
☐	PC35	Shawn Kemp	8.00	3.60	1.00
☐	PC36	Damon Stoudamire	12.00	5.50	1.50
☐	PC37	Greg Ostertag	1.25	.55	.16
☐	PC38	Bryant Reeves	3.00	1.35	.35
☐	PC39	Juwan Howard	6.00	2.70	.75
☐	PC40	Rasheed Wallace	2.50	1.10	.30

☐	PC1	Mookie Blaylock	8.00	3.60	1.00
☐	PC2	Eric Williams	6.00	2.70	.75
☐	PC3	Larry Johnson	12.00	5.50	1.50
☐	PC4	George Zidek	6.00	2.70	.75
☐	PC5	Michael Jordan	200.00	90.00	25.00
☐	PC6	Bob Sura	6.00	2.70	.75
☐	PC7	Jason Kidd	30.00	13.50	3.70
☐	PC8	Cherokee Parks	6.00	2.70	.75
☐	PC9	Antonio McDyess	25.00	11.00	3.10
☐	PC10	Grant Hill	50.00	22.00	6.25
☐	PC11	Theo Ratliff	6.00	2.70	.75
☐	PC12	Joe Smith	30.00	13.50	3.70
☐	PC13	Latrell Sprewell	8.00	3.60	1.00
☐	PC14	Hakeem Olajuwon	30.00	13.50	3.70
☐	PC15	Travis Best	6.00	2.70	.75
☐	PC16	Brent Barry	12.00	5.50	1.50
☐	PC17	Nick Van Exel	10.00	4.50	1.25
☐	PC18	Kurt Thomas	6.00	2.70	.75
☐	PC19	Shawn Respert	6.00	2.70	.75
☐	PC20	Glenn Robinson	15.00	6.75	1.85
☐	PC21	Christian Laettner	8.00	3.60	1.00
☐	PC22	Ed O'Bannon	10.00	4.50	1.25
☐	PC23	Patrick Ewing	12.00	5.50	1.50
☐	PC24	Anfernee Hardaway	100.00	45.00	12.50
☐	PC25	Shaquille O'Neal	70.00	32.00	8.75
☐	PC26	Jerry Stackhouse	50.00	22.00	6.25
☐	PC27	Mario Bennett	6.00	2.70	.75
☐	PC28	Michael Finley	30.00	13.50	3.70
☐	PC29	Randolph Childress	6.00	2.70	.75
☐	PC30	Brian Grant	6.00	2.70	.75
☐	PC31	Mitch Richmond	12.00	5.50	1.50
☐	PC32	Cory Alexander	6.00	2.70	.75
☐	PC33	David Robinson	25.00	11.00	3.10
☐	PC34	Sherell Ford	6.00	2.70	.75
☐	PC35	Shawn Kemp	40.00	18.00	5.00
☐	PC36	Damon Stoudamire	60.00	27.00	7.50
☐	PC37	Greg Ostertag	6.00	2.70	.75
☐	PC38	Bryant Reeves	15.00	6.75	1.85
☐	PC39	Juwan Howard	30.00	13.50	3.70
☐	PC40	Rasheed Wallace	12.00	5.50	1.50

1995-96 SP Holoview Die Cuts

Randomly inserted in packs at a rate of one in 76, this 40-card set parallels the more common Holoview inserts. Unlike the basic Holoview inserts, each Holoview Die Cut insert features a tiled, die cut top border.

	MINT	NRMT	EXC
COMP.SET (40)	900.00	400.00	110.00
COMMON CARD (PC1-PC40)	6.00	2.70	.75

1995-96 SP Jordan Collection

Randomly inserted at a rate of one in every 29 packs, these four cards cards continue the collection of Michael Jordan commemorative cards issued across all of Upper Deck's various 1995-96 brands.

	MINT	NRMT	EXC
COMPLETE SET (4)	40.00	18.00	5.00
COMMON CARD (JC17-JC20)	12.00	5.50	1.50

		MINT	NRMT	EXC
☐ JC17	Michael Jordan	12.00	5.50	1.50
☐ JC18	Michael Jordan	12.00	5.50	1.50
☐ JC19	Michael Jordan	12.00	5.50	1.50
☐ JC20	Michael Jordan	12.00	5.50	1.50

1994-95 SP Championship

The premier edition of the 1994-95 SP Championship series (made by Upper Deck) consists of 135 standard size cards issued in six-card foil packs, each with a suggested retail price of $2.99. SP Championship cards were shipped exclusively to retail outlets. Card fronts feature full-bleed, color action photos with a foil SP Championship logo. The player's name runs up the side of the card in small gold foil print. Team name is contained in a foil oval. After a Road to the Finals (1-27) subset, the cards are grouped alphabetically within team order. Rookie Cards of note in this set include Grant Hill, Juwan Howard, Eddie Jones, Jason Kidd and Glenn Robinson.

		MINT	NRMT	EXC
	COMPLETE SET (135)	30.00	13.50	3.70
	COMMON CARD (1-135)	.10	.05	.01
☐ 1	Mookie Blaylock RF	.10	.05	.01
☐ 2	Dominique Wilkins RF	.15	.07	.02
☐ 3	Alonzo Mourning RF	.25	.11	.03
☐ 4	Michael Jordan RF	4.00	1.80	.50
☐ 5	Mark Price RF	.10	.05	.01
☐ 6	Jamal Mashburn RF	.15	.07	.02
☐ 7	Dikembe Mutombo RF	.15	.07	.02
☐ 8	Grant Hill RF	2.00	.90	.25
☐ 9	Latrell Sprewell RF	.10	.05	.01
☐ 10	Hakeem Olajuwon RF	.50	.23	.06
☐ 11	Reggie Miller RF	.25	.11	.03
☐ 12	Loy Vaught RF	.10	.05	.01
☐ 13	Nick Van Exel RF	.60	.25	.07
☐ 14	Glen Rice RF	.10	.05	.01
☐ 15	Glenn Robinson RF	.60	.25	.07
☐ 16	Isaiah Rider RF	.10	.05	.01
☐ 17	Kenny Anderson RF	.10	.05	.01
☐ 18	Patrick Ewing RF	.25	.11	.03
☐ 19	Shaquille O'Neal RF	1.00	.45	.12
☐ 20	Dana Barros RF	.10	.05	.01
☐ 21	Charles Barkley RF	.30	.14	.04
☐ 22	Clifford Robinson RF	.10	.05	.01
☐ 23	Mitch Richmond RF	.10	.05	.01
☐ 24	David Robinson RF	.40	.18	.05
☐ 25	Shawn Kemp RF	.60	.25	.07
☐ 26	Karl Malone RF	.25	.11	.03
☐ 27	Chris Webber RF	.25	.11	.03
☐ 28	Stacey Augmon	.15	.07	.02
☐ 29	Mookie Blaylock	.15	.07	.02
☐ 30	Grant Long	.10	.05	.01
☐ 31	Steve Smith	.15	.07	.02
☐ 32	Dee Brown	.10	.05	.01
☐ 33	Eric Montross	.25	.11	.03
☐ 34	Dino Radja	.25	.11	.03
☐ 35	Dominique Wilkins	.25	.11	.03
☐ 36	Muggsy Bogues	.15	.07	.02
☐ 37	Scott Burrell	.10	.05	.01
☐ 38	Larry Johnson	.40	.18	.05
☐ 39	Alonzo Mourning	.50	.23	.06
☐ 40	B.J. Armstrong	.10	.05	.01
☐ 41	Michael Jordan	8.00	3.60	1.00
☐ 42	Toni Kukoc	.30	.14	.04
☐ 43	Scottie Pippen	1.25	.55	.16
☐ 44	Tyrone Hill	.10	.05	.01
☐ 45	Chris Mills	.25	.11	.03
☐ 46	Mark Price	.10	.05	.01
☐ 47	John Williams	.10	.05	.01
☐ 48	Jim Jackson	.75	.35	.09
☐ 49	Jason Kidd	3.00	1.35	.35
☐ 50	Jamal Mashburn	.30	.14	.04
☐ 51	Roy Tarpley	.10	.05	.01
☐ 52	Mahmoud Abdul-Rauf	.15	.07	.02
☐ 53	Dikembe Mutombo	.25	.11	.03
☐ 54	Rodney Rogers	.10	.05	.01
☐ 55	Bryant Stith	.10	.05	.01
☐ 56	Joe Dumars	.25	.11	.03
☐ 57	Grant Hill	5.00	2.20	.60
☐ 58	Lindsey Hunter	.10	.05	.01
☐ 59	Terry Mills	.10	.05	.01
☐ 60	Tim Hardaway	.25	.11	.03
☐ 61	Donyell Marshall	.15	.07	.02
☐ 62	Chris Mullin	.25	.11	.03
☐ 63	Latrell Sprewell	.75	.35	.09
☐ 64	Sam Cassell	.25	.11	.03
☐ 65	Clyde Drexler	.50	.23	.06
☐ 66	Vernon Maxwell	.10	.05	.01
☐ 67	Hakeem Olajuwon	1.00	.45	.12
☐ 68	Dale Davis	.10	.05	.01
☐ 69	Mark Jackson	.10	.05	.01
☐ 70	Reggie Miller	.50	.23	.06
☐ 71	Rik Smits	.25	.11	.03
☐ 72	Terry Dehere	.10	.05	.01
☐ 73	Lamond Murray	.15	.07	.02
☐ 74	Pooh Richardson	.10	.05	.01
☐ 75	Loy Vaught	.10	.05	.01
☐ 76	Cedric Ceballos	.25	.11	.03
☐ 77	Vlade Divac	.25	.11	.03
☐ 78	Eddie Jones	1.00	.45	.12

☐ 79	Nick Van Exel	.40	.18	.05
☐ 80	Bimbo Coles	.10	.05	.01
☐ 81	Billy Owens	.10	.05	.01
☐ 82	Glen Rice	.25	.11	.03
☐ 83	Kevin Willis	.10	.05	.01
☐ 84	Vin Baker	.50	.23	.06
☐ 85	Marty Conlon	.10	.05	.01
☐ 86	Eric Murdock	.10	.05	.01
☐ 87	Glenn Robinson	1.50	.70	.19
☐ 88	Tom Gugliotta	.25	.11	.03
☐ 89	Christian Laettner	.25	.11	.03
☐ 90	Isaiah Rider	.25	.11	.03
☐ 91	Doug West	.10	.05	.01
☐ 92	Kenny Anderson	.25	.11	.03
☐ 93	Benoit Benjamin	.10	.05	.01
☐ 94	Derrick Coleman	.10	.05	.01
☐ 95	Armon Gilliam	.10	.05	.01
☐ 96	Patrick Ewing	.40	.18	.05
☐ 97	Derek Harper	.10	.05	.01
☐ 98	Charles Oakley	.15	.07	.02
☐ 99	John Starks	.10	.05	.01
☐ 100	Nick Anderson	.25	.11	.03
☐ 101	Horace Grant	.25	.11	.03
☐ 102	Anfernee Hardaway	2.50	1.10	.30
☐ 103	Shaquille O'Neal	2.00	.90	.25
☐ 104	Dana Barros	.10	.05	.01
☐ 105	Shawn Bradley	.25	.11	.03
☐ 106	Clarence Weatherspoon	.15	.07	.02
☐ 107	Sharone Wright	.25	.11	.03
☐ 108	Charles Barkley	.60	.25	.07
☐ 109	Kevin Johnson	.25	.11	.03
☐ 110	Dan Majerle	.15	.07	.02
☐ 111	Wesley Person	1.00	.45	.12
☐ 112	Terry Porter	.10	.05	.01
☐ 113	Clifford Robinson	.25	.11	.03
☐ 114	Rod Strickland	.10	.05	.01
☐ 115	Buck Williams	.15	.07	.02
☐ 116	Brian Grant	.60	.25	.07
☐ 117	Mitch Richmond	.30	.14	.04
☐ 118	Spud Webb	.15	.07	.02
☐ 119	Walt Williams	.25	.11	.03
☐ 120	Vinny Del Negro	.10	.05	.01
☐ 121	Sean Elliott	.25	.11	.03
☐ 122	David Robinson	.75	.35	.09
☐ 123	Dennis Rodman	1.50	.70	.19
☐ 124	Kendall Gill	.10	.05	.01
☐ 125	Shawn Kemp	1.25	.55	.16
☐ 126	Gary Payton	.60	.25	.07
☐ 127	Detlef Schrempf	.15	.07	.02
☐ 128	David Benoit	.10	.05	.01
☐ 129	Jeff Hornacek	.15	.07	.02
☐ 130	Karl Malone	.40	.18	.05
☐ 131	John Stockton	.40	.18	.05
☐ 132	Rex Chapman	.10	.05	.01
☐ 133	Calbert Cheaney	.25	.11	.03
☐ 134	Juwan Howard	3.00	1.35	.35
☐ 135	Chris Webber	.50	.23	.06

1994-95 SP Championship Die Cuts

This 135-card parallel set is identical to the regular SP Championship series except for the die cut design on the cards as well as

the silver hologram on their backs. One die cut card was inserted in each pack. Please refer to the multipliers provide in the header to ascertain prices.

	MINT	NRMT	EXC
COMPLETE SET (135)	60.00	27.00	7.50
COMMON CARD (1-135)	.25	.11	.03
*DIE CUT STARS: 1.25X to 2.5X VALUE			
*DIE CUT ROOKIES: 1X to 2X VALUE			

1994-95 SP Championship Future Playoff Heroes

Randomly inserted at a rate of 1 in every 40 packs, this 10-card standard-size set spotlights up-and-coming NBA stars who figure to be Playoff Heroes in the coming years. Unlike, the glossy regular issue cards, these inserts feature a throwback design element incorporating basic cardboard-style backgrounds against glossy color player action photos. The set is sequenced in alphabetical order.

	MINT	NRMT	EXC
COMPLETE SET (10)	50.00	22.00	6.25
COMMON CARD (F1-F10)	1.25	.55	.16
☐ F1 Brian Grant	2.00	.90	.25
☐ F2 Anfernee Hardaway	15.00	6.75	1.85
☐ F3 Grant Hill	15.00	6.75	1.85
☐ F4 Eddie Jones	3.00	1.35	.35

		MINT	NRMT	EXC
☐ F5	Jamal Mashburn	2.00	.90	.25
☐ F6	Shaquille O'Neal	12.00	5.50	1.50
☐ F7	Isaiah Rider	1.25	.55	.16
☐ F8	Glenn Robinson	5.00	2.20	.60
☐ F9	Latrell Sprewell	1.25	.55	.16
☐ F10	Chris Webber	3.00	1.35	.35

1994-95 SP Championship Future Playoff Heroes Die Cuts

	MINT	NRMT	EXC
COMPLETE SET (10)	50.00	22.00	6.25
COMMON CARD (P1-P10)	1.00	.45	.12

		MINT	NRMT	EXC
☐ P1	Charles Barkley	4.00	1.80	.50
☐ P2	Michael Jordan	30.00	13.50	3.70
☐ P3	Shawn Kemp	8.00	3.60	1.00
☐ P4	Moses Malone	1.50	.70	.19
☐ P5	Reggie Miller	3.00	1.35	.35
☐ P6	Alonzo Mourning	3.00	1.35	.35
☐ P7	Dikembe Mutombo	1.00	.45	.12
☐ P8	Hakeem Olajuwon	6.00	2.70	.75
☐ P9	Robert Parish	1.00	.45	.12
☐ P10	John Stockton	2.50	1.10	.30

Randomly inserted at a rate of 1 in every 300 packs, this 10 card set parallels the more common non die cut cards. They differ from the basic inserts in their die cut design and the presence of silver (rather than gold) holograms on their backs. Please refer to the multiplier provided in the header to ascertain values.

	MINT	NRMT	EXC
COMPLETE SET (10)	325.00	145.00	40.00
COMMON CARD (F1-F10)	6.00	2.70	.75
*DIE CUTS: 3X to 6X VALUE			

1994-95 SP Championship Playoff Heroes

Randomly inserted at a rate of one in every 15 packs, this 10-card standard size set features active NBA Playoff performers. Unlike, the glossy regular issue cards, these inserts feature a throwback design element incorporating basic cardboard-style backgrounds against glossy color player action photos. A number of cards slipped through production with scuffed logos on front. In addition, some others also had "Future Playoff Heroes" logos rather than the regular "Playoff Heroes" logos. None of these variations trade for a premium. The set is sequenced in alphabetical order.

1994-95 SP Championship Playoff Heroes Die Cuts

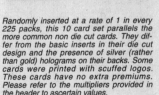

Randomly inserted at a rate of 1 in every 225 packs, this 10 card set parallels the more common non die cut cards. They differ from the basic inserts in their die cut design and the presence of silver (rather than gold) holograms on their backs. Some cards were printed with scuffed logos. These cards have no extra premiums. Please refer to the multipliers provided in the header to ascertain values.

	MINT	NRMT	EXC
COMPLETE SET (10)	250.00	110.00	31.00
COMMON CARD (P1-P10)	5.00	2.20	.60
*DIE CUTS: 2.5X to 5X VALUE			

1995-96 SP Championship

The 1995-96 SP Championship set was issued in one series totaling 146 cards. The 6-card packs retailed for $2.99 each. The set, issued in early-May, 1996 to retail outlets only, features full color action shots against an all-foil background with player name, team and a head shot along the front borders. The set is sequenced in alphabetical order by team and includes many of the top stars in the 1996 playoffs along with a special subset: Race for the Playoffs (118-146). Rookie Cards of note include Michael Finley, Kevin Garnett, Antonio McDyess, Jerry Stackhouse and Damon Stoudamire.

	MINT	NRMT	EXC
COMPLETE SET (146)	40.00	18.00	5.00
COMMON CARD (1-146)	.10	.05	.01

		MINT	NRMT	EXC
☐ 1	Stacey Augmon	.15	.07	.02
☐ 2	Mookie Blaylock	.20	.09	.03
☐ 3	Alan Henderson	.25	.11	.03
☐ 4	Steve Smith	.20	.09	.03
☐ 5	Dana Barros	.10	.05	.01
☐ 6	Dee Brown	.10	.05	.01
☐ 7	Eric Montross	.10	.05	.01
☐ 8	Dino Radja	.20	.09	.03
☐ 9	Eric Williams	.30	.14	.04
☐ 10	Kenny Anderson	.15	.07	.02
☐ 11	Larry Johnson	.40	.18	.05
☐ 12	Glen Rice	.20	.09	.03
☐ 13	George Zidek	.10	.05	.01
☐ 14	Toni Kukoc	.25	.11	.03
☐ 15	Scottie Pippen	1.25	.55	.16
☐ 16	Dennis Rodman Bulls	2.50	1.10	.30
☐ 17	Michael Jordan	5.00	2.20	.60
☐ 18	Terrell Brandon	.20	.09	.03
☐ 19	Danny Ferry	.10	.05	.01
☐ 20	Chris Mills	.10	.05	.01
☐ 21	Bobby Phills	.10	.05	.01
☐ 22	Jim Jackson	.20	.09	.03
☐ 23	Popeye Jones	.10	.05	.01
☐ 24	Jason Kidd	1.00	.45	.12
☐ 25	Jamal Mashburn	.25	.11	.03
☐ 26	Mahmoud Abdul-Rauf	.10	.05	.01
☐ 27	Dale Ellis	.10	.05	.01
☐ 28	Antonio McDyess	1.50	.70	.19
☐ 29	Dikembe Mutombo	.20	.09	.03
☐ 30	Joe Dumars	.20	.09	.03
☐ 31	Grant Hill	1.50	.70	.19
☐ 32	Allan Houston	.20	.09	.03
☐ 33	Otis Thorpe	.15	.07	.02
☐ 34	Tim Hardaway	.20	.09	.03
☐ 35	Chris Mullin	.15	.07	.02
☐ 36	Latrell Sprewell	.20	.09	.03
☐ 37	Joe Smith	2.00	.90	.25
☐ 38	Sam Cassell	.15	.07	.02
☐ 39	Clyde Drexler	.50	.23	.06
☐ 40	Robert Horry	.15	.07	.02
☐ 41	Hakeem Olajuwon	1.00	.45	.12
☐ 42	Dale Davis	.10	.05	.01
☐ 43	Derrick McKey	.10	.05	.01
☐ 44	Reggie Miller	.50	.23	.06
☐ 45	Rik Smits	.20	.09	.03
☐ 46	Brent Barry	.75	.35	.09
☐ 47	Lamond Murray	.10	.05	.01
☐ 48	Loy Vaught	.15	.07	.02
☐ 49	Brian Williams	.10	.05	.01
☐ 50	Cedric Ceballos	.20	.09	.03
☐ 51	Magic Johnson	1.25	.55	.16
☐ 52	Eddie Jones	.30	.14	.04
☐ 53	Nick Van Exel	.30	.14	.04
☐ 54	Sasha Danilovic	.10	.05	.01
☐ 55	Alonzo Mourning	.40	.18	.05
☐ 56	Billy Owens	.10	.05	.01
☐ 57	Kevin Willis	.10	.05	.01
☐ 58	Vin Baker	.40	.18	.05
☐ 59	Sherman Douglas	.10	.05	.01
☐ 60	Lee Mayberry	.10	.05	.01
☐ 61	Glenn Robinson	.50	.23	.06
☐ 62	Kevin Garnett	5.00	2.20	.60
☐ 63	Tom Gugliotta	.20	.09	.03
☐ 64	Christian Laettner	.15	.07	.02
☐ 65	Isaiah Rider	.20	.09	.03
☐ 66	Chris Childs	.10	.05	.01
☐ 67	Kendall Gill	.10	.05	.01
☐ 68	Armon Gilliam	.10	.05	.01
☐ 69	Ed O'Bannon	.60	.25	.07
☐ 70	Patrick Ewing	.40	.18	.05
☐ 71	Derek Harper	.15	.07	.02
☐ 72	Charles Oakley	.10	.05	.01
☐ 73	John Starks	.15	.07	.02
☐ 74	Horace Grant	.20	.09	.03
☐ 75	Anfernee Hardaway	2.50	1.10	.30
☐ 76	Shaquille O'Neal	2.00	.90	.25
☐ 77	Dennis Scott	.20	.09	.03
☐ 78	Derrick Coleman	.15	.07	.02
☐ 79	Trevor Ruffin	.10	.05	.01
☐ 80	Jerry Stackhouse	3.00	1.35	.35
☐ 81	Clarence Weatherspoon	.20	.09	.03
☐ 82	Charles Barkley	.60	.25	.07
☐ 83	Kevin Johnson	.20	.09	.03
☐ 84	Kevin Johnson	.20	.09	.03
☐ 85	Danny Manning	.15	.07	.02
☐ 86	Randolph Childress	.10	.05	.01
☐ 87	Clifford Robinson	.20	.09	.03
☐ 88	Arvydas Sabonis	1.25	.55	.16
☐ 89	Rod Strickland	.10	.05	.01
☐ 90	Tyus Edney	.75	.35	.09
☐ 91	Brian Grant	.10	.05	.01
☐ 92	Mitch Richmond	.30	.14	.04
☐ 93	Walt Williams	.15	.07	.02
☐ 94	Sean Elliott	.15	.07	.02
☐ 95	Avery Johnson	.15	.07	.02
☐ 96	Chuck Person	.10	.05	.01
☐ 97	David Robinson	.75	.35	.09
☐ 98	Shawn Kemp	1.25	.55	.16
☐ 99	Gary Payton	.60	.25	.07
☐ 100	Sam Perkins	.15	.07	.02
☐ 101	Detlef Schrempf	.20	.09	.03
☐ 102	Ed Pinckney	.10	.05	.01

			MINT	NRMT	EXC
☐ 103	Tracy Murray	.10	.05	.01
☐ 104	Alvin Robertson	.10	.05	.01
☐ 105	Damon Stoudamire	4.00	1.80	.50
☐ 106	Jeff Hornacek	.15	.07	.02
☐ 107	Karl Malone	.40	.18	.05
☐ 108	Chris Morris	.10	.05	.01
☐ 109	John Stockton	.40	.18	.05
☐ 110	Greg Anthony	.10	.05	.01
☐ 111	Blue Edwards	.10	.05	.01
☐ 112	Bryant Reeves	1.00	.45	.12
☐ 113	Byron Scott	.15	.07	.02
☐ 114	Juwan Howard	1.00	.45	.12
☐ 115	Gheorghe Muresan	.20	.09	.03
☐ 116	Rasheed Wallace	.75	.35	.09
☐ 117	Chris Webber	.40	.18	.05
☐ 118	Mookie Blaylock RP	.15	.07	.02
☐ 119	Dana Barros RP	.10	.05	.01
☐ 120	Larry Johnson RP	.15	.07	.02
☐ 121	Michael Jordan RP	2.50	1.10	.30
☐ 122	Terrell Brandon RP	.10	.05	.01
☐ 123	Jason Kidd RP	.50	.23	.06
☐ 124	Mahmoud Abdul-Rauf RP	.10	.05	.01
☐ 125	Grant Hill RP	.75	.35	.09
☐ 126	Latrell Sprewell RP	.15	.07	.02
☐ 127	Hakeem Olajuwon RP	.50	.23	.06
☐ 128	Reggie Miller RP	.25	.11	.03
☐ 129	Loy Vaught RP	.10	.05	.01
☐ 130	Magic Johnson RP	.60	.25	.07
☐ 131	Alonzo Mourning RP	.15	.07	.02
☐ 132	Vin Baker RP	.10	.05	.01
☐ 133	Tom Gugliotta RP	.15	.07	.02
☐ 134	Ed O'Bannon RP	.10	.05	.01
☐ 135	Patrick Ewing RP	.15	.07	.02
☐ 136	Anfernee Hardaway RP	1.25	.55	.16
☐ 137	Jerry Stackhouse RP	1.25	.55	.16
☐ 138	Charles Barkley RP	.30	.14	.04
☐ 139	Clifford Robinson RP	.15	.07	.02
☐ 140	Mitch Richmond RP	.15	.07	.02
☐ 141	David Robinson RP	.40	.18	.05
☐ 142	Shawn Kemp RP	.60	.25	.07
☐ 143	Damon Stoudamire RP	1.50	.70	.19
☐ 144	John Stockton RP	.15	.07	.02
☐ 145	Bryant Reeves RP	.40	.18	.05
☐ 146	Juwan Howard RP	.50	.23	.06

1995-96 SP Championship Champions of the Court

Randomly inserted in packs at a rate of one in 7, cards from this 30-card set feature one top star from each NBA team and an additional card of Michael Jordan. In this special horizontal design, there is one action color photo on the left side and the same action photo in black and white on the right side. The main feature of the card is a cel photo featuring a headshot with a protective film covering the cell photo on the front of the card. When you turn the card over you see the same photo of the player. Each card is printed on special transparent

chromium material. Unpeeled cards are priced below. Peeled cards are valued at about ten to twenty-five percent less.

		MINT	NRMT	EXC
COMPLETE SET (30)		125.00	55.00	15.50
COMMON CARD (C1-C30)		1.00	.45	.12
☐ C1	Steve Smith	1.00	.45	.12
☐ C2	Dino Radja	1.00	.45	.12
☐ C3	Glen Rice	1.50	.70	.19
☐ C4	Scottie Pippen	8.00	3.60	1.00
☐ C5	Terrell Brandon	1.00	.45	.12
☐ C6	Jason Kidd	6.00	2.70	.75
☐ C7	Dikembe Mutombo	1.50	.70	.19
☐ C8	Grant Hill	10.00	4.50	1.25
☐ C9	Joe Smith	6.00	2.70	.75
☐ C10	Hakeem Olajuwon	6.00	2.70	.75
☐ C11	Reggie Miller	3.00	1.35	.35
☐ C12	Loy Vaught	1.00	.45	.12
☐ C13	Magic Johnson	8.00	3.60	1.00
☐ C14	Alonzo Mourning	2.50	1.10	.30
☐ C15	Vin Baker	2.50	1.10	.30
☐ C16	Kevin Garnett	15.00	6.75	1.85
☐ C17	Ed O'Bannon	2.00	.90	.25
☐ C18	Patrick Ewing	2.50	1.10	.30
☐ C19	Shaquille O'Neal	12.00	5.50	1.50
☐ C20	Jerry Stackhouse	10.00	4.50	1.25
☐ C21	Charles Barkley	4.00	1.80	.50
☐ C22	Clifford Robinson	1.00	.45	.12
☐ C23	Mitch Richmond	2.00	.90	.25
☐ C24	David Robinson	5.00	2.20	.60
☐ C25	Shawn Kemp	8.00	3.60	1.00
☐ C26	Damon Stoudamire	12.00	5.50	1.50
☐ C27	John Stockton	2.50	1.10	.30
☐ C28	Bryant Reeves	3.00	1.35	.35
☐ C29	Juwan Howard	6.00	2.70	.75
☐ C30	Michael Jordan	30.00	13.50	3.70

1995-96 SP Championship Champions of the Court Die-Cut

Randomly inserted into packs at a rate of one in 75, this set is a parallel of the more common Champions of the Court inserts. The only difference is the borders contain two die-cut designs. Please refer to the multiplier provided below (coupled with the prices of the corresponding regular Champions of the Court inserts) for values on the die-cut cards. Unpeeled caards are priced below. Peeled cards are valued at about ten to twenty-five percent less.

	MINT	NRMT	EXC
COMPLETE SET (30)	800.00	350.00	100.00
COMMON CARD (C1-C30)	5.00	2.20	.60
*STARS: 2.5X to 5X VALUE			
*ROOKIES: 2X to 4X VALUE			

1995-96 SP Championship Championship Shots

Inserted at a rate of one per magazine and Wal-Mart pack, as well as randomly in one in every three regular retail packs, this 20-card set features intense, closeup shots of many of the top NBA stars. Despite their status as inserts, these cards are actually easier to pull from packs than regular-issue cards. The design is highlighted by a horizontal, silver-foil, saw-tooth die cut element on the side border.

	MINT	NRMT	EXC
COMPLETE SET (20)	30.00	13.50	3.70
COMMON CARD (S1-S20)	.25	.11	.03

		MINT	NRMT	EXC
☐ S1	Antonio McDyess	2.00	.90	.25
☐ S2	Nick Van Exel	.60	.25	.07
☐ S3	Michael Finley	2.50	1.10	.30
☐ S4	Anfernee Hardaway	5.00	2.20	.60
☐ S5	Latrell Sprewell	.35	.16	.04
☐ S6	Brian Grant	.25	.11	.03
☐ S7	Juwan Howard	2.00	.90	.25
☐ S8	Ed O'Bannon	.60	.25	.07
☐ S9	Kevin Garnett	6.00	2.70	.75
☐ S10	Charles Barkley	1.25	.55	.16
☐ S11	Joe Smith	2.50	1.10	.30
☐ S12	Patrick Ewing	.75	.35	.09
☐ S13	Brent Barry	1.00	.45	.12
☐ S14	Dennis Rodman Bulls	5.00	2.20	.60
☐ S15	Jerry Stackhouse	4.00	1.80	.50
☐ S16	Michael Jordan	10.00	4.50	1.25
☐ S17	Jalen Rose	.25	.11	.03
☐ S18	Jamal Mashburn	.50	.23	.06
☐ S19	Theo Ratliff	.25	.11	.03
☐ S20	Shaquille O'Neal	4.00	1.80	.50

1995-96 SP Championship Championship Shots Gold

Randomly inserted into one in every 62 packs, these 20 cards parallel the more common Championship Shots inserts. Their distinctive gold foil, saw-tooth front borders (instead of silver) differentiate them from the regular Championship Shots inserts. Please refer to the multiplier provided below (coupled with the prices of the corresponding regular Championship Shots inserts) to ascertain value for Gold singles.

	MINT	NRMT	EXC
COMPLETE SET (20)	300.00	135.00	38.00
COMMON CARD (S1-S20)	2.50	1.10	.30
*GOLD STARS: 5X to 10X BASIC CARDS			
*GOLD ROOKIES: 4X to 8X BASIC CARDS			

1995-96 SP Championship Jordan Collection

Randomly inserted in packs at a rate of one in 29, this 4-card set completes the run of Jordan cards across Upper Deck's 1995-96 brands.

		MINT	NRMT	EXC
COMPLETE SET (4)		40.00	18.00	5.00
COMMON CARD (JC21-JC24)		12.00	5.50	1.50

		MINT	NRMT	EXC
☐ JC17	Michael Jordan SPC	12.00	5.50	1.50
☐ JC18	Michael Jordan SPC	12.00	5.50	1.50
☐ JC19	Michael Jordan SPC	12.00	5.50	1.50
☐ JC20	Michael Jordan SPC	12.00	5.50	1.50

1996 SPx

The premier edition of Upper Deck's super-premium SPx basketball set contains 50

cards featuring only the top stars and youngsters in the NBA. The set marked a number of technological "firsts" in the basketball card market including first standalone all-Holoview set and first complete, perimeter die cut set. To create the holoview imagery, each athlete was videotaped while rotating on a turntable. The individual frames of videotape were then synthesized to produce a 50-degree, three-dimensional picture. Each card features super premium 32 point thick stock. Each pack contained only one card and carried a suggested retail price of $2.99. Each box contained 36 packs. In addition, to the 50 regular cards, a special Record Breaker card commemorating Michael Jordan's eighth scoring title (1:75 packs) and Tribute card commemorating Anfernee Hardaway's accomplishments in the NBA (1:24 packs) were issued. Also, two separate trade cards were available for signed Jordan and Hardaway cards. The odds of receiving a Jordan trade card were 1:34,560 packs. The Hardaway trade card was more than 25 times easier to pull at a rate of 1,345 packs.

	MINT	NRMT	EXC
COMPLETE SET (50)	100.00	45.00	12.50
COMMON CARD (1-50)	1.00	.45	.12
1 Stacey Augmon	1.25	.55	.16
2 Mookie Blaylock	1.25	.55	.16
3 Eric Montross	1.00	.45	.12
4 Eric Williams	1.00	.45	.12
5 Larry Johnson	2.00	.90	.25
6 George Zidek	1.00	.45	.12
7 Jason Caffey	1.00	.45	.12
8 Michael Jordan	25.00	11.00	3.10
9 Chris Mills	1.00	.45	.12
10 Bob Sura	1.00	.45	.12
11 Jason Kidd	5.00	2.20	.60
12 Jamal Mashburn	1.50	.70	.19
13 Antonio McDyess	3.00	1.35	.35
14 Jalen Rose	1.00	.45	.12
15 Grant Hill	8.00	3.60	1.00
16 Theo Ratliff	1.00	.45	.12
17 Joe Smith	4.00	1.80	.50
18 Latrell Sprewell	1.25	.55	.16
19 Hakeem Olajuwon	5.00	2.20	.60
20 Reggie Miller	2.50	1.10	.30
21 Rik Smits	1.25	.55	.16
22 Brent Barry	1.50	.70	.19
23 Lamond Murray	1.00	.45	.12
24 Magic Johnson	6.00	2.70	.75
25 Eddie Jones	1.50	.70	.19
26 Nick Van Exel	1.50	.70	.19
27 Alonzo Mourning	2.00	.90	.25
28 Kurt Thomas	1.00	.45	.12
29 Vin Baker	2.00	.90	.25
30 Glenn Robinson	2.50	1.10	.30
31 Kevin Garnett	12.00	5.50	1.50
32 Ed O'Bannon	1.00	.45	.12
33 Patrick Ewing	2.00	.90	.25
34 Anfernee Hardaway	12.00	5.50	1.50
35 Shaquille O'Neal	10.00	4.50	1.25
36 Jerry Stackhouse	6.00	2.70	.75
37 Charles Barkley	3.00	1.35	.35
38 Michael Finley	4.00	1.80	.50
39 Randolph Childress	1.00	.45	.12
40 Gary Trent	1.00	.45	.12
41 Brian Grant	1.00	.45	.12
42 Mitch Richmond	1.50	.70	.19
43 David Robinson	4.00	1.80	.50
44 Shawn Kemp	6.00	2.70	.75
45 Gary Payton	3.00	1.35	.35
46 Damon Stoudamire	8.00	3.60	1.00
47 Karl Malone	2.00	.90	.25
48 John Stockton	2.00	.90	.25
49 Bryant Reeves	2.00	.90	.25
50 Rasheed Wallace	1.50	.70	.19
R1 Michael Jordan RB	30.00	13.50	3.70
T1 Anfernee Hardaway TRIB	15.00	6.75	1.85
NNO M.Jordan AU Trade	3500.00	1600.00	450.00
NNO A.Hardaway AU Trade	250.00	110.00	31.00

1996 SPx Gold

Cards in this set of 50 were randomly issued in packs at a rate of one in seven and parallel the regular issue set. The cards are differentiated by gold borders on the front. Please refer to the multipliers provided below (coupled with the prices of the regular issue cards) to ascertain value for Gold singles.

	MINT	NRMT	EXC
COMPLETE SET (50)	350.00	160.00	45.00
COMMON CARD (1-50)	3.00	1.35	.35

*GOLD STARS: 1.25X to 3X VALUE .

1996 SPx Holoview Heroes

Cards in this set of ten were randomly issued at a rate of one in every 24 packs

and feature ten NBA players with the potential to be named to the NBA Hall of Fame. These die-cut cards feature a combination of lithograph and holoview technology.

	MINT	NRMT	EXC
COMPLETE SET (10)	175.00	80.00	22.00
COMMON CARD (H1-H10)	8.00	3.60	1.00
☐ H1 Michael Jordan	60.00	27.00	7.50
☐ H2 Jason Kidd	12.00	5.50	1.50
☐ H3 Grant Hill	20.00	9.00	2.50
☐ H4 Joe Smith	10.00	4.50	1.25
☐ H5 Magic Johnson	15.00	6.75	1.85
☐ H6 Antonio McDyess	8.00	3.60	1.00
☐ H7 Anfernee Hardaway	30.00	13.50	3.70
☐ H8 Jerry Stackhouse	15.00	6.75	1.85
☐ H9 Damon Stoudamire	20.00	9.00	2.50
☐ H10 Shaquille O'Neal	25.00	11.00	3.10

1992-93 Stadium Club

The complete 1992-93 Stadium Club basketball set (created by Topps) consists of 400 standard-size cards, having been issued in two 200-card series. Both first and second series packs contained 15 cards with a suggested retail price of $1.79 per pack. Topps also issued, late in the season, second series 23-card jumbo packs. A Stadium Club membership form was inserted in every 15-card pack. The basic card fronts feature full-bleed color action player photos. The team name and player's name appear in gold foil stripes that cut across the bottom of the card and intersect the Stadium Club logo. On a col-

orful background of a basketball in a net, the horizontal backs present biography, The Sporting News Skills Rating System, player evaluation, 1991-92 season and career statistics, and a miniature representation of the player's first Topps card, which is confusingly referenced as "Topps Rookie Card" by Topps. The first series closes and the second series begins with a Members Choice (191-211) subset. Rookie Cards of note include Tom Gugliotta, Robert Horry, Christian Laettner, Alonzo Mourning, Shaquille O'Neal, Latrell Sprewell and Clarence Weatherspoon.

	MINT	NRMT	EXC
COMPLETE SET (400)	60.00	27.00	7.50
COMPLETE SERIES 1 (200)	20.00	9.00	2.50
COMPLETE SERIES 2 (200)	40.00	18.00	5.00
COMMON CARD (1-400)	.10	.05	.01
☐ 1 Michael Jordan	8.00	3.60	1.00
☐ 2 Greg Anthony	.10	.05	.01
☐ 3 Otis Thorpe	.20	.09	.03
☐ 4 Jim Les	.10	.05	.01
☐ 5 Kevin Willis	.10	.05	.01
☐ 6 Derek Harper	.20	.09	.03
☐ 7 Elden Campbell	.20	.09	.03
☐ 8 A.J. English	.10	.05	.01
☐ 9 Kenny Gattison	.10	.05	.01
☐ 10 Drazen Petrovic	.20	.09	.03
☐ 11 Chris Mullin	.20	.09	.03
☐ 12 Mark Price	.10	.05	.01
☐ 13 Karl Malone	.60	.25	.07
☐ 14 Gerald Glass	.10	.05	.01
☐ 15 Negele Knight	.10	.05	.01
☐ 16 Mark Macon	.10	.05	.01
☐ 17 Michael Cage	.10	.05	.01
☐ 18 Kevin Edwards	.10	.05	.01
☐ 19 Sherman Douglas	.10	.05	.01
☐ 20 Ron Harper	.10	.05	.01
☐ 21 Clifford Robinson	.30	.14	.04
☐ 22 Byron Scott	.20	.09	.03
☐ 23 Antoine Carr	.10	.05	.01
☐ 24 Greg Dreiling	.10	.05	.01
☐ 25 Bill Laimbeer	.20	.09	.03
☐ 26 Hersey Hawkins	.20	.09	.03
☐ 27 Will Perdue	.10	.05	.01
☐ 28 Todd Lichti	.10	.05	.01
☐ 29 Gary Grant	.10	.05	.01
☐ 30 Sam Perkins	.20	.09	.03
☐ 31 Jayson Williams	.10	.05	.01
☐ 32 Magic Johnson	2.00	.90	.25
☐ 33 Larry Bird	2.50	1.10	.30
☐ 34 Chris Morris	.10	.05	.01
☐ 35 Nick Anderson	.15	.07	.02
☐ 36 Scott Hastings	.10	.05	.01
☐ 37 Ledell Eackles	.10	.05	.01
☐ 38 Robert Pack	.10	.05	.01
☐ 39 Dana Barros	.20	.09	.03
☐ 40 Anthony Bonner	.10	.05	.01
☐ 41 J.R. Reid	.10	.05	.01
☐ 42 Tyrone Hill	.10	.05	.01
☐ 43 Rik Smits	.30	.14	.04
☐ 44 Kevin Duckworth	.10	.05	.01
☐ 45 LaSalle Thompson	.10	.05	.01
☐ 46 Brian Williams	.10	.05	.01
☐ 47 Willie Anderson	.10	.05	.01
☐ 48 Ken Norman	.10	.05	.01
☐ 49 Mike Iuzzolino	.10	.05	.01
☐ 50 Isiah Thomas	.40	.18	.05

#	Player			
☐ 51	Alec Kessler	.10	.05	.01
☐ 52	Johnny Dawkins	.10	.05	.01
☐ 53	Avery Johnson	.10	.05	.01
☐ 54	Stacey Augmon	.20	.09	.03
☐ 55	Charles Oakley	.10	.05	.01
☐ 56	Rex Chapman	.10	.05	.01
☐ 57	Charles Shackleford	.10	.05	.01
☐ 58	Jeff Ruland	.10	.05	.01
☐ 59	Craig Ehlo	.10	.05	.01
☐ 60	Jon Koncak	.10	.05	.01
☐ 61	Danny Schayes	.10	.05	.01
☐ 62	David Benoit	.10	.05	.01
☐ 63	Robert Parish	.30	.14	.04
☐ 64	Mookie Blaylock	.20	.09	.03
☐ 65	Sean Elliott	.30	.14	.04
☐ 66	Mark Aguirre	.10	.05	.01
☐ 67	Scott Williams	.10	.05	.01
☐ 68	Doug West	.10	.05	.01
☐ 69	Kenny Anderson	.30	.14	.04
☐ 70	Randy Brown	.10	.05	.01
☐ 71	Muggsy Bogues	.20	.09	.03
☐ 72	Spud Webb	.20	.09	.03
☐ 73	Sedale Threatt	.10	.05	.01
☐ 74	Chris Gatling	.10	.05	.01
☐ 75	Derrick McKey	.10	.05	.01
☐ 76	Sleepy Floyd	.10	.05	.01
☐ 77	Chris Jackson	.20	.09	.03
☐ 78	Thurl Bailey	.10	.05	.01
☐ 79	Steve Smith	.50	.23	.06
☐ 80	Jerrod Mustaf	.10	.05	.01
☐ 81	Anthony Bowie	.10	.05	.01
☐ 82	John Williams	.10	.05	.01
☐ 83	Paul Graham	.10	.05	.01
☐ 84	Willie Burton	.10	.05	.01
☐ 85	Vernon Maxwell	.10	.05	.01
☐ 86	Stacey King	.10	.05	.01
☐ 87	B.J. Armstrong	.10	.05	.01
☐ 88	Kevin Gamble	.10	.05	.01
☐ 89	Terry Catledge	.10	.05	.01
☐ 90	Jeff Malone	.10	.05	.01
☐ 91	Sam Bowie	.10	.05	.01
☐ 92	Orlando Woolridge	.10	.05	.01
☐ 93	Steve Kerr	.10	.05	.01
☐ 94	Eric Leckner	.10	.05	.01
☐ 95	Loy Vaught	.20	.09	.03
☐ 96	Jud Buechler	.10	.05	.01
☐ 97	Doug Smith	.10	.05	.01
☐ 98	Sidney Green	.10	.05	.01
☐ 99	Jerome Kersey	.10	.05	.01
☐ 100	Patrick Ewing	.60	.25	.07
☐ 101	Ed Nealy	.10	.05	.01
☐ 102	Shawn Kemp	2.50	1.10	.30
☐ 103	Luc Longley	.10	.05	.01
☐ 104	George McCloud	.10	.05	.01
☐ 105	Ron Anderson	.10	.05	.01
☐ 106	Moses Malone UER	.40	.18	.05
	(Rookie Card is 1975-76, not 1976-77)			
☐ 107	Tony Smith	.10	.05	.01
☐ 108	Terry Porter	.10	.05	.01
☐ 109	Blair Rasmussen	.10	.05	.01
☐ 110	Bimbo Coles	.10	.05	.01
☐ 111	Grant Long	.10	.05	.01
☐ 112	John Battle	.10	.05	.01
☐ 113	Brian Oliver	.10	.05	.01
☐ 114	Tyrone Corbin	.10	.05	.01
☐ 115	Benoit Benjamin	.10	.05	.01
☐ 116	Rick Fox	.10	.05	.01
☐ 117	Rafael Addison	.10	.05	.01
☐ 118	Danny Young	.10	.05	.01
☐ 119	Fat Lever	.10	.05	.01
☐ 120	Terry Cummings	.10	.05	.01
☐ 121	Felton Spencer	.10	.05	.01
☐ 122	Joe Kleine	.10	.05	.01
☐ 123	Johnny Newman	.10	.05	.01
☐ 124	Gary Payton	1.25	.55	.16
☐ 125	Kurt Rambis	.10	.05	.01
☐ 126	Vlade Divac	.30	.14	.04
☐ 127	John Paxson	.20	.09	.03
☐ 128	Lionel Simmons	.10	.05	.01
☐ 129	Randy Wittman	.10	.05	.01
☐ 130	Winston Garland	.10	.05	.01
☐ 131	Jerry Reynolds	.10	.05	.01
☐ 132	Dell Curry	.10	.05	.01
☐ 133	Fred Roberts	.10	.05	.01
☐ 134	Michael Adams	.10	.05	.01
☐ 135	Charles Jones	.10	.05	.01
☐ 136	Frank Brickowski	.10	.05	.01
☐ 137	Alton Lister	.10	.05	.01
☐ 138	Horace Grant	.30	.14	.04
☐ 139	Greg Sutton	.10	.05	.01
☐ 140	John Starks	.30	.14	.04
☐ 141	Detlef Schrempf	.20	.09	.03
☐ 142	Rodney Monroe	.10	.05	.01
☐ 143	Pete Chilcutt	.10	.05	.01
☐ 144	Mike Brown	.10	.05	.01
☐ 145	Rony Seikaly	.10	.05	.01
☐ 146	Donald Hodge	.10	.05	.01
☐ 147	Kevin McHale	.30	.14	.04
☐ 148	Ricky Pierce	.10	.05	.01
☐ 149	Brian Shaw	.10	.05	.01
☐ 150	Reggie Williams	.10	.05	.01
☐ 151	Kendall Gill	.10	.05	.01
☐ 152	Tom Chambers	.10	.05	.01
☐ 153	Jack Haley	.10	.05	.01
☐ 154	Terrell Brandon	.50	.23	.06
☐ 155	Dennis Scott	.20	.09	.03
☐ 156	Mark Randall	.10	.05	.01
☐ 157	Kenny Payne	.10	.05	.01
☐ 158	Bernard King	.30	.14	.04
☐ 159	Tate George	.10	.05	.01
☐ 160	Scott Skiles	.10	.05	.01
☐ 161	Pervis Ellison	.10	.05	.01
☐ 162	Marcus Liberty	.10	.05	.01
☐ 163	Rumeal Robinson	.10	.05	.01
☐ 164	Anthony Mason	.30	.14	.04
☐ 165	Les Jepsen	.10	.05	.01
☐ 166	Kenny Smith	.10	.05	.01
☐ 167	Randy White	.10	.05	.01
☐ 168	Dee Brown	.10	.05	.01
☐ 169	Chris Dudley	.10	.05	.01
☐ 170	Armon Gilliam	.10	.05	.01
☐ 171	Eddie Johnson	.10	.05	.01
☐ 172	A.C. Green	.30	.14	.04
☐ 173	Darrell Walker	.10	.05	.01
☐ 174	Bill Cartwright	.10	.05	.01
☐ 175	Mike Gminski	.10	.05	.01
☐ 176	Tom Tolbert	.10	.05	.01
☐ 177	Buck Williams	.20	.09	.03
☐ 178	Mark Eaton	.10	.05	.01
☐ 179	Danny Manning	.20	.09	.03
☐ 180	Glen Rice	.30	.14	.04
☐ 181	Sarunas Marciulionis	.10	.05	.01
☐ 182	Danny Ferry	.10	.05	.01
☐ 183	Chris Corchiani	.10	.05	.01
☐ 184	Dan Majerle	.20	.09	.03
☐ 185	Alvin Robertson	.10	.05	.01
☐ 186	Vern Fleming	.10	.05	.01
☐ 187	Kevin Lynch	.10	.05	.01
☐ 188	John Williams	.10	.05	.01
☐ 189	Checklist 1-100	.10	.05	.01
☐ 190	Checklist 101-200	.10	.05	.01

☐ 191 David Robinson MC	.60	.25	.07
☐ 192 Larry Johnson MC	.60	.25	.07
☐ 193 Derrick Coleman MC	.10	.05	.01
☐ 194 Larry Bird MC	1.25	.55	.16
☐ 195 Billy Owens MC	.10	.05	.01
☐ 196 Dikembe Mutombo MC	.30	.14	.04
☐ 197 Charles Barkley MC	.50	.23	.06
☐ 198 Scottie Pippen MC	1.00	.45	.12
☐ 199 Clyde Drexler MC	.40	.18	.05
☐ 200 John Stockton MC	.30	.14	.04
☐ 201 Shaquille O'Neal MC	4.00	1.80	.50
☐ 202 Chris Mullin MC	.10	.05	.01
☐ 203 Glen Rice MC	.10	.05	.01
☐ 204 Isiah Thomas MC	.20	.09	.03
☐ 205 Karl Malone MC	.30	.14	.04
☐ 206 Christian Laettner MC	.40	.18	.05
☐ 207 Patrick Ewing MC	.30	.14	.04
☐ 208 Dominique Wilkins MC	.20	.09	.03
☐ 209 Alonzo Mourning MC	1.00	.45	.12
☐ 210 Michael Jordan MC	4.00	1.80	.50
☐ 211 Tim Hardaway MC	.10	.05	.01
☐ 212 Rodney McCray	.10	.05	.01
☐ 213 Larry Johnson	1.25	.55	.16
☐ 214 Charles Smith	.10	.05	.01
☐ 215 Kevin Brooks	.10	.05	.01
☐ 216 Kevin Johnson	.30	.14	.04
☐ 217 Duane Cooper	.10	.05	.01
☐ 218 Christian Laettner UER	1.00	.45	.12
(Missing '92 Draft			
Pick logo)			
☐ 219 Tim Perry	.10	.05	.01
☐ 220 Hakeem Olajuwon	1.50	.70	.19
☐ 221 Lee Mayberry	.10	.05	.01
☐ 222 Mark Bryant	.10	.05	.01
☐ 223 Robert Horry	1.25	.55	.16
☐ 224 Tracy Murray UER	.10	.05	.01
(Missing '92 Draft			
Pick logo)			
☐ 225 Greg Grant	.10	.05	.01
☐ 226 Rolando Blackman	.10	.05	.01
☐ 227 James Edwards UER	.10	.05	.01
(Rookie Card is 1978-79,			
not 1980-81)			
☐ 228 Sean Green	.10	.05	.01
☐ 229 Buck Johnson	.10	.05	.01
☐ 230 Andrew Lang	.10	.05	.01
☐ 231 Tracy Moore	.10	.05	.01
☐ 232 Adam Keefe UER	.20	.09	.03
(Missing '92 Draft			
Pick logo)			
☐ 233 Tony Campbell	.10	.05	.01
☐ 234 Rod Strickland	.10	.05	.01
☐ 235 Terry Mills	.10	.05	.01
☐ 236 Billy Owens	.10	.05	.01
☐ 237 Bryant Stith UER	.50	.23	.06
(Missing '92 Draft			
Pick logo)			
☐ 238 Tony Bennett UER	.10	.05	.01
(Missing '92 Draft			
Pick logo)			
☐ 239 David Wood	.10	.05	.01
☐ 240 Jay Humphries	.10	.05	.01
☐ 241 Doc Rivers	.10	.05	.01
☐ 242 Wayman Tisdale	.10	.05	.01
☐ 243 Litterial Green	.10	.05	.01
☐ 244 Jon Barry	.10	.05	.01
☐ 245 Brad Daugherty	.10	.05	.01
☐ 246 Nate McMillan	.10	.05	.01
☐ 247 Shaquille O'Neal	12.00	5.50	1.50
☐ 248 Chris Smith	.10	.05	.01
☐ 249 Duane Ferrell	.10	.05	.01
☐ 250 Anthony Peeler	.20	.09	.03
☐ 251 Gundars Vetra	.10	.05	.01
☐ 252 Danny Ainge	.30	.14	.04
☐ 253 Mitch Richmond	.50	.23	.06
☐ 254 Malik Sealy	.20	.09	.03
☐ 255 Brent Price	.10	.05	.01
☐ 256 Xavier McDaniel	.10	.05	.01
☐ 257 Bobby Phills	.75	.35	.09
☐ 258 Donald Royal	.10	.05	.01
☐ 259 Olden Polynice	.10	.05	.01
☐ 260 Dominique Wilkins UER	.30	.14	.04
(Scoring 10,000th point,			
should be 20,000th)			
☐ 261 Larry Krystkowiak	.10	.05	.01
☐ 262 Duane Causwell	.10	.05	.01
☐ 263 Todd Day	.20	.09	.03
☐ 264 Sam Mack	.10	.05	.01
☐ 265 John Stockton	.60	.25	.07
☐ 266 Eddie Lee Wilkins	.10	.05	.01
☐ 267 Gerald Glass	.10	.05	.01
☐ 268 Robert Pack	.10	.05	.01
☐ 269 Gerald Wilkins	.10	.05	.01
☐ 270 Reggie Lewis	.20	.09	.03
☐ 271 Scott Brooks	.10	.05	.01
☐ 272 Randy Woods UER	.10	.05	.01
(Missing '92 Draft			
Pick logo)			
☐ 273 Dikembe Mutombo	.60	.25	.07
☐ 274 Kiki Vandeweghe	.10	.05	.01
☐ 275 Rich King	.10	.05	.01
☐ 276 Jeff Turner	.10	.05	.01
☐ 277 Vinny Del Negro	.10	.05	.01
☐ 278 Marlon Maxey	.10	.05	.01
☐ 279 Elmore Spencer UER	.10	.05	.01
(Missing '92 Draft			
Pick logo)			
☐ 280 Cedric Ceballos	.25	.11	.03
☐ 281 Alex Blackwell	.10	.05	.01
☐ 282 Terry Davis	.10	.05	.01
☐ 283 Morlon Wiley	.10	.05	.01
☐ 284 Trent Tucker	.10	.05	.01
☐ 285 Carl Herrera	.10	.05	.01
☐ 286 Eric Anderson	.10	.05	.01
☐ 287 Clyde Drexler	.75	.35	.09
☐ 288 Tom Gugliotta	1.00	.45	.12
☐ 289 Dale Ellis	.10	.05	.01
☐ 290 Lance Blanks	.10	.05	.01
☐ 291 Tom Hammonds	.10	.05	.01
☐ 292 Eric Murdock	.10	.05	.01
☐ 293 Walt Williams	1.25	.55	.16
☐ 294 Gerald Paddio	.10	.05	.01
☐ 295 Brian Howard	.10	.05	.01
☐ 296 Ken Williams	.10	.05	.01
☐ 297 Alonzo Mourning	3.00	1.35	.35
☐ 298 Larry Nance	.10	.05	.01
☐ 299 Jeff Grayer	.10	.05	.01
☐ 300 Dave Johnson	.10	.05	.01
☐ 301 Bob McCann	.10	.05	.01
☐ 302 Bart Kofoed	.10	.05	.01
☐ 303 Anthony Cook	.10	.05	.01
☐ 304 Radisav Curcic	.10	.05	.01
☐ 305 John Crotty	.10	.05	.01
☐ 306 Brad Sellers	.10	.05	.01
☐ 307 Marcus Webb	.10	.05	.01
☐ 308 Winston Garland	.10	.05	.01
☐ 309 Walter Palmer	.10	.05	.01
☐ 310 Rod Higgins	.10	.05	.01
☐ 311 Travis Mays	.10	.05	.01
☐ 312 Alex Stivrins	.10	.05	.01
☐ 313 Greg Kite	.10	.05	.01
☐ 314 Dennis Rodman	2.50	1.10	.30

☐ 315 Mike Sanders	.10	.05	.01
☐ 316 Ed Pinckney	.10	.05	.01
☐ 317 Harold Miner	.20	.09	.03
☐ 318 Pooh Richardson	.10	.05	.01
☐ 319 Oliver Miller	.50	.23	.06
☐ 320 Latrell Sprewell	1.50	.70	.19
☐ 321 Anthony Pullard	.10	.05	.01
☐ 322 Mark Randall	.10	.05	.01
☐ 323 Jeff Hornacek	.10	.05	.01
☐ 324 Rick Mahorn UER	.10	.05	.01
(Rookie Card is 1981-82, not 1992-93)			
☐ 325 Sean Rooks	.10	.05	.01
☐ 326 Paul Pressey	.10	.05	.01
☐ 327 James Worthy	.30	.14	.04
☐ 328 Matt Bullard	.10	.05	.01
☐ 329 Reggie Smith	.10	.05	.01
☐ 330 Don MacLean UER	.20	.09	.03
(Missing '92 Draft Pick logo)			
☐ 331 John Williams UER	.10	.05	.01
(Rookie Card erroneously shows Hot Rod)			
☐ 332 Frank Johnson	.10	.05	.01
☐ 333 Hubert Davis UER	.20	.09	.03
(Missing '92 Draft Pick logo)			
☐ 334 Lloyd Daniels	.10	.05	.01
☐ 335 Steve Bardo	.10	.05	.01
☐ 336 Jeff Sanders	.10	.05	.01
☐ 337 Tree Rollins	.10	.05	.01
☐ 338 Micheal Williams	.10	.05	.01
☐ 339 Lorenzo Williams	.10	.05	.01
☐ 340 Harvey Grant	.10	.05	.01
☐ 341 Avery Johnson	.20	.09	.03
☐ 342 Bo Kimble	.10	.05	.01
☐ 343 LaPhonso Ellis UER	.50	.23	.06
(Missing '92 Draft Pick logo)			
☐ 344 Mookie Blaylock	.20	.09	.03
☐ 345 Isaiah Morris UER	.10	.05	.01
(Missing '92 Draft Pick logo)			
☐ 346 Clarence Weatherspoon	1.00	.45	.12
☐ 347 Manute Bol	.10	.05	.01
☐ 348 Victor Alexander	.10	.05	.01
☐ 349 Corey Williams	.10	.05	.01
☐ 350 Byron Houston	.10	.05	.01
☐ 351 Stanley Roberts	.10	.05	.01
☐ 352 Anthony Avent	.10	.05	.01
☐ 353 Vincent Askew	.10	.05	.01
☐ 354 Herb Williams	.10	.05	.01
☐ 355 J.R. Reid	.10	.05	.01
☐ 356 Brad Lohaus	.10	.05	.01
☐ 357 Reggie Miller	.75	.35	.09
☐ 358 Blue Edwards	.10	.05	.01
☐ 359 Tom Tolbert	.10	.05	.01
☐ 360 Charles Barkley	1.00	.45	.12
☐ 361 David Robinson	1.25	.55	.16
☐ 362 Dale Davis	.10	.05	.01
☐ 363 Robert Werdann UER	.10	.05	.01
(Missing '92 Draft Pick logo)			
☐ 364 Chuck Person	.10	.05	.01
☐ 365 Alaa Abdelnaby	.10	.05	.01
☐ 366 Dave Jamerson	.10	.05	.01
☐ 367 Scottie Pippen	2.00	.90	.25
☐ 368 Mark Jackson	.10	.05	.01
☐ 369 Keith Askins	.10	.05	.01
☐ 370 Marty Conlon	.10	.05	.01
☐ 371 Chucky Brown	.10	.05	.01

☐ 372 LaBradford Smith	.10	.05	.01
☐ 373 Tim Kempton	.10	.05	.01
☐ 374 Sam Mitchell	.10	.05	.01
☐ 375 John Salley	.10	.05	.01
☐ 376 Mario Elie	.10	.05	.01
☐ 377 Mark West	.10	.05	.01
☐ 378 David Wingate	.10	.05	.01
☐ 379 Jaren Jackson	.10	.05	.01
☐ 380 Rumeal Robinson	.10	.05	.01
☐ 381 Kennard Winchester	.10	.05	.01
☐ 382 Walter Bond	.10	.05	.01
☐ 383 Isaac Austin	.10	.05	.01
☐ 384 Derrick Coleman	.10	.05	.01
☐ 385 Larry Smith	.10	.05	.01
☐ 386 Joe Dumars	.30	.14	.04
☐ 387 Matt Geiger UER	.10	.05	.01
(Missing '92 Draft Pick logo)			
☐ 388 Stephen Howard	.10	.05	.01
☐ 389 William Bedford	.10	.05	.01
☐ 390 Jayson Williams	.10	.05	.01
☐ 391 Kurt Rambis	.10	.05	.01
☐ 392 Keith Jennings	.10	.05	.01
☐ 393 Steve Kerr UER	.10	.05	.01
(The words key stat are repeated on back)			
☐ 394 Larry Stewart	.10	.05	.01
☐ 395 Danny Young	.10	.05	.01
☐ 396 Doug Overton	.10	.05	.01
☐ 397 Mark Acres	.10	.05	.01
☐ 398 John Bagley	.10	.05	.01
☐ 399 Checklist 201-300	.10	.05	.01
☐ 400 Checklist 301-400	.10	.05	.01

1992-93 Stadium Club Beam Team

Comprised of some of the NBA's biggest stars, "Beam Team" cards commemorate Topps' 1993 sponsorship of a six-minute NBA laser animation show called Beams Above the Rim. The show premiered at the 1993 NBA All-Star Game. Afterwards, the laser show embarked on a ten-city tour and was featured in either the pre-game or half-time events in ten NBA arenas. These cards were randomly inserted in second series 15-card packs at a rate of one in 36. The color action player photos on the fronts are bordered on two sides by an angled silver light beam border design with a light refracting pattern. The player's name

appears on a white-outlined burnt orange bar superimposed over a basketball icon at the bottom. The backs present a color head shot and, on a basketball icon, career highlights.

	MINT	NRMT	EXC
COMPLETE SET (21)	250.00	110.00	31.00
COMMON CARD (1-21)	2.00	.90	.25

		MINT	NRMT	EXC
☐ 1	Michael Jordan	90.00	40.00	11.00
☐ 2	Dominique Wilkins	2.50	1.10	.30
☐ 3	Shawn Kemp	20.00	9.00	2.50
☐ 4	Clyde Drexler	8.00	3.60	1.00
☐ 5	Scottie Pippen	20.00	9.00	2.50
☐ 6	Chris Mullin	2.50	1.10	.30
☐ 7	Reggie Miller	8.00	3.60	1.00
☐ 8	Glen Rice	4.00	1.80	.50
☐ 9	Jeff Hornacek	2.50	1.10	.30
☐ 10	Jeff Malone	2.00	.90	.25
☐ 11	John Stockton	6.00	2.70	.75
☐ 12	Kevin Johnson	2.50	1.10	.30
☐ 13	Mark Price	2.00	.90	.25
☐ 14	Tim Hardaway	2.50	1.10	.30
☐ 15	Charles Barkley	10.00	4.50	1.25
☐ 16	Hakeem Olajuwon	15.00	6.75	1.85
☐ 17	Karl Malone	6.00	2.70	.75
☐ 18	Patrick Ewing	6.00	2.70	.75
☐ 19	Dennis Rodman	25.00	11.00	3.10
☐ 20	David Robinson	12.00	5.50	1.50
☐ 21	Shaquille O'Neal	120.00	55.00	15.00

1993-94 Stadium Club

The 1993-94 Stadium Club set consists of 360 standard-size cards issued in two series of 180 cards. Cards were issued in 12 and 20-card packs. There were 24 twelve-card packs per box. The full-bleed fronts feature glossy color action photos. The player's name is superimposed on the lower portion of the picture in white and gold foil lettering. The borderless backs are divided in half vertically with a torn effect. The left side sports a vertical player photo and on the right side, over a purple background, is biography and player's name and team. A brief section named "The Buzz" provides career highlights. A multicolored box lists the 1992-93 statistics, career statistics and a Topps Skills Rating

System that provides a score including player intimidation, mobility, shooting range and defense. Subsets featured are Triple Double (1-11, 101-111) and High Court (61-69, 170-178) and interspersed NBA Draft Picks. Card number 345 was never issued. Due to an error in numbering, both Toni Kukoc and Chris Corchiani are numbered 336. Corchiani is actually listed on the checklist card as number 345, thus we've listed him below in that order. Rookie Cards of note in this set include Vin Baker, Anfernee Hardaway, Allan Houston, Toni Kukoc, Jamal Mashburn, Nick Van Exel and Chris Webber.

	MINT	NRMT	EXC
COMPLETE SET (360)	40.00	18.00	5.00
COMPLETE SERIES 1 (180)	20.00	9.00	2.50
COMPLETE SERIES 2 (180)	20.00	9.00	2.50
COMMON CARD (1-180)	.10	.05	.01
COMMON CARD (181-360)	.05	.02	.01

		MINT	NRMT	EXC
☐ 1	Michael Jordan TD	2.50	1.10	.30
☐ 2	Kenny Anderson TD	.10	.05	.01
☐ 3	Steve Smith TD	.10	.05	.01
☐ 4	Kevin Gamble TD	.10	.05	.01
☐ 5	Detlef Schrempf TD	.10	.05	.01
☐ 6	Larry Johnson TD	.25	.11	.03
☐ 7	Brad Daugherty TD	.10	.05	.01
☐ 8	Rumeal Robinson TD	.10	.05	.01
☐ 9	Micheal Williams TD	.10	.05	.01
☐ 10	David Robinson TD	.40	.18	.05
☐ 11	Sam Perkins TD	.10	.05	.01
☐ 12	Thurl Bailey	.10	.05	.01
☐ 13	Sherman Douglas	.10	.05	.01
☐ 14	Larry Stewart	.10	.05	.01
☐ 15	Kevin Johnson	.20	.09	.03
☐ 16	Bill Cartwright	.10	.05	.01
☐ 17	Larry Nance	.10	.05	.01
☐ 18	P.J. Brown	.10	.05	.01
☐ 19	Tony Bennett	.10	.05	.01
☐ 20	Robert Parish	.20	.09	.03
☐ 21	David Benoit	.10	.05	.01
☐ 22	Detlef Schrempf	.15	.07	.02
☐ 23	Hubert Davis	.10	.05	.01
☐ 24	Donald Hodge	.10	.05	.01
☐ 25	Hersey Hawkins	.10	.05	.01
☐ 26	Mark Jackson	.10	.05	.01
☐ 27	Reggie Williams	.10	.05	.01
☐ 28	Lionel Simmons	.10	.05	.01
☐ 29	Ron Harper	.10	.05	.01
☐ 30	Chris Mills	.60	.25	.07
☐ 31	Danny Schayes	.10	.05	.01
☐ 32	J.R. Reid	.10	.05	.01
☐ 33	Willie Burton	.10	.05	.01
☐ 34	Greg Anthony	.10	.05	.01
☐ 35	Elden Campbell	.15	.07	.02
☐ 36	Ervin Johnson	.20	.09	.03
☐ 37	Scott Brooks	.10	.05	.01
☐ 38	Johnny Newman	.10	.05	.01
☐ 39	Rex Chapman	.10	.05	.01
☐ 40	Chuck Person	.10	.05	.01
☐ 41	John Williams	.10	.05	.01
☐ 42	Anthony Bowie	.10	.05	.01
☐ 43	Negele Knight	.10	.05	.01
☐ 44	Tyrone Corbin	.10	.05	.01
☐ 45	Jud Buechler	.10	.05	.01
☐ 46	Adam Keefe	.10	.05	.01
☐ 47	Glen Rice	.20	.09	.03
☐ 48	Tracy Murray	.10	.05	.01

☐ 49 Rick Mahorn	.10	.05	.01	☐ 120 Victor Alexander	.10	.05	.01

☐ 49	Rick Mahorn	.10	.05	.01
☐ 50	Vlade Divac	.20	.09	.03
☐ 51	Eric Murdock	.10	.05	.01
☐ 52	Isaiah Morris	.10	.05	.01
☐ 53	Bobby Hurley	.20	.09	.03
☐ 54	Mitch Richmond	.30	.14	.04
☐ 55	Danny Ainge	.20	.09	.03
☐ 56	Dikembe Mutombo	.20	.09	.03
☐ 57	Jeff Hornacek	.15	.07	.02
☐ 58	Tony Campbell	.10	.05	.01
☐ 59	Vinny Del Negro	.10	.05	.01
☐ 60	Xavier McDaniel HC	.10	.05	.01
☐ 61	Scottie Pippen HC	.60	.25	.07
☐ 62	Larry Nance HC	.10	.05	.01
☐ 63	Dikembe Mutombo HC	.15	.07	.02
☐ 64	Hakeem Olajuwon HC	.50	.23	.06
☐ 65	Dominique Wilkins HC	.15	.07	.02
☐ 66	Clarence Weatherspoon HC	.10	.05	.01
☐ 67	Chris Morris HC	.10	.05	.01
☐ 68	Patrick Ewing HC	.25	.11	.03
☐ 69	Kevin Willis HC	.10	.05	.01
☐ 70	Jon Barry	.10	.05	.01
☐ 71	Jerry Reynolds	.10	.05	.01
☐ 72	Sarunas Marciulionis	.10	.05	.01
☐ 73	Mark West	.10	.05	.01
☐ 74	B.J. Armstrong	.10	.05	.01
☐ 75	Greg Kite	.10	.05	.01
☐ 76	LaSalle Thompson	.10	.05	.01
☐ 77	Randy White	.10	.05	.01
☐ 78	Alaa Abdelnaby	.10	.05	.01
☐ 79	Kevin Brooks	.10	.05	.01
☐ 80	Vern Fleming	.10	.05	.01
☐ 81	Doc Rivers	.10	.05	.01
☐ 82	Shawn Bradley	.50	.23	.06
☐ 83	Wayman Tisdale	.10	.05	.01
☐ 84	Olden Polynice	.10	.05	.01
☐ 85	Michael Cage	.10	.05	.01
☐ 86	Harold Miner	.10	.05	.01
☐ 87	Doug Smith	.10	.05	.01
☐ 88	Tom Gugliotta	.20	.09	.03
☐ 89	Hakeem Olajuwon	1.00	.45	.12
☐ 90	Loy Vaught	.15	.07	.02
☐ 91	James Worthy	.20	.09	.03
☐ 92	John Paxson	.15	.07	.02
☐ 93	Jon Koncak	.10	.05	.01
☐ 94	Lee Mayberry	.10	.05	.01
☐ 95	Clarence Weatherspoon	.20	.09	.03
☐ 96	Mark Eaton	.10	.05	.01
☐ 97	Rex Walters	.10	.05	.01
☐ 98	Alvin Robertson	.10	.05	.01
☐ 99	Dan Majerle	.15	.07	.02
☐ 100	Shaquille O'Neal	2.50	1.10	.30
☐ 101	Derrick Coleman TD	.10	.05	.01
☐ 102	Hersey Hawkins TD	.10	.05	.01
☐ 103	Scottie Pippen TD	.60	.25	.07
☐ 104	Scott Skiles TD	.10	.05	.01
☐ 105	Rod Strickland TD	.10	.05	.01
☐ 106	Pooh Richardson TD	.10	.05	.01
☐ 107	Tom Gugliotta TD	.10	.05	.01
☐ 108	Mark Jackson TD	.10	.05	.01
☐ 109	Dikembe Mutombo TD	.15	.07	.02
☐ 110	Charles Barkley TD	.30	.14	.04
☐ 111	Otis Thorpe TD	.10	.05	.01
☐ 112	Malik Sealy	.10	.05	.01
☐ 113	Mark Macon	.10	.05	.01
☐ 114	Dee Brown	.10	.05	.01
☐ 115	Nate McMillan	.10	.05	.01
☐ 116	John Starks	.15	.07	.02
☐ 117	Clyde Drexler	.50	.23	.06
☐ 118	Antoine Carr	.10	.05	.01
☐ 119	Doug West	.10	.05	.01
☐ 120	Victor Alexander	.10	.05	.01
☐ 121	Kenny Gattison	.10	.05	.01
☐ 122	Spud Webb	.15	.07	.02
☐ 123	Rumeal Robinson	.10	.05	.01
☐ 124	Tim Kempton	.10	.05	.01
☐ 125	Karl Malone	.40	.18	.05
☐ 126	Randy Woods	.10	.05	.01
☐ 127	Calbert Cheaney	.40	.18	.05
☐ 128	Johnny Dawkins	.10	.05	.01
☐ 129	Dominique Wilkins	.20	.09	.03
☐ 130	Horace Grant	.20	.09	.03
☐ 131	Bill Laimbeer	.15	.07	.02
☐ 132	Kenny Smith	.10	.05	.01
☐ 133	Sedale Threatt	.10	.05	.01
☐ 134	Brian Shaw	.10	.05	.01
☐ 135	Dennis Scott	.15	.07	.02
☐ 136	Mark Bryant	.10	.05	.01
☐ 137	Xavier McDaniel	.10	.05	.01
☐ 138	David Wood	.10	.05	.01
☐ 139	Luther Wright	.10	.05	.01
☐ 140	Lloyd Daniels	.10	.05	.01
☐ 141	Marlon Maxey UER	.10	.05	.01
	(Name spelled Maxley on the front)			
☐ 142	Pooh Richardson	.10	.05	.01
☐ 143	Jeff Grayer	.10	.05	.01
☐ 144	LaPhonso Ellis	.10	.05	.01
☐ 145	Gerald Wilkins	.10	.05	.01
☐ 146	Dell Curry	.10	.05	.01
☐ 147	Duane Causwell	.10	.05	.01
☐ 148	Tim Hardaway	.20	.09	.03
☐ 149	Isiah Thomas	.25	.11	.03
☐ 150	Doug Edwards	.10	.05	.01
☐ 151	Anthony Peeler	.10	.05	.01
☐ 152	Tate George	.10	.05	.01
☐ 153	Terry Davis	.10	.05	.01
☐ 154	Sam Perkins	.10	.05	.01
☐ 155	John Salley	.10	.05	.01
☐ 156	Vernon Maxwell	.10	.05	.01
☐ 157	Anthony Avent	.10	.05	.01
☐ 158	Clifford Robinson	.20	.09	.03
☐ 159	Corie Blount	.10	.05	.01
☐ 160	Gerald Paddio	.10	.05	.01
☐ 161	Blair Rasmussen	.10	.05	.01
☐ 162	Carl Herrera	.10	.05	.01
☐ 163	Chris Smith	.10	.05	.01
☐ 164	Pervis Ellison	.10	.05	.01
☐ 165	Rod Strickland	.10	.05	.01
☐ 166	Jeff Malone	.10	.05	.01
☐ 167	Danny Ferry	.10	.05	.01
☐ 168	Kevin Lynch	.10	.05	.01
☐ 169	Michael Jordan	5.00	2.20	.60
☐ 170	Derrick Coleman HC	.10	.05	.01
☐ 171	Jerome Kersey HC	.10	.05	.01
☐ 172	David Robinson HC	.40	.18	.05
☐ 173	Shawn Kemp HC	.60	.25	.07
☐ 174	Karl Malone HC	.25	.11	.03
☐ 175	Shaquille O'Neal HC	1.25	.55	.16
☐ 176	Alonzo Mourning HC	.30	.14	.04
☐ 177	Charles Barkley HC	.30	.14	.04
☐ 178	Larry Johnson HC	.25	.11	.03
☐ 179	Checklist 1-90	.10	.05	.01
☐ 180	Checklist 91-180	.10	.05	.01
☐ 181	Michael Jordan FF	2.00	.90	.25
☐ 182	Dominique Wilkins FF	.10	.05	.01
☐ 183	Dennis Rodman FF	.60	.25	.07
☐ 184	Scottie Pippen FF	.50	.23	.06
☐ 185	Larry Johnson FF	.10	.05	.01
☐ 186	Karl Malone FF	.15	.07	.02
☐ 187	Clarence Weatherspoon FF	.05	.02	.01
☐ 188	Charles Barkley FF	.25	.11	.03
☐ 189	Patrick Ewing FF	.15	.07	.02

#	Player			
☐ 190	Derrick Coleman FF	.05	.02	.01
☐ 191	LaBradford Smith	.05	.02	.01
☐ 192	Derek Harper	.05	.02	.01
☐ 193	Ken Norman	.05	.02	.01
☐ 194	Rodney Rogers	.15	.07	.02
☐ 195	Chris Dudley	.05	.02	.01
☐ 196	Gary Payton	.50	.23	.06
☐ 197	Andrew Lang	.05	.02	.01
☐ 198	Billy Owens	.05	.02	.01
☐ 199	Bryon Russell	.05	.02	.01
☐ 200	Patrick Ewing	.30	.14	.04
☐ 201	Stacey King	.05	.02	.01
☐ 202	Grant Long	.05	.02	.01
☐ 203	Sean Elliott	.15	.07	.02
☐ 204	Muggsy Bogues	.10	.05	.01
☐ 205	Kevin Edwards	.05	.02	.01
☐ 206	Dale Davis	.05	.02	.01
☐ 207	Dale Ellis	.05	.02	.01
☐ 208	Terrell Brandon	.15	.07	.02
☐ 209	Kevin Gamble	.05	.02	.01
☐ 210	Robert Horry	.10	.05	.01
☐ 211	Moses Malone UER	.20	.09	.03
	Birthdate on back is 1993			
☐ 212	Gary Grant	.05	.02	.01
☐ 213	Bobby Hurley	.10	.05	.01
☐ 214	Larry Krystkowiak	.05	.02	.01
☐ 215	A.C. Green	.15	.07	.02
☐ 216	Christian Laettner	.15	.07	.02
☐ 217	Orlando Woolridge	.05	.02	.01
☐ 218	Craig Ehlo	.05	.02	.01
☐ 219	Terry Porter	.05	.02	.01
☐ 220	Jamal Mashburn	.75	.35	.09
☐ 221	Kevin Duckworth	.05	.02	.01
☐ 222	Shawn Kemp	1.00	.45	.12
☐ 223	Frank Brickowski	.05	.02	.01
☐ 224	Chris Webber	1.25	.55	.16
☐ 225	Charles Oakley	.10	.05	.01
☐ 226	Jay Humphries	.05	.02	.01
☐ 227	Steve Kerr	.10	.05	.01
☐ 228	Tim Perry	.05	.02	.01
☐ 229	Sleepy Floyd	.05	.02	.01
☐ 230	Bimbo Coles	.05	.02	.01
☐ 231	Eddie Johnson	.05	.02	.01
☐ 232	Terry Mills	.05	.02	.01
☐ 233	Danny Manning	.10	.05	.01
☐ 234	Isaiah Rider	.40	.18	.05
☐ 235	Darnell Mee	.05	.02	.01
☐ 236	Haywoode Workman	.05	.02	.01
☐ 237	Scott Skiles	.05	.02	.01
☐ 238	Otis Thorpe	.10	.05	.01
☐ 239	Mike Peplowski	.05	.02	.01
☐ 240	Eric Leckner	.05	.02	.01
☐ 241	Johnny Newman	.05	.02	.01
☐ 242	Benoit Benjamin	.05	.02	.01
☐ 243	Doug Christie	.05	.02	.01
☐ 244	Acie Earl	.05	.02	.01
☐ 245	Luc Longley	.05	.02	.01
☐ 246	Tyrone Hill	.05	.02	.01
☐ 247	Allan Houston	.60	.25	.07
☐ 248	Joe Kleine	.05	.02	.01
☐ 249	Mookie Blaylock	.10	.05	.01
☐ 250	Anthony Bonner	.05	.02	.01
☐ 251	Luther Wright	.05	.02	.01
☐ 252	Todd Day	.05	.02	.01
☐ 253	Kendall Gill	.05	.02	.01
☐ 254	Mario Elie	.05	.02	.01
☐ 255	Pete Myers UER	.05	.02	.01
	Card was born in 1993			
☐ 256	Jim Les	.05	.02	.01
☐ 257	Stanley Roberts	.05	.02	.01
☐ 258	Michael Adams	.05	.02	.01
☐ 259	Hersey Hawkins	.05	.02	.01
☐ 260	Shawn Bradley	.15	.07	.02
☐ 261	Scott Haskin	.05	.02	.01
☐ 262	Corie Blount	.05	.02	.01
☐ 263	Charles Smith	.05	.02	.01
☐ 264	Armon Gilliam	.05	.02	.01
☐ 265	Jamal Mashburn NW	.30	.14	.04
☐ 266	Anfernee Hardaway NW	2.50	1.10	.30
☐ 267	Shawn Bradley NW	.15	.07	.02
☐ 268	Chris Webber NW	.50	.23	.06
☐ 269	Bobby Hurley NW	.05	.02	.01
☐ 270	Isaiah Rider NW	.25	.11	.03
☐ 271	Dino Radja NW	.05	.02	.01
☐ 272	Chris Mills NW	.15	.07	.02
☐ 273	Nick Van Exel NW	.40	.18	.05
☐ 274	Lindsey Hunter NW	.05	.02	.01
☐ 275	Toni Kukoc NW	.30	.14	.04
☐ 276	Popeye Jones NW	.05	.02	.01
☐ 277	Chris Mills	.15	.07	.02
☐ 278	Ricky Pierce	.05	.02	.01
☐ 279	Negele Knight	.05	.02	.01
☐ 280	Kenny Walker	.05	.02	.01
☐ 281	Nick Van Exel	1.00	.45	.12
☐ 282	Derrick Coleman UER	.05	.02	.01
	(Career stats listed under '92-93)			
☐ 283	Popeye Jones	.15	.07	.02
☐ 284	Derrick McKey	.05	.02	.01
☐ 285	Rick Fox	.05	.02	.01
☐ 286	Jerome Kersey	.05	.02	.01
☐ 287	Steve Smith	.15	.07	.02
☐ 288	Brian Williams	.05	.02	.01
☐ 289	Chris Mullin	.10	.05	.01
☐ 290	Terry Cummings	.05	.02	.01
☐ 291	Donald Royal	.05	.02	.01
☐ 292	Alonzo Mourning	.50	.23	.06
☐ 293	Mike Brown	.05	.02	.01
☐ 294	Latrell Sprewell	.25	.11	.03
☐ 295	Oliver Miller	.05	.02	.01
☐ 296	Terry Dehere	.10	.05	.01
☐ 297	Detlef Schrempf	.10	.05	.01
☐ 298	Sam Bowie UER	.05	.02	.01
	(Last name Bowe on front)			
☐ 299	Chris Morris	.05	.02	.01
☐ 300	Scottie Pippen	1.00	.45	.12
☐ 301	Warren Kidd	.05	.02	.01
☐ 302	Don MacLean	.05	.02	.01
☐ 303	Sean Rooks	.05	.02	.01
☐ 304	Matt Geiger	.05	.02	.01
☐ 305	Dennis Rodman	1.25	.55	.16
☐ 306	Reggie Miller	.40	.18	.05
☐ 307	Vin Baker	1.25	.55	.16
☐ 308	Anfernee Hardaway	6.00	2.70	.75
☐ 309	Lindsey Hunter	.10	.05	.01
☐ 310	Stacey Augmon	.10	.05	.01
☐ 311	Randy Brown	.05	.02	.01
☐ 312	Anthony Mason	.10	.05	.01
☐ 313	John Stockton	.30	.14	.04
☐ 314	Sam Cassell	.50	.23	.06
☐ 315	Buck Williams	.10	.05	.01
☐ 316	Bryant Stith	.05	.02	.01
☐ 317	Brad Daugherty	.05	.02	.01
☐ 318	Dino Radja	.40	.18	.05
☐ 319	Rony Seikaly	.05	.02	.01
☐ 320	Charles Barkley	.50	.23	.06
☐ 321	Avery Johnson	.05	.02	.01
☐ 322	Mahmoud Abdul-Rauf.	.15	.07	.02
☐ 323	Larry Johnson	.40	.18	.05
☐ 324	Micheal Williams	.05	.02	.01
☐ 325	Mark Aguirre	.10	.05	.01
☐ 326	Jim Jackson	.40	.18	.05
☐ 327	Antonio Harvey	.05	.02	.01

☐ 328	David Robinson	.60	.25	.07
☐ 329	Calbert Cheaney	.15	.07	.02
☐ 330	Kenny Anderson	.15	.07	.02
☐ 331	Walt Williams	.15	.07	.02
☐ 332	Kevin Willis	.05	.02	.01
☐ 333	Nick Anderson	.15	.07	.02
☐ 334	Rik Smits	.15	.07	.02
☐ 335	Joe Dumars	.15	.07	.02
☐ 336	Toni Kukoc	.75	.35	.09
☐ 337	Harvey Grant	.05	.02	.01
☐ 338	Tom Chambers	.05	.02	.01
☐ 339	Blue Edwards	.05	.02	.01
☐ 340	Mark Price	.05	.02	.01
☐ 341	Ervin Johnson	.10	.05	.01
☐ 342	Rolando Blackman	.05	.02	.01
☐ 343	Scott Burrell	.15	.07	.02
☐ 344	Gheorghe Muresan	.50	.23	.06
☐ 345	Chris Corchiani UER 336	.05	.02	.01
☐ 346	Richard Petruska	.05	.02	.01
☐ 347	Dana Barros	.05	.02	.01.
☐ 348	Hakeem Olajuwon FF	.40	.18	.05
☐ 349	Dee Brown FF	.05	.02	.01
☐ 350	John Starks FF	.05	.02	.01
☐ 351	Ron Harper FF	.05	.02	.01
☐ 352	Chris Webber FF	.50	.23	.06
☐ 353	Dan Majerle FF	.05	.02	.01
☐ 354	Clyde Drexler FF	.15	.07	.02
☐ 355	Shawn Kemp FF	.50	.23	.06
☐ 356	David Robinson FF	.30	.14	.04
☐ 357	Chris Morris FF	.05	.02	.01
☐ 358	Shaquille O'Neal FF	1.00	.45	.12
☐ 359	Checklist	.05	.02	.01
☐ 360	Checklist	.05	.02	.01

1993-94 Stadium Club First Day Issue

Randomly inserted in first and second series foil packs at a rate of 1 in 24, the First Day Issue set parallels that of the basic Stadium Club set. Each of the 360 standard-size cards have a prismatic silver First Day logo in one upper corner. Topps announced that there were 1,000 of each card produced. Collectors should exercise caution when trading in these cards as some unscrupulous parties attempted to transfer the First Day logo from common First Day cards on to regular issue star cards. Only the top few cards in the set are individually priced below. Please refer to the multipliers provided below (coupled with

the price of the corresponding regular issue card) to ascertain value.

	MINT	NRMT	EXC
COMPLETE SET (360)	1800.00	800.00	220.00
COMPLETE SERIES 1 (180)	800.00	350.00	100.00
COMPLETE SERIES 2 (180)	1000.00	450.00	125.00
COMMON CARD (1-360)	2.50	1.10	.30
*SER.1 STARS: 20X TO 40X VALUE			
*SER.2 STARS: 25X TO 50X VALUE			
*SER.1 ROOKIES: 15X TO 30X VALUE			
*SER.2 ROOKIES: 20X TO 40X VALUE			

		MINT	NRMT	EXC
☐ 1	Michael Jordan TD	100.00	45.00	12.50
☐ 89	Hakeem Olajuwon	40.00	18.00	5.00
☐ 100	Shaquille O'Neal	100.00	45.00	12.50
☐ 169	Michael Jordan	200.00	90.00	25.00
☐ 175	Shaquille O'Neal HC	50.00	22.00	6.25
☐ 181	Michael Jordan FF	100.00	45.00	12.50
☐ 222	Shawn Kemp	50.00	22.00	6.25
☐ 224	Chris Webber	50.00	22.00	6.25
☐ 266	A.Hardaway NW	90.00	40.00	11.00
☐ 281	Nick Van Exel	40.00	18.00	5.00
☐ 300	Scottie Pippen	50.00	22.00	6.25
☐ 305	Dennis Rodman	60.00	27.00	7.50
☐ 307	Vin Baker	50.00	22.00	6.25
☐ 308	Anfernee Hardaway	225.00	100.00	28.00
☐ 358	Shaquille O'Neal FF	50.00	22.00	6.25

1993-94 Stadium Club Beam Team

Randomly inserted in first and second series 12-card and 20-card foil packs at a rate of one in 24, cards from this standard-size 27-card set features a selection of top NBA stars and rookies. Cards were issued in two series of 13 and 14, respectively. The design consists of borderless fronts with color player action photos set against game-crowd backgrounds. Silver metallic beams appear near the bottom above the player's name. The horizontal back carries a color action photo on one side, with player profile on the other. The cards are numbered on the back as "X of 27."

	MINT	NRMT	EXC
COMPLETE SET (27)	90.00	40.00	11.00
COMPLETE SERIES 1 (13)	30.00	13.50	3.70
COMPLETE SERIES 2 (14)	65.00	29.00	8.00
COMMON CARD (1-13)	.50	.23	.06
COMMON CARD (14-27)	1.00	.45	.12

		MINT	NRMT	EXC
☐ 1	Shaquille O'Neal	8.00	3.60	1.00
☐ 2	Mark Price	.50	.23	.06
☐ 3	Patrick Ewing	1.25	.55	.16
☐ 4	Michael Jordan	20.00	9.00	2.50
☐ 5	Charles Barkley	2.00	.90	.25
☐ 6	Reggie Miller	1.50	.70	.19
☐ 7	Derrick Coleman	.50	.23	.06
☐ 8	Dominique Wilkins	1.00	.45	.12
☐ 9	Karl Malone	1.25	.55	.16
☐ 10	Alonzo Mourning	2.00	.90	.25
☐ 11	Tim Hardaway	1.00	.45	.12
☐ 12	Hakeem Olajuwon	3.00	1.35	.35
☐ 13	David Robinson	2.50	1.10	.30
☐ 14	Dan Majerle	1.50	.70	.19
☐ 15	Larry Johnson	4.00	1.80	.50
☐ 16	LaPhonso Ellis	1.50	.70	.19
☐ 17	Nick Van Exel	6.00	2.70	.75
☐ 18	Scottie Pippen	10.00	4.50	1.25
☐ 19	John Stockton	3.00	1.35	.35
☐ 20	Bobby Hurley	1.00	.45	.12
☐ 21	Chris Webber	8.00	3.60	1.00
☐ 22	Jamal Mashburn	5.00	2.20	.60
☐ 23	Anfernee Hardaway	40.00	18.00	5.00
☐ 24	Isaiah Rider	2.50	1.10	.30
☐ 25	Ken Norman	1.00	.45	.12
☐ 26	Danny Manning	1.50	.70	.19
☐ 27	Calbert Cheaney	2.00	.90	.25

☐ 5	Cleveland Cavaliers	.25	.11	.03
☐ 6	Dallas Mavericks	.25	.11	.03
☐ 7	Denver Nuggets	.25	.11	.03
☐ 8	Detroit Pistons	.25	.11	.03
☐ 9	Golden State Warriors	.25	.11	.03
☐ 10	Houston Rockets	.25	.11	.03
☐ 11	Indiana Pacers	.25	.11	.03
☐ 12	Los Angeles Clippers	.25	.11	.03
☐ 13	Los Angeles Lakers	.25	.11	.03
☐ 14	Miami Heat	.25	.11	.03
☐ 15	Milwaukee Bucks	.25	.11	.03
☐ 16	Minnesota Timberwolves	.25	.11	.03
☐ 17	New Jersey Nets	.25	.11	.03
☐ 18	New York Knicks	.25	.11	.03
☐ 19	Orlando Magic	.25	.11	.03
☐ 20	Philadelphia 76ers	.25	.11	.03
☐ 21	Phoenix Suns	.25	.11	.03
☐ 22	Portland Trail Blazers	.25	.11	.03
☐ 23	Sacramento Kings	.25	.11	.03
☐ 24	San Antonio Spurs	.25	.11	.03
☐ 25	Seattle Supersonics	.25	.11	.03
☐ 26	Utah Jazz	.25	.11	.03
☐ 27	Washington Bullets	.25	.11	.03

1993-94 Stadium Club Big Tips

Randomly inserted about one in every four packs, these 27 team logo cards measure the standard size. The horizontal black fronts are framed by a thin white line and carry the words "NBA Showdown '94," the NBA logo and the team name and logo within a team-colored stripe across the bottom. The back carries game hints for the Electronic Arts NBA Showdown '94 and a videogame offer. The logo cards are unnumbered and checklisted below in alphabetical team order.

	MINT	NRMT	EXC
COMPLETE SET (27)	5.00	2.20	.60
COMMON CARD (1-27)	.25	.11	.03

☐ 1	Atlanta Hawks	.25	.11	.03
☐ 2	Boston Celtics	.25	.11	.03
☐ 3	Charlotte Hornets	.25	.11	.03
☐ 4	Chicago Bulls	.25	.11	.03

1993-94 Stadium Club Frequent Flyer Points

Randomly inserted in second series packs were 100 different Frequent Flyer point cards with 20 of the best NBA jumpshot stars each having five different point cards. The insertion rate was one in every six packs. Upon collecting 50 points or more for one particular player the collector could send the cards to Topps and receive a limited edition Frequent Flyer Upgrade card for the same player. The blue-bordered fronts features a rainbow colored map of the United States with a diagram of when, where and how many points the player scored. The players name appears in yellow in the upper right. The purple-bordered back features the rules on a ghosted sky background.

	MINT	NRMT	EXC
COMPLETE (50 PTS/CARD)	200.00	90.00	25.00
COMMON POINT	.10	.05	.01
C.BARKLEY (1) PER POINT	.40	.18	.05
DEE BROWN (2) PER POINT	.10	.05	.01

DERRICK COLEMAN (3) PER POINT .15 .07 .02
CLYDE DREXLER (4) PER POINT .15 .07 .02
PATRICK EWING (5) PER POINT .25 .11 .03
RON HARPER (6) PER POINT... .10 .05 .01
LARRY JOHNSON (7) PER POINT .25 .11 .03
SHAWN KEMP (8) PER POINT.... .25 .11 .03
DAN MAJERLE (9) PER POINT .. .10 .05 .01
KARL MALONE (10) PER POINT .20 .09 .03
CHRIS MORRIS (11) PER POINT .10 .05 .01
H.OLAJUWON (12) PER POINT . .50 .23 .06
SHAQUILLE O'NEAL (13)PER POINT 1.00 .45 .12
SCOTTIE PIPPEN (14) PER POINT .25 .11 .03
DAVID ROBINSON (15) PER POINT .40 .18 .05
DENNIS RODMAN (16) PER POINT .10 .05 .01
JOHN STARKS (17) PER POINT .10 .05 .01
C.W'SPOON (18) PER POINT.... .15 .07 .02
CHRIS WEBBER (19) PER POINT 1.00 .45 .12
D. WILKINS (20) PER POINT.... .20 .09 .03

Upgrades were available only through a mail offer based on Frequent Flyer Point cards which were randomly inserted at a rate of 1 in every 6 second series packs. Each of the 21 players featured in the Frequent Flyer subsets (except for Michael Jordan) had five different point cards (based upon point totals derived from actual games during the season) making for a total of 100 different point cards. Since none of the point cards feature player photos, none trade for a premium and are priced below as expired point cards. To obtain a Frequent Flyer Upgrade card, collectors had to accumulate 50 points or more of an individual player and redeem them by September 15, 1994.

		MINT	NRMT	EXC
COMPLETE SET (20)		75.00	34.00	9.50
COMMON (182-190/348-358)		1.00	.45	.12
☐ 182	Dominique Wilkins.....	2.50	1.10	.30
☐ 183	Dennis Rodman............	15.00	6.75	1.85
☐ 184	Scottie Pippen............	12.00	5.50	1.50
☐ 185	Larry Johnson............	5.00	2.20	.60
☐ 186	Karl Malone...............	4.00	1.80	.50
☐ 187	Clarence Weatherspoon	1.50	.70	.19
☐ 188	Charles Barkley............	6.00	2.70	.75
☐ 189	Patrick Ewing.............	4.00	1.80	.50
☐ 190	Derrick Coleman.........	1.00	.45	.12
☐ 348	Hakeem Olajuwon......	10.00	4.50	1.25
☐ 349	Dee Brown...............	1.00	.45	.12
☐ 350	John Starks...............	1.00	.45	.12
☐ 351	Ron Harper..............	1.00	.45	.12
☐ 352	Chris Webber.............	10.00	4.50	1.25
☐ 353	Dan Majerle...............	1.50	.70	.19
☐ 354	Clyde Drexler............	5.00	2.20	.60
☐ 355	Shawn Kemp..............	12.00	5.50	1.50
☐ 356	David Robinson.........	8.00	3.60	1.00
☐ 357	Chris Morris..............	1.00	.45	.12
☐ 358	Shaquille O'Neal........	25.00	11.00	3.10
☐ NNO	Expired Point Cards....	.25	.11	.03

☐ 1	Charles Barkley................	.40	.18	.05
☐ 2	Dee Brown......................	.10	.05	.01
☐ 3	Derrick Coleman	.15	.07	.02
☐ 4	Clyde Drexler	.15	.07	.02
☐ 5	Patrick Ewing	.25	.11	.03
☐ 6	Ron Harper	.10	.05	.01
☐ 7	Larry Johnson	.25	.11	.03
☐ 8	Shawn Kemp...................	.25	.11	.03
☐ 9	Dan Majerle....................	.10	.05	.01
☐ 10	Karl Malone....................	.20	.09	.03
☐ 11	Chris Morris	.10	.05	.01
☐ 12	Hakeem Olajuwon	.50	.23	.06
☐ 13	Shaquille O'Neal............	1.00	.45	.12
☐ 14	Scottie Pippen................	.25	.11	.03
☐ 15	David Robinson	.40	.18	.05
☐ 16	Dennis Rodman	.10	.05	.01
☐ 17	John Starks....................	.10	.05	.01
☐ 18	Clarence Weatherspoon..	.15	.07	.02
☐ 19	Chris Webber..................	1.00	.45	.12
☐ 20	Dominique Wilkins...........	.20	.09	.03

1993-94 Stadium Club Frequent Flyer Upgrades

Cards from this 20-card standard size set are based upon the Frequent Flyer subsets in the basic 1993-94 Stadium Club issue. Upgrades are identical to the basic cards with the exception of a chromium like metallic gloss and Upgrade logo on front.

1993-94 Stadium Club Rim Rockers

Randomly inserted in second series 12-card packs at a rate of one in 24, these six standard-size cards feature some of the NBA's top dunkers. Fronts contain color player action shots. The player's name *appears near the bottom. His first name is printed in white lowercase lettering; his last is gold-foil stamped in uppercase lettering. The back carries another borderless color player action shot, but its right side is ghosted, blue-screened, and overprinted with career highlights in white lettering. The cards are numbered on the back as "X of 6."*

	MINT	NRMT	EXC
COMPLETE SET (6)	8.00	3.60	1.00
COMMON CARD (1-6)	.25	.11	.03
☐ 1 Shaquille O'Neal	5.00	2.20	.60
☐ 2 Harold Miner	.25	.11	.03
☐ 3 Charles Barkley	1.25	.55	.16
☐ 4 Dominique Wilkins	.50	.23	.06
☐ 5 Shawn Kemp	2.50	1.10	.30
☐ 6 Robert Horry	.50	.23	.06

1993-94 Stadium Club Super Teams

Randomly inserted in first series 12 and 20-card foil packs at a rate of one in 24, cards from this standard-size 27-card set feature borderless fronts with color team action photos. The team name appears in gold-foil lettering at the bottom. The back features the NBA Super Team Card rules. If the team shown on the card won its division, conference or league championship, the collector could have redeemed it for special prizes until Nov. 1, 1994. Atlanta, Houston, New York and Seattle were all winners. Their cards are currently in shorter supply than non-winner Super Team cards. The four winning teams are designated below with a "W". In addition, Conference, Division and Finals winner cards have "C", "D" and "F" designations.

	MINT	NRMT	EXC
COMPLETE SET (27)	15.00	6.75	1.85
COMMON CARD (1-27)	.40	.18	.05
☐ 1 Atlanta Hawks WD (Kevin Willis Dominique Wilkins)	2.00	.90	.25
☐ 2 Boston Celtics (Xavier McDaniel Robert Parish)	2.00	.90	.25
☐ 3 Charlotte Hornets (Larry Johnson Alonzo Mourning)	2.50	1.10	.30
☐ 4 Chicago Bulls (Harvey Grant)	.40	.18	.05
☐ 5 Cleveland Cavaliers (Brad Daugherty John Williams)	.40	.18	.05
☐ 6 Dallas Mavericks (Group photo)	.40	.18	.05
☐ 7 Denver Nuggets (Dikembe Mutombo Kevin Brooks)	2.00	.90	.25
☐ 8 Detroit Pistons (Group photo)	.40	.18	.05
☐ 9 Golden State Warriors (Group photo)	.40	.18	.05
☐ 10 Houston Rockets WCDF (Group photo)	6.00	2.70	.75
☐ 11 Indiana Pacers (Group photo)	.40	.18	.05
☐ 12 Los Angeles Clippers (Danny Manning Ron Harper)	2.00	.90	.25
☐ 13 Los Angeles Lakers (Group photo)	.40	.18	.05
☐ 14 Miami Heat (John Salley Willie Burton)	.40	.18	.05
☐ 15 Milwaukee Bucks (Group photo)	.40	.18	.05
☐ 16 Minnesota Timberwolves (Christian Laettner Felton Spencer)	2.00	.90	.25
☐ 17 New Jersey Nets (Derrick Coleman)	.40	.18	.05
☐ 18 New York Knicks WCD (Patrick Ewing)	2.50	1.10	.30
☐ 19 Orlando Magic (Shaquille O'Neal)	8.00	3.60	1.00
☐ 20 Philadelphia 76ers (Clarence Weatherspoon Jeff Hornacek)	2.00	.90	.25
☐ 21 Phoenix Suns (Charles Barkley Dan Majerle)	1.25	.55	.16
☐ 22 Portland Trail Blazers (Buck Williams)	.40	.18	.05
☐ 23 Sacramento Kings (Lionel Simmons)	.40	.18	.05
☐ 24 San Antonio Spurs (David Robinson)	1.50	.70	.19
☐ 25 Seattle Supersonics WD (Shawn Kemp)	4.00	1.80	.50
☐ 26 Utah Jazz (Group photo)	.40	.18	.05
☐ 27 Washington Bullets (Group photo)	.40	.18	.05

1993-94 Stadium Club Super Teams Division Winners

Collectors who pulled either a Hawks, Knicks, Rockets or Sonics Super Team

	MINT	NRMT	EXC
☐ S341 Ervin Johnson............	.75	.35	.09
☐ HD1 Hawks DW Super Team	1.00	.45	.12
☐ KD18 Knicks DW Super Team	1.00	.45	.12
☐ RD10 Rockets DW Super Team	1.00	.45	.12
☐ SD25 Sonics DW Super Team	1.00	.45	.12

1993-94 Stadium Club Super Teams Master Photos

insert card (randomly inserted in 1993-94 Stadium Club series 1 packs) could exchange the card for an 11-card Division Winners team set. The offer expired November 1, 1994. The cards are identical to their regular issue counterparts, except for the gold-foil Division Winner logo on their fronts. In the listing below, the suffixes H, K, R, and S have been added to denote Hawks, Knicks, Rockets and Supersonics.

	MINT	NRMT	EXC
COMPLETE BAG HAWKS (11)	6.00	2.70	.75
COMPLETE BAG KNICKS (11)	6.00	2.70	.75
COMPLETE BAG ROCKETS (11)	10.00	4.50	1.25
COMPLETE BAG SONICS (11)	10.00	4.50	1.25
COMMON CARD	.50	.23	.06
☐ H46 Adam Keefe	.50	.23	.06
☐ H93 Jon Koncak	.50	.23	.06
☐ H129 Dominique Wilkins	1.50	.70	.19
☐ H150 Doug Edwards DP	.50	.23	.06
☐ H197 Andrew Lang	.50	.23	.06
☐ H218 Craig Ehlo	.50	.23	.06
☐ H233 Danny Manning	1.00	.45	.12
☐ H249 Mookie Blaylock	1.00	.45	.12
☐ H310 Stacey Augmon	1.00	.45	.12
☐ H332 Kevin Willis	1.00	.45	.12
☐ K23 Hubert Davis	.50	.23	.06
☐ K34 Greg Anthony	.50	.23	.06
☐ K81 Doc Rivers	.50	.23	.06
☐ K116 John Starks	1.00	.45	.12
☐ K192 Derek Harper	1.00	.45	.12
☐ K200 Patrick Ewing	3.00	1.35	.35
☐ K225 Charles Oakley	.75	.35	.09
☐ K250 Anthony Bonner	.50	.23	.06
☐ K263 Charles Smith	.50	.23	.06
☐ K312 Anthony Mason	1.00	.45	.12
☐ R37 Scott Brooks	.50	.23	.06
☐ R89 Hakeem Olajuwon	7.50	3.40	.95
☐ R132 Kenny Smith	.50	.23	.06
☐ R156 Vernon Maxwell	.50	.23	.06
☐ R162 Carl Herrera	.50	.23	.06
☐ R210 Robert Horry	1.50	.70	.19
☐ R238 Otis Thorpe	.75	.35	.09
☐ R254 Mario Elie	.50	.23	.06
☐ R314 Sam Cassell	2.50	1.10	.35
☐ R346 Richard Petruska	.50	.23	.06
☐ S85 Michael Cage	.50	.23	.06
☐ S115 Nate McMillan	.50	.23	.06
☐ S154 Sam Perkins	.75	.35	.09
☐ S173 Shawn Kemp HC	3.00	1.35	.35
☐ S196 Gary Payton	2.00	.90	.25
☐ S222 Shawn Kemp	6.00	2.70	.75
☐ S253 Kendall Gill	.50	.23	.06
☐ S278 Ricky Pierce	.50	.23	.06
☐ S297 Detlef Schrempf	.75	.35	.09

Collectors who pulled either a Knicks or Rockets Super Team insert card (randomly inserted in 1993-94 Stadium Club series 1 packs) could exchange the card via mail for a 11-card Master Photo set. The expiration date for the offer was November 1, 1994. Measuring 5" by 7", the cards are numbered on the back "X of 10." In the listing below, the suffixes K and R have been added to denote Knicks and Rockets.

	MINT	NRMT	EXC
COMPLETE BAG KNICKS (11)	10.00	4.50	1.25
COMPLETE BAG ROCKETS (11)	15.00	6.75	1.85
COMMON CARD	.75	.35	.09
COMMON MP TEAM CARD	1.50	.70	.19
☐ K1 Greg Anthony	.75	.35	.09
☐ K2 Anthony Bonner	.75	.35	.09
☐ K3 Hubert Davis	.75	.35	.09
☐ K4 Patrick Ewing	5.00	2.20	.60
☐ K5 Derek Harper	1.25	.55	.16
☐ K6 Anthony Mason	1.25	.55	.16
☐ K7 Charles Oakley	1.25	.55	.16
☐ K8 Doc Rivers	.75	.35	.09
☐ K9 Charles Smith	.75	.35	.09
☐ K10 John Starks	1.25	.55	.16
☐ KMP Knicks MP Superteam	1.50	.70	.19
☐ R1 Scott Brooks	.75	.35	.09
☐ R2 Sam Cassell	3.00	1.35	.35
☐ R3 Mario Elie	.75	.35	.09
☐ R4 Carl Herrera	.75	.35	.09
☐ R5 Robert Horry	2.50	1.10	.30
☐ R6 Vernon Maxwell	.75	.35	.09
☐ R7 Hakeem Olajuwon	10.00	4.50	1.25
☐ R8 Richard Petruska	.75	.35	.09
☐ R9 Kenny Smith	.75	.35	.09
☐ R10 Otis Thorpe	1.25	.55	.16
☐ RMP Rockets MP Superteam	1.50	.70	.19

1993-94 Stadium Club Super Teams NBA Finals

This parallel issue to the 1993-94 Stadium Club set was redeemable only by mail in exchange for the Houston Rockets Super Team card (randomly inserted into 1993-94 Stadium Club series 1 packs.) The card had to be mailed in before the Nov. 1st, 1994 deadline. A gold-foil NBA Finals logo on the front distinguishes these cards from their regular issue counterparts. Please refer to the multipliers provided below (coupled with the prices of the corresponding regular issue cards) to ascertain value.

	MINT	NRMT	EXC
COMPLETE SET (361)	60.00	27.00	7.50
COMMON CARD (1-360)	.15	.07	.02
*SER.1 STARS: 1.25X to 2.5X VALUE			
*SER.2 STARS: 1.5X to 3X VALUE...			
*SER.1 ROOKIES: 1X to 2X VALUE..			
*SER.2 ROOKIES: 1.25X to 2.5X VALUE			

1994-95 Stadium Club

The 362 standard size cards that comprise the 1994-95 Stadium Club set were issued in two separate series of 182 and 180 cards each. Cards were primarily distributed in 12-card packs, each with a suggested retail price of $2.00. Full-bleed fronts feature full-color action shots with player's name placed along the bottom in foil. Topical subsets featured are College Teammates (100-114), Draft Picks (172, 179-182), All-Import (201-205, 251-255), Back Court Tandem (226-230, 276-280, 326-330), and Faces of the Game (353-362). Other topical subsets, such as Thru the Glass as well as First and Second Round '94 Draft Picks, are scattered throughout the set. Autographed cards of Reggie Miller were randomly inserted one per box into special retail boxes. Rookie Cards of note include Grant Hill, Juwan Howard, Eddie Jones, Jason Kidd and Glenn Robinson.

		MINT	NRMT	EXC
	COMPLETE SET (362)	40.00	18.00	5.00
	COMPLETE SERIES 1 (182)	20.00	9.00	2.50
	COMPLETE SERIES 2 (180)	20.00	9.00	2.50
	COMMON CARD (1-362)	.10	.05	.01
☐ 1	Patrick Ewing	.40	.18	.05
☐ 2	Patrick Ewing TTG	.20	.09	.03
☐ 3	Bimbo Coles	.10	.05	.01
☐ 4	Elden Campbell	.15	.07	.02
☐ 5	Brent Price	.10	.05	.01
☐ 6	Hubert Davis	.10	.05	.01
☐ 7	Donald Royal	.10	.05	.01
☐ 8	Tim Perry	.10	.05	.01
☐ 9	Chris Webber	.50	.23	.06
☐ 10	Chris Webber TTG	.25	.11	.03
☐ 11	Brad Daugherty	.10	.05	.01
☐ 12	P.J. Brown	.10	.05	.01
☐ 13	Charles Barkley	.60	.25	.07
☐ 14	Mario Elie	.10	.05	.01
☐ 15	Tyrone Hill	.10	.05	.01
☐ 16	Anfernee Hardaway	2.50	1.10	.30
☐ 17	Anfernee Hardaway TTG	1.25	.55	.16
☐ 18	Toni Kukoc	.30	.14	.04
☐ 19	Chris Morris	.10	.05	.01
☐ 20	Gerald Wilkins	.10	.05	.01
☐ 21	David Benoit	.10	.05	.01
☐ 22	Kevin Duckworth	.10	.05	.01
☐ 23	Derrick Coleman	.10	.05	.01
☐ 24	Adam Keefe	.10	.05	.01
☐ 25	Marlon Maxey	.10	.05	.01
☐ 26	Vern Fleming	.10	.05	.01
☐ 27	Jeff Malone	.10	.05	.01
☐ 28	Rodney Rogers	.10	.05	.01
☐ 29	Terry Mills	.10	.05	.01
☐ 30	Doug West	.10	.05	.01
☐ 31	Doug West TTG	.10	.05	.01
☐ 32	Shaquille O'Neal	2.00	.90	.25
☐ 33	Scottie Pippen	1.25	.55	.16
☐ 34	Lee Mayberry	.10	.05	.01
☐ 35	Dale Ellis	.10	.05	.01
☐ 36	Cedric Ceballos	.15	.07	.02
☐ 37	Lionel Simmons	.10	.05	.01
☐ 38	Kenny Gattison	.10	.05	.01
☐ 39	Popeye Jones	.10	.05	.01
☐ 40	Jerome Kersey	.10	.05	.01
☐ 41	Jerome Kersey TTG	.10	.05	.01
☐ 42	Larry Stewart	.10	.05	.01
☐ 43	Rod Strickland	.10	.05	.01
☐ 44	Chris Mills	.20	.09	.03
☐ 45	Latrell Sprewell	.50	.23	.06
☐ 46	Haywoode Workman	.10	.05	.01
☐ 47	Charles Smith	.10	.05	.01
☐ 48	Detlef Schrempf	.15	.07	.02
☐ 49	Gary Grant	.10	.05	.01

☐ 50	Gary Grant TTG	.10	.05	.01
☐ 51	Tom Chambers	.10	.05	.01
☐ 52	J.R. Reid	.10	.05	.01
☐ 53	Mookie Blaylock	.15	.07	.02
☐ 54	Mookie Blaylock TTG	.10	.05	.01
☐ 55	Rony Seikaly	.10	.05	.01
☐ 56	Isaiah Rider	.20	.09	.03
☐ 57	Isaiah Rider TTG	.10	.05	.01
☐ 58	Nick Anderson	.15	.07	.02
☐ 59	Victor Alexander	.10	.05	.01
☐ 60	Lucious Harris	.10	.05	.01
☐ 61	Mark Macon	.10	.05	.01
☐ 62	Otis Thorpe	.15	.07	.02
☐ 63	Randy Woods	.10	.05	.01
☐ 64	Clyde Drexler	.50	.23	.06
☐ 65	Dikembe Mutombo	.20	.09	.03
☐ 66	Todd Day	.10	.05	.01
☐ 67	Greg Anthony	.10	.05	.01
☐ 68	Sherman Douglas	.10	.05	.01
☐ 69	Chris Mullin	.15	.07	.02
☐ 70	Kevin Johnson	.20	.09	.03
☐ 71	Kendall Gill	.10	.05	.01
☐ 72	Dennis Rodman	1.50	.70	.19
☐ 73	Dennis Rodman TG	.75	.35	.09
☐ 74	Jeff Turner	.10	.05	.01
☐ 75	John Stockton	.40	.18	.05
☐ 76	John Stockton TTG	.20	.09	.03
☐ 77	Doug Edwards	.10	.05	.01
☐ 78	Jim Jackson	.50	.23	.06
☐ 79	Hakeem Olajuwon	1.00	.45	.12
☐ 80	Glen Rice	.20	.09	.03
☐ 81	Christian Laettner	.20	.09	.03
☐ 82	Terry Porter	.10	.05	.01
☐ 83	Joe Dumars	.20	.09	.03
☐ 84	David Wingate	.10	.05	.01
☐ 85	B.J. Armstrong	.10	.05	.01
☐ 86	Derrick McKey	.10	.05	.01
☐ 87	Elmore Spencer	.10	.05	.01
☐ 88	Walt Williams	.20	.09	.03
☐ 89	Shawn Bradley	.20	.09	.03
☐ 90	Acie Earl	.10	.05	.01
☐ 91	Acie Earl TTG	.10	.05	.01
☐ 92	Randy Brown	.10	.05	.01
☐ 93	Grant Long	.10	.05	.01
☐ 94	Terry Dehere	.10	.05	.01
☐ 95	Spud Webb	.15	.07	.02
☐ 96	Lindsey Hunter	.10	.05	.01
☐ 97	Blair Rasmussen	.10	.05	.01
☐ 98	Tim Hardaway	.15	.07	.02
☐ 99	Kevin Edwards	.10	.05	.01
☐ 100	Patrick Ewing CT	.15	.07	.02
	Reggie Williams CT			
	Georgetown Hoyas			
☐ 101	Chuck Person CT	.15	.07	.02
	Charles Barkley CT			
	Auburn Tigers			
☐ 102	Mahmoud Abdul-Rauf CT	.50	.23	.06
	Shaquille O'Neal CT			
	LSU Tigers			
☐ 103	Rony Seikaly CT	.10	.05	.01
	Derrick Coleman CT			
	Syracuse Orangemen			
☐ 104	Hakeem Olajuwon CT	.50	.23	.06
	Clyde Drexler CT			
	Houston Cougars			
☐ 105	Chris Mullin CT	.10	.05	.01
	Mark Jackson CT			
	St. John Red Storm			
☐ 106	Robert Horry CT	.10	.05	.01
	Latrell Sprewell CT			
	Alabama Crimson Tide			
☐ 107	Pooh Richardson CT	.10	.05	.01
	Reggie Miller CT			
	UCLA Bruins			
☐ 108	Dennis Scott CT	.10	.05	.01
	Kenny Anderson CT			
	GA Tech Yellow Jackets			
☐ 109	Kendall Gill CT	.10	.05	.01
	Ken Norman CT			
	Illinois Fightin' Illini			
☐ 110	Scott Skiles CT	.10	.05	.01
	Kevin Willis CT			
	Michigan State Spartans			
☐ 111	Terry Mills CT	.10	.05	.01
	Glen Rice CT			
	Michigan Wolverines			
☐ 112	Christian Laettner CT	.20	.09	.03
	Bobby Hurley CT			
	Duke Blue Devils			
☐ 113	Stacey Augmon CT	.20	.09	.03
	Larry Johnson CT			
	UNLV Runnin' Rebels			
☐ 114	Sam Perkins CT	.15	.07	.02
	James Worthy CT			
	North Carolina Tar Heels			
☐ 115	Carl Herrera	.10	.05	.01
☐ 116	Sam Bowie	.10	.05	.01
☐ 117	Gary Payton	.60	.25	.07
☐ 118	Danny Ainge	.20	.09	.03
☐ 119	Danny Ainge TTG	.15	.07	.02
☐ 120	Luc Longley	.10	.05	.01
☐ 121	Antonio Davis	.10	.05	.01
☐ 122	Terry Cummings	.10	.05	.01
☐ 123	Terry Cummings TTG	.10	.05	.01
☐ 124	Mark Price	.10	.05	.01
☐ 125	Jamal Mashburn	.30	.14	.04
☐ 126	Mahmoud Abdul-Rauf	.15	.07	.02
☐ 127	Charles Oakley	.15	.07	.02
☐ 128	Steve Smith	.20	.09	.03
☐ 129	Vin Baker	.50	.23	.06
☐ 130	Robert Horry	.15	.07	.02
☐ 131	Doug Christie	.10	.05	.01
☐ 132	Wayman Tisdale	.10	.05	.01
☐ 133	Wayman Tisdale TTG	.10	.05	.01
☐ 134	Muggsy Bogues	.15	.07	.02
☐ 135	Dino Radja	.20	.09	.03
☐ 136	Jeff Hornacek	.15	.07	.02
☐ 137	Gheorghe Muresan	.20	.09	.03
☐ 138	Loy Vaught	.10	.05	.01
☐ 139	Loy Vaught TTG	.10	.05	.01
☐ 140	Benoit Benjamin	.10	.05	.01
☐ 141	Johnny Dawkins	.10	.05	.01
☐ 142	Allan Houston	.25	.11	.03
☐ 143	Jon Barry	.10	.05	.01
☐ 144	Reggie Miller	.50	.23	.06
☐ 145	Kevin Willis	.10	.05	.01
☐ 146	James Worthy	.20	.09	.03
☐ 147	James Worthy TTG	.15	.07	.02
☐ 148	Scott Burrell	.10	.05	.01
☐ 149	Tom Gugliotta	.20	.09	.03
☐ 150	LaPhonso Ellis	.10	.05	.01
☐ 151	Doug Smith	.10	.05	.01
☐ 152	A.C. Green	.20	.09	.03
☐ 153	A.C. Green TTG	.15	.07	.02
☐ 154	George Lynch	.10	.05	.01
☐ 155	Sam Perkins	.15	.07	.02
☐ 156	Corie Blount	.10	.05	.01
☐ 157	Xavier McDaniel	.10	.05	.01
☐ 158	Xavier McDaniel TTG	.10	.05	.01
☐ 159	Eric Murdock	.10	.05	.01
☐ 160	David Robinson	.75	.35	.09
☐ 161	Karl Malone	.40	.18	.05

☐ 162 Karl Malone TTG	.20	.09	.03
☐ 163 Clarence Weatherspoon	.15	.07	.02
☐ 164 Calbert Cheaney	.20	.09	.03
☐ 165 Tom Hammonds	.10	.05	.01
☐ 166 Tom Hammonds TTG	.10	.05	.01
☐ 167 Alonzo Mourning	.50	.23	.06
☐ 168 Clifford Robinson	.20	.09	.03
☐ 169 Micheal Williams	.10	.05	.01
☐ 170 Ervin Johnson	.10	.05	.01
☐ 171 Mike Gminski	.10	.05	.01
☐ 172 Jason Kidd	3.00	1.35	.35
☐ 173 Anthony Bonner	.10	.05	.01
☐ 174 Stacey King	.10	.05	.01
☐ 175 Rex Chapman	.10	.05	.01
☐ 176 Greg Anthony	.10	.05	.01
☐ 177 Stanley Roberts	.10	.05	.01
☐ 178 Mitch Richmond	.30	.14	.04
☐ 179 Eric Montross	.20	.09	.03
☐ 180 Eddie Jones	1.00	.45	.12
☐ 181 Grant Hill	5.00	2.20	.60
☐ 182 Donyell Marshall	.15	.07	.02
☐ 183 Glenn Robinson	1.50	.70	.19
☐ 184 Dominique Wilkins	.20	.09	.03
☐ 185 Mark Price	.10	.05	.01
☐ 186 Anthony Mason	.15	.07	.02
☐ 187 Tyrone Corbin	.10	.05	.01
☐ 188 Dale Davis	.10	.05	.01
☐ 189 Nate McMillan	.10	.05	.01
☐ 190 Jason Kidd	1.50	.70	.19
☐ 191 John Salley	.10	.05	.01
☐ 192 Keith Jennings	.10	.05	.01
☐ 193 Mark Bryant	.10	.05	.01
☐ 194 Sleepy Floyd	.10	.05	.01
☐ 195 Grant Hill	2.50	1.10	.30
☐ 196 Joe Kleine	.10	.05	.01
☐ 197 Anthony Peeler	.10	.05	.01
☐ 198 Malik Sealy	.10	.05	.01
☐ 199 Kenny Walker	.10	.05	.01
☐ 200 Donyell Marshall	.10	.05	.01
☐ 201 Vlade Divac Al	.15	.07	.02
☐ 202 Dino Radja Al	.10	.05	.01
☐ 203 Carl Herrera Al	.10	.05	.01
☐ 204 Olden Polynice Al	.10	.05	.01
☐ 205 Patrick Ewing Al	.20	.09	.03
☐ 206 Willie Anderson	.10	.05	.01
☐ 207 Mitch Richmond	.30	.14	.04
☐ 208 John Crotty	.10	.05	.01
☐ 209 Tracy Murray	.10	.05	.01
☐ 210 Juwan Howard	3.00	1.35	.35
☐ 211 Robert Parish	.20	.09	.03
☐ 212 Steve Kerr	.15	.07	.02
☐ 213 Anthony Bowie	.10	.05	.01
☐ 214 Tim Breaux	.10	.05	.01
☐ 215 Sharone Wright	.20	.09	.03
☐ 216 Brian Williams	.10	.05	.01
☐ 217 Rick Fox	.10	.05	.01
☐ 218 Harold Miner	.10	.05	.01
☐ 219 Duane Ferrell	.10	.05	.01
☐ 220 Lamond Murray	.15	.07	.02
☐ 221 Blue Edwards	.10	.05	.01
☐ 222 Bill Cartwright	.10	.05	.01
☐ 223 Sergei Bazarevich	.10	.05	.01
☐ 224 Herb Williams	.10	.05	.01
☐ 225 Brian Grant	.60	.25	.07
☐ 226 Derek Harper BCT	.10	.05	.01
John Starks			
☐ 227 Rod Strickland BCT	.15	.07	.02
Clyde Drexler			
☐ 228 Kevin Johnson BCT	.15	.07	.02
Dan Majerle			
☐ 229 Lindsey Hunter BCT	.10	.05	.01

Joe Dumars			
☐ 230 Tim Hardaway BCT	.10	.05	.01
Latrell Sprewell			
☐ 231 Bill Wennington	.10	.05	.01
☐ 232 Brian Shaw	.10	.05	.01
☐ 233 Jamie Watson	.10	.05	.01
☐ 234 Chris Whitney	.10	.05	.01
☐ 235 Eric Montross	.15	.07	.02
☐ 236 Kenny Smith	.10	.05	.01
☐ 237 Andrew Lang	.10	.05	.01
☐ 238 Lorenzo Williams	.10	.05	.01
☐ 239 Dana Barros	.10	.05	.01
☐ 240 Eddie Jones	.50	.23	.06
☐ 241 Harold Ellis	.10	.05	.01
☐ 242 James Edwards	.10	.05	.01
☐ 243 Don MacLean	.10	.05	.01
☐ 244 Ed Pinckney	.10	.05	.01
☐ 245 Carlos Rogers	.10	.05	.01
☐ 246 Michael Adams	.10	.05	.01
☐ 247 Rex Walters	.10	.05	.01
☐ 248 John Starks	.10	.05	.01
☐ 249 Terrell Brandon	.20	.09	.03
☐ 250 Khalid Reeves	.15	.07	.02
☐ 251 Dominique Wilkins Al	.15	.07	.02
☐ 252 Toni Kukoc Al	.15	.07	.02
☐ 253 Rick Fox Al	.10	.05	.01
☐ 254 Detlef Schrempf Al	.10	.05	.01
☐ 255 Rik Smits Al	.10	.05	.01
☐ 256 Johnny Dawkins	.10	.05	.01
☐ 257 Dan Majerle	.15	.07	.02
☐ 258 Mike Brown	.10	.05	.01
☐ 259 Byron Scott	.20	.09	.03
☐ 260 Jalen Rose	.40	.18	.05
☐ 261 Byron Houston	.10	.05	.01
☐ 262 Frank Brickowski	.10	.05	.01
☐ 263 Vernon Maxwell	.10	.05	.01
☐ 264 Craig Ehlo	.10	.05	.01
☐ 265 Yinka Dare	.10	.05	.01
☐ 266 Dee Brown	.10	.05	.01
☐ 267 Felton Spencer	.10	.05	.01
☐ 268 Harvey Grant	.10	.05	.01
☐ 269 Nick Van Exel	.40	.18	.05
☐ 270 Bob Martin	.10	.05	.01
☐ 271 Hersey Hawkins	.10	.05	.01
☐ 272 Scott Williams	.10	.05	.01
☐ 273 Sarunas Marciulionis	.10	.05	.01
☐ 274 Kevin Gamble	.10	.05	.01
☐ 275 Clifford Rozier	.15	.07	.02
☐ 276 B.J. Armstrong BCT	.10	.05	.01
Ron Harper			
☐ 277 John Stockton BCT	.20	.09	.03
Jeff Hornacek			
☐ 278 Bobby Hurley BCT	.10	.05	.01
Mitch Richmond			
☐ 279 Anfernee Hardaway BCT	.60	.25	.07
Dennis Scott			
☐ 280 Jason Kidd BCT	.60	.25	.07
Jim Jackson			
☐ 281 Ron Harper	.15	.07	.02
☐ 282 Chuck Person	.10	.05	.01
☐ 283 John Williams	.10	.05	.01
☐ 284 Robert Pack	.10	.05	.01
☐ 285 Aaron McKie	.20	.09	.03
☐ 286 Chris Smith	.10	.05	.01
☐ 287 Horace Grant	.20	.09	.03
☐ 288 Oliver Miller	.10	.05	.01
☐ 289 Derek Harper	.10	.05	.01
☐ 290 Eric Mobley	.15	.07	.02
☐ 291 Scott Skiles	.10	.05	.01
☐ 292 Olden Polynice	.10	.05	.01
☐ 293 Mark Jackson	.10	.05	.01

☐ 294 Wayman Tisdale	.10	.05	.01
☐ 295 Tony Dumas	.20	.09	.03
☐ 296 Bryon Russell	.10	.05	.01
☐ 297 Vlade Divac	.20	.09	.03
☐ 298 David Wesley	.10	.05	.01
☐ 299 Askia Jones	.10	.05	.01
☐ 300 B.J. Tyler	.10	.05	.01
☐ 301 Hakeem Olajuwon AI	.50	.23	.06
☐ 302 Luc Longley AI	.10	.05	.01
☐ 303 Rony Seikaly AI	.10	.05	.01
☐ 304 Sarunas Marciulionis AI	.10	.05	.01
☐ 305 Dikembe Mutombo AI	.15	.07	.02
☐ 306 Ken Norman	.10	.05	.01
☐ 307 Dell Curry	.10	.05	.01
☐ 308 Danny Ferry	.10	.05	.01
☐ 309 Shawn Kemp	1.25	.55	.16
☐ 310 Dickey Simpkins	.15	.07	.02
☐ 311 Johnny Newman	.10	.05	.01
☐ 312 Dwayne Schintzius	.10	.05	.01
☐ 313 Sean Elliott	.20	.09	.03
☐ 314 Sean Rooks	.10	.05	.01
☐ 315 Bill Curley	.10	.05	.01
☐ 316 Bryant Stith	.10	.05	.01
☐ 317 Pooh Richardson	.10	.05	.01
☐ 318 Jim McIlvaine	.15	.07	.02
☐ 319 Dennis Scott	.20	.09	.03
☐ 320 Wesley Person	.75	.35	.09
☐ 321 Bobby Hurley	.10	.05	.01
☐ 322 Armon Gilliam	.10	.05	.01
☐ 323 Rik Smits	.20	.09	.03
☐ 324 Tony Smith	.10	.05	.01
☐ 325 Monty Williams	.10	.05	.01
☐ 326 Gary Payton BCT	.15	.07	.02
Kendall Gill			
☐ 327 Mookie Blaylock BCT	.10	.05	.01
Stacey Augmon			
☐ 328 Mark Jackson BCT	.15	.07	.02
Reggie Miller			
☐ 329 Sam Cassell BCT	.10	.05	.01
Vernon Maxwell			
☐ 330 Harold Miner BCT	.10	.05	.01
Khalid Reeves			
☐ 331 Vinny Del Negro	.10	.05	.01
☐ 332 Billy Owens	.10	.05	.01
☐ 333 Mark West	.10	.05	.01
☐ 334 Matt Geiger	.10	.05	.01
☐ 335 Greg Minor	.10	.05	.01
☐ 336 Larry Johnson	.40	.18	.05
☐ 337 Donald Hodge	.10	.05	.01
☐ 338 Aaron Williams	.10	.05	.01
☐ 339 Jay Humphries	.10	.05	.01
☐ 340 Charlie Ward	.20	.09	.03
☐ 341 Scott Brooks	.10	.05	.01
☐ 342 Stacey Augmon	.15	.07	.02
☐ 343 Will Perdue	.10	.05	.01
☐ 344 Dale Ellis	.10	.05	.01
☐ 345 Brooks Thompson	.15	.07	.02
☐ 346 Manute Bol	.10	.05	.01
☐ 347 Kenny Anderson	.20	.09	.03
☐ 348 Willie Burton	.10	.05	.01
☐ 349 Michael Cage	.10	.05	.01
☐ 350 Danny Manning	.15	.07	.02
☐ 351 Ricky Pierce	.10	.05	.01
☐ 352 Sam Cassell	.20	.09	.03
☐ 353 Reggie Miller FG	.25	.11	.03
☐ 354 David Robinson FG	.40	.18	.05
☐ 355 Shaquille O'Neal FG	1.00	.45	.12
☐ 356 Scottie Pippen FG	.60	.25	.07
☐ 357 Alonzo Mourning FG	.25	.11	.03
☐ 358 Clarence Weatherspoon FG	.10	.05	.01
☐ 359 Derrick Coleman FG	.10	.05	.01

☐ 360 Charles Barkley FG	.30	.14	.04
☐ 361 Karl Malone FG	.20	.09	.03
☐ 362 Chris Webber FG	.25	.11	.03
☐ NNO Reggie Miller AU	30.00	13.50	3.70

1994-95 Stadium Club First Day Issue

This set parallels the basic issue 1994-95 Stadium Club set. First Day cards were randomly inserted into both series packs at a rate of one in 24. The cards differ from their regular issue counterparts in that each First Day card has a gold-foil "First Day Issue" logo on front. Please refer to the multipliers provided below (coupled with the values of the corresponding regular issue cards) to ascertain value of unlisted singles.

	MINT	NRMT	EXC
COMPLETE SET (362)	1200.00	550.00	150.00
COMP.SERIES 1 (182)	800.00	350.00	100.00
COMP.SERIES 2 (180)	400.00	180.00	50.00
COMMON CARD (1-362)	2.00	.90	.25
*STARS: 15X to 30X VALUE			
*ROOKIES: 10X to 20X VALUE			

☐ 16 Anfernee Hardaway	80.00	36.00	10.00
☐ 17 Anfernee Hardaway TTG	40.00	18.00	5.00
☐ 32 Shaquille O'Neal	60.00	27.00	7.50
☐ 33 Scottie Pippen	40.00	18.00	5.00
☐ 72 Dennis Rodman	50.00	22.00	6.25
☐ 79 Hakeem Olajuwon	30.00	13.50	3.70
☐ 172 Jason Kidd	60.00	27.00	7.50
☐ 181 Grant Hill	100.00	45.00	12.50
☐ 183 Glenn Robinson	30.00	13.50	3.70
☐ 190 Jason Kidd	30.00	13.50	3.70
☐ 195 Grant Hill	50.00	22.00	6.25
☐ 210 Juwan Howard	60.00	27.00	7.50
☐ 309 Shawn Kemp	40.00	18.00	5.00
☐ 355 Shaquille O'Neal FG	30.00	13.50	3.70

1994-95 Stadium Club Beam Team

Randomly inserted at a rate of 1 in every 24 second series packs, this 27-card standard-size set features a star player from

each NBA team spotlit with lazer light foil. The borderless fronts feature a player photo with his name in the upper left corner and the words "Beam Team" in funky lettering on the bottom. The backs are split between a player photo and some notes. Vital statistics are in the lower left corner and the cards are numbered in the lower corner as "X" of 27. The set is sequenced in alphabetical order by team.

	MINT	NRMT	EXC
COMPLETE SET (27)	75.00	34.00	9.50
COMMON CARD (1-27)	1.00	.45	.12

		MINT	NRMT	EXC
☐	1 Mookie Blaylock	1.00	.45	.12
☐	2 Dominique Wilkins	1.50	.70	.19
☐	3 Alonzo Mourning	4.00	1.80	.50
☐	4 Toni Kukoc	2.50	1.10	.30
☐	5 Mark Price	1.00	.45	.12
☐	6 Jason Kidd	12.00	5.50	1.50
☐	7 Jalen Rose	1.50	.70	.19
☐	8 Grant Hill	20.00	9.00	2.50
☐	9 Latrell Sprewell	1.50	.70	.19
☐	10 Hakeem Olajuwon	8.00	3.60	1.00
☐	11 Reggie Miller	4.00	1.80	.50
☐	12 Lamond Murray	1.00	.45	.12
☐	13 George Lynch	1.00	.45	.12
☐	14 Khalid Reeves	1.00	.45	.12
☐	15 Glenn Robinson	6.00	2.70	.75
☐	16 Donyell Marshall	1.00	.45	.12
☐	17 Derrick Coleman	1.00	.45	.12
☐	18 Patrick Ewing	2.50	1.10	.30
☐	19 Shaquille O'Neal	15.00	6.75	1.85
☐	20 Clarence Weatherspoon	1.50	.70	.19
☐	21 Charles Barkley	5.00	2.20	.60
☐	22 Clifford Robinson	1.50	.70	.19
☐	23 Bobby Hurley	1.00	.45	.12
☐	24 David Robinson	6.00	2.70	.75
☐	25 Shawn Kemp	10.00	4.50	1.25
☐	26 Karl Malone	3.00	1.35	.35
☐	27 Chris Webber	4.00	1.80	.50

1994-95 Stadium Club Clear Cut

Randomly inserted in all first series packs at a rate of one in 12, cards from this 27-card acetate set spotlight one key player from each NBA team. The set has "see through" fronts with some statistical information on the back. The player is identified

on the right side of the card and the words "Clear Cut" are located in the bottom right. The set is sequenced in alphabetical order by team.

	MINT	NRMT	EXC
COMPLETE SET (27)	35.00	16.00	4.40
COMMON CARD (1-27)	1.00	.45	.12

		MINT	NRMT	EXC
☐	1 Stacey Augmon	1.00	.45	.12
☐	2 Dino Radja	1.50	.70	.19
☐	3 Alonzo Mourning	4.00	1.80	.50
☐	4 Scottie Pippen	10.00	4.50	1.25
☐	5 Gerald Wilkins	1.00	.45	.12
☐	6 Jamal Mashburn	2.50	1.10	.30
☐	7 Dikembe Mutombo	1.50	.70	.19
☐	8 Lindsey Hunter	1.00	.45	.12
☐	9 Chris Mullin	1.50	.70	.19
☐	10 Hakeem Olajuwon	8.00	3.60	1.00
☐	11 Reggie Miller	4.00	1.80	.50
☐	12 Gary Grant	1.00	.45	.12
☐	13 Doug Christie	1.00	.45	.12
☐	14 Steve Smith	1.50	.70	.19
☐	15 Vin Baker	4.00	1.80	.50
☐	16 Christian Laettner	1.50	.70	.19
☐	17 Derrick Coleman	1.00	.45	.12
☐	18 Charles Oakley	1.00	.45	.12
☐	19 Dennis Scott	1.00	.45	.12
☐	20 Clarence Weatherspoon	1.50	.70	.19
☐	21 Charles Barkley	5.00	2.20	.60
☐	22 Clifford Robinson	1.50	.70	.19
☐	23 Mitch Richmond	2.50	1.10	.30
☐	24 David Robinson	6.00	2.70	.75
☐	25 Shawn Kemp	10.00	4.50	1.25
☐	26 Karl Malone	3.00	1.35	.35
☐	27 Don MacLean	1.00	.45	.12

1994-95 Stadium Club Dynasty and Destiny

This 20-card standard-size set was randomly inserted in first series foil packs at a rate of one in six and were also inserted one per first series rack pack. This set features a mixture of youthful phenoms paired up with a matching veteran star. The borderless fronts feature player photos, the player's name in the upper left corner and either the word "Destiny" or "Dynasty" in the lower right. The back has a player photo in a lower corner with a brief note and stats on the other side.

	MINT	NRMT	EXC
COMPLETE SET (20)	12.00	5.50	1.50
COMMON DYNASTY (1A-10A)	.25	.11	.03
COMMON DESTINY (1B-10B)	.25	.11	.03
☐ 1A Mark Price	.25	.11	.03
☐ 1B Kenny Anderson	.25	.11	.03
☐ 2A Karl Malone	.60	.25	.07
☐ 2B Derrick Coleman	.25	.11	.03
☐ 3A John Stockton	.60	.25	.07
☐ 3B Anfernee Hardaway	4.00	1.80	.50
☐ 4A Mitch Richmond	.40	.18	.05
☐ 4B Jim Jackson	.75	.35	.09
☐ 5A James Worthy	.40	.18	.05
☐ 5B Jamal Mashburn	.50	.23	.06
☐ 6A Patrick Ewing	.60	.25	.07
☐ 6B Alonzo Mourning	.75	.35	.09
☐ 7A Hakeem Olajuwon	1.50	.70	.19
☐ 7B Shaquille O'Neal	3.00	1.35	.35
☐ 8A Clyde Drexler	.75	.35	.09
☐ 8B Isaiah Rider	.25	.11	.03
☐ 9A Scottie Pippen	2.00	.90	.25
☐ 9B Latrell Sprewell	.40	.18	.05
☐ 10A Charles Barkley	1.00	.45	.12
☐ 10B Chris Webber	.75	.35	.09

1994-95 Stadium Club Rising Stars

Randomly inserted in all first series packs at a rate of one in 24, cards from this 10-card standard-size set feature a selection of young NBA stars. Card fronts feature full-color player action shots cut out against etched-foil backgrounds, with a prismatic galaxy design.

	MINT	NRMT	EXC
COMPLETE SET (12)	60.00	27.00	7.50
COMMON CARD (1-12)	1.00	.45	.12
☐ 1 Kenny Anderson	2.50	1.10	.30
☐ 2 Latrell Sprewell	2.50	1.10	.30
☐ 3 Jamal Mashburn	4.00	1.80	.50
☐ 4 Alonzo Mourning	6.00	2.70	.75
☐ 5 Shaquille O'Neal	25.00	11.00	3.10
☐ 6 LaPhonso Ellis	1.00	.45	.12
☐ 7 Chris Webber	6.00	2.70	.75
☐ 8 Isaiah Rider	1.00	.45	.12
☐ 9 Dikembe Mutombo	2.50	1.10	.30
☐ 10 Anfernee Hardaway	30.00	13.50	3.70
☐ 11 Antonio Davis	1.00	.45	.12
☐ 12 Robert Horry	2.50	1.10	.30

1994-95 Stadium Club Super Skills

Randomly inserted at a rate of 1 in every 24 second series 12-card packs and seeded one per second series retail rack pack, cards from this 25-card standard-size set feature Topps selection of the five top players at each position in the NBA. Card fronts feature a multi-hued rainbow foil background.

	MINT	NRMT	EXC
COMPLETE SET (25)	40.00	18.00	5.00
COMMON CARD (1-25)	.50	.23	.06
☐ 1 Mark Price	.50	.23	.06
☐ 2 Tim Hardaway	1.25	.55	.16
☐ 3 Kevin Johnson	1.25	.55	.16
☐ 4 John Stockton	2.00	.90	.25
☐ 5 Mookie Blaylock	.75	.35	.09
☐ 6 Reggie Miller	2.50	1.10	.30
☐ 7 Jeff Hornacek	.75	.35	.09
☐ 8 Latrell Sprewell	1.25	.55	.16
☐ 9 John Starks	.50	.23	.06
☐ 10 Nate McMillan	.50	.23	.06
☐ 11 Chris Mullin	1.25	.55	.16
☐ 12 Toni Kukoc	1.50	.70	.19
☐ 13 Anthony Mason	.75	.35	.09
☐ 14 Robert Horry	1.25	.55	.16
☐ 15 Scottie Pippen	6.00	2.70	.75
☐ 16 Charles Barkley	3.00	1.35	.35
☐ 17 Dennis Rodman	8.00	3.60	1.00
☐ 18 Karl Malone	2.00	.90	.25
☐ 19 Chris Webber	2.50	1.10	.30

		MINT	NRMT	EXC
☐ 20	Charles Oakley	.50	.23	.06
☐ 21	Patrick Ewing	2.00	.90	.25
☐ 22	Shaquille O'Neal	10.00	4.50	1.25
☐ 23	Dikembe Mutombo	1.25	.55	.16
☐ 24	David Robinson	4.00	1.80	.50
☐ 25	Hakeem Olajuwon	5.00	2.20	.60

1994-95 Stadium Club Super Teams

Randomly inserted in all first series packs at a rate of one in 24, cards from this 27-card standard-size set feature an action shot or group photo from each team in the league. Teams that won either their Division, their Conference or the NBA Finals were redeemable for special team sets or other prizes. The expiration date for Super Team cards was December 31st, 1995. The five winning cards (Houston, Indiana, Orlando, Phoenix and San Antonio) carry "W" designations. In addition "C", "D" and "F" designations are used to denote conference, division and finals winners.

		MINT	NRMT	EXC
COMPLETE SET (27)		40.00	18.00	5.00
COMMON TEAM (1-27)		1.00	.45	.12
☐ 1	Atlanta Hawks	1.00	.45	.12
	Kevin Willis			
☐ 2	Boston Celtics Group	1.00	.45	.12
☐ 3	Charlotte Hornets	1.00	.45	.12
	Muggsy Bogues			
☐ 4	Chicago Bulls Group	1.00	.45	.12
☐ 5	Cleveland Cavaliers	1.00	.45	.12
	Danny Ferry			
☐ 6	Dallas Mavericks	2.00	.90	.25
	Jim Jackson			
☐ 7	Denver Nuggets	1.00	.45	.12
	Rodney Rogers			
☐ 8	Detroit Pistons	1.50	.70	.19
	Joe Dumars			
☐ 9	Golden State Warriors	3.00	1.35	.35
	Chris Webber			
☐ 10	Houston Rockets WCF	15.00	6.75	1.85
	Hakeem Olajuwon			
☐ 11	Indiana Pacers WD	1.50	.70	.19
	Rik Smits			
☐ 12	LA Clippers/Group	1.00	.45	.12
☐ 13	L.A. Lakers	2.50	1.10	.30
	Nick Van Exel			
☐ 14	Miami Heat	1.00	.45	.12
	Glen Rice			
☐ 15	Milwaukee Bucks	3.00	1.35	.35
	Vin Baker			
☐ 16	Minnesota Timberwolves	1.50	.70	.19
	Christian Laettner			
☐ 17	New Jersey Nets	1.00	.45	.12
	Chris Morris			
☐ 18	New York Knicks/Group	1.00	.45	.12
☐ 19	Orlando Magic WCD	15.00	6.75	1.85
	Shaquille O'Neal			
☐ 20	Philadelphia 76ers	1.00	.45	.12
	Dana Barros			
☐ 21	Phoenix Suns WD	5.00	2.20	.60
	Charles Barkley			
☐ 22	Portland Trail Blazers	1.00	.45	.12
	Group			
☐ 23	Sacramento Kings	1.00	.45	.12
	Olden Polynice			
☐ 24	San Antonio Spurs WD	1.50	.70	.19
	Group			
☐ 25	Seattle Supersonics	1.00	.45	.12
	Group			
☐ 26	Utah Jazz	2.50	1.10	.30
	John Stockton			
☐ 27	Washington Bullets	1.00	.45	.12
	Group			

1994-95 Stadium Club Super Teams Division Winners

Each of these four team sets was available exclusively by mailing in the corresponding winning Super Team card before the December 31st, 1995 deadline. Super Team cards were randomly seeded in all first series Stadium Club packs at a rate of one in 24. The card design parallels the regular issue Stadium Club cards except for the gold foil "Division Winner" logo on each card front. The cards are listed below alphabetically according to teams; the prefixes M, P, SP, and SU have been added to denote Magic, Pacers, Spurs and Suns respectively.

	MINT	NRMT	EXC
COMP.BAG MAGIC (11)	12.00	5.50	1.50
COMP.BAG PACERS (11)	3.00	1.35	.35
COMP.BAG SPURS (11)	5.00	2.20	.60
COMP.BAG SUNS (11)	6.00	2.70	.75

COMMON CARD	.25	.11	.03
COMMON DW TEAM CARD	1.00	.45	.12

☐ M7 Donald Royal	.25	.11	.03
☐ M16 Anfernee Hardaway	6.00	2.70	.75
☐ M32 Shaquille O'Neal	5.00	2.20	.60
☐ M58 Nick Anderson	.50	.23	.06
☐ M74 Jeff Turner	.25	.11	.03
☐ M213 Anthony Bowie	.25	.11	.03
☐ M232 Brian Shaw	.25	.11	.03
☐ M287 Horace Grant	.50	.23	.06
☐ M319 Dennis Scott	.50	.23	.06
☐ M345 Brooks Thompson	.25	.11	.03
☐ MD19 Magic DW Super Team	1.00	.45	.12
☐ P26 Vern Fleming	.25	.11	.03
☐ P46 Haywoode Workman	.25	.11	.03
☐ P86 Derrick McKey	.25	.11	.03
☐ P121 Antonio Davis	.25	.11	.03
☐ P144 Reggie Miller	1.00	.45	.12
☐ P188 Dale Davis	.25	.11	.03
☐ P219 Duane Ferrell	.25	.11	.03
☐ P259 Byron Scott	.35	.16	.04
☐ P293 Mark Jackson	.25	.11	.03
☐ P323 Rik Smits	.50	.23	.06
☐ PD11 Pacers DW Super Team	1.00	.45	.12
☐ SP52 J.R. Reid	.25	.11	.03
☐ SP72 Dennis Rodman	2.00	.90	.25
☐ SP73 Dennis Rodman TG	1.00	.45	.12
☐ SP122 Terry Cummings	.25	.11	.03
☐ SP160 David Robinson	2.00	.90	.25
☐ SP206 Willie Anderson	.25	.11	.03
☐ SP282 Chuck Person	.25	.11	.03
☐ SP313 Sean Elliott	.50	.23	.06
☐ SP331 Vinny Del Negro	.35	.16	.04
☐ SP354 David Robinson FG	1.00	.45	.12
☐ SPD24 Spurs DW Super Team	1.00	.45	.12
☐ SU13 Charles Barkley	2.00	.90	.25
☐ SU70 Kevin Johnson	.50	.23	.06
☐ SU118 Danny Ainge	.50	.23	.06
☐ SU152 A.C. Green	.50	.23	.06
☐ SU196 Joe Kleine	.25	.11	.03
☐ SU257 Dan Majerle	.35	.16	.04
☐ SU294 Wayman Tisdale	.25	.11	.03
☐ SU320 Wesley Person	.50	.23	.06
☐ SU350 Danny Manning	.35	.16	.04
☐ SU360 Charles Barkley FG	1.00	.45	.12
☐ SUD21 Suns DW Super Team	1.00	.45	.12

1994-95 Stadium Club Super Teams Master Photos

Each of these two over-sized (5" by 7") team sets were available exclusively by mailing in the corresponding winning Super Team card before the December 31st, 1995 deadline. Super Team cards were randomly seeded in all first series Stadium Club packs at a rate of one in 24. The card design loosely parallels the corresponding regular issue Stadium Club cards but the bold, wildly designed borders and separate numbering sequences create distinctive differences. The cards are listed below alphabetically according to teams; the prefixes M and R have been added to denote Magic and Rockets respectively.

	MINT	NRMT	EXC
COMP.BAG MAGIC (11)	15.00	6.75	1.85
COMP.BAG ROCKETS (11)	8.00	3.60	1.00
COMMON CARD	.40	.18	.05
COMMON MP TEAM CARD	1.00	.45	.12

☐ M1 Nick Anderson	.75	.35	.09
☐ M2 Anthony Bowie	.40	.18	.05
☐ M3 Jeff Turner	.40	.18	.05
☐ M4 Dennis Scott	.40	.18	.05
☐ M5 Horace Grant	.75	.35	.09
☐ M6 Shaquille O'Neal	8.00	3.60	1.00
☐ M7 Brooks Thompson	.40	.18	.05
☐ M8 Anfernee Hardaway	8.00	3.60	1.00
☐ M9 Donald Royal	.40	.18	.05
☐ M10 Brian Shaw	.40	.18	.05
☐ MM19 Magic MP Super Team	1.00	.45	.12
☐ R1 Tim Breaux	.40	.18	.05
☐ R2 Scott Brooks	.40	.18	.05
☐ R3 Clyde Drexler	2.50	1.10	.30
Hakeem Olajuwon			
☐ R4 Hakeem Olajuwon	5.00	2.20	.60
☐ R5 Sam Cassell	.75	.35	.09
☐ R6 Vernon Maxwell	.40	.18	.05
☐ R7 Mario Elie	.40	.18	.05
☐ R8 Carl Herrera	.40	.18	.05
☐ R9 Kenny Smith	.40	.18	.05
☐ R10 Robert Horry	.75	.35	.09
☐ MR10 Rockets MP Super Team	1.00	.45	.12

1994-95 Stadium Club Super Teams NBA Finals

Available exclusively by redeeming the Stadium Club Super Teams Houston

Rockets card before the December 31st, 1995 deadline, this 362-card standard-size set parallels the basic issue 1994-95 Stadium Club set except for the gold foil NBA Finals logo placed on each card front. Please refer to the multipliers provided below (coupled with the value of the corresponding regular issue card) to ascertain value.

	MINT	NRMT	EXC
COMPLETE SET (363)		27.00	7.50
COMMON CARD (1-362)		.07	.02
*STARS: 1.25X to 2.5X VALUE			
*ROOKIES: 1X to 2X VALUE			

1994-95 Stadium Club Team of the Future

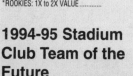

Randomly inserted at a rate of 1 in every 24 second series packs, this 10-card standard-size set is comprised of tomorrow's superstars. Card fronts feature color player action shots against brilliant gold, etched-foil backgrounds.

	MINT	NRMT	EXC
COMPLETE SET (10)	50.00	22.00	6.25
COMMON CARD (1-10)	1.25	.55	.16
☐ 1 Anfernee Hardaway	12.00	5.50	1.50
☐ 2 Latrell Sprewell	1.25	.55	.16
☐ 3 Grant Hill	12.00	5.50	1.50
☐ 4 Chris Webber	2.50	1.10	.30
☐ 5 Shaquille O'Neal	10.00	4.50	1.25
☐ 6 Jason Kidd	8.00	3.60	1.00
☐ 7 Jim Jackson	1.25	.55	.16
☐ 8 Jamal Mashburn	1.50	.70	.19
☐ 9 Glenn Robinson	4.00	1.80	.50
☐ 10 Alonzo Mourning	2.50	1.10	.30

1995-96 Stadium Club

The 1995-96 Stadium Club basketball set was issued in two series of 180 and 181

standard-size cards, for a total of 361. Cards were distributed in 13-card regular packs at a suggested retail price of $2.50, and in 24-card jumbo packs. The packs were distributed in 24-piece boxes. Fronts are full-bleed full-color action player shots. The player's name appears in etched foil against an exploding star background and his team's name is printed in gold foil at the bottom. Backs feature a close-up head shot and a full-color action photo with a blue background. The player's name is printed at the top as is his biography, player profile and '94-95 statistics. A category statistic chart appears on the lower right side of the chart. Second series cards included these variations. The "Rookie Cards" as well as other subset cards were issued in basic hobby and retail packs with a silver prismatic foil. These cards were also issued one per special retail pack with a gold/orange-type foil background. Subsets include 10 cards of players from the two expansion teams (Vancouver Grizzlies and Toronto Raptors), 29 "Extreme Corps" and six "Trans-Action" cards. A parallel version of every subset card was inserted in rack and jumbo packs. The parallel versions of the subset cards feature silver and blue diffraction foil around the player's name and team name. These foil variations are priced at equal value.

	MINT	NRMT	EXC
COMPLETE SET (361)	50.00	22.00	6.25
COMPLETE SERIES 1 (180)	25.00	11.00	3.10
COMPLETE SERIES 2 (181)	25.00	11.00	3.10
COMMON CARD (1-361)	.10	.05	.01
☐ 1 Michael Jordan	5.00	2.20	.60
☐ 2 Glenn Robinson	.50	.23	.06
☐ 3 Jason Kidd	1.00	.45	.12
☐ 4 Clyde Drexler	.50	.23	.06
☐ 5 Horace Grant	.20	.09	.03
☐ 6 Allan Houston	.20	.09	.03
☐ 7 Xavier McDaniel	.10	.05	.01
☐ 8 Jeff Hornacek	.15	.07	.02
☐ 9 Vlade Divac	.20	.09	.03
☐ 10 Juwan Howard	1.00	.45	.12
☐ 11 Keith Jennings EXP	.10	.05	.01
☐ 12 Grant Long	.10	.05	.01
☐ 13 Jalen Rose	.15	.07	.02
☐ 14 Malik Sealy	.10	.05	.01
☐ 15 Gary Payton	.60	.25	.07
☐ 16 Danny Ferry	.10	.05	.01
☐ 17 Glen Rice	.20	.09	.03
☐ 18 Randy Brown	.10	.05	.01

#	Player			
☐ 19	Greg Graham	.10	.05	.01
☐ 20	Kenny Anderson UER	.20	.09	.03
	Name is spelled Kenney			
☐ 21	Aaron McKie	.10	.05	.01
☐ 22	John Salley EXP	.10	.05	.01
☐ 23	Darrin Hancock	.10	.05	.01
☐ 24	Carlos Rogers	.10	.05	.01
☐ 25	Vin Baker	.40	.18	.05
☐ 26	Bill Wennington	.10	.05	.01
☐ 27	Kenny Smith	.10	.05	.01
☐ 28	Sherman Douglas	.10	.05	.01
☐ 29	Terry Davis	.10	.05	.01
☐ 30	Grant Hill	1.50	.70	.19
☐ 31	Reggie Miller	.50	.23	.06
☐ 32	Anfernee Hardaway	2.50	1.10	.30
☐ 33	Patrick Ewing	.40	.18	.05
☐ 34	Charles Barkley	.60	.25	.07
☐ 35	Eddie Jones	.30	.14	.04
☐ 36	Kevin Duckworth	.10	.05	.01
☐ 37	Tom Hammonds	.10	.05	.01
☐ 38	Craig Ehlo	.10	.05	.01
☐ 39	Micheal Williams	.10	.05	.01
☐ 40	Alonzo Mourning	.40	.18	.05
☐ 41	John Williams	.10	.05	.01
☐ 42	Felton Spencer	.10	.05	.01
☐ 43	Lamond Murray	.10	.05	.01
☐ 44	Dontonio Wingfield EXP.	.10	.05	.01
☐ 45	Rik Smits	.20	.09	.03
☐ 46	Donyell Marshall	.10	.05	.01
☐ 47	Clarence Weatherspoon	.10	.05	.01
☐ 48	Kevin Edwards	.10	.05	.01
☐ 49	Charlie Ward	.15	.07	.02
☐ 50	David Robinson	.75	.35	.09
☐ 51	James Robinson	.10	.05	.01
☐ 52	Bill Cartwright	.10	.05	.01
☐ 53	Bobby Hurley	.10	.05	.01
☐ 54	Kevin Gamble	.10	.05	.01
☐ 55	B.J. Tyler EXP	.10	.05	.01
☐ 56	Chris Smith	.10	.05	.01
☐ 57	Wesley Person	.15	.07	.02
☐ 58	Tim Breaux	.10	.05	.01
☐ 59	Mitchell Butler	.10	.05	.01
☐ 60	Toni Kukoc	.25	.11	.03
☐ 61	Roy Tarpley	.10	.05	.01
☐ 62	Todd Day	.10	.05	.01
☐ 63	Anthony Peeler	.10	.05	.01
☐ 64	Brian Williams	.10	.05	.01
☐ 65	Muggsy Bogues	.15	.07	.02
☐ 66	Jerome Kersey EXP	.10	.05	.01
☐ 67	Eric Piatkowski	.10	.05	.01
☐ 68	Tim Perry	.10	.05	.01
☐ 69	Chris Gatling	.10	.05	.01
☐ 70	Mark Price	.10	.05	.01
☐ 71	Terry Mills	.10	.05	.01
☐ 72	Anthony Avent	.10	.05	.01
☐ 73	Matt Geiger	.10	.05	.01
☐ 74	Walt Williams	.20	.09	.03
☐ 75	Sean Elliott	.20	.09	.03
☐ 76	Ken Norman	.10	.05	.01
☐ 77	Kendall Gill TA	.10	.05	.01
☐ 78	Byron Houston	.10	.05	.01
☐ 79	Rick Fox	.10	.05	.01
☐ 80	Derek Harper	.10	.05	.01
☐ 81	Rod Strickland	.10	.05	.01
☐ 82	Bryon Russell	.10	.05	.01
☐ 83	Antonio Davis	.10	.05	.01
☐ 84	Isaiah Rider	.20	.09	.03
☐ 85	Kevin Johnson	.20	.09	.03
☐ 86	Derrick Coleman	.10	.05	.01
☐ 87	Doug Overton	.10	.05	.01
☐ 88	Hersey Hawkins TA	.10	.05	.01
☐ 89	Popeye Jones	.10	.05	.01
☐ 90	Dickey Simpkins	.10	.05	.01
☐ 91	Rodney Rogers TA	.10	.05	.01
☐ 92	Rex Chapman TA	.10	.05	.01
☐ 93	Spud Webb TA	.15	.07	.02
☐ 94	Lee Mayberry	.10	.05	.01
☐ 95	Cedric Ceballos	.25	.11	.03
☐ 96	Tyrone Hill	.10	.05	.01
☐ 97	Bill Curley	.10	.05	.01
☐ 98	Jeff Turner	.10	.05	.01
☐ 99	Tyrone Corbin TA	.10	.05	.01
☐ 100	John Stockton	.40	.18	.05
☐ 101	Mookie Blaylock EC	.15	.07	.02
☐ 102	Dino Radja EC	.15	.07	.02
☐ 103	Alonzo Mourning EC	.40	.18	.05
☐ 104	Scottie Pippen EC	1.25	.55	.16
☐ 105	Terrell Brandon EC	.20	.09	.03
☐ 106	Jim Jackson EC	.25	.11	.03
☐ 107	Mahmoud Abdul-Rauf EC	.15	.07	.02
☐ 108	Grant Hill EC	1.50	.70	.19
☐ 109	Tim Hardaway EC	.20	.09	.03
☐ 110	Hakeem Olajuwon EC	1.00	.45	.12
☐ 111	Rik Smits EC	.20	.09	.03
☐ 112	Loy Vaught EC	.10	.05	.01
☐ 113	Vlade Divac EC	.20	.09	.03
☐ 114	Kevin Willis EC	.10	.05	.01
☐ 115	Glenn Robinson EC	.50	.23	.06
☐ 116	Christian Laettner EC	.20	.09	.03
☐ 117	Derrick Coleman EC	.10	.05	.01
☐ 118	Patrick Ewing EC	.40	.18	.05
☐ 119	Shaquille O'Neal EC	2.00	.90	.25
☐ 120	Dana Barros EC	.10	.05	.01
☐ 121	Charles Barkley EC	.60	.25	.07
☐ 122	Rod Strickland EC	.10	.05	.01
☐ 123	Brian Grant EC	.15	.07	.02
☐ 124	David Robinson EC	.75	.35	.09
☐ 125	Shawn Kemp EC	1.25	.55	.16
☐ 126	Oliver Miller EC	.10	.05	.01
☐ 127	Karl Malone EC	.40	.18	.05
☐ 128	Benoit Benjamin EC	.10	.05	.01
☐ 129	Chris Webber EC	.40	.18	.05
☐ 130	Dan Majerle	.15	.07	.02
☐ 131	Calbert Cheaney	.10	.05	.01
☐ 132	Mark Jackson	.10	.05	.01
☐ 133	Greg Anthony EXP	.10	.05	.01
☐ 134	Scott Burrell	.10	.05	.01
☐ 135	Detlef Schrempf	.15	.07	.02
☐ 136	Marty Conlon	.10	.05	.01
☐ 137	Rony Seikaly	.10	.05	.01
☐ 138	Olden Polynice	.10	.05	.01
☐ 139	Terry Cummings	.10	.05	.01
☐ 140	Stacey Augmon	.15	.07	.02
☐ 141	Bryant Stith	.10	.05	.01
☐ 142	Sean Higgins	.10	.05	.01
☐ 143	Antoine Carr	.10	.05	.01
☐ 144	Blue Edwards EXP	.10	.05	.01
☐ 145	A.C. Green	.20	.09	.03
☐ 146	Bobby Phills	.10	.05	.01
☐ 147	Terry Dehere	.10	.05	.01
☐ 148	Sharone Wright	.10	.05	.01
☐ 149	Nick Anderson	.20	.09	.03
☐ 150	Jim Jackson	.25	.11	.03
☐ 151	Eric Montross	.10	.05	.01
☐ 152	Doug West	.10	.05	.01
☐ 153	Charles Smith	.10	.05	.01
☐ 154	Will Perdue	.10	.05	.01
☐ 155	Gerald Wilkins EXP	.10	.05	.01
☐ 156	Robert Horry	.20	.09	.03
☐ 157	Robert Parish	.20	.09	.03
☐ 158	Lindsey Hunter	.10	.05	.01
☐ 159	Harvey Grant	.10	.05	.01

□					□				
□	160	Tim Hardaway	.20	.09	.03	□	232	Glen Rice	.10	.05	.01
□	161	Sarunas Marciulionis	.10	.05	.01	□	233	Terry Porter	.10	.05	.01
□	162	Khalid Reeves	.10	.05	.01	□	234	Mark Macon	.10	.05	.01
□	163	Bo Outlaw	.10	.05	.01	□	235	Michael Cage	.10	.05	.01
□	164	Dale Davis	.10	.05	.01	□	236	Eric Murdock	.10	.05	.01
□	165	Nick Van Exel	.30	.14	.04	□	237	Vinny Del Negro	.15	.07	.02
□	166	Byron Scott EXP	.20	.09	.03	□	238	Spud Webb	.15	.07	.02
□	167	Steve Smith	.20	.09	.03	□	239	Mario Elie	.10	.05	.01
□	168	Brian Grant	.20	.09	.03	□	240	Blue Edwards	.10	.05	.01
□	169	Avery Johnson	.15	.07	.02	□	241	Dontonio Wingfield	.10	.05	.01
□	170	Dikembe Mutombo	.20	.09	.03	□	242	Brooks Thompson	.10	.05	.01
□	171	Tom Gugliotta	.20	.09	.03	□	243	Alonzo Mourning	.40	.18	.05
□	172	Armon Gilliam	.15	.07	.02	□	244	Dennis Rodman Bulls	2.50	1.10	.30
□	173	Shawn Bradley	.20	.09	.03	□	245	Lorenzo Williams	.10	.05	.01
□	174	Herb Williams	.10	.05	.01	□	246	Haywoode Workman	.10	.05	.01
□	175	Dino Radja	.20	.09	.03	□	247	Loy Vaught	.10	.05	.01
□	176	Billy Owens	.10	.05	.01	□	248	Vernon Maxwell	.10	.05	.01
□	177	Kenny Gattison EXP	.10	.05	.01	□	249	Lionel Simmons	.10	.05	.01
□	178	J.R. Reid	.10	.05	.01	□	250	Chris Childs	.10	.05	.01
□	179	Otis Thorpe	.15	.07	.02	□	251	Mahmoud Abdul-Rauf	.10	.05	.01
□	180	Sam Cassell	.20	.09	.03	□	252	Vincent Askew	.10	.05	.01
□	182	Pooh Richardson	.10	.05	.01	□	253	Chris Morris	.10	.05	.01
□	183	Johnny Newman	.10	.05	.01	□	254	Elliot Perry	.10	.05	.01
□	184	Dennis Scott	.20	.09	.03	□	255	Dell Curry	.15	.07	.02
□	185	Will Perdue	.10	.05	.01	□	256	Dana Barros	.10	.05	.01
□	186	Andrew Lang	.10	.05	.01	□	257	Terrell Brandon	.20	.09	.03
□	187	Karl Malone	.40	.18	.05	□	258	Monty Williams	.10	.05	.01
□	188	Buck Williams	.15	.07	.02	□	259	Corie Blount	.10	.05	.01
□	189	P.J. Brown	.10	.05	.01	□	260	B.J. Armstrong	.10	.05	.01
□	190	Khalid Reeves	.10	.05	.01	□	261	Jim McIlvaine	.10	.05	.01
□	191	Kevin Willis	.10	.05	.01	□	262	Otis Thorpe	.15	.07	.02
□	192	Robert Pack	.10	.05	.01	□	263	Sean Rooks	.10	.05	.01
□	193	Joe Dumars	.20	.09	.03	□	264	Tony Massenburg	.10	.05	.01
□	194	Sam Perkins	.15	.07	.02	□	265	Steve Smith	.20	.09	.03
□	195	Dan Majerle	.15	.07	.02	□	266	Ron Harper	.10	.05	.01
□	196	John Williams	.10	.05	.01	□	267	Dale Ellis	.10	.05	.01
□	197	Reggie Williams	.10	.05	.01	□	268	Clyde Drexler	.50	.23	.06
□	198	Greg Anthony	.10	.05	.01	□	269	Jamie Watson	.10	.05	.01
□	199	Steve Kerr	.15	.07	.02	□	270	Doc Rivers	.10	.05	.01
□	200	Richard Dumas	.10	.05	.01	□	271	Derrick Alston	.10	.05	.01
□	201	Dee Brown	.10	.05	.01	□	272	Eric Mobley	.10	.05	.01
□	202	Zan Tabak	.10	.05	.01	□	273	Ricky Pierce	.10	.05	.01
□	203	David Wood	.10	.05	.01	□	274	David Wesley	.10	.05	.01
□	204	Duane Causwell	.10	.05	.01	□	275	John Starks	.10	.05	.01
□	205	Sedale Threatt	.10	.05	.01	□	276	Chris Mullin	.15	.07	.02
□	206	Hubert Davis	.10	.05	.01	□	277	Ervin Johnson	.10	.05	.01
□	207	Donald Hodge	.10	.05	.01	□	278	Jamal Mashburn	.25	.11	.03
□	208	Duane Ferrell	.10	.05	.01	□	279	Joe Kleine	.10	.05	.01
□	209	Sam Mitchell	.10	.05	.01	□	280	Mitch Richmond	.30	.14	.04
□	210	Adam Keefe	.10	.05	.01	□	281	Chris Mills	.10	.05	.01
□	211	Clifford Robinson	.20	.09	.03	□	282	Bimbo Coles	.10	.05	.01
□	212	Rodney Rogers	.10	.05	.01	□	283	Larry Johnson	.40	.18	.05
□	213	Jayson Williams	.10	.05	.01	□	284	Stanley Roberts	.10	.05	.01
□	214	Brian Shaw	.10	.05	.01	□	285	Rex Walters	.10	.05	.01
□	215	Luc Longley	.15	.07	.02	□	286	Donald Royal	.10	.05	.01
□	216	Don MacLean	.10	.05	.01	□	287	Benoit Benjamin	.10	.05	.01
□	217	Rex Chapman	.10	.05	.01	□	288	Chris Dudley	.10	.05	.01
□	218	Wayman Tisdale	.10	.05	.01	□	289	Elden Campbell	.15	.07	.02
□	219	Shawn Kemp	1.25	.55	.16	□	290	Mookie Blaylock	.20	.09	.03
□	220	Chris Webber	.40	.18	.05	□	291	Hersey Hawkins	.10	.05	.01
□	221	Antonio Harvey	.10	.05	.01	□	292	Anthony Mason	.10	.05	.01
□	222	Sarunas Marciulionis	.10	.05	.01	□	293	Latrell Sprewell	.20	.09	.03
□	223	Jeff Malone	.10	.05	.01	□	294	Harold Miner	.10	.05	.01
□	224	Chucky Brown	.10	.05	.01	□	295	Scott Williams	.10	.05	.01
□	225	Greg Minor	.10	.05	.01	□	296	David Benoit	.10	.05	.01
□	226	Clifford Rozier	.10	.05	.01	□	297	Christian Laettner	.15	.07	.02
□	227	Derrick McKey	.10	.05	.01	□	298	LaPhonso Ellis	.10	.05	.01
□	228	Tony Dumas	.10	.05	.01	□	299	Gheorghe Muresan	.20	.09	.03
□	229	Oliver Miller	.10	.05	.01	□	300	Kendall Gill	.10	.05	.01
□	230	Charles Oakley	.10	.05	.01	□	301	Eddie Johnson	.10	.05	.01
□	231	Fred Roberts	.10	.05	.01	□	302	Terry Cummings	.10	.05	.01

		MINT	NRMT	EXC

□ 303 Chuck Person .... .10 .05 .01
□ 304 Michael Smith .... .10 .05 .01
□ 305 Mark West .... .10 .05 .01
□ 306 Willie Anderson .... .10 .05 .01
□ 307 Pervis Ellison .... .10 .05 .01
□ 308 Brian Williams .... .10 .05 .01
□ 309 Danny Manning .... .10 .05 .01
□ 310 Hakeem Olajuwon .. 1.00 .45 .12
□ 311 Scottie Pippen .... 1.25 .55 .16
□ 312 Jon Koncak .... .10 .05 .01
□ 313 Sasha Danilovic .... .10 .05 .01
□ 314 Lucious Harris .... .10 .05 .01
□ 315 Yinka Dare .... .10 .05 .01
□ 316 Eric Williams .... .30 .14 .04
□ 317 Gary Trent .... .10 .05 .01
□ 318 Theo Ratliff .... .10 .05 .01
□ 319 Lawrence Moten .... .10 .05 .01
□ 320 Jerome Allen .... .10 .05 .01
□ 321 Tyus Edney .... .75 .35 .09
□ 322 Loren Meyer .... .10 .05 .01
□ 323 Michael Finley .... 2.00 .90 .25
□ 324 Alan Henderson .... .25 .11 .03
□ 325 Bob Sura .... .30 .14 .04
□ 326 Joe Smith .... 2.00 .90 .25
□ 327 Damon Stoudamire... 4.00 1.80 .50
□ 328 Sherell Ford .... .10 .05 .01
□ 329 Jerry Stackhouse ..... 3.00 1.35 .35
□ 330 George Zidek .... .10 .05 .01
□ 331 Brent Barry .... .75 .35 .09
□ 332 Shawn Respert .... .10 .05 .01
□ 333 Rasheed Wallace ...... .75 .35 .09
□ 334 Antonio McDyess .... 1.50 .70 .19
□ 335 David Vaughn .... .10 .05 .01
□ 336 Cory Alexander .... .10 .05 .01
□ 337 Jason Caffey .... .10 .05 .01
□ 338 Frankie King .... .10 .05 .01
□ 339 Travis Best .... .25 .11 .03
□ 340 Greg Ostertag .... .10 .05 .01
□ 341 Ed O'Bannon .... .60 .25 .07
□ 342 Kurt Thomas .... .50 .23 .06
□ 343 Kevin Garnett .... 5.00 2.20 .60
□ 344 Bryant Reeves .... 1.00 .45 .12
□ 345 Corliss Williamson .... .30 .14 .04
□ 346 Cherokee Parks .... .10 .05 .01
□ 347 Junior Burrough .... .10 .05 .01
□ 348 Randolph Childress .... .10 .05 .01
□ 349 Lou Roe .... .10 .05 .01
□ 350 Mario Bennett .... .10 .05 .01
□ 351 Dikembe Mutombo XP. .15 .07 .02
□ 352 Larry Johnson XP ..... .40 .18 .05
□ 353 Vlade Divac XP .... .15 .07 .02
□ 354 Karl Malone XP .... .40 .18 .05
□ 355 John Stockton XP ..... .40 .18 .05
□ 356 Alonzo Mourning TA .. .40 .18 .05
□ 357 Glen Rice TA .... .15 .07 .02
□ 358 Dan Majerle TA .... .10 .05 .01
□ 359 John Williams TA ...... .10 .05 .01
□ 360 Mark Price TA .... .10 .05 .01
□ 361 Magic Johnson .... 1.25 .55 .16

1995-96 Stadium Club Beam Team

Randomly inserted in all first and second series packs, this 20-card standard-size set features Topps' annual selection of their

Beam Team stars. First series cards were randomly seeded into one in every 18 hobby and retail packs. Second series cards were randomly seeded into one in every 36 hobby packs and one in every 72 retail packs. Card front design from first to second series is radically different. First series cards feature borderless fronts with full-color action player cutouts set against a dark background of laser beams. Second series cards feature very bright neon green, yellow and red die cut backgrounds set against a cut out action shot of the featured player.

	MINT	NRMT	EXC
COMPLETE SET (20)	90.00	40.00	11.00
COMPLETE SERIES 1 (10)....	15.00	6.75	1.85
COMPLETE SERIES 2 (10)....	75.00	34.00	9.50
COMMON CARD (BT1-BT10)..	1.50	.70	.19
COMMON CARD (BT11-BT20).	2.00	.90	.25

□ BT1 David Robinson .... 4.00 1.80 .50
□ BT2 Juwan Howard .... 5.00 2.20 .60
□ BT3 Mitch Richmond .... 2.00 .90 .25
□ BT4 Reggie Miller .... 2.50 1.10 .30
□ BT5 Glenn Robinson .... 2.50 1.10 .30
□ BT6 Shaquille O'Neal 10.00 4.50 1.25
□ BT7 Shawn Kemp .... 6.00 2.70 .75
□ BT8 Karl Malone .... 2.00 .90 .25
□ BT9 Jamal Mashburn .... 1.50 .70 .19
□ BT10 Alonzo Mourning ...... 2.00 .90 .25
□ BT11 Charles Barkley .... 6.00 2.70 .75
□ BT12 Hakeem Olajuwon.... 10.00 4.50 1.25
□ BT13 Kenny Anderson ...... 2.00 .90 .25
□ BT14 Michael Jordan 50.00 22.00 6.25
□ BT15 Dikembe Mutombo .. 2.00 .90 .25
□ BT16 Rod Strickland .... 2.00 .90 .25
□ BT17 Patrick Ewing .... 4.00 1.80 .50
□ BT18 Latrell Sprewell ...... 2.00 .90 .25
□ BT19 Grant Hill 15.00 6.75 1.85
□ BT20 Cedric Ceballos....... 2.00 .90 .25

1995-96 Stadium Club Draft Picks

Randomly inserted in series one packs, this set of 15 skip-numbered standard-size cards is numbered in the order of the 1995 NBA draft. Some draft picks are missing in the series one collection but those cards were not included in the second series. Full-bleed fronts picture the player in full-color action shots with the TSC logo at the top. "NBA Draft Pick" and the player's name are printed in red type at the bottom of the card. Blue and white backs are numbered according to place in draft with the player's name is printed in lower case white type at the top. The white areas resemble torn, crumpled paper and contain the player's biography, college statistics and a player profile, which is printed vertically in black type on the lower right side of the back.

	MINT	NRMT	EXC
COMPLETE SET (15)	10.00	4.50	1.25
COMMON CARD (2-6/8/9/11)	.25	.11	.03
COMMON CARD (12/15-19/22)	.25	.11	.03
☐ 2 Antonio McDyess	1.50	.70	.19
☐ 3 Jerry Stackhouse	3.00	1.35	.35
☐ 4 Rasheed Wallace	.75	.35	.09
☐ 5 Kevin Garnett	5.00	2.20	.60
☐ 6 Bryant Reeves	1.00	.45	.12
☐ 8 Shawn Respert	.25	.11	.03
☐ 9 Ed O'Bannon	.60	.25	.07
☐ 11 Gary Trent	.25	.11	.03
☐ 12 Cherokee Parks	.25	.11	.03
☐ 15 Brent Barry	.75	.35	.09
☐ 16 Alan Henderson	.25	.11	.03
☐ 17 Bob Sura	.25	.11	.03
☐ 18 Theo Ratliff	.25	.11	.03
☐ 19 Randolph Childress	.25	.11	.03
☐ 22 George Zidek	.25	.11	.03

1995-96 Stadium Club Nemeses

Randomly inserted in series one packs at a rate of one in 18, this 10-card standard-size set portrays arch rivals on each side of the card. Both sides are silver and blue etched foil with alternating full-color action cutouts of the players. Both sides carry a smaller full-color shot of each player's nemesis looking on. Each side carries a highlight of a game when one player got the better of the other. The "Nemeses" logo appears at the top of each side in gold etched foil.

	MINT	NRMT	EXC
COMPLETE SET (10)	80.00	36.00	10.00
COMMON CARD (N1-N10)	1.50	.70	.19
☐ N1 Hakeem Olajuwon David Robinson	12.00	5.50	1.50
☐ N2 Patrick Ewing Rik Smits	2.50	1.10	.30
☐ N3 John Stockton Kevin Johnson	2.50	1.10	.30
☐ N4 Shaquille O'Neal Alonzo Mourning	15.00	6.75	1.85
☐ N5 Charles Barkley Karl Malone	6.00	2.70	.75
☐ N6 Scottie Pippen Grant Hill	15.00	6.75	1.85
☐ N7 Anfernee Hardaway Kenny Anderson	15.00	6.75	1.85
☐ N8 R.Miller J.Starks	3.00	1.35	.35
☐ N9 Toni Kukoc Dino Radja	1.50	.70	.19
☐ N10 Michael Jordan Joe Dumars	30.00	13.50	3.70

1995-96 Stadium Club Power Zone

Randomly inserted in first and second series packs, this set of twelve standard-size cards feature the men who drive to the basket with authority. First series cards were randomly seeded into one in every 36 hobby and retail packs. Second series cards were randomly seeded into one in every 48 hobby and retail packs. First and second series card design differ radically. The first series cards feature borderless fronts with full-color action player cutouts set against a silver diffracted foil background. Second series cards contain a foil-etched background.

kings. Card fronts have a foil-etched background with the card name "Reign Men" running vertically along the right side. Card backs are horizontal with a head shot of the player, biographical information and a brief commentary. The cards are numbered with an "RM" prefix.

	MINT	NRMT	EXC
COMPLETE SET (10)	90.00	40.00	11.00
COMMON CARD (RM1-RM10)	2.00	.90	.25
☐ RM1 Shawn Kemp	12.00	5.50	1.50
☐ RM2 Michael Jordan	50.00	22.00	6.25
☐ RM3 Larry Johnson	4.00	1.80	.50
☐ RM4 Grant Hill	15.00	6.75	1.85
☐ RM5 Isaiah Rider	2.00	.90	.25
☐ RM6 Sean Elliott	2.00	.90	.25
☐ RM7 Scottie Pippen	12.00	5.50	1.50
☐ RM8 Robert Horry	2.00	.90	.25
☐ RM9 Kendall Gill	2.00	.90	.25
☐ RM10 Jerry Stackhouse	15.00	6.75	1.85

1995-96 Stadium Club Spike Says

Filmmaker Spike Lee picks his 10 favorite NBA players and tells us all about them in his inimitable style. Cards in this 10-piece set were randomly inserted at a rate of one in every 12 retail packs and one in every 24 hobby packs. Card fronts are full bleed action shots with the player's name and the set name in silver refractive foil. Spike Lee is also pictured on each card front in a small circle in the lower right. Card backs are horizontal with Spike Lee's commentary on the player. The cards are numbered with a "SS" prefix.

	MINT	NRMT	EXC
COMPLETE SET (10)	30.00	13.50	3.70
COMMON CARD (SS1-SS10)	.75	.35	.09
☐ SS1 Michael Jordan	20.00	9.00	2.50
☐ SS2 Alonzo Mourning	1.50	.70	.19
☐ SS3 Reggie Miller	2.00	.90	.25
☐ SS4 Patrick Ewing	1.50	.70	.19
☐ SS5 Charles Barkley	2.50	1.10	.30
☐ SS6 Kenny Anderson	.75	.35	.09
☐ SS7 Scottie Pippen	5.00	2.20	.60
☐ SS8 Jerry Stackhouse	6.00	2.70	.75

	MINT	NRMT	EXC
COMPLETE SET (12)	70.00	32.00	8.75
COMPLETE SERIES 1 (6)	30.00	13.50	3.70
COMPLETE SERIES 2 (6)	40.00	18.00	5.00
COMMON CARD (PZ1-PZ12)	1.50	.70	.19
☐ PZ1 Shaquille O'Neal	15.00	6.75	1.85
☐ PZ2 Charles Barkley	5.00	2.20	.60
☐ PZ3 Patrick Ewing	3.00	1.35	.35
☐ PZ4 Karl Malone	3.00	1.35	.35
☐ PZ5 Larry Johnson	3.00	1.35	.35
☐ PZ6 Derrick Coleman	1.50	.70	.19
☐ PZ8 David Robinson	8.00	3.60	1.00
☐ PZ9 Shawn Kemp	12.00	5.50	1.50
☐ PZ10 Dennis Rodman Bulls	20.00	9.00	2.50
☐ PZ11 Alonzo Mourning	4.00	1.80	.50
☐ PZ12 Vin Baker	4.00	1.80	.50

1995-96 Stadium Club Reign Men

Randomly inserted in second-series hobby and retail packs at a rate of one in 48, this 10-card set features the NBA's slam dunk

	MINT	NRMT	EXC
☐ SS9 Shaquille O'Neal	8.00	3.60	1.00
☐ SS10 John Starks	.75	.35	.09

1995-96 Stadium Club Warp Speed

Randomly inserted in first and second series packs, this 12-card standard-size set features the players with the quickest first steps in the league. First series cards were randomly seeded in hobby and retail packs at a rate of one in 36. Second series cards were randomnly seeded in hobby and retail packs at a rate of one in 48. First and second series card designs differ radically. First series features full-bleed fronts, a full-color action player cutout with a trailing ghost image set against a silver foil "outer space" background with shiny silver flecks. The "Warp Speed" logo appears vertically on the left side and the player's name printed in red at the bottom. Second series cards feature cur out action shots of each player set against a silver foil, vortex background.

	MINT	NRMT	EXC
COMPLETE SET (12)	125.00	55.00	15.50
COMPLETE SERIES 1 (6)	90.00	40.00	11.00
COMPLETE SERIES 2 (6)	35.00	16.00	4.40
COMMON CARD (WS1-WS12)	2.50	1.10	.30
☐ WS1 Michael Jordan	60.00	27.00	7.50
☐ WS2 Kevin Johnson	3.00	1.35	.35
☐ WS3 Gary Payton	8.00	3.60	1.00
☐ WS4 Anfernee Hardaway	30.00	13.50	3.70
☐ WS5 Mookie Blaylock	2.50	1.10	.30
☐ WS6 Tim Hardaway	3.00	1.35	.35

	MINT	NRMT	EXC
☐ WS8 Jason Kidd	12.00	5.50	1.50
☐ WS9 Grant Hill	20.00	9.00	2.50
☐ WS10 Nick Van Exel	4.00	1.80	.50
☐ WS11 Kenny Anderson	2.50	1.10	.30
☐ WS12 Latrell Sprewell	3.00	1.35	.35

1995-96 Stadium Club Wizards

Randomly inserted exclusively in series one hobby packs at a rate of one in 24, this 10-card standard-size set features the best ball handlers in the game. Borderless etched foil fronts feature the player in a full-action cutout with the Blue etched foil "Wizard" logo at the top. The player's name is stamped in gold foil at the bottom.

	MINT	NRMT	EXC
COMPLETE SET (10)	45.00	20.00	5.50
COMMON CARD (W1-W10)	2.00	.90	.25
☐ W1 Nick Van Exel	4.00	1.80	.50
☐ W2 Tim Hardaway	3.00	1.35	.35
☐ W3 Mookie Blaylock	2.00	.90	.25
☐ W4 Gary Payton	8.00	3.60	1.00
☐ W5 Jason Kidd	12.00	5.50	1.50
☐ W6 Kenny Anderson	3.00	1.35	.35
☐ W7 John Stockton	5.00	2.20	.60
☐ W8 Kevin Johnson	3.00	1.35	.35
☐ W9 Muggsy Bogues	2.00	.90	.25
☐ W10 Anfernee Hardaway	30.00	13.50	3.70

1995-96 Stadium Club X-2

Randomly inserted exclusively in second series hobby packs at a rate of one in 24 and second series retail packs at one in 48, this 10-card set showcases elite players who averaged double-doubles last season. Card fronts have an etched "X" in the background with an action shot. Card backs contain the same background with biographical and statistical information.

	MINT	NRMT	EXC
COMPLETE SET (10)	30.00	13.50	3.70
COMMON CARD (X1-X10)	1.50	.70	.19

		MINT	NRMT	EXC
☐ X1	Hakeem Olajuwon	8.00	3.60	1.00
☐ X2	Shaquille O'Neal	15.00	6.75	1.85
☐ X3	David Robinson	6.00	2.70	.75
☐ X4	Patrick Ewing	3.00	1.35	.35
☐ X5	Charles Barkley	5.00	2.20	.60
☐ X6	Karl Malone	3.00	1.35	.35
☐ X7	Derrick Coleman	1.50	.70	.19
☐ X8	Shawn Kemp	8.00	3.60	1.00
☐ X9	Vin Baker	3.00	1.35	.35
☐ X10	Vlade Divac	1.50	.70	.19

1996-97 Stadium Club

The 90-card Stadium Club Series I set features embossed, foil color action player photos printed on 20 pt. stock, making them noticeably sturdier than previous Stadium Club releases. Cards were distributed in eight-card packs with a suggested retail price of $2.50. Card fronts feature full-color game action phoptography with the players name running vertically up the right side of the card in an embossed foil strip. No subsets or Rookie Cards were included in the first series set. Two Moments or Rookies insert cards were guaranteed to be in each first series pack.

		MINT	NRMT	EXC
	COMPLETE SERIES 1 (90)	12.00	5.50	1.50
	COMMON CARD (1-90)	.10	.05	.01
☐ 1	Scottie Pippen	1.25	.55	.16
☐ 2	Dale Davis	.10	.05	.01
☐ 3	Horace Grant	.20	.09	.03
☐ 4	Gheorghe Muresan	.20	.09	.03
☐ 5	Elliot Perry	.10	.05	.01
☐ 6	Carlos Rogers	.10	.05	.01
☐ 7	Glenn Robinson	.40	.18	.05
☐ 8	Avery Johnson	.15	.07	.02
☐ 9	Dee Brown	.10	.05	.01
☐ 10	Grant Hill	1.25	.55	.16
☐ 11	Tyus Edney	.25	.11	.03
☐ 12	Patrick Ewing	.40	.18	.05
☐ 13	Jason Kidd	.75	.35	.09
☐ 14	Clifford Robinson	.10	.05	.01
☐ 15	Robert Horry	.10	.05	.01
☐ 16	Dell Curry	.10	.05	.01
☐ 17	Terry Porter	.10	.05	.01
☐ 18	Shaquille O'Neal Lakers	3.00	1.35	.35
☐ 19	Bryant Stith	.10	.05	.01
☐ 20	Shawn Kemp	1.25	.55	.16
☐ 21	Kurt Thomas	.10	.05	.01
☐ 22	Pooh Richardson	.10	.05	.01
☐ 23	Bob Sura	.10	.05	.01
☐ 24	Olden Polynice	.10	.05	.01
☐ 25	Lawrence Moten	.10	.05	.01
☐ 26	Kendall Gill	.10	.05	.01
☐ 27	Cedric Ceballos	.20	.09	.03
☐ 28	Latrell Sprewell	.20	.09	.03
☐ 29	Christian Laettner	.15	.07	.02
☐ 30	Jamal Mashburn	.20	.09	.03
☐ 31	Jerry Stackhouse	1.00	.45	.12
☐ 32	John Stockton	.40	.18	.05
☐ 33	Arvydas Sabonis	.40	.18	.05
☐ 34	Detlef Schrempf	.20	.09	.03
☐ 35	Toni Kukoc	.20	.09	.03
☐ 36	Sasha Danilovic	.10	.05	.01
☐ 37	Dana Barros	.10	.05	.01
☐ 38	Loy Vaught	.15	.07	.02
☐ 39	John Starks	.10	.05	.01
☐ 40	Marty Conlon	.10	.05	.01
☐ 41	Antonio McDyess	.50	.23	.06
☐ 42	Michael Finley	.60	.25	.07
☐ 43	Tom Gugliotta	.20	.09	.03
☐ 44	Terrell Brandon	.20	.09	.03
☐ 45	Derrick McKey	.10	.05	.01
☐ 46	Damon Stoudamire	1.25	.55	.16
☐ 47	Elden Campbell	.15	.07	.02
☐ 48	Luc Longley	.15	.07	.02
☐ 49	B.J. Armstrong	.10	.05	.01
☐ 50	Lindsey Hunter	.10	.05	.01
☐ 51	Glen Rice	.20	.09	.03
☐ 52	Shawn Respert	.10	.05	.01
☐ 53	Cory Alexander	.10	.05	.01
☐ 54	Tim Legler	.10	.05	.01
☐ 55	Bryant Reeves	.30	.14	.04
☐ 56	Anfernee Hardaway	2.50	1.10	.30
☐ 57	Charles Barkley	.60	.25	.07
☐ 58	Mookie Blaylock	.15	.07	.02
☐ 59	Kevin Garnett	1.50	.70	.19
☐ 60	Hersey Hawkins	.15	.07	.02
☐ 61	Ed O'Bannon	.10	.05	.01
☐ 62	George Zidek	.10	.05	.01
☐ 63	Mitch Richmond	.30	.14	.04
☐ 64	Derrick Coleman	.10	.05	.01
☐ 65	Chris Webber	.30	.14	.04
☐ 66	Bobby Phills	.10	.05	.01
☐ 67	Rik Smits	.20	.09	.03
☐ 68	Jeff Hornacek	.15	.07	.02
☐ 69	Sam Cassell	.15	.07	.02
☐ 70	Gary Trent	.10	.05	.01
☐ 71	LaPhonso Ellis	.10	.05	.01
☐ 72	Oliver Miller	.10	.05	.01
☐ 73	Rex Chapman	.10	.05	.01
☐ 74	Jim Jackson	.20	.09	.03
☐ 75	Eric Williams	.10	.05	.01

		MINT	NRMT	EXC
☐	76 Brent Barry	.25	.11	.03
☐	77 Nick Anderson	.15	.07	.02
☐	78 David Robinson	.75	.35	.09
☐	79 Calbert Cheaney	.15	.07	.02
☐	80 Joe Smith	.60	.25	.07
☐	81 Steve Kerr	.15	.07	.02
☐	82 Wayman Tisdale	.10	.05	.01
☐	83 Steve Smith	.15	.07	.02
☐	84 Clyde Drexler	.50	.23	.06
☐	85 Theo Ratliff	.10	.05	.01
☐	86 Charlie Ward	.15	.07	.02
☐	87 Karl Malone	.40	.18	.05
☐	88 Clarence Weatherspoon	.15	.07	.02
☐	89 Greg Anthony	.10	.05	.01
☐	90 Shawn Bradley	.10	.05	.01

1996-97 Stadium Club Moments

Comprised of two separate themes, five Golden Moment cards (GM1-M5) and fifteen Shining Moment cards (SM1-SM15), the 20-card Moments set highlights memorable events in the NBA from 1995 and 1996. The five Golden Moments cards feature record-breaking occasions and the fifteen Shining Moments cards showcase the slamming and jamming plays that made the '95-96 season memorable. The cards feature sturdy 20 pt. stock, actual event photography and were seeded at an approximate rate of one per first series pack.

		MINT	NRMT	EXC
	COMPLETE SET (20)	15.00	6.75	1.85
	COMMON CARD (1-20)	.15	.07	.02
☐	GM1 Robert Parish	.15	.07	.02
☐	GM2 John Stockton	.40	.18	.05
☐	GM3 Michael Jordan	4.00	1.80	.50
	Dennis Rodman			
☐	GM4 Dennis Scott	.15	.07	.02
☐	GM5 Hakeem Olajuwon	1.00	.45	.12
☐	SM1 Charles Barkley	.60	.25	.07
☐	SM2 Michael Jordan	5.00	2.20	.60
☐	SM3 Karl Malone	.40	.18	.05
☐	SM4 Hakeem Olajuwon	1.00	.45	.12
☐	SM5 John Stockton	.40	.18	.05
☐	SM6 Patrick Ewing	.40	.18	.05
☐	SM7 Reggie Miller	.50	.23	.06
☐	SM8 David Robinson	.75	.35	.09
☐	SM9 Dennis Rodman	2.00	.90	.25

		MINT	NRMT	EXC
☐	SM10 Damon Stoudamire	1.25	.55	.16
☐	SM11 Brent Barry	.25	.11	.03
☐	SM12 Tim Legler	.15	.07	.02
☐	SM13 Jason Kidd	.75	.35	.09
☐	SM14 Terrell Brandon	.15	.07	.02
☐	SM15 Allen Iverson	4.00	1.80	.50

1996-97 Stadium Club Rookies

This set of 25 standard-sized cards feature most of the top rookies selected in the first round of the 1996 NBA draft. These cards were seeded at an approximate rate of one per first series pack. Cards are printed on sturdy 20 pt. stock and were the first cards released to picture the rookies in their pro uniforms. Card fronts feature full color, borderless photographs with the word "Rookie" running down the side of the card. A number of the top foreign draft picks were excluded from the set.

		MINT	NRMT	EXC
	COMPLETE SET (25)	20.00	9.00	2.50
	COMMON CARD (1-25)	.25	.11	.03
☐	R1 Allen Iverson	4.00	1.80	.50
☐	R2 Marcus Camby	3.00	1.35	.35
☐	R3 Shareef Abdur-Rahim	2.00	.90	.25
☐	R4 Stephon Marbury	3.00	1.35	.35
☐	R5 Ray Allen	2.00	.90	.25
☐	R6 Antoine Walker	1.50	.70	.19
☐	R7 Lorenzen Wright	.60	.25	.07
☐	R8 Kerry Kittles	1.00	.45	.12
☐	R9 Samaki Walker	1.00	.45	.12
☐	R10 Erick Dampier	.25	.11	.03
☐	R11 Todd Fuller	.25	.11	.03
☐	R12 Kobe Bryant	4.00	1.80	.50
☐	R13 Steve Nash	.60	.25	.07
☐	R14 Tony Delk	.75	.35	.09
☐	R15 Jermaine O'Neal	.60	.25	.07
☐	R16 John Wallace	.60	.25	.07
☐	R17 Walter McCarty	.75	.35	.09
☐	R18 Dontae Jones	.25	.11	.03
☐	R19 Roy Rogers	.25	.11	.03
☐	R20 Derek Fisher	.25	.11	.03
☐	R21 Martin Muursepp	.25	.11	.03
☐	R22 Jerome Williams	.25	.11	.03
☐	R23 Brian Evans	.25	.11	.03
☐	R24 Priest Lauderdale	.25	.11	.03
☐	R25 Travis Knight	.25	.11	.03

1983 Star All-Star Game

This was the first NBA set issued by Star Company. The 30-card standard-size set was issued in a clear, sealed plastic bag and distributed through hobby dealers. According to information provided on the order forms, Star Company printed 15,000 sets. The sets originally retailed for $2.50 to $5.00 each. Each card has a blue border on the front and blue print on the back. The set commemorates the 1983 NBA All-Star Game held in Los Angeles. Many of the cards feature players in their All-Star uniforms. There are two unnumbered cards in the set listed at the end of the checklist below. The cards are numbered on the back with the order of the numbering essentially alphabetical according to the player's name. The set features the first professional card of Isiah Thomas.

	NRMT-MT	EXC	G-VG
COMPLETE BAG SET (32)	75.00	34.00	9.50
COMMON CARD (1-30)	2.00	.90	.25
OPENED SET: .75X to 1.0X			

		NRMT-MT	EXC	G-VG
☐ 1	Julius Erving CL	10.00	4.50	1.25
☐ 2	Larry Bird	30.00	13.50	3.70
☐ 3	Maurice Cheeks	3.00	1.35	.35
☐ 4	Julius Erving	12.00	5.50	1.50
☐ 5	Marques Johnson	3.00	1.35	.35
☐ 6	Bill Laimbeer	3.00	1.35	.35
☐ 7	Moses Malone	4.00	1.80	.50
☐ 8	Sidney Moncrief	3.00	1.35	.35
☐ 9	Robert Parish	4.00	1.80	.50
☐ 10	Reggie Theus	3.00	1.35	.35
☐ 11	Isiah Thomas	12.00	5.50	1.50
☐ 12	Andrew Toney	2.00	.90	.25
☐ 13	Buck Williams	3.00	1.35	.35
☐ 14	Kareem Abdul-Jabbar	12.00	5.50	1.50
☐ 15	Alex English	3.00	1.35	.35
☐ 16	George Gervin	6.00	2.70	.75
☐ 17	Artis Gilmore	3.00	1.35	.35
☐ 18	Magic Johnson	20.00	9.00	2.50
☐ 19	Maurice Lucas	3.00	1.35	.35
☐ 20	Jim Paxson	2.00	.90	.25
☐ 21	Jack Sikma	3.00	1.35	.35
☐ 22	David Thompson	6.00	2.70	.75
☐ 23	Kiki Vandeweghe	2.00	.90	.25
☐ 24	Jamaal Wilkes	3.00	1.35	.35
☐ 25	Gus Williams	2.00	.90	.25
☐ 26	Julius Erving MVP	10.00	4.50	1.25
☐ 27	Reggie Theus RB Moses Malone	3.00	1.35	.35
☐ 28	All-Star All-Time Leaders (East Coast Line)	2.00	.90	.25
☐ 29	Larry Bird Robert Parish	20.00	9.00	2.50
☐ 30	Sidney Moncrief IA	2.00	.90	.25
☐ xx	Kareem Abdul-Jabbar Artis Gilmore Alex English Ad on back	3.00	1.35	.35
☐ xx	Kareem Abdul-Jabbar (Uncut sheet offer on back)	12.00	5.50	1.50

1983-84 Star

This set of 276 standard-size cards was issued in four series during the first six months of 1984. Several teams in the first series (1-100) are difficult to obtain due to extensive miscuts (all of which, according to the company, were destroyed) in the initial production process. The team sets were issued in clear sealed bags. Many of the team bags were distributed to hobby dealers through a small group of Star Co. master distributors. According to Star Company's original sales materials and order forms, reportedly 5,000 team bags were printed for each team although quality control problems with the early sets apparently reduced that number considerably. The retail price per bag was $2.50 to $5 for most of the teams. Color borders around the fronts and color printing on the backs correspond to team colors. Cards are numbered according to team order: Philadelphia 76ers (1-12), Los Angeles Lakers (13-25), Boston Celtics (26-37), Milwaukee Bucks (38-48), Dallas Mavericks (49-60), New York Knicks (61-72), Houston Rockets (73-84), Detroit Pistons (85-96), Portland Trail Blazers (97-108), Phoenix Suns (109-120), San Diego Clippers (121-132), Utah Jazz (133-144), New Jersey Nets (145-156), Indiana Pacers (157-168), Chicago Bulls (169-180), Denver Nuggets (181-192), Seattle Supersonics (193-203), Washington Bullets (204-215), Kansas City Kings (216-227), Cleveland Cavaliers (228-240), San Antonio Spurs (241-251), Golden State Warriors (252-263), and Atlanta Hawks

(264-275). Extended Rookie Cards include Mark Aguirre, Danny Ainge, Rolando Blackman, Tom Chambers, Clyde Drexler, Dale Ellis, Derek Harper, Larry Nance, Rickey Pierce, Isiah Thomas, Dominique Wilkins, Buck Williams and James Worthy. A promotional card of Sidney Moncrief was produced in limited quantities, but it was numbered 39 rather than 38 as it was in the regular set. There is typically a slight discount on sales of opened team bags.

	NRMT-MT	EXC	G-VG
COMPLETE BAG SET (276)	2200.00	1000.00	275.00
COMP.BAG 76ERS (12)	110.00	50.00	14.00
COMP.BAG LAKERS (13)	175.00	80.00	22.00
COMP.BAG CELTICS (12)	550.00	250.00	70.00
COMP.BAG BUCKS (11)	55.00	25.00	7.00
COMP.BAG MAVS (12)	450.00	200.00	55.00
COMP.BAG KNICKS (12)	25.00	11.00	3.10
COMP.BAG ROCKETS (12)	20.00	9.00	2.50
COMP.BAG PISTONS (12)	150.00	70.00	19.00
COMP.BAG BLAZERS (12)	250.00	110.00	31.00
COMP.BAG SUNS (12)	60.00	27.00	7.50
COMP.BAG CLIPPERS (12)	60.00	27.00	7.50
COMP.BAG JAZZ (12)	20.00	9.00	2.50
COMP.BAG NETS (12)	20.00	9.00	2.50
COMP.BAG PACERS (12)	18.00	8.00	2.20
COMP.BAG BULLS (12)	25.00	11.00	3.10
COMP.BAG NUGGETS (12)	25.00	11.00	3.10
COMP.BAG SONICS (11)	50.00	22.00	6.25
COMP.BAG BULLETS (12)	25.00	11.00	3.10
COMP.BAG KINGS (12)	20.00	9.00	2.50
COMP.BAG CAVS (12)	18.00	8.00	2.20
COMP.BAG SPURS (11)	25.00	11.00	3.10
COMP.BAG WARRIORS (11)	20.00	9.00	2.50
COMP.BAG HAWKS (14)	160.00	70.00	20.00
COMMON SP (1-25/38-48)	4.00	1.80	.50
COMMON SP (26-37)	8.00	3.60	1.00
COMMON SP (49-60) !	18.00	8.00	2.20
COMMON CARD (61-276)	2.00	.90	.25

ABOVE PRICES ARE FOR SEALED BAGS
*OPENED TEAM SETS: .75X to 1.0...

☐ 1	Julius Erving SP	70.00	32.00	8.75
☐ 2	Maurice Cheeks SP	10.00	4.50	1.25
☐ 3	Franklin Edwards SP	4.00	1.80	.50
☐ 4	Marc Iavaroni SP	4.00	1.80	.50
☐ 5	Clemon Johnson SP	4.00	1.80	.50
☐ 6	Bobby Jones SP	10.00	4.50	1.25
☐ 7	Moses Malone SP	25.00	11.00	3.10
☐ 8	Leo Rautins SP	4.00	1.80	.50
☐ 9	Clint Richardson SP	4.00	1.80	.50
☐ 10	Sedale Threatt SP	12.00	5.50	1.50
☐ 11	Andrew Toney SP	10.00	4.50	1.25
☐ 12	Sam Williams SP	4.00	1.80	.50
☐ 13	Magic Johnson SP	110.00	50.00	14.00
☐ 14	Kareem Abdul-Jabbar SP	40.00	18.00	5.00
☐ 15	Michael Cooper SP	10.00	4.50	1.25
☐ 16	Calvin Garrett SP	4.00	1.80	.50
☐ 17	Mitch Kupchak SP	6.00	2.70	.75
☐ 18	Bob McAdoo SP	12.00	5.50	1.50
☐ 19	Mike McGee SP	4.00	1.80	.50
☐ 20	Swen Nater SP	6.00	2.70	.75
☐ 21	Kurt Rambis SP	8.00	3.60	1.00
☐ 22	Byron Scott SP	25.00	11.00	3.10
☐ 23	Larry Spriggs SP	4.00	1.80	.50
☐ 24	Jamaal Wilkes SP	8.00	3.60	1.00
☐ 25	James Worthy SP	45.00	20.00	5.50
☐ 26	Larry Bird SP	400.00	180.00	50.00
☐ 27	Danny Ainge SP	45.00	20.00	5.50
☐ 28	Quinn Buckner SP	9.00	4.00	1.10
☐ 29	M.L. Carr SP	9.00	4.00	1.10
☐ 30	Carlos Clark SP	8.00	3.60	1.00
☐ 31	Gerald Henderson SP	9.00	4.00	1.10
☐ 32	Dennis Johnson SP	18.00	8.00	2.20
☐ 33	Cedric Maxwell SP	10.00	4.50	1.25
☐ 34	Kevin McHale SP	60.00	27.00	7.50
☐ 35	Robert Parish SP	45.00	20.00	5.50
☐ 36	Scott Wedman SP	9.00	4.00	1.10
☐ 37	Greg Kite SP	8.00	3.60	1.00
☐ 38	Sidney Moncrief SP	15.00	6.75	1.85
☐ 39A	Sidney Moncrief SP (Promotional card)	30.00	13.50	3.70
☐ 39B	Nate Archibald SP	15.00	6.75	1.85
☐ 40	Randy Breuer SP	4.00	1.80	.50
☐ 41	Junior Bridgeman SP	5.00	2.20	.60
☐ 42	Harvey Catchings SP	4.00	1.80	.50
☐ 43	Kevin Grevey SP	4.00	1.80	.50
☐ 44	Marques Johnson SP	10.00	4.50	1.25
☐ 45	Bob Lanier SP	20.00	9.00	2.50
☐ 46	Alton Lister SP	4.00	1.80	.50
☐ 47	Paul Mokeski SP	4.00	1.80	.50
☐ 48	Paul Pressey SP	5.00	2.20	.60
☐ 49	Mark Aguirre SP	40.00	18.00	5.00
☐ 50	Rolando Blackman SP	40.00	18.00	5.00
☐ 51	Pat Cummings SP	20.00	9.00	2.50
☐ 52	Brad Davis SP	25.00	11.00	3.10
☐ 53	Dale Ellis SP	40.00	18.00	5.00
☐ 54	Bill Garnett SP	20.00	9.00	2.50
☐ 55	Derek Harper SP	75.00	34.00	9.50
☐ 56	Kurt Nimphius SP	20.00	9.00	2.50
☐ 57	Jim Spanarkel SP	20.00	9.00	2.50
☐ 58	Elston Turner SP	20.00	9.00	2.50
☐ 59	Jay Vincent SP	20.00	9.00	2.50
☐ 60	Mark West SP	20.00	9.00	2.50
☐ 61	Bernard King	8.00	3.60	1.00
☐ 62	Bill Cartwright	4.00	1.80	.50
☐ 63	Len Elmore	2.00	.90	.25
☐ 64	Eric Fernsten	2.00	.90	.25
☐ 65	Ernie Grunfeld	3.00	1.35	.35
☐ 66	Louis Orr	2.00	.90	.25
☐ 67	Leonard Robinson	2.00	.90	.25
☐ 68	Rory Sparrow	2.00	.90	.25
☐ 69	Trent Tucker	2.00	.90	.25
☐ 70	Darrell Walker	3.00	1.35	.35
☐ 71	Marvin Webster	2.00	.90	.25
☐ 72	Ray Williams	3.00	1.35	.35
☐ 73	Ralph Sampson	4.00	1.80	.50
☐ 74	James Bailey	2.00	.90	.25
☐ 75	Phil Ford	3.00	1.35	.35
☐ 76	Elvin Hayes	10.00	4.50	1.25
☐ 77	Caldwell Jones	3.00	1.35	.35
☐ 78	Major Jones	2.00	.90	.25
☐ 79	Allen Leavell	2.00	.90	.25
☐ 80	Lewis Lloyd	2.00	.90	.25
☐ 81	Rodney McCray	2.00	.90	.25
☐ 82	Robert Reid	2.00	.90	.25
☐ 83	Terry Teagle	2.00	.90	.25
☐ 84	Wally Walker	2.00	.90	.25
☐ 85	Kelly Tripucka	3.00	1.35	.35
☐ 86	Kent Benson	3.00	1.35	.35
☐ 87	Earl Cureton	2.00	.90	.25
☐ 88	Lionel Hollins	2.00	.90	.25
☐ 89	Vinnie Johnson	3.00	1.35	.35
☐ 90	Bill Laimbeer	4.00	1.80	.50
☐ 91	Cliff Levingston	2.00	.90	.25
☐ 92	John Long	2.00	.90	.25
☐ 93	David Thirdkill	2.00	.90	.25
☐ 94	Isiah Thomas	100.00	45.00	12.50
☐ 95	Ray Tolbert	2.00	.90	.25
☐ 96	Terry Tyler	2.00	.90	.25

☐ 97	Jim Paxson	3.00	1.35	.35	☐ 166	Jimmy Thomas	2.00	.90	.25
☐ 98	Kenny Carr	2.00	.90	.25	☐ 167	Granville Waiters	2.00	.90	.25
☐ 99	Wayne Cooper	2.00	.90	.25	☐ 168	Herb Williams	3.00	1.35	.35
☐ 100	Clyde Drexler	225.00	100.00	28.00	☐ 169	Dave Corzine	3.00	1.35	.35
☐ 101	Jeff Lamp	2.00	.90	.25	☐ 170	Wallace Bryant	2.00	.90	.25
☐ 102	Lafayette Lever	3.00	1.35	.35	☐ 171	Quintin Dailey	2.00	.90	.25
☐ 103	Calvin Natt	2.00	.90	.25	☐ 172	Sidney Green	3.00	1.35	.35
☐ 104	Audie Norris	2.00	.90	.25	☐ 173	David Greenwood	3.00	1.35	.35
☐ 105	Tom Piotrowski	2.00	.90	.25	☐ 174	Rod Higgins	2.00	.90	.25
☐ 106	Mychal Thompson	3.00	1.35	.35	☐ 175	Clarence Johnson	2.00	.90	.25
☐ 107	Darnell Valentine	2.00	.90	.25	☐ 176	Ronnie Lester	2.00	.90	.25
☐ 108	Pete Verhoeven	2.00	.90	.25	☐ 177	Jawann Oldham	2.00	.90	.25
☐ 109	Walter Davis	4.00	1.80	.50	☐ 178	Ennis Whatley	3.00	1.35	.35
☐ 110	Alvan Adams	3.00	1.35	.35	☐ 179	Mitchell Wiggins	2.00	.90	.25
☐ 111	James Edwards	3.00	1.35	.35	☐ 180	Orlando Woolridge	4.00	1.80	.50
☐ 112	Rod Foster	2.00	.90	.25	☐ 181	Kiki Vandeweghe	4.00	1.80	.50
☐ 113	Maurice Lucas	3.00	1.35	.35	☐ 182	Richard Anderson	2.00	.90	.25
☐ 114	Kyle Macy	3.00	1.35	.35	☐ 183	Howard Carter	2.00	.90	.25
☐ 115	Larry Nance	30.00	13.50	3.70	☐ 184	T.R. Dunn	2.00	.90	.25
☐ 116	Charles Pittman	2.00	.90	.25	☐ 185	Keith Edmonson	2.00	.90	.25
☐ 117	Rick Robey	3.00	1.35	.35	☐ 186	Alex English	8.00	3.60	1.00
☐ 118	Mike Sanders	2.00	.90	.25	☐ 187	Mike Evans	2.00	.90	.25
☐ 119	Alvin Scott	2.00	.90	.25	☐ 188	Bill Hanzlik	2.00	.90	.25
☐ 120	Paul Westphal	10.00	4.50	1.25	☐ 189	Dan Issel	10.00	4.50	1.25
☐ 121	Bill Walton	20.00	9.00	2.50	☐ 190	Anthony Roberts	2.00	.90	.25
☐ 122	Michael Brooks	2.00	.90	.25	☐ 191	Danny Schayes	3.00	1.35	.35
☐ 123	Terry Cummings	10.00	4.50	1.25	☐ 192	Rob Williams	2.00	.90	.25
☐ 124	James Donaldson	3.00	1.35	.35	☐ 193	Jack Sikma	3.00	1.35	.35
☐ 125	Craig Hodges	4.00	1.80	.50	☐ 194	Fred Brown	3.00	1.35	.35
☐ 126	Greg Kelser	3.00	1.35	.35	☐ 195	Tom Chambers	15.00	6.75	1.85
☐ 127	Hank McDowell	2.00	.90	.25	☐ 196	Steve Hawes	2.00	.90	.25
☐ 128	Billy McKinney	2.00	.90	.25	☐ 197	Steve Hayes	2.00	.90	.25
☐ 129	Norm Nixon	3.00	1.35	.35	☐ 198	Reggie King	2.00	.90	.25
☐ 130	Ricky Pierce UER	12.00	5.50	1.50	☐ 199	Scooter McCray	3.00	1.35	.35
	(Misspelled Rickey on both sides)				☐ 200	Jon Sundvold	2.00	.90	.25
					☐ 201	Danny Vranes	2.00	.90	.25
☐ 131	Derek Smith	2.00	.90	.25	☐ 202	Gus Williams	3.00	1.35	.35
☐ 132	Jerome Whitehead	2.00	.90	.25	☐ 203	Al Wood	2.00	.90	.25
☐ 133	Adrian Dantley	8.00	3.60	1.00	☐ 204	Jeff Ruland	3.00	1.35	.35
☐ 134	Mitch Anderson	2.00	.90	.25	☐ 205	Greg Ballard	2.00	.90	.25
☐ 135	Thurl Bailey	3.00	1.35	.35	☐ 206	Charles Davis	2.00	.90	.25
☐ 136	Tom Boswell	2.00	.90	.25	☐ 207	Darren Daye	2.00	.90	.25
☐ 137	John Drew	2.00	.90	.25	☐ 208	Michael Gibson	2.00	.90	.25
☐ 138	Mark Eaton	4.00	1.80	.50	☐ 209	Frank Johnson	3.00	1.35	.35
☐ 139	Jerry Eaves	2.00	.90	.25	☐ 210	Joe Kopicki	2.00	.90	.25
☐ 140	Rickey Green	3.00	1.35	.35	☐ 211	Rick Mahorn	3.00	1.35	.35
☐ 141	Darrell Griffith	3.00	1.35	.35	☐ 212	Jeff Malone	10.00	4.50	1.25
☐ 142	Bobby Hansen	2.00	.90	.25	☐ 213	Tom McMillen	3.00	1.35	.35
☐ 143	Rich Kelley	2.00	.90	.25	☐ 214	Ricky Sobers	2.00	.90	.25
☐ 144	Jeff Wilkins	2.00	.90	.25	☐ 215	Bryan Warrick	2.00	.90	.25
☐ 145	Buck Williams	15.00	6.75	1.85	☐ 216	Billy Knight	3.00	1.35	.35
☐ 146	Otis Birdsong	3.00	1.35	.35	☐ 217	Don Buse	3.00	1.35	.35
☐ 147	Darwin Cook	2.00	.90	.25	☐ 218	Larry Drew	3.00	1.35	.35
☐ 148	Darryl Dawkins	4.00	1.80	.50	☐ 219	Eddie Johnson	4.00	1.80	.50
☐ 149	Mike Gminski	3.00	1.35	.35	☐ 220	Joe Meriweather	2.00	.90	.25
☐ 150	Reggie Johnson	2.00	.90	.25	☐ 221	Larry Micheaux	2.00	.90	.25
☐ 151	Albert King	2.00	.90	.25	☐ 222	Ed Nealy	2.00	.90	.25
☐ 152	Mike O'Koren	3.00	1.35	.35	☐ 223	Mark Olberding	2.00	.90	.25
☐ 153	Kelvin Ransey	2.00	.90	.25	☐ 224	Dave Robisch	3.00	1.35	.35
☐ 154	Micheal Ray Richardson	2.00	.90	.25	☐ 225	Reggie Theus	3.00	1.35	.35
☐ 155	Clarence Walker	2.00	.90	.25	☐ 226	LaSalle Thompson	2.00	.90	.25
☐ 156	Bill Willoughby	2.00	.90	.25	☐ 227	Mike Woodson	2.00	.90	.25
☐ 157	Steve Stipanovich	3.00	1.35	.35	☐ 228	World B. Free	3.00	1.35	.35
☐ 158	Butch Carter	2.00	.90	.25	☐ 229	John Bagley	2.00	.90	.25
☐ 159	Edwin Leroy Combs	2.00	.90	.25	☐ 230	Jeff Cook	2.00	.90	.25
☐ 160	George L. Johnson	2.00	.90	.25	☐ 231	Geoff Crompton	2.00	.90	.25
☐ 161	Clark Kellogg	3.00	1.35	.35	☐ 232	John Garris	2.00	.90	.25
☐ 162	Sidney Lowe	3.00	1.35	.35	☐ 233	Stewart Granger	2.00	.90	.25
☐ 163	Kevin McKenna	2.00	.90	.25	☐ 234	Roy Hinson	2.00	.90	.25
☐ 164	Jerry Sichting	2.00	.90	.25	☐ 235	Phil Hubbard	2.00	.90	.25
☐ 165	Brook Steppe	2.00	.90	.25	☐ 236	Geoff Huston	2.00	.90	.25

		NRMT-MT	EXC	G-VG
☐ 237	Ben Poquette	2.00	.90	.25
☐ 238	Cliff Robinson	2.00	.90	.25
☐ 239	Lonnie Shelton	3.00	1.35	.35
☐ 240	Paul Thompson	2.00	.90	.25
☐ 241	George Gervin	16.00	7.25	2.00
☐ 242	Gene Banks	2.00	.90	.25
☐ 243	Ron Brewer	2.00	.90	.25
☐ 244	Artis Gilmore	4.00	1.80	.50
☐ 245	Edgar Jones	2.00	.90	.25
☐ 246	John Lucas	4.00	1.80	.50
☐ 247A	Mike Mitchell ERR (Photo actually Mark McNamara)	4.00	1.80	.50
☐ 247B	Mike Mitchell COR	6.00	2.70	.75
☐ 248A	Mark McNamara ERR (Photo actually Mike Mitchell)	4.00	1.80	.50
☐ 248B	Mark McNamara COR	6.00	2.70	.75
☐ 249	Johnny Moore	2.00	.90	.25
☐ 250	John Paxson	10.00	4.50	1.25
☐ 251	Fred Roberts	2.00	.90	.25
☐ 252	Joe Barry Carroll	3.00	1.35	.35
☐ 253	Mike Bratz	2.00	.90	.25
☐ 254	Don Collins	2.00	.90	.25
☐ 255	Lester Conner	2.00	.90	.25
☐ 256	Chris Engler	2.00	.90	.25
☐ 257	Sleepy Floyd	4.00	1.80	.50
☐ 258	Wallace Johnson	2.00	.90	.25
☐ 259	Pace Mannion	2.00	.90	.25
☐ 260	Purvis Short	2.00	.90	.25
☐ 261	Larry Smith	2.00	.90	.25
☐ 262	Darren Tillis	2.00	.90	.25
☐ 263	Dominique Wilkins	125.00	55.00	15.50
☐ 264	Rickey Brown	2.00	.90	.25
☐ 265	Johnny Davis	2.00	.90	.25
☐ 266	Mike Glenn	3.00	1.35	.35
☐ 267	Scott Hastings	2.00	.90	.25
☐ 268	Eddie Johnson	2.00	.90	.25
☐ 269	Mark Landsberger	2.00	.90	.25
☐ 270	Billy Paultz	3.00	1.35	.35
☐ 271	Doc Rivers	10.00	4.50	1.25
☐ 272	Tree Rollins	3.00	1.35	.35
☐ 273	Dan Roundfield	3.00	1.35	.35
☐ 274	Sly Williams	2.00	.90	.25
☐ 275	Randy Wittman	2.00	.90	.25

1983-84 Star All-Rookies

This set features the ten members of the 1982-83 NBA All-Rookie Team. The standard-size cards have a yellow border around the fronts of the cards. The set was issued in a sealed plastic bag and distributed through hobby dealers. It originally retailed for about $2.50 to $5. The set was issued late summer of 1983 and features the Star '84 logo on the front of each card. The cards are numbered on the backs with the order of the numbering alphabetical according to the player's last name.

	NRMT-MT	EXC	G-VG
COMPLETE BAG SET (10)	30.00	13.50	3.70
COMMON CARD (1-10)	2.00	.90	.25
*OPENED SET: .75X to 1.0X			

		NRMT-MT	EXC	G-VG
☐ 1	Terry Cummings	3.00	1.35	.35
☐ 2	Quintin Dailey	2.00	.90	.25
☐ 3	Roderick Higgins	2.00	.90	.25
☐ 4	Clark Kellogg	3.00	1.35	.35
☐ 5	Lafayette Lever	3.00	1.35	.35
☐ 6	Paul Pressey	2.00	.90	.25
☐ 7	Trent Tucker	2.00	.90	.25
☐ 8	Dominique Wilkins	15.00	6.75	1.85
☐ 9	Rob Williams	2.00	.90	.25
☐ 10	James Worthy	10.00	4.50	1.25

1983-84 Star Sixers Champs

This set of 25 standard-size cards is devoted to Philadelphia's NBA Championship victory over the Los Angeles Lakers in 1983. Reportedly 10,000 sets were printed. Majority of the distribution was done at the Spectrum, the 76ers home arena. The cards have a red border around the fronts of the cards and red printing on the backs. The set was issued in late summer of 1983 and features the Star '84 logo on the front of each card.

	NRMT-MT	EXC	G-VG
COMPLETE BAG SET (25)	40.00	18.00	5.00
COMMON CARD (1-25)	2.00	.90	.25
*OPENED SET: .75X to 1.0X			

		NRMT-MT	EXC	G-VG
☐ 1	Moses Malone CL	3.00	1.35	.35
☐ 2	Billy Cunningham CO	2.50	1.10	.30
☐ 3	Moses Malone Kareem Abdul-Jabbar	5.00	2.20	.60
☐ 4	Julius Erving IA	6.00	2.70	.75
☐ 5	Clint Richardson IA	2.00	.90	.25

		NRMT-MT	EXC	G-VG
☐ 6	Andrew Toney IA	2.00	.90	.25
☐ 7	Phila. 113, LA 107	2.00	.90	.25
	Game 1 Boxscore			
☐ 8	Bobby Jones IA	2.50	1.10	.30
☐ 9	Maurice Cheeks IA	2.50	1.10	.30
☐ 10	Julius Erving IA	6.00	2.70	.75
☐ 11	Andrew Toney IA	2.00	.90	.25
☐ 12	Phila. 103, LA 93	2.00	.90	.25
	Game 2 Boxscore			
☐ 13	Serious Sixers	2.00	.90	.25
	(Pre-Game Lineup)			
☐ 14	Moses Malone IA	3.00	1.35	.35
☐ 15	Clemon Johnson IA	2.00	.90	.25
☐ 16	Maurice Cheeks IA	2.50	1.10	.30
☐ 17	Phila. 111, LA 94	2.00	.90	.25
	Game 3 Boxscore			
☐ 18	Julius Erving IA	6.00	2.70	.75
☐ 19	Bobby Jones	2.50	1.10	.30
	Sixth Man of Year			
☐ 20	Moses Malone IA	3.00	1.35	.35
☐ 21	World Champs	2.00	.90	.25
	Phila. 115, LA 108			
	Game 4 Boxscore			
☐ 22	Julius Erving	6.00	2.70	.75
	Series Stats			
☐ 23	Moses Malone	3.00	1.35	.35
	Philly in a Sweep			
	Prior World Champs			
☐ 24	Julius Erving	6.00	2.70	.75
	Basking in Glory			
☐ 25	Moses Malone MVP	3.00	1.35	.35

		NRMT-MT	EXC	G-VG
☐ 3	Otis Birdsong	2.00	.90	.25
☐ 4	Julius Erving	16.00	7.25	2.00
☐ 5	Bernard King	3.00	1.35	.35
☐ 6	Bill Laimbeer	3.00	1.35	.35
☐ 7	Kevin McHale	10.00	4.50	1.25
☐ 8	Sidney Moncrief	3.00	1.35	.35
☐ 9	Robert Parish	6.00	2.70	.75
☐ 10	Jeff Ruland	2.00	.90	.25
☐ 11	Isiah Thomas	7.00	3.10	.85
	(Magic Johnson also			
	shown on card)			
☐ 12	Andrew Toney	2.00	.90	.25
☐ 13	Kelly Tripucka	2.00	.90	.25
☐ 14	Kareem Abdul-Jabbar	16.00	7.25	2.00
☐ 15	Mark Aguirre	3.00	1.35	.35
☐ 16	Adrian Dantley	3.00	1.35	.35
☐ 17	Walter Davis	3.00	1.35	.35
☐ 18	Alex English	3.00	1.35	.35
☐ 19	George Gervin	7.00	3.10	.85
☐ 20	Rickey Green	2.00	.90	.25
☐ 21	Magic Johnson	30.00	13.50	3.70
☐ 22	Jim Paxson	2.00	.90	.25
☐ 23	Ralph Sampson	3.00	1.35	.35
☐ 24	Jack Sikma	3.00	1.35	.35
☐ 25	Kiki Vandeweghe	3.00	1.35	.35

1984 Star All-Star Game

This set of 25 standard-size cards features participants in the 34th Annual NBA All-Star Game held in Denver. The cards have a white border around the fronts of the cards and blue printing on the backs. Cards feature the Star '84 logo on the front. The cards are ordered with the East All-Stars on cards 2-13 and the West All-Stars on cards 14-25. The cards are on the backs and are in alphabetical order by division.

	NRMT-MT	EXC	G-VG
COMPLETE BAG SET (25)	95.00	42.50	12.00
COMMON CARD (1-25)	2.00	.90	.25
OPENED SET: .75X to 1.0X			

		NRMT-MT	EXC	G-VG
☐ 1	Isiah Thomas CL	5.00	2.20	.60
☐ 2	Larry Bird	50.00	22.00	6.25

1984 Star All-Star Game Denver Police

This 34-card standard-size set was distributed as individual cards by the Denver Police in the months following the NBA All-Star Game held in Denver. Reportedly 10,000 sets were produced. The set was composed of participants in the All-Star Game (1-25) and the Slam Dunk contest (26-34). The cards have a white border around the fronts and blue printing on the backs. Cards feature the Star '84 logo on the fronts and safety tips on the backs.

	NRMT-MT	EXC	G-VG
COMPLETE SET (34)	200.00	90.00	25.00
COMMON CARD (1-25)	2.00	.90	.25
COMMON CARD (26-34)	2.00	.90	.25

		NRMT-MT	EXC	G-VG
☐ 1	Isiah Thomas CL	7.00	3.10	.85
☐ 2	Larry Bird	50.00	22.00	6.25
☐ 3	Otis Birdsong	2.00	.90	.25
☐ 4	Julius Erving	16.00	7.25	2.00
☐ 5	Bernard King	3.00	1.35	.35
☐ 6	Bill Laimbeer	3.00	1.35	.35

		NRMT-MT	EXC	G-VG
☐ 7	Kevin McHale	12.00	5.50	1.50
☐ 8	Sidney Moncrief	3.00	1.35	.35
☐ 9	Robert Parish	7.00	3.10	.85
☐ 10	Jeff Ruland	2.00	.90	.25
☐ 11	Isiah Thomas Magic Johnson	15.00	6.75	1.85
☐ 12	Andrew Toney	2.00	.90	.25
☐ 13	Kelly Tripucka	2.00	.90	.25
☐ 14	Kareem Abdul-Jabbar	16.00	7.25	2.00
☐ 15	Mark Aguirre	3.00	1.35	.35
☐ 16	Adrian Dantley	3.00	1.35	.35
☐ 17	Walter Davis	3.00	1.35	.35
☐ 18	Alex English	3.00	1.35	.35
☐ 19	George Gervin	7.00	3.10	.85
☐ 20	Rickey Green	2.00	.90	.25
☐ 21	Magic Johnson	35.00	16.00	4.40
☐ 22	Jim Paxson	2.00	.90	.25
☐ 23	Ralph Sampson	3.00	1.35	.35
☐ 24	Jack Sikma	3.00	1.35	.35
☐ 25	Kiki Vandeweghe	2.00	.90	.25
☐ 26	Michael Cooper	3.00	1.35	.35
☐ 27	Clyde Drexler	30.00	13.50	3.70
☐ 28	Julius Erving	16.00	7.25	2.00
☐ 29	Darrell Griffith	3.00	1.35	.35
☐ 30	Edgar Jones	2.00	.90	.25
☐ 31	Larry Nance	6.00	2.70	.75
☐ 32	Ralph Sampson	3.00	1.35	.35
☐ 33	Dominique Wilkins	10.00	4.50	1.25
☐ 34	Orlando Woolridge	2.00	.90	.25

1984 Star Award Banquet

This 24-card standard-size set was produced for the NBA to be given away at the Awards Banquet which took place following the conclusion of the 1983-84 season. According to a 1984 Star Company press release, only 3,000 sets were produced. The cards highlighted award winners from the 1983-84 season. Cards have a blue border around the fronts of the cards and pink and blue printing on the backs. The set was issued in June of 1984 and features the Star '84 logo on the front of each card.

	NRMT-MT	EXC	G-VG
COMPLETE BAG SET (24)	80.00	36.00	10.00
COMMON CARD (1-24)	2.00	.90	.25
*OPENED SET: .75X to 1.0X			

		NRMT-MT	EXC	G-VG
☐ 1	1984 Award Winners Checklist	2.00	.90	.25

		NRMT-MT	EXC	G-VG
☐ 2	Frank Layden CO	2.00	.90	.25
☐ 3	Ralph Sampson ROY	2.50	1.10	.30
☐ 4	Adrian Dantley Comeback Player of the Year	2.50	1.10	.30
☐ 5	Kevin McHale Sixth Man	6.00	2.70	.75
☐ 6	Magic Johnson Pivotal Player of the Year	16.00	7.25	2.00
☐ 7	Sidney Moncrief Defensive Player	2.50	1.10	.30
☐ 8	Larry Bird MVP	25.00	11.00	3.10
☐ 9	Larry Nance Slam Dunk Champ	4.00	1.80	.50
☐ 10	Larry Bird LL Darrell Griffith LL Artis Gilmore LL Adrian Dantley LL	12.00	5.50	1.50
☐ 11	Magic Johnson LL Rickey Green LL Mark Eaton LL Moses Malone LL	5.00	2.20	.60
☐ 12	Isiah Thomas All-Star Game MVP	5.00	2.20	.60
☐ 13	Adrian Dantley LL	2.50	1.10	.30
☐ 14	Artis Gilmore LL	2.50	1.10	.30
☐ 15	Larry Bird LL	25.00	11.00	3.10
☐ 16	Darrell Griffith LL	2.00	.90	.25
☐ 17	Magic Johnson LL	16.00	7.25	2.00
☐ 18	Rickey Green LL	2.00	.90	.25
☐ 19	Mark Eaton LL	2.00	.90	.25
☐ 20	Moses Malone LL	4.00	1.80	.50
☐ 21	Kareem Abdul-Jabbar David Stern	12.00	5.50	1.50
☐ 22	Bobby Jones Michael Cooper Tree Rollins#Sidney Moncrief Maurice Cheeks All-Defensive Team	2.50	1.10	.30
☐ 23	Ralph Sampson Steve Stipanovich Byron Scott Jeff Malone Thurl Bailey Darrell Walker All-Rookie Team	6.00	2.70	.75
☐ 24	Larry Bird Magic Johnson Isiah Thomas Kareem Abdul--Jabbar Bernard King All-NBA Team	15.00	6.75	1.85

1984 Star Larry Bird

This set contains 18 standard-size cards highlighting the career of basketball great Larry Bird. Cards have a green border around the fronts of the cards and green printing on the backs. Cards feature Star '84 logo on the front as they were released in May of 1984.

	NRMT-MT	EXC	G-VG
COMPLETE BAG SET (18)	80.00	36.00	10.00
COMMON L.BIRD (1-18)	7.00	3.10	.85
*OPENED SET: .75X to 1.0X			

☐ 1 Checklist	7.00	3.10	.85
☐ 2 Collegiate Stats	7.00	3.10	.85
☐ 3 1980 Rookie of the Year	7.00	3.10	.85
☐ 4 Regular Season Stats	7.00	3.10	.85
☐ 5 Playoff Stats	7.00	3.10	.85
☐ 6 All-Star Stats	7.00	3.10	.85
☐ 7 The 1979-80 Season	7.00	3.10	.85
☐ 8 The 1980-81 Season	7.00	3.10	.85
☐ 9 The 1981-82 Season	7.00	3.10	.85
☐ 10 The 1982-83 Season	7.00	3.10	.85
☐ 11 The 1983-84 Season	7.00	3.10	.85
☐ 12 The 1984 NBA MVP	7.00	3.10	.85
☐ 13 Member - 1984 All NBA Team	7.00	3.10	.85
☐ 14 World Champions 1981, 1984	7.00	3.10	.85
☐ 15 1984 Free Throw Percentage Leader	7.00	3.10	.85
☐ 16 Career Data	7.00	3.10	.85
☐ 17 Personal Data	7.00	3.10	.85
☐ 18 The Future	7.00	3.10	.85

☐ 1 Red Auerbach CL Cedric Maxwell David Stern	15.00	6.75	1.85
☐ 2 Kareem Abdul-Jabbar IA Robert Parish	10.00	4.50	1.25
☐ 3 Kevin McHale IA	8.00	3.60	1.00
☐ 4 Larry Bird IA	40.00	18.00	5.00
☐ 5 Magic Johnson IA	25.00	11.00	3.10
☐ 6 K.C. Jones CO Danny Ainge	7.00	3.10	.85
☐ 7 Larry Bird IA	40.00	18.00	5.00
☐ 8 Kareem Abdul-Jabbar IA Kevin McHale)	12.00	5.50	1.50
☐ 9 James Worthy IA	6.00	2.70	.75
☐ 10 Magic Johnson IA	25.00	11.00	3.10
☐ 11 Magic Johnson IA Larry Bird	70.00	32.00	8.75
☐ 12 Danny Ainge IA James Worthy	6.00	2.70	.75
☐ 13 M.L. Carr IA Cedric Maxwell	3.00	1.35	.35
☐ 14 Larry Bird IA	40.00	18.00	5.00
☐ 15 Pat Riley CO IA	6.00	2.70	.75
☐ 16 Kareem Abdul-Jabbar	14.00	6.25	1.75
☐ 17 Robert Parish IA	6.00	2.70	.75
☐ 18 Kareem Abdul-Jabbar IA	10.00	4.50	1.25
☐ 19 Dennis Johnson IA	4.00	1.80	.50
☐ 20 Kareem Abdul-Jabbar IA	10.00	4.50	1.25
☐ 21 K.C. Jones CO	4.00	1.80	.50
☐ 22 M.L. Carr IA	3.00	1.35	.35
☐ 23 Red Auerbach	10.00	4.50	1.25
☐ 24 Larry Bird MVP	45.00	20.00	5.50
☐ 25 Boston Garden The Road to the Title	15.00	6.75	1.85

1984 Star Celtics Champs

This set of 25 standard-size cards is devoted to Boston's NBA Championship victory over the Los Angeles Lakers in 1984. Cards have a green border around the fronts of the cards and green printing on the backs. The set was issued in summer of 1984 and features the Star '84 logo on the front of each card. The set includes two of the three Red Auerbach cards ever printed.

	NRMT-MT	EXC	G-VG
COMPLETE BAG SET (25)	325.00	145.00	40.00
COMMON CARD (1-25)	3.00	1.35	.35
*OPENED SET: .75X to 1.0X			

1984 Star Slam Dunk

An 11-card standard-size set highlighting the revival of the Slam Dunk contest (during the 1984 All-Star Weekend in Denver) was produced by the Star Company in 1984. The cards have a white border around the fronts and blue printing on the backs. The Star '84 logo are featured on the front.

	NRMT-MT	EXC	G-VG
COMPLETE BAG SET (11)	75.00	34.00	9.50
COMMON CARD (1-11)	2.00	.90	.25
*OPENED SET: .75X to 1.0X			

☐ 1	Group Photo 12.00	5.50	1.50
	(checklist back)		
☐ 2	Michael Cooper 3.00	1.35	.35
☐ 3	Clyde Drexler 25.00	11.00	3.10
☐ 4	Julius Erving 25.00	11.00	3.10
☐ 5	Darrell Griffith 3.00	1.35	.35
☐ 6	Edgar Jones 2.00	.90	.25
☐ 7	Larry Nance 6.00	2.70	.75
☐ 8	Ralph Sampson 3.00	1.35	.35
☐ 9	Dominique Wilkins 10.00	4.50	1.25
☐ 10	Orlando Woolridge 3.00	1.35	.35
☐ 11	Larry Nance 6.00	2.70	.75
	1984 Slam Dunk Champ		

1984-85 Star

This set of 288 standard-size cards was issued in three series during the first five months of 1985 by Star Company. The set is comprised of team sets that were issued in clear sealed bags. Many of these team bags were distributed to hobby dealers through a small group of Star Company master distributors and retailed for $2.50-$5. According to Star Company's original sales materials and order forms, reportedly 3,000 team bags were printed for each team. The cards have a colored border around the fronts of the cards according to the team with corresponding color printing on the backs. Cards are organized numerically by team, i.e., Boston Celtics (1-12), Los Angeles Clippers (13-24), New York Knicks (25-37), Phoenix Suns (38-51), Indiana Pacers (52-63), San Antonio Spurs (64-75), Atlanta Hawks (76-87), New Jersey Nets (88-100), Chicago Bulls (101-112), Seattle Supersonics (113-124), Milwaukee Bucks (125-136), Denver Nuggets (137-148), Golden State Warriors (149-160), Portland Trail Blazers (161-171), Los Angeles Lakers (172-184), Washington Bullets (185-194), Philadelphia 76ers (201-212), Cleveland Cavaliers (213-224), Utah Jazz (225-236), Houston Rockets (237-249), Dallas Mavericks (250-260), Detroit Pistons (261-269) and Sacramento Kings (270-280). The set also features a special subset (195-200) honoring Gold Medal-winning players from the 1984 Olympic basketball competition as well as a subset of NBA specials (281-288). Michael Jordan's Extended Rookie Card appears in this set. Other Extended Rookie's include Charles

Barkley, Craig Ehlo, Hakeem Olajuwon, Alvin Robertson, Sam Perkins, John Stockton and Otis Thorpe. There is typically a slight discount on sales of opened team bags.

	NRMT-MT	EXC	G-VG
COMPLETE BAG SET (288)	5500.00	2500.00	700.00
COMP.BAG CELTICS (12)	275.00	125.00	34.00
COMP.BAG CLIPPERS (12)	20.00	9.00	2.50
COMP.BAG KNICKS (13)	20.00	9.00	2.50
COMP.BAG SUNS (14)	25.00	11.00	3.10
COMP.BAG PACERS SP (12)	55.00	25.00	7.00
COMP.BAG SPURS (12)	25.00	11.00	3.10
COMP.BAG HAWKS (12)	110.00	50.00	14.00
COMP.BAG NETS (13)	18.00	8.00	2.20
COMP.BAG BULLS (12)	3200.00	1450.00	400.00
COMP.BAG SONICS (12)	20.00	9.00	2.50
COMP.BAG BUCKS (12)	18.00	8.00	2.20
COMP.BAG NUGGETS (12)	20.00	9.00	2.50
COMP.BAG WARRIORS (12)	18.00	8.00	2.20
COMP.BAG BLAZERS (11)	120.00	55.00	15.00
COMP.BAG LAKERS (13)	175.00	80.00	22.00
COMP.BAG BULLETS (10)	18.00	8.00	2.20
COMP.BAG SET OLY/SPC(14)	975.00	450.00	120.00
COMP.BAG 76ERS (12)	300.00	135.00	38.00
COMP.BAG CAVS (12)	18.00	8.00	2.20
COMP.BAG JAZZ (12)	250.00	110.00	31.00
COMP.BAG ROCKETS (13)	400.00	180.00	50.00
COMP.BAG MAVS (11)	50.00	22.00	6.25
COMP.BAG PISTONS (9)	50.00	22.00	6.25
COMP.BAG KINGS (11)	25.00	11.00	3.10
COMMON CARD (1-51/64-288)	2.00	.90	.25
COMMON SP (52-63)	5.00	2.20	.60
*OPENED TEAM SETS: .75X to 1.0...			

☐ 1	Larry Bird 175.00	80.00	22.00
☐ 2	Danny Ainge 12.00	5.50	1.50
☐ 3	Quinn Buckner 3.00	1.35	.35
☐ 4	Rick Carlisle 2.00	.90	.25
☐ 5	M.L. Carr 3.00	1.35	.35
☐ 6	Dennis Johnson 4.00	1.80	.50
☐ 7	Greg Kite 2.00	.90	.25
☐ 8	Cedric Maxwell 3.00	1.35	.35
☐ 9	Kevin McHale 16.00	7.25	2.00
☐ 10	Robert Parish 12.00	5.50	1.50
☐ 11	Scott Wedman 2.00	.90	.25
☐ 12	Larry Bird 100.00	45.00	12.50
	1983-84 NBA MVP		
☐ 13	Marques Johnson 3.00	1.35	.35
☐ 14	Junior Bridgeman 3.00	1.35	.35
☐ 15	Michael Cage 4.00	1.80	.50
☐ 16	Harvey Catchings 2.00	.90	.25
☐ 17	James Donaldson 2.00	.90	.25
☐ 18	Lancaster Gordon 2.00	.90	.25
☐ 19	Jay Murphy 2.00	.90	.25
☐ 20	Norm Nixon 3.00	1.35	.35
☐ 21	Derek Smith 2.00	.90	.25
☐ 22	Bill Walton 18.00	8.00	2.20
☐ 23	Bryan Warrick 2.00	.90	.25
☐ 24	Rory White 2.00	.90	.25
☐ 25	Bernard King 6.00	2.70	.75
☐ 26	James Bailey 2.00	.90	.25
☐ 27	Ken Bannister 2.00	.90	.25
☐ 28	Butch Carter 2.00	.90	.25
☐ 29	Bill Cartwright 3.00	1.35	.35
☐ 30	Pat Cummings 2.00	.90	.25
☐ 31	Ernie Grunfeld 3.00	1.35	.35
☐ 32	Louis Orr 2.00	.90	.25
☐ 33	Leonard Robinson 3.00	1.35	.35
☐ 34	Rory Sparrow 2.00	.90	.25

☐ 35	Trent Tucker	2.00	.90	.25
☐ 36	Darrell Walker	2.00	.90	.25
☐ 37	Eddie Lee Wilkins	2.00	.90	.25
☐ 38	Alvan Adams	3.00	1.35	.35
☐ 39	Walter Davis	4.00	1.80	.50
☐ 40	James Edwards	3.00	1.35	.35
☐ 41	Rod Foster	2.00	.90	.25
☐ 42	Michael Holton	2.00	.90	.25
☐ 43	Jay Humphries	3.00	1.35	.35
☐ 44	Charles Jones	2.00	.90	.25
☐ 45	Maurice Lucas	3.00	1.35	.35
☐ 46	Kyle Macy	3.00	1.35	.35
☐ 47	Larry Nance	10.00	4.50	1.25
☐ 48	Charles Pittman	2.00	.90	.25
☐ 49	Rick Robey	2.00	.90	.25
☐ 50	Mike Sanders	2.00	.90	.25
☐ 51	Alvin Scott	2.00	.90	.25
☐ 52	Clark Kellogg SP	6.00	2.70	.75
☐ 53	Tony Brown SP	5.00	2.20	.60
☐ 54	Devin Durrant SP	5.00	2.20	.60
☐ 55	Vern Fleming SP	7.00	3.10	.85
☐ 56	Bill Garnett	5.00	2.20	.60
☐ 57	Stuart Gray SP UER	5.00	2.20	.60
	(Photo actually			
	Tony Brown)			
☐ 58	Jerry Sichting SP	6.00	2.70	.75
☐ 59	Terence Stansbury SP	5.00	2.20	.60
☐ 60	Steve Stipanovich SP	6.00	2.70	.75
☐ 61	Jimmy Thomas SP	5.00	2.20	.60
☐ 62	Granville Waiters SP	5.00	2.20	.60
☐ 63	Herb Williams SP	6.00	2.70	.75
☐ 64	Artis Gilmore	4.00	1.80	.50
☐ 65	Gene Banks	2.00	.90	.25
☐ 66	Ron Brewer	2.00	.90	.25
☐ 67	George Gervin	15.00	6.75	1.85
☐ 68	Edgar Jones	2.00	.90	.25
☐ 69	Ozell Jones	2.00	.90	.25
☐ 70	Mark McNamara	2.00	.90	.25
☐ 71	Mike Mitchell	2.00	.90	.25
☐ 72	Johnny Moore	2.00	.90	.25
☐ 73	John Paxson	3.00	1.35	.35
☐ 74	Fred Roberts	2.00	.90	.25
☐ 75	Alvin Robertson	4.00	1.80	.50
☐ 76	Dominique Wilkins	60.00	27.00	7.50
☐ 77	Rickey Brown	2.00	.90	.25
☐ 78	Antoine Carr	3.00	1.35	.35
☐ 79	Mike Glenn	2.00	.90	.25
☐ 80	Scott Hastings	2.00	.90	.25
☐ 81	Eddie Johnson	2.00	.90	.25
☐ 82	Cliff Levingston	2.00	.90	.25
☐ 83	Leo Rautins	2.00	.90	.25
☐ 84	Doc Rivers	3.00	1.35	.35
☐ 85	Tree Rollins	3.00	1.35	.35
☐ 86	Randy Wittman	2.00	.90	.25
☐ 87	Sly Williams	2.00	.90	.25
☐ 88	Darryl Dawkins	4.00	1.80	.50
☐ 89	Otis Birdsong	3.00	1.35	.35
☐ 90	Darwin Cook	2.00	.90	.25
☐ 91	Mike Gminski	3.00	1.35	.35
☐ 92	George T. Johnson	2.00	.90	.25
☐ 93	Albert King	2.00	.90	.25
☐ 94	Mike O'Koren	2.00	.90	.25
☐ 95	Kelvin Ransey	2.00	.90	.25
☐ 96	M.R. Richardson	2.00	.90	.25
☐ 97	Wayne Sappleton	2.00	.90	.25
☐ 98	Jeff Turner	2.00	.90	.25
☐ 99	Buck Williams	4.00	1.80	.50
☐ 100	Michael Wilson	2.00	.90	.25
☐ 101	Michael Jordan	2900.00	1300.00	350.00
☐ 102	Dave Corzine	2.00	.90	.25
☐ 103	Quintin Dailey	2.00	.90	.25
☐ 104	Sidney Green	2.00	.90	.25
☐ 105	David Greenwood	3.00	1.35	.35
☐ 106	Rod Higgins	2.00	.90	.25
☐ 107	Steve Johnson	2.00	.90	.25
☐ 108	Caldwell Jones	3.00	1.35	.35
☐ 109	Wes Matthews	2.00	.90	.25
☐ 110	Jawann Oldham	2.00	.90	.25
☐ 111	Ennis Whatley	2.00	.90	.25
☐ 112	Orlando Woolridge	3.00	1.35	.35
☐ 113	Tom Chambers	4.00	1.80	.50
☐ 114	Cory Blackwell	2.00	.90	.25
☐ 115	Frank Brickowski	3.00	1.35	.35
☐ 116	Gerald Henderson	2.00	.90	.25
☐ 117	Reggie King	2.00	.90	.25
☐ 118	Tim McCormick	2.00	.90	.25
☐ 119	John Schweitz	2.00	.90	.25
☐ 120	Jack Sikma	3.00	1.35	.35
☐ 121	Ricky Sobers	2.00	.90	.25
☐ 122	Jon Sundvold	2.00	.90	.25
☐ 123	Danny Vranes	2.00	.90	.25
☐ 124	Al Wood	2.00	.90	.25
☐ 125	Terry Cummings UER	4.00	1.80	.50
	(Robert Cummings			
	on card back)			
☐ 126	Randy Breuer	2.00	.90	.25
☐ 127	Charles Davis	2.00	.90	.25
☐ 128	Mike Dunleavy	3.00	1.35	.35
☐ 129	Kenny Fields	2.00	.90	.25
☐ 130	Kevin Grevey	2.00	.90	.25
☐ 131	Craig Hodges	2.00	.90	.25
☐ 132	Alton Lister	2.00	.90	.25
☐ 133	Larry Micheaux	2.00	.90	.25
☐ 134	Paul Mokeski	2.00	.90	.25
☐ 135	Sidney Moncrief	4.00	1.80	.50
☐ 136	Paul Pressey	2.00	.90	.25
☐ 137	Alex English	6.00	2.70	.75
☐ 138	Wayne Cooper	2.00	.90	.25
☐ 139	T.R. Dunn	2.00	.90	.25
☐ 140	Mike Evans	2.00	.90	.25
☐ 141	Bill Hanzlik	2.00	.90	.25
☐ 142	Dan Issel	10.00	4.50	1.25
☐ 143	Joe Kopicki	2.00	.90	.25
☐ 144	Lafayette Lever	3.00	1.35	.35
☐ 145	Calvin Natt	2.00	.90	.25
☐ 146	Danny Schayes	3.00	1.35	.35
☐ 147	Elston Turner	2.00	.90	.25
☐ 148	Willie White	2.00	.90	.25
☐ 149	Purvis Short	2.00	.90	.25
☐ 150	Chuck Aleksinas	2.00	.90	.25
☐ 151	Mike Bratz	2.00	.90	.25
☐ 152	Steve Burtt	2.00	.90	.25
☐ 153	Lester Conner	2.00	.90	.25
☐ 154	Sleepy Floyd	3.00	1.35	.35
☐ 155	Mickey Johnson	2.00	.90	.25
☐ 156	Gary Plummer	2.00	.90	.25
☐ 157	Larry Smith	2.00	.90	.25
☐ 158	Peter Thibeaux	2.00	.90	.25
☐ 159	Jerome Whitehead	2.00	.90	.25
☐ 160	Othell Wilson	2.00	.90	.25
☐ 161	Kiki Vandeweghe	3.00	1.35	.35
☐ 162	Sam Bowie	4.00	1.80	.50
☐ 163	Kenny Carr	2.00	.90	.25
☐ 164	Steve Colter	2.00	.90	.25
☐ 165	Clyde Drexler	110.00	50.00	14.00
☐ 166	Audie Norris	2.00	.90	.25
☐ 167	Jim Paxson	3.00	1.35	.35
☐ 168	Tom Scheffler	2.00	.90	.25
☐ 169	Bernard Thompson	2.00	.90	.25
☐ 170	Mychal Thompson	3.00	1.35	.35
☐ 171	Darnell Valentine	2.00	.90	.25
☐ 172	Magic Johnson	110.00	50.00	14.00

☐ 173	Kareem Abdul-Jabbar	40.00	18.00	5.00
☐ 174	Michael Cooper	3.00	1.35	.35
☐ 175	Earl Jones	2.00	.90	.25
☐ 176	Mitch Kupchak	2.00	.90	.25
☐ 177	Ronnie Lester	2.00	.90	.25
☐ 178	Bob McAdoo	4.00	1.80	.50
☐ 179	Mike McGee	2.00	.90	.25
☐ 180	Kurt Rambis	2.00	.90	.25
☐ 181	Byron Scott	6.00	2.70	.75
☐ 182	Larry Spriggs	2.00	.90	.25
☐ 183	Jamaal Wilkes	3.00	1.35	.35
☐ 184	James Worthy	12.00	5.50	1.50
☐ 185	Gus Williams	3.00	1.35	.35
☐ 186	Greg Ballard	2.00	.90	.25
☐ 187	Dudley Bradley	2.00	.90	.25
☐ 188	Darren Daye	2.00	.90	.25
☐ 189	Frank Johnson	2.00	.90	.25
☐ 190	Charles Jones	2.00	.90	.25
☐ 191	Rick Mahorn	2.00	.90	.25
☐ 192	Jeff Malone	3.00	1.35	.35
☐ 193	Tom McMillen	3.00	1.35	.35
☐ 194	Jeff Ruland	2.00	.90	.25
☐ 195	Michael Jordan OLY	475.00	210.00	60.00
☐ 196	Vern Fleming OLY	3.00	1.35	.35
☐ 197	Sam Perkins OLY	6.00	2.70	.75
☐ 198	Alvin Robertson OLY	3.00	1.35	.35
☐ 199	Jeff Turner OLY	2.00	.90	.25
☐ 200	Leon Wood OLY	2.00	.90	.25
☐ 201	Moses Malone	12.00	5.50	1.50
☐ 202	Charles Barkley	225.00	100.00	28.00
☐ 203	Maurice Cheeks	4.00	1.80	.50
☐ 204	Julius Erving	40.00	18.00	5.00
☐ 205	Clemon Johnson	2.00	.90	.25
☐ 206	George L. Johnson	2.00	.90	.25
☐ 207	Bobby Jones	4.00	1.80	.50
☐ 208	Clint Richardson	2.00	.90	.25
☐ 209	Sedale Threatt	3.00	1.35	.35
☐ 210	Andrew Toney	2.00	.90	.25
☐ 211	Sam Williams	2.00	.90	.25
☐ 212	Leon Wood	2.00	.90	.25
☐ 213	Mel Turpin	2.00	.90	.25
☐ 214	Ron Anderson	2.00	.90	.25
☐ 215	John Bagley	2.00	.90	.25
☐ 216	Johnny Davis	2.00	.90	.25
☐ 217	World B. Free	3.00	1.35	.35
☐ 218	Roy Hinson	2.00	.90	.25
☐ 219	Phil Hubbard	2.00	.90	.25
☐ 220	Edgar Jones	2.00	.90	.25
☐ 221	Ben Poquette	2.00	.90	.25
☐ 222	Lonnie Shelton	2.00	.90	.25
☐ 223	Mark West	2.00	.90	.25
☐ 224	Kevin Williams	2.00	.90	.25
☐ 225	Mark Eaton	3.00	1.35	.35
☐ 226	Mitchell Anderson	2.00	.90	.25
☐ 227	Thurl Bailey	2.00	.90	.25
☐ 228	Adrian Dantley	6.00	2.70	.75
☐ 229	Rickey Green	3.00	1.35	.35
☐ 230	Darrell Griffith	3.00	1.35	.35
☐ 231	Rich Kelley	2.00	.90	.25
☐ 232	Pace Mannion	2.00	.90	.25
☐ 233	Billy Paultz	3.00	1.35	.35
☐ 234	Fred Roberts	2.00	.90	.25
☐ 235	John Stockton	200.00	90.00	25.00
☐ 236	Jeff Wilkins	2.00	.90	.25
☐ 237	Hakeem Olajuwon	375.00	170.00	47.50
☐ 238	Craig Ehlo	16.00	7.25	2.00
☐ 239	Lionel Hollins	2.00	.90	.25
☐ 240	Allen Leavell	2.00	.90	.25
☐ 241	Lewis Lloyd	2.00	.90	.25
☐ 242	John Lucas	3.00	1.35	.35
☐ 243	Rodney McCray	3.00	1.35	.35
☐ 244	Hank McDowell	2.00	.90	.25
☐ 245	Larry Micheaux	2.00	.90	.25
☐ 246	Jim Peterson	2.00	.90	.25
☐ 247	Robert Reid	2.00	.90	.25
☐ 248	Ralph Sampson	3.00	1.35	.35
☐ 249	Mitchell Wiggins	2.00	.90	.25
☐ 250	Mark Aguirre	4.00	1.80	.50
☐ 251	Rolando Blackman	3.00	1.35	.35
☐ 252	Wallace Bryant	2.00	.90	.25
☐ 253	Brad Davis	3.00	1.35	.35
☐ 254	Dale Ellis	3.00	1.35	.35
☐ 255	Derek Harper	8.00	3.60	1.00
☐ 256	Kurt Nimphius	2.00	.90	.25
☐ 257	Sam Perkins	15.00	6.75	1.85
☐ 258	Charlie Sitton	2.00	.90	.25
☐ 259	Tom Sluby	2.00	.90	.25
☐ 260	Jay Vincent	2.00	.90	.25
☐ 261	Isiah Thomas	35.00	16.00	4.40
☐ 262	Kent Benson	3.00	1.35	.35
☐ 263	Earl Cureton	2.00	.90	.25
☐ 264	Vinnie Johnson	3.00	1.35	.35
☐ 265	Bill Laimbeer	4.00	1.80	.50
☐ 266	John Long	3.00	1.35	.35
☐ 267	Dan Roundfield	3.00	1.35	.35
☐ 268	Kelly Tripucka	3.00	1.35	.35
☐ 269	Terry Tyler	2.00	.90	.25
☐ 270	Reggie Theus	3.00	1.35	.35
☐ 271	Don Buse	2.00	.90	.25
☐ 272	Larry Drew	3.00	1.35	.35
☐ 273	Eddie Johnson	2.00	.90	.25
☐ 274	Billy Knight	3.00	1.35	.35
☐ 275	Joe Meriweather	2.00	.90	.25
☐ 276	Mark Olberding	2.00	.90	.25
☐ 277	LaSalle Thompson	2.00	.90	.25
☐ 278	Otis Thorpe	15.00	6.75	1.85
☐ 279	Pete Verhoeven	2.00	.90	.25
☐ 280	Mike Woodson	2.00	.90	.25
☐ 281	Julius Erving	20.00	9.00	2.50
☐ 282	Kareem Abdul-Jabbar	20.00	9.00	2.50
☐ 283	Dan Issel	6.00	2.70	.75
☐ 284	Bernard King	3.00	1.35	.35
☐ 285	Moses Malone	8.00	3.60	1.00
☐ 286	Mark Eaton	3.00	1.35	.35
☐ 287	Isiah Thomas	15.00	6.75	1.85
☐ 288	Michael Jordan	475.00	210.00	60.00

1984-85 Star Arena

These sets were produced to be sold in the arena of each of the five teams featured in this set. The teams are Boston, Dallas, Milwaukee, Los Angeles Lakers and Philadelphia. Each set is different from the team's regular issue set in that the photog-

raphy and card backs are different. Shortly after distribution began, Bob Lanier announced his retirement and his cards were withdrawn from the Milwaukee set. Cards measure 2 1/2" by 3 1/2" and have a colored border around the fronts according to team. Corresponding color printing is on the backs. Celtics feature Star '85 logo on the front while the other four teams feature the Star '84 logo on the front. The cards are ordered alphabetically by team using prefixes A-E.

	NRMT-MT	EXC	G-VG
COMPLETE BAG SET (48) ...	300.00	135.00	38.00
COMPLETE SET (49) w/Lanier	550.00	250.00	70.00
COMP.BAG CELTICS (A1-A9)	110.00	50.00	14.00
COMP.BAG MAVS. (B1-B11)..	20.00	9.00	2.50
COMP.BAG BUCKS (C1-C8)..	20.00	9.00	2.50
COMP.BAG LAKERS (D1-D10)	100.00	45.00	12.50
COMP.BAG 76ERS (E1-E10)..	40.00	18.00	5.00
COMMON CARD	2.00	.90	.25
*OPENED TEAM SETS: .75X to 1.0...			

		NRMT-MT	EXC	G-VG
☐ A1	Larry Bird	60.00	27.00	7.50
☐ A2	Danny Ainge	8.00	3.60	1.00
☐ A3	Rick Carlisle...............	2.00	.90	.25
☐ A4	Dennis Johnson	4.00	1.80	.50
☐ A5	Cedric Maxwell	2.00	.90	.25
☐ A6	Kevin McHale.............	8.00	3.60	1.00
☐ A7	Robert Parish	6.00	2.70	.75
☐ A8	Scott Wedman	2.00	.90	.25
☐ A9	Robert Parish	40.00	18.00	5.00
	Larry Bird			
	Kevin McHale			
	Jimmy Rodgers CO			
	K.C. Jones CO			
	Chris Ford CO			
☐ B1	Mark Aguirre	4.00	1.80	.50
☐ B2	Rolando Blackman......	4.00	1.80	.50
☐ B3	Brad Davis	2.00	.90	.25
☐ B4	Dale Ellis	4.00	1.80	.50
☐ B5	Bill Garnett................	2.00	.90	.25
☐ B6	Derek Harper SP	5.00	2.20	.60
	(Mike Harper on both			
	sides with Mike's			
	birthdate ,etc.)			
☐ B7	Kurt Nimphius	2.00	.90	.25
☐ B8	Jim Spanarkel............	2.00	.90	.25
☐ B9	Elston Turner	2.00	.90	.25
☐ B10	Jay Vincent	2.00	.90	.25
☐ B11	Mark West	4.00	1.80	.50
☐ C1	Nate Archibald	6.00	2.70	.75
☐ C2	Junior Bridgeman	2.00	.90	.25
☐ C3	Mike Dunleavy............	2.00	.90	.25
☐ C4	Kevin Grevey..............	2.00	.90	.25
☐ C5	Marques Johnson	4.00	1.80	.50
☐ C6	Bob Lanier SP..........	300.00	135.00	38.00
☐ C7	Alton Lister	2.00	.90	.25
☐ C8	Sidney Moncrief	4.00	1.80	.50
☐ C9	Paul Pressey	2.00	.90	.25
☐ D1	Kareem Abdul-Jabbar	20.00	9.00	2.50
☐ D2	Michael Cooper	4.00	1.80	.50
☐ D3	Magic Johnson	45.00	20.00	5.50
☐ D4	Mike McGee	2.00	.90	.25
☐ D5	Swen Nater	2.00	.90	.25
☐ D6	Kurt Rambis	2.00	.90	.25
☐ D7	Byron Scott	3.00	1.35	.35
☐ D8	James Worthy	7.00	3.10	.85
☐ D9	Magic Johnson AS	40.00	18.00	5.00
	Kareem Abdul-Jabbar			

		NRMT-MT	EXC	G-VG
☐ D10	Kareem Abdul-Jabbar LL	18.00	8.00	2.20
☐ E1	Julius Erving	20.00	9.00	2.50
☐ E2	Maurice Cheeks	3.00	1.35	.35
☐ E3	Franklin Edwards	2.00	.90	.25
☐ E4	Marc Iavaroni	2.00	.90	.25
☐ E5	Clemon Johnson	2.00	.90	.25
☐ E6	Bobby Jones	3.00	1.35	.35
☐ E7	Moses Malone	8.00	3.60	1.00
☐ E8	Clint Richardson	2.00	.90	.25
☐ E9	Andrew Toney	2.00	.90	.25
☐ E10	Sam Williams..............	2.00	.90	.25

1984-85 Star Court Kings 5x7

This over-sized 50-card set was issued as two series of 25. Cards measure approximately 5" by 7" and have a yellow (first series 1-25) or blue (second series 26-50) colored border around the fronts of the cards and blue and yellow printing on the backs. These large cards feature the Star '85 logo on the front. The set features early professional cards of Charles Barkley, Michael Jordan and Hakeem Olajuwon.

		NRMT-MT	EXC	G-VG
COMPLETE BAG SET (50) ...		475.00	210.00	60.00
COMP.BAG SER.1 (25)		125.00	55.00	15.50
COMP.BAG SER.2 (25)		350.00	160.00	45.00
COMMON CARD (1-25)		2.00	.90	.25
COMMON CARD (26-50)		2.50	1.10	.30
*OPENED TEAM SETS: .75X to 1.0...				

		NRMT-MT	EXC	G-VG
☐ 1	Kareem Abdul-Jabbar ..	20.00	9.00	2.50
☐ 2	Jeff Ruland	2.00	.90	.25
☐ 3	Mark Aguirre	4.00	1.80	.50
☐ 4	Julius Erving	20.00	9.00	2.50
☐ 5	Kelly Tripucka	2.00	.90	.25
☐ 6	Buck Williams	2.00	.90	.25
☐ 7	Sidney Moncrief	4.00	1.80	.50
☐ 8	World B. Free	4.00	1.80	.50
☐ 9	Bill Walton	6.00	2.70	.75
☐ 10	Purvis Short................	2.00	.90	.25
☐ 11	Rickey Green	2.00	.90	.25
☐ 12	Dominique Wilkins.....	12.00	5.50	1.50
☐ 13	Jim Paxson	2.00	.90	.25
☐ 14	Ralph Sampson	4.00	1.80	.50
☐ 15	Magic Johnson	35.00	16.00	4.40
☐ 16	Reggie Theus	4.00	1.80	.50
☐ 17	Moses Malone	6.00	2.70	.75
☐ 18	Larry Bird..................	55.00	25.00	7.00

		NRMT-MT	EXC	G-VG
☐ 19	Larry Nance	2.00	.90	.25
☐ 20	Clark Kellogg	2.00	.90	.25
☐ 21	Jack Sikma	4.00	1.80	.50
☐ 22	Alex English	4.00	1.80	.50
☐ 23	Bernard King	4.00	1.80	.50
☐ 24	Dave Corzine	2.00	.90	.25
☐ 25	George Gervin	6.00	2.70	.75
☐ 26	Michael Jordan	275.00	125.00	34.00
☐ 27	Rolando Blackman	4.00	1.80	.50
☐ 28	Dan Issel	4.00	1.80	.50
☐ 29	Maurice Cheeks	4.00	1.80	.50
☐ 30	Isiah Thomas	12.00	5.50	1.50
☐ 31	Robert Parish	6.00	2.70	.75
☐ 32	Mark Eaton	4.00	1.80	.50
☐ 33	Sam Perkins	2.50	1.10	.30
☐ 34	Artis Gilmore	4.00	1.80	.50
☐ 35	Andrew Toney	2.50	1.10	.30
☐ 36	Adrian Dantley	4.00	1.80	.50
☐ 37	Terry Cummings	4.00	1.80	.50
☐ 38	Orlando Woolridge	2.50	1.10	.30
☐ 39	Tom Chambers	4.00	1.80	.50
☐ 40	Gus Williams	2.50	1.10	.30
☐ 41	Charles Barkley	45.00	20.00	5.50
☐ 42	Kevin McHale	8.00	3.60	1.00
☐ 43	Otis Birdsong	2.50	1.10	.30
☐ 44	Sam Bowie	2.50	1.10	.30
☐ 45	Darrell Griffith	2.50	1.10	.30
☐ 46	Kiki Vandeweghe	4.00	1.80	.50
☐ 47	Hakeem Olajuwon	60.00	27.00	7.50
☐ 48	Marques Johnson	4.00	1.80	.50
☐ 49	James Worthy	6.00	2.70	.75
☐ 50	Mel Turpin	2.50	1.10	.30

		NRMT-MT	EXC	G-VG
☐ 3	ABA Regular Season Stats	6.00	2.70	.75
☐ 4	NBA All-Star Eight Times	6.00	2.70	.75
☐ 5	ABA All-Star Five Times	6.00	2.70	.75
☐ 6	NBA Playoff Stats	6.00	2.70	.75
☐ 7	ABA Playoff Stats	6.00	2.70	.75
☐ 8	NBA MVP, 1981	6.00	2.70	.75
☐ 9	ABA MVP, 1974, 1975, and 1976	6.00	2.70	.75
☐ 10	Collegiate Stats	6.00	2.70	.75
☐ 11	NBA All-Star MVP, 1977 and 1983	6.00	2.70	.75
☐ 12	NBA Career Highlights	6.00	2.70	.75
☐ 13	ABA Career Highlights	6.00	2.70	.75
☐ 14	1983 World Champs	6.00	2.70	.75
☐ 15	ABA Champions 1974 and 1976	6.00	2.70	.75
☐ 16	All-Time Scoring	6.00	2.70	.75
☐ 17	Personal Data	6.00	2.70	.75
☐ 18	The Future	6.00	2.70	.75

1985 Star Kareem Abdul-Jabbar

The 1985 Star Kareem Abdul-Jabbar set is an 18-card standard-size tribute set. Most of the photos on the fronts are from the early 1980s. Card backs provide various statistics and tidbits of information about Abdul-Jabbar. The set's basic design is identical to those of the Star Company's regular NBA sets. The cards show a Star '85 logo in the upper right corner. The front borders are Lakers' purple.

1984-85 Star Julius Erving

This set contains 18 standard-size cards highlighting the career of basketball great Julius Erving. The cards have a red border around the fronts of the cards and red printing on the backs. Cards feature Star '85 logo on the front although they were released in the summer of 1984.

		NRMT-MT	EXC	G-VG
COMPLETE BAG SET (18)		80.00	36.00	10.00
COMMON J.ERVING (1-18)		6.00	2.70	.75
*OPENED SET: .75X to 1.0X				
☐ 1	Checklist	6.00	2.70	.75
☐ 2	NBA Regular Season Stats	6.00	2.70	.75

		NRMT-MT	EXC	G-VG
COMPLETE BAG SET (18)		50.00	22.00	6.25
COMMON JABBAR (1-18)		3.50	1.55	.45
*OPENED SET: .75X to 1.0X				
☐ 1	Checklist Card	3.50	1.55	.45
☐ 2	Collegiate Stats	3.50	1.55	.45
☐ 3	Regular Season Stats	3.50	1.55	.45
☐ 4	Playoff Stats	3.50	1.55	.45
☐ 5	All Star Stats	3.50	1.55	.45
☐ 6	All-Time Scoring King	3.50	1.55	.45
☐ 7	NBA MVP 71/72/74	3.50	1.55	.45
☐ 8	NBA MVP 76/77/80	3.50	1.55	.45
☐ 9	Defensive Star	3.50	1.55	.45
☐ 10	World Champs 71	3.50	1.55	.45
☐ 11	World Champs 80/82/85	3.50	1.55	.45
☐ 12	All-Time Records	3.50	1.55	.45

		NRMT-MT	EXC	G-VG
☐ 13	Rookie-of-the-Year 70	3.50	1.55	.45
☐ 14	Playoff MVP 71/85	3.50	1.55	.45
☐ 15	The League Leader	3.50	1.55	.45
☐ 16	Career Highlights	3.50	1.55	.45
☐ 17	Personal Data	3.50	1.55	.45
☐ 18	The Future	3.50	1.55	.45

1985 Star Coaches

The 1984-85 Star NBA Coaches set is a ten-card set depicting some of the NBA's best known coaches. The set's basic design is identical to those of the Star Company's regular NBA sets. The cards measure approximately 2 1/2" by 3 1/2". The front borders are royal blue, and the backs show each man's coaching records. Statistics for ex-players are NOT included. The cards show a Star '85 logo in the upper right corner. Coaching statistics on the card backs only go up through the 1983-84 NBA season. The cards are numbered on the back; the numbering is essentially alphabetical by name.

	NRMT-MT	EXC	G-VG
COMPLETE BAG SET (10)	18.00	8.00	2.20
COMMON CARD (1-10)	1.50	.70	.19
*OPENED SET: .75X to 1.0X			
☐ 1 John Bach	1.50	.70	.19
☐ 2 Hubie Brown	2.00	.90	.25
☐ 3 Cotton Fitzsimmons	1.50	.70	.19
☐ 4 Kevin Loughery	1.50	.70	.19
☐ 5 John MacLeod	1.50	.70	.19
☐ 6 Doug Moe	1.50	.70	.19
☐ 7 Don Nelson	2.50	1.10	.30
☐ 8 Jack Ramsey	1.50	.70	.19
☐ 9 Pat Riley	7.50	3.40	.95
☐ 10 Lenny Wilkens UER	5.00	2.20	.60
(Name misspelled on card back)			

1985 Star Crunch'n'Munch All-Stars

The 1985 Star Crunch'n'Munch NBA All-Stars set is an 11-card standard-size set featuring the ten starting players in the

1985 NBA All-Star Game plus a checklist card. The set was produced for the Crunch 'n' Munch Food Company and was originally available to the hobby exclusively through Don Guilbert of Woonsocket, Rhode Island. The set's basic design is identical to those of the Star Company's regular NBA sets. The cards show a Star '85 logo in the upper right corner. The front borders are yellowish orange and the backs show each player's All-Star Game record.

	NRMT-MT	EXC	G-VG
COMPLETE BAG SET (11)	525.00	240.00	65.00
COMMON CARD (1-11)	5.00	2.20	.60
*OPENED SET: .75X to 1.0X			
☐ 1 Checklist Card	10.00	4.50	1.25
☐ 2 Larry Bird	100.00	45.00	12.50
☐ 3 Julius Erving	25.00	11.00	3.10
☐ 4 Michael Jordan	375.00	170.00	47.50
☐ 5 Moses Malone	10.00	4.50	1.25
☐ 6 Isiah Thomas	10.00	4.50	1.25
☐ 7 Kareem Abdul-Jabbar	25.00	11.00	3.10
☐ 8 Adrian Dantley	6.00	2.70	.75
☐ 9 George Gervin	15.00	6.75	1.85
☐ 10 Magic Johnson	60.00	27.00	7.50
☐ 11 Ralph Sampson	5.00	2.20	.60

1985 Star Gatorade Slam Dunk

This nine-card set was given to the people who attended the 1985 All-Star Weekend Banquet at Indianapolis. Cards measure the standard size and have a green border around the fronts of the cards and green printing on the backs. Cards feature the

Star '85 and Gatorade logos on the fronts. Since Terence Stansbury was a late substitute in the Slam Dunk contest for Charles Barkley. Both cards were produced, but the Barkley card was never released. However, the card has since surfaced in the marketplace. The Barkley card is unnumbered and shows him dunking.

	NRMT-MT	EXC	G-VG
COMPLETE BAG SET (9)	325.00	145.00	40.00
COMMON CARD (1-9)	3.00	1.35	.35
*OPENED SET: .75X to 1.0X			

		NRMT-MT	EXC	G-VG
☐ 1	Gatorade 2nd Annual Slam Dunk Championship (Checklist back)	6.00	2.70	.75
☐ 2	Larry Nance	6.00	2.70	.75
☐ 3	Terence Stansbury	3.00	1.35	.35
☐ 4	Clyde Drexler	30.00	13.50	3.70
☐ 5	Julius Erving	25.00	11.00	3.10
☐ 6	Darrell Griffith	4.00	1.80	.50
☐ 7	Michael Jordan	275.00	125.00	34.00
☐ 8	Dominique Wilkins	10.00	4.50	1.25
☐ 9	Orlando Woolridge	4.00	1.80	.50
☐ NNO	Charles Barkley SP (Withdrawn)	125.00	55.00	15.50

1985 Star Last 11 ROY's

The 1985 Star Rookies of the Year set is an 11-card standard-size set depicting each of the NBA's ROY award winners from the 1974-75 through 1984-85 seasons. Michael Jordan's card only shows his collegiate statistics while all others provide NBA statistics up through the 1983-84 season. Cards of Darrell Griffith and Jamaal Wilkes show the Star '86 logo in the upper right corner while all others in the set show Star '85. The set's basic design is identical to those of the Star Company's regular NBA sets and the front borders are off-white. The set is sequenced in reverse chronological order according to when each player won the ROY.

	NRMT-MT	EXC	G-VG
COMPLETE BAG SET (11)	325.00	145.00	40.00
COMMON CARD (1-11)	3.00	1.35	.35
*OPENED SET: .75X to 1.0X			

		NRMT-MT	EXC	G-VG
☐ 1	Michael Jordan	275.00	125.00	34.00
☐ 2	Ralph Sampson	3.00	1.35	.35
☐ 3	Terry Cummings	3.00	1.35	.35
☐ 4	Buck Williams	5.00	2.20	.60
☐ 5	Darrell Griffith	3.00	1.35	.35
☐ 6	Larry Bird	100.00	45.00	12.50
☐ 7	Phil Ford	5.00	2.20	.60
☐ 8	Walter Davis	5.00	2.20	.60
☐ 9	Adrian Dantley	5.00	2.20	.60
☐ 10	Alvan Adams	5.00	2.20	.60
☐ 11	Keith/Jamaal Wilkes	5.00	2.20	.60

1985 Star Lite All-Stars

This 13-card standard-size set was given to the people who attended the 1985 All-Star Weekend Banquet at Indianapolis. The set was issued in a clear, sealed plastic bag. Cards have a blue border around the fronts of the cards and blue printing on the backs. Cards feature the Star '85 and Lite Beer logos on the fronts. Players featured are the 1985 NBA All-Star starting line-ups and coaches.

	NRMT-MT	EXC	G-VG
COMPLETE BAG SET (13)	375.00	170.00	47.50
COMMON CARD (1-13)	4.00	1.80	.50
*OPENED SET: .75X to 1.0X			

		NRMT-MT	EXC	G-VG
☐ 1	1985 NBA All-Stars Starting Line-Ups	4.00	1.80	.50
☐ 2	Larry Bird	90.00	40.00	11.00
☐ 3	Julius Erving	25.00	11.00	3.10
☐ 4	Michael Jordan	275.00	125.00	34.00
☐ 5	Moses Malone	8.00	3.60	1.00
☐ 6	Isiah Thomas	10.00	4.50	1.25
☐ 7	K.C. Jones CO	4.00	1.80	.50
☐ 8	Kareem Abdul-Jabbar	25.00	11.00	3.10
☐ 9	Adrian Dantley	5.00	2.20	.60
☐ 10	George Gervin	10.00	4.50	1.25
☐ 11	Magic Johnson	65.00	29.00	8.00
☐ 12	Ralph Sampson	4.00	1.80	.50
☐ 13	Pat Riley CO	8.00	3.60	1.00

1985 Star Schick Legends

This 24-card set was given to the people who attended the 1985 All-Star Weekend

Banquet at Indianapolis. Cards measure 2 1/2" by 3 1/2" and have a yellow border around the fronts of the cards and yellow and black printing on the backs. Cards feature the Star '85 and Schick logos on the fronts. Players featured were participants in the Schick NBA Legends Classic. The cards are numbered on the back; the numbering corresponds to alphabetical order by player.

	NRMT-MT	EXC	G-VG
COMPLETE BAG SET (25)	75.00	34.00	9.50
COMMON CARD (1-25)	2.00	.90	.25
*OPENED SET: .75X to 1.0X			
☐ 1 Schick NBA Legends Checklist	3.00	1.35	.35
☐ 2 Rick Barry	8.00	3.60	1.00
☐ 3 Zelmo Beaty	2.00	.90	.25
☐ 4 Walt Bellamy	5.00	2.20	.60
☐ 5 Dave Bing	6.00	2.70	.75
☐ 6 Roger Brown	2.00	.90	.25
☐ 7 Bob Cousy	12.00	5.50	1.50
☐ 8 Mel Daniels	2.00	.90	.25
☐ 9 Bob Davies	3.00	1.35	.35
☐ 10 Dave DeBusschere	6.00	2.70	.75
☐ 11 Walt Frazier	6.00	2.70	.75
☐ 12 John Havlicek	12.00	5.50	1.50
☐ 13 Connie Hawkins	10.00	4.50	1.25
☐ 14 Tom Heinsohn	6.00	2.70	.75
☐ 15 Red Holzman CO	2.50	1.10	.30
☐ 16 Johnny Kerr	2.50	1.10	.30
☐ 17 Bobby Leonard	2.00	.90	.25
☐ 18 Pete Maravich	25.00	11.00	3.10
☐ 19 Earl Monroe	6.00	2.70	.75
☐ 20 Bob Pettit	8.00	3.60	1.00
☐ 21 Oscar Robertson	12.00	5.50	1.50
☐ 22 Nate Thurmond	6.00	2.70	.75
☐ 23 Dick Van Arsdale	2.50	1.10	.30
☐ 24 Tom Van Arsdale	2.50	1.10	.30
☐ 25 George Yardley	2.50	1.10	.30

1985 Star Slam Dunk Supers 5x7

This ten-card set uses actual photography from the 1985 Slam Dunk contest in Indianapolis held during the NBA All-Star Weekend. Cards measure approximately 5" by 7" and have a red border around the fronts of the cards and red printing on the

backs. Cards feature Star '85 logo on the fronts. The set ordering for these numbered cards is alphabetical by subject's name.

	NRMT-MT	EXC	G-VG
COMPLETE BAG SET (10)	275.00	125.00	34.00
COMMON CARD (1-10)	2.00	.90	.25
*OPENED SET: .75X to 1.0X			
☐ 1 Checklist Card (Group photo)	50.00	22.00	6.25
☐ 2 Clyde Drexler	30.00	13.50	3.70
☐ 3 Julius Erving	20.00	9.00	2.50
☐ 4 Darrell Griffith	4.00	1.80	.50
☐ 5 Michael Jordan	250.00	110.00	31.00
☐ 6 Larry Nance	6.00	2.70	.75
☐ 7 Terence Stansbury	2.00	.90	.25
☐ 8 Dominique Wilkins	10.00	4.50	1.25
☐ 9 Orlando Woolridge	4.00	1.80	.50
☐ 10 Dominique Wilkins (1985 Slam Dunk Champ)	8.00	3.60	1.00

1985 Star Team Supers 5x7

This 40-card set is actually eight team sets of five each except for the Sixers having ten players included. Cards measure approximately 5" by 7" and have a colored border around the fronts of the cards according to the team with corresponding color printing on the backs. Cards feature Star '85 logo on the front. Cards are numbered below by assigning a team prefix based on the initials of the team, for example, BC for Boston Celtics.

	NRMT-MT	EXC	G-VG
COMPLETE BAG SET (40)	525.00	240.00	65.00
COMP.BAG CELTICS (5)	70.00	32.00	8.75

```
COMP.BAG BULLS (5)......... 260.00 115.00 32.00
COMP.BAG PISTONS (5)....... 25.00  11.00  3.10
COMP.BAG ROCKETS (5)....... 70.00  32.00  8.75
COMP.BAG LAKERS (5)........ 75.00  34.00  9.50
COMP.BAG BUCKS (5)......... 10.00   4.50  1.25
COMP.BAG 76ERS (10)........ 80.00  36.00 10.00
COMMON CARD ...............  2.00    .90   .25
ABOVE PRICES ARE FOR SEALED BAGS
*OPENED TEAM SETS: .75X to 1.0...
```

```
☐ BC1 Larry Bird........... 50.00  22.00  6.25
☐ BC2 Robert Parish........  5.00   2.20   .60
☐ BC3 Kevin McHale.........  7.00   3.10   .85
☐ BC4 Dennis Johnson.......  3.00   1.35   .35
☐ BC5 Danny Ainge..........  6.00   2.70   .75
☐ CB1 Michael Jordan...... 250.00 110.00 31.00
☐ CB2 Orlando Woolridge....  3.00   1.35   .35
☐ CB3 Quintin Dailey.......  2.00    .90   .25
☐ CB4 Dave Corzine.........  2.00    .90   .25
☐ CB5 Steve Johnson........  2.00    .90   .25
☐ DP1 Isiah Thomas......... 12.00   5.50  1.50
☐ DP2 Kelly Tripucka.......  3.00   1.35   .35
☐ DP3 Vinnie Johnson.......  3.00   1.35   .35
☐ DP4 Bill Laimbeer........  3.00   1.35   .35
☐ DP5 John Long............  2.00    .90   .25
☐ HR1 Ralph Sampson........  3.00   1.35   .35
☐ HR2 Hakeem Olajuwon...... 60.00  27.00  7.50
☐ HR3 Lewis Lloyd..........  2.00    .90   .25
☐ HR4 Rodney McCray........  3.00   1.35   .35
☐ HR5 Lionel Hollins.......  2.00    .90   .25
☐ LA1 Kareem Abdul-Jabbar.. 20.00   9.00  2.50
☐ LA2 Magic Johnson........ 35.00  16.00  4.40
☐ LA3 James Worthy.........  5.00   2.20   .60
☐ LA4 Byron Scott..........  3.00   1.35   .35
☐ LA5 Bob McAdoo...........  3.00   1.35   .35
☐ MB1 Terry Cummings.......  3.00   1.35   .35
☐ MB2 Sidney Moncrief......  3.00   1.35   .35
☐ MB3 Paul Pressey.........  2.00    .90   .25
☐ MB4 Mike Dunleavy........  3.00   1.35   .35
☐ MB5 Alton Lister.........  2.00    .90   .25
☐ PS1 Julius Erving........ 20.00   9.00  2.50
☐ PS2 Maurice Cheeks.......  3.00   1.35   .35
☐ PS3 Bobby Jones..........  3.00   1.35   .35
☐ PS4 Clemon Johnson.......  2.00    .90   .25
☐ PS5 Leon Wood............  2.00    .90   .25
☐ PS6 Moses Malone.........  5.00   2.20   .60
☐ PS7 Andrew Toney.........  2.00    .90   .25
☐ PS8 Charles Barkley...... 45.00  20.00  5.50
☐ PS9 Clint Richardson.....  2.00    .90   .25
☐ PS10 Sedale Threatt......  2.00    .90   .25
```

1985-86 Star

This 172-card standard-size set was produced by the Star Company and features players in the NBA. Cards were released in two groups, 1-94 and 95-172. The team sets were issued in clear sealed bags. Many of these team bags were distributed to hobby dealers through a small group of Star Company master distributors. The original wholesale price per bag was $2-$3 for most of the teams. According to Star Company's original sales materials and order forms, reportedly 2,000 team bags were printed for each team and an additional 2,200 team sets were printed for the more popular teams of that time. Cards are numbered in team order and measure the

standard 2 1/2" by 3 1/2". The team ordering is as follows, Philadelphia 76ers (1-9), Detroit Pistons (10-17), Houston Rockets (18-25), Los Angeles Lakers (26-33), Phoenix Suns (34-41), Atlanta Hawks (42-49), Denver Nuggets (50-57), New Jersey Nets (58-65), Seattle Supersonics (66-73), Sacramento Kings (74-80), Indiana Pacers (81-87), Los Angeles Clippers (88-94), Boston Celtics (95-102), Portland Trail Blazers (103-109), Washington Bullets (110-116), Chicago Bulls (117-123), Milwaukee Bucks (124-130), Golden State Warriors (131-136), Utah Jazz (137-144), San Antonio Spurs (145-151), Cleveland Cavaliers (152-158), Dallas Mavericks (159-165) and New York Knicks (166-172). Borders are colored according to team. Card backs are very similar to the other Star basketball sets except that the player statistics go up through the 1984-85 season. Extended Rookie Cards in this set include Patrick Ewing and Kevin Willis. There is typically a slight discount on opened team bags. Cards of Celtics players (95-102) have either green or white borders. Many cards in this set (particularly 95-176) have been counterfeited and are prevalent on the market. Among those affected are the Ewing Extended Rookie Card (166) and Jordan (117).

```
                          NRMT-MT   EXC  G-VG
COMPLETE BAG SET (172) 1600.00 700.00 200.00
COMP.BAG 76ERS (9) ....... 130.00  57.50  16.00
COMP.BAG PISTONS (8) .....  40.00  18.00   5.00
COMP.BAG ROCKETS (8) ..... 160.00  70.00  20.00
COMP.BAG LAKERS SP (8) .. 250.00 110.00  31.00
COMP.BAG SUNS(8) .........  15.00   6.75   1.85
COMP.BAG HAWKS(8) ........  70.00  32.00   8.75
COMP.BAG NUGGETS(8) ......  15.00   6.75   1.85
COMP.BAG NETS (8) ........  15.00   6.75   1.85
COMP.BAG SONICS (8) ......  15.00   6.75   1.85
COMP.BAG KINGS (7) .......  15.00   6.75   1.85
COMP.BAG PACERS (7) ......  15.00   6.75   1.85
COMP.BAG CLIPPERS (7) ....  15.00   6.75   1.85
COMP.BAG CELT.GRN.(8) ....  70.00  32.00   8.75
COMP.BAG CELT.WHT.(8) .. 120.00  55.00  15.00
COMP.BAG BLAZERS (7) .... 120.00  55.00  15.00
COMP.BAG BULLETS (7) .....  15.00   6.75   1.85
COMP.BAG BULLS (7)....... 975.00 450.00 120.00
COMP.BAG BUCKS ...........  15.00   6.75   1.85
COMP.BAG WARRIORS (7) ...  15.00   6.75   1.85
COMP.BAG JAZZ (7)........ 100.00  45.00  12.50
COMP.BAG SPURS (7) .......  15.00   6.75   1.85
COMP.BAG CAVS (7) ........  15.00   6.75   1.85
COMP.BAG MAVS(7) .........  15.00   6.75   1.85
```

COMP.BAG KNICKS (7)	200.00	90.00	25.00
COMMON CARD (1-25/34-172)	2.00	.90	.25
COMMON SP (26-33)	4.00	1.80	.50

*OPENED TEAM SETS: .75X to 1.0...
*GREEN/WHITE CELTICS: EQUAL VALUE
*GREEN CELTICS: EQUAL VALUE OF WHITE

☐ 1	Maurice Cheeks	4.00	1.80	.50
☐ 2	Charles Barkley	90.00	40.00	11.00
☐ 3	Julius Erving	35.00	16.00	4.40
☐ 4	Clemon Johnson	2.00	.90	.25
☐ 5	Bobby Jones	3.00	1.35	.35
☐ 6	Moses Malone	10.00	4.50	1.25
☐ 7	Sedale Threatt	3.00	1.35	.35
☐ 8	Andrew Toney	2.00	.90	.25
☐ 9	Leon Wood	2.00	.90	.25
☐ 10	Isiah Thomas UER	25.00	11.00	3.10
	(No Pistons logo on card front)			
☐ 11	Kent Benson	2.00	.90	.25
☐ 12	Earl Cureton	2.00	.90	.25
☐ 13	Vinnie Johnson	3.00	1.35	.35
☐ 14	Bill Laimbeer	3.00	1.35	.35
☐ 15	John Long	2.00	.90	.25
☐ 16	Rick Mahorn	2.00	.90	.25
☐ 17	Kelly Tripucka	3.00	1.35	.35
☐ 18	Hakeem Olajuwon	140.00	65.00	17.50
☐ 19	Allen Leavell	2.00	.90	.25
☐ 20	Lewis Lloyd	2.00	.90	.25
☐ 21	John Lucas	3.00	1.35	.35
☐ 22	Rodney McCray	2.00	.90	.25
☐ 23	Robert Reid	2.00	.90	.25
☐ 24	Ralph Sampson	3.00	1.35	.35
☐ 25	Mitchell Wiggins	2.00	.90	.25
☐ 26	K.Abdul-Jabbar SP	50.00	22.00	6.25
☐ 27	Michael Cooper SP	8.00	3.60	1.00
☐ 28	Magic Johnson SP	125.00	55.00	15.50
☐ 29	Mitch Kupchak SP	5.00	2.20	.60
☐ 30	Maurice Lucas SP	6.00	2.70	.75
☐ 31	Kurt Rambis SP	6.00	2.70	.75
☐ 32	Byron Scott SP	8.00	3.60	1.00
☐ 33	James Worthy SP	18.00	8.00	2.20
☐ 34	Larry Nance	8.00	3.60	1.00
☐ 35	Alvan Adams	3.00	1.35	.35
☐ 36	Walter Davis	3.00	1.35	.35
☐ 37	James Edwards	3.00	1.35	.35
☐ 38	Jay Humphries	2.00	.90	.25
☐ 39	Charles Pittman	2.00	.90	.25
☐ 40	Rick Robey	2.00	.90	.25
☐ 41	Mike Sanders	2.00	.90	.25
☐ 42	Dominique Wilkins	30.00	13.50	3.70
☐ 43	Scott Hastings	2.00	.90	.25
☐ 44	Eddie Johnson	2.00	.90	.25
☐ 45	Cliff Levingston	2.00	.90	.25
☐ 46	Tree Rollins	3.00	1.35	.35
☐ 47	Doc Rivers UER	3.00	1.35	.35
	(Ray Williams is pictured on the front)			
☐ 48	Kevin Willis	18.00	8.00	2.20
☐ 49	Randy Wittman	2.00	.90	.25
☐ 50	Alex English	4.00	1.80	.50
☐ 51	Wayne Cooper	2.00	.90	.25
☐ 52	T.R. Dunn	2.00	.90	.25
☐ 53	Mike Evans	2.00	.90	.25
☐ 54	Lafayette Lever	3.00	1.35	.35
☐ 55	Calvin Natt	2.00	.90	.25
☐ 56	Danny Schayes	3.00	1.35	.35
☐ 57	Elston Turner	2.00	.90	.25
☐ 58	Buck Williams	4.00	1.80	.50
☐ 59	Otis Birdsong	3.00	1.35	.35
☐ 60	Darwin Cook	2.00	.90	.25
☐ 61	Darryl Dawkins	3.00	1.35	.35
☐ 62	Mike Gminski	3.00	1.35	.35
☐ 63	Mickey Johnson	2.00	.90	.25
☐ 64	Mike O'Koren	3.00	1.35	.35
☐ 65	Micheal R. Richardson	2.00	.90	.25
☐ 66	Tom Chambers	4.00	1.80	.50
☐ 67	Gerald Henderson	2.00	.90	.25
☐ 68	Tim McCormick	2.00	.90	.25
☐ 69	Jack Sikma	3.00	1.35	.35
☐ 70	Ricky Sobers	2.00	.90	.25
☐ 71	Danny Vranes	2.00	.90	.25
☐ 72	Al Wood	2.00	.90	.25
☐ 73	Danny Young	2.00	.90	.25
☐ 74	Reggie Theus	3.00	1.35	.35
☐ 75	Larry Drew	3.00	1.35	.35
☐ 76	Eddie Johnson	3.00	1.35	.35
☐ 77	Mark Olberding	2.00	.90	.25
☐ 78	LaSalle Thompson	2.00	.90	.25
☐ 79	Otis Thorpe	6.00	2.70	.75
☐ 80	Mike Woodson	2.00	.90	.25
☐ 81	Clark Kellogg	3.00	1.35	.35
☐ 82	Quinn Buckner	3.00	1.35	.35
☐ 83	Vern Fleming	3.00	1.35	.35
☐ 84	Bill Garnett	2.00	.90	.25
☐ 85	Terence Stansbury	2.00	.90	.25
☐ 86	Steve Stipanovich	2.00	.90	.25
☐ 87	Herb Williams	3.00	1.35	.35
☐ 88	Marques Johnson	3.00	1.35	.35
☐ 89	Michael Cage	2.00	.90	.25
☐ 90	Franklin Edwards	2.00	.90	.25
☐ 91	Cedric Maxwell	3.00	1.35	.35
☐ 92	Derek Smith	2.00	.90	.25
☐ 93	Rory White	2.00	.90	.25
☐ 94	Jamaal Wilkes	3.00	1.35	.35
☐ 95G	Larry Bird Green	25.00	11.00	3.10
☐ 95W	Larry Bird White	100.00	45.00	12.50
☐ 96	Danny Ainge	10.00	4.50	1.25
☐ 97	Dennis Johnson	3.00	1.35	.35
☐ 98	Kevin McHale	14.00	6.25	1.75
☐ 99	Robert Parish	8.00	3.60	1.00
☐ 100	Jerry Sichting	2.00	.90	.25
☐ 101	Bill Walton	14.00	6.25	1.75
☐ 102	Scott Wedman	3.00	1.35	.35
☐ 103	Kiki Vandeweghe	3.00	1.35	.35
☐ 104	Sam Bowie	3.00	1.35	.35
☐ 105	Kenny Carr	2.00	.90	.25
☐ 106	Clyde Drexler	75.00	34.00	9.50
☐ 107	Jerome Kersey	3.00	1.35	.35
☐ 108	Jim Paxson	2.00	.90	.25
☐ 109	Mychal Thompson	3.00	1.35	.35
☐ 110	Gus Williams	3.00	1.35	.35
☐ 111	Darren Daye	2.00	.90	.25
☐ 112	Jeff Malone	3.00	1.35	.35
☐ 113	Tom McMillen	3.00	1.35	.35
☐ 114	Cliff Robinson	2.00	.90	.25
☐ 115	Dan Roundfield	3.00	1.35	.35
☐ 116	Jeff Ruland	3.00	1.35	.35
☐ 117	Michael Jordan	950.00	425.00	120.00
☐ 118	Gene Banks	2.00	.90	.25
☐ 119	Dave Corzine	2.00	.90	.25
☐ 120	Quintin Dailey	2.00	.90	.25
☐ 121	George Gervin	10.00	4.50	1.25
☐ 122	Jawann Oldham	2.00	.90	.25
☐ 123	Orlando Woolridge	3.00	1.35	.35
☐ 124	Terry Cummings	3.00	1.35	.35
☐ 125	Craig Hodges	2.00	.90	.25
☐ 126	Alton Lister	2.00	.90	.25
☐ 127	Paul Mokeski	2.00	.90	.25
☐ 128	Sidney Moncrief	3.00	1.35	.35
☐ 129	Ricky Pierce	3.00	1.35	.35
☐ 130	Paul Pressey	2.00	.90	.25

		NRMT-MT	EXC	G-VG
☐ 131	Purvis Short	2.00	.90	.25
☐ 132	Joe Barry Carroll	3.00	1.35	.35
☐ 133	Lester Conner	2.00	.90	.25
☐ 134	Sleepy Floyd	2.00	.90	.25
☐ 135	Geoff Huston	2.00	.90	.25
☐ 136	Larry Smith	2.00	.90	.25
☐ 137	Jerome Whitehead	2.00	.90	.25
☐ 138	Adrian Dantley	3.00	1.35	.35
☐ 139	Mitchell Anderson	2.00	.90	.25
☐ 140	Thurl Bailey	2.00	.90	.25
☐ 141	Mark Eaton	3.00	1.35	.35
☐ 142	Rickey Green	3.00	1.35	.35
☐ 143	Darrell Griffith	3.00	1.35	.35
☐ 144	John Stockton	90.00	40.00	11.00
☐ 145	Artis Gilmore	4.00	1.80	.50
☐ 146	Marc Iavaroni	2.00	.90	.25
☐ 147	Steve Johnson	2.00	.90	.25
☐ 148	Mike Mitchell	2.00	.90	.25
☐ 149	Johnny Moore	2.00	.90	.25
☐ 150	Alvin Robertson	3.00	1.35	.35
☐ 151	Jon Sundvold	2.00	.90	.25
☐ 152	World B. Free	3.00	1.35	.35
☐ 153	John Bagley	2.00	.90	.25
☐ 154	Johnny Davis	2.00	.90	.25
☐ 155	Roy Hinson	2.00	.90	.25
☐ 156	Phil Hubbard	2.00	.90	.25
☐ 157	Ben Poquette	2.00	.90	.25
☐ 158	Mel Turpin	2.00	.90	.25
☐ 159	Rolando Blackman	3.00	1.35	.35
☐ 160	Mark Aguirre	3.00	1.35	.35
☐ 161	Brad Davis	2.00	.90	.25
☐ 162	Dale Ellis	3.00	1.35	.35
☐ 163	Derek Harper	6.00	2.70	.75
☐ 164	Sam Perkins	4.00	1.80	.50
☐ 165	Jay Vincent	2.00	.90	.25
☐ 166	Patrick Ewing	160.00	70.00	20.00
☐ 167	Bill Cartwright	3.00	1.35	.35
☐ 168	Pat Cummings	2.00	.90	.25
☐ 169	Ernie Grunfeld	3.00	1.35	.35
☐ 170	Rory Sparrow	2.00	.90	.25
☐ 171	Trent Tucker	2.00	.90	.25
☐ 172	Darrell Walker	2.00	.90	.25

1985-86 Star All-Rookie Team

The 1985-86 Star NBA All-Rookie Team is an 11-card standard-size set that features 11 top rookies from the previous (1984-85) season. The set's basic design is identical to those of the Star Company's regular NBA sets. The front borders are red and the backs include each player's collegiate statistics. Alvin Robertson's card shows the Star '86 logo in the upper right corner. All others in the set show Star '85.

	NRMT-MT	EXC	G-VG
COMPLETE BAG SET (11) ...	475.00	210.00	60.00
COMMON CARD (1-11)	5.00	2.20	.60
*OPENED SET: .75X to 1.0X			

		NRMT-MT	EXC	G-VG
☐ 1	Hakeem Olajuwon	80.00	36.00	10.00
☐ 2	Michael Jordan	350.00	160.00	45.00
☐ 3	Charles Barkley	50.00	22.00	6.25
☐ 4	Sam Bowie	5.00	2.20	.60
☐ 5	Sam Perkins	5.00	2.20	.60
☐ 6	Vern Fleming	5.00	2.20	.60
☐ 7	Otis Thorpe	5.00	2.20	.60
☐ 8	John Stockton	50.00	22.00	6.25
☐ 9	Kevin Willis	5.00	2.20	.60
☐ 10	Tim McCormick	5.00	2.20	.60
☐ 11	Alvin Robertson	5.00	2.20	.60

1985-86 Star Lakers Champs

The 1985-86 Star Lakers NBA Champs set is an 18-card standard-size set commemorating the Los Angeles Lakers' 1985 NBA Championship. Each card depicts action from the Championship series. The front borders are off-white. The backs feature game and series summaries plus other related information. The set's basic design is identical to those of the Star Company's regular NBA sets. The cards show a Star '86 logo in the upper right corner.

	NRMT-MT	EXC	G-VG
COMPLETE BAG SET (18) ...	100.00	45.00	12.50
COMMON CARD (1-18)	2.00	.90	.25
*OPENED SET: .75X to 1.0X			

		NRMT-MT	EXC	G-VG
☐ 1	Kareem Abdul-Jabbar .. Jerry Buss	14.00	6.25	1.75
☐ 2	Larry Bird IA	30.00	13.50	3.70
☐ 3	Dennis Johnson IA	2.00	.90	.25
☐ 4	Danny Ainge IA	5.00	2.20	.60
☐ 5	Byron Scott IA	3.50	1.55	.45
☐ 6	Kevin McHale IA	7.00	3.10	.85
☐ 7	Magic Johnson IA	20.00	9.00	2.50
☐ 8	Kareem Abdul-Jabbar MVP Robert Parish	8.00	3.60	1.00

	NRMT-MT	EXC	G-VG
☐ 9 Larry Bird IA	30.00	13.50	3.70
☐ 10 Kareem Abdul-Jabbar IA	10.00	4.50	1.25
☐ 11 Danny Ainge IA	3.50	1.55	.45
Michael Cooper			
☐ 12 Pat Riley CO	6.00	2.70	.75
☐ 13 K.C. Jones CO	2.00	.90	.25
☐ 14 Magic Johnson IA	20.00	9.00	2.50
☐ 15 Boston Playoff Stats	3.50	1.55	.45
(action under basket)			
☐ 16 Road To The Title	2.00	.90	.25
☐ 17 Prior World Champs I	2.00	.90	.25
(riding on float)			
☐ 18 Ronald Reagan	35.00	16.00	4.40
Lakers Champs II			

		NRMT-MT	EXC	G-VG
☐ 8 Magic Johnson		35.00	16.00	4.40
☐ 9 Michael Jordan		200.00	90.00	25.00
☐ 10 Moses Malone		3.00	1.35	.35
☐ 11 Hakeem Olajuwon		40.00	18.00	5.00
☐ 12 John Stockton		25.00	11.00	3.10
☐ 13 Isiah Thomas		5.00	2.20	.60
☐ 14 Dominique Wilkins		4.00	1.80	.50
☐ 15 James Worthy		3.00	1.35	.35

1986 Star Best of the New/Old

It was reported that Star Company produced only 440 of these sets. They were distributed to dealers who purchased 1985-86 complete sets. Dealers received one set for every five regular sets purchased. The cards measure the standard size. The cards are unnumbered and checklisted below in alphabetical order. The Best of the New are numbered 1-4 and the Best of the Old are numbered 5-8. The numbering is alphabetical within each group. Counterfeiting has been a problem with Best of the New.

1986 Star Best of the Best

The Star Company reportedly produced only 1,400 sets and planned to release them in 1986. However, they were not issued until as late as 1990. This set and the Magic Johnson set were printed on the same uncut sheet. No factory-sealed bags exist for this set due to the fact that the sets were cut from the sheets years after the original printing. It is understood that the uncut sheets were sold to hobbyists who cut the sheets and packaged sets to be sold into the hobby. The cards measure the standard size. The fronts feature color action photos with white inner borders and a blue card face. The player's name, position, and team name appear at the bottom. The set title "Best of the Best" appears in a white circle at the lower left corner. The backs are white with blue borders and contain biography and statistics. The cards are numbered and arranged in alphabetical order.

	NRMT-MT	EXC	G-VG
COMPLETE SET (8)	750.00	350.00	95.00
COMPLETE NEW SET (4)	350.00	160.00	45.00
COMPLETE OLD SET (4)	400.00	180.00	50.00
COMMON NEW CARD (1-4)	6.00	2.70	.75
COMMON OLD CARD (5-8)	75.00	34.00	9.50
*BAGGED SETS: 1.0X to 1.5X			

	NRMT-MT	EXC	G-VG
☐ 1 Patrick Ewing	30.00	13.50	3.70
☐ 2 Michael Jordan	325.00	145.00	40.00
☐ 3 Hakeem Olajuwon	80.00	36.00	10.00
☐ 4 Ralph Sampson	6.00	2.70	.75
☐ 5 Kareem Abdul-Jabbar	140.00	65.00	17.50
☐ 6 Julius Erving	140.00	65.00	17.50
☐ 7 George Gervin	75.00	34.00	9.50
☐ 8 Bill Walton	75.00	34.00	9.50

	NRMT-MT	EXC	G-VG
COMPLETE SET (15)	275.00	125.00	34.00
COMMON CARD (1-15)	2.50	1.10	.30

	NRMT-MT	EXC	G-VG
☐ 1 Kareem Abdul-Jabbar	12.00	5.50	1.50
☐ 2 Charles Barkley	25.00	11.00	3.10
☐ 3 Larry Bird	60.00	27.00	7.50
☐ 4 Tom Chambers	2.50	1.10	.30
☐ 5 Terry Cummings	2.50	1.10	.30
☐ 6 Julius Erving	12.00	5.50	1.50
☐ 7 Patrick Ewing	18.00	8.00	2.20

1986 Star Court Kings

The 1986 Star Court Kings set contains 33 standard-size cards which feature many of the NBA's top players. The set's basic design is identical to those of the Star

Company's regular NBA sets. The front borders are yellow, and the backs have career narrative summaries of each player but no statistics. The cards show a Star '86 logo in the upper right corner. The cards are numbered in the upper left corner of the reverse. The numbering is alphabetical by last name.

		NRMT-MT	EXC	G-VG
COMPLETE BAG SET (33)		375.00	170.00	47.50
COMMON CARD (1-33)		2.00	.90	.25
*OPENED SET: .75X to 1.0X				

		NRMT-MT	EXC	G-VG
☐ 1	Mark Aguirre	3.50	1.55	.45
☐ 2	Kareem Abdul-Jabbar	15.00	6.75	1.85
☐ 3	Charles Barkley	30.00	13.50	3.70
☐ 4	Larry Bird	60.00	27.00	7.50
☐ 5	Rolando Blackman	3.50	1.55	.45
☐ 6	Tom Chambers	3.50	1.55	.45
☐ 7	Maurice Cheeks	3.50	1.55	.45
☐ 8	Terry Cummings	3.50	1.55	.45
☐ 9	Adrian Dantley	3.50	1.55	.45
☐ 10	Darryl Dawkins	3.50	1.55	.45
☐ 11	Mark Eaton	2.00	.90	.25
☐ 12	Alex English	3.50	1.55	.45
☐ 13	Julius Erving	15.00	6.75	1.85
☐ 14	Patrick Ewing	18.00	8.00	2.20
☐ 15	George Gervin	6.00	2.70	.75
☐ 16	Darrell Griffith	2.00	.90	.25
☐ 17	Magic Johnson	35.00	16.00	4.40
☐ 18	Michael Jordan	250.00	110.00	31.00
☐ 19	Clark Kellogg	3.50	1.55	.45
☐ 20	Bernard King	3.50	1.55	.45
☐ 21	Moses Malone	5.00	2.20	.60
☐ 22	Kevin McHale	7.00	3.10	.85
☐ 23	Sidney Moncrief	3.50	1.55	.45
☐ 24	Larry Nance	5.00	2.20	.60
☐ 25	Hakeem Olajuwon	50.00	22.00	6.25
☐ 26	Robert Parish	5.00	2.20	.60
☐ 27	Ralph Sampson	3.50	1.55	.45
☐ 28	Isiah Thomas	8.00	3.60	1.00
☐ 29	Andrew Toney	2.00	.90	.25
☐ 30	Kelly Tripucka	2.00	.90	.25
☐ 31	Kiki Vandeweghe	2.00	.90	.25
☐ 32	Dominique Wilkins	8.00	3.60	1.00
☐ 33	James Worthy	5.00	2.20	.60

1986 Star
Magic Johnson

This 10-card set highlights the career of Magic Johnson. The Star Company reportedly produced only 1,400 sets of these cards and planned to release them in 1986. However, they were not issued until perhaps as late as 1990. This set and the Best of the Best set were printed on the same uncut sheet. Star directly sold sheets to hobbyists who cut them and sold sets to the hobby. The cards measure the standard size. The cards are unnumbered and checklisted below in alphabetical order.

		NRMT-MT	EXC	G-VG
COMPLETE SET (10)		55.00	25.00	7.00
COMMON M.JOHNSON (1-10)		7.00	3.10	.85

		NRMT-MT	EXC	G-VG
☐ 1	Checklist	7.00	3.10	.85
☐ 2	Collegiate Stats	7.00	3.10	.85
☐ 3	Regular Season Stats	7.00	3.10	.85
☐ 4	Playoff Stats	7.00	3.10	.85
☐ 5	All-Star Stats	7.00	3.10	.85
☐ 6	Career Info 1	7.00	3.10	.85
☐ 7	Career Info 2	7.00	3.10	.85
☐ 8	Top Performance	7.00	3.10	.85
☐ 9	1980 Playoff MVP	7.00	3.10	.85
☐ 10	1982 Playoff MVP	7.00	3.10	.85

1986 Star
Michael Jordan

The 1986 Star Michael Jordan set contains ten cards highlighting his career. There were reportedly only 2,800 sets produced. They were originally available to the hobby exclusively through Dan Stickney of Michigan. Sets were originally issued in sealed plastic bags. The card backs contain various bits of information about Jordan. The set's basic design is identical to those of the Star Company's regular NBA sets. The front borders are red. The cards show a Star '86 logo in the upper right corner. The cards measure approximately 2 1/2" by 3 1/2". The cards are numbered in the upper left corner of the reverse. Collectors should beware of counterfeits.

	NRMT-MT	EXC	G-VG
COMPLETE BAG SET (10)	850.00	375.00	105.00
COMMON M.JORDAN (1-10)	90.00	40.00	11.00
*OPENED SET: .75X to 1.0X			

		NRMT-MT	EXC	G-VG
☐ 1	Michael Jordan	90.00	40.00	11.00
☐ 2	Collegiate Stats	90.00	40.00	11.00
☐ 3	1984 Olympian	90.00	40.00	11.00
☐ 4	Pro Stats	90.00	40.00	11.00
☐ 5	1985 All-Star	90.00	40.00	11.00
☐ 6	1985 Rookie of Year	90.00	40.00	11.00
☐ 7	Career Highlights	90.00	40.00	11.00
☐ 8	The 1986 Playoffs	90.00	40.00	11.00
☐ 9	Personal Data	90.00	40.00	11.00
☐ 10	The Future	90.00	40.00	11.00

1957-58 Topps

The 1957-58 Topps basketball set of 80 cards was Topps' first basketball issue. Topps did not produce another basketball set until it released a test issue in 1968. A major set followed in 1969. Cards were issued in 5-cent packs (six cards per pack, 24 per box) and measure the standard 2 1/2" by 3 1/2". A number of cards in the set were double printed (indicated by DP in checklist below). The set contains 49 double prints, 30 single prints and one quadruple print (No. 24 Bob Pettit). Card backs give statistical information from the 1956-57 NBA season. Bill Russell's Rookie Card is part of the set. Other Rookie Cards include Paul Arizin, Nat "Sweetwater" Clifton, Bob Cousy, Cliff Hagan, Tom Heinsohn, Rod Hundley, Red Kerr, Clyde Lovellette, Pettit, Dolph Schayes, Bill Sharman and Jack Twyman. The set contains the only card of Maurice Stokes. Topps also produced a three-card advertising panel featuring the fronts of Walt Davis, Joe Graboski and Cousy with an advertisement for the upcoming Topps basketball set on the combined reverse.

		EX-MT	VG-E	GOOD
COMPLETE SET (80)		5500.00	2500.00	700.00
COMMON CARD (1-80)		40.00	18.00	5.00
DP (9/11/14/20)		25.00	11.00	3.10
DP (31/38/46/47/52)		25.00	11.00	3.10
DP (55/57/64/65/68/79)		25.00	11.00	3.10
DP (6/7/8/18/21/25/34/66)		35.00	16.00	4.40
☐ 1	Nat Clifton DP	250.00	75.00	25.00
☐ 2	George Yardley DP	60.00	27.00	7.50
☐ 3	Neil Johnston DP	55.00	25.00	7.00
☐ 4	Carl Braun DP	50.00	22.00	6.25
☐ 5	Bill Sharman DP	175.00	80.00	22.00
☐ 6	George King DP	35.00	16.00	4.40
☐ 7	Kenny Sears DP	35.00	16.00	4.40
☐ 8	Dick Ricketts DP	35.00	16.00	4.40
☐ 9	Jack Nichols DP	25.00	11.00	3.10
☐ 10	Paul Arizin DP	110.00	50.00	14.00
☐ 11	Chuck Noble DP	25.00	11.00	3.10
☐ 12	Slater Martin DP	60.00	27.00	7.50
☐ 13	Dolph Schayes DP	135.00	60.00	17.00
☐ 14	Dick Atha DP	25.00	11.00	3.10
☐ 15	Frank Ramsey DP	75.00	34.00	9.50
☐ 16	Dick McGuire DP	50.00	22.00	6.25
☐ 17	Bob Cousy DP	500.00	220.00	60.00
☐ 18	Larry Foust DP	35.00	16.00	4.40
☐ 19	Tom Heinsohn	325.00	145.00	40.00
☐ 20	Bill Thieben DP	25.00	11.00	3.10
☐ 21	Don Meineke DP	35.00	16.00	4.40
☐ 22	Tom Marshall	40.00	18.00	5.00
☐ 23	Dick Garmaker	40.00	18.00	5.00
☐ 24	Bob Pettit QP	180.00	80.00	22.00
☐ 25	Jim Krebs DP	35.00	16.00	4.40
☐ 26	Gene Shue DP	55.00	25.00	7.00
☐ 27	Ed Macauley DP	55.00	25.00	7.00
☐ 28	Vern Mikkelsen	75.00	34.00	9.50
☐ 29	Willie Naulls	55.00	25.00	7.00
☐ 30	Walter Dukes DP	40.00	18.00	5.00
☐ 31	Dave Piontek DP	25.00	11.00	3.10
☐ 32	John Kerr	120.00	55.00	15.00
☐ 33	Larry Costello DP	50.00	22.00	6.25
☐ 34	Woody Sauldsberry DP	35.00	16.00	4.40
☐ 35	Ray Felix	40.00	18.00	5.00
☐ 36	Ernie Beck	40.00	18.00	5.00
☐ 37	Cliff Hagan	135.00	60.00	17.00
☐ 38	Guy Sparrow DP	25.00	11.00	3.10
☐ 39	Jim Loscutoff	45.00	20.00	5.50
☐ 40	Arnie Risen DP	45.00	20.00	5.50
☐ 41	Joe Graboski	40.00	18.00	5.00
☐ 42	Maurice Stokes DP UER	120.00	55.00	15.00
	(Text refers to			
	N.F.L. Record)			
☐ 43	Rod Hundley	135.00	60.00	17.00
☐ 44	Tom Gola DP	75.00	34.00	9.50
☐ 45	Med Park	40.00	18.00	5.00
☐ 46	Mel Hutchins DP	25.00	11.00	3.10
☐ 47	Larry Friend DP	25.00	11.00	3.10
☐ 48	Lennie Rosenbluth DP	55.00	25.00	7.00
☐ 49	Walt Davis	40.00	18.00	5.00
☐ 50	Richie Regan	40.00	18.00	5.00
☐ 51	Frank Selvy DP	50.00	22.00	6.25
☐ 52	Art Spoelstra DP	25.00	11.00	3.10
☐ 53	Bob Hopkins	40.00	18.00	5.00
☐ 54	Earl Lloyd	40.00	18.00	5.00
☐ 55	Phil Jordan DP	25.00	11.00	3.10
☐ 56	Bob Houbregs DP	40.00	18.00	5.00
☐ 57	Lou Tsioropoulos DP	25.00	11.00	3.10
☐ 58	Ed Conlin	40.00	18.00	5.00
☐ 59	Al Bianchi	75.00	34.00	9.50
☐ 60	George Dempsey	40.00	18.00	5.00
☐ 61	Chuck Share	40.00	18.00	5.00

☐ 62	Harry Gallatin DP	45.00	20.00	5.50
☐ 63	Bob Harrison	40.00	18.00	5.00
☐ 64	Bob Burrow DP	25.00	11.00	3.10
☐ 65	Win Wilfong DP	25.00	11.00	3.10
☐ 66	Jack McMahon DP	35.00	16.00	4.40
☐ 67	Jack George	40.00	18.00	5.00
☐ 68	Charlie Tyra DP	25.00	11.00	3.10
☐ 69	Ron Sobie	40.00	18.00	5.00
☐ 70	Jack Coleman	40.00	18.00	5.00
☐ 71	Jack Twyman DP	110.00	50.00	14.00
☐ 72	Paul Seymour	40.00	18.00	5.00
☐ 73	Jim Paxson DP	55.00	25.00	7.00
☐ 74	Bob Leonard	40.00	18.00	5.00
☐ 75	Andy Phillip	45.00	20.00	5.50
☐ 76	Joe Holup	40.00	18.00	5.00
☐ 77	Bill Russell	1800.00	800.00	220.00
☐ 78	Clyde Lovellette DP	120.00	55.00	15.00
☐ 79	Ed Fleming DP	25.00	11.00	3.10
☐ 80	Dick Schnittker	110.00	33.00	11.00

1969-70 Topps

The 1969-70 Topps set of 99 cards was Topps' first major basketball issue since 1957. Cards were issued in 10-cent packs (10 cards per pack, 24 packs per box) and measure 2 1/2" by 4 11/16". The set features the first card of Lew Alcindor (later Kareem Abdul-Jabbar). Other notable Rookie Cards in the set are Dave Bing, Bill Bradley, Billy Cunningham, Dave DeBusschere, Walt Frazier, John Havlicek, Connie Hawkins, Elvin Hayes, Jerry Lucas, Earl Monroe, Don Nelson, Willis Reed, Nate Thurmond and Wes Unseld. The set was printed on a sheet of 99 cards (nine rows of eleven across) with the checklist card occupying the lower right corner of the sheet. As a result, the checklist is prone to wear and very difficult to obtain in Near Mint or better condition.

	NRMT-MT	EXC	G-VG
COMPLETE SET (99)	1600.00	700.00	200.00
COMMON CARD (1-99)	4.00	1.80	.50

☐ 1	Wilt Chamberlain	180.00	55.00	18.00
☐ 2	Gail Goodrich	40.00	18.00	5.00
☐ 3	Cazzie Russell	15.00	6.75	1.85
☐ 4	Darrall Imhoff	5.00	2.20	.60
☐ 5	Bailey Howell	5.00	2.20	.60
☐ 6	Lucius Allen	7.00	3.10	.85
☐ 7	Tom Boerwinkle	6.00	2.70	.75
☐ 8	Jimmy Walker	8.00	3.60	1.00
☐ 9	John Block	5.00	2.20	.60
☐ 10	Nate Thurmond	30.00	13.50	3.70
☐ 11	Gary Gregor	4.00	1.80	.50
☐ 12	Gus Johnson	15.00	6.75	1.85
☐ 13	Luther Rackley	4.00	1.80	.50
☐ 14	Jon McGlocklin	6.00	2.70	.75
☐ 15	Connie Hawkins	45.00	20.00	5.50
☐ 16	Johnny Egan	4.00	1.80	.50
☐ 17	Jim Washington	4.00	1.80	.50
☐ 18	Dick Barnett	8.00	3.60	1.00
☐ 19	Tom Meschery	4.00	1.80	.50
☐ 20	John Havlicek	150.00	70.00	19.00
☐ 21	Eddie Miles	4.00	1.80	.50
☐ 22	Walt Wesley	4.00	1.80	.50
☐ 23	Rick Adelman	8.00	3.60	1.00
☐ 24	Al Attles	5.00	2.20	.60
☐ 25	Lew Alcindor	650.00	300.00	80.00
☐ 26	Jack Marin	8.00	3.60	1.00
☐ 27	Walt Hazzard	12.00	5.50	1.50
☐ 28	Connie Dierking	4.00	1.80	.50
☐ 29	Keith Erickson	10.00	4.50	1.25
☐ 30	Bob Rule	8.00	3.60	1.00
☐ 31	Dick Van Arsdale	10.00	4.50	1.25
☐ 32	Archie Clark	12.00	5.50	1.50
☐ 33	Terry Dischinger	4.00	1.80	.50
☐ 34	Henry Finkel	4.00	1.80	.50
☐ 35	Elgin Baylor	45.00	20.00	5.50
☐ 36	Ron Williams	4.00	1.80	.50
☐ 37	Loy Petersen	4.00	1.80	.50
☐ 38	Guy Rodgers	5.00	2.20	.60
☐ 39	Toby Kimball	4.00	1.80	.50
☐ 40	Billy Cunningham	50.00	22.00	6.25
☐ 41	Joe Caldwell	6.00	2.70	.75
☐ 42	Leroy Ellis	6.00	2.70	.75
☐ 43	Bill Bradley	130.00	57.50	16.00
☐ 44	Len Wilkens UER	40.00	18.00	5.00
	(Misspelled Wilkins on card back)			
☐ 45	Jerry Lucas	30.00	13.50	3.70
☐ 46	Neal Walk	6.00	2.70	.75
☐ 47	Emmette Bryant	5.00	2.20	.60
☐ 48	Bob Kauffman	4.00	1.80	.50
☐ 49	Mel Counts	5.00	2.20	.60
☐ 50	Oscar Robertson	60.00	27.00	7.50
☐ 51	Jim Barnett	5.00	2.20	.60
☐ 52	Don Smith	4.00	1.80	.50
☐ 53	Jim Davis	4.00	1.80	.50
☐ 54	Wally Jones	6.00	2.70	.75
☐ 55	Dave Bing	40.00	18.00	5.00
☐ 56	Wes Unseld	40.00	18.00	5.00
☐ 57	Joe Ellis	4.00	1.80	.50
☐ 58	John Tresvant	4.00	1.80	.50
☐ 59	Larry Siegfried	6.00	2.70	.75
☐ 60	Willis Reed	40.00	18.00	5.00
☐ 61	Paul Silas	15.00	6.75	1.85
☐ 62	Bob Weiss	8.00	3.60	1.00
☐ 63	Willie McCarter	4.00	1.80	.50
☐ 64	Don Kojis	4.00	1.80	.50
☐ 65	Lou Hudson	20.00	9.00	2.50
☐ 66	Jim King	4.00	1.80	.50
☐ 67	Luke Jackson	5.00	2.20	.60
☐ 68	Len Chappell	4.00	1.80	.50
☐ 69	Ray Scott	4.00	1.80	.50
☐ 70	Jeff Mullins	8.00	3.60	1.00
☐ 71	Howie Komives	4.00	1.80	.50
☐ 72	Tom Sanders	8.00	3.60	1.00
☐ 73	Dick Snyder	4.00	1.80	.50
☐ 74	Dave Stallworth	5.00	2.20	.60
☐ 75	Elvin Hayes	60.00	27.00	7.50
☐ 76	Art Harris	4.00	1.80	.50
☐ 77	Don Ohl	4.00	1.80	.50

		NRMT-MT	EXC	G-VG
☐ 78	Bob Love	30.00	13.50	3.70
☐ 79	Tom Van Arsdale	10.00	4.50	1.25
☐ 80	Earl Monroe	40.00	18.00	5.00
☐ 81	Greg Smith	4.00	1.80	.50
☐ 82	Don Nelson	35.00	16.00	4.40
☐ 83	Happy Hairston	8.00	3.60	1.00
☐ 84	Hal Greer	10.00	4.50	1.25
☐ 85	Dave DeBusschere	40.00	18.00	5.00
☐ 86	Bill Bridges	8.00	3.60	1.00
☐ 87	Herm Gilliam	5.00	2.20	.60
☐ 88	Jim Fox	4.00	1.80	.50
☐ 89	Bob Boozer	5.00	2.20	.60
☐ 90	Jerry West	90.00	40.00	11.00
☐ 91	Chet Walker	15.00	6.75	1.85
☐ 92	Flynn Robinson	5.00	2.20	.60
☐ 93	Clyde Lee	5.00	2.20	.60
☐ 94	Kevin Loughery	10.00	4.50	1.25
☐ 95	Walt Bellamy	10.00	4.50	1.25
☐ 96	Art Williams	4.00	1.80	.50
☐ 97	Adrian Smith	6.00	2.70	.75
☐ 98	Walt Frazier	60.00	27.00	7.50
☐ 99	Checklist 1-99	275.00	80.00	28.00

1970-71 Topps

The 1970-71 Topps basketball card set of 175 color cards continued the larger-size (2 1/2" by 4 11/16") format established the previous year. Cards were issued in 10-cent wax packs with 10 cards per pack and 24 packs per box. Cards numbered 106 to 115 contain the previous season's NBA first and second team All-Star selections. The first six cards in the set (1-6) feature the statistical league leaders from the previous season. The last eight cards in the set (168-175) summarize the results of the previous season's NBA championship playoff series won by the Knicks over the Lakers. The key Rookie Cards in this set are Pete Maravich, Calvin Murphy and Pat Riley. There are 22 short-printed cards in the first series which are marked SP in the checklist below.

	NRMT-MT	EXC	G-VG
COMPLETE SET (175)	1100.00	500.00	140.00
COMMON CARD (1-110)	2.50	1.10	.30
COMMON CARD (111-175)	3.00	1.35	.35

		NRMT-MT	EXC	G-VG
☐ 1	NBA Scoring Leaders	40.00	12.00	4.00
	Lew Alcindor			
	Jerry West			
	Elvin Hayes			
☐ 2	NBA Scoring SP	40.00	18.00	5.00
	Average Leaders			
	Jerry West			
	Lew Alcindor			
	Elvin Hayes			
☐ 3	NBA FG Pct Leaders	5.00	2.20	.60
	Johnny Green			
	Darrall Imhoff			
	Lou Hudson			
☐ 4	NBA FT Pct Leaders SP	10.00	4.50	1.25
	Flynn Robinson			
	Chet Walker			
	Jeff Mullins			
☐ 5	NBA Rebound Leaders	25.00	11.00	3.10
	Elvin Hayes			
	Wes Unseld			
	Lew Alcindor			
☐ 6	NBA Assist Leaders SP	10.00	4.50	1.25
	Len Wilkens			
	Walt Frazier			
	Clem Haskins			
☐ 7	Bill Bradley	40.00	18.00	5.00
☐ 8	Ron Williams	2.50	1.10	.30
☐ 9	Otto Moore	2.50	1.10	.30
☐ 10	John Havlicek SP	80.00	36.00	10.00
☐ 11	George Wilson	2.50	1.10	.30
☐ 12	John Trapp	2.50	1.10	.30
☐ 13	Pat Riley	55.00	25.00	7.00
☐ 14	Jim Washington	2.50	1.10	.30
☐ 15	Bob Rule	4.00	1.80	.50
☐ 16	Bob Weiss	4.00	1.80	.50
☐ 17	Neil Johnson	2.50	1.10	.30
☐ 18	Walt Bellamy	7.00	3.10	.85
☐ 19	McCoy McLemore	2.50	1.10	.30
☐ 20	Earl Monroe	12.00	5.50	1.50
☐ 21	Wally Anderzunas	2.50	1.10	.30
☐ 22	Guy Rodgers	4.00	1.80	.50
☐ 23	Rick Roberson	2.50	1.10	.30
☐ 24	Checklist 1-110	50.00	15.00	5.00
☐ 25	Jimmy Walker	4.00	1.80	.50
☐ 26	Mike Riordan	5.00	2.20	.60
☐ 27	Henry Finkel	2.50	1.10	.30
☐ 28	Joe Ellis	2.50	1.10	.30
☐ 29	Mike Davis	2.50	1.10	.30
☐ 30	Lou Hudson	6.00	2.70	.75
☐ 31	Lucius Allen SP	7.00	3.10	.85
☐ 32	Toby Kimball SP	5.00	2.20	.60
☐ 33	Luke Jackson SP	5.00	2.20	.60
☐ 34	Johnny Egan	2.50	1.10	.30
☐ 35	Leroy Ellis SP	5.00	2.20	.60
☐ 36	Jack Marin SP	7.00	3.10	.85
☐ 37	Joe Caldwell SP	7.00	3.10	.85
☐ 38	Keith Erickson	4.00	1.80	.50
☐ 39	Don Smith	2.50	1.10	.30
☐ 40	Flynn Robinson	4.00	1.80	.50
☐ 41	Bob Boozer	2.50	1.10	.30
☐ 42	Howie Komives	2.50	1.10	.30
☐ 43	Dick Barnett	4.00	1.80	.50
☐ 44	Stu Lantz	2.50	1.10	.30
☐ 45	Dick Van Arsdale	6.00	2.70	.75
☐ 46	Jerry Lucas	8.00	3.60	1.00
☐ 47	Don Chaney	8.00	3.60	1.00
☐ 48	Ray Scott	2.50	1.10	.30
☐ 49	Dick Cunningham SP	5.00	2.20	.60
☐ 50	Wilt Chamberlain	80.00	36.00	10.00
☐ 51	Kevin Loughery	4.00	1.80	.50
☐ 52	Stan McKenzie	2.50	1.10	.30
☐ 53	Fred Foster	2.50	1.10	.30
☐ 54	Jim Davis	2.50	1.10	.30
☐ 55	Walt Wesley	2.50	1.10	.30
☐ 56	Bill Hewitt	2.50	1.10	.30

☐ 57 Darrall Imhoff	2.50	1.10	.30
☐ 58 John Block	2.50	1.10	.30
☐ 59 Al Attles SP	8.00	3.60	1.00
☐ 60 Chet Walker	6.00	2.70	.75
☐ 61 Luther Rackley	2.50	1.10	.30
☐ 62 Jerry Chambers SP	6.00	2.70	.75
☐ 63 Bob Dandridge	8.00	3.60	1.00
☐ 64 Dick Snyder	2.50	1.10	.30
☐ 65 Elgin Baylor	25.00	11.00	3.10
☐ 66 Connie Dierking	2.50	1.10	.30
☐ 67 Steve Kuberski	2.50	1.10	.30
☐ 68 Tom Boerwinkle	2.50	1.10	.30
☐ 69 Paul Silas	6.00	2.70	.75
☐ 70 Elvin Hayes	25.00	11.00	3.10
☐ 71 Bill Bridges	4.00	1.80	.50
☐ 72 Wes Unseld	12.00	5.50	1.50
☐ 73 Herm Gilliam	2.50	1.10	.30
☐ 74 Bobby Smith SP	8.00	3.60	1.00
☐ 75 Lew Alcindor	110.00	50.00	14.00
☐ 76 Jeff Mullins	4.00	1.80	.50
☐ 77 Happy Hairston	4.00	1.80	.50
☐ 78 Dave Stallworth SP	5.00	2.20	.60
☐ 79 Fred Hetzel	2.50	1.10	.30
☐ 80 Len Wilkens SP	25.00	11.00	3.10
☐ 81 Johnny Green	5.00	2.20	.60
☐ 82 Erwin Mueller	2.50	1.10	.30
☐ 83 Wally Jones	4.00	1.80	.50
☐ 84 Bob Love	8.00	3.60	1.00
☐ 85 Dick Garrett	2.50	1.10	.30
☐ 86 Don Nelson SP	25.00	11.00	3.10
☐ 87 Neal Walk SP	5.00	2.20	.60
☐ 88 Larry Siegfried	2.50	1.10	.30
☐ 89 Gary Gregor	2.50	1.10	.30
☐ 90 Nate Thurmond	8.00	3.60	1.00
☐ 91 John Warren	2.50	1.10	.30
☐ 92 Gus Johnson	6.00	2.70	.75
☐ 93 Gail Goodrich	12.00	5.50	1.50
☐ 94 Dorie Murrey	2.50	1.10	.30
☐ 95 Cazzie Russell SP	10.00	4.50	1.25
☐ 96 Terry Dischinger	4.00	1.80	.50
☐ 97 Norm Van Lier SP	15.00	6.75	1.85
☐ 98 Jim Fox	2.50	1.10	.30
☐ 99 Tom Meschery	2.50	1.10	.30
☐ 100 Oscar Robertson	35.00	16.00	4.40
☐ 101A Checklist 111-175..	30.00	9.00	3.00
(1970-71 in black)			
☐ 101B Checklist 111-175..	30.00	9.00	3.00
(1970-71 in white)			
☐ 102 Rich Johnson	2.50	1.10	.30
☐ 103 Mel Counts	4.00	1.80	.50
☐ 104 Bill Hosket SP	6.00	2.70	.75
☐ 105 Archie Clark	4.00	1.80	.50
☐ 106 Walt Frazier AS	10.00	4.50	1.25
☐ 107 Jerry West AS	30.00	13.50	3.70
☐ 108 Bill Cunningham AS	12.00	5.50	1.50
☐ 109 Connie Hawkins AS..	8.00	3.60	1.00
☐ 110 Willis Reed AS	8.00	3.60	1.00
☐ 111 Nate Thurmond AS	5.00	2.20	.60
☐ 112 John Havlicek AS	25.00	11.00	3.10
☐ 113 Elgin Baylor AS	18.00	8.00	2.20
☐ 114 Oscar Robertson AS	20.00	9.00	2.50
☐ 115 Lou Hudson AS	4.00	1.80	.50
☐ 116 Emmette Bryant	3.00	1.35	.35
☐ 117 Greg Howard	3.00	1.35	.35
☐ 118 Rick Adelman	4.50	2.00	.55
☐ 119 Barry Clemens	3.00	1.35	.35
☐ 120 Walt Frazier	25.00	11.00	3.10
☐ 121 Jim Barnes	3.00	1.35	.35
☐ 122 Bernie Williams	3.00	1.35	.35
☐ 123 Pete Maravich	250.00	110.00	31.00
☐ 124 Matt Guokas	8.00	3.60	1.00

☐ 125 Dave Bing	12.00	5.50	1.50
☐ 126 John Tresvant	3.00	1.35	.35
☐ 127 Shaler Halimon	3.00	1.35	.35
☐ 128 Don Ohl	3.00	1.35	.35
☐ 129 Fred Carter	5.00	2.20	.60
☐ 130 Connie Hawkins	15.00	6.75	1.85
☐ 131 Jim King	3.00	1.35	.35
☐ 132 Ed Manning	5.00	2.20	.60
☐ 133 Adrian Smith	3.00	1.35	.35
☐ 134 Walt Hazzard	5.00	2.20	.60
☐ 135 Dave DeBusschere	12.00	5.50	1.50
☐ 136 Don Kojis	3.00	1.35	.35
☐ 137 Calvin Murphy	30.00	13.50	3.70
☐ 138 Nate Bowman	3.00	1.35	.35
☐ 139 Jon McGlocklin	4.50	2.00	.55
☐ 140 Billy Cunningham	15.00	6.75	1.85
☐ 141 Willie McCarter	3.00	1.35	.35
☐ 142 Jim Barnett	3.00	1.35	.35
☐ 143 JoJo White	18.00	8.00	2.20
☐ 144 Clyde Lee	3.00	1.35	.35
☐ 145 Tom Van Arsdale	6.00	2.70	.75
☐ 146 Len Chappell	3.00	1.35	.35
☐ 147 Lee Winfield	3.00	1.35	.35
☐ 148 Jerry Sloan	15.00	6.75	1.85
☐ 149 Art Harris	3.00	1.35	.35
☐ 150 Willis Reed	15.00	6.75	1.85
☐ 151 Art Williams	3.00	1.35	.35
☐ 152 Don May	3.00	1.35	.35
☐ 153 Loy Petersen	3.00	1.35	.35
☐ 154 Dave Gambee	3.00	1.35	.35
☐ 155 Hal Greer	6.00	2.70	.75
☐ 156 Dave Newmark	3.00	1.35	.35
☐ 157 Jimmy Collins	3.00	1.35	.35
☐ 158 Bill Turner	3.00	1.35	.35
☐ 159 Eddie Miles	3.00	1.35	.35
☐ 160 Jerry West	50.00	22.00	6.25
☐ 161 Bob Quick	3.00	1.35	.35
☐ 162 Fred Crawford	3.00	1.35	.35
☐ 163 Tom Sanders	5.00	2.20	.60
☐ 164 Dale Schlueter	3.00	1.35	.35
☐ 165 Clem Haskins	8.00	3.60	1.00
☐ 166 Greg Smith	3.00	1.35	.35
☐ 167 Rod Thorn	8.00	3.60	1.00
☐ 168 Willis Reed PO	8.00	3.60	1.00
☐ 169 Dick Garnett PO	5.00	2.20	.60
☐ 170 Dave DeBusschere PO	8.00	3.60	1.00
☐ 171 Jerry West PO	15.00	6.75	1.85
☐ 172 Bill Bradley PO	15.00	6.75	1.85
☐ 173 Wilt Chamberlain PO	18.00	8.00	2.20
☐ 174 Walt Frazier PO	10.00	4.50	1.25
☐ 175 Knicks Celebrate	20.00	6.00	2.00
(New York Knicks,			
World Champs)			

1971-72 Topps

The 1971-72 Topps basketball set of 233 witnessed a return to the standard-sized card, i.e., 2 1/2" by 3 1/2". Cards were issued in 10-card, 10 cent packs with 24 packs per box. National Basketball Association players are depicted on cards 1 to 144 and American Basketball Association players are depicted on cards 145 to 233. The set was produced on two sheets. The second production sheet contained the ABA players (145-233) as well as 31 double-printed cards (NBA players) from

LARRY BROWN
ROCKETS' GUARD

the first sheet. These DP's are indicated in the checklist below. Subsets include NBA Playoffs (133-137), NBA Statistical Leaders (138-143) and ABA Statistical Leaders (146-151). The key Rookie Cards in this set are Nate Archibald, Rick Barry, Larry Brown, Dave Cowens, Spencer Haywood, Dan Issel, Bob Lanier, Rudy Tomjanovich and Doug Moe.

	NRMT-MT	EXC	G-VG
COMPLETE SET (233)	750.00	350.00	95.00
COMMON NBA CARD (1-144)	1.50	.70	.19
COMMON ABA CARD (145-233)	2.00	.90	.25

☐ 1	Oscar Robertson	35.00	10.50	3.50
☐ 2	Bill Bradley	25.00	11.00	3.10
☐ 3	Jim Fox	1.50	.70	.19
☐ 4	John Johnson	2.00	.90	.25
☐ 5	Luke Jackson	2.00	.90	.25
☐ 6	Don May DP	1.50	.70	.19
☐ 7	Kevin Loughery	2.00	.90	.25
☐ 8	Terry Dischinger	1.50	.70	.19
☐ 9	Neal Walk	2.00	.90	.25
☐ 10	Elgin Baylor	25.00	11.00	3.10
☐ 11	Rick Adelman	2.00	.90	.25
☐ 12	Clyde Lee	1.50	.70	.19
☐ 13	Jerry Chambers	1.50	.70	.19
☐ 14	Fred Carter	2.00	.90	.25
☐ 15	Tom Boerwinkle DP	1.50	.70	.19
☐ 16	John Block	1.50	.70	.19
☐ 17	Dick Barnett	2.00	.90	.25
☐ 18	Henry Finkel	1.50	.70	.19
☐ 19	Norm Van Lier	4.00	1.80	.50
☐ 20	Spencer Haywood	12.00	5.50	1.50
☐ 21	George Johnson	1.50	.70	.19
☐ 22	Bobby Lewis	1.50	.70	.19
☐ 23	Bill Hewitt	1.50	.70	.19
☐ 24	Walt Hazzard DP	3.00	1.35	.35
☐ 25	Happy Hairston	2.00	.90	.25
☐ 26	George Wilson	1.50	.70	.19
☐ 27	Lucius Allen	2.00	.90	.25
☐ 28	Jim Washington	1.50	.70	.19
☐ 29	Nate Archibald	20.00	9.00	2.50
☐ 30	Willis Reed	10.00	4.50	1.25
☐ 31	Erwin Mueller	1.50	.70	.19
☐ 32	Art Harris	1.50	.70	.19
☐ 33	Pete Cross	1.50	.70	.19
☐ 34	Geoff Petrie	5.00	2.20	.60
☐ 35	John Havlicek	30.00	13.50	3.70
☐ 36	Larry Siegfried	1.50	.70	.19
☐ 37	John Tresvant	1.50	.70	.19
☐ 38	Ron Williams	1.50	.70	.19
☐ 39	Lamar Green DP	1.50	.70	.19
☐ 40	Bob Rule DP	1.50	.70	.19
☐ 41	Jim McMillian	2.00	.90	.25
☐ 42	Wally Jones	1.50	.70	.19
☐ 43	Bob Boozer	1.50	.70	.19
☐ 44	Eddie Miles	1.50	.70	.19
☐ 45	Bob Love DP	5.00	2.20	.60
☐ 46	Claude English	1.50	.70	.19
☐ 47	Dave Cowens	45.00	20.00	5.50
☐ 48	Emmette Bryant	1.50	.70	.19
☐ 49	Dave Stallworth	1.50	.70	.19
☐ 50	Jerry West	40.00	18.00	5.00
☐ 51	Joe Ellis	1.50	.70	.19
☐ 52	Walt Wesley DP	1.50	.70	.19
☐ 53	Howie Komives	1.50	.70	.19
☐ 54	Paul Silas	4.00	1.80	.50
☐ 55	Pete Maravich DP	45.00	20.00	5.50
☐ 56	Gary Gregor	1.50	.70	.19
☐ 57	Sam Lacey	3.00	1.35	.35
☐ 58	Calvin Murphy DP	6.00	2.70	.75
☐ 59	Bob Dandridge	2.00	.90	.25
☐ 60	Hal Greer	4.00	1.80	.50
☐ 61	Keith Erickson	2.00	.90	.25
☐ 62	Joe Cooke	1.50	.70	.19
☐ 63	Bob Lanier	40.00	18.00	5.00
☐ 64	Don Kojis	1.50	.70	.19
☐ 65	Walt Frazier	12.00	5.50	1.50
☐ 66	Chet Walker DP	3.00	1.35	.35
☐ 67	Dick Garrett	1.50	.70	.19
☐ 68	John Trapp	2.00	.90	.25
☐ 69	JoJo White	6.00	2.70	.75
☐ 70	Wilt Chamberlain	40.00	18.00	5.00
☐ 71	Dave Sorenson	1.50	.70	.19
☐ 72	Jim King	1.50	.70	.19
☐ 73	Cazzie Russell	4.00	1.80	.50
☐ 74	Jon McGlocklin	2.00	.90	.25
☐ 75	Tom Van Arsdale	2.00	.90	.25
☐ 76	Dale Schlueter	1.50	.70	.19
☐ 77	Gus Johnson DP	2.00	.90	.25
☐ 78	Dave Bing	8.00	3.60	1.00
☐ 79	Billy Cunningham	10.00	4.50	1.25
☐ 80	Len Wilkens	10.00	4.50	1.25
☐ 81	Jerry Lucas DP	5.00	2.20	.60
☐ 82	Don Chaney	2.00	.90	.25
☐ 83	McCoy McLemore	1.50	.70	.19
☐ 84	Bob Kauffman DP	1.50	.70	.19
☐ 85	Dick Van Arsdale	2.00	.90	.25
☐ 86	Johnny Green	1.50	.70	.19
☐ 87	Jerry Sloan	4.00	1.80	.50
☐ 88	Luther Rackley DP	1.50	.70	.19
☐ 89	Shaler Halimon	1.50	.70	.19
☐ 90	Jimmy Walker	2.00	.90	.25
☐ 91	Rudy Tomjanovich	25.00	11.00	3.10
☐ 92	Levi Fontaine	1.50	.70	.19
☐ 93	Bobby Smith	2.00	.90	.25
☐ 94	Bob Arnzen	1.50	.70	.19
☐ 95	Wes Unseld DP	6.00	2.70	.75
☐ 96	Clem Haskins DP	2.00	.90	.25
☐ 97	Jim Davis	1.50	.70	.19
☐ 98	Steve Kuberski	1.50	.70	.19
☐ 99	Mike Davis DP	1.50	.70	.19
☐ 100	Lew Alcindor	55.00	25.00	7.00
☐ 101	Willie McCarter	1.50	.70	.19
☐ 102	Charlie Paulk	1.50	.70	.19
☐ 103	Lee Winfield	1.50	.70	.19
☐ 104	Jim Barnett	1.50	.70	.19
☐ 105	Connie Hawkins DP	8.00	3.60	1.00
☐ 106	Archie Clark DP	2.00	.90	.25
☐ 107	Dave DeBusschere	8.00	3.60	1.00
☐ 108	Stu Lantz DP	2.00	.90	.25
☐ 109	Don Smith	1.50	.70	.19
☐ 110	Lou Hudson	3.00	1.35	.35
☐ 111	Leroy Ellis	2.00	.90	.25
☐ 112	Jack Marin	2.00	.90	.25
☐ 113	Matt Guokas	2.00	.90	.25

☐ 114	Don Nelson	6.00	2.70	.75
☐ 115	Jeff Mullins DP	2.00	.90	.25
☐ 116	Walt Bellamy	4.00	1.80	.50
☐ 117	Bob Quick	1.50	.70	.19
☐ 118	John Warren	1.50	.70	.19
☐ 119	Barry Clemens	1.50	.70	.19
☐ 120	Elvin Hayes DP	10.00	4.50	1.25
☐ 121	Gail Goodrich	8.00	3.60	1.00
☐ 122	Ed Manning	2.00	.90	.25
☐ 123	Herm Gilliam DP	1.50	.70	.19
☐ 124	Dennis Awtrey	2.00	.90	.25
☐ 125	John Hummer	1.50	.70	.19
☐ 126	Mike Riordan	2.00	.90	.25
☐ 127	Mel Counts	2.00	.90	.25
☐ 128	Bob Weiss DP	1.50	.70	.19
☐ 129	Greg Smith DP	1.50	.70	.19
☐ 130	Earl Monroe	8.00	3.60	1.00
☐ 131	Nate Thurmond DP	4.00	1.80	.50
☐ 132	Bill Bridges DP	2.00	.90	.25
☐ 133	Lew Alcindor PO	12.00	5.50	1.50
☐ 134	NBA Playoffs G2 Bucks make it Two Straight	3.00	1.35	.35
☐ 135	Bob Dandridge PO	3.00	1.35	.35
☐ 136	Oscar Robertson PO	8.00	3.60	1.00
☐ 137	NBA Champs Celebrate Bucks sweep Bullets	3.50	1.55	.45
☐ 138	NBA Scoring Leaders Lew Alcindor Elvin Hayes John Havlicek	20.00	9.00	2.50
☐ 139	NBA Scoring Average Leaders Lew Alcindor John Havlicek Elvin Hayes	20.00	9.00	2.50
☐ 140	NBA FG Pct Leaders Johnny Green Lew Alcindor Wilt Chamberlain	18.00	8.00	2.20
☐ 141	NBA FT Pct Leaders Chet Walker Oscar Robertson Ron Williams	3.00	1.35	.35
☐ 142	NBA Rebound Leaders Wilt Chamberlain Elvin Hayes Lew Alcindor	25.00	11.00	3.10
☐ 143	NBA Assist Leaders Norm Van Lier Oscar Robertson Jerry West	12.00	5.50	1.50
☐ 144A	NBA Checklist 1-144 (Copyright notation extends up to card 110)	18.00	5.50	1.80
☐ 144B	NBA Checklist 1-144 (Copyright notation extends up to card 108)	18.00	5.50	1.80
☐ 145	ABA Checklist 145-233	18.00	5.50	1.80
☐ 146	ABA Scoring Leaders Dan Issel John Brisker Charlie Scott	8.00	3.60	1.00
☐ 147	ABA Scoring Average Leaders Dan Issel Rick Barry John Brisker	12.00	5.50	1.50
☐ 148	ABA 2pt FG Pct Leaders	4.00	1.80	.50
☐ 149	ABA FT Pct Leaders Rick Barry Darrell Carrier Billy Keller	10.00	4.50	1.25
☐ 150	ABA Rebound Leaders Mel Daniels Julius Keye Mike Lewis	4.00	1.80	.50
☐ 151	ABA Assist Leaders Bill Melchionni Mack Calvin Charlie Scott	4.00	1.80	.50
☐ 152	Larry Brown	25.00	11.00	3.10
☐ 153	Bob Bedell	2.00	.90	.25
☐ 154	Merv Jackson	2.00	.90	.25
☐ 155	Joe Caldwell	2.50	1.10	.30
☐ 156	Billy Paultz	4.00	1.80	.50
☐ 157	Les Hunter	2.00	.90	.25
☐ 158	Charlie Williams	2.00	.90	.25
☐ 159	Stew Johnson	2.00	.90	.25
☐ 160	Mack Calvin	5.00	2.20	.60
☐ 161	Don Sidle	2.00	.90	.25
☐ 162	Mike Barrett	2.00	.90	.25
☐ 163	Tom Workman	2.00	.90	.25
☐ 164	Joe Hamilton	2.00	.90	.25
☐ 165	Zelmo Beaty	8.00	3.60	1.00
☐ 166	Dan Hester	2.00	.90	.25
☐ 167	Bob Verga	2.00	.90	.25
☐ 168	Wilbert Jones	2.00	.90	.25
☐ 169	Skeeter Swift	2.00	.90	.25
☐ 170	Rick Barry	45.00	20.00	5.50
☐ 171	Billy Keller	4.00	1.80	.50
☐ 172	Ron Franz	2.00	.90	.25
☐ 173	Roland Taylor	2.00	.90	.25
☐ 174	Julian Hammond	2.00	.90	.25
☐ 175	Steve Jones	5.00	2.20	.60
☐ 176	Gerald Govan	2.00	.90	.25
☐ 177	Darrell Carrier	2.00	.90	.25
☐ 178	Ron Boone	4.00	1.80	.50
☐ 179	George Peeples	2.00	.90	.25
☐ 180	John Brisker	2.50	1.10	.30
☐ 181	Doug Moe	6.00	2.70	.75
☐ 182	Ollie Taylor	2.00	.90	.25
☐ 183	Bob Netolicky	2.50	1.10	.30
☐ 184	Sam Robinson	2.00	.90	.25
☐ 185	James Jones	2.50	1.10	.30
☐ 186	Julius Keye	2.00	.90	.25
☐ 187	Wayne Hightower	2.00	.90	.25
☐ 188	Warren Armstrong	2.50	1.10	.30
☐ 189	Mike Lewis	2.00	.90	.25
☐ 190	Charlie Scott	8.00	3.60	1.00
☐ 191	Jim Ard	2.00	.90	.25
☐ 192	George Lehmann	2.00	.90	.25
☐ 193	Ira Harge	2.00	.90	.25
☐ 194	Willie Wise	5.00	2.20	.60
☐ 195	Mel Daniels	8.00	3.60	1.00
☐ 196	Larry Cannon	2.00	.90	.25
☐ 197	Jim Eakins	2.00	.90	.25
☐ 198	Rich Jones	2.00	.90	.25
☐ 199	Bill Melchionni	4.00	1.80	.50
☐ 200	Dan Issel	35.00	16.00	4.40
☐ 201	George Stone	2.00	.90	.25
☐ 202	George Thompson	2.00	.90	.25
☐ 203	Craig Raymond	2.00	.90	.25
☐ 204	Freddie Lewis	2.50	1.10	.30
☐ 205	George Carter	2.00	.90	.25
☐ 206	Lonnie Wright	2.00	.90	.25
☐ 207	Cincy Powell	2.00	.90	.25

		NRMT-MT	EXC	G-VG
☐ 208	Larry Miller	2.00	.90	.25
☐ 209	Sonny Dove	2.00	.90	.25
☐ 210	Byron Beck	2.50	1.10	.30
☐ 211	John Beasley	2.00	.90	.25
☐ 212	Lee Davis	2.00	.90	.25
☐ 213	Rick Mount	6.00	2.70	.75
☐ 214	Walt Simon	2.00	.90	.25
☐ 215	Glen Combs	2.00	.90	.25
☐ 216	Neil Johnson	2.00	.90	.25
☐ 217	Manny Leaks	2.00	.90	.25
☐ 218	Chuck Williams	2.00	.90	.25
☐ 219	Warren Davis	2.00	.90	.25
☐ 220	Donnie Freeman	2.50	1.10	.30
☐ 221	Randy Mahaffey	2.00	.90	.25
☐ 222	John Barnhill	2.00	.90	.25
☐ 223	Al Cueto	2.00	.90	.25
☐ 224	Louie Dampier	8.00	3.60	1.00
☐ 225	Roger Brown	2.50	1.10	.30
☐ 226	Joe DePre	2.00	.90	.25
☐ 227	Ray Scott	2.00	.90	.25
☐ 228	Arvesta Kelly	2.00	.90	.25
☐ 229	Vann Williford	2.00	.90	.25
☐ 230	Larry Jones	2.50	1.10	.30
☐ 231	Gene Moore	2.00	.90	.25
☐ 232	Ralph Simpson	2.50	1.10	.30
☐ 233	Red Robbins	4.00	1.20	.40

1972-73 Topps

The 1972-73 Topps set of 264 standard size cards contains NBA players (1-176) and ABA players (177-264). Cards were issued in 10-card packs with 24 packs per box. All-Star selections are depicted for the NBA on cards 161-170 and for the ABA on cards 249-258. Subsets include NBA Playoffs (154-159), NBA Statistical Leaders (171-176), ABA Playoffs (241-247) and ABA Statistical Leaders (259-264). The key Rookie Card is Julius Erving. Other Rookie Cards include Artis Gilmore and Phil Jackson.

	NRMT-MT	EXC	G-VG
COMPLETE SET (264)	750.00	350.00	95.00
COMMON NBA CARD (1-176)	1.00	.45	.12
COMMON ABA CARD (177-264)	1.50	.70	.19

		NRMT-MT	EXC	G-VG
☐ 1	Wilt Chamberlain	40.00	12.00	4.00
☐ 2	Stan Love	1.00	.45	.12
☐ 3	Geoff Petrie	1.50	.70	.19
☐ 4	Curtis Perry	1.50	.70	.19
☐ 5	Pete Maravich	40.00	18.00	5.00
☐ 6	Gus Johnson	1.50	.70	.19
☐ 7	Dave Cowens	18.00	8.00	2.20
☐ 8	Randy Smith	4.00	1.80	.50
☐ 9	Matt Guokas	1.50	.70	.19
☐ 10	Spencer Haywood	4.00	1.80	.50
☐ 11	Jerry Sloan	1.50	.70	.19
☐ 12	Dave Sorenson	1.00	.45	.12
☐ 13	Howie Komives	1.00	.45	.12
☐ 14	Joe Ellis	1.00	.45	.12
☐ 15	Jerry Lucas	4.00	1.80	.50
☐ 16	Stu Lantz	1.50	.70	.19
☐ 17	Bill Bridges	1.50	.70	.19
☐ 18	Leroy Ellis	1.50	.70	.19
☐ 19	Art Williams	1.00	.45	.12
☐ 20	Sidney Wicks	8.00	3.60	1.00
☐ 21	Wes Unseld	6.00	2.70	.75
☐ 22	Jim Washington	1.00	.45	.12
☐ 23	Fred Hilton	1.00	.45	.12
☐ 24	Curtis Rowe	1.00	.45	.12
☐ 25	Oscar Robertson	18.00	8.00	2.20
☐ 26	Larry Steele	1.50	.70	.19
☐ 27	Charlie Davis	1.00	.45	.12
☐ 28	Nate Thurmond	4.00	1.80	.50
☐ 29	Fred Carter	1.50	.70	.19
☐ 30	Connie Hawkins	7.00	3.10	.85
☐ 31	Calvin Murphy	5.00	2.20	.60
☐ 32	Phil Jackson	35.00	16.00	4.40
☐ 33	Lee Winfield	1.00	.45	.12
☐ 34	Jim Fox	1.00	.45	.12
☐ 35	Dave Bing	6.00	2.70	.75
☐ 36	Gary Gregor	1.00	.45	.12
☐ 37	Mike Riordan	1.50	.70	.19
☐ 38	George Trapp	1.00	.45	.12
☐ 39	Mike Davis	1.00	.45	.12
☐ 40	Bob Rule	1.00	.45	.12
☐ 41	John Block	1.00	.45	.12
☐ 42	Bob Dandridge	1.50	.70	.19
☐ 43	John Johnson	1.50	.70	.19
☐ 44	Rick Barry	15.00	6.75	1.85
☐ 45	JoJo White	3.00	1.35	.35
☐ 46	Cliff Meely	1.00	.45	.12
☐ 47	Charlie Scott	2.50	1.10	.30
☐ 48	Johnny Green	1.00	.45	.12
☐ 49	Pete Cross	1.00	.45	.12
☐ 50	Gail Goodrich	6.00	2.70	.75
☐ 51	Jim Davis	1.00	.45	.12
☐ 52	Dick Barnett	1.50	.70	.19
☐ 53	Bob Christian	1.00	.45	.12
☐ 54	Jon McGlocklin	1.50	.70	.19
☐ 55	Paul Silas	3.00	1.35	.35
☐ 56	Hal Greer	3.00	1.35	.35
☐ 57	Barry Clemens	1.00	.45	.12
☐ 58	Nick Jones	1.00	.45	.12
☐ 59	Cornell Warner	1.00	.45	.12
☐ 60	Walt Frazier	10.00	4.50	1.25
☐ 61	Dorie Murrey	1.00	.45	.12
☐ 62	Dick Cunningham	1.00	.45	.12
☐ 63	Sam Lacey	1.50	.70	.19
☐ 64	John Warren	1.00	.45	.12
☐ 65	Tom Boerwinkle	1.00	.45	.12
☐ 66	Fred Foster	1.00	.45	.12
☐ 67	Mel Counts	1.50	.70	.19
☐ 68	Toby Kimball	1.00	.45	.12
☐ 69	Dale Schlueter	1.00	.45	.12
☐ 70	Jack Marin	1.50	.70	.19
☐ 71	Jim Barnett	1.00	.45	.12
☐ 72	Clem Haskins	1.50	.70	.19
☐ 73	Earl Monroe	6.00	2.70	.75
☐ 74	Tom Sanders	1.50	.70	.19
☐ 75	Jerry West	25.00	11.00	3.10
☐ 76	Elmore Smith	1.50	.70	.19

☐ 77 Don Adams	1.00	.45	.12	
☐ 78 Wally Jones	1.00	.45	.12	
☐ 79 Tom Van Arsdale	1.50	.70	.19	
☐ 80 Bob Lanier	10.00	4.50	1.25	
☐ 81 Len Wilkens	8.00	3.60	1.00	
☐ 82 Neal Walk	1.50	.70	.19	
☐ 83 Kevin Loughery	1.50	.70	.19	
☐ 84 Stan McKenzie	1.00	.45	.12	
☐ 85 Jeff Mullins	1.50	.70	.19	
☐ 86 Otto Moore	1.00	.45	.12	
☐ 87 John Tresvant	1.00	.45	.12	
☐ 88 Dean Meminger	1.00	.45	.12	
☐ 89 Jim McMillian	1.50	.70	.19	
☐ 90 Austin Carr	6.00	2.70	.75	
☐ 91 Clifford Ray	1.00	.45	.12	
☐ 92 Don Nelson	4.00	1.80	.50	
☐ 93 Mahdi Abdul-Rahman..	1.50	.70	.19	
(formerly Walt Hazzard)				
☐ 94 Willie Norwood	1.00	.45	.12	
☐ 95 Dick Van Arsdale	1.50	.70	.19	
☐ 96 Don May	1.00	.45	.12	
☐ 97 Walt Bellamy	2.50	1.10	.30	
☐ 98 Garfield Heard	4.00	1.80	.50	
☐ 99 Dave Wohl	1.00	.45	.12	
☐ 100 Kareem Abdul-Jabbar	40.00	18.00	5.00	
☐ 101 Ron Knight	1.00	.45	.12	
☐ 102 Phil Chenier	4.00	1.80	.50	
☐ 103 Rudy Tomjanovich	8.00	3.60	1.00	
☐ 104 Flynn Robinson	1.00	.45	.12	
☐ 105 Dave DeBusschere	6.00	2.70	.75	
☐ 106 Dennis Layton	1.00	.45	.12	
☐ 107 Bill Hewitt	1.00	.45	.12	
☐ 108 Dick Garrett	1.00	.45	.12	
☐ 109 Walt Wesley	1.00	.45	.12	
☐ 110 John Havlicek	20.00	9.00	2.50	
☐ 111 Norm Van Lier	1.50	.70	.19	
☐ 112 Cazzie Russell	2.50	1.10	.30	
☐ 113 Herm Gilliam	1.00	.45	.12	
☐ 114 Greg Smith	1.00	.45	.12	
☐ 115 Nate Archibald	6.00	2.70	.75	
☐ 116 Don Kojis	1.00	.45	.12	
☐ 117 Rick Adelman	1.50	.70	.19	
☐ 118 Luke Jackson	1.50	.70	.19	
☐ 119 Lamar Green	1.00	.45	.12	
☐ 120 Archie Clark	1.50	.70	.19	
☐ 121 Happy Hairston	1.50	.70	.19	
☐ 122 Bill Bradley	16.00	7.25	2.00	
☐ 123 Ron Williams	1.00	.45	.12	
☐ 124 Jimmy Walker	1.50	.70	.19	
☐ 125 Bob Kauffman	1.00	.45	.12	
☐ 126 Rick Roberson	1.00	.45	.12	
☐ 127 Howard Porter	1.50	.70	.19	
☐ 128 Mike Newlin	1.50	.70	.19	
☐ 129 Willis Reed	7.00	3.10	.85	
☐ 130 Lou Hudson	2.50	1.10	.30	
☐ 131 Don Chaney	1.50	.70	.19	
☐ 132 Dave Stallworth	1.00	.45	.12	
☐ 133 Charlie Yelverton	1.00	.45	.12	
☐ 134 Ken Durrett	1.00	.45	.12	
☐ 135 John Brisker	1.00	.45	.12	
☐ 136 Dick Snyder	1.00	.45	.12	
☐ 137 Jim McDaniels	1.00	.45	.12	
☐ 138 Clyde Lee	1.00	.45	.12	
☐ 139 Dennis Awtrey UER..	1.50	.70	.19	
(Misspelled Awtry				
on card front)				
☐ 140 Keith Erickson	1.50	.70	.19	
☐ 141 Bob Weiss	1.00	.45	.12	
☐ 142 Butch Beard	3.00	1.35	.35	
☐ 143 Terry Dischinger	1.00	.45	.12	
☐ 144 Pat Riley	15.00	6.75	1.85	
☐ 145 Lucius Allen	1.50	.70	.19	
☐ 146 John Mengelt	1.00	.45	.12	
☐ 147 John Hummer	1.00	.45	.12	
☐ 148 Bob Love	4.00	1.80	.50	
☐ 149 Bobby Smith	1.50	.70	.19	
☐ 150 Elvin Hayes	10.00	4.50	1.25	
☐ 151 Nate Williams	1.00	.45	.12	
☐ 152 Chet Walker	2.50	1.10	.30	
☐ 153 Steve Kuberski	1.00	.45	.12	
☐ 154 Earl Monroe PO	3.00	1.35	.35	
☐ 155 NBA Playoffs G2	2.50	1.10	.30	
Lakers Come Back				
(under the basket)				
☐ 156 NBA Playoffs G3	2.50	1.10	.30	
Two in a Row				
(under the basket)				
☐ 157 Leroy Ellis PO	2.50	1.10	.30	
☐ 158 Jerry West PO	8.00	3.60	1.00	
☐ 159 Wilt Chamberlain PO	10.00	4.50	1.25	
☐ 160 NBA Checklist 1-176	16.00	4.80	1.60	
UER (135 Jim King)				
☐ 161 John Havlicek AS	10.00	4.50	1.25	
☐ 162 Spencer Haywood AS	2.00	.90	.25	
☐ 163 Kareem Abdul-Jabbar AS	25.00	11.00	3.10	
☐ 164 Jerry West AS	15.00	6.75	1.85	
☐ 165 Walt Frazier AS	5.00	2.20	.60	
☐ 166 Bob Love AS	2.00	.90	.25	
☐ 167 Billy Cunningham AS.	4.00	1.80	.50	
☐ 168 Wilt Chamberlain AS	20.00	9.00	2.50	
☐ 169 Nate Archibald AS	4.00	1.80	.50	
☐ 170 Archie Clark AS	2.00	.90	.25	
☐ 171 NBA Scoring Leaders	14.00	6.25	1.75	
Kareem Abdul-Jabbar				
John Havlicek				
Nate Archibald				
☐ 172 NBA Scoring Average	14.00	6.25	1.75	
Leaders				
Kareem Abdul-Jabbar				
Nate Archibald				
John Havlicek				
☐ 173 NBA FG Pct Leaders.	15.00	6.75	1.85	
Wilt Chamberlain				
Kareem Abdul-Jabbar				
Walt Bellamy				
☐ 174 NBA FT Pct Leaders ..	2.50	1.10	.30	
Jack Marin				
Calvin Murphy				
Gail Goodrich				
☐ 175 NBA Rebound Leaders	15.00	6.75	1.85	
Wilt Chamberlain				
Kareem Abdul-Jabbar				
Wes Unseld				
☐ 176 NBA Assist Leaders .	12.00	5.50	1.50	
Len Wilkens				
Jerry West				
Nate Archibald				
☐ 177 Roland Taylor	1.50	.70	.19	
☐ 178 Art Becker	1.50	.70	.19	
☐ 179 Mack Calvin	2.00	.90	.25	
☐ 180 Artis Gilmore	20.00	9.00	2.50	
☐ 181 Collis Jones	1.50	.70	.19	
☐ 182 John Roche	2.00	.90	.25	
☐ 183 George McGinnis	12.00	5.50	1.50	
☐ 184 Johnny Neumann	2.00	.90	.25	
☐ 185 Willie Wise	2.00	.90	.25	
☐ 186 Bernie Williams	1.50	.70	.19	
☐ 187 Byron Beck	2.00	.90	.25	
☐ 188 Larry Miller	1.50	.70	.19	
☐ 189 Cincy Powell	1.50	.70	.19	
☐ 190 Donnie Freeman	2.00	.90	.25	
☐ 191 John Baum	1.50	.70	.19	

		NRMT-MT	EXC	G-VG
☐ 192	Billy Keller	2.00	.90	.25
☐ 193	Wilbert Jones	1.50	.70	.19
☐ 194	Glen Combs	1.50	.70	.19
☐ 195	Julius Erving	275.00	125.00	34.00
	(Forward on front, but Center on back)			
☐ 196	Al Smith	1.50	.70	.19
☐ 197	George Carter	1.50	.70	.19
☐ 198	Louie Dampier	3.00	1.35	.35
☐ 199	Rich Jones	1.50	.70	.19
☐ 200	Mel Daniels	3.00	1.35	.35
☐ 201	Gene Moore	1.50	.70	.19
☐ 202	Randy Denton	1.50	.70	.19
☐ 203	Larry Jones	1.50	.70	.19
☐ 204	Jim Ligon	1.50	.70	.19
☐ 205	Warren Jabali	2.00	.90	.25
☐ 206	Joe Caldwell	2.00	.90	.25
☐ 207	Darrell Carrier	1.50	.70	.19
☐ 208	Gene Kennedy	1.50	.70	.19
☐ 209	Ollie Taylor	1.50	.70	.19
☐ 210	Roger Brown	2.00	.90	.25
☐ 211	George Lehmann	1.50	.70	.19
☐ 212	Red Robbins	1.50	.70	.19
☐ 213	Jim Eakins	1.50	.70	.19
☐ 214	Willie Long	1.50	.70	.19
☐ 215	Billy Cunningham	8.00	3.60	1.00
☐ 216	Steve Jones	2.00	.90	.25
☐ 217	Les Hunter	1.50	.70	.19
☐ 218	Billy Paultz	2.00	.90	.25
☐ 219	Freddie Lewis	2.00	.90	.25
☐ 220	Zelmo Beaty	2.00	.90	.25
☐ 221	George Thompson	1.50	.70	.19
☐ 222	Neil Johnson	1.50	.70	.19
☐ 223	Dave Robisch	2.00	.90	.25
☐ 224	Walt Simon	1.50	.70	.19
☐ 225	Bill Melchionni	2.00	.90	.25
☐ 226	Wendell Ladner	2.00	.90	.25
☐ 227	Joe Hamilton	1.50	.70	.19
☐ 228	Bob Netolicky	2.00	.90	.25
☐ 229	James Jones	2.00	.90	.25
☐ 230	Dan Issel	10.00	4.50	1.25
☐ 231	Charlie Williams	1.50	.70	.19
☐ 232	Willie Sojourner	1.50	.70	.19
☐ 233	Merv Jackson	1.50	.70	.19
☐ 234	Mike Lewis	1.50	.70	.19
☐ 235	Ralph Simpson	2.00	.90	.25
☐ 236	Darnell Hillman	2.00	.90	.25
☐ 237	Rick Mount	3.00	1.35	.35
☐ 238	Gerald Govan	1.50	.70	.19
☐ 239	Ron Boone	2.00	.90	.25
☐ 240	Tom Washington	1.50	.70	.19
☐ 241	ABA Playoffs G1	2.50	1.10	.30
	Pacers take lead (under the basket)			
☐ 242	Rick Barry PO	5.00	2.20	.60
☐ 243	George McGinnis PO	4.00	1.80	.50
☐ 244	Rick Barry PO	5.00	2.20	.60
☐ 245	Billy Keller PO	2.50	1.10	.30
☐ 246	ABA Playoffs G6	2.50	1.10	.30
	Tight Defense			
☐ 247	ABA Champs: Pacers	3.00	1.35	.35
☐ 248	ABA Checklist 177-264	16.00	4.80	1.60
	UER (236 John Brisker)			
☐ 249	Dan Issel AS	6.00	2.70	.75
☐ 250	Rick Barry AS	8.00	3.60	1.00
☐ 251	Artis Gilmore AS	6.00	2.70	.75
☐ 252	Donnie Freeman AS	2.00	.90	.25
☐ 253	Bill Melchionni AS	2.00	.90	.25
☐ 254	Willie Wise AS	2.50	1.10	.30
☐ 255	Julius Erving AS	50.00	22.00	6.25
☐ 256	Zelmo Beaty AS	2.50	1.10	.30

		NRMT-MT	EXC	G-VG
☐ 257	Ralph Simpson AS	2.50	1.10	.30
☐ 258	Charlie Scott AS	2.50	1.10	.30
☐ 259	ABA Scoring Average.	8.00	3.60	1.00
	Leaders			
	Charlie Scott			
	Rick Barry			
	Dan Issel			
☐ 260	ABA 2pt FG Pct.	4.00	1.80	.50
	Leaders			
	Artis Gilmore			
	Tom Washington			
	Larry Jones			
☐ 261	ABA 3pt FG Pct.	2.50	1.10	.30
	Leaders			
	Glen Combs			
	Louie Dampier			
	Warren Jabali			
☐ 262	ABA FT Pct Leaders	4.00	1.80	.50
	Rick Barry			
	Mack Calvin			
	Steve Jones			
☐ 263	ABA Rebound Leaders	20.00	9.00	2.50
	Artis Gilmore			
	Julius Erving			
	Mel Daniels			
☐ 264	ABA Assist Leaders	6.00	1.80	.60
	Bill Melchionni			
	Larry Brown			
	Louie Dampier			

1973-74 Topps

The 1973-74 Topps set of 264 standard-size cards contains NBA players on cards numbered 1 to 176 and ABA players on cards numbered 177 to 264. Cards were issued in 10-card packs with 24 packs per box. All-Star selections (first and second team) for both leagues are noted on the respective player's regular cards. Card backs are printed in red and green on gray card stock. The backs feature year-by-year ABA and NBA statistics. Subsets include NBA Playoffs (62-68), NBA League Leaders (153-158), ABA Playoffs (202-208) and ABA League Leaders (234-239). The only notable Rookie Cards in this set are Chris Ford, Bob McAdoo, and Paul Westphal.

	NRMT-MT	EXC	G-VG
COMPLETE SET (264)	325.00	145.00	40.00
COMMON NBA CARD (1-176)	.50	.23	.06
COMMON ABA CARD (177-264)	1.00	.45	.12

☐	1 Nate Archibald AS1	8.00	2.40	.80
☐	2 Steve Kuberski	.50	.23	.06
☐	3 John Mengelt	.50	.23	.06
☐	4 Jim McMillian	1.00	.45	.12
☐	5 Nate Thurmond	3.00	1.35	.35
☐	6 Dave Wohl	.50	.23	.06
☐	7 John Brisker	.50	.23	.06
☐	8 Charlie Davis	.50	.23	.06
☐	9 Lamar Green	.50	.23	.06
☐	10 Walt Frazier AS2	6.00	2.70	.75
☐	11 Bob Christian	.50	.23	.06
☐	12 Cornell Warner	.50	.23	.06
☐	13 Calvin Murphy	4.00	1.80	.50
☐	14 Dave Sorenson	.50	.23	.06
☐	15 Archie Clark	1.00	.45	.12
☐	16 Clifford Ray	1.00	.45	.12
☐	17 Terry Driscoll	.50	.23	.06
☐	18 Matt Guokas	1.00	.45	.12
☐	19 Elmore Smith	1.00	.45	.12
☐	20 John Havlicek AS1	15.00	6.75	1.85
☐	21 Pat Riley	6.00	2.70	.75
☐	22 George Trapp	.50	.23	.06
☐	23 Ron Williams	.50	.23	.06
☐	24 Jim Fox	.50	.23	.06
☐	25 Dick Van Arsdale	1.00	.45	.12
☐	26 John Tresvant	.50	.23	.06
☐	27 Rick Adelman	1.00	.45	.12
☐	28 Eddie Mast	.50	.23	.06
☐	29 Jim Cleamons	.50	.23	.06
☐	30 Dave DeBusschere AS2	5.00	2.20	.60
☐	31 Norm Van Lier	1.00	.45	.12
☐	32 Stan McKenzie	.50	.23	.06
☐	33 Bob Dandridge	1.00	.45	.12
☐	34 Leroy Ellis	1.00	.45	.12
☐	35 Mike Riordan	1.00	.45	.12
☐	36 Fred Hilton	.50	.23	.06
☐	37 Toby Kimball	.50	.23	.06
☐	38 Jim Price	.50	.23	.06
☐	39 Willie Norwood	.50	.23	.06
☐	40 Dave Cowens AS2	10.00	4.50	1.25
☐	41 Cazzie Russell	1.00	.45	.12
☐	42 Lee Winfield	.50	.23	.06
☐	43 Connie Hawkins	5.00	2.20	.60
☐	44 Mike Newlin	1.00	.45	.12
☐	45 Chet Walker	1.00	.45	.12
☐	46 Walt Bellamy	2.50	1.10	.30
☐	47 John Johnson	1.00	.45	.12
☐	48 Henry Bibby	3.00	1.35	.35
☐	49 Bobby Smith	1.00	.45	.12
☐	50 K.Abdul-Jabbar AS1	30.00	13.50	3.70
☐	51 Mike Price	.50	.23	.06
☐	52 John Hummer	.50	.23	.06
☐	53 Kevin Porter	5.00	2.20	.60
☐	54 Nate Williams	.50	.23	.06
☐	55 Gail Goodrich	4.00	1.80	.50
☐	56 Fred Foster	.50	.23	.06
☐	57 Don Chaney	1.00	.45	.12
☐	58 Bud Stallworth	.50	.23	.06
☐	59 Clem Haskins	1.00	.45	.12
☐	60 Bob Love AS2	3.00	1.35	.35
☐	61 Jimmy Walker	1.00	.45	.12
☐	62 NBA Eastern Semis Knicks shoot down Bullets in 5	1.00	.45	.12
☐	63 NBA Eastern Semis Celts oust Hawks 2nd Straight Year	1.00	.45	.12
☐	64 Wilt Chamberlain PO	8.00	3.60	1.00
☐	65 NBA Western Semis Warriors over- whelm Milwaukee	1.00	.45	.12
☐	66 Willis Reed PO Henry Finkel	3.00	1.35	.35
☐	67 NBA Western Finals Lakers Breeze Past Golden State	1.00	.45	.12
☐	68 NBA Championship Knicks Do It, Repeat '70 Miracle (W.Frazier/Erickson)	4.00	1.80	.50
☐	69 Larry Steele	1.00	.45	.12
☐	70 Oscar Robertson	12.00	5.50	1.50
☐	71 Phil Jackson	12.00	5.50	1.50
☐	72 John Wetzel	.50	.23	.06
☐	73 Steve Patterson	1.00	.45	.12
☐	74 Manny Leaks	.50	.23	.06
☐	75 Jeff Mullins	1.00	.45	.12
☐	76 Stan Love	.50	.23	.06
☐	77 Dick Garrett	.50	.23	.06
☐	78 Don Nelson	3.00	1.35	.35
☐	79 Chris Ford	3.00	1.35	.35
☐	80 Wilt Chamberlain	25.00	11.00	3.10
☐	81 Dennis Layton	.50	.23	.06
☐	82 Bill Bradley	10.00	4.50	1.25
☐	83 Jerry Sloan	1.00	.45	.12
☐	84 Cliff Meely	.50	.23	.06
☐	85 Sam Lacey	.50	.23	.06
☐	86 Dick Snyder	.50	.23	.06
☐	87 Jim Washington	.50	.23	.06
☐	88 Lucius Allen	1.00	.45	.12
☐	89 LaRue Martin	.50	.23	.06
☐	90 Rick Barry	8.00	3.60	1.00
☐	91 Fred Boyd	.50	.23	.06
☐	92 Barry Clemens	.50	.23	.06
☐	93 Dean Meminger	.50	.23	.06
☐	94 Henry Finkel	.50	.23	.06
☐	95 Elvin Hayes	6.00	2.70	.75
☐	96 Stu Lantz	1.00	.45	.12
☐	97 Bill Hewitt	.50	.23	.06
☐	98 Neal Walk	.50	.23	.06
☐	99 Garfield Heard	1.00	.45	.12
☐	100 Jerry West AS1	20.00	9.00	2.50
☐	101 Otto Moore	.50	.23	.06
☐	102 Don Kojis	.50	.23	.06
☐	103 Fred Brown	4.00	1.80	.50
☐	104 Dwight Davis	.50	.23	.06
☐	105 Willis Reed	5.00	2.20	.60
☐	106 Herm Gilliam	.50	.23	.06
☐	107 Mickey Davis	.50	.23	.06
☐	108 Jim Barnett	.50	.23	.06
☐	109 Ollie Johnson	.50	.23	.06
☐	110 Bob Lanier	6.00	2.70	.75
☐	111 Fred Carter	1.00	.45	.12
☐	112 Paul Silas	1.50	.70	.19
☐	113 Phil Chenier	1.00	.45	.12
☐	114 Dennis Awtrey	.50	.23	.06
☐	115 Austin Carr	1.50	.70	.19
☐	116 Bob Kauffman	.50	.23	.06
☐	117 Keith Erickson	1.00	.45	.12
☐	118 Walt Wesley	.50	.23	.06
☐	119 Steve Bracey	.50	.23	.06
☐	120 Spencer Haywood AS1	2.50	1.10	.30
☐	121 NBA Checklist 1-176	12.00	3.60	1.20
☐	122 Jack Marin	.50	.23	.06
☐	123 Jon McGlocklin	.50	.23	.06
☐	124 Johnny Green	.50	.23	.06
☐	125 Jerry Lucas	3.00	1.35	.35
☐	126 Paul Westphal	18.00	8.00	2.20
☐	127 Curtis Rowe	1.00	.45	.12
☐	128 Mahdi Abdul-Rahman (formerly Walt Hazzard)	1.00	.45	.12
☐	129 Lloyd Neal	.50	.23	.06

130	Pete Maravich AS1	30.00	13.50	3.70
131	Don May	.50	.23	.06
132	Bob Weiss	.50	.23	.06
133	Dave Stallworth	.50	.23	.06
134	Dick Cunningham	.50	.23	.06
135	Bob McAdoo	20.00	9.00	2.50
136	Butch Beard	1.00	.45	.12
137	Happy Hairston	1.00	.45	.12
138	Bob Rule	.50	.23	.06
139	Don Adams	.50	.23	.06
140	Charlie Scott	1.00	.45	.12
141	Ron Riley	.50	.23	.06
142	Earl Monroe	4.00	1.80	.50
143	Clyde Lee	.50	.23	.06
144	Rick Roberson	.50	.23	.06
145	Rudy Tomjanovich	6.00	2.70	.75
	(Printed without Houston on basket)			
146	Tom Van Arsdale	1.00	.45	.12
147	Art Williams	.50	.23	.06
148	Curtis Perry	.50	.23	.06
149	Rich Rinaldi	.50	.23	.06
150	Lou Hudson	1.00	.45	.12
151	Mel Counts	.50	.23	.06
152	Jim McDaniels	.50	.23	.06
153	NBA Scoring Leaders	8.00	3.60	1.00
	Nate Archibald			
	Kareem Abdul-Jabbar			
	Spencer Haywood			
154	NBA Scoring Average Leaders	8.00	3.60	1.00
	Nate Archibald			
	Kareem Abdul-Jabbar			
	Spencer Haywood			
155	NBA FG Pct Leaders	12.00	5.50	1.50
	Wilt Chamberlain			
	Matt Guokas			
	Kareem Abdul-Jabbar			
156	NBA FT Pct Leaders	4.00	1.80	.50
	Rick Barry			
	Calvin Murphy			
	Mike Newlin			
157	NBA Rebound Leaders	8.00	3.60	1.00
	Wilt Chamberlain			
	Nate Thurmond			
	Dave Cowens			
158	NBA Assist Leaders	4.00	1.80	.50
	Nate Archibald			
	Len Wilkens			
	Dave Bing			
159	Don Smith	.50	.23	.06
160	Sidney Wicks	2.50	1.10	.30
161	Howie Komives	.50	.23	.06
162	John Gianelli	.50	.23	.06
163	Jeff Halliburton	.50	.23	.06
164	Kennedy McIntosh	.50	.23	.06
165	Len Wilkens	6.00	2.70	.75
166	Corky Calhoun	.50	.23	.06
167	Howard Porter	1.00	.45	.12
168	JoJo White	2.50	1.10	.30
169	John Block	.50	.23	.06
170	Dave Bing	4.00	1.80	.50
171	Joe Ellis	.50	.23	.06
172	Chuck Terry	.50	.23	.06
173	Randy Smith	1.00	.45	.12
174	Bill Bridges	1.00	.45	.12
175	Geoff Petrie	1.00	.45	.12
176	Wes Unseld	4.00	1.80	.50
177	Skeeter Swift	1.00	.45	.12
178	Jim Eakins	1.00	.45	.12
179	Steve Jones	1.50	.70	.19
180	George McGinnis AS1	3.00	1.35	.35
181	Al Smith	1.00	.45	.12
182	Tom Washington	1.00	.45	.12
183	Louie Dampier	1.50	.70	.19
184	Simmie Hill	1.00	.45	.12
185	George Thompson	1.00	.45	.12
186	Cincy Powell	1.00	.45	.12
187	Larry Jones	1.00	.45	.12
188	Neil Johnson	1.00	.45	.12
189	Tom Owens	1.00	.45	.12
190	Ralph Simpson AS2	1.50	.70	.19
191	George Carter	1.00	.45	.12
192	Rick Mount	1.50	.70	.19
193	Red Robbins	1.00	.45	.12
194	George Lehmann	1.00	.45	.12
195	Mel Daniels AS2	1.50	.70	.19
196	Bob Warren	1.00	.45	.12
197	Gene Kennedy	1.00	.45	.12
198	Mike Barr	1.00	.45	.12
199	Dave Robisch	1.00	.45	.12
200	Billy Cunningham AS1	5.00	2.20	.60
201	John Roche	1.00	.45	.12
202	ABA Western Semis..	2.00	.90	.25
	Pacers Oust Injured Rockets			
203	ABA Western Semis..	2.00	.90	.25
	Stars sweep Q's in Four Straight			
204	Dan Issel PO	2.00	.90	.25
205	ABA Eastern Semis ..	2.00	.90	.25
	Cougars in strong finish over Nets			
206	ABA Western Finals ..	2.00	.90	.25
	Pacers nip bitter rival, Stars			
207	Artis Gilmore PO	3.00	1.35	.35
208	George McGinnis PO .	2.00	.90	.25
209	Glen Combs	1.00	.45	.12
210	Dan Issel AS2	6.00	2.70	.75
211	Randy Denton	1.00	.45	.12
212	Freddie Lewis	1.50	.70	.19
213	Stew Johnson	1.00	.45	.12
214	Roland Taylor	1.00	.45	.12
215	Rich Jones	1.00	.45	.12
216	Billy Paultz	1.50	.70	.19
217	Ron Boone	1.50	.70	.19
218	Walt Simon	1.00	.45	.12
219	Mike Lewis	1.00	.45	.12
220	Warren Jabali AS1	1.50	.70	.19
221	Wilbert Jones	1.00	.45	.12
222	Don Buse	2.00	.90	.25
223	Gene Moore	1.00	.45	.12
224	Joe Hamilton	1.00	.45	.12
225	Zelmo Beaty	1.50	.70	.19
226	Brian Taylor	2.00	.90	.25
227	Julius Keye	1.00	.45	.12
228	Mike Gale	1.50	.70	.19
229	Warren Davis	1.00	.45	.12
230	Mack Calvin AS2	1.50	.70	.19
231	Roger Brown	1.50	.70	.19
232	Chuck Williams	1.00	.45	.12
233	Gerald Govan	1.00	.45	.12
234	ABA Scoring Average Leaders	10.00	4.50	1.25
	Julius Erving			
	George McGinnis			
	Dan Issel			
235	ABA 2 Pt. Pct. Leaders	2.50	1.10	.30
	Artis Gilmore			
	Gene Kennedy			

	Tom Owens			
☐ 236	ABA 3 Pt. Pct.	2.00	.90	.25
	Leaders			
	Glen Combs			
	Roger Brown			
	Louie Dampier			
☐ 237	ABA F.T. Pct. Leaders	2.00	.90	.25
	Billy Keller			
	Ron Boone			
	Bob Warren			
☐ 238	ABA Rebound Leaders	2.50	1.10	.30
	Artis Gilmore			
	Mel Daniels			
	Bill Paultz			
☐ 239	ABA Assist Leaders	2.00	.90	.25
	Bill Melchionni			
	Chuck Williams			
	Warren Jabali			
☐ 240	Julius Erving AS2	50.00	22.00	6.25
☐ 241	Jimmy O'Brien	1.00	.45	.12
☐ 242	ABA Checklist 177-264	12.00	3.60	1.20
☐ 243	Johnny Neumann	1.00	.45	.12
☐ 244	Darnell Hillman	1.50	.70	.19
☐ 245	Willie Wise	1.50	.70	.19
☐ 246	Collis Jones	1.00	.45	.12
☐ 247	Ted McClain	1.00	.45	.12
☐ 248	George Irvine	1.00	.45	.12
☐ 249	Bill Melchionni	1.50	.70	.19
☐ 250	Artis Gilmore AS1	6.00	2.70	.75
☐ 251	Willie Long	1.00	.45	.12
☐ 252	Larry Miller	1.00	.45	.12
☐ 253	Lee Davis	1.00	.45	.12
☐ 254	Donnie Freeman	1.00	.45	.12
☐ 255	Joe Caldwell	1.50	.70	.19
☐ 256	Bob Netolicky	1.50	.70	.19
☐ 257	Bernie Williams	1.00	.45	.12
☐ 258	Byron Beck	1.50	.70	.19
☐ 259	Jim Chones	3.00	1.35	.35
☐ 260	James Jones AS1	1.50	.70	.19
☐ 261	Wendell Ladner	1.00	.45	.12
☐ 262	Ollie Taylor	1.00	.45	.12
☐ 263	Les Hunter	1.00	.45	.12
☐ 264	Billy Keller	2.50	.75	.25

1974-75 Topps

The 1974-75 Topps set of 264 standard-size cards contains NBA players on cards numbered 1 to 176 and ABA players on cards numbered 177 to 264. For the first time Team Leader (TL) cards are provided for each team. The cards were issued in 10-card packs with 24 packs per box. All-Star selections (first and second team) for

both leagues are noted on the respective player's regular cards. The card backs are printed in blue and red on gray card stock. Subsets include NBA Team Leaders (81-98), NBA Statistical Leaders (144-149), NBA Playoffs (161-164), ABA Statistical Leaders (207-212), ABA Team Leaders (221-230) and ABA Playoffs (246-249). The key Rookie Cards in this set are Doug Collins, George Gervin and Bill Walton.

		NRMT-MT	EXC	G-VG
COMPLETE SET (264)		325.00	145.00	40.00
COMMON NBA CARD (1-176)		.50	.23	.06
COMMON ABA CARD (177-264)		1.00	.45	.12

☐ 1	Kareem Abdul-Jabbar AS1	35.00	10.50	3.50
☐ 2	Don May	.50	.23	.06
☐ 3	Bernie Fryer	1.00	.45	.12
☐ 4	Don Adams	.50	.23	.06
☐ 5	Herm Gilliam	.50	.23	.06
☐ 6	Jim Chones	1.00	.45	.12
☐ 7	Rick Adelman	1.00	.45	.12
☐ 8	Randy Smith	1.00	.45	.12
☐ 9	Paul Silas	2.00	.90	.25
☐ 10	Pete Maravich	20.00	9.00	2.50
☐ 11	Ron Behagen	.50	.23	.06
☐ 12	Kevin Porter	1.00	.45	.12
☐ 13	Bill Bridges	1.00	.45	.12
	(On back team shown as			
	Los And., should			
	be Los Ang.)			
☐ 14	Charles Johnson	.50	.23	.06
☐ 15	Bob Love	1.50	.70	.19
☐ 16	Henry Bibby	1.00	.45	.12
☐ 17	Neal Walk	.50	.23	.06
☐ 18	John Brisker	.50	.23	.06
☐ 19	Lucius Allen	.50	.23	.06
☐ 20	Tom Van Arsdale	1.00	.45	.12
☐ 21	Larry Steele	.50	.23	.06
☐ 22	Curtis Rowe	1.00	.45	.12
☐ 23	Dean Meminger	.50	.23	.06
☐ 24	Steve Patterson	.50	.23	.06
☐ 25	Earl Monroe	3.00	1.35	.35
☐ 26	Jack Marin	.50	.23	.06
☐ 27	JoJo White	2.00	.90	.25
☐ 28	Rudy Tomjanovich	6.00	2.70	.75
☐ 29	Otto Moore	.50	.23	.06
☐ 30	Elvin Hayes AS2	5.00	2.20	.60
☐ 31	Pat Riley	6.00	2.70	.75
☐ 32	Clyde Lee	.50	.23	.06
☐ 33	Bob Weiss	.50	.23	.06
☐ 34	Jim Fox	.50	.23	.06
☐ 35	Charlie Scott	1.00	.45	.12
☐ 36	Cliff Meely	.50	.23	.06
☐ 37	Jon McGlocklin	.50	.23	.06
☐ 38	Jim McMillian	1.00	.45	.12
☐ 39	Bill Walton	60.00	27.00	7.50
☐ 40	Dave Bing AS2	3.00	1.35	.35
☐ 41	Jim Washington	.50	.23	.06
☐ 42	Jim Cleamons	.50	.23	.06
☐ 43	Mel Davis	.50	.23	.06
☐ 44	Garfield Heard	1.00	.45	.12
☐ 45	Jimmy Walker	1.00	.45	.12
☐ 46	Don Nelson	1.00	.45	.12
☐ 47	Jim Barnett	.50	.23	.06
☐ 48	Manny Leaks	.50	.23	.06
☐ 49	Elmore Smith	1.00	.45	.12
☐ 50	Rick Barry AS1	6.00	2.70	.75
☐ 51	Jerry Sloan	1.00	.45	.12
☐ 52	John Hummer	.50	.23	.06

☐ 53	Keith Erickson	1.00	.45	.12
☐ 54	George E. Johnson	.50	.23	.06
☐ 55	Oscar Robertson	10.00	4.50	1.25
☐ 56	Steve Mix	1.00	.45	.12
☐ 57	Rick Roberson	.50	.23	.06
☐ 58	John Mengelt	.50	.23	.06
☐ 59	Dwight Jones	1.00	.45	.12
☐ 60	Austin Carr	1.50	.70	.19
☐ 61	Nick Weatherspoon	1.00	.45	.12
☐ 62	Clem Haskins	1.00	.45	.12
☐ 63	Don Kojis	.50	.23	.06
☐ 64	Paul Westphal	5.00	2.20	.60
☐ 65	Walt Bellamy	2.00	.90	.25
☐ 66	John Johnson	1.00	.45	.12
☐ 67	Butch Beard	1.00	.45	.12
☐ 68	Happy Hairston	1.00	.45	.12
☐ 69	Tom Boerwinkle	.50	.23	.06
☐ 70	Spencer Haywood AS2	2.00	.90	.25
☐ 71	Gary Melchionni	.50	.23	.06
☐ 72	Ed Ratleff	1.00	.45	.12
☐ 73	Mickey Davis	.50	.23	.06
☐ 74	Dennis Awtrey	.50	.23	.06
☐ 75	Fred Carter	1.00	.45	.12
☐ 76	George Trapp	.50	.23	.06
☐ 77	John Wetzel	.50	.23	.06
☐ 78	Bobby Smith	1.00	.45	.12
☐ 79	John Gianelli	.50	.23	.06
☐ 80	Bob McAdoo AS2	6.00	2.70	.75
☐ 81	Atlanta Hawks TL	5.00	2.20	.60
	Pete Maravich			
	Lou Hudson			
	Walt Bellamy			
	Pete Maravich			
☐ 82	Boston Celtics TL	5.00	2.20	.60
	John Havlicek			
	JoJo White			
	Dave Cowens			
	JoJo White			
☐ 83	Buffalo Braves TL	1.50	.70	.19
	Bob McAdoo			
	Ernie DiGregorio			
	Bob McAdoo			
	Ernie DiGregorio			
☐ 84	Chicago Bulls TL	2.50	1.10	.30
	Bob Love			
	Chet Walker			
	Clifford Ray			
	Norm Van Lier			
☐ 85	Cleveland Cavs TL	1.50	.70	.19
	Austin Carr			
	Austin Carr			
	Dwight Davis			
	Len Wilkens			
☐ 86	Detroit Pistons TL	1.50	.70	.19
	Bob Lanier			
	Stu Lantz			
	Bob Lanier			
	Dave Bing			
☐ 87	Golden State	2.50	1.10	.30
	Warriors TL			
	Rick Barry			
	Rick Barry			
	Nate Thurmond			
	Rick Barry			
☐ 88	Houston Rockets TL	1.50	.70	.19
	Rudy Tomjanovich			
	Calvin Murphy			
	Don Smith			
	Calvin Murphy			
☐ 89	Kansas City Omaha TL	1.00	.45	.12
	Jimmy Walker			
	Jimmy Walker			
	Sam Lacey			
	Jimmy Walker			
☐ 90	Los Angeles Lakers TL	1.00	.45	.12
	Gail Goodrich			
	Gail Goodrich			
	Happy Hairston			
	Gail Goodrich			
☐ 91	Milwaukee Bucks TL	12.00	5.50	1.50
	Kareem Abdul-Jabbar			
	Oscar Robertson			
	Kareem Abdul-Jabbar			
	Oscar Robertson			
☐ 92	New Orleans Jazz	1.00	.45	.12
	Emblem; Expansion			
	Draft Picks on Back			
☐ 93	New York Knicks	5.00	2.20	.60
	Walt Frazier			
	Bill Bradley			
	Dave DeBusschere			
	Walt Frazier			
☐ 94	Philadelphia 76ers TL	1.50	.70	.19
	Fred Carter			
	Tom Van Arsdale			
	Leroy Ellis			
	Fred Carter			
☐ 95	Phoenix Suns TL	1.50	.70	.19
	Charlie Scott			
	Dick Van Arsdale			
	Neal Walk			
	Neal Walk			
☐ 96	Portland Trail	1.50	.70	.19
	Blazers TL			
	Geoff Petrie			
	Geoff Petrie			
	Rick Roberson			
	Sidney Wicks			
☐ 97	Seattle Supersonics TL	1.50	.70	.19
	Spencer Haywood			
	Dick Snyder			
	Spencer Haywood			
	Fred Brown			
☐ 98	Capitol Bullets TL	1.50	.70	.19
	Phil Chenier			
	Phil Chenier			
	Elvin Hayes			
	Kevin Porter			
☐ 99	Sam Lacey	.50	.23	.06
☐ 100	John Havlicek AS1	10.00	4.50	1.25
☐ 101	Stu Lantz	1.00	.45	.12
☐ 102	Mike Riordan	.50	.23	.06
☐ 103	Larry Jones	.50	.23	.06
☐ 104	Connie Hawkins	4.00	1.80	.50
☐ 105	Nate Thurmond	2.00	.90	.25
☐ 106	Dick Gibbs	.50	.23	.06
☐ 107	Corky Calhoun	.50	.23	.06
☐ 108	Dave Wohl	.50	.23	.06
☐ 109	Cornell Warner	.50	.23	.06
☐ 110	Geoff Petrie UER	1.00	.45	.12
	(Misspelled Patrie on card front)			
☐ 111	Leroy Ellis	1.00	.45	.12
☐ 112	Chris Ford	1.00	.45	.12
☐ 113	Bill Bradley	8.00	3.60	1.00
☐ 114	Clifford Ray	1.00	.45	.12
☐ 115	Dick Snyder	.50	.23	.06
☐ 116	Nate Williams	.50	.23	.06
☐ 117	Matt Guokas	1.00	.45	.12
☐ 118	Henry Finkel	.50	.23	.06
☐ 119	Curtis Perry	.50	.23	.06
☐ 120	Gail Goodrich AS1	3.00	1.35	.35

☐ 121	Wes Unseld	3.00	1.35	.35
☐ 122	Howard Porter	1.00	.45	.12
☐ 123	Jeff Mullins	.50	.23	.06
☐ 124	Mike Bantom	1.00	.45	.12
☐ 125	Fred Brown	1.50	.70	.19
☐ 126	Bob Dandridge	1.00	.45	.12
☐ 127	Mike Newlin	1.00	.45	.12
☐ 128	Greg Smith	.50	.23	.06
☐ 129	Doug Collins	15.00	6.75	1.85
☐ 130	Lou Hudson	1.00	.45	.12
☐ 131	Bob Lanier	5.00	2.20	.60
☐ 132	Phil Jackson	8.00	3.60	1.00
☐ 133	Don Chaney	1.00	.45	.12
☐ 134	Jim Brewer	1.00	.45	.12
☐ 135	Ernie DiGregorio	2.50	1.10	.30
☐ 136	Steve Kuberski	.50	.23	.06
☐ 137	Jim Price	.50	.23	.06
☐ 138	Mike D'Antoni	.50	.23	.06
☐ 139	John Brown	.50	.23	.06
☐ 140	Norm Van Lier AS2	1.00	.45	.12
☐ 141	NBA Checklist 1-176	10.00	3.00	1.00
☐ 142	Don Slick Watts	1.50	.70	.19
☐ 143	Walt Wesley	.50	.23	.06
☐ 144	NBA Scoring Leaders	12.00	5.50	1.50
	Bob McAdoo			
	Kareem Abdul-Jabbar			
	Pete Maravich			
☐ 145	NBA Scoring	12.00	5.50	1.50
	Average Leaders			
	Bob McAdoo			
	Pete Maravich			
	Kareem Abdul-Jabbar			
☐ 146	NBA F.G. Pct. Leaders	10.00	4.50	1.25
	Bob McAdoo			
	Kareem Abdul-Jabbar			
	Rudy Tomjanovich			
☐ 147	NBA F.T. Pct. Leaders	1.00	.45	.12
	Ernie DiGregorio			
	Rick Barry			
	Jeff Mullins			
☐ 148	NBA Rebound Leaders	4.00	1.80	.50
	Elvin Hayes			
	Dave Cowens			
	Bob McAdoo			
☐ 149	NBA Assist Leaders	1.00	.45	.12
	Ernie DiGregorio			
	Calvin Murphy			
	Len Wilkens			
☐ 150	Walt Frazier AS1	5.00	2.20	.60
☐ 151	Cazzie Russell	1.00	.45	.12
☐ 152	Calvin Murphy	3.00	1.35	.35
☐ 153	Bob Kauffman	.50	.23	.06
☐ 154	Fred Boyd	.50	.23	.06
☐ 155	Dave Cowens	6.00	2.70	.75
☐ 156	Willie Norwood	.50	.23	.06
☐ 157	Lee Winfield	.50	.23	.06
☐ 158	Dwight Davis	.50	.23	.06
☐ 159	George T. Johnson	.50	.23	.06
☐ 160	Dick Van Arsdale	1.00	.45	.12
☐ 161	NBA Eastern Semis	1.00	.45	.12
	Celts over Braves			
	Knicks edge Bullets			
☐ 162	NBA Western Semis	1.00	.45	.12
	Bucks over Lakers			
	Bulls edge Pistons			
☐ 163	NBA Div. Finals	1.00	.45	.12
	Celts over Knicks			
	Bucks sweep Bulls			
☐ 164	NBA Championship	1.50	.70	.19
	Celtics over Bucks			
☐ 165	Phil Chenier	1.00	.45	.12
☐ 166	Kermit Washington	1.50	.70	.19
☐ 167	Dale Schlueter	.50	.23	.06
☐ 168	John Block	.50	.23	.06
☐ 169	Don Smith	.50	.23	.06
☐ 170	Nate Archibald	4.00	1.80	.50
☐ 171	Chet Walker	1.00	.45	.12
☐ 172	Archie Clark	1.00	.45	.12
☐ 173	Kennedy McIntosh	.50	.23	.06
☐ 174	George Thompson	.50	.23	.06
☐ 175	Sidney Wicks	2.00	.90	.25
☐ 176	Jerry West	20.00	9.00	2.50
☐ 177	Dwight Lamar	1.00	.45	.12
☐ 178	George Carter	1.00	.45	.12
☐ 179	Wil Robinson	1.00	.45	.12
☐ 180	Artis Gilmore AS1	4.00	1.80	.50
☐ 181	Brian Taylor	1.50	.70	.19
☐ 182	Darnell Hillman	1.50	.70	.19
☐ 183	Dave Robisch	1.00	.45	.12
☐ 184	Gene Littles	1.50	.70	.19
☐ 185	Willie Wise AS2	1.50	.70	.19
☐ 186	James Silas	2.50	1.10	.30
☐ 187	Caldwell Jones	3.00	1.35	.35
☐ 188	Roland Taylor	1.00	.45	.12
☐ 189	Randy Denton	1.00	.45	.12
☐ 190	Dan Issel AS2	5.00	2.20	.60
☐ 191	Mike Gale	1.00	.45	.12
☐ 192	Mel Daniels	1.50	.70	.19
☐ 193	Steve Jones	1.50	.70	.19
☐ 194	Marv Roberts	1.00	.45	.12
☐ 195	Ron Boone AS2	1.50	.70	.19
☐ 196	George Gervin	50.00	22.00	6.25
☐ 197	Flynn Robinson	1.00	.45	.12
☐ 198	Cincy Powell	1.00	.45	.12
☐ 199	Glen Combs	1.00	.45	.12
☐ 200	Julius Erving AS1 UER	45.00	20.00	5.50
	(Misspelled Irving			
	on card back)			
☐ 201	Billy Keller	1.50	.70	.19
☐ 202	Willie Long	1.00	.45	.12
☐ 203	ABA Checklist 177-264	10.00	3.00	1.00
☐ 204	Joe Caldwell	1.50	.70	.19
☐ 205	Swen Nater AS2	2.00	.90	.25
☐ 206	Rick Mount	1.00	.45	.12
☐ 207	ABA Scoring	10.00	4.50	1.25
	Avg. Leaders			
	Julius Erving			
	George McGinnis			
	Dan Issel			
☐ 208	ABA Two-Point Field	2.00	.90	.25
	Goal Percent Leaders			
	Swen Nater			
	James Jones			
	Tom Owens			
☐ 209	ABA Three-Point Field	2.00	.90	.25
	Goal Percent Leaders			
	Louie Dampier			
	Billy Keller			
	Roger Brown			
☐ 210	ABA Free Throw	2.00	.90	.25
	Percent Leaders			
	James Jones			
	Mack Calvin			
	Ron Boone			
☐ 211	ABA Rebound Leaders	2.50	1.10	.30
	Artis Gilmore			
	George McGinnis			
	Caldwell Jones			
☐ 212	ABA Assist Leaders	2.00	.90	.25
	Al Smith			
	Chuck Williams			
	Louie Dampier			

☐ 213	Larry Miller	1.00	.45	.12
☐ 214	Stew Johnson	1.00	.45	.12
☐ 215	Larry Finch	2.00	.90	.25
☐ 216	Larry Kenon	3.00	1.35	.35
☐ 217	Joe Hamilton	1.00	.45	.12
☐ 218	Gerald Govan	1.00	.45	.12
☐ 219	Ralph Simpson	1.50	.70	.19
☐ 220	George McGinnis AS1	2.50	1.10	.30
☐ 221	Carolina Cougars TL	2.50	1.10	.30
	Billy Cunningham			
	Mack Calvin			
	Tom Owens			
	Joe Caldwell			
☐ 222	Denver Nuggets TL	2.50	1.10	.30
	Ralph Simpson			
	Byron Beck			
	Dave Robisch			
	Al Smith			
☐ 223	Indiana Pacers TL	2.50	1.10	.30
	George McGinnis			
	Billy Keller			
	George McGinnis			
	Freddie Lewis			
☐ 224	Kentucky Colonels TL	3.00	1.35	.35
	Dan Issel			
	Louie Dampier			
	Artis Gilmore			
	Louie Dampier			
☐ 225	Memphis Sounds TL	2.00	.90	.25
	George Thompson			
	Larry Finch			
	Randy Denton			
	George Thompson			
☐ 226	New York Nets TL	10.00	4.50	1.25
	Julius Erving			
	John Roche			
	Larry Kenon			
	Julius Erving			
☐ 227	San Antonio Spurs TL	5.00	2.20	.60
	George Gervin			
	George Gervin			
	Swen Nater			
	James Silas			
☐ 228	San Diego Conq. TL	2.00	.90	.25
	Dwight Lamar			
	Stew Johnson			
	Caldwell Jones			
	Chuck Williams			
☐ 229	Utah Stars TL	2.50	1.10	.30
	Willie Wise			
	James Jones			
	Gerald Govan			
	James Jones			
☐ 230	Virginia Squires TL	2.00	.90	.25
	George Carter			
	George Irvine			
	Jim Eakins			
	Roland Taylor			
☐ 231	Bird Averitt	1.00	.45	.12
☐ 232	John Roche	1.00	.45	.12
☐ 233	George Irvine	1.00	.45	.12
☐ 234	John Williamson	1.50	.70	.19
☐ 235	Billy Cunningham	4.00	1.80	.50
☐ 236	Jimmy O'Brien	1.00	.45	.12
☐ 237	Wilbert Jones	1.00	.45	.12
☐ 238	Johnny Neumann	1.00	.45	.12
☐ 239	Al Smith	1.00	.45	.12
☐ 240	Roger Brown	1.50	.70	.19
☐ 241	Chuck Williams	1.00	.45	.12
☐ 242	Rich Jones	1.00	.45	.12
☐ 243	Dave Twardzik	2.00	.90	.25

☐ 244	Wendell Ladner	1.00	.45	.12
☐ 245	Mack Calvin AS1	1.50	.70	.19
☐ 246	ABA Eastern Semis	2.00	.90	.25
	Nets over Squires			
	Colonels sweep Cougars			
☐ 247	ABA Western Semis...	2.00	.90	.25
	Stars over Conquistadors			
	Pacers over Spurs			
☐ 248	ABA Div. Finals	2.00	.90	.25
	Nets sweep Colonels			
	Stars edge Pacers			
☐ 249	Julius Erving PO	12.00	5.50	1.50
☐ 250	Wilt Chamberlain CO	25.00	11.00	3.10
☐ 251	Ron Robinson	1.00	.45	.12
☐ 252	Zelmo Beaty	1.50	.70	.19
☐ 253	Donnie Freeman	1.00	.45	.12
☐ 254	Mike Green	1.00	.45	.12
☐ 255	Louie Dampier AS2	1.50	.70	.19
☐ 256	Tom Owens	1.00	.45	.12
☐ 257	George Karl	6.00	2.70	.75
☐ 258	Jim Eakins	1.00	.45	.12
☐ 259	Travis Grant	1.50	.70	.19
☐ 260	James Jones AS1	1.50	.7C	.19
☐ 261	Mike Jackson	1.00	.45	.12
☐ 262	Billy Paultz	1.50	.70	.19
☐ 263	Freddie Lewis	1.50	.70	.19
☐ 264	Byron Beck	2.00	.60	.20
	(Back refers to ANA,			
	should be ABA)			

1975-76 Topps

The 1975-76 Topps basketball card set of 330 standard-size cards was the largest basketball set ever produced up to that time. Cards were issued in 10-card packs with 24 packs per box. NBA players are depicted on cards 1-220 and ABA players on cards 221-330. Team Leaders (TL) cards are 116-133 (NBA teams) and 278-287 (ABA). Other subsets include NBA Statistical Leaders (1-6), NBA Playoffs (188-189), NBA Team Checklists (203-220), ABA Statistical Leaders (221-226), ABA Playoffs (309-310) and ABA Team Checklists (321-330). All-Star selections (first and second team) for both leagues are noted on the respective player's regular cards. Card backs are printed in blue and green on gray card stock. The set is particularly hard to sort numerically, as the small card number on the back is printed in blue on a dark green background. The set was printed on three large sheets each containing 110 different cards. Investigation of the second (series) sheet reveals that 22 of the cards were double printed; they are marked DP in the checklist below. Rookie Cards in this set include Bobby Jones, Maurice Lucas, Moses Malone and Keith (Jamaal) Wilkes.

	NRMT-MT	EXC	G-VG
COMPLETE SET (330)	450.00	200.00	55.00
COMMON NBA CARD (1-110)	.75	.35	.09
COMMON NBA CARD (111-220)	.35	.09	
COMMON ABA CARD (221-330)	1.50	.70	.19
☐ 1 NBA Scoring Average	14.00	4.20	1.40
Leaders			
Bob McAdoo			
Rick Barry			
Kareem Abdul-Jabbar			
☐ 2 NBA Field Goal	4.00	1.80	.50
Percentage Leaders			
Don Nelson			
Butch Beard			
Rudy Tomjanovich			
☐ 3 NBA Free Throw	5.00	2.20	.60
Percentage Leaders			
Rick Barry			
Calvin Murphy			
Bill Bradley			
☐ 4 NBA Rebounds Leaders	1.50	.70	.19
Wes Unseld			
Dave Cowens			
Sam Lacey			
☐ 5 NBA Assists Leaders	3.00	1.35	.35
Kevin Porter			
Dave Bing			
Nate Archibald			
☐ 6 NBA Steals Leaders	4.00	1.80	.50
Rick Barry			
Walt Frazier			
Larry Steele			
☐ 7 Tom Van Arsdale	1.25	.55	.16
☐ 8 Paul Silas	1.25	.55	.16
☐ 9 Jerry Sloan	1.25	.55	.16
☐ 10 Bob McAdoo AS1	6.00	2.70	.75
☐ 11 Dwight Davis	.75	.35	.09
☐ 12 John Mengelt	.75	.35	.09
☐ 13 George Johnson	.75	.35	.09
☐ 14 Ed Ratleff	.75	.35	.09
☐ 15 Nate Archibald AS1	4.00	1.80	.50
☐ 16 Elmore Smith	.75	.35	.09
☐ 17 Bob Dandridge	1.25	.55	.16
☐ 18 Louie Nelson	.75	.35	.09
☐ 19 Neal Walk	.75	.35	.09
☐ 20 Billy Cunningham	4.00	1.80	.50
☐ 21 Gary Melchionni	.75	.35	.09
☐ 22 Barry Clemens	.75	.35	.09
☐ 23 Jimmy Jones	.75	.35	.09
☐ 24 Tom Burleson	2.00	.90	.25
☐ 25 Lou Hudson	1.25	.55	.16
☐ 26 Henry Finkel	.75	.35	.09
☐ 27 Jim McMillian	1.25	.55	.16
☐ 28 Matt Guokas	1.25	.55	.16
☐ 29 Fred Foster DP	.75	.35	.09
☐ 30 Bob Lanier	5.00	2.20	.60
☐ 31 Jimmy Walker	1.25	.55	.16
☐ 32 Cliff Meely	.75	.35	.09
☐ 33 Butch Beard	1.25	.55	.16
☐ 34 Cazzie Russell	1.25	.55	.16
☐ 35 Jon McGlocklin	.75	.35	.09
☐ 36 Bernie Fryer	1.25	.55	.16
☐ 37 Bill Bradley	6.00	2.70	.75
☐ 38 Fred Carter	1.25	.55	.16
☐ 39 Dennis Awtrey DP	.75	.35	.09
☐ 40 Sidney Wicks	2.00	.90	.25
☐ 41 Fred Brown	1.25	.55	.16
☐ 42 Rowland Garrett	.75	.35	.09
☐ 43 Herm Gilliam	.75	.35	.09
☐ 44 Don Nelson	1.25	.55	.16
☐ 45 Ernie DiGregorio	1.25	.55	.16
☐ 46 Jim Brewer	.75	.35	.09
☐ 47 Chris Ford	1.25	.55	.16
☐ 48 Nick Weatherspoon	.75	.35	.09
☐ 49 Zaid Abdul-Aziz	.75	.35	.09
(formerly Don Smith)			
☐ 50 Keith Wilkes	7.00	3.10	.85
☐ 51 Ollie Johnson DP	.75	.35	.09
☐ 52 Lucius Allen	.75	.35	.09
☐ 53 Mickey Davis	.75	.35	.09
☐ 54 Otto Moore	.75	.35	.09
☐ 55 Walt Frazier AS1	5.00	2.20	.60
☐ 56 Steve Mix	1.25	.55	.16
☐ 57 Nate Hawthorne	.75	.35	.09
☐ 58 Lloyd Neal	.75	.35	.09
☐ 59 Don Slick Watts	1.25	.55	.16
☐ 60 Elvin Hayes	5.00	2.20	.60
☐ 61 Checklist 1-110	8.00	2.40	.80
☐ 62 Mike Sojourner	.75	.35	.09
☐ 63 Randy Smith	1.25	.55	.16
☐ 64 John Block DP	.75	.35	.09
☐ 65 Charlie Scott	1.25	.55	.16
☐ 66 Jim Chones	1.25	.55	.16
☐ 67 Rick Adelman	1.25	.55	.16
☐ 68 Curtis Rowe	.75	.35	.09
☐ 69 Derrek Dickey	2.00	.90	.25
☐ 70 Rudy Tomjanovich	5.00	2.20	.60
☐ 71 Pat Riley	5.00	2.20	.60
☐ 72 Cornell Warner	.75	.35	.09
☐ 73 Earl Monroe	3.00	1.35	.35
☐ 74 Allan Bristow	3.00	1.35	.35
☐ 75 Pete Maravich DP	16.00	7.25	2.00
☐ 76 Curtis Perry	.75	.35	.09
☐ 77 Bill Walton	18.00	8.00	2.20
☐ 78 Leonard Gray	.75	.35	.09
☐ 79 Kevin Porter	1.25	.55	.16
☐ 80 John Havlicek AS2	10.00	4.50	1.25
☐ 81 Dwight Jones	.75	.35	.09
☐ 82 Jack Marin	.75	.35	.09
☐ 83 Dick Snyder	.75	.35	.09
☐ 84 George Trapp	.75	.35	.09
☐ 85 Nate Thurmond	2.50	1.10	.30
☐ 86 Charles Johnson	.75	.35	.09
☐ 87 Ron Riley	.75	.35	.09
☐ 88 Stu Lantz	.75	.35	.09
☐ 89 Scott Wedman	2.00	.90	.25
☐ 90 Kareem Abdul-Jabbar	25.00	11.00	3.10
☐ 91 Aaron James	.75	.35	.09
☐ 92 Jim Barnett	.75	.35	.09
☐ 93 Clyde Lee	.75	.35	.09
☐ 94 Larry Steele	.75	.35	.09
☐ 95 Mike Riordan	.75	.35	.09
☐ 96 Archie Clark	1.25	.55	.16
☐ 97 Mike Bantom	.75	.35	.09
☐ 98 Bob Kauffman	.75	.35	.09
☐ 99 Kevin Stacom	.75	.35	.09
☐ 100 Rick Barry AS1	6.00	2.70	.75
☐ 101 Ken Charles	.75	.35	.09
☐ 102 Tom Boerwinkle	.75	.35	.09
☐ 103 Mike Newlin	1.25	.55	.16
☐ 104 Leroy Ellis	1.25	.55	.16
☐ 105 Austin Carr	1.25	.55	.16
☐ 106 Ron Behagen	.75	.35	.09

☐ 107	Jim Price...................... .75	.35	.09
☐ 108	Bud Stallworth.............. .75	.35	.09
☐ 109	Earl Williams................ .75	.35	.09
☐ 110	Gail Goodrich............ 3.00	1.35	.35
☐ 111	Phil Jackson............... 7.00	3.10	.85
☐ 112	Rod Derline................. .75	.35	.09
☐ 113	Keith Erickson............. .75	.35	.09
☐ 114	Phil Lumpkin............... .75	.35	.09
☐ 115	Wes Unseld............. 3.00	1.35	.35
☐ 116	Atlanta Hawks TL....... 1.50	.70	.19
	Lou Hudson		
	Lou Hudson		
	John Drew		
	Dean Meminger		
☐ 117	Boston Celtics TL...... 3.00	1.35	.35
	Dave Cowens		
	Kevin Stacom		
	Paul Silas		
	JoJo White		
☐ 118	Buffalo Braves TL...... 2.00	.90	.25
	Bob McAdoo		
	Jack Marin		
	Bob McAdoo		
	Randy Smith		
☐ 119	Chicago Bulls TL....... 2.50	1.10	.30
	Bob Love		
	Chet Walker		
	Nate Thurmond		
	Norm Van Lier		
☐ 120	Cleveland Cavs TL...... 1.50	.70	.19
	Bobby Smith		
	Dick Snyder		
	Jim Chones		
	Jim Cleamons		
☐ 121	Detroit Pistons TL...... 3.00	1.35	.35
	Bob Lanier		
	John Mengelt		
	Bob Lanier		
	Dave Bing		
☐ 122	Golden State TL......... 3.00	1.35	.35
	Rick Barry		
	Rick Barry		
	Clifford Ray		
	Rick Barry		
☐ 123	Houston Rockets TL .. 2.00	.90	.25
	Rudy Tomjanovich		
	Calvin Murphy		
	Kevin Kunnert		
	Mike Newlin		
☐ 124	Kansas City Kings TL . 2.00	.90	.25
	Nate Archibald		
	Ollie Johnson		
	Sam Lacey UER		
	(Lacy on front)		
	Nate Archibald		
☐ 125	Los Angeles Lakers TL 1.50	.70	.19
	Gail Goodrich		
	Cazzie Russell		
	Happy Hairston		
	Gail Goodrich		
☐ 126	Milwaukee Bucks TL .. 8.00	3.60	1.00
	Kareem Abdul-Jabbar		
	Mickey Davis		
	Kareem Abdul-Jabbar		
	Kareem Abdul-Jabbar		
☐ 127	New Orleans Jazz TL.. 8.00	3.60	1.00
	Pete Maravich		
	Stu Lantz		
	E.C. Coleman		
	Pete Maravich		
☐ 128	New York Knicks TL DP 3.00	1.35	.35

	Walt Frazier		
	Bill Bradley		
	John Gianelli		
	Walt Frazier		
☐ 129	Phila. 76ers TL DP..... 2.00	.90	.25
	Fred Carter		
	Doug Collins		
	Billy Cunningham		
	Billy Cunningham		
☐ 130	Phoenix Suns TL DP .. 1.50	.70	.19
	Charlie Scott		
	Keith Erickson		
	Curtis Perry		
	Dennis Awtrey		
☐ 131	Portland Blazers TL DP 1.50	.70	.19
	Sidney Wicks		
	Geoff Petrie		
	Sidney Wicks		
	Geoff Petrie		
☐ 132	Seattle Sonics TL....... 2.00	.90	.25
	Spencer Haywood		
	Archie Clark		
	Spencer Haywood		
	Don Watts		
☐ 133	Washington Bullets TL 3.00	1.35	.35
	Elvin Hayes		
	Clem Haskins		
	Wes Unseld		
	Kevin Porter		
☐ 134	John Drew 2.00	.90	.25
☐ 135	JoJo White AS2 .... 2.00	.90	.25
☐ 136	Garfield Heard 1.25	.55	.16
☐ 137	Jim Cleamons.............. .75	.35	.09
☐ 138	Howard Porter 1.25	.55	.16
☐ 139	Phil Smith................. 1.25	.55	.16
☐ 140	Bob Love.................... 2.00	.90	.25
☐ 141	John Gianelli DP .... .75	.35	.09
☐ 142	Larry McNeill............... .75	.35	.09
☐ 143	Brian Winters 3.00	1.35	.35
☐ 144	George Thompson......... .75	.35	.09
☐ 145	Kevin Kunnert .... .75	.35	.09
☐ 146	Henry Bibby............... 1.25	.55	.16
☐ 147	John Johnson.............. .75	.35	.09
☐ 148	Doug Collins 4.00	1.80	.50
☐ 149	John Brisker................ .75	.35	.09
☐ 150	Dick Van Arsdale........ 1.25	.55	.16
☐ 151	Leonard Robinson....... 2.50	1.10	.30
☐ 152	Dean Meminger............ .75	.35	.09
☐ 153	Phil Hankinson............. .75	.35	.09
☐ 154	Dale Schlueter............. .75	.35	.09
☐ 155	Norm Van Lier 1.25	.55	.16
☐ 156	Campy Russell............ 3.00	1.35	.35
☐ 157	Jeff Mullins................. .75	.35	.09
☐ 158	Sam Lacey.................. .75	.35	.09
☐ 159	Happy Hairston........... 1.25	.55	.16
☐ 160	Dave Bing DP.............. 2.50	1.10	.30
☐ 161	Kevin Restani............... .75	.35	.09
☐ 162	Dave Wohl................... .75	.35	.09
☐ 163	E.C. Coleman.............. .75	.35	.09
☐ 164	Jim Fox...................... .75	.35	.09
☐ 165	Geoff Petrie............... 1.25	.55	.16
☐ 166	Hawthorne Wingo UER .75	.35	.09
	(Misspelled Harthorne		
	on card front)		
☐ 167	Fred Boyd .... .75	.35	.09
☐ 168	Willie Norwood .... .75	.35	.09
☐ 169	Bob Wilson .... .75	.35	.09
☐ 170	Dave Cowens 6.00	2.70	.75
☐ 171	Tom Henderson........... .75	.35	.09
☐ 172	Jim Washington........... .75	.35	.09
☐ 173	Clem Haskins 1.25	.55	.16

☐ 174	Jim Davis	.75	.35	.09
☐ 175	Bobby Smith DP	.75	.35	.09
☐ 176	Mike D'Antoni	.75	.35	.09
☐ 177	Zelmo Beaty	1.25	.55	.16
☐ 178	Gary Brokaw	.75	.35	.09
☐ 179	Mel Davis	.75	.35	.09
☐ 180	Calvin Murphy	3.00	1.35	.35
☐ 181	Checklist 111-220 DP	8.00	2.40	.80
☐ 182	Nate Williams	.75	.35	.09
☐ 183	LaRue Martin	.75	.35	.09
☐ 184	George McGinnis	2.50	1.10	.30
☐ 185	Clifford Ray	.75	.35	.09
☐ 186	Paul Westphal	4.00	1.80	.50
☐ 187	Talvin Skinner	.75	.35	.09
☐ 188	NBA Playoff Semis DP	1.50	.70	.19
	Warriors edge Bulls			
	Bullets over Celts			
☐ 189	Clifford Ray PO	1.50	.70	.19
☐ 190	Phil Chenier AS2 DP	1.25	.55	.16
☐ 191	John Brown	.75	.35	.09
☐ 192	Lee Winfield	.75	.35	.09
☐ 193	Steve Patterson	.75	.35	.09
☐ 194	Charles Dudley	.75	.35	.09
☐ 195	Connie Hawkins DP	3.00	1.35	.35
☐ 196	Leon Benbow	.75	.35	.09
☐ 197	Don Kojis	.75	.35	.09
☐ 198	Ron Williams	.75	.35	.09
☐ 199	Mel Counts	.75	.35	.09
☐ 200	Spencer Haywood AS2	2.00	.90	.25
☐ 201	Greg Jackson	.75	.35	.09
☐ 202	Tom Kozelko DP	.75	.35	.09
☐ 203	Atlanta Hawks Checklist	1.50	.70	.19
☐ 204	Boston Celtics Checklist	3.00	1.35	.35
☐ 205	Buffalo Braves Checklist	1.50	.70	.19
☐ 206	Chicago Bulls Checklist	2.50	1.10	.30
☐ 207	Cleveland Cavs Checklist	1.50	.70	.19
☐ 208	Detroit Pistons Checklist	1.50	.70	.19
☐ 209	Golden State Checklist	1.50	.70	.19
☐ 210	Houston Rockets Checklist	1.50	.70	.19
☐ 211	Kansas City Kings DP Checklist	1.50	.70	.19
☐ 212	Los Angeles Lakers DP Checklist	1.50	.70	.19
☐ 213	Milwaukee Bucks Checklist	1.50	.70	.19
☐ 214	New Orleans Jazz Checklist	1.50	.70	.19
☐ 215	New York Knicks Checklist	1.50	.70	.19
☐ 216	Philadelphia 76ers Checklist	1.50	.70	.19
☐ 217	Phoenix Suns DP Checklist	1.50	.70	.19
☐ 218	Portland Blazers Checklist	1.50	.70	.19
☐ 219	Seattle Sonics DP Checklist	10.00	4.50	1.25
☐ 220	Washington Bullets Checklist	1.50	.70	.19
☐ 221	ABA Scoring Average Leaders George McGinnis Julius Erving	8.00	3.60	1.00
	Ron Boone			
☐ 222	ABA 2 Pt. Field Goal Percentage Leaders Bobby Jones Artis Gilmore Moses Malone	8.00	3.60	1.00
☐ 223	ABA 3 Pt. Field Goal Percentage Leaders Billy Shepherd Louie Dampier Al Smith	2.00	.90	.25
☐ 224	ABA Free Throw Percentage Leaders Mack Calvin James Silas Dave Robisch	2.00	.90	.25
☐ 225	ABA Rebounds Leaders Swen Nater Artis Gilmore Marvin Barnes	2.00	.90	.25
☐ 226	ABA Assists Leaders Mack Calvin Chuck Williams George McGinnis	2.00	.90	.25
☐ 227	Mack Calvin AS1	2.00	.90	.25
☐ 228	Billy Knight AS1	3.00	1.35	.35
☐ 229	Bird Averitt	1.50	.70	.19
☐ 230	George Carter	1.50	.70	.19
☐ 231	Swen Nater AS2	2.00	.90	.25
☐ 232	Steve Jones	2.00	.90	.25
☐ 233	George Gervin	16.00	7.25	2.00
☐ 234	Lee Davis	1.50	.70	.19
☐ 235	Ron Boone AS1	2.00	.90	.25
☐ 236	Mike Jackson	1.50	.70	.19
☐ 237	Kevin Joyce	1.50	.70	.19
☐ 238	Marv Roberts	1.50	.70	.19
☐ 239	Tom Owens	1.50	.70	.19
☐ 240	Ralph Simpson	2.00	.90	.25
☐ 241	Gus Gerard	1.50	.70	.19
☐ 242	Brian Taylor AS2	1.50	.70	.19
☐ 243	Rich Jones	1.50	.70	.19
☐ 244	John Roche	1.50	.70	.19
☐ 245	Travis Grant	2.00	.90	.25
☐ 246	Dave Twardzik	2.00	.90	.25
☐ 247	Mike Green	1.50	.70	.19
☐ 248	Billy Keller	2.00	.90	.25
☐ 249	Stew Johnson	1.50	.70	.19
☐ 250	Artis Gilmore AS1	4.00	1.80	.50
☐ 251	John Williamson	2.00	.90	.25
☐ 252	Marvin Barnes AS2	4.00	1.80	.50
☐ 253	James Silas AS2	2.00	.90	.25
☐ 254	Moses Malone	45.00	20.00	5.50
☐ 255	Willie Wise	2.00	.90	.25
☐ 256	Dwight Lamar	1.50	.70	.19
☐ 257	Checklist 221-330	8.00	2.40	.80
☐ 258	Byron Beck	2.00	.90	.25
☐ 259	Len Elmore	3.00	1.35	.35
☐ 260	Dan Issel	5.00	2.20	.60
☐ 261	Rick Mount	1.50	.70	.19
☐ 262	Billy Paultz	2.00	.90	.25
☐ 263	Donnie Freeman	1.50	.70	.19
☐ 264	George Adams	1.50	.70	.19
☐ 265	Don Chaney	2.00	.90	.25
☐ 266	Randy Denton	1.50	.70	.19
☐ 267	Don Washington	1.50	.70	.19
☐ 268	Roland Taylor	1.50	.70	.19
☐ 269	Charlie Edge	1.50	.70	.19
☐ 270	Louie Dampier	2.00	.90	.25
☐ 271	Collis Jones	1.50	.70	.19
☐ 272	Al Skinner	1.50	.70	.19
☐ 273	Coby Dietrick	1.50	.70	.19

☐ 274	Tim Bassett	1.50	.70	.19
☐ 275	Freddie Lewis	2.00	.90	.25
☐ 276	Gerald Govan	1.50	.70	.19
☐ 277	Ron Thomas	1.50	.70	.19
☐ 278	Denver Nuggets TL	2.00	.90	.25
	Ralph Simpson			
	Mack Calvin			
	Mike Green			
	Mack Calvin			
☐ 279	Indiana Pacers TL	2.50	1.10	.30
	George McGinnis			
	Billy Keller			
	George McGinnis			
	George McGinnis			
☐ 280	Kentucky Colonels TL	2.50	1.10	.30
	Artis Gilmore			
	Louie Dampier			
	Artis Gilmore			
	Louie Dampier			
☐ 281	Memphis Sounds TL	2.00	.90	.25
	George Carter			
	Larry Finch			
	Tom Owens			
	Chuck Williams			
☐ 282	New York Nets TL	10.00	4.50	1.25
	Julius Erving			
	John Williamson			
	Julius Erving			
	Julius Erving			
☐ 283	St. Louis Spirits TL	2.50	1.10	.30
	Marvin Barnes			
	Freddie Lewis			
	Marvin Barnes			
	Freddie Lewis			
☐ 284	San Antonio Spurs TL	5.00	2.20	.60
	George Gervin			
	James Silas			
	Swen Nater			
	James Silas			
☐ 285	San Diego Sails TL	2.00	.90	.25
	Travis Grant			
	Jimmy O'Brien			
	Caldwell Jones			
	Jimmy O'Brien			
☐ 286	Utah Stars TL	8.00	3.60	1.00
	Ron Boone			
	Ron Boone			
	Moses Malone			
	Al Smith			
☐ 287	Virginia Squires TL	2.00	.90	.25
	Willie Wise			
	Red Robbins			
	Dave Vaughn			
	Dave Twardzik			
☐ 288	Claude Terry	1.50	.70	.19
☐ 289	Wilbert Jones	1.50	.70	.19
☐ 290	Darnell Hillman	2.00	.90	.25
☐ 291	Bill Melchionni	2.00	.90	.25
☐ 292	Mel Daniels	2.00	.90	.25
☐ 293	Fly Williams	2.00	.90	.25
☐ 294	Larry Kenon	2.00	.90	.25
☐ 295	Red Robbins	1.50	.70	.19
☐ 296	Warren Jabali	1.50	.70	.19
☐ 297	Jim Eakins	1.50	.70	.19
☐ 298	Bobby Jones	12.00	5.50	1.50
☐ 299	Don Buse	2.00	.90	.25
☐ 300	Julius Erving AS1	45.00	20.00	5.50
☐ 301	Billy Shepherd	1.50	.70	.19
☐ 302	Maurice Lucas	6.00	2.70	.75
☐ 303	George Karl	3.00	1.35	.35
☐ 304	Jim Bradley	1.50	.70	.19

☐ 305	Caldwell Jones	2.00	.90	.25
☐ 306	Al Smith	1.50	.70	.19
☐ 307	Jan Van Breda Kolff	2.00	.90	.25
☐ 308	Darrell Elston	1.50	.70	.19
☐ 309	ABA Playoff Semifinals	2.00	.90	.25
	Colonels over Spirits;			
	Pacers edge Nuggets			
☐ 310	Artis Gilmore PO	2.50	1.10	.30
☐ 311	Ted McClain	1.50	.70	.19
☐ 312	Willie Sojourner	1.50	.70	.19
☐ 313	Bob Warren	1.50	.70	.19
☐ 314	Bob Netolicky	2.00	.90	.25
☐ 315	Chuck Williams	1.50	.70	.19
☐ 316	Gene Kennedy	1.50	.70	.19
☐ 317	Jimmy O'Brien	1.50	.70	.19
☐ 318	Dave Robisch	1.50	.70	.19
☐ 319	Wali Jones	1.50	.70	.19
☐ 320	George Irvine	1.50	.70	.19
☐ 321	Denver Nuggets Checklist	2.00	.90	.25
☐ 322	Indiana Pacers Checklist	2.00	.90	.25
☐ 323	Kentucky Colonels Checklist	2.00	.90	.25
☐ 324	Memphis Sounds Checklist	2.00	.90	.25
☐ 325	New York Nets Checklist	2.00	.90	.25
☐ 326	St. Louis Spirits Checklist (Spirits of St. Louis on card back)	2.00	.90	.25
☐ 327	San Antonio Spurs Checklist	2.00	.90	.25
☐ 328	San Diego Sails Checklist	2.00	.90	.25
☐ 329	Utah Stars Checklist	2.00	.90	.25
☐ 330	Virginia Squires Checklist	4.00	1.20	.40

1976-77 Topps

Perhaps the most popular set of the seventies, the 144-card 1976-77 Topps set witnessed a return to the larger-size at 3 1/8" by 5 1/4". The larger size and excellent photo quality are appealing to collectors. Also, because of the size, they are attractive to autograph collectors. Cards were issued in 10-card packs with 24 packs per box. The fronts have a large color photo with the team name vertical on the left border. The player's name and position are at *the bottom. Backs have statistical and biographical data. Cards numbered 126-135 are the previous season's NBA All-Star selections. The cards were printed on two large sheets, each with eight rows and nine columns. The checklist card was located in the lower right corner of the second sheet. Card No. 1, Julius Erving, is rarely found centered. Rookie Cards include Alvan Adams, Lloyd Free, Gus Williams and David Thompson.*

	NRMT-MT	EXC	G-VG
COMPLETE SET (144)	350.00	160.00	45.00
COMMON CARD (1-144)	1.75	.80	.22

		NRMT-MT	EXC	G-VG
☐	1 Julius Erving	70.00	21.00	7.00
☐	2 Dick Snyder	1.75	.80	.22
☐	3 Paul Silas	2.50	1.10	.30
☐	4 Keith Erickson	1.75	.80	.22
☐	5 Wes Unseld	4.00	1.80	.50
☐	6 Butch Beard	2.00	.90	.25
☐	7 Lloyd Neal	1.75	.80	.22
☐	8 Tom Henderson	1.75	.80	.22
☐	9 Jim McMillian	2.00	.90	.25
☐	10 Bob Lanier	6.00	2.70	.75
☐	11 Junior Bridgeman	2.50	1.10	.30
☐	12 Corky Calhoun	1.75	.80	.22
☐	13 Billy Keller	2.00	.90	.25
☐	14 Mickey Johnson	2.00	.90	.25
☐	15 Fred Brown	2.00	.90	.25
☐	16 Jamaal Wilkes	3.00	1.35	.35
☐	17 Louie Nelson	1.75	.80	.22
☐	18 Ed Ratleff	1.75	.80	.22
☐	19 Billy Paultz	2.00	.90	.25
☐	20 Nate Archibald	5.00	2.20	.60
☐	21 Steve Mix	2.00	.90	.25
☐	22 Ralph Simpson	1.75	.80	.22
☐	23 Campy Russell	2.00	.90	.25
☐	24 Charlie Scott	2.00	.90	.25
☐	25 Artis Gilmore	5.00	2.20	.60
☐	26 Dick Van Arsdale	2.00	.90	.25
☐	27 Phil Chenier	2.00	.90	.25
☐	28 Spencer Haywood	3.00	1.35	.35
☐	29 Chris Ford	2.00	.90	.25
☐	30 Dave Cowens	10.00	4.50	1.25
☐	31 Sidney Wicks	2.50	1.10	.30
☐	32 Jim Price	1.75	.80	.22
☐	33 Dwight Jones	1.75	.80	.22
☐	34 Lucius Allen	1.75	.80	.22
☐	35 Marvin Barnes	2.00	.90	.25
☐	36 Henry Bibby	2.00	.90	.25
☐	37 Joe Meriweather	1.75	.80	.22
☐	38 Doug Collins	5.00	2.20	.60
☐	39 Garfield Heard	2.00	.90	.25
☐	40 Randy Smith	2.00	.90	.25
☐	41 Tom Burleson	2.00	.90	.25
☐	42 Dave Twardzik	2.00	.90	.25
☐	43 Bill Bradley	12.00	5.50	1.50
☐	44 Calvin Murphy	4.00	1.80	.50
☐	45 Bob Love	2.50	1.10	.30
☐	46 Brian Winters	2.50	1.10	.30
☐	47 Glenn McDonald	1.75	.80	.22
☐	48 Checklist 1-144	30.00	9.00	3.00
☐	49 Bird Averitt	1.75	.80	.22
☐	50 Rick Barry	10.00	4.50	1.25
☐	51 Ticky Burden	1.75	.80	.22
☐	52 Rich Jones	1.75	.80	.22
☐	53 Austin Carr	2.00	.90	.25
☐	54 Steve Kuberski	1.75	.80	.22
☐	55 Paul Westphal	5.00	2.20	.60
☐	56 Mike Riordan	1.75	.80	.22
☐	57 Bill Walton	25.00	11.00	3.10
☐	58 Eric Money	1.75	.80	.22
☐	59 John Drew	2.00	.90	.25
☐	60 Pete Maravich	35.00	16.00	4.40
☐	61 John Shumate	2.50	1.10	.30
☐	62 Mack Calvin	2.00	.90	.25
☐	63 Bruce Seals	1.75	.80	.22
☐	64 Walt Frazier	6.00	2.70	.75
☐	65 Elmore Smith	1.75	.80	.22
☐	66 Rudy Tomjanovich	6.00	2.70	.75
☐	67 Sam Lacey	1.75	.80	.22
☐	68 George Gervin	25.00	11.00	3.10
☐	69 Gus Williams	5.00	2.20	.60
☐	70 George McGinnis	2.50	1.10	.30
☐	71 Len Elmore	1.75	.80	.22
☐	72 Jack Marin	1.75	.80	.22
☐	73 Brian Taylor	1.75	.80	.22
☐	74 Jim Brewer	1.75	.80	.22
☐	75 Alvan Adams	6.00	2.70	.75
☐	76 Dave Bing	4.00	1.80	.50
☐	77 Phil Jackson	8.00	3.60	1.00
☐	78 Geoff Petrie	2.00	.90	.25
☐	79 Mike Sojourner	1.75	.80	.22
☐	80 James Silas	2.00	.90	.25
☐	81 Bob Dandridge	2.00	.90	.25
☐	82 Ernie DiGregorio	2.00	.90	.25
☐	83 Cazzie Russell	2.00	.90	.25
☐	84 Kevin Porter	2.00	.90	.25
☐	85 Tom Boerwinkle	1.75	.80	.22
☐	86 Darnell Hillman	2.00	.90	.25
☐	87 Herm Gilliam	1.75	.80	.22
☐	88 Nate Williams	1.75	.80	.22
☐	89 Phil Smith	2.00	.90	.25
☐	90 John Havlicek	16.00	7.25	2.00
☐	91 Kevin Kunnert	1.75	.80	.22
☐	92 Jimmy Walker	2.00	.90	.25
☐	93 Billy Cunningham	5.00	2.20	.60
☐	94 Dan Issel	6.00	2.70	.75
☐	95 Ron Boone	2.00	.90	.25
☐	96 Lou Hudson	2.00	.90	.25
☐	97 Jim Chones	2.00	.90	.25
☐	98 Earl Monroe	4.00	1.80	.50
☐	99 Tom Van Arsdale	2.00	.90	.25
☐	100 Kareem Abdul-Jabbar	35.00	16.00	4.40
☐	101 Moses Malone	18.00	8.00	2.20
☐	102 Ricky Sobers	1.75	.80	.22
☐	103 Swen Nater	2.00	.90	.25
☐	104 Leonard Robinson	2.50	1.10	.30
☐	105 Don Slick Watts	2.00	.90	.25
☐	106 Otto Moore	1.75	.80	.22
☐	107 Maurice Lucas	2.50	1.10	.30
☐	108 Norm Van Lier	2.00	.90	.25
☐	109 Clifford Ray	1.75	.80	.22
☐	110 David Thompson	45.00	20.00	5.50
☐	111 Fred Carter	2.00	.90	.25
☐	112 Caldwell Jones	2.00	.90	.25
☐	113 John Williamson	2.00	.90	.25
☐	114 Bobby Smith	1.75	.80	.22
☐	115 JoJo White	2.50	1.10	.30
☐	116 Curtis Perry	1.75	.80	.22
☐	117 John Gianelli	1.75	.80	.22
☐	118 Curtis Rowe	1.75	.80	.22
☐	119 Lionel Hollins	2.50	1.10	.30
☐	120 Elvin Hayes	6.00	2.70	.75
☐	121 Ken Charles	1.75	.80	.22
☐	122 Dave Meyers	2.50	1.10	.30
☐	123 Jerry Sloan	2.00	.90	.25
☐	124 Billy Knight	2.00	.90	.25
☐	125 Gail Goodrich	2.50	1.10	.30
☐	126 Kareem Abdul-Jabbar AS	20.00	9.00	2.50

		NRMT-MT	EXC	G-VG
☐ 127	Julius Erving AS	25.00	11.00	3.10
☐ 128	George McGinnis AS	2.75	1.25	.35
☐ 129	Nate Archibald AS	3.00	1.35	.35
☐ 130	Pete Maravich AS	20.00	9.00	2.50
☐ 131	Dave Cowens AS	5.00	2.20	.60
☐ 132	Rick Barry AS	5.00	2.20	.60
☐ 133	Elvin Hayes AS	4.00	1.80	.50
☐ 134	James Silas AS	2.00	.90	.25
☐ 135	Randy Smith AS	2.00	.90	.25
☐ 136	Leonard Gray	1.75	.80	.22
☐ 137	Charles Johnson	1.75	.80	.22
☐ 138	Ron Behagen	1.75	.80	.22
☐ 139	Mike Newlin	2.00	.90	.25
☐ 140	Bob McAdoo	6.00	2.70	.75
☐ 141	Mike Gale	1.75	.80	.22
☐ 142	Scott Wedman	2.00	.90	.25
☐ 143	Lloyd Free	5.00	2.20	.60
☐ 144	Bobby Jones	6.00	1.80	.60

1977-78 Topps

The 1977-78 Topps basketball card set consists of 132 standard-size cards. Cards were issued in 10-card packs with 24 packs per box. Fronts feature team and player name at the bottom with the player's position in a basketball at bottom left of the photo. Card backs are printed in green and black on either white or gray card stock. The white card stock is considered more desirable by most collectors and may even be a little tougher to find. However, there is no difference in value for either card stock. Rookie Cards include Adrian Dantley, Darryl Dawkins, John Lucas, Tom McMillen and Robert Parish.

	NRMT-MT	EXC	G-VG
COMPLETE SET (132)	90.00	40.00	11.00
COMMON CARD (1-132)	.30	.14	.04
*GRAY AND WHITE BACKS: EQUAL VALUE			

☐ 1	Kareem Abdul-Jabbar	15.00	4.50	1.50
☐ 2	Henry Bibby	.40	.18	.05
☐ 3	Curtis Rowe	.30	.14	.04
☐ 4	Norm Van Lier	.40	.18	.05
☐ 5	Darnell Hillman	.40	.18	.05
☐ 6	Earl Monroe	1.50	.70	.19
☐ 7	Leonard Gray	.30	.14	.04
☐ 8	Bird Averitt	.30	.14	.04
☐ 9	Jim Brewer	.30	.14	.04
☐ 10	Paul Westphal	1.25	.55	.16
☐ 11	Bob Gross	.40	.18	.05
☐ 12	Phil Smith	.30	.14	.04
☐ 13	Dan Roundfield	.60	.25	.07
☐ 14	Brian Taylor	.30	.14	.04
☐ 15	Rudy Tomjanovich	2.00	.90	.25
☐ 16	Kevin Porter	.40	.18	.05
☐ 17	Scott Wedman	.40	.18	.05
☐ 18	Lloyd Free	.60	.25	.07
☐ 19	Tom Boswell	.30	.14	.04
☐ 20	Pete Maravich	12.00	5.50	1.50
☐ 21	Cliff Poindexter	.30	.14	.04
☐ 22	Bubbles Hawkins	.40	.18	.05
☐ 23	Kevin Grevey	.75	.35	.09
☐ 24	Ken Charles	.30	.14	.04
☐ 25	Bob Dandridge	.40	.18	.05
☐ 26	Lonnie Shelton	.30	.14	.04
☐ 27	Don Chaney	.40	.18	.05
☐ 28	Larry Kenon	.40	.18	.05
☐ 29	Checklist 1-132	3.00	.90	.25
☐ 30	Fred Brown	.40	.18	.05
☐ 31	John Gianelli UER	.30	.14	.04
	(Listed as Cavaliers,			
	should be Buffalo Braves)			
☐ 32	Austin Carr	.40	.18	.05
☐ 33	Jamaal Wilkes	.60	.25	.07
☐ 34	Caldwell Jones	.40	.18	.05
☐ 35	JoJo White	.60	.25	.07
☐ 36	Scott May	.75	.35	.09
☐ 37	Mike Newlin	.30	.14	.04
☐ 38	Mel Davis	.30	.14	.04
☐ 39	Lionel Hollins	.60	.25	.07
☐ 40	Elvin Hayes	2.50	1.10	.30
☐ 41	Dan Issel	2.00	.90	.25
☐ 42	Ricky Sobers	.30	.14	.04
☐ 43	Don Ford	.30	.14	.04
☐ 44	John Williamson	.30	.14	.04
☐ 45	Bob McAdoo	2.00	.90	.25
☐ 46	Geoff Petrie	.40	.18	.05
☐ 47	M.L. Carr	3.00	1.35	.35
☐ 48	Brian Winters	.60	.25	.07
☐ 49	Sam Lacey	.30	.14	.04
☐ 50	George McGinnis	.60	.25	.07
☐ 51	Don Slick Watts	.40	.18	.05
☐ 52	Sidney Wicks	.60	.25	.07
☐ 53	Wilbur Holland	.30	.14	.04
☐ 54	Tim Bassett	.30	.14	.04
☐ 55	Phil Chenier	.40	.18	.05
☐ 56	Adrian Dantley	8.00	3.60	1.00
☐ 57	Jim Chones	.40	.18	.05
☐ 58	John Lucas	4.00	1.80	.50
☐ 59	Cazzie Russell	.40	.18	.05
☐ 60	David Thompson	5.00	2.20	.60
☐ 61	Bob Lanier	2.00	.90	.25
☐ 62	Dave Twardzik	.40	.18	.05
☐ 63	Wilbert Jones	.30	.14	.04
☐ 64	Clifford Ray	.30	.14	.04
☐ 65	Doug Collins	1.50	.70	.19
☐ 66	Tom McMillen	2.50	1.10	.30
☐ 67	Rich Kelley	.30	.14	.04
☐ 68	Mike Bantom	.30	.14	.04
☐ 69	Tom Boerwinkle	.30	.14	.04
☐ 70	John Havlicek	6.00	2.70	.75
☐ 71	Marvin Webster	.40	.18	.05
☐ 72	Curtis Perry	.30	.14	.04
☐ 73	George Gervin	6.00	2.70	.75
☐ 74	Leonard Robinson	.60	.25	.07
☐ 75	Wes Unseld	1.50	.70	.19
☐ 76	Dave Meyers	.40	.18	.05
☐ 77	Gail Goodrich	.60	.25	.07
☐ 78	Richard Washington	.60	.25	.07
☐ 79	Mike Gale	.30	.14	.04
☐ 80	Maurice Lucas	.60	.25	.07

		NRMT-MT	EXC	G-VG
☐ 81	Harvey Catchings	.30	.14	.04
☐ 82	Randy Smith	.30	.14	.04
☐ 83	Campy Russell	.40	.18	.05
☐ 84	Al Skinner	.30	.14	.04
☐ 85	Lou Hudson	.40	.18	.05
☐ 86	Mickey Johnson	.30	.14	.04
☐ 87	Lucius Allen	.30	.14	.04
☐ 88	Spencer Haywood	1.00	.45	.12
☐ 89	Gus Williams	.60	.25	.07
☐ 90	Dave Cowens	3.00	1.35	.35
☐ 91	Al Skinner	.30	.14	.04
☐ 92	Swen Nater	.30	.14	.04
☐ 93	Tom Henderson	.30	.14	.04
☐ 94	Don Buse	.40	.18	.05
☐ 95	Alvan Adams	.60	.25	.07
☐ 96	Mack Calvin	.40	.18	.05
☐ 97	Tom Burleson	.30	.14	.04
☐ 98	John Drew	.40	.18	.05
☐ 99	Mike Green	.30	.14	.04
☐ 100	Julius Erving	15.00	6.75	1.85
☐ 101	John Mengelt	.30	.14	.04
☐ 102	Howard Porter	.40	.18	.05
☐ 103	Billy Paultz	.40	.18	.05
☐ 104	John Shumate	.40	.18	.05
☐ 105	Calvin Murphy	1.50	.70	.19
☐ 106	Elmore Smith	.30	.14	.04
☐ 107	Jim McMillian	.30	.14	.04
☐ 108	Kevin Stacom	.30	.14	.04
☐ 109	Jan Van Breda Kolff	.30	.14	.04
☐ 110	Billy Knight	.40	.18	.05
☐ 111	Robert Parish	30.00	13.50	3.70
☐ 112	Larry Wright	.30	.14	.04
☐ 113	Bruce Seals	.30	.14	.04
☐ 114	Junior Bridgeman	.40	.18	.05
☐ 115	Artis Gilmore	1.50	.70	.19
☐ 116	Steve Mix	.40	.18	.05
☐ 117	Ron Lee	.30	.14	.04
☐ 118	Bobby Jones	.60	.25	.07
☐ 119	Ron Boone	.40	.18	.05
☐ 120	Bill Walton	8.00	3.60	1.00
☐ 121	Chris Ford	.40	.18	.05
☐ 122	Earl Tatum	.30	.14	.04
☐ 123	E.C. Coleman	.30	.14	.04
☐ 124	Moses Malone	6.00	2.70	.75
☐ 125	Charlie Scott	.40	.18	.05
☐ 126	Bobby Smith	.30	.14	.04
☐ 127	Nate Archibald	1.50	.70	.19
☐ 128	Mitch Kupchak	.75	.35	.09
☐ 129	Walt Frazier	2.50	1.10	.30
☐ 130	Rick Barry	3.00	1.35	.35
☐ 131	Ernie DiGregorio	.40	.18	.05
☐ 132	Darryl Dawkins	8.00	2.40	.80

1978-79 Topps

The 1978-79 Topps basketball card set contains 132 standard-size cards. Cards were issued in 10-card packs with 36 packs per box. Card fronts feature the player and team name down the left border and a small head shot inserted at bottom right. Card backs are printed in orange and brown on gray card stock. The key Rookie Cards in this set inlcude Quinn Buckner, Walter Davis, James "Buddha" Edwards, Dennis Johnson, Marques Johnson, Bernard King, Norm Nixon and Jack Sikma.

		NRMT-MT	EXC	G-VG
	COMPLETE SET (132)	70.00	32.00	8.75
	COMMON CARD (1-132)	.30	.14	.04
☐ 1	Bill Walton	10.00	3.00	1.00
☐ 2	Doug Collins	1.50	.70	.19
☐ 3	Jamaal Wilkes	.75	.35	.09
☐ 4	Wilbur Holland	.30	.14	.04
☐ 5	Bob McAdoo	1.25	.55	.16
☐ 6	Lucius Allen	.30	.14	.04
☐ 7	Wes Unseld	1.25	.55	.16
☐ 8	Dave Meyers	.50	.23	.06
☐ 9	Austin Carr	.50	.23	.06
☐ 10	Walter Davis	7.00	3.10	.85
☐ 11	John Williamson	.30	.14	.04
☐ 12	E.C. Coleman	.30	.14	.04
☐ 13	Calvin Murphy	1.00	.45	.12
☐ 14	Bobby Jones	.75	.35	.09
☐ 15	Chris Ford	.50	.23	.06
☐ 16	Kermit Washington	.50	.23	.06
☐ 17	Butch Beard	.50	.23	.06
☐ 18	Steve Mix	.30	.14	.04
☐ 19	Marvin Webster	.50	.23	.06
☐ 20	George Gervin	6.00	2.70	.75
☐ 21	Steve Hawes	.30	.14	.04
☐ 22	Johnny Davis	.30	.14	.04
☐ 23	Swen Nater	.30	.14	.04
☐ 24	Lou Hudson	.50	.23	.06
☐ 25	Elvin Hayes	1.50	.70	.19
☐ 26	Nate Archibald	1.00	.45	.12
☐ 27	James Edwards	3.00	1.35	.35
☐ 28	Howard Porter	.50	.23	.06
☐ 29	Quinn Buckner	1.25	.55	.16
☐ 30	Leonard Robinson	.50	.23	.06
☐ 31	Jim Cleamons	.30	.14	.04
☐ 32	Campy Russell	.50	.23	.06
☐ 33	Phil Smith	.30	.14	.04
☐ 34	Darryl Dawkins	1.50	.70	.19
☐ 35	Don Buse	.50	.23	.06
☐ 36	Mickey Johnson	.30	.14	.04
☐ 37	Mike Gale	.30	.14	.04
☐ 38	Moses Malone	4.00	1.80	.50
☐ 39	Gus Williams	.75	.35	.09
☐ 40	Dave Cowens	2.00	.90	.25
☐ 41	Bobby Wilkerson	.50	.23	.06
☐ 42	Wilbert Jones	.30	.14	.04
☐ 43	Charlie Scott	.50	.23	.06
☐ 44	John Drew	.50	.23	.06
☐ 45	Earl Monroe	1.25	.55	.16
☐ 46	John Shumate	.50	.23	.06
☐ 47	Earl Tatum	.30	.14	.04
☐ 48	Mitch Kupchak	.50	.23	.06
☐ 49	Ron Boone	.50	.23	.06
☐ 50	Maurice Lucas	.75	.35	.09
☐ 51	Louie Dampier	.50	.23	.06
☐ 52	Aaron James	.30	.14	.04

		NRMT-MT	EXC	G-VG

☐	53 John Mengelt	.30	.14	.04
☐	54 Garfield Heard	.50	.23	.06
☐	55 George Johnson	.30	.14	.04
☐	56 Junior Bridgeman	.30	.14	.04
☐	57 Elmore Smith	.30	.14	.04
☐	58 Rudy Tomjanovich	1.50	.70	.19
☐	59 Fred Brown	.50	.23	.06
☐	60 Rick Barry UER	2.00	.90	.25
	(reversed negative)			
☐	61 Dave Bing	1.25	.55	.16
☐	62 Anthony Roberts	.30	.14	.04
☐	63 Norm Nixon	2.00	.90	.25
☐	64 Leon Douglas	.30	.14	.04
☐	65 Henry Bibby	.50	.23	.06
☐	66 Lonnie Shelton	.30	.14	.04
☐	67 Checklist 1-132	2.00	.60	.20
☐	68 Tom Henderson	.30	.14	.04
☐	69 Dan Roundfield	.50	.23	.06
☐	70 Armond Hill	.50	.23	.06
☐	71 Larry Kenon	.50	.23	.06
☐	72 Billy Knight	.50	.23	.06
☐	73 Artis Gilmore	1.00	.45	.12
☐	74 Lionel Hollins	.50	.23	.06
☐	75 Bernard King	7.00	3.10	.85
☐	76 Brian Winters	.75	.35	.09
☐	77 Alvan Adams	.75	.35	.09
☐	78 Dennis Johnson	8.00	3.60	1.00
☐	79 Scott Wedman	.30	.14	.04
☐	80 Pete Maravich	7.00	3.10	.85
☐	81 Dan Issel	1.50	.70	.19
☐	82 M.L. Carr	.75	.35	.09
☐	83 Walt Frazier	1.50	.70	.19
☐	84 Dwight Jones	.30	.14	.04
☐	85 JoJo White	.75	.35	.09
☐	86 Robert Parish	5.00	2.20	.60
☐	87 Charlie Criss	.50	.23	.06
☐	88 Jim McMillian	.30	.14	.04
☐	89 Chuck Williams	.30	.14	.04
☐	90 George McGinnis	.75	.35	.09
☐	91 Billy Paultz	.50	.23	.06
☐	92 Bob Dandridge	.50	.23	.06
☐	93 Ricky Sobers	.30	.14	.04
☐	94 Paul Silas	.50	.23	.06
☐	95 Gail Goodrich	.75	.35	.09
☐	96 Tim Bassett	.30	.14	.04
☐	97 Ron Lee	.30	.14	.04
☐	98 Bob Gross	.50	.23	.06
☐	99 Sam Lacey	.30	.14	.04
☐	100 David Thompson	3.00	1.35	.35
	(College North Carolina, should be NC State)			
☐	101 John Gianelli	.30	.14	.04
☐	102 Norm Van Lier	.50	.23	.06
☐	103 Caldwell Jones	.50	.23	.06
☐	104 Eric Money	.30	.14	.04
☐	105 Jim Chones	.50	.23	.06
☐	106 John Lucas	1.50	.70	.19
☐	107 Spencer Haywood	.75	.35	.09
☐	108 Eddie Johnson	.30	.14	.04
☐	109 Sidney Wicks	.75	.35	.09
☐	110 Kareem Abdul-Jabbar	10.00	4.50	1.25
☐	111 Sonny Parker	.30	.14	.04
☐	112 Randy Smith	.30	.14	.04
☐	113 Kevin Grevey	.50	.23	.06
☐	114 Rich Kelley	.30	.14	.04
☐	115 Scott May	.50	.23	.06
☐	116 Lloyd Free	.75	.35	.09
☐	117 Jack Sikma	2.00	.90	.25
☐	118 Kevin Porter	.50	.23	.06
☐	119 Darnell Hillman	.50	.23	.06
☐	120 Paul Westphal	1.00	.45	.12
☐	121 Richard Washington	.30	.14	.04
☐	122 Dave Twardzik	.50	.23	.06
☐	123 Mike Bantom	.30	.14	.04
☐	124 Mike Newlin	.30	.14	.04
☐	125 Bob Lanier	1.50	.70	.19
☐	126 Marques Johnson	3.50	1.55	.45
☐	127 Foots Walker	.50	.23	.06
☐	128 Cedric Maxwell	1.25	.55	.16
☐	129 Ray Williams	.30	.14	.04
☐	130 Julius Erving	10.00	4.50	1.25
☐	131 Clifford Ray	.30	.14	.04
☐	132 Adrian Dantley	3.00	.90	.30

1979-80 Topps

The 1979-80 Topps basketball set contains 132 standard-size cards. Cards were issued in 12-card packs along with a stick of bubble gum. The player's name, team and position are at the bottom. The team name is wrapped around a basketball. Card backs are printed in red and black on gray card stock. All-Star selections are designated as AS1 for first team selections and AS2 for second team selections and are denoted on the front of the player's regular card. Notable Rookie Cards in this set include Alex English, Reggie Theus, and Mychal Thompson.

		NRMT-MT	EXC	G-VG
	COMPLETE SET (132)	70.00	32.00	8.75
	COMMON CARD (1-132)	.30	.14	.04
☐	1 George Gervin	6.00	2.70	.75
☐	2 Mitch Kupchak	.40	.18	.05
☐	3 Henry Bibby	.40	.18	.05
☐	4 Bob Gross	.40	.18	.05
☐	5 Dave Cowens	2.00	.90	.25
☐	6 Dennis Johnson	1.50	.70	.19
☐	7 Scott Wedman	.30	.14	.04
☐	8 Earl Monroe	1.25	.55	.16
☐	9 Mike Bantom	.30	.14	.04
☐	10 Kareem Abdul-Jabbar AS	10.00	4.50	1.25
☐	11 JoJo White	.60	.25	.07
☐	12 Spencer Haywood	.60	.25	.07
☐	13 Kevin Porter	.40	.18	.05
☐	14 Bernard King	1.50	.70	.19
☐	15 Mike Newlin	.30	.14	.04
☐	16 Sidney Wicks	.60	.25	.07
☐	17 Dan Issel	1.25	.55	.16
☐	18 Tom Henderson	.30	.14	.04
☐	19 Jim Chones	.40	.18	.05

☐ 20 Julius Erving	10.00	4.50	1.25
☐ 21 Brian Winters	.60	.25	.07
☐ 22 Billy Paultz	.40	.18	.05
☐ 23 Cedric Maxwell	.40	.18	.05
☐ 24 Eddie Johnson	.30	.14	.04
☐ 25 Artis Gilmore	.75	.35	.09
☐ 26 Maurice Lucas	.60	.25	.07
☐ 27 Gus Williams	.60	.25	.07
☐ 28 Sam Lacey	.30	.14	.04
☐ 29 Toby Knight	.30	.14	.04
☐ 30 Paul Westphal AS1	.75	.35	.09
☐ 31 Alex English	8.00	3.60	1.00
☐ 32 Gail Goodrich	.60	.25	.07
☐ 33 Caldwell Jones	.40	.18	.05
☐ 34 Kevin Grevey	.40	.18	.05
☐ 35 Jamaal Wilkes	.60	.25	.07
☐ 36 Sonny Parker	.30	.14	.04
☐ 37 John Gianelli	.30	.14	.04
☐ 38 John Long	.40	.18	.05
☐ 39 George Johnson	.30	.14	.04
☐ 40 Lloyd Free AS2	.60	.25	.07
☐ 41 Rudy Tomjanovich	1.25	.55	.16
☐ 42 Foots Walker	.40	.18	.05
☐ 43 Dan Roundfield	.40	.18	.05
☐ 44 Reggie Theus	3.00	1.35	.35
☐ 45 Bill Walton	3.00	1.35	.35
☐ 46 Fred Brown	.40	.18	.05
☐ 47 Darnell Hillman	.40	.18	.05
☐ 48 Ray Williams	.30	.14	.04
☐ 49 Larry Kenon	.40	.18	.05
☐ 50 David Thompson	2.00	.90	.25
☐ 51 Billy Knight	.40	.18	.05
☐ 52 Alvan Adams	.60	.25	.07
☐ 53 Phil Smith	.30	.14	.04
☐ 54 Adrian Dantley	1.25	.55	.16
☐ 55 John Williamson	.30	.14	.04
☐ 56 Campy Russell	.40	.18	.05
☐ 57 Armond Hill	.40	.18	.05
☐ 58 Bob Lanier	1.25	.55	.16
☐ 59 Mickey Johnson	.30	.14	.04
☐ 60 Pete Maravich	7.00	3.10	.85
☐ 61 Nick Weatherspoon	.30	.14	.04
☐ 62 Robert Reid	.60	.25	.07
☐ 63 Mychal Thompson	1.50	.70	.19
☐ 64 Doug Collins	1.00	.45	.12
☐ 65 Wes Unseld	1.25	.55	.16
☐ 66 Jack Sikma	.60	.25	.07
☐ 67 Bobby Wilkerson	.30	.14	.04
☐ 68 Bill Robinzine	.30	.14	.04
☐ 69 Joe Meriweather	.30	.14	.04
☐ 70 Marques Johnson AS1	.40	.18	.05
☐ 71 Ricky Sobers	.30	.14	.04
☐ 72 Clifford Ray	.30	.14	.04
☐ 73 Tim Bassett	.30	.14	.04
☐ 74 James Silas	.40	.18	.05
☐ 75 Bob McAdoo	.75	.35	.09
☐ 76 Austin Carr	.40	.18	.05
☐ 77 Don Ford	.30	.14	.04
☐ 78 Steve Hawes	.30	.14	.04
☐ 79 Ron Brewer	.30	.14	.04
☐ 80 Walter Davis	1.00	.45	.12
☐ 81 Calvin Murphy	.75	.35	.09
☐ 82 Tom Boswell	.30	.14	.04
☐ 83 Lonnie Shelton	.30	.14	.04
☐ 84 Terry Tyler	.30	.14	.04
☐ 85 Randy Smith	.30	.14	.04
☐ 86 Rich Kelley	.30	.14	.04
☐ 87 Otis Birdsong	.40	.18	.05
☐ 88 Marvin Webster	.30	.14	.04
☐ 89 Eric Money	.30	.14	.04
☐ 90 Elvin Hayes AS1	1.50	.70	.19

☐ 91 Junior Bridgeman	.30	.14	.04
☐ 92 Johnny Davis	.30	.14	.04
☐ 93 Robert Parish	3.00	1.35	.35
☐ 94 Eddie Jordan	.40	.18	.05
☐ 95 Leonard Robinson	.40	.18	.05
☐ 96 Rick Robey	.40	.18	.05
☐ 97 Norm Nixon	.60	.25	.07
☐ 98 Mark Olberding	.30	.14	.04
☐ 99 Wilbur Holland	.30	.14	.04
☐ 100 Moses Malone AS1	3.00	1.35	.35
☐ 101 Checklist 1-132	2.00	.60	.20
☐ 102 Tom Owens	.30	.14	.04
☐ 103 Phil Chenier	.40	.18	.05
☐ 104 John Johnson	.30	.14	.04
☐ 105 Darryl Dawkins	.75	.35	.09
☐ 106 Charlie Scott	.40	.18	.05
☐ 107 M.L. Carr	.60	.25	.07
☐ 108 Phil Ford	2.00	.90	.25
☐ 109 Swen Nater	.30	.14	.04
☐ 110 Nate Archibald	1.25	.55	.16
☐ 111 Aaron James	.30	.14	.04
☐ 112 Jim Cleamons	.30	.14	.04
☐ 113 James Edwards	.60	.25	.07
☐ 114 Don Buse	.40	.18	.05
☐ 115 Steve Mix	.30	.14	.04
☐ 116 Charles Johnson	.30	.14	.04
☐ 117 Elmore Smith	.30	.14	.04
☐ 118 John Drew	.30	.14	.04
☐ 119 Lou Hudson	.40	.18	.05
☐ 120 Rick Barry	2.00	.90	.25
☐ 121 Kent Benson	.30	.14	.04
☐ 122 Mike Gale	.30	.14	.04
☐ 123 Jan Van Breda Kolff	.30	.14	.04
☐ 124 Chris Ford	.40	.18	.05
☐ 125 George McGinnis	.60	.25	.07
☐ 126 Leon Douglas	.30	.14	.04
☐ 127 John Lucas	.60	.25	.07
☐ 128 Kermit Washington	.40	.18	.05
☐ 129 Lionel Hollins	.40	.18	.05
☐ 130 Bob Dandridge AS2	.40	.18	.05
☐ 131 James McElroy	.30	.14	.04
☐ 132 Bobby Jones	1.50	.70	.19

1980-81 Topps

The 1980-81 Topps basketball card set contains 264 different individual players (1 1/6" by 2 1/2") on 176 different panels of three (2 1/2" by 3 1/2"). This set was issued in packs of eight cards with 36 packs per box. The cards come with three individual players per standard card. A perforation line segments each card into three players. In all, there are 176 different complete cards, however, the same player will be on more than one card. The variations stem from the fact that the cards in this set were printed on two separate sheets. In the checklist below, the first 88 cards comprise a complete set of all 264 players. The second 88 cards (89-176) provide a slight rearrangement of players within the card, but still contain the same 264 players. The cards are numbered within each series of 88 by any ordering of the left-hand player's number when the card is viewed from the back. In the checklist below, SD refers to a "Slam Dunk" star card. The letters AS in the checklist refer to an All-Star selection pictured on the front of the checklist card. There are a number of Team Leader (TL) cards which depict the team's leader in assists, scoring or rebounds. Prices given below are for complete panels, as that is the typical way these cards are collected. Cards which have been separated into the three parts are relatively valueless. The key card in this set features Larry Bird, Julius Erving and Magic Johnson. It the Rookie Card for Bird and Magic. In addition to Bird and Magic, other noteworthy players making their first card appearance in this set include Bill Cartwright, Maurice Cheeks, Michael Cooper, Sidney Moncrief and Tree Rollins. Other lesser-known players making their first card appearance include James Bailey, Greg Ballard, Dudley Bradley, Mike Bratz, Joe Bryant, Kenny Carr, Wayne Cooper, David Greenwood, Phil Hubbard, Geoff Huston, Abdul Jeelani, Greg Kelser, Reggie King, Tom LaGarde, Mark Landsberger, Allen Leavell, Calvin Natt, Roger Phegley, Ben Poquette, Micheal Ray Richardson, Cliff Robinson, Purvis Short, Jerome Whitehead, and Freeman Williams.

	NRMT-MT	EXC	G-VG
COMPLETE SET (176)	525.00	240.00	65.00
COMMON PANEL (1-176)	.30	.14	.04

□ 1	3 Dan Roundfield AS 181 Julius Erving 258 Ron Brewer SD	5.00	2.20	.60
□ 2	7 Moses Malone AS 185 Steve Mix 92 Robert Parish TL	1.50	.70	.19
□ 3	12 Gus Williams AS 67 Geoff Huston 5 John Drew AS	.40	.18	.05
□ 4	24 Steve Hawes 32 Nate Archibald TL 248 Elvin Hayes	1.00	.45	.12
□ 5	29 Dan Roundfield 73 Dan Issel TL 152 Brian Winters	.60	.25	.07
□ 6	34 Larry Bird 174 Julius Erving 139 Magic Johnson	425.00	190.00	52.50
□ 7	36 Dave Cowens 186 Paul Westphal TL 142 Jamaal Wilkes	1.00	.45	.12
□ 8	38 Pete Maravich 264 Lloyd Free SD 194 Dennis Johnson	5.00	2.20	.60
□ 9	40 Rick Robey	.60	.25	.07
□ 10	47 Scott May 196 K.Washington TL 177 Henry Bibby	.30	.14	.04
□ 11	55 Don Ford 145 Quinn Buckner TL 138 Brad Holland	.30	.14	.04
□ 12	58 Campy Russell 247 Kevin Grevey 52 Dave Robisch TL	.30	.14	.04
□ 13	60 Foots Walker 113 Mick.Johnson TL 130 Bill Robinzine	.30	.14	.04
□ 14	61 Austin Carr 8 Kareem Abdul-Jabbar AS 200 Calvin Natt	3.00	1.35	.35
□ 15	63 Jim Cleamons 256 Robert Reid SD 2 Charlie Criss	.30	.14	.04
□ 16	69 Tom LaGarde 215 Swen Nater TL 213 James Silas	.30	.14	.04
□ 17	71 Jerome Whitehead 259 Artis Gilmore SD 184 Caldwell Jones	.60	.25	.07
□ 18	74 John Roche 99 Clifford Ray 235 Ben Poquette TL	.30	.14	.04
□ 19	75 Alex English 2 Marques Johnson AS 68 Jeff Judkins	1.50	.70	.19
□ 20	82 Terry Tyler TL 21 Armond Hill TL 171 M.R. Richardson	.30	.14	.04
□ 21	84 Kent Benson 212 John Shumate 229 Paul Westphal	.60	.25	.07
□ 22	86 Phil Hubbard 93 Robert Parish TL 126 Tom Burleson	1.50	.70	.19
□ 23	88 John Long 1 Julius Erving SD 49 Ricky Sobers	3.00	1.35	.35
□ 24	90 Eric Money 57 Dave Robisch 254 Rick Robey SD	.30	.14	.04
□ 25	95 Wayne Cooper 226 John Johnson TL 45 David Greenwood	.30	.14	.04
□ 26	97 Robert Parish 187 Leon.Robinson TL 46 Dwight Jones	2.50	1.10	.30
□ 27	98 Sonny Parker 197 Dave Twardzik TL 39 Cedric Maxwell	.30	.14	.04
□ 28	105 Rick Barry 122 Otis Birdsong TL 48 John Mengelt	1.00	.45	.12
□ 29	106 Allen Leavell 53 Foots Walker TL 223 Freeman Williams	.30	.14	.04
□ 30	108 Calvin Murphy 176 Maur.Cheeks TL 87 Greg Kelser	.60	.25	.07
□ 31	110 Robert Reid 243 Wes Unseld TL 50 Reggie Theus	.60	.25	.07
□ 32	111 Rudy Tomjanovich 13 Eddie Johnson AS 179 Doug Collins	.60	.25	.07

234 Ad.Dantley TL
26 Eddie Johnson

☐ 33 112 Mickey Johnson TL .30 | .14 | .04
28 Wayne Rollins
15 M.R.Richardson AS
☐ 34 115 Mike Bantom .40 | .18 | .05
6 Adrian Dantley AS
227 James Bailey
☐ 35 116 Dudley Bradley .30 | .14 | .04
155 Eddie Jordan TL
239 Allan Bristow
☐ 36 118 James Edwards .30 | .14 | .04
153 Mike Newlin TL
182 Lionel Hollins
☐ 37 119 Mickey Johnson .30 | .14 | .04
154 Geo.Johnson TL
193 Leonard Robinson
☐ 38 120 Billy Knight .60 | .25 | .07
16 Paul Westphal AS
59 Randy Smith
☐ 39 121 George McGinnis .40 | .18 | .05
83 Eric Money TL
65 Mike Bratz
☐ 40 124 Phil Ford TL .30 | .14 | .04
101 Phil Smith
224 Gus Williams TL
☐ 41 127 Phil Ford .30 | .14 | .04
19 John Drew TL
209 Larry Kenon
☐ 42 131 Scott Wedman .40 | .18 | .05
164 B.Cartwright TL
23 John Drew
☐ 43 132 K.Abdul-Jabbar TL 3.00 | 1.35 | .35
56 Mike Mitchell
81 Terry Tyler TL
☐ 44 135 K.Abdul-Jabbar 5.00 | 2.20 | .60
79 David Thompson
216 Brian Taylor TL
☐ 45 137 Michael Cooper 2.00 | .90 | .25
103 Moses Malone TL
148 George Johnson
☐ 46 140 Mark Landsberger 1.50 | .70 | .19
10 Bob Lanier AS
222 Bill Walton
☐ 47 141 Norm Nixon .30 | .14 | .04
123 Sam Lacey TL
54 Kenny Carr
☐ 48 143 Marq.Johnson TL 15.00 | 6.75 | 1.85
30 Larry Bird TL
232 Jack Sikma
☐ 49 146 Junior Bridgeman 15.00 | 6.75 | 1.85
31 Larry Bird TL
198 Ron Brewer
☐ 50 147 Quinn Buckner 3.00 | 1.35 | .35
133 K.Abdul-Jabbar TL
207 Mike Gale
☐ 51 149 Marques Johnson 3.00 | 1.35 | .35
262 Julius Erving SD
62 Abdul Jeelani
☐ 52 151 Sidney Moncrief 2.50 | 1.10 | .30
260 Lonnie Shelton SD
220 Paul Silas
☐ 53 156 George Johnson .40 | .18 | .05
9 Bill Cartwright TL
199 Bob Gross
☐ 54 158 Maurice Lucas .40 | .18 | .05
261 James Edwards SD
157 Eddie Jordan
☐ 55 159 Mike Newlin .30 | .14 | .04
134 Norm Nixon TL
180 Darryl Dawkins
☐ 56 160 Roger Phegley .30 | .14 | .04
206 James Silas TL

91 Terry Tyler UER
(First name spelled Jams)
☐ 57 161 Cliff Robinson .30 | .14 | .04
51 Mike Mitchell
80 Bobby Wilkerson
☐ 58 162 Jan V.Breda Kolff .40 | .18 | .05
204 George Gervin TL
117 Johnny Davis
☐ 59 165 M.R.Richardson TL .30 | .14 | .04
214 Lloyd Free TL
44 Artis Gilmore
☐ 60 166 Bill Cartwright 1.50 | .70 | .19
244 Kevin Porter TL
25 Armond Hill
☐ 61 168 Toby Knight .30 | .14 | .04
14 Lloyd Free AS
240 Adrian Dantley
☐ 62 169 Joe Meriweather .40 | .18 | .05
218 Lloyd Free
42 D.Greenwood TL
☐ 63 170 Earl Monroe .60 | .25 | .07
27 James McElroy
85 Leon Douglas
☐ 64 172 Marvin Webster .40 | .18 | .05
175 Caldwell Jones TL
129 Sam Lacey
☐ 65 173 Ray Williams .30 | .14 | .04
94 John Lucas TL
202 Dave Twardzik
☐ 66 178 Maurice Cheeks 12.00 | 5.50 | 1.50
18 Magic Johnson AS
237 Ron Boone
☐ 67 183 Bobby Jones .60 | .25 | .07
37 Chris Ford
66 Joe Hassett
☐ 68 189 Alvan Adams .60 | .25 | .07
163 B.Cartwright TL
76 Dan Issel
☐ 69 190 Don Buse .40 | .18 | .05
242 Elvin Hayes TL
35 M.L. Carr
☐ 70 191 Walter Davis .60 | .25 | .07
11 George Gervin AS
136 Jim Chones
☐ 71 192 Rich Kelley 1.00 | .45 | .12
102 Moses Malone TL
64 Winford Boynes
☐ 72 201 Tom Owens .30 | .14 | .04
225 Jack Sikma TL
100 Purvis Short
☐ 73 208 George Gervin 1.50 | .70 | .19
72 Dan Issel TL
249 Mitch Kupchak
☐ 74 217 Joe Bryant 1.50 | .70 | .19
263 Bobby Jones SD
107 Moses Malone
☐ 75 219 Swen Nater .40 | .18 | .05
17 Calvin Murphy AS
70 Rich.Washington
☐ 76 221 Brian Taylor .30 | .14 | .04
253 John Shumate SD
167 Larry Demic
☐ 77 228 Fred Brown .30 | .14 | .04
205 Larry Kenon TL
203 Kerm.Washington
☐ 78 230 John Johnson .60 | .25 | .07
4 Walter Davis AS
33 Nate Archibald
☐ 79 231 Lonnie Shelton .40 | .18 | .05
104 Allen Leavell TL
96 John Lucas

□ 80	233 Gus Williams............	.30	.14	.04
	20 Dan Roundfield TL			
	211 Kevin Restani			
□ 81	236 Allan Bristow TL......	.30	.14	.04
	210 Mark Olberding			
	255 James Bailey SD			
□ 82	238 Tom Boswell............	.60	.25	.07
	109 Billy Paultz			
	150 Bob Lanier			
□ 83	241 Ben Poquette...........	.60	.25	.07
	188 Paul Westphal TL			
	77 Charlie Scott			
□ 84	245 Greg Ballard............	.30	.14	.04
	43 Reggie Theus TL			
	252 John Williamson			
□ 85	246 Bob Dandridge........	.40	.18	.05
	41 Reggie Theus TL			
	128 Reggie King			
□ 86	250 Kevin Porter............	.30	.14	.04
	114 Johnny Davis TL			
	125 Otis Birdsong			
□ 87	251 Wes Unseld.............	.40	.18	.05
	195 Tom Owens TL			
	78 John Roche			
□ 88	257 Elvin Hayes SD........	.40	.18	.05
	144 Marq.Johnson TL			
	89 Bob McAdoo			
□ 89	3 Dan Roundfield	.40	.18	.05
	218 Lloyd Free			
	42 D.Greenwood TL			
□ 90	7 Moses Malone	1.00	.45	.12
	247 Kevin Grevey			
	52 Dave Robisch TL			
□ 91	12 Gus Williams..............	.30	.14	.04
	210 Mark Olberding			
	255 James Bailey SD			
□ 92	24 Steve Hawes.............	.30	.14	.04
	226 John Johnson TL			
	45 David Greenwood			
□ 93	29 Dan Roundfield	.30	.14	.04
	113 Mick.Johnson TL			
	130 Bill Robinzine			
□ 94	34 Larry Bird	50.00	22.00	6.25
	164 B.Cartwright TL			
	23 John Drew			
□ 95	36 Dave Cowens	1.00	.45	.12
	16 Paul Westphal AS			
	59 Randy Smith			
□ 96	38 Pete Maravich...........	4.00	1.80	.50
	187 Leon.Robinson TL			
	46 Dwight Jones			
□ 97	40 Rick Robey	.40	.18	.05
	37 Chris Ford			
	66 Joe Hassett			
□ 98	47 Scott May	15.00	6.75	1.85
	30 Larry Bird TL			
	232 Jack Sikma			
□ 99	55 Don Ford....................	.60	.25	.07
	144 Marq.Johnson TL			
	89 Bob McAdoo			
□ 100	58 Campy Russell...........	.40	.18	.05
	21 Armond Hill TL			
	171 M.R.Richardson			
□ 101	60 Foots Walker.............	.30	.14	.04
	122 Otis Birdsong TL			
	48 John Mengelt			
□ 102	61 Austin Carr.................	.30	.14	.04
	56 Mike Mitchell			
	81 Terry Tyler TL			
□ 103	63 Jim Cleamons	.30	.14	.04
	261 James Edwards SD			

	157 Eddie Jordan			
□ 104	69 Tom LaGarde	.60	.25	.07
	109 Billy Paultz			
	150 Bob Lanier			
□ 105	71 Jerome Whitehead....	.40	.18	.05
	17 Calvin Murphy AS			
	70 Rich.Washington			
□ 106	74 John Roche TL...........	.30	.14	.04
	28 Wayne Rollins			
	15 M.R.Richardson AS			
□ 107	75 Alex English	1.50	.70	.19
	102 Moses Malone TL			
	64 Winford Boynes			
□ 108	82 Terry Tyler TL	.30	.14	.04
	79 David Thompson			
	216 Brian Taylor TL			
□ 109	84 Kent Benson	.40	.18	.05
	259 Artis Gilmore SD			
	184 Caldwell Jones			
□ 110	86 Phil Hubbard.............	.30	.14	.04
	195 Tom Owens TL			
	78 John Roche			
□ 111	88 John Long.............	10.00	4.50	1.25
	18 Magic Johnson TL			
	237 Ron Boone			
□ 112	90 Eric Money................	.30	.14	.04
	215 Swen Nater TL			
	213 James Silas			
□ 113	95 Wayne Cooper	.30	.14	.04
	154 Geo.Johnson TL			
	193 Leon.Robinson			
□ 114	97 Robert Parish	2.50	1.10	.30
	103 Moses Malone TL			
	148 George Johnson			
□ 115	98 Sonny Parker	.40	.18	.05
	94 John Lucas TL			
	202 Dave Twardzik			
□ 116	105 Rick Barry	1.00	.45	.12
	123 Sam Lacey TL			
	54 Kenny Carr			
□ 117	106 Allen Leavell............	.30	.14	.04
	197 Dave Twardzik TL			
	39 Cedric Maxwell			
□ 118	108 Calvin Murphy........	.40	.18	.05
	51 Mike Mitchell TL			
	80 Bobby Wilkerson			
□ 119	110 Robert Reid............	.40	.18	.05
	153 Mike Newlin TL			
	182 Lionel Hollins			
□ 120	111 Rudy Tomjanovich	.60	.25	.07
	73 Dan Issel TL			
	152 Brian Winters			
□ 121	112 Mick.Johnson TL ..	.60	.25	.07
	264 Lloyd Free SD			
	194 Dennis Johnson			
□ 122	115 Mike Bantom...........	.40	.18	.05
	204 George Gervin TL			
	117 Johnny Davis			
□ 123	116 Dudley Bradley.......	.60	.25	.07
	186 Paul Westphal TL			
	142 Jamaal Wilkes			
□ 124	118 James Edwards...	1.00	.45	.12
	32 Nate Archibald TL			
	248 Elvin Hayes			
□ 125	119 Mickey Johnson....	.60	.25	.07
	72 Dan Issel TL			
	249 Mitch Kupchak			
□ 126	120 Billy Knight.............	.30	.14	.04
	104 Allen Leavell TL			
	96 John Lucas			
□ 127	121 George McGinnis	1.50	.70	.19

10 Bob Lanier AS
222 Bill Walton

□ 128	124 Phil Ford TL	.40	.18	.05
	234 Adr.Dantley TL			
	26 Eddie Johnson			
□ 129	127 Phil Ford	.40	.18	.05
	43 Reggie Theus TL			
	252 John Williamson			
□ 130	131 Scott Wedman	.30	.14	.04
	244 Kevin Porter TL			
	25 Armond Hill			
□ 131	132 K.Abdul-Jabbar TL	4.00	1.80	.50
	93 Robert Parish TL			
	126 Tom Burleson			
□ 132	135 K.Abdul-Jabbar	5.00	2.20	.60
	253 John Shumate SD			
	167 Larry Demic			
□ 133	137 Michael Cooper	1.00	.45	.12
	212 John Shumate			
	229 Paul Westphal			
□ 134	140 Mark Landsberger	.40	.18	.05
	214 Lloyd Free TL			
	44 Artis Gilmore			
□ 135	141 Norm Nixon	.40	.18	.05
	242 Elvin Hayes TL			
	35 M.L. Carr			
□ 136	143 Marq.Johnson TL..	.30	.14	.04
	57 Dave Robisch			
	254 Rick Robey SD			
□ 137	146 Junior Bridgeman	3.00	1.35	.35
	1 Julius Erving AS			
	49 Ricky Sobers			
□ 138	147 Quinn Buckner	.40	.18	.05
	2 Marques Johnson AS			
	68 Jeff Judkins			
□ 139	149 Marques Johnson	.30	.14	.04
	83 Eric Money TL			
	65 Mike Bratz			
□ 140	151 Sidney Moncrief..	4.00	1.80	.50
	133 K.Abdul-Jabbar TL			
	207 Mike Gale			
□ 141	156 George Johnson	.30	.14	.04
	175 Caldw.Jones TL			
	129 Sam Lacey			
□ 142	158 Maurice Lucas	3.00	1.35	.35
	262 Julius Erving SD			
	62 Abdul Jeelani			
□ 143	159 Mike Newlin	.40	.18	.05
	243 Wes Unseld TL			
	50 Reggie Theus			
□ 144	160 Roger Phegley	.30	.14	.04
	145 Quinn Buckner TL			
	138 Brad Holland			
□ 145	161 Cliff Robinson	.30	.14	.04
	114 Johnny Davis TL			
	125 Otis Birdsong			
□ 146	162 Jan V.Breda Kolff	40.00	18.00	5.00
	174 Julius Erving TL			
	139 Magic Johnson			
□ 147	165 M.R.Richardson TL	1.00	.45	.12
	185 Steve Mix			
	92 Robert Parish TL			
□ 148	166 Bill Cartwright...	1.00	.45	.12
	13 Eddie Johnson AS			
	179 Doug Collins			
□ 149	168 Toby Knight	.60	.25	.07
	188 Paul Westphal TL			
	77 Charlie Scott			
□ 150	169 Joe Meriweather ...	.30	.14	.04
	196 K.Washington TL			
	177 Henry Bibby			
□ 151	170 Earl Monroe	.30	.14	.04
	206 James Silas TL			
	91 Terry Tyler			
□ 152	172 Marvin Webster	.40	.18	.05
	155 Eddie Jordan TL			
	239 Allan Bristow			
□ 153	173 Ray Williams	.30	.14	.04
	225 Jack Sikma TL			
	100 Purvis Short			
□ 154	178 Maurice Cheeks	4.00	1.80	.50
	11 George Gervin AS			
	136 Jim Chones			
□ 155	183 Bobby Jones	.40	.18	.05
	99 Clifford Ray			
	235 Ben Poquette TL			
□ 156	189 Alvan Adams	.40	.18	.05
	14 Lloyd Free AS			
	240 Adrian Dantley			
□ 157	190 Don Buse	.40	.18	.05
	6 Adrian Dantley AS			
	227 James Bailey			
□ 158	191 Walter Davis	.40	.18	.05
	9 Bill Cartwright AS			
	199 Bob Gross			
□ 159	192 Rich Kelley	1.50	.70	.19
	263 Bobby Jones SD			
	107 Moses Malone			
□ 160	201 Tom Owens	.40	.18	.05
	134 Norm Nixon TL			
	180 Darryl Dawkins			
□ 161	202 George Gervin	1.50	.70	.19
	53 Foots Walker TL			
	223 Freeman Williams			
□ 162	217 Joe Bryant	3.00	1.35	.35
	8 K.Abdul-Jabbar AS			
	200 Calvin Natt			
□ 163	219 Swen Nater	.30	.14	.04
	101 Phil Smith			
	224 Gus Williams TL			
□ 164	221 Brian Taylor	.30	.14	.04
	256 Robert Reid SD			
	22 Charlie Criss			
□ 165	228 Fred Brown	15.00	6.75	1.85
	31 Larry Bird TL			
	198 Ron Brewer			
□ 166	230 John Johnson	.60	.25	.07
	163 B.Cartwright TL			
	76 Dan Issel			
□ 167	231 Lonnie Shelton	.30	.14	.04
	205 Larry Kenon TL			
	203 Kermit Washington			
□ 168	233 Gus Williams	.40	.18	.05
	41 Reggie Theus TL			
	128 Reggie King			
□ 169	236 Allan Bristow TL...	.30	.14	.04
	260 Lonnie Shelton SD			
	220 Paul Silas			
□ 170	238 Tom Boswell	.30	.14	.04
	27 James McElroy			
	85 Leon Douglas			
□ 171	241 Ben Poquette	.60	.25	.07
	176 Maurice Cheeks TL			
	87 Greg Kelser			
□ 172	245 Greg Ballard	.60	.25	.07
	4 Walter Davis AS			
	33 Nate Archibald			
□ 173	246 Bob Dandridge	.30	.14	.04
	19 John Drew TL			
	209 Larry Kenon			
□ 174	250 Kevin Porter	.30	.14	.04
	20 Dan Roundfield TL			

211 Kevin Restani
☐ 175 251 Wes Unseld........... .60 .25 .07
67 Geoff Huston
5 John Drew AS
☐ 176 257 Elvin Hayes SD.... 5.00 2.20 .60
181 Julius Erving
258 Ron Brewer SD

1981-82 Topps

The 1981-82 Topps basketball card set contains a total of 198 standard-size cards that were issued in 13-card, 30-cent wax packs with 36 packs per box. These cards are numbered depending upon the regional distribution used in the issue. A 66-card national set was issued to all parts of the country, however, subsets of 44 cards each were issued in the East, Midwest and West. The national set is easier to acquire than any of the regional issues. Card numbers over 66 are prefaced on the card by the region in which they were distributed, e.g., East 96. The cards feature the Topps logo in the frame line and a quarter-round sun-burst in the lower left-hand corner which lists the name, position and team of the player depicted. Cards 44-66 are Team Leader (TL) cards picturing each team's statistical leaders. The back, printed in orange and brown on gray stock, features standard Topps biographical data and career statistics. There are a number of Super Action (SA) cards in the set. Rookie Cards include Joe Barry Carroll, Mike Dunleavy, Mike Gminski, Darrell Griffith, Ernie Grunfeld, Vinnie Johnson, Bill Laimbeer, Rick Mahorn, Kevin McHale, Jim Paxson and Larry Smith. The card numbering sequence is alphabetical within team within each series. This was Topps' last basketball card issue until 1992.

	NRMT-MT	EXC	G-VG
COMPLETE SET (198)	75.00	34.00	9.50
COMMON CARD (1-66)	.10	.05	.01
COMMON CARD (E67-E110)	.15	.07	.02
COMMON CARD (MW67-MW110)	.15	.07	.02
COMMON CARD (W67-W110)...	.15	.07	.02

☐	1 John Drew	.20	.09	.03
☐	2 Dan Roundfield	.20	.09	.03
☐	3 Nate Archibald	.60	.25	.07
☐	4 Larry Bird......................	25.00	11.00	3.10
☐	5 Cedric Maxwell	.20	.09	.03
☐	6 Robert Parish...................	1.50	.70	.19
☐	7 Artis Gilmore...................	.60	.25	.07
☐	8 Ricky Sobers....................	.10	.05	.01
☐	9 Mike Mitchell	.20	.09	.03
☐	10 Tom LaGarde	.10	.05	.01
☐	11 Dan Issel	.75	.35	.09
☐	12 David Thompson	.75	.35	.09
☐	13 Lloyd Free	.25	.11	.03
☐	14 Moses Malone	1.50	.70	.19
☐	15 Calvin Murphy	.25	.11	.03
☐	16 Johnny Davis	.10	.05	.01
☐	17 Otis Birdsong	.25	.11	.03
☐	18 Phil Ford	.20	.09	.03
☐	19 Scott Wedman	.10	.05	.01
☐	20 Kareem Abdul-Jabbar ..	4.00	1.80	.50
☐	21 Magic Johnson	16.00	7.25	2.00
☐	22 Norm Nixon	.25	.11	.03
☐	23 Jamaal Wilkes	.25	.11	.03
☐	24 Marques Johnson	.25	.11	.03
☐	25 Bob Lanier	.75	.35	.09
☐	26 Bill Cartwright	.50	.23	.06
☐	27 Michael Ray Richardson	.20	.09	.03
☐	28 Ray Williams	.20	.09	.03
☐	29 Darryl Dawkins	.25	.11	.03
☐	30 Julius Erving	4.00	1.80	.50
☐	31 Lionel Hollins	.10	.05	.01
☐	32 Bobby Jones	.25	.11	.03
☐	33 Walter Davis	.50	.23	.06
☐	34 Dennis Johnson	.50	.23	.06
☐	35 Leonard Robinson	.25	.11	.03
☐	36 Mychal Thompson	.25	.11	.03
☐	37 George Gervin	1.50	.70	.19
☐	38 Swen Nater	.10	.05	.01
☐	39 Jack Sikma	.25	.11	.03
☐	40 Adrian Dantley	.60	.25	.07
☐	41 Darrell Griffith	1.00	.45	.12
☐	42 Elvin Hayes	.75	.35	.09
☐	43 Fred Brown	.25	.11	.03
☐	44 Atlanta Hawks TL	.15	.07	.02
	John Drew			
	Dan Roundfield			
	Eddie Johnson			
☐	45 Boston Celtics TL..........	2.00	.90	.25
	Larry Bird			
	Larry Bird			
	Nate Archibald			
☐	46 Chicago Bulls TL............	.25	.11	.03
	Reggie Theus			
	Artis Gilmore			
	Reggie Theus			
☐	47 Cleveland Cavs TL..........	.15	.07	.02
	Mike Mitchell			
	Kenny Carr			
	Mike Bratz			
☐	48 Dallas Mavericks TL........	.15	.07	.02
	Jim Spanarkel			
	Tom LaGarde			
	Brad Davis			
☐	49 Denver Nuggets TL..........	.25	.11	.03
	David Thompson			
	Dan Issel			
	Kenny Higgs			
☐	50 Detroit Pistons TL..........	.15	.07	.02
	John Long			
	Phil Hubbard			
	Ron Lee			
☐	51 Golden State TL	.25	.11	.03
	Lloyd Free			
	Larry Smith			
	John Lucas			

☐ 52 Houston Rockets TL	.40	.18	.05
Moses Malone			
Moses Malone			
Allen Leavell			
☐ 53 Indiana Pacers TL	.25	.11	.03
Billy Knight			
James Edwards			
Johnny Davis			
☐ 54 Kansas City Kings TL	.15	.07	.02
Otis Birdsong			
Reggie King			
Phil Ford			
☐ 55 Los Angeles Lakers TL	1.00	.45	.12
Kareem Abdul-Jabbar			
Kareem Abdul-Jabbar			
Norm Nixon			
☐ 56 Milwaukee Bucks TL	.25	.11	.03
Marques Johnson			
Mickey Johnson			
Quinn Buckner			
☐ 57 New Jersey Nets TL	.15	.07	.02
Mike Newlin			
Maurice Lucas			
Mike Newlin			
☐ 58 New York Knicks TL	.25	.11	.03
Bill Cartwright			
Bill Cartwright			
M.R. Richardson			
☐ 59 Philadelphia 76ers TL ..	1.25	.55	.16
Julius Erving			
Caldwell Jones			
Maurice Cheeks			
☐ 60 Phoenix Suns TL	.25	.11	.03
Truck Robinson			
Truck Robinson			
Alvan Adams			
☐ 61 Portland Blazers TL	.15	.07	.02
Jim Paxson			
Mychal Thompson			
Kermit Washington			
Kelvin Ransey			
☐ 62 San Antonio Spurs TL	.25	.11	.03
George Gervin			
Dave Corzine			
Johnny Moore			
☐ 63 San Diego Clippers TL	.15	.07	.02
Freeman Williams			
Swen Nater			
Brian Taylor			
☐ 64 Seattle Sonics TL	.25	.11	.03
Jack Sikma			
Jack Sikma			
Vinnie Johnson			
☐ 65 Utah Jazz TL	.25	.11	.03
Adrian Dantley			
Ben Poquette			
Allan Bristow			
☐ 66 Washington Bullets TL	.25	.11	.03
Elvin Hayes			
Elvin Hayes			
Kevin Porter			
☐ E67 Charlie Criss	.25	.11	.03
☐ E68 Eddie Johnson	.15	.07	.02
☐ E69 Wes Matthews	.15	.07	.02
☐ E70 Tom McMillen	.40	.18	.05
☐ E71 Tree Rollins	.40	.18	.05
☐ E72 M.L. Carr	.25	.11	.03
☐ E73 Chris Ford	.25	.11	.03
☐ E74 Gerald Henderson	.40	.18	.05
☐ E75 Kevin McHale	22.00	10.00	2.70
☐ E76 Rick Robey	.25	.11	.03
☐ E77 Darwin Cook	.15	.07	.02
☐ E78 Mike Gminski	.75	.35	.09
☐ E79 Maurice Lucas	.25	.11	.03
☐ E80 Mike Newlin	.25	.11	.03
☐ E81 Mike O'Koren	.25	.11	.03
☐ E82 Steve Hawes	.15	.07	.02
☐ E83 Foots Walker	.25	.11	.03
☐ E84 Campy Russell	.25	.11	.03
☐ E85 DeWayne Scales	.15	.07	.02
☐ E86 Randy Smith	.25	.11	.03
☐ E87 Marvin Webster	.25	.11	.03
☐ E88 Sly Williams	.15	.07	.02
☐ E89 Mike Woodson	.25	.11	.03
☐ E90 Maurice Cheeks	1.50	.70	.19
☐ E91 Caldwell Jones	.25	.11	.03
☐ E92 Steve Mix	.25	.11	.03
☐ E93A Checklist 1-110 ERR	2.00	.60	.20
(WEST above card number)			
☐ E93B Checklist 1-110 COR	1.00	.30	.10
☐ E94 Greg Ballard	.15	.07	.02
☐ E95 Don Collins	.15	.07	.02
☐ E96 Kevin Grevey	.25	.11	.03
☐ E97 Mitch Kupchak	.25	.11	.03
☐ E98 Rick Mahorn	.75	.35	.09
☐ E99 Kevin Porter	.25	.11	.03
☐ E100 Nate Archibald	.25	.11	.03
☐ E101 Larry Bird SA	12.00	5.50	1.50
☐ E102 Bill Cartwright SA	.15	.07	.02
☐ E103 Darryl Dawkins SA	.25	.11	.03
☐ E104 Julius Erving SA	2.50	1.10	.30
☐ E105 Kevin Porter SA	.25	.11	.03
☐ E106 Bobby Jones SA	.25	.11	.03
☐ E107 Cedric Maxwell SA	.25	.11	.03
☐ E108 Robert Parish SA	1.00	.45	.12
☐ E109 M.R.Richardson SA	.25	.11	.03
☐ E110 Dan Roundfield SA	.25	.11	.03
☐ W67 T.R. Dunn	.15	.07	.02
☐ W68 Alex English	1.50	.70	.19
☐ W69 Billy McKinney	.25	.11	.03
☐ W70 Dave Robisch	.25	.11	.03
☐ W71 Joe Barry Carroll	.40	.18	.05
☐ W72 Bernard King	1.00	.45	.12
☐ W73 Sonny Parker	.15	.07	.02
☐ W74 Purvis Short	.25	.11	.03
☐ W75 Larry Smith	.40	.18	.05
☐ W76 Jim Chones	.25	.11	.03
☐ W77 Michael Cooper	.75	.35	.09
☐ W78 Mark Landsberger	.15	.07	.02
☐ W79 Alvan Adams	.25	.11	.03
☐ W80 Jeff Cook	.15	.07	.02
☐ W81 Rich Kelley	.15	.07	.02
☐ W82 Kyle Macy	.40	.18	.05
☐ W83 Billy Ray Bates	.40	.18	.05
☐ W84 Bob Gross	.25	.11	.03
☐ W85 Calvin Natt	.25	.11	.03
☐ W86 Lonnie Shelton	.25	.11	.03
☐ W87 Jim Paxson	.75	.35	.09
☐ W88 Kelvin Ransey	.15	.07	.02
☐ W89 Kermit Washington	.25	.11	.03
☐ W90 Henry Bibby	.25	.11	.03
☐ W91 Michael Brooks	.15	.07	.02
☐ W92 Joe Bryant	.15	.07	.02
☐ W93 Phil Smith	.15	.07	.02
☐ W94 Brian Taylor	.15	.07	.02
☐ W95 Freeman Williams	.25	.11	.03
☐ W96 James Bailey	.15	.07	.02
☐ W97 Checklist 1-110	1.00	.30	.10
☐ W98 John Johnson	.15	.07	.02
☐ W99 Vinnie Johnson	1.50	.70	.19
☐ W100 Wally Walker	.25	.11	.03
☐ W101 Paul Westphal	.25	.11	.03

☐ W102	Allan Bristow	.25	.11	.03
☐ W103	Wayne Cooper	.15	.07	.02
☐ W104	Carl Nicks	.15	.07	.02
☐ W105	Ben Poquette	.15	.07	.02
☐ W106	Kareem Abdul-Jabbar SA	2.50	1.10	.30
☐ W107	Dan Issel SA	.50	.23	.06
☐ W108	Dennis Johnson SA	.25	.11	.03
☐ W109	Magic Johnson SA	8.00	3.60	1.00
☐ W110	Jack Sikma SA	.25	.11	.03
☐ MW67	David Greenwood	.25	.11	.03
☐ MW68	Dwight Jones	.15	.07	.02
☐ MW69	Reggie Theus	.25	.11	.03
☐ MW70	Bobby Wilkerson	.15	.07	.02
☐ MW71	Mike Bratz	.15	.07	.02
☐ MW72	Kenny Carr	.15	.07	.02
☐ MW73	Geoff Huston	.15	.07	.02
☐ MW74	Bill Laimbeer	3.00	1.35	.35
☐ MW75	Roger Phegley	.15	.07	.02
☐ MW76	Checklist 1-110	1.00	.30	.10
☐ MW77	Abdul Jeelani	.15	.07	.02
☐ MW78	Bill Robinzine	.15	.07	.02
☐ MW79	Jim Spanarkel	.15	.07	.02
☐ MW80	Kent Benson	.25	.11	.03
☐ MW81	Keith Herron	.15	.07	.02
☐ MW82	Phil Hubbard	.15	.07	.02
☐ MW83	John Long	.15	.07	.02
☐ MW84	Terry Tyler	.15	.07	.02
☐ MW85	Mike Dunleavy	1.00	.45	.12
☐ MW86	Tom Henderson	.15	.07	.02
☐ MW87	Billy Paultz	.25	.11	.03
☐ MW88	Robert Reid	.15	.07	.02
☐ MW89	Mike Bantom	.15	.07	.02
☐ MW90	James Edwards	.25	.11	.03
☐ MW91	Billy Knight	.25	.11	.03
☐ MW92	George McGinnis	.25	.11	.03
☐ MW93	Louis Orr	.15	.07	.02
☐ MW94	Ernie Grunfeld	.40	.18	.05
☐ MW95	Reggie King	.15	.07	.02
☐ MW96	Sam Lacey	.15	.07	.02
☐ MW97	Junior Bridgeman	.25	.11	.03
☐ MW98	Mickey Johnson	.25	.11	.03
☐ MW99	Sidney Moncrief	.75	.35	.09
☐ MW100	Brian Winters	.25	.11	.03
☐ MW101	Dave Corzine	.15	.07	.02
☐ MW102	Paul Griffin	.15	.07	.02
☐ MW103	Johnny Moore	.25	.11	.03
☐ MW104	Mark Olberding	.15	.07	.02
☐ MW105	James Silas	.25	.11	.03
☐ MW106	George Gervin SA	.75	.35	.09
☐ MW107	Artis Gilmore SA	.25	.11	.03
☐ MW108	Marques Johnson SA	.25	.11	.03
☐ MW109	Bob Lanier SA	.50	.23	.06
☐ MW110	Moses Malone SA	1.00	.45	.12

1992-93 Topps

The complete 1992-93 Topps basketball set consists of 396 standard-size cards, issued in two 198-card series. Cards were issued in 15-card plastic wrap packs (suggested retail 79 cents, 36 packs per box), 18-card mini-jumbo packs, 45-card retail packs and 41-card magazine jumbo packs. In addition, factory sets were also released. On a white card face, the fronts display color action player photos framed by two-color border stripes. The player's name and team name appear in two different colored bars across the bottom of the picture. In addition to a color close-up photo, the horizontal backs have biography on a light blue panel as well as statistics and brief player profile on a yellow panel. Most Rookie Cards have the a gold-foil "92 Draft Pix" emblem on their card fronts. Topical subsets included are Highlight (2-4), All-Star (100-126), 50 Point Club (199-215), and 20 Assist Club (216-224). Rookie Cards of note include Tom Gugliotta, Robert Horry, Christian Laettner, Alonzo Mourning, Shaquille O'Neal, Latrell Sprewell and Clarence Weatherspoon.

	MINT	NRMT	EXC
COMPLETE SET (396)	12.00	5.50	1.50
COMPLETE FACTORY SET (408)	15.00	6.75	1.85
COMPLETE SERIES 1 (198)	4.00	1.80	.50
COMPLETE SERIES 2 (198)	8.00	3.60	1.00
COMMON CARD (1-396)	.05	.02	.01

☐ 1	Larry Bird	.60	.25	.07
☐ 2	Magic Johnson HL	.25	.11	.03
	Earvin's Magical Moment 2/9/92			
☐ 3	Michael Jordan HL	1.00	.45	.12
	Michael Lights It Up 6/3/92			
☐ 4	David Robinson HL	.15	.07	.02
	Admiral Ranks High In Five 4/19/92			
☐ 5	Johnny Newman	.05	.02	.01
☐ 6	Mike Iuzzolino	.05	.02	.01
☐ 7	Ken Norman	.05	.02	.01
☐ 8	Chris Jackson	.08	.04	.01
☐ 9	Duane Ferrell	.05	.02	.01
☐ 10	Sean Elliott	.08	.04	.01
☐ 11	Bernard King	.08	.04	.01
☐ 12	Armon Gilliam	.05	.02	.01
☐ 13	Reggie Williams	.05	.02	.01
☐ 14	Steve Kerr	.05	.02	.01
☐ 15	Anthony Bowie	.05	.02	.01
☐ 16	Alton Lister	.05	.02	.01
☐ 17	Dee Brown	.05	.02	.01
☐ 18	Tom Chambers	.05	.02	.01
☐ 19	Otis Thorpe	.08	.04	.01
☐ 20	Karl Malone	.15	.07	.02
☐ 21	Kenny Gattison	.05	.02	.01
☐ 22	Lionel Simmons UER	.05	.02	.01
	(Misspelled Lionell on card front)			
☐ 23	Vern Fleming	.05	.02	.01
☐ 24	John Paxson	.08	.04	.01
☐ 25	Mitch Richmond	.15	.07	.02
☐ 26	Danny Schayes	.05	.02	.01
☐ 27	Derrick McKey	.05	.02	.01

☐	28	Mark Randall	.05	.02	.01
☐	29	Bill Laimbeer	.05	.02	.01
☐	30	Chris Morris	.05	.02	.01
☐	31	Alec Kessler	.05	.02	.01
☐	32	Vlade Divac	.08	.04	.01
☐	33	Rick Fox	.05	.02	.01
☐	34	Charles Shackleford	.05	.02	.01
☐	35	Dominique Wilkins	.08	.04	.01
☐	36	Sleepy Floyd	.05	.02	.01
☐	37	Doug West	.05	.02	.01
☐	38	Pete Chilcutt	.05	.02	.01
☐	39	Orlando Woolridge	.05	.02	.01
☐	40	Eric Leckner	.05	.02	.01
☐	41	Joe Kleine	.05	.02	.01
☐	42	Scott Skiles	.05	.02	.01
☐	43	Jerrod Mustaf	.05	.02	.01
☐	44	John Starks	.08	.04	.01
☐	45	Sedale Threatt	.05	.02	.01
☐	46	Doug Smith	.05	.02	.01
☐	47	Byron Scott	.08	.04	.01
☐	48	Willie Anderson	.05	.02	.01
☐	49	David Benoit	.05	.02	.01
☐	50	Scott Hastings	.05	.02	.01
☐	51	Terry Porter	.05	.02	.01
☐	52	Sidney Green	.05	.02	.01
☐	53	Danny Young	.05	.02	.01
☐	54	Magic Johnson	.50	.23	.06
☐	55	Brian Williams	.05	.02	.01
☐	56	Randy Wittman	.05	.02	.01
☐	57	Kevin McHale	.08	.04	.01
☐	58	Dana Barros	.05	.02	.01
☐	59	Thurl Bailey	.05	.02	.01
☐	60	Kevin Duckworth	.05	.02	.01
☐	61	John Williams	.05	.02	.01
☐	62	Willie Burton	.05	.02	.01
☐	63	Spud Webb	.08	.04	.01
☐	64	Detlef Schrempf	.08	.04	.01
☐	65	Sherman Douglas	.05	.02	.01
☐	66	Patrick Ewing	.15	.07	.02
☐	67	Michael Adams	.05	.02	.01
☐	68	Vernon Maxwell	.05	.02	.01
☐	69	Terrell Brandon	.08	.04	.01
☐	70	Terry Catledge	.05	.02	.01
☐	71	Mark Eaton	.05	.02	.01
☐	72	Tony Smith	.05	.02	.01
☐	73	B.J. Armstrong	.05	.02	.01
☐	74	Moses Malone	.10	.05	.01
☐	75	Anthony Bonner	.05	.02	.01
☐	76	George McCloud	.05	.02	.01
☐	77	Glen Rice	.08	.04	.01
☐	78	Jon Koncak	.05	.02	.01
☐	79	Michael Cage	.05	.02	.01
☐	80	Ron Harper	.05	.02	.01
☐	81	Tom Tolbert	.05	.02	.01
☐	82	Brad Sellers	.05	.02	.01
☐	83	Winston Garland	.05	.02	.01
☐	84	Negele Knight	.05	.02	.01
☐	85	Ricky Pierce	.05	.02	.01
☐	86	Mark Aguirre	.08	.04	.01
☐	87	Ron Anderson	.05	.02	.01
☐	88	Loy Vaught	.05	.02	.01
☐	89	Luc Longley	.05	.02	.01
☐	90	Jerry Reynolds	.05	.02	.01
☐	91	Terry Cummings	.05	.02	.01
☐	92	Rony Seikaly	.05	.02	.01
☐	93	Derek Harper	.05	.02	.01
☐	94	Clifford Robinson	.08	.04	.01
☐	95	Kenny Anderson	.08	.04	.01
☐	96	Chris Gatling	.05	.02	.01
☐	97	Stacey Augmon	.08	.04	.01
☐	98	Chris Corchiani	.05	.02	.01
☐	99	Pervis Ellison	.05	.02	.01
☐	100	Larry Bird AS	.30	.14	.04
☐	101	John Stockton AS UER	.08	.04	.01
		(Listed as Center			
		on card back)			
☐	102	Clyde Drexler AS	.08	.04	.01
☐	103	Scottie Pippen AS	.25	.11	.03
☐	104	Reggie Lewis AS	.05	.02	.01
☐	105	Hakeem Olajuwon AS	.20	.09	.03
☐	106	David Robinson AS	.15	.07	.02
☐	107	Charles Barkley AS	.15	.07	.02
☐	108	James Worthy AS	.08	.04	.01
☐	109	Kevin Willis AS	.05	.02	.01
☐	110	Dikembe Mutombo AS	.08	.04	.01
☐	111	Joe Dumars AS	.08	.04	.01
☐	112	Jeff Hornacek AS UER	.05	.02	.01
		(5 or 7 shots should			
		be 5 of 7 shots)			
☐	113	Mark Price AS	.05	.02	.01
☐	114	Michael Adams AS	.05	.02	.01
☐	115	Michael Jordan AS	1.00	.45	.12
☐	116	Brad Daugherty AS	.05	.02	.01
☐	117	Dennis Rodman AS	.30	.14	.04
☐	118	Isiah Thomas AS	.08	.04	.01
☐	119	Tim Hardaway AS	.08	.04	.01
☐	120	Chris Mullin AS	.05	.02	.01
☐	121	Patrick Ewing AS	.08	.04	.01
☐	122	Dan Majerle AS	.05	.02	.01
☐	123	Karl Malone AS	.08	.04	.01
☐	124	Otis Thorpe AS	.05	.02	.01
☐	125	Dominique Wilkins AS	.08	.04	.01
☐	126	Magic Johnson AS	.25	.11	.03
☐	127	Charles Oakley	.05	.02	.01
☐	128	Robert Pack	.05	.02	.01
☐	129	Billy Owens	.05	.02	.01
☐	130	Jeff Malone	.05	.02	.01
☐	131	Danny Ferry	.05	.02	.01
☐	132	Sam Bowie	.05	.02	.01
☐	133	Avery Johnson	.05	.02	.01
☐	134	Jayson Williams	.05	.02	.01
☐	135	Fred Roberts	.05	.02	.01
☐	136	Greg Sutton	.05	.02	.01
☐	137	Dennis Rodman	.60	.25	.07
☐	138	John Williams	.05	.02	.01
☐	139	Greg Dreiling	.05	.02	.01
☐	140	Rik Smits	.08	.04	.01
☐	141	Michael Jordan	2.00	.90	.25
☐	142	Nick Anderson	.08	.04	.01
☐	143	Jerome Kersey	.05	.02	.01
☐	144	Fat Lever	.05	.02	.01
☐	145	Tyrone Corbin	.05	.02	.01
☐	146	Robert Parish	.08	.04	.01
☐	147	Steve Smith	.08	.04	.01
☐	148	Chris Dudley	.05	.02	.01
☐	149	Antoine Carr	.05	.02	.01
☐	150	Elden Campbell	.08	.04	.01
☐	151	Randy White	.05	.02	.01
☐	152	Felton Spencer	.05	.02	.01
☐	153	Cedric Ceballos	.08	.04	.01
☐	154	Mark Macon	.05	.02	.01
☐	155	Jack Haley	.05	.02	.01
☐	156	Bimbo Coles	.05	.02	.01
☐	157	A.J. English	.05	.02	.01
☐	158	Kendall Gill	.05	.02	.01
☐	159	A.C. Green	.08	.04	.01
☐	160	Mark West	.05	.02	.01
☐	161	Benoit Benjamin	.05	.02	.01
☐	162	Tyrone Hill	.05	.02	.01
☐	163	Larry Nance	.05	.02	.01
☐	164	Gary Grant	.05	.02	.01
☐	165	Bill Cartwright	.05	.02	.01

☐	166	Greg Anthony	.05	.02	.01
☐	167	Jim Les	.05	.02	.01
☐	168	Johnny Dawkins	.05	.02	.01
☐	169	Alvin Robertson	.05	.02	.01
☐	170	Kenny Smith	.05	.02	.01
☐	171	Gerald Glass	.05	.02	.01
☐	172	Harvey Grant	.05	.02	.01
☐	173	Paul Graham	.05	.02	.01
☐	174	Sam Perkins	.05	.02	.01
☐	175	Manute Bol	.05	.02	.01
☐	176	Muggsy Bogues	.08	.04	.01
☐	177	Mike Brown	.05	.02	.01
☐	178	Donald Hodge	.05	.02	.01
☐	179	Dave Jamerson	.05	.02	.01
☐	180	Mookie Blaylock	.08	.04	.01
☐	181	Randy Brown	.05	.02	.01
☐	182	Todd Lichti	.05	.02	.01
☐	183	Kevin Gamble	.05	.02	.01
☐	184	Gary Payton	.30	.14	.04
☐	185	Brian Shaw	.05	.02	.01
☐	186	Grant Long	.05	.02	.01
☐	187	Frank Brickowski	.05	.02	.01
☐	188	Tim Hardaway	.08	.04	.01
☐	189	Danny Manning	.08	.04	.01
☐	190	Kevin Johnson	.08	.04	.01
☐	191	Craig Ehlo	.05	.02	.01
☐	192	Dennis Scott	.08	.04	.01
☐	193	Reggie Miller	.20	.09	.03
☐	194	Darrell Walker	.05	.02	.01
☐	195	Anthony Mason	.08	.04	.01
☐	196	Buck Williams	.08	.04	.01
☐	197	Checklist 1-99	.05	.02	.01
☐	198	Checklist 100-198	.05	.02	.01
☐	199	Karl Malone 50P	.08	.04	.01
☐	200	Dominique Wilkins 50P	.08	.04	.01
☐	201	Tom Chambers 50P	.05	.02	.01
☐	202	Bernard King 50P	.08	.04	.01
☐	203	Kiki Vandeweghe 50P	.05	.02	.01
☐	204	Dale Ellis 50P	.05	.02	.01
☐	205	Michael Jordan 50P	1.00	.45	.12
☐	206	Michael Adams 50P	.05	.02	.01
☐	207	Charles Smith 50P	.05	.02	.01
☐	208	Moses Malone 50P	.08	.04	.01
☐	209	Terry Cummings 50P	.05	.02	.01
☐	210	Vernon Maxwell 50P	.05	.02	.01
☐	211	Patrick Ewing 50P	.08	.04	.01
☐	212	Clyde Drexler 50P	.08	.04	.01
☐	213	Kevin McHale 50P	.08	.04	.01
☐	214	Hakeem Olajuwon 50P	.20	.09	.03
☐	215	Reggie Miller 50P	.10	.05	.01
☐	216	Gary Grant 20A	.05	.02	.01
☐	217	Doc Rivers 20A	.05	.02	.01
☐	218	Mark Price 20A	.05	.02	.01
☐	219	Isiah Thomas 20A	.08	.04	.01
☐	220	Nate McMillan 20A	.05	.02	.01
☐	221	Fat Lever 20A	.05	.02	.01
☐	222	Kevin Johnson 20A	.08	.04	.01
☐	223	John Stockton 20A	.08	.04	.01
☐	224	Scott Skiles 20A	.05	.02	.01
☐	225	Kevin Brooks	.05	.02	.01
☐	226	Bobby Phills	.20	.09	.03
☐	227	Oliver Miller	.15	.07	.02
☐	228	John Williams	.05	.02	.01
☐	229	Brad Lohaus	.05	.02	.01
☐	230	Derrick Coleman	.05	.02	.01
☐	231	Ed Pinckney	.05	.02	.01
☐	232	Trent Tucker	.05	.02	.01
☐	233	Lance Blanks	.05	.02	.01
☐	234	Drazen Petrovic	.08	.04	.01
☐	235	Mark Bryant	.05	.02	.01
☐	236	Lloyd Daniels	.05	.02	.01
☐	237	Dale Davis	.05	.02	.01
☐	238	Jayson Williams	.05	.02	.01
☐	239	Mike Sanders	.05	.02	.01
☐	240	Mike Gminski	.05	.02	.01
☐	241	William Bedford	.05	.02	.01
☐	242	Dell Curry	.05	.02	.01
☐	243	Gerald Paddio	.05	.02	.01
☐	244	Chris Smith	.05	.02	.01
☐	245	Jud Buechler	.05	.02	.01
☐	246	Walter Palmer	.05	.02	.01
☐	247	Larry Krystkowiak	.05	.02	.01
☐	248	Marcus Liberty	.05	.02	.01
☐	249	Sam Mitchell	.05	.02	.01
☐	250	Kiki Vandeweghe	.05	.02	.01
☐	251	Vincent Askew	.05	.02	.01
☐	252	Travis Mays	.05	.02	.01
☐	253	Charles Smith	.05	.02	.01
☐	254	John Bagley	.05	.02	.01
☐	255	James Worthy	.08	.04	.01
☐	256	Paul Pressey P/CO	.05	.02	.01
☐	257	Rumeal Robinson	.05	.02	.01
☐	258	Tom Gugliotta	.25	.11	.03
☐	259	Eric Anderson	.05	.02	.01
☐	260	Hersey Hawkins	.08	.04	.01
☐	261	Terry Davis	.05	.02	.01
☐	262	Rex Chapman	.05	.02	.01
☐	263	Chucky Brown	.05	.02	.01
☐	264	Danny Young	.05	.02	.01
☐	265	Olden Polynice	.05	.02	.01
☐	266	Kevin Willis	.05	.02	.01
☐	267	Shawn Kemp	.60	.25	.07
☐	268	Mookie Blaylock	.08	.04	.01
☐	269	Malik Sealy	.08	.04	.01
☐	270	Charles Barkley	.25	.11	.03
☐	271	Corey Williams	.05	.02	.01
☐	272	Stephen Howard	.05	.02	.01
		(See also card 286)			
☐	273	Keith Askins	.05	.02	.01
☐	274	Matt Bullard	.05	.02	.01
☐	275	John Battle	.05	.02	.01
☐	276	Andrew Lang	.05	.02	.01
☐	277	David Robinson	.30	.14	.04
☐	278	Harold Miner	.08	.04	.01
☐	279	Tracy Murray	.08	.04	.01
☐	280	Pooh Richardson	.05	.02	.01
☐	281	Dikembe Mutombo	.15	.07	.02
☐	282	Wayman Tisdale	.05	.02	.01
☐	283	Larry Johnson	.30	.14	.04
☐	284	Todd Day	.08	.04	.01
☐	285	Stanley Roberts	.05	.02	.01
☐	286	Randy Woods UER	.05	.02	.01
		(Card misnumbered 272; run he show should be run the show)			
☐	287	Avery Johnson	.08	.04	.01
☐	288	Anthony Peeler	.08	.04	.01
☐	289	Mario Elie	.05	.02	.01
☐	290	Doc Rivers	.05	.02	.01
☐	291	Blue Edwards	.05	.02	.01
☐	292	Sean Rooks	.05	.02	.01
☐	293	Xavier McDaniel	.05	.02	.01
☐	294	Clarence Weatherspoon	.25	.11	.03
☐	295	Morlon Wiley	.05	.02	.01
☐	296	LaBradford Smith	.05	.02	.01
☐	297	Reggie Lewis	.08	.04	.01
☐	298	Chris Mullin	.08	.04	.01
☐	299	Litterial Green	.05	.02	.01
☐	300	Elmore Spencer	.05	.02	.01
☐	301	John Stockton	.15	.07	.02
☐	302	Walt Williams	.30	.14	.04
☐	303	Anthony Pullard	.05	.02	.01

☐ 304	Gundars Vetra	.05	.02	.01
☐ 305	LaSalle Thompson	.05	.02	.01
☐ 306	Nate McMillan	.05	.02	.01
☐ 307	Steve Bardo	.05	.02	.01
☐ 308	Robert Horry	.30	.14	.04
☐ 309	Scott Williams	.05	.02	.01
☐ 310	Bo Kimble	.05	.02	.01
☐ 311	Tree Rollins	.05	.02	.01
☐ 312	Tim Perry	.05	.02	.01
☐ 313	Isaac Austin	.05	.02	.01
☐ 314	Tate George	.05	.02	.01
☐ 315	Kevin Lynch	.05	.02	.01
☐ 316	Victor Alexander	.05	.02	.01
☐ 317	Doug Overton	.05	.02	.01
☐ 318	Tom Hammonds	.05	.02	.01
☐ 319	LaPhonso Ellis	.15	.07	.02
☐ 320	Scott Brooks	.05	.02	.01
☐ 321	Anthony Avent UER	.05	.02	.01
	(Front photo actually Blue Edwards)			
☐ 322	Matt Geiger	.05	.02	.01
☐ 323	Duane Causwell	.05	.02	.01
☐ 324	Horace Grant	.08	.04	.01
☐ 325	Mark Jackson	.05	.02	.01
☐ 326	Dan Majerle	.08	.04	.01
☐ 327	Chuck Person	.05	.02	.01
☐ 328	Buck Johnson	.05	.02	.01
☐ 329	Duane Cooper	.05	.02	.01
☐ 330	Rod Strickland	.05	.02	.01
☐ 331	Isiah Thomas	.10	.05	.01
☐ 332	Greg Kite	.05	.02	.01
	(See also card 387)			
☐ 333	Don MacLean	.08	.04	.01
☐ 334	Christian Laettner	.25	.11	.03
☐ 335	John Crotty	.05	.02	.01
☐ 336	Tracy Moore	.05	.02	.01
☐ 337	Hakeem Olajuwon	.40	.18	.05
☐ 338	Byron Houston	.05	.02	.01
☐ 339	Walter Bond	.05	.02	.01
☐ 340	Brent McCray	.05	.02	.01
☐ 341	Bryant Stith	.15	.07	.02
☐ 342	Will Perdue	.05	.02	.01
☐ 343	Jeff Hornacek	.05	.02	.01
☐ 344	Adam Keefe	.08	.04	.01
☐ 345	Rafael Addison	.05	.02	.01
☐ 346	Marlon Maxey	.05	.02	.01
☐ 347	Joe Dumars	.08	.04	.01
☐ 348	Jon Barry	.05	.02	.01
☐ 349	Marty Conlon	.05	.02	.01
☐ 350	Alaa Abdelnaby	.05	.02	.01
☐ 351	Micheal Williams	.05	.02	.01
☐ 352	Brad Daugherty	.05	.02	.01
☐ 353	Tony Bennett	.05	.02	.01
☐ 354	Clyde Drexler	.20	.09	.03
☐ 355	Rolando Blackman	.05	.02	.01
☐ 356	Tom Tolbert	.05	.02	.01
☐ 357	Sarunas Marciulionis	.05	.02	.01
☐ 358	Jaren Jackson	.05	.02	.01
☐ 359	Stacey King	.05	.02	.01
☐ 360	Danny Ainge	.08	.04	.01
☐ 361	Dale Ellis	.05	.02	.01
☐ 362	Shaquille O'Neal	4.00	1.80	.50
☐ 363	Bob McCann	.05	.02	.01
☐ 364	Reggie Smith	.05	.02	.01
☐ 365	Vinny Del Negro	.05	.02	.01
☐ 366	Robert Pack	.05	.02	.01
☐ 367	David Wood	.05	.02	.01
☐ 368	Rodney McCray	.05	.02	.01
☐ 369	Terry Mills	.05	.02	.01
☐ 370	Eric Murdock UER	.05	.02	.01
	(Jazz on back spelled Jass)			
☐ 371	Alex Blackwell	.05	.02	.01
☐ 372	Jay Humphries	.05	.02	.01
☐ 373	Eddie Lee Wilkins	.05	.02	.01
☐ 374	James Edwards	.05	.02	.01
☐ 375	Tim Kempton	.05	.02	.01
☐ 376	J.R. Reid	.05	.02	.01
☐ 377	Sam Mack	.05	.02	.01
☐ 378	Donald Royal	.05	.02	.01
☐ 379	Mark Price	.05	.02	.01
☐ 380	Mark Acres	.05	.02	.01
☐ 381	Hubert Davis	.08	.04	.01
☐ 382	Dave Johnson	.05	.02	.01
☐ 383	John Salley	.05	.02	.01
☐ 384	Eddie Johnson	.05	.02	.01
☐ 385	Brian Howard	.05	.02	.01
☐ 386	Isaiah Morris	.05	.02	.01
☐ 387	Frank Johnson	.05	.02	.01
	(Card misnumbered 332)			
☐ 388	Rick Mahorn	.05	.02	.01
☐ 389	Scottie Pippen	.50	.23	.06
☐ 390	Lee Mayberry	.06	.03	.01
☐ 391	Tony Campbell	.05	.02	.01
☐ 392	Latrell Sprewell	.40	.18	.05
☐ 393	Alonzo Mourning	.75	.35	.09
☐ 394	Robert Werdann	.05	.02	.01
☐ 395	Checklist 199-297 UER	.05	.02	.01
	(286 Kennard Winchester; should be Randy Woods)			
☐ 396	Checklist 298-396	.05	.02	.01

1992-93 Topps Gold

Gold foil versions of the regular cards were inserted one per 15-card plastic-wrap pack, except if the pack contained a randomly inserted Topps Beam Team card. Gold foil cards were also inserted two per 18-card mini-jumbo pack, three per 45-card retail rack pack, five per 41-card magazine jumbo pack, and 12 per factory set. In addition, complete Gold factory sets were made at the end of the season. These sets include all 396 cards, plus a seven-card Gold Beam Team insert set. The cards are identical in design to the regular issue, except that on the fronts the team color-coded stripes carrying player information are replaced by gold foil stripes. The cards are numbered on the back without a "G" suffix. Reportedly, only 10,000 factory sets were produced. Four different player cards replaced the checklist cards found in the regular 396-card set. Please refer to the multiplier provided below (coupled with the prices of the corresponding regular issue cards) to ascertain the value.

	MINT	NRMT	EXC
COMPLETE GOLD SET (396)	60.00	27.00	7.50
COMPLETE FACTORY SET (403)	75.00	34.00	9.50
COMPLETE SERIES 1 (198)	20.00	9.00	2.50
COMPLETE SERIES 2 (198)	40.00	18.00	5.00
COMMON CARD (1-396)	.10	.05	.01
*STARS: 2.5X to 5X VALUE			
*ROOKIES: 1.5X to 3X VALUE			
☐ 197G Jeff Sanders	.50	.23	.06
☐ 198G Elliott Perry UER	.75	.35	.09
(Misspelled Elliot on front)			
☐ 395G David Wingate	.50	.23	.06
☐ 396G Carl Herrera	.50	.23	.06

1992-93 Topps Beam Team

Comprised of some of the NBA's biggest stars, the Topps Beam Team set contains seven standard size cards. Inserted in 15-card second series packs at a ratio of one in 18, these special "Topps Beam Team" bonus cards commemorate Topps' 1993 sponsorship of a six-minute NBA laser animation show. Called Beams Above the Rim, the show premiered at the NBA All-Star Game on Feb. 21. Afterwards, the laser show embarked on a ten-city tour and was featured in either the pre-game or half-time events in ten NBA arenas. Three players are featured on each Topps Beam Team card. The horizontal fronts display three color action player photos on a dark blue background with a grid of brightly colored light beams. The set title "Beam Team" appears in pastel green block lettering across the top. The backs carry three light blue panels, with a close-up color photo, biography, and player profile on each panel.

	MINT	NRMT	EXC
COMPLETE SET (7)	10.00	4.50	1.25
COMMON TRIO (1-7)	.50	.23	.06
☐ 1 Reggie Miller	1.00	.45	.12
Charles Barkley			
Clyde Drexler			
☐ 2 Patrick Ewing	.50	.23	.06
Tim Hardaway			
Jeff Hornacek			
☐ 3 Kevin Johnson	5.00	2.20	.60
Michael Jordan			
Dennis Rodman			
☐ 4 Dominique Wilkins	.50	.23	.06
John Stockton			
Karl Malone			
☐ 5 Hakeem Olajuwon	1.50	.70	.19
Mark Price			
Shawn Kemp			
☐ 6 Scottie Pippen	1.00	.45	.12
David Robinson			
Jeff Malone			
☐ 7 Chris Mullin	4.00	1.80	.50
Shaquille O'Neal			
Glen Rice			

1992-93 Topps Beam Team Gold

Topps also produced a 7-card gold parallel version to the regular issue Beam Team series. These gold cards command 1.5 to 3 times the values of their nongold counterparts. One of these gold Beam Team sets was included with the purchase of a 1992-93 Topps Gold factory set. Please refer to the multiplier provided below (coupled with the prices of the corresponding regular Beam Team inserts) to ascertain value.

	MINT	NRMT	EXC
COMPLETE SET (7)	25.00	11.00	3.10
COMMON CARD (1-7)	1.50	.70	.19
*GOLD: 1.5X to 3X VALUE			

1993-94 Topps

The complete 1993-94 Topps basketball set consists of 396 standard-size cards issued in two 198-card series. Cards were issued in 12, 15 and 29-card packs. Factory sets contain 410 cards including 10 Gold, three Black Gold and one Finest Redemption card. The Finest Redemption card enabled a collector to mail away for two random Finest cards. The redemption deadline was July 31, 1994. The white bordered fronts display color action player photos with a team color coded inner border. The player's name is printed in white script at the lower left corner with the team name appearing on a team color coded bar at the very bottom. The horizontal backs carry a

close-up player photo on the right with complete NBA statistics, biography, and career highlights on the left on a beige panel. Subsets featured are Highlights (1-5), 50 Point Club (50, 57, 64), Topps All-Star 1st Team (100-104), Topps All-Star 2nd Team (115-119), Topps All-Star 3rd Team (130-134), Topps All-Rookie 1st Team (150-154), Topps All-Rookie 2nd Team (175-179), Future Playoff MVP's (199-209) and Future Scoring Leaders (384-394). Rookie Cards of note in this set include Vin Baker, Anfernee Hardaway, Allan Houston, Jamal Mashburn, Nick Van Exel and Chris Webber.

	MINT	NRMT	EXC
COMPLETE SET (396)	20.00	9.00	2.50
COMPLETE FACT.SET (410)	25.00	11.00	3.10
COMPLETE SERIES 1 (198)	10.00	4.50	1.25
COMPLETE SERIES 2 (198)	10.00	4.50	1.25
COMMON CARD (1-396)	.05	.02	.01

☐ 1	Charles Barkley HL	.20	.09	.03
☐ 2	Hakeem Olajuwon HL	.30	.14	.04
☐ 3	Shaquille O'Neal HL	.75	.35	.09
☐ 4	Chris Jackson HL	.10	.05	.01
☐ 5	Clifford Robinson HL	.10	.05	.01
☐ 6	Donald Hodge	.05	.02	.01
☐ 7	Victor Alexander	.05	.02	.01
☐ 8	Chris Morris	.05	.02	.01
☐ 9	Muggsy Bogues	.10	.05	.01
☐ 10	Steve Smith UER	.10	.05	.01
	(Listed with Kings in '90-91; was not in NBA that year)			
☐ 11	Dave Johnson	.05	.02	.01
☐ 12	Tom Gugliotta	.10	.05	.01
☐ 13	Doug Edwards	.05	.02	.01
☐ 14	Vlade Divac	.05	.02	.01
☐ 15	Corie Blount	.05	.02	.01
☐ 16	Derek Harper	.10	.05	.01
☐ 17	Matt Bullard	.05	.02	.01
☐ 18	Terry Catledge	.05	.02	.01
☐ 19	Mark Eaton	.05	.02	.01
☐ 20	Mark Jackson	.05	.02	.01
☐ 21	Terry Mills	.05	.02	.01
☐ 22	Johnny Dawkins	.05	.02	.01
☐ 23	Michael Jordan UER	3.00	1.35	.35
	(Listed as a forward with birthdate of 1968; he is a guard with bithdate of 1963)			
☐ 24	Rick Fox UER	.05	.02	.01
	(Listed with Kings in '91-92)			
☐ 25	Charles Oakley	.10	.05	.01
☐ 26	Derrick McKey	.05	.02	.01
☐ 27	Christian Laettner	.10	.05	.01
☐ 28	Todd Day	.05	.02	.01
☐ 29	Danny Ferry	.05	.02	.01
☐ 30	Kevin Johnson	.10	.05	.01
☐ 31	Vinny Del Negro	.05	.02	.01
☐ 32	Kevin Brooks	.05	.02	.01
☐ 33	Pete Chilcutt	.05	.02	.01
☐ 34	Larry Stewart	.05	.02	.01
☐ 35	Dave Jamerson	.05	.02	.01
☐ 36	Sidney Green	.05	.02	.01
☐ 37	J.R. Reid	.05	.02	.01
☐ 38	Jimmy Jackson	.30	.14	.04
☐ 39	Micheal Williams UER	.05	.02	.01
	(350.2 minutes per game)			
☐ 40	Rex Walters	.05	.02	.01
☐ 41	Shawn Bradley	.30	.14	.04

☐ 42	Jon Koncak	.05	.02	.01
☐ 43	Byron Houston	.05	.02	.01
☐ 44	Brian Shaw	.05	.02	.01
☐ 45	Bill Cartwright	.05	.02	.01
☐ 46	Jerome Kersey	.05	.02	.01
☐ 47	Danny Schayes	.05	.02	.01
☐ 48	Olden Polynice	.05	.02	.01
☐ 49	Anthony Peeler	.05	.02	.01
☐ 50	Nick Anderson 50	.10	.05	.01
☐ 51	David Benoit	.05	.02	.01
☐ 52	David Robinson	.25	.11	.03
☐ 53	Greg Kite	.05	.02	.01
☐ 54	Gerald Paddio	.05	.02	.01
☐ 55	Don MacLean	.05	.02	.01
☐ 56	Randy Woods	.05	.02	.01
☐ 57	Reggie Miller 50	.15	.07	.02
☐ 58	Kevin Gamble	.05	.02	.01
☐ 59	Sean Green	.05	.02	.01
☐ 60	Jeff Hornacek	.10	.05	.01
☐ 61	John Starks	.05	.02	.01
☐ 62	Gerald Wilkins	.05	.02	.01
☐ 63	Jim Les	.05	.02	.01
☐ 64	Michael Jordan 50	1.50	.70	.19
☐ 65	Alvin Robertson	.05	.02	.01
☐ 66	Tim Kempton	.05	.02	.01
☐ 67	Bryant Stith	.05	.02	.01
☐ 68	Jeff Turner	.05	.02	.01
☐ 69	Malik Sealy	.05	.02	.01
☐ 70	Dell Curry	.05	.02	.01
☐ 71	Brent Price	.05	.02	.01
☐ 72	Kevin Lynch	.05	.02	.01
☐ 73	Bimbo Coles	.05	.02	.01
☐ 74	Larry Nance	.05	.02	.01
☐ 75	Luther Wright	.05	.02	.01
☐ 76	Willie Anderson	.05	.02	.01
☐ 77	Dennis Rodman	1.00	.45	.12
☐ 78	Anthony Mason	.10	.05	.01
☐ 79	Chris Gatling	.05	.02	.01
☐ 80	Antoine Carr	.05	.02	.01
☐ 81	Kevin Willis	.05	.02	.01
☐ 82	Thurl Bailey	.05	.02	.01
☐ 83	Reggie Williams	.05	.02	.01
☐ 84	Rod Strickland	.05	.02	.01
☐ 85	Rolando Blackman	.05	.02	.01
☐ 86	Bobby Hurley	.10	.05	.01
☐ 87	Jeff Malone	.05	.02	.01
☐ 88	James Worthy	.10	.05	.01
☐ 89	Alaa Abdelnaby	.05	.02	.01
☐ 90	Duane Ferrell	.05	.02	.01
☐ 91	Anthony Avent	.05	.02	.01
☐ 92	Scottie Pippen	.75	.35	.09
☐ 93	Ricky Pierce	.05	.02	.01
☐ 94	P.J. Brown	.05	.02	.01
☐ 95	Jeff Grayer	.05	.02	.01
☐ 96	Jerrod Mustaf	.05	.02	.01
☐ 97	Elmore Spencer	.05	.02	.01
☐ 98	Walt Williams	.10	.05	.01
☐ 99	Otis Thorpe	.10	.05	.01
☐ 100	Patrick Ewing AS	.15	.07	.01
☐ 101	Michael Jordan AS	1.50	.70	.19
☐ 102	John Stockton AS	.10	.05	.01
☐ 103	Dominique Wilkins AS	.10	.05	.01
☐ 104	Charles Barkley AS	.20	.09	.03
☐ 105	Lee Mayberry	.05	.02	.01
☐ 106	James Edwards	.05	.02	.01
☐ 107	Scott Brooks	.05	.02	.01
☐ 108	John Battle	.05	.02	.01
☐ 109	Kenny Gattison	.05	.02	.01
☐ 110	Pooh Richardson	.05	.02	.01
☐ 111	Rony Seikaly	.05	.02	.01
☐ 112	Mahmoud Abdul-Rauf	.10	.05	.01

☐ 113 Nick Anderson	.10	.05	.01
☐ 114 Gundars Vetra	.05	.02	.01
☐ 115 Joe Dumars AS	.10	.05	.01
☐ 116 Hakeem Olajuwon AS	.30	.14	.04
☐ 117 Scottie Pippen AS	.40	.18	.05
☐ 118 Mark Price AS	.05	.02	.01
☐ 119 Karl Malone AS	.10	.05	.01
☐ 120 Michael Cage	.05	.02	.01
☐ 121 Ed Pinckney	.05	.02	.01
☐ 122 Jay Humphries	.05	.02	.01
☐ 123 Dale Davis	.05	.02	.01
☐ 124 Sean Rooks	.05	.02	.01
☐ 125 Mookie Blaylock	.10	.05	.01
☐ 126 Buck Williams	.10	.05	.01
☐ 127 John Williams	.05	.02	.01
☐ 128 Stacey King	.05	.02	.01
☐ 129 Tim Perry	.05	.02	.01
☐ 130 Tim Hardaway AS	.05	.02	.01
☐ 131 Larry Johnson AS	.10	.05	.01
☐ 132 Detlef Schrempf AS	.05	.02	.01
☐ 133 Reggie Miller AS	.15	.07	.02
☐ 134 Shaquille O'Neal	.75	.35	.09
☐ 135 Dale Ellis	.05	.02	.01
☐ 136 Duane Causwell	.05	.02	.01
☐ 137 Rumeal Robinson	.05	.02	.01
☐ 138 Billy Owens	.05	.02	.01
☐ 139 Malcolm Mackey	.05	.02	.01
☐ 140 Vernon Maxwell	.05	.02	.01
☐ 141 LaPhonso Ellis	.05	.02	.01
☐ 142 Robert Parish	.10	.05	.01
☐ 143 LaBradford Smith	.05	.02	.01
☐ 144 Charles Smith	.05	.02	.01
☐ 145 Terry Porter	.05	.02	.01
☐ 146 Elden Campbell	.05	.02	.01
☐ 147 Bill Laimbeer	.10	.05	.01
☐ 148 Chris Mills	.40	.18	.05
☐ 149 Brad Lohaus	.05	.02	.01
☐ 150 Jimmy Jackson ART	.15	.07	.02
☐ 151 Tom Gugliotta ART	.05	.02	.01
☐ 152 Shaquille O'Neal ART	.75	.35	.09
☐ 153 Latrell Sprewell ART	.10	.05	.01
☐ 154 Walt Williams ART	.05	.02	.01
☐ 155 Gary Payton	.40	.18	.05
☐ 156 Orlando Woolridge	.05	.02	.01
☐ 157 Adam Keefe	.05	.02	.01
☐ 158 Calbert Cheaney	.25	.11	.03
☐ 159 Rick Mahorn	.05	.02	.01
☐ 160 Robert Horry	.10	.05	.01
☐ 161 John Salley	.05	.02	.01
☐ 162 Sam Mitchell	.05	.02	.01
☐ 163 Stanley Roberts	.05	.02	.01
☐ 164 Clarence Weatherspoon	.10	.05	.01
☐ 165 Anthony Bowie	.05	.02	.01
☐ 166 Derrick Coleman	.05	.02	.01
☐ 167 Negele Knight	.05	.02	.01
☐ 168 Marlon Maxey	.05	.02	.01
☐ 169 Spud Webb UER	.10	.05	.01
(Listed as center instead of guard)			
☐ 170 Alonzo Mourning	.40	.18	.05
☐ 171 Ervin Johnson	.10	.05	.01
☐ 172 Sedale Threatt	.05	.02	.01
☐ 173 Mark Macon	.05	.02	.01
☐ 174 B.J. Armstrong	.05	.02	.01
☐ 175 Harold Miner ART	.05	.02	.01
☐ 176 Anthony Peeler ART	.05	.02	.01
☐ 177 Alonzo Mourning ART	.20	.09	.03
☐ 178 Christian Laettner ART	.05	.02	.01
☐ 179 C. Weatherspoon ART	.05	.02	.01
☐ 180 Dee Brown	.05	.02	.01
☐ 181 Shaquille O'Neal	1.50	.70	.19
☐ 182 Loy Vaught	.05	.02	.01

☐ 183 Terrell Brandon	.10	.05	.01
☐ 184 Lionel Simmons	.05	.02	.01
☐ 185 Mark Aguirre	.10	.05	.01
☐ 186 Danny Ainge	.10	.05	.01
☐ 187 Reggie Miller	.30	.14	.04
☐ 188 Terry Davis	.05	.02	.01
☐ 189 Mark Bryant	.05	.02	.01
☐ 190 Tyrone Corbin	.05	.02	.01
☐ 191 Chris Mullin	.10	.05	.01
☐ 192 Johnny Newman	.05	.02	.01
☐ 193 Doug West	.05	.02	.01
☐ 194 Keith Askins	.05	.02	.01
☐ 195 Bo Kimble	.05	.02	.01
☐ 196 Sean Elliott	.10	.05	.01
☐ 197 Checklist 1-99 UER	.05	.02	.01
(No. 18 listed as Terry Mills			
instead of Terry Cummings and			
No. 23 listed as Sam Mitchell			
instead of Michael Jordan)			
☐ 198 Checklist 100-198	.05	.02	.01
☐ 199 Michael Jordan FPM	1.50	.70	.19
☐ 200 Patrick Ewing FPM	.10	.05	.01
☐ 201 John Stockton FPM	.10	.05	.01
☐ 202 Shawn Kemp FPM	.40	.18	.05
☐ 203 Mark Price FPM	.05	.02	.01
☐ 204 Charles Barkley FPM	.20	.09	.03
☐ 205 Hakeem Olajuwon FPM	.30	.14	.04
☐ 206 Clyde Drexler FPM	.10	.05	.01
☐ 207 Kevin Johnson FPM	.10	.05	.01
☐ 208 John Starks FPM	.05	.02	.01
☐ 209 Chris Mullin FPM	.05	.02	.01
☐ 210 Doc Rivers	.05	.02	.01
☐ 211 Kenny Walker	.05	.02	.01
☐ 212 Doug Christie	.05	.02	.01
☐ 213 James Robinson	.10	.05	.01
☐ 214 Larry Krystkowiak	.05	.02	.01
☐ 215 Manute Bol	.05	.02	.01
☐ 216 Carl Herrera	.05	.02	.01
☐ 217 Paul Graham	.05	.02	.01
☐ 218 Jud Buechler	.05	.02	.01
☐ 219 Mike Brown	.05	.02	.01
☐ 220 Tom Chambers	.05	.02	.01
☐ 221 Kendall Gill	.05	.02	.01
☐ 222 Kenny Anderson	.10	.05	.01
☐ 223 Larry Johnson	.30	.14	.04
☐ 224 Chris Webber	1.00	.45	.12
☐ 225 Randy White	.05	.02	.01
☐ 226 Rik Smits	.10	.05	.01
☐ 227 A.C. Green	.10	.05	.01
☐ 228 David Robinson	.50	.23	.06
☐ 229 Sean Elliott	.10	.05	.01
☐ 230 Gary Grant	.05	.02	.01
☐ 231 Dana Barros	.05	.02	.01
☐ 232 Bobby Hurley	.05	.02	.01
☐ 233 Blue Edwards	.05	.02	.01
☐ 234 Tom Hammonds	.05	.02	.01
☐ 235 Pete Myers UER	.05	.02	.01
Card says born in 1993			
☐ 236 Acie Earl	.05	.02	.01
☐ 237 Tony Smith	.05	.02	.01
☐ 238 Bill Wennington	.05	.02	.01
☐ 239 Andrew Lang	.05	.02	.01
☐ 240 Ervin Johnson	.05	.02	.01
☐ 241 Byron Scott	.10	.05	.01
☐ 242 Eddie Johnson	.05	.02	.01
☐ 243 Anthony Bonner	.05	.02	.01
☐ 244 Luther Wright	.05	.02	.01
☐ 245 LaSalle Thompson	.05	.02	.01
☐ 246 Harold Miner	.05	.02	.01
☐ 247 Chris Smith	.05	.02	.01
☐ 248 John Williams	.05	.02	.01

☐	249 Clyde Drexler	.30	.14	.04
☐	250 Calbert Cheaney	.10	.05	.01
☐	251 Avery Johnson	.05	.02	.01
☐	252 Steve Kerr	.10	.05	.01
☐	253 Warren Kidd	.05	.02	.01
☐	254 Wayman Tisdale	.05	.02	.01
☐	255 Bob Martin	.05	.02	.01
☐	256 Popeye Jones	.10	.05	.01
☐	257 Jimmy Oliver	.05	.02	.01
☐	258 Kevin Edwards	.05	.02	.01
☐	259 Dan Majerle	.10	.05	.01
☐	260 Jon Barry	.05	.02	.01
☐	261 Allan Houston	.50	.23	.06
☐	262 Dikembe Mutombo	.10	.05	.01
☐	263 Sleepy Floyd	.05	.02	.01
☐	264 George Lynch	.05	.02	.01
☐	265 Stacey Augmon UER	.10	.05	.01
	(Listed with Heat in stats)			
☐	266 Hakeem Olajuwon	.60	.25	.07
☐	267 Scott Skiles	.05	.02	.01
☐	268 Detlef Schrempf	.10	.05	.01
☐	269 Brian Davis	.05	.02	.01
☐	270 Tracy Murray	.05	.02	.01
☐	271 Gheorghe Muresan	.40	.18	.05
☐	272 Terry Dehere	.10	.05	.01
☐	273 Terry Cummings	.05	.02	.01
☐	274 Keith Jennings	.05	.02	.01
☐	275 Tyrone Hill	.05	.02	.01
☐	276 Hersey Hawkins	.05	.02	.01
☐	277 Grant Long	.05	.02	.01
☐	278 Herb Williams	.05	.02	.01
☐	279 Karl Malone	.25	.11	.03
☐	280 Mitch Richmond	.20	.09	.03
☐	281 Derek Strong	.05	.02	.01
☐	282 Dino Radja	.30	.14	.04
☐	283 Jack Haley	.05	.02	.01
☐	284 Derek Harper	.05	.02	.01
☐	285 Dwayne Schintzius	.05	.02	.01
☐	286 Michael Curry	.05	.02	.01
☐	287 Rodney Rogers	.10	.05	.01
☐	288 Horace Grant	.10	.05	.01
☐	289 Oliver Miller	.05	.02	.01
☐	290 Luc Longley	.05	.02	.01
☐	291 Walter Bond	.05	.02	.01
☐	292 Dominique Wilkins	.10	.05	.01
☐	293 Vern Fleming	.05	.02	.01
☐	294 Mark Price	.05	.02	.01
☐	295 Mark Aguirre	.10	.05	.01
☐	296 Shawn Kemp	.75	.35	.09
☐	297 Pervis Ellison	.05	.02	.01
☐	298 Josh Grant	.05	.02	.01
☐	299 Scott Burrell	.10	.05	.01
☐	300 Patrick Ewing	.25	.11	.03
☐	301 Sam Cassell	.40	.18	.05
☐	302 Nick Van Exel	.75	.35	.09
☐	303 Clifford Robinson	.10	.05	.01
☐	304 Frank Johnson	.05	.02	.01
☐	305 Matt Geiger	.05	.02	.01
☐	306 Vin Baker	1.00	.45	.12
☐	307 Benoit Benjamin	.05	.02	.01
☐	308 Shawn Bradley	.10	.05	.01
☐	309 Chris Whitney	.05	.02	.01
☐	310 Eric Riley	.05	.02	.01
☐	311 Isiah Thomas	.15	.07	.02
☐	312 Jamal Mashburn	.60	.25	.07
☐	313 Xavier McDaniel	.05	.02	.01
☐	314 Mike Peplowski	.05	.02	.01
☐	315 Darnell Mee	.05	.02	.01
☐	316 Toni Kukoc	.60	.25	.07
☐	317 Felton Spencer	.05	.02	.01
☐	318 Sam Bowie	.05	.02	.01
☐	319 Mario Elie	.05	.02	.01
☐	320 Tim Hardaway	.10	.05	.01
☐	321 Ken Norman	.05	.02	.01
☐	322 Isaiah Rider	.30	.14	.04
☐	323 Rex Chapman	.05	.02	.01
☐	324 Dennis Rodman	1.00	.45	.12
☐	325 Derrick McKey	.05	.02	.01
☐	326 Corie Blount	.05	.02	.01
☐	327 Fat Lever	.05	.02	.01
☐	328 Ron Harper	.05	.02	.01
☐	329 Eric Anderson	.05	.02	.01
☐	330 Armon Gilliam	.05	.02	.01
☐	331 Lindsey Hunter	.05	.02	.01
☐	332 Eric Leckner	.05	.02	.01
☐	333 Chris Corchiani	.05	.02	.01
☐	334 Anfernee Hardaway	5.00	2.20	.60
☐	335 Randy Brown	.05	.02	.01
☐	336 Sam Perkins	.05	.02	.01
☐	337 Glen Rice	.10	.05	.01
☐	338 Orlando Woolridge	.05	.02	.01
☐	339 Mike Gminski	.05	.02	.01
☐	340 Latrell Sprewell	.20	.09	.03
☐	341 Harvey Grant	.05	.02	.01
☐	342 Doug Smith	.05	.02	.01
☐	343 Kevin Duckworth	.05	.02	.01
☐	344 Cedric Ceballos	.10	.05	.01
☐	345 Chuck Person	.05	.02	.01
☐	346 Scott Haskin	.05	.02	.01
☐	347 Frank Brickowski	.05	.02	.01
☐	348 Scott Williams	.05	.02	.01
☐	349 Brad Daugherty	.05	.02	.01
☐	350 Willie Burton	.05	.02	.01
☐	351 Joe Dumars	.10	.05	.01
☐	352 Craig Ehlo	.05	.02	.01
☐	353 Lucious Harris	.10	.05	.01
☐	354 Danny Manning	.10	.05	.01
☐	355 Litterial Green	.05	.02	.01
☐	356 John Stockton	.25	.11	.03
☐	357 Nate McMillan	.05	.02	.01
☐	358 Greg Graham	.05	.02	.01
☐	359 Rex Walters	.05	.02	.01
☐	360 Lloyd Daniels	.05	.02	.01
☐	361 Antonio Harvey	.05	.02	.01
☐	362 Brian Williams	.05	.02	.01
☐	363 LeRon Ellis	.05	.02	.01
☐	364 Chris Dudley	.05	.02	.01
☐	365 Hubert Davis	.05	.02	.01
☐	366 Evers Burns	.05	.02	.01
☐	367 Sherman Douglas	.05	.02	.01
☐	368 Sarunas Marciulionis	.05	.02	.01
☐	369 Tom Tolbert	.05	.02	.01
☐	370 Robert Pack	.05	.02	.01
☐	371 Michael Adams	.05	.02	.01
☐	372 Negele Knight	.05	.02	.01
☐	373 Charles Barkley	.40	.18	.05
☐	374 Bryon Russell	.05	.02	.01
☐	375 Greg Anthony	.05	.02	.01
☐	376 Ken Williams	.05	.02	.01
☐	377 John Paxson	.10	.05	.01
☐	378 Corey Gaines	.05	.02	.01
☐	379 Eric Murdock	.05	.02	.01
☐	380 Kevin Thompson	.05	.02	.01
☐	381 Moses Malone	.15	.07	.02
☐	382 Kenny Smith	.05	.02	.01
☐	383 Dennis Scott	.10	.05	.01
☐	384 Michael Jordan FSL	1.50	.70	.19
☐	385 Hakeem Olajuwon FSL	.30	.14	.04
☐	386 Shaquille O'Neal FSL	.75	.35	.09
☐	387 David Robinson FSL	.25	.11	.03
☐	388 Derrick Coleman FSL	.05	.02	.01
☐	389 Karl Malone FSL	.10	.05	.01

		MINT	NRMT	EXC
☐ 390	Patrick Ewing FSL	.10	.05	.01
☐ 391	Scottie Pippen FSL	.40	.18	.05
☐ 392	Dominique Wilkins FSL	.10	.05	.01
☐ 393	Charles Barkley FSL	.20	.09	.03
☐ 394	Larry Johnson FSL	.10	.05	.01
☐ 395	Checklist	.05	.02	.01
☐ 396	Checklist	.05	.02	.01
☐ NNO	Expired Finest Redemption Card	1.00	.45	.12

1993-94 Topps Gold

The cards of this parallel set were distributed through various means. Each pack of '93-94 Topps contained one Gold card with two Gold cards inserted in every fourth pack. Three Gold cards were inserted in every rack pack and 10 in every factory set. Aside from the gold-foil highlights, the 396 standard-size Gold cards are identical to their regular issue counterparts, except the four regular issue checklist cards were replaced by Gold cards featuring the players listed below. Please refer to the multipliers provided below (coupled with the prices of the corresponding regular issue card) to ascertain value.

	MINT	NRMT	EXC
COMPLETE SET (396)	70.00	32.00	8.75
COMPLETE SERIES 1 (198)	30.00	13.50	3.70
COMPLETE SERIES 2 (198)	40.00	18.00	5.00
COMMON CARD (1-396)	.10	.05	.01
*STARS: 2X to 4X VALUE			
*ROOKIES: 1.25X to 2.5X VALUE			

		MINT	NRMT	EXC
☐ 197G	Frank Johnson	.50	.23	.06
☐ 198G	David Wingate	.50	.23	.06
☐ 395G	Will Perdue	.50	.23	.06
☐ 396G	Mark West	.50	.23	.06

1993-94 Topps Black Gold

Randomly inserted in first and second series packs and three per factory set, this 25-card standard size set features the top five draft picks each year from 1989-1993. Thirteen cards were inserts in series one

and 12 in series two. They were inserted at a rate of one in 72 for 12-card packs and one in 18 for 29-card packs. Winner A cards, redeemable for a series 1 set, were randomly inserted into 1 in every 144 series 1 packs. Winner B cards, redeemable for a series 2 set, were randomly inserted into 1 in every 144 series 2 packs. The A/B Winner card (randomly inserted in 1 in every 288 series 2 packs only) was redeemable for a complete set. Each white-bordered front displays a color action player shot with the background tinted in black. Gold prismatic wavy stripes appear above and below the photo with the player's name reversed out of the black bar near the bottom. The white-bordered horizontal backs carry a close-up color cutout on a black background with white concentric stripes. The player's name appears in gold-foil lettering on a wood textured bar with the team name directly to the right in black lettering. Player statistics appear below in an orange background.

	MINT	NRMT	EXC
COMPLETE SET (25)	35.00	16.00	4.40
COMPLETE SERIES 1 (13)	5.00	2.20	.60
COMPLETE SERIES 2 (12)	30.00	13.50	3.70
COMMON CARD (1-25)	.25	.11	.03

		MINT	NRMT	EXC
☐ 1	Sean Elliott	.75	.35	.09
☐ 2	Dennis Scott	.50	.23	.06
☐ 3	Kenny Anderson	.50	.23	.06
☐ 4	Alonzo Mourning	1.50	.70	.19
☐ 5	Glen Rice	.50	.23	.06
☐ 6	Billy Owens	.25	.11	.03
☐ 7	Jim Jackson	1.25	.55	.16
☐ 8	Derrick Coleman	.25	.11	.03
☐ 9	Larry Johnson	1.25	.55	.16
☐ 10	Gary Payton	2.00	.90	.25
☐ 11	Christian Laettner	.75	.35	.09
☐ 12	Dikembe Mutombo	.75	.35	.09
☐ 13	Mahmoud Abdul-Rauf	.50	.23	.06
☐ 14	Isaiah Rider	1.00	.45	.12
☐ 15	Steve Smith	.50	.23	.06
☐ 16	LaPhonso Ellis	.25	.11	.03
☐ 17	Danny Ferry	.25	.11	.03
☐ 18	Shaquille O'Neal	6.00	2.70	.75
☐ 19	Anfernee Hardaway	15.00	6.75	1.85
☐ 20	J.R. Reid	.25	.11	.03
☐ 21	Shawn Bradley	.75	.35	.09
☐ 22	Pervis Ellison	.25	.11	.03
☐ 23	Chris Webber	3.00	1.35	.35
☐ 24	Jamal Mashburn	2.00	.90	.25
☐ 25	Kendall Gill	.25	.11	.03
☐ A	Expired Winner A	.75	.35	.09

☐ B Expired Winner B	.75	.35	.09
☐ AX Redeemed Winner A	.25	.11	.03
☐ BX Redeemed Winner B	.25	.11	.03
☐ AB Expired Winner A/B	1.50	.70	.19

1994-95 Topps

The 396 standard-size cards that comprise the 1994-95 Topps set were issued in two separate series of 198 cards each. Cards were distributed primarily in 12-card packs that carried a suggested retail price of $1.00 each. Fronts feature full-color action photos framed by a jagged white border. Player's name and team are placed in gold foil along the bottom. The following subsets are included in this set: Eastern All-Star (1-13), Paint Patrol (100-109), and Western All-Star (183-195). In addition, various "From the Roof" subsets cards are intermingled within the set. Rookie Cards of note in this set include Grant Hill, Juwan Howard, Eddie Jones, Jason Kidd and Glenn Robinson.

	MINT	NRMT	EXC
COMPLETE SET (396)	30.00	13.50	3.70
COMPLETE SERIES 1 (198)	12.00	5.50	1.50
COMPLETE SERIES 2 (198)	18.00	8.00	2.20
COMMON CARD (1-396)	.05	.02	.01

☐ 1	Patrick Ewing AS	.10	.05	.01
☐ 2	Mookie Blaylock AS	.05	.02	.01
☐ 3	Charles Oakley AS	.05	.02	.01
☐ 4	Mark Price AS	.05	.02	.01
☐ 5	John Starks AS	.05	.02	.01
☐ 6	Dominique Wilkins AS	.10	.05	.01
☐ 7	Horace Grant AS	.05	.02	.01
☐ 8	Alonzo Mourning AS	.15	.07	.02
☐ 9	B.J. Armstrong AS	.05	.02	.01
☐ 10	Kenny Anderson AS	.05	.02	.01
☐ 11	Scottie Pippen AS	.40	.18	.05
☐ 12	Derrick Coleman AS	.05	.02	.01
☐ 13	Shaquille O'Neal AS	.60	.25	.07
☐ 14	Anfernee Hardaway SPEC	.75	.35	.09
☐ 15	Isaiah Rider SPEC	.05	.02	.01
☐ 16	John Williams	.05	.02	.01
☐ 17	Todd Day	.05	.02	.01
☐ 18	Dale Davis	.05	.02	.01
☐ 19	Sean Rooks	.05	.02	.01
☐ 20	George Lynch	.05	.02	.01
☐ 21	Mitchell Butler	.05	.02	.01
☐ 22	Stacey King	.05	.02	.01
☐ 23	Sherman Douglas	.05	.02	.01
☐ 24	Derrick McKey	.05	.02	.01
☐ 25	Joe Dumars	.10	.05	.01
☐ 26	Scott Brooks	.05	.02	.01
☐ 27	Clarence Weatherspoon	.05	.02	.01
☐ 28	Jayson Williams	.05	.02	.01
☐ 29	Scottie Pippen	.75	.35	.09
☐ 30	John Starks	.05	.02	.01
☐ 31	Robert Pack	.05	.02	.01
☐ 32	Donald Royal	.05	.02	.01
☐ 33	Haywoode Workman	.05	.02	.01
☐ 34	Greg Graham	.05	.02	.01
☐ 35	Terry Cummings	.05	.02	.01
☐ 36	Andrew Lang	.05	.02	.01
☐ 37	Jason Kidd	2.00	.90	.25
☐ 38	Terry Mills	.05	.02	.01
☐ 39	Alonzo Mourning	.30	.14	.04
☐ 40	Shawn Kemp	.75	.35	.09
☐ 41	Kevin Willis FTR	.05	.02	.01
☐ 42	Kevin Willis	.05	.02	.01
☐ 43	Armon Gilliam	.05	.02	.01
☐ 44	Bobby Hurley	.05	.02	.01
☐ 45	Jerome Kersey	.05	.02	.01
☐ 46	Xavier McDaniel	.05	.02	.01
☐ 47	Chris Webber	.30	.14	.04
☐ 48	Chris Webber FTR	.15	.07	.02
☐ 49	Jeff Malone	.05	.02	.01
☐ 50	Dikembe Mutombo SPEC	.10	.05	.01
☐ 51	Dan Majerle SPEC	.10	.05	.01
☐ 52	Dee Brown SPEC	.05	.02	.01
☐ 53	John Stockton SPEC	.10	.05	.01
☐ 54	Dennis Rodman SPEC	.50	.23	.06
☐ 55	Eric Murdock SPEC	.05	.02	.01
☐ 56	Glen Rice	.10	.05	.01
☐ 57	Glen Rice FTR	.05	.02	.01
☐ 58	Dino Radja	.10	.05	.01
☐ 59	Billy Owens	.05	.02	.01
☐ 60	Doc Rivers	.05	.02	.01
☐ 61	Don MacLean	.05	.02	.01
☐ 62	Lindsey Hunter	.05	.02	.01
☐ 63	Sam Cassell	.10	.05	.01
☐ 64	James Worthy	.10	.05	.01
☐ 65	Christian Laettner	.10	.05	.01
☐ 66	Wesley Person	.50	.23	.06
☐ 67	Rich King	.05	.02	.01
☐ 68	Jon Koncak	.05	.02	.01
☐ 69	Muggsy Bogues	.10	.05	.01
☐ 70	Jamal Mashburn	.20	.09	.03
☐ 71	Gary Grant	.05	.02	.01
☐ 72	Eric Murdock	.05	.02	.01
☐ 73	Scott Burrell	.05	.02	.01
☐ 74	Scott Burrell FTR	.05	.02	.01
☐ 75	Anfernee Hardaway	1.50	.70	.19
☐ 76	Anfernee Hardaway FTR.	.75	.35	.09
☐ 77	Yinka Dare	.05	.02	.01
☐ 78	Anthony Avent	.05	.02	.01
☐ 79	Jon Barry	.05	.02	.01
☐ 80	Rodney Rogers	.05	.02	.01
☐ 81	Chris Mills	.10	.05	.01
☐ 82	Antonio Davis	.05	.02	.01
☐ 83	Steve Smith	.10	.05	.01
☐ 84	Buck Williams	.10	.05	.01
☐ 85	Spud Webb	.10	.05	.01
☐ 86	Stacey Augmon	.05	.02	.01
☐ 87	Allan Houston	.15	.07	.02
☐ 88	Will Perdue	.05	.02	.01
☐ 89	Chris Gatling	.05	.02	.01
☐ 90	Danny Ainge	.10	.05	.01
☐ 91	Rick Mahorn	.05	.02	.01
☐ 92	Elmore Spencer	.05	.02	.01
☐ 93	Vin Baker	.30	.14	.04
☐ 94	Rex Chapman	.05	.02	.01
☐ 95	Dale Ellis	.05	.02	.01

☐ 96	Doug Smith	.05	.02	.01
☐ 97	Tim Perry	.05	.02	.01
☐ 98	Toni Kukoc	.20	.09	.03
☐ 99	Terry Dehere	.05	.02	.01
☐ 100	Shaquille O'Neal PP	.60	.25	.07
☐ 101	Shawn Kemp PP	.40	.18	.05
☐ 102	Hakeem Olajuwon PP	.30	.14	.04
☐ 103	Derrick Coleman PP	.05	.02	.01
☐ 104	Alonzo Mourning PP	.15	.07	.02
☐ 105	Dikembe Mutombo PP	.10	.05	.01
☐ 106	Chris Webber PP	.15	.07	.02
☐ 107	Dennis Rodman PP	.50	.23	.06
☐ 108	David Robinson PP	.25	.11	.03
☐ 109	Charles Barkley PP	.20	.09	.03
☐ 110	Brad Daugherty	.05	.02	.01
☐ 111	Derek Harper	.05	.02	.01
☐ 112	Detlef Schrempf	.10	.05	.01
☐ 113	Harvey Grant	.05	.02	.01
☐ 114	Vlade Divac	.10	.05	.01
☐ 115	Isaiah Rider	.10	.05	.01
☐ 116	Mitch Richmond	.20	.09	.03
☐ 117	Tom Chambers	.05	.02	.01
☐ 118	Kenny Gattison	.05	.02	.01
☐ 119	Kenny Gattison FTR	.05	.02	.01
☐ 120	Vernon Maxwell	.05	.02	.01
☐ 121	Reggie Williams	.05	.02	.01
☐ 122	Chris Mullin	.10	.05	.01
☐ 123	Harold Miner	.05	.02	.01
☐ 124	Harold Miner FTR	.05	.02	.01
☐ 125	Calbert Cheaney	.05	.02	.01
☐ 126	Randy Woods	.05	.02	.01
☐ 127	Mike Gminski	.05	.02	.01
☐ 128	Willie Anderson	.05	.02	.01
☐ 129	Mark Macon	.05	.02	.01
☐ 130	Avery Johnson	.10	.05	.01
☐ 131	Bimbo Coles	.05	.02	.01
☐ 132	Kenny Smith	.05	.02	.01
☐ 133	Dennis Scott	.10	.05	.01
☐ 134	Lionel Simmons	.05	.02	.01
☐ 135	Nate McMillan	.05	.02	.01
☐ 136	Eric Montross	.10	.05	.01
☐ 137	Sedale Threatt	.05	.02	.01
☐ 138	Kenny Anderson	.10	.05	.01
☐ 139	Micheal Williams	.05	.02	.01
☐ 140	Grant Long	.05	.02	.01
☐ 141	Grant Long FTR	.05	.02	.01
☐ 142	Tyrone Corbin	.05	.02	.01
☐ 143	Craig Ehlo	.05	.02	.01
☐ 144	Gerald Wilkins	.05	.02	.01
☐ 145	LaPhonso Ellis	.05	.02	.01
☐ 146	Reggie Miller	.30	.14	.04
☐ 147	Tracy Murray	.05	.02	.01
☐ 148	Victor Alexander	.05	.02	.01
☐ 149	Victor Alexander FTR	.05	.02	.01
☐ 150	Clifford Robinson	.10	.05	.01
☐ 151	Anthony Mason FTR	.05	.02	.01
☐ 152	Anthony Mason	.10	.05	.01
☐ 153	Jim Jackson	.30	.14	.04
☐ 154	Jeff Hornacek	.10	.05	.01
☐ 155	Nick Anderson	.10	.05	.01
☐ 156	Mike Brown	.05	.02	.01
☐ 157	Kevin Johnson	.10	.05	.01
☐ 158	John Paxson	.10	.05	.01
☐ 159	Loy Vaught	.05	.02	.01
☐ 160	Carl Herrera	.05	.02	.01
☐ 161	Shawn Bradley	.10	.05	.01
☐ 162	Hubert Davis	.05	.02	.01
☐ 163	David Benoit	.05	.02	.01
☐ 164	Dell Curry	.05	.02	.01
☐ 165	Dee Brown	.05	.02	.01
☐ 166	LaSalle Thompson	.05	.02	.01
☐ 167	Eddie Jones	.60	.25	.07
☐ 168	Walt Williams	.10	.05	.01
☐ 169	A.C. Green	.10	.05	.01
☐ 170	Kendall Gill	.05	.02	.01
☐ 171	Kendall Gill FTR	.05	.02	.01
☐ 172	Danny Ferry	.05	.02	.01
☐ 173	Bryant Stith	.05	.02	.01
☐ 174	John Salley	.05	.02	.01
☐ 175	Cedric Ceballos	.10	.05	.01
☐ 176	Derrick Coleman	.05	.02	.01
☐ 177	Tony Bennett	.05	.02	.01
☐ 178	Kevin Duckworth	.05	.02	.01
☐ 179	Jay Humphries	.05	.02	.01
☐ 180	Sean Elliott	.10	.05	.01
☐ 181	Sam Perkins	.05	.02	.01
☐ 182	Luc Longley	.05	.02	.01
☐ 183	Mitch Richmond AS	.05	.02	.01
☐ 184	Clyde Drexler AS	.10	.05	.01
☐ 185	Karl Malone AS	.10	.05	.01
☐ 186	Shawn Kemp AS	.40	.18	.05
☐ 187	Hakeem Olajuwon AS	.30	.14	.04
☐ 188	Danny Manning AS	.05	.02	.01
☐ 189	Kevin Johnson AS	.10	.05	.01
☐ 190	John Stockton AS	.10	.05	.01
☐ 191	Latrell Sprewell AS	.05	.02	.01
☐ 192	Gary Payton AS	.20	.09	.03
☐ 193	Clifford Robinson AS	.05	.02	.01
☐ 194	David Robinson AS	.25	.11	.03
☐ 195	Charles Barkley AS	.20	.09	.03
☐ 196	Mark Price SPEC	.05	.02	.01
☐ 197	Checklist 1-99	.05	.02	.01
☐ 198	Checklist 100-198	.05	.02	.01
☐ 199	Patrick Ewing	.25	.11	.03
☐ 200	Patrick Ewing FTR	.10	.05	.01
☐ 201	Tracy Murray PP	.05	.02	.01
☐ 202	Craig Ehlo PP	.05	.02	.01
☐ 203	Nick Anderson PP	.05	.02	.01
☐ 204	John Starks PP	.05	.02	.01
☐ 205	Rex Chapman PP	.05	.02	.01
☐ 206	Hersey Hawkins PP	.05	.02	.01
☐ 207	Glen Rice PP	.05	.02	.01
☐ 208	Jeff Malone PP	.05	.02	.01
☐ 209	Dan Majerle PP	.05	.02	.01
☐ 210	Chris Mullin PP	.05	.02	.01
☐ 211	Grant Hill	3.00	1.35	.35
☐ 212	Bobby Phills	.05	.02	.01
☐ 213	Dennis Rodman	1.00	.45	.12
☐ 214	Doug West	.05	.02	.01
☐ 215	Harold Ellis	.05	.02	.01
☐ 216	Kevin Edwards	.05	.02	.01
☐ 217	Lorenzo Williams	.05	.02	.01
☐ 218	Rick Fox	.05	.02	.01
☐ 219	Mookie Blaylock	.10	.05	.01
☐ 220	Mookie Blaylock FTR	.05	.02	.01
☐ 221	John Williams	.05	.02	.01
☐ 222	Keith Jennings	.05	.02	.01
☐ 223	Nick Van Exel	.25	.11	.03
☐ 224	Gary Payton	.40	.18	.05
☐ 225	John Stockton	.25	.11	.03
☐ 226	Ron Harper	.10	.05	.01
☐ 227	Monty Williams	.05	.02	.01
☐ 228	Marty Conlon	.05	.02	.01
☐ 229	Hersey Hawkins	.05	.02	.01
☐ 230	Rik Smits	.10	.05	.01
☐ 231	James Robinson	.05	.02	.01
☐ 232	Malik Sealy	.05	.02	.01
☐ 233	Sergei Bazarevich	.05	.02	.01
☐ 234	Brad Lohaus	.05	.02	.01
☐ 235	Olden Polynice	.05	.02	.01
☐ 236	Brian Williams	.05	.02	.01
☐ 237	Tyrone Hill	.05	.02	.01

#	Player			
☐ 238	Jim McIlvaine	.10	.05	.01
☐ 239	Latrell Sprewell	.30	.14	.04
☐ 240	Latrell Sprewell FTR	.05	.02	.01
☐ 241	Popeye Jones	.05	.02	.01
☐ 242	Scott Williams	.05	.02	.01
☐ 243	Eddie Jones	.30	.14	.04
☐ 244	Moses Malone	.15	.07	.02
☐ 245	B.J. Armstrong	.05	.02	.01
☐ 246	Jim Les	.05	.02	.01
☐ 247	Greg Grant	.05	.02	.01
☐ 248	Lee Mayberry	.05	.02	.01
☐ 249	Mark Jackson	.05	.02	.01
☐ 250	Larry Johnson	.25	.11	.03
☐ 251	Terrell Brandon	.10	.05	.01
☐ 252	Ledell Eackles	.05	.02	.01
☐ 253	Yinka Dare	.05	.02	.01
☐ 254	Dontonio Wingfield	.05	.02	.01
☐ 255	Clyde Drexler	.30	.14	.04
☐ 256	Andres Guibert	.05	.02	.01
☐ 257	Gheorghe Muresan	.10	.05	.01
☐ 258	Tom Hammonds	.05	.02	.01
☐ 259	Charles Barkley	.40	.18	.05
☐ 260	Charles Barkley FTR	.20	.09	.03
☐ 261	Acie Earl	.05	.02	.01
☐ 262	Lamond Murray	.05	.02	.01
☐ 263	Dana Barros	.05	.02	.01
☐ 264	Greg Anthony	.05	.02	.01
☐ 265	Dan Majerle	.10	.05	.01
☐ 266	Zan Tabak	.05	.02	.01
☐ 267	Ricky Pierce	.05	.02	.01
☐ 268	Eric Leckner	.05	.02	.01
☐ 269	Duane Ferrell	.05	.02	.01
☐ 270	Mark Price	.05	.02	.01
☐ 271	Anthony Peeler	.05	.02	.01
☐ 272	Adam Keefe	.05	.02	.01
☐ 273	Rex Walters	.05	.02	.01
☐ 274	Scott Skiles	.05	.02	.01
☐ 275	Glenn Robinson	1.00	.45	.12
☐ 276	Tony Dumas	.10	.05	.01
☐ 277	Elliot Perry	.05	.02	.01
☐ 278	Bo Outlaw	.05	.02	.01
☐ 279	Karl Malone	.25	.11	.03
☐ 280	Karl Malone FTR	.10	.05	.01
☐ 281	Herb Williams	.05	.02	.01
☐ 282	Vincent Askew	.05	.02	.01
☐ 283	Askia Jones	.05	.02	.01
☐ 284	Shawn Bradley	.10	.05	.01
☐ 285	Tim Hardaway	.10	.05	.01
☐ 286	Mark West	.05	.02	.01
☐ 287	Chuck Person	.05	.02	.01
☐ 288	James Edwards	.05	.02	.01
☐ 289	Antonio Lang	.05	.02	.01
☐ 290	Dominique Wilkins	.10	.05	.01
☐ 291	Khalid Reeves	.05	.02	.01
☐ 292	Jamie Watson	.05	.02	.01
☐ 293	Darnell Mee	.05	.02	.01
☐ 294	Brian Grant	.40	.18	.05
☐ 295	Hakeem Olajuwon	.60	.25	.07
☐ 296	Dickey Simpkins	.10	.05	.01
☐ 297	Tyrone Corbin	.05	.02	.01
☐ 298	David Wingate	.05	.02	.01
☐ 299	Shaquille O'Neal	1.25	.55	.16
☐ 300	Shaquille O'Neal FTR	.60	.25	.07
☐ 301	B.J. Armstrong PP	.05	.02	.01
☐ 302	Mitch Richmond PP	.05	.02	.01
☐ 303	Jim Jackson PP	.10	.05	.01
☐ 304	Jeff Hornacek PP	.05	.02	.01
☐ 305	Mark Price PP	.05	.02	.01
☐ 306	Kendall Gill PP	.05	.02	.01
☐ 307	Dale Ellis PP	.05	.02	.01
☐ 308	Vernon Maxwell PP	.05	.02	.01
☐ 309	Joe Dumars PP	.10	.05	.01
☐ 310	Reggie Miller PP	.15	.07	.02
☐ 311	Geert Hammink	.05	.02	.01
☐ 312	Charles Smith	.05	.02	.01
☐ 313	Bill Cartwright	.05	.02	.01
☐ 314	Aaron McKie	.10	.05	.01
☐ 315	Tom Gugliotta	.10	.05	.01
☐ 316	P.J. Brown	.05	.02	.01
☐ 317	David Wesley	.05	.02	.01
☐ 318	Felton Spencer	.05	.02	.01
☐ 319	Robert Horry	.10	.05	.01
☐ 320	Robert Horry FR	.05	.02	.01
☐ 321	Larry Krystkowiak	.05	.02	.01
☐ 322	Eric Piatkowski	.05	.02	.01
☐ 323	Anthony Bonner	.05	.02	.01
☐ 324	Keith Askins	.05	.02	.01
☐ 325	Mahmoud Abdul-Rauf	.10	.05	.01
☐ 326	Darrin Hancock	.05	.02	.01
☐ 327	Vern Fleming	.05	.02	.01
☐ 328	Wayman Tisdale	.05	.02	.01
☐ 329	Sam Bowie	.05	.02	.01
☐ 330	Billy Owens	.05	.02	.01
☐ 331	Donald Hodge	.05	.02	.01
☐ 332	Derrick Alston	.05	.02	.01
☐ 333	Doug Edwards	.05	.02	.01
☐ 334	Johnny Newman	.05	.02	.01
☐ 335	Otis Thorpe	.10	.05	.01
☐ 336	Bill Curley	.05	.02	.01
☐ 337	Michael Cage	.05	.02	.01
☐ 338	Chris Smith	.05	.02	.01
☐ 339	Dikembe Mutombo	.10	.05	.01
☐ 340	Dikembe Mutombo FTR	.10	.05	.01
☐ 341	Duane Causwell	.05	.02	.01
☐ 342	Sean Higgins	.05	.02	.01
☐ 343	Steve Kerr	.10	.05	.01
☐ 344	Eric Montross	.10	.05	.01
☐ 345	Charles Oakley	.10	.05	.01
☐ 346	Brooks Thompson	.10	.05	.01
☐ 347	Rony Seikaly	.05	.02	.01
☐ 348	Chris Dudley	.05	.02	.01
☐ 349	Sharone Wright	.10	.05	.01
☐ 350	Sarunas Marciulionis	.05	.02	.01
☐ 351	Anthony Miller	.05	.02	.01
☐ 352	Pooh Richardson	.05	.02	.01
☐ 353	Byron Scott	.10	.05	.01
☐ 354	Michael Adams	.05	.02	.01
☐ 355	Ken Norman	.05	.02	.01
☐ 356	Clifford Rozier	.10	.05	.01
☐ 357	Tim Breaux	.05	.02	.01
☐ 358	Derek Strong	.05	.02	.01
☐ 359	David Robinson	.50	.23	.06
☐ 360	David Robinson FR	.25	.11	.03
☐ 361	Benoit Benjamin	.05	.02	.01
☐ 362	Terry Porter	.05	.02	.01
☐ 363	Ervin Johnson	.05	.02	.01
☐ 364	Alaa Abdelnaby	.05	.02	.01
☐ 365	Robert Parish	.10	.05	.01
☐ 366	Mario Elie	.05	.02	.01
☐ 367	Antonio Harvey	.05	.02	.01
☐ 368	Charlie Ward	.10	.05	.01
☐ 369	Kevin Gamble	.05	.02	.01
☐ 370	Rod Strickland	.05	.02	.01
☐ 371	Jason Kidd	1.00	.45	.12
☐ 372	Oliver Miller	.05	.02	.01
☐ 373	Eric Mobley	.10	.05	.01
☐ 374	Brian Shaw	.05	.02	.01
☐ 375	Horace Grant	.10	.05	.01
☐ 376	Corie Blount	.05	.02	.01
☐ 377	Sam Mitchell	.05	.02	.01
☐ 378	Jalen Rose	.25	.11	.03
☐ 379	Elden Campbell	.10	.05	.01

		MINT	NRMT	EXC
☐ 380	Elden Campbell FTR	.05	.02	.01
☐ 381	Donyell Marshall	.10	.05	.01
☐ 382	Frank Brickowski	.05	.02	.01
☐ 383	B.J. Tyler	.05	.02	.01
☐ 384	Bryon Russell	.05	.02	.01
☐ 385	Danny Manning	.10	.05	.01
☐ 386	Manute Bol	.05	.02	.01
☐ 387	Brent Price	.05	.02	.01
☐ 388	J.R. Reid	.05	.02	.01
☐ 389	Byron Houston	.05	.02	.01
☐ 390	Blue Edwards	.05	.02	.01
☐ 391	Adrian Caldwell	.05	.02	.01
☐ 392	Wesley Person	.10	.05	.01
☐ 393	Juwan Howard	2.00	.90	.25
☐ 394	Chris Morris	.05	.02	.01
☐ 395	Checklist 199-296	.05	.02	.01
☐ 396	Checklist 297-396	.05	.02	.01

1994-95 Topps
Spectralight

Randomly inserted into both first and second series packs at a rate of one in four, cards from this standard-size set parallel the basic issue 1994-95 Topps set. Unlike the basic issue cards, fronts feature a full foil-treatment on the pictures. Also, card numbers 197-198 and 395-396 feature players on them (in replacement of the checklist cards that are part of the regular issue set). Please refer to the multipliers provided below (coupled with the prices of the corresponding regular issue card) to ascertain value.

	MINT	NRMT	EXC
COMPLETE SET (396)	300.00	135.00	38.00
COMPLETE SERIES 1 (198)	125.00	55.00	15.50
COMPLETE SERIES 2 (198)	175.00	80.00	22.00
COMMON CARD (1-396)	.25	.11	.03
*STARS: 5X to 10X VALUE			
*ROOKIES: 4X to 8X VALUE			

		MINT	NRMT	EXC
☐ 197	Keith Jennings	.50	.23	.06
☐ 198	Mark Price	1.00	.45	.12
☐ 395	Chris Webber	3.00	1.35	.35
☐ 396	Mitch Richmond	2.00	.90	.25

1994-95 Topps
Franchise/Futures

Randomly inserted into all second series packs at a rate of one in 18, cards from this

20-card set feature a selection of promising youngsters coupled with established stars from the same team. Card fronts feature full-color action shots surrounded by a white border.

		MINT	NRMT	EXC
COMPLETE SET (20)		60.00	27.00	7.50
COMMON CARD (1-20)		1.00	.45	.12
☐ 1	Mookie Blaylock	1.00	.45	.12
☐ 2	Stacey Augmon	1.00	.45	.12
☐ 3	Dominique Wilkins	1.50	.70	.19
☐ 4	Eric Montross	1.00	.45	.12
☐ 5	Dikembe Mutombo	1.50	.70	.19
☐ 6	Jalen Rose	1.00	.45	.12
☐ 7	Joe Dumars	1.50	.70	.19
☐ 8	Grant Hill	20.00	9.00	2.50
☐ 9	Chris Mullin	1.50	.70	.19
☐ 10	Latrell Sprewell	1.50	.70	.19
☐ 11	Glen Rice	1.50	.70	.19
☐ 12	Khalid Reeves	1.00	.45	.12
☐ 13	Derrick Coleman	1.00	.45	.12
☐ 14	Yinka Dare	1.00	.45	.12
☐ 15	Patrick Ewing	3.00	1.35	.35
☐ 16	Monty Williams	1.00	.45	.12
☐ 17	Shaquille O'Neal	15.00	6.75	1.85
☐ 18	Anfernee Hardaway	20.00	9.00	2.50
☐ 19	Charles Barkley	5.00	2.20	.60
☐ 20	Wesley Person	1.50	.70	.19

1994-95 Topps
Own the Game

Randomly inserted in all first series packs (12-card packs one in 18, jumbo packs one in 9), cards from this 50-card standard-size unnumbered set featured nine top players

in five different statistical categories (Super Passers, Super Rebounders, Super Scorers, Super Stealers and Super Swatters) in addition to five Field Cards. If the player pictured on the card (Field Card represented all other players in the league) led the league in that respective category, it became redeemable for a special 10-card Own the Game redemption set for that category. The Own the Game redemption expired on February 7th, 1996. Cards are listed below in alphabetical order with a number assigned to them for checklisting purposes. Exchange cards began shipping in October, 1995. According to Topps, only 8,000 exchange sets were shipped. The 10-card exchange sets consists of the top two players that finished in each category: O'Neal and Olajuwon for Scoring, Stockton and Anderson for Passing, Rodman and Mutombo for Rebounds, Pippen and Blaylock for Steals and Mutombo and Olajuwon for Blocks. Please refer to the multipliers provided below for values on individual exchange cards.

	MINT	NRMT	EXC
COMPLETE SET (50)	25.00	11.00	3.10
COMMON CARD (1-50)	.15	.07	.02
COMPLETE EXCHANGE SET (10)	10.00	4.50	1.25
*EXCHANGE CARDS: 1X VALUE.......			

		MINT	NRMT	EXC
☐ 1	Kenny Anderson PASS	.30	.14	.04
☐ 2	Charles Barkley SCORE	1.00	.45	.12
☐ 3	Mookie Blaylock PASS	.30	.14	.04
☐ 4	Mookie Blaylock STEAL	.30	.14	.04
☐ 5	Muggsy Bogues PASS	.30	.14	.04
☐ 6	Shawn Bradley SWAT	.30	.14	.04
☐ 7	Derrick Coleman REB	.15	.07	.02
☐ 8	Sherman Douglas PASS	.15	.07	.02
☐ 9	Patrick Ewing REB	.60	.25	.07
☐ 10	Patrick Ewing SCORE	.60	.25	.07
☐ 11	Patrick Ewing SWAT	.60	.25	.07
☐ 12	Tom Gugliotta STEAL	.30	.14	.04
☐ 13	A.Hardaway STEAL	4.00	1.80	.50
☐ 14	Mark Jackson PASS	.15	.07	.02
☐ 15	Kevin Johnson PASS	.30	.14	.04
☐ 16	Karl Malone REB	.60	.25	.07
☐ 17	Karl Malone SCORE	.60	.25	.07
☐ 18	Nate McMillan STEAL	.15	.07	.02
☐ 19	Oliver Miller SWAT	.15	.07	.02
☐ 20	Alonzo Mourning SWAT	.75	.35	.09
☐ 21	Eric Murdock STEAL	.15	.07	.02
☐ 22	D.Mutombo REB	.30	.14	.04
☐ 23	D.Mutombo SWAT W	.50	.23	.06
☐ 24	Charles Oakley REB	.15	.07	.02
☐ 25	H.Olajuwon REB	1.50	.70	.19
☐ 26	H.Olajuwon SCORE	1.50	.70	.19
☐ 27	H.Olajuwon SWAT	1.50	.70	.19
☐ 28	S. O'Neal REB	3.00	1.35	.35
☐ 29	S.O'Neal SCORE W	4.00	1.80	.50
☐ 30	S.O'Neal SWAT	3.00	1.35	.35
☐ 31	Gary Payton STEAL	1.00	.45	.12
☐ 32	Scottie Pippen SCORE	2.00	.90	.25
☐ 33	Scottie Pippen STEAL W	2.00	1.10	.30
☐ 34	Mark Price PASS	.15	.07	.02
☐ 35	Mitch Richmond SCORE	.30	.14	.04
☐ 36	David Robinson SCORE	1.25	.55	.16
☐ 37	David Robinson SWAT	1.25	.55	.16
☐ 38	Dennis Rodman REB W	3.00	1.35	.35
☐ 39	Latrell Sprewell STEAL	.30	.14	.04
☐ 40	John Stockton PASS W	.75	.35	.09
☐ 41	John Stockton STEAL	.60	.25	.07
☐ 42	Rod Strickland PASS	.15	.07	.02
☐ 43	Chris Webber SWAT	.75	.35	.09
☐ 44	Kevin Willis REB	.15	.07	.02
☐ 45	D.Wilkins SCORE	.30	.14	.04
☐ 46	Passers Field Card	.15	.07	.02
☐ 47	Rebounders Field Card	.15	.07	.02
☐ 48	Scorers Field Card	.15	.07	.02
☐ 49	Stealers Field Card	.15	.07	.02
☐ 50	Swatters Field Card	.15	.07	.02

1994-95 Topps Super Sophomores

Randomly inserted into all second series packs at a rate of one in 36, cards from this 10-card standard-size set spotlight a selection of young phenoms in their second NBA season. Fronts feature full-color player action shots cut out against silver-foil backgrounds.

		MINT	NRMT	EXC
COMPLETE SET (10)		50.00	22.00	6.25
COMMON CARD (1-10)		1.50	.70	.19

		MINT	NRMT	EXC
☐ 1	Chris Webber	6.00	2.70	.75
☐ 2	Anfernee Hardaway	30.00	13.50	3.70
☐ 3	Vin Baker	6.00	2.70	.75
☐ 4	Sam Cassell	2.50	1.10	.30
☐ 5	Jamal Mashburn	4.00	1.80	.50
☐ 6	Isaiah Rider	2.50	1.10	.30
☐ 7	Chris Mills	2.50	1.10	.30
☐ 8	Antonio Davis	1.50	.70	.19
☐ 9	Nick Van Exel	5.00	2.20	.60
☐ 10	Lindsey Hunter	1.50	.70	.19

1995-96 Topps

The 1995-96 Topps Basketball set was issued in two separate series of 181 and 110 standard-size cards for a total of 291. Both first and second series cards were issued in 12-card hobby and retail packs (SRP $1.29). The white bordered fronts have a full-color action photo with the player's name in gold set against a black shadow. Horizontal backs have color head-shots

with statistics and information. Subsets include Active Leaders (1-5), Scoring Leaders (6-10), Rebound Leaders (11-15), Assist Leaders (16-20), Steal Leaders (21-25) and Block Leaders (26-30). Rookie Cards of note in this set include Michael Finley, Kevin Garnett, Antonio McDyess, Joe Smith, Jerry Stackhouse and Damon Stoudamire.

	MINT	NRMT	EXC
COMPLETE SET (291)	30.00	13.50	3.70
COMPLETE SERIES 1 (181)	15.00	6.75	1.85
COMPLETE SERIES 2 (110)	15.00	6.75	1.85
COMMON CARD (1-291)	.05	.02	.01

☐	1 Michael Jordan AL	1.50	.70	.19
☐	2 Dennis Rodman AL	.50	.23	.06
☐	3 John Stockton AL	.10	.05	.01
☐	4 Michael Jordan AL	1.50	.70	.19
☐	5 David Robinson AL	.25	.11	.03
☐	6 Shaquille O'Neal LL	.60	.25	.07
☐	7 Hakeem Olajuwon LL	.30	.14	.04
☐	8 David Robinson LL	.25	.11	.03
☐	9 Karl Malone LL	.10	.05	.01
☐	10 Jamal Mashburn LL	.10	.05	.01
☐	11 Dennis Rodman LL	.50	.23	.06
☐	12 Dikembe Mutombo LL	.10	.05	.01
☐	13 Shaquille O'Neal LL	.60	.25	.07
☐	14 Patrick Ewing LL	.10	.05	.01
☐	15 Tyrone Hill LL	.05	.02	.01
☐	16 John Stockton LL	.10	.05	.01
☐	17 Kenny Anderson LL	.05	.02	.01
☐	18 Tim Hardaway LL	.05	.02	.01
☐	19 Rod Strickland LL	.05	.02	.01
☐	20 Muggsy Bogues LL	.05	.02	.01
☐	21 Scottie Pippen LL	.40	.18	.05
☐	22 Mookie Blaylock LL	.05	.02	.01
☐	23 Gary Payton LL	.20	.09	.03
☐	24 John Stockton LL	.10	.05	.01
☐	25 Nate McMillan LL	.05	.02	.01
☐	26 Dikembe Mutombo LL	.10	.05	.01
☐	27 Hakeem Olajuwon LL	.30	.14	.04
☐	28 Shawn Bradley LL	.05	.02	.01
☐	29 David Robinson LL	.25	.11	.03
☐	30 Alonzo Mourning LL	.10	.05	.01
☐	31 Reggie Miller	.30	.14	.04
☐	32 Karl Malone	.25	.11	.03
☐	33 Grant Hill	1.00	.45	.12
☐	34 Charles Barkley	.40	.18	.05
☐	35 Cedric Ceballos	.10	.05	.01
☐	36 Gheorghe Muresan	.10	.05	.01
☐	37 Doug West	.05	.02	.01
☐	38 Tony Dumas	.05	.02	.01
☐	39 Kenny Gattison	.05	.02	.01
☐	40 Chris Mullin	.10	.05	.01
☐	41 Pervis Ellison	.05	.02	.01
☐	42 Vinny Del Negro	.05	.02	.01
☐	43 Mario Elie	.05	.02	.01
☐	44 Todd Day	.05	.02	.01
☐	45 Scottie Pippen	.75	.35	.09
☐	46 Buck Williams	.10	.05	.01
☐	47 P.J. Brown	.05	.02	.01
☐	48 Bimbo Coles	.05	.02	.01
☐	49 Terrell Brandon	.05	.02	.01
☐	50 Charles Oakley	.10	.05	.01
☐	51 Sam Perkins	.05	.02	.01
☐	52 Dale Ellis	.05	.02	.01
☐	53 Andrew Lang	.05	.02	.01
☐	54 Harold Ellis	.05	.02	.01
☐	55 Clarence Weatherspoon	.05	.02	.01
☐	56 Bill Curley	.05	.02	.01
☐	57 Robert Parish	.10	.05	.01
☐	58 David Benoit	.05	.02	.01
☐	59 Anthony Avent	.05	.02	.01
☐	60 Jamal Mashburn	.15	.07	.02
☐	61 Duane Ferrell	.05	.02	.01
☐	62 Elden Campbell	.10	.05	.01
☐	63 Rex Chapman	.05	.02	.01
☐	64 Wesley Person	.10	.05	.01
☐	65 Mitch Richmond	.20	.09	.03
☐	66 Micheal Williams	.05	.02	.01
☐	67 Clifford Rozier	.05	.02	.01
☐	68 Eric Montross	.05	.02	.01
☐	69 Dennis Rodman	1.00	.45	.12
☐	70 Vin Baker	.25	.11	.03
☐	71 Tyrone Hill	.05	.02	.01
☐	72 Tyrone Corbin	.05	.02	.01
☐	73 Chris Dudley	.05	.02	.01
☐	74 Nate McMillan	.05	.02	.01
☐	75 Kenny Anderson	.10	.05	.01
☐	76 Monty Williams	.05	.02	.01
☐	77 Kenny Smith	.05	.02	.01
☐	78 Rodney Rogers	.05	.02	.01
☐	79 Corie Blount	.05	.02	.01
☐	80 Glen Rice	.10	.05	.01
☐	81 Walt Williams	.10	.05	.01
☐	82 Scott Williams	.05	.02	.01
☐	83 Michael Adams	.05	.02	.01
☐	84 Terry Mills	.05	.02	.01
☐	85 Horace Grant	.10	.05	.01
☐	86 Chuck Person	.05	.02	.01
☐	87 Adam Keefe	.05	.02	.01
☐	88 Scott Brooks	.05	.02	.01
☐	89 George Lynch	.05	.02	.01
☐	90 Kevin Johnson	.10	.05	.01
☐	91 Armon Gilliam	.05	.02	.01
☐	92 Greg Minor	.05	.02	.01
☐	93 Derrick McKey	.05	.02	.01
☐	94 Victor Alexander	.05	.02	.01
☐	95 B.J. Armstrong	.05	.02	.01
☐	96 Terry Dehere	.05	.02	.01
☐	97 Christian Laettner	.10	.05	.01
☐	98 Hubert Davis	.05	.02	.01
☐	99 Aaron McKie	.05	.02	.01
☐	100 Hakeem Olajuwon	.60	.25	.07
☐	101 Michael Cage	.05	.02	.01
☐	102 Grant Long	.05	.02	.01
☐	103 Calbert Cheaney	.05	.02	.01
☐	104 Olden Polynice	.05	.02	.01
☐	105 Sharone Wright	.05	.02	.01
☐	106 Lee Mayberry	.05	.02	.01
☐	107 Robert Pack	.05	.02	.01
☐	108 Loy Vaught	.05	.02	.01
☐	109 Khalid Reeves	.05	.02	.01
☐	110 Shawn Kemp	.75	.35	.09
☐	111 Lindsey Hunter	.05	.02	.01
☐	112 Dell Curry	.05	.02	.01

☐ 113	Dan Majerle	.10	.05	.01	☐ 184	Ervin Johnson	.05	.02	.01
☐ 114	Bryon Russell	.05	.02	.01	☐ 185	Chucky Brown	.05	.02	.01
☐ 115	John Starks	.05	.02	.01	☐ 186	Luc Longley	.05	.02	.01
☐ 116	Roy Tarpley	.05	.02	.01	☐ 187	Anthony Miller	.05	.02	.01
☐ 117	Dale Davis	.05	.02	.01	☐ 188	Ed O'Bannon	.40	.18	.05
☐ 118	Nick Anderson	.10	.05	.01	☐ 189	Bobby Hurley	.05	.02	.01
☐ 119	Rex Walters	.05	.02	.01	☐ 190	Dikembe Mutombo	.10	.05	.01
☐ 120	Dominique Wilkins	.10	.05	.01	☐ 191	Robert Horry	.10	.05	.01
☐ 121	Sam Cassell	.10	.05	.01	☐ 192	George Zidek	.15	.07	.02
☐ 122	Sean Elliott	.10	.05	.01	☐ 193	Rasheed Wallace	.50	.23	.06
☐ 123	B.J. Tyler	.05	.02	.01	☐ 194	Marty Conlon	.05	.02	.01
☐ 124	Eric Mobley	.05	.02	.01	☐ 195	A.C. Green	.10	.05	.01
☐ 125	Toni Kukoc	.15	.07	.02	☐ 196	Mike Brown	.05	.02	.01
☐ 126	Pooh Richardson	.05	.02	.01	☐ 197	Oliver Miller	.05	.02	.01
☐ 127	Isaiah Rider	.10	.05	.01	☐ 198	Charles Smith	.05	.02	.01
☐ 128	Steve Smith	.10	.05	.01	☐ 199	Eric Williams	.20	.09	.03
☐ 129	Chris Mills	.10	.05	.01	☐ 200	Rik Smits	.10	.05	.01
☐ 130	Detlef Schrempf	.10	.05	.01	☐ 201	Donald Royal	.05	.02	.01
☐ 131	Donyell Marshall	.05	.02	.01	☐ 202	Bryant Reeves	.60	.25	.07
☐ 132	Eddie Jones	.20	.09	.03	☐ 203	Danny Ferry	.05	.02	.01
☐ 133	Otis Thorpe	.10	.05	.01	☐ 204	Brian Williams	.05	.02	.01
☐ 134	Lionel Simmons	.05	.02	.01	☐ 205	Joe Smith	1.25	.55	.16
☐ 135	Jeff Hornacek	.10	.05	.01	☐ 206	Gary Trent	.20	.09	.03
☐ 136	Jalen Rose	.05	.02	.01	☐ 207	Greg Ostertag	.05	.02	.01
☐ 137	Kevin Willis	.05	.02	.01	☐ 208	Ken Norman	.05	.02	.01
☐ 138	Don MacLean	.05	.02	.01	☐ 209	Avery Johnson	.10	.05	.01
☐ 139	Dee Brown	.05	.02	.01	☐ 210	Theo Ratliff UER	.20	.09	.03
☐ 140	Glenn Robinson	.30	.14	.04		Card has no draft pick logo			
☐ 141	Joe Kleine	.05	.02	.01	☐ 211	Corie Blount	.05	.02	.01
☐ 142	Ron Harper	.10	.05	.01	☐ 212	Hersey Hawkins	.05	.02	.01
☐ 143	Antonio Davis	.05	.02	.01	☐ 213	Loren Meyer	.10	.05	.01
☐ 144	Jeff Malone	.05	.02	.01	☐ 214	Mario Bennett	.05	.02	.01
☐ 145	Joe Dumars	.10	.05	.01	☐ 215	Randolph Childress	.05	.02	.01
☐ 146	Jason Kidd	.60	.25	.07	☐ 216	Spud Webb	.10	.05	.01
☐ 147	J.R. Reid	.05	.02	.01	☐ 217	Popeye Jones	.05	.02	.01
☐ 148	Lamond Murray	.05	.02	.01	☐ 218	Shawn Respert	.20	.09	.03
☐ 149	Derrick Coleman	.05	.02	.01	☐ 219	Malik Sealy	.05	.02	.01
☐ 150	Alonzo Mourning	.25	.11	.03	☐ 220	Dino Radja	.10	.05	.01
☐ 151	Clifford Robinson	.10	.05	.01	☐ 221	James Robinson	.05	.02	.01
☐ 152	Kendall Gill	.05	.02	.01	☐ 222	David Vaughn	.05	.02	.01
☐ 153	Doug Christie	.05	.02	.01	☐ 223	Michael Smith	.05	.02	.01
☐ 154	Stacey Augmon	.10	.05	.01	☐ 224	Jamie Watson	.05	.02	.01
☐ 155	Anfernee Hardaway	1.50	.70	.19	☐ 225	LaPhonso Ellis	.05	.02	.01
☐ 156	Mahmoud Abdul-Rauf	.10	.05	.01	☐ 226	Kevin Gamble	.05	.02	.01
☐ 157	Latrell Sprewell	.10	.05	.01	☐ 227	Dennis Rodman Bulls	1.50	.70	.19
☐ 158	Mark Price	.05	.02	.01	☐ 228	B.J. Armstrong	.05	.02	.01
☐ 159	Brian Grant	.10	.05	.01	☐ 229	Jerry Stackhouse	2.00	.90	.25
☐ 160	Clyde Drexler	.30	.14	.04	☐ 230	Muggsy Bogues	.10	.05	.01
☐ 161	Juwan Howard	.60	.25	.07	☐ 231	Lawrence Moten	.05	.02	.01
☐ 162	Tom Gugliotta	.10	.05	.01	☐ 232	Cory Alexander	.05	.02	.01
☐ 163	Nick Van Exel	.20	.09	.03	☐ 233	Carlos Rogers	.05	.02	.01
☐ 164	Billy Owens	.05	.02	.01	☐ 234	Tyus Edney	.50	.23	.06
☐ 165	Brooks Thompson	.05	.02	.01	☐ 235	Doc Rivers	.05	.02	.01
☐ 166	Acie Earl	.05	.02	.01	☐ 236	Antonio Harvey	.05	.02	.01
☐ 167	Ed Pinckney	.05	.02	.01	☐ 237	Kevin Garnett	3.00	1.35	.35
☐ 168	Oliver Miller	.05	.02	.01	☐ 238	Derek Harper	.05	.02	.01
☐ 169	John Salley	.05	.02	.01	☐ 239	Kevin Edwards	.05	.02	.01
☐ 170	Jerome Kersey	.05	.02	.01	☐ 240	Chris Smith	.05	.02	.01
☐ 171	Willie Anderson	.05	.02	.01	☐ 241	Haywoode Workman	.05	.02	.01
☐ 172	Keith Jennings	.05	.02	.01	☐ 242	Bobby Phills	.05	.02	.01
☐ 173	Doug Smith	.05	.02	.01	☐ 243	Sherell Ford	.05	.02	.01
☐ 174	Gerald Wilkins	.05	.02	.01	☐ 244	Corliss Williamson	.20	.09	.03
☐ 175	Byron Scott	.10	.05	.01	☐ 245	Shawn Bradley	.10	.05	.01
☐ 176	Benoit Benjamin	.05	.02	.01	☐ 246	Jason Caffey	.05	.02	.01
☐ 177	Blue Edwards	.05	.02	.01	☐ 247	Bryant Stith	.05	.02	.01
☐ 178	Greg Anthony	.05	.02	.01	☐ 248	Mark West	.05	.02	.01
☐ 179	Trevor Ruffin	.05	.02	.01	☐ 249	Dennis Scott	.10	.05	.01
☐ 180	Kenny Gattison	.05	.02	.01	☐ 250	Jim Jackson	.15	.07	.02
☐ 181	Checklist 1-181	.05	.02	.01	☐ 251	Travis Best	.15	.07	.02
☐ 182	Cherokee Parks	.20	.09	.03	☐ 252	Sean Rooks	.05	.02	.01
☐ 183	Kurt Thomas	.30	.14	.04	☐ 253	Yinka Dare	.05	.02	.01

☐ 254 Felton Spencer	.05	.02	.01
☐ 255 Vlade Divac	.10	.05	.01
☐ 256 Michael Finley	1.25	.55	.16
☐ 257 Damon Stoudamire	2.50	1.10	.30
☐ 258 Mark Bryant	.05	.02	.01
☐ 259 Brent Barry	.50	.23	.06
☐ 260 Rony Seikaly	.05	.02	.01
☐ 261 Alan Henderson	.15	.07	.02
☐ 262 Kendall Gill	.05	.02	.01
☐ 263 Rex Chapman	.05	.02	.01
☐ 264 Eric Murdock	.05	.02	.01
☐ 265 Rodney Rogers	.05	.02	.01
☐ 266 Greg Graham	.05	.02	.01
☐ 267 Jayson Williams	.05	.02	.01
☐ 268 Antonio McDyess	1.00	.45	.12
☐ 269 Sedale Threatt	.05	.02	.01
☐ 270 Danny Manning	.10	.05	.01
☐ 271 Pete Chilcutt	.05	.02	.01
☐ 272 Bob Sura	.20	.09	.03
☐ 273 Dana Barros	.05	.02	.01
☐ 274 Allan Houston	.10	.05	.01
☐ 275 Tracy Murray	.05	.02	.01
☐ 276 Anthony Mason	.05	.02	.01
☐ 277 Michael Jordan	3.00	1.35	.35
☐ 278 Patrick Ewing	.25	.11	.03
☐ 279 Shaquille O'Neal	1.25	.55	.16
☐ 280 Larry Johnson	.25	.11	.03
☐ 281 Mark Jackson	.05	.02	.01
☐ 282 Chris Webber	.25	.11	.03
☐ 283 David Robinson	.50	.23	.06
☐ 284 John Stockton	.25	.11	.03
☐ 285 Mookie Blaylock	.05	.02	.01
☐ 286 Mark Price	.05	.02	.01
☐ 287 Tim Hardaway	.10	.05	.01
☐ 288 Rod Strickland	.05	.02	.01
☐ 289 Sherman Douglas	.05	.02	.01
☐ 290 Gary Payton	.40	.18	.05
☐ 291 Checklist (182-291)			

1995-96 Topps Draft Redemption

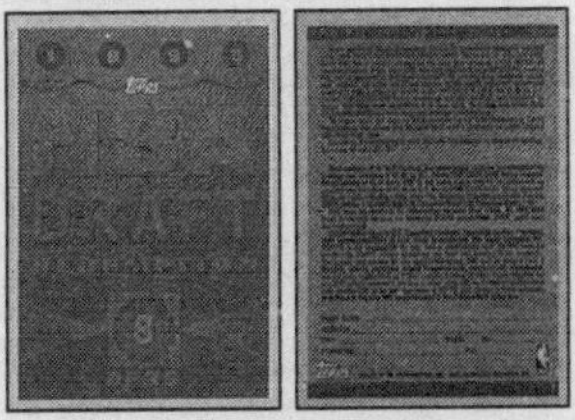

These 29 draft pick cards (covering the entire first round of the 1995 NBA draft) were available exclusively by redeeming one of the Topps Draft Redemption insert cards (randomly inserted in series one packs at a rate of one in 18). These cards feature all foil silver bordered fronts with a full-color action shot of the featured rookie. The first series exchange cards each featured a large number on the card front representing the player that was chosen at that slot in the 1995 NBA draft. Collectors had to then mail the card in to Topps to receive their player card. The redemption deadline for these cards was April 1, 1996.

	MINT	NRMT	EXC
COMPLETE SET (29)	100.00	45.00	12.50
COMMON CARD (1-29)	1.50	.70	.19
☐ 1 Joe Smith	10.00	4.50	1.25
☐ 2 Antonio McDyess	8.00	3.60	1.00
☐ 3 Jerry Stackhouse	15.00	6.75	1.85
☐ 4 Rasheed Wallace	4.00	1.80	.50
☐ 5 Kevin Garnett	30.00	13.50	3.70
☐ 6 Bryant Reeves	5.00	2.20	.60
☐ 7 Damon Stoudamire	20.00	9.00	2.50
☐ 8 Shawn Respert	2.50	1.10	.30
☐ 9 Ed O'Bannon	3.00	1.35	.35
☐ 10 Kurt Thomas	2.50	1.10	.30
☐ 11 Gary Trent	2.50	1.10	.30
☐ 12 Cherokee Parks	2.50	1.10	.30
☐ 13 Corliss Williamson	2.50	1.10	.30
☐ 14 Eric Williams	2.50	1.10	.30
☐ 15 Brent Barry	4.00	1.80	.50
☐ 16 Alan Henderson	2.50	1.10	.30
☐ 17 Bob Sura	2.50	1.10	.30
☐ 18 Theo Ratliff	2.50	1.10	.30
☐ 19 Randolph Childress	1.50	.70	.19
☐ 20 Jason Caffey	1.50	.70	.19
☐ 21 Michael Finley	10.00	4.50	1.25
☐ 22 George Zidek	1.50	.70	.19
☐ 23 Travis Best	1.50	.70	.19
☐ 24 Loren Meyer	1.50	.70	.19
☐ 25 David Vaughn	1.50	.70	.19
☐ 26 Sherell Ford	1.50	.70	.19
☐ 27 Mario Bennett	1.50	.70	.19
☐ 28 Greg Ostertag	1.50	.70	.19
☐ 29 Cory Alexander	1.50	.70	.19
☐ NNO Expired Trade Cards	1.00	.45	.12

1995-96 Topps Mystery Finest

Randomly inserted into all second series packs at a rate of one in 36, cards from this 22-card standard-size insert set spotlight a selection of top forwards and guards in the league. Each Mystery Finest card was inserted into packs with a black plastic coating on front. Hence, the "mystery" was to peel off the coating to see whether one

had a basic card or a parallel refractor. Card fronts featur a silver foil border and a player action photo cut out against a galaxy design background. These cards are often found poorly centered.

	MINT	NRMT	EXC
COMPLETE SET (22)	125.00	55.00	15.50
COMMON CARD (M1-M22)	2.00	.90	.25

		MINT	NRMT	EXC
☐ M1	Michael Jordan	60.00	27.00	7.50
☐ M2	Anfernee Hardaway	25.00	11.00	3.10
☐ M3	Clyde Drexler	5.00	2.20	.60
☐ M4	Mark Price	2.00	.90	.25
☐ M5	Steve Smith	2.00	.90	.25
☐ M6	Jim Jackson	2.50	1.10	.30
☐ M7	Nick Anderson	2.00	.90	.25
☐ M8	Kenny Anderson	2.00	.90	.25
☐ M9	Mookie Blaylock	2.00	.90	.25
☐ M10	Jason Kidd	10.00	4.50	1.25
☐ M11	Tim Hardaway	2.00	.90	.25
☐ M12	Kevin Johnson	2.00	.90	.25
☐ M13	Gary Payton	6.00	2.70	.75
☐ M14	John Stockton	4.00	1.80	.50
☐ M15	Rod Strickland	2.00	.90	.25
☐ M16	Jamal Mashburn	2.50	1.10	.30
☐ M17	Danny Manning	2.00	.90	.25
☐ M18	Billy Owens	2.00	.90	.25
☐ M19	Grant Hill	15.00	6.75	1.85
☐ M20	Scottie Pippen	12.00	5.50	1.50
☐ M21	Isaiah Rider	2.00	.90	.25
☐ M22	Latrell Sprewell	2.00	.90	.25

☐ M1	Michael Jordan	250.00	110.00	31.00
☐ M2	Anfernee Hardaway	135.00	60.00	17.00
☐ M3	Clyde Drexler	25.00	11.00	3.10
☐ M4	Mark Price	10.00	4.50	1.25
☐ M5	Steve Smith	12.50	5.50	1.55
☐ M6	Jim Jackson	12.50	5.50	1.55
☐ M7	Nick Anderson	12.50	5.50	1.55
☐ M8	Kenny Anderson	12.50	5.50	1.55
☐ M9	Mookie Blaylock	10.00	4.50	1.25
☐ M10	Jason Kidd	50.00	22.00	6.25
☐ M11	Tim Hardaway	12.50	5.50	1.55
☐ M12	Kevin Johnson	12.50	5.50	1.55
☐ M13	Gary Payton	30.00	13.50	3.70
☐ M14	John Stockton	20.00	9.00	2.50
☐ M15	Rod Strickland	10.00	4.50	1.25
☐ M16	Jamal Mashburn	15.00	6.75	1.85
☐ M17	Danny Manning	10.00	4.50	1.25
☐ M18	Billy Owens	10.00	4.50	1.25
☐ M19	Grant Hill	80.00	36.00	10.00
☐ M20	Scottie Pippen	60.00	27.00	7.50
☐ M21	Isaiah Rider	10.00	4.50	1.25
☐ M22	Latrell Sprewell	12.50	5.50	1.55

1995-96 Topps Pan For Gold

Randomly inserted in first series retail packs only at a rate of one in eight, this 15-card standard-size set chronicles the play of NBA stars who came from small colleges and were drafted late. White-bordered fronts feature a full-color player cutout set against a mine shaft background. The player's team name is printed in silver across the top and his name is stamped in gold foil across the bottom. Horizontal backs have a full-color player head shot on the left third of the card with his name, biography and details of his draft and school information on the right. Pieces of gold serve as a background for the back. These cards are numbered with a "PFG" prefix.

1995-96 Topps Mystery Finest Refractors

These twenty-two cards parallel the Topps Mystery Finest inserts. The only difference is the refractive coating on the card fronts. Mystery Finest Refractors are randomly seeded into one in every 36 second series hobby packs and one in every 216 second series retail packs. Many of the cards are found off-center and are considered condition sensitive.

	MINT	NRMT	EXC
COMPLETE SET (22)	600.00	275.00	75.00
COMMON CARD (M1-M22)	10.00	4.50	1.25

	MINT	NRMT	EXC
COMPLETE SET (15)	40.00	18.00	5.00
COMMON CARD (1-15)	1.00	.45	.12

		MINT	NRMT	EXC
☐ 1	Vin Baker	4.00	1.80	.50
☐ 2	John Stockton	4.00	1.80	.50
☐ 3	Dan Majerle	2.00	.90	.25
☐ 4	Joe Dumars	2.00	.90	.25
☐ 5	Rik Smits	2.00	.90	.25

		MINT	NRMT	EXC
☐ 6	Tim Hardaway	2.00	.90	.25
☐ 7	Charles Oakley	1.00	.45	.12
☐ 8	Cedric Ceballos	2.50	1.10	.30
☐ 9	Karl Malone	4.00	1.80	.50
☐ 10	Scottie Pippen	12.00	5.50	1.50
☐ 11	David Robinson	8.00	3.60	1.00
☐ 12	Gary Payton	6.00	2.70	.75
☐ 13	Mitch Richmond	3.00	1.35	.35
☐ 14	Antonio Davis	1.00	.45	.12
☐ 15	Dennis Rodman	15.00	6.75	1.85

1995-96 Topps Power Boosters

This 45-card insert standard-size set is printed on 28-point stock and features the leaders in points, rebounds, assists, steals and blocks paralleling the regular issue subset cards. The first 30 cards in the set (1-30) were seeded into first series packs at a rate of 1 in 36. The last 15 cards in the set (276-290) were seeded into second series packs also at a rate of one in 36. A Power Boosters card replaced two regular cards in every they came in. Full-bleed fronts carry a full-color action player cutout set against diffraction foil background with the player's name stamped in gold foil across the top. The Power Boosters logo appears at the bottom of the card with the individual's category listed above the logo. Borderless backs are one-color background with a full-color player head shot boxed on the right. Player name, team name, profile and biography appear on the back.

	MINT	NRMT	EXC
COMPLETE SET (45)	400.00	180.00	50.00
COMPLETE SERIES 1 (30)	300.00	135.00	38.00
COMPLETE SERIES 2 (15)	100.00	45.00	12.50
COMMON CARD (1-30)	2.00	.90	.25
COMMON CARD (276-290)	1.50	.70	.19

☐ 1	Michael Jordan	80.00	36.00	10.00
☐ 2	Dennis Rodman	20.00	9.00	2.50
☐ 3	John Stockton	5.00	2.20	.60
☐ 4	Michael Jordan	80.00	36.00	10.00
☐ 5	David Robinson	10.00	4.50	1.25
☐ 6	Shaquille O'Neal	25.00	11.00	3.10
☐ 7	Hakeem Olajuwon	12.00	5.50	1.50
☐ 8	David Robinson	10.00	4.50	1.25
☐ 9	Karl Malone	5.00	2.20	.60

☐ 10	Jamal Mashburn	3.00	1.35	.35
☐ 11	Dennis Rodman	20.00	9.00	2.50
☐ 12	Dikembe Mutombo	3.00	1.35	.35
☐ 13	Shaquille O'Neal	25.00	11.00	3.10
☐ 14	Patrick Ewing	5.00	2.20	.60
☐ 15	Tyrone Hill	2.00	.90	.25
☐ 16	John Stockton	5.00	2.20	.60
☐ 17	Kenny Anderson	3.00	1.35	.35
☐ 18	Tim Hardaway	3.00	1.35	.35
☐ 19	Rod Strickland	2.00	.90	.25
☐ 20	Muggsy Bogues	3.00	1.35	.35
☐ 21	Scottie Pippen	15.00	6.75	1.85
☐ 22	Mookie Blaylock	3.00	1.35	.35
☐ 23	Gary Payton	8.00	3.60	1.00
☐ 24	John Stockton	5.00	2.20	.60
☐ 25	Nate McMillan	2.00	.90	.25
☐ 26	Dikembe Mutombo	3.00	1.35	.35
☐ 27	Hakeem Olajuwon	12.00	5.50	1.50
☐ 28	Shawn Bradley	3.00	1.35	.35
☐ 29	David Robinson	10.00	4.50	1.25
☐ 30	Alonzo Mourning	5.00	2.20	.60
☐ 276	Anthony Mason	2.00	.90	.25
☐ 277	Michael Jordan	60.00	27.00	7.50
☐ 278	Patrick Ewing	4.00	1.80	.50
☐ 279	Shaquille O'Neal	20.00	9.00	2.50
☐ 280	Larry Johnson	4.00	1.80	.50
☐ 281	Mark Jackson	2.00	.90	.25
☐ 282	Chris Webber	4.00	1.80	.50
☐ 283	David Robinson	8.00	3.60	1.00
☐ 284	John Stockton	4.00	1.80	.50
☐ 285	Mookie Blaylock	2.00	.90	.25
☐ 286	Mark Price	2.00	.90	.25
☐ 287	Tim Hardaway	3.00	1.35	.35
☐ 288	Rod Strickland	2.00	.90	.25
☐ 289	Sherman Douglas	2.00	.90	.25
☐ 290	Gary Payton	6.00	2.70	.75

1995-96 Topps Rattle and Roll

Randomly inserted in second series retail packs only at a rate of one in 12, this 10-card set takes aim at the power mongers of the NBA. Fronts are bordered in silver foil with a blue and red silver swirl pattern for a background. A full-color player cutout appears on the front with his name printed in a copper foil at the bottom. White-bordered backs contain a player head shot and his name printed underneath in red type. The blue and red swirl pattern continues and the player's biography and profile are printed in white type.

	MINT	NRMT	EXC
COMPLETE SET (10)	25.00	11.00	3.10
COMMON CARD (R1-R10)	1.00	.45	.12
☐ R1 Juwan Howard	5.00	2.20	.60
☐ R2 Glenn Robinson	2.50	1.10	.30
☐ R3 Grant Hill	8.00	3.60	1.00
☐ R4 Sharone Wright	1.00	.45	.12
☐ R5 Brian Grant	1.00	.45	.12
☐ R6 Antonio McDyess	4.00	1.80	.50
☐ R7 Bryant Reeves	2.50	1.10	.30
☐ R8 Gary Trent	1.00	.45	.12
☐ R9 Jerry Stackhouse	8.00	3.60	1.00
☐ R10 Joe Smith	5.00	2.20	.60

1995-96 Topps Show Stoppers

Cards in this set of ten were randomly issued in first series hobby packs only at a rate of one in 24 and feature the top players of the NBA. Fronts are white bordered with silver foil and a full-color player action cutout. The player's name is printed in gold foil at the bottom. Backs have a player head shot with a spotlight description, a game high feature and a show stopper highlight.

	MINT	NRMT	EXC
COMPLETE SET (10)	80.00	36.00	10.00
COMMON CARD (1-10)	1.50	.70	.19
☐ SS1 Michael Jordan	40.00	18.00	5.00
☐ SS2 Grant Hill	12.00	5.50	1.50
☐ SS3 Glenn Robinson	4.00	1.80	.50
☐ SS4 Anfernee Hardaway	20.00	9.00	2.50
☐ SS5 Charles Barkley	5.00	2.20	.60
☐ SS6 Patrick Ewing	3.00	1.35	.35
☐ SS7 Shaquille O'Neal	15.00	6.75	1.85
☐ SS8 Jason Kidd	8.00	3.60	1.00
☐ SS9 Glen Rice	1.50	.70	.19
☐ SS10 Karl Malone	3.00	1.35	.35

1995-96 Topps Spark Plugs

Randomly inserted in all second series retail packs at a rate of one in 8, cards from

this 10-card chase set highlight NBA scorers on full-foil fronts. Silver foil serves as a border and a blue and silver foil are background for a full-color action player cutout. A spark plug with sparks flying out and the player's name are printed in silver foil. Horizontal backs are white bordered with a full-color action shot on one side and a player biography and '94-95 season highlights on the other.

	MINT	NRMT	EXC
COMPLETE SET (10)	30.00	13.50	3.70
COMMON CARD (SP1-SP10)	.50	.23	.06
☐ SP1 Shaquille O'Neal	6.00	2.70	.75
☐ SP2 Michael Jordan	15.00	6.75	1.85
☐ SP3 Reggie Miller	1.50	.70	.19
☐ SP4 Anfernee Hardaway	8.00	3.60	1.00
☐ SP5 John Stockton	1.25	.55	.16
☐ SP6 David Robinson	2.50	1.10	.30
☐ SP7 Hakeem Olajuwon	3.00	1.35	.35
☐ SP8 Tim Hardaway	.50	.23	.06
☐ SP9 Grant Hill	5.00	2.20	.60
☐ SP10 Scottie Pippen	4.00	1.80	.50

1995-96 Topps Sudden Impact

Sudden Impact is a hobby-exclusive insert set of ten rookies that were expected to make a significant impact on their teams. The horizontally designed "all foil" cards were randomly inserted at a rate of 1 in 72 second series hobby packs. The cards are numbered on the back with an "S" prefix.

	MINT	NRMT	EXC
COMPLETE SET (10)	100.00	45.00	12.50
COMMON CARD (S1-S10)	3.00	1.35	.35

		MINT	NRMT	EXC
☐	S1 Damon Stoudamire....	30.00	13.50	3.70
☐	S2 Cherokee Parks.............	3.00	1.35	.35
☐	S3 Kurt Thomas.................	3.00	1.35	.35
☐	S4 Gary Trent...................	3.00	1.35	.35
☐	S5 Bryant Reeves.............	8.00	3.60	1.00
☐	S6 Ed O'Bannon..............	5.00	2.20	.60
☐	S7 Shawn Respert...........	3.00	1.35	.35
☐	S8 Antonio McDyess......	12.00	5.50	1.50
☐	S9 Joe Smith.................	15.00	6.75	1.85
☐	S10 Jerry Stackhouse.....	25.00	11.00	3.10

1995-96 Topps
Top Flight

Cards in this 20-piece set feature the high flyers of the NBA and were inserted one per retail pack. The white bordered fronts have a full-color player action cutout set against a background with two fighter jets. The player's name is printed in gold foil near the bottom above a gold foil swooshing jet whose vapor spells out "Top Flight." Backs have a ful-coor head shot inset within a sky background of a jet in flight. A biography and special abilities box appear on the back.

		MINT	NRMT	EXC
COMPLETE SET (20)		70.00	32.00	8.75
COMMON CARD (TF1-TF20)....		1.00	.45	.12
☐	TF1 Michael Jordan......	40.00	18.00	5.00
☐	TF2 Isaiah Rider................	2.00	.90	.25
☐	TF3 Harold Miner............	1.00	.45	.12
☐	TF4 Dominique Wilkins....	2.00	.90	.25
☐	TF5 Clyde Drexler..........	4.00	1.80	.50
☐	TF6 Scottie Pippen.........	10.00	4.50	1.25
☐	TF7 Shawn Kemp............	10.00	4.50	1.25
☐	TF8 Chris Webber...........	3.00	1.35	.35
☐	TF9 Anfernee Hardaway..	20.00	9.00	2.50
☐	TF10 Grant Hill...............	12.00	5.50	1.50
☐	TF11 Kevin Johnson........	2.00	.90	.25
☐	TF12 John Starks............	1.00	.45	.12
☐	TF13 Dan Majerle...........	2.00	.90	.25
☐	TF14 Latrell Sprewell	2.00	.90	.25
☐	TF15 Dee Brown.............	1.00	.45	.12
☐	TF16 Stacey Augmon.......	1.00	.45	.12
☐	TF17 David Benoit...........	1.00	.45	.12
☐	TF18 Sean Elliott.............	2.00	.90	.25
☐	TF19 Cedric Ceballos.......	2.00	.90	.25
☐	TF20 Robert Horry..........	2.00	.90	.25

1995-96 Topps
Whiz Kids

Randomly inserted in all first series packs at a rate of one in 24, this set of 12 standard-size cards highlights the young power of the NBA. Etched silver foil fronts have a basketball court background and a full-color player action cutout. "Whiz Kids" is spelled out in children's letter blocks on the top. The players name is printed in red at the bottom. Borderless backs are numbered with the prefix "WK" and continue with a basketball court background. A full-color player head shot appears inside the key of the court and his name appears underneath the photo in red print on a blue banner. Career stats, biography and a trivia question appear on the lower half and the answer to the question on the preceding card appears at the bottom.

		MINT	NRMT	EXC
COMPLETE SET (12)		50.00	22.00	6.25
COMMON CARD (WK1-WK12)		1.00	.45	.12
☐	WK1 Grant Hill..............	12.00	5.50	1.50
☐	WK2 Nick Van Exel	2.50	1.10	.30
☐	WK3 Juwan Howard	8.00	3.60	1.00
☐	WK4 Chris Webber	3.00	1.35	.35
☐	WK5 Brian Grant..............	2.00	.90	.25
☐	WK6 Glenn Robinson	4.00	1.80	.50
☐	WK7 Donyell Marshall	1.00	.45	.12
☐	WK8 Jason Kidd	8.00	3.60	1.00
☐	WK9 Anfernee Hardaway ..	20.00	9.00	2.50
☐	WK10 Jamal Mashburn	2.00	.90	.25
☐	WK11 Vin Baker..............	3.00	1.35	.35
☐	WK12 Eddie Jones...........	2.50	1.10	.30

1996-97 Topps

The 1996-97 Topps basketball set was issued in two series with the first series containing 111 standard-size cards. First series cards were issued in 11-card hobby and retail packs carrying a suggested retail price of $1.29. The white-bordered fronts have a full-color action photo with the player's name in gold set against the blazing trail of a moving basketball. Horizontal backs have color head shots with career

statistics and information. The checklist card (#111) actually looks more like a premium Finest brand card than a Topps issue. No Rookie Cards are included in the first series set.

	MINT	NRMT	EXC
COMPLETE SERIES 1 (111)...	10.00	4.50	1.25
COMMON CARD (1-110)	.05	.02	.01

		MINT	NRMT	EXC
☐ 1	Patrick Ewing	.25	.11	.03
☐ 2	Christian Laettner	.10	.05	.01
☐ 3	Mahmoud Abdul-Rauf	.05	.02	.01
☐ 4	Chris Webber	.20	.09	.03
☐ 5	Jason Kidd	.50	.23	.06
☐ 6	Clifford Rozier	.05	.02	.01
☐ 7	Elden Campbell	.10	.05	.01
☐ 8	Chuck Person	.05	.02	.01
☐ 9	Jeff Hornacek	.10	.05	.01
☐ 10	Rik Smits	.10	.05	.01
☐ 11	Kurt Thomas	.05	.02	.01
☐ 12	Rod Strickland	.10	.05	.01
☐ 13	Kendall Gill	.05	.02	.01
☐ 14	Brian Williams	.05	.02	.01
☐ 15	Tom Gugliotta	.10	.05	.01
☐ 16	Ron Harper	.10	.05	.01
☐ 17	Eric Williams	.05	.02	.01
☐ 18	A.C. Green	.05	.02	.01
☐ 19	Scott Williams	.05	.02	.01
☐ 20	Damon Stoudamire	.75	.35	.09
☐ 21	Bryant Reeves	.20	.09	.03
☐ 22	Bob Sura	.05	.02	.01
☐ 23	Mitch Richmond	.20	.09	.03
☐ 24	Larry Johnson	.25	.11	.03
☐ 25	Vin Baker	.20	.09	.03
☐ 26	Mark Bryant	.05	.02	.01
☐ 27	Horace Grant	.10	.05	.01
☐ 28	Allan Houston	.10	.05	.01
☐ 29	Sam Perkins	.05	.02	.01
☐ 30	Antonio McDyess	.30	.14	.04
☐ 31	Rasheed Wallace	.15	.07	.02
☐ 32	Malik Sealy	.05	.02	.01
☐ 33	Scottie Pippen	.75	.35	.09
☐ 34	Charles Barkley	.40	.18	.05
☐ 35	Hakeem Olajuwon	.60	.25	.07
☐ 36	John Starks	.10	.05	.01
☐ 37	Byron Scott	.05	.02	.01
☐ 38	Arvydas Sabonis	.25	.11	.03
☐ 39	Vlade Divac	.10	.05	.01
☐ 40	Joe Dumars	.10	.05	.01
☐ 41	Danny Ferry	.05	.02	.01
☐ 42	Jerry Stackhouse	.60	.25	.07
☐ 43	B.J. Armstrong	.05	.02	.01
☐ 44	Shawn Bradley	.10	.05	.01
☐ 45	Kevin Garnett	1.00	.45	.12
☐ 46	Dee Brown	.05	.02	.01
☐ 47	Michael Smith	.05	.02	.01
☐ 48	Doug Christie	.05	.02	.01
☐ 49	Mark Jackson	.05	.02	.01
☐ 50	Shawn Kemp	.75	.35	.09
☐ 51	Sasha Danilovic	.05	.02	.01
☐ 52	Nick Anderson	.10	.05	.01
☐ 53	Matt Geiger	.05	.02	.01
☐ 54	Charles Smith	.05	.02	.01
☐ 55	Mookie Blaylock	.10	.05	.01
☐ 56	Johnny Newman	.05	.02	.01
☐ 57	George McCloud	.05	.02	.01
☐ 58	Greg Ostertag	.05	.02	.01
☐ 59	Reggie Williams	.05	.02	.01
☐ 60	Brent Barry	.05	.02	.01
☐ 61	Doug West	.05	.02	.01
☐ 62	Donald Royal	.05	.02	.01
☐ 63	Randy Brown	.05	.02	.01
☐ 64	Vincent Askew	.05	.02	.01
☐ 65	John Stockton	.25	.11	.03
☐ 66	Joe Kleine	.05	.02	.01
☐ 67	Keith Askins	.05	.02	.01
☐ 68	Bobby Phills	.05	.02	.01
☐ 69	Chris Mullin	.05	.02	.01
☐ 70	Nick Van Exel	.15	.07	.02
☐ 71	Rick Fox	.05	.02	.01
☐ 72	Chicago Bulls - 72 Wins	1.50	.70	.19
☐ 73	Shawn Respert	.05	.02	.01
☐ 74	Hubert Davis	.05	.02	.01
☐ 75	Jim Jackson	.10	.05	.01
☐ 76	Olden Polynice	.05	.02	.01
☐ 77	Gheorghe Muresan	.10	.05	.01
☐ 78	Theo Ratliff	.05	.02	.01
☐ 79	Khalid Reeves	.05	.02	.01
☐ 80	David Robinson	.50	.23	.06
☐ 81	Lawrence Moten	.05	.02	.01
☐ 82	Sam Cassell	.10	.05	.01
☐ 83	George Zidek	.05	.02	.01
☐ 84	Sharone Wright	.05	.02	.01
☐ 85	Clarence Weatherspoon	.10	.05	.01
☐ 86	Alan Henderson	.05	.02	.01
☐ 87	Chris Dudley	.05	.02	.01
☐ 88	Ed O'Bannon	.05	.02	.01
☐ 89	Calbert Cheaney	.05	.02	.01
☐ 90	Cedric Ceballos	.10	.05	.01
☐ 91	Michael Cage	.05	.02	.01
☐ 92	Ervin Johnson	.05	.02	.01
☐ 93	Gary Trent	.05	.02	.01
☐ 94	Sherman Douglas	.05	.02	.01
☐ 95	Joe Smith	.40	.18	.05
☐ 96	Dale Davis	.05	.02	.01
☐ 97	Tony Dumas	.05	.02	.01
☐ 98	Muggsy Bogues	.10	.05	.01
☐ 99	Toni Kukoc	.10	.05	.01
☐ 100	Grant Hill	.75	.35	.09
☐ 101	Michael Finley	.40	.18	.05
☐ 102	Isaiah Rider	.10	.05	.01
☐ 103	Bryant Stith	.05	.02	.01
☐ 104	Pooh Richardson	.05	.02	.01
☐ 105	Karl Malone	.25	.11	.03
☐ 106	Brian Grant	.05	.02	.01
☐ 107	Sean Elliott	.10	.05	.01
☐ 108	Charles Oakley	.05	.02	.01
☐ 109	Pervis Ellison	.05	.02	.01
☐ 110	Anfernee Hardaway	1.50	.70	.19
☐ 111	Checklist	1.25	.55	.16

1996-97 Topps NBA at 50

Randomly inserted into one in every three 11-card first series packs, these 110 cards parallel the regular issue set. The only difference in design is a striking gold foil treatment to each card front with a stamp commemorating the NBA at 50. Please refer to the multipliers provided below (coupled with the prices of the corresponding regular issue cards) to ascertain values for individual NBA at 50 cards.

	MINT	NRMT	EXC
COMPLETE SERIES 1 (110)...	70.00	32.00	8.75
COMMON CARD (1-110)	.25	.11	.03
SEMISTARS.................................	.50	.23	.06
*NBA 50 STARS: 3X to 6X VALUE....			

1996-97 Topps Draft Redemption

These trade cards were randomly inserted in first series packs at a rate of one in 18. Each trade card has a number printed on front that corresponds to each draft position of the first round of the 1996 NBA draft. Collectors that exchanged their trade card would then receive an exchange card picturing the player selected at that spot in the draft. The Draft Redemption trade deadline is April 1, 1997.

	MINT	NRMT	EXC
COMPLETE SET (29)	110.00	50.00	14.00
COMMON CARD (1-29)	2.00	.90	.25
☐ 1 Allen Iverson Trade......	20.00	9.00	2.50
☐ 2 Marcus Camby Trade...	15.00	6.75	1.85
☐ 3 S.Abdur-Rahim Trade ..	10.00	4.50	1.25
☐ 4 Stephon Marbury Trade	15.00	6.75	1.85
☐ 5 Ray Allen Trade.............	10.00	4.50	1.25

☐ 6 Antoine Walker Trade.....	8.00	3.60	1.00
☐ 7 Lorenzen Wright Trade ..	3.00	1.35	.35
☐ 8 Kerry Kittles Trade	5.00	2.20	.60
☐ 9 Samaki Walker Trade......	5.00	2.20	.60
☐ 10 Erick Dampier Trade	2.00	.90	.25
☐ 11 Todd Fuller Trade...........	2.00	.90	.25
☐ 12 Vitaly Potapenko Trade	2.00	.90	.25
☐ 13 Kobe Bryant Trade........	20.00	9.00	2.50
☐ 14 P.Stojakovic Trade........	2.00	.90	.25
☐ 15 Steve Nash Trade.........	3.00	1.35	.35
☐ 16 Tony Delk Trade............	4.00	1.80	.50
☐ 17 Jermaine O'Neal Trade.	3.00	1.35	.35
☐ 18 John Wallace Trade	4.00	1.80	.50
☐ 19 Walter McCarty Trade ...	4.00	1.80	.50
☐ 20 Z.Ilgauskas Trade.........	2.00	.90	.25
☐ 21 Dontae Jones Trade......	2.00	.90	.25
☐ 22 Roy Rogers Trade........	2.00	.90	.25
☐ 23 Efthimis Retzias Trade .	2.00	.90	.25
☐ 24 Derek Fisher Trade.......	2.00	.90	.25
☐ 25 Martin Muursepp Trade	2.00	.90	.25
☐ 26 Jerome Williams Trade	2.00	.90	.25
☐ 27 Brian Evans Trade.........	2.00	.90	.25
☐ 28 Priest Lauderdale Trade	2.00	.90	.25
☐ 29 Travis Knight Trade......	2.00	.90	.25

1996-97 Topps Hobby Masters

Randomly inserted exclusively into one in every 36 first series hobby packs, these inserts feature a selection of ten top NBA stars as determined by Topps hobby dealer network. In addition to player selection, the dealers also determined the rate of insertion. Each card features 28 point full diffraction foil stock. Due to the thickness, a Hobby Masters insert replaced two regular issue cards within the packs they were seeded into. The card backs are numbered with an "HM" prefix. The cards are numbered 21-30 due to the fact that they are part of a cross-sport (football, baseball and basketball) insert program by Topps.

	MINT	NRMT	EXC
COMPLETE SET (10)	100.00	45.00	12.50
COMMON CARD (HM21-HM30)	5.00	2.20	.60
☐ HM21 Grant Hill................	15.00	6.75	1.85
☐ HM22 Scottie Pippen.......	15.00	6.75	1.85
☐ HM23 Karl Malone	5.00	2.20	.60
☐ HM24 Patrick Ewing	5.00	2.20	.60

		MINT	NRMT	EXC
☐ HM25	Shawn Kemp	15.00	6.75	1.85
☐ HM26	Anfernee Hardaway	30.00	13.50	3.70
☐ HM27	Charles Barkley	8.00	3.60	1.00
☐ HM28	Jason Kidd	10.00	4.50	1.25
☐ HM29	Hakeem Olajuwon	12.00	5.50	1.50
☐ HM30	Larry Johnson	5.00	2.20	.60

1996-97 Topps Holding Court

Cards in this set of fifteen were randomly inserted in hobby and retail packs at a rate of one in 36 and feature the undeniable members of the NBA royalty, crowned "kings of the court" due to their impact on the game. Each card is printed utilizing Topps' exclusive Finest technology. Card backs are numbered with an "HC" prefix. Prices below refer to unpeeled cards. Peeled cards generally trade for 75% of the values listed below.

		MINT	NRMT	EXC
COMPLETE SET (15)		125.00	55.00	15.50
COMMON CARD (HC1-HC15)		2.00	.90	.25
☐ HC1	Larry Johnson	4.00	1.80	.50
☐ HC2	Michael Jordan	50.00	22.00	6.25
☐ HC3	Cedric Ceballos	2.00	.90	.25
☐ HC4	Grant Hill	12.00	5.50	1.50
☐ HC5	Anfernee Hardaway	25.00	11.00	3.10
☐ HC6	Reggie Miller	5.00	2.20	.60
☐ HC7	Glenn Robinson	4.00	1.80	.50
☐ HC8	Patrick Ewing	4.00	1.80	.50
☐ HC9	Chris Webber	3.00	1.35	.35
☐ HC10	Shaquille O'Neal	20.00	9.00	2.50
☐ HC11	John Stockton	4.00	1.80	.50
☐ HC12	Mitch Richmond	3.00	1.35	.35
☐ HC13	David Robinson	8.00	3.60	1.00
☐ HC14	Gary Payton	6.00	2.70	.75
☐ HC15	Karl Malone	4.00	1.80	.50

1996-97 Topps Holding Court Refractors

Cards in this set parallel the fifteen of the more common Holding Court inserts. The scarce Refractor versions were seeded at a rate of one in every 108 first series hobby and retail packs. Refractors are distinguished by their rainbow-like appearance that refracts with light. Please refer to the multiplier provided below (coupled with the price of the corresponding regular issue card) to ascertain values for Refractor singles. Prices below refer to unpeeled cards. Peeled cards generally trade for 75% of the values listed below.

		MINT	NRMT	EXC
COMPLETE SET (15)		500.00	220.00	60.00
COMMON CARD (HC1-HC15)		6.00	2.70	.75
☐ HC1	Larry Johnson	12.00	5.50	1.50
☐ HC2	Michael Jordan	225.00	100.00	28.00
☐ HC3	Cedric Ceballos	6.00	2.70	.75
☐ HC4	Grant Hill	50.00	22.00	6.25
☐ HC5	Anfernee Hardaway	100.00	45.00	12.50
☐ HC6	Reggie Miller	15.00	6.75	1.85
☐ HC7	Glenn Robinson	12.00	5.50	1.50
☐ HC8	Patrick Ewing	12.00	5.50	1.50
☐ HC9	Chris Webber	20.00	9.00	2.50
☐ HC10	Shaquille O'Neal	60.00	27.00	7.50
☐ HC11	John Stockton	12.00	5.50	1.50
☐ HC12	Mitch Richmond	10.00	4.50	1.25
☐ HC13	David Robinson	25.00	11.00	3.10
☐ HC14	Gary Payton	20.00	9.00	2.50
☐ HC15	Karl Malone	12.00	5.50	1.50

1996-97 Topps Pro Files

Cards in this set of ten were randomly issued in first series hobby and retail packs at a rate of one in 12. Topps' basketball *spokesperson David Robinson was handed the assignment of writing all of the card backs for this insert set. "The Admiral" came through with flying colors as he gets up close and peronal with ten of the NBA's top stars. Card fronts contain a prismatic foil background with an action shot of the player and a head shot of David Robinson in the bottom left corner. Card backs are numbered with a "PF" prefix.*

	MINT	NRMT	EXC
COMPLETE SET (10)	25.00	11.00	3.10
COMMON CARD (PF1-PF10)	.75	.35	.09
☐ PF1 Grant Hill	3.00	1.35	.35
☐ PF2 Shawn Kemp	3.00	1.35	.35
☐ PF3 Michael Jordan	12.00	5.50	1.50
☐ PF4 Vin Baker	.75	.35	.09
☐ PF5 Chris Webber	1.00	.45	.12
☐ PF6 Joe Smith	1.50	.70	.19
☐ PF7 Shaquille O'Neal	5.00	2.20	.60
☐ PF8 Patrick Ewing	1.00	.45	.12
☐ PF9 Scottie Pippen	3.00	1.35	.35
☐ PF10 Damon Stoudamire	3.00	1.35	.35

1996-97 Topps
Season's Best

Cards in this set of 25 were randomly issued in first series hobby and retail packs at a rate of one in eight and feature five players who have excelled in the five key statistical categories of the game: Points - En Fuego; Rebounds - Board Members; Steals - Sticky Fingers; Assists - Dish Men and Blocks - Swat Team. Card fronts feature a prismatic background with the statistical theme title located around the action shot. Card backs are numbered with a "Season's Best" prefix.

	MINT	NRMT	EXC
COMPLETE SET (25)	60.00	27.00	7.50
COMMON CARD (SB1-SB25)	.40	.18	.05
☐ SB1 Michael Jordan	15.00	6.75	1.85
☐ SB2 Hakeem Olajuwon	3.00	1.35	.35
☐ SB3 Shaquille O'Neal	6.00	2.70	.75
☐ SB4 Karl Malone	1.25	.55	.16
☐ SB5 David Robinson	2.50	1.10	.30
☐ SB6 Dennis Rodman	6.00	2.70	.75
☐ SB7 David Robinson	2.50	1.10	.30
☐ SB8 Dikembe Mutombo	1.00	.45	.12
☐ SB9 Charles Barkley	2.00	.90	.25
☐ SB10 Shawn Kemp	4.00	1.80	.50
☐ SB11 John Stockton	1.25	.55	.16
☐ SB12 Jason Kidd	2.50	1.10	.30
☐ SB13 Avery Johnson	.40	.18	.05
☐ SB14 Rod Strickland	.40	.18	.05
☐ SB15 Damon Stoudamire	4.00	1.80	.50
☐ SB16 Gary Payton	2.00	.90	.25
☐ SB17 Mookie Blaylock	.40	.18	.05
☐ SB18 Michael Jordan	15.00	6.75	1.85
☐ SB19 Jason Kidd	2.50	1.10	.30
☐ SB20 Alvin Robertson	.40	.18	.05
☐ SB21 Dikembe Mutombo	1.00	.45	.12
☐ SB22 Shawn Bradley	.40	.18	.05
☐ SB23 David Robinson	2.50	1.10	.30
☐ SB24 Hakeem Olajuwon	3.00	1.35	.35
☐ SB25 Alonzo Mourning	1.25	.55	.16

1996-97 Topps
Super Teams

After a one-year hiatus, Topps decided to transfer this insert set concept from their Stadium Club brand which had featured interactive Super Team inserts in 1993-94 and 1994-95. Cards from this set of 29 were randomly issued in first series hobby and retail packs at a rate of one in 36 and featured an action shot or group photo from each team in the league. Cards that feature teams that won either their division, their conference or the NBA finals or was the team selected to have the first draft pick in the 1997 NBA Draft are redeemable for various special Mystery Finest cards. The expiration date for Super Team cards is February 10, 1997.

	MINT	NRMT	EXC
COMPLETE SET (29)	225.00	100.00	28.00
COMMON CARD (ST1-ST29)	5.00	2.20	.60
☐ ST1 Atlanta Hawks	5.00	2.20	.60
Stacy Augmon			
Grant Long			
Ken Norman			
☐ ST2 Boston Celtics	5.00	2.20	.60
Dino Radja			
Dana Barros			
Eric Williams			

☐ ST3 Charlotte Hornets ...... 5.00 2.20 .60
    Robert Parish
    Glen Rice
    Kenny Anderson
    Larry Johnson
    Dell Curry
    Muggsy Bogues
☐ ST4 Chicago Bulls........... 75.00 34.00 9.50
    Michael Jordan
    Scottie Pippen
    Dennis Rodman
    Luc Longley
    Ron Harper
☐ ST5 Cleveland Cavaliers..., 5.00 2.20 .60
    Bob Sura
    Dan Majerle
    Donny Marshall
☐ ST6 Dallas Mavericks........ 5.00 2.20 .60
    Jason Kidd
    Jamal Mashburn
    Jim Jackson
    Popeye Jones
☐ ST7 Denver Nuggets .... 5.00 2.20 .60
    Dikembe Mutombo
    Bryant Stith
    Don MacLean)
☐ ST8 Detroit Pistons........... 5.00 2.20 .60
    Mark West
    Theo Ratliff
    Lindsey Hunter
    Joe Dumars
    Terry Cummings
    Grant Hill
    Lou Roe
☐ ST9 Golden State Warriors 5.00 2.20 .60
    B.J. Armstrong
    Latrell Sprewell
    Joe Smith)
☐ ST10 Houston Rockets ... 20.00 9.00 2.50
    Hakeem Olajuwon
    Robert Horry
    Chucky Brown
    Eldridge Recasner
    Clyde Drexler
☐ ST11 Indiana Pacers......... 8.00 3.60 1.00
    Rik Smits
    Reggie Miller
    Dale Davis
    Mark Jackson)
☐ ST12 Los Angeles Clippers 10.00 4.50 1.25
    Malik Sealy
    Terry Dehere
☐ ST13 Los Angeles Lakers 20.00 9.00 2.50
    Elden Campbell
    Sedale Threatt
    Vlade Divac
    Anthony Peeler
    Eddie Jones
    Derek Strong
    Frankie King)
☐ ST14 Miami Heat .... 5.00 2.20 .60
    Veshon Lenard
    Alonzo Mourning
    Rex Chapman
    Keith Askins
    Dan Schayes
    Jeff Malone
    Tony Smith
☐ ST15 Milwaukee Bucks..... 5.00 2.20 .60
    Glenn Robinson
    Vin Baker

    Benoit Benjamin
    Lee Mayberry
    Johnny Newman
☐ ST16 Minnesota Timberwolves 10.00 4.50 1.25
    Doug West,
    Tom Gugliotta
    Kevin Garnett
    Sam Mitchell
☐ ST17 New Jersey Nets 10.00 4.50 1.25
    P.J. Brown
    Armon Gilliam
    Ed O'Bannon
    Chris Childs
    Vern Fleming
☐ ST18 New York Knicks 10.00 4.50 1.25
    J.R. Reid
    Anthony Mason
    Hubert Davis
☐ ST19 Orlando Magic 10.00 4.50 1.25
    Anfernee Hardaway
    Shaquille O'Neal
    Dennis Scott)
☐ ST20 Philadelphia 76ers . 10.00 4.50 1.25
    Trevor Ruffin
    Derrick Alston
    LaSalle Thompson)
☐ ST21 Phoenix Suns .... 5.00 2.20 .60
    Joe Kleine
    Charles Barkley
    Wayman Tisdale
    Michael Finley
    Elliot Perry
☐ ST22 Portland Trail Blazers 5.00 2.20 .60
    Arvydas Sabonis
    Chris Dudley
    Clifford Robinson
    James Robinson
    Gary Trent
    Aaron McKie
☐ ST23 Sacramento Kings ... 5.00 2.20 .60
    Bobby Hurley
    Sarunas Marciulionis
    Mitch Richmond
    Olden Polynice
    Brian Grant
☐ ST24 San Antonio Spurs... 8.00 3.60 1.00
    Vinny Del Negro
    David Robinson
    Doc Rivers
    Dell Demps
☐ ST25 Seattle Supersonics 20.00 9.00 2.50
    Ervin Johnson
    Gary Payton
    Shawn Kemp
☐ ST26 Toronto Raptors ...... 5.00 2.20 .60
    Acie Earl
    Carlos Rogers
    Alvin Robertson
    B.J. Tyler
☐ ST27 Utah Jazz 8.00 3.60 1.00
    John Stockton
    Karl Malone
    David Benoit
    Felton Spencer)
☐ ST28 Vancouver Grizzlies . 5.00 2.20 .60
    Eric Murdock
    Eric Mobley
    Lawrence Moten
    Blue Edwards
    Doug Edwards
    Ashraf Amaya

Literrial Green)
☐ ST29 Washington Bullets.. 8.00   3.60   1.00
   Juwan Howard
   Gheorghe Muresan
   Chris Webber
   Ledell Eackles

1992-93 Topps Archives

Featuring the missing years of Topps basketball from 1981 through 1991, this 150-card set consists of 139 current NBA players and an 11-card subset of the Number One draft picks from 1981 to 1991. Production was limited to 10,000 24-box cases (24 packs per box). Each pack contained 14 cards and one Stadium Club membership card. Since Topps did not produce basketball cards when the photos were taken, the front designs are patterned after the Topps baseball cards issued during the same year. The horizontal backs display a small, square, current action player photo that overlaps a red, yellow, and white box containing biographical information, and statistics from college and the NBA. The set name, player's name, and team are printed in the upper left portion. The background is in varying shades of blue with a light beam design. After opening with a No. 1 Draft Pick (1-11) subset, the player cards are arranged by year in ascending chronological order and alphabetically within each season. The set closes with checklist (149-150) cards.

	MINT	NRMT	EXC
COMPLETE SET (150)	8.00	3.60	1.00
COMMON CARD (1-150)	.05	.02	.01

☐ 1 Mark Aguirre FDP	.10	.05	.01
☐ 2 James Worthy FDP	.15	.07	.02
☐ 3 Ralph Sampson FDP	.05	.02	.01
☐ 4 Hakeem Olajuwon FDP	.40	.18	.05
☐ 5 Patrick Ewing FDP	.15	.07	.02
☐ 6 Brad Daugherty FDP	.05	.02	.01
☐ 7 David Robinson FDP	.30	.14	.04
☐ 8 Danny Manning FDP	.10	.05	.01
☐ 9 Pervis Ellison FDP UER....	.05	.02	.01
(Text on back: Clippers not Lakers had 2nd pick)			

☐ 10 Derrick Coleman FDP	.05	.02	.01
☐ 11 Larry Johnson FDP	.30	.14	.04
☐ 12 Mark Aguirre	.10	.05	.01
☐ 13 Danny Ainge	.15	.07	.02
☐ 14 Rolando Blackman	.05	.02	.01
☐ 15 Tom Chambers	.05	.02	.01
☐ 16 Eddie Johnson	.05	.02	.01
☐ 17 Alton Lister	.05	.02	.01
☐ 18 Larry Nance	.05	.02	.01
☐ 19 Kurt Rambis	.05	.02	.01
☐ 20 Isiah Thomas	.20	.09	.03
☐ 21 Buck Williams	.10	.05	.01
☐ 22 Orlando Woolridge	.05	.02	.01
☐ 23 John Bagley	.05	.02	.01
☐ 24 Terry Cummings	.05	.02	.01
☐ 25 Mark Eaton	.05	.02	.01
☐ 26 Sleepy Floyd	.05	.02	.01
☐ 27 Fat Lever	.05	.02	.01
☐ 28 Ricky Pierce	.05	.02	.01
☐ 29 Trent Tucker	.05	.02	.01
☐ 30 Dominique Wilkins	.15	.07	.02
☐ 31 James Worthy	.15	.07	.02
☐ 32 Thurl Bailey	.05	.02	.01
☐ 33 Clyde Drexler	.40	.18	.05
☐ 34 Dale Ellis	.05	.02	.01
☐ 35 Sidney Green	.05	.02	.01
☐ 36 Derek Harper	.05	.02	.01
☐ 37 Jeff Malone	.05	.02	.01
☐ 38 Rodney McCray	.05	.02	.01
☐ 39 John Paxson	.10	.05	.01
☐ 40 Doc Rivers	.10	.05	.01
☐ 41 Byron Scott	.10	.05	.01
☐ 42 Sedale Threatt	.05	.02	.01
☐ 43 Ron Anderson	.05	.02	.01
☐ 44 Charles Barkley	.50	.23	.06
☐ 45 Sam Bowie	.05	.02	.01
☐ 46 Michael Cage	.05	.02	.01
☐ 47 Tony Campbell	.05	.02	.01
☐ 48 Antoine Carr	.05	.02	.01
☐ 49 Craig Ehlo	.05	.02	.01
☐ 50 Vern Fleming	.05	.02	.01
☐ 51 Jay Humphries	.05	.02	.01
☐ 52 Michael Jordan	4.00	1.80	.50
☐ 53 Jerome Kersey	.05	.02	.01
☐ 54 Hakeem Olajuwon	.75	.35	.09
☐ 55 Sam Perkins	.05	.02	.01
☐ 56 Alvin Robertson	.05	.02	.01
☐ 57 John Stockton	.30	.14	.04
☐ 58 Otis Thorpe	.10	.05	.01
☐ 59 Kevin Willis	.05	.02	.01
☐ 60 Michael Adams	.05	.02	.01
☐ 61 Benoit Benjamin	.05	.02	.01
☐ 62 Terry Catledge	.05	.02	.01
☐ 63 Joe Dumars	.15	.07	.02
☐ 64 Patrick Ewing	.30	.14	.04
☐ 65 A.C. Green	.15	.07	.02
☐ 66 Karl Malone	.30	.14	.04
☐ 67 Reggie Miller	.40	.18	.05
☐ 68 Chris Mullin	.10	.05	.01
☐ 69 Xavier McDaniel	.05	.02	.01
☐ 70 Charles Oakley	.05	.02	.01
☐ 71 Terry Porter	.05	.02	.01
☐ 72 Jerry Reynolds	.05	.02	.01
☐ 73 Detlef Schrempf	.10	.05	.01
☐ 74 Wayman Tisdale	.05	.02	.01
☐ 75 Spud Webb	.05	.02	.01
☐ 76 Gerald Wilkins	.05	.02	.01
☐ 77 Dell Curry	.05	.02	.01
☐ 78 Brad Daugherty	.05	.02	.01
☐ 79 Johnny Dawkins	.05	.02	.01
☐ 80 Kevin Duckworth	.05	.02	.01

☐ 81	Ron Harper	.05	.02	.01
☐ 82	Jeff Hornacek	.10	.05	.01
☐ 83	Johnny Newman	.05	.02	.01
☐ 84	Chuck Person	.05	.02	.01
☐ 85	Mark Price	.05	.02	.01
☐ 86	Dennis Rodman	1.25	.55	.16
☐ 87	John Salley	.05	.02	.01
☐ 88	Scott Skiles	.05	.02	.01
☐ 89	Muggsy Bogues	.10	.05	.01
☐ 90	Armon Gilliam	.05	.02	.01
☐ 91	Horace Grant	.15	.07	.02
☐ 92	Mark Jackson	.05	.02	.01
☐ 93	Kevin Johnson	.15	.07	.02
☐ 94	Reggie Lewis	.10	.05	.01
☐ 95	Derrick McKey	.05	.02	.01
☐ 96	Ken Norman	.05	.02	.01
☐ 97	Scottie Pippen	1.00	.45	.12
☐ 98	Olden Polynice	.05	.02	.01
☐ 99	Kenny Smith	.05	.02	.01
☐ 100	John Williams	.05	.02	.01
☐ 101	Willie Anderson	.05	.02	.01
☐ 102	Rex Chapman	.05	.02	.01
☐ 103	Harvey Grant	.05	.02	.01
☐ 104	Hersey Hawkins	.05	.02	.01
☐ 105	Dan Majerle	.10	.05	.01
☐ 106	Danny Manning	.10	.05	.01
☐ 107	Vernon Maxwell	.05	.02	.01
☐ 108	Chris Morris	.05	.02	.01
☐ 109	Mitch Richmond UER	.25	.11	.03
	(Tim Hardaway pictured on front)			
☐ 110	Rony Seikaly	.05	.02	.01
☐ 111	Brian Shaw	.05	.02	.01
☐ 112	Charles Smith	.05	.02	.01
☐ 113	Rod Strickland	.05	.02	.01
☐ 114	Micheal Williams	.05	.02	.01
☐ 115	Nick Anderson	.10	.05	.01
☐ 116	B.J. Armstrong	.05	.02	.01
☐ 117	Mookie Blaylock	.10	.05	.01
☐ 118	Vlade Divac	.10	.05	.01
☐ 119	Sherman Douglas	.05	.02	.01
☐ 120	Blue Edwards	.05	.02	.01
☐ 121	Sean Elliott	.15	.07	.02
☐ 122	Pervis Ellison	.05	.02	.01
☐ 123	Tim Hardaway	.10	.05	.01
☐ 124	Sarunas Marciulionis	.05	.02	.01
☐ 125	Drazen Petrovic	.10	.05	.01
☐ 126	J.R. Reid	.05	.02	.01
☐ 127	Glen Rice	.10	.05	.01
☐ 128	Pooh Richardson	.05	.02	.01
☐ 129	Clifford Robinson	.15	.07	.02
☐ 130	David Robinson	.60	.25	.07
☐ 131	Dee Brown	.05	.02	.01
☐ 132	Cedric Ceballos	.10	.05	.01
☐ 133	Derrick Coleman	.10	.05	.01
☐ 134	Kendall Gill	.05	.02	.01
☐ 135	Chris Jackson	.10	.05	.01
☐ 136	Shawn Kemp	1.25	.55	.16
☐ 137	Gary Payton	.60	.25	.07
☐ 138	Dennis Scott	.10	.05	.01
☐ 139	Lionel Simmons	.05	.02	.01
☐ 140	Kenny Anderson	.15	.07	.02
☐ 141	Greg Anthony	.05	.02	.01
☐ 142	Stacey Augmon	.05	.02	.01
☐ 143	Rick Fox	.05	.02	.01
☐ 144	Larry Johnson	.60	.25	.07
☐ 145	Luc Longley	.05	.02	.01
☐ 146	Dikembe Mutombo	.30	.14	.04
☐ 147	Billy Owens	.05	.02	.01
☐ 148	Steve Smith	.10	.05	.01
☐ 149	Checklist 1-75	.05	.02	.01
☐ 150	Checklist 76-150	.05	.02	.01

1992-93 Topps Archives Gold

10,000 factory sets were made of the 1992-93 Topps Archives Gold. The factory sets were sold to dealers in eight-set cases. The 150 cards comprising this set have identical player selection and numbering as the regular-issue Topps Archives set, except that the checklist cards from the regular Archives set (149 and 150) have been replaced by cards of Rumeal Robinson and Shaquille O'Neal. Like the regular-issue Archive cards, the fronts are designed to mimic the layouts of several Topps' baseball issues of the 1980s; the only differences being that the Topps Archives logo, which doesn't appear on the regular-issue set, and the player's name are stamped in gold foil. The horizontal backs, however, all have the same design, with player action photos displayed in the upper right, the NBA and Topps Archives logos to the left of the picture, and the player's name and team beneath the logos. A brief biography is printed within a red rectangle, a complete college record appears beneath within a yellow rectangle, and the player's record of his NBA rookie year on the bottom rounds out the back. Please refer to the multiplier provided below (coupled with the prices of the corresponding regular issue card) to ascertain value.

	MINT	NRMT	EXC
COMPLETE FACTORY SET (150)	40.00	18.00	5.00
COMMON CARD (1-150)	.10	.05	.01
*STARS: 1.5X to 3X BASIC CARDS..			

☐ 149G	Rumeal Robinson	.50	.23	.06
☐ 150G	Shaquille O'Neal	15.00	6.75	1.85

1992-93 Topps Archives Master Photos

In one out of 24 '92-93 Archives packs, the Stadium Club membership card was

replaced by a mini-Master Photo Trade card (2 1/2" by 3 1/2") good for three of these full-size (5" by 7") Master Photos. The expiration date was January 31, 1994. Showcasing the 11 No. 1 NBA draft picks from 1981 through 1991, these 12 over-sized cards feature white-bordered color player action shots framed by prismatic sil-ver-foil lines. The player's name, team name and year of his being the No. 1 pick appear in diagonal red, yellow, and blue stripes near the bottom. The words "#1 Draft Pick" followed by a curving comet like prismatic silver-foil tail appear in one of the photo's upper corners. Aside from the Topps and NBA trademarks, the backs are blank. The cards are numbered on the front by year. The mini Master Photo cards are presently valued the same as the large.

	MINT	NRMT	EXC
COMPLETE SET (12)	8.00	3.60	1.00
COMMON CARD (1981-1991)	.25	.11	.03
☐ 1981 Mark Aguirre	.25	.11	.03
1981 No. 1 Draft Pick			
☐ 1982 James Worthy	.50	.23	.06
1982 No. 1 Draft Pick			
☐ 1983 Ralph Sampson	.25	.11	.03
1983 No. 1 Draft Pick			
☐ 1984 Hakeem Olajuwon	3.00	1.35	.35
1984 No. 1 Draft Pick			
☐ 1985 Patrick Ewing	1.25	.55	.16
1985 No. 1 Draft Pick			
☐ 1986 Brad Daugherty	.25	.11	.03
1986 No. 1 Draft Pick			
☐ 1987 David Robinson	2.50	1.10	.30
1987 No. 1 Draft Pick			
☐ 1988 Danny Manning	.50	.23	.06
1988 No. 1 Draft Pick			
☐ 1989 Pervis Ellison	.25	.11	.03
1989 No. 1 Draft Pick			
☐ 1990 Derrick Coleman	.25	.11	.03
1990 No. 1 Draft Pick			
☐ 1991 Larry Johnson	1.50	.70	.19
1991 No. 1 Draft Pick			
☐ NNO First Picks 1981-91	.50	.23	.06

1995-96 Topps Gallery

The 1995-96 Topps Gallery set was issued in one series of 144 cards. The 8-card packs, offered exclusively to hobby outlets, retailed for $3.00 each. The set features the topical subsets: The Masters (1-18), The Modernists (19-36), New Editions (37-84) and The Classics (85-144). Each card is printed on 24-point stock, covered with an exclusive high-gloss film and etch stamped with one or more foils. Rookie Cards of note in this set include Michael Finley, Kevin Garnett, Antonio McDyess, Jerry Stackhouse and Damon Stoudamire.

		MINT	NRMT	EXC
COMPLETE SET (144)		30.00	13.50	3.70
COMMON CARD (1-144)		.10	.05	.01
☐ 1	Shaquille O'Neal	2.00	.90	.25
☐ 2	Shawn Kemp	1.25	.55	.16
☐ 3	Reggie Miller	.50	.23	.06
☐ 4	Mitch Richmond	.30	.14	.04
☐ 5	Grant Hill	1.50	.70	.19
☐ 6	Magic Johnson	1.25	.55	.16
☐ 7	Vin Baker	.40	.18	.05
☐ 8	Charles Barkley	.60	.25	.07
☐ 9	Hakeem Olajuwon	1.00	.45	.12
☐ 10	Michael Jordan	6.00	2.70	.75
☐ 11	Patrick Ewing	.40	.18	.05
☐ 12	David Robinson	.75	.35	.09
☐ 13	Alonzo Mourning	.40	.18	.05
☐ 14	Karl Malone	.40	.18	.05
☐ 15	Chris Webber	.40	.18	.05
☐ 16	Dikembe Mutombo	.20	.09	.03
☐ 17	Larry Johnson	.40	.18	.05
☐ 18	Jamal Mashburn	.25	.11	.03
☐ 19	Anfernee Hardaway	3.00	1.35	.35
☐ 20	Bryant Stith	.10	.05	.01
☐ 21	Juwan Howard	1.00	.45	.12
☐ 22	Jason Kidd	1.00	.45	.12
☐ 23	Sharone Wright	.10	.05	.01
☐ 24	Tom Gugliotta	.20	.09	.03
☐ 25	Eric Montross	.10	.05	.01
☐ 26	Allan Houston	.10	.05	.01
☐ 27	Antonio Davis	.10	.05	.01
☐ 28	Brian Grant	.10	.05	.01
☐ 29	Terrell Brandon	.20	.09	.03
☐ 30	Eddie Jones	.30	.14	.04
☐ 31	James Robinson	.10	.05	.01
☐ 32	Wesley Person	.10	.05	.01
☐ 33	Glenn Robinson	.50	.23	.06
☐ 34	Donyell Marshall	.10	.05	.01
☐ 35	Sam Cassell	.10	.05	.01
☐ 36	Lamond Murray	.10	.05	.01
☐ 37	Damon Stoudamire RC	4.00	1.80	.50
☐ 38	Tyus Edney RC	.75	.35	.09
☐ 39	Jerry Stackhouse RC	3.00	1.35	.35
☐ 40	Arvydas Sabonis RC	1.25	.55	.16
☐ 41	Kevin Garnett RC	5.00	2.20	.60

☐ 42	Brent Barry RC	.75	.35	.09
☐ 43	Alan Henderson RC	.25	.11	.03
☐ 44	Bryant Reeves RC	1.00	.45	.12
☐ 45	Shawn Respert RC	.10	.05	.01
☐ 46	Michael Finley RC	2.00	.90	.25
☐ 47	Gary Trent RC	.10	.05	.01
☐ 48	Antonio McDyess RC	1.50	.70	.19
☐ 49	George Zidek RC	.10	.05	.01
☐ 50	Joe Smith RC	2.00	.90	.25
☐ 51	Ed O'Bannon RC	.60	.25	.07
☐ 52	Rasheed Wallace RC	.75	.35	.09
☐ 53	Eric Williams RC	.30	.14	.04
☐ 54	Kurt Thomas RC	.50	.23	.06
☐ 55	Mookie Blaylock	.15	.07	.02
☐ 56	Robert Pack	.10	.05	.01
☐ 57	Dana Barros	.10	.05	.01
☐ 58	Eric Murdock	.10	.05	.01
☐ 59	Glen Rice	.20	.09	.03
☐ 60	John Stockton	.40	.18	.05
☐ 61	Scottie Pippen	1.25	.55	.16
☐ 62	Oliver Miller	.10	.05	.01
☐ 63	Tyrone Hill	.10	.05	.01
☐ 64	Gary Payton	.60	.25	.07
☐ 65	Jim Jackson	.20	.09	.03
☐ 66	Avery Johnson	.15	.07	.02
☐ 67	Mahmoud Abdul-Rauf	.10	.05	.01
☐ 68	Olden Polynice	.10	.05	.01
☐ 69	Joe Dumars	.20	.09	.03
☐ 70	Rod Strickland	.10	.05	.01
☐ 71	Chris Mullin	.15	.07	.02
☐ 72	Kevin Johnson	.20	.09	.03
☐ 73	Derrick Coleman	.15	.07	.02
☐ 74	Clyde Drexler	.50	.23	.06
☐ 75	Dale Davis	.10	.05	.01
☐ 76	Horace Grant	.20	.09	.03
☐ 77	Loy Vaught	.15	.07	.02
☐ 78	Armon Gilliam	.10	.05	.01
☐ 79	Nick Van Exel	.30	.14	.04
☐ 80	Charles Oakley	.10	.05	.01
☐ 81	Kevin Willis	.10	.05	.01
☐ 82	Sherman Douglas	.10	.05	.01
☐ 83	Isaiah Rider	.10	.05	.01
☐ 84	Steve Smith	.20	.09	.03
☐ 85	Dee Brown	.10	.05	.01
☐ 86	Dell Curry	.10	.05	.01
☐ 87	Calbert Cheaney	.15	.07	.02
☐ 88	Greg Anthony	.10	.05	.01
☐ 89	Jeff Hornacek	.15	.07	.02
☐ 90	Dennis Rodman Bulls	2.50	1.10	.30
☐ 91	Willie Anderson	.10	.05	.01
☐ 92	Chris Mills	.10	.05	.01
☐ 93	Hersey Hawkins	.15	.07	.02
☐ 94	Popeye Jones	.10	.05	.01
☐ 95	Chuck Person	.10	.05	.01
☐ 96	Reggie Williams	.10	.05	.01
☐ 97	A.C. Green	.15	.07	.02
☐ 98	Otis Thorpe	.15	.07	.02
☐ 99	Walt Williams	.10	.05	.01
☐ 100	Latrell Sprewell	.20	.09	.03
☐ 101	Buck Williams	.15	.07	.02
☐ 102	Robert Horry	.15	.07	.02
☐ 103	Clarence Weatherspoon	.15	.07	.02
☐ 104	Dennis Scott	.20	.09	.03
☐ 105	Rik Smits	.20	.09	.03
☐ 106	Jayson Williams	.10	.05	.01
☐ 107	Pooh Richardson	.10	.05	.01
☐ 108	Anthony Mason	.10	.05	.01
☐ 109	Cedric Ceballos	.15	.07	.02
☐ 110	Billy Owens	.10	.05	.01
☐ 111	Johnny Newman	.10	.05	.01
☐ 112	Christian Laettner	.15	.07	.02

☐ 113	Stacey Augmon	.15	.07	.02
☐ 114	Chris Morris	.10	.05	.01
☐ 115	Detlef Schrempf	.20	.09	.03
☐ 116	Dino Radja	.15	.07	.02
☐ 117	Sean Elliott	.20	.09	.03
☐ 118	Muggsy Bogues	.15	.07	.02
☐ 119	Toni Kukoc	.25	.11	.03
☐ 120	Clifford Robinson	.20	.09	.03
☐ 121	Bobby Hurley	.10	.05	.01
☐ 122	Lorenzo Williams	.10	.05	.01
☐ 123	Wayman Tisdale	.10	.05	.01
☐ 124	Bobby Phills	.10	.05	.01
☐ 125	Nick Anderson	.10	.05	.01
☐ 126	LaPhonso Ellis	.10	.05	.01
☐ 127	Scott Williams	.10	.05	.01
☐ 128	Mark West	.10	.05	.01
☐ 129	P.J. Brown	.10	.05	.01
☐ 130	Tim Hardaway	.15	.07	.02
☐ 131	Derek Harper	.10	.05	.01
☐ 132	Mario Elie	.10	.05	.01
☐ 133	Benoit Benjamin	.10	.05	.01
☐ 134	Terry Porter	.10	.05	.01
☐ 135	Derrick McKey	.10	.05	.01
☐ 136	Bimbo Coles	.10	.05	.01
☐ 137	John Salley	.10	.05	.01
☐ 138	Malik Sealy	.10	.05	.01
☐ 139	Byron Scott	.15	.07	.02
☐ 140	Vlade Divac	.20	.09	.03
☐ 141	Mark Price	.10	.05	.01
☐ 142	Rony Seikaly	.10	.05	.01
☐ 143	Mark Jackson	.10	.05	.01
☐ 144	John Starks	.10	.05	.01

1995-96 Topps Gallery Players Private Issue

Randomly inserted into 1 in every 12 packs, cards from this 126 card set parallel cards 19-144 from the basic Topps Gallery issue. Each Player's Private Issue card is marked with a special holographic silver foil stamp on front, differentiating them from their regular-issue counterparts. According to Topps media literature, half of the cards printed were sent to the actual NBA players featured in the set and the rest were seeded into packs. Only the top level stars are listed below. Please refer to the multipliers for all other card values. Quite a hullabaloo was made over the discovery that Topps

had never released the first 18 cards in this set (the Masters subset) due to an unannounced production flaw at the printing plant. For many months, it was believed that Private Issue parallels existed for these first eighteen cards (as was stated on Topps media literature) but the cards were simply not turning up on the open market as wholesale dealer buy offers skyrocketed. The book is still open as to whether or not a few copies actually survived the production gaffes, but if they do, their scarcity pushes them out of the mainstream arena of cards commonly traded.

	MINT	NRMT	EXC
COMPLETE SET (126)	800.00	350.00	100.00
COMMON CARD (19-144)	4.00	1.80	.50
☐ 19 Anfernee Hardaway	125.00	55.00	15.50
☐ 21 Juwan Howard	30.00	13.50	3.70
☐ 22 Jason Kidd	25.00	11.00	3.10
☐ 26 Allan Houston	10.00	4.50	1.25
☐ 30 Eddie Jones	10.00	4.50	1.25
☐ 33 Glenn Robinson	15.00	6.75	1.85
☐ 37 Damon Stoudamire	50.00	22.00	6.25
☐ 38 Tyus Edney	10.00	4.50	1.25
☐ 39 Jerry Stackhouse	40.00	18.00	5.00
☐ 40 Arvydas Sabonis	15.00	6.75	1.85
☐ 41 Kevin Garnett	90.00	40.00	11.00
☐ 42 Brent Barry	10.00	4.50	1.25
☐ 44 Bryant Reeves	12.00	5.50	1.50
☐ 46 Michael Finley	25.00	11.00	3.10
☐ 48 Antonio McDyess	20.00	9.00	2.50
☐ 50 Joe Smith	25.00	11.00	3.10
☐ 52 Rasheed Wallace	10.00	4.50	1.25
☐ 60 John Stockton	12.00	5.50	1.50
☐ 61 Scottie Pippen	40.00	18.00	5.00
☐ 64 Gary Payton	20.00	9.00	2.50
☐ 74 Clyde Drexler	15.00	6.75	1.85
☐ 79 Nick Van Exel	10.00	4.50	1.25
☐ 90 Dennis Rodman Bulls	80.00	36.00	10.00

1995-96 Topps Gallery Expressionists

Randomly inserted into 1 in every 24 packs, these inserts feature a collection of fifteen NBA team leaders. Each card attempts to capture the intensity and spirit of the featured player incorporating an embossed, textured, brush stroke effect.

	Mint	Good	Poor
COMPLETE SET (15)	110.00	50.00	14.00
COMMON CARD (EX1-EX15)	1.00	.45	.12
☐ EX1 Shawn Kemp	10.00	4.50	1.25
☐ EX2 Michael Jordan	45.00	20.00	5.50
☐ EX3 Reggie Miller	4.00	1.80	.50
☐ EX4 Kevin Willis	1.00	.45	.12
☐ EX5 Jason Kidd	8.00	3.60	1.00
☐ EX6 Larry Johnson	3.00	1.35	.35
☐ EX7 Patrick Ewing	3.00	1.35	.35
☐ EX8 Rasheed Wallace	3.00	1.35	.35
☐ EX9 Karl Malone	3.00	1.35	.35
☐ EX10 Shaquille O'Neal	15.00	6.75	1.85
☐ EX11 Joe Smith	8.00	3.60	1.00
☐ EX12 Jerry Stackhouse	12.00	5.50	1.50
☐ EX13 Glen Rice	1.50	.70	.19
☐ EX14 Clyde Drexler	4.00	1.80	.50
☐ EX15 Grant Hill	12.00	5.50	1.50

1995-96 Topps Gallery Photo Gallery

Randomly inserted into 1 in every 30 packs, this seventeen card set features a selection of premium quality photographs, chronicling classic moments from some of the NBA's biggest stars. Each card is custom-designed to compliment the photography. Multiple foils were also used on each card.

	Mint	Good	Poor
COMPLETE SET (17)	160.00	70.00	20.00
COMMON CARD (PG1-PG17)	2.50	1.10	.30
☐ PG1 Vin Baker	5.00	2.20	.60
☐ PG2 Brian Grant	2.50	1.10	.30
☐ PG3 George Zidek	2.50	1.10	.30
☐ PG4 Hakeem Olajuwon	12.00	5.50	1.50
☐ PG5 Stacey Augmon	2.50	1.10	.30
☐ PG6 Oliver Miller	2.50	1.10	.30
☐ PG7 Kenny Gattison	2.50	1.10	.30
☐ PG8 Dikembe Mutombo	4.00	1.80	.50
☐ PG9 Rony Seikaly	2.50	1.10	.30
☐ PG10 Tom Gugliotta	4.00	1.80	.50
☐ PG11 Scottie Pippen	15.00	6.75	1.85

	MINT	NRMT	EXC
☐ PG12 David Robinson.....	10.00	4.50	1.25
☐ PG13 Anfernee Hardaway	35.00	16.00	4.40
☐ PG14 Dennis Rodman Bulls	30.00	13.50	3.70
☐ PG15 Kevin Garnett	30.00	13.50	3.70
☐ PG16 Damon Stoudamire	25.00	11.00	3.10
☐ PG17 Charles Barkley	8.00	3.60	1.00

1992-93 Ultra

The complete premier 1992-93 Ultra basketball set (made by Fleer) consists of 375 standard-size cards. The set was released in two series of 200 and 175 cards, respectively. Both series packs contained 14 cards each with 36 packs to a box. Suggested retail pack price was 1.79. The glossy color action player photos on the fronts are full-bleed except at the bottom where a diagonal gold-foil stripe edges a pale green variegated border. The player's name and team appear on two team color-coded bars that overlay the bottom border. The horizontal backs display action and close-up cut-out player photos against a basketball court background. The team logo and biographical information appear in a pale green bar like that on the front that edges the right side, while the player's name and statistics are given in bars running across the card bottom. The cards are numbered on the back and grouped alphabetically within team order. The first series closes with an NBA Draft Picks subset (193-198) and both series close with checklists (199-200/373-375). The second series contains more than 40 rookies, 30 trade cards, free agent signings, and other veterans omitted from the first series. The second series opens with an NBA Jam Session (201-220) subset. Three players from this Jam Session subset, Duane Causwell, Pervis Ellison, and Stacey Augmon, autographed a total of more than 2,500 cards that were randomly inserted in second series foil packs. These cards were embossed with Fleer logos for authenticity. On each series two pack, a mail-in offer provided the opportunity to acquire two more exclusive Jam Session cards, showing all 20 players in the set, for ten wrappers and 1.00 for postage and handling. According to Fleer, they anticipated about 100,000 requests. Key Rookie Cards include Tom Gugliotta, Robert Horry, Christian Laettner, Alonzo Mourning, Shaquille O'Neal, Latrell Sprewell and Clarence Weatherspoon.

	MINT	NRMT	EXC
COMPLETE SET (375)	30.00	13.50	3.70
COMPLETE SERIES 1 (200)......	15.00	6.75	1.85
COMPLETE SERIES 2 (175)......	15.00	6.75	1.85
COMMON CARD (1-200)	.10	.05	.01
COMMON CARD (201-375)	.05	.02	.01
☐ 1 Stacey Augmon..............	.20	.09	.03
☐ 2 Duane Ferrell................	.10	.05	.01
☐ 3 Paul Graham................	.10	.05	.01
☐ 4 Blair Rasmussen.............	.10	.05	.01
☐ 5 Rumeal Robinson...........	.10	.05	.01
☐ 6 Dominique Wilkins...........	.20	.09	.03
☐ 7 Kevin Willis................	.10	.05	.01
☐ 8 John Bagley................	.10	.05	.01
☐ 9 Dee Brown................	.10	.05	.01
☐ 10 Rick Fox................	.10	.05	.01
☐ 11 Kevin Gamble.............	.10	.05	.01
☐ 12 Joe Kleine................	.10	.05	.01
☐ 13 Reggie Lewis..............	.15	.07	.02
☐ 14 Kevin McHale.............	.20	.09	.03
☐ 15 Robert Parish.............	.20	.09	.03
☐ 16 Ed Pinckney..............	.10	.05	.01
☐ 17 Muggsy Bogues..........	.15	.07	.02
☐ 18 Dell Curry................	.10	.05	.01
☐ 19 Kenny Gattison.............	.10	.05	.01
☐ 20 Kendall Gill................	.10	.05	.01
☐ 21 Larry Johnson.............	1.00	.45	.12
☐ 22 Johnny Newman............	.10	.05	.01
☐ 23 J.R. Reid................	.10	.05	.01
☐ 24 B.J. Armstrong.............	.10	.05	.01
☐ 25 Bill Cartwright.............	.10	.05	.01
☐ 26 Horace Grant..............	.20	.09	.03
☐ 27 Michael Jordan	6.00	2.70	.75
☐ 28 Stacey King.............	.10	.05	.01
☐ 29 John Paxson.............	.15	.07	.02
☐ 30 Will Perdue.............	.10	.05	.01
☐ 31 Scottie Pippen.............	1.50	.70	.19
☐ 32 Scott Williams.............	.10	.05	.01
☐ 33 John Battle................	.10	.05	.01
☐ 34 Terrell Brandon.............	.20	.09	.03
☐ 35 Brad Daugherty.............	.10	.05	.01
☐ 36 Craig Ehlo................	.10	.05	.01
☐ 37 Larry Nance................	.10	.05	.01
☐ 38 Mark Price................	.10	.05	.01
☐ 39 Mike Sanders.............	.10	.05	.01
☐ 40 John Williams.............	.10	.05	.01
☐ 41 Terry Davis................	.10	.05	.01
☐ 42 Derek Harper..............	.15	.07	.02
☐ 43 Donald Hodge.............	.10	.05	.01
☐ 44 Mike Iuzzolino.............	.10	.05	.01
☐ 45 Fat Lever................	.10	.05	.01
☐ 46 Doug Smith.............	.10	.05	.01
☐ 47 Randy White.............	.10	.05	.01
☐ 48 Winston Garland.............	.10	.05	.01
☐ 49 Chris Jackson..............	.15	.07	.02
☐ 50 Marcus Liberty.............	.10	.05	.01
☐ 51 Todd Lichti................	.10	.05	.01
☐ 52 Mark Macon.............	.10	.05	.01
☐ 53 Dikembe Mutombo...........	.50	.23	.06
☐ 54 Reggie Williams.............	.10	.05	.01
☐ 55 Mark Aguirre..............	.15	.07	.02
☐ 56 Joe Dumars..............	.20	.09	.03
☐ 57 Bill Laimbeer..............	.15	.07	.02
☐ 58 Dennis Rodman.............	2.00	.90	.25
☐ 59 Isiah Thomas.............	.30	.14	.04
☐ 60 Darrell Walker..............	.10	.05	.01
☐ 61 Orlando Woolridge........	.10	.05	.01

☐	62	Victor Alexander	.10	.05	.01
☐	63	Chris Gatling	.10	.05	.01
☐	64	Tim Hardaway	.15	.07	.02
☐	65	Tyrone Hill	.10	.05	.01
☐	66	Sarunas Marciulionis	.10	.05	.01
☐	67	Chris Mullin	.15	.07	.02
☐	68	Billy Owens	.10	.05	.01
☐	69	Sleepy Floyd	.10	.05	.01
☐	70	Avery Johnson	.15	.07	.02
☐	71	Vernon Maxwell	.10	.05	.01
☐	72	Hakeem Olajuwon	1.25	.55	.16
☐	73	Kenny Smith	.10	.05	.01
☐	74	Otis Thorpe	.15	.07	.02
☐	75	Dale Davis	.10	.05	.01
☐	76	Vern Fleming	.10	.05	.01
☐	77	George McCloud	.10	.05	.01
☐	78	Reggie Miller	.60	.25	.07
☐	79	Detlef Schrempf	.15	.07	.02
☐	80	Rik Smits	.20	.09	.03
☐	81	LaSalle Thompson	.10	.05	.01
☐	82	Gary Grant	.10	.05	.01
☐	83	Ron Harper	.10	.05	.01
☐	84	Mark Jackson	.10	.05	.01
☐	85	Danny Manning	.15	.07	.02
☐	86	Ken Norman	.10	.05	.01
☐	87	Stanley Roberts	.10	.05	.01
☐	88	Loy Vaught	.15	.07	.02
☐	89	Elden Campbell	.15	.07	.02
☐	90	Vlade Divac	.20	.09	.03
☐	91	A.C. Green	.20	.09	.03
☐	92	Sam Perkins	.15	.07	.02
☐	93	Byron Scott	.20	.09	.03
☐	94	Tony Smith	.10	.05	.01
☐	95	Sedale Threatt	.10	.05	.01
☐	96	James Worthy	.20	.09	.03
☐	97	Willie Burton	.10	.05	.01
☐	98	Bimbo Coles	.10	.05	.01
☐	99	Kevin Edwards	.10	.05	.01
☐	100	Grant Long	.10	.05	.01
☐	101	Glen Rice	.20	.09	.03
☐	102	Rony Seikaly	.10	.05	.01
☐	103	Brian Shaw	.10	.05	.01
☐	104	Steve Smith	.20	.09	.03
☐	105	Frank Brickowski	.10	.05	.01
☐	106	Moses Malone	.30	.14	.04
☐	107	Fred Roberts	.10	.05	.01
☐	108	Alvin Robertson	.10	.05	.01
☐	109	Thurl Bailey	.10	.05	.01
☐	110	Gerald Glass	.10	.05	.01
☐	111	Luc Longley	.10	.05	.01
☐	112	Felton Spencer	.10	.05	.01
☐	113	Doug West	.10	.05	.01
☐	114	Kenny Anderson	.20	.09	.03
☐	115	Mookie Blaylock	.15	.07	.02
☐	116	Sam Bowie	.10	.05	.01
☐	117	Derrick Coleman	.10	.05	.01
☐	118	Chris Dudley	.10	.05	.01
☐	119	Chris Morris	.10	.05	.01
☐	120	Drazen Petrovic	.15	.07	.02
☐	121	Greg Anthony	.10	.05	.01
☐	122	Patrick Ewing	.50	.23	.06
☐	123	Anthony Mason	.20	.09	.03
☐	124	Charles Oakley	.15	.07	.02
☐	125	Doc Rivers	.10	.05	.01
☐	126	Charles Smith	.10	.05	.01
☐	127	John Starks	.15	.07	.02
☐	128	Nick Anderson	.20	.09	.03
☐	129	Anthony Bowie	.10	.05	.01
☐	130	Terry Catledge	.10	.05	.01
☐	131	Jerry Reynolds	.10	.05	.01
☐	132	Dennis Scott	.15	.07	.02
☐	133	Scott Skiles	.10	.05	.01
☐	134	Brian Williams	.10	.05	.01
☐	135	Ron Anderson	.10	.05	.01
☐	136	Manute Bol	.10	.05	.01
☐	137	Johnny Dawkins	.10	.05	.01
☐	138	Armon Gilliam	.15	.07	.02
☐	139	Hersey Hawkins	.15	.07	.02
☐	140	Jeff Ruland	.10	.05	.01
☐	141	Charles Shackleford	.10	.05	.01
☐	142	Cedric Ceballos	.20	.09	.03
☐	143	Tom Chambers	.15	.07	.02
☐	144	Kevin Johnson	.20	.09	.03
☐	145	Negele Knight	.10	.05	.01
☐	146	Dan Majerle	.15	.07	.02
☐	147	Mark West	.10	.05	.01
☐	148	Mark Bryant	.10	.05	.01
☐	149	Clyde Drexler	.60	.25	.07
☐	150	Kevin Duckworth	.10	.05	.01
☐	151	Jerome Kersey	.10	.05	.01
☐	152	Robert Pack	.10	.05	.01
☐	153	Terry Porter	.10	.05	.01
☐	154	Clifford Robinson	.20	.09	.03
☐	155	Buck Williams	.15	.07	.02
☐	156	Anthony Bonner	.10	.05	.01
☐	157	Duane Causwell	.10	.05	.01
☐	158	Mitch Richmond	.40	.18	.05
☐	159	Lionel Simmons	.10	.05	.01
☐	160	Wayman Tisdale	.10	.05	.01
☐	161	Spud Webb	.15	.07	.02
☐	162	Willie Anderson	.10	.05	.01
☐	163	Antoine Carr	.10	.05	.01
☐	164	Terry Cummings	.10	.05	.01
☐	165	Sean Elliott	.20	.09	.03
☐	166	Sidney Green	.10	.05	.01
☐	167	David Robinson	1.00	.45	.12
☐	168	Dana Barros	.10	.05	.01
☐	169	Benoit Benjamin	.10	.05	.01
☐	170	Michael Cage	.10	.05	.01
☐	171	Eddie Johnson	.10	.05	.01
☐	172	Shawn Kemp	2.00	.90	.25
☐	173	Derrick McKey	.10	.05	.01
☐	174	Nate McMillan	.10	.05	.01
☐	175	Gary Payton	1.00	.45	.12
☐	176	Ricky Pierce	.10	.05	.01
☐	177	David Benoit	.10	.05	.01
☐	178	Mike Brown	.10	.05	.01
☐	179	Tyrone Corbin	.10	.05	.01
☐	180	Mark Eaton	.10	.05	.01
☐	181	Jeff Malone	.10	.05	.01
☐	182	Karl Malone	.50	.23	.06
☐	183	John Stockton	.50	.23	.06
☐	184	Michael Adams	.10	.05	.01
☐	185	Ledell Eackles	.10	.05	.01
☐	186	Pervis Ellison	.10	.05	.01
☐	187	A.J. English	.10	.05	.01
☐	188	Harvey Grant	.10	.05	.01
☐	189	Buck Johnson	.10	.05	.01
☐	190	LaBradford Smith	.10	.05	.01
☐	191	Larry Stewart	.10	.05	.01
☐	192	David Wingate	.10	.05	.01
☐	193	Alonzo Mourning	2.50	1.10	.30
☐	194	Adam Keefe	.20	.09	.03
☐	195	Robert Horry	1.00	.45	.12
☐	196	Anthony Peeler	.15	.07	.02
☐	197	Tracy Murray	.20	.09	.03
☐	198	Dave Johnson	.10	.05	.01
☐	199	Checklist 1-104	.10	.05	.01
☐	200	Checklist 105-200	.10	.05	.01
☐	201	David Robinson JS	.30	.14	.04
☐	202	Dikembe Mutombo JS	.20	.09	.03
☐	203	Otis Thorpe JS	.05	.02	.01

□	#	Name			
□	204	Hakeem Olajuwon JS	.40	.18	.05
□	205	Shawn Kemp JS	.60	.25	.07
□	206	Charles Barkley JS	.25	.11	.03
□	207	Pervis Ellison JS	.05	.02	.01
□	208	Chris Morris JS	.05	.02	.01
□	209	Brad Daugherty JS	.05	.02	.01
□	210	Derrick Coleman JS	.05	.02	.01
□	211	Tim Perry JS	.05	.02	.01
□	212	Duane Causwell JS	.05	.02	.01
□	213	Scottie Pippen JS	.50	.23	.06
□	214	Robert Parish JS	.10	.05	.01
□	215	Stacey Augmon JS	.05	.02	.01
□	216	Michael Jordan JS	2.00	.90	.25
□	217	Karl Malone JS	.20	.09	.03
□	218	John Williams JS	.05	.02	.01
□	219	Horace Grant JS	.05	.02	.01
□	220	Orlando Woolridge JS	.05	.02	.01
□	221	Mookie Blaylock	.10	.05	.01
□	222	Greg Foster	.05	.02	.01
□	223	Steve Henson	.05	.02	.01
□	224	Adam Keefe	.05	.02	.01
□	225	Jon Koncak	.05	.02	.01
□	226	Travis Mays	.05	.02	.01
□	227	Alaa Abdelnaby	.05	.02	.01
□	228	Sherman Douglas	.05	.02	.01
□	229	Xavier McDaniel	.05	.02	.01
□	230	Marcus Webb	.05	.02	.01
□	231	Tony Bennett	.05	.02	.01
□	232	Mike Gminski	.05	.02	.01
□	233	Kevin Lynch	.05	.02	.01
□	234	Alonzo Mourning	.75	.35	.09
□	235	David Wingate	.05	.02	.01
□	236	Rodney McCray	.05	.02	.01
□	237	Trent Tucker	.05	.02	.01
□	238	Corey Williams	.05	.02	.01
□	239	Danny Ferry	.05	.02	.01
□	240	Jay Guidinger	.05	.02	.01
□	241	Jerome Lane	.05	.02	.01
□	242	Bobby Phills	.40	.18	.05
□	243	Gerald Wilkins	.05	.02	.01
□	244	Walter Bond	.05	.02	.01
□	245	Dexter Cambridge	.05	.02	.01
□	246	Radisav Curcic UER	.05	.02	.01
		(Misspelled Radislav on card front)			
□	247	Brian Howard	.05	.02	.01
□	248	Tracy Moore	.05	.02	.01
□	249	Sean Rooks	.05	.02	.01
□	250	Kevin Brooks	.05	.02	.01
□	251	LaPhonso Ellis	.25	.11	.03
□	252	Scott Hastings	.05	.02	.01
□	253	Robert Pack	.05	.02	.01
□	254	Gary Plummer	.05	.02	.01
□	255	Bryant Stith	.25	.11	.03
□	256	Robert Werdann	.05	.02	.01
□	257	Gerald Glass	.05	.02	.01
□	258	Terry Mills	.05	.02	.01
□	259	Olden Polynice	.05	.02	.01
□	260	Danny Young	.05	.02	.01
□	261	Jud Buechler	.05	.02	.01
□	262	Jeff Grayer	.05	.02	.01
□	263	Bryon Houston	.05	.02	.01
□	264	Keith Jennings	.05	.02	.01
□	265	Ed Nealy	.05	.02	.01
□	266	Latrell Sprewell	.75	.35	.09
□	267	Scott Brooks	.05	.02	.01
□	268	Matt Bullard	.05	.02	.01
□	269	Winston Garland	.05	.02	.01
□	270	Carl Herrera	.05	.02	.01
□	271	Robert Horry	.30	.14	.04
□	272	Tree Rollins	.05	.02	.01
□	273	Greg Dreiling	.05	.02	.01
□	274	Sean Green	.05	.02	.01
□	275	Sam Mitchell	.05	.02	.01
□	276	Pooh Richardson	.05	.02	.01
□	277	Malik Sealy	.20	.09	.03
□	278	Kenny Williams	.05	.02	.01
□	279	Mark Jackson	.05	.02	.01
□	280	Stanley Roberts	.05	.02	.01
□	281	Elmore Spencer	.05	.02	.01
□	282	Kiki Vandeweghe	.05	.02	.01
□	283	John S. Williams	.05	.02	.01
□	284	Randy Woods	.05	.02	.01
□	285	Alex Blackwell	.05	.02	.01
□	286	Duane Cooper	.05	.02	.01
□	287	James Edwards	.05	.02	.01
□	288	Jack Haley	.05	.02	.01
□	289	Anthony Peeler	.05	.02	.01
□	290	Keith Askins	.05	.02	.01
□	291	Matt Geiger	.05	.02	.01
□	292	Alec Kessler	.05	.02	.01
□	293	Harold Miner	.25	.11	.03
□	294	John Salley	.05	.02	.01
□	295	Anthony Avent	.05	.02	.01
□	296	Jon Barry	.05	.02	.01
□	297	Todd Day	.10	.05	.01
□	298	Blue Edwards	.05	.02	.01
□	299	Brad Lohaus	.05	.02	.01
□	300	Lee Mayberry	.05	.02	.01
□	301	Eric Murdock	.05	.02	.01
□	302	Dan Schayes	.05	.02	.01
□	303	Lance Blanks	.05	.02	.01
□	304	Christian Laettner	.50	.23	.06
□	305	Marlon Maxey	.05	.02	.01
□	306	Bob McCann	.05	.02	.01
□	307	Chuck Person	.05	.02	.01
□	308	Brad Sellers	.05	.02	.01
□	309	Chris Smith	.05	.02	.01
□	310	Gundars Vetra	.05	.02	.01
□	311	Micheal Williams	.05	.02	.01
□	312	Rafael Addison	.05	.02	.01
□	313	Chucky Brown	.05	.02	.01
□	314	Maurice Cheeks	.20	.09	.03
□	315	Tate George	.05	.02	.01
□	316	Rick Mahorn	.05	.02	.01
□	317	Rumeal Robinson	.05	.02	.01
□	318	Eric Anderson	.05	.02	.01
□	319	Rolando Blackman	.05	.02	.01
□	320	Tony Campbell	.05	.02	.01
□	321	Hubert Davis	.20	.09	.03
□	322	Doc Rivers	.05	.02	.01
□	323	Charles Smith	.05	.02	.01
□	324	Herb Williams	.05	.02	.01
□	325	Litterial Green	.05	.02	.01
□	326	Steve Kerr	.05	.02	.01
□	327	Greg Kite	.05	.02	.01
□	328	Shaquille O'Neal	6.00	2.70	.75
□	329	Tom Tolbert	.05	.02	.01
□	330	Jeff Turner	.05	.02	.01
□	331	Greg Grant	.05	.02	.01
□	332	Jeff Hornacek	.10	.05	.01
□	333	Andrew Lang	.05	.02	.01
□	334	Tim Perry	.05	.02	.01
□	335	Clarence Weatherspoon	.50	.23	.06
□	336	Danny Ainge	.20	.09	.03
□	337	Charles Barkley	.50	.23	.06
□	338	Richard Dumas	.05	.02	.01
□	339	Frank Johnson	.05	.02	.01
□	340	Tim Kempton	.05	.02	.01
□	341	Oliver Miller	.25	.11	.03
□	342	Jerrod Mustaf	.05	.02	.01
□	343	Mario Elie	.05	.02	.01

☐	344	Dave Johnson	.05	.02	.01
☐	345	Tracy Murray	.05	.02	.01
☐	346	Rod Strickland	.05	.02	.01
☐	347	Randy Brown	.05	.02	.01
☐	348	Pete Chilcutt	.05	.02	.01
☐	349	Marty Conlon	.05	.02	.01
☐	350	Jim Les	.05	.02	.01
☐	351	Kurt Rambis	.05	.02	.01
☐	352	Walt Williams	.60	.25	.07
☐	353	Lloyd Daniels	.05	.02	.01
☐	354	Vinny Del Negro	.05	.02	.01
☐	355	Dale Ellis	.05	.02	.01
☐	356	Avery Johnson	.10	.05	.01
☐	357	Sam Mack	.05	.02	.01
☐	358	J.R. Reid	.05	.02	.01
☐	359	David Wood	.05	.02	.01
☐	360	Vincent Askew	.05	.02	.01
☐	361	Isaac Austin	.05	.02	.01
☐	362	John Crotty	.05	.02	.01
☐	363	Stephen Howard	.05	.02	.01
☐	364	Jay Humphries	.05	.02	.01
☐	365	Larry Krystkowiak	.05	.02	.01
☐	366	Rex Chapman	.05	.02	.01
☐	367	Tom Gugliotta	.50	.23	.06
☐	368	Buck Johnson	.05	.02	.01
☐	369	Charles Jones	.05	.02	.01
☐	370	Don MacLean	.10	.05	.01
☐	371	Doug Overton	.05	.02	.01
☐	372	Brent Price	.05	.02	.01
☐	373	Checklist 201-266	.05	.02	.01
☐	374	Checklist 267-330	.05	.02	.01
☐	375	Checklist 331-375	.05	.02	.01
☐	JS207	Pervis Ellison AU	20.00	9.00	2.50
		(Certified Autograph)			
☐	JS212	Duane Causwell AU	15.00	6.75	1.85
		(Certified Autograph)			
☐	JS215	Stacey Augmon AU	40.00	18.00	5.00
		(Certified Autograph)			
☐	NNO	Jam Session Rank 1-10	2.50	1.10	.30

David Robinson
Dikembe Mutombo
Otis Thorpe
Hakeem Olajuwon
Shawn Kemp
Charles Barkley
Pervis Ellison
Chris Morris
Brad Daugherty
Derrick Coleman

☐ NNO Jam Session Rank 11-20 2.50 1.10 .30

Tim Perry
Duane Causwell
Scottie Pippen
Robert Parish
Stacey Augmon
Michael Jordan
Karl Malone
John Williams
Horace Grant
Orlando Woolridge

1992-93 Ultra
All-NBA

This set features 15 standard-size cards, one for each All-NBA first, second, and

third-team player. The cards were randomly inserted into approximately one out of every 14 first series foil packs. The fronts feature color action player photos which are full-bleed except at the bottom, where a gold foil stripe separates a marbleized diagonal bottom border. A crest showing which All-NBA team the player was on overlaps the border and picture. The player's name is gold-foil stamped at the bottom. The horizontal backs carry a cut-out player close-up and career highlights on a marbleized background.

	MINT	NRMT	EXC
COMPLETE SET (15)	50.00	22.00	6.25
COMMON CARD (1-15)	.50	.23	.06

☐	1	Karl Malone	2.50	1.10	.30
☐	2	Chris Mullin	1.00	.45	.12
☐	3	David Robinson	5.00	2.20	.60
☐	4	Michael Jordan	30.00	13.50	3.70
☐	5	Clyde Drexler	3.00	1.35	.35
☐	6	Scottie Pippen	8.00	3.60	1.00
☐	7	Charles Barkley	4.00	1.80	.50
☐	8	Patrick Ewing	2.50	1.10	.30
☐	9	Tim Hardaway	1.00	.45	.12
☐	10	John Stockton	2.50	1.10	.30
☐	11	Dennis Rodman	10.00	4.50	1.25
☐	12	Kevin Willis	.50	.23	.06
☐	13	Brad Daugherty	.50	.23	.06
☐	14	Mark Price	.50	.23	.06
☐	15	Kevin Johnson	1.00	.45	.12

1992-93 Ultra
All-Rookies

Randomly inserted in second series foil packs at a reported rate of approximately one card per nine packs, this ten-card standard-size set focuses on the 1992-93 class of outstanding rookies. A color action shot on the front has been cut out and superimposed on grid of identical close-up shots of the player, which resemble the effect produced by a wall of TV sets displaying the same image. The "All-Rookie" logo and the player's name are gold-foil stamped across the bottom of the picture. On the backs, a wheat-colored panel carrying a player profile overlays a second full-bleed color action photo. The set is sequenced in alphabetical order.

	MINT	NRMT	EXC
COMPLETE SET (10)	25.00	11.00	3.10
COMMON CARD (1-10)	.25	.11	.03

		MINT	NRMT	EXC
☐ 1	LaPhonso Ellis	.75	.35	.09
☐ 2	Tom Gugliotta	1.25	.55	.16
☐ 3	Robert Horry	1.50	.70	.19
☐ 4	Christian Laettner	1.25	.55	.16
☐ 5	Harold Miner	.25	.11	.03
☐ 6	Alonzo Mourning	4.00	1.80	.50
☐ 7	Shaquille O'Neal	15.00	6.75	1.85
☐ 8	Latrell Sprewell	2.00	.90	.25
☐ 9	Clarence Weatherspoon	1.25	.55	.16
☐ 10	Walt Williams	1.50	.70	.19

1992-93 Ultra Award Winners

This five-card standard-size Ultra Award Winners insert set spotlights the 1991-92 MVP, Rookie of the Year, Defensive Player of the Year, top "6th Man" and Most Improved Player. These cards were randomly inserted into first series packs at a rate of one card in every 42 packs according to information printed on the wrappers. Card fronts feature an action photo with the player's name and Award Winners logo at the bottom. Backs have career highlights and a photo.

	MINT	NRMT	EXC
COMPLETE SET (5)	40.00	18.00	5.00
COMMON CARD (1-5)	1.00	.45	.12

		MINT	NRMT	EXC
☐ 1	Michael Jordan	30.00	13.50	3.70
☐ 2	David Robinson	5.00	2.20	.60

		MINT	NRMT	EXC
☐ 3	Larry Johnson	3.00	1.35	.35
☐ 4	Detlef Schrempf	2.00	.90	.25
☐ 5	Pervis Ellison	1.00	.45	.12

1992-93 Ultra Scottie Pippen

This 12-card standard-size "Career Highlights" set chronicles Scottie Pippen's rise to NBA stardom. The cards were inserted at a rate of one card per 21 first series packs according to information printed on the wrappers. Pippen autographed more than 2,000 of these cards for random insertion in first series packs. These autograph cards have embossed Fleer logos for authenticity. Through a special mail-in offer only, two additional Pippen cards were made available to collectors who sent in ten wrappers and 1.00 for postage and handling. On the front, the cards feature color action player photos with brownish-green marbleized borders. The player's name and the words "Career Highlights" are stamped in gold foil below the picture. On the same marbleized background, the backs carry a color head shot as well as biography and career summary.

	MINT	NRMT	EXC
COMPLETE SET (10)	15.00	6.75	1.85
COMMON S.PIPPEN (1-10)	1.50	.70	.19
COMMON SEND-OFF (11-12)	1.50	.70	.19

		MINT	NRMT	EXC
☐ 1	Scottie Pippen (Dribbling, right index finger pointing down)	1.50	.70	.19
☐ 2	Scottie Pippen (Dribbling, Magnavox ad in background)	1.50	.70	.19
☐ 3	Scottie Pippen (Preparing to dunk)	1.50	.70	.19
☐ 4	Scottie Pippen (Dribbling, defender's hand reaching in)	1.50	.70	.19
☐ 5	Scottie Pippen (In air, ball in both hands, vs. Bucks)	1.50	.70	.19
☐ 6	Scottie Pippen (Driving toward basket, vs. Nuggets)	1.50	.70	.19
☐ 7	Scottie Pippen	1.50	.70	.19

		MINT	NRMT	EXC
	(Shooting over McDaniel of the Knicks)			
☐ 8	Scottie Pippen.............. (Dribbling, Laker cheerleader in background)	1.50	.70	.19
☐ 9	Scottie Pippen.............. (Defending against McDaniel of the Knicks)	1.50	.70	.19
☐ 10	Scottie Pippen.............. (Driving toward basket, vs. Nets)	1.50	.70	.19
☐ 11	Scottie Pippen.............. (Defended by Rodman; ball in left hand)	1.50	.70	.19
☐ 12	Scottie Pippen.............. (Dunking over Nugget player)	1.50	.70	.19
☐ AU	Scottie Pippen.............. (Certified autograph)	200.00	90.00	25.00

1992-93 Ultra Playmakers

Randomly inserted in second series foil packs at a reported rate of one card per 13 packs, this ten-card standard-size set features the NBA's top point guards. The glossy color action photos on the fronts are full-bleed except at the bottom where a lavender stripe edges the picture. The "Playmaker" logo and the player's name are gold-foil stamped across the bottom of the picture. On the backs, a wheat-colored panel carrying a player profile overlays a second full-bleed color action photo. The cards are numbered in the lower left corner of the panel.

		MINT	NRMT	EXC
	COMPLETE SET (10)	4.00	1.80	.50
	COMMON CARD (1-10)	.25	.11	.03
☐ 1	Kenny Anderson	.75	.35	.09
☐ 2	Muggsy Bogues	.50	.23	.06
☐ 3	Tim Hardaway	.50	.23	.06
☐ 4	Mark Jackson	.25	.11	.03
☐ 5	Kevin Johnson	.50	.23	.06
☐ 6	Mark Price	.25	.11	.03
☐ 7	Terry Porter	.25	.11	.03
☐ 8	Scott Skiles	.25	.11	.03
☐ 9	John Stockton	1.50	.70	.19
☐ 10	Isiah Thomas	1.00	.45	.12

1992-93 Ultra Rejectors

Randomly inserted in second series foil packs at a reported rate of one in 26, this five-card standard-size set showcases defensive big men who are aptly dubbed "Rejectors." The glossy color action photos on the fronts are full-bleed except at the bottom where a gold stripe edges the picture. The player's name and the "Rejector" logo are gold-foil stamped across the bottom of the picture. On a black panel inside gold borders, the horizontal backs carry text describing the player's defensive accomplishments and a color close-up photo. The set is sequenced in alphabetical order.

		MINT	NRMT	EXC
	COMPLETE SET (5)	15.00	6.75	1.85
	COMMON CARD (1-5)	.50	.23	.06
☐ 1	Alonzo Mourning	2.50	1.10	.30
☐ 2	Dikembe Mutombo	.50	.23	.06
☐ 3	Hakeem Olajuwon	2.00	.90	.25
☐ 4	Shaquille O'Neal	10.00	4.50	1.25
☐ 5	David Robinson	1.50	.70	.19

1993-94 Ultra

The complete 1993-94 Ultra basketball set consists of 375 standard-size cards that were issued in series of 200 and 175 respectively. Cards were issued in 14 and 19-card packs. There are 36 packs per box. The glossy color action player photos on the fronts are full-bleed except at the bottom. The bottom of the front consists of player name, team name and a peach colored border. The horizontal backs feature a player photo against a basketball court background. The team logo and biographical information appear a pale peach bar, while the player's name and statistics are printed in team color-coded bars running across the card bottom. The cards are alphabetically arranged by team and are numbered alphabetically within team order. A USA Basketball subset contains cards 361-372. Ten second series wrappers and

$1.50 could be redeemed for USA cards of Reggie Miller (M1), Shaquille O'Neal (M2) and a team photo (M3). The offer was good through June 10, 1994. These cards are not considered part of the basic set. Rookie Cards of note in this set include Vin Baker, Anfernee Hardaway, Allan Houston, Toni Kukoc, Jamal Mashburn, Nick Van Exel and Chris Webber.

	MINT	NRMT	EXC
COMPLETE SET (375)	30.00	13.50	3.70
COMPLETE SERIES 1 (200)	15.00	6.75	1.85
COMPLETE SERIES 2 (175)	15.00	6.75	1.85
COMMON CARD (1-375)	.05	.02	.01

		MINT	NRMT	EXC
☐ 1	Stacey Augmon	.10	.05	.01
☐ 2	Mookie Blaylock	.10	.05	.01
☐ 3	Doug Edwards	.05	.02	.01
☐ 4	Duane Ferrell	.05	.02	.01
☐ 5	Paul Graham	.05	.02	.01
☐ 6	Adam Keefe	.05	.02	.01
☐ 7	Dominique Wilkins	.15	.07	.02
☐ 8	Kevin Willis	.05	.02	.01
☐ 9	Alaa Abdelnaby	.05	.02	.01
☐ 10	Dee Brown	.05	.02	.01
☐ 11	Sherman Douglas	.05	.02	.01
☐ 12	Rick Fox	.05	.02	.01
☐ 13	Kevin Gamble	.05	.02	.01
☐ 14	Xavier McDaniel	.05	.02	.01
☐ 15	Robert Parish	.15	.07	.02
☐ 16	Muggsy Bogues	.10	.05	.01
☐ 17	Scott Burrell	.15	.07	.02
☐ 18	Dell Curry	.05	.02	.01
☐ 19	Kenny Gattison	.05	.02	.01
☐ 20	Hersey Hawkins	.05	.02	.01
☐ 21	Eddie Johnson	.05	.02	.01
☐ 22	Larry Johnson	.40	.18	.05
☐ 23	Alonzo Mourning	.50	.23	.06
☐ 24	Johnny Newman	.05	.02	.01
☐ 25	David Wingate	.05	.02	.01
☐ 26	B.J. Armstrong	.05	.02	.01
☐ 27	Corie Blount	.05	.02	.01
☐ 28	Bill Cartwright	.05	.02	.01
☐ 29	Horace Grant	.15	.07	.02
☐ 30	Michael Jordan	4.00	1.80	.50
☐ 31	Stacey King	.05	.02	.01
☐ 32	John Paxson	.10	.05	.01
☐ 33	Will Perdue	.05	.02	.01
☐ 34	Scottie Pippen	1.00	.45	.12
☐ 35	Terrell Brandon	.15	.07	.02
☐ 36	Brad Daugherty	.05	.02	.01
☐ 37	Danny Ferry	.05	.02	.01
☐ 38	Chris Mills	.50	.23	.06
☐ 39	Larry Nance	.05	.02	.01
☐ 40	Mark Price	.05	.02	.01
☐ 41	Gerald Wilkins	.05	.02	.01
☐ 42	John Williams	.05	.02	.01
☐ 43	Terry Davis	.05	.02	.01
☐ 44	Derek Harper	.10	.05	.01
☐ 45	Donald Hodge	.05	.02	.01
☐ 46	Jim Jackson	.40	.18	.05
☐ 47	Sean Rooks	.05	.02	.01
☐ 48	Doug Smith	.05	.02	.01
☐ 49	Mahmoud Abdul-Rauf	.10	.05	.01
☐ 50	LaPhonso Ellis	.05	.02	.01
☐ 51	Mark Macon	.05	.02	.01
☐ 52	Dikembe Mutombo	.15	.07	.02
☐ 53	Bryant Stith	.05	.02	.01
☐ 54	Reggie Williams	.05	.02	.01
☐ 55	Mark Aguirre	.10	.05	.01
☐ 56	Joe Dumars	.15	.07	.02
☐ 57	Bill Laimbeer	.10	.05	.01
☐ 58	Terry Mills	.05	.02	.01
☐ 59	Olden Polynice	.05	.02	.01
☐ 60	Alvin Robertson	.05	.02	.01
☐ 61	Sean Elliott	.15	.07	.02
☐ 62	Isiah Thomas	.20	.09	.03
☐ 63	Victor Alexander	.05	.02	.01
☐ 64	Chris Gatling	.05	.02	.01
☐ 65	Tim Hardaway	.15	.07	.02
☐ 66	Byron Houston	.05	.02	.01
☐ 67	Sarunas Marciulionis	.05	.02	.01
☐ 68	Chris Mullin	.15	.07	.02
☐ 69	Billy Owens	.10	.05	.01
☐ 70	Latrell Sprewell	.25	.11	.03
☐ 71	Matt Bullard	.05	.02	.01
☐ 72	Sam Cassell	.50	.23	.06
☐ 73	Carl Herrera	.05	.02	.01
☐ 74	Robert Horry	.10	.05	.01
☐ 75	Vernon Maxwell	.05	.02	.01
☐ 76	Hakeem Olajuwon	.75	.35	.09
☐ 77	Kenny Smith	.05	.02	.01
☐ 78	Otis Thorpe	.10	.05	.01
☐ 79	Dale Davis	.05	.02	.01
☐ 80	Vern Fleming	.05	.02	.01
☐ 81	Reggie Miller	.40	.18	.05
☐ 82	Sam Mitchell	.05	.02	.01
☐ 83	Pooh Richardson	.05	.02	.01
☐ 84	Detlef Schrempf	.10	.05	.01
☐ 85	Rik Smits	.15	.07	.02
☐ 86	Ron Harper	.05	.02	.01
☐ 87	Mark Jackson	.05	.02	.01
☐ 88	Danny Manning	.10	.05	.01
☐ 89	Stanley Roberts	.05	.02	.01
☐ 90	Loy Vaught	.10	.05	.01
☐ 91	John Williams	.05	.02	.01
☐ 92	Sam Bowie	.05	.02	.01
☐ 93	Doug Christie	.05	.02	.01
☐ 94	Vlade Divac	.15	.07	.02
☐ 95	George Lynch	.05	.02	.01
☐ 96	Anthony Peeler	.05	.02	.01
☐ 97	James Worthy	.15	.07	.02
☐ 98	Bimbo Coles	.05	.02	.01
☐ 99	Grant Long	.05	.02	.01
☐ 100	Harold Miner	.05	.02	.01
☐ 101	Glen Rice	.15	.07	.02
☐ 102	Rony Seikaly	.05	.02	.01
☐ 103	Brian Shaw	.05	.02	.01
☐ 104	Steve Smith	.15	.07	.02
☐ 105	Anthony Avent	.05	.02	.01
☐ 106	Vin Baker	1.25	.55	.16
☐ 107	Frank Brickowski	.05	.02	.01
☐ 108	Todd Day	.05	.02	.01
☐ 109	Blue Edwards	.05	.02	.01
☐ 110	Lee Mayberry	.05	.02	.01
☐ 111	Eric Murdock	.05	.02	.01
☐ 112	Orlando Woolridge	.05	.02	.01

#	Player			
☐ 113	Thurl Bailey	.05	.02	.01
☐ 114	Christian Laettner	.15	.07	.02
☐ 115	Chuck Person	.05	.02	.01
☐ 116	Doug West	.05	.02	.01
☐ 117	Micheal Williams	.05	.02	.01
☐ 118	Kenny Anderson	.15	.07	.02
☐ 119	Derrick Coleman	.05	.02	.01
☐ 120	Rick Mahorn	.05	.02	.01
☐ 121	Chris Morris	.05	.02	.01
☐ 122	Rumeal Robinson	.05	.02	.01
☐ 123	Rex Walters	.05	.02	.01
☐ 124	Greg Anthony	.05	.02	.01
☐ 125	Rolando Blackman	.05	.02	.01
☐ 126	Hubert Davis	.05	.02	.01
☐ 127	Patrick Ewing	.30	.14	.04
☐ 128	Anthony Mason	.10	.05	.01
☐ 129	Charles Oakley	.10	.05	.01
☐ 130	Doc Rivers	.05	.02	.01
☐ 131	Charles Smith	.05	.02	.01
☐ 132	John Starks	.10	.05	.01
☐ 133	Nick Anderson	.15	.07	.02
☐ 134	Anthony Bowie	.05	.02	.01
☐ 135	Shaquille O'Neal	2.00	.90	.25
☐ 136	Dennis Scott	.10	.05	.01
☐ 137	Scott Skiles	.05	.02	.01
☐ 138	Jeff Turner	.05	.02	.01
☐ 139	Shawn Bradley	.40	.18	.05
☐ 140	Johnny Dawkins	.05	.02	.01
☐ 141	Jeff Hornacek	.10	.05	.01
☐ 142	Tim Perry	.05	.02	.01
☐ 143	Clarence Weatherspoon	.15	.07	.02
☐ 144	Danny Ainge	.15	.07	.02
☐ 145	Charles Barkley	.50	.23	.06
☐ 146	Cedric Ceballos	.15	.07	.02
☐ 147	Kevin Johnson	.15	.07	.02
☐ 148	Negele Knight	.05	.02	.01
☐ 149	Malcolm Mackey	.05	.02	.01
☐ 150	Dan Majerle	.10	.05	.01
☐ 151	Oliver Miller	.05	.02	.01
☐ 152	Mark West	.05	.02	.01
☐ 153	Mark Bryant	.05	.02	.01
☐ 154	Clyde Drexler	.40	.18	.05
☐ 155	Jerome Kersey	.05	.02	.01
☐ 156	Terry Porter	.05	.02	.01
☐ 157	Clifford Robinson	.15	.07	.02
☐ 158	Rod Strickland	.05	.02	.01
☐ 159	Buck Williams	.10	.05	.01
☐ 160	Duane Causwell	.05	.02	.01
☐ 161	Bobby Hurley	.15	.07	.02
☐ 162	Mitch Richmond	.25	.11	.03
☐ 163	Lionel Simmons	.05	.02	.01
☐ 164	Wayman Tisdale	.05	.02	.01
☐ 165	Spud Webb	.10	.05	.01
☐ 166	Walt Williams	.10	.05	.01
☐ 167	Willie Anderson	.05	.02	.01
☐ 168	Antoine Carr	.05	.02	.01
☐ 169	Lloyd Daniels	.05	.02	.01
☐ 170	Dennis Rodman	1.25	.55	.16
☐ 171	Dale Ellis	.05	.02	.01
☐ 172	Avery Johnson	.10	.05	.01
☐ 173	J.R. Reid	.05	.02	.01
☐ 174	David Robinson	.60	.25	.07
☐ 175	Michael Cage	.05	.02	.01
☐ 176	Kendall Gill	.05	.02	.01
☐ 177	Ervin Johnson	.05	.02	.01
☐ 178	Shawn Kemp	1.00	.45	.12
☐ 179	Derrick McKey	.05	.02	.01
☐ 180	Nate McMillan	.05	.02	.01
☐ 181	Gary Payton	.50	.23	.06
☐ 182	Sam Perkins	.10	.05	.01
☐ 183	Ricky Pierce	.05	.02	.01
☐ 184	David Benoit	.05	.02	.01
☐ 185	Tyrone Corbin	.05	.02	.01
☐ 186	Mark Eaton	.05	.02	.01
☐ 187	Jay Humphries	.05	.02	.01
☐ 188	Jeff Malone	.05	.02	.01
☐ 189	Karl Malone	.30	.14	.04
☐ 190	John Stockton	.30	.14	.04
☐ 191	Luther Wright	.05	.02	.01
☐ 192	Michael Adams	.05	.02	.01
☐ 193	Calbert Cheaney	.30	.14	.04
☐ 194	Pervis Ellison	.05	.02	.01
☐ 195	Tom Gugliotta	.15	.07	.02
☐ 196	Buck Johnson	.05	.02	.01
☐ 197	LaBradford Smith	.05	.02	.01
☐ 198	Larry Stewart	.05	.02	.01
☐ 199	Checklist	.05	.02	.01
☐ 200	Checklist	.05	.02	.01
☐ 201	Doug Edwards	.05	.02	.01
☐ 202	Craig Ehlo	.05	.02	.01
☐ 203	Jon Koncak	.05	.02	.01
☐ 204	Andrew Lang	.05	.02	.01
☐ 205	Ennis Whatley	.05	.02	.01
☐ 206	Chris Corchiani	.05	.02	.01
☐ 207	Acie Earl	.05	.02	.01
☐ 208	Jimmy Oliver	.05	.02	.01
☐ 209	Ed Pinckney	.05	.02	.01
☐ 210	Dino Radja	.40	.18	.05
☐ 211	Matt Wenstrom	.05	.02	.01
☐ 212	Tony Bennett	.05	.02	.01
☐ 213	Scott Burrell	.05	.02	.01
☐ 214	LeRon Ellis	.05	.02	.01
☐ 215	Hersey Hawkins	.05	.02	.01
☐ 216	Eddie Johnson	.05	.02	.01
☐ 217	Rumeal Robinson	.05	.02	.01
☐ 218	Corie Blount	.05	.02	.01
☐ 219	Dave Johnson	.05	.02	.01
☐ 220	Steve Kerr	.10	.05	.01
☐ 221	Toni Kukoc	.75	.35	.09
☐ 222	Pete Myers	.05	.02	.01
☐ 223	Bill Wennington	.05	.02	.01
☐ 224	Scott Williams	.05	.02	.01
☐ 225	John Battle	.05	.02	.01
☐ 226	Tyrone Hill	.05	.02	.01
☐ 227	Gerald Madkins	.05	.02	.01
☐ 228	Chris Mills	.15	.07	.02
☐ 229	Bobby Phills	.15	.07	.02
☐ 230	Greg Dreiling	.05	.02	.01
☐ 231	Lucious Harris	.10	.05	.01
☐ 232	Popeye Jones	.15	.07	.02
☐ 233	Tim Legler	.05	.02	.01
☐ 234	Fat Lever	.05	.02	.01
☐ 235	Jamal Mashburn	.75	.35	.09
☐ 236	Tom Hammonds	.05	.02	.01
☐ 237	Darnell Mee	.05	.02	.01
☐ 238	Robert Pack	.05	.02	.01
☐ 239	Rodney Rogers	.10	.05	.01
☐ 240	Brian Williams	.05	.02	.01
☐ 241	Greg Anderson	.05	.02	.01
☐ 242	Sean Elliott	.15	.07	.02
☐ 243	Allan Houston	.60	.25	.07
☐ 244	Lindsey Hunter	.10	.05	.01
☐ 245	Mark Macon	.05	.02	.01
☐ 246	David Wood	.05	.02	.01
☐ 247	Jud Buechler	.05	.02	.01
☐ 248	Josh Grant	.05	.02	.01
☐ 249	Jeff Grayer	.05	.02	.01
☐ 250	Keith Jennings	.05	.02	.01
☐ 251	Avery Johnson	.10	.05	.01
☐ 252	Chris Webber	1.25	.55	.16
☐ 253	Scott Brooks	.05	.02	.01
☐ 254	Sam Cassell	.15	.07	.02

☐ 255	Mario Elie	.05	.02	.01
☐ 256	Richard Petruska	.05	.02	.01
☐ 257	Eric Riley	.05	.02	.01
☐ 258	Antonio Davis	.05	.02	.01
☐ 259	Scott Haskin	.05	.02	.01
☐ 260	Derrick McKey	.05	.02	.01
☐ 261	Byron Scott	.15	.07	.02
☐ 262	Malik Sealy	.05	.02	.01
☐ 263	Kenny Williams	.05	.02	.01
☐ 264	Haywoode Workman	.05	.02	.01
☐ 265	Mark Aguirre	.10	.05	.01
☐ 266	Terry Dehere	.10	.05	.01
☐ 267	Harold Ellis	.05	.02	.01
☐ 268	Gary Grant	.05	.02	.01
☐ 269	Bob Martin	.05	.02	.01
☐ 270	Elmore Spencer	.05	.02	.01
☐ 271	Tom Tolbert	.05	.02	.01
☐ 272	Sam Bowie	.05	.02	.01
☐ 273	Elden Campbell	.10	.05	.01
☐ 274	Antonio Harvey	.05	.02	.01
☐ 275	George Lynch	.05	.02	.01
☐ 276	Tony Smith	.05	.02	.01
☐ 277	Sedale Threatt	.05	.02	.01
☐ 278	Nick Van Exel	1.00	.45	.12
☐ 279	Willie Burton	.05	.02	.01
☐ 280	Matt Geiger	.05	.02	.01
☐ 281	John Salley	.05	.02	.01
☐ 282	Vin Baker	.60	.25	.07
☐ 283	Jon Barry	.05	.02	.01
☐ 284	Brad Lohaus	.05	.02	.01
☐ 285	Ken Norman	.05	.02	.01
☐ 286	Derek Strong	.05	.02	.01
☐ 287	Mike Brown	.05	.02	.01
☐ 288	Brian Davis	.05	.02	.01
☐ 289	Tellis Frank	.05	.02	.01
☐ 290	Luc Longley	.05	.02	.01
☐ 291	Marlon Maxey	.05	.02	.01
☐ 292	Isaiah Rider	.40	.18	.05
☐ 293	Chris Smith	.05	.02	.01
☐ 294	P.J. Brown	.05	.02	.01
☐ 295	Kevin Edwards	.05	.02	.01
☐ 296	Armon Gilliam	.05	.02	.01
☐ 297	Johnny Newman	.05	.02	.01
☐ 298	Rex Walters	.05	.02	.01
☐ 299	David Wesley	.05	.02	.01
☐ 300	Jayson Williams	.05	.02	.01
☐ 301	Anthony Bonner	.05	.02	.01
☐ 302	Derek Harper	.05	.02	.01
☐ 303	Herb Williams	.05	.02	.01
☐ 304	Litterial Green	.05	.02	.01
☐ 305	Anfernee Hardaway	6.00	2.70	.75
☐ 306	Greg Kite	.05	.02	.01
☐ 307	Larry Krystkowiak	.05	.02	.01
☐ 308	Keith Tower	.05	.02	.01
☐ 309	Dana Barros	.05	.02	.01
☐ 310	Shawn Bradley	.15	.07	.02
☐ 311	Greg Graham	.05	.02	.01
☐ 312	Sean Green	.05	.02	.01
☐ 313	Warren Kidd	.05	.02	.01
☐ 314	Eric Leckner	.05	.02	.01
☐ 315	Moses Malone	.20	.09	.03
☐ 316	Orlando Woolridge	.05	.02	.01
☐ 317	Duane Cooper	.05	.02	.01
☐ 318	Joe Courtney	.05	.02	.01
☐ 319	A.C. Green	.15	.07	.02
☐ 320	Frank Johnson	.05	.02	.01
☐ 321	Joe Kleine	.05	.02	.01
☐ 322	Chris Dudley	.05	.02	.01
☐ 323	Harvey Grant	.05	.02	.01
☐ 324	Jaren Jackson	.05	.02	.01
☐ 325	Tracy Murray	.05	.02	.01

☐ 326	James Robinson	.10	.05	.01
☐ 327	Reggie Smith	.05	.02	.01
☐ 328	Kevin Thompson	.05	.02	.01
☐ 329	Randy Brown	.05	.02	.01
☐ 330	Evers Burns	.05	.02	.01
☐ 331	Pete Chilcutt	.05	.02	.01
☐ 332	Bobby Hurley	.10	.05	.01
☐ 333	Mike Peplowski	.05	.02	.01
☐ 334	LaBradford Smith	.05	.02	.01
☐ 335	Trevor Wilson	.05	.02	.01
☐ 336	Terry Cummings	.05	.02	.01
☐ 337	Vinny Del Negro	.05	.02	.01
☐ 338	Sleepy Floyd	.05	.02	.01
☐ 339	Negele Knight	.05	.02	.01
☐ 340	Dennis Rodman	1.25	.55	.16
☐ 341	Chris Whitney	.05	.02	.01
☐ 342	Vincent Askew	.05	.02	.01
☐ 343	Kendall Gill	.05	.02	.01
☐ 344	Ervin Johnson	.05	.02	.01
☐ 345	Chris King	.05	.02	.01
☐ 346	Detlef Schrempf	.10	.05	.01
☐ 347	Walter Bond	.05	.02	.01
☐ 348	Tom Chambers	.05	.02	.01
☐ 349	John Crotty	.05	.02	.01
☐ 350	Bryon Russell	.05	.02	.01
☐ 351	Felton Spencer	.05	.02	.01
☐ 352	Mitchell Butler	.05	.02	.01
☐ 353	Rex Chapman	.05	.02	.01
☐ 354	Calbert Cheaney	.15	.07	.02
☐ 355	Kevin Duckworth	.05	.02	.01
☐ 356	Don MacLean	.05	.02	.01
☐ 357	Gheorghe Muresan	.50	.23	.06
☐ 358	Doug Overton	.05	.02	.01
☐ 359	Brent Price	.05	.02	.01
☐ 360	Kenny Walker	.05	.02	.01
☐ 361	Derrick Coleman USA	.05	.02	.01
☐ 362	Joe Dumars USA	.10	.05	.01
☐ 363	Tim Hardaway USA	.05	.02	.01
☐ 364	Larry Johnson USA	.10	.05	.01
☐ 365	Shawn Kemp USA	.50	.23	.06
☐ 366	Dan Majerle USA	.05	.02	.01
☐ 367	Alonzo Mourning USA	.25	.11	.03
☐ 368	Mark Price USA	.05	.02	.01
☐ 369	Steve Smith USA	.05	.02	.01
☐ 370	Isiah Thomas USA	.10	.05	.01
☐ 371	Dominique Wilkins USA	.10	.05	.01
☐ 372	Don Nelson USA Don Chaney	.05	.02	.01
☐ 373	Jamal Mashburn CL	.25	.11	.03
☐ 374	Checklist	.05	.02	.01
☐ 375	Checklist	.05	.02	.01
☐ M1	Reggie Miller USA	1.00	.45	.12
☐ M2	Shaquille O'Neal USA	5.00	2.20	.60
☐ M3	Team Checklist USA	2.00	.90	.25

1993-94 Ultra
All-Defensive

Randomly inserted in 1 of 24 first series 19-card jumbo packs, this standard-size ten-card set features members of the first (1-5) and second (6-10) All-NBA defensive teams. The design features a borderless front and color player action cutout set against a background of an enlarged and ghosted version of the same photo. The

player's name appears in gold-foil lettering at the bottom. The back features a color player photo at the lower left, along with his career highlights set against the same ghosted photo background. The cards are numbered on the back as "X of 10."

	MINT	NRMT	EXC
COMPLETE SET (10)	150.00	70.00	19.00
COMMON CARD (1-10)	2.50	1.10	.30
☐ 1 Joe Dumars	4.00	1.80	.50
☐ 2 Michael Jordan	100.00	45.00	12.50
☐ 3 Hakeem Olajuwon	20.00	9.00	2.50
☐ 4 Scottie Pippen	25.00	11.00	3.10
☐ 5 Dennis Rodman	30.00	13.50	3.70
☐ 6 Horace Grant	4.00	1.80	.50
☐ 7 Dan Majerle	4.00	1.80	.50
☐ 8 Larry Nance	2.50	1.10	.30
☐ 9 David Robinson	15.00	6.75	1.85
☐ 10 John Starks	2.50	1.10	.30

1993-94 Ultra All-NBA

Randomly inserted in 14-card first series packs at a rate of approximately one in 16, this 14-card standard-size set features one card for each All-NBA first (1-5), second (6-10) and third (11-14) team player from the 1992-93 season. Drazen Petrovic was named to the third team. Due to his death following the '92-93 season, a card was not produced. The fronts display full-bleed glossy color action photos with a series of three smaller photos along the left side. The player's name appears in gold-foil lettering at the lower right. The back carries a

hardwood floor-design background with three small photos along the left side that progressively zoom in on the player. Career highlights appear alongside. The cards are numbered on the back as "X of 14."

	MINT	NRMT	EXC
COMPLETE SET (14)	50.00	22.00	6.25
COMMON CARD (1-14)	1.00	.45	.12
☐ 1 Charles Barkley	4.00	1.80	.50
☐ 2 Michael Jordan	30.00	13.50	3.70
☐ 3 Karl Malone	2.50	1.10	.30
☐ 4 Hakeem Olajuwon	6.00	2.70	.75
☐ 5 Mark Price	1.00	.45	.12
☐ 6 Joe Dumars	1.50	.70	.19
☐ 7 Patrick Ewing	2.50	1.10	.30
☐ 8 Larry Johnson	3.00	1.35	.35
☐ 9 John Stockton	2.50	1.10	.30
☐ 10 Dominique Wilkins	1.50	.70	.19
☐ 11 Derrick Coleman	1.00	.45	.12
☐ 12 Tim Hardaway	1.50	.70	.19
☐ 13 Scottie Pippen	8.00	3.60	1.00
☐ 14 David Robinson	5.00	2.20	.60

1993-94 Ultra All-Rookie Series

Randomly inserted in 14-card second series packs at an approximate rate of one in seven, this 15-card standard-size set features some of the NBA's top draft picks of 1993-94. Each borderless front features a color action photo. The player's name appears in silver foil near the bottom. The horizontal borderless back carries a color player action shot on one side and career highlights on the other. The cards are numbered on the back as "X of 15" and are sequenced in alphabetical order.

	MINT	NRMT	EXC
COMPLETE SET (15)	40.00	18.00	5.00
COMMON CARD (1-15)	.75	.35	.09
☐ 1 Vin Baker	5.00	2.20	.60
☐ 2 Shawn Bradley	1.50	.70	.19
☐ 3 Calbert Cheaney	1.25	.55	.16
☐ 4 Anfernee Hardaway	25.00	11.00	3.10
☐ 5 Lindsey Hunter	.75	.35	.09
☐ 6 Bobby Hurley	.75	.35	.09
☐ 7 Popeye Jones	.75	.35	.09

		MINT	NRMT	EXC
☐ 8	Toni Kukoc	3.00	1.35	.35
☐ 9	Jamal Mashburn	3.00	1.35	.35
☐ 10	Chris Mills	2.00	.90	.25
☐ 11	Dino Radja	1.50	.70	.19
☐ 12	Isaiah Rider	1.50	.70	.19
☐ 13	Rodney Rogers	.75	.35	.09
☐ 14	Nick Van Exel	4.00	1.80	.50
☐ 15	Chris Webber	5.00	2.20	.60

1993-94 Ultra All-Rookie Team

Randomly inserted in series one 14-card packs at an approximate rate of one in 24, this five-card standard-size set features the NBA's 1992-93 All-Rookie Team. Fronts feature borderless fronts with color player action cutouts breaking out of hardwood floor backgrounds. The player's name appears in gold-foil lettering at the bottom. The horizontal borderless back carries a color player cutout and career highlights on a hardwood floor background. The cards are numbered on the back as "X of 5" and are sequenced in alphabetical order.

	MINT	NRMT	EXC
COMPLETE SET (5)	12.00	5.50	1.50
COMMON CARD (1-5)	.50	.23	.06
☐ 1 LaPhonso Ellis	.50	.23	.06
☐ 2 Tom Gugliotta	1.00	.45	.12
(with Michael Jordan)			
☐ 3 Christian Laettner	1.00	.45	.12
☐ 4 Alonzo Mourning	2.50	1.10	.30
☐ 5 Shaquille O'Neal	10.00	4.50	1.25

1993-94 Ultra Award Winners

Randomly inserted in first series 19-card jumbo packs at a rate of one in 36, this five-card standard-size set features NBA award winners from the 1992-93 season. Borderless fronts feature color player action cutouts on metallic backgrounds. The player's name appears in silver-foil lettering at

the bottom. The back carries a color player close-up and career highlights. The cards are numbered on the back as "X of 5." and are sequenced in alphabetical order.

	MINT	NRMT	EXC
COMPLETE SET (5)	25.00	11.00	3.10
COMMON CARD (1-5)	1.00	.45	.12
☐ 1 Mahmoud Abdul-Rauf	1.00	.45	.12
☐ 2 Charles Barkley	4.00	1.80	.50
☐ 3 Hakeem Olajuwon	6.00	2.70	.75
☐ 4 Shaquille O'Neal	15.00	6.75	1.85
☐ 5 Clifford Robinson	1.00	.45	.12

1993-94 Ultra Famous Nicknames

Randomly inserted into 14-card second series packs at a rate of one in five, this 15-card standard-size set features popular nicknames of today's stars. Borderless fronts feature color action cutouts on hardwood-floor and basket-net backgrounds. The player's nickname appears in silver-foil lettering on the right. The borderless back carries a color player photo on one side. On the other, the shot's game background blends into a hardwood-floor background for the player's name in vertical silver-foil lettering and his career highlights. The cards are numbered on the back as "X of 15" and are sequenced in alphabetical order.

	MINT	NRMT	EXC
COMPLETE SET (15)	75.00	34.00	9.50
COMMON CARD (1-15)	.50	.23	.06

☐ 1	Charles Barkley Sir Charles	3.00	1.35	.35
☐ 2	Tyrone Bogues Muggsy	.75	.35	.09
☐ 3	Derrick Coleman D.C.	.50	.23	.06
☐ 4	Clyde Drexler The Glide	2.50	1.10	.30
☐ 5	Anfernee Hardaway Penny	25.00	11.00	3.10
☐ 6	Larry Johnson L.J.	2.50	1.10	.30
☐ 7	Michael Jordan Air	25.00	11.00	3.10
☐ 8	Toni Kukoc The Pink Panther	3.00	1.35	.35
☐ 9	Karl Malone The Mailman	2.00	.90	.25
☐ 10	Harold Miner Baby Jordan	.50	.23	.06
☐ 11	Alonzo Mourning Zo	3.00	1.35	.35
☐ 12	Hakeem Olajuwon The Dream	5.00	2.20	.60
☐ 13	Shaquille O'Neal Shaq	12.00	5.50	1.50
☐ 14	David Robinson The Admiral	4.00	1.80	.50
☐ 15	Dominique Wilkins Human Highlight Film	1.00	.45	.12

1993-94 Ultra
Inside/Outside

Randomly inserted in 14-card second series packs, this 10-card standard-size set features on each borderless front a color player action cutout over a shot of a comet like basketball going through the basket, all on a black background. The player's name appears in gold foil near the bottom. This design, but with a different action cutout, is mirrored somewhat on the borderless back, which also carries to the left of the player photo his career highlights within a ghosted box framed by a purple line. The cards are numbered on the back as "X of 10" and are sequenced in alphabetical order.

	MINT	NRMT	EXC
COMPLETE SET (10)	12.00	5.50	1.50
COMMON CARD (1-10)	.25	.11	.03

☐ 1	Patrick Ewing	.60	.25	.07
☐ 2	Jim Jackson	.75	.35	.09
☐ 3	Larry Johnson	.75	.35	.09
☐ 4	Michael Jordan	8.00	3.60	1.00
☐ 5	Dan Majerle	.40	.18	.05
☐ 6	Hakeem Olajuwon	1.50	.70	.19
☐ 7	Scottie Pippen	2.00	.90	.25
☐ 8	Latrell Sprewell	.50	.23	.06
☐ 9	John Starks	.25	.11	.03
☐ 10	Walt Williams	.40	.18	.05

1993-94 Ultra
Jam City

Randomly inserted in 19-card second series jumbo packs at a rate of one in 37, this 9-card standard-size set features borderless fronts with color player action cutouts on black and purple metallic cityscape backgrounds. The player's name appears in gold foil in a lower corner. The borderless back carries a color player action cutout on a non-metallic cityscape background otherwise similar to the front. The player's name and career highlights appear in a ghosted box to the left of the photo. The cards are numbered on the back as "X of 10" and are sequenced in alphabetical order.

	MINT	NRMT	EXC
COMPLETE SET (9)	80.00	36.00	10.00
COMMON CARD (1-9)	1.50	.70	.19

☐ 1	Charles Barkley	10.00	4.50	1.25
☐ 2	Derrick Coleman	1.50	.70	.19
☐ 3	Clyde Drexler	8.00	3.60	1.00
☐ 4	Patrick Ewing	6.00	2.70	.75
☐ 5	Shawn Kemp	20.00	9.00	2.50
☐ 6	Harold Miner	1.50	.70	.19
☐ 7	Shaquille O'Neal	40.00	18.00	5.00
☐ 8	David Robinson	12.00	5.50	1.50
☐ 9	Dominique Wilkins	3.00	1.35	.35

1993-94 Ultra
Karl Malone

This ten-card standard-size set of Career Highlights spotlights Utah Jazz forward Karl

Malone. The cards were randomly inserted
in 14-card first series packs at a rate of
approximately one in 16. The full-bleed
color card fronts have purple tinted ghosted
backgrounds with Malone portrayed in nor-
mal color action and posed photos. Across
the bottom edge is a marbleized border
with the subset title "Career Highlights",
above the lower border is a silver and black
box containing Malone's name. The backs
carry information about Malone within a
purple tinted ghosted box that is superimposed over a color photo. More than 2,000
autographed cards were randomly inserted
in packs. These card have embossed Fleer
logos for authenticity. An additional two
cards (Nos.11 and 12) were available
through a mail-in offer. Prior to June 10,
1994, collectors had to send 10 first series
Ultra wrappers and $1.50 to receive the
cards. The set is considered complete without these cards.

1993-94 Ultra Power In The Key

Randomly inserted in 14-card second
series packs at a rate of one in 37, this
nine-card standard-size features some of
the NBA's top power players. Card fronts
feature borderless color player action
cutouts on multicolored metallic court illustration backgrounds. The player's name
appears in gold-foil lettering at the lower
right. The borderless horizontal back carries
on its right side a color player close-up on a
nonmetallic background otherwise similar to
the front. The player's name and career
highlights appear in a ghosted box to the
left of the photo. The cards are numbered
on the back as "X of 9" and are sequenced
in alphabetical order.

	MINT	NRMT	EXC
COMPLETE SET (10)	8.00	3.60	1.00
COMMON MALONE (1-10)	1.00	.45	.12
COMMON SEND-OFF (11-12)	2.00	.90	.25
☐ 1 Karl Malone Power Rig	1.00	.45	.12
☐ 2 Karl Malone Summerfield	1.00	.45	.12
☐ 3 Karl Malone Mailman-Born	1.00	.45	.12
☐ 4 Karl Malone Luck of the Draw	1.00	.45	.12
☐ 5 Karl Malone Double-Double	1.00	.45	.12
☐ 6 Karl Malone Dynamic Duo	1.00	.45	.12
☐ 7 Karl Malone Mt. Malone	1.00	.45	.12
☐ 8 Karl Malone Salt Lake Slammer	1.00	.45	.12
☐ 9 Karl Malone Overhead Delivery	1.00	.45	.12
☐ 10 Karl Malone Truckin'	1.00	.45	.12
☐ 11 Karl Malone Role Player	2.00	.90	.25
☐ 12 Karl Malone Rigged	2.00	.90	.25
☐ AU Karl Malone Certified Autograph	100.00	45.00	12.50

	MINT	NRMT	EXC
COMPLETE SET (9)	80.00	36.00	10.00
COMMON CARD (1-9)	1.00	.45	.12
☐ 1 Larry Johnson	4.00	1.80	.50
☐ 2 Michael Jordan	40.00	18.00	5.00
☐ 3 Karl Malone	3.00	1.35	.35
☐ 4 Oliver Miller	1.00	.45	.12
☐ 5 Alonzo Mourning	5.00	2.20	.60
☐ 6 Hakeem Olajuwon	8.00	3.60	1.00
☐ 7 Shaquille O'Neal	20.00	9.00	2.50
☐ 8 Otis Thorpe	2.00	.90	.25
☐ 9 Chris Webber	8.00	3.60	1.00

1993-94 Ultra Rebound Kings

Randomly inserted in 14-card second
series packs at a rate of one in four, this
10-card standard-size set features some of
the NBA's top rebounders. Borderless
fronts feature color player action shots on
backgrounds that blend from the actual
action background at the bottom to a ghosted and color-screened player close-up at
the top. The player's name appears vertically in gold foil on one side. The borderless
horizontal back carries a color player cutout
on one side and the player's name in gold

foil and career highlights on the other, all on a ghosted and color-screened background. The cards are numbered on the back as "X of 10" and are sequenced in alphabetical order.

	MINT	NRMT	EXC
COMPLETE SET (10)	10.00	4.50	1.25
COMMON CARD (1-10)	.25	.11	.03
☐ 1 Charles Barkley	1.00	.45	.12
☐ 2 Derrick Coleman	.25	.11	.03
☐ 3 Shawn Kemp	2.00	.90	.25
☐ 4 Karl Malone	.60	.25	.07
☐ 5 Alonzo Mourning	1.00	.45	.12
☐ 6 Dikembe Mutombo	.35	.16	.04
☐ 7 Charles Oakley	.25	.11	.03
☐ 8 Hakeem Olajuwon	1.50	.70	.19
☐ 9 Shaquille O'Neal	4.00	1.80	.50
☐ 10 Dennis Rodman	2.50	1.10	.30

1993-94 Ultra Scoring Kings

Randomly inserted in first series hobby packs at a rate of one in 36, this 10-card standard-size set features some of the NBA's top scorers. Card fronts feature color player action cutouts on borderless metallic backgrounds highlighted by lightning filaments. The player's name appears in silver-foil lettering in a lower corner. The horizontal back carries a color player close-up on the right, with the player's name appearing in silver-foil lettering at the upper left, followed below by career highlights, all on a dark borderless background again highlighted by lightning filaments. The cards are numbered on the back as "X of 10" and are sequenced in alphabetical order.

	MINT	NRMT	EXC
COMPLETE SET (10)	200.00	90.00	25.00
COMMON CARD (1-10)	4.00	1.80	.50
☐ 1 Charles Barkley	15.00	6.75	1.85
☐ 2 Joe Dumars	4.00	1.80	.50
☐ 3 Patrick Ewing	10.00	4.50	1.25
☐ 4 Larry Johnson	12.00	5.50	1.50
☐ 5 Michael Jordan	125.00	55.00	15.50
☐ 6 Karl Malone	10.00	4.50	1.25
☐ 7 Alonzo Mourning	15.00	6.75	1.85
☐ 8 Shaquille O'Neal	50.00	22.00	6.25
☐ 9 David Robinson	20.00	9.00	2.50
☐ 10 Dominique Wilkins	4.00	1.80	.50

1994-95 Ultra

The 350 standard-size cards comprising the 1994-95 Ultra set were issued in two separate series of 200 and 150 cards each. Cards were distributed in 14-card ($1.99) and 17-card ($2.69) retail packs. Borderless fronts feature color player action shots. The player's name, team name, and position appear in vertical silver-foil lettering in an upper corner. The borderless back carries multiple player images, with the player's name and team logo appearing in gold foil, followed by biography and statistics near the bottom. The cards are numbered on the back and grouped alphabetically within team order. Unlike previous years, there are no subset cards in this set. Rookie Cards of note include Grant Hill, Juwan Howard, Jason Kidd, Eddie Jones, and Glenn Robinson. There is an insert in every pack. Every 72nd pack is a Hot Pack that contains inserts only.

	MINT	NRMT	EXC
COMPLETE SET (350)	35.00	16.00	4.40
COMPLETE SERIES 1 (200)	20.00	9.00	2.50
COMPLETE SERIES 2 (150)	15.00	6.75	1.85
COMMON CARD (1-350)	.10	.05	.01
☐ 1 Stacey Augmon	.15	.07	.02
☐ 2 Mookie Blaylock	.15	.07	.02
☐ 3 Craig Ehlo	.10	.05	.01
☐ 4 Adam Keefe	.10	.05	.01
☐ 5 Andrew Lang	.10	.05	.01

#	Player			
☐ 6	Ken Norman	.10	.05	.01
☐ 7	Kevin Willis	.10	.05	.01
☐ 8	Dee Brown	.10	.05	.01
☐ 9	Sherman Douglas	.10	.05	.01
☐ 10	Acie Earl	.10	.05	.01
☐ 11	Pervis Ellison	.10	.05	.01
☐ 12	Rick Fox	.10	.05	.01
☐ 13	Xavier McDaniel	.10	.05	.01
☐ 14	Eric Montross	.15	.07	.02
☐ 15	Dino Radja	.20	.09	.03
☐ 16	Dominique Wilkins	.20	.09	.03
☐ 17	Michael Adams	.10	.05	.01
☐ 18	Muggsy Bogues	.15	.07	.02
☐ 19	Dell Curry	.10	.05	.01
☐ 20	Kenny Gattison	.10	.05	.01
☐ 21	Hersey Hawkins	.10	.05	.01
☐ 22	Larry Johnson	.40	.18	.05
☐ 23	Alonzo Mourning	.50	.23	.06
☐ 24	Robert Parish	.20	.09	.03
☐ 25	B.J. Armstrong	.10	.05	.01
☐ 26	Steve Kerr	.15	.07	.02
☐ 27	Toni Kukoc	.30	.14	.04
☐ 28	Luc Longley	.10	.05	.01
☐ 29	Pete Myers	.10	.05	.01
☐ 30	Will Perdue	.10	.05	.01
☐ 31	Scottie Pippen	1.25	.55	.16
☐ 32	Terrell Brandon	.20	.09	.03
☐ 33	Brad Daugherty	.10	.05	.01
☐ 34	Tyrone Hill	.10	.05	.01
☐ 35	Chris Mills	.20	.09	.03
☐ 36	Bobby Phills	.10	.05	.01
☐ 37	Mark Price	.10	.05	.01
☐ 38	Gerald Wilkins	.10	.05	.01
☐ 39	John Williams	.10	.05	.01
☐ 40	Terry Davis	.10	.05	.01
☐ 41	Jim Jackson	.50	.23	.06
☐ 42	Popeye Jones	.10	.05	.01
☐ 43	Jason Kidd	3.00	1.35	.35
☐ 44	Jamal Mashburn	.30	.14	.04
☐ 45	Sean Rooks	.10	.05	.01
☐ 46	Doug Smith	.10	.05	.01
☐ 47	Mahmoud Abdul-Rauf	.15	.07	.02
☐ 48	LaPhonso Ellis	.10	.05	.01
☐ 49	Dikembe Mutombo	.20	.09	.03
☐ 50	Robert Pack	.10	.05	.01
☐ 51	Rodney Rogers	.10	.05	.01
☐ 52	Bryant Stith	.10	.05	.01
☐ 53	Brian Williams	.10	.05	.01
☐ 54	Reggie Williams	.10	.05	.01
☐ 55	Greg Anderson	.10	.05	.01
☐ 56	Joe Dumars	.20	.09	.03
☐ 57	Allan Houston	.25	.11	.03
☐ 58	Lindsey Hunter	.10	.05	.01
☐ 59	Terry Mills	.10	.05	.01
☐ 60	Tim Hardaway	.20	.09	.03
☐ 61	Chris Mullin	.20	.09	.03
☐ 62	Billy Owens	.10	.05	.01
☐ 63	Latrell Sprewell	.50	.23	.06
☐ 64	Chris Webber	.50	.23	.06
☐ 65	Sam Cassell	.20	.09	.03
☐ 66	Carl Herrera	.10	.05	.01
☐ 67	Robert Horry	.15	.07	.02
☐ 68	Vernon Maxwell	.10	.05	.01
☐ 69	Hakeem Olajuwon	1.00	.45	.12
☐ 70	Kenny Smith	.10	.05	.01
☐ 71	Otis Thorpe	.15	.07	.02
☐ 72	Antonio Davis	.10	.05	.01
☐ 73	Dale Davis	.10	.05	.01
☐ 74	Mark Jackson	.10	.05	.01
☐ 75	Derrick McKey	.10	.05	.01
☐ 76	Reggie Miller	.50	.23	.06
☐ 77	Byron Scott	.20	.09	.03
☐ 78	Rik Smits	.20	.09	.03
☐ 79	Haywoode Workman	.10	.05	.01
☐ 80	Gary Grant	.10	.05	.01
☐ 81	Ron Harper	.10	.05	.01
☐ 82	Elmore Spencer	.10	.05	.01
☐ 83	Loy Vaught	.10	.05	.01
☐ 84	Elden Campbell	.15	.07	.02
☐ 85	Doug Christie	.10	.05	.01
☐ 86	Vlade Divac	.20	.09	.03
☐ 87	Eddie Jones	1.00	.45	.12
☐ 88	George Lynch	.10	.05	.01
☐ 89	Anthony Peeler	.10	.05	.01
☐ 90	Sedale Threatt	.10	.05	.01
☐ 91	Nick Van Exel	.40	.18	.05
☐ 92	James Worthy	.20	.09	.03
☐ 93	Bimbo Coles	.10	.05	.01
☐ 94	Matt Geiger	.10	.05	.01
☐ 95	Grant Long	.10	.05	.01
☐ 96	Harold Miner	.10	.05	.01
☐ 97	Glen Rice	.20	.09	.03
☐ 98	John Salley	.10	.05	.01
☐ 99	Rony Seikaly	.10	.05	.01
☐ 100	Brian Shaw	.10	.05	.01
☐ 101	Steve Smith	.20	.09	.03
☐ 102	Vin Baker	.50	.23	.06
☐ 103	Jon Barry	.10	.05	.01
☐ 104	Todd Day	.10	.05	.01
☐ 105	Lee Mayberry	.10	.05	.01
☐ 106	Eric Murdock	.10	.05	.01
☐ 107	Thurl Bailey	.10	.05	.01
☐ 108	Stacey King	.10	.05	.01
☐ 109	Christian Laettner	.20	.09	.03
☐ 110	Isaiah Rider	.20	.09	.03
☐ 111	Chris Smith	.10	.05	.01
☐ 112	Doug West	.10	.05	.01
☐ 113	Micheal Williams	.10	.05	.01
☐ 114	Kenny Anderson	.20	.09	.03
☐ 115	Benoit Benjamin	.10	.05	.01
☐ 116	P.J. Brown	.10	.05	.01
☐ 117	Derrick Coleman	.10	.05	.01
☐ 118	Yinka Dare	.10	.05	.01
☐ 119	Kevin Edwards	.10	.05	.01
☐ 120	Armon Gilliam	.10	.05	.01
☐ 121	Chris Morris	.10	.05	.01
☐ 122	Greg Anthony	.10	.05	.01
☐ 123	Anthony Bonner	.10	.05	.01
☐ 124	Hubert Davis	.10	.05	.01
☐ 125	Patrick Ewing	.40	.18	.05
☐ 126	Derek Harper	.10	.05	.01
☐ 127	Anthony Mason	.15	.07	.02
☐ 128	Charles Oakley	.15	.07	.02
☐ 129	Doc Rivers	.10	.05	.01
☐ 130	John Starks	.10	.05	.01
☐ 131	Nick Anderson	.20	.09	.03
☐ 132	Anthony Avent	.10	.05	.01
☐ 133	Anthony Bowie	.10	.05	.01
☐ 134	Anfernee Hardaway	2.50	1.10	.30
☐ 135	Shaquille O'Neal	2.00	.90	.25
☐ 136	Dennis Scott	.15	.07	.02
☐ 137	Jeff Turner	.10	.05	.01
☐ 138	Dana Barros	.10	.05	.01
☐ 139	Shawn Bradley	.20	.09	.03
☐ 140	Greg Graham	.10	.05	.01
☐ 141	Jeff Malone	.10	.05	.01
☐ 142	Tim Perry	.10	.05	.01
☐ 143	Clarence Weatherspoon	.15	.07	.02
☐ 144	Scott Williams	.10	.05	.01
☐ 145	Danny Ainge	.20	.09	.03
☐ 146	Charles Barkley	.60	.25	.07
☐ 147	Cedric Ceballos	.15	.07	.02

#	Player			
☐ 148	A.C. Green	.20	.09	.03
☐ 149	Frank Johnson	.10	.05	.01
☐ 150	Kevin Johnson	.20	.09	.03
☐ 151	Dan Majerle	.15	.07	.02
☐ 152	Oliver Miller	.10	.05	.01
☐ 153	Wesley Person	.75	.35	.09
☐ 154	Mark Bryant	.10	.05	.01
☐ 155	Clyde Drexler	.50	.23	.06
☐ 156	Harvey Grant	.10	.05	.01
☐ 157	Jerome Kersey	.10	.05	.01
☐ 158	Tracy Murray	.10	.05	.01
☐ 159	Terry Porter	.10	.05	.01
☐ 160	Clifford Robinson	.20	.09	.03
☐ 161	James Robinson	.10	.05	.01
☐ 162	Rod Strickland	.10	.05	.01
☐ 163	Buck Williams	.15	.07	.02
☐ 164	Duane Causwell	.10	.05	.01
☐ 165	Olden Polynice	.10	.05	.01
☐ 166	Mitch Richmond	.30	.14	.04
☐ 167	Lionel Simmons	.10	.05	.01
☐ 168	Walt Williams	.20	.09	.03
☐ 169	Willie Anderson	.10	.05	.01
☐ 170	Terry Cummings	.10	.05	.01
☐ 171	Sean Elliott	.20	.09	.03
☐ 172	Avery Johnson	.15	.07	.02
☐ 173	J.R. Reid	.10	.05	.01
☐ 174	David Robinson	.75	.35	.09
☐ 175	Dennis Rodman	1.50	.70	.19
☐ 176	Kendall Gill	.10	.05	.01
☐ 177	Shawn Kemp	1.25	.55	.16
☐ 178	Nate McMillan	.10	.05	.01
☐ 179	Gary Payton	.60	.25	.07
☐ 180	Sam Perkins	.15	.07	.02
☐ 181	Detlef Schrempf	.15	.07	.02
☐ 182	David Benoit	.10	.05	.01
☐ 183	Tyrone Corbin	.10	.05	.01
☐ 184	Jeff Hornacek	.15	.07	.02
☐ 185	Jay Humphries	.10	.05	.01
☐ 186	Karl Malone	.40	.18	.05
☐ 187	Bryon Russell	.10	.05	.01
☐ 188	Felton Spencer	.10	.05	.01
☐ 189	John Stockton	.40	.18	.05
☐ 190	Mitchell Butler	.10	.05	.01
☐ 191	Rex Chapman	.10	.05	.01
☐ 192	Calbert Cheaney	.20	.09	.03
☐ 193	Kevin Duckworth	.10	.05	.01
☐ 194	Tom Gugliotta	.20	.09	.03
☐ 195	Don MacLean	.10	.05	.01
☐ 196	Gheorghe Muresan	.20	.09	.03
☐ 197	Scott Skiles	.10	.05	.01
☐ 198	Checklist	.10	.05	.01
☐ 199	Checklist	.10	.05	.01
☐ 200	Checklist	.10	.05	.01
☐ 201	Tyrone Corbin	.10	.05	.01
☐ 202	Doug Edwards	.10	.05	.01
☐ 203	Jim Les	.10	.05	.01
☐ 204	Grant Long	.10	.05	.01
☐ 205	Ken Norman	.10	.05	.01
☐ 206	Steve Smith	.20	.09	.03
☐ 207	Blue Edwards	.10	.05	.01
☐ 208	Greg Minor	.10	.05	.01
☐ 209	Eric Montross	.15	.07	.02
☐ 210	Derek Strong	.10	.05	.01
☐ 211	David Wesley	.10	.05	.01
☐ 212	Tony Bennett	.10	.05	.01
☐ 213	Scott Burrell	.10	.05	.01
☐ 214	Darrin Hancock	.10	.05	.01
☐ 215	Greg Sutton	.10	.05	.01
☐ 216	Corie Blount	.10	.05	.01
☐ 217	Jud Buechler	.10	.05	.01
☐ 218	Ron Harper	.15	.07	.02
☐ 219	Larry Krystkowiak	.10	.05	.01
☐ 220	Dickey Simpkins	.15	.07	.02
☐ 221	Bill Wennington	.10	.05	.01
☐ 222	Michael Cage	.10	.05	.01
☐ 223	Tony Campbell	.10	.05	.01
☐ 224	Steve Colter	.10	.05	.01
☐ 225	Greg Dreiling	.10	.05	.01
☐ 226	Danny Ferry	.10	.05	.01
☐ 227	Tony Dumas	.20	.09	.03
☐ 228	Lucious Harris	.10	.05	.01
☐ 229	Donald Hodge	.10	.05	.01
☐ 230	Jason Kidd	1.50	.70	.19
☐ 231	Lorenzo Williams	.10	.05	.01
☐ 232	Dale Ellis	.10	.05	.01
☐ 233	Tom Hammonds	.10	.05	.01
☐ 234	Jalen Rose	.40	.18	.05
☐ 235	Reggie Slater	.10	.05	.01
☐ 236	Rafael Addison	.10	.05	.01
☐ 237	Bill Curley	.10	.05	.01
☐ 238	Johnny Dawkins	.10	.05	.01
☐ 239	Grant Hill	5.00	2.20	.60
☐ 240	Eric Leckner	.10	.05	.01
☐ 241	Mark Macon	.10	.05	.01
☐ 242	Oliver Miller	.10	.05	.01
☐ 243	Mark West	.10	.05	.01
☐ 244	Victor Alexander	.10	.05	.01
☐ 245	Chris Gatling	.10	.05	.01
☐ 246	Tom Gugliotta	.20	.09	.03
☐ 247	Keith Jennings	.10	.05	.01
☐ 248	Ricky Pierce	.10	.05	.01
☐ 249	Carlos Rogers	.10	.05	.01
☐ 250	Clifford Rozier	.15	.07	.02
☐ 251	Rony Seikaly	.10	.05	.01
☐ 252	David Wood	.10	.05	.01
☐ 253	Tim Breaux	.10	.05	.01
☐ 254	Scott Brooks	.10	.05	.01
☐ 255	Zan Tabak	.10	.05	.01
☐ 256	Duane Ferrell	.10	.05	.01
☐ 257	Mark Jackson	.10	.05	.01
☐ 258	Sam Mitchell	.10	.05	.01
☐ 259	John Williams	.10	.05	.01
☐ 260	Terry Dehere	.10	.05	.01
☐ 261	Harold Ellis	.10	.05	.01
☐ 262	Matt Fish	.10	.05	.01
☐ 263	Tony Massenburg	.10	.05	.01
☐ 264	Lamond Murray	.10	.05	.01
☐ 265	Charles Outlaw	.10	.05	.01
☐ 266	Eric Piatkowski	.10	.05	.01
☐ 267	Pooh Richardson	.10	.05	.01
☐ 268	Malik Sealy	.10	.05	.01
☐ 269	Randy Woods	.10	.05	.01
☐ 270	Sam Bowie	.10	.05	.01
☐ 271	Cedric Ceballos	.15	.07	.02
☐ 272	Antonio Harvey	.10	.05	.01
☐ 273	Eddie Jones	.50	.23	.06
☐ 274	Anthony Miller	.10	.05	.01
☐ 275	Tony Smith	.10	.05	.01
☐ 276	Ledell Eackles	.10	.05	.01
☐ 277	Kevin Gamble	.10	.05	.01
☐ 278	Brad Lohaus	.10	.05	.01
☐ 279	Billy Owens	.10	.05	.01
☐ 280	Khalid Reeves	.10	.05	.01
☐ 281	Kevin Willis	.10	.05	.01
☐ 282	Marty Conlon	.10	.05	.01
☐ 283	Alton Lister	.10	.05	.01
☐ 284	Eric Mobley	.15	.07	.02
☐ 285	Johnny Newman	.10	.05	.01
☐ 286	Ed Pinckney	.10	.05	.01
☐ 287	Glenn Robinson	1.50	.70	.19
☐ 288	Howard Eisley	.10	.05	.01
☐ 289	Winston Garland	.10	.05	.01

☐	290	Andres Guibert	.10	.05	.01
☐	291	Donyell Marshall	.15	.07	.02
☐	292	Sean Rooks	.10	.05	.01
☐	293	Yinka Dare	.10	.05	.01
☐	294	Sleepy Floyd	.10	.05	.01
☐	295	Sean Higgins	.10	.05	.01
☐	296	Rex Walters	.10	.05	.01
☐	297	Jayson Williams	.10	.05	.01
☐	298	Charles Smith	.10	.05	.01
☐	299	Charlie Ward	.20	.09	.03
☐	300	Herb Williams	.10	.05	.01
☐	301	Monty Williams	.10	.05	.01
☐	302	Horace Grant	.20	.09	.03
☐	303	Geert Hammink	.10	.05	.01
☐	304	Tree Rollins	.10	.05	.01
☐	305	Donald Royal	.10	.05	.01
☐	306	Brian Shaw	.10	.05	.01
☐	307	Brooks Thompson	.15	.07	.02
☐	308	Derrick Alston	.10	.05	.01
☐	309	Willie Burton	.10	.05	.01
☐	310	Jaren Jackson	.10	.05	.01
☐	311	B.J. Tyler	.10	.05	.01
☐	312	Scott Williams	.10	.05	.01
☐	313	Sharone Wright	.20	.09	.03
☐	314	Joe Kleine	.10	.05	.01
☐	315	Danny Manning	.15	.07	.02
☐	316	Elliot Perry	.10	.05	.01
☐	317	Wesley Person	.20	.09	.03
☐	318	Trevor Ruffin	.20	.09	.03
☐	319	Dan Schayes	.10	.05	.01
☐	320	Wayman Tisdale	.10	.05	.01
☐	321	Chris Dudley	.10	.05	.01
☐	322	James Edwards	.10	.05	.01
☐	323	Alaa Abdelnaby	.10	.05	.01
☐	324	Randy Brown	.10	.05	.01
☐	325	Brian Grant	.60	.25	.07
☐	326	Bobby Hurley	.10	.05	.01
☐	327	Michael Smith	.15	.07	.02
☐	328	Henry Turner	.10	.05	.01
☐	329	Trevor Wilson	.10	.05	.01
☐	330	Vinny Del Negro	.10	.05	.01
☐	331	Moses Malone	.25	.11	.03
☐	332	Julius Nwosu	.10	.05	.01
☐	333	Chuck Person	.10	.05	.01
☐	334	Chris Whitney	.10	.05	.01
☐	335	Vincent Askew	.10	.05	.01
☐	336	Bill Cartwright	.10	.05	.01
☐	337	Ervin Johnson	.10	.05	.01
☐	338	Sarunas Marciulionis	.10	.05	.01
☐	339	Antoine Carr	.10	.05	.01
☐	340	Tom Chambers	.10	.05	.01
☐	341	John Crotty	.10	.05	.01
☐	342	Jamie Watson	.10	.05	.01
☐	343	Juwan Howard	3.00	1.35	.35
☐	344	Jim McIlvaine	.15	.07	.02
☐	345	Doug Overton	.10	.05	.01
☐	346	Scott Skiles	.10	.05	.01
☐	347	Anthony Tucker	.10	.05	.01
☐	348	Chris Webber	.50	.23	.06
☐	349	Checklist	.10	.05	.01
☐	350	Checklist	.10	.05	.01

1994-95 Ultra All-NBA

Randomly inserted into approximately one in every three first series packs, cards from

this 15-card standard-size set feature members of the All-NBA first (1-5), second (6-10), and third (11-15) teams. The fronts are laid out horizontally and have a color action photo and three photos that look like they were taken in a room with a black light. On the right side is the player's first name in white behind his last name in the color of his team. At the bottom in gold-foil are the words "ALL-NBA" and the corresponding team he made. On the backs are a color photo in front of the same photo with the black light look. Their is also player information and the cards are numbered "X of 15."

	MINT	NRMT	EXC
COMPLETE SET (15)	15.00	6.75	1.85
COMMON CARD (1-15)	.40	.18	.05

☐	1	Karl Malone	1.00	.45	.12
☐	2	Hakeem Olajuwon	2.50	1.10	.30
☐	3	Scottie Pippen	3.00	1.35	.35
☐	4	Latrell Sprewell	.75	.35	.09
☐	5	John Stockton	1.00	.45	.12
☐	6	Charles Barkley	1.50	.70	.19
☐	7	Kevin Johnson	.75	.35	.09
☐	8	Shawn Kemp	3.00	1.35	.35
☐	9	Mitch Richmond	.75	.35	.09
☐	10	David Robinson	2.00	.90	.25
☐	11	Derrick Coleman	.40	.18	.05
☐	12	Shaquille O'Neal	5.00	2.20	.60
☐	13	Gary Payton	1.50	.70	.19
☐	14	Mark Price	.40	.18	.05
☐	15	Dominique Wilkins	.75	.35	.09

1994-95 Ultra All-Rookie Team

Randomly inserted exclusively into first series jumbo packs at a rate of one in 36, cards from this 10-card standard-size set feature some of the top rookies from the 1993-94 season. Fronts feature a full-color action shot aside a bold, gold-foil All-Rookie logo with the player's name.

	MINT	NRMT	EXC
COMPLETE SET (10)	125.00	55.00	15.50
COMMON CARD (1-10)	2.50	1.10	.30

☐	1	Vin Baker	15.00	6.75	1.85
☐	2	Anfernee Hardaway	75.00	34.00	9.50

		MINT	NRMT	EXC
☐ 3	Jamal Mashburn	10.00	4.50	1.25
☐ 4	Isaiah Rider	2.50	1.10	.30
☐ 5	Chris Webber	15.00	6.75	1.85
☐ 6	Shawn Bradley	5.00	2.20	.60
☐ 7	Lindsey Hunter	2.50	1.10	.30
☐ 8	Toni Kukoc	10.00	4.50	1.25
☐ 9	Dino Radja	5.00	2.20	.60
☐ 10	Nick Van Exel	12.00	5.50	1.50

1994-95 Ultra
All-Rookies

Randomly inserted at a rate of one in every five second series packs, this 15-card standard-size set captures the best first-year players from the 1994-95 season. The fronts have a full-color photo with a hardwood floor background. The words "All-Rookie" and the player's name are on the left side in gold-foil. The backs a full-color photo with his name and a hardwood floor in the background. There is also player information and the cards are numbered "X of 15." The set is sequenced in alphabetical order.

		MINT	NRMT	EXC
COMPLETE SET (15)		25.00	11.00	3.10
COMMON CARD (1-15)		.50	.23	.06
☐ 1	Brian Grant	1.25	.55	.16
☐ 2	Grant Hill	10.00	4.50	1.25
☐ 3	Juwan Howard	6.00	2.70	.75
☐ 4	Eddie Jones	2.00	.90	.25
☐ 5	Jason Kidd	6.00	2.70	.75
☐ 6	Donyell Marshall	1.00	.45	.12
☐ 7	Eric Montross	1.00	.45	.12

☐ 8	Lamond Murray	.50	.23	.06
☐ 9	Wesley Person	1.00	.45	.12
☐ 10	Khalid Reeves	.50	.23	.06
☐ 11	Glenn Robinson	3.00	1.35	.35
☐ 12	Carlos Rogers	.50	.23	.06
☐ 13	Jalen Rose	1.00	.45	.12
☐ 14	B.J. Tyler	.50	.23	.06
☐ 15	Sharone Wright	1.00	.45	.12

1994-95 Ultra
Award Winners

Randomly inserted into approximately one in every four first series packs, cards from this four-card standard-size set feature players who won individual awards during the 1993-94 season. The fronts are laid out horizontally and have a color-action photo with the backgrounds having a black and white head shot with horizontal white lines across the card. At on of the bottom corners are the words "NBA Award Winner" with a basketball in gold-foil. The backs have a color photo from the chest up with a similar background to the front. There is also player information and the cards are numbered "X of 4." The set is sequenced in alphabetical order.

		MINT	NRMT	EXC
COMPLETE SET (4)		4.00	1.80	.50
COMMON CARD (1-4)		.25	.11	.03
☐ 1	Dell Curry	.25	.11	.03
	Sixth Man Award			
☐ 2	Don MacLean	.25	.11	.03
	Most Improved			
☐ 3	Hakeem Olajuwon	2.50	1.10	.30
	MVP and Defensive POY			
☐ 4	Chris Webber	1.25	.55	.16
	Rookie of the Year			

1994-95 Ultra
Defensive Gems

Randomly inserted at a rate of one in every 37 second-series packs, this 6-card standard-size set focuses on six NBA stars who play standout defense. The borderless fronts feature 100% etched-foil backgrounds. The player's name is located at the bottom while the words "Defensive Gems" surrounding a diamond are in the lower right. The backs are split between another player photo and some information about the player's defensive prowess. The cards are numbered in the lower left as "X" of 6. The set is sequenced in alphabetical order.

	MINT	NRMT	EXC
COMPLETE SET (6)	40.00	18.00	5.00
COMMON CARD (1-6)	2.00	.90	.25
☐ 1 Mookie Blaylock	2.00	.90	.25
☐ 2 Hakeem Olajuwon	12.00	5.50	1.50
☐ 3 Gary Payton	8.00	3.60	1.00
☐ 4 Scottie Pippen	15.00	6.75	1.85
☐ 5 David Robinson	10.00	4.50	1.25
☐ 6 Latrell Sprewell	3.00	1.35	.35

1994-95 Ultra Double Trouble

Randomly inserted into approximately one in every five first series packs, cards from this 10-card standard-size set feature a selection of multi-skilled NBA stars. The fronts feature two photos of the player in a split player design. The words "Double Trouble" and player's name are printed in silver foil on the bottom. The borderless backs are split between an explanation of the the player's skills as well as a photo.

The cards are numbered "X" of 10 in the lower left corner. The set is sequenced in alphabetical order.

	MINT	NRMT	EXC
COMPLETE SET (10)	12.00	5.50	1.50
COMMON CARD (1-10)	.40	.18	.05
☐ 1 Derrick Coleman	.40	.18	.05
☐ 2 Patrick Ewing	1.00	.45	.12
☐ 3 Anfernee Hardaway	6.00	2.70	.75
☐ 4 Jamal Mashburn	.75	.35	.09
☐ 5 Reggie Miller	1.25	.55	.16
☐ 6 Alonzo Mourning	1.25	.55	.16
☐ 7 Scottie Pippen	3.00	1.35	.35
☐ 8 David Robinson	2.00	.90	.25
☐ 9 Latrell Sprewell	.50	.23	.06
☐ 10 John Stockton	1.00	.45	.12

1994-95 Ultra Inside/Outside

Randomly inserted exclusively into one in every seven second series hobby packs, cards from this 10-card standard-size set focus on players who can score from anywhere on the court. The borderless fronts feature dual player photos against a gray background. The player's name is in the lower left corner while the words "Inside/Outside" are in the lower right corner. The backs describe the player's shooting ability and have a small photo as well. The cards are numbered in the lower right as "X" of 10. The set is sequenced in alphabetical order.

	MINT	NRMT	EXC
COMPLETE SET (10)	10.00	4.50	1.25
COMMON CARD (1-10)	.25	.11	.03
☐ 1 Sam Cassell	.50	.23	.06
☐ 2 Cedric Ceballos	.50	.23	.06
☐ 3 Calbert Cheaney	.25	.11	.03
☐ 4 Anfernee Hardaway	8.00	3.60	1.00
☐ 5 Jim Jackson	.50	.23	.06
☐ 6 Dan Majerle	.50	.23	.06
☐ 7 Robert Pack	.25	.11	.03
☐ 8 Scottie Pippen	4.00	1.80	.50
☐ 9 Mitch Richmond	1.00	.45	.12
☐ 10 Latrell Sprewell	.50	.23	.06

1994-95 Ultra
Jam City

Randomly inserted exclusively into one in every seven second series jumbo packs, cards from this 10-card standard size set spotlight ten well known dunkers. The borderless fronts feature color player action cutouts on a multi colored metallic cityscape background. The words "Jam City" and the player's name are printed in gold foil on the bottom of the card. The back features another cutout photo against a different skyscraper background with the player's name in the middle in gold foil. A brief blurb about the player is inset at the bottom. The cards are numbered "X" of 10 in the bottom right. The set is sequenced in alphabetical order.

	MINT	NRMT	EXC
COMPLETE SET (10)	10.00	4.50	1.25
COMMON CARD (1-10)	.25	.11	.03
☐ 1 Charles Barkley	1.25	.55	.16
☐ 2 Derrick Coleman	.25	.11	.03
☐ 3 Larry Johnson	.75	.35	.09
☐ 4 Shawn Kemp	2.50	1.10	.30
☐ 5 Karl Malone	.75	.35	.09
☐ 6 Dikembe Mutombo	.50	.23	.06
☐ 7 Charles Oakley	.25	.11	.03
☐ 8 Shaquille O'Neal	4.00	1.80	.50
☐ 9 Dennis Rodman	3.00	1.35	.35
☐ 10 Chris Webber	1.00	.45	.12

	MINT	NRMT	EXC
COMPLETE SET (10)	65.00	29.00	8.00
COMMON CARD (1-10)	1.50	.70	.19
☐ 1 Vin Baker	5.00	2.20	.60
☐ 2 Grant Hill	25.00	11.00	3.10
☐ 3 Robert Horry	1.50	.70	.19
☐ 4 Shawn Kemp	12.00	5.50	1.50
☐ 5 Jamal Mashburn	3.00	1.35	.35
☐ 6 Alonzo Mourning	5.00	2.20	.60
☐ 7 Dikembe Mutombo	1.50	.70	.19
☐ 8 Shaquille O'Neal	20.00	9.00	2.50
☐ 9 Glenn Robinson	8.00	3.60	1.00
☐ 10 Dominique Wilkins	2.00	.90	.25

1994-95 Ultra Power

Randomly inserted in all first series packs at an approximate rate of one in three, cards from this 10-card standard-size set feature a selection of the NBA's most powerful stars. This set features color player action cutouts set on a colorful and sparkly starburst background design. The player's name appears in gold lettering in a lower corner. The colorful starburst design continues on the borderless horizontal back, which carries a color player head shot on one side, and career highlights on the other. The cards are numbered on the back as "X of 10." The set is sequenced in alphabetical order.

1994-95 Ultra
Power In The Key

Randomly inserted exclusively into one in every seven second series retail packs, cards from this 10-card standard-size set feature ten players who are effective playing near the basket. The front feature a player cutout against a multicolored basketball court design. The words "Power in the Key" are on either side, with the player's name directly underneath those words. The backs contain biographical information along with an inset photo of the player. The cards are numbered in the lower right as "X" of 10. The set is sequenced in alphabetical order.

	MINT	NRMT	EXC
COMPLETE SET (10)	25.00	11.00	3.10
COMMON CARD (1-10)	.50	.23	.06

		MINT	NRMT	EXC
☐ 1	Charles Barkley	3.00	1.35	.35
☐ 2	Patrick Ewing	2.00	.90	.25
☐ 3	Horace Grant	1.25	.55	.16
☐ 4	Larry Johnson	2.00	.90	.25
☐ 5	Karl Malone	2.00	.90	.25
☐ 6	Hakeem Olajuwon	5.00	2.20	.60
☐ 7	Shaquille O'Neal	10.00	4.50	1.25
☐ 8	David Robinson	4.00	1.80	.50
☐ 9	Chris Webber	2.50	1.10	.30
☐ 10	Kevin Willis	.50	.23	.06

1994-95 Ultra Rebound Kings

Randomly inserted at a rate of one in every two second-series packs, cards from this 10-card standard-size set focus on league's top rebounders. The fronts have a color-action photo and a color picture of his head at the bottom along with a gold-foil crown. The words "Rebound King" are at the top and side with rebound behind king at the top and vice-versa on the side, each card uses different colors for the words. The backs have a color photo with his name in gold-foil and information on why he is a top rebounder. The cards are numbered "X of 10." The set is sequenced in alphabetical order.

		MINT	NRMT	EXC
COMPLETE SET (10)		4.00	1.80	.50
COMMON CARD (1-10)		.15	.07	.02
☐ 1	Derrick Coleman	.15	.07	.02
☐ 2	A.C. Green	.25	.11	.03
☐ 3	Alonzo Mourning	.50	.23	.06
☐ 4	Dikembe Mutombo	.25	.11	.03
☐ 5	Charles Oakley	.15	.07	.02
☐ 6	Hakeem Olajuwon	1.00	.45	.12
☐ 7	Shaquille O'Neal	2.00	.90	.25
☐ 8	David Robinson	.75	.35	.09
☐ 9	Chris Webber	.50	.23	.06
☐ 10	Kevin Willis	.15	.07	.02

1994-95 Ultra Scoring Kings

Randomly inserted exclusively into one in every 37 first series hobby packs, cards

from this 10-card standard-size set feature a selection of perennial NBA scoring leaders. Fronts feature full-color player action shots cut out against 100% etched-foil backgrounds. The set is sequenced in alphabetical order.

		MINT	NRMT	EXC
COMPLETE SET (10)		90.00	40.00	11.00
COMMON CARD (1-10)		3.00	1.35	.35
☐ 1	Charles Barkley	10.00	4.50	1.25
☐ 2	Patrick Ewing	6.00	2.70	.75
☐ 3	Karl Malone	6.00	2.70	.75
☐ 4	Hakeem Olajuwon	15.00	6.75	1.85
☐ 5	Shaquille O'Neal	30.00	13.50	3.70
☐ 6	Scottie Pippen	20.00	9.00	2.50
☐ 7	Mitch Richmond	5.00	2.20	.60
☐ 8	David Robinson	12.00	5.50	1.50
☐ 9	Latrell Sprewell	4.00	1.80	.50
☐ 10	Dominique Wilkins	3.00	1.35	.35

1995-96 Ultra

The 1995-96 Ultra set was issued in two series of 200 and 150 for a total of 350 standard-size cards. They were issued in 12-card hobby and retail packs (SRP $2.49) in addition to 17-card pre-priced packs (SRP $2.99). Each 12-card pack contains two insert cards and one in every 72 packs contains nothing but insert cards (referred to as a "Hot Pack"). Fleer upgraded the stock of the 1995-96 cards by making them 40% thicker than the previous year's Ultra release. The fronts have a full-color action photo with the player's name and team at the bottom in gold-foil. The backs have two-color photos and one full black-and-white with statistics at the bot-

tom. The basic issue cards are grouped alphabetically within teams and checklisted below alphabetically according to city. Subsets featured are Rookies (263-298) and Encore (299-348). Rookie Cards of note in this set include Michael Finley, Kevin Garnett, Antonio McDyess, Joe Smith, Jerry Stackhouse and Damon Stoudamire.

	MINT	NRMT	EXC
COMPLETE SET (350)	40.00	18.00	5.00
COMPLETE SERIES 1 (200)	20.00	9.00	2.50
COMPLETE SERIES 2 (150)	20.00	9.00	2.50
COMMON CARD (1-350)	.10	.05	.01

☐ 1	Stacey Augmon	.15	.07	.02
☐ 2	Mookie Blaylock	.15	.07	.02
☐ 3	Craig Ehlo	.10	.05	.01
☐ 4	Andrew Lang	.10	.05	.01
☐ 5	Grant Long	.10	.05	.01
☐ 6	Ken Norman	.10	.05	.01
☐ 7	Steve Smith	.20	.09	.03
☐ 8	Spud Webb	.20	.09	.03
☐ 9	Dee Brown	.10	.05	.01
☐ 10	Sherman Douglas	.10	.05	.01
☐ 11	Pervis Ellison	.10	.05	.01
☐ 12	Rick Fox	.10	.05	.01
☐ 13	Eric Montross	.10	.05	.01
☐ 14	Dino Radja	.15	.07	.02
☐ 15	David Wesley	.10	.05	.01
☐ 16	Dominique Wilkins	.20	.09	.03
☐ 17	Muggsy Bogues	.15	.07	.02
☐ 18	Scott Burrell	.10	.05	.01
☐ 19	Dell Curry	.10	.05	.01
☐ 20	Kendall Gill	.10	.05	.01
☐ 21	Larry Johnson	.40	.18	.05
☐ 22	Alonzo Mourning	.40	.18	.05
☐ 23	Robert Parish	.20	.09	.03
☐ 24	Ron Harper	.15	.07	.02
☐ 25	Michael Jordan	5.00	2.20	.60
☐ 26	Toni Kukoc	.25	.11	.03
☐ 27	Will Perdue	.10	.05	.01
☐ 28	Scottie Pippen	1.25	.55	.16
☐ 29	Terrell Brandon	.20	.09	.03
☐ 30	Michael Cage	.10	.05	.01
☐ 31	Tyrone Hill	.10	.05	.01
☐ 32	Chris Mills	.20	.09	.03
☐ 33	Bobby Phills	.10	.05	.01
☐ 34	Mark Price	.10	.05	.01
☐ 35	John Williams	.10	.05	.01
☐ 36	Lucious Harris	.10	.05	.01
☐ 37	Jim Jackson	.40	.18	.05
☐ 38	Popeye Jones	.10	.05	.01
☐ 39	Jason Kidd	1.00	.45	.12
☐ 40	Jamal Mashburn	.25	.11	.03
☐ 41	George McCloud	.10	.05	.01
☐ 42	Roy Tarpley	.10	.05	.01
☐ 43	Lorenzo Williams	.10	.05	.01
☐ 44	Mahmoud Abdul-Rauf	.15	.07	.02
☐ 45	Dikembe Mutombo	.20	.09	.03
☐ 46	Robert Pack	.10	.05	.01
☐ 47	Jalen Rose	.10	.05	.01
☐ 48	Bryant Stith	.10	.05	.01
☐ 49	Brian Williams	.10	.05	.01
☐ 50	Reggie Williams	.10	.05	.01
☐ 51	Joe Dumars	.20	.09	.03
☐ 52	Grant Hill	1.50	.70	.19
☐ 53	Allan Houston	.20	.09	.03
☐ 54	Lindsey Hunter	.10	.05	.01
☐ 55	Terry Mills	.10	.05	.01
☐ 56	Mark West	.10	.05	.01
☐ 57	Chris Gatling	.10	.05	.01
☐ 58	Tim Hardaway	.20	.09	.03
☐ 59	Donyell Marshall	.10	.05	.01
☐ 60	Chris Mullin	.20	.09	.03
☐ 61	Carlos Rogers	.10	.05	.01
☐ 62	Clifford Rozier	.10	.05	.01
☐ 63	Rony Seikaly	.10	.05	.01
☐ 64	Latrell Sprewell	.20	.09	.03
☐ 65	Sam Cassell	.20	.09	.03
☐ 66	Clyde Drexler	.50	.23	.06
☐ 67	Mario Elie	.10	.05	.01
☐ 68	Carl Herrera	.10	.05	.01
☐ 69	Robert Horry	.20	.09	.03
☐ 70	Hakeem Olajuwon	1.00	.45	.12
☐ 71	Kenny Smith	.10	.05	.01
☐ 72	Antonio Davis	.10	.05	.01
☐ 73	Dale Davis	.10	.05	.01
☐ 74	Mark Jackson	.10	.05	.01
☐ 75	Derrick McKey	.10	.05	.01
☐ 76	Reggie Miller	.50	.23	.06
☐ 77	Rik Smits	.20	.09	.03
☐ 78	Terry Dehere	.10	.05	.01
☐ 79	Lamond Murray	.10	.05	.01
☐ 80	Charles Outlaw	.10	.05	.01
☐ 81	Pooh Richardson	.10	.05	.01
☐ 82	Rodney Rogers	.10	.05	.01
☐ 83	Malik Sealy	.10	.05	.01
☐ 84	Loy Vaught	.10	.05	.01
☐ 85	Sam Bowie	.10	.05	.01
☐ 86	Elden Campbell	.15	.07	.02
☐ 87	Cedric Ceballos	.20	.09	.03
☐ 88	Vlade Divac	.20	.09	.03
☐ 89	Eddie Jones	.30	.14	.04
☐ 90	Anthony Peeler	.10	.05	.01
☐ 91	Sedale Threatt	.10	.05	.01
☐ 92	Nick Van Exel	.30	.14	.04
☐ 93	Rex Chapman	.10	.05	.01
☐ 94	Bimbo Coles	.10	.05	.01
☐ 95	Matt Geiger	.10	.05	.01
☐ 96	Billy Owens	.10	.05	.01
☐ 97	Khalid Reeves	.10	.05	.01
☐ 98	Glen Rice	.20	.09	.03
☐ 99	Kevin Willis	.10	.05	.01
☐ 100	Vin Baker	.40	.18	.05
☐ 101	Marty Conlon	.10	.05	.01
☐ 102	Todd Day	.10	.05	.01
☐ 103	Eric Murdock	.10	.05	.01
☐ 104	Glenn Robinson	.50	.23	.06
☐ 105	Winston Garland	.10	.05	.01
☐ 106	Tom Gugliotta	.20	.09	.03
☐ 107	Christian Laettner	.20	.09	.03
☐ 108	Isaiah Rider	.20	.09	.03
☐ 109	Sean Rooks	.10	.05	.01
☐ 110	Doug West	.10	.05	.01
☐ 111	Kenny Anderson	.20	.09	.03
☐ 112	P.J. Brown	.10	.05	.01
☐ 113	Derrick Coleman	.20	.09	.03
☐ 114	Armon Gilliam	.15	.07	.02
☐ 115	Chris Morris	.10	.05	.01
☐ 116	Anthony Bonner	.10	.05	.01
☐ 117	Patrick Ewing	.40	.18	.05
☐ 118	Derek Harper	.10	.05	.01
☐ 119	Anthony Mason	.15	.07	.02
☐ 120	Charles Oakley	.15	.07	.02
☐ 121	Charles Smith	.10	.05	.01
☐ 122	John Starks	.10	.05	.01
☐ 123	Nick Anderson	.20	.09	.03
☐ 124	Horace Grant	.20	.09	.03
☐ 125	Anfernee Hardaway	2.50	1.10	.30
☐ 126	Shaquille O'Neal	2.00	.90	.25

#	Player			
☐	127	Donald Royal	.10	.05	.01
☐	128	Dennis Scott	.20	.09	.03
☐	129	Brian Shaw	.10	.05	.01
☐	130	Derrick Alston	.10	.05	.01
☐	131	Dana Barros	.10	.05	.01
☐	132	Shawn Bradley	.20	.09	.03
☐	133	Willie Burton	.10	.05	.01
☐	134	Jeff Malone	.10	.05	.01
☐	135	Clarence Weatherspoon	.10	.05	.01
☐	136	Scott Williams	.10	.05	.01
☐	137	Sharone Wright	.15	.07	.02
☐	138	Danny Ainge	.20	.09	.03
☐	139	Charles Barkley	.60	.25	.07
☐	140	A.C. Green	.20	.09	.03
☐	141	Kevin Johnson	.20	.09	.03
☐	142	Dan Majerle	.15	.07	.02
☐	143	Danny Manning	.15	.07	.02
☐	144	Elliot Perry	.10	.05	.01
☐	145	Wesley Person	.15	.07	.02
☐	146	Wayman Tisdale	.10	.05	.01
☐	147	Chris Dudley	.10	.05	.01
☐	148	Harvey Grant	.10	.05	.01
☐	149	Aaron McKie	.10	.05	.01
☐	150	Terry Porter	.10	.05	.01
☐	151	Clifford Robinson	.20	.09	.03
☐	152	Rod Strickland	.10	.05	.01
☐	153	Otis Thorpe	.15	.07	.02
☐	154	Buck Williams	.15	.07	.02
☐	155	Brian Grant	.20	.09	.03
☐	156	Bobby Hurley	.10	.05	.01
☐	157	Olden Polynice	.10	.05	.01
☐	158	Mitch Richmond	.30	.14	.04
☐	159	Michael Smith	.10	.05	.01
☐	160	Walt Williams	.20	.09	.03
☐	161	Vinny Del Negro	.10	.05	.01
☐	162	Sean Elliott	.20	.09	.03
☐	163	Avery Johnson	.15	.07	.02
☐	164	Chuck Person	.10	.05	.01
☐	165	J.R. Reid	.10	.05	.01
☐	166	Doc Rivers	.10	.05	.01
☐	167	David Robinson	.75	.35	.09
☐	168	Dennis Rodman	1.50	.70	.19
☐	169	Vincent Askew	.10	.05	.01
☐	170	Hersey Hawkins	.15	.07	.02
☐	171	Shawn Kemp	1.25	.55	.16
☐	172	Sarunas Marciulionis	.10	.05	.01
☐	173	Nate McMillan	.10	.05	.01
☐	174	Gary Payton	.60	.25	.07
☐	175	Sam Perkins	.15	.07	.02
☐	176	Detlef Schrempf	.15	.07	.02
☐	177	B.J. Armstrong	.10	.05	.01
☐	178	Jerome Kersey	.10	.05	.01
☐	179	Tony Massenburg	.10	.05	.01
☐	180	Oliver Miller	.10	.05	.01
☐	181	John Salley	.10	.05	.01
☐	182	David Benoit	.10	.05	.01
☐	183	Antoine Carr	.10	.05	.01
☐	184	Jeff Hornacek	.15	.07	.02
☐	185	Karl Malone	.40	.18	.05
☐	186	Felton Spencer	.10	.05	.01
☐	187	John Stockton	.40	.18	.05
☐	188	Greg Anthony	.10	.05	.01
☐	189	Benoit Benjamin	.10	.05	.01
☐	190	Byron Scott	.20	.09	.03
☐	191	Calbert Cheaney	.10	.05	.01
☐	192	Juwan Howard	1.00	.45	.12
☐	193	Don MacLean	.10	.05	.01
☐	194	Gheorghe Muresan	.20	.09	.03
☐	195	Doug Overton	.10	.05	.01
☐	196	Scott Skiles	.10	.05	.01
☐	197	Chris Webber	.40	.18	.05
☐	198	Checklist (1-94)	.10	.05	.01
☐	199	Checklist (95-190)	.10	.05	.01
☐	200	Checklist (191-200)	.10	.05	.01
☐	201	Stacey Augmon	.15	.07	.02
☐	202	Mookie Blaylock	.15	.07	.02
☐	203	Grant Long	.10	.05	.01
☐	204	Steve Smith	.20	.09	.03
☐	205	Dana Barros	.10	.05	.01
☐	206	Kendall Gill	.10	.05	.01
☐	207	Khalid Reeves	.10	.05	.01
☐	208	Glen Rice	.20	.09	.03
☐	209	Luc Longley	.10	.05	.01
☐	210	Dennis Rodman Bulls	2.50	1.10	.30
☐	211	Dan Majerle	.15	.07	.02
☐	212	Tony Dumas	.10	.05	.01
☐	213	Elmore Spencer	.10	.05	.01
☐	214	Otis Thorpe	.15	.07	.02
☐	215	B.J. Armstrong	.10	.05	.01
☐	216	Sam Cassell	.20	.09	.03
☐	217	Clyde Drexler	.50	.23	.06
☐	218	Robert Horry	.20	.09	.03
☐	219	Hakeem Olajuwon	1.00	.45	.12
☐	220	Eddie Johnson	.10	.05	.01
☐	221	Ricky Pierce	.10	.05	.01
☐	222	Eric Piatkowski	.10	.05	.01
☐	223	Rodney Rogers	.10	.05	.01
☐	224	Brian Williams	.10	.05	.01
☐	225	George Lynch	.10	.05	.01
☐	226	Alonzo Mourning	.40	.18	.05
☐	227	Benoit Benjamin	.10	.05	.01
☐	228	Terry Porter	.10	.05	.01
☐	229	Shawn Bradley	.20	.09	.03
☐	230	Kevin Edwards	.10	.05	.01
☐	231	Jayson Williams	.10	.05	.01
☐	232	Charlie Ward	.15	.07	.02
☐	233	Jon Koncak	.10	.05	.01
☐	234	Derrick Coleman	.10	.05	.01
☐	235	Richard Dumas	.10	.05	.01
☐	236	Vernon Maxwell	.10	.05	.01
☐	237	John Williams	.10	.05	.01
☐	238	Dontonio Wingfield	.10	.05	.01
☐	239	Tyrone Corbin	.10	.05	.01
☐	240	Will Perdue	.10	.05	.01
☐	241	Shawn Kemp	1.25	.55	.16
☐	242	Gary Payton	.60	.25	.07
☐	243	Sam Perkins	.15	.07	.02
☐	244	Detlef Schrempf	.15	.07	.02
☐	245	Chris Morris	.10	.05	.01
☐	246	Robert Pack	.10	.05	.01
☐	247	Willie Anderson EXP	.10	.05	.01
☐	248	Oliver Miller EXP	.10	.05	.01
☐	249	Tracy Murray EXP	.10	.05	.01
☐	250	Alvin Robertson EXP	.10	.05	.01
☐	251	Carlos Rogers EXP	.10	.05	.01
☐	252	John Salley EXP	.10	.05	.01
☐	253	Damon Stoudamire EXP	1.50	.70	.19
☐	254	Zan Tabak EXP	.10	.05	.01
☐	255	Greg Anthony EXP	.10	.05	.01
☐	256	Blue Edwards EXP	.10	.05	.01
☐	257	Kenny Gattison EXP	.10	.05	.01
☐	258	Chris King EXP	.10	.05	.01
☐	259	Lawrence Moten EXP	.10	.05	.01
☐	260	Eric Murdock EXP	.10	.05	.01
☐	261	Bryant Reeves EXP	.40	.18	.05
☐	262	Byron Scott EXP	.20	.09	.03
☐	263	Cory Alexander	.10	.05	.01
☐	264	Brent Barry	.75	.35	.09
☐	265	Mario Bennett	.10	.05	.01
☐	266	Travis Best	.25	.11	.03
☐	267	Junior Burrough	.10	.05	.01
☐	268	Jason Caffey	.15	.07	.02

☐ 269	Randolph Childress	.10	.05	.01
☐ 270	Sasha Danilovic	.25	.11	.03
☐ 271	Tyus Edney	.75	.35	.09
☐ 272	Michael Finley	2.00	.90	.25
☐ 273	Sherell Ford	.10	.05	.01
☐ 274	Kevin Garnett	5.00	2.20	.60
☐ 275	Alan Henderson	.25	.11	.03
☐ 276	Donny Marshall	.10	.05	.01
☐ 277	Antonio McDyess	1.50	.70	.19
☐ 278	Loren Meyer	.20	.09	.03
☐ 279	Lawrence Moten	.10	.05	.01
☐ 280	Ed O'Bannon	.60	.25	.07
☐ 281	Greg Ostertag	.10	.05	.01
☐ 282	Cherokee Parks	.30	.14	.04
☐ 283	Theo Ratliff	.30	.14	.04
☐ 284	Bryant Reeves	1.00	.45	.12
☐ 285	Shawn Respert	.30	.14	.04
☐ 286	Lou Roe	.10	.05	.01
☐ 287	Arvydas Sabonis	1.25	.55	.16
☐ 288	Joe Smith	2.00	.90	.25
☐ 289	Jerry Stackhouse	3.00	1.35	.35
☐ 290	Damon Stoudamire	4.00	1.80	.50
☐ 291	Bob Sura	.30	.14	.04
☐ 292	Kurt Thomas	.50	.23	.06
☐ 293	Gary Trent	.30	.14	.04
☐ 294	David Vaughn	.10	.05	.01
☐ 295	Rasheed Wallace	.75	.35	.09
☐ 296	Eric Williams	.30	.14	.04
☐ 297	Corliss Williamson	.30	.14	.04
☐ 298	George Zidek	.25	.11	.03
☐ 299	Mahmoud Abdul-Rauf ENC	.15	.07	.02
☐ 300	Kenny Anderson ENC	.15	.07	.02
☐ 301	Vin Baker ENC	.20	.09	.03
☐ 302	Charles Barkley ENC	.30	.14	.04
☐ 303	Mookie Blaylock ENC	.10	.05	.01
☐ 304	Cedric Ceballos ENC	.10	.05	.01
☐ 305	Vlade Divac ENC	.20	.09	.03
☐ 306	Clyde Drexler ENC	.20	.09	.03
☐ 307	Joe Dumars ENC	.20	.09	.03
☐ 308	Sean Elliott ENC	.20	.09	.03
☐ 309	Patrick Ewing ENC	.20	.09	.03
☐ 310	Anfernee Hardaway ENC	1.25	.55	.16
☐ 311	Tim Hardaway ENC	.20	.09	.03
☐ 312	Grant Hill ENC	.75	.35	.09
☐ 313	Tyrone Hill ENC	.10	.05	.01
☐ 314	Robert Horry ENC	.15	.07	.02
☐ 315	Juwan Howard ENC	.50	.23	.06
☐ 316	Jim Jackson ENC	.20	.09	.03
☐ 317	Kevin Johnson ENC	.20	.09	.03
☐ 318	Larry Johnson ENC	.20	.09	.03
☐ 319	Eddie Jones ENC	.10	.05	.01
☐ 320	Shawn Kemp ENC	.60	.25	.07
☐ 321	Jason Kidd ENC	.50	.23	.06
☐ 322	Christian Laettner ENC	.20	.09	.03
☐ 323	Karl Malone ENC	.20	.09	.03
☐ 324	Jamal Mashburn ENC	.15	.07	.02
☐ 325	Reggie Miller ENC	.20	.09	.03
☐ 326	Alonzo Mourning ENC	.20	.09	.03
☐ 327	Dikembe Mutombo ENC	.20	.09	.03
☐ 328	Hakeem Olajuwon ENC	.50	.23	.06
☐ 329	Gary Payton ENC	.30	.14	.04
☐ 330	Scottie Pippen ENC	.60	.25	.07
☐ 331	Dino Radja ENC	.15	.07	.02
☐ 332	Glen Rice ENC	.10	.05	.01
☐ 333	Mitch Richmond ENC	.10	.05	.01
☐ 334	Clifford Robinson ENC	.20	.09	.03
☐ 335	David Robinson ENC	.40	.18	.05
☐ 336	Glenn Robinson ENC	.25	.11	.03
☐ 337	D.Rodman ENC Bulls	1.25	.55	.16
☐ 338	Carlos Rogers ENC	.10	.05	.01
☐ 339	Detlef Schrempf ENC	.15	.07	.02

☐ 340	Byron Scott ENC	.15	.07	.02
☐ 341	Rik Smits ENC	.20	.09	.03
☐ 342	Latrell Sprewell ENC	.20	.09	.03
☐ 343	John Stockton ENC	.20	.09	.03
☐ 344	Nick Van Exel ENC	.20	.09	.03
☐ 345	Loy Vaught ENC	.10	.05	.01
☐ 346	Clarence Weatherspoon ENC	.10	.05	.01
☐ 347	Chris Webber ENC	.20	.09	.03
☐ 348	Kevin Willis ENC	.10	.05	.01
☐ 349	Checklist (201-298)	.10	.05	.01
☐ 350	Checklist (299-350/inserts)	.10	.05	.01

1995-96 Ultra Gold Medallion

One card from this 200-card parallel set was inserted in every first series pack. Due to lack of collector reponse the set was discontinued for the second series, and is thus considered complete at 200 cards. The attractive fronts feature borderless, full gold foil backgrounds with a full-color player cutout. Backs are identical to the regular cards. Please refer to the multipliers provided in the header to ascertain values for singles.

	MINT	NRMT	EXC
COMPLETE SET (200)	125.00	55.00	15.50
COMMON CARD (1-200)	.25	.11	.03
* STARS: 3X to 6X BASIC CARDS			

1995-96 Ultra All-NBA

Randomly inserted in all series one packs at a rate of one in five, this 15-card set features the league's best and is divided into three standard-size sets of five (first, second and third team NBA All-Stars). Borderless fronts picture the player in a full-color action cutout with a black and gold metallic streak background. The "All NBA" box is printed in reverse-type metallic foil on the bottom left with the player's name printed in gold foil across the bottom right.

Full-bleed backs continue with the black and gold metallic streaks and another full-color action player cutout. A screened box highlights the player's accomplishments and includes his name in gold foil.

	MINT	NRMT	EXC
COMPLETE SET (15)	20.00	9.00	2.50
COMMON CARD (1-15)	.40	.18	.05

		MINT	NRMT	EXC
☐ 1	Anfernee Hardaway	6.00	2.70	.75
☐ 2	Karl Malone	1.00	.45	.12
☐ 3	Scottie Pippen	3.00	1.35	.35
☐ 4	David Robinson	2.00	.90	.25
☐ 5	John Stockton	1.00	.45	.12
☐ 6	Charles Barkley	1.50	.70	.19
☐ 7	Shawn Kemp	3.00	1.35	.35
☐ 8	Shaquille O'Neal	5.00	2.20	.60
☐ 9	Gary Payton	1.50	.70	.19
☐ 10	Mitch Richmond	.50	.23	.06
☐ 11	Clyde Drexler	1.25	.55	.16
☐ 12	Reggie Miller	1.25	.55	.16
☐ 13	Hakeem Olajuwon	2.50	1.10	.30
☐ 14	Dennis Rodman	4.00	1.80	.50
☐ 15	Detlef Schrempf	.40	.18	.05

1995-96 Ultra All-NBA Gold Medallion

This parallel set is identical to the more common All-NBA basic insert set with the exception of a gold foil medallion on the card front. They were seeded in all first series packs at 10 percent the rate of the basic inserts (approximately one in every 50 first series packs). Please refer to the multiplier provided below for values on Gold Medallion singles.

	MINT	NRMT	EXC
COMPLETE SET (15)	50.00	22.00	6.25
COMMON CARD (1-15)	1.00	.45	.12

*GOLD MEDALLION: 1.5X to 3X VALUE

1995-96 Ultra All-Rookie Team

Randomly inserted in first series retail cello packs at a rate of one in seven, this 10-card set is divided into first team rookies (1-5) and second team rookies (6-10). Borderless fronts feature a full-color action player cutout set against a dark background with multicolored basketballs. All-Rookie team and the player's name are printed in gold foil across the bottom. Borderless backs continue with the multicolored basketball backgrounds and a full-color cutout of the player. A tan-screened box profiles the player and his name is printed in gold foil script across the top of the screen.

	MINT	NRMT	EXC
COMPLETE SET (10)	30.00	13.50	3.70
COMMON CARD (1-10)	1.00	.45	.12

		MINT	NRMT	EXC
☐ 1	Brian Grant	2.00	.90	.25
☐ 2	Grant Hill	12.00	5.50	1.50
☐ 3	Eddie Jones	2.50	1.10	.30
☐ 4	Jason Kidd	8.00	3.60	1.00
☐ 5	Glenn Robinson	4.00	1.80	.50
☐ 6	Juwan Howard	8.00	3.60	1.00
☐ 7	Donyell Marshall Sharone Wright	1.00	.45	.12
☐ 8	Eric Montross	1.00	.45	.12
☐ 9	Wesley Person	2.00	.90	.25
☐ 10	Jalen Rose	2.00	.90	.25

1995-96 Ultra All-Rookie Team Gold Medallion

This parallel set is identical to the more common All-Rookie Team basic insert set with the exception of a gold foil medallion on the card front. They were seeded in all first series packs at 10 percent the rate of the basic inserts (approximately one in every 70 first series retail cello packs). Please refer to the multiplier provided below for values on Gold Medallion singles.

	MINT	NRMT	EXC
COMPLETE SET (10)	80.00	36.00	10.00
COMMON CARD (1-10)	3.00	1.35	.35

*GOLD MEDALLION: 1.5X to 3X VALUE

1995-96 Ultra All-Rookies

Randomly inserted in all second series packs at a rate of one in 30, this set of 10 standard-size cards focuses on the play of the hot rookies of the '95 draft. Borderless fronts have a team color spectrum background with a full-color action cutout. The player's name and position are printed in gold foil near the bottom and "All Rookies" appears at the top. Backs have another full-color action cutout set against a color spectrum background. A screened box holds the player's name and a player profile. Card #'s 4 and 8 (McDyess and Stoudamire) were featured on an unperforated promo sheet of Ultra cards saluting card stores across America. The sheets were distributed to shop owners nationwide. Unfortunately, some unscrupulous parties cut up a number of the sheets and distributed the cut cards into the hobby market under false pretenses. The cut up cards are identical to the real inserts, thus supply has been altered and we've applied a "DP" designation to signify a double-print on this card.

	MINT	NRMT	EXC
COMPLETE SET (10)	80.00	36.00	10.00
COMMON CARD (1-10)	2.00	.90	.25
☐ 1 Tyus Edney	4.00	1.80	.50
☐ 2 Michael Finley	10.00	4.50	1.25
☐ 3 Kevin Garnett	25.00	11.00	3.10
☐ 4 Antonio McDyess DP	4.00	1.80	.50
☐ 5 Ed O'Bannon	2.50	1.10	.30
☐ 6 Joe Smith	10.00	4.50	1.25
☐ 7 Jerry Stackhouse	15.00	6.75	1.85

☐ 8 Damon Stoudamire DP	10.00	4.50	1.25
☐ 9 Rasheed Wallace	4.00	1.80	.50
☐ 10 Eric Williams	2.00	.90	.25

1995-96 Ultra Double Trouble

Randomly inserted in all first series packs at a rate of one in five, this 10-card standard-size set celebrates the players who perform well in more than one category. Full-bleed fronts feature a full-color action player cutout and a one-color action shot that serves as a background. "Double Trouble" is repeatedly printed in the background with a shadow effect. The player's name and "Double Trouble" are printed in alternating black and gold foil at the bottom. Another full-color action cutout appears on the back against the repeating "Double Trouble" colored background. A light screened box appears on the back with the player's abilities and accomplishments printed in black type. The player's name is printed in gold foil above the screened box. The set is sequenced in alphabetical order.

	MINT	NRMT	EXC
COMPLETE SET (10)	15.00	6.75	1.85
COMMON CARD (1-10)	.25	.11	.03
☐ 1 Charles Barkley	1.00	.45	.12
☐ 2 Anfernee Hardaway	4.00	1.80	.50
☐ 3 Michael Jordan	8.00	3.60	1.00
☐ 4 Alonzo Mourning	.60	.25	.07
☐ 5 Hakeem Olajuwon	1.50	.70	.19
☐ 6 Shaquille O'Neal	3.00	1.35	.35
☐ 7 Gary Payton	1.00	.45	.12
☐ 8 Scottie Pippen	2.00	.90	.25
☐ 9 David Robinson	1.25	.55	.16
☐ 10 John Stockton	.60	.25	.07

1995-96 Ultra Double Trouble Gold Medallion

This parallel set is identical to the more common Double Trouble basic insert set

		MINT	NRMT	EXC
☐ 1	Dana Barros	.25	.11	.03
☐ 2	Willie Burton	.25	.11	.03
☐ 3	Cedric Ceballos	.75	.35	.09
☐ 4	Jim Jackson	.75	.35	.09
☐ 5	Michael Jordan	15.00	6.75	1.85
☐ 6	Jamal Mashburn	.75	.35	.09
☐ 7	Glen Rice	.25	.11	.03

with the exception of a gold foil medallion on the card front. They were seeded in all first series packs at 10 percent the rate of the inserts (approximately one in every 50 first series packs). Please refer to the multiplier provided below for values on Gold Medallion singles.

	MINT	NRMT	EXC
COMPLETE SET (10)	40.00	18.00	5.00
COMMON CARD (1-10)	.75	.35	.09
*GOLD MEDALLION: 1.5X to 3X VALUE			

1995-96 Ultra Fabulous Fifties

Randomly inserted in first series hobby packs at a rate of one in 12, this seven-card standard-size set spotlights players who scored 50 or more points in a 94/95 NBA single game. The horizontal fronts feature a full-color action player cutout set against a two-color background with basketball nets and "Fabulous 50's" printed in alternating red boxes. Player's name and "Fabulous 50's" are printed in silver foil across the bottom left. A one-color picture of a basketball net serves as a backdrop on the back with the player's name and team printed in silver foil on the top. A full-color action cutout appears with a story of how and when the player reached his 50-point scoring mark. The set is sequenced in alphabetical order.

	MINT	NRMT	EXC
COMPLETE SET (7)	18.00	8.00	2.20
COMMON CARD (1-7)	.25	.11	.03

1995-96 Ultra Fabulous Fifties Gold Medallion

This parallel set is identical to the Fabulous Fifties basic card with the exception of a silver foil medallion on the card front. They were seeded in all first series packs at 10 percent the rate of the inserts (approximately one in every 120 first series packs). Please refer to the multiplier provided below for values on Gold Medallion singles.

	MINT	NRMT	EXC
COMPLETE SET (10)	50.00	22.00	6.25
COMMON CARD (1-10)	.75	.35	.09
*GOLD MEDALLION: 1.5X to 3X VALUE			

1995-96 Ultra Jam City

Randomly inserted exclusively in second series retail packs at a rate of one in 12, cards from this 12-card standard-size set focus on the NBA's most powerful dunkers. Borderless fronts have full-color action cutouts set against a one-color etched foil background. "Jam City" is printed in gold foil vertically along one side and the player's name is printed in silver foil vertically. Borderless backs feature a full-color player cutout with a halo effect set against a skyline background and a player profile. The set is sequenced in alphabetical order. A full parallel Hot Pack set could be found in one of every 72 packs (known appropriately as "Hot Packs"). These Hot Pack parallels are two times easier to obtain than corresponding regular issue Jam City inserts. Please refer to the percentage provided below for values on individual Hot Pack parallel cards.

	MINT	NRMT	EXC
COMPLETE SET (12)	80.00	36.00	10.00
COMMON CARD (1-12)	1.00	.45	.12
COMP.HOT PACK SET (12)	30.00	13.50	3.70
HOT PACK CARDS: 33% VALUE			
☐ 1 Grant Hill	10.00	4.50	1.25
☐ 2 Robert Horry	1.00	.45	.12
☐ 3 Michael Jordan	30.00	13.50	3.70
☐ 4 Shawn Kemp	8.00	3.60	1.00
☐ 5 Jamal Mashburn	1.50	.70	.19
☐ 6 Antonio McDyess	5.00	2.20	.60
☐ 7 Alonzo Mourning	2.50	1.10	.30
☐ 8 Hakeem Olajuwon	6.00	2.70	.75
☐ 9 Shaquille O'Neal	12.00	5.50	1.50
☐ 10 David Robinson	5.00	2.20	.60
☐ 11 Joe Smith	6.00	2.70	.75
☐ 12 Jerry Stackhouse	10.00	4.50	1.25

1995-96 Ultra Power

Randomly inserted in all first series packs at a rate of one in four, this 10-card standard-size set features the big rebounders and strong inside men of the NBA. A multicolored kaleidoscopic front serves as a background for a full-color action shot. The "Ultra Power" logo and player's name are stamped at the bottom left in gold foil. Backs continue with the kaleidoscopic background and another full-color action cutout. A screened box holds the player's name in gold foil along with a synopsis of the player's abilities and accomplishments. Gold Medallion editions were seeded in

packs at 10 percent the rate of regular cards. Backs are identical to regular inserts.

	MINT	NRMT	EXC
COMPLETE SET (10)	8.00	3.60	1.00
COMMON CARD (1-10)	.40	.18	.05
☐ 1 Charles Barkley	1.00	.45	.12
☐ 2 Patrick Ewing	.60	.25	.07
☐ 3 Larry Johnson	.60	.25	.07
☐ 4 Shawn Kemp	2.00	.90	.25
☐ 5 Karl Malone	.60	.25	.07
☐ 6 Alonzo Mourning	.60	.25	.07
☐ 7 Dikembe Mutombo	.40	.18	.05
☐ 8 Hakeem Olajuwon	1.50	.70	.19
☐ 9 Shaquille O'Neal	3.00	1.35	.35
☐ 10 David Robinson	1.25	.55	.16

1995-96 Ultra Power Gold Medallion

This parallel set is identical to the more common basic Power insert set with the exception of a gold foil medallion on the card front. They were seeded in all first series packs at 10 percent the rate of the inserts (approximately one in every 40 first series packs). Please refer to the multiplier provided below for values on Gold Medallion singles.

	MINT	NRMT	EXC
COMPLETE SET (10)	20.00	9.00	2.50
COMMON CARD (1-10)	1.00	.45	.12
*GOLD MEDALLION: 1.5X to 3X VALUE			

1995-96 Ultra Rising Stars

Randomly inserted in all first series packs at a rate of one in 37, this nine-card standard-size set features promising youngsters of the NBA. Etched foil fronts feature multicolored basketballs and a full-color action cutout. The "Rising Star" logo and player's name are printed in silver foil on the fronts. Backs include a screened player informa-

tion box and a full-color action cutout set against a multicolored basketball background. The set is sequenced in alphabetical order.

	MINT	NRMT	EXC
COMPLETE SET (9)	120.00	55.00	15.00
COMMON CARD (1-9)	4.00	1.80	.50
☐ 1 Vin Baker	6.00	2.70	.75
☐ 2 Anfernee Hardaway	40.00	18.00	5.00
☐ 3 Grant Hill	25.00	11.00	3.10
☐ 4 Jason Kidd	15.00	6.75	1.85
☐ 5 Jamal Mashburn	4.00	1.80	.50
☐ 6 Shaquille O'Neal	30.00	13.50	3.70
☐ 7 Glenn Robinson	8.00	3.60	1.00
☐ 8 Nick Van Exel	5.00	2.20	.60
☐ 9 Chris Webber	6.00	2.70	.75

1995-96 Ultra Rising Stars Gold Medallion

This parallel set is identical to the more common basic Rising Stars insert set with the exception of a gold foil medallion on the card front. They were seeded in all first series packs at 10 percent the rate of the inserts (approximately one in every 370 first series packs). Please refer to the multiplier provided below for values on Gold Medallion singles.

	MINT	NRMT	EXC
COMPLETE SET (9)	300.00	135.00	38.00
COMMON CARD (1-9)	10.00	4.50	1.25
*GOLD MEDALLION: 1.5X to 3X VALUE			

1995-96 Ultra Scoring Kings

Randomly inserted at a rate of one in 24 hobby packs only, this 12-card standard-size set spotlights the number crunchers of the NBA. Borderless fronts have full color player action shots and are stamped with

gold foil. Backs have another full-color action shot and include a player profile. The set is sequenced in alphabetical order. A full parallel Hot Pack set could be found in one of every 72 packs (known appropriately as "Hot Packs"). These Hot Pack parallels are four times easier to obtain than corresponding regular issue Jam City inserts. Please refer to the percentage provided below for values on individual Hot Pack parallel cards.

	MINT	NRMT	EXC
COMPLETE SET (12)	125.00	55.00	15.50
COMMON CARD (1-12)	2.50	1.10	.30
COMP.HOT PACK SET (12)	30.00	13.50	3.70
HP CARDS: 25% VALUE			
☐ 1 Patrick Ewing	4.00	1.80	.50
☐ 2 Grant Hill	15.00	6.75	1.85
☐ 3 Jim Jackson	2.50	1.10	.30
☐ 4 Michael Jordan	50.00	22.00	6.25
☐ 5 Karl Malone	4.00	1.80	.50
☐ 6 Reggie Miller	5.00	2.20	.60
☐ 7 Hakeem Olajuwon	10.00	4.50	1.25
☐ 8 Shaquille O'Neal	20.00	9.00	2.50
☐ 9 Scottie Pippen	12.00	5.50	1.50
☐ 10 David Robinson	8.00	3.60	1.00
☐ 11 Glenn Robinson	5.00	2.20	.60
☐ 12 Jerry Stackhouse	15.00	6.75	1.85

1995-96 Ultra Stackhouse's Scrapbook

Randomly inserted into one in every 24 second series packs, these two cards con-

tinue the eight-card, cross-brand set devoted to Fleer spokesperson Jerry Stackhouse. Card #S3 was featured on an unperforated promo sheet of Ultra cards saluting card stores across America. The sheets were distributed to shop owners nationwide. Unfortunately, some unscrupulous parties cut up a number of the sheets and distributed the cut cards into the hobby market under false pretenses. The cut up cards are identical to the real inserts, thus supply has been altered and we've applied a "DP" designation to signify a double-print on this card.

	MINT	NRMT	EXC
COMPLETE SET (2)	4.00	1.80	.50
COMMON CARD (S3-S4)	1.50	.70	.19
☐ S3 Jerry Stackhouse Ultra DP	1.50	.70	.19
☐ S4 Jerry Stackhouse Ultra	3.00	1.35	.35

1995-96 Ultra USA Basketball

Randomly inserted into all second series packs at a rate of one in 54, cards from this 10-card standard-size set capture the first 10 members named to the USA Olympic team in their new red, white and blue jerseys. Borderless fronts feature the player in full-color action set against an American flag backdrop. The player's name, position and the USA basketball logo are stamped in gold foil at the bottom. Backs have a full-color action shot on one side and a player profile set against a red and white stripe background with blue stars on the other side. The set is sequenced in alphabetical order.

	MINT	NRMT	EXC
COMPLETE SET (10)	180.00	80.00	22.00
COMMON CARD (1-10)	8.00	3.60	1.00
☐ 1 Anfernee Hardaway	50.00	22.00	6.25
☐ 2 Grant Hill	30.00	13.50	3.70
☐ 3 Karl Malone	8.00	3.60	1.00
☐ 4 Reggie Miller	10.00	4.50	1.25
☐ 5 Hakeem Olajuwon	20.00	9.00	2.50
☐ 6 Shaquille O'Neal	40.00	18.00	5.00
☐ 7 Scottie Pippen	25.00	11.00	3.10
☐ 8 David Robinson	15.00	6.75	1.85
☐ 9 Glenn Robinson	10.00	4.50	1.25
☐ 10 John Stockton	8.00	3.60	1.00

1991-92 Upper Deck

The 1991-92 set marks Upper Deck's debut in the basketball card industry. The set contains 500 standard-size cards. The set was released in two series of 400 and 100 cards, respectively. High series cards are in relatively shorter supply because high series packs contained a mix of both high and low series cards. High series lockers contained seven 12-card packs of cards 1-500 and a special "Rookie Standouts" card. Both low and high series were offered in a 500-card factory set. The fronts feature glossy color player photos, bordered below and on the right by a hardwood basketball floor design. The player's name appears beneath the picture, while the team name is printed vertically alongside the picture. The backs display a second color player photo as well as biographical and statistical information. Special subsets featured include Draft Choices (1-21), Classic Confrontations (30-34), All-Rookie Team (35-39), All-Stars (49-72), and Team Checklists (73-99). The fronts feature glossy color player photos, bordered below and on the right by a hardwood basketball floor design. The player's name appears beneath the picture, while the team name is printed vertically alongside the picture. The backs display a second color player photo as well as biographical and statistical information. In addition to rookie and traded players, the high series includes the following topical subsets: Top Prospects (438-448), All-Star Skills (476-484), capturing players who participated in the slam dunk competition as well as the three-point shootout winner, Eastern All-Star Team (449, 451-462), and Western All-Star Team (450, 463-475). Rookie Cards of note include Kenny Anderson, Stacey Augmon, Terrell Brandon, Larry Johnson, Anthony Mason, Dikembe Mutombo, Steve Smith, and John Starks.

	MINT	NRMT	EXC
COMPLETE SET (500)	20.00	9.00	2.50
COMPLETE FACT.SET (500)	20.00	9.00	2.50
COMPLETE SERIES 1 (400)	12.00	5.50	1.50

COMPLETE SERIES 2 (100)	8.00	3.60	1.00
COMMON CARD (1-400)	.05	.02	.01
COMMON CARD (401-500)	.10	.05	.01
☐ 1 Stacey Augmon CL	.05	.02	.01
Rodney Monroe			
☐ 2 Larry Johnson UER	1.50	.70	.19
(Career FG Percentage			
is .643, not .648)			
☐ 3 Dikembe Mutombo	.75	.35	.09
☐ 4 Steve Smith	.60	.25	.07
☐ 5 Stacey Augmon	.30	.14	.04
☐ 6 Terrell Brandon	.60	.25	.07
☐ 7 Greg Anthony	.25	.11	.03
☐ 8 Rich King	.05	.02	.01
☐ 9 Chris Gatling	.10	.05	.01
☐ 10 Victor Alexander	.05	.02	.01
☐ 11 John Turner	.05	.02	.01
☐ 12 Eric Murdock	.10	.05	.01
☐ 13 Mark Randall	.05	.02	.01
☐ 14 Rodney Monroe	.05	.02	.01
☐ 15 Myron Brown	.05	.02	.01
☐ 16 Mike Iuzzolino	.05	.02	.01
☐ 17 Chris Corchiani	.05	.02	.01
☐ 18 Elliot Perry	.15	.07	.02
☐ 19 Jimmy Oliver	.05	.02	.01
☐ 20 Doug Overton	.05	.02	.01
☐ 21 Steve Hood UER	.05	.02	.01
(Card has NBA record,			
but he's a rookie)			
☐ 22 Michael Jordan	.75	.35	.09
Stay In School			
☐ 23 Kevin Johnson	.10	.05	.01
Stay In School			
☐ 24 Kurk Lee	.05	.02	.01
☐ 25 Sean Higgins	.05	.02	.01
☐ 26 Morlon Wiley	.05	.02	.01
☐ 27 Derek Smith	.05	.02	.01
☐ 28 Kenny Payne	.05	.02	.01
☐ 29 Magic Johnson	.40	.18	.05
Assist Record			
☐ 30 Larry Bird CC	.25	.11	.03
and Chuck Person			
☐ 31 Karl Malone CC	.15	.07	.02
and Charles Barkley			
☐ 32 Kevin Johnson CC	.10	.05	.01
and John Stockton			
☐ 33 Hakeem Olajuwon CC	.25	.11	.03
and Patrick Ewing			
☐ 34 Magic Johnson CC	1.00	.45	.12
and Michael Jordan			
☐ 35 Derrick Coleman ART	.05	.02	.01
☐ 36 Lionel Simmons ART	.05	.02	.01
☐ 37 Dee Brown ART	.05	.02	.01
☐ 38 Dennis Scott ART	.10	.05	.01
☐ 39 Kendall Gill ART	.05	.02	.01
☐ 40 Winston Garland	.05	.02	.01
☐ 41 Danny Young	.05	.02	.01
☐ 42 Rick Mahorn	.05	.02	.01
☐ 43 Michael Adams	.05	.02	.01
☐ 44 Michael Jordan	3.00	1.35	.35
☐ 45 Magic Johnson	.75	.35	.09
☐ 46 Doc Rivers	.05	.02	.01
☐ 47 Moses Malone	.15	.07	.02
☐ 48 Michael Jordan AS CL	1.50	.70	.19
☐ 49 James Worthy AS	.10	.05	.01
☐ 50 Tim Hardaway AS	.10	.05	.01
☐ 51 Karl Malone AS	.10	.05	.01
☐ 52 John Stockton AS	.10	.05	.01
☐ 53 Clyde Drexler AS	.10	.05	.01
☐ 54 Terry Porter AS	.05	.02	.01

☐ 55 Kevin Duckworth AS	.05	.02	.01
☐ 56 Tom Chambers AS	.05	.02	.01
☐ 57 Magic Johnson AS	.40	.18	.05
☐ 58 David Robinson AS	.30	.14	.04
☐ 59 Kevin Johnson AS	.10	.05	.01
☐ 60 Chris Mullin AS	.05	.02	.01
☐ 61 Joe Dumars AS	.10	.05	.01
☐ 62 Kevin McHale AS	.10	.05	.01
☐ 63 Brad Daugherty AS	.05	.02	.01
☐ 64 Alvin Robertson AS	.05	.02	.01
☐ 65 Bernard King AS	.10	.05	.01
☐ 66 Dominique Wilkins AS	.10	.05	.01
☐ 67 Ricky Pierce AS	.05	.02	.01
☐ 68 Patrick Ewing AS	.10	.05	.01
☐ 69 Michael Jordan AS	1.50	.70	.19
☐ 70 Charles Barkley AS	.20	.09	.03
☐ 71 Hersey Hawkins AS	.05	.02	.01
☐ 72 Robert Parish AS	.10	.05	.01
☐ 73 Alvin Robertson TC	.05	.02	.01
☐ 74 Bernard King TC	.10	.05	.01
☐ 75 Michael Jordan TC	1.50	.70	.19
☐ 76 Brad Daugherty TC	.05	.02	.01
☐ 77 Larry Bird TC	.50	.23	.06
☐ 78 Ron Harper TC	.05	.02	.01
☐ 79 Dominique Wilkins TC	.10	.05	.01
☐ 80 Rony Seikaly TC	.05	.02	.01
☐ 81 Rex Chapman TC	.05	.02	.01
☐ 82 Mark Eaton TC	.05	.02	.01
☐ 83 Lionel Simmons TC	.05	.02	.01
☐ 84 Gerald Wilkins TC	.05	.02	.01
☐ 85 James Worthy TC	.10	.05	.01
☐ 86 Scott Skiles TC	.05	.02	.01
☐ 87 Rolando Blackman TC	.05	.02	.01
☐ 88 Derrick Coleman TC	.05	.02	.01
☐ 89 Chris Jackson TC	.05	.02	.01
☐ 90 Reggie Miller TC	.15	.07	.02
☐ 91 Isiah Thomas TC	.10	.05	.01
☐ 92 Hakeem Olajuwon TC	.30	.14	.04
☐ 93 Hersey Hawkins TC	.05	.02	.01
☐ 94 David Robinson TC	.30	.14	.04
☐ 95 Tom Chambers TC	.05	.02	.01
☐ 96 Shawn Kemp TC	.60	.25	.07
☐ 97 Pooh Richardson TC	.05	.02	.01
☐ 98 Clyde Drexler TC	.10	.05	.01
☐ 99 Chris Mullin TC	.05	.02	.01
☐ 100 Checklist 1-100	.05	.02	.01
☐ 101 John Shasky	.05	.02	.01
☐ 102 Dana Barros	.05	.02	.01
☐ 103 Stojko Vrankovic	.05	.02	.01
☐ 104 Larry Drew	.05	.02	.01
☐ 105 Randy White	.05	.02	.01
☐ 106 Dave Corzine	.05	.02	.01
☐ 107 Joe Kleine	.05	.02	.01
☐ 108 Lance Blanks	.05	.02	.01
☐ 109 Rodney McCray	.05	.02	.01
☐ 110 Sedale Threatt	.05	.02	.01
☐ 111 Ken Norman	.05	.02	.01
☐ 112 Rickey Green	.05	.02	.01
☐ 113 Andy Toolson	.05	.02	.01
☐ 114 Bo Kimble	.05	.02	.01
☐ 115 Mark West	.05	.02	.01
☐ 116 Mark Eaton	.05	.02	.01
☐ 117 John Paxson	.10	.05	.01
☐ 118 Mike Brown	.05	.02	.01
☐ 119 Brian Oliver	.05	.02	.01
☐ 120 Will Perdue	.05	.02	.01
☐ 121 Michael Smith	.05	.02	.01
☐ 122 Sherman Douglas	.05	.02	.01
☐ 123 Reggie Lewis	.10	.05	.01
☐ 124 James Donaldson	.05	.02	.01
☐ 125 Scottie Pippen	.75	.35	.09

#	Name				#	Name		
126	Elden Campbell	.10	.05	.01	197	Delaney Rudd	.05	.02	.01
127	Michael Cage	.05	.02	.01	198	Alan Ogg	.05	.02	.01
128	Tony Smith	.05	.02	.01	199	Blue Edwards	.05	.02	.01
129	Ed Pinckney	.05	.02	.01	200	Checklist 101-200	.05	.02	.01
130	Keith Askins	.05	.02	.01	201	Mark Acres	.05	.02	.01
131	Darrell Griffith	.10	.05	.01	202	Craig Ehlo	.05	.02	.01
132	Vinnie Johnson	.05	.02	.01	203	Anthony Cook	.05	.02	.01
133	Ron Harper	.05	.02	.01	204	Eric Leckner	.05	.02	.01
134	Andre Turner	.05	.02	.01	205	Terry Catledge	.05	.02	.01
135	Jeff Hornacek	.10	.05	.01	206	Reggie Williams	.05	.02	.01
136	John Stockton	.25	.11	.03	207	Greg Kite	.05	.02	.01
137	Derek Kerr	.05	.02	.01	208	Steve Kerr	.05	.02	.01
138	Loy Vaught	.10	.05	.01	209	Kenny Battle	.05	.02	.01
139	Thurl Bailey	.05	.02	.01	210	John Morton	.05	.02	.01
140	Olden Polynice	.05	.02	.01	211	Kenny Williams	.05	.02	.01
141	Kevin Edwards	.05	.02	.01	212	Mark Jackson	.05	.02	.01
142	Byron Scott	.10	.05	.01	213	Alaa Abdelnaby	.05	.02	.01
143	Dee Brown	.05	.02	.01	214	Rod Strickland	.05	.02	.01
144	Sam Perkins	.10	.05	.01	215	Micheal Williams	.05	.02	.01
145	Rony Seikaly	.05	.02	.01	216	Kevin Duckworth	.05	.02	.01
146	James Worthy	.10	.05	.01	217	David Wingate	.05	.02	.01
147	Glen Rice	.15	.07	.02	218	LaSalle Thompson	.05	.02	.01
148	Craig Hodges	.05	.02	.01	219	John Starks	.30	.14	.04
149	Bimbo Coles	.05	.02	.01	220	Clifford Robinson	.10	.05	.01
150	Mychal Thompson	.05	.02	.01	221	Jeff Grayer	.05	.02	.01
151	Xavier McDaniel	.05	.02	.01	222	Marcus Liberty	.05	.02	.01
152	Roy Tarpley	.05	.02	.01	223	Larry Nance	.05	.02	.01
153	Gary Payton	.60	.25	.07	224	Michael Ansley	.05	.02	.01
154	Rolando Blackman	.05	.02	.01	225	Kevin McHale	.10	.05	.01
155	Hersey Hawkins	.10	.05	.01	226	Scott Skiles	.05	.02	.01
156	Ricky Pierce	.05	.02	.01	227	Darnell Valentine	.05	.02	.01
157	Fat Lever	.05	.02	.01	228	Nick Anderson	.10	.05	.01
158	Andrew Lang	.05	.02	.01	229	Brad Davis	.05	.02	.01
159	Benoit Benjamin	.05	.02	.01	230	Gerald Paddio	.05	.02	.01
160	Cedric Ceballos	.10	.05	.01	231	Sam Bowie	.05	.02	.01
161	Charles Smith	.05	.02	.01	232	Sam Vincent	.05	.02	.01
162	Jeff Martin	.05	.02	.01	233	George McCloud	.10	.05	.01
163	Robert Parish	.10	.05	.01	234	Gerald Wilkins	.05	.02	.01
164	Danny Manning	.10	.05	.01	235	Mookie Blaylock	.10	.05	.01
165	Mark Aguirre	.10	.05	.01	236	Jon Koncak	.05	.02	.01
166	Jeff Malone	.05	.02	.01	237	Danny Ferry	.05	.02	.01
167	Bill Laimbeer	.10	.05	.01	238	Vern Fleming	.05	.02	.01
168	Willie Burton	.05	.02	.01	239	Mark Price	.05	.02	.01
169	Dennis Hopson	.05	.02	.01	240	Sidney Moncrief	.10	.05	.01
170	Kevin Gamble	.05	.02	.01	241	Jay Humphries	.05	.02	.01
171	Terry Teagle	.05	.02	.01	242	Muggsy Bogues	.10	.05	.01
172	Dan Majerle	.10	.05	.01	243	Tim Hardaway	.10	.05	.01
173	Shawn Kemp	1.25	.55	.16	244	Alvin Robertson	.05	.02	.01
174	Tom Chambers	.05	.02	.01	245	Chris Mullin	.10	.05	.01
175	Vlade Divac	.10	.05	.01	246	Pooh Richardson	.05	.02	.01
176	Johnny Dawkins	.05	.02	.01	247	Winston Bennett	.05	.02	.01
177	A.C. Green	.10	.05	.01	248	Kelvin Upshaw	.05	.02	.01
178	Manute Bol	.05	.02	.01	249	John Williams	.05	.02	.01
179	Terry Davis	.05	.02	.01	250	Steve Alford	.10	.05	.01
180	Ron Anderson	.05	.02	.01	251	Spud Webb	.10	.05	.01
181	Horace Grant	.10	.05	.01	252	Sleepy Floyd	.05	.02	.01
182	Stacey King	.05	.02	.01	253	Chuck Person	.05	.02	.01
183	William Bedford	.05	.02	.01	254	Hakeem Olajuwon	.60	.25	.07
184	B.J. Armstrong	.05	.02	.01	255	Dominique Wilkins	.10	.05	.01
185	Dennis Rodman	1.00	.45	.12	256	Reggie Miller	.30	.14	.04
186	Nate McMillan	.05	.02	.01	257	Dennis Scott	.10	.05	.01
187	Cliff Levingston	.05	.02	.01	258	Charles Oakley	.05	.02	.01
188	Quintin Dailey	.05	.02	.01	259	Sidney Green	.05	.02	.01
189	Bill Cartwright	.05	.02	.01	260	Detlef Schrempf	.10	.05	.01
190	John Salley	.05	.02	.01	261	Rod Higgins	.05	.02	.01
191	Jayson Williams	.05	.02	.01	262	J.R. Reid	.05	.02	.01
192	Grant Long	.05	.02	.01	263	Tyrone Hill	.10	.05	.01
193	Negele Knight	.05	.02	.01	264	Reggie Theus	.10	.05	.01
194	Alec Kessler	.05	.02	.01	265	Mitch Richmond	.25	.11	.03
195	Gary Grant	.05	.02	.01	266	Dale Ellis	.10	.05	.01
196	Billy Thompson	.05	.02	.01	267	Terry Cummings	.05	.02	.01

#	Player			
268	Johnny Newman	.05	.02	.01
269	Doug West	.05	.02	.01
270	Jim Petersen	.05	.02	.01
271	Otis Thorpe	.10	.05	.01
272	John Williams	.05	.02	.01
273	Kennard Winchester	.05	.02	.01
274	Duane Ferrell	.05	.02	.01
275	Vernon Maxwell	.05	.02	.01
276	Kenny Smith	.05	.02	.01
277	Jerome Kersey	.05	.02	.01
278	Kevin Willis	.05	.02	.01
279	Danny Ainge	.10	.05	.01
280	Larry Smith	.05	.02	.01
281	Maurice Cheeks	.10	.05	.01
282	Willie Anderson	.05	.02	.01
283	Tom Tolbert	.05	.02	.01
284	Jerrod Mustaf	.05	.02	.01
285	Randolph Keys	.05	.02	.01
286	Jerry Reynolds	.05	.02	.01
287	Sean Elliott	.15	.07	.02
288	Otis Smith	.05	.02	.01
289	Terry Mills	.10	.05	.01
290	Kelly Tripucka	.05	.02	.01
291	Jon Sundvold	.05	.02	.01
292	Rumeal Robinson	.05	.02	.01
293	Fred Roberts	.05	.02	.01
294	Rik Smits	.10	.05	.01
295	Jerome Lane	.05	.02	.01
296	Dave Jamerson	.05	.02	.01
297	Joe Wolf	.05	.02	.01
298	David Wood	.05	.02	.01
299	Todd Lichti	.05	.02	.01
300	Checklist 201-300	.05	.02	.01
301	Randy Breuer	.05	.02	.01
302	Buck Johnson	.05	.02	.01
303	Scott Brooks	.05	.02	.01
304	Jeff Turner	.05	.02	.01
305	Felton Spencer	.05	.02	.01
306	Greg Dreiling	.05	.02	.01
307	Gerald Glass	.05	.02	.01
308	Tony Brown	.05	.02	.01
309	Sam Mitchell	.05	.02	.01
310	Adrian Caldwell	.05	.02	.01
311	Chris Dudley	.05	.02	.01
312	Blair Rasmussen	.05	.02	.01
313	Antoine Carr	.05	.02	.01
314	Greg Anderson	.05	.02	.01
315	Drazen Petrovic	.10	.05	.01
316	Alton Lister	.05	.02	.01
317	Jack Haley	.05	.02	.01
318	Bobby Hansen	.05	.02	.01
319	Chris Jackson	.05	.02	.01
320	Herb Williams	.05	.02	.01
321	Kendall Gill	.05	.02	.01
322	Tyrone Corbin	.05	.02	.01
323	Kiki Vandeweghe	.05	.02	.01
324	David Robinson	.60	.25	.07
325	Rex Chapman	.05	.02	.01
326	Tony Campbell	.05	.02	.01
327	Dell Curry	.05	.02	.01
328	Charles Jones	.05	.02	.01
329	Kenny Gattison	.05	.02	.01
330	Haywoode Workman	.05	.02	.01
331	Travis Mays	.05	.02	.01
332	Derrick Coleman	.05	.02	.01
333	Isiah Thomas	.15	.07	.02
334	Jud Buechler	.05	.02	.01
335	Joe Dumars	.10	.05	.01
336	Tate George	.05	.02	.01
337	Mike Sanders	.05	.02	.01
338	James Edwards	.05	.02	.01
339	Chris Morris	.05	.02	.01
340	Scott Hastings	.05	.02	.01
341	Trent Tucker	.05	.02	.01
342	Harvey Grant	.05	.02	.01
343	Patrick Ewing	.25	.11	.03
344	Larry Bird	1.00	.45	.12
345	Charles Barkley	.40	.18	.05
346	Brian Shaw	.05	.02	.01
347	Kenny Walker	.05	.02	.01
348	Danny Schayes	.05	.02	.01
349	Tom Hammonds	.05	.02	.01
350	Frank Brickowski	.05	.02	.01
351	Terry Porter	.05	.02	.01
352	Orlando Woolridge	.05	.02	.01
353	Buck Williams	.10	.05	.01
354	Sarunas Marciulionis	.05	.02	.01
355	Karl Malone	.25	.11	.03
356	Kevin Johnson	.10	.05	.01
357	Clyde Drexler	.30	.14	.04
358	Duane Causwell	.05	.02	.01
359	Paul Pressey	.05	.02	.01
360	Jim Les	.05	.02	.01
361	Derrick McKey	.05	.02	.01
362	Scott Williams	.05	.02	.01
363	Mark Alarie	.05	.02	.01
364	Brad Daugherty	.05	.02	.01
365	Bernard King	.10	.05	.01
366	Steve Henson	.05	.02	.01
367	Darrell Walker	.05	.02	.01
368	Larry Krystkowiak	.05	.02	.01
369	Henry James UER	.05	.02	.01
	(Scored 20 points vs.			
	Pistons, not Jazz)			
370	Jack Sikma	.10	.05	.01
371	Eddie Johnson	.05	.02	.01
372	Wayman Tisdale	.05	.02	.01
373	Joe Barry Carroll	.05	.02	.01
374	David Greenwood	.05	.02	.01
375	Lionel Simmons	.05	.02	.01
376	Dwayne Schintzius	.05	.02	.01
377	Tod Murphy	.05	.02	.01
378	Wayne Cooper	.05	.02	.01
379	Anthony Bonner	.05	.02	.01
380	Walter Davis	.10	.05	.01
381	Lester Conner	.05	.02	.01
382	Ledell Eackles	.05	.02	.01
383	Brad Lohaus	.05	.02	.01
384	Derrick Gervin	.05	.02	.01
385	Pervis Ellison	.05	.02	.01
386	Tim McCormick	.05	.02	.01
387	A.J. English	.05	.02	.01
388	John Battle	.05	.02	.01
389	Roy Hinson	.05	.02	.01
390	Armon Gilliam	.05	.02	.01
391	Kurt Rambis	.05	.02	.01
392	Mark Bryant	.05	.02	.01
393	Chucky Brown	.05	.02	.01
394	Avery Johnson	.10	.05	.01
395	Rory Sparrow	.05	.02	.01
396	Mario Elie	.10	.05	.01
397	Ralph Sampson	.05	.02	.01
398	Mike Gminski	.05	.02	.01
399	Bill Wennington	.05	.02	.01
400	Checklist 301-400	.05	.02	.01
401	David Wingate	.10	.05	.01
402	Moses Malone	.30	.14	.04
403	Darrell Walker	.10	.05	.01
404	Antoine Carr	.10	.05	.01
405	Charles Shackleford	.10	.05	.01
406	Orlando Woolridge	.10	.05	.01
407	Robert Pack	.15	.07	.02

☐ 408 Bobby Hansen	.10	.05	.01
☐ 409 Dale Davis	.50	.23	.06
☐ 410 Vincent Askew	.10	.05	.01
☐ 411 Alexander Volkov	.10	.05	.01
☐ 412 Dwayne Schintzius	.10	.05	.01
☐ 413 Tim Perry	.10	.05	.01
☐ 414 Tyrone Corbin	.10	.05	.01
☐ 415 Pete Chilcutt	.10	.05	.01
☐ 416 James Edwards	.10	.05	.01
☐ 417 Jerrod Mustaf	.10	.05	.01
☐ 418 Thurl Bailey	.10	.05	.01
☐ 419 Spud Webb	.15	.07	.02
☐ 420 Doc Rivers	.10	.05	.01
☐ 421 Sean Green	.10	.05	.01
☐ 422 Walter Davis	.15	.07	.02
☐ 423 Terry Davis	.10	.05	.01
☐ 424 John Battle	.10	.05	.01
☐ 425 Vinnie Johnson	.10	.05	.01
☐ 426 Sherman Douglas	.10	.05	.01
☐ 427 Kevin Brooks	.10	.05	.01
☐ 428 Greg Sutton	.10	.05	.01
☐ 429 Rafael Addison	.10	.05	.01
☐ 430 Anthony Mason	.75	.35	.09
☐ 431 Paul Graham	.10	.05	.01
☐ 432 Anthony Frederick	.10	.05	.01
☐ 433 Dennis Hopson	.10	.05	.01
☐ 434 Rory Sparrow	.10	.05	.01
☐ 435 Michael Adams	.10	.05	.01
☐ 436 Kevin Lynch	.10	.05	.01
☐ 437 Randy Brown	.10	.05	.01
☐ 438 Larry Johnson CL	.40	.18	.05
Billy Owens			
☐ 439 Stacey Augmon TP	.15	.07	.02
☐ 440 Larry Stewart TP	.10	.05	.01
☐ 441 Terrell Brandon TP	.30	.14	.04
☐ 442 Billy Owens TP	.50	.23	.06
☐ 443 Rick Fox TP	.30	.14	.04
☐ 444 Kenny Anderson TP	1.00	.45	.12
☐ 445 Larry Johnson TP	.75	.35	.09
☐ 446 Dikembe Mutombo TP	.40	.18	.05
☐ 447 Steve Smith TP	.30	.14	.04
☐ 448 Greg Anthony TP	.10	.05	.01
☐ 449 East All-Star	.10	.05	.01
Checklist			
☐ 450 West All-Star	.10	.05	.01
Checklist			
☐ 451 Isiah Thomas AS	.25	.11	.03
(Magic Johnson			
also shown)			
☐ 452 Michael Jordan AS	3.00	1.35	.35
☐ 453 Scottie Pippen AS	.75	.35	.09
☐ 454 Charles Barkley AS	.40	.18	.05
☐ 455 Patrick Ewing AS	.25	.11	.03
☐ 456 Michael Adams AS	.10	.05	.01
☐ 457 Dennis Rodman AS	1.00	.45	.12
☐ 458 Reggie Lewis AS	.15	.07	.02
☐ 459 Joe Dumars AS	.15	.07	.02
☐ 460 Mark Price AS	.10	.05	.01
☐ 461 Brad Daugherty AS	.10	.05	.01
☐ 462 Kevin Willis AS	.10	.05	.01
☐ 463 Clyde Drexler AS	.30	.14	.04
☐ 464 Magic Johnson AS	.75	.35	.09
☐ 465 Chris Mullin AS	.10	.05	.01
☐ 466 Karl Malone AS	.25	.11	.03
☐ 467 David Robinson AS	.60	.25	.07
☐ 468 Tim Hardaway AS	.15	.07	.02
☐ 469 Jeff Hornacek AS	.10	.05	.01
☐ 470 John Stockton AS	.25	.11	.03
☐ 471 Dikembe Mutombo AS UER	.25	.11	.03
(Drafted in 1992,			
should be 1991)			

☐ 472 Hakeem Olajuwon AS	.60	.25	.07
☐ 473 James Worthy AS	.15	.07	.02
☐ 474 Otis Thorpe AS	.10	.05	.01
☐ 475 Dan Majerle AS	.10	.05	.01
☐ 476 Cedric Ceballos CL	.10	.05	.01
All-Star Skills			
☐ 477 Nick Anderson SD	.10	.05	.01
☐ 478 Stacey Augmon SD	.10	.05	.01
☐ 479 Cedric Ceballos SD	.15	.07	.02
☐ 480 Larry Johnson SD	.60	.25	.07
☐ 481 Shawn Kemp SD	1.25	.55	.16
☐ 482 John Starks SD	.10	.05	.01
☐ 483 Doug West SD	.10	.05	.01
☐ 484 Craig Hodges	.10	.05	.01
Long Distance Shoot Out			
☐ 485 LaBradford Smith	.10	.05	.01
☐ 486 Winston Garland	.10	.05	.01
☐ 487 David Benoit	.15	.07	.02
☐ 488 John Bagley	.10	.05	.01
☐ 489 Mark Macon	.10	.05	.01
☐ 490 Mitch Richmond	.50	.23	.06
☐ 491 Luc Longley	.60	.25	.07
☐ 492 Sedale Threatt	.10	.05	.01
☐ 493 Doug Smith	.10	.05	.01
☐ 494 Travis Mays	.10	.05	.01
☐ 495 Xavier McDaniel	.10	.05	.01
☐ 496 Brian Shaw	.10	.05	.01
☐ 497 Stanley Roberts	.10	.05	.01
☐ 498 Blair Rasmussen	.10	.05	.01
☐ 499 Brian Williams	.30	.14	.04
☐ 500 Checklist Card	.10	.05	.01

1991-92 Upper Deck Award Winner Holograms

These holograms feature NBA statistical leaders in nine different categories. The first six holograms were random inserts in 1991-92 Upper Deck low series foil and jumbo packs, while the last three were inserted in high series foil and jumbo packs. The standard-size holograms have the player's name and award received in the lower right corner on the front. The back has a color player photo and a summary of the player's performance. The cards are numbered on the back with an "AW" prefix before the number.

	MINT	NRMT	EXC
COMPLETE SET (9)	35.00	16.00	4.40
COMMON CARD (AW1-AW9)	.50	.23	.06

		MINT	NRMT	EXC
☐ AW1	Michael Jordan....... Scoring Leader	15.00	6.75	1.85
☐ AW2	Alvin Robertson.......... Steals Leader	.50	.23	.06
☐ AW3	John Stockton.......... Assists Leader	1.00	.45	.12
☐ AW4	Michael Jordan....... MVP	15.00	6.75	1.85
☐ AW5	Detlef Schrempf .... Sixth Man	.75	.35	.09
☐ AW6	David Robinson....... Rebounds Leader	2.50	1.10	.30
☐ AW7	Derrick Coleman....... Rookie of the Year	.50	.23	.06
☐ AW8	Hakeem Olajuwon ..... Blocked Shots Leader	2.50	1.10	.30
☐ AW9	Dennis Rodman....... Defensive POY	4.00	1.80	.50

1991-92 Upper Deck Rookie Standouts

Inserted one per jumbo and locker pack in both the low and high series, fronts of this standard-size 40-card set feature color action player photos, bordered on the right and below by a hardwood basketball court and with the "'91-92 Rookie Standouts" emblem in the lower right corner. The back features a second color player photo and player profile.

		MINT	NRMT	EXC
COMPLETE SET (40)		15.00	6.75	1.85
COMPLETE SERIES 1 (20)......		5.00	2.20	.60
COMPLETE SERIES 2 (20)		10.00	4.50	1.25
COMMON CARD (R1-R40)		.25	.11	.03

		MINT	NRMT	EXC
☐ R1	Gary Payton....................	2.50	1.10	.30
☐ R2	Dennis Scott	.50	.23	.06
☐ R3	Kendall Gill	.50	.23	.06
☐ R4	Felton Spencer	.25	.11	.03
☐ R5	Bo Kimble	.25	.11	.03
☐ R6	Willie Burton..................	.25	.11	.03
☐ R7	Tyrone Hill	.75	.35	.09
☐ R8	Loy Vaught	.75	.35	.09
☐ R9	Travis Mays	.25	.11	.03
☐ R10	Derrick Coleman..........	.50	.23	.06
☐ R11	Duane Causwell............	.25	.11	.03
☐ R12	Dee Brown	.75	.35	.09
☐ R13	Gerald Glass	.25	.11	.03
☐ R14	Jayson Williams	.40	.18	.05

☐ R15	Elden Campbell	.75	.35	.09
☐ R16	Negele Knight	.25	.11	.03
☐ R17	Chris Jackson	.50	.23	.06
☐ R18	Danny Ferry	.40	.18	.05
☐ R19	Tony Smith	.25	.11	.03
☐ R20	Cedric Ceballos	1.00	.45	.12
☐ R21	Victor Alexander	.25	.11	.03
☐ R22	Terrell Brandon............	1.50	.70	.19
☐ R23	Rick Fox	.50	.23	.06
☐ R24	Stacey Augmon............	.75	.35	.09
☐ R25	Mark Macon	.25	.11	.03
☐ R26	Larry Johnson	4.00	1.80	.50
☐ R27	Paul Graham	.25	.11	.03
☐ R28	Stanley Roberts UER ... (Not the Magic's 1st pick in 1991)	.25	.11	.03
☐ R29	Dikembe Mutombo........	2.00	.90	.25
☐ R30	Robert Pack	.25	.11	.03
☐ R31	Doug Smith	.25	.11	.03
☐ R32	Steve Smith	1.50	.70	.19
☐ R33	Billy Owens..................	.60	.25	.07
☐ R34	David Benoit	.40	.18	.05
☐ R35	Brian Williams	.50	.23	.06
☐ R36	Kenny Anderson	1.25	.55	.16
☐ R37	Greg Anthony	.50	.23	.06
☐ R38	Dale Davis	.60	.25	.07
☐ R39	Larry Stewart	.25	.11	.03
☐ R40	Mike Iuzzolino	.25	.11	.03

1991-92 Upper Deck Jerry West Heroes

This ten-card insert set was randomly inserted in Upper Deck's high series basketball foil packs. Also included in the packs were 2,500 checklist cards autographed by West. The fronts of the standard-size cards capture memorable moments from his college and professional career. The player photos are cut out and superimposed over a jump ball circle on a hardwood basketball floor design. The card backs present commentary.

		MINT	NRMT	EXC
COMPLETE SET (10)		6.00	2.70	.75
COMMON J.WEST (1-9)		1.00	.45	.12

☐ 1	Jerry West .... 1959 NCAA Tournament MVP	1.00	.45	.12
☐ 2	Jerry West	1.00	.45	.12

			MINT	NRMT	EXC
		1960 U.S. Team			
☐ 3	Jerry West	1968-69 NBA Playoff MVP	1.00	.45	.12
☐ 4	Jerry West	1969-70 NBA Scoring Leader	1.00	.45	.12
☐ 5	Jerry West	1972 NBA World Championship	1.00	.45	.12
☐ 6	Jerry West	1973-74 25,000 Points	1.00	.45	.12
☐ 7	Jerry West	1979 Basketball Hall of Fame	1.00	.45	.12
☐ 8	Jerry West	1982 to the present Front Office Success	1.00	.45	.12
☐ 9	Jerry West	Portrait Card	1.00	.45	.12
☐ AU	Jerry West AU/2500 (Certified autograph)		175.00	80.00	22.00
☐ NNO	Jerry West	Cover/Title Card	1.50	.70	.19

1991-92 Upper Deck Jerry West Box Bottoms

These oversized cards, measuring approximately 5" by 7", are actually the bottom panel of the 1991-92 Upper Deck high number series basketball wax/foil boxes. Except for the size and the blank backs, these waxbox bottoms are identical to the first eight cards in the Jerry West Basketball Heroes insert set.

			MINT	NRMT	EXC
COMPLETE SET (8)			5.00	2.20	.60
COMMON CARD (1-8)			.75	.35	.09
☐ 1	Jerry West	1959 NCAA Tournament MVP	.75	.35	.09
☐ 2	Jerry West	1960 U.S. Team	.75	.35	.09
☐ 3	Jerry West	1968-69 NBA Playoff MVP	.75	.35	.09
☐ 4	Jerry West	1969-70 NBA Scoring Leader	.75	.35	.09
☐ 5	Jerry West		.75	.35	.09

		1972 NBA World Championship			
☐ 6	Jerry West	1973-74 25,000 Points	.75	.35	.09
☐ 7	Jerry West	1979 Basketball Hall of Fame	.75	.35	.09
☐ 8	Jerry West	1982 to the present Front Office Success	.75	.35	.09

1992-93 Upper Deck

The complete 1992-93 Upper Deck basketball set consists of 510 standard-size cards issued in two series of 310 and 200 cards, respectively. High series cards are slightly tougher to find (compared to the low numbers) because high series packs contained a mix of high and low series cards. For both series, cards were issued in 15-card hobby and retail foil packs, 27-card locker packs and 27-card jumbo packs. No factory sets were produced by Upper Deck for this issue. Both series were also distributed through 27-card Locker packs. Card number 1A (available only in low series packs) is a "Trade Upper Deck" card that the collector could trade to Upper Deck for a Shaquille O'Neal mail-away trade card beginning on Jan. 1, 1993. The offer expired June 30, 1993. The fronts feature color action player photos with white borders. The team name is gold-foil stamped across the top of the picture. The border design at the bottom consists of a team colored stripe that shades from one team color to the other with diagonal stripes within the larger stripe that add texture. The entire design is edged in gold foil. The right end is off-set slightly by the Upper Deck logo. The backs show an action player photo that runs down the left side of the card. The right side displays statistics printed on a ghosted NBA logo. Topical subsets featured include NBA Draft (2-21), Team Checklists (35-61), and Scoring Threats (62-66). The set also includes two art cards (67-68) and one Stay in School card (69). Second series subsets featured are Team Fact Cards (350-376), NBA East All-Star Game (421-433), NBA West All-Star Game (434-445), In Your Face (446-454), Top Prospects (455-482), NBA Game Faces

(483-497), Scoring Threats (498-505), and Fanimation (506-510). The cards are numbered on the back. Rookie Cards of note include Doug Christie (second series SP), Tom Gugliotta, Jim Jackson (second series SP), Christian Laettner, Alonzo Mourning, Shaquille O'Neal (second series SP), Latrell Sprewell and Clarence Weatherspoon. A card commemorating the retirement of Larry Bird and Magic Johnson (SP1) and the 20,000th point scored by Dominique Wilkins and Michael Jordan (SP2) were first and second series inserts, respectively. There were inserted at a rate of one in 72 packs. The basic card numbers of Jordan (23), Magic (32) and Bird (33) represent their uniform numbers.

	MINT	NRMT	EXC
COMPLETE SET (514)	50.00	22.00	6.25
COMPLETE LO SERIES (311)	20.00	9.00	2.50
COMPLETE HI SERIES (203)	30.00	13.50	3.70
COMMON CARD (1-510)	.05	.02	.01
COMMON CARD (311-510)			

		MINT	NRMT	EXC
☐ 1	Shaquille O'Neal SP NBA First Draft Pick	15.00	6.75	1.85
☐ 1A	1992 NBA Draft Trade Card SP	.15	.07	.02
☐ 1B	Shaquille O'Neal TRADE	6.00	2.70	.75
☐ 1AX	1992 NBA Draft Trade Card (Stamped)	.10	.05	.01
☐ 2	Alonzo Mourning	1.50	.70	.19
☐ 3	Christian Laettner	.50	.23	.06
☐ 4	LaPhonso Ellis	.25	.11	.03
☐ 5	Clarence Weatherspoon	.50	.23	.06
☐ 6	Adam Keefe	.10	.05	.01
☐ 7	Robert Horry	.60	.25	.07
☐ 8	Harold Miner	.10	.05	.01
☐ 9	Bryant Stith	.25	.11	.03
☐ 10	Malik Sealy	.10	.05	.01
☐ 11	Anthony Peeler	.05	.02	.01
☐ 12	Randy Woods	.05	.02	.01
☐ 13	Tracy Murray	.10	.05	.01
☐ 14	Tom Gugliotta	.50	.23	.06
☐ 15	Hubert Davis	.10	.05	.01
☐ 16	Don MacLean	.10	.05	.01
☐ 17	Lee Mayberry	.05	.02	.01
☐ 18	Corey Williams	.05	.02	.01
☐ 19	Sean Rooks	.05	.02	.01
☐ 20	Todd Day	.10	.05	.01
☐ 21	Bryant Stith CL LaPhonso Ellis	.05	.02	.01
☐ 22	Jeff Hornacek	.10	.05	.01
☐ 23	Michael Jordan	4.00	1.80	.50
☐ 24	John Salley	.05	.02	.01
☐ 25	Andre Turner	.05	.02	.01
☐ 26	Charles Barkley	.50	.23	.06
☐ 27	Anthony Frederick	.05	.02	.01
☐ 28	Mario Elie	.05	.02	.01
☐ 29	Olden Polynice	.05	.02	.01
☐ 30	Rodney Monroe	.05	.02	.01
☐ 31	Tim Perry	.05	.02	.01
☐ 32	Doug Christie SP	.20	.09	.03
☐ 32A	Magic Johnson SP	2.00	.90	.25
☐ 33	Jim Jackson SP	5.00	2.20	.60
☐ 33A	Larry Bird SP	2.50	1.10	.30
☐ 34	Randy White	.05	.02	.01
☐ 35	Frank Brickowski TC	.05	.02	.01
☐ 36	Michael Adams TC	.05	.02	.01
☐ 37	Scottie Pippen TC	.50	.23	.06
☐ 38	Mark Price TC	.05	.02	.01
☐ 39	Robert Parish TC	.10	.05	.01
☐ 40	Danny Manning TC	.10	.05	.01
☐ 41	Kevin Willis TC	.05	.02	.01
☐ 42	Glen Rice TC	.10	.05	.01
☐ 43	Kendall Gill TC	.05	.02	.01
☐ 44	Karl Malone TC	.15	.07	.02
☐ 45	Mitch Richmond TC	.10	.05	.01
☐ 46	Patrick Ewing TC	.15	.07	.02
☐ 47	Sam Perkins TC	.05	.02	.01
☐ 48	Dennis Scott TC	.10	.05	.01
☐ 49	Derek Harper TC	.05	.02	.01
☐ 50	Drazen Petrovic TC	.10	.05	.01
☐ 51	Reggie Williams TC	.05	.02	.01
☐ 52	Rik Smits TC	.10	.05	.01
☐ 53	Joe Dumars TC	.10	.05	.01
☐ 54	Otis Thorpe TC	.05	.02	.01
☐ 55	Johnny Dawkins TC	.05	.02	.01
☐ 56	Sean Elliott TC	.05	.02	.01
☐ 57	Kevin Johnson TC	.10	.05	.01
☐ 58	Ricky Pierce TC	.05	.02	.01
☐ 59	Doug West TC	.05	.02	.01
☐ 60	Terry Porter TC	.05	.02	.01
☐ 61	Tim Hardaway TC	.05	.02	.01
☐ 62	Michael Jordan ST Scottie Pippen	1.00	.45	.12
☐ 63	Kendall Gill ST Larry Johnson	.05	.02	.01
☐ 64	Tom Chambers ST Kevin Johnson	.05	.02	.01
☐ 65	Tim Hardaway ST Chris Mullin	.05	.02	.01
☐ 66	Karl Malone ST John Stockton	.15	.07	.02
☐ 67	Michael Jordan MVP	2.00	.90	.25
☐ 68	Stacey Augmon Six Million Point Man	.05	.02	.01
☐ 69	Bob Lanier Stay in School	.15	.07	.02
☐ 70	Alaa Abdelnaby	.05	.02	.01
☐ 71	Andrew Lang	.05	.02	.01
☐ 72	Larry Krystkowiak	.05	.02	.01
☐ 73	Gerald Wilkins	.05	.02	.01
☐ 74	Rod Strickland	.05	.02	.01
☐ 75	Danny Ainge	.15	.07	.02
☐ 76	Chris Corchiani	.05	.02	.01
☐ 77	Jeff Grayer	.05	.02	.01
☐ 78	Eric Murdock	.05	.02	.01
☐ 79	Rex Chapman	.05	.02	.01
☐ 80	LaBradford Smith	.05	.02	.01
☐ 81	Jay Humphries	.05	.02	.01
☐ 82	David Robinson	.60	.25	.07
☐ 83	William Bedford	.05	.02	.01
☐ 84	James Edwards	.05	.02	.01
☐ 85	Dan Schayes	.05	.02	.01
☐ 86	Lloyd Daniels	.05	.02	.01
☐ 87	Blue Edwards	.05	.02	.01
☐ 88	Dale Ellis	.05	.02	.01
☐ 89	Rolando Blackman	.05	.02	.01
☐ 90	Michael Jordan CL	.25	.11	.03
☐ 91	Rik Smits	.15	.07	.02
☐ 92	Terry Davis	.05	.02	.01
☐ 93	Bill Cartwright	.05	.02	.01
☐ 94	Avery Johnson	.05	.02	.01
☐ 95	Micheal Williams	.05	.02	.01
☐ 96	Spud Webb	.10	.05	.01
☐ 97	Benoit Benjamin	.05	.02	.01
☐ 98	Derek Harper	.10	.05	.01
☐ 99	Matt Bullard	.05	.02	.01
☐ 100A	Tyrone Corbin ERR (Heat on front)	1.00	.45	.12

#	Player			
☐ 100B	Tyrone Corbin COR	.05	.02	.01
☐ 101	Doc Rivers	.05	.02	.01
☐ 102	Tony Smith	.05	.02	.01
☐ 103	Doug West	.05	.02	.01
☐ 104	Kevin Duckworth	.05	.02	.01
☐ 105	Luc Longley	.05	.02	.01
☐ 106	Antoine Carr	.05	.02	.01
☐ 107	Clifford Robinson	.15	.07	.02
☐ 108	Grant Long	.05	.02	.01
☐ 109	Terry Porter	.05	.02	.01
☐ 110A	Steve Smith ERR	4.00	1.80	.50
	(Jazz on front)			
☐ 110B	Steve Smith COR	.15	.07	.02
☐ 111	Brian Williams	.05	.02	.01
☐ 112	Karl Malone	.30	.14	.04
☐ 113	Reggie Williams	.05	.02	.01
☐ 114	Tom Chambers	.05	.02	.01
☐ 115	Winston Garland	.05	.02	.01
☐ 116	John Stockton	.30	.14	.04
☐ 117	Chris Jackson	.10	.05	.01
☐ 118	Mike Brown	.05	.02	.01
☐ 119	Kevin Johnson	.15	.07	.02
☐ 120	Reggie Lewis	.10	.05	.01
☐ 121	Bimbo Coles	.05	.02	.01
☐ 122	Drazen Petrovic	.10	.05	.01
☐ 123	Reggie Miller	.40	.18	.05
☐ 124	Derrick Coleman	.05	.02	.01
☐ 125	Chuck Person	.05	.02	.01
☐ 126	Glen Rice	.15	.07	.02
☐ 127	Kenny Anderson	.15	.07	.02
☐ 128	Willie Burton	.05	.02	.01
☐ 129	Chris Morris	.05	.02	.01
☐ 130	Patrick Ewing	.30	.14	.04
☐ 131	Sean Elliott	.15	.07	.02
☐ 132	Clyde Drexler	.40	.18	.05
☐ 133	Scottie Pippen	1.00	.45	.12
☐ 134	Pooh Richardson	.05	.02	.01
☐ 135	Horace Grant	.15	.07	.02
☐ 136	Hakeem Olajuwon	.75	.35	.09
☐ 137	John Paxson	.10	.05	.01
☐ 138	Kendall Gill	.05	.02	.01
☐ 139	Michael Adams	.05	.02	.01
☐ 140	Otis Thorpe	.10	.05	.01
☐ 141	Dennis Scott	.10	.05	.01
☐ 142	Stacey Augmon	.10	.05	.01
☐ 143	Robert Pack	.05	.02	.01
☐ 144	Kevin Willis	.05	.02	.01
☐ 145	Jerome Kersey	.05	.02	.01
☐ 146	Paul Graham	.05	.02	.01
☐ 147	Stanley Roberts	.05	.02	.01
☐ 148	Dominique Wilkins	.15	.07	.02
☐ 149	Scott Skiles	.05	.02	.01
☐ 150	Rumeal Robinson	.05	.02	.01
☐ 151	Mookie Blaylock	.10	.05	.01
☐ 152	Elden Campbell	.10	.05	.01
☐ 153	Chris Dudley	.05	.02	.01
☐ 154	Sedale Threatt	.05	.02	.01
☐ 155	Tate George	.05	.02	.01
☐ 156	James Worthy	.15	.07	.02
☐ 157	B.J. Armstrong	.05	.02	.01
☐ 158	Gary Payton	.60	.25	.07
☐ 159	Ledell Eackles	.05	.02	.01
☐ 160	Sam Perkins	.10	.05	.01
☐ 161	Nick Anderson	.15	.07	.02
☐ 162	Mitch Richmond	.25	.11	.03
☐ 163	Buck Williams	.10	.05	.01
☐ 164	Blair Rasmussen	.05	.02	.01
☐ 165	Vern Fleming	.05	.02	.01
☐ 166	Duane Ferrell	.05	.02	.01
☐ 167	George McCloud	.05	.02	.01
☐ 168	Terry Cummings	.05	.02	.01
☐ 169	Detlef Schrempf	.10	.05	.01
☐ 170	Willie Anderson	.05	.02	.01
☐ 171	Scott Williams	.05	.02	.01
☐ 172	Vernon Maxwell	.05	.02	.01
☐ 173	Todd Lichti	.05	.02	.01
☐ 174	David Benoit	.05	.02	.01
☐ 175	Marcus Liberty	.05	.02	.01
☐ 176	Kenny Smith	.05	.02	.01
☐ 177	Dan Majerle	.10	.05	.01
☐ 178	Jeff Malone	.05	.02	.01
☐ 179	Robert Parish	.15	.07	.02
☐ 180	Mark Eaton	.05	.02	.01
☐ 181	Rony Seikaly	.05	.02	.01
☐ 182	Tony Campbell	.05	.02	.01
☐ 183	Kevin McHale	.15	.07	.02
☐ 184	Thurl Bailey	.05	.02	.01
☐ 185	Kevin Edwards	.05	.02	.01
☐ 186	Gerald Glass	.05	.02	.01
☐ 187	Hersey Hawkins	.10	.05	.01
☐ 188	Sam Mitchell	.05	.02	.01
☐ 189	Brian Shaw	.05	.02	.01
☐ 190	Felton Spencer	.05	.02	.01
☐ 191	Mark Macon	.05	.02	.01
☐ 192	Jerry Reynolds	.05	.02	.01
☐ 193	Dale Davis	.05	.02	.01
☐ 194	Sleepy Floyd	.05	.02	.01
☐ 195	A.C. Green	.15	.07	.02
☐ 196	Terry Catledge	.05	.02	.01
☐ 197	Byron Scott	.15	.07	.02
☐ 198	Sam Bowie	.05	.02	.01
☐ 199	Vlade Divac	.10	.05	.01
☐ 200	Michael Jordan CL	.25	.11	.03
☐ 201	Brad Lohaus	.05	.02	.01
☐ 202	Johnny Newman	.05	.02	.01
☐ 203	Gary Grant	.05	.02	.01
☐ 204	Sidney Green	.05	.02	.01
☐ 205	Frank Brickowski	.05	.02	.01
☐ 206	Anthony Bowie	.05	.02	.01
☐ 207	Duane Causwell	.05	.02	.01
☐ 208	A.J. English	.05	.02	.01
☐ 209	Mark Aguirre	.10	.05	.01
☐ 210	Jon Koncak	.05	.02	.01
☐ 211	Kevin Gamble	.05	.02	.01
☐ 212	Craig Ehlo	.05	.02	.01
☐ 213	Herb Williams	.05	.02	.01
☐ 214	Cedric Ceballos	.10	.05	.01
☐ 215	Mark Jackson	.05	.02	.01
☐ 216	John Bagley	.05	.02	.01
☐ 217	Ron Anderson	.05	.02	.01
☐ 218	John Battle	.05	.02	.01
☐ 219	Kevin Lynch	.05	.02	.01
☐ 220	Donald Hodge	.05	.02	.01
☐ 221	Chris Gatling	.05	.02	.01
☐ 222	Muggsy Bogues	.10	.05	.01
☐ 223	Bill Laimbeer	.10	.05	.01
☐ 224	Anthony Bonner	.05	.02	.01
☐ 225	Fred Roberts	.05	.02	.01
☐ 226	Larry Stewart	.05	.02	.01
☐ 227	Darrell Walker	.05	.02	.01
☐ 228	Larry Smith	.05	.02	.01
☐ 229	Billy Owens	.05	.02	.01
☐ 230	Vinnie Johnson	.05	.02	.01
☐ 231	Johnny Dawkins	.05	.02	.01
☐ 232	Rick Fox	.05	.02	.01
☐ 233	Travis Mays	.05	.02	.01
☐ 234	Mark Price	.05	.02	.01
☐ 235	Derrick McKey	.05	.02	.01
☐ 236	Greg Anthony	.05	.02	.01
☐ 237	Doug Smith	.05	.02	.01
☐ 238	Alec Kessler	.05	.02	.01
☐ 239	Anthony Mason	.15	.07	.02

☐ 240	Shawn Kemp	1.25	.55	.16
☐ 241	Jim Les	.05	.02	.01
☐ 242	Dennis Rodman	1.25	.55	.16
☐ 243	Lionel Simmons	.05	.02	.01
☐ 244	Pervis Ellison	.05	.02	.01
☐ 245	Terrell Brandon	.15	.07	.02
☐ 246	Mark Bryant	.05	.02	.01
☐ 247	Brad Daugherty	.05	.02	.01
☐ 248	Scott Brooks	.05	.02	.01
☐ 249	Sarunas Marciulionis	.05	.02	.01
☐ 250	Danny Ferry	.05	.02	.01
☐ 251	Loy Vaught	.10	.05	.01
☐ 252	Dee Brown	.05	.02	.01
☐ 253	Alvin Robertson	.05	.02	.01
☐ 254	Charles Smith	.05	.02	.01
☐ 255	Dikembe Mutombo	.30	.14	.04
☐ 256	Greg Kite	.05	.02	.01
☐ 257	Ed Pinckney	.05	.02	.01
☐ 258	Ron Harper	.05	.02	.01
☐ 259	Elliot Perry	.05	.02	.01
☐ 260	Rafael Addison	.05	.02	.01
☐ 261	Tim Hardaway	.15	.07	.02
☐ 262	Randy Brown	.05	.02	.01
☐ 263	Isiah Thomas	.20	.09	.03
☐ 264	Victor Alexander	.05	.02	.01
☐ 265	Wayman Tisdale	.05	.02	.01
☐ 266	Harvey Grant	.05	.02	.01
☐ 267	Mike Iuzzolino	.05	.02	.01
☐ 268	Joe Dumars	.15	.07	.02
☐ 269	Xavier McDaniel	.05	.02	.01
☐ 270	Jeff Sanders	.05	.02	.01
☐ 271	Danny Manning	.10	.05	.01
☐ 272	Jayson Williams	.05	.02	.01
☐ 273	Ricky Pierce	.05	.02	.01
☐ 274	Will Perdue	.05	.02	.01
☐ 275	Dana Barros	.05	.02	.01
☐ 276	Randy Breuer	.05	.02	.01
☐ 277	Manute Bol	.05	.02	.01
☐ 278	Negele Knight	.05	.02	.01
☐ 279	Rodney McCray	.05	.02	.01
☐ 280	Greg Sutton	.05	.02	.01
☐ 281	Larry Nance	.05	.02	.01
☐ 282	John Starks	.10	.05	.01
☐ 283	Pete Chilcutt	.05	.02	.01
☐ 284	Kenny Gattison	.05	.02	.01
☐ 285	Stacey King	.05	.02	.01
☐ 286	Bernard King	.15	.07	.02
☐ 287	Larry Johnson	.60	.25	.07
☐ 288	John Williams	.05	.02	.01
☐ 289	Dell Curry	.05	.02	.01
☐ 290	Orlando Woolridge	.05	.02	.01
☐ 291	Nate McMillan	.05	.02	.01
☐ 292	Terry Mills	.05	.02	.01
☐ 293	Sherman Douglas	.05	.02	.01
☐ 294	Charles Shackleford	.05	.02	.01
☐ 295	Ken Norman	.05	.02	.01
☐ 296	LaSalle Thompson	.05	.02	.01
☐ 297	Chris Mullin	.10	.05	.01
☐ 298	Eddie Johnson	.05	.02	.01
☐ 299	Armon Gilliam	.05	.02	.01
☐ 300	Michael Cage	.05	.02	.01
☐ 301	Moses Malone	.20	.09	.03
☐ 302	Charles Oakley	.10	.05	.01
☐ 303	David Wingate	.05	.02	.01
☐ 304	Steve Kerr	.05	.02	.01
☐ 305	Tyrone Hill	.05	.02	.01
☐ 306	Mark West	.05	.02	.01
☐ 307	Fat Lever	.05	.02	.01
☐ 308	J.R. Reid	.05	.02	.01
☐ 309	Ed Nealy	.05	.02	.01
☐ 310	Michael Jordan CL	.25	.11	.03
☐ 311	Alaa Abdelnaby	.05	.02	.01
☐ 312	Stacey Augmon	.10	.05	.01
☐ 313	Anthony Avent	.05	.02	.01
☐ 314	Walter Bond	.05	.02	.01
☐ 315	Byron Houston	.05	.02	.01
☐ 316	Rick Mahorn	.05	.02	.01
☐ 317	Sam Mitchell	.05	.02	.01
☐ 318	Mookie Blaylock	.10	.05	.01
☐ 319	Lance Blanks	.05	.02	.01
☐ 320	John Williams	.05	.02	.01
☐ 321	Rolando Blackman	.05	.02	.01
☐ 322	Danny Ainge	.15	.07	.02
☐ 323	Gerald Glass	.05	.02	.01
☐ 324	Robert Pack	.05	.02	.01
☐ 325	Oliver Miller	.25	.11	.03
☐ 326	Charles Smith	.05	.02	.01
☐ 327	Duane Ferrell	.05	.02	.01
☐ 328	Pooh Richardson	.05	.02	.01
☐ 329	Scott Brooks	.05	.02	.01
☐ 330	Walt Williams	.60	.25	.07
☐ 331	Andrew Lang	.05	.02	.01
☐ 332	Eric Murdock	.05	.02	.01
☐ 333	Vinny Del Negro	.05	.02	.01
☐ 334	Charles Barkley	.50	.23	.06
☐ 335	James Edwards	.05	.02	.01
☐ 336	Xavier McDaniel	.05	.02	.01
☐ 337	Paul Graham	.05	.02	.01
☐ 338	David Wingate	.05	.02	.01
☐ 339	Richard Dumas	.05	.02	.01
☐ 340	Jay Humphries	.05	.02	.01
☐ 341	Mark Jackson	.05	.02	.01
☐ 342	John Salley	.05	.02	.01
☐ 343	Jon Koncak	.05	.02	.01
☐ 344	Rodney McCray	.05	.02	.01
☐ 345	Chuck Person	.05	.02	.01
☐ 346	Mario Elie	.05	.02	.01
☐ 347	Frank Johnson	.05	.02	.01
☐ 348	Rumeal Robinson	.05	.02	.01
☐ 349	Terry Mills	.05	.02	.01
☐ 350	Kevin Willis TFC	.05	.02	.01
☐ 351	Dee Brown TFC	.05	.02	.01
☐ 352	Muggsy Bogues TFC	.10	.05	.01
☐ 353	B.J. Armstrong TFC	.05	.02	.01
☐ 354	Larry Nance TFC	.05	.02	.01
☐ 355	Doug Smith TFC	.05	.02	.01
☐ 356	Robert Pack TFC	.05	.02	.01
☐ 357	Joe Dumars TFC	.10	.05	.01
☐ 358	Sarunas Marciulionis TFC	.05	.02	.01
☐ 359	Kenny Smith TFC	.05	.02	.01
☐ 360	Pooh Richardson TFC	.05	.02	.01
☐ 361	Mark Jackson TFC	.05	.02	.01
☐ 362	Sedale Threatt TFC	.05	.02	.01
☐ 363	Grant Long TFC	.05	.02	.01
☐ 364	Eric Murdock TFC	.05	.02	.01
☐ 365	Doug West TFC	.05	.02	.01
☐ 366	Kenny Anderson TFC	.10	.05	.01
☐ 367	Anthony Mason TFC	.10	.05	.01
☐ 368	Nick Anderson TFC	.10	.05	.01
☐ 369	Jeff Hornacek TFC	.05	.02	.01
☐ 370	Dan Majerle TFC	.10	.05	.01
☐ 371	Clifford Robinson TFC	.10	.05	.01
☐ 372	Lionel Simmons TFC	.05	.02	.01
☐ 373	Dale Ellis TFC	.05	.02	.01
☐ 374	Gary Payton TFC	.30	.14	.04
☐ 375	David Benoit TFC	.05	.02	.01
☐ 376	Harvey Grant TFC	.05	.02	.01
☐ 377	Buck Johnson	.05	.02	.01
☐ 378	Brian Howard	.05	.02	.01
☐ 379	Travis Mays	.05	.02	.01
☐ 380	Jud Buechler	.05	.02	.01
☐ 381	Matt Geiger	.05	.02	.01

☐ 382	Bob McCann	.05	.02	.01
☐ 383	Cedric Ceballos	.10	.05	.01
☐ 384	Rod Strickland	.05	.02	.01
☐ 385	Kiki Vandeweghe	.05	.02	.01
☐ 386	Latrell Sprewell	.75	.35	.09
☐ 387	Larry Krystkowiak	.05	.02	.01
☐ 388	Dale Ellis	.05	.02	.01
☐ 389	Trent Tucker	.05	.02	.01
☐ 390	Negele Knight	.05	.02	.01
☐ 391	Stanley Roberts	.05	.02	.01
☐ 392	Tony Campbell	.05	.02	.01
☐ 393	Tim Perry	.05	.02	.01
☐ 394	Doug Overton	.05	.02	.01
☐ 395	Dan Majerle	.10	.05	.01
☐ 396	Duane Cooper	.05	.02	.01
☐ 397	Kevin Willis	.05	.02	.01
☐ 398	Micheal Williams	.05	.02	.01
☐ 399	Avery Johnson	.10	.05	.01
☐ 400	Dominique Wilkins	.15	.07	.02
☐ 401	Chris Smith	.05	.02	.01
☐ 402	Blair Rasmussen	.05	.02	.01
☐ 403	Jeff Hornacek	.05	.02	.01
☐ 404	Blue Edwards	.05	.02	.01
☐ 405	Olden Polynice	.05	.02	.01
☐ 406	Jeff Grayer	.05	.02	.01
☐ 407	Tony Bennett	.05	.02	.01
☐ 408	Don MacLean	.05	.02	.01
☐ 409	Tom Chambers	.05	.02	.01
☐ 410	Keith Jennings	.05	.02	.01
☐ 411	Gerald Wilkins	.05	.02	.01
☐ 412	Kennard Winchester	.05	.02	.01
☐ 413	Doc Rivers	.05	.02	.01
☐ 414	Brent Price	.05	.02	.01
☐ 415	Mark West	.05	.02	.01
☐ 416	J.R. Reid	.05	.02	.01
☐ 417	Jon Barry	.05	.02	.01
☐ 418	Kevin Johnson	.15	.07	.02
☐ 419	Michael Jordan CL	.25	.11	.03
☐ 420	Michael Jordan CL	.25	.11	.03
☐ 421	Brad Daugherty CL	.05	.02	.01
	Mark Price			
	Larry Nance			
☐ 422	Scottie Pippen AS	.50	.23	.06
☐ 423	Larry Johnson AS	.30	.14	.04
☐ 424	Shaquille O'Neal AS	2.00	.90	.25
☐ 425	Michael Jordan AS	2.00	.90	.25
☐ 426	Isiah Thomas AS	.10	.05	.01
☐ 427	Brad Daugherty AS	.05	.02	.01
☐ 428	Joe Dumars AS	.10	.05	.01
☐ 429	Patrick Ewing AS	.15	.07	.02
☐ 430	Larry Nance AS	.05	.02	.01
☐ 431	Mark Price AS	.05	.02	.01
☐ 432	Detlef Schrempf AS	.05	.02	.01
☐ 433	Dominique Wilkins AS	.10	.05	.01
☐ 434	Karl Malone AS	.15	.07	.02
☐ 435	Charles Barkley AS	.25	.11	.03
☐ 436	David Robinson AS	.30	.14	.04
☐ 437	John Stockton AS	.15	.07	.02
☐ 438	Clyde Drexler AS	.15	.07	.02
☐ 439	Sean Elliott AS	.10	.05	.01
☐ 440	Tim Hardaway AS	.10	.05	.01
☐ 441	Shawn Kemp AS	.60	.25	.07
☐ 442	Dan Majerle AS	.05	.02	.01
☐ 443	Danny Manning AS	.05	.02	.01
☐ 444	Hakeem Olajuwon AS	.40	.18	.05
☐ 445	Terry Porter AS	.05	.02	.01
☐ 446	Harold Miner FACE	.05	.02	.01
☐ 447	David Benoit FACE	.05	.02	.01
☐ 448	Cedric Ceballos FACE	.05	.02	.01
☐ 449	Chris Jackson FACE	.10	.05	.01
☐ 450	Tim Perry FACE	.05	.02	.01

☐ 451	Kenny Smith FACE	.05	.02	.01
☐ 452	Clarence Weatherspoon	.15	.07	.02
	FACE			
☐ 453A	Michael Jordan	25.00	11.00	3.10
	FACE ERR (Slam Dunk Champ			
	in 1985 and 1990)			
☐ 453B	Michael Jordan	2.00	.90	.25
	FACE COR (Slam Dunk Champ			
	in 1987 and 1988)			
☐ 454A	Dominique Wilkins	3.00	1.35	.35
	FACE ERR (Slam Dunk Champ			
	in 1987 and 1988)			
☐ 454B	Dominique Wilkins	.15	.07	.02
	FACE COR (Slam Dunk Champ			
	in 1985 and 1990)			
☐ 455	Anthony Peeler	.05	.02	.01
	Duane Cooper CL			
☐ 456	Adam Keefe TP	.15	.07	.02
☐ 457	Alonzo Mourning TP	.50	.23	.06
☐ 458	Jim Jackson TP	.60	.25	.07
☐ 459	Sean Rooks TP	.05	.02	.01
☐ 460	LaPhonso Ellis TP	.10	.05	.01
☐ 461	Bryant Stith TP	.05	.02	.01
☐ 462	Byron Houston TP	.05	.02	.01
☐ 463	Latrell Sprewell TP	.25	.11	.03
☐ 464	Robert Horry TP	.20	.09	.03
☐ 465	Malik Sealy TP	.05	.02	.01
☐ 466	Doug Christie TP	.10	.05	.01
☐ 467	Duane Cooper TP	.05	.02	.01
☐ 468	Anthony Peeler TP	.05	.02	.01
☐ 469	Harold Miner TP	.05	.02	.01
☐ 470	Todd Day TP	.10	.05	.01
☐ 471	Lee Mayberry TP	.05	.02	.01
☐ 472	Christian Laettner TP	.20	.09	.03
☐ 473	Hubert Davis TP	.10	.05	.01
☐ 474	Shaquille O'Neal TP	2.00	.90	.25
☐ 475	Clarence Weatherspoon TP	.15	.07	.02
☐ 476	Richard Dumas TP	.05	.02	.01
☐ 477	Oliver Miller TP	.05	.02	.01
☐ 478	Tracy Murray TP	.05	.02	.01
☐ 479	Walt Williams TP	.15	.07	.02
☐ 480	Lloyd Daniels TP	.05	.02	.01
☐ 481	Tom Gugliotta TP	.15	.07	.02
☐ 482	Brent Price TP	.05	.02	.01
☐ 483	Mark Aguirre GF	.10	.05	.01
☐ 484	Frank Brickowski GF	.05	.02	.01
☐ 485	Derrick Coleman GF	.05	.02	.01
☐ 486	Clyde Drexler GF	.15	.07	.02
☐ 487	Harvey Grant GF	.05	.02	.01
☐ 488	Michael Jordan GF	2.00	.90	.25
☐ 489	Karl Malone GF	.15	.07	.02
☐ 490	Xavier McDaniel GF	.05	.02	.01
☐ 491	Drazen Petrovic GF	.10	.05	.01
☐ 492	John Starks GF	.05	.02	.01
☐ 493	Robert Parish GF	.10	.05	.01
☐ 494	Christian Laettner GF	.20	.09	.03
☐ 495	Ron Harper GF	.05	.02	.01
☐ 496	David Robinson GF	.30	.14	.04
☐ 497	John Salley GF	.05	.02	.01
☐ 498	Brad Daugherty ST	.05	.02	.01
	Mark Price			
☐ 499	Dikembe Mutombo ST	.10	.05	.01
	Chris Jackson			
☐ 500	Isiah Thomas ST	.10	.05	.01
	Joe Dumars			
☐ 501	Hakeem Olajuwon ST	.10	.05	.01
	Otis Thorpe ST			
☐ 502	Derrick Coleman ST	.05	.02	.01
	Drazen Petrovic			
☐ 503	Terry Porter ST	.10	.05	.01
	Clyde Drexler			

		MINT	NRMT	EXC
☐ 504	Lionel Simmons ST	.05	.02	.01
	Mitch Richmond			
☐ 505	Sean Elliott ST	.10	.05	.01
	Sean Elliott			
☐ 506	Michael Jordan FAN	2.00	.90	.25
☐ 507	Larry Bird FAN	.60	.25	.07
☐ 508	Karl Malone FAN	.15	.07	.02
☐ 509	Dikembe Mutombo FAN	.15	.07	.02
☐ 510	Larry Bird FAN	1.00	.45	.12
	Michael Jordan			
☐ SP1	Larry Bird	3.00	1.35	.35
	Magic Johnson			
	Retirement			
☐ SP2	20,000 Points	8.00	3.60	1.00
	Dominique Wilkins			
	Nov. 6, 1992			
	Michael Jordan			
	Jan. 8, 1993			

1992-93 Upper Deck All-Division

Inserted one per second series red or gray jumbo pack, this 20-card standard-size set consists of Upper Deck's selection of the top five players in each of the NBA's four divisions. There is a special logo representing each division. The cards are arranged according to division as follows: Atlantic (1-5), Central (6-10), Midwest (11-15), and Pacific (16-20). The cards are numbered with an "AD" prefix. The fronts feature full-bleed, color, action player photos. A black and team color-coded bar outlined with gold foil carries the player's name and position. These cards can be distinguished by an All-Division Team icon in the lower left corner above the player's name. The backs display career highlights against a light blue panel. A U.S. map shows the player's division.

	MINT	NRMT	EXC
COMPLETE SET (20)	20.00	9.00	2.50
COMMON CARD (AD1-AD20)	.25	.11	.03
☐ AD1 Shaquille O'Neal	10.00	4.50	1.25
☐ AD2 Derrick Coleman	.25	.11	.03
☐ AD3 Glen Rice	.50	.23	.06
☐ AD4 Reggie Lewis	.50	.23	.06
☐ AD5 Kenny Anderson	.50	.23	.06
☐ AD6 Brad Daugherty	.25	.11	.03
☐ AD7 Dominique Wilkins	.50	.23	.06
☐ AD8 Larry Johnson	1.00	.45	.12
☐ AD9 Michael Jordan	10.00	4.50	1.25
☐ AD10 Mark Price	.25	.11	.03
☐ AD11 David Robinson	1.50	.70	.19
☐ AD12 Karl Malone	.75	.35	.09
☐ AD13 Sean Elliott	.50	.23	.06
☐ AD14 John Stockton	.75	.35	.09
☐ AD15 Derek Harper	.25	.11	.03
☐ AD16 Kevin Duckworth	.25	.11	.03
☐ AD17 Chris Mullin	.50	.23	.06
☐ AD18 Charles Barkley	1.25	.55	.16
☐ AD19 Tim Hardaway	.50	.23	.06
☐ AD20 Clyde Drexler	1.00	.45	.12

1992-93 Upper Deck All-NBA

This ten-card standard-size set featuring the 1991-92 All-NBA team was issued one per 27-card low series Locker pack. Each plastic locker box contained four specially wrapped. The fronts feature full-bleed color action player photos with black bottom borders. The player's name is foil-stamped in the border, and the words "All-NBA Team" are foil-stamped at the top. Gold and silver foil stamping are used to designate the First (1-5) and Second Teams (6-10) respectively. The backs carry a close-up player photo and career summary. The cards are numbered on the back with an "AN" prefix.

	MINT	NRMT	EXC
COMPLETE SET (10)	75.00	34.00	9.50
COMMON CARD (AN1-AN10)	2.00	.90	.25
☐ AN1 Michael Jordan	50.00	22.00	6.25
☐ AN2 Clyde Drexler	5.00	2.20	.60
☐ AN3 David Robinson	8.00	3.60	1.00
☐ AN4 Karl Malone	4.00	1.80	.50
☐ AN5 Chris Mullin	2.00	.90	.25
☐ AN6 John Stockton	4.00	1.80	.50
☐ AN7 Tim Hardaway	2.00	.90	.25
☐ AN8 Patrick Ewing	4.00	1.80	.50
☐ AN9 Scottie Pippen	12.00	5.50	1.50
☐ AN10 Charles Barkley	6.00	2.70	.75

1992-93 Upper Deck All-Rookies

Randomly inserted in low series 15-card retail foil packs at a reported rate of one

card for every nine packs, this ten-card standard-size insert set features the top first-year players of the 1991-92 season. Card numbers 1-5 present the first team and card numbers 6-10 the second team. The cards are numbered with an "AR" prefix. The fronts feature full-bleed, color, action player photos. A gold and red bottom border design carries the player's name, position, the number team (first or second), and an NBA All-Rookie Team icon. The backs carry player profiles.

	MINT	NRMT	EXC
COMPLETE SET (10)	10.00	4.50	1.25
COMMON CARD (AR1-AR10)	.50	.23	.06
☐ AR1 Larry Johnson	4.00	1.80	.50
☐ AR2 Dikembe Mutombo	2.00	.90	.25
☐ AR3 Billy Owens	1.00	.45	.12
☐ AR4 Steve Smith	1.50	.70	.19
☐ AR5 Stacey Augmon	.75	.35	.09
☐ AR6 Rick Fox	.50	.23	.06
☐ AR7 Terrell Brandon	1.50	.70	.19
☐ AR8 Larry Stewart	.50	.23	.06
☐ AR9 Stanley Roberts	.50	.23	.06
☐ AR10 Mark Macon	.50	.23	.06

1992-93 Upper Deck Award Winner Holograms

The 1992-93 Upper Deck Award Winner Holograms set features nine holograms depicting league leaders in various statistical categories. The set also honors 1991-92 award winners such as top Sixth Man, Rookie of the Year, Defensive Player of the Year and Most Valuable Player. Card numbers 1-6 were randomly inserted in all forms of low series packs while card numbers 7-9 were included in all forms of high series packs. The card numbers have an "AW" prefix. The fronts feature holographic cutout images of the player against a game-action photo of the player. The player's name and award are displayed at the bottom. The backs carry vertical, color player photos. A light blue plaque-style panel contains information about the player and the award won.

	MINT	NRMT	EXC
COMPLETE SET (9)	35.00	16.00	4.40
COMPLETE LO SERIES (6)	18.00	8.00	2.20
COMPLETE HI SERIES (3)	20.00	9.00	2.50
COMMON CARD (AW1-AW9)	.50	.23	.06
☐ AW1 Michael Jordan Scoring	15.00	6.75	1.85
☐ AW2 John Stockton Steals	1.00	.45	.12
☐ AW3 Dennis Rodman Rebounds	4.00	1.80	.50
☐ AW4 Detlef Schrempf Sixth Man	.50	.23	.06
☐ AW5 Larry Johnson Rookie of the Year	1.25	.55	.16
☐ AW6 David Robinson Blocked Shots	2.00	.90	.25
☐ AW7 David Robinson Def. Player of Year	2.00	.90	.25
☐ AW8 John Stockton Assists	1.00	.45	.12
☐ AW9 Michael Jordan Most Valuable Player	15.00	6.75	1.85

1992-93 Upper Deck Larry Bird Heroes

Randomly inserted into all forms of high series packs, this ten-card standard-size set chronicles the career of Larry Bird from his college days at Indiana State University to pro stardom with the Boston Celtics. The color action player photos on the fronts are bordered on the left and bottom by black borders that carry the card subtitle and "Basketball Heroes, Larry Bird" respectively. On a background shading from white to green, brief summaries of Bird's career are *presented on a center panel. The cards are numbered on the back in continuation of the Upper Deck Basketball Heroes.*

	MINT	NRMT	EXC
COMPLETE SET (10)	10.00	4.50	1.25
COMMON BIRD (19-27)	1.00	.45	.12
☐ 19 Larry Bird 1979 College Player of the Year	1.00	.45	.12
☐ 20 Larry Bird 1979-80 Rookie of the Year	1.00	.45	.12
☐ 21 Larry Bird 1980-92 12-Time NBA All-Star	1.00	.45	.12
☐ 22 Larry Bird 1981-86 Three NBA Championships	1.00	.45	.12
☐ 23 Larry Bird 1984-86 3-Time NBA MVP	1.00	.45	.12
☐ 24 Larry Bird 1986-88 3-Point King	1.00	.45	.12
☐ 25 Larry Bird 1990 20,000 Points Larry Legend	1.00	.45	.12
☐ 26 Larry Bird Larry Legend	1.00	.45	.12
☐ 27 Larry Bird (Portrait by Alan Studt)	1.00	.45	.12
☐ NNO Larry Bird Title/Header Card	2.00	.90	.25

1992-93 Upper Deck Wilt Chamberlain Heroes

Randomly inserted in all types of low series packs, this ten-card standard-size set honors Wilt Chamberlain by highlighting various points in his career. Circular photos on the fronts depict Wilt from college, to the Globetrotter's to pro basketball. Information on the back corresponds to the portion of his career that is represented on front. The set is numbered in continuation of Upper Deck's Hero series.

	MINT	NRMT	EXC
COMPLETE SET (10)	5.00	2.20	.60
COMMON CHAMBERLAIN (10-18)	.50	.23	.06

☐ 10	1956-58 College Star	.50	.23	.06
☐ 11	1958-59 Harlem Globetrotter	.50	.23	.06
☐ 12	1960 NBA ROY	.50	.23	.06
☐ 13	1962 100-Point Game	.50	.23	.06
☐ 14	1960-68 Four-time NBA MVP	.50	.23	.06
☐ 15	1960-66 Seven consecutive scoring titles	.50	.23	.06
☐ 16	1971-72 30,000-Point Plateau	.50	.23	.06
☐ 17	1978 Basketball HOF	.50	.23	.06
☐ 18	Basketball Heroes CL	.50	.23	.06
☐ NNO	Basketball Heroes (Header card)	1.00	.45	.12

1992-93 Upper Deck Wilt Chamberlain Box Bottom

Measuring approximately 5" by 7", this box bottom displays a color painting by artist Alan Studt. Four different images of Chamberlain are presented, each showing Wilt at a different stage of his career according to uniform (Kansas, Harlem Globetrotters, Philadelphia 76ers, and Los Angeles Lakers). The back is blank. The box bottom is unnumbered.

	MINT	NRMT	EXC
COMPLETE SET (1)	.75	.35	.09
COMMON CARD	.75	.35	.09
☐ NNO Wilt Chamberlain	.75	.35	.09

1992-93 Upper Deck 15000 Point Club

Randomly inserted in 15-card high series hobby packs at a reported rate of one card per nine packs, this 20-card standard-size set spotlights then-active NBA players who had scored more than 15,000 points in their career. The fronts feature full-bleed color action player photos accented at the top and bottom by team color-coded stripes carrying the phrase "15,000 Point Club" and the player's name respectively. A gold 15,000-Point club logo at the lower left corner carries the season the player joined this

elite club. The backs display a small player photo and year-by-year scoring totals. The cards are numbered with an "PC" prefix.

	MINT	NRMT	EXC
COMPLETE SET (20)	70.00	32.00	8.75
COMMON CARD (PC1-PC20)	1.00	.45	.12
☐ PC1 Dominique Wilkins	2.00	.90	.25
☐ PC2 Kevin McHale	2.00	.90	.25
☐ PC3 Robert Parish	2.00	.90	.25
☐ PC4 Michael Jordan	50.00	22.00	6.25
☐ PC5 Isiah Thomas	2.50	1.10	.30
☐ PC6 Mark Aguirre	1.50	.70	.19
☐ PC7 Kiki Vandeweghe	1.00	.45	.12
☐ PC8 James Worthy	2.00	.90	.25
☐ PC9 Rolando Blackman	1.00	.45	.12
☐ PC10 Moses Malone	2.50	1.10	.30
☐ PC11 Charles Barkley	6.00	2.70	.75
☐ PC12 Tom Chambers	1.00	.45	.12
☐ PC13 Clyde Drexler	5.00	2.20	.60
☐ PC14 Terry Cummings	1.00	.45	.12
☐ PC15 Eddie Johnson	1.00	.45	.12
☐ PC16 Karl Malone	4.00	1.80	.50
☐ PC17 Bernard King	2.00	.90	.25
☐ PC18 Larry Nance	1.00	.45	.12
☐ PC19 Jeff Malone	1.00	.45	.12
☐ PC20 Hakeem Olajuwon	10.00	4.50	1.25

1992-93 Upper Deck Foreign Exchange

Inserted one card per pack in second series 4-pack locker boxes, this ten-card standard-size set showcases foreign born players who are stars in the NBA. Each card uses the colors of the flag from the player's homeland as well as a "Foreign Exchange" logo. The cards are numbered with an "FE" prefix. The fronts carry full-bleed, color, action player photos. The player's name, position, and place of birth appear in border stripes at the bottom. The backs display either an action or close-up player photo on a pale beige panel along with a player profile. A small representation of the player's home flag appears at the lower right corner of the picture. The set is sequenced in alphabetical order.

	MINT	NRMT	EXC
COMPLETE SET (10)	20.00	9.00	2.50
COMMON CARD (FE1-FE10)	1.00	.45	.12
☐ FE1 Manute Bol	1.00	.45	.12
☐ FE2 Vlade Divac	2.00	.90	.25
☐ FE3 Patrick Ewing	4.00	1.80	.50
☐ FE4 Sarunas Marciulionis	1.00	.45	.12
☐ FE5 Dikembe Mutombo	2.50	1.10	.30
☐ FE6 Hakeem Olajuwon	10.00	4.50	1.25
☐ FE7 Drazen Petrovic	1.50	.70	.19
☐ FE8 Detlef Schrempf	1.50	.70	.19
☐ FE9 Rik Smits	2.00	.90	.25
☐ FE10 Dominique Wilkins	2.00	.90	.25

1992-93 Upper Deck Rookie Standouts

Randomly inserted in high series retail and high series red jumbo packs at a reported rate of one card per nine packs, this 20-card standard-size set honors top rookies who made the most impact during the 1992-93 NBA season. The cards are numbered on the back with an "RS" prefix. The fronts feature full-bleed, color, action player photos. The player's name and position appear in a teal stripe across the bottom. A "Rookie Standouts" icon overlaps the stripe and the picture at the lower right corner. The backs have a vertical action photo and career highlights within a gold box. A red banner over a gold basketball icon accent the top of the box.

	MINT	NRMT	EXC
COMPLETE SET (20)	25.00	11.00	3.10
COMMON CARD (RS1-RS20)	.25	.11	.03
☐ RS1 Adam Keefe	.25	.11	.03
☐ RS2 Alonzo Mourning	4.00	1.80	.50
☐ RS3 Sean Rooks	.25	.11	.03

☐ RS4	LaPhonso Ellis	.25	.11	.03
☐ RS5	Latrell Sprewell	2.00	.90	.25
☐ RS6	Robert Horry	1.50	.70	.19
☐ RS7	Malik Sealy	.50	.23	.06
☐ RS8	Anthony Peeler	.25	.11	.03
☐ RS9	Harold Miner	.25	.11	.03
☐ RS10	Anthony Avent	.25	.11	.03
☐ RS11	Todd Day	.25	.11	.03
☐ RS12	Lee Mayberry	.25	.11	.03
☐ RS13	Christian Laettner	1.25	.55	.16
☐ RS14	Hubert Davis	.50	.23	.06
☐ RS15	Shaquille O'Neal	15.00	6.75	1.85
☐ RS16	Clarence Weatherspoon	1.25	.55	.16
☐ RS17	Richard Dumas	.25	.11	.03
☐ RS18	Walt Williams	1.25	.55	.16
☐ RS19	Lloyd Daniels	.25	.11	.03
☐ RS20	Tom Gugliotta	1.25	.55	.16

☐ TM17	Pooh Richardson	.50	.23	.06
☐ TM18	Derrick Coleman	.50	.23	.06
☐ TM19	Patrick Ewing	2.50	1.10	.30
☐ TM20	Scott Skiles	.50	.23	.06
☐ TM21	Hersey Hawkins	1.00	.45	.12
☐ TM22	Kevin Johnson	1.50	.70	.19
☐ TM23	Clyde Drexler	3.00	1.35	.35
☐ TM24	Mitch Richmond	2.00	.90	.25
☐ TM25	David Robinson	5.00	2.20	.60
☐ TM26	Ricky Pierce	.50	.23	.06
☐ TM27	John Stockton	2.50	1.10	.30
☐ TM28	Pervis Ellison	.50	.23	.06

1992-93 Upper Deck Team MVPs

This 28-card standard-size set honors a top player from each NBA team. One "Team MVP" card was inserted into each 1992-93 Upper Deck low series 27-card jumbo pack. Card fronts feature a photo that takes up most of the front. The only other feature on front is the player's name within a bottom border. Backs contain a photo with highlights. These cards are numbered on the back with a "TM" prefix.

	MINT	NRMT	EXC
COMPLETE SET (28)	75.00	34.00	9.50
COMMON CARD (TM1-TM28)	.50	.23	.06

☐ TM1	Michael Jordan CL	30.00	13.50	3.70
☐ TM2	Dominique Wilkins	1.50	.70	.19
☐ TM3	Reggie Lewis	1.00	.45	.12
☐ TM4	Kendall Gill	.50	.23	.06
☐ TM5	Michael Jordan	30.00	13.50	3.70
☐ TM6	Brad Daugherty	.50	.23	.06
☐ TM7	Derek Harper	.50	.23	.06
☐ TM8	Dikembe Mutombo	1.50	.70	.19
☐ TM9	Isiah Thomas	1.50	.70	.19
☐ TM10	Chris Mullin	1.00	.45	.12
☐ TM11	Hakeem Olajuwon	6.00	2.70	.75
☐ TM12	Reggie Miller	3.00	1.35	.35
☐ TM13	Ron Harper	.50	.23	.06
☐ TM14	James Worthy	1.50	.70	.19
☐ TM15	Rony Seikaly	.50	.23	.06
☐ TM16	Alvin Robertson	.50	.23	.06

1992-93 Upper Deck Jerry West Selects

Randomly inserted in 15-card low series hobby packs at a reported rate of one card per nine packs, this 20-card standard-size set pays tribute to Jerry West's selection of NBA players who are the most dominant (or projected to be) in ten different basketball skills. The cards feature color action player photos bordered on the right edge by a white stripe containing the player's name. Two stripes border the bottom of the cards, a black stripe containing a gold foil facsimile autograph of Jerry West and the word "Select," and a gradated team-colored stripe. This second stripe contains the player's specific achievement. The backs show a smaller color action shot of the player above a pale gray panel containing comments by West. The right edge of the card has a 1/2" white border containing the player's name. A small cut-out action image of Jerry West appears at the lower right corner. Card numbers 1-10 feature his present selections for best in ten different categories while card numbers 11-20 are his future selections. The cards are numbered on the back with a "JW" prefix. The set includes four cards of Michael Jordan.

	MINT	NRMT	EXC
COMPLETE SET (20)	80.00	36.00	10.00
COMMON CARD (JW1-JW20)	.75	.35	.09

☐ JW1	Michael Jordan Best Shooter	20.00	9.00	2.50
☐ JW2	Dennis Rodman Best Rebounder	8.00	3.60	1.00

		MINT	NRMT	EXC
☐ JW3	David Robinson .... Best Shot Blocker	4.00	1.80	.50
☐ JW4	Michael Jordan .... Best Defender	20.00	9.00	2.50
☐ JW5	Magic Johnson .... Best Point Guard	3.00	1.35	.35
☐ JW6	Detlef Schrempf ..... Best Sixth Man	1.50	.70	.19
☐ JW7	Magic Johnson .... Most Inspirational Player	3.00	1.35	.35
☐ JW8	Michael Jordan .... Best All-Around Player	20.00	9.00	2.50
☐ JW9	Michael Jordan .... Best Clutch Player	20.00	9.00	2.50
☐ JW10	Magic Johnson .... Best Court Leader	3.00	1.35	.35
☐ JW11	Glen Rice .... Best Shooter	2.00	.90	.25
☐ JW12	Dikembe Mutombo . Best Rebounder	1.25	.55	.16
☐ JW13	Dikembe Mutombo . Best Shot Blocker	1.25	.55	.16
☐ JW14	Stacey Augmon .... Best Defender	.75	.35	.09
☐ JW15	Tim Hardaway .... Best Point Guard	1.50	.70	.19
☐ JW16	Shawn Kemp .... Best Sixth Man	8.00	3.60	1.00
☐ JW17	Danny Manning ...... Most Inspirational Player	1.50	.70	.19
☐ JW18	Larry Johnson .... Best All-Around Player	2.50	1.10	.30
☐ JW19	Reggie Lewis .... Best Clutch Player	1.50	.70	.19
☐ JW20	Tim Hardaway .... Best Court Leader	1.50	.70	.19

1993-94 Upper Deck

This 510-card standard-size UV-coated set was issued in two series of 255. The cards were issued in 12-card hobby and retail packs (36 per box), 22-card green and blue retail jumbo packs (first series only), 22-card red and purple retail jumbo packs (second series only) and 22-card hobby locker packs for both series. Card fronts feature glossy color player action photos on the fronts. The left and bottom borders (team colors) contain the team and player's name respectively. The backs feature another color action player photo at the top.

At bottom, player stats are shaded in team colors. Topical subsets featured are the following: Season Leaders (166-177), NBA Playoffs Highlights (178-197), NBA Finals Highlights (198-209), Schedules (210-236), Signature Moves (237-251), Executive Board (421-435), Breakaway Threats (436-455), Game Images (456-465), Skylights (467-480), Top Prospects (482-497) and McDonald's Open (498-507). The cards are numbered on the back. The SP3 card was inserted randomly in all forms of first series packaging with the SP4 in the second series. Both cards were inserted at a rate of 1 in 72 packs. Rookie Cards of note include Vin Baker, Anfernee Hardaway, Allan Houston, Toni Kukoc, Jamal Mashburn, Nick Van Exel and Chris Webber.

		MINT	NRMT	EXC
COMPLETE SET (510)		30.00	13.50	3.70
COMPLETE SERIES 1 (255)...		15.00	6.75	1.85
COMPLETE SERIES 2 (255)...		15.00	6.75	1.85
COMMON CARD (1-510)		.05	.02	.01
☐ 1	Muggsy Bogues	.10	.05	.01
☐ 2	Kenny Anderson	.15	.07	.02
☐ 3	Dell Curry.....................	.05	.02	.01
☐ 4	Charles Smith	.05	.02	.01
☐ 5	Chuck Person	.05	.02	.01
☐ 6	Chucky Brown................	.05	.02	.01
☐ 7	Kevin Johnson	.15	.07	.02
☐ 8	Winston Garland	.05	.02	.01
☐ 9	John Salley	.05	.02	.01
☐ 10	Dale Ellis	.05	.02	.01
☐ 11	Otis Thorpe	.10	.05	.01
☐ 12	John Stockton	.30	.14	.04
☐ 13	Kendall Gill	.05	.02	.01
☐ 14	Randy White	.05	.02	.01
☐ 15	Mark Jackson	.05	.02	.01
☐ 16	Vlade Divac	.15	.07	.02
☐ 17	Scott Skiles	.05	.02	.01
☐ 18	Xavier McDaniel	.05	.02	.01
☐ 19	Jeff Hornacek	.10	.05	.01
☐ 20	Stanley Roberts	.05	.02	.01
☐ 21	Harold Miner	.05	.02	.01
☐ 22	Terrell Brandon	.15	.07	.02
☐ 23	Michael Jordan	4.00	1.80	.50
☐ 24	Jim Jackson	.40	.18	.05
☐ 25	Keith Askins	.05	.02	.01
☐ 26	Corey Williams	.05	.02	.01
☐ 27	David Benoit	.05	.02	.01
☐ 28	Charles Oakley	.10	.05	.01
☐ 29	Michael Adams	.05	.02	.01
☐ 30	Clarence Weatherspoon.	.15	.07	.02
☐ 31	Jon Koncak	.05	.02	.01
☐ 32	Gerald Wilkins	.05	.02	.01
☐ 33	Anthony Bowie	.05	.02	.01
☐ 34	Willie Burton	.05	.02	.01
☐ 35	Stacey Augmon	.10	.05	.01
☐ 36	Doc Rivers	.05	.02	.01
☐ 37	Luc Longley	.05	.02	.01
☐ 38	Dee Brown	.05	.02	.01
☐ 39	Litteral Green	.05	.02	.01
☐ 40	Dan Majerle	.10	.05	.01
☐ 41	Doug West.....................	.05	.02	.01
☐ 42	Joe Dumars	.15	.07	.02
☐ 43	Dennis Scott	.10	.05	.01
☐ 44	Mahmoud Abdul-Rauf.. (formerly Chris Jackson)	.10	.05	.01
☐ 45	Mark Eaton	.05	.02	.01

#	Player			
46	Danny Ferry	.05	.02	.01
47	Kenny Smith	.05	.02	.01
48	Ron Harper	.05	.02	.01
49	Adam Keefe	.05	.02	.01
50	David Robinson	.60	.25	.07
51	John Starks	.10	.05	.01
52	Jeff Malone	.05	.02	.01
53	Vern Fleming	.05	.02	.01
54	Olden Polynice	.05	.02	.01
55	Dikembe Mutombo	.15	.07	.02
56	Chris Morris	.05	.02	.01
57	Paul Graham	.05	.02	.01
58	Richard Dumas	.05	.02	.01
59	J.R. Reid	.05	.02	.01
60	Brad Daugherty	.05	.02	.01
61	Blue Edwards	.05	.02	.01
62	Mark Macon	.05	.02	.01
63	Latrell Sprewell	.25	.11	.03
64	Mitch Richmond	.25	.11	.03
65	David Wingate	.05	.02	.01
66	LaSalle Thompson	.05	.02	.01
67	Sedale Threatt	.05	.02	.01
68	Larry Krystkowiak	.05	.02	.01
69	John Paxson	.10	.05	.01
70	Frank Brickowski	.05	.02	.01
71	Duane Causwell	.05	.02	.01
72	Fred Roberts	.05	.02	.01
73	Rod Strickland	.05	.02	.01
74	Willie Anderson	.05	.02	.01
75	Thurl Bailey	.05	.02	.01
76	Ricky Pierce	.05	.02	.01
77	Todd Day	.05	.02	.01
78	Hot Rod Williams	.05	.02	.01
79	Danny Ainge	.15	.07	.02
80	Mark West	.05	.02	.01
81	Marcus Liberty	.05	.02	.01
82	Keith Jennings	.05	.02	.01
83	Derrick Coleman	.05	.02	.01
84	Larry Stewart	.05	.02	.01
85	Tracy Murray	.05	.02	.01
86	Robert Horry	.10	.05	.01
87	Derek Harper	.10	.05	.01
88	Scott Hastings	.05	.02	.01
89	Sam Perkins	.05	.02	.01
90	Clyde Drexler	.40	.18	.05
91	Brent Price	.05	.02	.01
92	Chris Mullin	.15	.07	.02
93	Rafael Addison	.05	.02	.01
94	Tyrone Corbin	.05	.02	.01
95	Sarunas Marciulionis	.05	.02	.01
96	Antoine Carr	.05	.02	.01
97	Tony Bennett	.05	.02	.01
98	Sam Mitchell	.05	.02	.01
99	Lionel Simmons	.05	.02	.01
100	Tim Perry	.05	.02	.01
101	Horace Grant	.15	.07	.02
102	Tom Hammonds	.05	.02	.01
103	Walter Bond	.05	.02	.01
104	Detlef Schrempf	.10	.05	.01
105	Terry Porter	.05	.02	.01
106	Dan Schayes	.05	.02	.01
107	Rumeal Robinson	.05	.02	.01
108	Gerald Glass	.05	.02	.01
109	Mike Gminski	.05	.02	.01
110	Terry Mills	.05	.02	.01
111	Loy Vaught	.10	.05	.01
112	Jim Les	.05	.02	.01
113	Byron Houston	.05	.02	.01
114	Randy Brown	.05	.02	.01
115	Anthony Avent	.05	.02	.01
116	Donald Hodge	.05	.02	.01
117	Kevin Willis	.05	.02	.01
118	Robert Pack	.05	.02	.01
119	Dale Davis	.05	.02	.01
120	Grant Long	.05	.02	.01
121	Anthony Bonner	.05	.02	.01
122	Chris Smith	.05	.02	.01
123	Elden Campbell	.10	.05	.01
124	Clifford Robinson	.15	.07	.02
125	Sherman Douglas	.05	.02	.01
126	Alvin Robertson	.05	.02	.01
127	Rolando Blackman	.05	.02	.01
128	Malik Sealy	.05	.02	.01
129	Ed Pinckney	.05	.02	.01
130	Anthony Peeler	.05	.02	.01
131	Scott Brooks	.05	.02	.01
132	Rik Smits	.15	.07	.02
133	Derrick McKey	.05	.02	.01
134	Alaa Abdelnaby	.05	.02	.01
135	Rex Chapman	.05	.02	.01
136	Tony Campbell	.05	.02	.01
137	John Williams	.05	.02	.01
138	Vincent Askew	.05	.02	.01
139	LaBradford Smith	.05	.02	.01
140	Vinny Del Negro	.05	.02	.01
141	Darrell Walker	.05	.02	.01
142	James Worthy	.15	.07	.02
143	Jeff Turner	.05	.02	.01
144	Duane Ferrell	.05	.02	.01
145	Larry Smith	.05	.02	.01
146	Eddie Johnson	.05	.02	.01
147	Chris Gatling	.05	.02	.01
148	Buck Williams	.10	.05	.01
149	Donald Royal	.05	.02	.01
150	Dino Radja	.40	.18	.05
151	Johnny Dawkins	.05	.02	.01
152	Tim Legler	.05	.02	.01
153	Bill Laimbeer	.10	.05	.01
154	Glen Rice	.15	.07	.02
155	Bill Cartwright	.05	.02	.01
156	Luther Wright	.05	.02	.01
157	Rex Walters	.05	.02	.01
158	Doug Edwards	.05	.02	.01
159	George Lynch	.05	.02	.01
160	Chris Mills	.50	.23	.06
161	Sam Cassell	.50	.23	.06
162	Nick Van Exel	1.00	.45	.12
163	Shawn Bradley	.40	.18	.05
164	Calbert Cheaney	.30	.14	.04
165	Corie Blount	.05	.02	.01
166	Michael Jordan SL Scoring	2.00	.90	.25
167	Dennis Rodman SL Rebounds	.60	.25	.07
168	John Stockton SL Assists	.15	.07	.02
169	B.J. Armstrong SL 3-pt. field goals	.05	.02	.01
170	Hakeem Olajuwon SL Blocked shots	.40	.18	.05
171	Michael Jordan SL Steals	2.00	.90	.25
172	Cedric Ceballos SL Field goal percentage	.05	.02	.01
173	Mark Price SL Free-throw percentage	.05	.02	.01
174	Charles Barkley SL MVP	.25	.11	.03
175	Clifford Robinson SL Sixth man	.05	.02	.01
176	Hakeem Olajuwon SL Defensive player	.40	.18	.05

☐ 177	Shaquille O'Neal SL ... ROY	1.00	.45	.12
☐ 178	Reggie Miller................. Charles Oakley PO	.10	.05	.01
☐ 179	Rick Fox..................... Kenny Gattison PO	.05	.02	.01
☐ 180	Michael Jordan .... Stackey Augmon PO	1.00	.45	.12
☐ 181	Brad Daugherty PO	.05	.02	.01
☐ 182	Oliver Miller .... Byron Scott PO	.05	.02	.01
☐ 183	David Robinson .... Sean Elliott PO	.15	.07	.02
☐ 184	Kenny Smith .... Mark Jackson PO	.05	.02	.01
☐ 185	Eddie Johnson PO	.05	.02	.01
☐ 186	Anthony Mason........... Patrick Ewing A Mourning PO	.15	.07	.02
☐ 187	Michael Jordan .... Gerald Wilkins PO	1.00	.45	.12
☐ 188	Oliver Miller PO...........	.05	.02	.01
☐ 189	Sam Perkins .... Hakeem Olajuwon PO	.15	.07	.02
☐ 190	Bill Cartwright PO	.05	.02	.01
☐ 191	Kevin Johnson PO	.10	.05	.01
☐ 192	Dan Majerle PO...........	.05	.02	.01
☐ 193	Michael Jordan PO.......	2.00	.90	.25
☐ 194	Larry Johnson .... Muggsy Bogues PO	.10	.05	.01
☐ 195	Reggie Miller PO.........	.15	.07	.02
☐ 196	John Starks................. Scottie Pippen PO	.15	.07	.02
☐ 197	Charles Barkley PO	.15	.07	.02
☐ 198	Michael Jordan FIN......	2.00	.90	.25
☐ 199	Scottie Pippen FIN......	.50	.23	.06
☐ 200	Kevin Johnson FIN......	.10	.05	.01
☐ 201	Michael Jordan FIN......	2.00	.90	.25
☐ 202	Richard Dumas FIN......	.05	.02	.01
☐ 203	Horace Grant FIN	.10	.05	.01
☐ 204	Michael Jordan FIN...... 1993 Finals MVP	2.00	.90	.25
☐ 205	Scottie Pippen FIN...... Charles Barkley	.25	.11	.03
☐ 206	John Paxson FIN......... Hits 3 for title	.10	.05	.01
☐ 207	B.J. Armstrong FIN...... Finals records	.05	.02	.01
☐ 208	1992-93 Bulls FIN....... Road to 1993 Finals	.05	.02	.01
☐ 209	1992-93 Suns FIN....... Road to 1993 Finals	.05	.02	.01
☐ 210	Atlanta Hawks Sked ...... Kevin Willis	.05	.02	.01
☐ 211	Boston Celtics Sked...... Brian Shaw	.05	.02	.01
☐ 212	Charlotte Hornets Sked	.05	.02	.01
☐ 213	Chicago Bulls Sked...... Michael Jordan	1.00	.45	.12
☐ 214	Cleveland Cavaliers ..... Sked (Mark Price)	.05	.02	.01
☐ 215	Dallas Mavericks Sked. (Jim Jackson Sean Rooks)	.15	.07	.02
☐ 216	Denver Nuggets Sked .. Dikembe Mutombo	.05	.02	.01
☐ 217	Detroit Pistons Sked .... Isiah Thomas Bill Laimbeer Terry Mills	.10	.05	.01
☐ 218	Golden State Warriors .	.05	.02	.01
	Sked			
☐ 219	Houston Rockets Sked. (Hakeem Olajuwon)	.20	.09	.03
☐ 220	Indiana Pacers Sked .... Rik Smits Detlef Schrempf	.05	.02	.01
☐ 221	L.A. Clippers Sked ...... Ron Harper Danny Manning Mark Jackson	.05	.02	.01
☐ 222	L.A. Lakers Sked...........	.05	.02	.01
☐ 223	Miami Heat Sked........... Steve Smith Harold Miner Rony Seikaly	.05	.02	.01
☐ 224	Milwaukee Bucks Sked	.05	.02	.01
☐ 225	Minnesota Timberwolves Sked	.05	.02	.01
☐ 226	New Jersey Nets Sked . Kenny Anderson	.05	.02	.01
☐ 227	New York Knicks Sked. Rolando Blackmon	.05	.02	.01
☐ 228	Orlando Magic Sked..... (Shaquille O'Neal)	.60	.25	.07
☐ 229	Philadelphia 76ers ...... Sked Hersey Hawkins Jeff Hornacek	.05	.02	.01
☐ 230	Phoenix Suns Sked....... (Charles Barkley)	.15	.07	.02
☐ 231	Portland Trail Blazers .. Sked Buck Williams Jerome Kersey Terry Porter)	.05	.02	.01
☐ 232	Sacramento Kings Sked	.05	.02	.01
☐ 233	San Antonio Spurs Sked David Robinson Avery Johnson Sean Elliott	.15	.07	.02
☐ 234	Seattle Supersonics Sked Gary Payton Shawn Kemp	.30	.14	.04
☐ 235	Utah Jazz Sked.............	.05	.02	.01
☐ 236	Washington Bullets ...... Sked Tom Gugliotta Michael Adams	.05	.02	.01
☐ 237	Michael Jordan SM......	2.00	.90	.25
☐ 238	Clyde Drexler SM	.15	.07	.02
☐ 239	Tim Hardaway SM	.05	.02	.01
☐ 240	Dominique Wilkins SM	.10	.05	.01
☐ 241	Brad Daugherty SM	.05	.02	.01
☐ 242	Chris Mullin SM...........	.05	.02	.01
☐ 243	Kenny Anderson SM	.05	.02	.01
☐ 244	Patrick Ewing SM	.15	.07	.02
☐ 245	Isiah Thomas SM..........	.10	.05	.01
☐ 246	Dikembe Mutombo SM	.05	.02	.01
☐ 247	Danny Manning SM	.05	.02	.01
☐ 248	David Robinson SM	.30	.14	.04
☐ 249	Karl Malone SM	.15	.07	.02
☐ 250	James Worthy SM	.10	.05	.01
☐ 251	Shawn Kemp SM	.50	.23	.06
☐ 252	Checklist 1-64.............	.05	.02	.01
☐ 253	Checklist 65-128..........	.05	.02	.01
☐ 254	Checklist 129-192........	.05	.02	.01
☐ 255	Checklist 193-255........	.05	.02	.01
☐ 256	Patrick Ewing	.30	.14	.04
☐ 257	B.J. Armstrong	.05	.02	.01
☐ 258	Oliver Miller	.05	.02	.01
☐ 259	Jud Buechler...............	.05	.02	.01

☐	260	Pooh Richardson	.05	.02	.01	☐	331	Greg Kite	.05	.02	.01
☐	261	Victor Alexander	.05	.02	.01	☐	332	Michael Cage	.05	.02	.01
☐	262	Kevin Gamble	.05	.02	.01	☐	333	Alonzo Mourning	.50	.23	.06
☐	263	Doug Smith	.05	.02	.01	☐	334	Acie Earl	.05	.02	.01
☐	264	Isiah Thomas	.20	.09	.03	☐	335	Terry Dehere	.10	.05	.01
☐	265	Doug Christie	.05	.02	.01	☐	336	Negele Knight	.05	.02	.01
☐	266	Mark Bryant	.05	.02	.01	☐	337	Gerald Madkins	.05	.02	.01
☐	267	Lloyd Daniels	.05	.02	.01	☐	338	Lindsey Hunter	.10	.05	.01
☐	268	Micheal Williams	.05	.02	.01	☐	339	Luther Wright	.05	.02	.01
☐	269	Nick Anderson	.15	.07	.02	☐	340	Mike Peplowski	.05	.02	.01
☐	270	Tom Gugliotta	.15	.07	.02	☐	341	Gerald Paddio	.20	.09	.03
☐	271	Kenny Gattison	.05	.02	.01	☐	342	Danny Manning	.10	.05	.01
☐	272	Vernon Maxwell	.05	.02	.01	☐	343	Chris Mills	.05	.02	.01
☐	273	Terry Cummings	.05	.02	.01	☐	344	Kevin Lynch	.05	.02	.01
☐	274	Karl Malone	.30	.14	.04	☐	345	Shawn Bradley	.15	.07	.02
☐	275	Rick Fox	.05	.02	.01	☐	346	Evers Burns	.05	.02	.01
☐	276	Matt Bullard	.05	.02	.01	☐	347	Rodney Rogers	.15	.07	.02
☐	277	Johnny Newman	.05	.02	.01	☐	348	Cedric Ceballos	.15	.07	.02
☐	278	Mark Price	.05	.02	.01	☐	349	Warren Kidd	.05	.02	.01
☐	279	Mookie Blaylock	.10	.05	.01	☐	350	Darnell Mee	.05	.02	.01
☐	280	Charles Barkley	.50	.23	.06	☐	351	Matt Geiger	.05	.02	.01
☐	281	Larry Nance	.05	.02	.01	☐	352	Jamal Mashburn	.75	.35	.09
☐	282	Walt Williams	.15	.07	.02	☐	353	Antonio Davis	.05	.02	.01
☐	283	Brian Shaw	.05	.02	.01	☐	354	Calbert Cheaney	.15	.07	.02
☐	284	Robert Parish	.15	.07	.02	☐	355	George Lynch	.05	.02	.01
☐	285	Pervis Ellison	.05	.02	.01	☐	356	Derrick McKey	.05	.02	.01
☐	286	Spud Webb	.10	.05	.01	☐	357	Jerry Reynolds	.05	.02	.01
☐	287	Hakeem Olajuwon	.75	.35	.09	☐	358	Don MacLean	.05	.02	.01
☐	288	Jerome Kersey	.05	.02	.01	☐	359	Scott Haskin	.05	.02	.01
☐	289	Carl Herrera	.05	.02	.01	☐	360	Malcolm Mackey	.05	.02	.01
☐	290	Dominique Wilkins	.15	.07	.02	☐	361	Isaiah Rider	.40	.18	.05
☐	291	Billy Owens	.05	.02	.01	☐	362	Detlef Schrempf	.10	.05	.01
☐	292	Greg Anthony	.05	.02	.01	☐	363	Josh Grant	.05	.02	.01
☐	293	Nate McMillan	.05	.02	.01	☐	364	Richard Petruska	.05	.02	.01
☐	294	Christian Laettner	.15	.07	.02	☐	365	Larry Johnson	.40	.18	.05
☐	295	Gary Payton	.50	.23	.06	☐	366	Felton Spencer	.05	.02	.01
☐	296	Steve Smith	.15	.07	.02	☐	367	Ken Norman	.05	.02	.01
☐	297	Anthony Mason	.10	.05	.01	☐	368	Anthony Cook	.05	.02	.01
☐	298	Sean Rooks	.05	.02	.01	☐	369	James Robinson	.10	.05	.01
☐	299	Toni Kukoc	.75	.35	.09	☐	370	Kevin Duckworth	.05	.02	.01
☐	300	Shaquille O'Neal	2.00	.90	.25	☐	371	Chris Whitney	.05	.02	.01
☐	301	Jay Humphries	.05	.02	.01	☐	372	Moses Malone	.20	.09	.03
☐	302	Sleepy Floyd	.05	.02	.01	☐	373	Nick Van Exel	.50	.23	.06
☐	303	Bimbo Coles	.05	.02	.01	☐	374	Scott Burrell	.15	.07	.02
☐	304	John Battle	.05	.02	.01	☐	375	Harvey Grant	.05	.02	.01
☐	305	Shawn Kemp	1.00	.45	.12	☐	376	Benoit Benjamin	.05	.02	.01
☐	306	Scott Williams	.05	.02	.01	☐	377	Henry James	.05	.02	.01
☐	307	Wayman Tisdale	.05	.02	.01	☐	378	Craig Ehlo	.05	.02	.01
☐	308	Rony Seikaly	.05	.02	.01	☐	379	Ennis Whatley	.05	.02	.01
☐	309	Reggie Miller	.40	.18	.05	☐	380	Sean Green	.05	.02	.01
☐	310	Scottie Pippen	1.00	.45	.12	☐	381	Eric Murdock	.05	.02	.01
☐	311	Chris Webber	1.25	.55	.16	☐	382	Anfernee Hardaway	6.00	2.70	.75
☐	312	Trevor Wilson	.05	.02	.01	☐	383	Gheorghe Muresan	.50	.23	.06
☐	313	Derek Strong	.05	.02	.01	☐	384	Kendall Gill	.05	.02	.01
☐	314	Bobby Hurley	.15	.07	.02	☐	385	David Wood	.05	.02	.01
☐	315	Herb Williams	.05	.02	.01	☐	386	Mario Elie	.05	.02	.01
☐	316	Rex Walters	.05	.02	.01	☐	387	Chris Corchiani	.05	.02	.01
☐	317	Doug Edwards	.05	.02	.01	☐	388	Greg Graham	.05	.02	.01
☐	318	Ken Williams	.05	.02	.01	☐	389	Hersey Hawkins	.05	.02	.01
☐	319	Jon Barry	.05	.02	.01	☐	390	Mark Aguirre	.10	.05	.01
☐	320	Joe Courtney	.05	.02	.01	☐	391	LaPhonso Ellis	.05	.02	.01
☐	321	Ervin Johnson	.10	.05	.01	☐	392	Anthony Bonner	.05	.02	.01
☐	322	Sam Cassell	.05	.02	.01	☐	393	Lucious Harris	.10	.05	.01
☐	323	Tim Hardaway	.15	.07	.02	☐	394	Andrew Lang	.05	.02	.01
☐	324	Ed Stokes	.05	.02	.01	☐	395	Chris Dudley	.05	.02	.01
☐	325	Steve Kerr	.10	.05	.01	☐	396	Dennis Rodman	1.25	.55	.16
☐	326	Doug Overton	.05	.02	.01	☐	397	Larry Krystkowiak	.05	.02	.01
☐	327	Reggie Williams	.05	.02	.01	☐	398	A.C. Green	.15	.07	.02
☐	328	Avery Johnson	.05	.02	.01	☐	399	Eddie Johnson	.05	.02	.01
☐	329	Stacey King	.05	.02	.01	☐	400	Kevin Edwards	.05	.02	.01
☐	330	Vin Baker	1.25	.55	.16	☐	401	Tyrone Hill	.05	.02	.01

☐ 402 Greg Anderson	.05	.02	.01
☐ 403 P.J. Brown	.05	.02	.01
☐ 404 Dana Barros	.05	.02	.01
☐ 405 Allan Houston	.60	.25	.07
☐ 406 Mike Brown	.05	.02	.01
☐ 407 Lee Mayberry	.05	.02	.01
☐ 408 Fat Lever	.05	.02	.01
☐ 409 Tony Smith	.05	.02	.01
☐ 410 Tom Chambers	.05	.02	.01
☐ 411 Manute Bol	.05	.02	.01
☐ 412 Joe Kleine	.05	.02	.01
☐ 413 Bryant Stith	.05	.02	.01
☐ 414 Eric Riley	.05	.02	.01
☐ 415 JoJo English	.05	.02	.01
☐ 416 Sean Elliott	.15	.07	.02
☐ 417 Sam Bowie	.05	.02	.01
☐ 418 Armon Gilliam	.05	.02	.01
☐ 419 Brian Williams	.05	.02	.01
☐ 420 Popeye Jones	.15	.07	.02
☐ 421 Dennis Rodman EB	.60	.25	.07
☐ 422 Karl Malone EB	.15	.07	.02
☐ 423 Tom Gugliotta EB	.05	.02	.01
☐ 424 Kevin Willis EB	.05	.02	.01
☐ 425 Hakeem Olajuwon EB	.40	.18	.05
☐ 426 Charles Oakley EB	.05	.02	.01
☐ 427 Clarence Weatherspoon EB	.05	.02	.01
☐ 428 Derrick Coleman EB	.05	.02	.01
☐ 429 Buck Williams EB	.05	.02	.01
☐ 430 Christian Laettner EB	.05	.02	.01
☐ 431 Dikembe Mutombo EB	.10	.05	.01
☐ 432 Rony Seikaly EB	.05	.02	.01
☐ 433 Brad Daugherty EB	.05	.02	.01
☐ 434 Horace Grant EB	.05	.02	.01
☐ 435 Larry Johnson EB	.10	.05	.01
☐ 436 Dee Brown EB	.05	.02	.01
☐ 437 Muggsy Bogues BT	.05	.02	.01
☐ 438 Michael Jordan BT	2.00	.90	.25
☐ 439 Tim Hardaway BT	.05	.02	.01
☐ 440 Micheal Williams BT	.05	.02	.01
☐ 441 Gary Payton BT	.25	.11	.03
☐ 442 Mookie Blaylock BT	.05	.02	.01
☐ 443 Doc Rivers BT	.05	.02	.01
☐ 444 Kenny Smith BT	.05	.02	.01
☐ 445 John Stockton BT	.15	.07	.02
☐ 446 Alvin Robertson BT	.05	.02	.01
☐ 447 Mark Jackson BT	.05	.02	.01
☐ 448 Kenny Anderson BT	.05	.02	.01
☐ 449 Scottie Pippen BT	.50	.23	.06
☐ 450 Isiah Thomas BT	.15	.07	.02
☐ 451 Mark Price BT	.05	.02	.01
☐ 452 Latrell Sprewell BT	.10	.05	.01
☐ 453 Sedale Threatt BT	.05	.02	.01
☐ 454 Nick Anderson BT	.05	.02	.01
☐ 455 Rod Strickland BT	.05	.02	.01
☐ 456 Oliver Miller GI	.05	.02	.01
☐ 457 James Worthy GI	.05	.02	.01
Vlade Divac GI			
☐ 458 Robert Horry GI	.05	.02	.01
☐ 459 Rockets Shoot-Around GI	.05	.02	.01
☐ 460 Sean Rooks	.10	.05	.01
Jim Jackson			
Tim Legler GI			
☐ 461 Mitch Richmond GI	.05	.02	.01
☐ 462 Chris Morris GI	.05	.02	.01
☐ 463 Mark Jackson	.05	.02	.01
Gary Grant GI			
☐ 464 David Robinson GI	.30	.14	.04
☐ 465 Danny Ainge GI	.05	.02	.01
☐ 466 Michael Jordan SL	2.00	.90	.25
☐ 467 Dominique Wilkins SL	.10	.05	.01
☐ 468 Alonzo Mourning SL	.25	.11	.03

☐ 469 Shaquille O'Neal SL	1.00	.45	.12
☐ 470 Tim Hardaway SL	.05	.02	.01
☐ 471 Patrick Ewing SL	.15	.07	.02
☐ 472 Kevin Johnson SL	.10	.05	.01
☐ 473 Clyde Drexler SL	.15	.07	.02
☐ 474 David Robinson SL	.30	.14	.04
☐ 475 Shawn Kemp SL	.50	.23	.06
☐ 476 Dee Brown SL	.05	.02	.01
☐ 477 Jim Jackson SL	.20	.09	.03
☐ 478 John Stockton SL	.15	.07	.02
☐ 479 Robert Horry SL	.05	.02	.01
☐ 480 Glen Rice SL	.10	.05	.01
☐ 481 Micheal Williams SIS	.05	.02	.01
☐ 482 George Lynch	.05	.02	.01
Terry Dehere CL			
☐ 483 Chris Webber TP	.50	.23	.06
☐ 484 Anfernee Hardaway TP	2.50	1.10	.30
☐ 485 Shawn Bradley TP	.15	.07	.02
☐ 486 Jamal Mashburn TP	.30	.14	.04
☐ 487 Calbert Cheaney TP	.15	.07	.02
☐ 488 Isaiah Rider TP	.25	.11	.03
☐ 489 Bobby Hurley TP	.05	.02	.01
☐ 490 Vin Baker TP	.50	.23	.06
☐ 491 Rodney Rogers TP	.05	.02	.01
☐ 492 Lindsey Hunter TP	.05	.02	.01
☐ 493 Allan Houston TP	.25	.11	.03
☐ 494 Terry Dehere TP	.05	.02	.01
☐ 495 George Lynch TP	.05	.02	.01
☐ 496 Scott Burrell TP	.30	.14	.04
☐ 497 Nick Van Exel TP	.40	.18	.05
☐ 498 Charles Barkley MO	.25	.11	.03
☐ 499 A.C. Green MO	.05	.02	.01
☐ 500 Dan Majerle MO	.05	.02	.01
☐ 501 Jerrod Mustaf MO	.05	.02	.01
☐ 502 Kevin Johnson MO	.10	.05	.01
☐ 503 Negele Knight MO	.05	.02	.01
☐ 504 Danny Ainge MO	.10	.05	.01
☐ 505 Oliver Miller MO	.05	.02	.01
☐ 506 Joe Courtney MO	.05	.02	.01
☐ 507 Checklist	.05	.02	.01
☐ 508 Checklist	.05	.02	.01
☐ 509 Checklist	.05	.02	.01
☐ 510 Checklist	.05	.02	.01
☐ SP3 Michael Jordan	8.00	3.60	1.00
Wilt Chamberlain			
☐ SP4 Chicago Bulls' Third	8.00	3.60	1.00
NBA Championship			

1993-94 Upper Deck All-NBA

Inserted one per blue and green first series retail 22-card jumbo packs, this 15-card standard-size set spotlights All-NBA first, second and third teams. The cards feature a borderless front with a color action photo set against a game-crowd background. The player's name appears in a red vertical stripe along the right side. The All NBA Team appears in a blue vertical stripe along the right side. The back features a color action photo along the left side with player's statistics along the right side.

	MINT	NRMT	EXC
COMPLETE SET (15)	15.00	6.75	1.85
COMMON CARD (AN1-AN15)	.25	.11	.03

			MINT	NRMT	EXC
☐	AN1	Charles Barkley	1.00	.45	.12
☐	AN2	Karl Malone	.60	.25	.07
☐	AN3	Hakeem Olajuwon	1.50	.70	.19
☐	AN4	Michael Jordan	8.00	3.60	1.00
☐	AN5	Mark Price	.25	.11	.03
☐	AN6	Dominique Wilkins	.40	.18	.05
☐	AN7	Larry Johnson	.75	.35	.09
☐	AN8	Patrick Ewing	.60	.25	.07
☐	AN9	John Stockton	.60	.25	.07
☐	AN10	Joe Dumars	.40	.18	.05
☐	AN11	Scottie Pippen	2.00	.90	.25
☐	AN12	Derrick Coleman	.25	.11	.03
☐	AN13	David Robinson	1.25	.55	.16
☐	AN14	Tim Hardaway	.40	.18	.05
☐	AN15	Michael Jordan CL	4.00	1.80	.50

☐	AR1	Shaquille O'Neal	15.00	6.75	1.85
☐	AR2	Alonzo Mourning	4.00	1.80	.50
☐	AR3	Christian Laettner	1.50	.70	.19
☐	AR4	Tom Gugliotta	1.50	.70	.19
☐	AR5	LaPhonso Ellis	1.00	.45	.12
☐	AR6	Walt Williams	1.00	.45	.12
☐	AR7	Robert Horry	1.50	.70	.19
☐	AR8	Latrell Sprewell	2.00	.90	.25
☐	AR9	Clarence Weatherspoon	1.00	.45	.12
☐	AR10	Richard Dumas	.50	.23	.06

1993-94 Upper Deck Box Bottoms

Measuring approximately 5" by 7", these box bottoms display enlarged versions of the fronts of regular series cards. The backs are blank. The box bottoms are unnumbered and checklisted below in alphabetical order.

	MINT	NRMT	EXC
COMPLETE SET (2)	1.25	.55	.16
COMMON CARD (1-2)	.25	.11	.03
☐ 1 Bobby Hurley	.25	.11	.03
☐ 2 Michael Jordan	1.00	.45	.12

1993-94 Upper Deck All-Rookies

Randomly inserted in first series 12-card retail packs at a rate of one in 30, this 10-card standard-size set features the NBA All-Rookie first (1-5) and second (6-10) teams from 1992-93. The cards feature color game-action player photos on their fronts. They are borderless, except at the top, where a red stripe edges the cards of the first team and a blue one edges those of the second. The player's name appears in white lettering within a red or blue stripe near the bottom. The back carries a color player action photo on the left and career highlights on the right.

	MINT	NRMT	EXC
COMPLETE SET (10)	20.00	9.00	2.50
COMMON CARD (AR1-AR10)	.50	.23	.06

1993-94 Upper Deck Flight Team

Michael Jordan selected the league's best dunkers for this 20-card insert set. The

cards are randomly inserted in first series 12-card hobby packs at a rate of one in 30. The standard-size cards feature on their fronts full-bleed color action player photos. The words "Michael Jordan's Flight Team" appear in ghosted block lettering over the background. The player's name is gold-foil stamped at the bottom, with the Flight Team insignia displayed immediately above carrying his team's city name and the his uniform number. On a background consisting of blue sky and clouds, the back carries a color player action cutout and an evaluative quote by Jordan. The set is sequenced in alphabetical order.

	MINT	NRMT	EXC
COMPLETE SET (20)	90.00	40.00	11.00
COMMON CARD (FT1-FT20)	1.50	.70	.19
☐ FT1 Stacey Augmon	3.00	1.35	.35
☐ FT2 Charles Barkley	10.00	4.50	1.25
☐ FT3 David Benoit	1.50	.70	.19
☐ FT4 Dee Brown	1.50	.70	.19
☐ FT5 Cedric Ceballos	2.50	1.10	.30
☐ FT6 Derrick Coleman	1.50	.70	.19
☐ FT7 Clyde Drexler	8.00	3.60	1.00
☐ FT8 Sean Elliott	3.00	1.35	.35
☐ FT9 LaPhonso Ellis	1.50	.70	.19
☐ FT10 Kendall Gill	1.50	.70	.19
☐ FT11 Larry Johnson	8.00	3.60	1.00
☐ FT12 Shawn Kemp	20.00	9.00	2.50
☐ FT13 Karl Malone	6.00	2.70	.75
☐ FT14 Harold Miner	1.50	.70	.19
☐ FT15 Alonzo Mourning	10.00	4.50	1.25
☐ FT16 Shaquille O'Neal	40.00	18.00	5.00
☐ FT17 Scottie Pippen	20.00	9.00	2.50
☐ FT18 Clarence Weatherspoon	3.00	1.35	.35
☐ FT19 Spud Webb	3.00	1.35	.35
☐ FT20 Dominique Wilkins	3.00	1.35	.35

1993-94 Upper Deck Future Heroes

Inserted one per first series locker pack, this set continues Upper Deck's year-by-year basketball Heroes program. Unlike previous sets devoted to individual players, the 1993-94 set features a selection of young phenoms destined to be stars. This 10-card standard-size set features color player action shots on its fronts. The photos

are bordered on the left and bottom by gray and team color-coded stripes. The player's name and position appear in white lettering in the color-coded stripe at the bottom. An embossed silver-foil basketball appears at the lower left. The white back carries the player's career highlights. The set is numbered in continuation of Upper Deck's Hero Series and is sequenced in alphabetical order.

	MINT	NRMT	EXC
COMPLETE SET (10)	30.00	13.50	3.70
COMMON CARD (28-36)	1.00	.45	.12
☐ 28 Derrick Coleman	1.00	.45	.12
☐ 29 LaPhonso Ellis	1.00	.45	.12
☐ 30 Jim Jackson	4.00	1.80	.50
☐ 31 Larry Johnson	4.00	1.80	.50
☐ 32 Shawn Kemp	10.00	4.50	1.25
☐ 33 Christian Laettner	1.50	.70	.19
☐ 34 Alonzo Mourning	5.00	2.20	.60
☐ 35 Shaquille O'Neal	20.00	9.00	2.50
☐ 36 Walt Williams	1.50	.70	.19
☐ NNO LaPhonso Ellis CL	1.00	.45	.12
Christian Laettner			

1993-94 Upper Deck Locker Talk

Inserted one per Series II locker pack, this 15-card standard-size set features color player action photos on their fronts. The player's name appears in white lettering within the gold stripe that edges the left side. A personal player quote appears in white lettering within the photo's "torn" lower right corner. The back carries the same quote at the upper right, within a shot of a locker that has a print of the front's action shot taped to the door. Another player photo and more personal player quotes round out the back.

	MINT	NRMT	EXC
COMPLETE SET (15)	75.00	34.00	9.50
COMMON CARD (LT1-LT15)	1.00	.45	.12
☐ LT1 Michael Jordan	40.00	18.00	5.00
☐ LT2 Stacey Augmon	1.50	.70	.19
☐ LT3 Shaquille O'Neal	20.00	9.00	2.50
☐ LT4 Alonzo Mourning	5.00	2.20	.60

		MINT	NRMT	EXC
☐	LT5 Harold Miner	1.00	.45	.12
☐	LT6 Clarence Weatherspoon	1.50	.70	.19
☐	LT7 Derrick Coleman	1.00	.45	.12
☐	LT8 Charles Barkley	5.00	2.20	.60
☐	LT9 David Robinson	6.00	2.70	.75
☐	LT10 Chuck Person	1.00	.45	.12
☐	LT11 Karl Malone	3.00	1.35	.35
☐	LT12 Muggsy Bogues	1.50	.70	.19
☐	LT13 Latrell Sprewell	2.50	1.10	.30
☐	LT14 John Starks	1.00	.45	.12
☐	LT15 Jim Jackson	4.00	1.80	.50

1993-94 Upper Deck Mr. June

Randomly inserted in series two 12-card hobby packs at a rate of one in 30, this 10-card standard-size set focuses on Michael Jordan's performance while leading his team to three consecutive NBA Championships. The front features a color action shot of Michael Jordan with his name, accomplishment, and year thereof printed in the team-colored (Chicago Bulls) stripe at bottom. The back features a color action photo at the upper right with a description of his accomplishments printed alongside and below.

		MINT	NRMT	EXC
	COMPLETE SET (10)	180.00	80.00	22.00
	COMMON JORDAN (1-10)		9.00	2.50
☐	MJ1 Michael Jordan Jordan's a Steal	20.00	9.00	2.50
☐	MJ2 Michael Jordan M.J.'s High Five	20.00	9.00	2.50
☐	MJ3 Michael Jordan 1991 NBA Finals MVP	20.00	9.00	2.50
☐	MJ4 Michael Jordan 35 Points in One Half	20.00	9.00	2.50
☐	MJ5 Michael Jordan Three-Points King	20.00	9.00	2.50
☐	MJ6 Michael Jordan Back-To-Back Finals MVP	20.00	9.00	2.50
☐	MJ7 Michael Jordan 55-Point Game	20.00	9.00	2.50
☐	MJ8 Michael Jordan Record Scoring Average	20.00	9.00	2.50
☐	MJ9 Michael Jordan Jordan's Three-Peat	20.00	9.00	2.50
☐	MJ10 Checklist	20.00	9.00	2.50

1993-94 Upper Deck Rookie Exchange

This 10-card standard-size set features the top ten players from the 1993 NBA Draft. The set could only be obtained by mail in exchange for the Silver Trade card that was randomly inserted in first series 12-card packs at a rate of one in 72. The Silver Exchange expiration date was 12/31/93. The borderless front features a color player action photo with his name printed in white lettering within a red stripe near the bottom. The word "Exchange" runs vertically along the left side in silver-foil lettering. The white and gray back carries a color player photo at the upper left and career highlights and statistics alongside and below. The set is sequenced in draft order.

		MINT	NRMT	EXC
	COMPLETE SILVER SET (10)	8.00	3.60	1.00
	COMMON SILVER (RE1-RE10)	.15	.07	.02
☐	RE1 Chris Webber	1.25	.55	.16
☐	RE2 Shawn Bradley	.40	.18	.05
☐	RE3 Anfernee Hardaway	6.00	2.70	.75
☐	RE4 Jamal Mashburn	.75	.35	.09
☐	RE5 Isaiah Rider	.40	.18	.05
☐	RE6 Calbert Cheaney	.30	.14	.04
☐	RE7 Bobby Hurley	.15	.07	.02
☐	RE8 Vin Baker	1.25	.55	.16
☐	RE9 Rodney Rogers	.15	.07	.02
☐	RE10 Lindsey Hunter	.15	.07	.02
☐	TC2 Redeemed Silver Trade	.25	.11	.03
☐	TC2 Unredeemed Silver Trade	.10	.05	.01

1993-94 Upper Deck Rookie Exchange Gold

This 10-card standard-size (2 1/2" by 3 1/2") set features the top ten players from the 1993 NBA Draft. The set could only be obtained by mail in exchange for the Gold Trade Card that was randomly inserted (one in 288) in 12-card first series packs. The Gold Trade expiration date was

		MINT	NRMT	EXC
☐ RS5	Toni Kukoc	3.00	1.35	.35
☐ RS6	Shawn Bradley	1.50	.70	.19
☐ RS7	Allan Houston	2.50	1.10	.30
☐ RS8	Chris Mills	2.00	.90	.25
☐ RS9	Jamal Mashburn	3.00	1.35	.35
☐ RS10	Acie Earl	.50	.23	.06
☐ RS11	George Lynch	.50	.23	.06
☐ RS12	Scott Burrell	1.00	.45	.12
☐ RS13	Calbert Cheaney	1.25	.55	.16
☐ RS14	Lindsey Hunter	.50	.23	.06
☐ RS15	Nick Van Exel	4.00	1.80	.50
☐ RS16	Rex Walters	.50	.23	.06
☐ RS17	Anfernee Hardaway	25.00	11.00	3.10
☐ RS18	Sam Cassell	2.00	.90	.25
☐ RS19	Vin Baker	5.00	2.20	.60
☐ RS20	Rodney Rogers	1.00	.45	.12

12/31/93. The cards are identical to the basic "Rookie Exchange" inserts except for the word "Exchange" on the card front, which is featured in gold-foil instead of silver. Please refer to the multiplier listed below for card values.

	MINT	NRMT	EXC
COMPLETE SET (10)	15.00	6.75	1.85
COMMON CARD (RE1-RE10)	.30	.14	.04
*GOLD CARDS: 1X to 2X VALUE			

		MINT	NRMT	EXC
☐ TC1	Redeemed Gold Trade	.50	.23	.06
☐ TC1	Unredeemed Gold Trade	2.00	.90	.25

1993-94 Upper Deck Rookie Standouts

Randomly inserted at a rate of one in 30 second series 12-card retail packs and inserted one per second series 22-card purple jumbo pack, this 20-card standard-size set showcases top rookies of the 1993-94 NBA season. The borderless front features a color player action photo with his name printed in a gold-foil banner beneath the silver-foil set logo in a lower corner. The gray back carries a color player photo on one side and career highlights on the other.

	MINT	NRMT	EXC
COMPLETE SET (20)	50.00	22.00	6.25
COMMON CARD (RS1-RS20)	.50	.23	.06

		MINT	NRMT	EXC
☐ RS1	Chris Webber	5.00	2.20	.60
☐ RS2	Bobby Hurley	1.00	.45	.12
☐ RS3	Isaiah Rider	1.50	.70	.19
☐ RS4	Terry Dehere	.50	.23	.06

1993-94 Upper Deck Team MVPs

Cards from this 27-card standard-size set were issued one per second series red and purple 22-card jumbo packs. The set highlights one key "Team MVP" from each of the 27 NBA teams. The white and prismatic team-colored foil-bordered front features a color player action shot, with the player's name printed vertically in the foil border at the upper right. The horizontal back is bordered in white and a team color and carries a color action shot on the left with career highlights appearing in a gray panel alongside on the right. The set is sequenced in team alphabetical order.

	MINT	NRMT	EXC
COMPLETE SET (27)	20.00	9.00	2.50
COMMON CARD (TM1-TM27)	.25	.11	.03

		MINT	NRMT	EXC
☐ TM1	Dominique Wilkins	.40	.18	.05
☐ TM2	Robert Parish	.40	.18	.05
☐ TM3	Larry Johnson	1.00	.45	.12
☐ TM4	Scottie Pippen	2.50	1.10	.30
☐ TM5	Mark Price	.25	.11	.03
☐ TM6	Jim Jackson	1.00	.45	.12
☐ TM7	Mahmoud Abdul-Rauf	.25	.11	.03
☐ TM8	Joe Dumars	.40	.18	.05
☐ TM9	Chris Mullin	.40	.18	.05
☐ TM10	Hakeem Olajuwon	2.00	.90	.25
☐ TM11	Reggie Miller	1.00	.45	.12
☐ TM12	Danny Manning	.40	.18	.05
☐ TM13	James Worthy	.40	.18	.05

		MINT	NRMT	EXC
☐ TM14	Glen Rice	.40	.18	.05
☐ TM15	Blue Edwards	.25	.11	.03
☐ TM16	Christian Laettner	.40	.18	.05
☐ TM17	Derrick Coleman	.25	.11	.03
☐ TM18	Patrick Ewing	.75	.35	.09
☐ TM19	Shaquille O'Neal	5.00	2.20	.60
☐ TM20	Clarence Weatherspoon	.40	.18	.05
☐ TM21	Charles Barkley	1.25	.55	.16
☐ TM22	Clyde Drexler	1.00	.45	.12
☐ TM23	Mitch Richmond	.40	.18	.05
☐ TM24	David Robinson	1.50	.70	.19
☐ TM25	Shawn Kemp	2.50	1.10	.30
☐ TM26	John Stockton	.75	.35	.09
☐ TM27	Tom Gugliotta	.40	.18	.05

1993-94 Upper Deck Triple Double

This 10-card standard-size set features the NBA leaders in triple-doubles from the 1992-93 season. Cards were randomly inserted at a rate of 1 in 20 first series 12-card hobby and retail packs, 1 in 20 first series 22-card blue jumbo packs, one per first series 22-card green jumbo pack and approximately 1 in every 11 first series 22-card locker packs. The standard-size horizontal hologram cards feature one color player action cutout and two hologram action shots on their fronts. Each of the three images show the player performing three different skills (scoring, rebounding, passing or blocking) necessary to achieve a triple-double. The words "Triple Double" appear vertically on the left. The player's name appears at the upper right of the hologram. The horizontal back displays another color player action shot on the left, with a story of the player's triple-double feat on the right. The player's name appears in a team-colored bar at the bottom.

		MINT	NRMT	EXC
COMPLETE SET (10)		20.00	9.00	2.50
COMMON CARD (TD1-TD10)		.50	.23	.06
☐ TD1	Charles Barkley	2.00	.90	.25
☐ TD2	Michael Jordan	15.00	6.75	1.85
☐ TD3	Scottie Pippen	4.00	1.80	.50
☐ TD4	Detlef Schrempf	1.00	.45	.12
☐ TD5	Mark Jackson	.50	.23	.06
☐ TD6	Kenny Anderson	1.00	.45	.12

		MINT	NRMT	EXC
☐ TD7	Larry Johnson	1.50	.70	.19
☐ TD8	Dikembe Mutombo	1.00	.45	.12
☐ TD9	Rumeal Robinson	.50	.23	.06
☐ TD10	Micheal Williams	.50	.23	.06

1994-95 Upper Deck

The 1994-95 Upper Deck basketball set consists of 360 standard-size cards, released in two separate 180-card series. Cards were primarily distributed in 12-card packs, each of which carried a suggested retail price of $1.99. Fronts feature full-color action photos with player's name and team running in color-coded bars along the side. Topical subsets featured are All-Rookie Team (1-10), All-NBA (11-25), USA Basketball (167-180), Draft Analysis (181-198), and Then and Now (352-360). Rookie Cards of note include Grant Hill, Juwan Howard, Eddie Jones, Jason Kidd and Glenn Robinson.

		MINT	NRMT	EXC
COMPLETE SET (360)		45.00	20.00	5.50
COMPLETE SERIES 1 (180)		25.00	11.00	3.10
COMPLETE SERIES 2 (180)		20.00	9.00	2.50
COMMON CARD (1-360)		.10	.05	.01
☐ 1	Chris Webber ART	.25	.11	.03
☐ 2	Anfernee Hardaway ART	1.25	.55	.16
☐ 3	Vin Baker ART	.20	.09	.03
☐ 4	Jamal Mashburn ART	.15	.07	.02
☐ 5	Isaiah Rider ART	.10	.05	.01
☐ 6	Dino Radja ART	.10	.05	.01
☐ 7	Nick Van Exel ART	.40	.18	.05
☐ 8	Shawn Bradley ART	.10	.05	.01
☐ 9	Toni Kukoc ART	.15	.07	.02
☐ 10	Lindsey Hunter ART	.10	.05	.01
☐ 11	Scottie Pippen AN	.60	.25	.07
☐ 12	Karl Malone AN	.20	.09	.03
☐ 13	Hakeem Olajuwon AN	.50	.23	.06
☐ 14	John Stockton AN	.20	.09	.03
☐ 15	Latrell Sprewell AN	.10	.05	.01
☐ 16	Shawn Kemp AN	.60	.25	.07
☐ 17	Charles Barkley AN	.30	.14	.04
☐ 18	David Robinson AN	.40	.18	.05
☐ 19	Mitch Richmond AN	.15	.07	.02
☐ 20	Kevin Johnson AN	.15	.07	.02
☐ 21	Derrick Coleman AN	.10	.05	.01
☐ 22	Dominique Wilkins AN	.15	.07	.02
☐ 23	Shaquille O'Neal AN	1.00	.45	.12
☐ 24	Mark Price AN	.10	.05	.01

☐ 25	Gary Payton AN	.30	.14	.04
☐ 26	Dan Majerle	.15	.07	.02
☐ 27	Vernon Maxwell	.10	.05	.01
☐ 28	Matt Geiger	.10	.05	.01
☐ 29	Jeff Turner	.10	.05	.01
☐ 30	Vinny Del Negro	.10	.05	.01
☐ 31	B.J. Armstrong	.10	.05	.01
☐ 32	Chris Gatling	.10	.05	.01
☐ 33	Tony Smith	.10	.05	.01
☐ 34	Doug West	.10	.05	.01
☐ 35	Clyde Drexler	.50	.23	.06
☐ 36	Keith Jennings	.10	.05	.01
☐ 37	Steve Smith	.20	.09	.03
☐ 38	Kendall Gill	.10	.05	.01
☐ 39	Bob Martin	.10	.05	.01
☐ 40	Calbert Cheaney	.20	.09	.03
☐ 41	Terrell Brandon	.20	.09	.03
☐ 42	Pete Chilcutt	.10	.05	.01
☐ 43	Avery Johnson	.15	.07	.02
☐ 44	Tom Gugliotta	.20	.09	.03
☐ 45	LaBradford Smith	.10	.05	.01
☐ 46	Sedale Threatt	.10	.05	.01
☐ 47	Chris Smith	.10	.05	.01
☐ 48	Kevin Edwards	.10	.05	.01
☐ 49	Lucious Harris	.10	.05	.01
☐ 50	Tim Perry	.10	.05	.01
☐ 51	Lloyd Daniels	.10	.05	.01
☐ 52	Dee Brown	.10	.05	.01
☐ 53	Sean Elliott	.20	.09	.03
☐ 54	Tim Hardaway	.20	.09	.03
☐ 55	Christian Laettner	.20	.09	.03
☐ 56	Charles Outlaw	.10	.05	.01
☐ 57	Kevin Johnson	.20	.09	.03
☐ 58	Duane Ferrell	.10	.05	.01
☐ 59	Jo Jo English	.10	.05	.01
☐ 60	Stanley Roberts	.10	.05	.01
☐ 61	Kevin Willis	.10	.05	.01
☐ 62	Dana Barros	.10	.05	.01
☐ 63	Gheorghe Muresan	.20	.09	.03
☐ 64	Vern Fleming	.10	.05	.01
☐ 65	Anthony Peeler	.10	.05	.01
☐ 66	Negele Knight	.10	.05	.01
☐ 67	Harold Ellis	.10	.05	.01
☐ 68	Vincent Askew	.10	.05	.01
☐ 69	Ennis Whatley	.10	.05	.01
☐ 70	Elden Campbell	.15	.07	.02
☐ 71	Sherman Douglas	.10	.05	.01
☐ 72	Luc Longley	.10	.05	.01
☐ 73	Lorenzo Williams	.10	.05	.01
☐ 74	Jay Humphries	.10	.05	.01
☐ 75	Chris King	.10	.05	.01
☐ 76	Tyrone Corbin	.10	.05	.01
☐ 77	Bobby Hurley	.10	.05	.01
☐ 78	Dell Curry	.10	.05	.01
☐ 79	Dino Radja	.20	.09	.03
☐ 80	A.C. Green	.20	.09	.03
☐ 81	Craig Ehlo	.10	.05	.01
☐ 82	Gary Payton	.60	.25	.07
☐ 83	Sleepy Floyd	.10	.05	.01
☐ 84	Rodney Rogers	.10	.05	.01
☐ 85	Brian Shaw	.10	.05	.01
☐ 86	Kevin Gamble	.10	.05	.01
☐ 87	John Stockton	.40	.18	.05
☐ 88	Hersey Hawkins	.10	.05	.01
☐ 89	Johnny Newman	.10	.05	.01
☐ 90	Larry Johnson	.40	.18	.05
☐ 91	Robert Pack	.10	.05	.01
☐ 92	Willie Burton	.10	.05	.01
☐ 93	Bobby Phills	.10	.05	.01
☐ 94	David Benoit	.10	.05	.01
☐ 95	Harold Miner	.10	.05	.01
☐ 96	David Robinson	.75	.35	.09
☐ 97	Nate McMillan	.10	.05	.01
☐ 98	Chris Mills	.20	.09	.03
☐ 99	Hubert Davis	.10	.05	.01
☐ 100	Shaquille O'Neal	2.00	.90	.25
☐ 101	Loy Vaught	.10	.05	.01
☐ 102	Kenny Smith	.10	.05	.01
☐ 103	Terry Dehere	.10	.05	.01
☐ 104	Carl Herrera	.10	.05	.01
☐ 105	LaPhonso Ellis	.10	.05	.01
☐ 106	Armon Gilliam	.10	.05	.01
☐ 107	Greg Graham	.10	.05	.01
☐ 108	Eric Murdock	.10	.05	.01
☐ 109	Ron Harper	.10	.05	.01
☐ 110	Andrew Lang	.10	.05	.01
☐ 111	Johnny Dawkins	.10	.05	.01
☐ 112	David Wingate	.10	.05	.01
☐ 113	Tom Hammonds	.10	.05	.01
☐ 114	Brad Daugherty	.10	.05	.01
☐ 115	Charles Smith	.10	.05	.01
☐ 116	Dale Ellis	.10	.05	.01
☐ 117	Bryant Stith	.10	.05	.01
☐ 118	Lindsey Hunter	.10	.05	.01
☐ 119	Patrick Ewing	.40	.18	.05
☐ 120	Kenny Anderson	.20	.09	.03
☐ 121	Charles Barkley	.60	.25	.07
☐ 122	Harvey Grant	.10	.05	.01
☐ 123	Anthony Bowie	.10	.05	.01
☐ 124	Shawn Kemp	1.25	.55	.16
☐ 125	Lee Mayberry	.10	.05	.01
☐ 126	Reggie Miller	.50	.23	.06
☐ 127	Scottie Pippen	1.25	.55	.16
☐ 128	Spud Webb	.15	.07	.02
☐ 129	Antonio Davis	.10	.05	.01
☐ 130	Greg Anderson	.10	.05	.01
☐ 131	Jim Jackson	.50	.23	.06
☐ 132	Dikembe Mutombo	.20	.09	.03
☐ 133	Terry Porter	.10	.05	.01
☐ 134	Mario Elie	.10	.05	.01
☐ 135	Vlade Divac	.20	.09	.03
☐ 136	Robert Horry	.15	.07	.02
☐ 137	Popeye Jones	.10	.05	.01
☐ 138	Brad Lohaus	.10	.05	.01
☐ 139	Anthony Bonner	.10	.05	.01
☐ 140	Doug Christie	.10	.05	.01
☐ 141	Rony Seikaly	.10	.05	.01
☐ 142	Allan Houston	.25	.11	.03
☐ 143	Tyrone Hill	.10	.05	.01
☐ 144	Latrell Sprewell	.50	.23	.06
☐ 145	Andres Guibert	.10	.05	.01
☐ 146	Dominique Wilkins	.20	.09	.03
☐ 147	Jon Barry	.10	.05	.01
☐ 148	Tracy Murray	.10	.05	.01
☐ 149	Mike Peplowski	.10	.05	.01
☐ 150	Mike Brown	.10	.05	.01
☐ 151	Cedric Ceballos	.15	.07	.02
☐ 152	Stacey King	.10	.05	.01
☐ 153	Trevor Wilson	.10	.05	.01
☐ 154	Anthony Avent	.10	.05	.01
☐ 155	Horace Grant	.20	.09	.03
☐ 156	Bill Curley	.10	.05	.01
☐ 157	Grant Hill	5.00	2.20	.60
☐ 158	Charlie Ward	.20	.09	.03
☐ 159	Jalen Rose	.40	.18	.05
☐ 160	Jason Kidd	3.00	1.35	.35
☐ 161	Yinka Dare	.10	.05	.01
☐ 162	Eric Montross	.20	.09	.03
☐ 163	Donyell Marshall	.15	.07	.02
☐ 164	Tony Dumas	.20	.09	.03
☐ 165	Wesley Person	.75	.35	.09
☐ 166	Eddie Jones	1.00	.45	.12

☐ 167	Tim Hardaway USA	.10	.05	.01	☐ 238	Eric Mobley	.15	.07	.02
☐ 168	Isiah Thomas USA	.15	.07	.02	☐ 239	Brian Williams	.10	.05	.01
☐ 169	Joe Dumars USA	.15	.07	.02	☐ 240	Eric Piatkowski	.10	.05	.01
☐ 170	Mark Price USA	.10	.05	.01	☐ 241	Karl Malone	.40	.18	.05
☐ 171	Derrick Coleman USA	.10	.05	.01	☐ 242	Wayman Tisdale	.10	.05	.01
☐ 172	Shawn Kemp USA	.60	.25	.07	☐ 243	Sarunas Marciulionis	.10	.05	.01
☐ 173	Steve Smith USA	.10	.05	.01	☐ 244	Sean Rooks	.10	.05	.01
☐ 174	Dan Majerle USA	.10	.05	.01	☐ 245	Ricky Pierce	.10	.05	.01
☐ 175	Reggie Miller USA	.25	.11	.03	☐ 246	Don MacLean	.10	.05	.01
☐ 176	Kevin Johnson USA	.15	.07	.02	☐ 247	Aaron McKie	.15	.07	.02
☐ 177	Dominique Wilkins USA	.15	.07	.02	☐ 248	Kenny Gattison	.10	.05	.01
☐ 178	Shaquille O'Neal USA	1.00	.45	.12	☐ 249	Derek Harper	.10	.05	.01
☐ 179	Alonzo Mourning USA	.25	.11	.03	☐ 250	Michael Smith	.15	.07	.02
☐ 180	Larry Johnson USA	.20	.09	.03	☐ 251	John Williams	.10	.05	.01
☐ 181	Brian Grant DA	.20	.09	.03	☐ 252	Pooh Richardson	.10	.05	.01
☐ 182	Darrin Hancock DA	.10	.05	.01	☐ 253	Sergei Bazarevich	.10	.05	.01
☐ 183	Grant Hill DA	2.00	.90	.25	☐ 254	Brian Grant	.60	.25	.07
☐ 184	Jalen Rose DA	.20	.09	.03	☐ 255	Ed Pinckney	.10	.05	.01
☐ 185	Lamond Murray DA	.10	.05	.01	☐ 256	Ken Norman	.10	.05	.01
☐ 186	Jason Kidd DA	1.25	.55	.16	☐ 257	Marty Conlon	.10	.05	.01
☐ 187	Donyell Marshall DA	.10	.05	.01	☐ 258	Matt Fish	.10	.05	.01
☐ 188	Eddie Jones DA	.40	.18	.05	☐ 259	Darrin Hancock	.10	.05	.01
☐ 189	Eric Montross DA	.10	.05	.01	☐ 260	Mahmoud Abdul-Rauf	.15	.07	.02
☐ 190	Khalid Reeves DA	.10	.05	.01	☐ 261	Roy Tarpley	.10	.05	.01
☐ 191	Sharone Wright DA	.10	.05	.01	☐ 262	Chris Morris	.10	.05	.01
☐ 192	Wesley Person DA	.20	.09	.03	☐ 263	Sharone Wright	.15	.07	.02
☐ 193	Glenn Robinson DA	.60	.25	.07	☐ 264	Jamal Mashburn	.30	.14	.04
☐ 194	Carlos Rogers DA	.10	.05	.01	☐ 265	John Starks	.10	.05	.01
☐ 195	Aaron McKie DA	.10	.05	.01	☐ 266	Rod Strickland	.10	.05	.01
☐ 196	Juwan Howard DA	1.25	.55	.16	☐ 267	Adam Keefe	.10	.05	.01
☐ 197	Charlie Ward DA	.15	.07	.02	☐ 268	Scott Burrell	.10	.05	.01
☐ 198	Brooks Thompson DA	.10	.05	.01	☐ 269	Eric Riley	.10	.05	.01
☐ 199	Tony Massenburg	.10	.05	.01	☐ 270	Sam Perkins	.15	.07	.02
☐ 200	James Robinson	.10	.05	.01	☐ 271	Stacey Augmon	.15	.07	.02
☐ 201	Dickey Simpkins	.15	.07	.02	☐ 272	Kevin Willis	.10	.05	.01
☐ 202	Johnny Dawkins	.10	.05	.01	☐ 273	Lamond Murray	.10	.05	.01
☐ 203	Joe Kleine	.10	.05	.01	☐ 274	Derrick Coleman	.10	.05	.01
☐ 204	Bill Wennington	.10	.05	.01	☐ 275	Scott Skiles	.10	.05	.01
☐ 205	Sean Higgins	.10	.05	.01	☐ 276	Buck Williams	.15	.07	.02
☐ 206	Larry Krystkowiak	.10	.05	.01	☐ 277	Sam Cassell	.20	.09	.03
☐ 207	Winston Garland	.10	.05	.01	☐ 278	Rik Smits	.20	.09	.03
☐ 208	Muggsy Bogues	.15	.07	.02	☐ 279	Dennis Rodman	1.50	.70	.19
☐ 209	Charles Oakley	.15	.07	.02	☐ 280	Olden Polynice	.10	.05	.01
☐ 210	Vin Baker	.50	.23	.06	☐ 281	Glenn Robinson	1.50	.70	.19
☐ 211	Malik Sealy	.10	.05	.01	☐ 282	Clarence Weatherspoon	.15	.07	.02
☐ 212	Willie Anderson	.10	.05	.01	☐ 283	Monty Williams	.10	.05	.01
☐ 213	Dale Davis	.10	.05	.01	☐ 284	Terry Mills	.10	.05	.01
☐ 214	Grant Long	.10	.05	.01	☐ 285	Oliver Miller	.10	.05	.01
☐ 215	Danny Ainge	.20	.09	.03	☐ 286	Dennis Scott	.15	.07	.02
☐ 216	Toni Kukoc	.30	.14	.04	☐ 287	Micheal Williams	.10	.05	.01
☐ 217	Doug Smith	.10	.05	.01	☐ 288	Moses Malone	.25	.11	.03
☐ 218	Danny Manning	.15	.07	.02	☐ 289	Donald Royal	.10	.05	.01
☐ 219	Otis Thorpe	.15	.07	.02	☐ 290	Mark Jackson	.10	.05	.01
☐ 220	Mark Price	.10	.05	.01	☐ 291	Walt Williams	.20	.09	.03
☐ 221	Victor Alexander	.10	.05	.01	☐ 292	Bimbo Coles	.10	.05	.01
☐ 222	Brent Price	.10	.05	.01	☐ 293	Derrick Alston	.10	.05	.01
☐ 223	Howard Eisley	.10	.05	.01	☐ 294	Scott Williams	.10	.05	.01
☐ 224	Chris Mullin	.20	.09	.03	☐ 295	Acie Earl	.10	.05	.01
☐ 225	Nick Van Exel	.40	.18	.05	☐ 296	Jeff Hornacek	.15	.07	.02
☐ 226	Xavier McDaniel	.10	.05	.01	☐ 297	Kevin Duckworth	.10	.05	.01
☐ 227	Khalid Reeves	.10	.05	.01	☐ 298	Dontonio Wingfield	.10	.05	.01
☐ 228	Anfernee Hardaway	2.50	1.10	.30	☐ 299	Danny Ferry	.10	.05	.01
☐ 229	B.J. Tyler	.10	.05	.01	☐ 300	Mark West	.10	.05	.01
☐ 230	Elmore Spencer	.10	.05	.01	☐ 301	Jayson Williams	.10	.05	.01
☐ 231	Rick Fox	.10	.05	.01	☐ 302	David Wesley	.10	.05	.01
☐ 232	Alonzo Mourning	.50	.23	.06	☐ 303	Jim McIlvaine	.15	.07	.02
☐ 233	Hakeem Olajuwon	1.00	.45	.12	☐ 304	Michael Adams	.10	.05	.01
☐ 234	Blue Edwards	.10	.05	.01	☐ 305	Greg Minor	.10	.05	.01
☐ 235	P.J. Brown	.10	.05	.01	☐ 306	Jeff Malone	.10	.05	.01
☐ 236	Ron Harper	.15	.07	.02	☐ 307	Pervis Ellison	.10	.05	.01
☐ 237	Isaiah Rider	.20	.09	.03	☐ 308	Clifford Rozier	.15	.07	.02

☐ 309	Billy Owens	.10	.05	.01
☐ 310	Duane Causwell	.10	.05	.01
☐ 311	Rex Chapman	.10	.05	.01
☐ 312	Detlef Schrempf	.15	.07	.02
☐ 313	Mitch Richmond	.30	.14	.04
☐ 314	Carlos Rogers	.10	.05	.01
☐ 315	Byron Scott	.20	.09	.03
☐ 316	Dwayne Morton	.10	.05	.01
☐ 317	Bill Cartwright	.10	.05	.01
☐ 318	J.R. Reid	.10	.05	.01
☐ 319	Derrick McKey	.10	.05	.01
☐ 320	Jamie Watson	.10	.05	.01
☐ 321	Mookie Blaylock	.15	.07	.02
☐ 322	Chris Webber	.50	.23	.06
☐ 323	Joe Dumars	.20	.09	.03
☐ 324	Shawn Bradley	.20	.09	.03
☐ 325	Chuck Person	.10	.05	.01
☐ 326	Haywoode Workman	.10	.05	.01
☐ 327	Benoit Benjamin	.10	.05	.01
☐ 328	Will Perdue	.10	.05	.01
☐ 329	Sam Mitchell	.10	.05	.01
☐ 330	George Lynch	.10	.05	.01
☐ 331	Juwan Howard	3.00	1.35	.35
☐ 332	Robert Parish	.20	.09	.03
☐ 333	Glen Rice	.20	.09	.03
☐ 334	Michael Cage	.10	.05	.01
☐ 335	Brooks Thompson	.15	.07	.02
☐ 336	Rony Seikaly	.10	.05	.01
☐ 337	Steve Kerr	.15	.07	.02
☐ 338	Anthony Miller	.10	.05	.01
☐ 339	Nick Anderson	.20	.09	.03
☐ 340	Clifford Robinson	.20	.09	.03
☐ 341	Todd Day	.10	.05	.01
☐ 342	Jon Koncak	.10	.05	.01
☐ 343	Felton Spencer	.10	.05	.01
☐ 344	Willie Burton	.10	.05	.01
☐ 345	Ledell Eackles	.10	.05	.01
☐ 346	Anthony Mason	.15	.07	.02
☐ 347	Derek Strong	.10	.05	.01
☐ 348	Reggie Williams	.10	.05	.01
☐ 349	Johnny Newman	.10	.05	.01
☐ 350	Terry Cummings	.10	.05	.01
☐ 351	Anthony Tucker	.10	.05	.01
☐ 352	Junior Bridgeman TN	.10	.05	.01
☐ 353	Jerry West TN	.50	.23	.06
☐ 354	Harvey Catchings TN	.10	.05	.01
☐ 355	John Lucas TN	.10	.05	.01
☐ 356	Bill Bradley TN	.25	.11	.03
☐ 357	Bill Walton TN	.25	.11	.03
☐ 358	Don Nelson TN	.15	.07	.02
☐ 359	Michael Jordan TN	2.50	1.10	.30
☐ 360	Tom(Satch) Sanders TN	.15	.07	.02

1994-95 Upper Deck Draft Trade

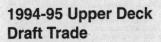

This set was available exclusively by redeeming the Upper Deck Draft Trade card before the June 30th, 1995 deadline. Draft Trade cards were randomly seeded into one in every 240 first series Upper Deck packs. The first ten players selected in the 1994 NBA Draft are featured within this set. The fronts feature the words NBA Draft Lottery Picks 1994 on the top of the card with the player vertically identified on

the front left. The NBA draft logo is in the lower left corner. All of this surrounds a playerr cutout photo against a shaded background. The backs contain player information as well as a player photo. The cards are numbered with a "D" prefix in the upper left corner.

	MINT	NRMT	EXC
COMPLETE SET (10)	25.00	11.00	3.10
COMMON CARD (D1-D10)	.50	.23	.06
☐ D1 Glenn Robinson	3.00	1.35	.35
☐ D2 Jason Kidd	6.00	2.70	.75
☐ D3 Grant Hill	10.00	4.50	1.25
☐ D4 Donyell Marshall	.50	.23	.06
☐ D5 Juwan Howard	6.00	2.70	.75
☐ D6 Sharone Wright	1.00	.45	.12
☐ D7 Lamond Murray	.50	.23	.06
☐ D8 Brian Grant	1.25	.55	.16
☐ D9 Eric Montross	1.00	.45	.12
☐ D10 Eddie Jones	2.00	.90	.25
☐ NNO Draft Trade Card	1.00	.45	.12

1994-95 Upper Deck Jordan He's Back

The nine standard-size cards were reissued to celebrate the return of Michael Jordan. These cards parallel earlier Upper Deck Michael Jordan cards, the difference being that each is stamped with a foil "He's Back" logo on front. The cards were distributed one per second series rack pack.

	MINT	NRMT	EXC
COMPLETE SET (9)	15.00	6.75	1.85
COMMON CARD (1-9)	2.00	.90	.25

COMPLETE JUMBO SET (3) ..	15.00	6.75	1.85
COMMON JUMBO (1-3)...........	5.00	2.20	.60
☐ 23 Michael Jordan .... (92-93 Upper Deck)	2.00	.90	.25
☐ 23 Michael Jordan .... (93-94 Upper Deck)	2.00	.90	.25
☐ 41 Michael Jordan .... (94-95 SP Championship)	2.00	.90	.25
☐ 44 Michael Jordan .... (91-92 Upper Deck)	2.00	.90	.25
☐ 204 Michael Jordan .... (93-94 Upper Deck)	2.00	.90	.25
☐ 237 Michael Jordan .... (93-94 Upper Deck)	2.00	.90	.25
☐ 402 Michael Jordan .... (94-95 Collector's Choice)	2.00	.90	.25
☐ 425 Michael Jordan .... (92-93 Upper Deck)	2.00	.90	.25
☐ 453 Michael Jordan .... (92-93 Upper Deck)	2.00	.90	.25

	MINT	NRMT	EXC
COMPLETE SET (10)	90.00	40.00	11.00
COMMON JORDAN (37-45)...	10.00	4.50	1.25
☐ 37 Michael Jordan .... 1985 NBA Rookie of the Year	10.00	4.50	1.25
☐ 38 Michael Jordan .... 1986 63-Point Game	10.00	4.50	1.25
☐ 39 Michael Jordan .... 1987-88 Air Raid	10.00	4.50	1.25
☐ 40 Michael Jordan 1988	10.00	4.50	1.25
☐ 41 Michael Jordan .... 1985-93 9-Time NBA All-Star	10.00	4.50	1.25
☐ 42 Michael Jordan 1984	10.00	4.50	1.25
☐ 43 Michael Jordan .... 1991-93 MJOs Highlight Zone	10.00	4.50	1.25
☐ 44 Michael Jordan .... 1984-93 Rare Air	10.00	4.50	1.25
☐ 45 Checklist....................	10.00	4.50	1.25
☐ NNO Header Card..............	10.00	4.50	1.25

1994-95 Upper Deck Jordan Heroes

Randomly inserted in 12-card first series hobby and retail packs at a rate of one in 30, these 10 (nine numbered cards and one unnumbered header card) standard-size cards spotlight Michael Jordan's outstanding career. The fronts feature color action shots of Jordan from different stages in his career. His name appears in gold-foil lettering in the bottom margin and also as a facsimile autograph in gold foil in the upper margin. The card's subtitle appears in vertical gold-foil lettering in the left margin. The right side is full-bleed. The back carries a color action shot of Jordan on a ghosted background. A small color action shot appears at the lower left. Career highlights appear in a colored panel set off to one side. The cards are numbered on the back 37-45, a continuation of previous Heroes sets which included Jerry West, Wilt Chamberlain, Larry Bird, and Future Heroes. A 3" by 5" jumbo version of the entire set was also issued one card per blister pack sold at retail outlets. These cards are valued at approximately 50% of the values of the standard-size cards.

1994-95 Upper Deck Predictor Award Winners

Randomly inserted exclusively into one in every 25 first and second series hobby packs, cards from this 40-card standard-size set are subdivided into All-Star MVP (H1-H10), Defensive Player of the Year (H11-H20), MVP (H21-H30) and ROY (H31-H40) subsets. If the featured player placed first or second in his respective category, the card was redeemable before the June 30th, 1995 deadline for a special Predictors exchange set (of which mailing was delayed until late October, 1995). Winner cards have been designated below with a "W1" (good for a 20-card exchange set) or "W2" (good for a 10-card exchange set) listing. The fronts feature the player photo for most of the card. The award that the card is good for is vertically on the left side of the card. The player's name, team and position is in the lower right corner and is printed in white. The backs of the card contain contest information. The cards are numbered with an "H" prefix. To ascertain the values of those exchange sets, please see header.

	MINT	NRMT	EXC
COMPLETE SET (40)	125.00	55.00	15.50
COMPLETE SERIES 1 (20)....	50.00	22.00	6.25
COMPLETE SERIES 2 (20)....	75.00	34.00	9.50
COMMON AS MVP (H1-H10)	1.00	.45	.12
COMMON DEF POY (H11-H20).	.75	.35	.09
COMMON MVP (H21-H30)	.75	.35	.09
COMMON ROY (H31-H40)	.75	.35	.09
COMP. AS MVP EXCH. SET (10)	15.00	6.75	1.85
COMP. DEF. POY EXCH. SET (10)	10.00	4.50	1.25
COMPLETE MVP EXCH.SET (10)	15.00	6.75	1.85
COMPLETE ROY EXCH.SET (10)	15.00	6.75	1.85
*AW. WIN. REDEMP. CARDS: 50% VALUE			

		MINT	NRMT	EXC
☐	H1 Charles Barkley............	3.00	1.35	.35
☐	H2 Hakeem Olajuwon......	5.00	2.20	.60
☐	H3 Shaquille O'Neal	10.00	4.50	1.25
☐	H4 Scottie Pippen	6.00	2.70	.75
☐	H5 David Robinson........	4.00	1.80	.50
☐	H6 Shawn Kemp W2.....	6.00	2.70	.75
☐	H7 Alonzo Mourning......	2.50	1.10	.30
☐	H8 Larry Johnson..........	2.00	.90	.25
☐	H9 Patrick Ewing	2.00	.90	.25
☐	H10 AS-MVP Wild Card W1	1.00	.45	.12
☐	H11 Hakeem Olajuwon.....	5.00	2.20	.60
☐	H12 Dikembe Mutombo W1	1.50	.70	.19
☐	H13 Nate McMillan	.75	.35	.09
☐	H14 Dennis Rodman......	8.00	3.60	1.00
☐	H15 Shaquille O'Neal	2.50	1.10	.30
☐	H16 Patrick Ewing	2.00	.90	.25
☐	H17 Charles Barkley......	3.00	1.35	.35
☐	H18 David Robinson	4.00	1.80	.50
☐	H19 John Stockton	2.00	.90	.25
☐	H20 DEF-POY Wild Card W2	.75	.35	.09
☐	H21 Shaquille O'Neal W2	10.00	4.50	1.25
☐	H22 Hakeem Olajuwon....	5.00	2.20	.60
☐	H23 David Robinson W1..	4.00	1.80	.50
☐	H24 Scottie Pippen	6.00	2.70	.75
☐	H25 Alonzo Mourning	2.50	1.10	.30
☐	H26 Shawn Kemp	6.00	2.70	.75
☐	H27 Charles Barkley......	3.00	1.35	.35
☐	H28 Patrick Ewing	2.00	.90	.25
☐	H29 Larry Johnson	2.00	.90	.25
☐	H30 MVP Wild Card	.75	.35	.09
☐	H31 Jason Kidd W1	8.00	3.60	1.00
☐	H32 Grant Hill W1	12.00	5.50	1.50
☐	H33 Glenn Robinson......	4.00	1.80	.50
☐	H34 Eddie Jones	2.50	1.10	.30
☐	H35 Donyell Marshall.....	.75	.35	.09
☐	H36 Eric Montross.........	.75	.35	.09
☐	H37 Sharone Wright	.75	.35	.09
☐	H38 Juwan Howard	8.00	3.60	1.00
☐	H39 Carlos Rogers........	.75	.35	.09
☐	H40 ROY Wild Card W1	.75	.35	.09

1994-95 Upper Deck Predictor League Leaders

Randomly inserted exclusively into one in every 25 first and second series retail packs, cards from this 40-card standard-size set are subdivided into Scoring (R1-R10), Assists (R11-R20), Rebounds (R21-R30) and Blocks (R31-R40) subsets. If the

featured player placed first or second in his respective category, the card was redeemable before the June 30th, 1995 deadline for a special Predictors exchange set (of which mailing was delayed until late October, 1995). Winner cards have been designated below with a "W1" (good for a 20-card exchange set) or "W2" (good for a 10-card exchange set) listing. Card design is identical to the Predictor Award Winners inserts. To ascertain values for exchange cards, please see header.

	MINT	NRMT	EXC
COMPLETE SET (40)	100.00	45.00	12.50
COMPLETE SERIES 1 (20).....	50.00	22.00	6.25
COMPLETE SERIES 2 (20)....	50.00	22.00	6.25
COMMON SCORERS (R1-R10)..	.75	.35	.09
COMMON ASSISTS (R11-R20).	.75	.35	.09
COMMON REB.(R21-R30)	.75	.35	.09
COMMON BLOCKS (R31-R40) .	.75	.35	.09
COMP. SCO. EXCH. SET (10).	12.00	5.50	1.50
COMP. AST.EXCH. SET (10)..	6.00	2.70	.75
COMP. REB. EXCH. SET (10).	4.50	4.50	1.25
COMP.BLOCKS EXCH.SET (10)	12.00	5.50	1.50
*LEAGUE LEADERS REDEMPTION CARDS: 50% VALUE			

		MINT	NRMT	EXC
☐	R1 David Robinson...........	4.00	1.80	.50
☐	R2 Shaquille O'Neal W1...	10.00	4.50	1.25
☐	R3 Hakeem Olajuwon W2.	5.00	2.20	.60
☐	R4 Scottie Pippen	6.00	2.70	.75
☐	R5 Chris Webber	2.50	1.10	.30
☐	R6 Karl Malone	2.00	.90	.25
☐	R7 Patrick Ewing	2.00	.90	.25
☐	R8 Mitch Richmond	1.50	.70	.19
☐	R9 Charles Barkley.........	3.00	1.35	.35
☐	R10 Scorers Wild Card	.75	.35	.09
☐	R11 John Stockton W1.....	2.00	.90	.25
☐	R12 Mookie Blaylock	.75	.35	.09
☐	R13 Kenny Anderson W2.	1.25	.55	.16
☐	R14 Kevin Johnson	1.25	.55	.16
☐	R15 Muggsy Bogues	.75	.35	.09
☐	R16 Tim Hardaway	1.25	.55	.16
☐	R17 Anfernee Hardaway .	12.00	5.50	1.50
☐	R18 Rod Strickland	.75	.35	.09
☐	R19 Sherman Douglas.....	.75	.35	.09
☐	R20 Assists Wild Card	.75	.35	.09
☐	R21 Shaquille O'Neal	10.00	4.50	1.25
☐	R22 Hakeem Olajuwon.....	5.00	2.20	.60
☐	R23 Dennis Rodman W1 ..	8.00	3.60	1.00
☐	R24 Dikembe Mutombo W2	1.25	.55	.16
☐	R25 Karl Malone	2.00	.90	.25
☐	R26 Kevin Willis.............	.75	.35	.09
☐	R27 Chris Webber	2.50	1.10	.30
☐	R28 Alonzo Mourning	2.50	1.10	.30
☐	R29 Derrick Coleman.......	.75	.35	.09

		MINT	NRMT	EXC
☐ R30	Rebounds Wild Card ...	.75	.35	.09
☐ R31	Dikembe Mutombo W1	1.25	.55	.16
☐ R32	Hakeem Olajuwon W2	5.00	2.20	.60
☐ R33	David Robinson	4.00	1.80	.50
☐ R34	Shawn Bradley	1.25	.55	.16
☐ R35	Shaquille O'Neal	10.00	4.50	1.25
☐ R36	Patrick Ewing	2.00	.90	.25
☐ R37	Alonzo Mourning	2.50	1.10	.30
☐ R38	Shawn Kemp	6.00	2.70	.75
☐ R39	Derrick Coleman	.75	.35	.09
☐ R40	Blocks Wild Card	.75	.35	.09

1994-95 Upper Deck Rookie Standouts

Randomly inserted into one in every 30 second series packs, cards from this 20-card standard size set feature a selection of the top rookies from the 1994-95 season. The borderless fronts feature a color photo in the middle. The words "Rookie Standouts" are in gold foil in the bottom left corner. The hard to read player's names are in the upper left corner. The backs have player information and are numbered with a RS prefix in the upper left corner. The set is sequenced in 1994 NBA draft order.

		MINT	NRMT	EXC
	COMPLETE SET (20)	80.00	36.00	10.00
	COMMON CARD (RS1-RS20)	1.00	.45	.12
☐ RS1	Glenn Robinson	10.00	4.50	1.25
☐ RS2	Jason Kidd	20.00	9.00	2.50
☐ RS3	Grant Hill	30.00	13.50	3.70
☐ RS4	Donyell Marshall	1.00	.45	.12
☐ RS5	Juwan Howard	20.00	9.00	2.50
☐ RS6	Sharone Wright	2.00	.90	.25
☐ RS7	Lamond Murray	1.00	.45	.12
☐ RS8	Brian Grant	4.00	1.80	.50
☐ RS9	Eric Montross	2.00	.90	.25
☐ RS10	Eddie Jones	6.00	2.70	.75
☐ RS11	Carlos Rogers	1.00	.45	.12
☐ RS12	Khalid Reeves	1.00	.45	.12
☐ RS13	Jalen Rose	2.00	.90	.25
☐ RS14	Michael Smith	1.00	.45	.12
☐ RS15	Eric Piatkowski	1.00	.45	.12
☐ RS16	Clifford Rozier	2.00	.90	.25
☐ RS17	Aaron McKie	2.00	.90	.25
☐ RS18	Eric Mobley	1.00	.45	.12
☐ RS19	Bill Curley	1.00	.45	.12
☐ RS20	Wesley Person	2.00	.90	.25

1994-95 Upper Deck Slam Dunk Stars

Randomly inserted into one in every 30 second series packs, cards from this 20-card standard-size set feature Upper Deck spokesperson Shawn Kemp's selections of the top dunkers. The fronts feature the words "Kemp Slam Dunk Stars" as well as a sculpture of Kemp in gold foil on the left. The rest of the card is dedicated to a photo of the player dunking. The back has Kemp's opinion of each player. There is also a small inset photo of Kemp as well as a cutout of the featured player. The set is sequenced in alphabetical order.

		MINT	NRMT	EXC
	COMPLETE SET (20)	130.00	57.50	16.00
	COMMON CARD (S1-S20)	1.50	.70	.19
☐ S1	Vin Baker	8.00	3.60	1.00
☐ S2	Charles Barkley	10.00	4.50	1.25
☐ S3	Derrick Coleman	1.50	.70	.19
☐ S4	Clyde Drexler	8.00	3.60	1.00
☐ S5	LaPhonso Ellis	1.50	.70	.19
☐ S6	Larry Johnson	6.00	2.70	.75
☐ S7	Shawn Kemp	20.00	9.00	2.50
☐ S8	Donyell Marshall	1.50	.70	.19
☐ S9	Jamal Mashburn	5.00	2.20	.60
☐ S10	Gheorghe Muresan	3.00	1.35	.35
☐ S11	Alonzo Mourning	8.00	3.60	1.00
☐ S12	Shaquille O'Neal	30.00	13.50	3.70
☐ S13	Hakeem Olajuwon	15.00	6.75	1.85
☐ S14	Scottie Pippen	20.00	9.00	2.50
☐ S15	Isaiah Rider	1.50	.70	.19
☐ S16	David Robinson	12.00	5.50	1.50
☐ S17	Clarence Weatherspoon	3.00	1.35	.35
☐ S18	Chris Webber	8.00	3.60	1.00
☐ S19	Dominique Wilkins	3.00	1.35	.35
☐ S20	Rik Smits	3.00	1.35	.35

1994-95 Upper Deck Special Edition

Inserted one per pack into both first and second series 12-card packs and four per second series rack pack, cards from this 180-card standard-size set (issued in two

separate 90-card series) are comprised of a wide selection of the top stars and prospects in the NBA. Fronts feature full-color player action shots against silver-foil backgrounds. The players are categorized by team name as follows: Atlanta Hawks (1-3, 91, 93-94), Boston Celtics (4-6, 95-97), Charlotte Hornets (5-7, 98-100), Chicago Bulls (10-12, 101-103), Cleveland Cavaliers (13-15, 104-106), Dallas Mavericks (16-19, 107-109, 116), Denver Nuggets (20-23, 113-115), Detroit Pistons (24-26, 110-112), Golden State Warriors (27-30, 117-121), Houston Rockets (31-34, 122-124), Indiana Pacers (35-37, 125-127), Los Angeles Clippers (38-40, 128-130, 134), Los Angeles Lakers (41-44, 131-133), Miami Heat (45-48, 135-137), Milwaukee Bucks (49-51, 138-140), Minnesota Timberwolves (52-54, 141-143), New Jersey Nets (55-57, 144-146), New York Knicks (58-62, 148-150), Orlando Magic (63-65, 151-154), Philadelphia 76ers (66-68, 147, 155-157), Phoenix Suns (69-71, 158-161), Portland Trail Blazers (72-74, 162-164), Sacramento Kings (75-77, 165-167, 174), San Antonio Spurs (78-81, 168-170), Seattle Supersonics (82-84, 171-173), Utah Jazz (85-87, 175-177), Washington Bullets (88-90, 92, 178-180). Cards are numbered with an SE prefix on back.

	MINT	NRMT	EXC
COMPLETE SET (180)	50.00	22.00	6.25
COMPLETE SERIES 1 (90)	15.00	6.75	1.85
COMPLETE SERIES 2 (90)	35.00	16.00	4.40
COMMON CARD (1-180)	.15	.07	.02

		MINT	NRMT	EXC
☐ 1	Stacey Augmon	.25	.11	.03
☐ 2	Kevin Willis	.15	.07	.02
☐ 3	Mookie Blaylock	.25	.11	.03
☐ 4	Rick Fox	.15	.07	.02
☐ 5	Xavier McDaniel	.15	.07	.02
☐ 6	Dee Brown	.15	.07	.02
☐ 7	Muggsy Bogues	.25	.11	.03
☐ 8	Kenny Gattison	.15	.07	.02
☐ 9	Alonzo Mourning	1.00	.45	.12
☐ 10	B.J. Armstrong	.15	.07	.02
☐ 11	Bill Cartwright	.15	.07	.02
☐ 12	Toni Kukoc	.60	.25	.07
☐ 13	Mark Price	.15	.07	.02
☐ 14	Gerald Wilkins	.15	.07	.02
☐ 15	John Williams	.15	.07	.02
☐ 16	Jamal Mashburn	.60	.25	.07
☐ 17	Sean Rooks	.15	.07	.02
☐ 18	Doug Smith	.15	.07	.02
☐ 19	Jim Jackson	.40	.18	.05
☐ 20	Mahmoud Abdul-Rauf	.15	.07	.02
☐ 21	Rodney Rogers	.15	.07	.02
☐ 22	Reggie Williams	.15	.07	.02
☐ 23	LaPhonso Ellis	.15	.07	.02
☐ 24	Allan Houston	.50	.23	.06
☐ 25	Terry Mills	.15	.07	.02
☐ 26	Joe Dumars	.40	.18	.05
☐ 27	Chris Mullin	.40	.18	.05
☐ 28	Billy Owens	.15	.07	.02
☐ 29	Latrell Sprewell	.40	.18	.05
☐ 30	Chris Webber	1.00	.45	.12
☐ 31	Sam Cassell	.40	.18	.05
☐ 32	Vernon Maxwell	.15	.07	.02
☐ 33	Hakeem Olajuwon	2.00	.90	.25
☐ 34	Otis Thorpe	.25	.11	.03
☐ 35	Rik Smits	.40	.18	.05
☐ 36	Derrick McKey	.15	.07	.02
☐ 37	Haywoode Workman	.15	.07	.02
☐ 38	Charles Outlaw	.15	.07	.02
☐ 39	Elmore Spencer	.15	.07	.02
☐ 40	Loy Vaught	.25	.11	.03
☐ 41	George Lynch	.15	.07	.02
☐ 42	Nick Van Exel	.75	.35	.09
☐ 43	James Worthy	.40	.18	.05
☐ 44	Elden Campbell	.25	.11	.03
☐ 45	Grant Long	.15	.07	.02
☐ 46	Harold Miner	.15	.07	.02
☐ 47	Glen Rice	.40	.18	.05
☐ 48	Steve Smith	.40	.18	.05
☐ 49	Todd Day	.15	.07	.02
☐ 50	Eric Murdock	.15	.07	.02
☐ 51	Vin Baker	1.00	.45	.12
☐ 52	Christian Laettner	.40	.18	.05
☐ 53	Isaiah Rider	.15	.07	.02
☐ 54	Micheal Williams	.15	.07	.02
☐ 55	Benoit Benjamin	.15	.07	.02
☐ 56	Derrick Coleman	.15	.07	.02
☐ 57	Chris Morris	.15	.07	.02
☐ 58	Charles Smith	.15	.07	.02
☐ 59	Greg Anthony	.15	.07	.02
☐ 60	Doc Rivers	.15	.07	.02
☐ 61	Derek Harper	.15	.07	.02
☐ 62	John Starks	.15	.07	.02
☐ 63	Anfernee Hardaway	5.00	2.20	.60
☐ 64	Dennis Scott	.25	.11	.03
☐ 65	Nick Anderson	.40	.18	.05
☐ 66	Shawn Bradley	.40	.18	.05
☐ 67	Clarence Weatherspoon	.25	.11	.03
☐ 68	Jeff Malone	.15	.07	.02
☐ 69	Cedric Ceballos	.30	.14	.04
☐ 70	Kevin Johnson	.40	.18	.05
☐ 71	Oliver Miller	.15	.07	.02
☐ 72	Clifford Robinson	.40	.18	.05
☐ 73	Rod Strickland	.15	.07	.02
☐ 74	Buck Williams	.25	.11	.03
☐ 75	Mitch Richmond	.60	.25	.07
☐ 76	Walt Williams	.40	.18	.05
☐ 77	Lionel Simmons	.15	.07	.02
☐ 78	Willie Anderson	.15	.07	.02
☐ 79	Terry Cummings	.15	.07	.02
☐ 80	J.R. Reid	.15	.07	.02
☐ 81	Dennis Rodman	3.00	1.35	.35
☐ 82	Kendall Gill	.15	.07	.02
☐ 83	Sam Perkins	.25	.11	.03
☐ 84	Detlef Schrempf	.25	.11	.03
☐ 85	Jeff Hornacek	.25	.11	.03
☐ 86	Karl Malone	.75	.35	.09
☐ 87	Felton Spencer	.15	.07	.02
☐ 88	Calbert Cheaney	.25	.11	.03

☐ 89 Don MacLean	.15	.07	.02
☐ 90 Brent Price	.15	.07	.02
☐ 91 Tyrone Corbin	.15	.07	.02
☐ 92 Rex Chapman	.15	.07	.02
☐ 93 Ken Norman	.15	.07	.02
☐ 94 Steve Smith	.40	.18	.05
☐ 95 Eric Montross	.40	.18	.05
☐ 96 Dino Radja	.40	.18	.05
☐ 97 Dominique Wilkins	.40	.18	.05
☐ 98 Scott Burrell	.25	.11	.03
☐ 99 Hersey Hawkins	.25	.11	.03
☐ 100 Larry Johnson	.75	.35	.09
☐ 101 Ron Harper	.25	.11	.03
☐ 102 Scottie Pippen	2.50	1.10	.30
☐ 103 Dickey Simpkins	.25	.11	.03
☐ 104 Tyrone Hill	.15	.07	.02
☐ 105 Chris Mills	.40	.18	.05
☐ 106 Bobby Phills	.15	.07	.02
☐ 107 Lorenzo Williams	.15	.07	.02
☐ 108 Popeye Jones	.15	.07	.02
☐ 109 Jason Kidd	5.00	2.20	.60
☐ 110 Dikembe Mutombo	.40	.18	.05
☐ 111 Robert Pack	.15	.07	.02
☐ 112 Jalen Rose	.60	.25	.07
☐ 113 Bill Curley	.15	.07	.02
☐ 114 Grant Hill	8.00	3.60	1.00
☐ 115 Lindsey Hunter	.15	.07	.02
☐ 116 Roy Tarpley	.15	.07	.02
☐ 117 Tim Hardaway	.40	.18	.05
☐ 118 Ricky Pierce	.15	.07	.02
☐ 119 Carlos Rogers	.15	.07	.02
☐ 120 Clifford Rozier	.25	.11	.03
☐ 121 Rony Seikaly	.15	.07	.02
☐ 122 Mario Elie	.15	.07	.02
☐ 123 Robert Horry	.40	.18	.05
☐ 124 Kenny Smith	.15	.07	.02
☐ 125 Antonio Davis	.15	.07	.02
☐ 126 Dale Davis	.15	.07	.02
☐ 127 Reggie Miller	1.00	.45	.12
☐ 128 Lamond Murray	.15	.07	.02
☐ 129 Eric Piatkowski	.15	.07	.02
☐ 130 Pooh Richardson	.15	.07	.02
☐ 131 Cedric Ceballos	.40	.18	.05
☐ 132 Vlade Divac	.40	.18	.05
☐ 133 Eddie Jones	1.50	.70	.19
☐ 134 Mark Jackson	.15	.07	.02
☐ 135 Matt Geiger	.15	.07	.02
☐ 136 Khalid Reeves	.15	.07	.02
☐ 137 Kevin Willis	.15	.07	.02
☐ 138 Lee Mayberry	.15	.07	.02
☐ 139 Eric Mobley	.15	.07	.02
☐ 140 Glenn Robinson	2.50	1.10	.30
☐ 141 Doug West	.15	.07	.02
☐ 142 Donyell Marshall	.25	.11	.03
☐ 143 Chris Smith	.15	.07	.02
☐ 144 Kenny Anderson	.40	.18	.05
☐ 145 Chris Morris	.15	.07	.02
☐ 146 Armon Gilliam	.15	.07	.02
☐ 147 Dana Barros	.15	.07	.02
☐ 148 Patrick Ewing	.75	.35	.09
☐ 149 Charles Oakley	.25	.11	.03
☐ 150 Charlie Ward	.40	.18	.05
☐ 151 Horace Grant	.40	.18	.05
☐ 152 Shaquille O'Neal	4.00	1.80	.50
☐ 153 Brian Shaw	.15	.07	.02
☐ 154 Brooks Thompson	.25	.11	.03
☐ 155 B.J. Tyler	.15	.07	.02
☐ 156 Scott Williams	.15	.07	.02
☐ 157 Sharone Wright	.40	.18	.05
☐ 158 Charles Barkley	1.25	.55	.16
☐ 159 Dan Majerle	.25	.11	.03

☐ 160 Danny Manning	.25	.11	.03
☐ 161 Wesley Person	.40	.18	.05
☐ 162 Clyde Drexler	1.00	.45	.12
☐ 163 Harvey Grant	.15	.07	.02
☐ 164 Terry Porter	.15	.07	.02
☐ 165 Brian Grant	1.00	.45	.12
☐ 166 Bobby Hurley	.15	.07	.02
☐ 167 Olden Polynice	.15	.07	.02
☐ 168 Sean Elliott	.40	.18	.05
☐ 169 Chuck Person	.15	.07	.02
☐ 170 David Robinson	1.50	.70	.19
☐ 171 Shawn Kemp	2.50	1.10	.30
☐ 172 Nate McMillan	.15	.07	.02
☐ 173 Gary Payton	1.25	.55	.16
☐ 174 Michael Smith	.15	.07	.02
☐ 175 David Benoit	.15	.07	.02
☐ 176 Jay Humphries	.15	.07	.02
☐ 177 John Stockton	.75	.35	.09
☐ 178 Juwan Howard	5.00	2.20	.60
☐ 179 Chris Webber	1.00	.45	.12
☐ 180 Scott Skiles	.15	.07	.02

1994-95 Upper Deck Special Edition Gold

Randomly inserted at the rate of one per 35 first and second series packs, these 180 standard-size cards are similar in design to their regular Special Edition counterparts, except that their fronts are gold foil instead of silver foil, and their backs have a gold-hued background for the area that carries the team logo. Only the top few cards from the set are individually priced below. Please refer to the multipliers provided below (coupled with the prices for the corresponding basic Special Edition inserts) to ascertain value for unlisted cards. Cards are numbered with an SE prefix on back.

	MINT	NRMT	EXC
COMPLETE SET (180)	500.00	220.00	60.00
COMPLETE SERIES 1 (90)	150.00	70.00	19.00
COMPLETE SERIES 2 (90)	350.00	160.00	45.00
COMMON CARD (1-180)	1.00	.45	.12
*STARS: 4X to 8X BASIC CARDS			
*ROOKIES: 3X to 6X BASIC CARDS			

☐ 33 Hakeem Olajuwon	15.00	6.75	1.85
☐ 63 Anfernee Hardaway	40.00	18.00	5.00
☐ 81 Dennis Rodman	25.00	11.00	3.10
☐ 102 Scottie Pippen	20.00	9.00	2.50
☐ 109 Jason Kidd	30.00	13.50	3.70
☐ 114 Grant Hill	50.00	22.00	6.25

		MINT	NRMT	EXC
☐ 140	Glenn Robinson	15.00	6.75	1.85
☐ 152	Shaquille O'Neal	30.00	13.50	3.70
☐ 171	Shawn Kemp	20.00	9.00	2.50
☐ 178	Juwan Howard	30.00	13.50	3.70

1994-95 Upper Deck Special Edition Jumbos

One of these twenty-seven different over-sized Special Edition Jumbo cards was inserted into each Upper Deck second series hobby box. The cards parallel their corresponding basic Special Edition inserts except for their size and numbering.

a total of 360 cards. Twelve-card packs carried a suggested retail price of $1.99. The fronts are borderless full-color player action shots with the player's name printed in gold foil at the bottom. The backs feature another player color action shot with a graph of the player's career stats. The player's name and biography are printed vertically on the left side of the back in white type. The set features the following topical subsets: The Rookie Years (136-154), All-Rookie team (155-165), All NBA Team (166-180), USAI '96 (316-325), Images of '95 (326-335), Major Attractions (336-346) and Slams and Jams (347-360). Rookie Cards of note include Michael Finley, Kevin Garnett, Antonio McDyess, Jerry Stackhouse and Damon Stoudamire.

		MINT	NRMT	EXC
	COMPLETE SET (27)	60.00	27.00	7.50
	COMMON CARD (1-27)	1.00	.45	.12
☐ 1	Steve Smith	1.00	.45	.12
☐ 2	Dominique Wilkins	1.50	.70	.19
☐ 3	Larry Johnson	3.00	1.35	.35
☐ 4	Scottie Pippen	10.00	4.50	1.25
☐ 5	Chris Mills	1.00	.45	.12
☐ 6	Jason Kidd	12.00	5.50	1.50
☐ 7	Jalen Rose	1.50	.70	.19
☐ 8	Lindsey Hunter	1.00	.45	.12
☐ 9	Tim Hardaway	1.50	.70	.19
☐ 10	Kenny Smith	1.00	.45	.12
☐ 11	Mark Jackson	1.00	.45	.12
☐ 12	Lamond Murray	1.00	.45	.12
☐ 13	Cedric Ceballos	1.50	.70	.19
☐ 14	Kevin Willis	1.00	.45	.12
☐ 15	Glenn Robinson	6.00	2.70	.75
☐ 16	Doug West	1.00	.45	.12
☐ 17	Kenny Anderson	1.50	.70	.19
☐ 18	Patrick Ewing	3.00	1.35	.35
☐ 19	Horace Grant	1.50	.70	.19
☐ 20	Sharone Wright	1.00	.45	.12
☐ 21	Charles Barkley	5.00	2.20	.60
☐ 22	Clyde Drexler	4.00	1.80	.50
☐ 23	Brian Grant	2.50	1.10	.30
☐ 24	Sean Elliott	1.50	.70	.19
☐ 25	Shawn Kemp	10.00	4.50	1.25
☐ 26	John Stockton	3.00	1.35	.35
☐ 27	Juwan Howard	12.00	5.50	1.50

1995-96 Upper Deck

The 1995-96 Upper Deck set was issued in two separate series of 180 cards each, for

		MINT	NRMT	EXC
	COMPLETE SET (360)	50.00	22.00	6.25
	COMPLETE SERIES 1 (180)	25.00	11.00	3.10
	COMPLETE SERIES 2 (180)	25.00	11.00	3.10
	COMMON CARD (1-360)	.10	.05	.01
☐ 1	Eddie Jones	.30	.14	.04
☐ 2	Hubert Davis	.10	.05	.01
☐ 3	Latrell Sprewell	.20	.09	.03
☐ 4	Stacey Augmon	.15	.07	.02
☐ 5	Mario Elie	.10	.05	.01
☐ 6	Tyrone Hill	.10	.05	.01
☐ 7	Dikembe Mutombo	.20	.09	.03
☐ 8	Antonio Davis	.10	.05	.01
☐ 9	Horace Grant	.20	.09	.03
☐ 10	Ken Norman	.10	.05	.01
☐ 11	Aaron McKie	.10	.05	.01
☐ 12	Vinny Del Negro	.10	.05	.01
☐ 13	Glenn Robinson	.50	.23	.06
☐ 14	Allan Houston	.20	.09	.03
☐ 15	Bryon Russell	.10	.05	.01
☐ 16	Tony Dumas	.10	.05	.01
☐ 17	Gary Payton	.60	.25	.07
☐ 18	Rik Smits	.20	.09	.03
☐ 19	Dino Radja	.15	.07	.02
☐ 20	Robert Pack	.10	.05	.01
☐ 21	Calbert Cheaney	.10	.05	.01
☐ 22	Clarence Weatherspoon	.10	.05	.01
☐ 23	Michael Jordan	5.00	2.20	.60
☐ 24	Felton Spencer	.10	.05	.01
☐ 25	J.R. Reid	.10	.05	.01
☐ 26	Cedric Ceballos	.25	.11	.03
☐ 27	Dan Majerle	.15	.07	.02
☐ 28	Donald Hodge	.10	.05	.01
☐ 29	Nate McMillan	.10	.05	.01
☐ 30	Bimbo Coles	.10	.05	.01
☐ 31	Mitch Richmond	.30	.14	.04
☐ 32	Scott Brooks	.10	.05	.01

#	Player			
33	Patrick Ewing	.40	.18	.05
34	Carl Herrera	.10	.05	.01
35	Rick Fox	.10	.05	.01
36	James Robinson	.10	.05	.01
37	Donald Royal	.10	.05	.01
38	Joe Dumars	.20	.09	.03
39	Rony Seikaly	.10	.05	.01
40	Dennis Rodman	1.50	.70	.19
41	Muggsy Bogues	.15	.07	.02
42	Gheorghe Muresan	.20	.09	.03
43	Ervin Johnson	.10	.05	.01
44	Todd Day	.10	.05	.01
45	Rex Walters	.10	.05	.01
46	Terrell Brandon	.20	.09	.03
47	Wesley Person	.20	.09	.03
48	Terry Dehere	.10	.05	.01
49	Steve Smith	.20	.09	.03
50	Brian Grant	.20	.09	.03
51	Eric Piatkowski	.10	.05	.01
52	Lindsey Hunter	.10	.05	.01
53	Chris Webber	.40	.18	.05
54	Antoine Carr	.10	.05	.01
55	Chris Dudley	.10	.05	.01
56	Clyde Drexler	.50	.23	.06
57	P.J. Brown	.10	.05	.01
58	Kevin Willis	.10	.05	.01
59	Jeff Turner	.10	.05	.01
60	Sean Elliott	.20	.09	.03
61	Kevin Johnson	.20	.09	.03
62	Scott Skiles	.10	.05	.01
63	Charles Smith	.10	.05	.01
64	Derrick McKey	.10	.05	.01
65	Danny Ferry	.10	.05	.01
66	Detlef Schrempf	.15	.07	.02
67	Shawn Bradley	.20	.09	.03
68	Isaiah Rider	.20	.09	.03
69	Karl Malone	.40	.18	.05
70	Will Perdue	.10	.05	.01
71	Terry Mills	.10	.05	.01
72	Glen Rice	.20	.09	.03
73	Tim Breaux	.10	.05	.01
74	Malik Sealy	.10	.05	.01
75	Walt Williams	.20	.09	.03
76	Bobby Phills	.10	.05	.01
77	Anthony Avent	.10	.05	.01
78	Jamal Mashburn UER	.25	.11	.03
	Career FG percentage is wrong			
79	Vlade Divac	.20	.09	.03
80	Reggie Williams	.10	.05	.01
81	Xavier McDaniel	.10	.05	.01
82	Avery Johnson	.15	.07	.02
83	Derek Harper	.10	.05	.01
84	Don MacLean	.10	.05	.01
85	Tom Gugliotta	.20	.09	.03
86	Craig Ehlo	.10	.05	.01
87	Robert Horry	.20	.09	.03
88	Kevin Edwards	.10	.05	.01
89	Chuck Person	.10	.05	.01
90	Sharone Wright	.10	.05	.01
91	Steve Kerr	.15	.07	.02
92	Marty Conlon	.10	.05	.01
93	Jalen Rose	.10	.05	.01
94	Bryant Reeves	1.00	.45	.12
95	Shaquille O'Neal	2.00	.90	.25
96	David Wesley	.10	.05	.01
97	Chris Mills	.10	.05	.01
98	Rod Strickland	.10	.05	.01
99	Pooh Richardson	.10	.05	.01
100	Sam Perkins	.15	.07	.02
101	Dell Curry	.10	.05	.01
102	David Benoit	.10	.05	.01
103	Christian Laettner	.20	.09	.03
104	Duane Causwell	.10	.05	.01
105	Jason Kidd	1.00	.45	.12
106	Mark West	.10	.05	.01
107	Lee Mayberry	.10	.05	.01
108	John Salley	.10	.05	.01
109	Jeff Malone	.10	.05	.01
110	George Zidek	.25	.11	.03
111	Kenny Smith	.10	.05	.01
112	George Lynch	.10	.05	.01
113	Toni Kukoc	.25	.11	.03
114	A.C. Green	.20	.09	.03
115	Kenny Anderson	.20	.09	.03
116	Robert Parish	.20	.09	.03
117	Chris Mullin	.15	.07	.02
118	Loy Vaught	.10	.05	.01
119	Olden Polynice	.10	.05	.01
120	Clifford Robinson	.20	.09	.03
121	Eric Mobley	.10	.05	.01
122	Doug West	.10	.05	.01
123	Sam Cassell	.20	.09	.03
124	Nick Anderson	.20	.09	.03
125	Matt Geiger	.10	.05	.01
126	Elden Campbell	.15	.07	.02
127	Alonzo Mourning	.40	.18	.05
128	Bryant Stith	.10	.05	.01
129	Mark Jackson	.10	.05	.01
130	Cherokee Parks	.30	.14	.04
131	Shawn Respert	.30	.14	.04
132	Alan Henderson	.25	.11	.03
133	Jerry Stackhouse	3.00	1.35	.35
134	Rasheed Wallace	.75	.35	.09
135	Antonio McDyess	1.50	.70	.19
136	Charles Barkley ROO	.30	.14	.04
137	Michael Jordan	2.50	1.10	.30
138	Hakeem Olajuwon	.50	.23	.06
139	Joe Dumars	.20	.09	.03
140	Patrick Ewing	.20	.09	.03
141	A.C. Green	.20	.09	.03
142	Karl Malone	.20	.09	.03
143	Detlef Schrempf	.15	.07	.02
144	Chuck Person	.10	.05	.01
145	Muggsy Bogues	.15	.07	.02
146	Horace Grant	.20	.09	.03
147	Mark Jackson	.10	.05	.01
148	Kevin Johnson ROO	.15	.07	.02
149	Mitch Richmond	.15	.07	.02
150	Rik Smits	.20	.09	.03
151	Nick Anderson	.20	.09	.03
152	Tim Hardaway	.20	.09	.03
153	Shawn Kemp	.60	.25	.07
154	David Robinson	.40	.18	.05
155	Jason Kidd	.50	.23	.06
156	Grant Hill	.75	.35	.09
157	Glenn Robinson	.25	.11	.03
158	Eddie Jones	.15	.07	.02
159	Brian Grant	.10	.05	.01
160	Juwan Howard	.15	.07	.02
161	Eric Montross	.10	.05	.01
162	Wesley Person	.10	.05	.01
163	Jalen Rose	.10	.05	.01
164	Donyell Marshall	.10	.05	.01
165	Sharone Wright	.10	.05	.01
166	Karl Malone	.20	.09	.03
167	Scottie Pippen	.60	.25	.07
168	David Robinson	.40	.18	.05
169	John Stockton	.20	.09	.03
170	Anfernee Hardaway	1.25	.55	.16
171	Charles Barkley	.30	.14	.04
172	Shawn Kemp	.60	.25	.07
173	Shaquille O'Neal	1.00	.45	.12

#	Player			
174	Gary Payton	.30	.14	.04
175	Mitch Richmond	.15	.07	.02
176	Dennis Rodman	.75	.35	.09
177	Detlef Schrempf	.15	.07	.02
178	Hakeem Olajuwon	.50	.23	.06
179	Reggie Miller	.25	.11	.03
180	Clyde Drexler	.25	.11	.03
181	Hakeem Olajuwon	1.00	.45	.12
182	Vin Baker	.40	.18	.05
183	Jeff Hornacek	.15	.07	.02
184	Popeye Jones	.10	.05	.01
185	Sedale Threatt	.10	.05	.01
186	Scottie Pippen	1.25	.55	.16
187	Terry Porter	.10	.05	.01
188	Dan Majerle	.15	.07	.02
189	Clifford Rozier	.10	.05	.01
190	Greg Minor	.10	.05	.01
191	Dennis Scott	.20	.09	.03
192	Hersey Hawkins	.10	.05	.01
193	Chris Gatling	.10	.05	.01
194	Charles Oakley	.15	.07	.02
195	Dale Davis	.10	.05	.01
196	Robert Pack	.10	.05	.01
197	Lamond Murray	.10	.05	.01
198	Mookie Blaylock	.15	.07	.02
199	Dickey Simpkins	.10	.05	.01
200	Kevin Gamble	.10	.05	.01
201	Lorenzo Williams	.10	.05	.01
202	Scott Burrell	.10	.05	.01
203	Armon Gilliam	.15	.07	.02
204	Doc Rivers	.10	.05	.01
205	Blue Edwards	.10	.05	.01
206	Billy Owens	.10	.05	.01
207	Juwan Howard	1.00	.45	.12
208	Harvey Grant	.10	.05	.01
209	Richard Dumas	.10	.05	.01
210	Anthony Peeler	.10	.05	.01
211	Matt Geiger	.10	.05	.01
212	Lucious Harris	.10	.05	.01
213	Grant Long	.10	.05	.01
214	Sasha Danilovic	.25	.11	.03
215	Chris Morris	.10	.05	.01
216	Donyell Marshall	.10	.05	.01
217	Alonzo Mourning	.40	.18	.05
218	John Stockton	.40	.18	.05
219	Khalid Reeves	.10	.05	.01
220	Mahmoud Abdul-Rauf	.15	.07	.02
221	Sean Rooks	.10	.05	.01
222	Shawn Kemp	1.25	.55	.16
223	John Williams	.10	.05	.01
224	Dee Brown	.10	.05	.01
225	Jim Jackson	.25	.11	.03
226	Harold Miner	.10	.05	.01
227	B.J. Armstrong	.10	.05	.01
228	Elliot Perry	.10	.05	.01
229	Anthony Miller	.10	.05	.01
230	Donny Marshall	.10	.05	.01
231	Tyrone Corbin	.10	.05	.01
232	Anthony Mason	.15	.07	.02
233	Grant Hill	1.50	.70	.19
234	Buck Williams	.15	.07	.02
235	Brian Shaw	.10	.05	.01
236	Dale Ellis	.10	.05	.01
237	Magic Johnson	1.25	.55	.16
238	Eric Montross	.10	.05	.01
239	Rex Chapman	.10	.05	.01
240	Otis Thorpe	.15	.07	.02
241	Tracy Murray	.10	.05	.01
242	Sarunas Marciulionis	.10	.05	.01
243	Luc Longley	.10	.05	.01
244	Elmore Spencer	.10	.05	.01
245	Terry Cummings	.10	.05	.01
246	Sam Mitchell	.10	.05	.01
247	Terrence Rencher	.10	.05	.01
248	Byron Houston	.10	.05	.01
249	Pervis Ellison	.10	.05	.01
250	Carlos Rogers	.10	.05	.01
251	Kendall Gill	.10	.05	.01
252	Sherell Ford	.10	.05	.01
253	Michael Finley	2.00	.90	.25
254	Kurt Thomas	.50	.23	.06
255	Joe Smith	2.00	.90	.25
256	Bobby Hurley	.10	.05	.01
257	Greg Anthony	.10	.05	.01
258	Willie Anderson	.10	.05	.01
259	Theo Ratliff	.30	.14	.04
260	Duane Ferrell	.10	.05	.01
261	Antonio Harvey	.10	.05	.01
262	Gary Grant	.10	.05	.01
263	Brian Williams	.10	.05	.01
264	Danny Manning	.15	.07	.02
265	Micheal Williams	.10	.05	.01
266	Dennis Rodman Bulls	2.50	1.10	.30
267	Arvydas Sabonis	1.25	.55	.16
268	Don MacLean	.10	.05	.01
269	Keith Askins	.10	.05	.01
270	Reggie Miller	.50	.23	.06
271	Ed Pinckney	.10	.05	.01
272	Bob Sura	.30	.14	.04
273	Kevin Garnett	5.00	2.20	.60
274	Byron Scott	.20	.09	.03
275	Mario Bennett	.10	.05	.01
276	Junior Burrough	.10	.05	.01
277	Anfernee Hardaway	2.50	1.10	.30
278	George McCloud	.10	.05	.01
279	Loren Meyer	.20	.09	.03
	Beckett staff member			
	Mary Campana in background			
280	Ed O'Bannon	.60	.25	.07
281	Lawrence Moten	.10	.05	.01
282	Dana Barros	.10	.05	.01
283	Damon Stoudamire	4.00	1.80	.50
284	Eric Williams	.30	.14	.04
285	Wayman Tisdale	.10	.05	.01
286	Rodney Rogers	.10	.05	.01
287	Sherman Douglas	.10	.05	.01
288	Greg Ostertag	.10	.05	.01
289	Alvin Robertson	.10	.05	.01
290	Tim Legler	.10	.05	.01
291	Zan Tabak	.10	.05	.01
292	Gary Trent	.30	.14	.04
293	Haywoode Workman	.10	.05	.01
294	Charles Barkley	.60	.25	.07
295	Derrick Coleman	.10	.05	.01
296	Ricky Pierce	.10	.05	.01
297	Benoit Benjamin	.10	.05	.01
298	Larry Johnson	.40	.18	.05
299	Travis Best	.25	.11	.03
300	Jason Caffey	.10	.05	.01
301	Cory Alexander	.10	.05	.01
302	Nick Van Exel	.30	.14	.04
303	Corliss Williamson	.30	.14	.04
304	Eric Murdock	.10	.05	.01
305	Tyus Edney	.75	.35	.09
306	Lou Roe	.10	.05	.01
307	John Salley	.10	.05	.01
308	Spud Webb	.15	.07	.02
309	Brent Barry	.75	.35	.09
310	David Robinson	.75	.35	.09
311	Glen Rice	.20	.09	.03
312	Chris King	.10	.05	.01
313	David Vaughn	.10	.05	.01

			MINT	NRMT	EXC

☐ 314 Kenny Gattison .... .10 .05 .01
☐ 315 Randolph Childress...... .10 .05 .01
☐ 316 Anfernee Hardaway USA 1.25 .55 .16
☐ 317 Grant Hill USA.............. .75 .35 .09
☐ 318 Karl Malone USA.......... .20 .09 .03
☐ 319 Reggie Miller USA........ .25 .11 .03
☐ 320 Hakeem Olajuwon USA .50 .23 .06
☐ 321 Shaquille O'Neal USA. 1.00 .45 .12
☐ 322 Scottie Pippen USA...... .60 .25 .07
☐ 323 David Robinson USA .... .40 .18 .05
☐ 324 Glenn Robinson USA .... .25 .11 .03
☐ 325 John Stockton USA....... .20 .09 .03
☐ 326 Cedric Ceballos I95...... .10 .05 .01
☐ 327 Shaquille O'Neal I95 .. 1.00 .45 .12
☐ 328 Glenn Robinson I95...... .25 .11 .03
☐ 329 Shawn Kemp I95.......... .60 .25 .07
☐ 330 Nick Anderson I95........ .15 .07 .02
☐ 331 Shawn Bradley I95........ .15 .07 .02
☐ 332 Horace Grant I95.......... .15 .07 .02
         Brooks Thompson
☐ 333 Robert Horry I95........... .15 .07 .02
☐ 334 NBA Expansion I95....... .10 .05 .01
         Grizzlies/Raptors
☐ 335 Michael Jordan I95 ... 2.50 1.10 .30
☐ 336 Nick Van Exel .... .15 .07 .02
         Dyan Cannon MA
☐ 337 Michael Jordan .... 1.25 .55 .16
         David Hanson MA
☐ 338 Scottie Pippen .... .25 .11 .03
         Jenna Von Oy MA
☐ 339 Michael Jordan .... 1.25 .55 .16
         Charlie Sheen MA
☐ 340 Jason Kidd .... .25 .11 .03
         Christopher "Kid" Reid MA
☐ 341 Michael Jordan .... 1.25 .55 .16
         Queen Latifah MA
☐ 342 Charles Barkley .... .15 .07 .02
         Don Johnson MA
☐ 343 Hakeem Olajuwon .... .25 .11 .03
         Corbin Bernsen MA
☐ 344 Ahmad Rashad MA....... .10 .05 .01
☐ 345 Willow Bay MA............. .10 .05 .01
☐ 346 Gary Payton .... .10 .05 .01
         Mark Curry MA
☐ 347 Horace Grant SJ.......... .15 .07 .02
☐ 348 Juwan Howard SJ........ .20 .09 .03
☐ 349 David Robinson SJ....... .40 .18 .05
☐ 350 Reggie Miller SJ.......... .25 .11 .03
☐ 351 Brian Grant SJ .... .15 .07 .02
☐ 352 Michael Jordan SJ..... 2.50 1.10 .30
☐ 353 Cedric Ceballos SJ...... .10 .05 .01
☐ 354 Blue Edwards SJ......... .10 .05 .01
☐ 355 Acie Earl SJ................ .10 .05 .01
☐ 356 Dennis Rodman SJ Bulls 1.25 .55 .16
☐ 357 Shawn Kemp SJ.......... .60 .25 .07
☐ 358 Jerry Stackhouse SJ.. 1.25 .55 .16
☐ 359 Jamal Mashburn SJ..... .10 .05 .01
☐ 360 Antonio McDyess SJ.... .60 .25 .07

1995-96 Upper Deck Electric Court

One card from this 180-card parallel set was inserted into each retail pack. The cards are distinguished from their regular issue counterparts by a thicker card stock,

a new logo, and special foil treatment. Please refer to the multipliers in the header to ascertain values.

	MINT	NRMT	EXC
COMPLETE SET (360)	100.00	45.00	12.50
COMPLETE SERIES 1 (180)...	50.00	22.00	6.25
COMPLETE SERIES 2 (180)...	50.00	22.00	6.25
COMMON CARD (1-360)	.15	.07	.02

*STARS: 1.25X to 2.5X VALUE............
*ROOKIES: 1X to 2X VALUE.............

1995-96 Upper Deck Electric Court Gold

Parallel to the basic set, Electric Court Gold differs in design with their refractive "Electric Court" logo on each card front. The cards were randomly seeded in both series retail packs at an approximate rate of one in thirty-six. Please refer to the multipliers in the header to ascertain values.

	MINT	NRMT	EXC
COMPLETE SET (360)	1200.00	550.00	150.00
COMP.SERIES 1 (180)	600.00	275.00	75.00
COMP.SERIES 2 (180).........	600.00	275.00	75.00
COMMON CARD (1-360)	2.00	.90	.25

*STARS: 12.5X to 25X VALUE............
*ROOKIES: 7.5X to 15X VALUE............

☐ 23 Michael Jordan 160.00 70.00 20.00
☐ 40 Dennis Rodman 40.00 18.00 5.00
☐ 95 Shaquille O'Neal....... 50.00 22.00 6.25
☐ 105 Jason Kidd 25.00 11.00 3.10
☐ 133 Jerry Stackhouse...... 50.00 22.00 6.25
☐ 135 Antonio McDyess...... 25.00 11.00 3.10
☐ 137 Michael Jordan ROO 75.00 34.00 9.50

		MINT	NRMT	EXC
☐ 170	A.Hardaway AN	30.00	13.50	3.70
☐ 181	Hakeem Olajuwon	25.00	11.00	3.10
☐ 186	Scottie Pippen	30.00	13.50	3.70
☐ 207	Juwan Howard	25.00	11.00	3.10
☐ 222	Shawn Kemp	30.00	13.50	3.70
☐ 233	Grant Hill	40.00	18.00	5.00
☐ 237	Magic Johnson	30.00	13.50	3.70
☐ 253	Michael Finley	30.00	13.50	3.70
☐ 255	Joe Smith	30.00	13.50	3.70
☐ 266	Dennis Rodman Bulls	60.00	27.00	7.50
☐ 273	Kevin Garnett	110.00	50.00	14.00
☐ 277	Anfernee Hardaway	60.00	27.00	7.50
☐ 283	Damon Stoudamire	60.00	27.00	7.50
☐ 316	A.Hardaway USA	30.00	13.50	3.70
☐ 335	Michael Jordan I95	75.00	34.00	9.50
☐ 337	M.Jordan/Hansen MA	40.00	18.00	5.00
☐ 339	M.Jordan/C.Sheen MA	40.00	18.00	5.00
☐ 341	M.Jordan/Q.Latifah MA	40.00	18.00	5.00
☐ 352	Michael Jordan SJ	75.00	34.00	9.50

		MINT	NRMT	EXC
☐ AS8	Vin Baker	5.00	2.20	.60
☐ AS9	Alonzo Mourning	5.00	2.20	.60
☐ AS10	Joe Dumars	2.50	1.10	.30
☐ AS11	Patrick Ewing	5.00	2.20	.60
☐ AS12	Tyrone Hill	1.50	.70	.19
☐ AS13	Latrell Sprewell	2.50	1.10	.30
☐ AS14	Dan Majerle	2.50	1.10	.30
☐ AS15	Shawn Kemp	15.00	6.75	1.85
☐ AS16	Karl Malone	5.00	2.20	.60
☐ AS17	Hakeem Olajuwon	12.00	5.50	1.50
☐ AS18	Gary Payton	8.00	3.60	1.00
☐ AS19	Mitch Richmond	4.00	1.80	.50
☐ AS20	David Robinson	10.00	4.50	1.25
☐ AS21	Detlef Schrempf	2.50	1.10	.30
☐ AS22	Cedric Ceballos	3.00	1.35	.35
☐ AS23	John Stockton	5.00	2.20	.60
☐ AS24	Dikembe Mutombo	2.50	1.10	.30
☐ AS25	Charles Barkley	8.00	3.60	1.00

1995-96 Upper Deck All-Star Class

Randomly inserted in first series packs at a rate of one in 17, this 25-card standard-size set highlights the play of the NBA's best in the 1995 All Star Game. Borderless foil fronts feature the player in full-color action and include the Upper Deck logo stamped in blue foil on the upper right. "1995 NBA All Star Class" is printed in blue foil and centered at the bottom. On either side of the logo are gold pyramids which feature the player's name, team and position printed in black type. Blue backs have a copper bordered posed player shot with game highlights. The Phoenix All Star Weekend logo is printed at the top of the picture and the player's name, team and position are printed over the logo.

	MINT	NRMT	EXC
COMPLETE SET (25)	150.00	70.00	19.00
COMMON CARD (AS1-AS25)	1.50	.70	.19
☐ AS1 Anfernee Hardaway	30.00	13.50	3.70
☐ AS2 Reggie Miller	6.00	2.70	.75
☐ AS3 Grant Hill	20.00	9.00	2.50
☐ AS4 Scottie Pippen	15.00	6.75	1.85
☐ AS5 Shaquille O'Neal	25.00	11.00	3.10
☐ AS6 Larry Johnson	5.00	2.20	.60
☐ AS7 Dana Barros	1.50	.70	.19

1995-96 Upper Deck Jordan Collection

Upper Deck spokesperson and NBA legend Michael Jordan is featured on these eight, multi-series insert cards. Cards JC5-JC8 were randomly inserted into one in every 29 first series packs. Cards JC13-JC16 were randomly inserted into one in every 29 second series packs. The eight cards actually represent two segments of a twenty-four card set issued in six different series across all of Upper Deck's 1995-96 products (except SPx). Full-bleed, silver-foil fronts feature Jordan in full color in both posed and action shots. Backs feature Jordan in a spectacular action shot with alternating boxes of separated colors. A "Jordan Collection" box appears at the mid-left of the card with an explanation of the award that was featured on the front.

	MINT	NRMT	EXC
COMPLETE SET (8)	60.00	27.00	7.50
COMPLETE SERIES 1 (4)	30.00	13.50	3.70
COMPLETE SERIES 2 (4)	30.00	13.50	3.70
COMMON CARD (JC5-JC8)	10.00	4.50	1.25
COMMON CARD (JC13-JC16)	10.00	4.50	1.25
☐ JC5 Michael Jordan	10.00	4.50	1.25
☐ JC6 Michael Jordan	10.00	4.50	1.25
☐ JC7 Michael Jordan	10.00	4.50	1.25
☐ JC8 Michael Jordan	10.00	4.50	1.25

1995-96 Upper Deck Predictor MVP

1995-96 Upper Deck Predictor Player of the Month

Randomly inserted exclusively into second series retail packs at a rate of one in 30, this 10-card standard-size set features five Michael Jordan cards, four top NBA stars and a Long Shot card (representing all other NBA players). In addition, Upper Deck offered dealers a 5-card Predictor pack with the purchase of one case (20 boxes) of second series product. Dealers were given all 20 second series Predictor cards (retail MVP and hobby Scoring) with the purchase of two cases. Black and red basketball court fronts frame a full-color action player cutout. A black border surrounds the player's name, team and the month of the predicted award, all of which are stamped in gold foil. The outer border of the front is a black marble texture. Numbered backs are printed on white, have the prefix "R" and explain the rules of the game. Those holding a winning Predictor card redeemed the cards through a mail-in offer for a full set of the Predictor MVP cards. The expiration date to redeem winning cards was July 8, 1996. Exchange cards differ from the regular cards with their holographic silver foil text on front (replacing the gold foil on the regular cards) and player text on back (replacing the Predictor rules). Please refer to the header for values on the exchange singles.

	MINT	NRMT	EXC
COMPLETE SET (10)	50.00	22.00	6.25
COMMON CARD (R1-R10)	.75	.35	.09
COMP. MVP EXCH. SET (10) .	15.00	6.75	1.85
*MVP EXCH. CARDS: 50% VALUE ...			

☐ R1	M.Jordan MVP W	8.00	3.60	1.00
☐ R2	M.Jordan All-NBA W ...	8.00	3.60	1.00
☐ R3	M.Jordan Def. POY L ...	8.00	3.60	1.00
☐ R4	M.Jordan All-Def. W ...	8.00	3.60	1.00
☐ R5	M.Jordan Finals MVP W	8.00	3.60	1.00
☐ R6	Hakeem Olajuwon L	3.00	1.35	.35
☐ R7	Charles Barkley L	2.00	.90	.25
☐ R8	Karl Malone L	1.25	.55	.16
☐ R9	Anfernee Hardaway L ..	8.00	3.60	1.00
☐ R10	Long Shot Card L	.75	.35	.09

Randomly inserted exclusively into first series retail packs at a rate of one in 30, this 10-card standard-size set features five Michael Jordan cards, four top NBA stars and a Long Shot card (representing all other NBA players). In addition, Upper Deck offered dealers a 5-card Predictor pack with the purchase of one case (20 boxes) of first series product. Dealers were given all 20 first series Predictor cards (retail Player of the Month and hobby Player of the Week) with the purchase of two cases. Each card lists months that the featured player might win Player of the Month honors. Black and red basketball court fronts frame a full-color action player cutout. A black border surrounds the player's name, team and the month of the predicted award, all of which are stamped in gold foil. The outer border of the front is a black marble texture. Numbered backs are printed on white, have the prefix "R" and explain the rules of the game. Those holding a winning Predictor card redeemed the cards through a mail-in offer for a full set of the Predictor Player of the Month cards. The expiration date to redeem winning cards was July 1, 1996. Exchange cards differ from the regular cards with their holographic silver foil text on front (replacing the gold foil on the regular cards) and player text on back (replacing the Predictor rules). Please refer to the header for values on the exchange singles.

	MINT	NRMT	EXC
COMPLETE SET (10)	40.00	18.00	5.00
COMMON CARD (R1-R10)	.75	.35	.09
COMP. POM EXCH. SET (10).	15.00	6.75	1.85
*POM EXCH. CARDS: 50% VALUE ...			

☐ R1	M.Jordan Nov./Dec. L.	8.00	3.60	1.00
☐ R2	M.Jordan Jan. W	8.00	3.60	1.00
☐ R3	M.Jordan Feb. L	8.00	3.60	1.00
☐ R4	M.Jordan Mar. L	8.00	3.60	1.00
☐ R5	M.Jordan Apr. L	8.00	3.60	1.00
☐ R6	Jamal Mashburn L	.75	.35	.09
☐ R7	David Robinson W.......	2.50	1.10	.30

		MINT	NRMT	EXC
☐ R8	Latrell Sprewell L	.75	.35	.09
☐ R9	Chris Webber L	1.25	.55	.16
☐ R10	Long Shot Card W	.75	.35	.09

1995-96 Upper Deck Predictor Player of the Week

Randomly inserted exclusively into first series hobby packs at a rate of one in 30, this 10-card standard-sized set features five Michael Jordan cards, four top NBA stars and a Long Shot card (representing all other NBA players). In addition, Upper Deck offered dealers a 5-card Predictor pack with the purchase of one case (20 boxes) of first series product. Dealers were given all 20 first series Predictor cards (retail Player of the Month and hobby Player of the Week) with the purchase of two cases. Each card lists weeks that the featured player might win Player of the Week honors. The fronts feature the player in a full color cutout set against a red court background and a black border surrounding the red. The player's name, team name and predictor category are printed in gold foil. Card edges are trimmed with a black marble texture. Those holding a winning Predictor card redeemed the cards through a mail-in offer for a full set of the Predictor Player of the Week cards. The expiration date to redeem winning cards was July 1, 1996. Exchange cards differ from the regular cards with their holographic silver foil text on front (replacing the gold foil on the regular cards) and player text on back (replacing the Predictor rules). Please refer to the header for values on the exchange singles.

	MINT	NRMT	EXC
COMPLETE SET (10)	50.00	22.00	6.25
COMMON CARD (H1-H10)	.75	.35	.09
COMP. POW EXCH. SET (10)	15.00	6.75	1.85
*POW EXCH. CARDS: 50% VALUE...			
☐ H1 M.Jordan Nov./Dec. W	8.00	3.60	1.00
☐ H2 M.Jordan Jan. W	8.00	3.60	1.00
☐ H3 M.Jordan Feb. L	8.00	3.60	1.00
☐ H4 M.Jordan Mar.	8.00	3.60	1.00

		MINT	NRMT	EXC
☐ H5	M.Jordan Apr. L	8.00	3.60	1.00
☐ H6	Anfernee Hardaway W.	8.00	3.60	1.00
☐ H7	Hakeem Olajuwon W.	3.00	1.35	.35
☐ H8	Scottie Pippen W.	4.00	1.80	.50
☐ H9	Glenn Robinson L	1.50	.70	.19
☐ H10	Long Shot Card W	.75	.35	.09

1995-96 Upper Deck Predictor Scoring

Randomly inserted in second series hobby packs at a rate of one in 30, cards from this 10-card insert set feature five Michael Jordan cards, four top NBA stars and a Long Shot card (representing all other NBA players). In addition, Upper Deck offered dealers a 5-card Predictor pack with the purchase of one case (20 boxes) of second series product. Dealers were given all 20 second series Predictor cards (retail MVP and hobby Scoring) with the purchase of two cases. Card fronts feature the player in a full color cutout set against a red court background and a black border surrounding the red. The player's name, team name and predictor category are printed in gold foil. Card edges are trimmed with a black marble texture. If the player pictured won the NBA scoring title, the card was redeemable for a special version of the hobby Predictor Scoring set. The expiration date to redeem winning cards was July 8, 1996. Exchange cards differ from the regular cards with their holographic silver foil text on front (replacing the gold foil on the regular cards) and player text on back (replacing the Predictor rules). Please refer to the header for values on the exchange singles.

	MINT	NRMT	EXC
COMPLETE SET (10)	50.00	22.00	6.25
COMMON CARD (H1-H10)	.75	.35	.09
COMP.SCORING EXCH. SET (10)	15.00	6.75	1.85
*SCO. EXCH. CARDS: 50% VALUE...			
☐ H1 M.Jordan Scoring W	8.00	3.60	1.00
☐ H2 M.Jordan Assists L	8.00	3.60	1.00
☐ H3 M.Jordan Steals L	8.00	3.60	1.00
☐ H4 M.Jordan 3-pt. L	8.00	3.60	1.00
☐ H5 M.Jordan Playoff W	8.00	3.60	1.00
☐ H6 David Robinson L	2.50	1.10	.30

		MINT	NRMT	EXC
☐ H7	Scottie Pippen L	4.00	1.80	.50
☐ H8	Jerry Stackhouse L	5.00	2.20	.60
☐ H9	Glenn Robinson L	1.50	.70	.19
☐ H10	Long Shot Card L	.75	.35	.09

1995-96 Upper Deck Special Edition

These 180 standard-size cards were insert-ed at a rate of one per hobby pack only and were printed on a silver foil front. The cards were issued in two separate series of 90 (1-90 in first series packs and 91-180 in sec-ond series). Only the top veterans and rookies were selected for inclusion in this set. The player is featured in an action shot but only he is singled out for color. The rest of the shot is faded out to black and white. The player's name is stamped in silver foil at the bottom and the Special Edition logo is stamped in silver foil at the top right. "SE" is stamped in silver foil and runs vertically down the left side of the front. Backs are printed on a white and gray background and include a player biography, career sta-tistics and player highlights. A color player action shot appears on the upper left side and includes the card number.

	MINT	NRMT	EXC
COMPLETE SET (180)	90.00	40.00	11.00
COMPLETE SERIES 1 (90)	30.00	13.50	3.70
COMPLETE SERIES 2 (90)	60.00	27.00	7.50
COMMON CARD (1-180)	.25	.11	.03

		MINT	NRMT	EXC
☐ 1	Mookie Blaylock	.25	.11	.03
☐ 2	Tryone Corbin	.25	.11	.03
☐ 3	Grant Long	.25	.11	.03
☐ 4	Dee Brown	.35	.16	.04
☐ 5	Sherman Douglas	.25	.11	.03
☐ 6	Eric Montross	.25	.11	.03
☐ 7	Scott Burrell	.25	.11	.03
☐ 8	Dell Curry	.25	.11	.03
☐ 9	Larry Johnson	1.25	.55	.16
☐ 10	Will Perdue	.25	.11	.03
☐ 11	Scottie Pippen	4.00	1.80	.50
☐ 12	Dickey Simpkins	.25	.11	.03
☐ 13	Michael Cage	.25	.11	.03
☐ 14	Mark Price	.25	.11	.03
☐ 15	John Williams	.25	.11	.03
☐ 16	Lucious Harris	.25	.11	.03
☐ 17	Jim Jackson	.75	.35	.09
☐ 18	Popeye Jones	.25	.11	.03
☐ 19	Mahmoud Abdul-Rauf	.35	.16	.04
☐ 20	LaPhonso Ellis	.25	.11	.03
☐ 21	Robert Pack	.25	.11	.03
☐ 22	Bill Curley	.25	.11	.03
☐ 23	Grant Hill	5.00	2.20	.60
☐ 24	Allan Houston	.50	.23	.06
☐ 25	Chris Gatling	.25	.11	.03
☐ 26	Tim Hardaway	.50	.23	.06
☐ 27	Donyell Marshall	.25	.11	.03
☐ 28	Clifford Rozier	.25	.11	.03
☐ 29	Mario Elie	.25	.11	.03
☐ 30	Robert Horry	.50	.23	.06
☐ 31	Hakeem Olajuwon	3.00	1.35	.35
☐ 32	Kenny Smith	.25	.11	.03
☐ 33	Dale Davis	.25	.11	.03
☐ 34	Duane Ferrell	.25	.11	.03
☐ 35	Derrick McKey	.25	.11	.03
☐ 36	Reggie Miller	1.50	.70	.19
☐ 37	Lamond Murray	.25	.11	.03
☐ 38	Charles Outlaw	.25	.11	.03
☐ 39	Eric Piatkowski	.25	.11	.03
☐ 40	Anthony Peeler	.25	.11	.03
☐ 41	Sedale Threatt	.25	.11	.03
☐ 42	Nick Van Exel	1.00	.45	.12
☐ 43	Kevin Gamble	.25	.11	.03
☐ 44	Matt Geiger	.25	.11	.03
☐ 45	Billy Owens	.25	.11	.03
☐ 46	Khalid Reeves	.25	.11	.03
☐ 47	Vin Baker	1.25	.55	.16
☐ 48	Lee Mayberry	.25	.11	.03
☐ 49	Eric Murdock	.25	.11	.03
☐ 50	Christian Laettner	.50	.23	.06
☐ 51	Sean Rooks	.25	.11	.03
☐ 52	Doug West	.25	.11	.03
☐ 53	P.J. Brown	.25	.11	.03
☐ 54	Derrick Coleman	.50	.23	.06
☐ 55	Armon Gilliam	.35	.16	.04
☐ 56	Hubert Davis	.25	.11	.03
☐ 57	Charles Oakley	.35	.16	.04
☐ 58	John Starks	.25	.11	.03
☐ 59	Monty Williams	.25	.11	.03
☐ 60	Anfernee Hardaway	8.00	3.60	1.00
☐ 61	Donald Royal	.25	.11	.03
☐ 62	Dennis Scott	.50	.23	.06
☐ 63	Jeff Turner	.25	.11	.03
☐ 64	Clarence Weatherspoon	.25	.11	.03
☐ 65	Jeff Malone	.25	.11	.03
☐ 66	Scott Williams	.25	.11	.03
☐ 67	A.C. Green	.50	.23	.06
☐ 68	Kevin Johnson	.50	.23	.06
☐ 69	Elliot Perry	.25	.11	.03
☐ 70	Wesley Person	.35	.16	.04
☐ 71	Harvey Grant	.25	.11	.03
☐ 72	Aaron McKie	.25	.11	.03
☐ 73	Rod Strickland	.25	.11	.03
☐ 74	Buck Williams	.35	.16	.04
☐ 75	Randy Brown	.25	.11	.03
☐ 76	Bobby Hurley	.25	.11	.03
☐ 77	Lionel Simmons	.25	.11	.03
☐ 78	Terry Cummings	.25	.11	.03
☐ 79	Vinny Del Negro	.25	.11	.03
☐ 80	Avery Johnson	.35	.16	.04
☐ 81	David Robinson	2.50	1.10	.30
☐ 82	Vincent Askew	.25	.11	.03
☐ 83	Shawn Kemp	4.00	1.80	.50
☐ 84	Nate McMillan	.25	.11	.03
☐ 85	David Benoit	.25	.11	.03
☐ 86	Jeff Hornacek	.35	.16	.04
☐ 87	John Stockton	1.25	.55	.16
☐ 88	Juwan Howard	3.00	1.35	.35

☐ 89	Gheorghe Muresan	.50	.23	.06
☐ 90	Doug Overton	.25	.11	.03
☐ 91	Stacey Augmon	.35	.16	.04
☐ 92	Alan Henderson	.75	.35	.09
☐ 93	Steve Smith	.50	.23	.06
☐ 94	Rick Fox	.25	.11	.03
☐ 95	Dino Radja	.35	.16	.04
☐ 96	Eric Williams	.75	.35	.09
☐ 97	Muggsy Bogues	.35	.16	.04
☐ 98	Kendall Gill	.25	.11	.03
☐ 99	Glen Rice	.50	.23	.06
☐ 100	Michael Jordan	12.00	5.50	1.50
☐ 101	Toni Kukoc	.35	.16	.04
☐ 102	Dennis Rodman Bulls	6.00	2.70	.75
☐ 103	Terrell Brandon	.50	.23	.06
☐ 104	Tyrone Hill	.25	.11	.03
☐ 105	Dan Majerle	.35	.16	.04
☐ 106	Jason Kidd	2.50	1.10	.30
☐ 107	Jamal Mashburn	.60	.25	.07
☐ 108	Cherokee Parks	.50	.23	.06
☐ 109	Antonio McDyess	4.00	1.80	.50
☐ 110	Dikembe Mutombo	.50	.23	.06
☐ 111	Reggie Williams	.25	.11	.03
☐ 112	Joe Dumars	.50	.23	.06
☐ 113	Lindsey Hunter	.25	.11	.03
☐ 114	Otis Thorpe	.35	.16	.04
☐ 115	Chris Mullin	.50	.23	.06
☐ 116	Joe Smith	4.00	1.80	.50
☐ 117	Latrell Sprewell	.50	.23	.06
☐ 118	Chucky Brown	.25	.11	.03
☐ 119	Sam Cassell	.50	.23	.06
☐ 120	Clyde Drexler	1.25	.55	.16
☐ 121	Travis Best	.25	.11	.03
☐ 122	Mark Jackson	.25	.11	.03
☐ 123	Rik Smits	.50	.23	.06
☐ 124	Brent Barry	1.50	.70	.19
☐ 125	Rodney Rogers	.25	.11	.03
☐ 126	Loy Vaught	.25	.11	.03
☐ 127	Cedric Ceballos	.60	.25	.07
☐ 128	Vlade Divac	3.00	1.35	.35
☐ 129	Eddie Jones	.60	.25	.07
☐ 130	Alonzo Mourning	1.00	.45	.12
☐ 131	Kurt Thomas	1.00	.45	.12
☐ 132	Kevin Willis	.25	.11	.03
☐ 133	Sherman Douglas	.25	.11	.03
☐ 134	Shawn Respert	.50	.23	.06
☐ 135	Glenn Robinson	1.25	.55	.16
☐ 136	Kevin Garnett	10.00	4.50	1.25
☐ 137	Tom Gugliotta	.50	.23	.06
☐ 138	Isaiah Rider	.50	.23	.06
☐ 139	Kenny Anderson	.50	.23	.06
☐ 140	Ed O'Bannon	1.25	.55	.16
☐ 141	Jayson Williams	.25	.11	.03
☐ 142	Patrick Ewing	1.00	.45	.12
☐ 143	Derek Harper	.25	.11	.03
☐ 144	Charles Smith	.25	.11	.03
☐ 145	Nick Anderson	.50	.23	.06
☐ 146	Horace Grant	.25	.11	.03
☐ 147	Shaquille O'Neal	5.00	2.20	.60
☐ 148	Vernon Maxwell	.25	.11	.03
☐ 149	Jerry Stackhouse	6.00	2.70	.75
☐ 150	Sharone Wright	.25	.11	.03
☐ 151	Charles Barkley	1.50	.70	.19
☐ 152	Michael Finley	4.00	1.80	.50
☐ 153	Danny Manning	.35	.16	.04
☐ 154	John Williams	.25	.11	.03
☐ 155	Clifford Robinson	.50	.23	.06
☐ 156	Arvydas Sabonis	2.50	1.10	.30
☐ 157	Gary Trent	.50	.23	.06
☐ 158	Brian Grant	.50	.23	.06
☐ 159	Mitch Richmond	.75	.35	.09

☐ 160	Corliss Williamson	.50	.23	.06
☐ 161	Sean Elliott	.50	.23	.06
☐ 162	Will Perdue	.25	.11	.03
☐ 163	Doc Rivers	.25	.11	.03
☐ 164	Gary Payton	1.50	.70	.19
☐ 165	Sam Perkins	.35	.16	.04
☐ 166	Detlef Schrempf	.35	.16	.04
☐ 167	Tracy Murray	.25	.11	.03
☐ 168	Ed Pinckney	.25	.11	.03
☐ 169	Carlos Rogers	.25	.11	.03
☐ 170	Damon Stoudamire	8.00	3.60	1.00
☐ 171	Karl Malone	1.00	.45	.12
☐ 172	Chris Morris	.25	.11	.03
☐ 173	Greg Ostertag	.25	.11	.03
☐ 174	Greg Anthony	.25	.11	.03
☐ 175	Lawrence Moten	.25	.11	.03
☐ 176	Bryant Reeves	2.00	.90	.25
☐ 177	Byron Scott	.50	.23	.06
☐ 178	Calbert Cheaney	.25	.11	.03
☐ 179	Rasheed Wallace	1.50	.70	.19
☐ 180	Chris Webber	1.00	.45	.12

1995-96 Upper Deck Special Edition Gold

Randomly inserted in hobby packs only at a rate of one in 35, this 180-card set parallels the more common Special Edition insert set. The Gold foil wording on the front of each card (instead of silver) differentiate them. Only the top few cards are listed individually. Please refer to the multipliers provided below (coupled with the values of the corresponding regular Special Edition cards) for prices on all other Gold singles.

	MINT	NRMT	EXC
COMPLETE SET (180)	600.00	275.00	75.00
COMP.SERIES 1 (90)	200.00	90.00	25.00
COMP.SERIES 2 (90)	400.00	180.00	50.00
COMMON CARD (SE1-SE180)	1.50	.70	.19
*STARS: 4X to 8X VALUE			
*ROOKIES: 2.5X to 5X VALUE			

☐ 11	Scottie Pippen	30.00	13.50	3.70
☐ 23	Grant Hill	40.00	18.00	5.00
☐ 31	Hakeem Olajuwon	25.00	11.00	3.10
☐ 60	Anfernee Hardaway	60.00	27.00	7.50
☐ 83	Shawn Kemp	30.00	13.50	3.70
☐ 88	Juwan Howard	25.00	11.00	3.10
☐ 100	Michael Jordan	125.00	55.00	15.50
☐ 102	Dennis Rodman Bulls	50.00	22.00	6.25

		MINT	NRMT	EXC
☐	106 Jason Kidd	20.00	9.00	2.50
☐	109 Antonio McDyess	15.00	6.75	1.85
☐	116 Joe Smith	20.00	9.00	2.50
☐	128 Vlade Divac	25.00	11.00	3.10
☐	136 Kevin Garnett	50.00	22.00	6.25
☐	147 Shaquille O'Neal	40.00	18.00	5.00
☐	149 Jerry Stackhouse	30.00	13.50	3.70
☐	152 Michael Finley	20.00	9.00	2.50
☐	170 Damon Stoudamire	40.00	18.00	5.00

1993-94 Upper Deck Pro View

This 110-card standard-size set was distributed in 5-card packs (48 per box) that included 3-D glasses with which to see the 3-D effect. Fronts feature white-bordered color player action shots, with the player's name appearing within a vertical ghosted strip on the left. The back carries a color player action shot on the left, with career highlights horizontally printed alongside on the right. The set closes with the following subsets: 3-D Playground Legends (71-79), 3-D Rookie (80-88) and 3-D Jams (89-108). Rookie Cards of note include Vin Baker, Anfernee Hardaway, Jamal Mashburn and Chris Webber.

		MINT	NRMT	EXC
	COMPLETE SET (110)	25.00	11.00	3.10
	COMMON CARD (1-110)	.05	.02	.01
☐	1 Karl Malone	.30	.14	.04
☐	2 Chuck Person	.05	.02	.01
☐	3 Latrell Sprewell	.25	.11	.03
☐	4 Dominique Wilkins	.15	.07	.02
☐	5 Reggie Miller	.40	.18	.05
☐	6 Vlade Divac	.15	.07	.02
☐	7 Otis Thorpe	.10	.05	.01
☐	8 Patrick Ewing	.30	.14	.04
☐	9 Ron Harper	.05	.02	.01
☐	10 Brad Daugherty	.05	.02	.01
☐	11 Robert Parish	.15	.07	.02
☐	12 Glen Rice	.15	.07	.02
☐	13 Kevin Johnson	.15	.07	.02
☐	14 Christian Laettner	.15	.07	.02
☐	15 Ricky Pierce	.05	.02	.01
☐	16 Joe Dumars	.15	.07	.02
☐	17 James Worthy	.15	.07	.02
☐	18 John Stockton	.30	.14	.04
☐	19 Robert Horry	.10	.05	.01
☐	20 John Starks	.05	.02	.01
☐	21 Danny Manning	.10	.05	.01
☐	22 Alonzo Mourning	.50	.23	.06
☐	23 Michael Jordan	4.00	1.80	.50
☐	24 Hakeem Olajuwon	.75	.35	.09
☐	25 Scott Skiles	.05	.02	.01
☐	26 Stacey Augmon	.10	.05	.01
☐	27 Mitch Richmond	.25	.11	.03
☐	28 Derrick Coleman	.05	.02	.01
☐	29 Jeff Malone	.05	.02	.01
☐	30 Larry Johnson	.40	.18	.05
☐	31 Sam Perkins	.10	.05	.01
☐	32 Shaquille O'Neal	2.00	.90	.25
☐	33 Walt Williams	.15	.07	.02
☐	34 Doug West	.05	.02	.01
☐	35 Mark Price	.05	.02	.01
☐	36 Rony Seikaly	.05	.02	.01
☐	37 Michael Adams	.05	.02	.01
☐	38 Anthony Peeler	.05	.02	.01
☐	39 Larry Nance	.05	.02	.01
☐	40 Shawn Kemp	1.00	.45	.12
☐	41 Terry Porter	.05	.02	.01
☐	42 Dan Majerle	.10	.05	.01
☐	43 Dennis Rodman	1.25	.55	.16
☐	44 Isiah Thomas	.20	.09	.03
☐	45 Spud Webb	.10	.05	.01
☐	46 Pooh Richardson	.05	.02	.01
☐	47 Tim Hardaway	.15	.07	.02
☐	48 Derek Harper	.10	.05	.01
☐	49 Pervis Ellison	.05	.02	.01
☐	50 Xavier McDaniel	.05	.02	.01
☐	51 Jeff Hornacek	.10	.05	.01
☐	52 Ken Norman	.05	.02	.01
☐	53 LaPhonso Ellis	.05	.02	.01
☐	54 Charles Barkley	.50	.23	.06
☐	55 Tom Gugliotta	.15	.07	.02
☐	56 Clifford Robinson	.15	.07	.02
☐	57 Mark Jackson	.05	.02	.01
☐	58 Mahmoud Abdul-Rauf	.10	.05	.01
☐	59 Todd Day	.05	.02	.01
☐	60 Kenny Anderson	.15	.07	.02
☐	61 Jim Jackson	.40	.18	.05
☐	62 Chris Mullin	.15	.07	.02
☐	63 Scottie Pippen	1.00	.45	.12
☐	64 Dikembe Mutombo	.15	.07	.02
☐	65 Sean Elliott	.15	.07	.02
☐	66 Clarence Weatherspoon	.15	.07	.02
☐	67 Chris Morris	.05	.02	.01
☐	68 Clyde Drexler	.40	.18	.05
☐	69 Dennis Scott	.10	.05	.01
☐	70 David Robinson	.60	.25	.07
☐	71 Larry Johnson PL	.15	.07	.02
☐	72 Chris Webber PL	.50	.23	.06
☐	73 Alonzo Mourning PL	.25	.11	.03
☐	74 Lloyd Daniels PL	.05	.02	.01
☐	75 Derrick Coleman PL	.05	.02	.01
☐	76 Tim Hardaway PL	.05	.02	.01
☐	77 Isiah Thomas PL	.10	.05	.01
☐	78 Chris Mullin PL	.05	.02	.01
☐	79 Shaquille O'Neal PL	1.00	.45	.12
☐	80 Shawn Bradley	.40	.18	.05
☐	81 Chris Webber	1.25	.55	.16
☐	82 Jamal Mashburn	.75	.35	.09
☐	83 Anfernee Hardaway	6.00	2.70	.75
☐	84 Calbert Cheaney	.30	.14	.04
☐	85 Vin Baker	1.25	.55	.16
☐	86 Isaiah Rider	.40	.18	.05
☐	87 Lindsey Hunter	.10	.05	.01
☐	88 Bobby Hurley	.15	.07	.02
☐	89 Dominique Wilkins 3DJ	.10	.05	.01
☐	90 Charles Barkley 3DJ	.25	.11	.03
☐	91 Michael Jordan 3DJ	2.00	.90	.25

		MINT	NRMT	EXC
☐ 92	Derrick Coleman 3DJ	.05	.02	.01
☐ 93	Scottie Pippen 3DJ	.50	.23	.06
☐ 94	Karl Malone 3DJ	.15	.07	.02
☐ 95	Larry Johnson 3DJ	.15	.07	.02
☐ 96	Cedric Ceballos 3DJ	.05	.02	.01
☐ 97	David Robinson 3DJ	.30	.14	.04
☐ 98	Patrick Ewing 3DJ	.15	.07	.02
☐ 99	Clarence Weatherspoon 3DJ	.05	.02	.01
☐ 100	Alonzo Mourning 3DJ	.25	.11	.03
☐ 101	Stacey Augmon 3DJ	.05	.02	.01
☐ 102	Shaquille O'Neal 3DJ	1.00	.45	.12
☐ 103	Clyde Drexler 3DJ	.15	.07	.02
☐ 104	Shawn Kemp 3DJ	.50	.23	.06
☐ 105	Harold Miner 3DJ	.05	.02	.01
☐ 106	Chris Webber 3DJ	.50	.23	.06
☐ 107	Dikembe Mutombo 3DJ	.05	.02	.01
☐ 108	Doug West 3DJ	.05	.02	.01
☐ 109	Michael Jordan CL	.25	.11	.03
☐ 110	Michael Jordan CL	.25	.11	.03

1993-94 Upper Deck SE

This 225-card standard-size set was distributed in 12-card hobby East, hobby West, retail and 10-card magazine retail packs. There are 36 packs per box. Card fronts feature color player action shots that are borderless, except on the left, where a strip carries the player's name in gold foil along with his position and a vertically distorted black-and-white version of the action shot. The player's team name appears in vertical gold-foil lettering near the right edge. The back carries a color player action photo, with his name, position, and brief biography appearing in stripes across the top. Statistics and career highlights are displayed horizontally in a ghosted panel on the left. The set closes with the following topical subsets: NBA All-Star Weekend Highlights (181-198) and Team Headlines (199-225). Two Michael Jordan insert cards are a Kilroy card (JK1) and a retirement tribute card (MJR1). These were inserted at a rate of 1 in 72 packs. Rookie Cards of note in this set include Vin Baker, Anfernee Hardaway, Jamal Mashburn, Nick Van Exel and Chris Webber.

	MINT	NRMT	EXC
COMPLETE SET (225)	15.00	6.75	1.85
COMMON CARD (1-225)	.05	.02	.01

		MINT	NRMT	EXC
☐ 1	Scottie Pippen	1.00	.45	.12
☐ 2	Todd Day	.05	.02	.01
☐ 3	Detlef Schrempf	.10	.05	.01
☐ 4	Chris Webber	1.25	.55	.16
☐ 5	Michael Adams	.05	.02	.01
☐ 6	Loy Vaught	.10	.05	.01
☐ 7	Doug West	.05	.02	.01
☐ 8	A.C. Green	.15	.07	.02
☐ 9	Anthony Mason	.10	.05	.01
☐ 10	Clyde Drexler	.40	.18	.05
☐ 11	Popeye Jones	.15	.07	.02
☐ 12	Vlade Divac	.15	.07	.02
☐ 13	Armon Gilliam	.05	.02	.01
☐ 14	Hersey Hawkins	.05	.02	.01
☐ 15	Dennis Scott	.10	.05	.01
☐ 16	Bimbo Coles	.05	.02	.01
☐ 17	Blue Edwards	.05	.02	.01
☐ 18	Negele Knight	.05	.02	.01
☐ 19	Dale Davis	.05	.02	.01
☐ 20	Isiah Thomas	.20	.09	.03
☐ 21	Latrell Sprewell	.25	.11	.03
☐ 22	Kenny Smith	.05	.02	.01
☐ 23	Bryant Stith	.05	.02	.01
☐ 24	Terry Porter	.05	.02	.01
☐ 25	Spud Webb	.10	.05	.01
☐ 26	John Battle	.05	.02	.01
☐ 27	Jeff Malone	.05	.02	.01
☐ 28	Olden Polynice	.05	.02	.01
☐ 29	Kevin Willis	.05	.02	.01
☐ 30	Robert Parish	.15	.07	.02
☐ 31	Kevin Johnson	.15	.07	.02
☐ 32	Shaquille O'Neal	2.00	.90	.25
☐ 33	Willie Anderson	.05	.02	.01
☐ 34	Micheal Williams	.05	.02	.01
☐ 35	Steve Smith	.15	.07	.02
☐ 36	Rik Smits	.15	.07	.02
☐ 37	Pete Myers	.05	.02	.01
☐ 38	Oliver Miller	.05	.02	.01
☐ 39	Eddie Johnson	.05	.02	.01
☐ 40	Calbert Cheaney	.30	.14	.04
☐ 41	Vernon Maxwell	.05	.02	.01
☐ 42	James Worthy	.15	.07	.02
☐ 43	Dino Radja	.40	.18	.05
☐ 44	Derrick Coleman	.05	.02	.01
☐ 45	Reggie Williams	.05	.02	.01
☐ 46	Dale Ellis	.05	.02	.01
☐ 47	Clifford Robinson	.15	.07	.02
☐ 48	Doug Christie	.05	.02	.01
☐ 49	Ricky Pierce	.05	.02	.01
☐ 50	Sean Elliott	.15	.07	.02
☐ 51	Anfernee Hardaway	6.00	2.70	.75
☐ 52	Dana Barros	.05	.02	.01
☐ 53	Reggie Miller	.40	.18	.05
☐ 54	Brian Williams	.05	.02	.01
☐ 55	Otis Thorpe	.10	.05	.01
☐ 56	Jerome Kersey	.05	.02	.01
☐ 57	Larry Johnson	.40	.18	.05
☐ 58	Rex Chapman	.05	.02	.01
☐ 59	Kevin Edwards	.05	.02	.01
☐ 60	Nate McMillan	.05	.02	.01
☐ 61	Chris Mullin	.15	.07	.02
☐ 62	Bill Cartwright	.05	.02	.01
☐ 63	Dennis Rodman	1.25	.55	.16
☐ 64	Pooh Richardson	.05	.02	.01
☐ 65	Tyrone Hill	.05	.02	.01
☐ 66	Scott Brooks	.05	.02	.01
☐ 67	Brad Daugherty	.05	.02	.01
☐ 68	Joe Dumars	.15	.07	.02
☐ 69	Vin Baker	1.25	.55	.16
☐ 70	Rod Strickland	.05	.02	.01

☐ 71	Tom Chambers	.05	.02	.01
☐ 72	Charles Oakley	.05	.02	.01
☐ 73	Craig Ehlo	.05	.02	.01
☐ 74	LaPhonso Ellis	.05	.02	.01
☐ 75	Kevin Gamble	.05	.02	.01
☐ 76	Shawn Bradley	.40	.18	.05
☐ 77	Kendall Gill	.05	.02	.01
☐ 78	Hakeem Olajuwon	.75	.35	.09
☐ 79	Nick Anderson	.15	.07	.02
☐ 80	Anthony Peeler	.05	.02	.01
☐ 81	Wayman Tisdale	.05	.02	.01
☐ 82	Danny Manning	.10	.05	.01
☐ 83	John Starks	.05	.02	.01
☐ 84	Jeff Hornacek	.05	.02	.01
☐ 85	Victor Alexander	.05	.02	.01
☐ 86	Mitch Richmond	.25	.11	.03
☐ 87	Mookie Blaylock	.10	.05	.01
☐ 88	Harvey Grant	.05	.02	.01
☐ 89	Doug Smith	.05	.02	.01
☐ 90	John Stockton	.30	.14	.04
☐ 91	Charles Barkley	.50	.23	.06
☐ 92	Gerald Wilkins	.05	.02	.01
☐ 93	Mario Elie	.05	.02	.01
☐ 94	Ken Norman	.05	.02	.01
☐ 95	B.J. Armstrong	.05	.02	.01
☐ 96	John Williams	.05	.02	.01
☐ 97	Rony Seikaly	.05	.02	.01
☐ 98	Sean Rooks	.05	.02	.01
☐ 99	Shawn Kemp	1.00	.45	.12
☐ 100	Danny Ainge	.15	.07	.02
☐ 101	Terry Mills	.05	.02	.01
☐ 102	Doc Rivers	.05	.02	.01
☐ 103	Chuck Person	.05	.02	.01
☐ 104	Sam Cassell	.50	.23	.06
☐ 105	Kevin Duckworth	.05	.02	.01
☐ 106	Dan Majerle	.10	.05	.01
☐ 107	Mark Jackson	.05	.02	.01
☐ 108	Steve Kerr	.10	.05	.01
☐ 109	Sam Perkins	.10	.05	.01
☐ 110	Clarence Weatherspoon	.15	.07	.02
☐ 111	Felton Spencer	.05	.02	.01
☐ 112	Greg Anthony	.05	.02	.01
☐ 113	Pete Chilcutt	.05	.02	.01
☐ 114	Malik Sealy	.05	.02	.01
☐ 115	Horace Grant	.15	.07	.02
☐ 116	Chris Morris	.05	.02	.01
☐ 117	Xavier McDaniel	.05	.02	.01
☐ 118	Lionel Simmons	.05	.02	.01
☐ 119	Dell Curry	.05	.02	.01
☐ 120	Moses Malone	.20	.09	.03
☐ 121	Lindsey Hunter	.05	.02	.01
☐ 122	Buck Williams	.10	.05	.01
☐ 123	Mahmoud Abdul-Rauf	.10	.05	.01
☐ 124	Rumeal Robinson	.05	.02	.01
☐ 125	Chris Mills	.50	.23	.06
☐ 126	Scott Skiles	.05	.02	.01
☐ 127	Derrick McKey	.05	.02	.01
☐ 128	Avery Johnson	.05	.02	.01
☐ 129	Harold Miner	.05	.02	.01
☐ 130	Frank Brickowski	.05	.02	.01
☐ 131	Gary Payton	.50	.23	.06
☐ 132	Don MacLean	.05	.02	.01
☐ 133	Thurl Bailey	.05	.02	.01
☐ 134	Nick Van Exel	1.00	.45	.12
☐ 135	Matt Geiger	.05	.02	.01
☐ 136	Stacey Augmon	.10	.05	.01
☐ 137	Sedale Threatt	.05	.02	.01
☐ 138	Patrick Ewing	.30	.14	.04
☐ 139	Tyrone Corbin	.05	.02	.01
☐ 140	Jim Jackson	.40	.18	.05
☐ 141	Christian Laettner	.15	.07	.02
☐ 142	Robert Horry	.10	.05	.01
☐ 143	J.R. Reid	.05	.02	.01
☐ 144	Eric Murdock	.05	.02	.01
☐ 145	Alonzo Mourning	.50	.23	.06
☐ 146	Sherman Douglas	.05	.02	.01
☐ 147	Tom Gugliotta	.15	.07	.02
☐ 148	Glen Rice	.15	.07	.02
☐ 149	Mark Price	.05	.02	.01
☐ 150	Dikembe Mutombo	.15	.07	.02
☐ 151	Derek Harper	.05	.02	.01
☐ 152	Karl Malone	.30	.14	.04
☐ 153	Byron Scott	.15	.07	.02
☐ 154	Reggie Jordan	.05	.02	.01
☐ 155	Dominique Wilkins	.15	.07	.02
☐ 156	Bobby Hurley	.15	.07	.02
☐ 157	Ron Harper	.05	.02	.01
☐ 158	Bryon Russell	.05	.02	.01
☐ 159	Frank Johnson	.05	.02	.01
☐ 160	Toni Kukoc	.75	.35	.09
☐ 161	Lloyd Daniels	.05	.02	.01
☐ 162	Jeff Turner	.05	.02	.01
☐ 163	Muggsy Bogues	.10	.05	.01
☐ 164	Chris Gatling	.05	.02	.01
☐ 165	Kenny Anderson	.15	.07	.02
☐ 166	Elmore Spencer	.05	.02	.01
☐ 167	Jamal Mashburn	.75	.35	.09
☐ 168	Tim Perry	.05	.02	.01
☐ 169	Antonio Davis	.05	.02	.01
☐ 170	Isaiah Rider	.40	.18	.05
☐ 171	Dee Brown	.05	.02	.01
☐ 172	Walt Williams	.15	.07	.02
☐ 173	Elden Campbell	.10	.05	.01
☐ 174	Benoit Benjamin	.05	.02	.01
☐ 175	Billy Owens	.05	.02	.01
☐ 176	Andrew Lang	.05	.02	.01
☐ 177	David Robinson	.60	.25	.07
☐ 178	Checklist 1	.05	.02	.01
☐ 179	Checklist 2	.05	.02	.01
☐ 180	Checklist 3	.05	.02	.01
☐ 181	Shawn Bradley AS	.15	.07	.02
☐ 182	Calbert Cheaney AS	.15	.07	.02
☐ 183	Toni Kukoc AS	.30	.14	.04
☐ 184	Popeye Jones AS	.05	.02	.01
☐ 185	Lindsey Hunter AS	.05	.02	.01
☐ 186	Chris Webber AS	.50	.23	.06
☐ 187	Bryon Russell AS	.05	.02	.01
☐ 188	Anfernee Hardaway AS	2.50	1.10	.30
☐ 189	Nick Van Exel AS	.40	.18	.05
☐ 190	P.J. Brown AS	.05	.02	.01
☐ 191	Isaiah Rider AS	.25	.11	.03
☐ 192	Chris Mills AS	.05	.02	.01
☐ 193	Antonio Davis AS	.05	.02	.01
☐ 194	Jamal Mashburn AS	.30	.14	.04
☐ 195	Dino Radja AS	.15	.07	.02
☐ 196	Sam Cassell AS	.15	.07	.02
☐ 197	Isaiah Rider ASW	.25	.11	.03
☐ 198	Mark Price ASW	.05	.02	.01
☐ 199	Stacey Augmon TH	.05	.02	.01
☐ 200	Celtics Team TH	.05	.02	.01
☐ 201	Eddie Johnson TH	.05	.02	.01
☐ 202	Scottie Pippen TH	.50	.23	.06
☐ 203	Brad Daugherty TH	.05	.02	.01
☐ 204	Jamal Mashburn TH	.20	.09	.03
☐ 205	Dikembe Mutombo TH	.15	.07	.02
☐ 206	Lindsey Hunter TH	.05	.02	.01
☐ 207	Chris Webber TH	.30	.14	.04
☐ 208	Rockets Team TH	.05	.02	.01
☐ 209	Derrick McKey TH	.05	.02	.01
☐ 210	Danny Manning TH	.05	.02	.01
☐ 211	Doug Christie HDL	.05	.02	.01
☐ 212	Glen Rice TH	.05	.02	.01

		MINT	NRMT	EXC
☐ 213	Todd Day TH	.05	.02	.01
	Ken Norman TH			
	Vin Baker TH			
	Jon Barry TH			
☐ 214	Isaiah Rider TH	.05	.02	.01
☐ 215	Kenny Anderson TH	.05	.02	.01
☐ 216	Patrick Ewing TH	.15	.07	.02
☐ 217	Anfernee Hardaway TH	1.50	.70	.19
☐ 218	Moses Malone TH	.10	.05	.01
☐ 219	Kevin Johnson TH	.10	.05	.01
☐ 220	Clifford Robinson TH	.05	.02	.01
☐ 221	Wayman Tisdale TH	.05	.02	.01
☐ 222	David Robinson TH	.30	.14	.04
☐ 223	Sonics Team TH	.05	.02	.01
☐ 224	John Stockton TH	.15	.07	.02
☐ 225	Don MacLean TH	.05	.02	.01
☐ JK1	Johnny Kilroy	5.00	2.20	.60
☐ MJR1	Michael Jordan Retirement Card	10.00	4.50	1.25

1993-94 Upper Deck SE Electric Court

This 225-card set parallels that of the 1993-94 Upper Deck SE. The only difference in design is an "Electric Court" logo that appears on the fronts and the thicker stock that these cards feature. These cards were distributed one per 12-card hobby East, hobby West and retail pack and two per 10-card magazine pack. Please refer to the multipliers provided below (coupled with the prices of the corresponding regular issue cards) to ascertain values.ersion of the action shot. The player's team name appears in vertical gold-foil lettering near the right edge. The Electric Court set name appears in prismatic silver foil lettering near the bottom. The back carries a color player action photo, with his name, position, and brief biography appearing in stripes across the top. Statistics and career highlights are displayed horizontally in a ghosted panel on the left. The cards are numbered on the back.

	MINT	NRMT	EXC
COMPLETE SET (225)	60.00	27.00	7.50
COMMON CARD (1-225)	.15	.07	.02
*STARS: 1.25X to 2.5X VALUE			
*ROOKIES: 1X to 2X VALUE			

1993-94 Upper Deck SE Electric Gold

Randomly inserted in hobby East, hobby West and retail packs at a rate of one in 36, this is a parallel set to '93-94 Upper Deck SE. The Electric Gold set name appears in gold foil lettering near the bottom. Only the top few cards in the set are individually priced below. Please refer to the multipliers listed below (coupled with the prices of the corresponding regular issue cards) to ascertain values.

	MINT	NRMT	EXC
COMPLETE SET (225)	500.00	220.00	60.00
COMMON CARD (1-225)	1.50	.70	.19
*STARS: 12.5X to 25X BASIC CARDS			
*ROOKIES: 10X to 20X BASIC CARDS			

		MINT	NRMT	EXC
☐ 1	Scottie Pippen	25.00	11.00	3.10
☐ 4	Chris Webber	30.00	13.50	3.70
☐ 32	Shaquille O'Neal	50.00	22.00	6.25
☐ 51	Anfernee Hardaway	125.00	55.00	15.50
☐ 63	Dennis Rodman	30.00	13.50	3.70
☐ 69	Vin Baker	25.00	11.00	3.10
☐ 78	Hakeem Olajuwon	20.00	9.00	2.50
☐ 99	Shawn Kemp	25.00	11.00	3.10
☐ 134	Nick Van Exel	20.00	9.00	2.50
☐ 188	Anfernee Hardaway AS	50.00	22.00	6.25

1993-94 Upper Deck SE Behind the Glass

Randomly inserted in 12-card retail packs at a rate of one in 30, cards from this 15-card standard-size set capture some of the NBA's best dunkers from the unique camera angle behind the backboard glass. A gold-foil "Behind the Glass Trade Card" was randomly inserted in retail and hobby packs at a rate of one in 360. The collector could redeem the card for the complete 15-card "Behind the Glass" set. The redemption deadline was August 31, 1994. The borderless front features a color player action shot on a gold metallic finish. The

player's name and position appear vertically along the right side. The back features a color player action shot on the right side with career highlights appearing alongside on the left.

	MINT	NRMT	EXC
COMPLETE SET (15)	50.00	22.00	6.25
COMMON CARD (G1-G15)	.75	.35	.09
☐ G1 Shawn Kemp	6.00	2.70	.75
☐ G2 Patrick Ewing	2.00	.90	.25
☐ G3 Dikembe Mutombo	1.25	.55	.16
☐ G4 Charles Barkley	3.00	1.35	.35
☐ G5 Hakeem Olajuwon	5.00	2.20	.60
☐ G6 Larry Johnson	2.50	1.10	.30
☐ G7 Chris Webber	5.00	2.20	.60
☐ G8 John Starks	.75	.35	.09
☐ G9 Kevin Willis	.75	.35	.09
☐ G10 Scottie Pippen	6.00	2.70	.75
☐ G11 Michael Jordan	25.00	11.00	3.10
☐ G12 Alonzo Mourning	3.00	1.35	.35
☐ G13 Shaquille O'Neal	12.00	5.50	1.50
☐ G14 Shawn Bradley	1.50	.70	.19
☐ G15 Ron Harper	.75	.35	.09
☐ NNO Behind the Glass	1.50	.70	.19
Trade Card			
☐ NNO Redeemed BHG Trade	.25	.11	.03

1993-94 Upper Deck SE Die Cut All-Stars

In these two 15-card insert standard-size sets, Upper Deck saluted a selection of current and potential future all-stars. The cards were available in East hobby and West hobby packs at a rate of one in 30 packs. Hobby dealers in the East received cases containing players from the Eastern conference, while hobby dealers in the West received cases containing players from the Western conference. These die-cut cards were inserted in hobby packs only. This unique card design features a partial gold-foil border at the top only. Centered is a color player action photo. The player's name and team appear in red vertical lettering along the left side. The back features brief statistics. Each set is sequenced in alphabetical team order.

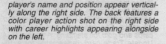

	MINT	NRMT	EXC
COMPLETE SET (30)	700.00	325.00	90.00
COMP.EAST SET (15)	375.00	170.00	47.50
COMP.WEST SET (15)	325.00	145.00	40.00
COMMON EAST (E1-E15)	5.00	2.20	.60
COMMON WEST (W1-W15)	5.00	2.20	.60
☐ E1 Dominique Wilkins	5.00	2.20	.60
☐ E2 Alonzo Mourning	25.00	11.00	3.10
☐ E3 B.J. Armstrong	5.00	2.20	.60
☐ E4 Scottie Pippen	50.00	22.00	6.25
☐ E5 Mark Price	5.00	2.20	.60
☐ E6 Isiah Thomas	10.00	4.50	1.25
☐ E7 Harold Miner	5.00	2.20	.60
☐ E8 Vin Baker	40.00	18.00	5.00
☐ E9 Kenny Anderson	5.00	2.20	.60
☐ E10 Derrick Coleman	5.00	2.20	.60
☐ E11 Patrick Ewing	15.00	6.75	1.85
☐ E12 Anfernee Hardaway	175.00	80.00	22.00
☐ E13 Shaquille O'Neal	100.00	45.00	12.50
☐ E14 Shawn Bradley	12.00	5.50	1.50
☐ E15 Calbert Cheaney	10.00	4.50	1.25
☐ W1 Jim Jackson	20.00	9.00	2.50
☐ W2 Jamal Mashburn	25.00	11.00	3.10
☐ W3 Dikembe Mutombo	10.00	4.50	1.25
☐ W4 Latrell Sprewell	12.00	5.50	1.50
☐ W5 Chris Webber	40.00	18.00	5.00
☐ W6 Hakeem Olajuwon	40.00	18.00	5.00
☐ W7 Danny Manning	5.00	2.20	.60
☐ W8 Nick Van Exel	30.00	13.50	3.70
☐ W9 Isaiah Rider	12.00	5.50	1.50
☐ W10 Charles Barkley	25.00	11.00	3.10
☐ W11 Clyde Drexler	20.00	9.00	2.50
☐ W12 Mitch Richmond	15.00	6.75	1.85
☐ W13 David Robinson	30.00	13.50	3.70
☐ W14 Shawn Kemp	50.00	22.00	6.25
☐ W15 Karl Malone	15.00	6.75	1.85

1993-94 Upper Deck SE USA Trade

This 24-card standard-size set was only available by exchanging the Upper Deck SE USA Trade card (random insert at one in 360 packs) before August 31, 1994. The set previewed the USA Basketball set that was released in the summer of 1994. The cards depict the 12 players selected by USA Basketball for "Dream Team II" plus Tim Hardaway, who was originally selected to the team was unable to participate due to

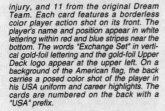

injury, and 11 from the original Dream Team. Each card features a borderless color player action shot on its front. The player's name and position appear in white lettering within red and blue stripes near the bottom. The words "Exchange Set" in vertical gold-foil lettering and the gold-foil Upper Deck logo appear at the upper left. On a background of the American flag, the back carries a posed color shot of the player in his USA uniform and career highlights. The cards are numbered on the back with a "USA" prefix.

	MINT	NRMT	EXC
COMPLETE SET (24)	50.00	22.00	6.25
COMMON CARD (1-24)	.50	.23	.06
☐ 1 Charles Barkley	3.00	1.35	.35
☐ 2 Larry Bird	8.00	3.60	1.00
☐ 3 Clyde Drexler	2.50	1.10	.30
☐ 4 Patrick Ewing	2.00	.90	.25
☐ 5 Michael Jordan	25.00	11.00	3.10
☐ 6 Christian Laettner	1.00	.45	.12
☐ 7 Karl Malone	2.00	.90	.25
☐ 8 Chris Mullin	1.00	.45	.12
☐ 9 Scottie Pippen	6.00	2.70	.75
☐ 10 David Robinson	4.00	1.80	.50
☐ 11 John Stockton	2.00	.90	.25
☐ 12 Dominique Wilkins	1.00	.45	.12
☐ 13 Isiah Thomas	1.00	.45	.12
☐ 14 Dan Majerle	1.00	.45	.12
☐ 15 Steve Smith	1.00	.45	.12
☐ 16 Alonzo Mourning	3.00	1.35	.35
☐ 17 Shawn Kemp	6.00	2.70	.75
☐ 18 Larry Johnson	2.50	1.10	.30
☐ 19 Tim Hardaway	1.00	.45	.12
☐ 20 Joe Dumars	1.00	.45	.12
☐ 21 Mark Price	.50	.23	.06
☐ 22 Derrick Coleman	.50	.23	.06
☐ 23 Reggie Miller	2.50	1.10	.30
☐ 24 Shaquille O'Neal	12.00	5.50	1.50
☐ NNO Exp. USA Trade Card	1.50	.70	.19
☐ NNO Red. USA Trade Card	.25	.11	.03

1996 Upper Deck USA

This 62-card, skip-numbered set features the first 10 team members of the 1996 men's and complete 1996 USA women's basketball teams. The cards were released during the summer of 1996. Each pack contained twelve cards and sold for a suggested retail price of $2.29. Each box contained 32 packs. The entire set features die-cut cards and gold foil stamping. A special USA Update Trade card, redeemable for a 10-card set featuring Charles Barkley (#'s 41-44 and 59) and Mitch Richmond (#'s 45-48 and 60) to finish off the set, was randomly seeded into one in every ten packs. The expiration of the trade card was October 31, 1996.

	MINT	NRMT	EXC
COMPLETE SET (62)	12.00	5.50	1.50
COMMON CARD (1-40/)	.10	.05	.01
COMMON CARD (61-72)	.10	.05	.01
☐ 1 Anfernee Hardaway	.75	.35	.09
☐ 2 Anfernee Hardaway	.75	.35	.09
☐ 3 Anfernee Hardaway	.75	.35	.09
☐ 4 Anfernee Hardaway	.75	.35	.09
☐ 5 Grant Hill	.40	.18	.05
☐ 6 Grant Hill	.40	.18	.05
☐ 7 Grant Hill	.40	.18	.05
☐ 8 Grant Hill	.40	.18	.05
☐ 9 Karl Malone	.15	.07	.02
☐ 10 Karl Malone	.15	.07	.02
☐ 11 Karl Malone	.15	.07	.02
☐ 12 Karl Malone	.15	.07	.02
☐ 13 Reggie Miller	.15	.07	.02
☐ 14 Reggie Miller	.15	.07	.02
☐ 15 Reggie Miller	.15	.07	.02
☐ 16 Reggie Miller	.15	.07	.02
☐ 17 Shaquille O'Neal	.60	.25	.07
☐ 18 Shaquille O'Neal	.60	.25	.07
☐ 19 Shaquille O'Neal	.60	.25	.07
☐ 20 Shaquille O'Neal	.60	.25	.07
☐ 21 Hakeem Olajuwon	.30	.14	.04
☐ 22 Hakeem Olajuwon	.30	.14	.04
☐ 23 Hakeem Olajuwon	.30	.14	.04
☐ 24 Hakeem Olajuwon	.30	.14	.04
☐ 25 Scottie Pippen	.40	.18	.05
☐ 26 Scottie Pippen	.40	.18	.05
☐ 27 Scottie Pippen	.40	.18	.05
☐ 28 Scottie Pippen	.40	.18	.05
☐ 29 David Robinson	.25	.11	.03
☐ 30 David Robinson	.25	.11	.03
☐ 31 David Robinson	.25	.11	.03
☐ 32 David Robinson	.25	.11	.03
☐ 33 Glenn Robinson	.15	.07	.02
☐ 34 Glenn Robinson	.15	.07	.02
☐ 35 Glenn Robinson	.15	.07	.02
☐ 36 Glenn Robinson	.15	.07	.02
☐ 37 John Stockton	.15	.07	.02
☐ 38 John Stockton	.15	.07	.02
☐ 39 John Stockton	.15	.07	.02

☐ 40 John Stockton	.15	.07	.02
☐ 41 Charles Barkley	.20	.09	.03
☐ 42 Charles Barkley	.20	.09	.03
☐ 43 Charles Barkley	.20	.09	.03
☐ 44 Charles Barkley	.20	.09	.03
☐ 45 Mitch Richmond	.10	.05	.01
☐ 46 Mitch Richmond	.10	.05	.01
☐ 47 Mitch Richmond	.10	.05	.01
☐ 48 Mitch Richmond	.10	.05	.01
☐ 49 Anfernee Hardaway	.75	.35	.09
☐ 50 Grant Hill	.40	.18	.05
☐ 51 Karl Malone	.15	.07	.02
☐ 52 Reggie Miller	.15	.07	.02
☐ 53 Shaquille O'Neal	.60	.25	.07
☐ 54 Hakeem Olajuwon	.30	.14	.04
☐ 55 Scottie Pippen	.40	.18	.05
☐ 56 David Robinson	.25	.11	.03
☐ 57 Glenn Robinson	.15	.07	.02
☐ 58 John Stockton	.15	.07	.02
☐ 59 Charles Barkley	.25	.11	.03
☐ 60 Mitch Richmond	.10	.05	.01
☐ 61 Jennifer Azzi	.10	.05	.01
☐ 62 Ruthie Bolton	.10	.05	.01
☐ 63 Teresa Edwards	.10	.05	.01
☐ 64 Lisa Leslie	.25	.11	.03
☐ 65 Rebecca Lobo	.25	.11	.03
☐ 66 Katrina McClain	.10	.05	.01
☐ 67 Nikki McCray	.10	.05	.01
☐ 68 Carla McGhee	.10	.05	.01
☐ 69 Dawn Staley	.10	.05	.01
☐ 70 Katy Stedling	.10	.05	.01
☐ 71 Sheryl Swoopes	.10	.05	.01
☐ 72 Tara VanDerveer CO	.10	.05	.01
☐ NNO USA Trade Card	2.00	.90	.25

1996 Upper Deck USA Follow Your Dreams

Randomly inserted in packs at a rate of one in 6, this 11-card insert set features the first 10 members selected to the team, plus a special "Field Card" representing Charles Barkley, Gary Payton and Mitch Richmond. Card front designs featured a full-color player cut out set against a red and white striped background. If a collector had the card of the USAB 1996 Olympics scoring leader, a 12-card gold commemorative set was awarded; collectors with second place scoring leader cards received a 12-card silver commemorative set. The expiration date for the exchange was October 31, 1996.

	MINT	NRMT	EXC
COMPLETE SET (11)	25.00	11.00	3.10
COMMON CARD (F1-F11)	.50	.23	.06
☐ F1 Anfernee Hardaway	6.00	2.70	.75
☐ F2 Grant Hill	4.00	1.80	.50
☐ F3 Karl Malone	1.00	.45	.12
☐ F4 Reggie Miller	4.00	1.80	.50
☐ F5 Shaquille O'Neal	5.00	2.20	.60
☐ F6 Hakeem Olajuwon	2.50	1.10	.30
☐ F7 Scottie Pippen	3.00	1.35	.35
☐ F8 David Robinson	4.00	1.80	.50
☐ F9 Glenn Robinson	1.25	.55	.16
☐ F10 John Stockton	1.00	.45	.12
☐ F11 Eleventh , Twelfth Men	.50	.23	.06

1996 Upper Deck USA Anfernee Hardaway American Made

Randomly inserted in packs at a rate of one in 56, this 4-card die cut insert set focuses on Orlando guard Penny Hardaway. Each card looks at a particular aspect of Hardaway's abilities - scoring, defense, smoothness and versatility.

	MINT	NRMT	EXC
COMPLETE SET (4)	50.00	22.00	6.25
COMMON CARD (A1-A4)	15.00	6.75	1.85
☐ A1 A.Hardaway Scoring	15.00	6.75	1.85
☐ A2 A.Hardaway Defense	15.00	6.75	1.85
☐ A3 A.Hardaway Smooth	15.00	6.75	1.85
☐ A4 A.Hardaway Versatility	15.00	6.75	1.85

1996 Upper Deck USA Michael Jordan American Made

Randomly inserted in packs at a rate of one in 55, this 4-card die cut insert set looks at basketball legend Michael Jordan. Each card focuses on a particular part of Jordan's game - scoring, defense, desire and leadership.

	MINT	NRMT	EXC
COMPLETE SET (4)	90.00	40.00	11.00
COMMON CARD (M1-M4)	25.00	11.00	3.10
☐ M1 M.Jordan Scoring	25.00	11.00	3.10
☐ M2 M.Jordan Defense	25.00	11.00	3.10
☐ M3 M.Jordan Desire	25.00	11.00	3.10
☐ M4 M.Jordan Leadership	25.00	11.00	3.10

1996 Upper Deck USA SP Career Statistics

Inserted one in every pack, this 10-card die cut insert set features a card of each 1996 USAB player outlining their career stats and accomplishments. Each card is printed on premium stock and features Upper Deck's special silver "Light F/X" technology.

	MINT	NRMT	EXC
COMPLETE SILVER SET (10)	8.00	3.60	1.00
COMMON SILVER (S1-S10)	.40	.18	.05
☐ S1 Anfernee Hardaway	2.50	1.10	.30
☐ S2 Grant Hill	1.50	.70	.19
☐ S3 Karl Malone	.40	.18	.05
☐ S4 Reggie Miller	.50	.23	.06
☐ S5 Shaquille O'Neal	2.00	.90	.25
☐ S6 Hakeem Olajuwon	1.00	.45	.12
☐ S7 Scottie Pippen	1.25	.55	.16
☐ S8 David Robinson	.75	.35	.09
☐ S9 Glenn Robinson	.50	.23	.06
☐ S10 John Stockton	.40	.18	.05
☐ S11 Eleventh,Twelfth Men	.40	.18	.05
☐ S12 Mitch Richmond	.40	.18	.05

1996 Upper Deck USA SP Career Statistics Gold

Randomly inserted into one in every 27 packs, these 12 die cut cards parallel the more common silver SP Career Highlights inserts. The major difference in design is the gold (rather than silver) "Light F/X" printing on the card fronts. Please refer to the multiplier provided below (coupled with the price of the corresponding silver cards listed above) to ascertain value for Gold cards.

	MINT	NRMT	EXC
COMPLETE SET (10)	80.00	36.00	10.00
COMMON CARD (S1-S10)	5.00	2.20	.60
*GOLD CARDS: 6X to 12X VALUE			

Acknowledgments

A great deal of diligence, hard work, and dedicated effort went into this year's volume. The high standards to which we hold ourselves, however, could not have been met without the expert input and generous amount of time contributed by many people. Our sincere thanks are extended to each and every one of you.

Each year we refine the process of developing the most accurate and up-to-date information for this book. I believe this year's Price Guide is our best yet. Thanks again to all of the contributors nationwide (listed below) as well as our staff here in Dallas.

Those who have worked closely with us on this and many other books, have again proven themselves invaluable in every aspect of producing this book: Rich Altman, Randy Archer, Mike Aronstein, Jerry Bell, Chris Benjamin, Mike Blaisdell, Bill Bossert (Mid-Atlantic Coin Exchange), Classic (Ken Goldin and Mark Pokedoff), Todd Crosner (California Sportscard Exchange), Bud Darland, Bill and Diane Dodge, Rick Donohoo, Willie Erving, Fleer/SkyBox International (Doug Drotman and Ted Taylor), Gervise Ford, Steve Freedman, Larry and Jeff Fritsch, Jim Galusha, Dick Gariepy, Dick Gilkeson, Mike and Howard Gordon, Sally Grace, George Grauer, John Greenwald, Wayne Grove, Bill Haber, George Henn, Mike Hersh, John Inouye, Steven L. Judd, Edward J. Kabala, Judy and Norman Kay, Robert Levin (The Star Company), Lew Lipset, Dave Lucey, Paul Marchant, Brian Marcy (Scottsdale Baseball Cards), Dr. John McCue, Mike Mosier (Columbia City Collectibles Co.), Clark Muldavin, B.A. Murry, Pacific Trading Cards (Mike Cramer and Bob Wilke), Earl N. Petersen (U.S.A. Coins), Pinnacle (Laurie Goldberg), Jack Pollard, Jonathan Pullano, Tom Reid, Henry M. Reizes, Gavin Riley, Alan Rosen (Mr. Mint), Rotman Productions, John Rumierz, San Diego Sport Collectibles (Bill Goepner and Nacho Arredondo), Kevin Savage (Sports Gallery), Mike Schechter (MSA), Dan Sherlock, Bill Shonscheck, Glen J. Sidler, John Spalding, Spanky's, Nigel Spill (Oldies and Goodies), Sports Collectors Store (Pat Quinn and Don Steinbach), Frank Steele, Murvin Sterling, Dan Stickney, Steve Taft, Ed Taylor, Lee Temanson, Topps (Marty Appel, Sy Berger and Melissa Rosen), Upper Deck (Rich Bradley), Bill Vizas, Bill Wesslund (Portland Sports Card Co.), Jim Woods, Kit Young, Robert Zanze, and Bill Zimpleman.

Many other individuals have provided price input, illustrative material, checklist verifications, errata, and/or background information. At the risk of inadvertently overlooking or omitting these many contributors, we should like to personally thank Joseph A. Abram, Jerry Adamic, Tom Akins, Anthony Amada Jr., Dennis Anderson, Ellis Anmuth, Toni Axtell, Darryl B. Baker, Earle Baldwin, Baseball Cards Plus, Baseball Hobby News (Frank and Vivian Barning), William E. Baxendale, Bay State Cards (Lenny DeAngelico), John Beaman, Glen Beram (Lakeside National Cards, Inc.), Philip Berg, Carl Bergstrom, Beulah Sports, Brian Bigelow (Candl), Walter Bird, Theodore Bodnar, Keith and Ryan Bonner, Gary Boyd, Dan Brandenburg, Briggs Sportscards, Fritz Brogan, Douglas J. Brown (Doug's Dugout), George and Donald Brown, Jason Brown, Dan Bruner (The Card King), Bob Bubnick, Buckhead Baseball Cards (Marc Spector), Terry L. Bunt, Virgil Burns, California Card Co., David Cadelina, Mark Cantin, Danny Cariseo, Cee Tim's Cards, N. Garrett Chan (The Greatest Moment), Dwight Chapin, Philip L. Chapman, Manfred Chiu, Judy Chung (The Sportsman's Gallery), Michael Chung, Shane Cohen (Grand Slam), Barry Colla, Collectors Edge, Matt

Collett, Jose E. Conde, H. William Cook, Joe Court, Steve Crane, Rob Croft, Robert Curtis, Herb Dallas Jr., David Diehl, Byron Dittamore, Bill Dodson, Cliff Dolgins, Discount Dorothy, Robin Doty, Eagle Collectibles, Ed Emmitt, Mark Enger, Tom England, Michael Estreicher, Karen Eudaley, Gary Farbstein, L.V. Fischer (The Collectors Den), G.E. Forst, Steve Foster, Mark Franke, Doug French, Rob Gagnon, Steve Galletta, Tony Galovich, Ron Gerencher, Michael R. Gionet, Steve Gold (AU Sports), Jeff Goldstein, Mark Goodman, Arthur Goyette, Gary W. Graber (Minden Games), David Grauf (Cards for the Connoisseur), Don Guilbert, Hall's Nostalgia, Monty Hamilton, Wynn Hansen, Lenny Helicher, Bill Henderson, Jerry and Etta Hersh, Clay Hill, Alisa Hills, H.L.T. and T. Sports (Harold and Todd Nelkin), Will Ho, Russell Hoffman, Home Plate of Provo (Ken Edick), Chris Hooper, James R. Hopper III, Keith Hora, Gene Horvath, Steve Johnson, Barbara-Lee Jordan, James Jordan (Squeeze Play), Jay and Mary Kasper, Alan Kaye, Koinz and Kardz, George Koziol, Roger Krafve, Thomas Kunnecke, Tim Landis, William Langley, Ted Larkins (The Card Clubhouse), Dan Lavin, John Law, Stephen M. Lawson, Henry Lee, Irv Lerner, Howie Levy, Scott Lewandowski, Kendall Loyd (Orlando Sportscards South), Brian Luther, Jim Macie, Ben Macre, Jack Maiden, Larry Marks, Robert Matonis, Jack Mayes, Mike McDonald (Sports Page), Brad McNail (ACCI Sports Cards), James McNaughton, Patrick Menasche, Blake Meyer, Deron Milligan, Pat Mills, Ronald Moermond, J.L. Montgomery Inc. (Colorado Cards), William Moorhead, Joe Morano, Michael Moretto, Brian Morris, John G. Most, Jeff Mowers, Randy Munn, Michael J. Nadeau, Dr. Richard Neel, Robert Neff, No Gum Just Cards, Lon J. Normandin, Efrain Ochoa, John O'Hara, G. Michael Oyster, Russ Palmer, Ed Parkin (Home Front), Clay Pasternack, Bill Pekarik (Pastime Hobbies), Daren Pelletier, Richard Pellizzer, G.N. Perkins (Illini Sportscards), Michael Petruso, Tom Pfirrmann, Wesley Philpott, Roger Porter, Adam Price, Lee Prince (Time Out Sports Shop), Randy Ramuglia, Richard H. Ranck, Phil Regli, David Renshaw, Rocky Mountain Sports Cards, Chuck Roethel, Terry Sack, Joe Sak, Dale A. Sakamoto, Jennifer Salems, Garret Salomon, Ron Sanders, Ray Sandlin, Bob Santos, Guy Scebat, Nathan Schank, Jason Schubert, Sebring Sports, Steven Senft, Rob Shilt, Greg Sholes (Hall of Fame Sportscards), Ryan Shrimplin, Darrin Silverman, Tom Skinner, Ron Smith, Steve Smith (Sports Memories, Inc.), David Snider, Bob Snyder, Carl Specht, Sports Legends, Paul M. Stefani, Allen Stengel (Perfect Image), Cary Stephenson, Arnold Stern, Rao Tadikonda, George Tahinos, Mark Tanaka (Front Row), Chad Taniguchi, Chris Tateosian, Paul S. Taylor, Steve Taylor, Harold Teller, Nick Teresi, Bud Tompkins (Minnesota Connection), Felix F. Torres (Ponce Card & Memorabilia), Huy Tran, Jeffrey K. Tsai, Peter Tsang, Carlo Tulloch, University Trading Cards (Mike Livingston), Mark Velger (Trade Mark SportsCards), Steve Verkman (Baseball Cards & Sports Memorabilia), Adam Wandy, Howard Weissman, Adam B. Weldaz, Richard West, Paul Wetterau, Brian Wilkie, Ali Raza Williams, Jeff Williams, Mark Williams, Opry Winston, Matt Winters, John L. Witcher, Mike Woods (The Dugout), World Series Cards (Neil Armstrong), Scot York, Zards Cards, Dean Zindler, and Adam Zuwerink.

Every year we make active solicitations for expert input. We are particularly appreciative of the help (however extensive or cursory) provided for this volume. We receive many inquiries, comments and questions regarding material within this book. In fact, each and every one is read and digested. Time constraints, however, prevent us from personally replying. But keep sharing your knowledge. Your letters and input are part of the "big picture" of hobby information we can pass along to readers of our books and magazines. Even though we cannot respond to each letter, you are making significant contributions to the hobby through your interest and comments.

The effort to continually refine and improve this book also involves a growing number of people and types of expertise on our home team. Our company boasts a substantial Sport Data Publishing team, which strengthens our ability to provide comprehensive analysis of the marketplace. Sport Data Publishing capably handled numerous technical details and provided able assistance in the preparation of this edition.

Our basketball analysts played a major part in compiling this year's book, travelling thousands of miles during the past year to attend sports card shows and visit card shops around the United States and Canada. The Beckett basketball specialists are Randy Barning, Pat Blandford, Grant Sandground (Assistant Manager, Pricing Analysis) and Rob Springs (Price Guide Editor). Their baseline analysis and careful proofreading were key contributions to the accuracy of this annual.

Rob Springs' coordination of input as *Beckett Basketball Monthly* Price Guide Editor helped immeasurably, as did Rich Klein's encyclopedic knowledge and meticulous attention to detail. Grant Sandground and Pat Blandford also contributed many hours of painstaking analysis in the specialist role as did Randy Barning.

The effort was led by Senior Manager of Sports Data Publishing Pepper Hastings and the Manager of Sports Data Publishing Dan Hitt. They were ably assisted by the rest of the Price Guide analysts: Theo Chen, Ben Ecklar, Mike Jaspersen, Steven Judd, Eddie Kelly and Allan Muir. Also contributing to Sports Data Publishing functions were Jeany Finch, Gabriel Rangel and Beverly Mills.

The price gathering and analytical talents of this fine group of hobbyists have helped make our Beckett team stronger, while making this guide and its companion monthly Price Guide more widely recognized as the hobby's most reliable and relied upon sources of pricing information.

The Information Services department, ably headed by Mark Harwell, again played a crucial role in technology. David Schneider and Eric Best also spent countless hours programming, testing and implementing it to simplify the handling of thousands of prices that must be checked and updated for each section.

In the Production department, Paul Kerutis supervised the formatting and card illustration of the price guide. He was ably assisted by Marlon DePaula.

Loretta Gibbs attended to the wishes of our dealer advertisers under the direction of Customer Service assistant manager Patti Harris. Once the ad specifications were delivered to our offices, Phaedra Strecher turned raw copy into attractive display advertisements.

In the years since this guide debuted, Beckett Publications has grown beyond any rational expectation. A great many talented and hard working individuals have been instrumental in this growth and success. Our whole team is to be congratulated for what we together have accomplished. Our Beckett Publications team is led by Executive Vice President Jeff Amano, Vice Presidents Claire Backus, Joe Galindo and Fred Reed, Directors Mark Harwell, Jay Johnson and Reed Poole, and Senior Managers Jeff Anthony, Beth Harwell and Pepper Hastings. They are ably assisted by Dana Alecknavage, Kelly Atkins, Kaye Ball, Airey Baringer, Barbara Barry, Rob Barry, Therese Bellar, Julie Binion, Louise Bird, Amy Brougher, Bob Brown,

Chris Calandro, Randall Calvert, Emily Camp, Mary Campana, Susan Catka, Jud Chappell, Albert Chavez, Marty Click, Laura Corley, Andy Costilla, Belinda Cross, Randy Cummings, Eric Evans, Marcelo Gomez DeSouza, Lauren Drewes, Denise Ellison, Barbara Faraldo, Craig Ferris, Gean Paul Figari, Carol Fowler, Gayle Gasperin, Steve Genusa, Rosanna Gonzalez-Olaechea, Duane Green, Jeff Greer, Mary Gregory, Robert Gregory, Jenifer Grellhesl, Julie Grove, Tracy Hackler, Patti Harris, Brent Hawkins, Joanna Hayden, Chris Hellem, Melissa Herzog, Tim Jaksa, Wendy Kizer, Rudy J. Klancnik, Brian Kosley, Tom Layberger, Jane Ann Layton, Sara Leeman, Benedito Leme, Lori Lindsey, Stanley Lira, Kirk Lockhart, Sara Maneval, Louis Marroquin, John Marshall, Mike McAllister, Teri McGahey, Omar Mediano, Lisa McQuilkin Monaghan, Sherry Monday, Mila Morante, Daniel Moscoso Jr., Mike Moss, Randy Mosty, Hugh Murphy, Shawn Murphy, Mike Obert, Stacy Olivieri, Lisa O'Neill. Mike Pagel, Wendy Pallugna, Laura Patterson, Mike Payne, Tim Polzer, Will Pry, Bob Richardson, Tina Riojas, Susan Sainz, Evan Salituro, Gary Santaniello, Brett Setter, Dave Sliepka, Judi Smalling, Sheri Smith, Jeff Stanton, Margaret Steele, Marcia Stoesz, Dawn Sturgeon, Doree Tate, Jim Tereschuk, Doug Williams, Steve Wilson and Mark Zeske. The whole Beckett Publications team has my thanks for jobs well done. Thank you, everyone.

NOTES

NOTES

NOTES

NOTES

NOTES